The Ashmolean Museum

COMPLETE ILLUSTRATED CATALOGUE
OF PAINTINGS

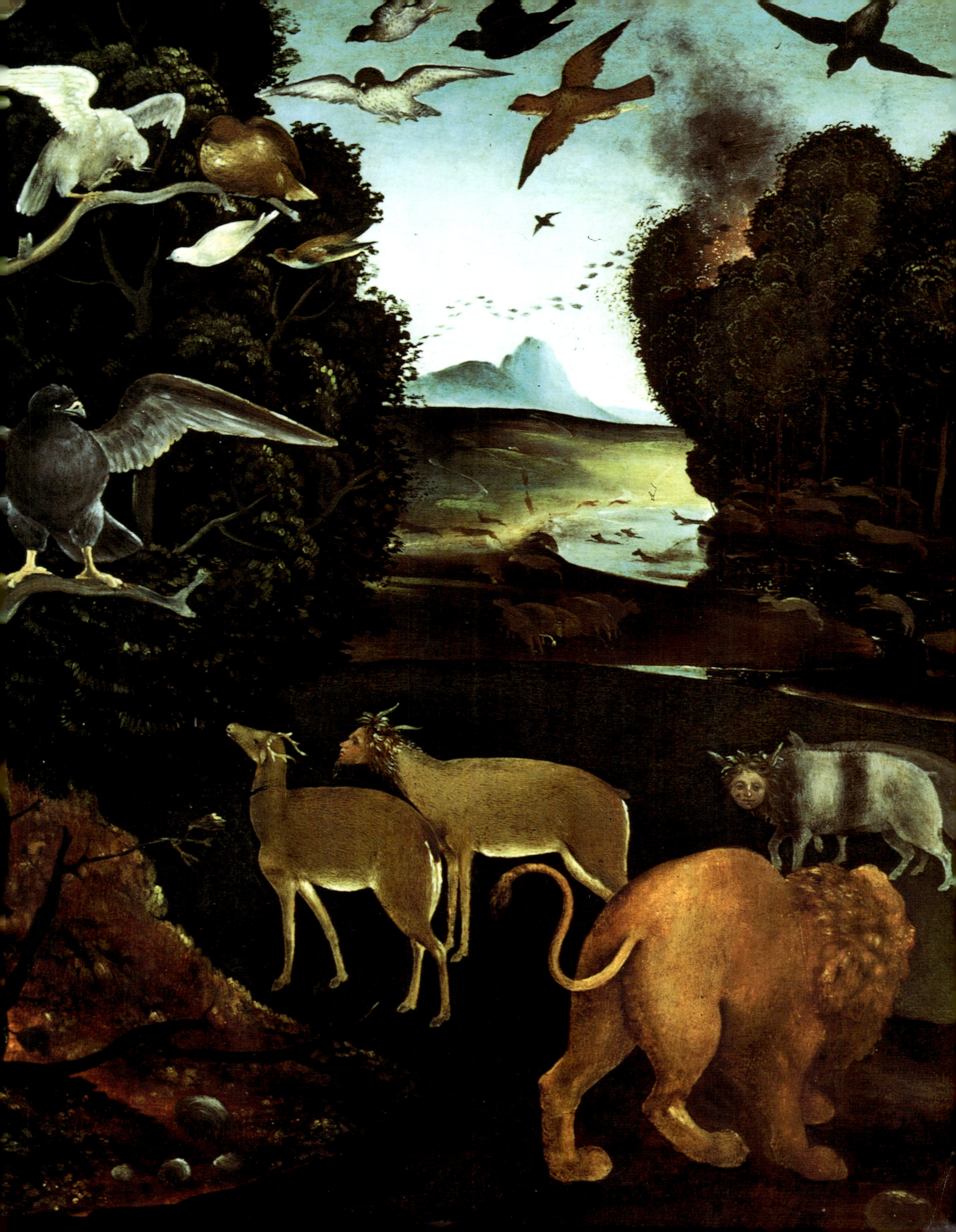

The Ashmolean Museum

COMPLETE ILLUSTRATED CATALOGUE OF PAINTINGS

CONTRIBUTORS

Colin Harrison
Cyril Mango
Marlia Mundell Mango
Timothy Newbery
Christian Rümelin
Catherine Whistler
Jon Whiteley
Timothy Wilson

CO-ORDINATING EDITORS

Catherine Casley, Colin Harrison and Jon Whiteley

Oxford 2004

First published in the United Kingdom in 2004 by the Ashmolean Museum, Publications Department, Beaumont Street, Oxford OX1 2PH

ISBN 1 85444 187 6 (hardback)

ISBN 1 85444 188 4 (paperback)

British Library Cataloguing in Publication Data

A catalogue record for this book is available from the British Library

Catalogue designed by Tim Harvey
Typeset in FF Scala

Printed and bound in the United Kingdom by Cambridge University Press

A list of photographic acknowledgements appears on page 335

frontispiece: Piero di Cosimo *The Forest Fire* (detail)

CONTENTS

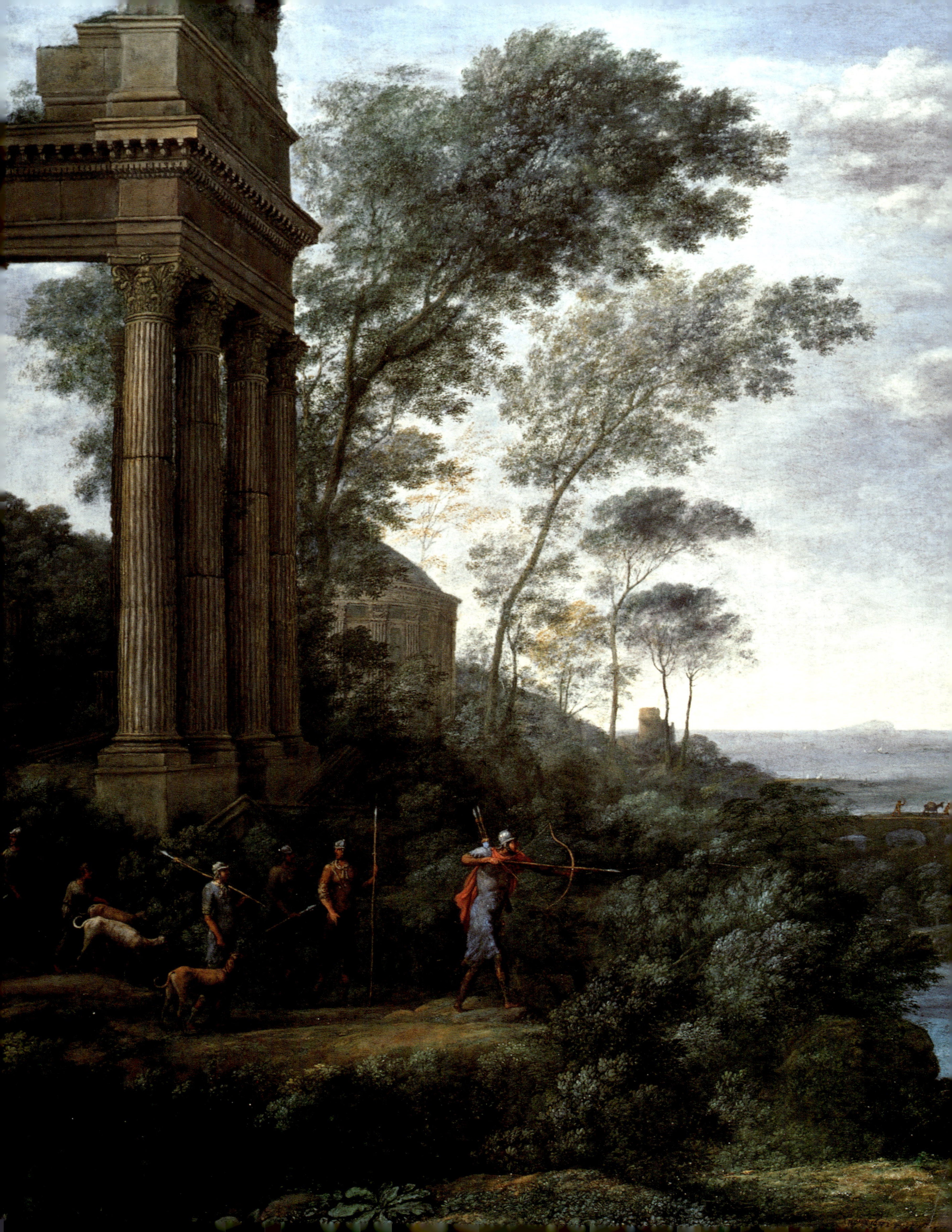

DIRECTOR'S PREFACE

THE FIRST CATALOGUE of Oxford University's art collection was written in the 1750s by the janitor of the Bodleian Library. The next, compiled by one of his successors, appeared in 1840. Since then, summary catalogues have appeared every twenty years or so, growing in thickness and in scholarship as the collection has increased in size and as research into the paintings has advanced. The present catalogue and its recent predecessors have relied heavily on the series of specialized catalogues dealing with parts of the collection which have been published at intervals since 1950. The compilers of the present Summary Catalogue would like to acknowledge a large debt to the authors of these books – Jan van Gelder, Gerald Taylor, Christopher Lloyd, Sir Christopher White, and Fred Meijer – who have provided much of the material on which the entries of this catalogue are based. Large areas of the collection, however, remain unpublished except in summary form. This is the case with all the French, Spanish, and British paintings, as well as the later Italians. Summary catalogues, as a rule, are generated from existing publications but, because over half of the Ashmolean's collection of paintings has not yet been published in any depth, this catalogue contains a good deal of new material, deriving from catalogues in hand but not yet completed. Meanwhile, visitors to the Ashmolean have a right to expect to find an accessible, comprehensive guide to the paintings, including all those which are not on view, fully illustrated and accompanied by brief notes on each. I hope this book will be useful to scholars, but it is intended for everyone.

Jon Whiteley was in overall charge of the planning of the catalogue, while Colin Harrison has been involved in editorial decisions at all stages and, with Timothy Wilson, has taken on the arduous task of editing the texts into uniformity of format. The entries have been written by Colin Harrison (British artists before 1945, and the Pissarro Family); Catherine Whistler (Italian and Spanish artists and French artists born before *c.* 1800); Jon Whiteley (Dutch, Flemish, German and Russian and 19th-century French artists, excluding the Pissarro Family); Christian Rümelin (most of the 20th-century paintings); Marlia and Cyril Mango (icons); and Timothy Newbery (frames). The artists' biographies were written by Catherine Whistler, Jon Whiteley, and Timothy Wilson. David Gowers and his staff in the Photography Studio have coped brilliantly with the multifarious demands of photographing a large number of paintings in different locations and varying degrees of conservation. Declan McCarthy of the Publications Department has managed all the practicalities of the publication and seen the book through the press. Catherine Casley, Documentation Officer in the Department of Western Art, has co-ordinated the whole project with exemplary calm and efficiency; she has also compiled the concordances.

Finally, it would not have been possible to publish such an ambitious catalogue without the generous support of the Michael Marks Charitable Trust. We very much hope that the Trustees will share in the pleasure and instruction which this book is intended to bring to our many audiences.

Christopher Brown DIRECTOR, ASHMOLEAN MUSEUM

opposite: Fig. 1 CLAUDE GELLÉE (LE LORRAIN) *Landscape with Ascanius Shooting the Stag of Sylvia* (detail)

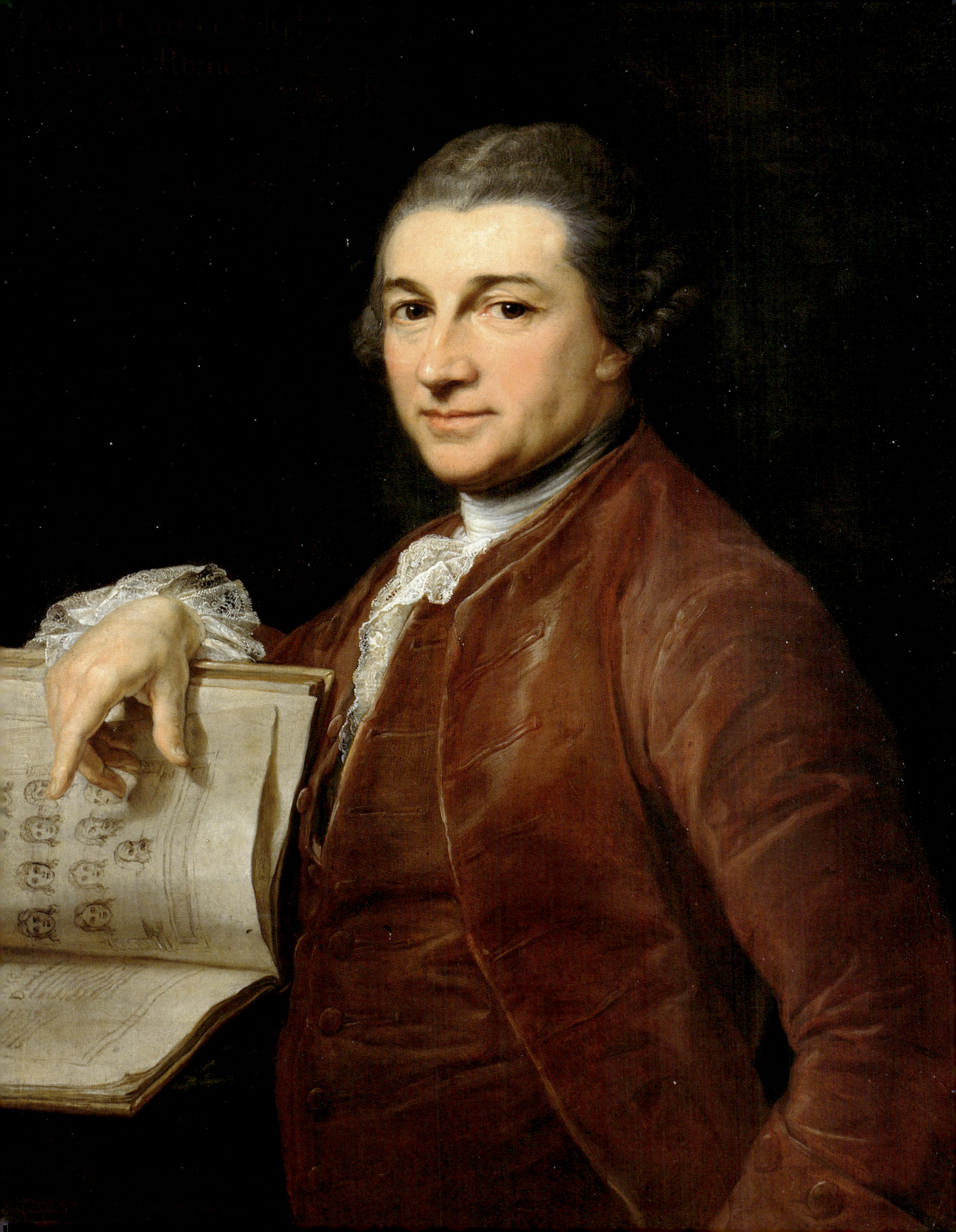

A SHORT HISTORY OF THE ASHMOLEAN'S PAINTING COLLECTION

Jon Whiteley

The Ashmolean Museum is based on two ancient University collections, the works of art from the Bodleian Library and the artefacts from the Old Ashmolean in Broad Street. These collections were already old when they were transferred to the present building in the 19th century. The original Ashmolean was founded in 1683 while the Bodleian Picture Gallery, where the University at one time kept most of its artefacts and works of art, dates from about 1620. The Bodleian collection was not the first museum of its kind – libraries and scholars' cabinets had included coins, antiquities, exotic artefacts and portraits since the early 1500s – but, as a collection which has been accessible to the public for nearly four hundred years, first in the Bodleian and later in the Ashmolean, it constitutes the oldest surviving public museum in Britain and one of the oldest in existence.

The Picture Gallery (fig. 3) was installed in rooms on three sides of the second storey of the Bodleian Quadrangle. These rooms, now occupied by the Upper Library, were built between 1613 and 1619 with funds bequeathed by Sir Thomas Bodley who intended that they should be used, in due course, for the storage of books. However, before the need for a book store became apparent, the new rooms had been taken over for the purpose of displaying a museum of 'curiosities', a collection of man-made and natural objects of a kind commonly brought together in the 17th century for a variety of scholarly and scientific purposes. The collection was well established by the 1630s and continued to expand by way of gifts. In 1636, the arrival of Archbishop Laud's collection of coins formed the basis of the Coin Room, a collection of the greatest importance which was inserted into an angle of the Picture Gallery and is now incorporated into the Ashmolean. Other gifts included a 'Muscovite coat', a crocodile from Jamaica, a chair made from the timbers of Drake's *Golden Hind*, and Guy Fawkes's lantern. Several of these, including the

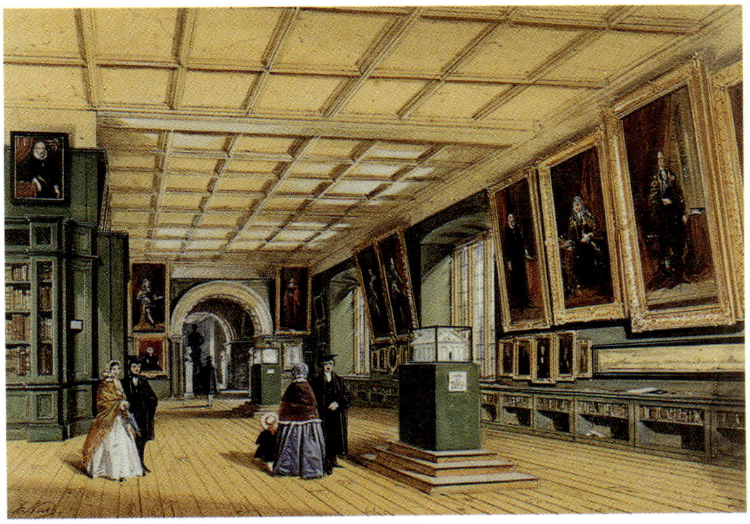

Fig. 3 J. Nash The Bodleian picture gallery shortly before the opening of the University Galleries Reproduced by kind permission of the Bodleian Library, University of Oxford.

opposite: Fig. 2 Pompeo Batoni *David Garrick*

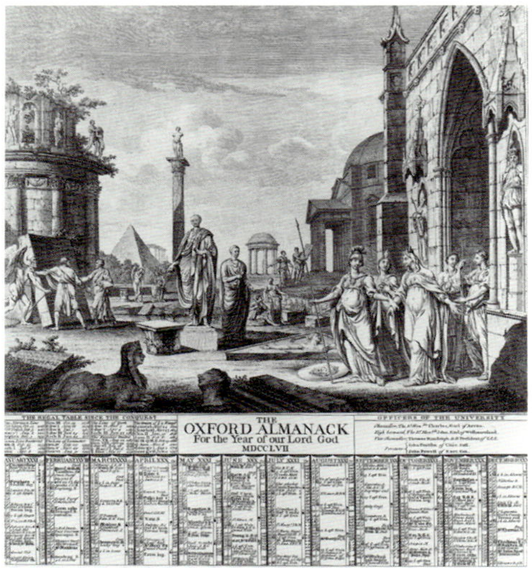

Fig. 4 University Almanack for 1757

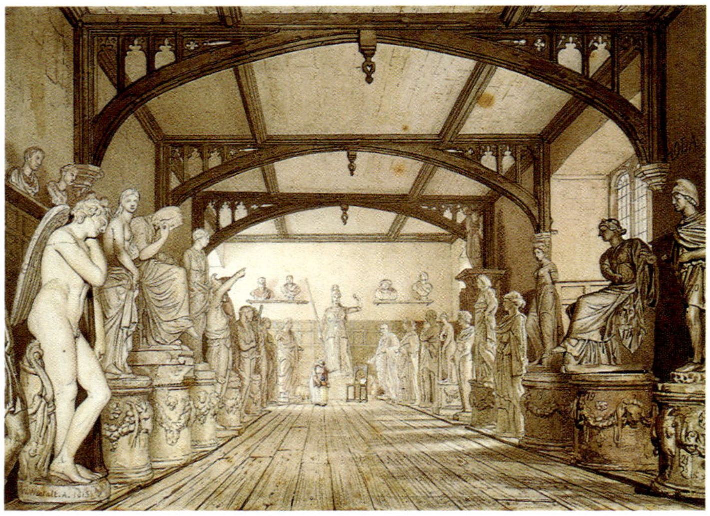

Fig. 5 William Westall Sculptures displayed at the Bodleian, 1813

famous lantern, survive in the present Ashmolean while others, including the coat and the crocodile, have long since disappeared. After 1683 when the Ashmolean Museum opened in Broad Street as a home for the collection of curiosities donated by Elias Ashmole, gifts of this kind tended to go to the Ashmolean while the Bodleian Gallery, which had better wall space for pictures than the Ashmolean, developed into a museum of art.

From the earliest years, the Gallery had received gifts of portraits. The pace of acquisition increased after 1660 and by the early 1700s, the Picture Gallery had become a portrait museum of considerable interest, representing writers, in particular, as well as benefactors and librarians but including also portraits of travellers, painters, scientists and other people who had contributed to the common stock of art and learning. It had the disadvantage which is common to collections of portraits that the chief interest lay in the sitters and not in the painters, so that it acquired a great deal of second-rate art. Many of the attributions were also ambitious. We now know that Holbein's portrait of Martin Luther, Federico Zuccaro's portrait of Elizabeth I, Rubens's portrait of Louis XIII and self-portraits of Raphael and Rembrandt are nothing of the sort. There was, nonetheless, much of artistic interest and by the early 19th century, the visitor could see a series of fine portraits, including *Flora Macdonald* by Allan Ramsay, *James Paine and his Son* and *The Duke of Grafton* by Reynolds, *Francis Junius* by Van Dyck and *David Garrick* by Pompeo Batoni and a number of distinguished busts, most of which have since been transferred to the new galleries in the present Ashmolean.

In the course of the 18th century, the scope of the Gallery expanded to become an art museum in the modern sense. Dr John King's bequest in 1739 added a group of thirteen paintings which modified the emphasis on portraits. These included seapieces by Adam Willaerts and Cornelis van Wieringhen, a painting of boys stealing fruit, then attributed to 'Old Frank Hall' (i.e. Frans Hals) but now attributed to the lesser known Claes Moeyaert, and two large paintings, then attributed to Jordaens, now given to his minor contemporary, Arnout Vinckenborch. Several gifts and a bequest, received in 1755, from Dr Richard Rawlinson – a generous benefactor to the library – brought in a number of similar pictures, including a seapiece by Minderhout, a good portrait by Pieter Nason, a fair number of spurious Holbeins and a charming picture of an officer, now attributed to Peter Codde. These collections were sober, Northern and Protestant, not uncharacteristic, perhaps, of contemporary academic taste. Although Italian art was much collected at this time in England, it was hardly represented in the Picture Gallery. If John Guise had bequeathed his art collection to the Bodleian in 1762 and not to Christ Church, the collection would have been transformed by the addition of a number of major paintings by Italian artists among others and a collection of Italian drawings of matchless rarity; but Guise's sense of allegiance towards the University, like that of many graduates before and since, was directed towards his former college and, as a consequence, once Christ Church had fitted up the ground floor of the college library as a home for

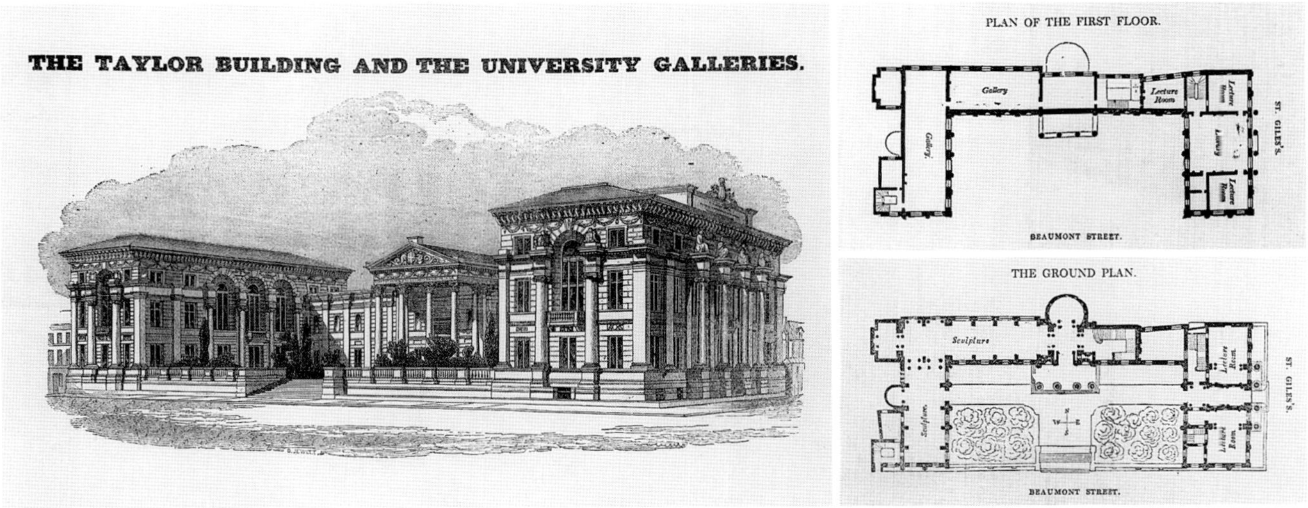

Fig. 6 Proposed elevation and floor plans of the University Galleries and Taylor Institution

the Guise collection, the University became home to two picture galleries, both of which continued to attract gifts.

Some contemporary art came to the Bodleian through commissioned portraits but most came as gifts, sometimes from the artists themselves. Sir Godfrey Kneller, Sir James Thornhill, Edward Penny and others donated portraits and a few historical compositions, followed in the late 18th and early 19th centuries by a number of amateur painters with University connections – Oldfield Bowles, Lord Harcourt, Edward Hamilton, William Cowden, Sir William Elford and Sir George Beaumont – who donated a series of landscape paintings. These landscapes, although not important in themselves, mark a stage in changing attitudes towards art within the University, as interest in the subjects of paintings lost ground to the idea that art might be important in its own right.

The character of the Bodleian collection was affected profoundly by the Countess of Pomfret's gift of a large part of Lord Arundel's famous collection of Greek and Roman marbles in 1755. The gift reunited Arundel's busts and figures with a group of inscribed stones from Arundel's collection which were already in the Bodleian. The inscriptions, given in 1677, were, at first, built into the boundary wall between the library and Sheldonian Theatre. In 1714, they were moved into the Picture Gallery and remained there until 1749 when they were transferred to a ground floor room during a refurbishment of the Gallery. They were not moved to the present museum until 1888. The inscriptions were not out of place in a library which is why, no doubt, they were left in the Bodleian precinct long after the busts and figures had been removed to the museum in Beaumont Street. The busts and figures, however, were chiefly important as works of art and required better premises than the library could offer. The need 'to build a temple on purpose to receive them' along with other art works which might be given to the University was immediately acknowledged by the Vice-Chancellor. In 1757, the University's annual Almanack was published with a print which included allegorical figures of Architecture and Geometry discussing plans for a new museum (fig. 4). This, however, was no more than wishful thinking. The University did not have funds to construct a 'temple' of the kind then proposed and the Pomfret marbles were installed instead in a ground floor room on the south-east corner of the quadrangle (fig. 5). These premises were too dark, too small and generally ill-suited for exhibiting a collection of classical statuary, but at least the evident inadequacy of this arrangement ensured that the plan for a new gallery of art, launched with much enthusiasm in the mid-1750s, was not forgotten.

In 1797, the University received a bequest of £1,000 in the will of Dr Francis Randolph, Principal of St Alban Hall, towards the cost of building a museum for the marbles and other works of art. This was not enough to allow work to begin and as further funds were not forthcoming the new museum was not put in hand until 1839. That it was begun at all was only due to an ingenious scheme, devised by the University Registrar, Dr Philip Bliss, to amalgamate Randolph's money with a much larger sum received

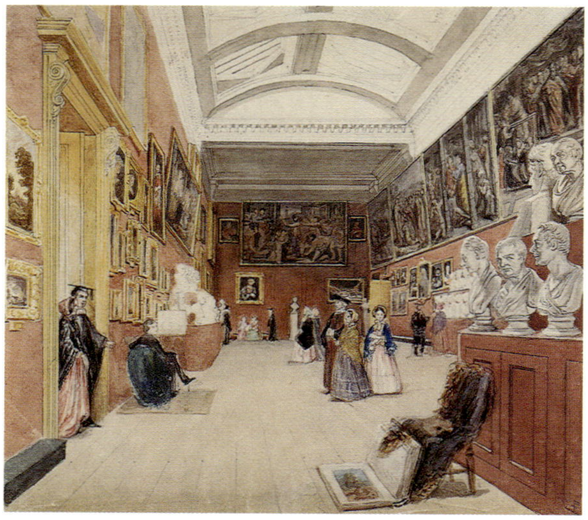

Fig. 7 Joseph Fisher *First-floor gallery in the west wing of the University Galleries, c. 1850*
Reproduced by kind permission of the Bodleian Library, University of Oxford.

in 1835 for building an institution for teaching Modern Languages and to combine the institution and the art gallery within a single building. Following a competition, Charles Robert Cockerell, the most distinguished of the competing architects, was given the commission. His art gallery on Beaumont Street, joined to the Taylorian Institute for Modern Languages on the east side, was divided into two floors with two galleries for sculptures on the ground floor and two galleries for paintings and drawings above (fig. 6). When the University Galleries opened to the public in 1846, the first of the two upstairs rooms (the present Fox-Strangways Gallery) was used to exhibit a collection of drawings by Raphael and Michelangelo, bought for the new museum on the initiative of Dr Henry Wellesley, nephew of the Duke of Wellington and one of the three curators appointed to take care of the works of art. The second room, the Great Gallery, a large and very high gallery, long since subdivided into six smaller rooms in two storeys, was filled with paintings from the Bodleian (fig. 7). The Picture Gallery, which had been elegantly refurbished in 1831 by Robert Smirke, did not close but became more exclusively a gallery of portraits while the paintings which were thought to be chiefly interesting as works of art were sent to the Galleries in Beaumont Street. There were good things among the works transferred but the average quality was mild. The contrast with other early museums of art in Britain, such as the gallery in Dulwich or the Fitzwilliam in Cambridge, or with similar museums on the continent, founded on collections of masterpieces, is striking. The Great Gallery, dominated by a series of seven full-size copies of Raphael's famous

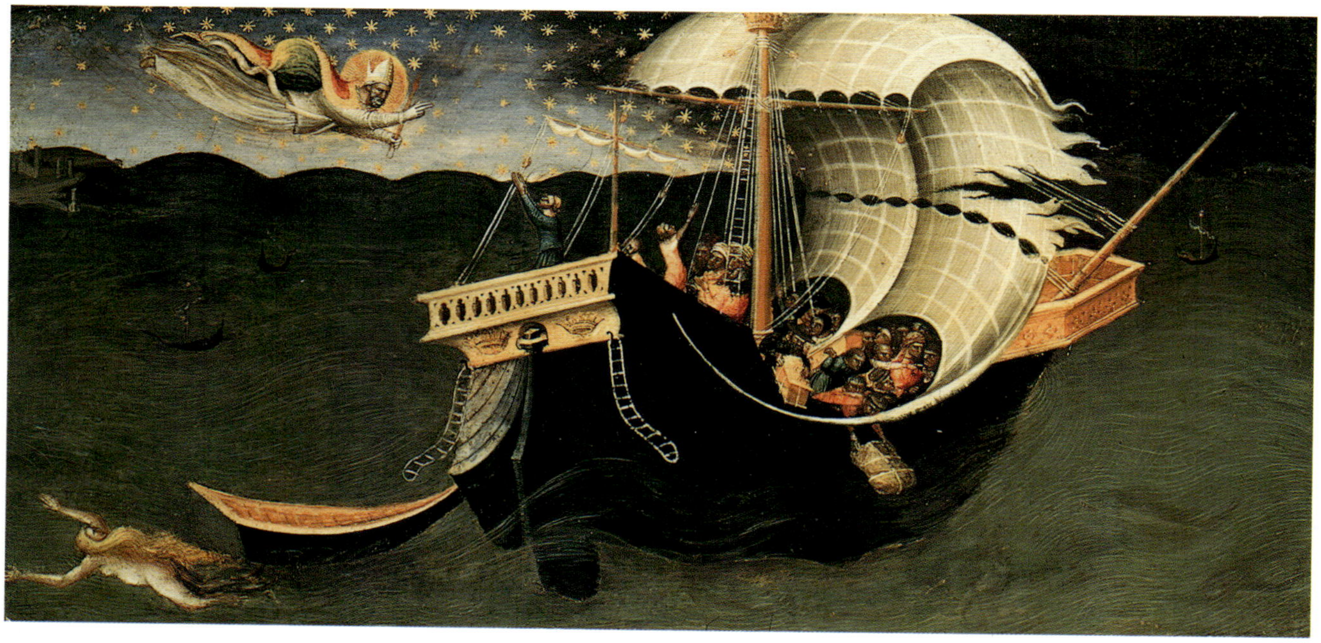

Fig. 8 Bicci di Lorenzo *St Nicholas of Bari Banishing the Storm*

opposite: Fig. 9 Paolo di Dono, called Uccello *The Hunt in the Forest* (detail)

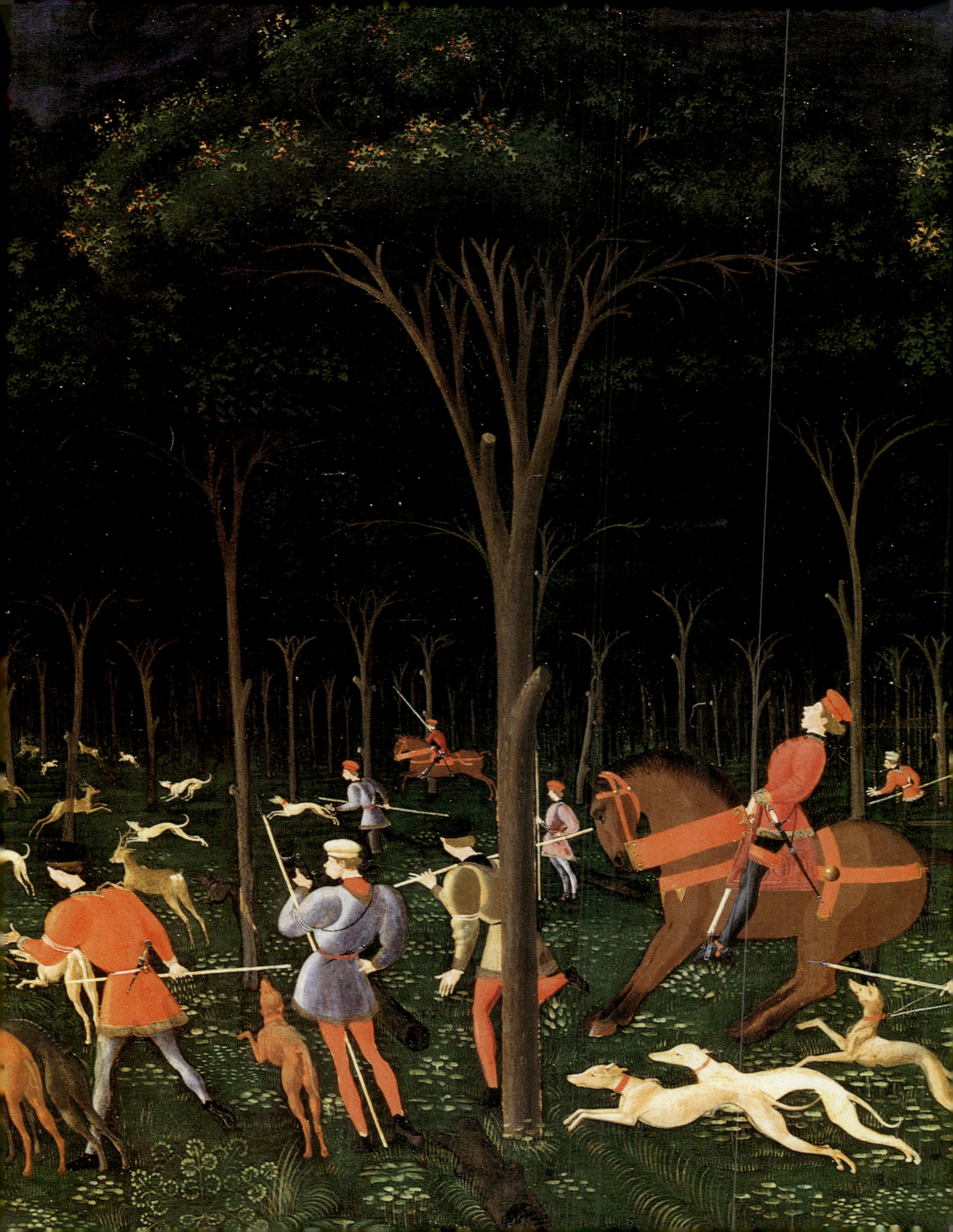

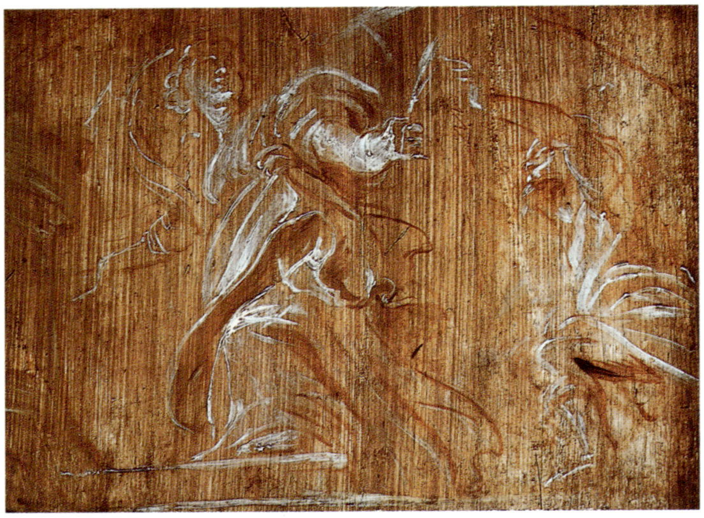

Fig. 10 Sir Peter Paul Rubens *St Barbara pursued by her Father*

cartoons, transferred from the Bodleian, was encumbered by worthy but dull originals and many misattributions and copies. From the start, the greater interest of the 'Raffaello Gallery' where the drawings by Raphael and Michelangelo were exhibited, was generally recognised. Connoisseurs came to the University Galleries chiefly to see the drawings. It was the hope of the founders, however, that the new building would encourage gifts. These began to arrive within a few years of the opening, gradually taking the place of the works of art originally exhibited in the Great Gallery so that, nowadays, most of the paintings which the visitor will see in the museum galleries have been acquired since 1846.

News of the first major gift was received by Wellesley in 1850 in a letter from the Hon. William

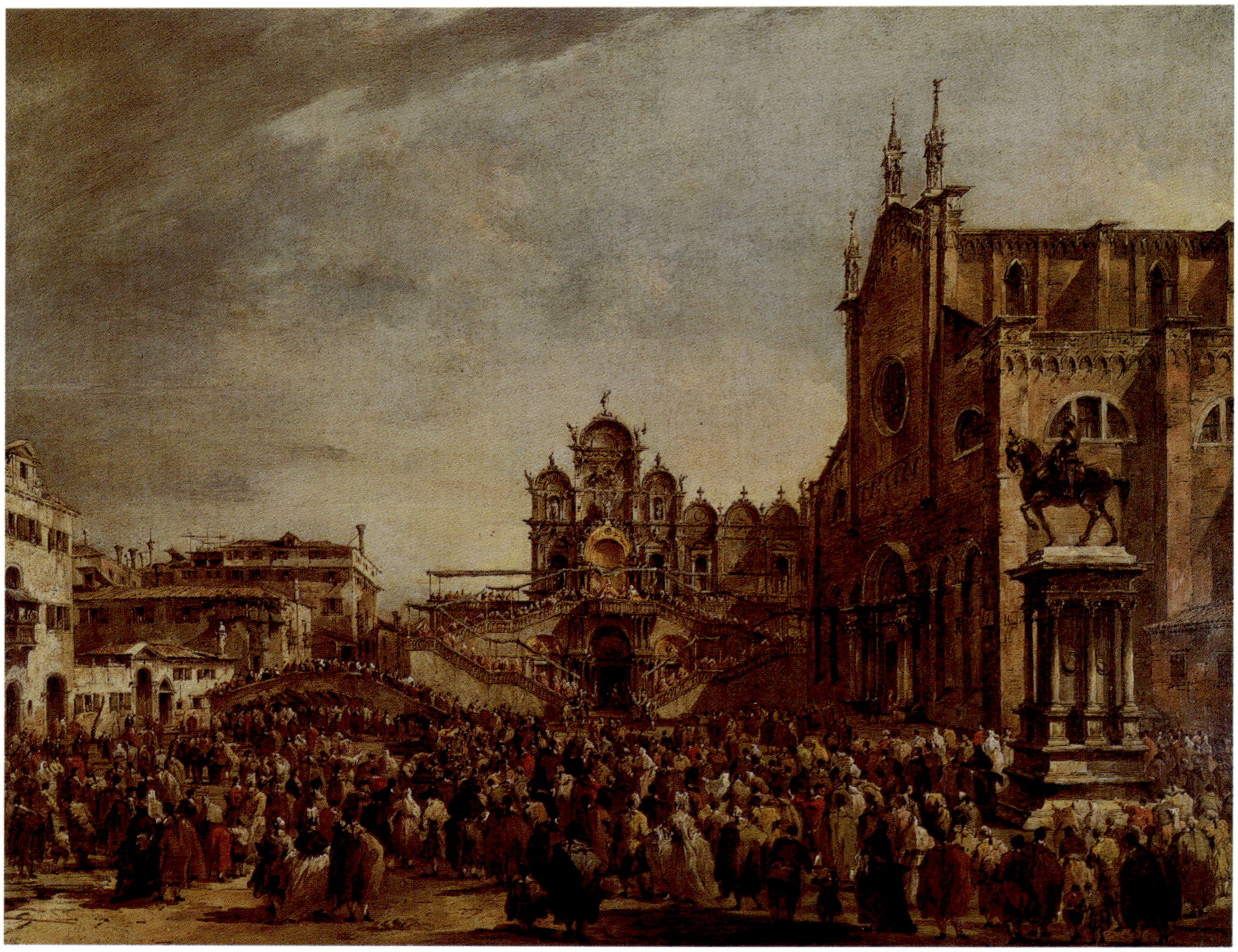

Fig. 11 Francesco Guardi *Pope Pius VI blessing the Crowd at Campo SS Giovanni e Paolo, Venice*

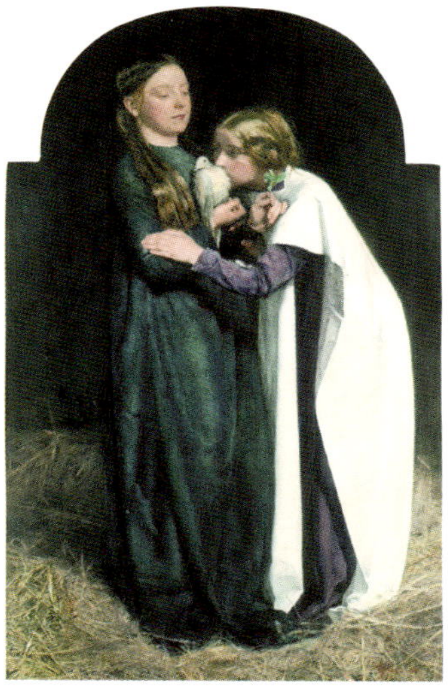

Fig. 12 Sir John Everett Millais Bt *The Return of the Dove to the Ark*

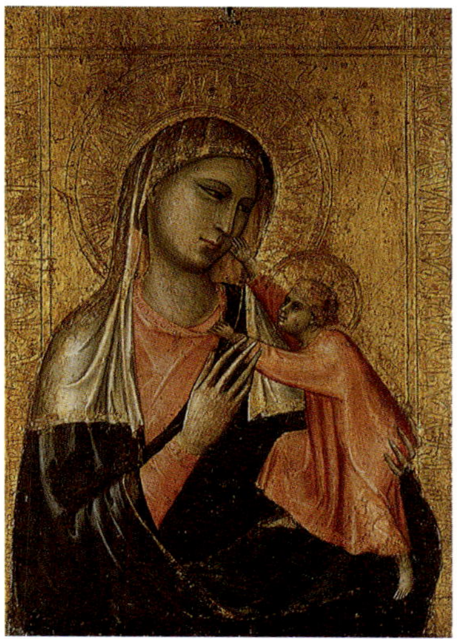

Fig. 13 Studio of Giotto di Bondone *The Virgin and Child*

Thomas Horner Fox-Strangways, indicating that he wished to donate a collection of paintings by early Italian painters to the Galleries, similar to those which he had presented some twenty years earlier to Christ Church. These paintings, collected by Fox-Strangways in Italy between 1827 and 1832, seem to have been acquired with the purpose of illustrating the development of art in central Italy from Giotto to the age of Raphael. Fox-Strangways was a diplomat but his passion was botany and he collected pictures as he might have collected plants, keeping many of them in packing cases until they were transferred to Oxford. This was an area with opportunities for a collector in the late 1820s but it also had many pitfalls, especially for a voracious collector like Fox-Strangways who was, it seems, looking out principally for names. Scholarship in this area was rudimentary and very few of the forty-one paintings given by Fox-Strangways to the Galleries are now attributed to the artists to whom they were then attributed. Nevertheless, he bought his paintings with a discriminating eye. They include Uccello's *Hunt in the Forest* (attributed by Fox-Strangways to Benozzo Gozzoli), now perhaps the most famous painting in the museum, (fig. 9) and many other works of charm and quality (fig. 8).

The second major gift, received in 1855, was made by Wellesley's friend, Chambers Hall, a collector from Southampton with eclectic tastes and a marked liking for paintings by Rubens, van Dyck, Guardi (fig. 11) and Canaletto, drawings and etchings by Claude and Ostade, and small antique bronzes. He was an amateur painter and had a painter's eye for technical effects. Much of his collection is small in scale and while he might not have had house room for the largest works by Rubens, his taste suggests a preference for Rubens's sketches of which he had a group of remarkable importance (fig. 10).

The works donated by other collectors singly or in groups during the remainder of the century gradually displaced the lesser works to the point at which space in the Great Gallery became a problem. The Chambers Hall gift, at first exhibited separately in what is now the Founder's Room, was moved in due course into the Great Gallery when the room they had occupied was hung with Herkomer's portraits of the keeper and curators. From this time onwards, the need for additional space arose with every major gift. Mrs Combe's bequest of paintings by the Pre-Raphaelites, received in 1894, including important works by Millais (fig. 12), Holman Hunt and Collins, was installed in 1907 in a room on the first floor of a small wing, added on the north end of the Great Gallery. The paintings were arranged with help from Holman Hunt, the walls were hung with Morris paper and the room was lit by electricity. This was the first of several extensions added piecemeal to Cockerell's building to cater for the steady influx of accessions. More ambitious schemes came and went. Money was always a problem but the greatest difficulty lay in the restricted nature of the site.

The arrival of the Combe bequest, purchased, for the most part, from the artists by Thomas Combe, superintendent of the University Press, seems to mark a shift towards the collecting of contemporary art. John Ruskin had energetically promoted the cause of modern artists while he held the post of Slade

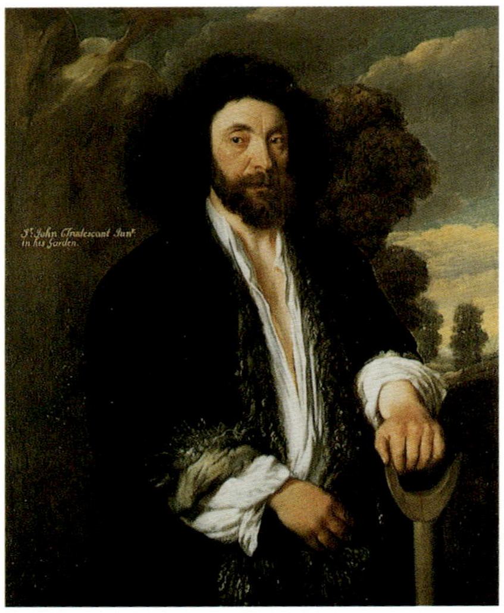

Fig. 14 Attributed to THOMAS DE CRITZ
John Tradescant the Younger as a Gardener

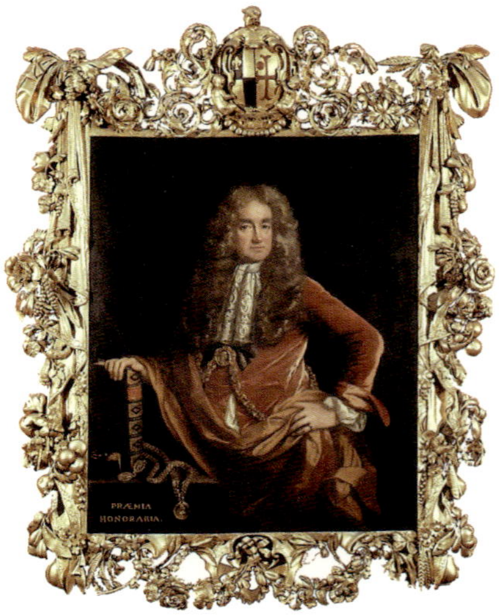

FIG. 15 JOHN RILEY *Elias Ashmole*

Professor at the University. His gift of watercolours by J.M.W. Turner in 1861 was intended to set the balance right alongside the drawings by Michelangelo and Raphael. This, however, did not become a trend. Few paintings by living artists were added before 1936, when the arrival of Mrs Weldon's bequest brought in a large number of works by contemporary and near-contemporary painters. In reality, the character of the collection of paintings owed more to the tastes of benefactors than it did to a policy of acquisition and the tastes of the benefactors were extremely varied. If Ruskin had an effect upon the evolution of the collection of paintings, it was felt indirectly, through the gifts of those who had felt his influence. The ten paintings belonging to James Reddie Anderson, presented in part by his widow in 1913 and in part by his daughters in 1947 in memory of their father, represent a taste for the early Italians which Anderson had acquired from Ruskin. It was not an unusual taste by the mid-19th century but Anderson had been an undergraduate when Ruskin was Slade Professor and he became a devoted follower. His paintings, which merge imperceptibly with Fox-Strangways's collection (which must have been very familiar to him) include a beautiful Virgin and Child by a follower of Giotto (fig. 13) and an important panel by the anonymous Master of the Bielefeld Altarpiece.

The period from 1892 to 1908 saw fundamental changes in the character and administration of the Galleries. The Ashmolean building in Broad Street had long outgrown its narrow premises and could not cope with the influx of acquisitions coming into the collection from recent excavations. Following a campaign by Dr Henry Acland, Ruskin's friend and Wellesley's successor at the Galleries, the collection of natural history had moved from the Ashmolean to a new museum built in 1855-60 on the edge of the University Parks. Something similar would have served archaeology equally well; but, instead, through the sustained efforts of Arthur Evans, Keeper of the Ashmolean, and paid for by an endowment of £10,000 from C.D.E. Fortnum, the Ashmolean collections were moved into somewhat utilitarian premises built onto the back of the Galleries in Beaumont Street on a site recently acquired by the University. From 1894, the Visitors of the Ashmolean (as the Ashmolean's Governing Body is known) and the Curators of the Galleries met as a joint body until, on Evans's recommendation, they were merged into a single committee in 1908. From this date, the joint institution became known as the Ashmolean Museum of Art and Archaeology. The move restricted space for expanding the galleries of art northwards, as had been the hope of the curators, and there was much resentment at the manner in which the Ashmolean had colonised the site and thrust unwanted changes on the Galleries. Evans and his Assistant Keeper, Charles Bell, retaliated vigorously in the face of opposition from the 'brutes' and 'fools who will never see their folly', as Bell described the unfortunate curators and their allies. The scheme, however, had a willing sponsor and, as Bell rightly predicted, the prospect of saving money by the proposed changes ensured the support of the University.

The merger brought a number of paintings into the Galleries which had previously been displayed on

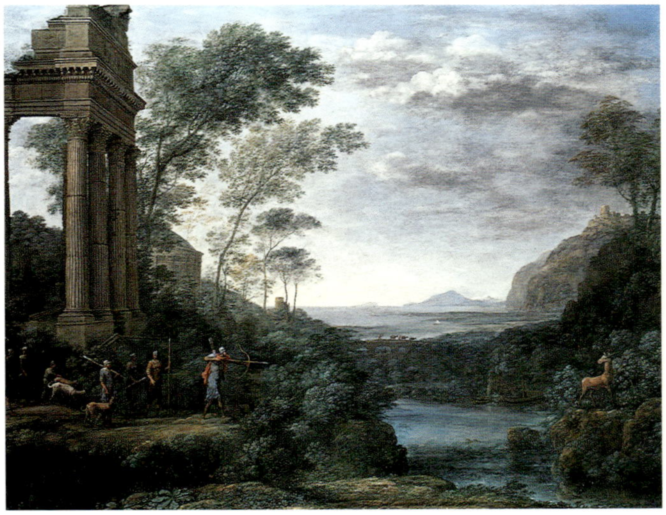

Fig. 16 Claude Gellée (Le Lorrain) *Landscape with Ascanius Shooting the Stag of Sylvia*

the staircase of the Old Ashmolean. These included a group of striking portraits of the Tradescant family, of uncertain attribution, of which the finest and most unusual is the portrait of the gardener, John Tradescant the Younger, his hair unkempt, his shirt open, holding his spade as a sign of his profession (fig. 14). By contrast, the portrait of his friend, Elias Ashmole, who donated Tradescant's collection to the University, is a portrait of the donor as a man of fame and substance, painted by the court painter, John Riley, and enclosed within an elaborate surround, carved in lime-wood by Grinling Gibbons (fig. 15). There were, in all, 72 paintings in the Ashmolean by the middle of the 19th century but many vanished at the time of the move, including an intriguing *Dead Christ*, attributed to Annibale Carraci, which had been

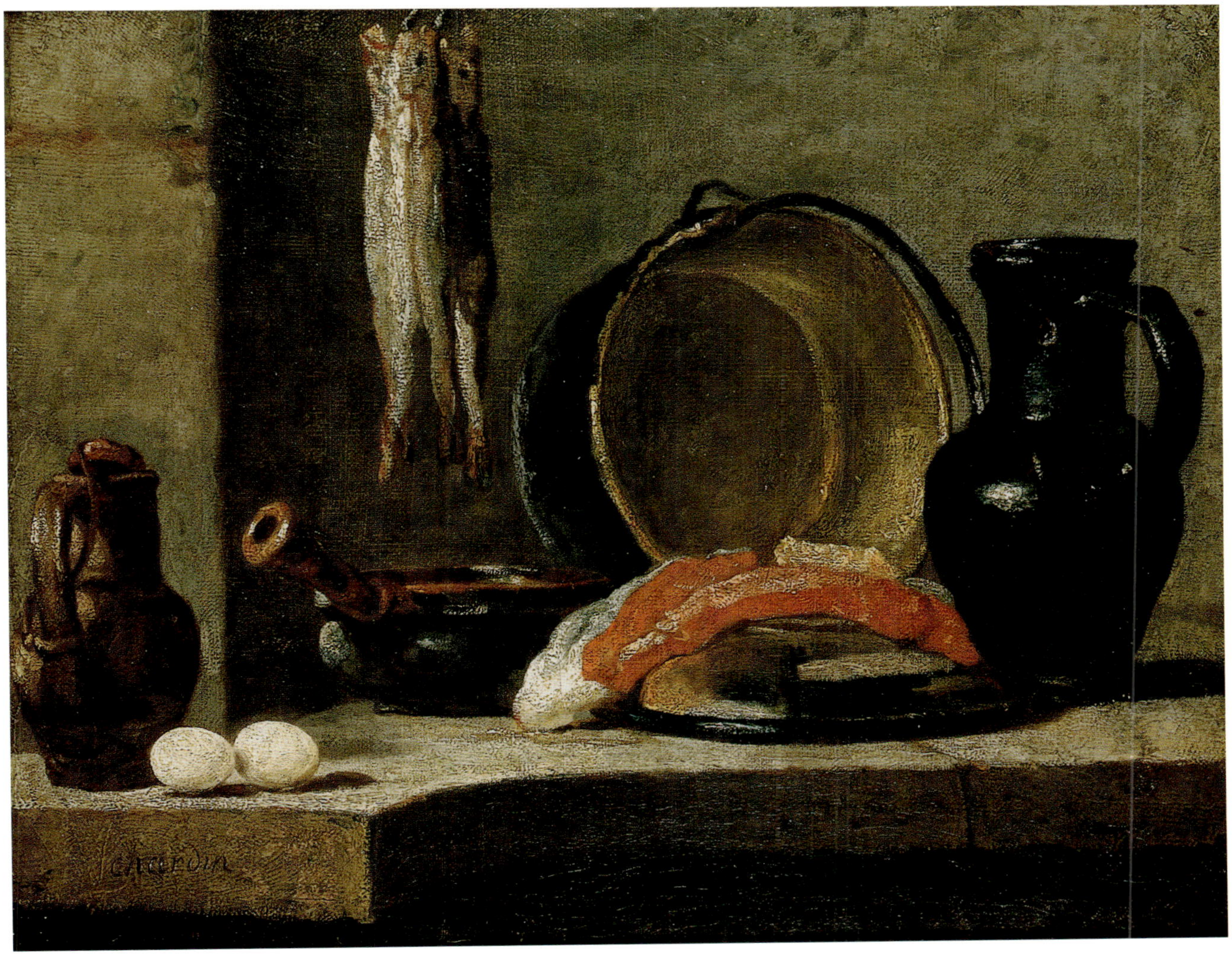

Fig. 17 Jean-Siméon Chardin *Still life of Kitchen Utensils*

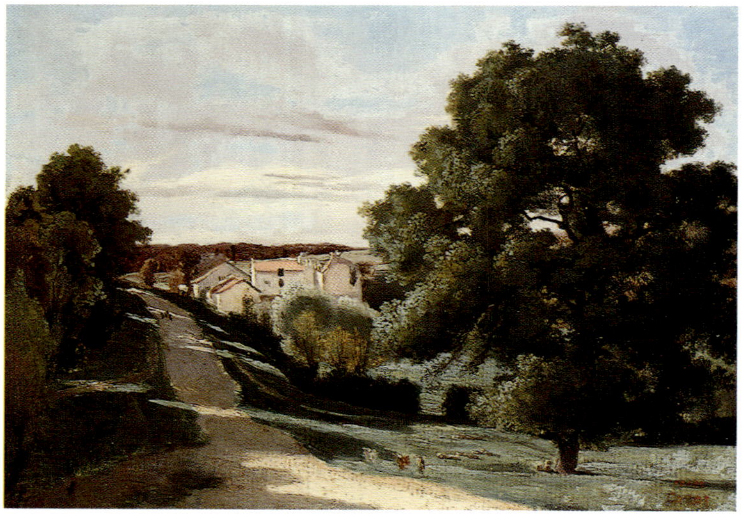

Fig. 18 Jean-Baptiste-Camille Corot *Le Petit Chaville, near Ville-d'Avray*

given to the Ashmolean in 1757. They were, it seems, mostly very minor and may still survive in some forgotten attic in the University.

During the period from 1908 to 1931 when Charles Bell was Keeper of the Department of Fine Art, a few fine paintings were added to the collection. The best were given by Mrs Weldon (née Florence Tebb) who had inherited much wealth from her father, a property developer in London, and who seems to have begun collecting after the death of her husband, Walter Frank Raphael Weldon, Linacre Professor of Comparative Anatomy, in 1906. Her first gift, a landscape by G.F. Watts, was made in 1915 and she continued to present the occasional choice work, mostly by Old Masters, over the following twenty years: an allegory by Nicolaes Maes in 1917, works by Watteau and Chardin (fig. 17) in 1927, Drost's *Ruth and Naomi* in 1929; a painting by Georges Michel in 1934; above all, Claude's *Ascanius shooting the Stag of Sylvia* (fig. 16), the artist's last painting and one of his most poetical, given by Mrs Weldon in 1926 after it had been on loan for a number of years. She was, no doubt, prompted by Bell whose affection for the Pre-Raphaelites may explain her gift of Brown's *Seeds and Fruit of English Poetry* in 1920. The pictures which she donated in her life-time, at any rate, are, on the whole, not the kind of paintings which she bought for her own collection. All but one of the sixty paintings received through her bequest in 1936 are works by 19th- and 20th-century artists, most of whom worked in the tradition which leads by way of Corot (fig. 18) and the Impressionists to the New English Art Club. Her bequest, which included an imposing view of the gardens of the Tuileries by Camille Pissarro and a number of works by contemporary British painters, brought into the collection works of art from the period from the 1890s to the 1930s when French art and the French manner of painting were in high fashion

At this time, the Ashmolean staff were involved in the Oxford Arts Club, founded in 1920 to encourage interest in the arts on the lines of the Burlington Fine Arts Club in London. Under the direction of Sir Michael Sadler, Master of University College, the Oxford club became a centre for promoting interest in contemporary art. Sadler had attended Ruskin's lectures as an undergraduate and he responded to Ruskin's appeal on behalf of modern artists by taking up the cause of contemporary modernists. Works by Picasso and Matisse appeared at the club's exhibitions in 1923, 1924 and 1937. Exhibitions of van Gogh and Cézanne were held in 1924 and 1934 and works by Calder, Gabo, Mondrian and Kandinsky were exhibited in 1938. These exhibitions left little mark on the Ashmolean until 1939 when the picture dealer, Percy Moore Turner, allocated a major part of Frank Hindley Smith's collection of contemporary art to the Ashmolean. Turner had been Hindley Smith's chief adviser and supplier and was appointed his executor when he left his collection to be divided between a number of museums. Turner had also been involved for many years with the work of the Oxford Arts Club and became a long-standing friend and benefactor of the Ashmolean.

Hindley Smith's taste, formed chiefly, it seems, through his friendship with Turner, were less

opposite: Fig. 19 Claude Gellée (Le Lorrain) *Landscape with a Goatherd* (detail)

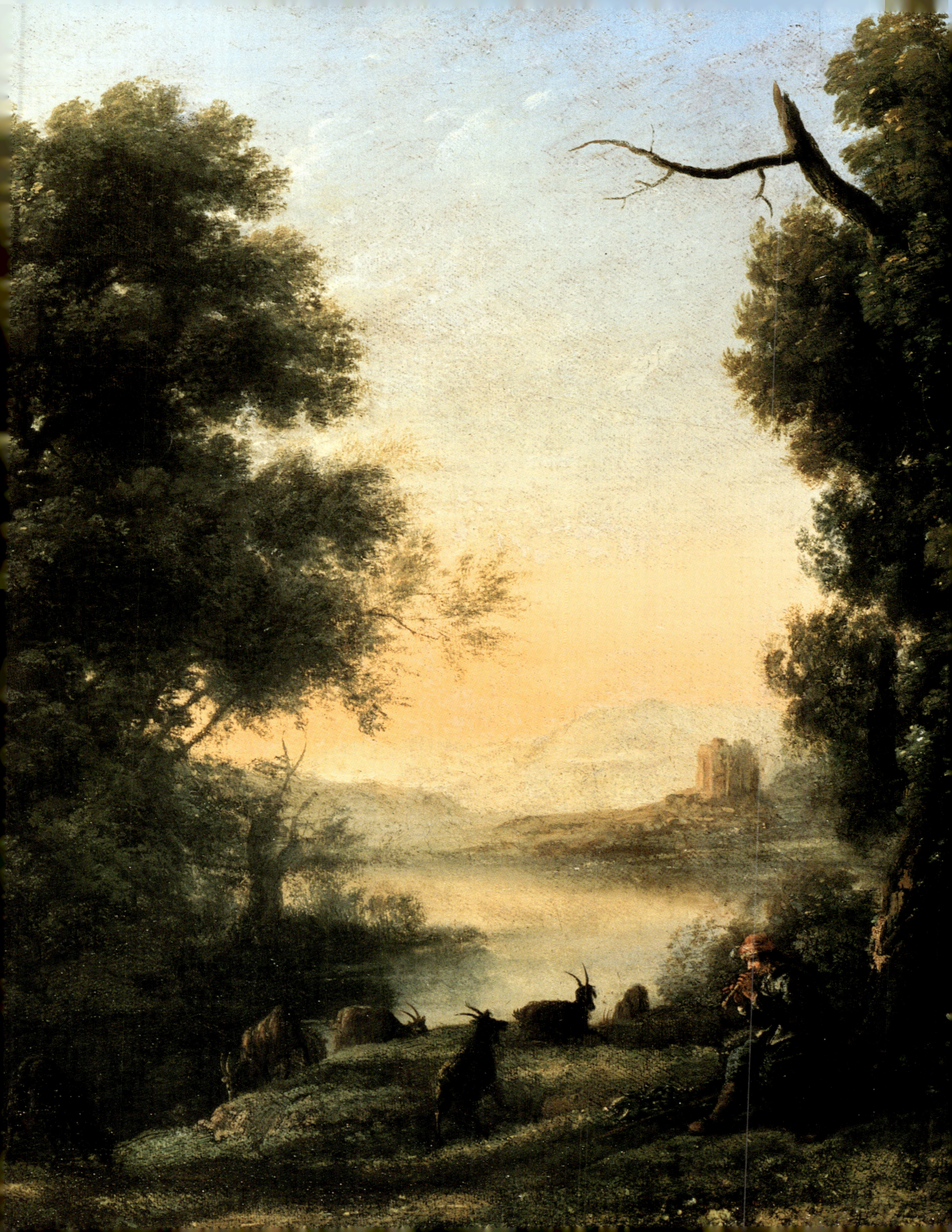

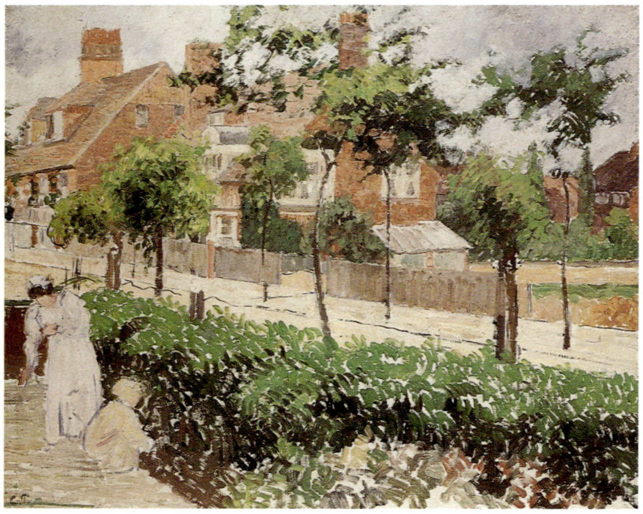

Fig. 20 Camille Pissarro *Bath Road, London*

adventurous than Sadler's. It began with Corot and although it included works by the milder followers of Cézanne (who were particularly promoted by Turner) as well as works by members of the Bloomsbury group, it did not extend as far as Cubism or Surrealism (his one Picasso is a work of the Blue Period). This was, nevertheless, the most important collection of contemporary painting ever given to the Ashmolean and for many years, it largely marked the limits of the 20th century in the museum. Other important gifts of 20th-century British art – works by Robert Bevan and the Camden Town School, given by Bevan's son in 1957, and works by Mark Gertler, Charles Ginner, Stanley Spencer and others, given by the writer and collector, Thomas Balston in 1959 – complemented Hindley Smith's bequest. Benefactors did not think of the Ashmolean as a museum of modern art in its more extreme forms: nor, probably, did Bell and the curators who succeeded him. When Sadler and P.M. Turner donated works of art from their own collections, they confined their gifts mainly to artists of the past. The only painting by a living artist donated by Sadler, Wilson Steer's fine *View of Richmond*, given in memory of his wife in 1931, was a safe choice. Francis Falconer Madan, who took up Mrs Weldon's role in the museum by making annual gifts of prints, drawings, paintings and purchase funds – including a small, beautiful landscape by Claude (fig. 19) – bought nothing by an artist of the 20th century.

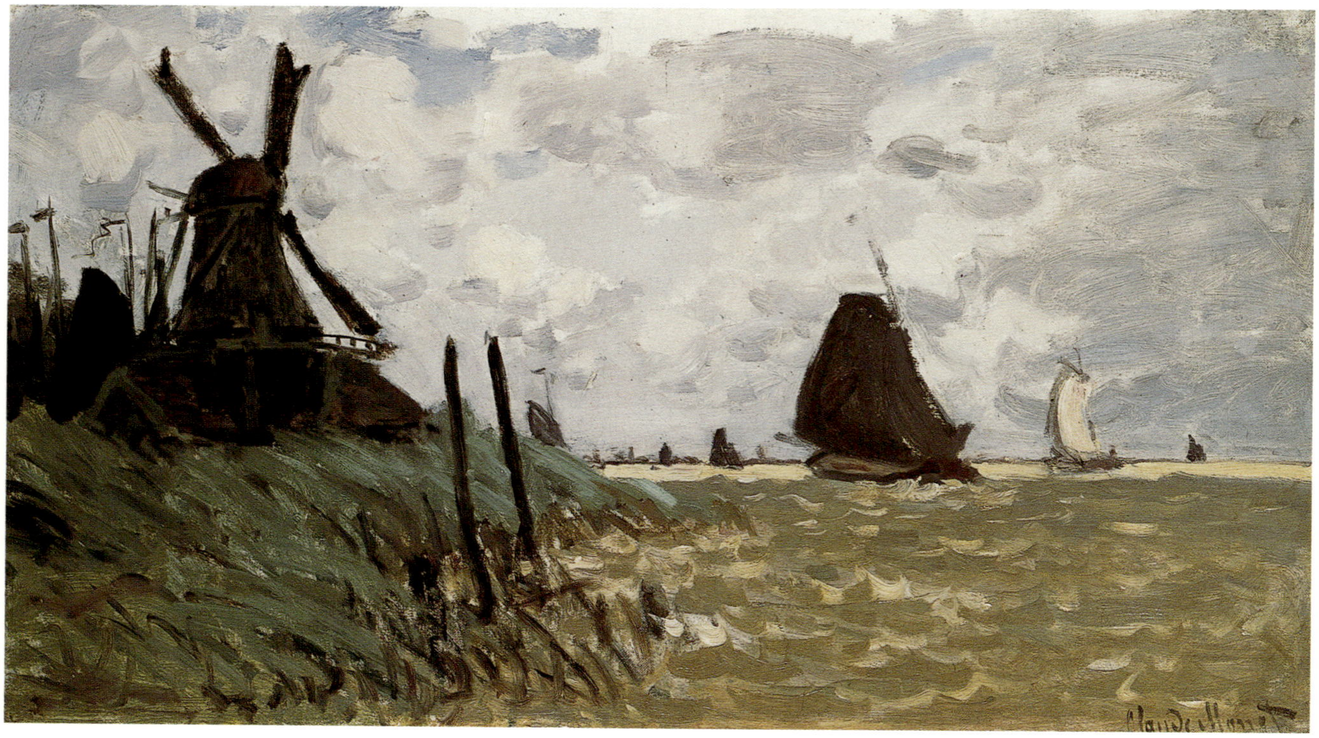

Fig. 21 Claude Monet *A Mill near Zaandam*

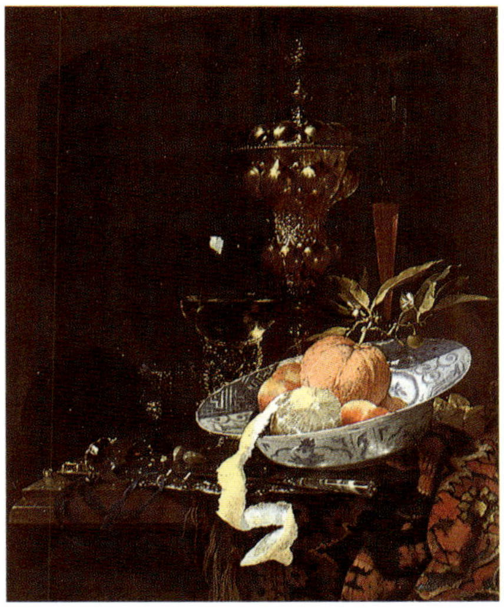

Fig. 22 WILLEM KALF *Still life with an Oriental Rug*

The handful of works by the Impressionists in the Weldon and Hindley Smith bequests did not make the Ashmolean a place of importance for the study of Impressionism. This changed radically in 1950 when the Keeper, K.T. Parker, agreed to accept a gift of paintings, drawings, prints, books and archives from the studio of Lucien Pissarro, much of which had been inherited from Lucien's father, Camille Pissarro, in 1903. Lucien had settled in England in 1883 and died in London in 1944. It was his widow's wish that the collection should be taken as whole and should be maintained for the purpose of commemorating the Pissarro family. In addition to eleven paintings by Camille (fig. 20), the gift included many paintings by his sons, Félix, Lucien and Ludovico-Rodolphe, as well as works by Lucien's daughter, Orovida. The size and scope of the collection would have created difficulties for most museums at this time, but Parker had recently taken possession of a substantial Print Room, added to the museum along Beaumont Street after the Keeper's house had been demolished in 1939, and this enabled him to accept the books, archives and works on paper. Part of the collection arrived in 1950 and transfers to the museum continued until 1952; important additions were made by Orovida in 1968 and the collection has steadily increased through gifts from other members of the family – the most recent in 2003 – in keeping with Esther Pissarro's wish that it should become a centre for the study of the work of Camille and his descendants.

The collection of Impressionists, by now somewhat unbalanced in favour of Pissarro, was enhanced in 1980 by the bequest of a collection of paintings and watercolours from Sophie and Richard Walzer which included fine works by Monet (fig. 21), Manet and Cézanne. These had been brought to England from Germany in 1933 by Mrs Walzer's father, Bruno Cassirer, whose brother, Paul, owned an important art firm in Berlin. The museum's single work by van Gogh, bequeathed by Dr Erich Alport in 1972, was also brought out of Germany in the 1930s when Dr Alport and his family settled in England. Similarly, Dr Grete Ring who had worked at one time at Paul Cassirer's gallery in Berlin, brought her collection of German Romantic and French Impressionist drawings to London in 1938 and these too came to the Ashmolean in 1954 in the form of a bequest. In this way, the taste for French Impressionist art in Germany in the 1920s and 1930s, which was then more deeply rooted than it was in England, brought a number of significant works to the Ashmolean by way of the refugees who arrived here in the 1930s.

As always, these increases brought about a need for new space. In 1957, the Pissarro collection, the Hindley Smith paintings and the Pre-Raphaelites were installed in a sequence of three rooms built onto the west end of the Weldon Gallery. By the late 1980s, however, the 20th-century British pictures, in particular, had been squeezed out by the additions. The offer of an important collection of ten works by Walter Sickert, which had once belonged to Sickert's friends, Ethel and Morton Sands, provided the impetus to add one final room in this corner of the site, filling the space on the first floor between the museum and the new Sackler Library. The Sands Gallery, completed in 2000 with a large contribution

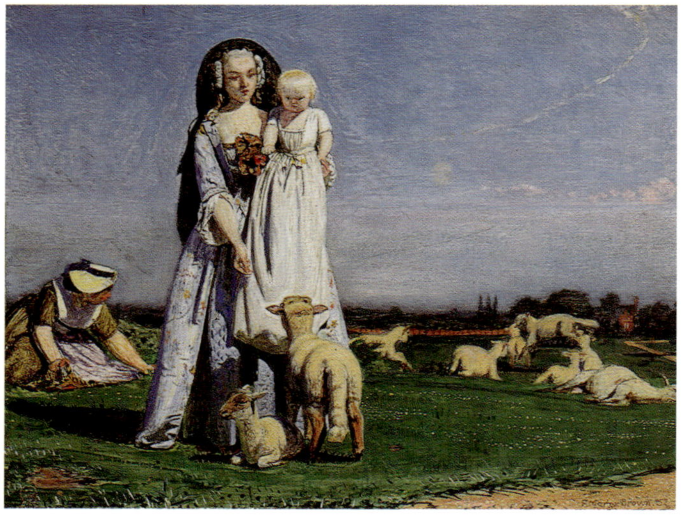

Fig. 23 Ford Madox Brown *The pretty Baa-Lambs*

from the Heritage Lottery Fund, now provides space for the British 20th-century collection, beginning with a group of works by Sickert, painted across a period of twenty years, and ending with a number of works by contemporary artists, given mostly through the National Art Collections Fund by an anonymous benefactor.

The Sands Gallery was not the first occasion when a promised gift has been linked to the construction of a gallery. In 1939, Theodore Ward agreed to donate his collection of Dutch and Flemish still-life paintings to the museum only after the museum had given an undertaking to vacate and convert the rooms formerly occupied by the Hope Library (fig. 22). The collection was given in memory of the donor's wife, Daisy Linda Ward (*née* Travers), herself a painter who had trained at the Slade School and had some success as an opera singer. Why Ward wished to give the collection to the Ashmolean is not clear. Neither he nor his wife seems to have had a connection with Oxford but it may be that the strict conditions which he attached to the gift might have limited his choice: the collection had to be exhibited in its entirety; it had to be shown in its own gallery; it had to be top lit; it was to be known as the Daisy Linda Ward Bequest (although, strictly speaking, it was a gift) and within a reasonable time, the museum had to provide a scholarly catalogue for sale to the public. As a result, the collection has remained intact and on permanent display in a dedicated gallery and two catalogues of the Ward paintings have been published, one in 1950 and another in 2003, by leading scholars of the subject. As Daisy Linda Ward was a painter of still-life – the collection includes two paintings by her – one might assume that she took a hand in forming the collection, but it seems that most of the paintings were bought by Ward himself. He had inherited a successful paint business from his father, Albert Charles Holzapfel (Theodore changed his name to Ward during World War I), and could well afford to purchase fine works by famous artists as well as works of a more scholarly interest.

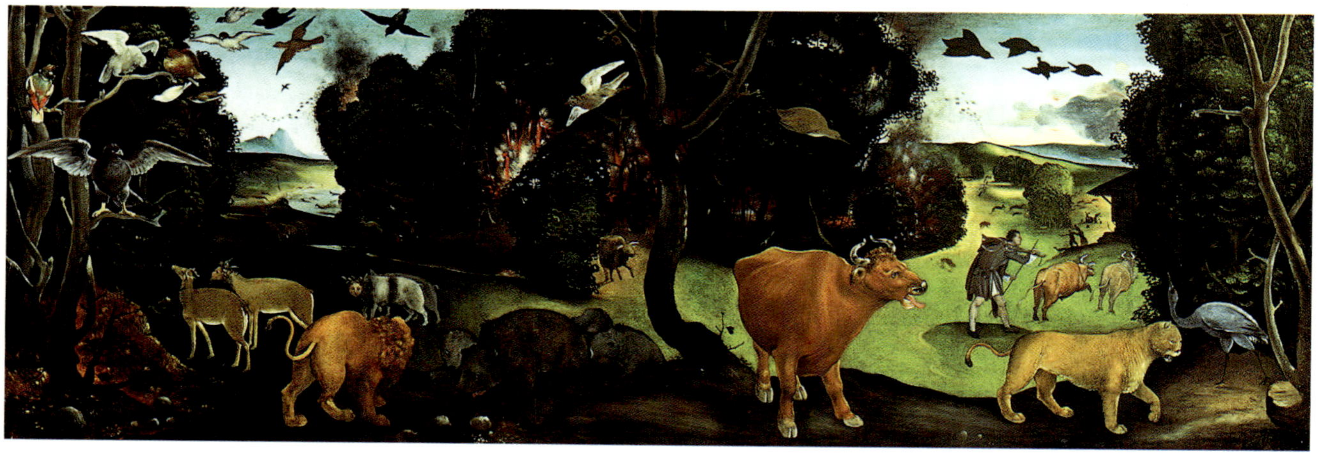

Fig. 24 Piero di Cosimo *The Forest Fire*

opposite: Fig. 25 Giovanni Battista Tiepolo *A Young Woman with a Macaw*

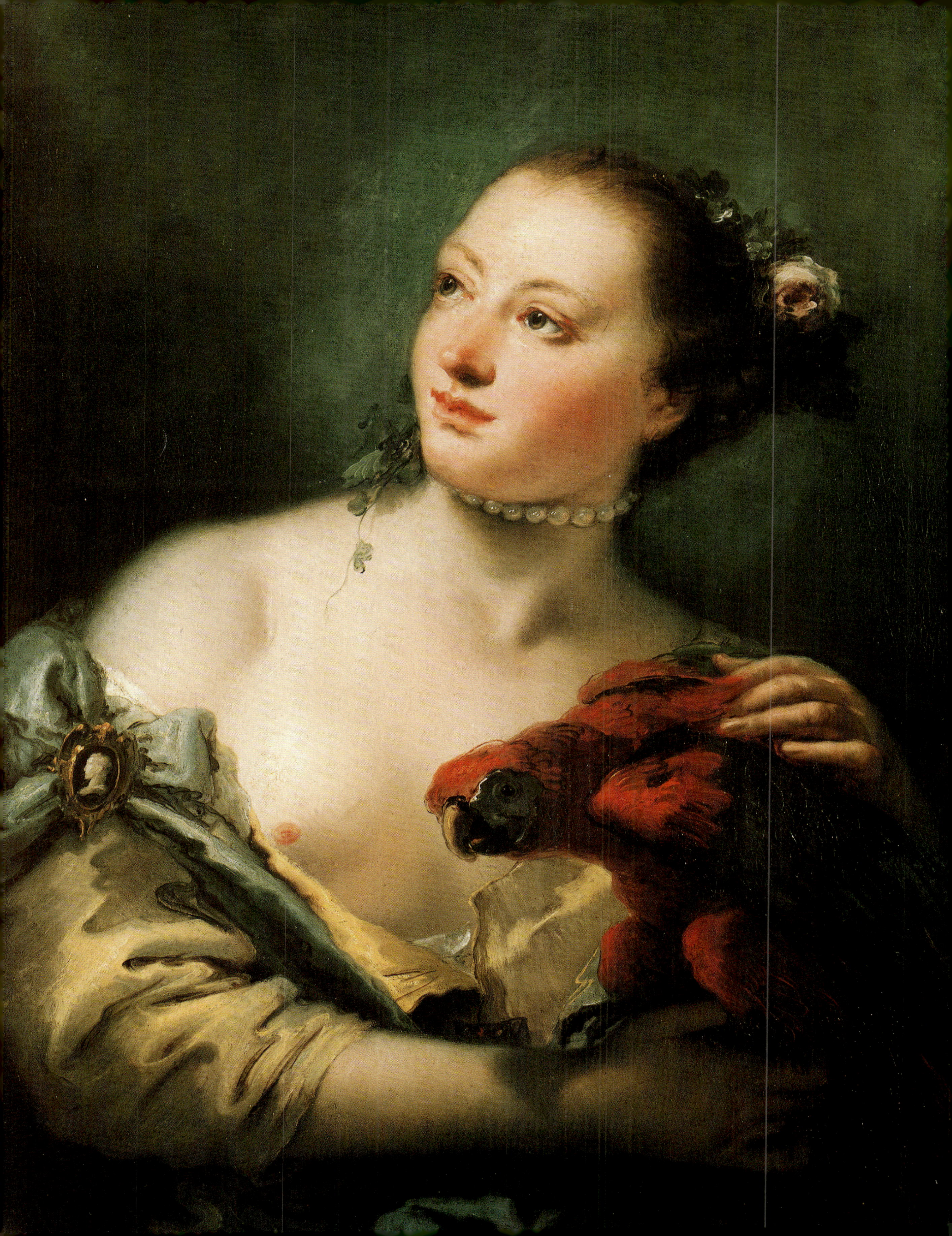

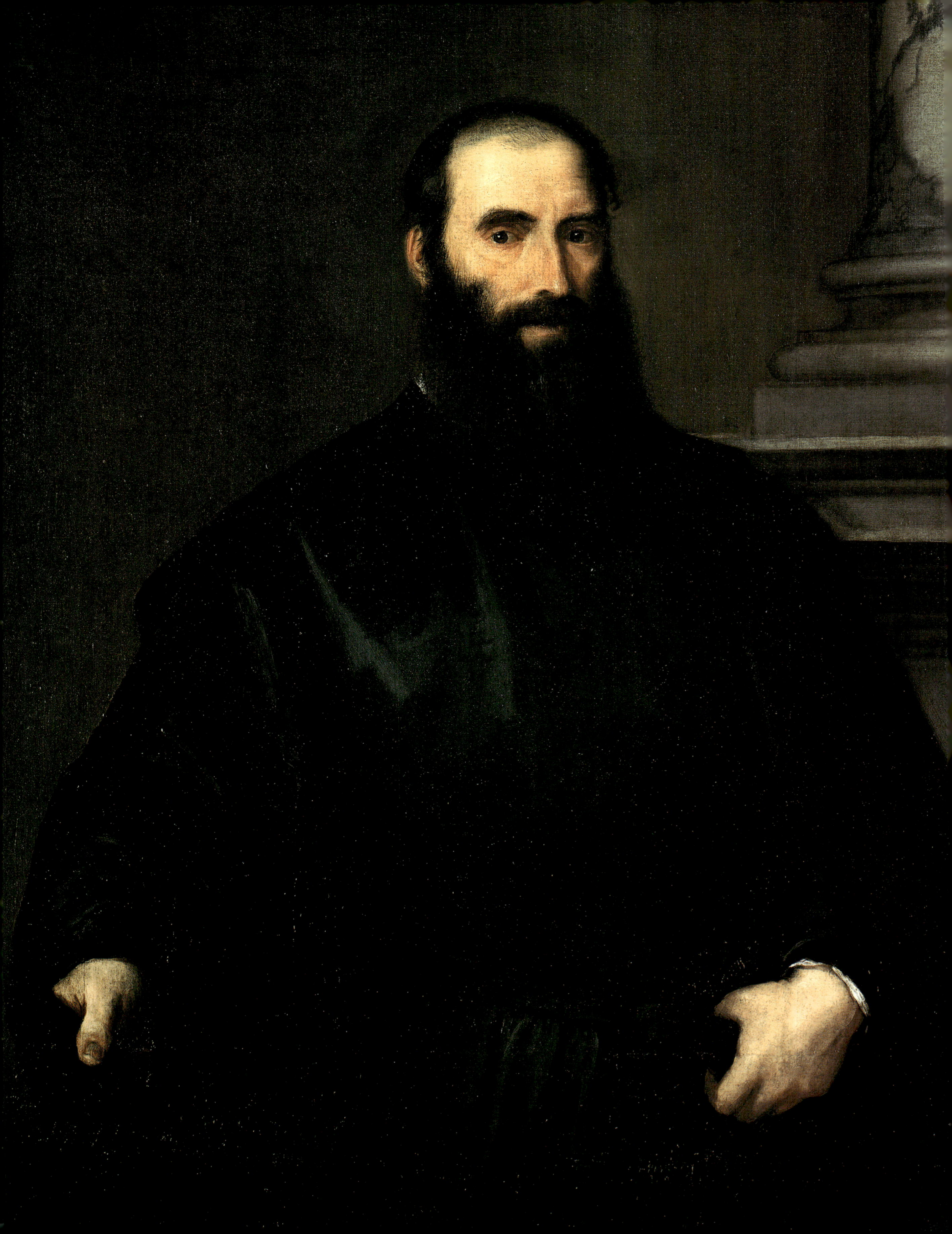

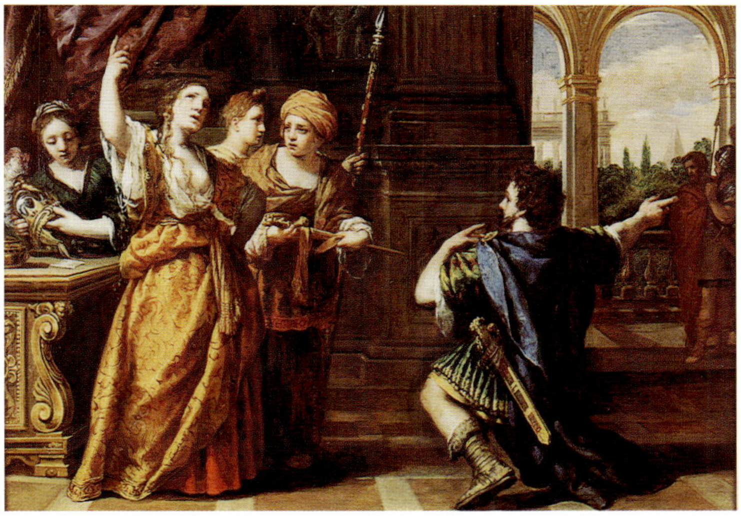

Fig. 26 Pietro da Cortona *The Oath of Semiramis*

It was never easy for the keepers to purchase paintings for the collection. Funds were very limited, particularly in the early days, although Bell persuaded Magdalen College to make a small annual grant with which he made a handful of acquisitions. The most interesting work acquired from the Magdalen Fund, Ford Madox Brown's study in sunlight, *Pretty Baa Lambs* (fig. 23), was bought in 1909. In 1932, Bell's successor, Kenneth Clark, persuaded the National Art Collections Fund to purchase Samuel Palmer's *Rest on the Flight* for £300 and present it to the museum. He followed this sensationally in 1933 when he acquired Piero di Cosimo's *Forest Fire* (fig. 24) which the Fund had bought from Prince Paul of Yugoslavia on behalf of the museum for £3,000. These were not the first gifts made by the Fund to the Ashmolean: in 1917, it purchased a statue from the Deepdene sale for the museum and in 1919 donated three watercolours by William Blake from a group bought by the Fund from the family of John Linnell.

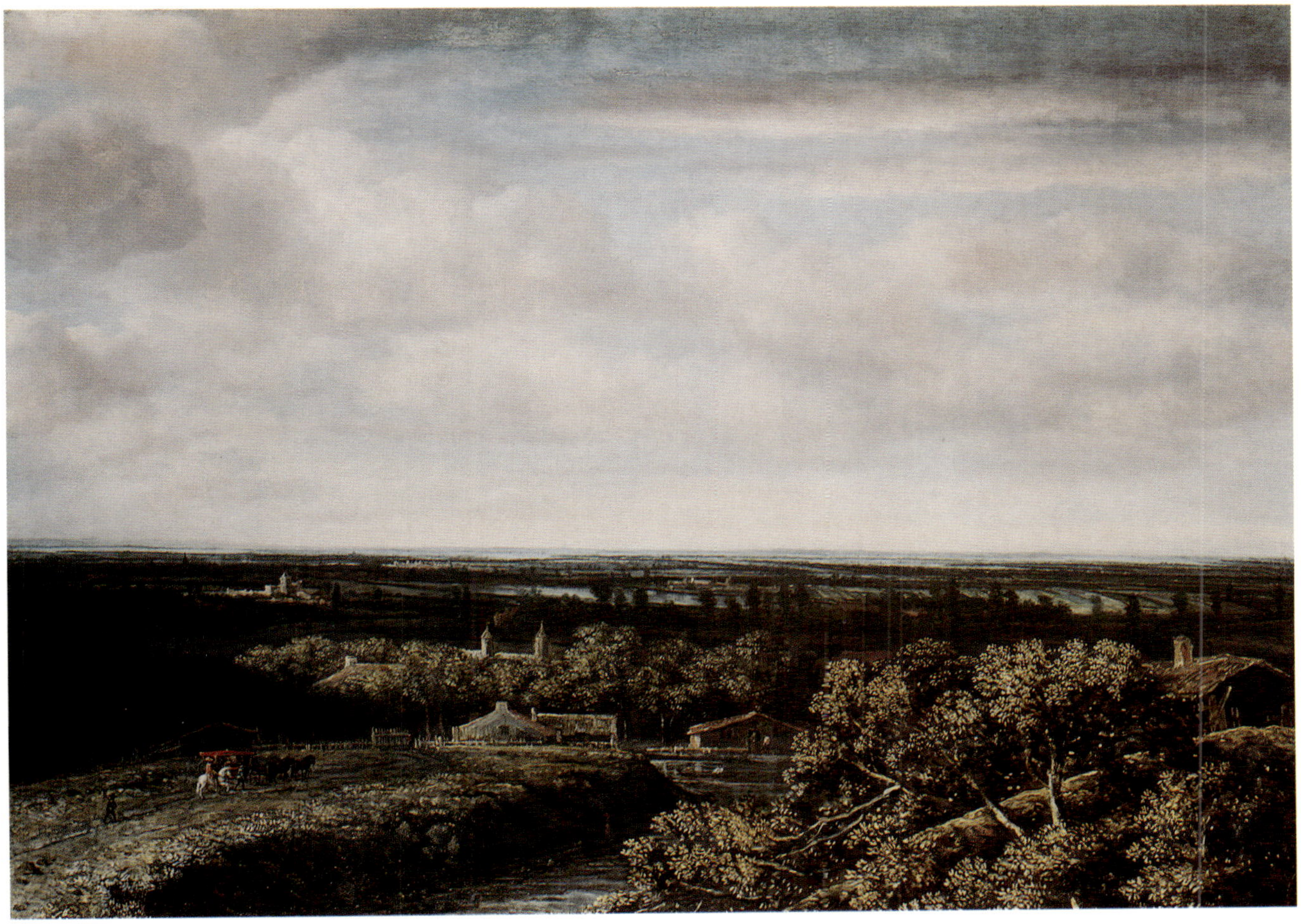

Fig. 27 Philips Koninck *A View over Flat Country*

opposite: Fig. 28 Tiziano Vecellio, called Titian *Portrait of Giacomo Doria*

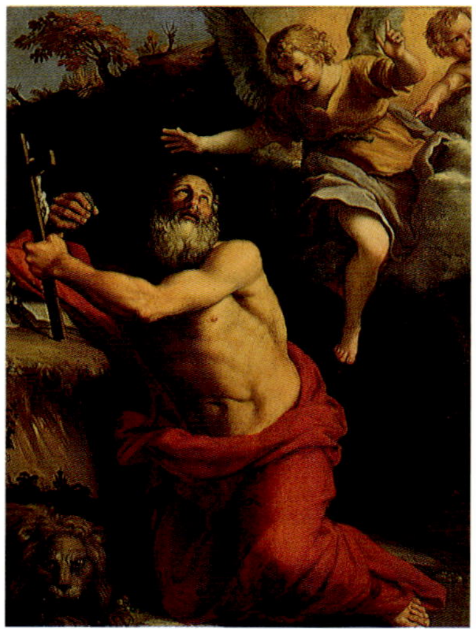

Fig. 29 Domenico Zampieri, called Domenichino *The Vision of St Jerome*

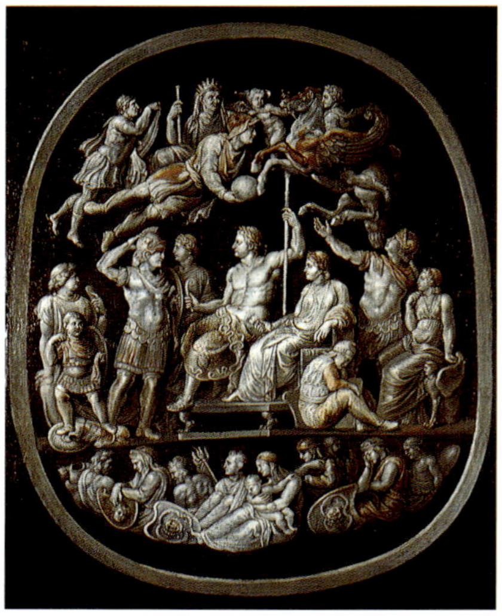

Fig. 30 Sir Peter Paul Rubens *The 'Apotheosis of Germanicus'*: copy after an Antique Cameo *(The 'Gemma Tiberiana')*

The Palmer and the Piero di Cosimo were the first of many paintings which entered the Ashmolean with the help of the National Art Collections Fund. In 1934, the Fund presented a dramatic still-life by Ruoppolo; in 1936, a little roundel of the *Destruction of Sodom and Gomorrah* by a follower of Patenir; in 1942, a beautiful *Madonna and Child* attributed to Vanni; in 1951, a portrait by Cristofano Allori; in 1955, four exceptional paintings – Gainsborough's portrait of George Drummond, a landscape by Ruisdael, Boonen's portrait of van Huysum and Tiepolo's *Woman with a Macaw* (fig. 25) – were allocated from the collection of E.E. Cook. In recent years, the Fund has more often contributed a large part of the cost of purchase which the museum has made up from trust funds as well as from sums donated by the Friends of the Ashmolean and grants from various public bodies, including the Lottery, which have become available in recent decades. The list of purchases made with the help of the Fund is too long to list here in its

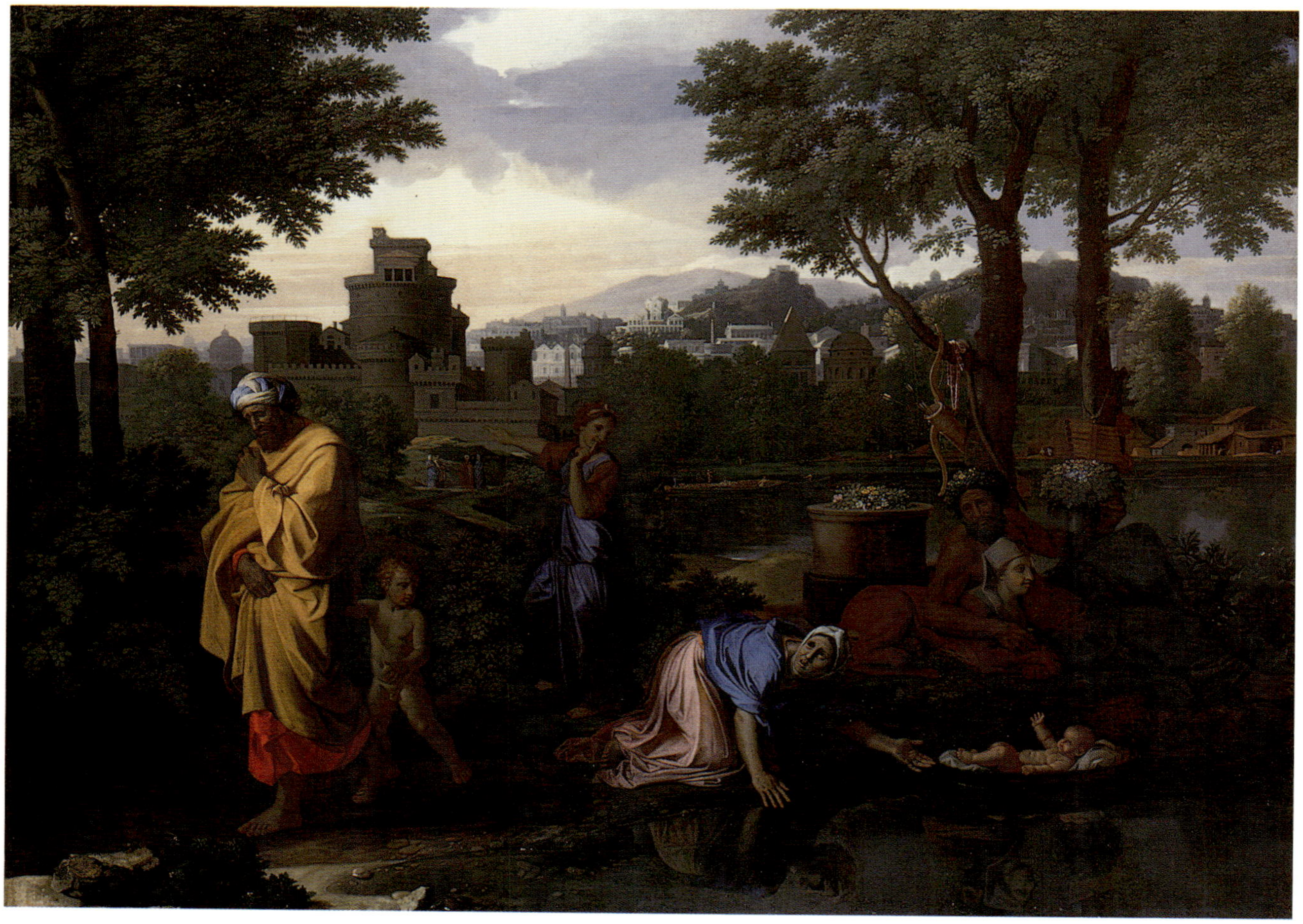

Fig. 31 Nicolas Poussin *The Exposition of Moses*

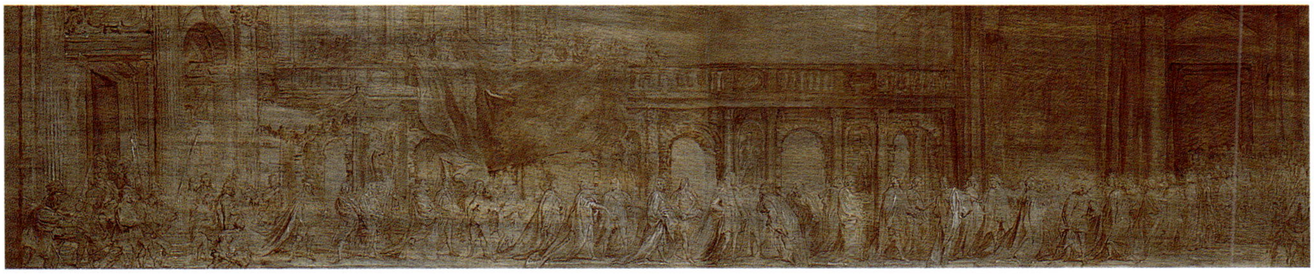

Fig. 32 Sir Anthony van Dyck *Charles I and the Knights of the Garter in procession*

entirety but it includes a memorable, now unattributed *Allegory of Vanity* (bought in 1939), Poussin's *Exposition of Moses* (fig. 31) (bought on generous terms in 1950), Luca Giordano's *Raising of the Cross* (bought in 1970), Mengs's portrait of *William Fermor* (bought in 1978), Paolo de' Matteis's *Choice of Hercules* (bought in 1980), Allessandro Allori's *Portrait of a young Man* (bought in 1983), Giambono's *Bishop Saint* (bought in 1985), Lucian Freud's *Small naked Portrait* (bought in 1989), Titian's portrait of *Giacomo Doria* (fig. 28) (bought in 2000 in memory of Professor Francis Haskell with a large contribution from the Heritage Lottery Fund) and many others.

Many paintings, drawings and artefacts have also been donated to the museum through the National Art Collections Fund by benefactors who support its work. Gaspard O. Farrer's bequest, which included major paintings by Koninck (fig. 27), Licinio, Montagna and Tintoretto, came to the museum in 1946 by this route. Mattia Preti's *Game of Draughts* was presented in 1978 through the Fund by a body of subscribers in memory of Benedict Nicolson. Thomas Balston bequeathed his collection of works by Gertler and his contemporaries through the Fund in 1959. In 1999, through a variant of this process, the museum received an important group of 17th-century paintings by Guercino, Pietro da Cortona (fig. 26), Paul Bril, Domenichino (fig. 29), Cerquozzi, Giuseppe Maria Crespi, Pierre Patel I, Romanelli, Lo Scarsellino, Gaspard Dughet and Bernardo Strozzi from the collection of Sir Denis Mahon which Sir Denis intends to leave on permanent loan to the museum via the Fund. Sir Denis's interest in the Carracci and their followers was initially directed by Kenneth Clark when Clark was at the Ashmolean and Sir Denis was at Christ Church. This was a pioneering interest at a time when the contempt which Ruskin and his contemporaries felt towards the Bolognese School was still commonplace.

Other major acquisitions have been made across the years by means of a concession which allows benefactors to discount all or part of the value of a gift against inheritance tax. By this means, Rubens's famous painting of the *Gemma Tiberiana* (fig. 30) was acquired in 1990 from the estate of Christopher Norris and a little *Madonna and Child* attributed to Giovanni Bellini came to the museum in 1992 from the estate of Kenneth Clark. The Impressionist paintings from the estate of Mr and Mrs Walzer were entirely discounted under the same arrangement. So was van Dyck's important sketch showing a procession of the Order of the Garter, which was once in the collection of Charles I and which was allocated to the Ashmolean in 2002 (fig. 32). Tax concessions, along with grants from the National Art Collections Fund, Resource (the government body with responsibility for libraries and museums), the Heritage Lottery Fund and other sources, have enabled the museum to acquire works of art which it could not have purchased otherwise. Despite financial difficulties and prices which would have astonished our predecessors, it is now possible to acquire works of art of the highest importance which would have been beyond the reach of former keepers even at prices which, in retrospect, seem very modest.

ACKNOWLEDGEMENTS

In addition to those thanked in the Director's preface, the compilers of the catalogue would like to acknowledge with gratitude the assistance of the following:

Mercedes Agueda Villar, Brian Allen, Sivigliano Alloisi, Babette Ball, Davide Banzati, William Barcham, Juliet Bareau, Liliana Barroero, Patricia Bascom, Paola Pacht Bassani, Charles Beddington, Daniele Benati, Sergio Benedetti, Giuseppe Bertini, Anne Bertrand, Donatella Biagi Maino, Rachel Billinge, Bonnie J. Blackburn, Linda Borean, Barbara Brejon, Julian Brooks, Christopher Brown, Duncan Bull, Vittorio Casali, Ian Charlton, Marco Chiarini, Keith Christiansen, Irene Cioffi, Julie Clements, Ximo Company, Richard Cocke, David Connell, Emmanuel Coquery, Philip Cottrell, Ladislav Daniel, Matías Díaz Padrón, Fernando Benito Doménech, Elizabeth Einberg, Regina Erbentraut, Everett Fahy, Marzia Faietti, Gabriele Finaldi, Jennifer Fletcher, Fausta Franchini Guelfi, Klara Gáras, Christa Gardner von Teuffel, Kenneth Garlick, Nigel Glendinning, Dillian Gordon, Mina Gregori, Enriqueta Harris, Charles Hope, Peter Humfrey, John Ingamells, Ronda Kasl, Laurence Kanter, Alan Kitchen and the workshop, George Knox, Bozena Anna Kowalczyk, Alastair Laing, Simon Lee, Rees Lloyd-Jones, Stéphane Loire, Christopher Lloyd, Denis Mahon, Sergio Marinelli, Giorgio Marini, Adriano Mariuz, David Marshall, Isabel Mateo Gómez, Elizabeth McGrath, Manuela Mena Márquez, Sue Moss, Mary Newcome Schleier, Alexander Newson, Edward J. Olszewski, Giuseppe Pavanello, Nicholas Penny, D. Stephen Pepper, Alfonso E. Perez Sánchez, Giuliana Pieri, Catherine Puglisi, W. Roger Rearick, Pierre Rosenberg, Anthony Rowland-Jones, Stella Rudolph, Dietulf Sander, Erich Schleier, Verity Shaw, Jeffrey Spier, John Spike, Claudio Strinati, Ann Sutherland Harris, Nicola Spinosa, Robert Upstone, Marc Rudolf de Vrij, Malcolm Warner, Aidan Weston-Lewis, Clovis Whitfield, Martin Wyld.

ABBREVIATED BENEFACTIONS

Bywater Bequest, 1915	Professor Ingram Bywater (1840–1914)
Combe Bequest, 1893	Thomas Combe (1797–1872)
Fortnum Bequest, 1899	Charles Drury Edward Fortnum (1820–1899)
Fox-Strangways Gift, 1850	William Thomas Horner Fox-Strangways, later 4th Earl of Ilchester (1795–1865)
Chambers Hall Gift, 1855	Chambers Hall (1786–1855)
Hindley Smith Bequest, 1939	Frank Hindley Smith (d. 1939)
Madan Bequest, 1962	Francis Falconer Madan (1886–1961)
Mahon Loan, 1999	Lent by Sir Denis Mahon, C.H., C.B.E., F.B.A., through the National Art Collections Fund
Pierrepont Barnard Bequest, 1931	Professor Francis Pierrepont Barnard (1854–1931)
Russell Bequest, 1958	Archibald G.B. Russell, C.V.O. (1879–1955)
Daisy Linda Ward Bequest, 1939	Daisy Linda Ward (1883–1937)
Weldon Bequest, 1937	Mrs W.F.R. Weldon (d. 1936)

ORGANIZATION OF CATALOGUE

This catalogue includes details of all paintings in the Department of Western Art in the Ashmolean Museum, acquired before July 2003, along with a number of paintings, similar in type, which are kept in other Departments. It includes icons, which have been separately listed, but excludes miniatures, drawings and watercolours, and painted furniture. It also includes a handful of works which have been recorded as missing or stolen. Works are listed alphabetically under the name of the artist. Where more than one painting is listed under the name of an artist, those which are firmly attributed are arranged, as far as possible, in chronological order, followed by doubtful attributions, works in the style of the artist and copies. Anonymous works are listed in the alphabetical sequence under their national school, or, in the case of some early Italian paintings, under their regional school. Literary references are limited to a small number of major sources, including previous museum catalogues to which the reader is referred for more detailed information. The provenance notes on each painting summarize the known history of ownership but exclude auction sales. All measurements are given in centimetres, height before width.

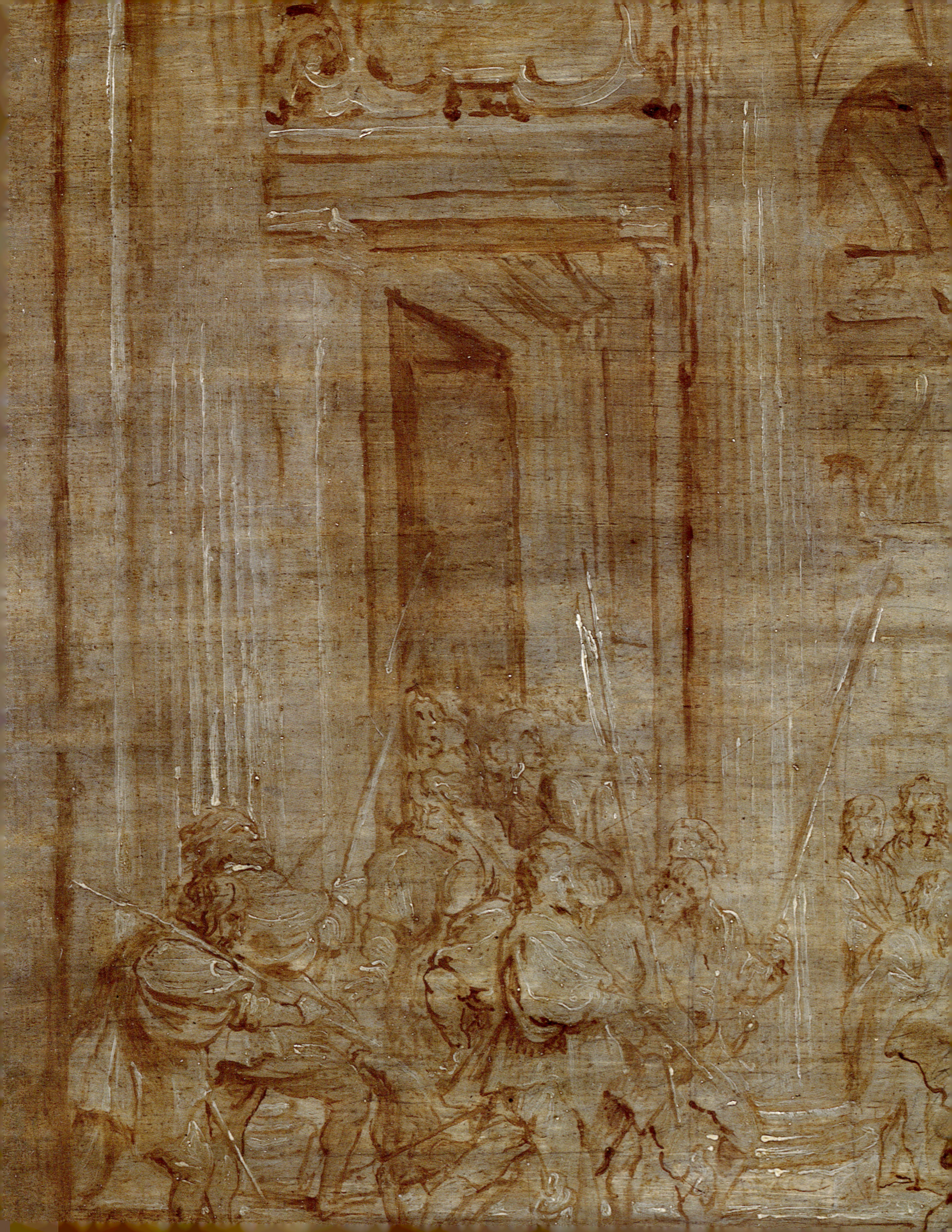

COMPLETE ILLUSTRATED CATALOGUE OF PAINTINGS

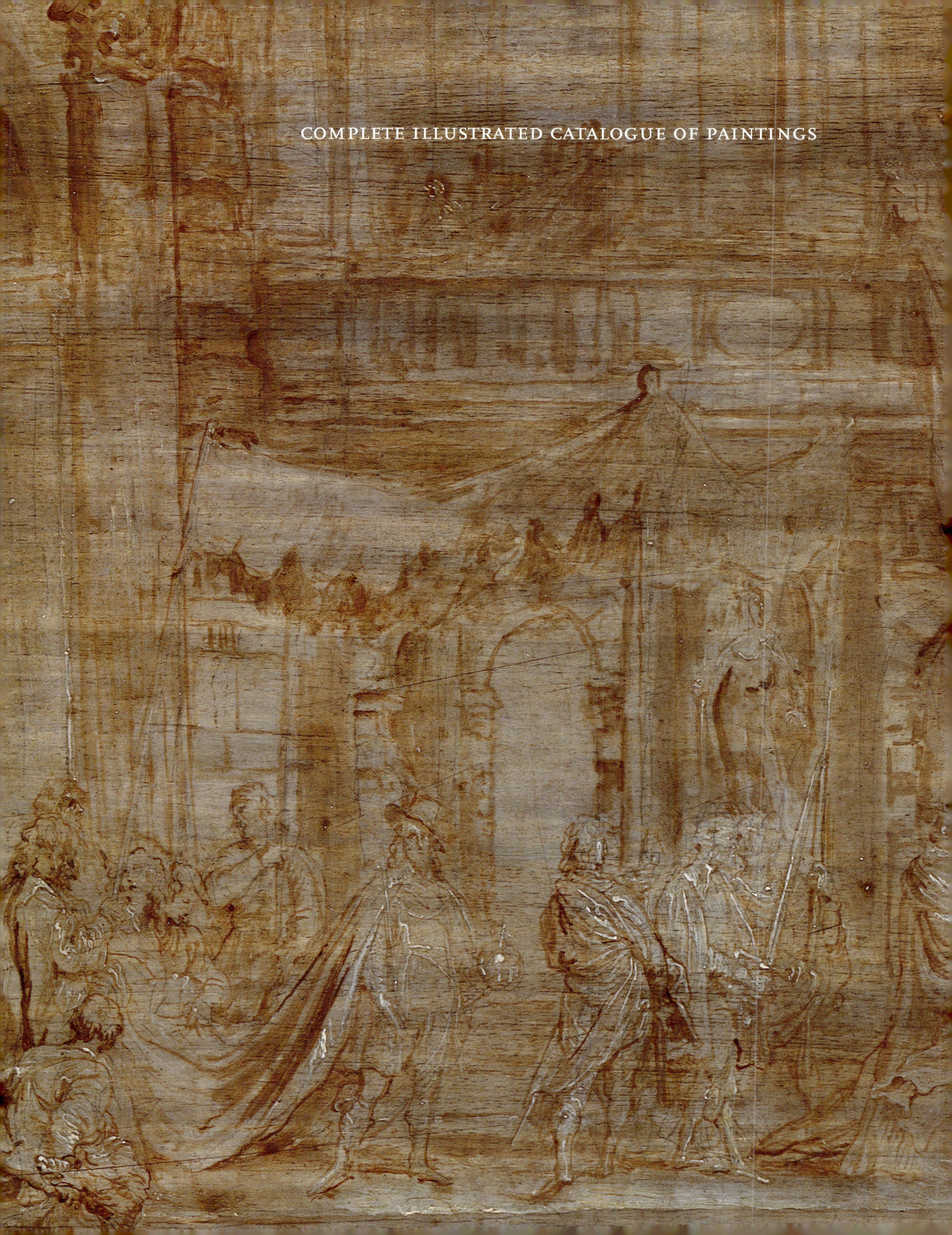

John White Abbott
(1764 – 1851)

Landscape: Houses at the Edge of a Wood

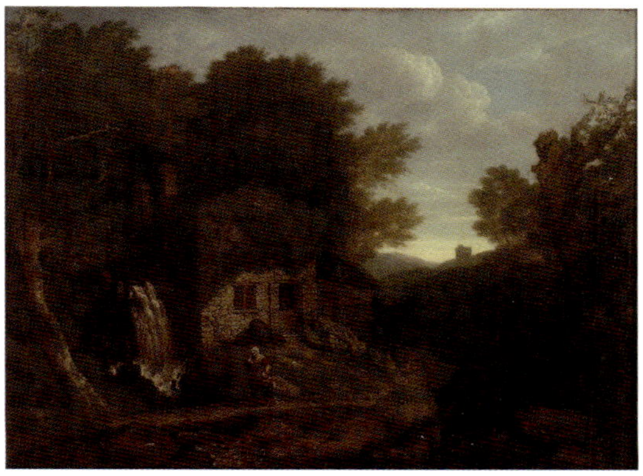

A522a; oil on canvas, 61 × 81 cm
Signed in monogram and dated: *1835*
Presented by the Executors of Miss Mabel Price in accordance with her wishes, 1939; WA1939.18.1

Abbott was the most distinctive follower of Francis Towne and like him, exhibited mostly watercolours. Apart from a few views of his native Exeter, his oil paintings are rarely of identified sites and most include picturesque cottages and staffage.

Willem van Aelst
(1627 – in or after 1683)

Still Life of Fruit

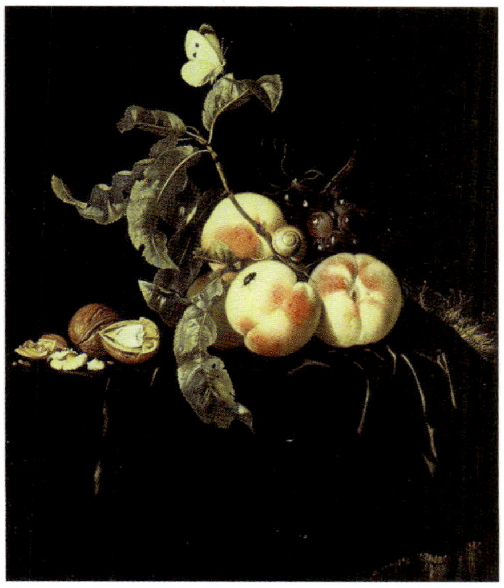

A528; oil on canvas, 47 × 39 cm
Prov.: Dr Seligmann
Daisy Linda Ward Bequest, 1939; WA1940.2.4

Meijer 2003, no. 2

The existence of a copy of this painting (last recorded in a sale in Cologne in 1933) with wider margins, particularly along the upper edge, suggests that the Oxford painting has been cut down on all sides. It probably dates from a time close to a very similar painting of peaches in Budapest dated 1667. Velvet cloths, similarly painted, are found in paintings by van Aelst dating from between 1667 and 1674.

Copy after Willem van Aelst
(1627 – in or after 1683)

A Vase of Flowers with a Watch

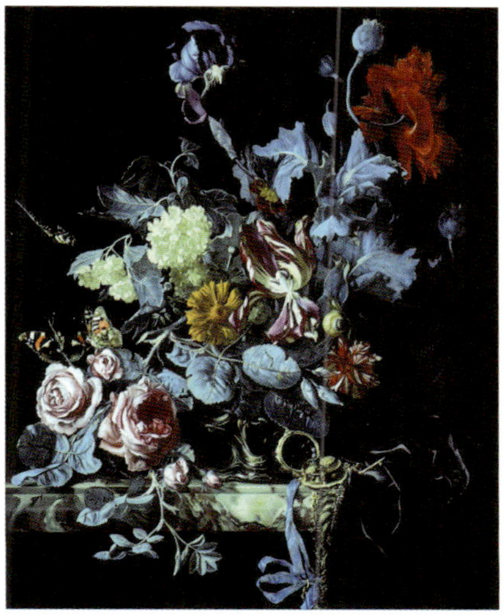

A527; oil on canvas, 66 × 53 cm
Prov.: (?)Pieter Locquet
Daisy Linda Ward Bequest, 1939; WA1940.2.3

Meijer 2003, no. 4

Comparison with a nearly identical version of this composition in the Fine Art Museums of San Francisco suggests that A527 is a very careful copy, probably by a close follower of the artist, possibly painted in his studio. Hendrick de Fromantiou and Nicolaes Lachtropius have both been proposed as the copyist.

Willem van Aelst
(1627 – in or after 1683)

A Vase of Flowers

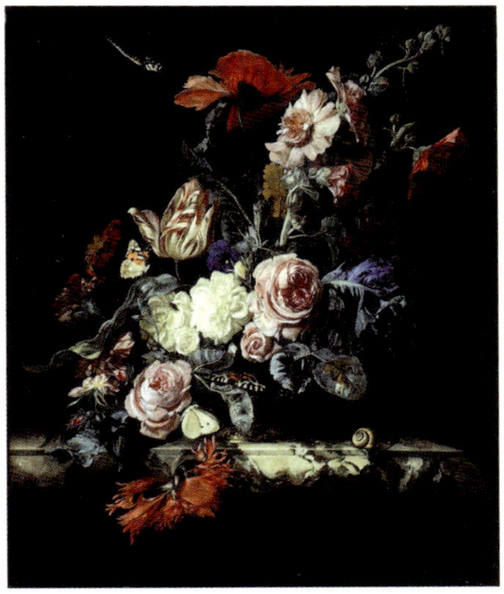

A526; oil on canvas, 67 × 55 cm
Signed: *Guill.mo van Aelst. 1663*
Prov.: (?)Sir John Austen; C.H.T. Hawkins
Daisy Linda Ward Bequest, 1939; WA1940.2.2

Meijer 2003, no. 1

Van Aelst was one of the most successful and influential still-life painters of the 17th century. His flower paintings, composed with a sinuous asymmetry and lavishly detailed, brought a new decorative elegance into Dutch still-life painting. The vase in this painting was one of the artist's favourite accessories, first appearing in a still life in 1649.

Willem van Aelst
(1627 – in or after 1683)

Still Life of Flowers

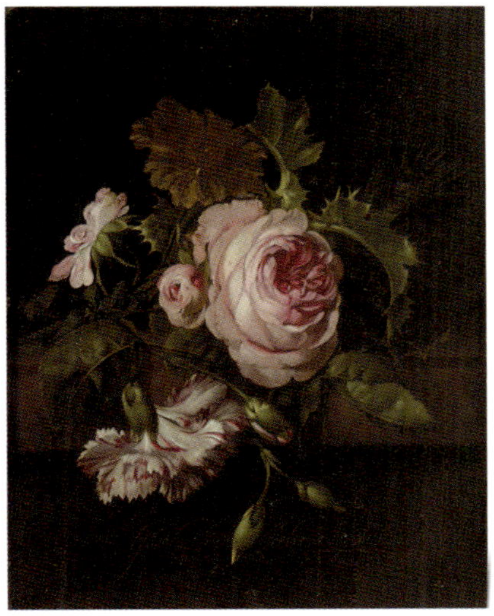

A435; oil on canvas, 32 × 26 cm
Signed and dated: *Guillmo va. Aelst 1677*
Presented by Francis Falconer Madan, 1934; WA1934.11

White 1999, p. 7

There is a similar painting of a bouquet on a marble ledge in the Fitzwilliam Museum, Cambridge, signed and dated 1675. Both are signed with the Italian form of van Aelst's Christian name.

Style of Willem van Aelst
(1627 – in or after 1683)

Still Life with a dead Jay

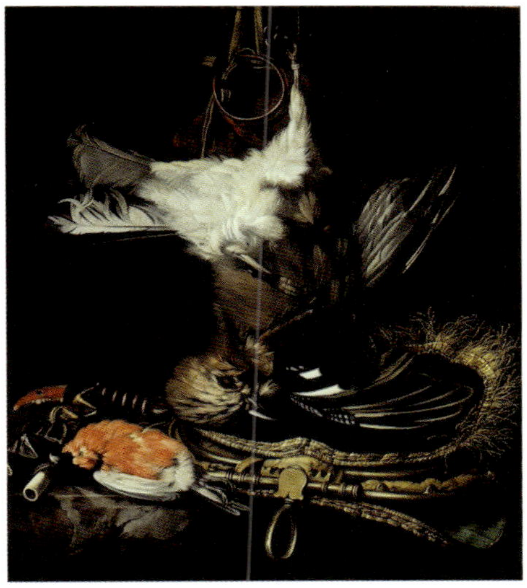

A525; oil on canvas, 43 × 37 cm
Prov.: J. Herbrand, Paris
Daisy Linda Ward Bequest, 1939; WA1940.2.1

Meijer 2003, no. 3

The bird's plumage is not painted as smoothly as one might expect in a work by van Aelst and the composition lacks his habitual elegance. It has been attributed to one of his followers, several of whom were capable of imitating his art closely. Isaac Derues (1647–1690) has been suggested as a possible candidate.

Agnolo di Domenico di Donnino
(1466 – *c.* 1513)

Sts Bartholomew and Julian the Hospitaler

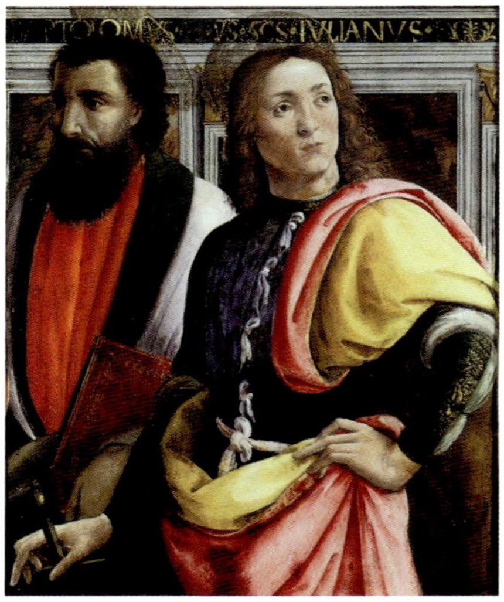

A99; tempera (and oil?) and gold on panel, 77.9 × 64 cm
Inscribed: *BARTOLOMUS.APLUS.SCS.JULIANUS*
Fox-Strangways Gift, 1850; WA1850.14

Lloyd 1977, pp. 112–3; Fahy 1993

A99 belongs to a lost altar-piece of which two other fragments are known showing *The Virgin and Child* and *Sts Leonard and James the Great*. The apostle Bartholomew is usually depicted with a knife, the instrument of his martyrdom. St Julian, a nobleman who accidentally murdered his parents, founded a hospice for travellers in atonement. The artist formerly known as the Master of Santo Spirito has been plausibly identified as Agnolo di Domenico.

Charles Alexander
(exhibited 1893 – 94)

C. Drury E. Fortnum, Esq., D.C.L.

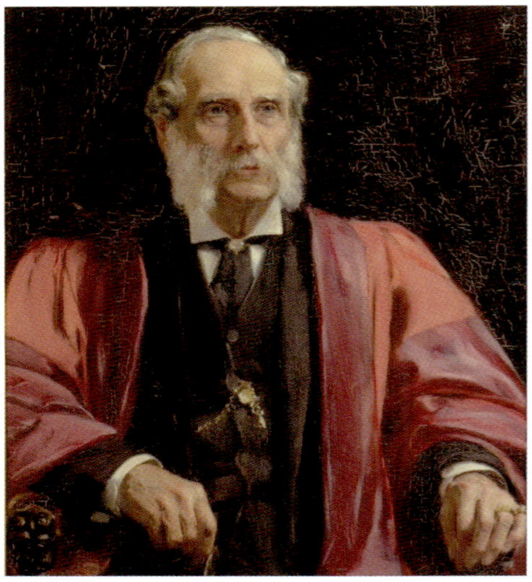

A299b; oil on canvas, 74 × 66 cm
Signed and dated: *CHARLES ALEXANDER 1893*
Fortnum Bequest, 1899; WA1899.4

Poole 1912, no. 497

Charles Drury Edward Fortnum (1820–1899) was one of the most generous benefactors to the Ashmolean Museum. This portrait of him was exhibited at the Royal Academy in 1893. It shows him wearing the gown of a Doctor of Civil Law at Oxford, a degree he was awarded in 1889.

William T. Howell Allchin
(1844 – 1883)

Still Life with an open Book and Spectacles

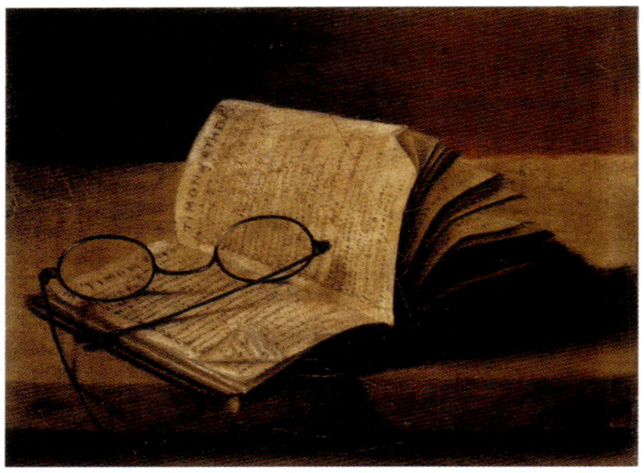

Oil on canvas, mounted as a drawing, 14.9 × 20 cm
Signed with monogram
Presented by the artist's daughter, 1966; WA1966.20.2

Allchin was organist of St John's College, Oxford, between 1876 and his death.

Joseph van Aken
(*c.* 1699 – 1749)

Saying Grace

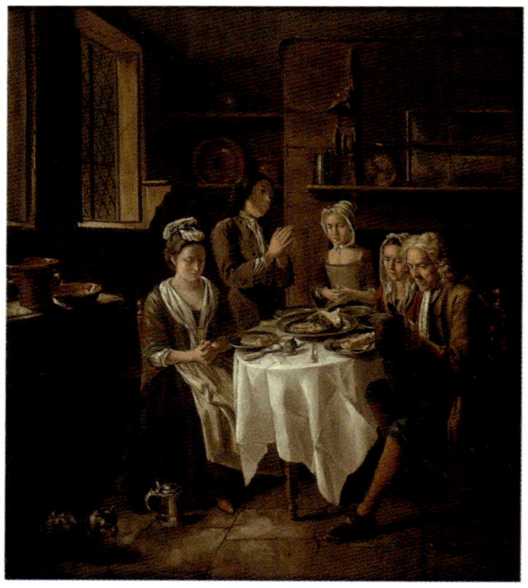

A962; oil on canvas, 35 × 30 cm
Madan Bequest, 1962; WA1962.17.4

Although best known as a drapery painter, van Aken began his career in Flanders, painting genre pictures. Judging from the accessories, this middle-class interior seems to be English and to date from about 1720, shortly after van Aken had settled permanently in London. He tended to re-employ the same figures and accessories in different compositions. The detail and the figures in this painting reappear in other works.

Charles Alexander
(exhibited 1893 – 94)

L'amateur chez lui

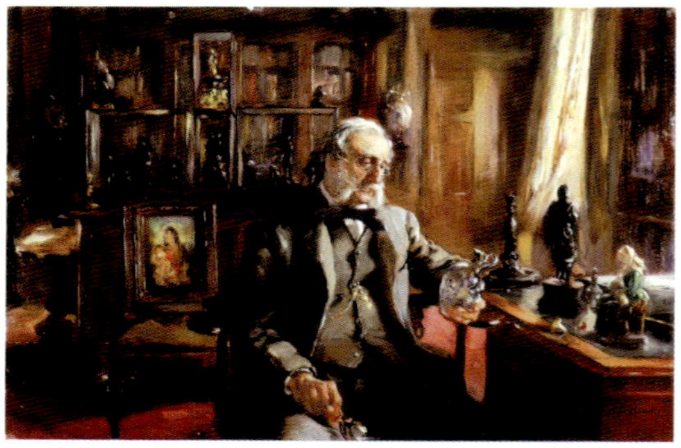

A299a; oil on panel, 38 × 56 cm
Signed: *Charles Alexander*
Fortnum Bequest, 1899; WA1899.3

Poole 1912, no. 500

In this portrait of Fortnum, he is seen in his house at Stanmore, surrounded by some of the collections he would later give or bequeath to the Ashmolean. He holds a jug of Medici porcelain; on the desk is one of his Palissy figures, a bronze of St John the Baptist and a bronze candlestick, while on the chair is propped up the *Virgin and Child* by Pintoricchio (A303).

Alessandro Allori
(1535 – 1607)

Portrait of a young Man

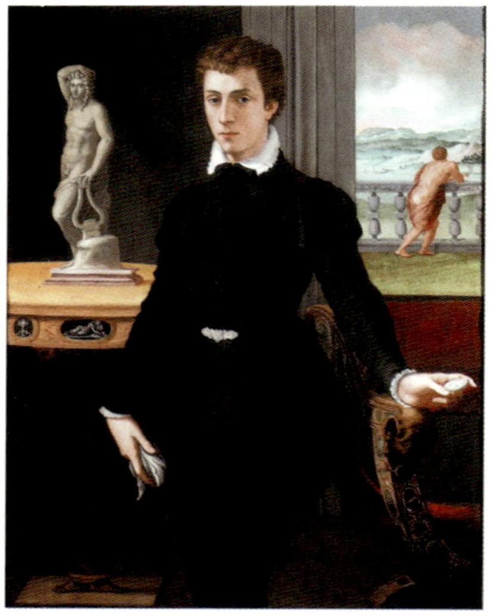

A1123; oil on panel, 133 × 140 cm
Inscribed: *AS.AL.B.P.F.M. DLXI*, the date repeated above
Prov.: probably Baron Mayer Amschel de Rothschild (d. 1874); Hannah de Rothschild; 5th Earl of Rosebery and by descent until 1977
Purchased with the assistance of the Victoria & Albert Museum Purchase Grant Fund and the National Art Collections Fund, 1982; WA1982.38

Lecchini Giovannoni 1991, no. 183

The young collector holds a medal showing a profile head of a woman in classical costume. His arm rests on an ornate chair with carved and inlaid decoration. A replica of the antique statue of Apollo Citharoedos stands on the elaborate table; the original was in the della Valle collection in Rome in 1561. Different identifications have been proposed for the aristocratic sitter, including that of Paolo Capranica, related to the Della Valle family, or a member of the Palma di Cesnola family, because their motto *Oppraesa Resurgam* appears on a scroll across a palm tree in the table inlay. The view of an imaginary landscape with a classically-draped figure leaning on a mannerist balcony gives the portrait an enigmatic air. Allori was a pupil of Bronzino and shares his ideal of polished refinement in portraiture. A1123 was painted soon after Allori's return from Rome, where he had studied antique and modern art from 1554 to 1560 and had established himself as a portraitist.

Cristofano Allori
(1577 – 1621)

Bernardo Davanzati Bostichi

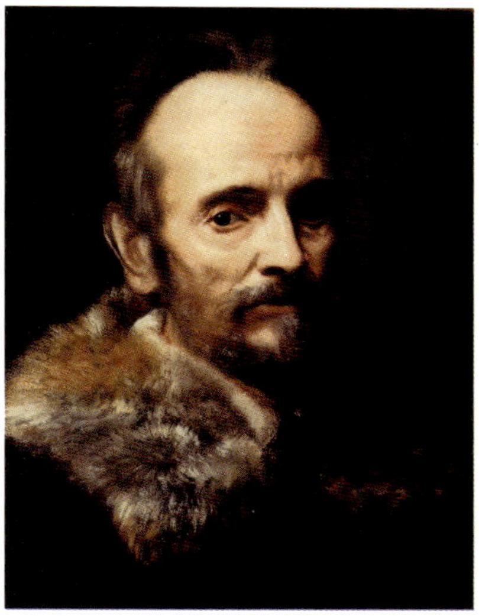

A797b; oil on canvas, 48 × 37 cm
Prov.: Carlo Davanzati Bostichi; Incontri family, Florence; Lord Nelson
Presented by the National Art Collections Fund, 1951; WA1951.50

Chappell 1984, no. 11

The sitter (1529–1606) was an antiquarian and scholar. Baldinucci recorded that Bostichi's son, Carlo, a patron and friend of Allori, owned a bust-length portrait of Bernardo by the artist. Engraved by Francesco Rondinelli, A797b may have served as the model for the portrait of Bernardo included in a ceiling in the Uffizi by Agnolo Gori of 1658 (repainted after 1762).

Sir Lawrence Alma-Tadema
(1836 – 1912)

A Hearty Welcome

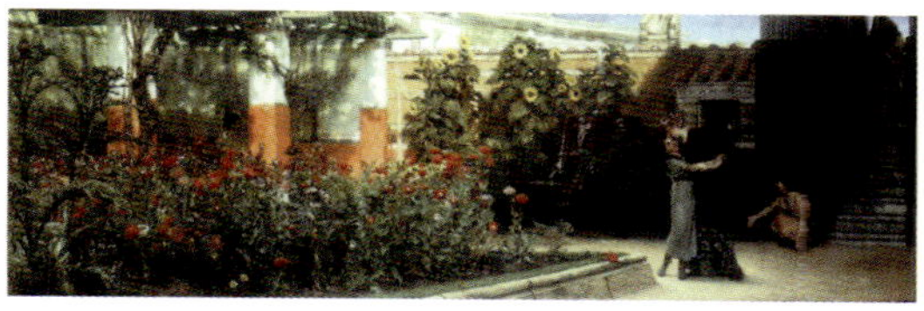

A881; oil on canvas, 30 × 91 cm
Signed and inscribed: *L. Alma-Tadema Op. CXC*
Prov.: Sir Henry Thompson, Bt and by descent
Presented by the Misses H.G. and G.E.G. Watkins, 1955; WA1955.60

Swanson 1990, no. 236

An ancient Roman family returns home to a warm welcome. The figures represent Alma-Tadema's own family: the father is the artist, the girl below, his daughter Laurense. The central group comprises his younger daughter, Anna, embracing her step-mother, Laura. On the left, a nurse, modelled on Alice Search, carries the baby Pieter Rodeck.

Sir Lawrence Alma-Tadema
(1836 – 1912)

A Corner of the Gardens of the Villa Borghese

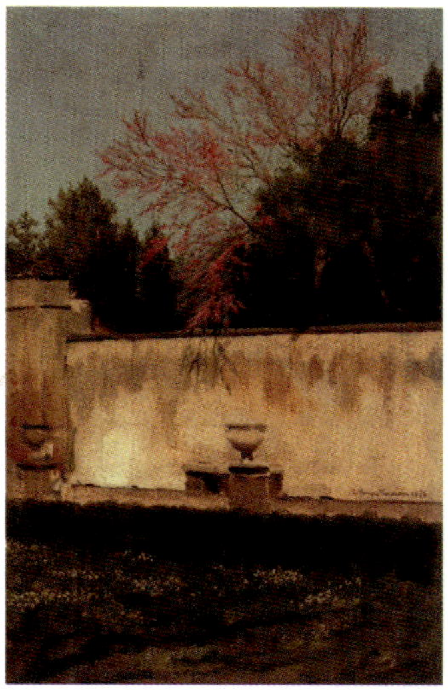

A1022a; oil on canvas, mounted as a drawing, 34.9 × 22 cm
Signed and dated: *L. Alma-Tadema 1876*
Prov.: George Henschel; Lord Blanesburgh
Presented by Miss Sylvia Gosse, 1966; WA1966.13.1

Swanson 1990, no. 202

During a visit to Rome from December 1875 to April 1876, Alma-Tadema collected material for future paintings and made three studies of unassuming parts of the city, including two in the gardens of the Villa Borghese. This one, completed on 2 April 1876, is reminiscent of Velàzquez's celebrated study in the same garden (Prado).

Jacopo Amigoni
(*c.* 1685 – 1752)

Abraham and the three Angels

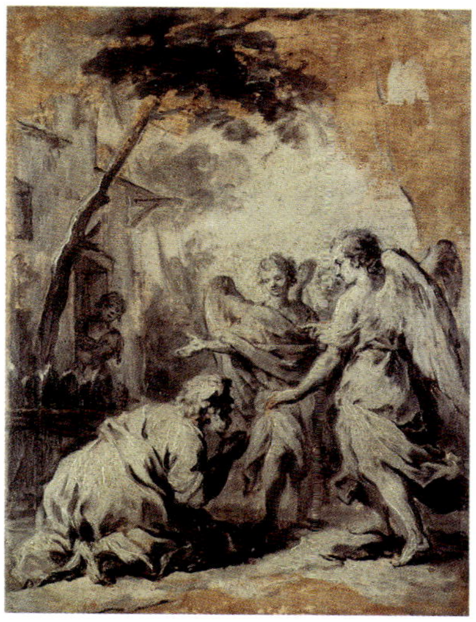

A1015a; oil on paper, mounted as a drawing, 43.9 × 32.6 cm
Prov.: Miss M.V. Taylor
Purchased, 1964; WA1964.48

Macandrew 1980, no. 965-2

Abraham was visited by three angels, who prophesied that his wife would bear a son (Genesis 18:2). A1015a is the *modello* for one of a set of six prints of Old Testament subjects engraved by Francesco Bartolozzi after Amigoni and published by Giuseppe Wagner in 1758. As with three other extant *modelli* (Graphische Sammlung, Munich), it is painted on the back of a print by Wagner after Amigoni. The artist prepared the oil sketches before his departure from Venice for Madrid in 1747.

Albert André
(1869 – 1954)

Woman sewing at a Window

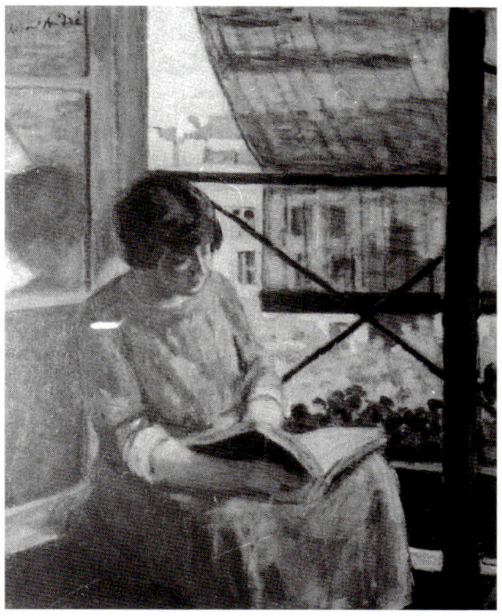

A454; oil on canvas, 60 × 49 cm
Signed: *Albert André*
Weldon Bequest, 1937; WA1937.34

André developed his sense of colour and his interest in contemporary themes through contact with the Impressionists. This painting shows the view from André's studio in the Boulevard de Clichy looking north. The church of the Sacré Coeur is hidden by the blind. The work dates from about 1913.

Andrea di Bartolo Cini
(*c.* 1358–64 – 1428)

St Lucy

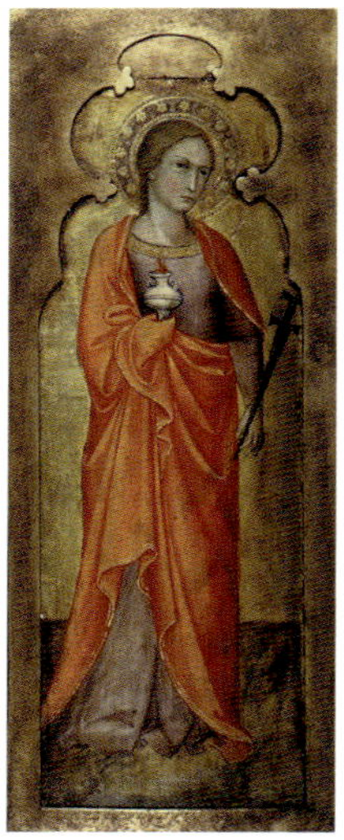

A75; tempera and gilding on panel, 63.5 × 20.5 cm
Fox-Strangways Gift, 1850; WA1850.19

Lloyd 1977, pp. 2–3

A75 was part of a large altar-piece, now dismembered, of which five other similarly shaped panels of individual saints are known. St Lucy, an early Christian martyr, holds her attributes of a dagger, with which she was executed and an oil-lamp, referring to her name, Lucia (light). A leading painter in Siena, Andrea also worked on manuscript illumination and stained-glass designs and was prominent in public life. He developed a refined, conservative style which changed little during his career, making his work difficult to date.

Henrick Andriessen
(1607 – 1655)

Still Life with Mask

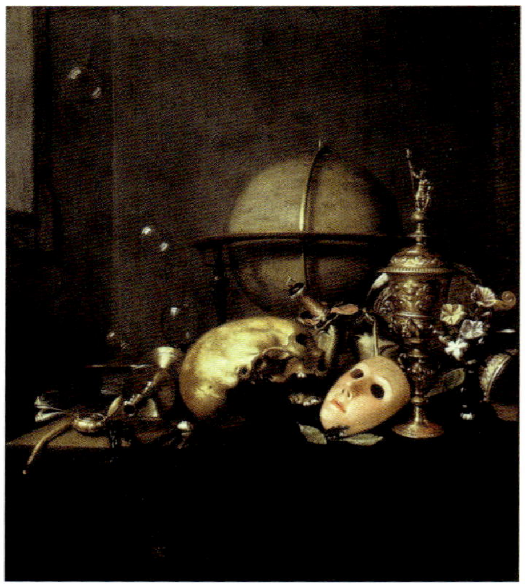

A529; oil on canvas, 48 × 43 cm
Signed (?): *h. andriessens fecit*
Daisy Linda Ward Bequest, 1939; WA1940.2.5

Meijer 2003, no. 5

This painting is a *vanitas*, a still-life painting of impermanent things. The violin, whose sound fades, the soap bubbles, the burning taper and the watch recall the transience of the world (the globe) and the brevity of life (the skull). The appearance of the same skull in three paintings by Pieter van Willigen and similar links in other works has led to the attribution of works by Andriessen to van Willigen, who may have been his pupil.

Studio of Fra Angelico
(*c.* 1395–1400 – 1455)

Virgin and Child with Angels and a Dominican Saint; St Peter (left); *St Paul* (right)

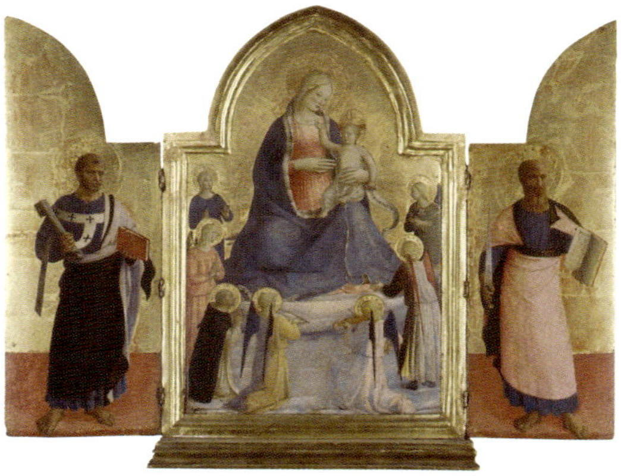

A77; tempera and gilding on panel, 41 × 26.8 (arched); 44.9 × 16.3 (left wing); 44.8 × 15.2 (right wing) cm
Inscribed on the scroll: *DISCITE AME QUIA MITIS SUM SUM* (Matthew 11:29)
Fox-Strangways Gift, 1850; WA1850.5

Lloyd 1977, pp. 5–6; Bonsanti 1998, no. 87

This portable folding triptych was made for private devotion. The side panels have been cut down and may have belonged to a different small altar-piece so that the triptych was assembled, or altered, at a later date. The artist was close to Benozzo Gozzoli. St Peter holds his attribute of a key and St Paul a sword, the instrument of his martyrdom. The saintly friar is probably St Dominic.

Attributed to Andrea del Brescianino
(*c.* 1487 – after 1525)

Portrait of a young Woman

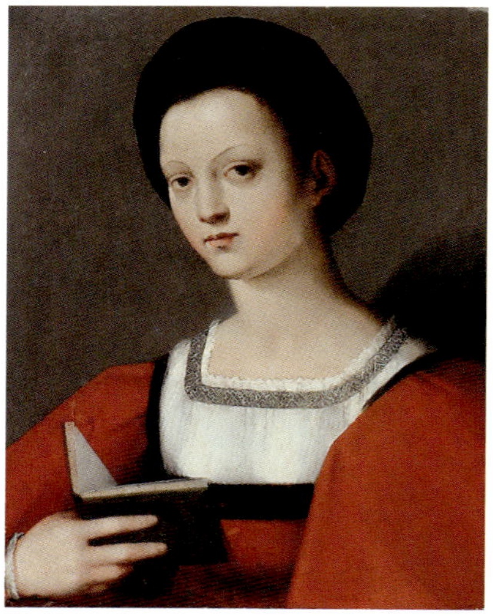

A370; oil on panel, 58.3 × 45 cm
Bequeathed by the Revd Robert Finch, 1830; WA1921.7

Lloyd 1977, pp. 3–4

Although damaged, this portrait of an unknown woman is of fine quality and has affinities with the work of Andrea in the 1520s. Apart from a short stay in Rome *c.* 1516, Andrea spent most of his career in Siena and in Florence, where he collaborated with his brother Raffaello Piccinelli.

Philips Angel
(1616 – after 1683)

Still Life of Game with four Plovers

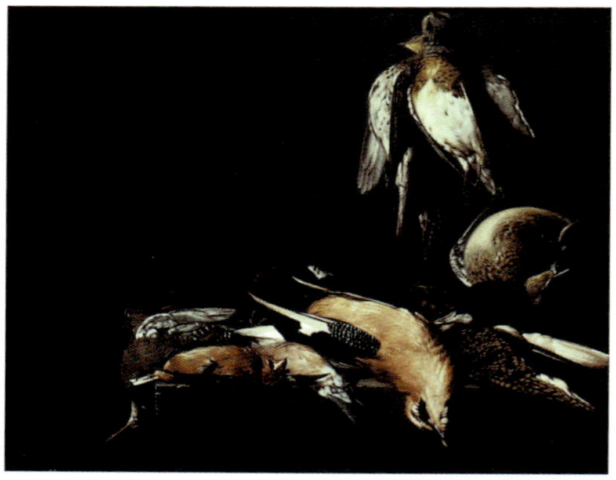

A615; oil on panel, 57 × 73 cm
Daisy Linda Ward Bequest, 1939; WA1940.2.91

Meijer 2003, no. 6

Long attributed to Jan Vonck, a painter who specialized in paintings of dead birds, this still life is now attributed to Philips Angel, a painter from Middelburg who painted live birds as well as dead game and also barn interiors with a strong element of still life. Parallels for the type of composition, the texture of the feathers and careful attention to the detail of the table can be found in firmly attributed works by Angel.

Follower of Fra Angelico
(*c.* 1395/1400 – 1455)

The Annunciation

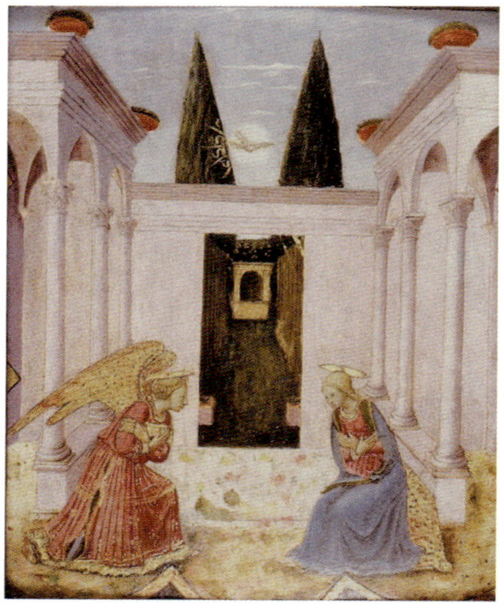

A78; tempera and gilding on panel, 23.2 × 19.6 cm
Fox-Strangways Gift, 1850; WA1850.25

Lloyd 1977, pp. 6–8

The Angel Gabriel announces to the Virgin that she will bear the son of God (Luke 1: 26–8); the walled garden and closed gate are symbols of Mary's purity. The inspiration for this composition was Fra Angelico's small *Annunciation* of *c.* 1450–52 (Museo di San Marco, Florence), one of a series of scenes decorating the doors of the silver reliquary chest in SS Annunziata. A78 has clear affinities with the work of Zanobi Strozzi (1412–1468).

ANONYMOUS ANGLO-FLEMISH ARTIST
(*c.* 1630)

Portrait of a young Woman

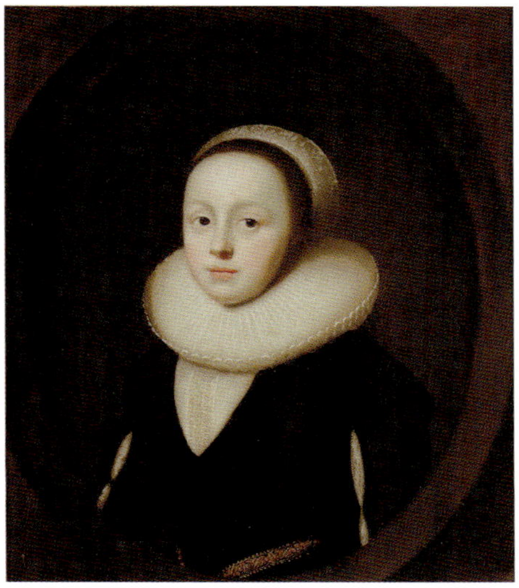

A183; oil on canvas, 69 × 59 cm
Chambers Hall Gift, 1855; WA1855.196

The format of a feigned oval was a favourite with Cornelius Jonson, but the attribution remains uncertain.

APOLLONIO DI GIOVANNI (*c.* 1416 – 1465) and MARCO DEL BUONO GIAMBERTI
(?1403 – after 1480)

The Assassination and Funeral of Julius Caesar

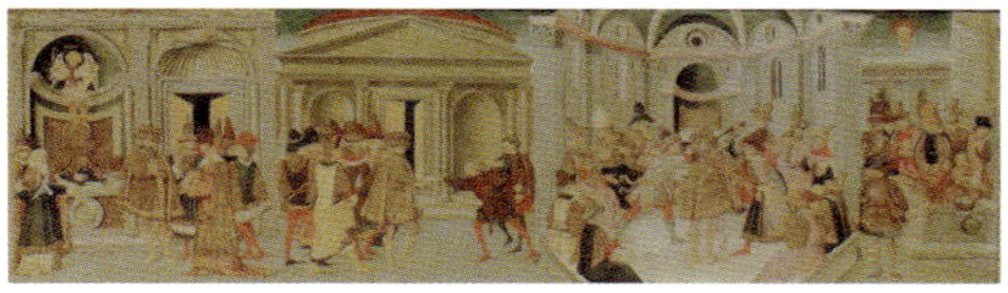

A90; tempera (?) and gilding on panel, 38.5 × 134.5 cm
Inscribed: *APPOLLO, CESARE, CHASCHA, BRUTO*
Fox-Strangways Gift, 1850; WA1850.27

Lloyd 1977, pp. 8–10; Lloyd 1993, p. 14

Made for the front of a *cassone*, this would have been commissioned on the occasion of a marriage *c.* 1455–60. Following Plutarch's *Lives* (lxii–lxviii), Caesar is seen on the left sacrificing to Apollo; he is then shown on his way to the Forum and, in front of the Pantheon, being handed the message of warning. To the right, his murder in the Senate is depicted and his body is burnt on a pyre in front of Trajan's column; above the wall his spirit watches.

Attributed to ARCANGELO DI JACOPO DEL SELLAIO
(1478 – 1531)

St John the Baptist

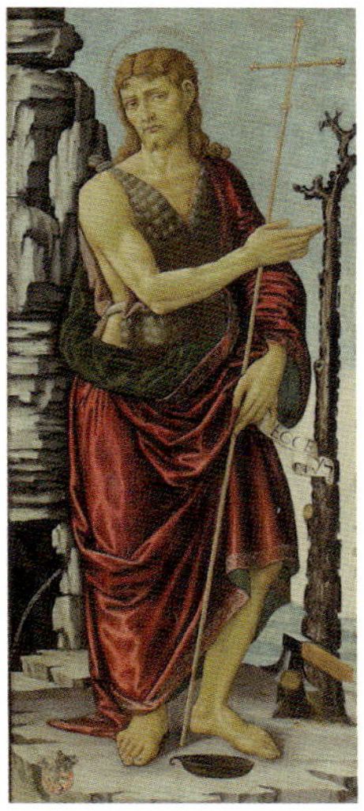

A85; tempera on panel, 156 × 66 cm
Inscribed: *ECCE (AG)NUS (DEI)*
Fox-Strangways Gift, 1850; WA1850.1

Lloyd 1977, pp. 37–8

The text held by the saint comes from Matthew 3: 10 where St John identified Christ as the Saviour with the words 'behold the lamb of God'. There is a very abraded coat of arms lower left. A85 has recently been plausibly attributed to the Master of the Miller Tondo, now identified as Arcangelo di Jacopo del Sellaio. Having inherited the studio of his father, Jacopo, he continued to work in his manner, which was based on that of Botticelli and Lippi.

JOSÉ ANTOLINEZ
(1635 – 1675)

The Immaculate Conception

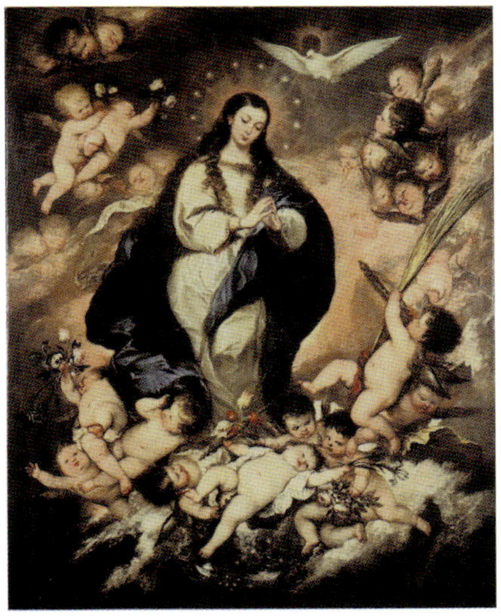

A690; oil on canvas, 213 × 170 cm
Prov.: 6th Marquess of Lansdowne; Louis Lyon, New York
Purchased, 1941; WA1941.159

Angulo Iñiguez 1957, p. 20

The Virgin with a halo of stars stands on a globe, with the Holy Spirit above; cherubs bear her attributes: the flowers symbolise purity, the palm victory, the mirror spotless virtue and the sceptre alludes to her title of Queen of Heaven. A popular subject in 17th-century Spain, the Immaculate Conception signifies Mary's freedom from original sin. A690 is one of over twenty-five renditions by Antolinez and dates from the late 1660s.

APOLLONIO DI GIOVANNI (*c.* 1416 – 1465) and MARCO DEL BUONO GIAMBERTI
(?1403 – after 1480)

The Rape of the Sabine Women

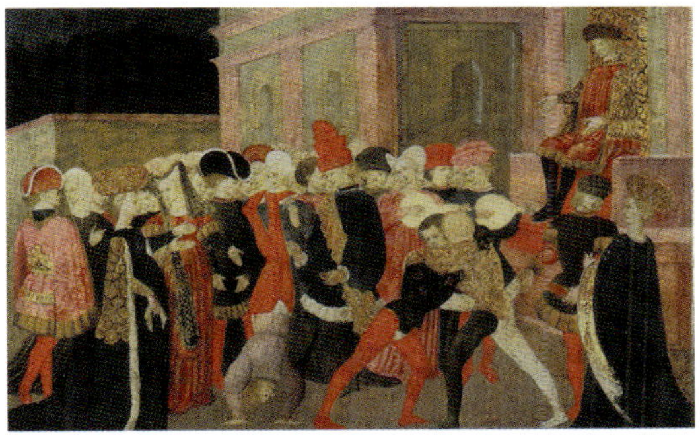

A92; tempera (?) and gilding on panel, trimmed on all sides and cut down on the left, 38.2 × 60.3 cm
Fox-Strangways Gift, 1850; WA1850.30

Lloyd 1977, pp. 10–11; Filippini 1992, pp. 233, 236

Probably a fragment from the right-hand side of a *cassone* front, this panel may represent Romulus, king of Rome about to order the abduction of the Sabine women while they are attending the games in honour of Neptune. This act and its consequences as narrated by Livy (*Ab Urbe condita* I, 9–13) was seen by Renaissance commentators as leading to the institution of marriage in ancient Rome, thus the scene was appropriate for wedding celebrations.

DAVID ADOLPHE CONSTANT ARTZ
(1837 – 1890)

Two Girls on the Dunes, bleaching

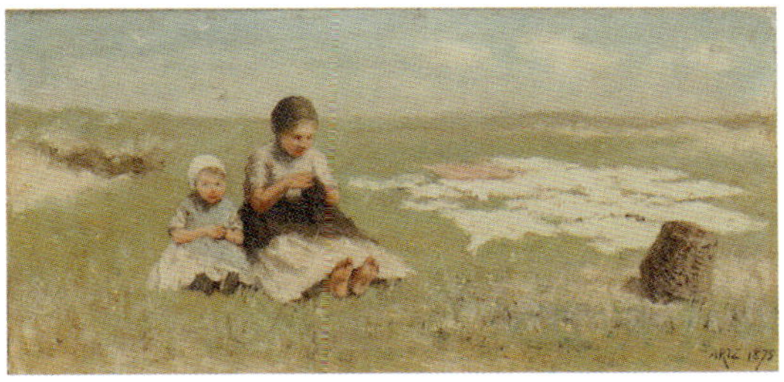

A1179; oil on panel, 16.5 × 23 cm
Bequeathed by Professor Edith Bulbring, 1993; WA1993.416

White 1999, p. 8

Artz was the most gifted pupil of Jozef Israels, uncle of the donor, and a prominent member of the Hague School of painters in the second half of the 19th century. An inscribed label on the back of the panel suggests the subject might be an illustration of a book of poems by the popular Dutch writer Nicolaas Beets.

Geneviève Asse
(b. 1923)

Distance

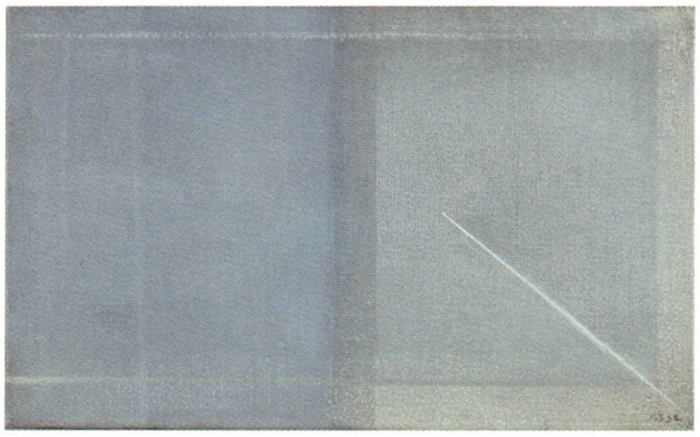

A1151; oil on canvas, 14 × 22 cm
Signed: *Asse*; inscribed on the stretcher: *Distance;* signed and dated on the back of canvas: *Asse 71*
Prov.: Christopher Hewett
Presented by the Family of Christopher Hewett, 1987; WA1987.87

Oxford 1987, no. 19

In the early 1970s Asse began to examine ways of creating space through colour. This small painting from 1971 is typical of her work at this time. She used white lines and two different tones of a light blue to create what she calls 'an internal architecture'.

Geneviève Asse
(b. 1923)

Composition

A1152; oil on canvas, 16 × 22 cm
Signed and dated on the back and on the stretcher: *Asse 72*
Prov.: Christopher Hewett
Presented by the Family of Christopher Hewett, 1987; WA1987.88

Oxford 1987, no. 20

In this painting of 1972, Asse concentrates on creating a sense of space through colour and line. Here colour is reduced to a very light translucent blue while the linear structure, suggested by a few diagonal lines, is barely visible.

Balthasar van der Ast
(?1593–4 – *c.* 1657)

A Vase of Flowers

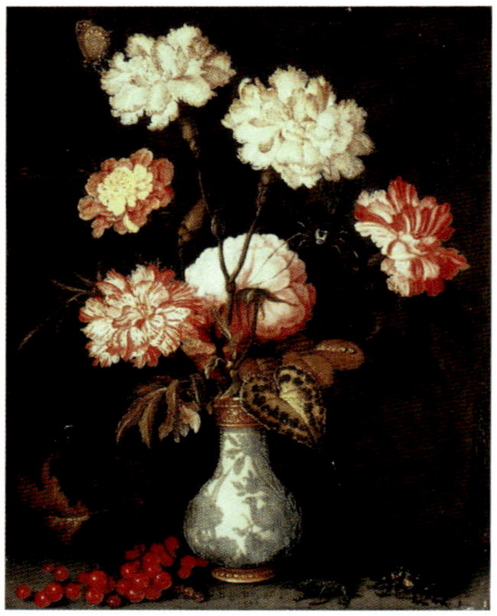

A530; oil on panel, 30 × 24 cm
Signed and dated: *B. vander.ast fe./.i.6.2.3.*
Prov.: Miss Hill, Leamington Spa
Daisy Linda Ward Bequest, 1939; WA1940.2.6

Meijer 2003, no. 7

Van der Ast's prolific output ranges from small coppers to large, complex compositions. He was trained by Ambrosius Bosschaert and developed his teacher's compositions with added sea-shells, fruit and other accessories. This panel from the 1620s combines a central porcelain flask of flowers in the manner of Bosschaert with beetles and a spider which may have been inspired by of the work of Roelant Savery.

Etienne Aubry
(1745 – 1781)

Portrait of a Gentleman

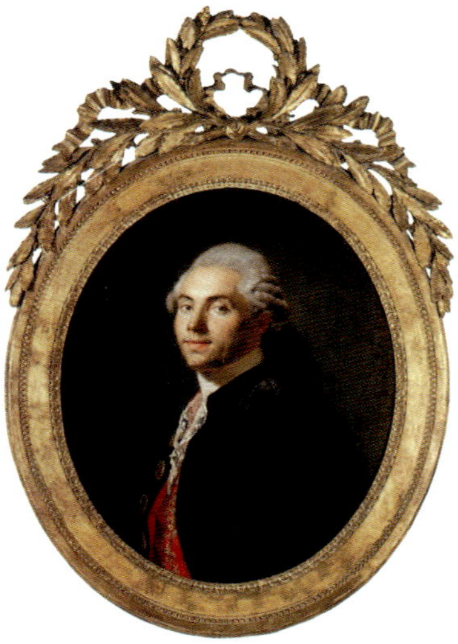

A1139; oil on canvas, 65 × 54 cm
Faintly signed: *Et Aubry 17..*
Purchased (Blakiston Fund) to mark the Directorship of Sir David Piper with the assistance of the Friends of the Ashmolean, 1986; WA1986.76

Aubry is best known for his attractive genre scenes and his portraits are relatively rare. A date of *c.* 1777 has been suggested for A1139 on the basis of the large buttons and style of formal wig. The handsome Louis XVI frame is not original to the painting but is contemporary.

Robert Austin
(1895 – 1973)

Landscape with dead Trees

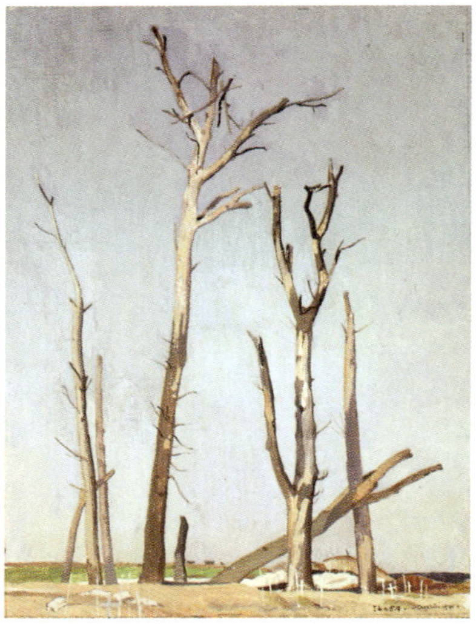

A1135; tempera on canvas on cardboard, 26.7 × 19.8 cm
Signed and dated: *Austin 1920;* inscribed: *I4a5.9*
Presented by Miss Sara Sproule, 1985; WA1985.174

Better known as a printmaker and as President of the Royal Society of Painter-Etchers, Robert Austin was also a painter and draughtsman and in this capacity was active as an official War Artist. This painting from his earlier years shows a group of trees, entirely leafless. The very low horizon accentuates their nakedness.

Attributed to Francesco Ubertini, called Bacchiacca
(1494 – 1557)

Holy Family with the young St John

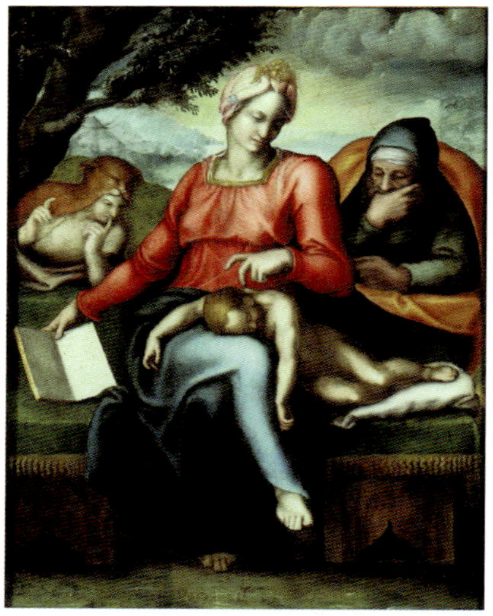

A67; oil on slate, 52.5 × 41.2 cm
Prov.: Ganucci, Florence
Bequeathed by George Fairholme, 1846; WA1846.11

Lloyd 1977, pp. 13–14

A famous presentation drawing by Michelangelo of *c.* 1538–40 was the basis for painted versions by his followers, of which this is the only example with an extensive landscape. Known as *Il Silenzio* (Silence) because of the gesture of St John, A67 shows the Holy Family contemplating the sleeping Christ, foreshadowing the Lamentation. The Virgin holds a book open at Psalm 85.11 and lifts a transparent veil from the Child's body, a reference to the revelation of Truth.

Jakob Adriaensz. Backer
(1608 – 1651)

A young Man wearing a Wreath of Vine Leaves

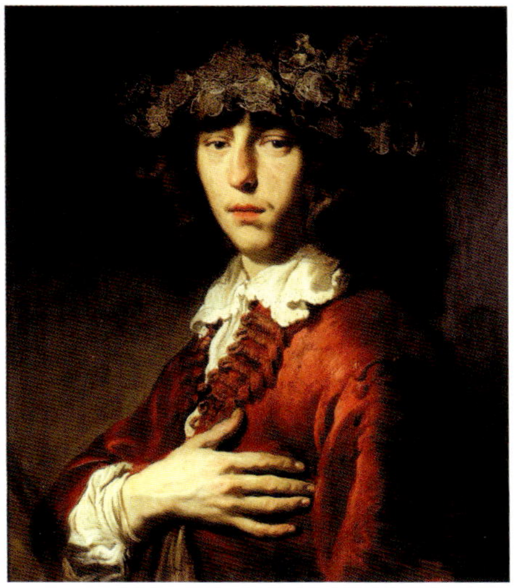

A668; oil on panel, 64 × 54 cm
Bequeathed by Sir Arthur Evans, 1941; WA1941.1

White 1999, p. 8

Formerly attributed to Ferdinand Bol but now given to Jakob Backer, a painter who came under the influence of Rembrandt after he had settled in Amsterdam in the early 1630s. It is probably not a conventional portrait but a fanciful head study, albeit based closely on the model.

Sisto Badalocchio
(1585 – after 1619)

St Francis of Assisi consoled by Angels

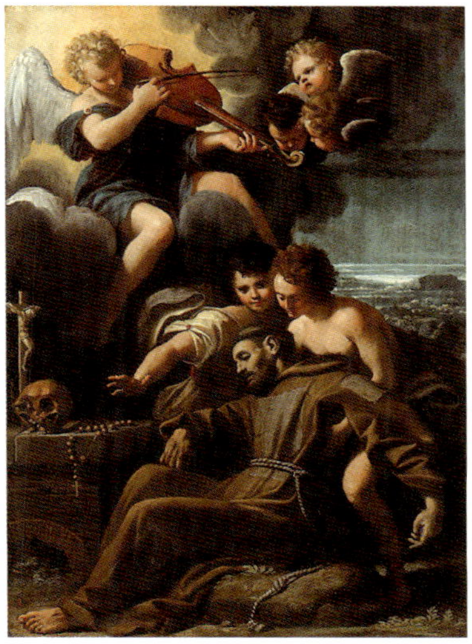

A742; oil on panel, 72 × 51.5 cm
Prov.: probably Margherita de' Medici; Maria Maddalena Farnese, Farnese Collection, Parma, 1708; Marquis of Stafford and by descent until 1946
Purchased, 1947; WA1947.161

Negro and Pirondini 1995, p. 93–4

St Francis received the stigmata, or the wounds of the Passion of Christ, in 1224. Variations on the subject became popular in the Counter-Reformation period and A742 illustrates a moment when the agonized saint was consoled by angelic music. For a long time thought to be by Ludovico Carracci or Giovanni Lanfranco, A742 with its attractive nocturnal landscape dates from *c.* 1610–13.

Thomas Balston
(1883 – 1967)

The Reservoir

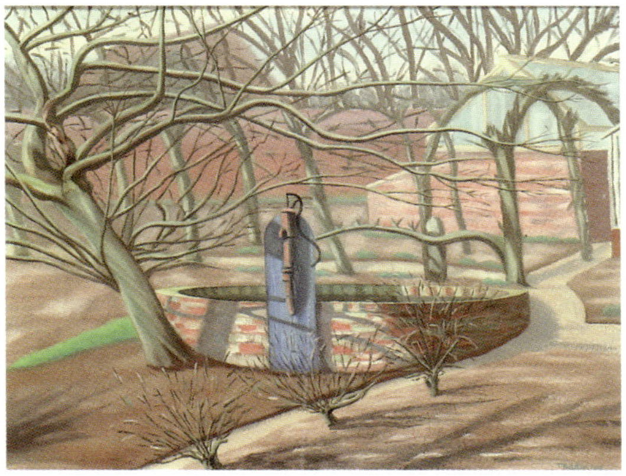

A924b; oil on canvas, 40.5 × 51 cm
Signed and dated: *TBalston 1938*
Presented by A.H. Smith, Warden of New College, 1959; WA1959.43.1

Thomas Balston was not only a prolific collector and writer but also a painter. He studied painting for a short period in the 1930s with Mark Gertler, from whom he acquired several paintings. This landscape is painted in his typical, somewhat idealised and atmospheric style.

Sir Nathaniel Bacon
(1585 – 1627)

Landscape

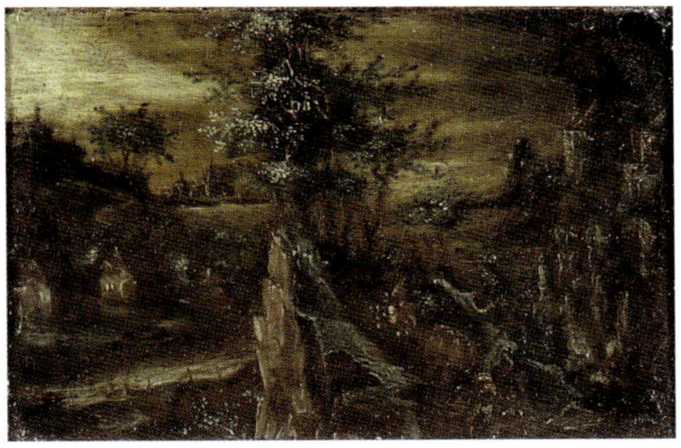

F635; oil on unprimed copper, backed with oak panel, 7 × 11 cm
Signed: *NB*
Presented by Elias Ashmole, 1683; WA1908.224

MacGregor 1983, no. 254

This small painting can be identified with a reference in the *Musaeum Tradescantianum* of 1656 as a landscape by Sir Nathaniel Bacon, an amateur artist otherwise known for his large, flamboyant portraits and still lifes. It is the earliest surving landscape painted by a native artist in Britain, but is indebted to Flemish models for the technique and Italian for the style.

Thomas Baker
(1809 – 1869)

View looking towards Offchurch Bury with Men reaping

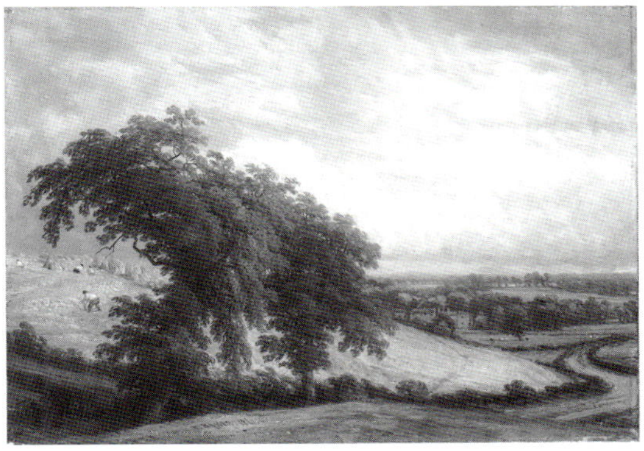

A1007; oil on canvas, 25 × 35 cm
Signed and dated: *T.BAKER. 1861.*
Bequeathed by Major Thomas Bouch, 1963; WA1963.150.4

The house at Offchurch Bury, south-east of Leamington Spa in Warwickshire, was a favourite subject of Baker's from 1854 onwards. This view was painted during the harvest in August 1861.

Thomas Balston
(1883 – 1967)

Interior with an Arum Lily

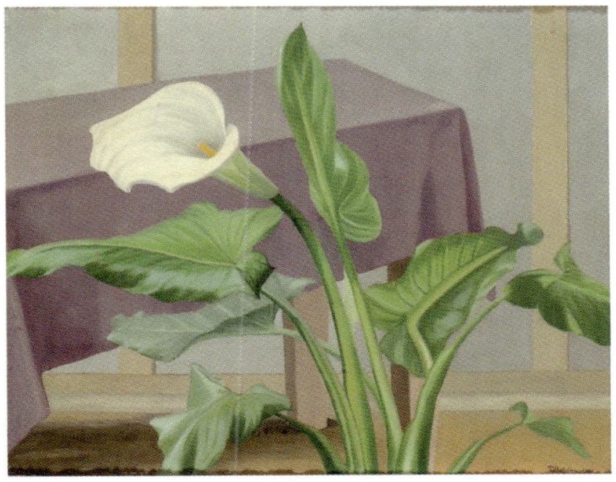

A928; oil on canvas, 41 × 51 cm
Signed and dated: *TBalston 1939*
Presented by the artist, 1959; WA1959.54.4

In this still life, Balston does not concentrate exclusively on the arrangement of flowers but on the setting and the representation of the room behind. The uniform, blended paint surface somewhat recalls Gertler's manner.

Thomas Bardwell
(1704 – 1767)

Thomas Fermor, 1st Earl of Pomfret and Henrietta Louisa, Countess of Pomfret

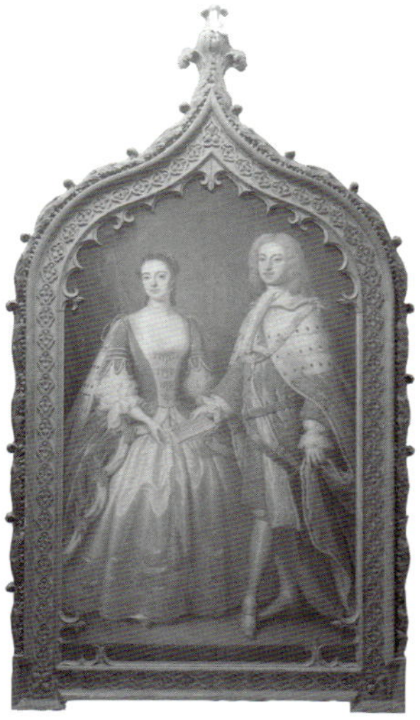

A30; oil on canvas, 216 × 124 cm
Signed: *TBardwell.f.* and inscribed: *Thomas Farmor, Earl of Pomfret, and Henrietta Louisa Jeffreys, his Wife.*
Presented by the Countess of Pomfret, 1759; WA1845.30

Poole 1912, no. 456; Talley 1976–8, pp. 142–3

Thomas Fermor (1698–1753) succeeded as 2nd Baron Leominster in 1711 and was created Earl of Pomfret in 1721. He was Master of Horse to Queen Caroline from 1727 to 1737. He married Henrietta Louisa Jeffreys (1703–1761) in 1720. This portrait of the couple in peer's robes may have been painted to commemorate thirty years of married life and the parchment he is handing to her would have been the marriage settlement. After the death of her husband, Lady Pomfret bought the celebrated Arundel marbles from her son and presented them to the University of Oxford in 1755. Around 1757, she built a large town house in Arlington Street, designed by Sanderson Miller in the Gothic style. The frame was designed for Pomfret House.

Thomas Barker of Bath
(1769 – 1847)

Three Girls asleep under a Tent – Morning

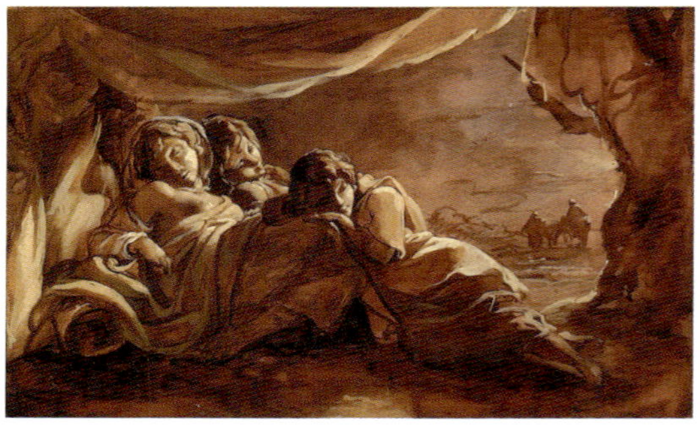

A955; oil on canvas, 42 × 66 cm
Purchased, 1961; WA1961.47

A study for a picture exhibited at the British Institution in 1815 (untraced). The literary source has not been identified.

Thomas Barker of Bath
(1769 – 1847)

Hannah Mary de Cardonnel Lawson

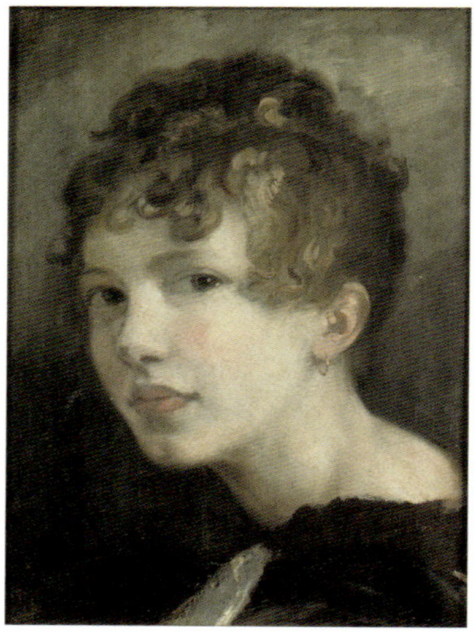

A1103; oil on canvas, 39.5 × 29.5 cm
Russell Bequest, 1958; WA1958.119

The donor identified this sketch as a portrait of Hannah Mary, daughter of Adam Mansfeldt de Cardonnel Lawson of Chirton and Cramlington, Northumberland, who married Joseph Elmsell of Woodlands, near Doncaster in 1824. However, it has more the appearance of a freely painted head study than a portrait.

'Barna da Siena'
(active *c.* 1330 – 1350)

The Crucifixion and Lamentation

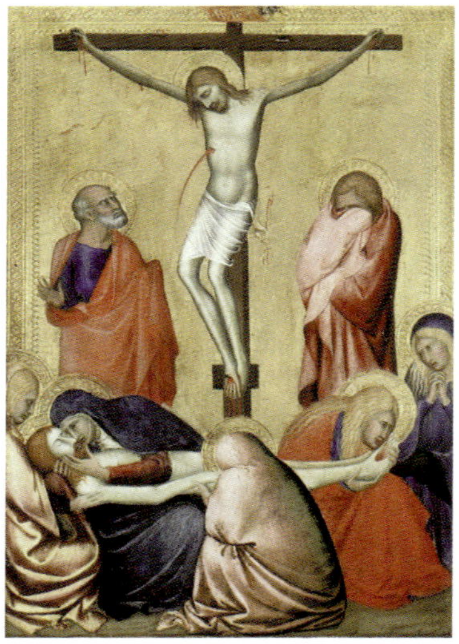

A73; tempera and gilding on panel, integral frame, 53 × 38 cm
Fox-Strangways Gift, 1850; WA1850.9

Lloyd 1977 pp. 15–16; Boskovits and Schleier 1988, under no. 32; Kanter 1994, p. 94

The right-hand part of a diptych, this panel once had as its companion an *Annunciation with a Donor, and six Saints below* (Gemäldegalerie, Berlin). It is very rare to find the subjects of the Crucifixion and Lamentation depicted in one scene, which makes for a highly charged devotional image. Christ on the Cross is flanked, unusually, by St Peter and St John the Evangelist and the body of Christ is mourned by women, with the Virgin Mary at his head and Mary Madgalen at his feet. A73 is one of a group of panel paintings by the hand of an artist traditionally known as 'Barna da Siena'; this master was a close follower of the great Sienese artist Simone Martini (*c.* 1284–1344) and is sometimes thought to be Lippo Memmi or his brother Federico.

Federico Barocci
(*c.* 1535 – 1612)

St Dominic de Guzmán receiving the Rosary

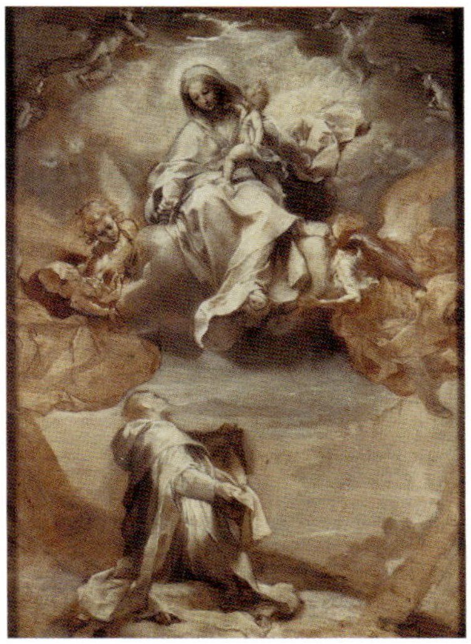

A709; oil sketch with pen and brown ink over black chalk on paper, 54.5 × 38.5 cm
Prov.: Nourri, Paris, 1785; Lord Nugent; Sir Francis Boileau
Purchased, 1944; WA1944.100

Parker 1956, no. 94; Turner 2000, p. 99

The prayer of the Rosary is traditionally said to have been instituted by St Dominic (1170–1221). A709 is preparatory for the *Madonna del Rosario* painted between 1588 and 1591 for the Confraternity of the Assumption and the Rosary at Senigallia (now in the Palazzo Vescovile). This monochrome oil-sketch came at a relatively late stage of preparation and is a dynamic study of light and shadow.

Bartolomeo and Agnolo degli Erri
(active 1430 – 1479) (active 1442 – 1497)

St Vincent Ferrer preaching before a Pope

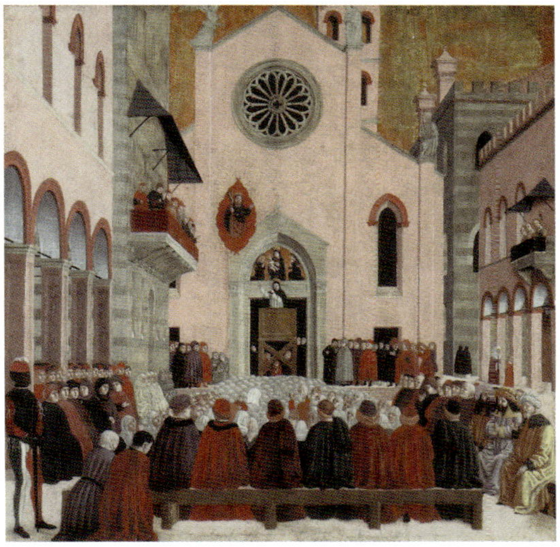

A93; tempera and gilding on panel, 62 × 61.5 cm
Fox-Strangways Gift, 1850; WA1850.18

Lloyd 1977 pp. 18–21; Benati 1988, pp. 135, 139, 168

Originally part of a large altar-piece, A93 is one of thirteen panels illustrating scenes from the life of St Vincent Ferrer (*c.* 1350–1419) who was canonised in 1455. The altar-piece was made for the church of S. Domenico in Modena: Bartolomeo worked on this and on other commissions there from 1450 in collaboration with his brother Agnolo. The pope may be Benedict XIII, the Avignonese pope of the Great Schism (when there were three claimants to the papal throne) before whom St Vincent preached in his attempts to resolve the Schism.

Attributed to Bartolomeo di Fruosino
(1366 – 1441)

The Virgin
St John the Evangelist

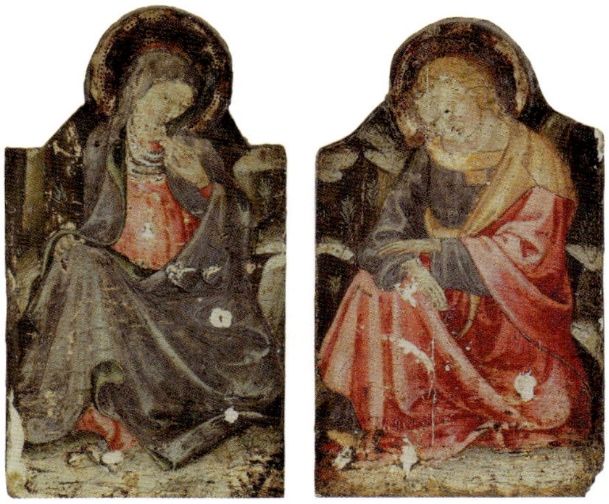

A736c; tempera and gilding on panel, 32.5 × 17.7 cm
A736d; tempera and gilding on panel, 32.5 × 18.2 cm
Presented by the daughters of James Reddie Anderson, 1947; WA1947.202.1

Lloyd 1977, pp. 213–4

These are pinnacle panels that once belonged to the same unknown altar-piece, which may have been crowned with a central pinnacle panel showing Christ on the Cross. The artist was Florentine, working in a late Gothic manner and an attribution to Bartolomeo di Fruosino has recently been suggested. A painter and miniaturist, Bartolomeo was a pupil of Agnolo Gaddi.

George Barret the Elder
(*c.* 1728 – 1784)

Horse-ferry: Sunset

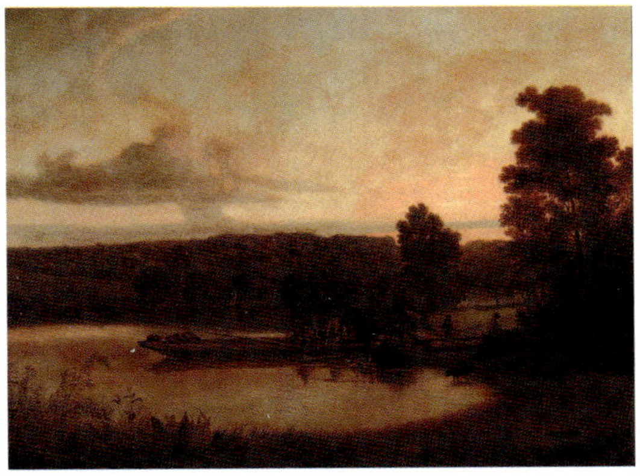

A247; oil on canvas, 65 × 85 cm
Signed: *George Barret*
Bequeathed by John Frederick Boyes, 1879; WA1879.1

The painting is now difficult to see owing to the thick yellow varnish. However, it appears to be a characteristic work by Barret of the 1770s. It has also been attributed to Barret's son, George Barret Junior (1767–1842), who, however, painted exclusively in watercolour.

Copy after Fra Bartolomeo
(1472 – 1517)

The Holy Family

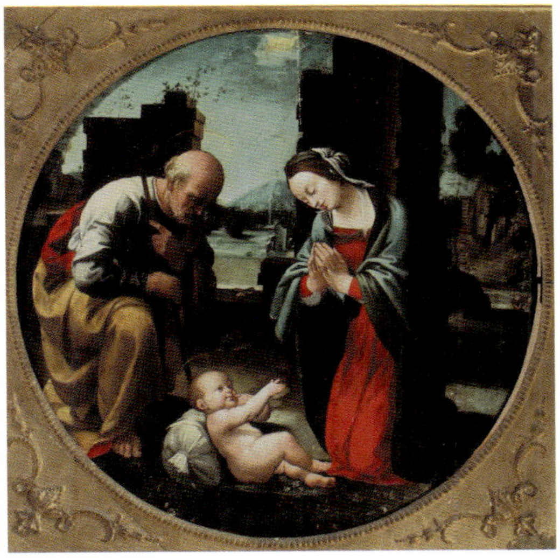

A104; oil on panel, 86 cm in diameter
Prov.: Capponi-Pasquali, Florence
Fox-Strangways Gift, 1850; WA1850.3

Lloyd 1977, pp. 22–3

An exact and good-quality copy, though smaller in size, of the roundel by Fra Bartolomeo of *c.* 1495 now in the Borghese Gallery, Rome, A104 may have been painted in the mid-16th century.

Attributed to Marco Basaiti
(active 1496 – 1530)

Head of the Virgin (fragment)

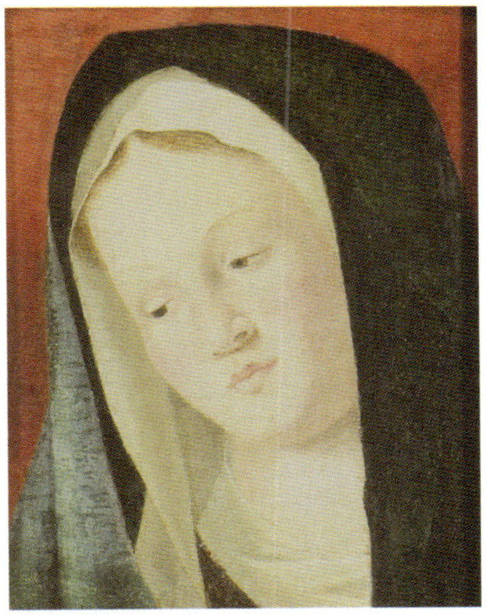

A735; oil on panel, 24.2 × 18.5 cm
Presented by the daughters of James Reddie Anderson, 1947; WA1947.202

Lloyd 1977, pp. 23–4

The attribution to Basaiti has been made on the basis of comparison with *The Virgin and Child* in the National Gallery (NG 2499), which dates from *c.* 1496–1505. As a fragment of a much larger panel, A735 may have been part of an *Annunciation*. A conservative artist, Marco was close to Cima da Conegliano and Giovanni Bellini.

Jacopo da Ponte, called Bassano
(*c.* 1510 – 1592)

Christ among the Doctors

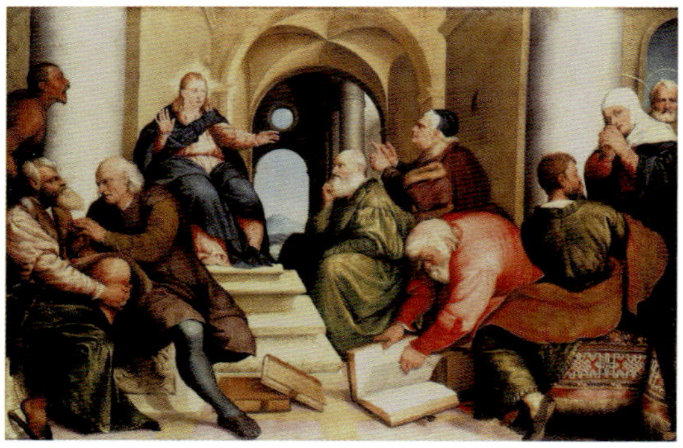

A771; oil on canvas, 116 × 174 cm
Prov.: Marco Pizzamano, Venice; Sir John Oxenden; by descent to Lady Capel Cure, *née* Dixwell-Oxenden; Christopher Blunt
Purchased, 1949; WA1949.5

Lloyd 1977, pp. 24–7; Muraro 1992, pp. 30, 180, 368

Painted in late 1539 for the Venetian nobleman Marco Pizzamano, A771 displays Bassano's interest in dramatic narrative and his knowledge of the art of Giorgione, Leonardo and Dürer. Christ engages in a learned discussion in the Temple of Jerusalem, bewildering the elders, who are so individually characterized that they have the appearance of portraits, (Luke 2: 41–51).

Leandro Bassano
(1557 – 1622)

Procurator of San Marco

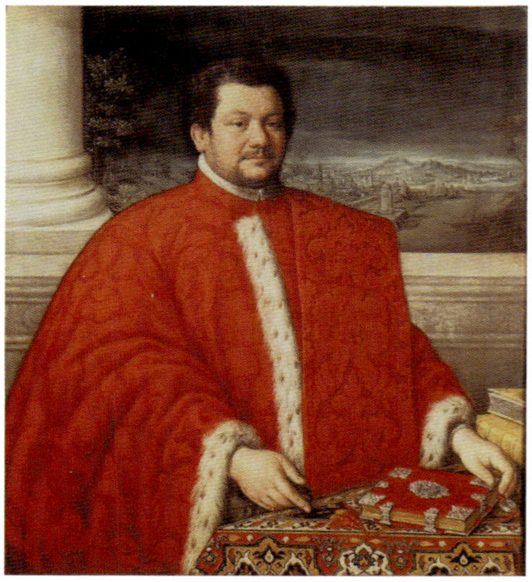

A445; oil on canvas, 113.9 × 101 cm
Purchased, 1935; WA1935.97

Lloyd 1977, pp. 28–9

While the sitter wears the official robes of a Procurator of San Marco, these were also worn by noblemen holding other offices of state. The harbour in the background cannot be definitively located. The costume and the style of the hair and beard suggest a date in the later 1590s. Trained by his father Jacopo, Leandro settled in Venice in 1588 where he worked on religious and historical paintings and became famous as a portraitist.

Pompeo Batoni
(1708 – 1787)

David Garrick

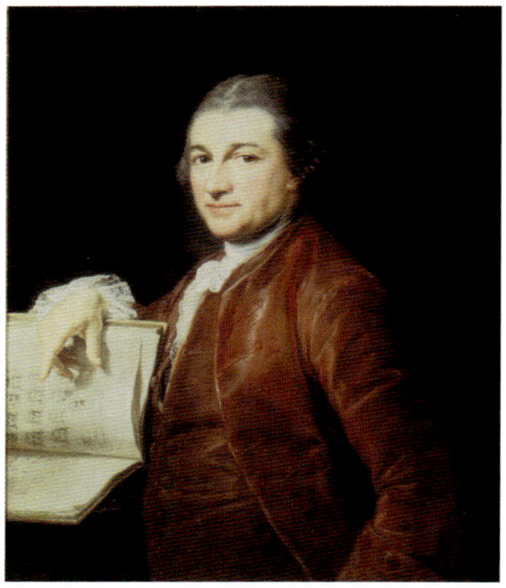

A61; oil on canvas, 76 × 63 cm
Inscribed: *David Garrick Esq.r / given at Rome / 1764*
Prov.: given by Garrick to Richard Kaye, 1764
Acquired by 1827: WA1845.61

Clark and Bowron 1985, no. 266; Whistler 1997

David Garrick (1717–1779), a celebrated actor and playwright, travelled in Italy in 1763–5; his portrait by Batoni was made as a gift for Richard Kaye, in exchange for an antique gem that Kaye had found at the Baths of Caracalla. Garrick holds an illustrated edition (1736) of Terence's *Comedies*, with a page showing the masks for the *Andria* copied from a manuscript in the Vatican Library. Various copies of A61 are known.

Copy after Jacopo Bassano
(*c.* 1510 – 1592)

The Annunciation to the Shepherds

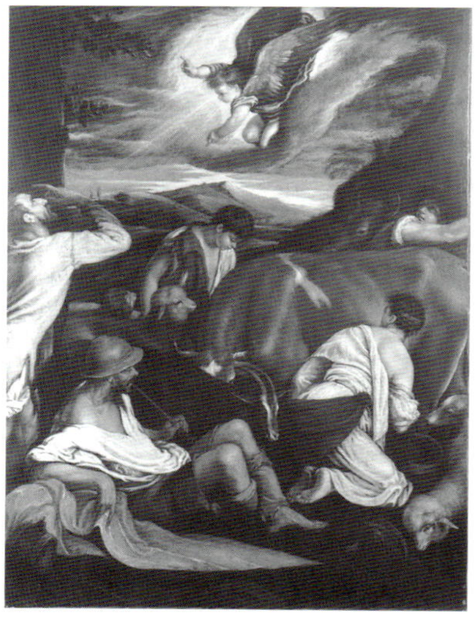

A905; oil on canvas, 131 × 97.5 cm
Presented by Francis Falconer Madan, 1957; WA1957.89

Lloyd 1977, p. 27; Ballarin 1995–6, I, Part II, pp. 326–68

While shepherds watched their flocks at night, an angel appeared to announce the birth of Christ (Luke 2: 8–18). One of a large number of copies of an influential composition, this may date from the 17th century. The prototype may be the version formerly in the collection of the Duke of Rutland, of *c.* 1560, rather than that in the National Gallery of Art, Washington, of *c.* 1558. A905 has been on loan to the University Church, Oxford, since 1988.

Jules Bastien-Lepage
(1848 – 1884)

Laura, Lady Alma-Tadema

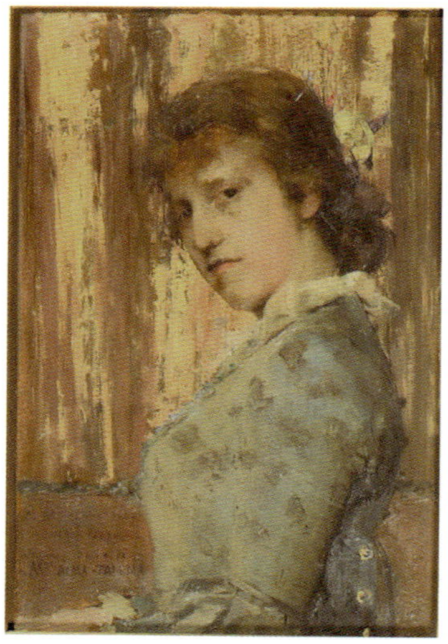

A1020; oil on copper, 22 × 15 cm
Signed and dated: *J. BASTIEN-LEPAGE / LONDRES 1879*; and inscribed: *Affectueux souvenir à Mme ALMA-TADEMA*
Presented by Miss Sylvia Gosse, 1965; WA1965.15.2

Aubrun 1985, no. 226

The sitter, Laura Epps *(1852–1899)*, wife of the painter, Lawrence Alma-Tadema and herself a painter, was the donor's aunt. Bastien-Lepage is best known as a painter of peasant subjects but was also a skilled painter of portraits. This little panel is painted with characteristic bravura. Bastien-Lepage's technique was much admired by his contemporaries.

Walter John Bayes
(1869 – 1956)

Interior with a Woman dressing

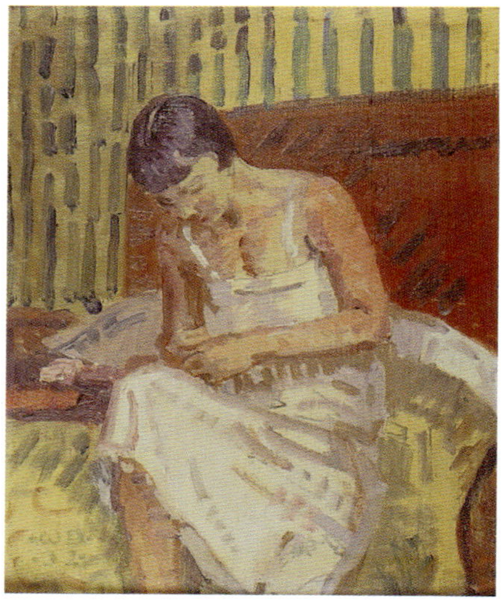

A1032; oil on canvas laid down on board, 35 × 30 cm
Signed and dated: *WB 32*
Presented by Professor J. Anthony Betts, 1967; WA1967.34.1

Bayes was a founder member of the Allied Artists Association (1908), the Camden Town Group (1911) and the London Group (1913–15). From 1918 to 1934, he was Principal of the Westminster School of Art, a position he owed to Sickert's influence. His later pictures continued the themes of the Camden Town Group, but were painted in a looser style.

Walter John Bayes
(1869 – 1956)

Two Men on a Beach

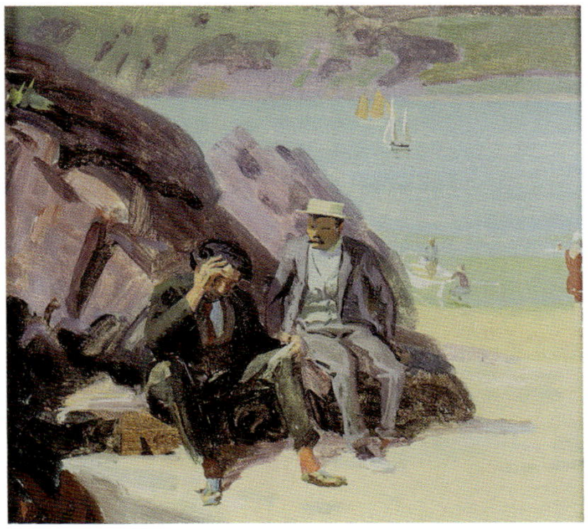

A1032a; oil on canvas, laid on board, mounted as a drawing, 26.4 × 29.1 cm
Presented by Professor J. Anthony Betts, 1967; WA1967.34.2

One of a number of beach scenes by Bayes, this may have been painted on a family holiday in Brittany shortly before the First World War.

Sir George Howland Beaumont, Bt
(1753 – 1827)

Woodland Scene with Gipsies

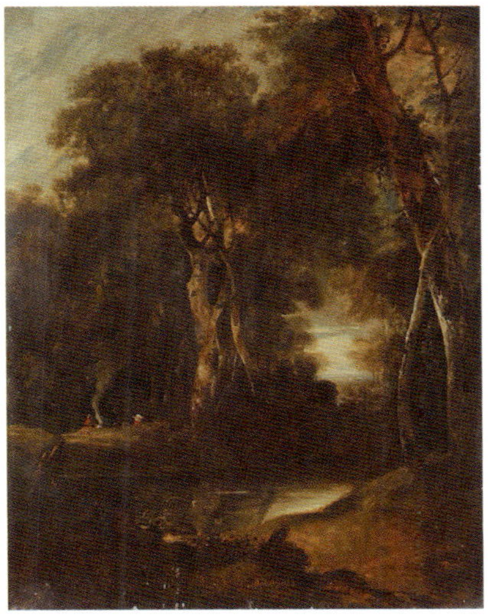

A42; oil on canvas, 90 × 70 cm
Presented by the artist, 1801; WA1845.42

Owen and Brown 1987, p. 138; Kidson 1999, p. 38

In addition to being one of the most important collectors and patrons of his day, Beaumont exhibited as an amateur artist at the Royal Academy between 1779 and 1825, showing exclusively landscapes in the manner of Richard Wilson. This example may have been shown in 1800. It was engraved by John Browne (1741–1801) as *The Forest.*

Cornelis Bega
(1631/2 – 1664)

The Blind Fiddler

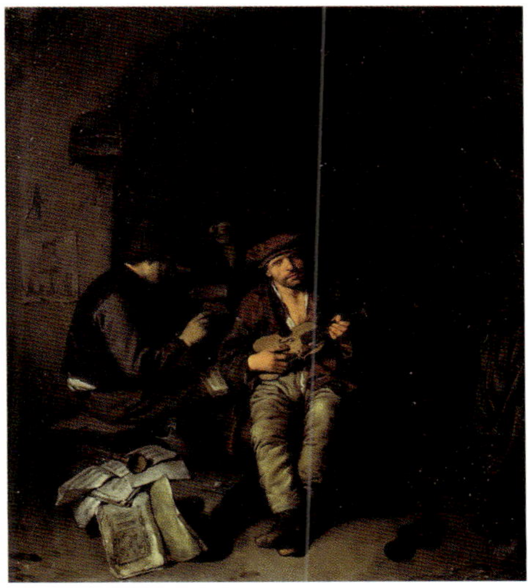

A288; oil on canvas, 35 × 30 cm
Presented by the Revd Henry George Woods, 1897; WA1897.11

White 1999, p. 10

Like his master, Adriaen van Ostade, Bega was a painter of taverns and peasant subjects. A drawing or print of an owl is fixed to the wall on the left. As owls do not see well by day, it has been suggested that this may refer to the blindness of the fiddler, plucking the strings of his instrument.

Keith Baynes
(1887 – 1977)

Landscape, St Clair

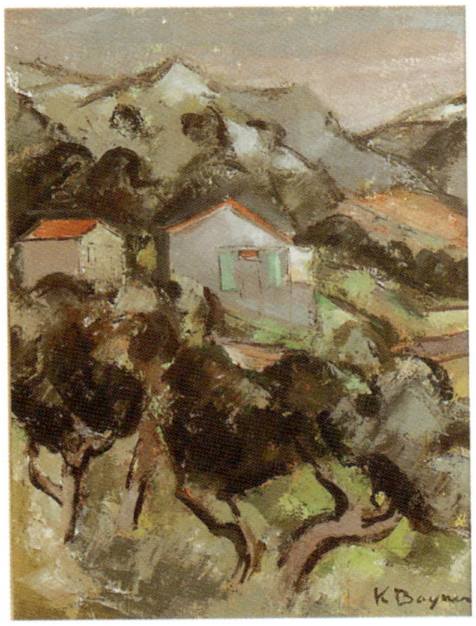

A750; oil on canvas, 41 × 33 cm
Signed: *K Baynes*
Presented by John Dodgson, 1948; WA1948.72

Educated at Trinity College, Cambridge and the Slade School of Fine Art in London, Baynes first exhibited in 1924 with the London Group. This landscape, painted in broad, vivid brush-strokes using rather dry paint, reflects the manner of Cézanne.

Style of Osias Beert the Elder
(*c.* 1580 – 1623)

A Vase of Flowers

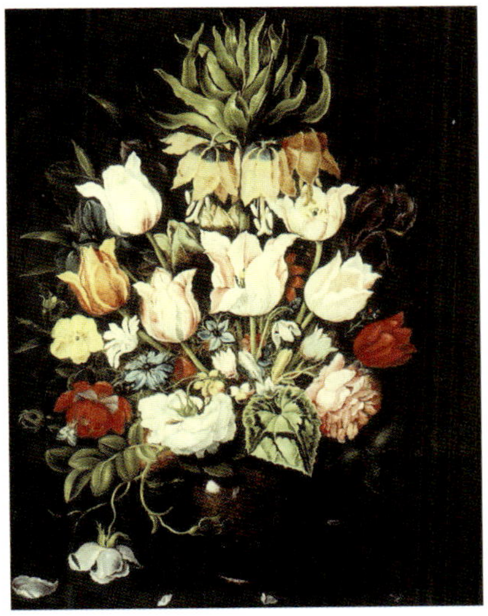

A531; oil on panel, 61 × 45 cm
Daisy Linda Ward Bequest, 1939; WA1940.2.7

Meijer 2003, no. 8

One of a number of works traditionally attributed to Osias Beerts which is too uneven in execution and too coarse in parts to be autograph. Otherwise, the motif of a bunch of fairly large blooms, filling the picture plane, the lighting and the choice of flowers (tulips, iris, crown imperial lily, love-in-a-mist, crocus, pansy, jonquil, snowdrop, roses, forget-me-not and cyclamen) is typical of Beert and some parts, notably the tulips, are quite close to his manner. It is generally believed to date from about 1616.

Vanessa Bell
(1879 – 1961)

Le Pont Neuf, Paris

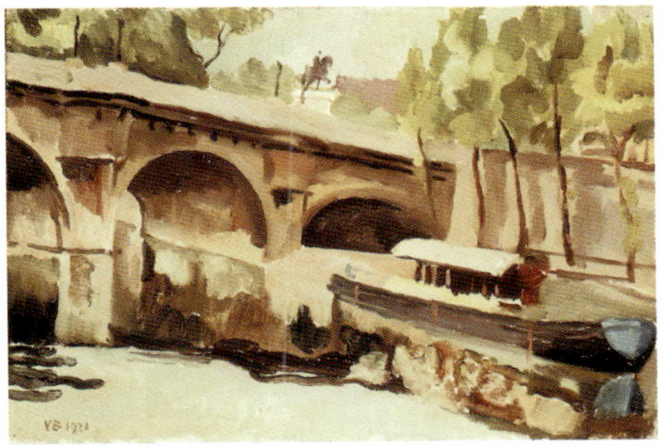

A644; oil on canvas, 38 × 55 cm
Signed in monogram and dated: *VB 1921*
Hindley Smith Bequest, 1939; WA1940.1.26

After the First World War, Bell reverted to a more naturalistic style. This cityscape of Paris, painted in 1921, indicates the direction of her art. At first glance, the painting seems to be a exact depiction of the Pont Neuf in Paris. The aim, however, is not to give a naturalistic description of the bridge but to examine the effects of light and movement and the patterns which result from both. The brushwork is fast and broad and develops its own dynamic, taking the work to the edge of pure abstraction.

Giovanni Bellini
(*c.* 1431–6 – 1516)

Madonna and Child

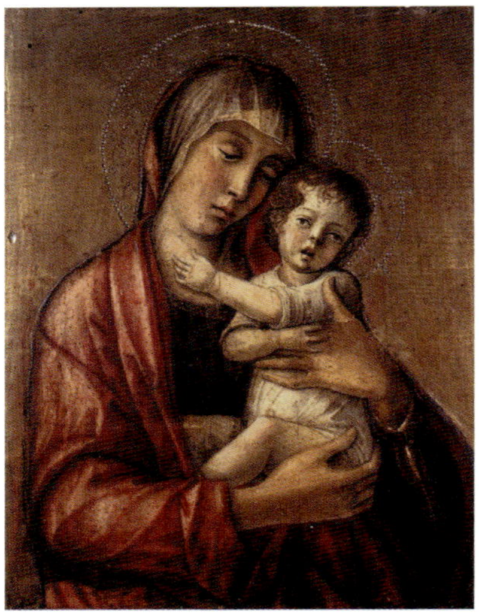

A1145; tempera and gilding on panel, 33.5 × 27.2 cm
Prov.: Portalupi, Verona; J.P. Richter; Ludwig Mond; Lord Melchett; Lord Clark of Saltwood
Accepted by H.M. Government in lieu of inheritance tax and allocated to the Ashmolean Museum, 1987; WA1987.26

Tempestini 1992, no. 28

Trained by his father Jacopo, Giovanni began his career by producing numerous small devotional works and A1145 may date from the late 1460s to early 1470s. However, the gold ground dates from the early 20th century and the figures may originally have been placed against a curtain or a landscape; the painting has been heavily restored.

Antonio Bellucci
(1654 – 1726)

Self-portrait

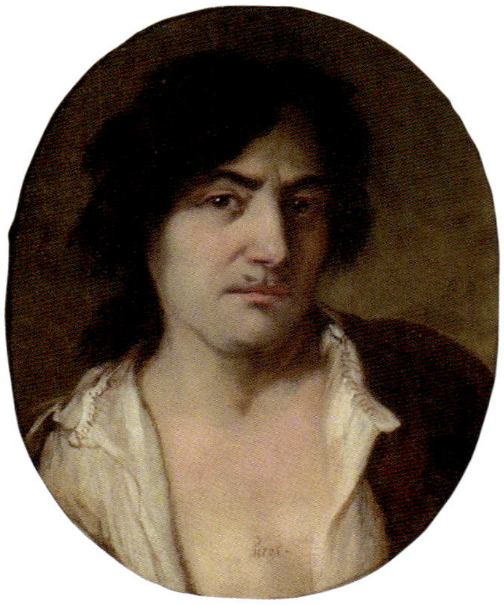

A1027; oil on canvas, 49 × 40 cm
Inscribed: *Pictor* (centre); *Antonius / Belluccius* (on the collar)
Purchased, 1966; WA1966.43

Magani 1995, no. 10

The artist may be around thirty years old, dating the picture to *c.* 1684, when Bellucci, a former soldier who trained with Antonio Zanchi, was establishing his artistic reputation in Venice. Later self-portraits are in the Uffizi and on the far left of the *Marriage of the Elector Palatine* (Alte Pinakothek, Munich), painted at the court of Düsseldorf, where Bellucci worked from 1705 to 1716.

Circle of Giovanni Bellini
(*c.* 1431/6 – 1516)

St Jerome reading in a Landscape

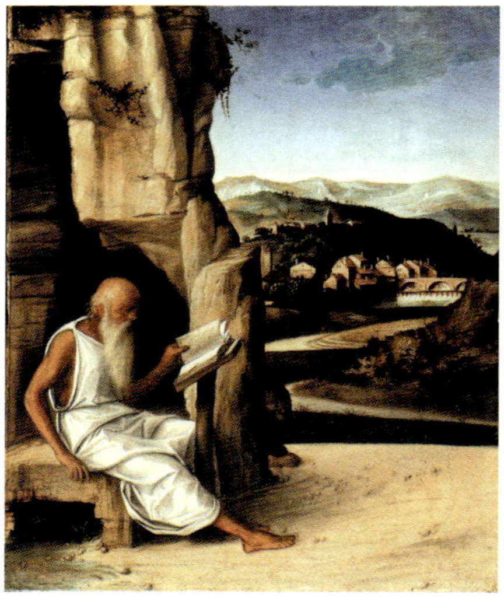

A302; tempera and oil (?) on panel, 26.6 × 21.7 cm
Prov.: purchased in Florence, 1864
Fortnum Bequest, 1899; WA1899.CDEF.P1

Lloyd 1977, pp. 29–31

The learned St Jerome retired to the desert *c.* 374–6 to lead a life of prayer and contemplation; he befriended a lion by removing a thorn from its paw. Suggested attributions for A302 have included Andrea Previtali and Vittore Carpaccio, the author of a related drawing in Berlin, although the composition may well derive from Bellini.

Antonio Bellucci
(1654 – 1726)

The Family of Darius before Alexander the Great

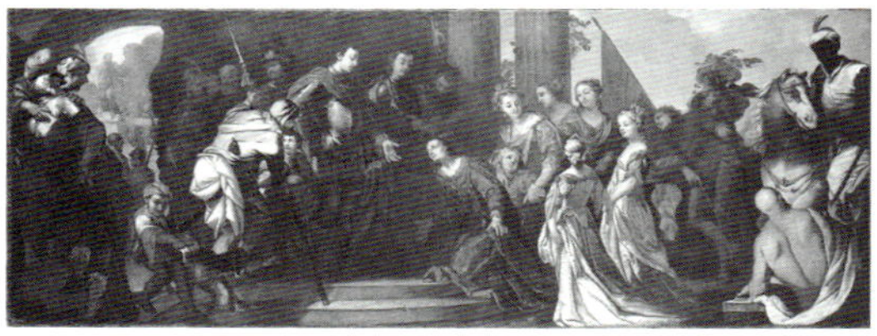

A140; oil on canvas, 213 × 564 cm
Prov.: Joseph Franz Anton Graf von Waldberg-Zeil-Wurzach, Vienna; Truchsessian Gallery sales, London 1803–6
Presented by the Hon. G.C. Percival, 1854; WA1854.2

Magani 1995, no. R81

The family of the defeated Persian king, Darius, kneel before Alexander but mistakenly address their pleas to his companion, Hephaestion: Alexander displays modesty and magnanimity in his response (Quintus Curtius Rufus, *History of Alexander* III, xii, 13–26). Bellucci's main source was the painting by Veronese for Ca' Pisani, Venice, now in the National Gallery.

Traditionally A140 was assumed to have been painted in England, where Bellucci worked from 1716 to 1722. Some scholars have rightly argued it is stylistically incongruous for that period and have questioned or rejected the attribution. In fact, A140 is clearly an early work, probably for the *portego* or main reception room of a Venetian palace. Little is known of Bellucci's early career and patrons.

Wilhelm Bendz
(1804 – 1832)

The Church of Ramsau, Austria

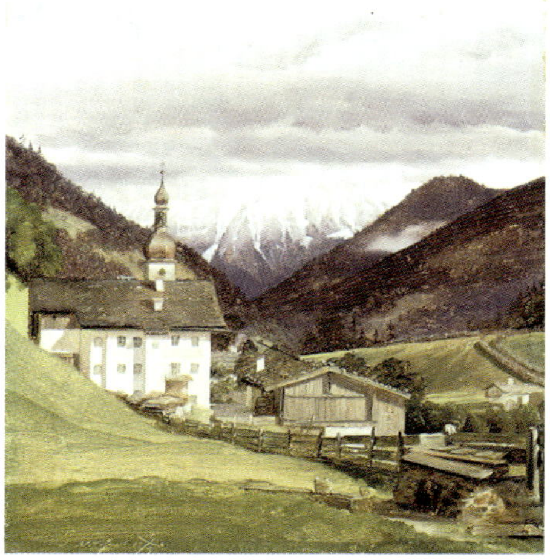

A1244; oil on paper, 28.9 × 24.5 cm
Dated: *Ramsau 18-9-1830*
Purchased (Miller Fund), 2002; WA2002.44

Bendz was principally a painter of figure subjects; his landscapes are rare. This view was painted in September 1832 when he was making his way from Copenhagen to Rome. He stopped briefly at Ramsau in Austria and made a number of lively sketches of the church and mountains. Shortly after, he fell ill and died in Vicenza on 14 November.

Ambrosius Benson
(active 1521 – d. 1550)

The Holy Family in a Landscape

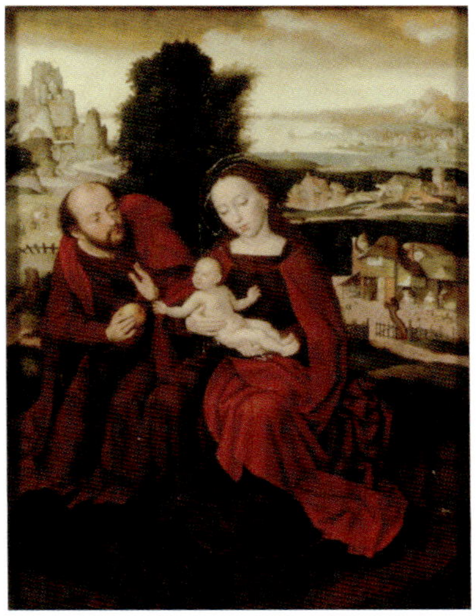

A712; oil on panel, 69 × 52 cm
Bequeathed by Miss Emily G. Kemp, 1940; WA1945.62

White 1999, p. 10

The background, crowded with incident, is characteristic of Benson's work. The treatment of the landscape with the tree is somewhat Italianate. A variant of the landscape appears in the background of a painting of the Virgin and Child in Campion Hall, Oxford. Benson was based in Bruges. His art developed initially under the influence of Gerard David in Bruges but his colour is more subdued and his interest in detail is less marked than they are in the work of his master.

Ambrosius Benson
(active 1521 – d. 1550)

The Holy Family

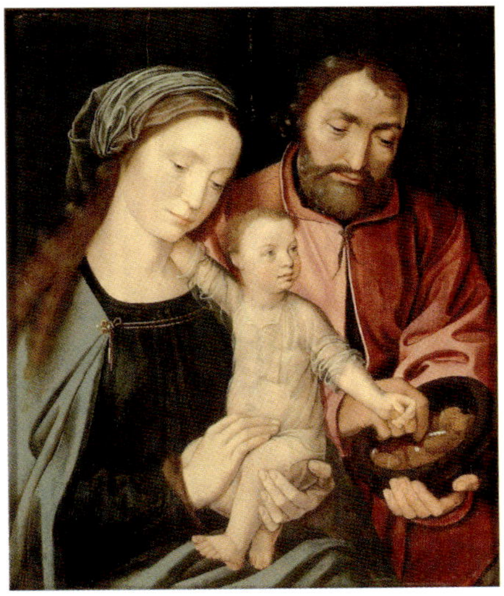

A814; oil on panel, 55 × 46 cm
Bequeathed by J. Reginald Jones, 1951; WA1951.51.8

White 1999, p. 11

The mixture of Flemish detail and Italian monumentality is typical of Benson's work. The Christ Child reaches down to take a handful of nuts or fruits from St Joseph's hat. This probably represents an episode from a legend which first appears in an apocryphal Gospel, known as the Pseudo-Matthew, which tells how a palm tree bent over to supply the Holy Family with fruit during the Flight into Egypt.

Nicolaes Pietersz. Berchem
(1620 – 1683)

Peasants with Cattle fording a Stream

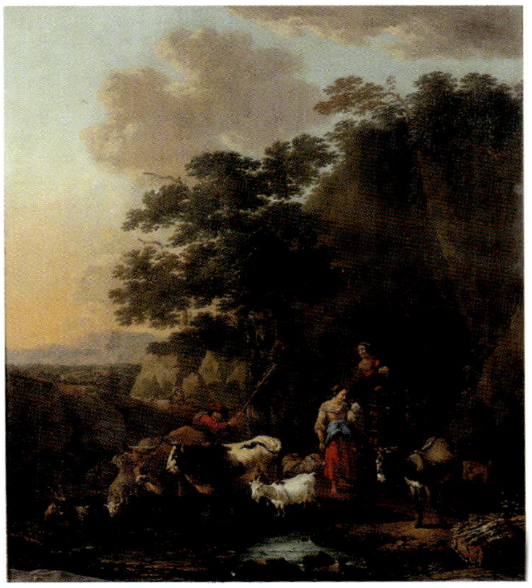

A808; oil on canvas, 103 × 90 cm
Signed and dated: *N Berchem ft / 1674*
Bequeathed by J. Reginald Jones, 1951; WA1951.51.2

White 1999, p. 13

One of the few late dated paintings by Berchem. He was living at the time in Haarlem. His early works are tonal landscapes of the kind developed by van Goyen but during the 1650s his style changed, perhaps as the result of a visit to Italy. Like many landscape paintings from the second half of his career, this composition is brightly lit and features peasants in an Italianate landscape.

Copy after Nicolaes Pietersz. Berchem
(baptized 1620 – 1683)

Landscape with Figures and Animals before a Castle

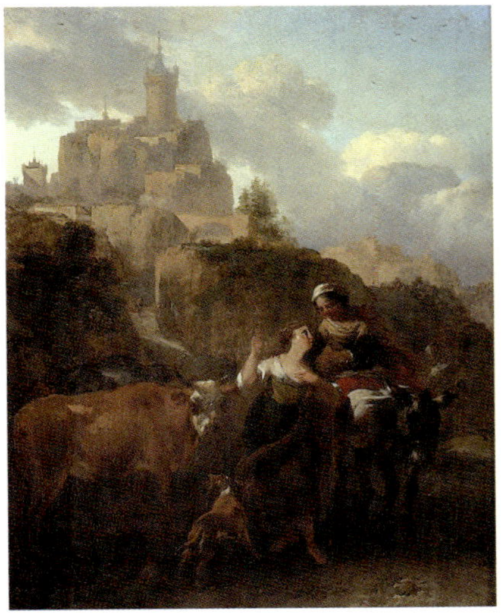

A289; oil on panel, 28 × 22 cm
Presented by the Revd Henry George Woods, 1897; WA1897.12

White 1999, p. 14

A loosely painted copy after a lost painting by Berchem, whose work was at one time highly regarded and much imitated.

Attributed to Niccolò Berrettoni
(1637 – 1682)

The Rape of Europa

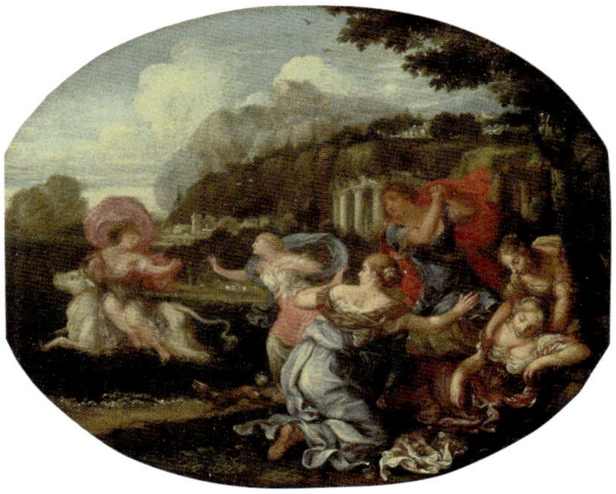

A919 ; oil on canvas, 33 × 41 cm
Russell Bequest, 1958; WA1958.57.2

Europa was abducted by the god Zeus in the form of a bull (Ovid, *Metamorphoses* II. 845–75). Traditionally attributed to Berrettoni, a talented associate of Carlo Maratta, this charming painting also has affinities in the treatment of the draperies and the female types with the work of Giuseppe Nicola Nasini (1657–1736), who was particularly impressed by the art of Maratta in the 1680s.

Jean-Victor Bertin
(1767 – 1842)

An Italian Villa

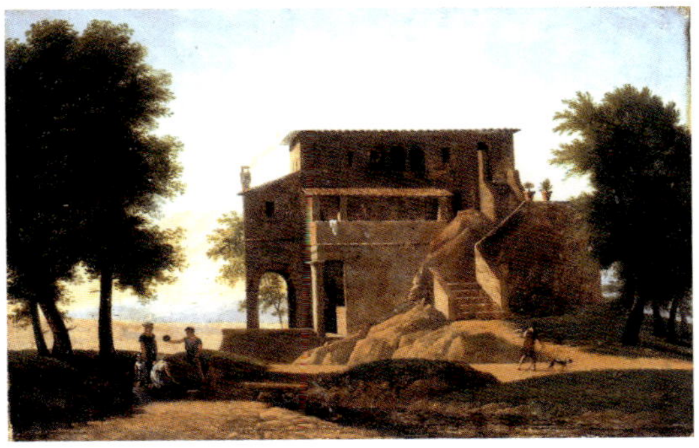

A1178; oil on canvas, 20.5 × 30.5 cm
Inscribed on the stretcher: *Edouard Bertin / 1823 No.1072*
Purchased with the aid of donations in memory of Margaret Grinyer, 1993; WA1993.328

A version of this composition entitled *Vue prise à Palestrine* was exhibited at the Salon of 1808 and an engraving made after it, which differs from A1178 in some details; another version is known, signed and dated 1807. Bertin specialised in Italianate classical landscapes. He was an important teacher, with Achille Michallon and Jean-Baptiste-Camille Corot amongst his pupils. The inscription refers to Edouard Bertin who entered the studio of Jean-Victor in 1823.

Robert Polhill Bevan
(1865 – 1925)

In the Downs near Lewes

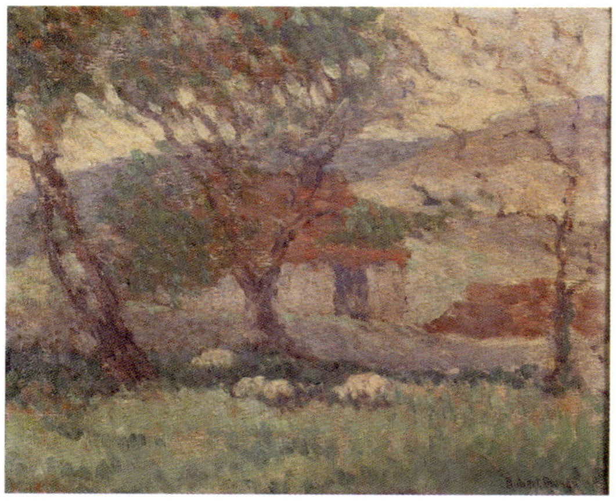

A945; oil on canvas, 34 × 46 cm
Signed: *Robert Bevan*
Prov.: R.A. Bevan
Purchased (Bevan Fund), 1961; WA1961.15

Baron 1979, p. 363

In 1905 and 1906, Bevan spent periods alone at St Ives, Kingston, near Lewes in the Sussex Downs. This landscape, painted in 1906, is characteristic of his work at that period: both the colouring and the handling are reminiscent of the painters around Gauguin at Pont Aven, where Bevan had stayed in 1893–4.

Robert Polhill Bevan
(1865 – 1925)

Queen's Grove, St John's Wood

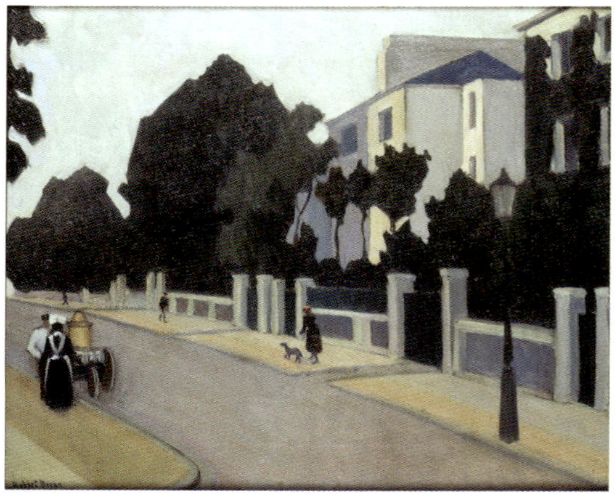

A897; oil on canvas, 50 × 60 cm
Signed: *Robert Bevan*
Presented by R.A. Bevan, the artist's son, 1957; WA1957.14.2

Bevan 1965, pl. 67; London 1988, no. 188

Between 1900 and 1922, Bevan lived at 14 Adamson Road, Swiss Cottage, in a house with a top floor studio built for Sir Alfred East. He painted a number of views in the neighbouring suburbs of Belsize Park and St John's Wood. This painting, which has been dated 1918, probably shows Queen's Grove, St John's Wood, though the anonymity of the scene is deliberate.

Abraham van Beyeren
(1620/1 – 1690)

Still Life with a Lobster

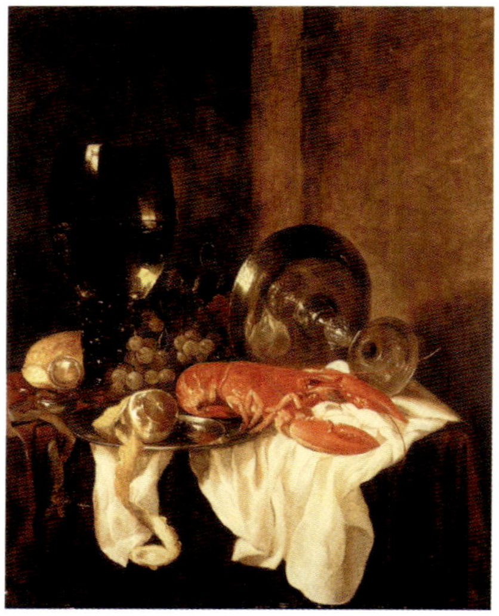

A533; oil on panel, 80 × 63 cm
Prov.: Marquis of Stafford; Brig.-Gen. Godfrey Meynell; Daisy Linda Ward Bequest, 1939; WA1940.2.9

Meijer 2003, no. 9

Van Beyeren painted fish and lavish banquet pictures with vessels of silver and gold from early in his career. This is thought to be one of his earlier pictures of a banquet, dating perhaps from the 1640s. No dated still-life paintings before 1652 are known but the somewhat transparent paint and thinly painted background are thought to be characteristic of his early work.

Robert Polhill Bevan
(1865 – 1925)

The Chestnut Tree

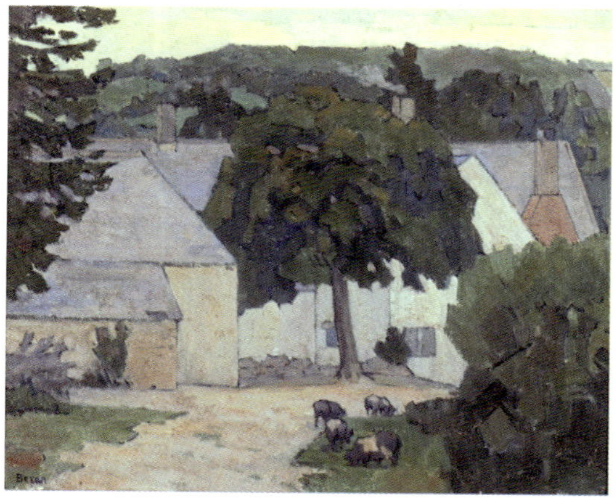

A896; oil on canvas, 50 × 60 cm
Signed: *Bevan*
Presented by R.A. Bevan, the artist's son, 1957; WA1957.14.1

Bevan 1965, pl. 63

Gore, Ginner and Bevan enjoyed visiting Harold Harrison, who kept a farm at Clayhidon, Devonshire. During the First World War, the Harrisons were unable to offer hospitality and between 1916 and 1919, Bevan rented a nearby cottage called Lytchetts, at Clayhidon. Here, he painted a number of landscapes.

Robert Polhill Bevan
(1865 – 1925)

Showing at Tattersalls

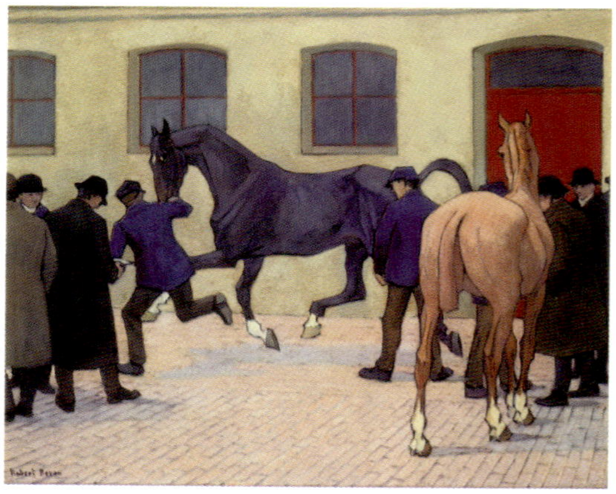

A898; oil on canvas, 58 × 71 cm
Signed: *Robert Bevan*
Presented by R.A. Bevan, the artist's son, 1957; WA1957.14.3

Bevan 1965, pl. 75; London 1988, no. 193; Eustace 1999, no. 15

The subject matter of cab-yards, mews and horse sales in London was suggested to Bevan by Sickert and was in keeping with the tenets of the Camden Town Group. This painting, of *c.* 1919, shows how Bevan's mature technique had developed into an angular style in which colour fused into broad masses of a subdued and subtle tone.

Abraham van Beyeren
(1620–1 – 1690)

Still Life with a Lobster and Turkey

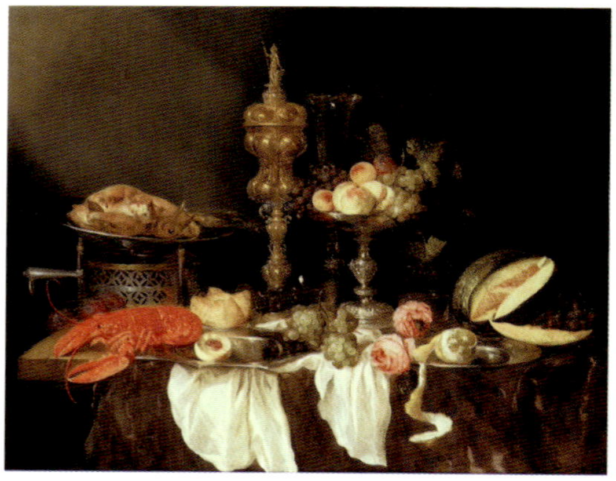

A535; oil on canvas, 91 × 112 cm
Daisy Linda Ward Bequest, 1939; WA1940.2.11

Meijer 2003, no. 10

This sumptuous composition includes a number of accessories which appear in different arrangements in many of van Beyeren's paintings. The silver-gilt standing cup-and-cover appears frequently throughout his work. The lobster, a similar cup-and-cover, lemon, dish, melon and tazza all reappear in a still life in the Metropolitan Museum, New York which is also undated but, like this still life, may predate his earliest dated work of 1653.

Abraham van Beyeren
(1620/1 – 1690)

Still Life with a silver Wine-jar and a reflected portrait of the artist

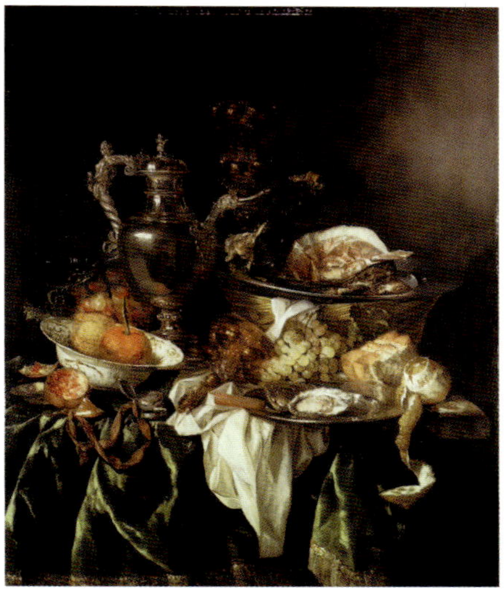

A534; oil on canvas, 102 × 85 cm
Signed in monogram: *AvB*
Prov.: M. van Eyck; Earl of Clancarty; Rodolfe Kann; Carl von Hollitscher, Berlin; Clement Bayard
Daisy Linda Ward Bequest, 1939; WA1940.2.10

Meijer 2003, no. 12

This abundant still life includes a pewter dish with two oysters, a half-peeled lemon, bread, a pomegranate, grapes, a watch with key-ribbon, a Wan-li porcelain bowl containing an orange and a lemon, a gilt cup, a silver wine-jar, a glass of white wine and pewter dish and cut ham on a plaited straw basket. These objects can be found in different combinations in the artist's work from 1655 onwards. A similar still life in a private collection, dated 1657, may be contemporary. The silver wine-jar reflecting the artist at work wearing a hat is seen in a number of still lifes, including a particularly sumptuous example in The Mauritshuis in The Hague. It has been noted that the pitcher appears in all these works in exactly the same position, suggesting that the artist did not own this expensive vessel but relied upon a drawing as a model for each of these works. Unlike a normal reflection which reverses the image, van Beyeren's image on the jar shows an artist painting with his right hand, ie. a reflection of a left-handed artist. It may be that van Beyeren was left-handed but it may also be that he improvised his reflection without troubling to reverse the image.

Abraham van Beyeren
(1620/1 – 1690)

Still Life with Fruit

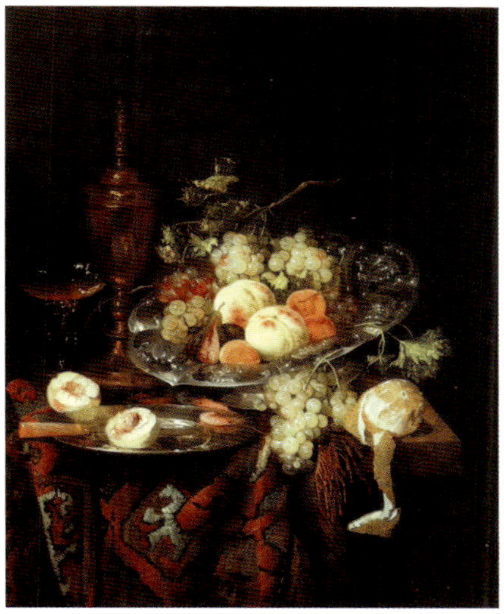

A536; oil on canvas, 75 × 60 cm
Signed: *AVB f* (AVB in monogram)
Daisy Linda Ward Bequest, 1939; WA1940.2.12

Meijer 2003, no. 13

Dated on grounds of style to the 1660s. The accessories – the peeled lemon, grapes, pewter dish with knife, the cut peach, prawns and the oriental rug – appear in other still lifes by van Beyeren, although the oriental rug is not as common as the others.

Abraham van Beyeren
(1620/1 – 1690)

Interior with Still Life of Fish

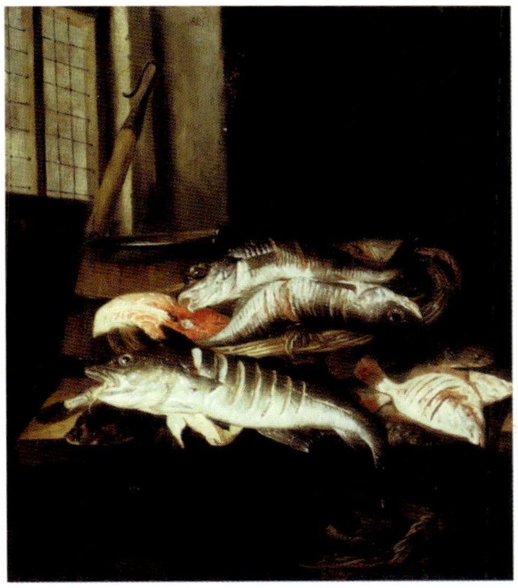

A532; oil on canvas, 104 × 89 cm
Daisy Linda Ward Bequest, 1939; WA1940.2.8

Meijer 2003, no. 11

Like most of van Beyeren's many still-life paintings of fish, this composition depicts sea fish. He sometimes showed them out of doors, usually on a beach, and sometimes indoors on a table before a window which opens onto a fish market on a beach, or as here before a closed window. He painted fish paintings throughout his career. This one is difficult to date but there are similar still-life paintings of fish in the Staatliche Museen, Berlin (dated 1655) and in the Akademie der bildenden Künste, Vienna (dated 1666).

Biagio di Antonio Tucci
(1446 – 1516)

The Flight of the Vestal Virgins

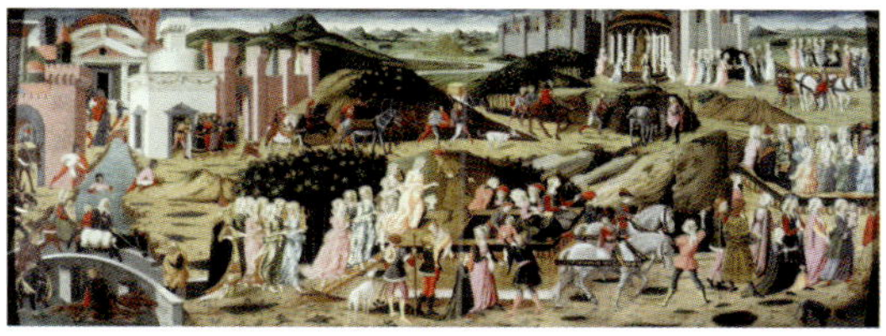

A82; tempera and gilding on panel, 67.3 × 174 cm
Fox-Strangways Gift, 1850; WA1850.28

Lloyd 1977, pp. 175–8; Bartoli 1999, pp. 153–4 and no. 14

Livy's history of Rome (*Ab urbe condita* V, 40–42) was the source for these scenes of the Gauls attacking Rome (390BC), with the escape of the Vestal Virgins in the carriage of the Roman citizen Lucius Albinus in the foreground; on the right they approach the safety of the Temple of Caere. Dating from the early 1480s, probably when Biagio was working in Rome, this *spalliera* panel was intended to be seen at eye-level, perhaps inserted into the panelling of a room.

Ferdinando Galli Bibiena
(1657 – 1743)

Design for an allegorical ceiling painting

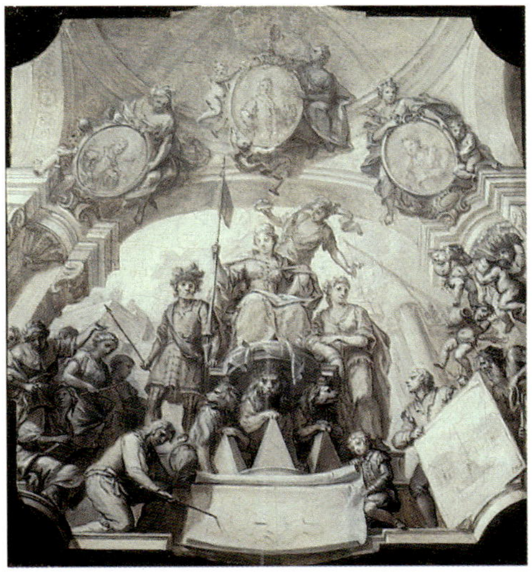

A1022; oil on canvas, 60.2 × 56.5 cm
Inscribed: *F.B.*
Prov.: (?)Elizabeth-Christine of Braunschweig-Lüneburg
Purchased, 1965; WA1965.62

The Bibiena family of architects and theatre designers worked for the courts of north Italy and central Europe. Paintings by Ferdinando are rare. Three family members are shown in the foreground, probably Ferdinando, his brother Francesco (1659–1739) and eldest son Alessandro (1686–1748). Accompanied by allegorical figures on the left including History and Painting, they present their plans to a ruler, represented by an enthroned female flanked by a warrior and by an allegory of abundance, with three crowned lions above pyramids, signifying three dukedoms. This ruling house is also represented by three framed male portraits of the late 17th century, accompanied respectively by Justice, Prudence and Peace. The horned river god on the right, with numerous *putti* bearing urns of water, is the River Po. The Bibiena worked for the Farnese family at Parma in the 1690s however; the regal family cannot be conclusively identified as the Farnese and may well be a German or Austrian house.

(three gold balls, his traditional attribute); and banishing the storm. The panels probably originally had quatrefoil frames. Bicci based the design of A89 on Gentile da Fabriano's Quaratesi altar-piece of 1425 for S. Niccolò oltr'Arno.

Style of Jan Frans van Bloemen, called Orizzonte
(1662 – 1749)

Extensive Landscape

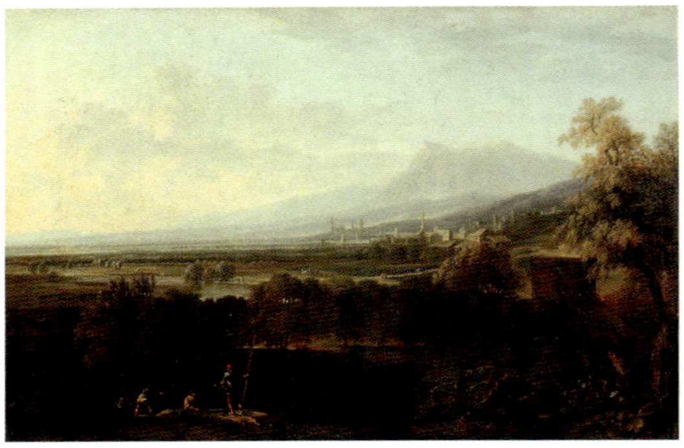

A670; oil on canvas, 64 × 94 cm
Bequeathed by Sir Arthur Evans, 1941; WA1941.3

White 1999, p. 15

Painted somewhat in the style of Jan Frans van Bloemen but by an imitator, perhaps working long after van Bloemen's lifetime. Van Bloemen's pastoral and Italianate landscapes, painted during and after a period spent in Rome (*c.* 1688–92), had a marked influence on the development of landscape painting in early 18th-century Rome and were much imitated.

Bicci di Lorenzo
(active late 1380s – 1452)

St Nicholas of Bari banishing the Storm

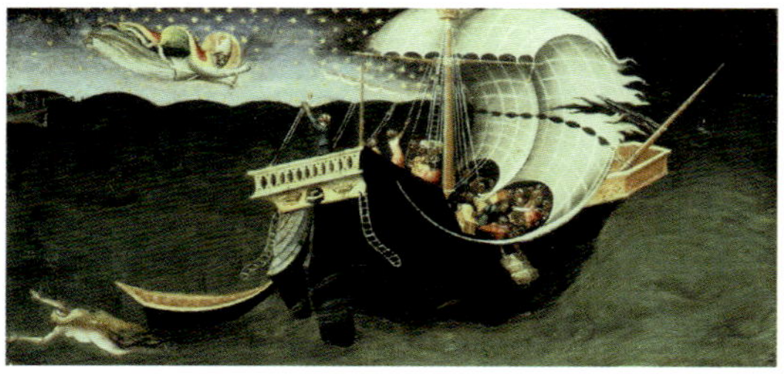

A89; tempera and gilding on panel, 29 × 59 cm
Fox-Strangways Gift, 1850; WA1850.26

Lloyd 1977, pp. 31–4; Thomas 1995, pp. 223–6

This panel comes from the predella of a large altar-piece of 1433–35 for S. Niccolò in Cafaggio, Florence, whose parts are now scattered in various collections. The *Virgin and Child with Four Angels* in the centre was flanked by pairs of saints (*Sts Benedict and Nicholas of Bari* and *St John the Baptist and an Evangelist*, probably St Matthew). The predella showed scenes from the life of St Nicholas, of which five are known: the birth of the saint; pilgrims at the shrine of the saint; St Nicholas resuscitating three youths; the saint providing dowries for three sisters

Jacques-Émile Blanche
(1861 – 1942)

Sir Max Beerbohm

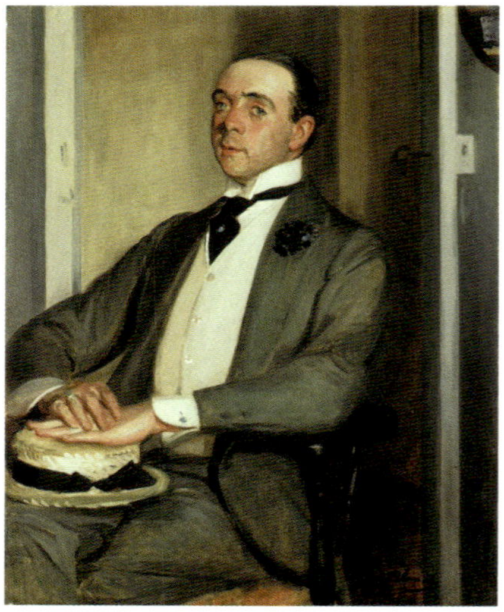

A739; oil on canvas, 100.8 × 82.1 cm
Signed and dated: *J.E.Blanche / 1903*
Presented by M. Mévil-Blanche (the artist's nephew) through the Contemporary Art Society, 1947; WA1947.233

Blanche moved from Paris to London in 1903, taking a studio in William Street, in Knightsbridge where this portrait was probably painted. Blanche had been a friend of Max Beerbohm (1872–1956), at least since the mid-1890s, when they frequented the colony of writers and artists in Dieppe. Beerbohm is posed as an Oxford student with the arms of the University on upper right and a boater on his knees. By the date of this portrait, he had already made his reputation as an essayist and humourist.

Pieter Boel
(1622 – 1674)

Study of Dogs and a Monkey on the Edge of a Wood

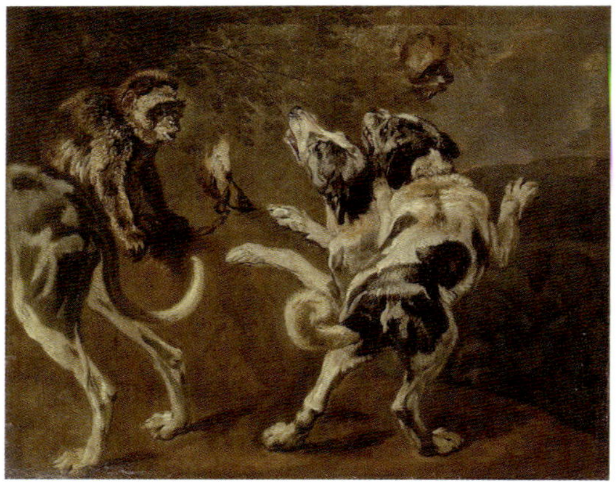

A180; oil on canvas, 83 × 104 cm
Chambers Hall Gift, 1855; WA1855.181

White 1999, p. 16

This painting was formerly attributed to Jan Fijt but is now identified as the work of Fijt's pupil, Pieter Boel, who specialised in painting animals and still life, occasionally in collaboration with other artists. Boel worked mainly in Antwerp but moved to Paris in 1668 where he was employed as a designer of animals for the Gobelins tapestry works.

Pieter Boel
(1622 – 1674)

Still Life of Game

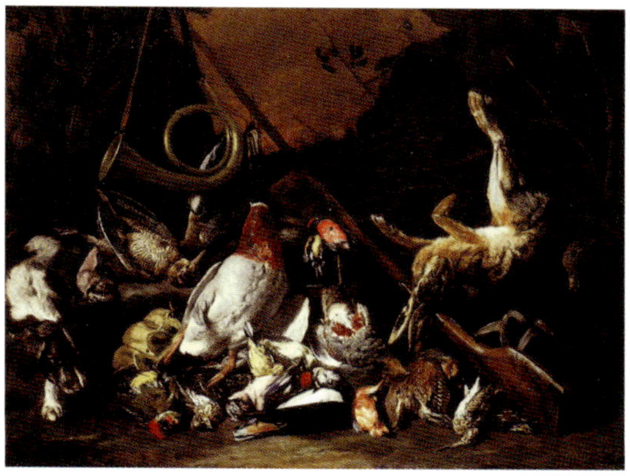

A551; oil on canvas, 104 × 135.5 cm
Daisy Linda Ward Bequest, 1939; WA1940.2.27

Meijer 2003, no. 14

This still life, like the previous, was formerly attributed to Boel's teacher, Jan Fijt. Boel rarely signed his works and many have been misattributed to Fijt. Boel's compositions tend to be quieter than those of his master. The gun dog in this picture is less nervously alert than he would be in a painting by Fijt. This may be a relatively early work dating from 1650–55.

Hans Bollongier
(*c.* 1600 – 1650)

A Vase of Flowers

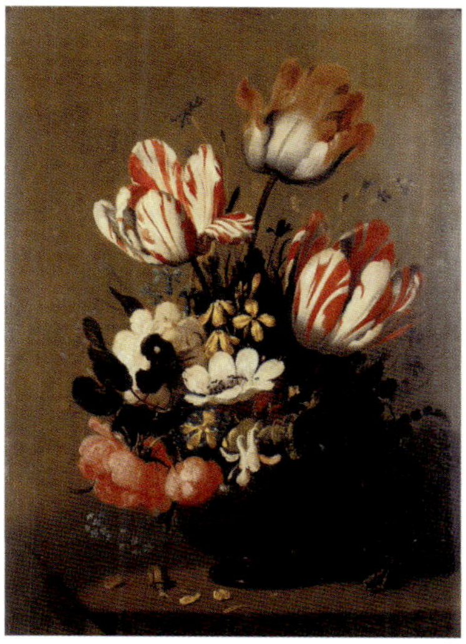

A537; oil on panel, 45 × 32 cm
Signed: *Ano 1636. HB.* (HB in monogram)
Daisy Linda Ward Bequest, 1939; WA1940.2.13

Meijer 2003, no. 15

Bollongier was one of the few painters of the first half of the 17th century in Haarlem who specialised in painting flowers. His work seems to have been influenced by the Bosschaert school but with an added naturalism in the arrangement of the flowers. The glass container in this painting was a favourite accessory. It appears first in a work of 1627 and for the last time in a flower piece of 1639 (Rijksmuseum, Amsterdam).

Anonymous Bolognese Artist
(*c.* 1610)

The Infant Christ with the Instruments of the Passion

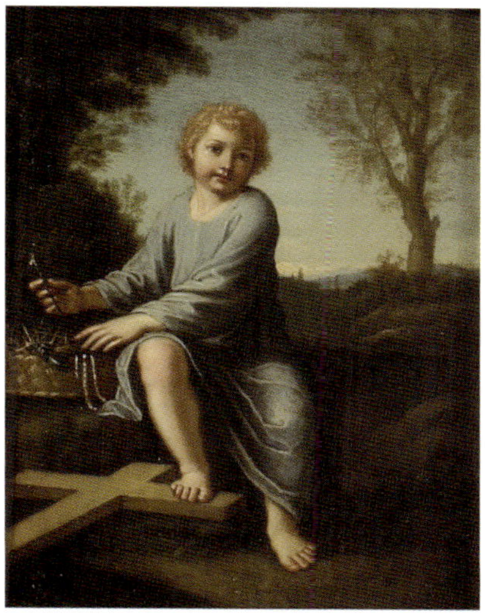

A647; oil on copper, 23 × 17.9 cm
Prov.: Dr Robert Bragge; Benjamin West; W.G. Coesvelt; Samuel Rogers; Baroness Burdett-Coutts
Hindley Smith Bequest 1939; WA1940.1.29

Spear 1982, I, p. 231

The Infant Christ with the instruments of the Passion was a popular subject in the Counter-Reformation, with Christ most commonly shown either sleeping, or in prayer; A647 is unusual in showing the attitude of Christ in Judgement. A replica on panel was in the Northbrook collection. A plausible attribution has been suggested to Innocenzo Tacconi (1575–post 1625).

Anonymous Bohemian (?) Artist
(*c.* 1720)

Self-portrait

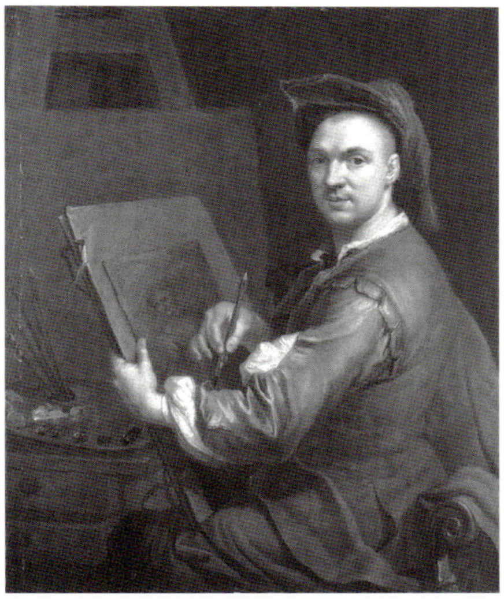

A418; oil on canvas, 98 × 81 cm
Purchased, 1932; WA1932.199

The artist is drawing a portrait of a woman in black chalk on blue paper. Acquired as an anonymous self-portrait of *c.* 1720, A418 was subsequently attributed to Johann Kupecký (1667–1740). Kupecký's likeness is known, however and the style is not his. While A418 may be by a Bohemian artist close to Kupecký, there are also affinities with north Italian portraiture.

Anonymous Bolognese Artist
(*c.* 1600)

Head of an old Man

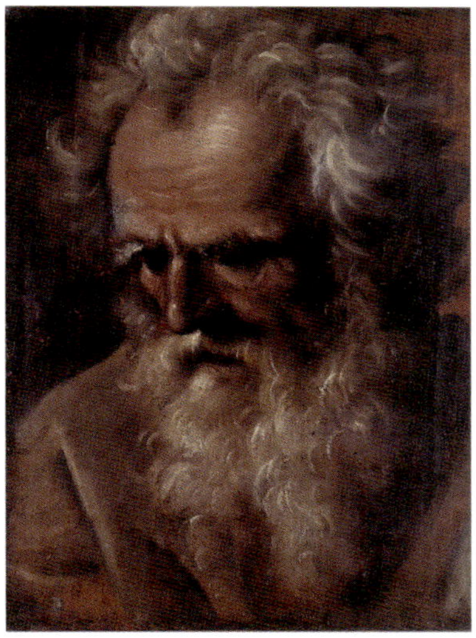

Oil on paper, laid on canvas, mounted as a drawing, 28.7 × 20.9 cm
Prov.: H.D. Molesworth
Purchased, 1955; WA1955.31

Formerly attributed to Beccafumi, this oil-sketch may be a study for the figure of a prophet or saint such as St Joseph in a *Holy Family*. A similar expressive head in oil on paper from the same model (and with the same provenance) was on the art market in 1979.

Anonymous Bolognese Artist
(*c.* 1730 – 40)

Diana and Endymion

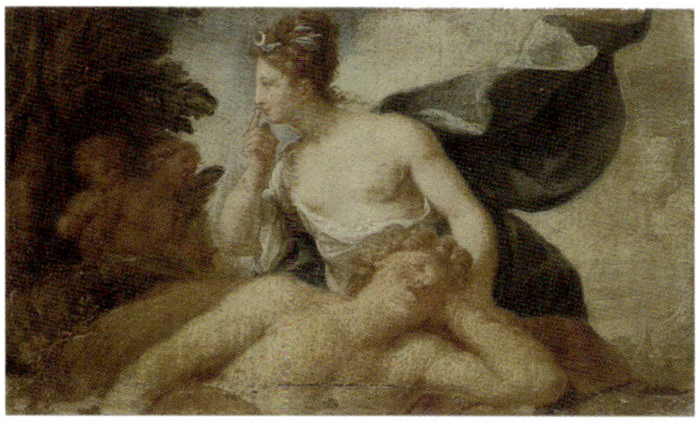

A145; oil on canvas, 16 × 25 cm
Chambers Hall Gift, 1855; WA1855.208

In Greek myth, Selene, goddess of the moon, loved Endymion, whom she kissed in his eternal sleep. Diana, the chaste goddess of the hunt in Roman myth, was also identified with the moon and her attribute of the crescent moon is visible here. Traditionally attributed to Francesco Albani, this fragment, no doubt once forming part of a decorative ensemble, may be from *c.* 1730–40 by a Bolognese artist close to Donato Creti or to Ercole Graziani.

Anonymous Bolognese Artist
(*c.* 1750)

A saintly Cleric with a Crucifix

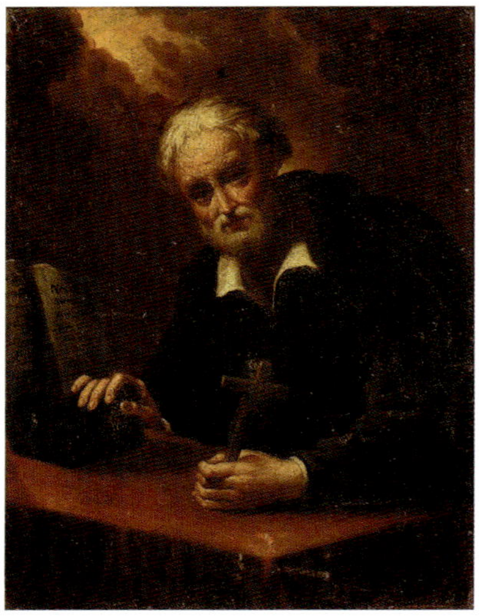

A258; oil on canvas, 29 × 22 cm
Bequeathed by the Revd Greville John Chester, 1892; WA1892.3

The cleric holds a crucifix, with an open book before him; he has no halo, but heavenly light is evoked on the left, so that he may have been a recently beatified or venerable priest. A plausible attribution has recently been suggested to Antonio Crespi (1712–81).

David Bomberg
(1890 – 1957)

Procession

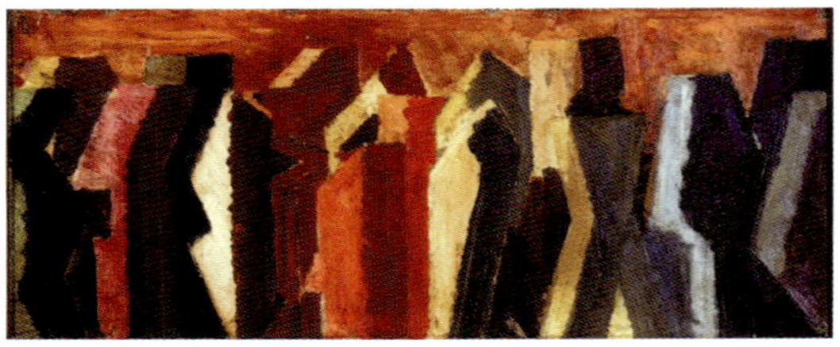

A1120; oil on paper laid on panel, 28.9 × 68.8 cm
Signed: *DAVID BOMBERG*
Presented by Mr and Mrs James Newmark, in memory of the artist, through the Contemporary Art Society, 1981; WA1981.604

Lipke 1967; Eustace 1999, no. 9

This painting cannot be exactly dated, but must have been made between 1912 and 1914. One preparatory drawing for this work is known. Reduced to black and white and some shades of red, it already shows Bomberg's later interest in the substance of paint and in the movement of figures.

Studio of Bonifazio de' Pitati
(1487 – 1553)

Moses brought before Pharaoh's Daughter

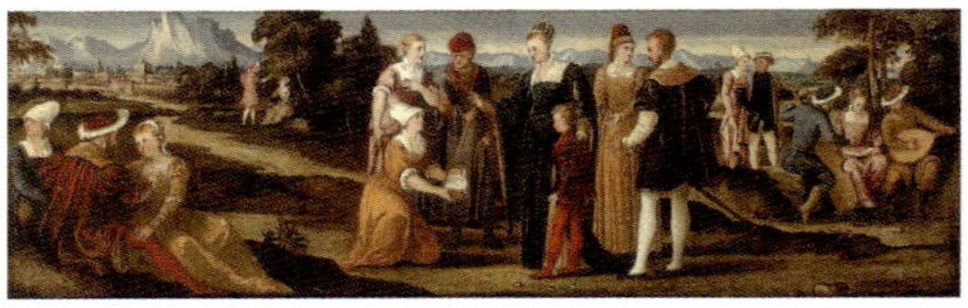

A451a; oil on canvas laid on panel, 27 × 81 cm
Prov.: Capt. James W. St L. Wheble; Revd E. Moodie
Purchased, 1936; WA1936.170

Lloyd 1977, pp. 34–5; Simonetti 1986, p. 124, A120

Pharoah had ordered that all first-born Hebrew sons be killed and to avoid this fate, the baby Moses was placed in a rush basket in the river Nile, where he was rescued and brought before Pharoah's daughter (Exodus 2:3–10). A451a is probably a companion painting to A430. The elongated forms in both pictures are reminiscent of the work of Antonio Palma, Bonifazio's senior assistant.

Giacomo Bolognini
(?1664 – 1734/37)

Perseus and Andromeda

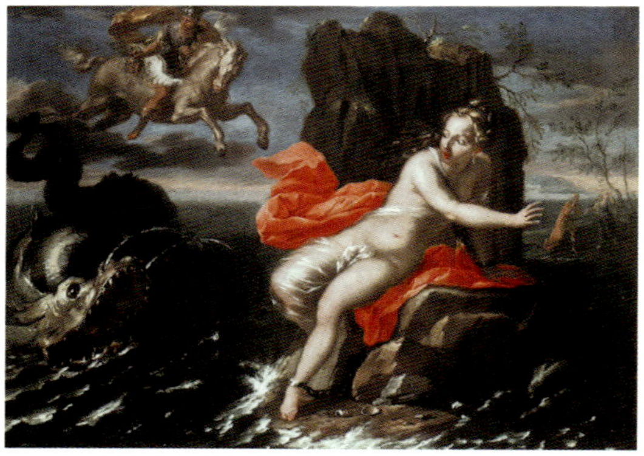

A1102; oil on canvas, 40.8 × 51.2 cm
Signed: *G.B.f*
Prov.: John, Earl of Abergavenny until 1849; Sir Shafto Adair; Major General Sir Allan Adair
Presented by M.V.B. Hill, 1978; WA1978.106

Biagi Maino 1996, pp. 35–6

Perseus on his winged horse liberates Andromeda from a sea-monster (Ovid, *Metamorphosis* IV, 669). A1102 had a variety of attributions to Bolognese artists with the initials G.B., including Giacomo Bolognini. However, little comparable work was known by that rare artist until the publication of a painting of *Tancred and Erminia* which confirmed that A1102 is by the same hand.

David Bomberg
(1890 – 1957)

Circus (Abstract Composition)

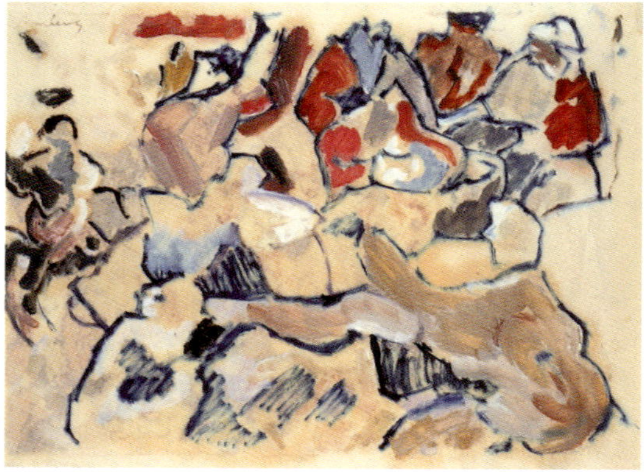

Oil on paper, laid on cardboard, mounted as a drawing, 32.8 × 43 cm
Signed: *Bomberg*
Presented by Mr and Mrs James Newmark, in memory of the artist, through the Contemporary Art Society, 1981; WA1981.605

This sketch-like work shows Bomberg's lifelong interest in form. In his early career he claimed to be interested only in pure form, but later developed a style which combines a fascination for mechanics and structure with a free use of the paint. Paint is applied in an extremely dynamic manner, combining outlines and colour and creating a simple and abstract pattern.

Studio of Bonifazio de' Pitati
(1487 – 1553)

The Trial of Moses

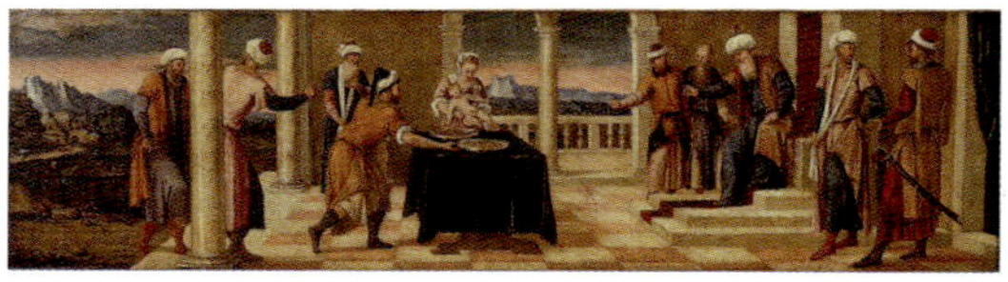

A730; oil on canvas laid on panel, 27.4 × 96.9 cm
Bequeathed by F.P.M. Schiller, 1946; WA1946.270

Lloyd 1977, pp. 34–5; Simonetti 1986, p. 124, A121

In this apocryphal subject, Pharoah, worried about his future, tests the intentions of the baby Moses, who demonstrates his innocence. The two pictures, in their subjects, dimensions and handling, seem to be companion pieces, perhaps *cassone* panels. Bonifazio, who had probably been a pupil of Palma Vecchio, ran a large and important studio in Venice, which produced much domestic and furniture painting.

Studio of Bonifazio de' Pitati
(1487 – 1553)

The Judgement of Solomon

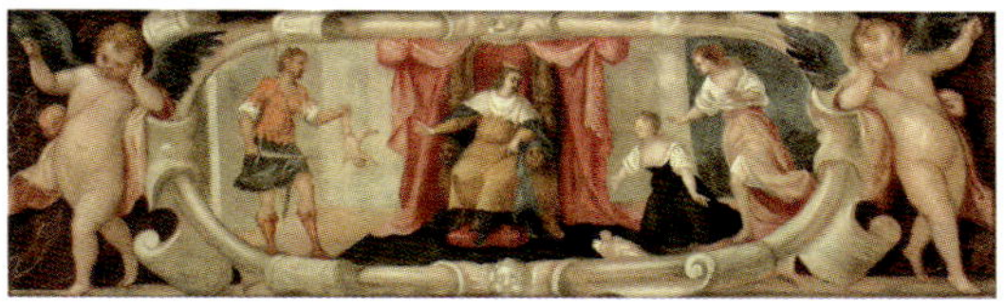

A914; oil on panel, 27.5 × 86.5 cm
Prov.: Susan, Duchess of Somerset
Russell Bequest, 1958; WA1958.57.1

Lloyd 1977, p. 36; Simonetti 1986, p. 124, A122

Solomon, famous for his wisdom, solved a dispute where two women claimed to be the mother of the same child, revealing the true mother's identity when the baby's life was threatened (I Kings 3: 16–28). The narrative is framed by a strapwork cartouche with two winged *putti*. The panel may have been part of a decorative frieze in the cornice of a room.

Richard Parkes Bonington
(1802 – 1828)

Amy Robsart and the Earl of Leicester

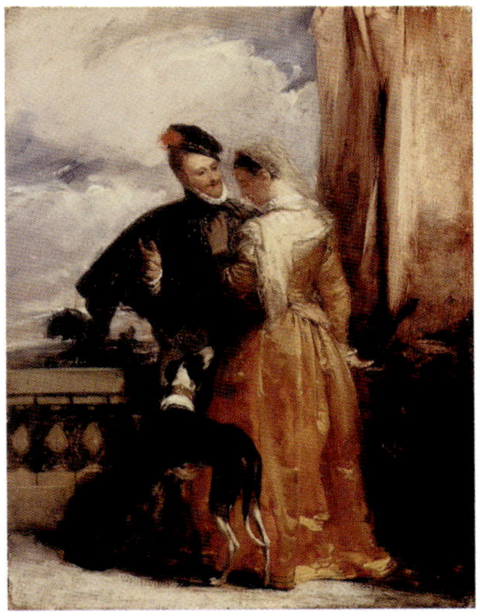

A421; oil on canvas, 35 × 27 cm
Prov.: Alexander Hamilton Douglas, 10th Duke of Hamilton and by descent
Presented by Mrs W.F.R. Weldon, 1933; WA1933.3

Noon 1991, no. 141

The story of Amy Robsart is told in chapter 5 of Sir Walter Scott's *Kenilworth*: the tragic heroine has made a secret marriage to Lord Leicester and here is seen pleading with him to make public their vows. He later prefers to satisfy his political ambition rather than fulfil his private obligations. This painting was probably made in Paris in 1827 and was inspired not only by the contemporary vogue for Scott's novel, but by the production of Victor Hugo's new play, with scenery and costumes designed by Delacroix. The figure of Leicester is based on Clouet's portrait of Charles X in the Louvre.

Copy after Richard Parkes Bonington
(1802 – 1828)

Coast scene: Morning

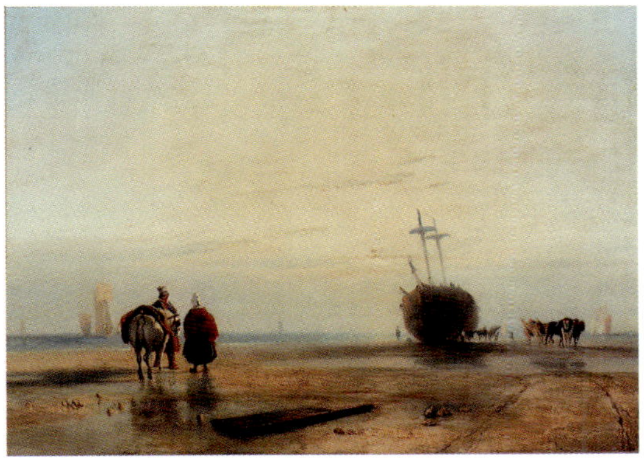

A276; oil on canvas, 54 × 76 cm
Combe Bequest, 1893; WA1894.12.2

Long accepted as autograph, this is a copy after an orginal of *c.* 1826 (private collection), which may have been painted on the northern coast of France.

Style of Richard Parkes Bonington
(1802 – 1828)

Coast Scene

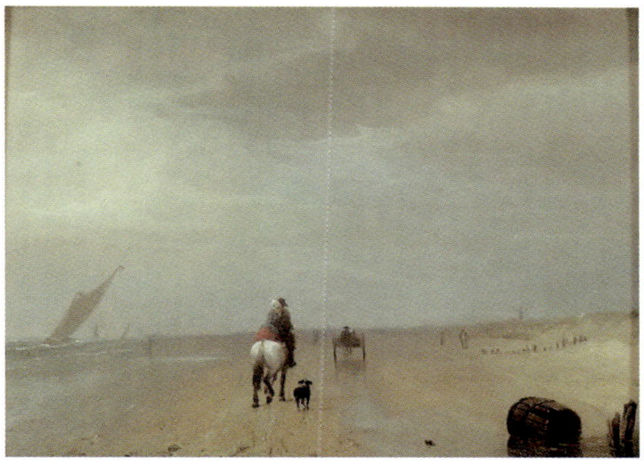

A480; oil on panel, 31.4 × 41.3 cm
Prov.: Alfred Elmore, R.A.; Charles Strut; Lindsay Hammond
Weldon Bequest, 1937; WA1937.61

Style of Richard Parkes Bonington
(1802 – 1828)

River scene near Dordrecht

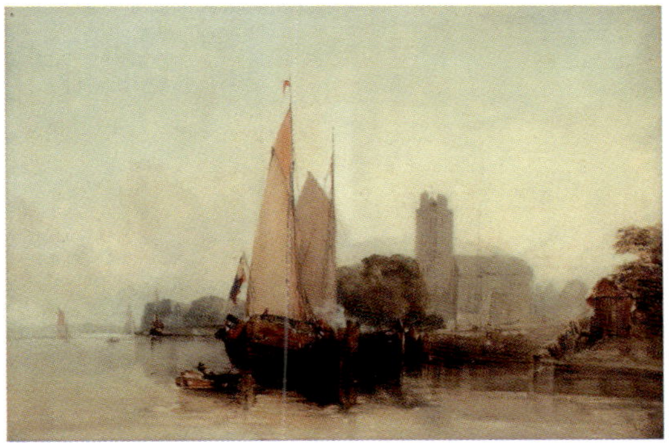

A459; oil on board, 36 × 26 cm
Prov.: R.K. Hodgson
Weldon Bequest, 1937; WA1937.39

Pierre Bonnard
(1867 – 1947)

Interior with Nude Figure

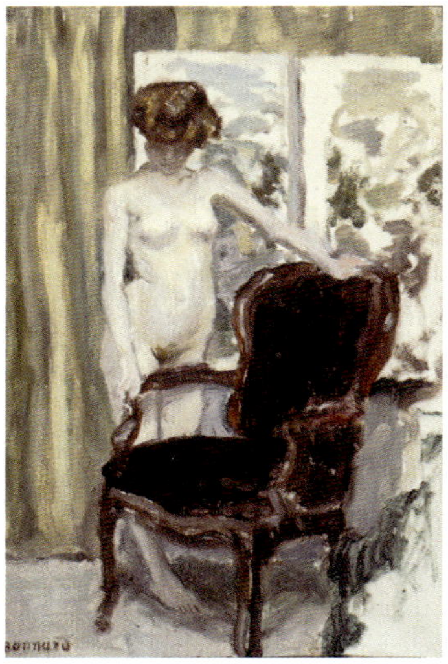

A627; oil on canvas, 54.1 × 35.8 cm
Signed: *Bonnard*
Hindley Smith Bequest, 1939; WA1940.1.9

Dauberville 1965–74, no. 371

Painted in about 1905. The canvas is inscribed on the back: *65, rue Doudé*, the address of Bonnard's studio from 1893 to 1907. The freedom with which it is painted recalls the work of the Impressionists but the colour is relatively subdued. The strong, luminous colour with which his art is chiefly associated did not become a major preoccupation until 1910.

Arnold Boonen
(1669 – 1729)

Jan van Huysum

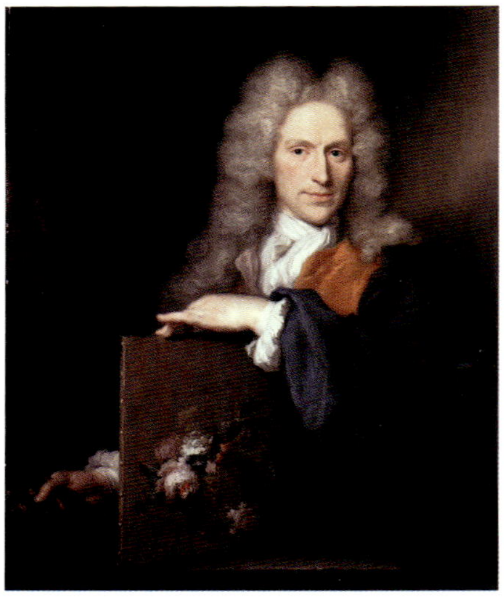

A877; oil on canvas, 93 × 76 cm
Prov.: 6th Duke of Newcastle and by descent to the 9th Duke; Earl of Lincoln
Presented by the National Art Collections Fund from the collection of Ernest E. Cook, 1955; WA1955.63

White 1999, p. 17

Formerly considered a self-portrait of Jan van Os, this has been identified as a portrait of the still-life painter, Jan van Huysum, painted between 1710 and 1729

Johannes Borman
(active 1653 – in or after 1660)

Still Life of Fruit

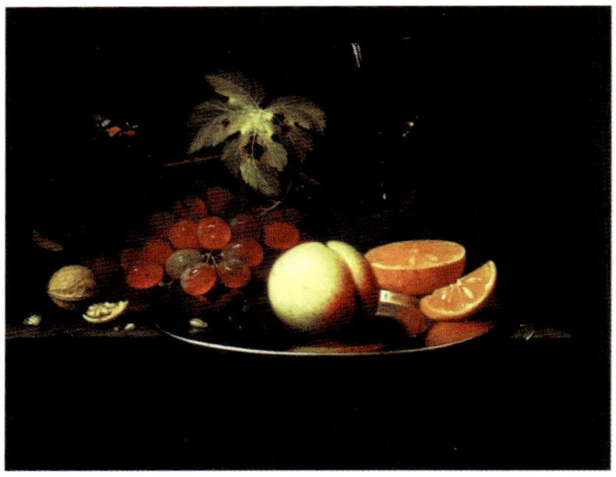

A538; oil on panel, 32 × 41 cm
Signed: *J Borman f.*
Daisy Linda Ward Bequest, 1939; WA1940.2.14

Meijer 2003, no. 16

Borman's work consists mainly of fruit pieces, although a few flower paintings are known. He was active in Leiden in The Hague. This fairly modest still life is characteristic of his work. A pewter plate with a peach and cut orange is placed on a ledge. Beside and behind are walnuts, a bunch of grapes and a glass of white wine. A butterfly hovers over the grapes.

Pierre Bonnard
(1867 – 1947)

A Path in the Forest

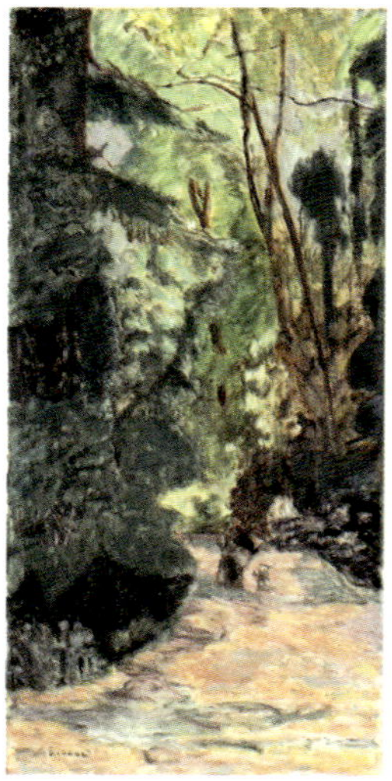

A628; oil on canvas, 86 × 41.5 cm
Signed: *Bonnard*
Hindley Smith Bequest, 1939; WA1940.1.10

Dauberville 1965–74, no. 983

Painted in about 1919 in a tall format which Vuillard, Bonnard's friend and colleague, also used on occasion. The shape suggests a decorative wall panel. It was presumably painted for a specific location.

Francisco Borès
(1898 – 1972)

Nature morte (Still Life)

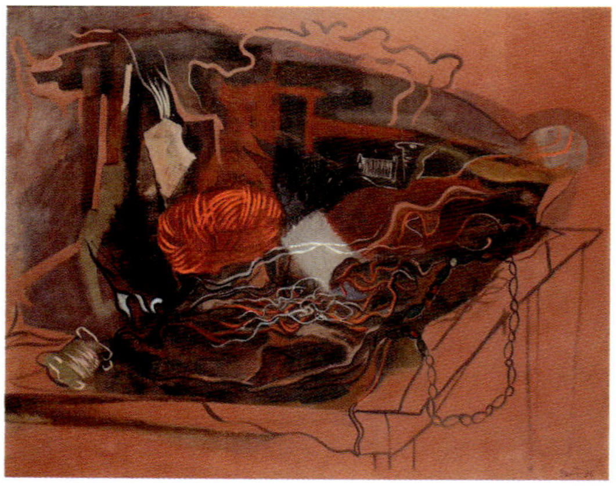

A996; oil on canvas, 65 × 81 cm
Signed and dated: *Borès 34*
Presented by Miss Elizabeth Watt, 1962; WA1962.78

Borès settled in Paris, where he became associated with other Spanish painters, such as Picasso and Gris, but also with Matisse and Derain. While his art derives from Cubism, he adds a new sense of colour and a synthetic treatment of space.

Johannes Bosboom
(1817 – 1891)

Church Interior

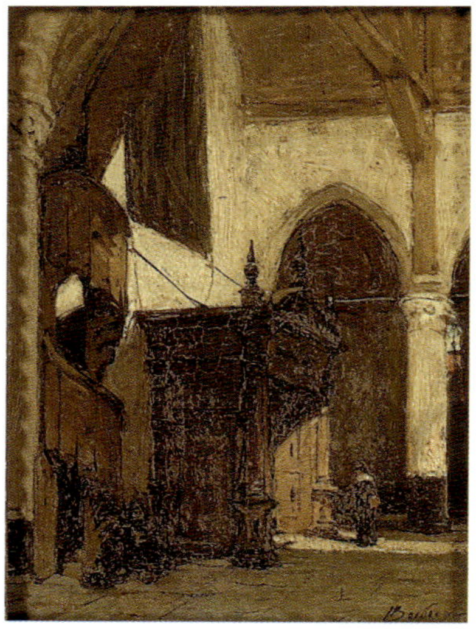

A1180; oil on mahogany panel, 21 × 15.5 cm
Signed: *Bosboom*
Bequeathed by Professor Edith Bulbring, 1993; WA1993.417

White 1999, p. 18

Bosboom specialised in painting the interiors of Dutch Protestant Churches somewhat in the manner of the 17th-century Dutch painter, Emanuel de Witte. This interior has not been identified. To judge by the sketchy manner, which is a characteristic of his later work, it was probably painted after 1865.

Ambrosius Bosschaert
(1573 – 1621)

A Vase of Flowers

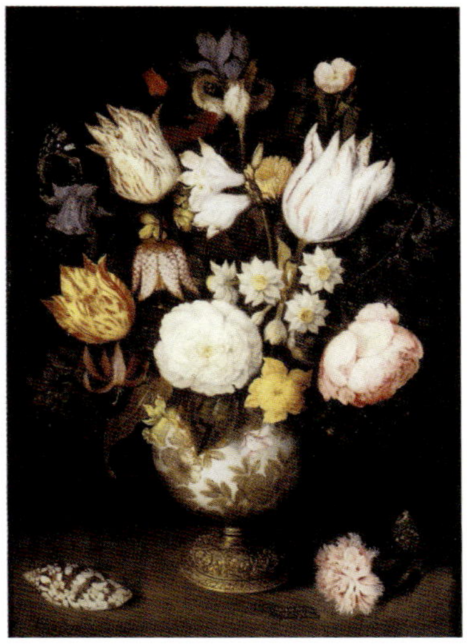

A539; oil on copper, 37.5 × 26.9 cm
Signed in monogram: *AB*
Daisy Linda Ward Bequest, 1939; WA1940.2.15

Meijer 2003, no. 17

When Bosschaert was about thirty, he took up painting still life, a genre in which he became an important influence on other painters, including his brother-in-law and pupil, Balthasar van der Ast. He used a variety of blooms, painting them carefully and separately in a central arrangement. The general design of this still life is similar to a flower piece, dated 1609, in the Kunsthistorisches Museum, Vienna. The two paintings are probably contemporary.

Studio of Sandro Botticelli
(*c.* 1444–5 – 1510)

The Virgin and Child

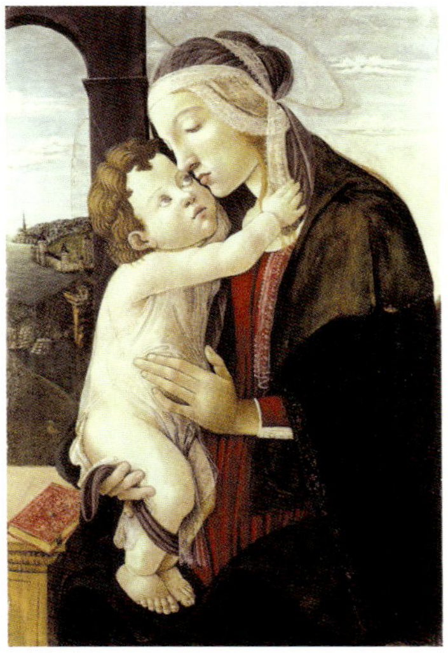

A413; oil (?) on panel, 88 × 57.9 cm
Prov.: John Ruskin
Presented by the National Art Collections Fund, 1932; WA1932.1

Lloyd 1977, pp. 36–7; Lightbown 1978, II, C23 (∠)

One of a number of studio variations based on an early composition by Botticelli now in the Musée du Louvre, this picture differs from the prototype in omitting the figure of the young St John, while the background is considerably altered. A413 was owned by John Ruskin, whose admiration for Botticelli did much to revive interest in that artist in late 19th-century Britain.

Eugène Boudin
(1824 – 1898)

The Estuary

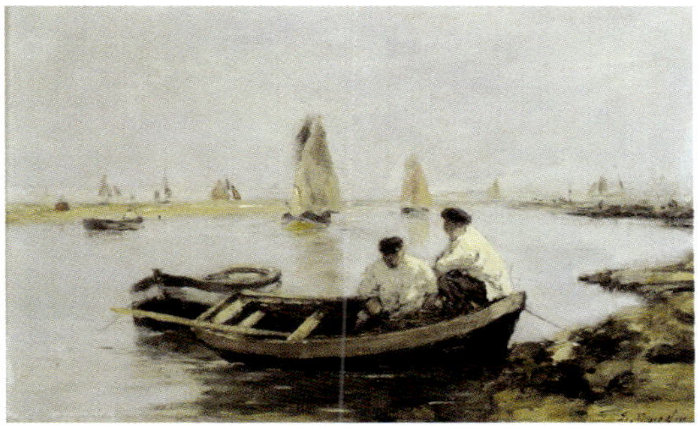

A633; oil on panel, 21 × 48 cm
Signed: *E. Boudin*
Hindley Smith Bequest, 1939; WA1940.1.15

Schmit 1973, no. 1378

Boudin strongly advocated the practice of painting out of doors. He advised the young Monet to work in the open air. The bright colour and atmospheric effects of compositions like this, painted on the north coast of France, link these little pictures to the work of the Impressionists.

Jan Both
(*c.* 1618 – 1652)

Italianate Landscape with Muleteers

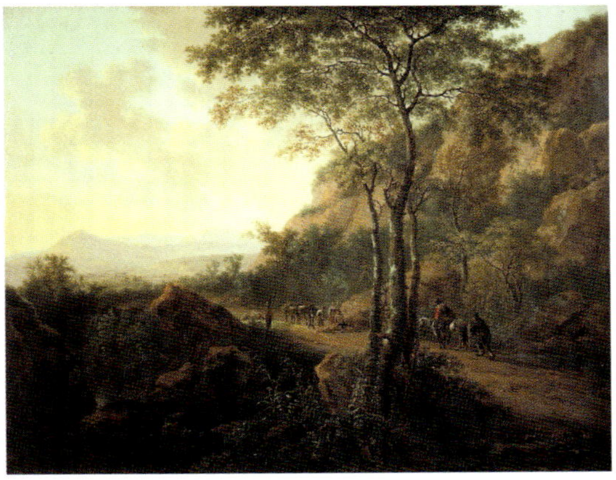

A704; oil on canvas, 127.5 × 160.5 cm
Prov.: Frederick Perkins and by descent; Walter de Zoete; Collings
Presented by Francis Falconer Madan, 1943; WA1943.1

White 1999, pp. 19–20

Jan Both spent his life in Utrecht but based much of his work on the landscape of Italy where he stayed from *c.* 1638 until *c.* 1641. His expansive landscapes, bathed in golden light, often featuring a diagonal road with figures and detailed foreground vegetation, were very influential. This characteristic work probably dates from late in his career.

Eugène Boudin
(1824 – 1898)

The Jetty at Trouville: Sunset

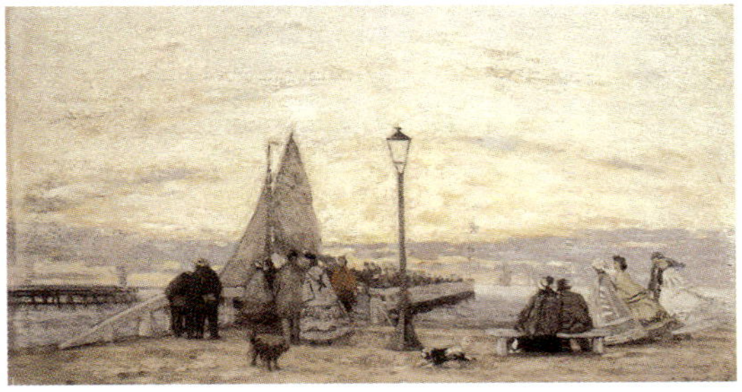

A475; oil on panel, 26 × 48 cm
Signed and dated: *E. Boudin 62*
Prov.: H.W.B. Davies
Weldon Bequest, 1937; WA1937.55

Schmit 1973, no. 259

Boudin specialised in painting the coastal regions of northern France. In the 1860s, he painted many views of the Channel resorts, featuring the visitors who brought prosperity to the district where he had been brought up. He went to Trouville in 1861 and returned every year throughout his career. The Trouville jetty was a favourite subject of his in the 1860s.

Eugène Boudin
(1824 – 1898)

A Beach Scene at Trouville

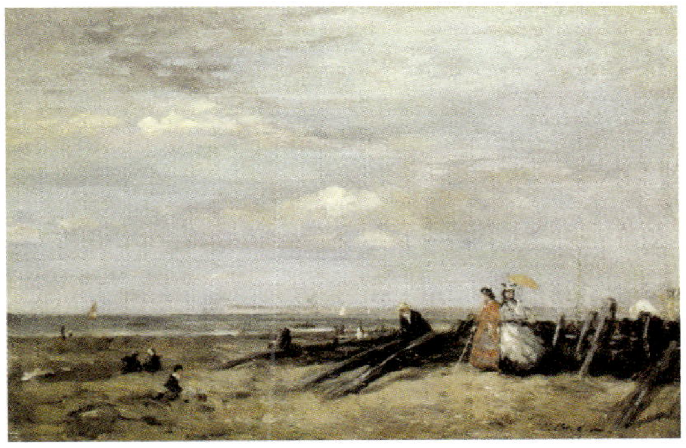

A963; oil on card laid on panel, 21 × 31 cm
Madan Bequest, 1962; WA1962.17.5

The beach at Trouville was one of Boudin's favourite locations in the 1860s.

Eugène Boudin
(1824 – 1898)

Berck, cloudy Landscape

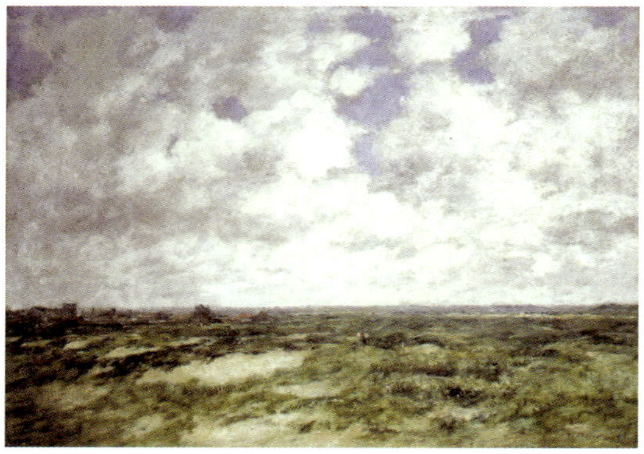

A1163; oil on canvas, 55 × 75 cm
Signed and dated: *E. Boudin 82*; and inscribed: *Berck 19 Juillet*
Bequeathed by Mr and Mrs Francis Hock through the National Art Collections Fund, 1988; WA1988.291

Schmit 1973, no. 1667

Views in and around the village of Berck in northern France appear in many of the artist's paintings from 1870 until his death in 1898. This view across the dunes is precisely dated. The unbroken horizon and solitary figure in the foreground emphasize the windswept emptiness of the site.

Georges Braque
(1882 – 1963)

The Tobacco Packet

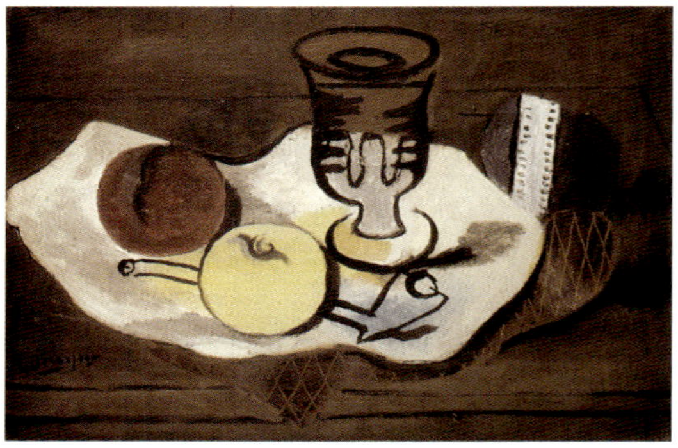

A639; oil on canvas, 24 × 35 cm
Signed: *G Braque*
Hindley Smith Bequest, 1939; WA1940.1.21

Eustace 1999, no. 25

When he painted this still life in 1931, Georges Braque enjoyed a considerable reputation as a founding member of Fauvism and Cubism. Still-lifes allowed him to explore the relation of everyday objects in varied arrangements. This painting recalls Braque's Cubist paintings from 1911, although the paint, applied rather dry, the scratched background and fragmented form are treated differently.

John Brett
(1831 – 1902)

Mrs Coventry Patmore

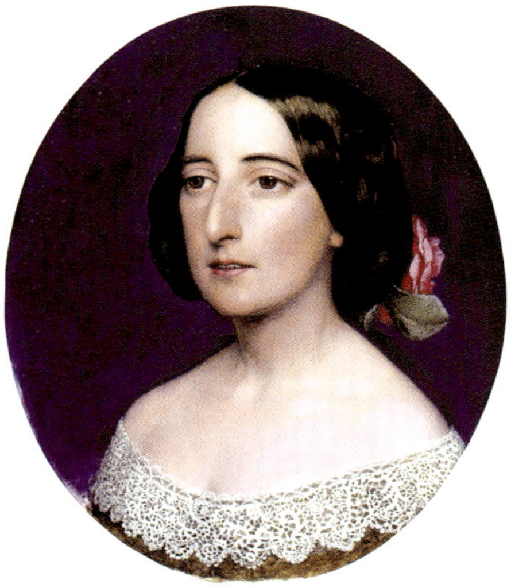

A1217; oil on card, 34.6 × 29.5 cm
Prov.: by descent
Presented by the executors of Mary Patmore, 1998; WA1998.217

Coventry Patmore (1823–1896) was an influential friend of the early Pre-Raphaelites and was instrumental in introducing them to their greatest champion, John Ruskin. He married Emily Augusta Andrews (1824–1862) in 1847. Brett's portrait of Mrs Patmore, exhibited at the Royal Academy in 1856, followed an earlier and less successful portrait by Millais of 1851 (now in the Fitzwilliam Museum, Cambridge).

Oldfield Bowles
(1739 – 1810)

Landscape with a small Lake and a Tower

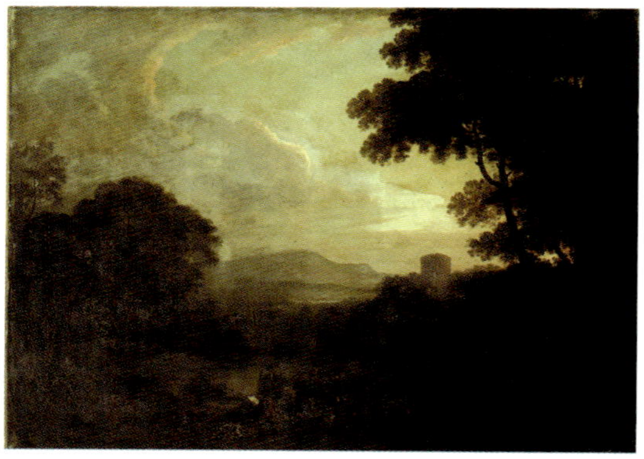

A51; oil on canvas, 109 × 147 cm
Presented by the artist, 1807; WA1845.51

This is one of a group of works by amateur artists presented to the Bodleian Library following the example of Sir George Beaumont. Bowles was a landowner at North Aston, Oxon, and a patron of Reynolds and Gainsborough. His paintings are strongly influenced by Richard Wilson.

William Breakspeare
(1855 – 1914)

Self-portrait

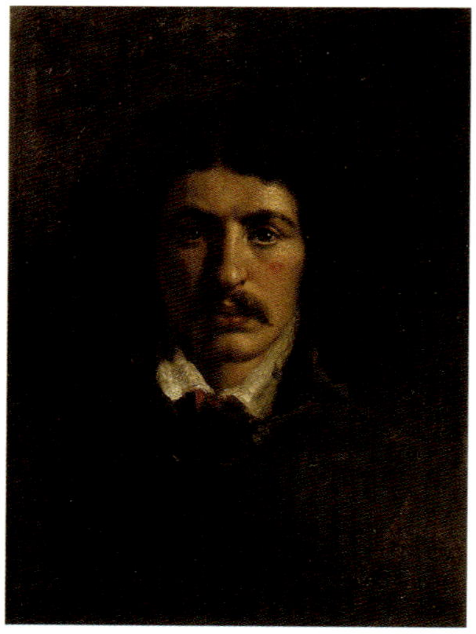

A1022c; oil on canvas, mounted as a drawing, 58.9 × 43 cm
Signed and dated: *W. Breakspeare 1876*
Presented by K.E.G. Bonfiglioli, 1966; WA1966.24

Painted when the artist was twenty or twenty-one and showing the influence of Thomas Couture, whose work he studied in Paris.

John Brett
(1831 – 1902)

Kennack Sands, Cornwall, at Low Tide

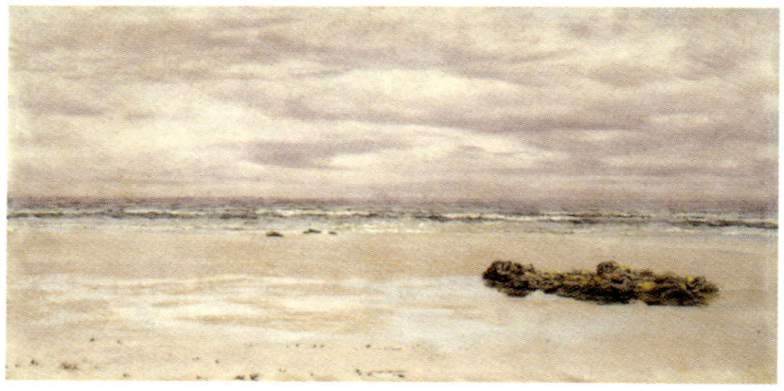

Oil on board, mounted as a drawing, 17.9 × 35.4 cm
Inscribed: *Kennack Jul 25 77*
Prov.: by descent from the artist
Purchased, 1966; WA1966.22

This is a characteristic example of the type of oil-sketch Brett produced in vast numbers during his summer holidays on board a yacht cruising round the coast of Britain. Instead of the Pre-Raphaelite technique of his early work, it is rapidly painted to capture fleeting effects of cloud and light.

Paul Bril
(1554 – 1626)

Mythological Landscape with Nymphs and Satyrs

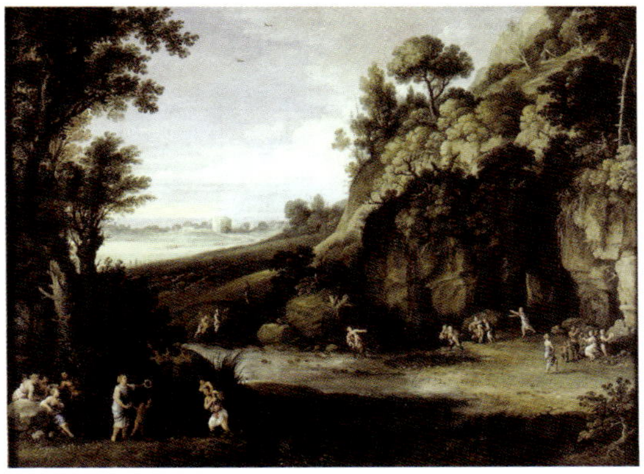

Oil on canvas, 70.6 × 92.8 cm
Signed: *P.BRILLI / 1621*
Prov.: Ducs d'Orléans by 1727; Wilson, London 1793; Lucy Copeman, Norfolk, 1898
Mahon loan, 1999; WA.L.99.6

Finaldi and Kitson 1997, no. 6

This carefully structured landscape, based on the Roman Campagna, provides a setting for a scene of nymphs and satyrs dancing and making music. Bril collaborated with figure painters and here the figures are probably by Pietro Paolo Bonzi (*c.* 1576–1636).

Anonymous British Artist
(*c.* 1500)

Elizabeth Woodville, Queen of Edward IV

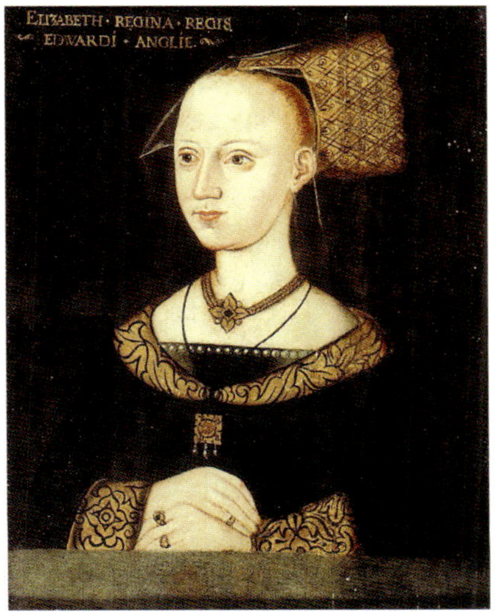

F680; oil on panel, 41 × 32 cm
Inscribed: *ELIZABETH.REGINA.REGIS / EDWARDI.ANGLIE*
Prov.: (?)Tradescant
Presented by Elias Ashmole, 1683; WA1898.1

Poole 1912, no. 402; MacGregor 1983, no. 273

Elizabeth Woodville (?1437–1492) married King Edward IV privately in 1464. She suffered numerous vicissitudes in the political turmoil of the late 15th century, but, among other achievements, refounded and endowed Queens' College, Cambridge. This portrait was derived from one in the Royal Collection at Windsor Castle.

Anonymous British Artist
(1562)

Edward Fiennes de Clinton, later 1st Earl of Lincoln

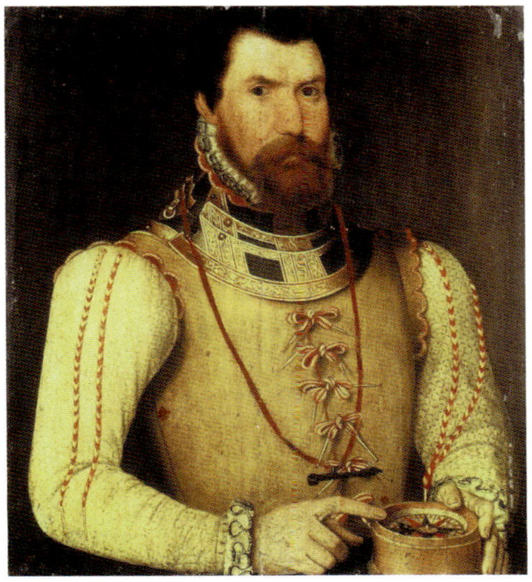

A4; oil on panel, 57 × 51 cm
Dated: *1562*
Presented by Bernard Mould, 1707; WA1845.4

Poole 1912, no. 404

Edward Fiennes de Clinton (1512–1585) served as Lord High Admiral, 1550–53 and 1558–85, and was appointed a Knight of the Garter in 1551. He was created Earl of Lincoln in 1572. The sitter has been identified from his attributes: the compass he points at and the Whistle of Honour of the Lord High Admiral he wears round his neck.

Copy after Paul Bril
(1554 – 1626)

Wooded Landscape with Duck Shooting

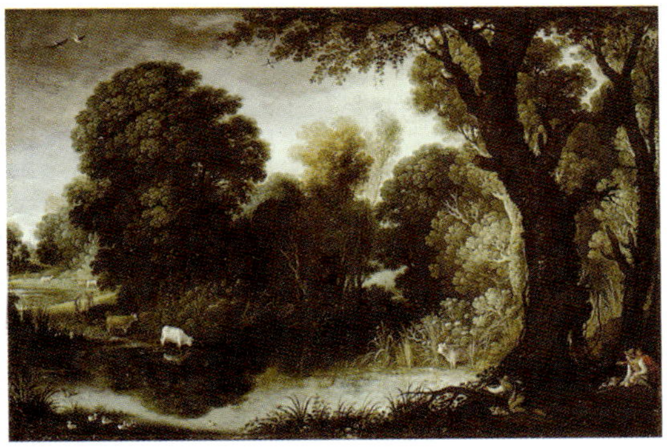

A964; oil on canvas, 48 × 72 cm
Prov.: 2nd Viscount Palmerston; Mrs G. Blois
Madan Bequest, 1962; WA1962.17.6

White 1999, p. 21

Copied from a larger painting by Bril, now in the Louvre. The original is believed to date from after 1620 when Bril adopted a lower viewpoint and a more naturalistic approach to landscape.

Anonymous British Artist
(*c.* 1555)

Portrait of a Lady

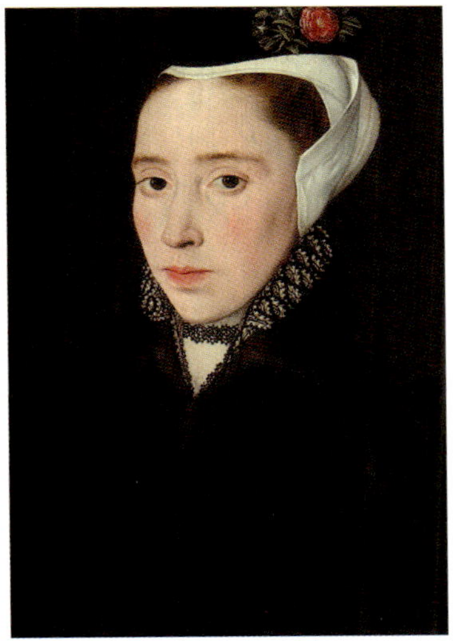

A429; oil on panel, 40 × 29 cm
Prov.: Lord North
Purchased, 1933; WA1933.25

Anonymous British Artist
(*c.* 1580?)

Portrait of a Lady holding a Book

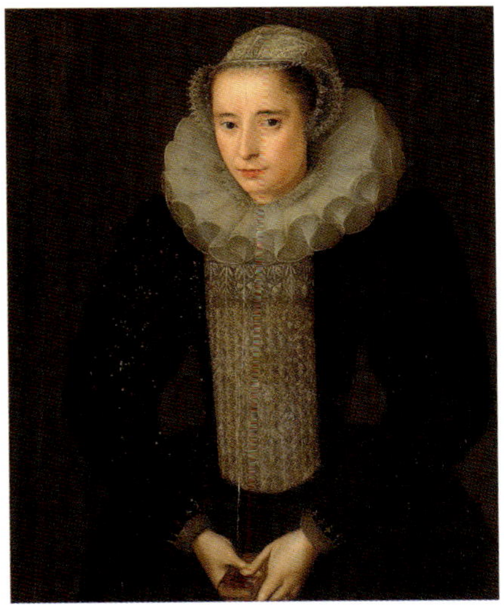

?F691; oil on panel, 78 × 62 cm
Prov.: (?)Tradescant
Probably presented by Elias Ashmole, 1683; WA1898.3

Poole 1912, no. 406; MacGregor 1983, no. 285

The sitter has been identified as Hester Puckering (d. 1592), who married Edward Wotton in 1575. He had a garden at Canterbury where he employed John Tradescant the Elder. This may be the portrait of Lady Wotton from the Founder's Collection, which is otherwise unidentified. The costume and style would suggest a date of *c.* 1580.

Anonymous British Artist
(*c.* 1575 – 1600)

Portrait of a Man, perhaps Charles Howard, 2nd Baron Howard of Effingham

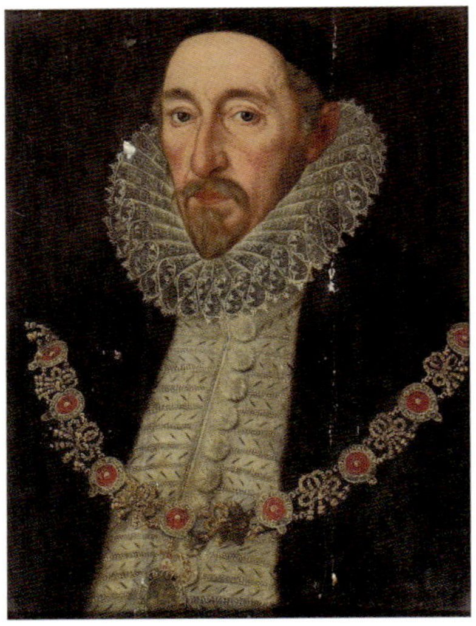

F672; oil on panel, 56 × 42 cm
?Presented by Elias Ashmole, 1683; WA1898.6

Poole 1912, no. 408; MacGregor 1983, no. 270

The sitter wears the collar of the Order of the Garter and on this basis has been identified as Charles Howard (1536–1624), who succeeded his father as Baron Howard of Effingham in 1573 and was installed as a Knight of the Garter in 1574. As Lord High Admiral, he commanded the forces which defeated the Spanish Armada in 1588. He was created Earl of Nottingham in 1597.

Anonymous British Artist
(*c.* 1594)

John Dee

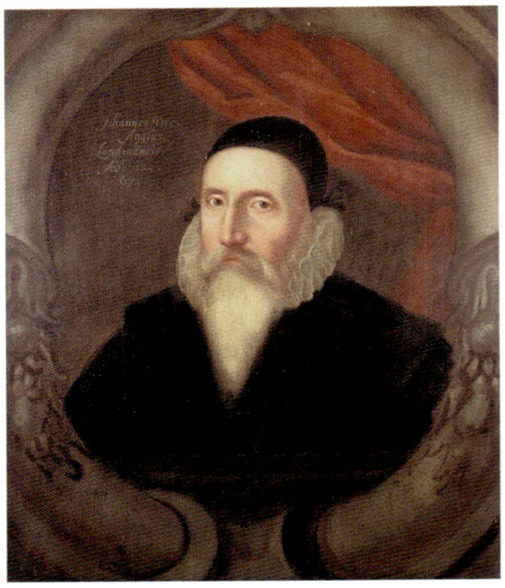

F746; oil on canvas, 76 × 63.5 cm
Inscribed: *Johannes Dee / Anglus, / Londinensis / AEt. suae / 67*
Bequeathed by Elias Ashmole, 1692; WA1898.18

Poole 1912, no. 407; MacGregor 1983, no. 291

John Dee (1527–1608) was one of the most influential figures of the Elizabethan age. He studied mathematics and astrology and from an early age was supposed to practise magic. Ashmole owned a number of Dee's manuscripts (now in the British Library) and obtained this portrait while gathering material for a biography, which, however, he never wrote.

Anonymous British Artist
(17th century)

St Peter

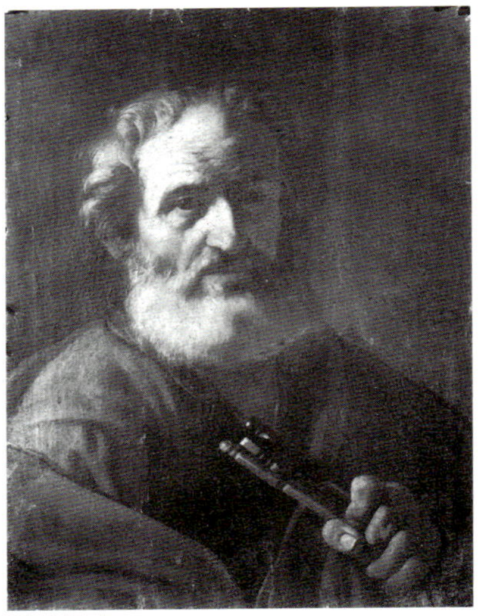

A15; oil on canvas, rolled, 66 × 49 cm
Bequeathed by the Revd Dr John King, 1737; WA1845.15

Anonymous British Artist
(1587)

Portrait of a Man, called Sir Francis Drake

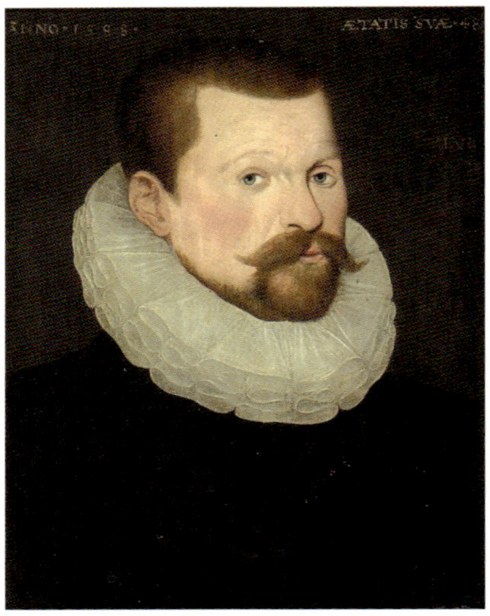

A21a; oil on panel, 47 × 37 cm
Inscribed: *ANNO.1588 / AETATIS SUAE 48 / AETATIS XLVII / A⁰ 1587*
Provenance unknown; WA1845.68

Poole 1912, no. 405; MacGregor 1983, no. 286

Sir Francis Drake (*c.* 1540–1596), responsible for the defeat of the Spanish Armada in 1588 and other notable naval exploits. The identification is doubtful when compared with authenticated portraits of Drake.

Anonymous British Artist
(*c.* 1680?)

St Andrew?

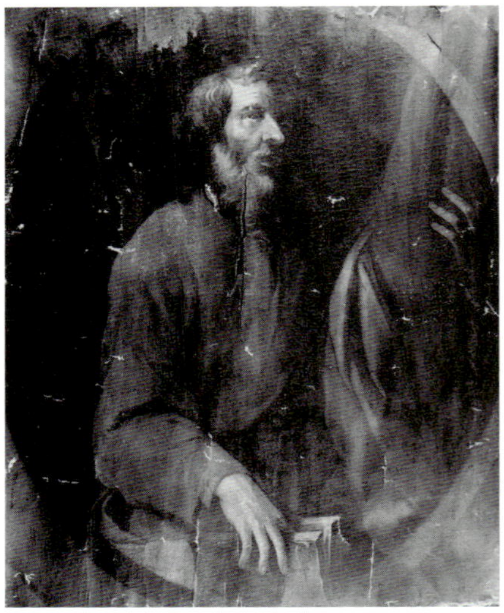

A13; oil on canvas, rolled, 123 × 98 cm
Bequeathed by the Revd Dr John King, 1737; WA1845.13

Anonymous British Artist
(*c.* 1680?)

St Paul

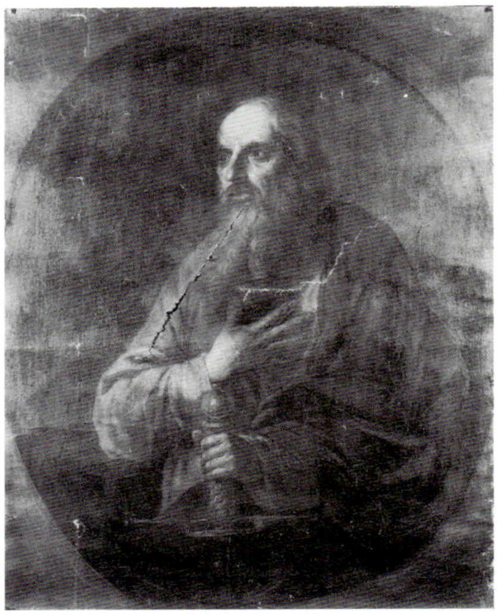

A14; oil on canvas, rolled, 124 × 98.5 cm
Bequeathed by the Revd Dr John King, 1737; WA1845.14

Anonymous British Artist
(17th century)

Portrait of a Lady

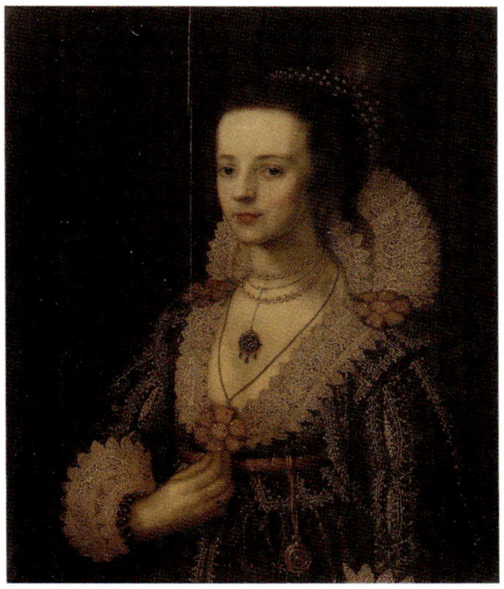

A298; oil on panel, 79 × 64 cm
Dated: *1621*
Bequeathed by John D. Chambers, 1897; WA1897.17

Formerly described as a portrait of Elisabeth Stuart, Queen of Bohemia (1596–1662) by the Flemish artist, Paul van Somer (*c.* 1576–*c.* 1621), but it is neither of her nor by him.

Anonymous British Artist
(*c.* 1620?)

Anne Harington, Lady Molyneux

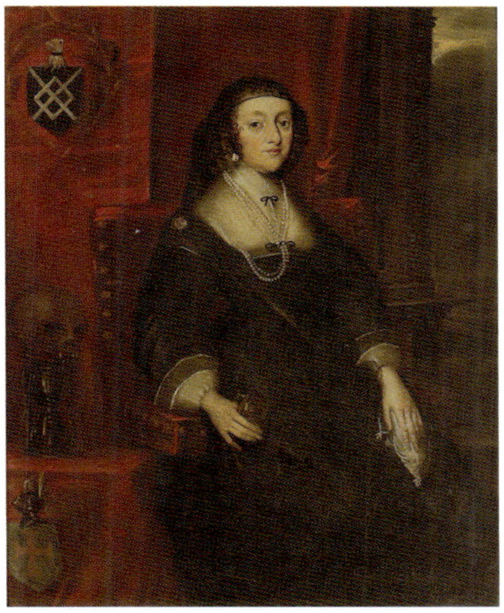

F656; oil on canvas, 127 × 102 cm
Presented by Elias Ashmole, 1683; WA1898.35

Poole 1912, no. 417; MacGregor 1983, no. 257

The arms and crest at upper left are those of Harington, below a skull on an hourglass, and Molyneux, with a helm. On this basis, the sitter has been identified as Anne (*c.* 1590–1644), daughter of Sir James Harington of Exton, Rutland, who married secondly, as his second wife, Sir John Molyneux, Bt, of Teversal, Notts. (d. 1618). Her widow's weeds suggest that the portrait may date from shortly after 1618.

Anonymous British Artist
(*c.* 1630?)

Portrait of a Couple, said to be John Tradescant the Elder and his Wife Elizabeth

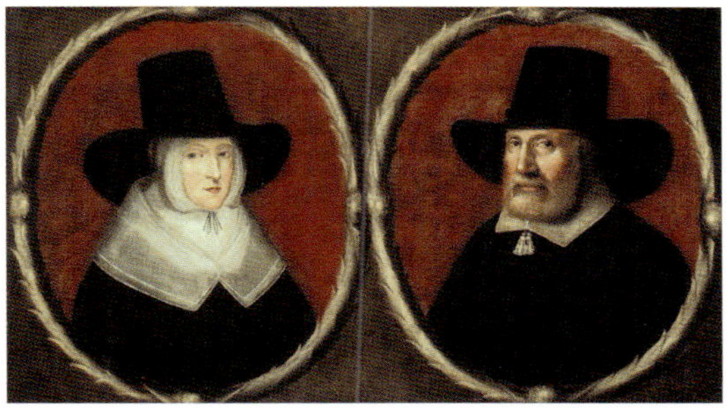

A374b; oil on canvas, 73 × 117 cm
Prov.: E.G. Thorne
Presented by the Misses E.D. and A.C. Thorne, 1924; WA1924.12

MacGregor 1983, no. 294

This portrait is said to have been in Tradescant's house in Lambeth before it was demolished in 1881. Here, John Tradescant the Elder (d. 1638) established the first physic garden in England. Elizabeth Day (b. 1573/86) married John Tradescant the Elder in 1607. No other portraits of Mrs Tradescant survive and the identification of both sitters remains doubtful.

Anonymous British Artist
(*c.* 1620)

Portrait of a Lady

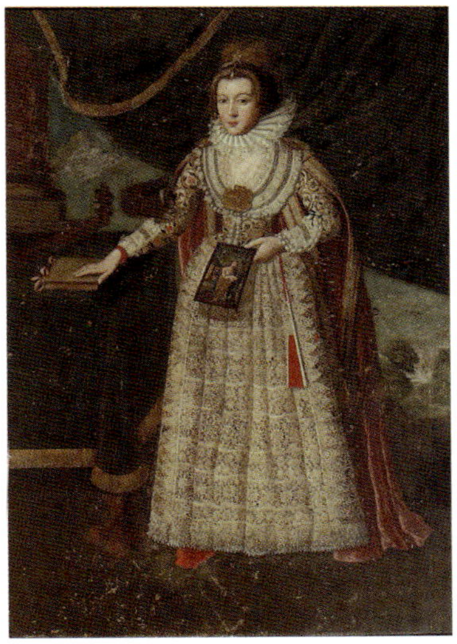

A2; oil on canvas, 195 × 136 cm
Acquired before 1706; WA1845.2

Poole 1912, no. 429

The sitter has been identified as Elizabeth, daughter of Sir Christopher Kenn of Kenn Court, who married John Poulett and died in 1663. However, in early Bodleian catalogues, she is described as a member of the Duke of Bolton's family (Orde-Powlett), who presented to the Library on 9 July 1636 needlework of her own working representing scenes from the gospels, together with her own portrait. She is holding a panel of the Penitent Magdalen and has a pet squirrel on her arm.

Anonymous British Artist
(*c.* 1625 – 1640)

Portrait of a Youth, said to be Sir John Suckling

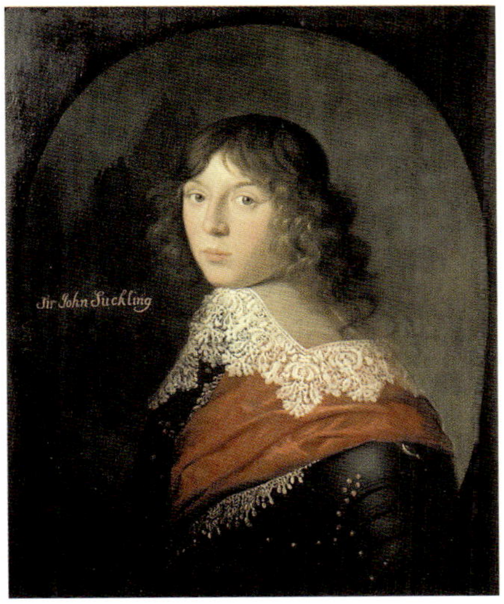

F676; oil on canvas, 84 × 69 cm
Inscribed: *Sir John Suckling*
Presented by Elias Ashmole, 1683; WA1898.27

Poole 1912, no. 416; MacGregor 1983, no. 271

John Suckling (1609–1642) came from an old Norfolk family and inherited large estates on the death of his father in 1627. He was one of Charles I's leading courtiers, known as a gamester (he invented the game of cribbage) and for his sparkling wit. He was the author of plays and numerous poems, collected as *Fragmenta Aurea* in 1646. He died, perhaps by his own hand, in Paris. The identification is by no means certain.

Anonymous British Artist
(*c.* 1630)

Jane, first Wife of John Tradescant the Younger

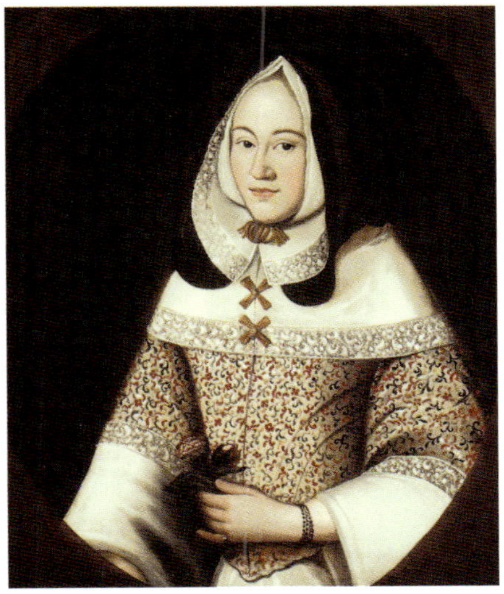

A374a; oil on canvas, 74 × 61 cm
Prov.: E.G. Thorne
Presented by the Misses E.D. and A.C. Thorne, 1924; WA1924.11

Like the preceding, this painting is supposed to have come from the Tradescant house at Lambeth. No other portrait of the sitter exists, so the identification cannot be confirmed. Jane Hurte (d. 1634) married John Tradescant the Younger in 1627 and was the mother of Frances and John III.

Anonymous British Artist
(*c*. 1630)

Richard Napier

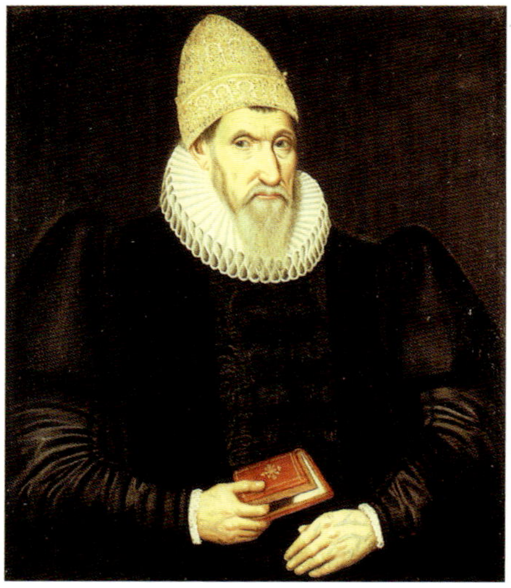

F747; oil on canvas, 76 × 64 cm
Bequeathed by Elias Ashmole, 1692; WA1898.19

Poole 1912, no. 411; MacGregor 1983, no. 292

The son of Sir Richard Napier of Luton Hoo, Richard Napier (1559–1634) was the rector of Great Linford, Bucks and a celebrated physician and astrologer. It was widely believed that he conversed with the angel Raphael in order to obtain correct prognoses, and that he was so devout that he had horny knees. After his death, his papers were obtained by Elias Ashmole and are now in the Bodleian Library.

Anonymous British Artist
(1638)

John Tradescant the Elder on his Deathbed

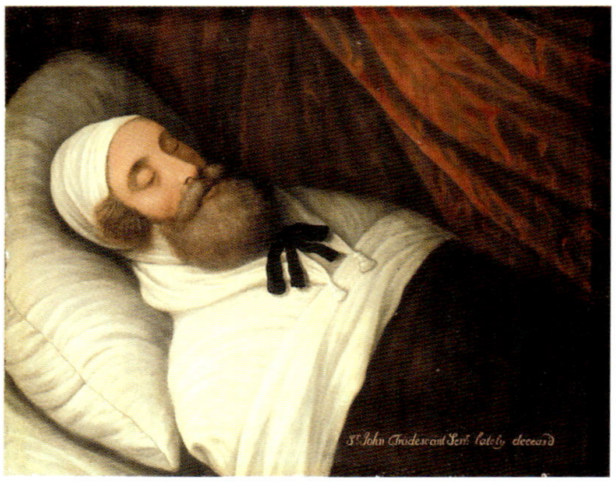

F692; oil on canvas, 61 × 74 cm
Inscribed: *Sr John Tradescant Senr lately deceased*
Presented by Elias Ashmole, 1683; WA1898.9

Poole 1912, no. 415; MacGregor 1983, no. 276

The funeral of the elder Tradescant was held on 17 April 1638 and this painting, or at least the preparatory studies, was presumably begun before then. Such images were not uncommon in Northern Europe and generally commissioned by the family of the deceased.

Anonymous British Artist
(*c*. 1638)

Frances Tradescant

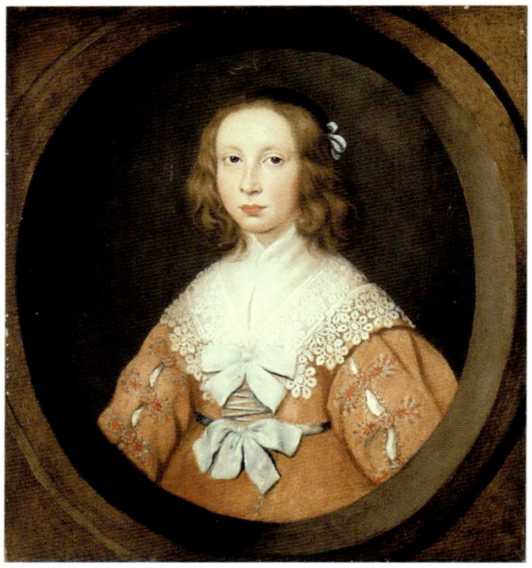

F704; oil on canvas, 68 × 61 cm
Presented by Elias Ashmole, 1683; WA1898.17

Poole 1912, no. 441; MacGregor 1983, no. 278

Frances Tradescant (*c*. 1628–after 1661) was the daughter of John Tradescant the Younger. She married Alexander Norman in 1644. She is portrayed with her brother and step-mother in another painting (see F671). Like its pendant, this portrait has recently been attributed to Johan Priwitzer (active 1626–1635), but may be by an artist from the de Critz/de Neve circle.

Anonymous British Artist
(*c*. 1635)

Thomas Parr

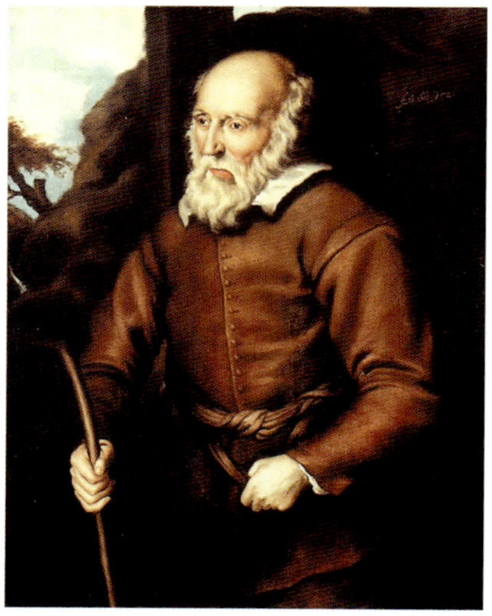

F685; oil on canvas, 104 × 80 cm
Inscribed: *AEtis sue 152*
Prov.: Tradescant
Presented by Elias Ashmole, 1683; WA1898.26

Poole 1912, no. 412; MacGregor 1983, no. 275

Thomas Parr, known as 'Old Parr', was reputedly born in 1483 and thus lived under the reigns of ten monarchs. He was taken to London from Shropshire in 1635, presented to the king and enjoyed brief fame as the subject of John Taylor's pamphlet, 'The Old, Old, Very Old Man or the Age and Long Life of Thomas Parr'. He survived only a few months and died on 15 November 1635.

Anonymous British Artist
(*c*. 1638)

John Tradescant III

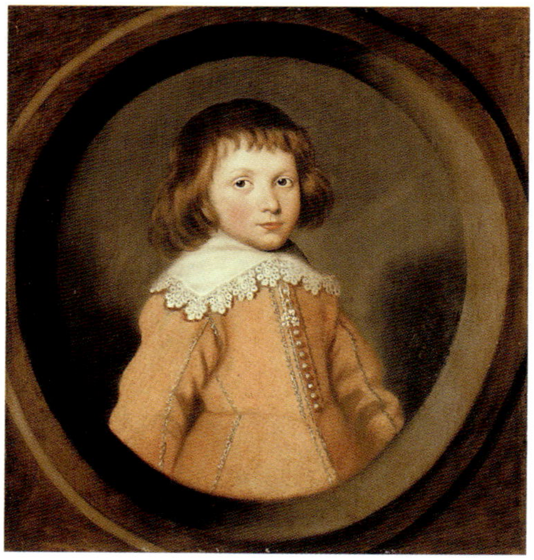

F703; oil on canvas, 66 × 61 cm
Presented by Elias Ashmole, 1683; WA1898.16

Poole 1912, no. 422; MacGregor 1983, no. 277

It was the premature death of John Tradescant III (1633–1652) which left the Tradescant family collections without a secure future and ultimately led to their gift to Elias Ashmole in 1659. The portrait and its pendant have recently been attributed to Johan Priwitzer (active 1626–1635), but may well be from the de Critz/de Neve circle.

Anonymous British Artist
(1640)

John Lowin

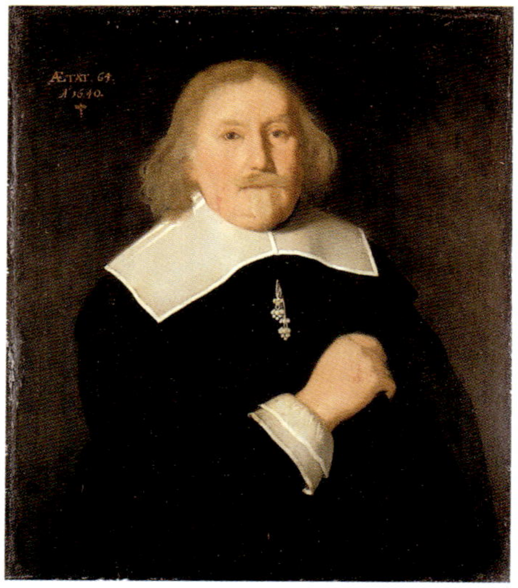

F741; oil on canvas, 76 × 65 cm
Inscribed: *Aetat 64 Ao 1640*
Bequeathed by Elias Ashmole, 1692; WA1898.22

Poole 1912, no. 425; MacGregor 1983, no. 289

John Lowin (1576–1659) was a celebrated actor and associate of Shakespeare. He managed the King's Players from 1623 to 1642. No attribution has been proposed.

Anonymous British Artist
(*c.* 1640)

Edward Montagu, 2nd Earl of Manchester

F677; oil on canvas, 64 × 56 cm
Presented by Elias Ashmole, 1683; WA1898.34

Poole 1912, no. 437; MacGregor 1983, no. 272

Edward Montagu (1602–1671) succeeded his father as Earl of Manchester in 1642 and commanded the Puritan forces at the Battle of Marston Moor in 1644. He is shown in his late thirties or early forties, wearing a breastplate, and therefore presumably before his resignation in 1645.

Anonymous British Artist
(*c.* 1645)

Hester Pookes, second Wife of John Tradescant the Younger

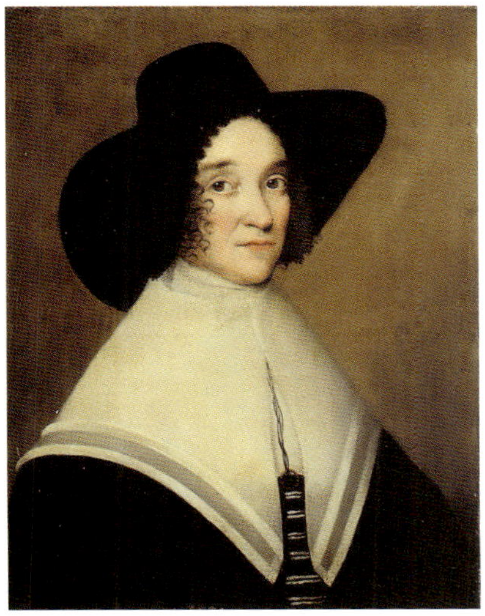

F662; oil on canvas, 60 × 44 cm
Presented by Elias Ashmole, 1683; WA1898.15

Poole 1912, no. 442; MacGregor 1983, no. 261

This portrait of Hester Tradescant (*c.* 1608–1678) may have been made at the time of her marriage to John Tradescant the Younger in 1638.

Anonymous British Artist
(*c.* 1650)

Portrait of a Sculptor

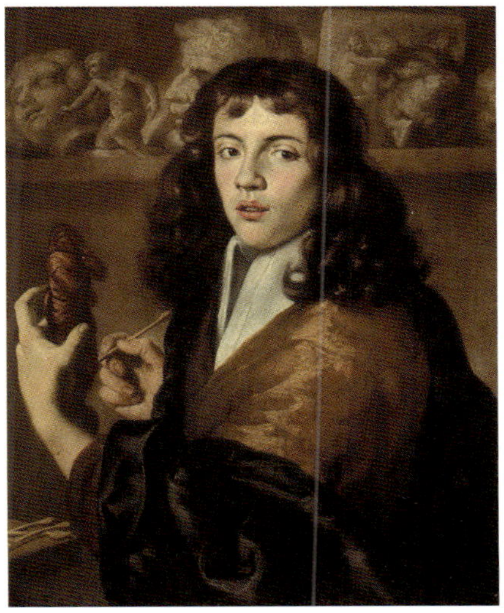

A860; oil on canvas, 71 × 57 cm
Prov.: Robert Ross
Bequeathed by Sir Robert Witt through the National Art Collections Fund, 1952; WA1952.66

Cust 1917

This is clearly the portrait of a professional sculptor, shown in his studio with some of his work on the shelf behind. He holds a terracotta figure of a saint, perhaps the Virgin Mary. The painting has been tentatively attributed to the circle of the de Critz family.

Anonymous British Artist
(*c.* 1644)

Hester Tradescant and her Stepchildren, John and Frances

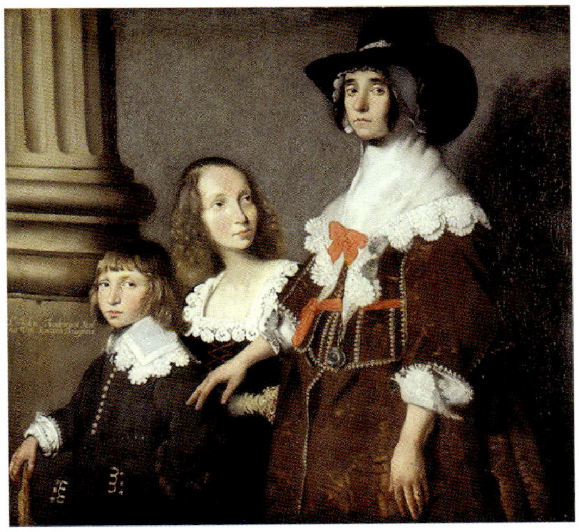

F671; oil on canvas, 109 × 117 cm
Inscribed: *Sr John Tradescant Senr his Wife Son and Daughter*
Presented by Elias Ashmole, 1683; WA1898.13

Poole 1912, no. 440; MacGregor 1983, no. 269

Hester Pookes (*c.* 1608–1678) married John Tradescant the Younger as his second wife in 1638. She is shown with her husband's children by his first marriage, John Tradescant (1633–1652) and Frances, who was born *c.* 1628. From the ages of the sitters, the painting was probably made in the early 1640s, before Frances's wedding to Alexander Norman in 1644.

Anonymous British Artist
(1646)

William Lilly

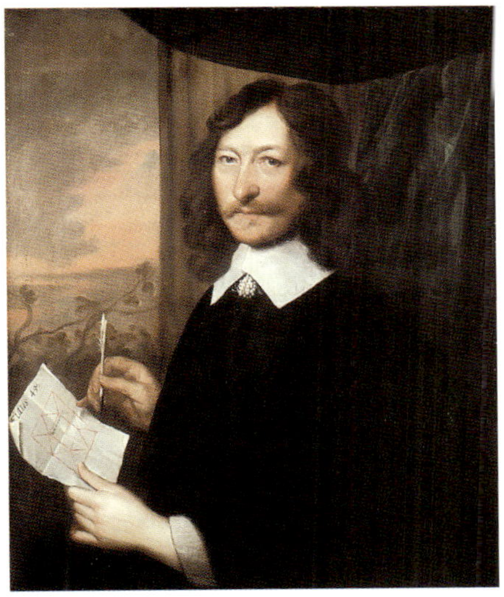

F748; oil on canvas, 74 × 61 cm
Dated: *1646*; and inscribed: *Aetatis 45;* and, in the horoscope: *non cogunt*
Bequeathed by Elias Ashmole, 1692; WA1898.20

Poole 1912, no. 444; MacGregor 1983, no. 293

William Lilly (1602–1681) was one of the most eminent astrologers of his day, publishing an annual almanac from 1644 until his death, many pamphlets of prophecy and other works. He is portrayed holding a horoscope, which is blank apart from the words *non cogunt* ('they do not compel'), which are found in arguments directed against fatalism. This portrait was probably given to Ashmole in 1652.

Anonymous British Artist
(*c.* 1660)

Portrait of a Man

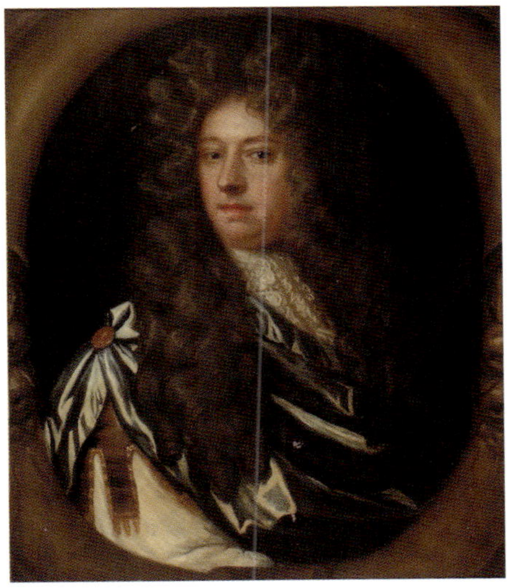

A307; oil on canvas, 74 × 62 cm
Fortnum Bequest, 1899; WA1899.CDEF.P7

Poole 1912, no. 436

This undistinguished portrait was formerly ascribed to an artist in the circle of Lely.

Anonymous British Artist
(*c.* 1670 – 79)

An unknown Man

F665; oil on canvas, 56 × 52 cm
Inscribed: *AEtat . . . / 107*
Presented by Elias Ashmole, 1683; WA1898.30

Poole 1912, no. 421; MacGregor 1983, no. 264

The subject has been identified as Robert Montgomery, on the basis of the inscription which seems to read, *AEtats 107*, the only supposed centenarian recorded at a date suitable for the painting, who died aged 127 in 1671. 1651 is also the date of the portrait of Fiske (see F740).

Anonymous British Artist
(late 17th century)

St Jerome

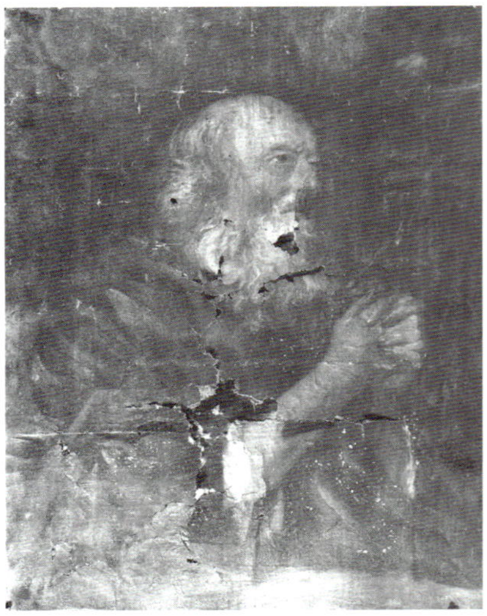

A5; oil on canvas, rolled, 93 × 72 cm
Acquired by the Bodleian Library by 1700; WA1845.5

Anonymous British Artist
(*c.* 1700)

Oxford from the South-West

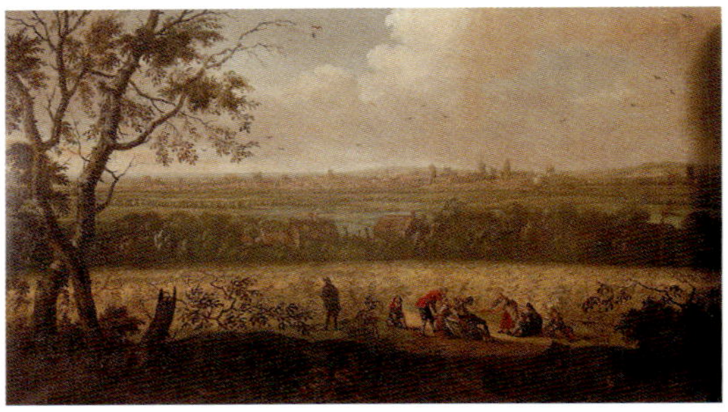

A3; oil on canvas, 168 × 323 cm
Acquired by 1795; WA1845.3

Although an early inventory of the paintings in the Bodleian Library gives the artist as 'Summers', which may have been intended for William Sonmans (d. 1708), no other attribution has been proposed. The approximate date can be deduced from the presence of Tom Tower at Christ Church, which was constructed in 1681–2, and from the absence of the steeple of All Saints' Church, erected in 1707–8.

Anonymous British Artist
(*c.* 1670 – 80)

Charles II

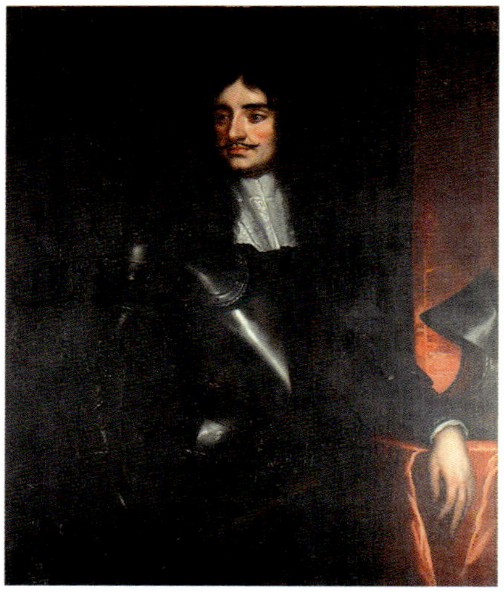

A1050d; oil on canvas, 121 × 95 cm
Prov.: 4th Earl of Harrington
Bequeathed by Miss Orovida Pissarro, 1968; WA1968.474.2

Anonymous British Artist
(18th century)

Death leading a pagan Woman

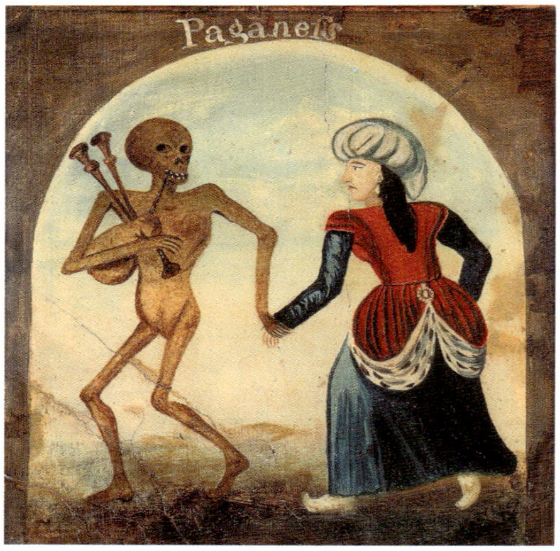

Painted plaster on panel, 54.5cm × 54.5 cm (inc. frame)
Inscribed: *Paganefs*
ANT1990.101

Oxoniensia 2 1937, pp. 179–186

Part of a cycle of forty related images. Based on a 16th century 'Dance of Death' scene – salvaged in 1937 from 46 Broad Street, Oxford and executed for Alderman William Fletcher (*c.* 1738–1826) who lived at this address.

Anonymous British(?) Artist
(*c.* 1700)

Still Life with Books and Astronomical instruments

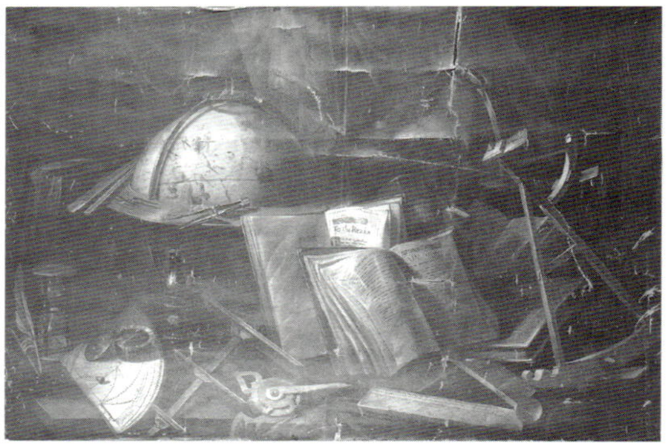

A12; oil on canvas, rolled, 115 × 169 cm
Bequeathed by the Revd Dr John King, 1737; WA1845.12

Perhaps designed as an overdoor. The English texts suggest that the artist was either British or an artist from the Netherlands working in Britain.

Anonymous British Artist
(1711)

Sir John Chardin

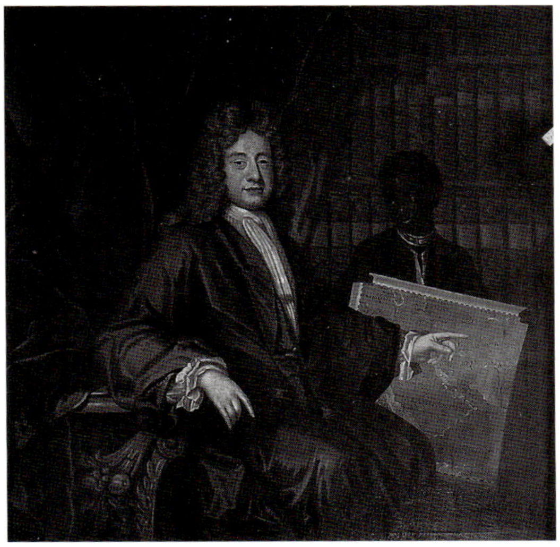

A17; oil on canvas, 138 × 138 cm
Inscribed: *Anno 1711 / AEtatis 68*
Presented by the sitter's son, Sir John Chardin, Bt, 1746; WA1845.17

Poole 1912, no. 453

Sir John Chardin (1643–1713) was born in Paris but settled in England as a Huguenot refugee. He was a jewel merchant who travelled extensively in Persia and India, 1664–70 and 1671–7. His published voyages contain valuable information on the history and customs of Islam. He was appointed court jeweller and knighted in 1681 and became a Fellow of the Royal Society in 1682. In this portrait, he is seen pointing to a map of Persia.

Anonymous British Artist
(*c.* 1760)

Portrait of a young Man

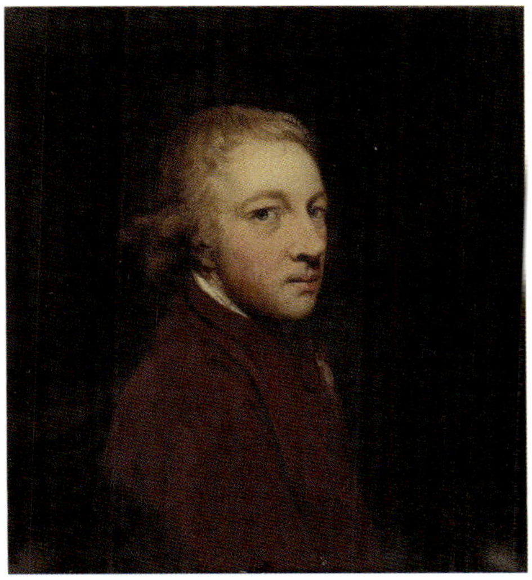

A65; oil on canvas, 61 × 54 cm
Provenance unknown; WA1845.65

This is perhaps a portrait of an undergraduate in the University of Oxford. An old attribution to Wright of Derby can be dismissed.

Anonymous British Artist
(*c.* 1775)

Landscape with a Sportsman

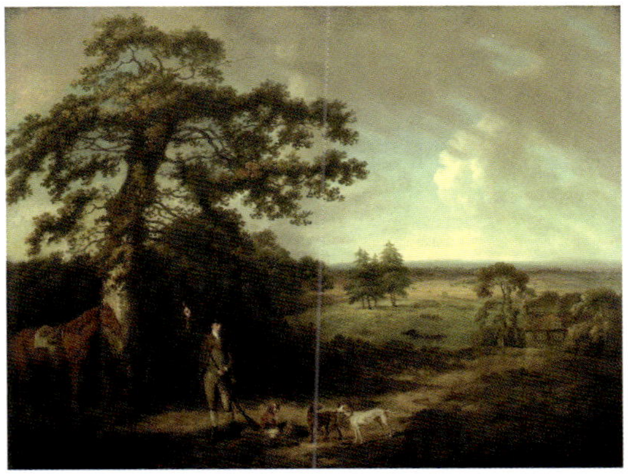

A131; oil on canvas, 95 × 122 cm
Bequeathed by the Revd Dr Thomas Penrose, 1851; WA1851.2

An old label records the unlikely story that this is *The Portrait of Captain Phillips of Culham. Painted by Richard Wilson R.A., and presented to him by the Artist.* It has more recently been suggested that the landscape is by George Barret (*c.* 1728–1784), the animals by Sawrey Gilpin (1733–1807), and the figure by Philip Reinagle (1749–1833).

Anonymous British (?) Artist
(*c.* 1720)

The Finding of Moses

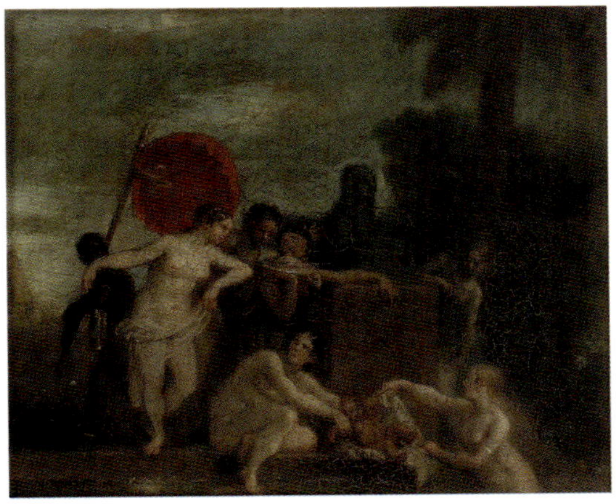

A201; oil on canvas, 25 × 30 cm
Chambers Hall Gift, 1855; WA1855.584

A feeble work of uncertain nationality in poor condition.

Anonymous British Artist
(*c.* 1765)

The Revd John Kinderley

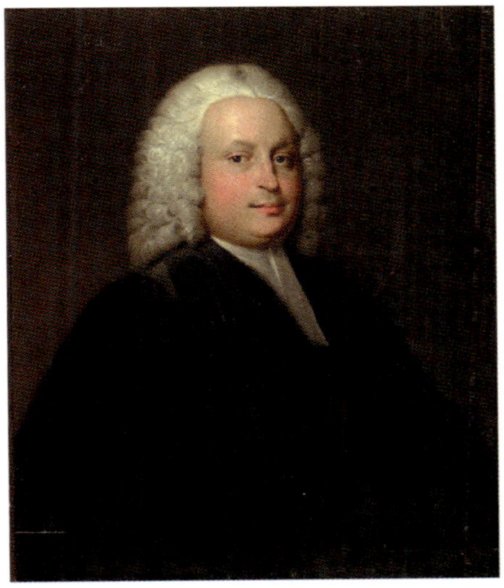

A438g; oil on canvas, 76 × 64 cm
Pierrepont Barnard Bequest, 1934; WA1934.65.249

John Kinderley (1705–1775) was the father of Mrs Smith, the subject of A438d.

Anonymous British Artist
(*c.* 1780)

Bay on a Sea Coast

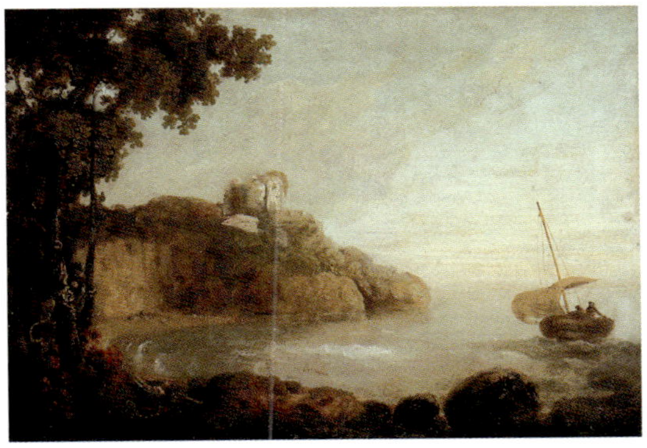

A198; oil on canvas, 43 × 60 cm
Chambers Hall Gift, 1855; WA1855.203

This painting was attributed to Richard Wilson by the donor, but the quality and style make this attribution implausible. It is characteristic of decorative Italianate landscape, popular in the late 18th century.

Anonymous British Artist
(*c.* 1780)

Mountain Torrent and Bridge

A411; oil on panel, 31 × 38 cm
Prov.: J.S. Valentine
Bequeathed by the Very Revd W. H. Hutton, Dean of Winchester, 1931; WA1931.58

Mitchell 1999, p. 116

This was formerly attributed to Julius Caesar Ibbetson (1759–1817), but is stylistically dissimilar to his work.

Anonymous British Artist
(*c.* 1790)

The Milkmaid and the Snail

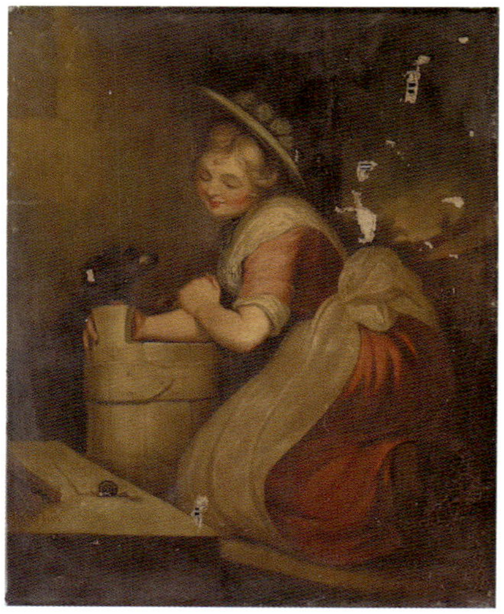

A311; oil on canvas, 29 × 23 cm
Prov.: (?)Charles Fortnum
Fortnum Bequest, 1899; WA1899.CDEF.P8

Formerly associated with George Morland, this feeble and damaged work was presumably copied after an unknown original.

Anonymous British Artist
(19th Century)

Still Life with a dead Pigeon

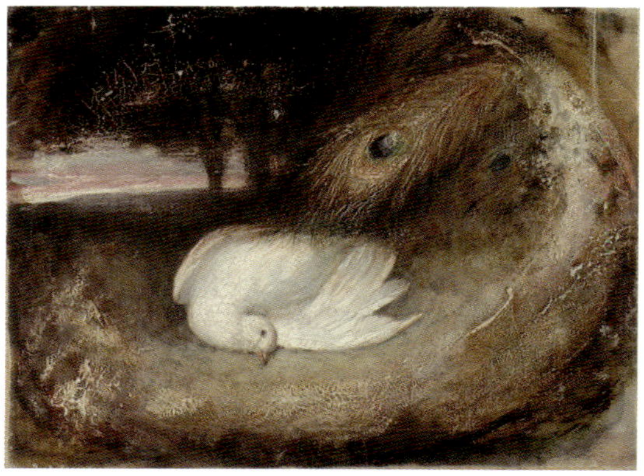

A320; oil on canvas, 38 × 51 cm
Provenance unknown; WA.OA906

Anonymous British Artist
(*c.* 1790)

Portrait of a young Lady in a pink Dress

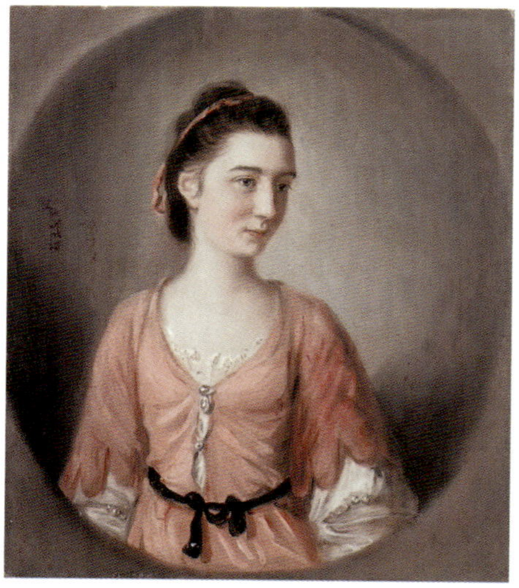

A936; oil on canvas, 35 × 30 cm
Presented by Francis Falconer Madan, 1960; WA1960.52

Formerly attributed to Francis Cotes (1726–1770) and to Hugh Douglas Hamilton (1740–1808).

Anonymous British Artist
(1794)

The Revd Dr Francis Randolph

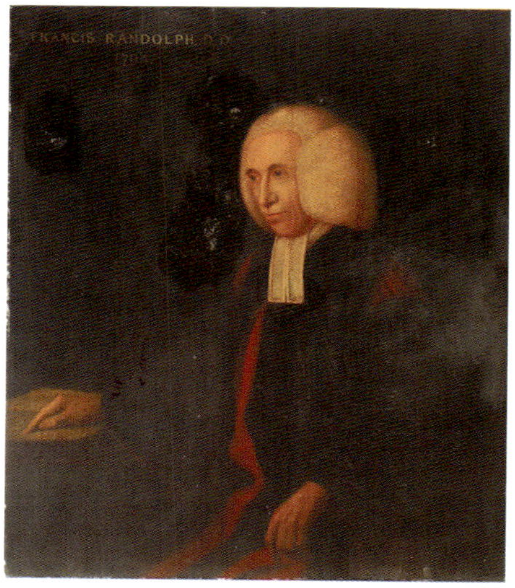

A68; oil on canvas, 99 × 85 cm
Inscribed: *Francis Randolph D.D. 1794*
Presented by the Revd Edward Cardwell D.D., 1847; WA1847.2

Poole 1912, no. 465

Francis Randolph (*c.* 1714–1797) was elected Principal of St Alban Hall, Oxford, in 1759. He bequeathed £1,000 to the University to open a fund for building a gallery. This was eventually opened as the University Galleries in 1846.

Anonymous British Artist
(19th century)

View of Jerusalem

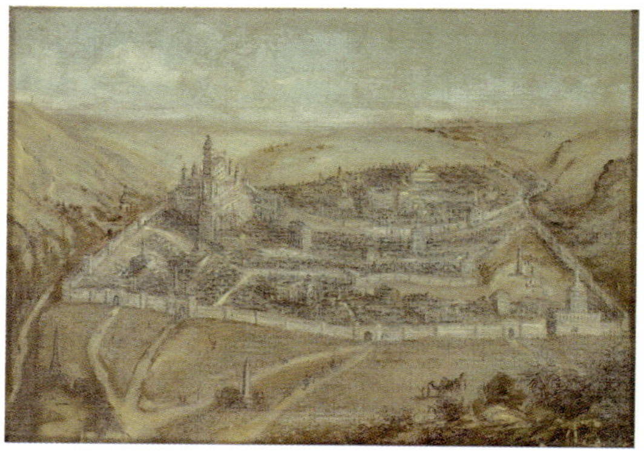

A245a; oil on canvas, 25 × 35 cm
Presented by the Revd John Rigaud, 1887; ANT3179.1887

Anonymous British Artist
(*c.* 1800)

Allegory of Youth and Age

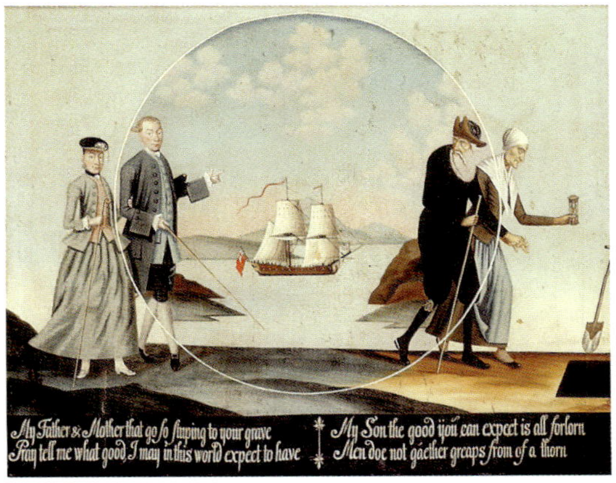

A1091; oil on canvas, 62 × 78 cm
Inscribed in two couplets beneath the image:
My Father and Mother that go stuping to your grave
Pray tell me what good I may in this world expect to have,
My son the good you can expext is forlorn
Men doe not gaether greaps from of a thorn.
Presented by Gerald Reitlinger, 1972; WA1978.32

On the left, a young man escorts his wife and points to a naval ship. A stooped old couple walk towards a grave on the far right. An English verse is written below to explain the allegory. A painting of almost identical composition and with a similar rhyme is signed 'H.G. Howlett' (Sotheby's, London, 22 July 1986, lot 94).

Anonymous British Artist
(*c.* 1830)

Princess Mary Tudor

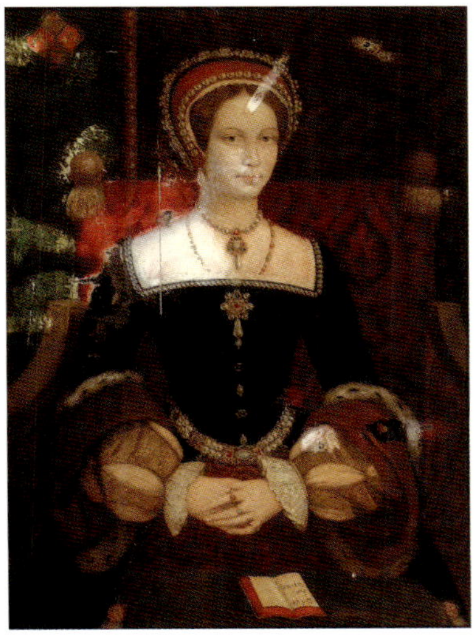

A152, oil on panel, 102 × 72 cm
Chambers Hall Gift, 1855; WA1855.197

Poole 1912, no. 403

Mary Tudor (1516–1558) succeeded as Queen of England in 1553 and married Philip II of Spain in the following year. A disastrous cleaning in 1976 revealed that the painting is substantially a 19th-century pastiche, perhaps over a 17th-century original.

Anonymous British Artist
(*c.* 1830)

Landscape with a River and Bridge

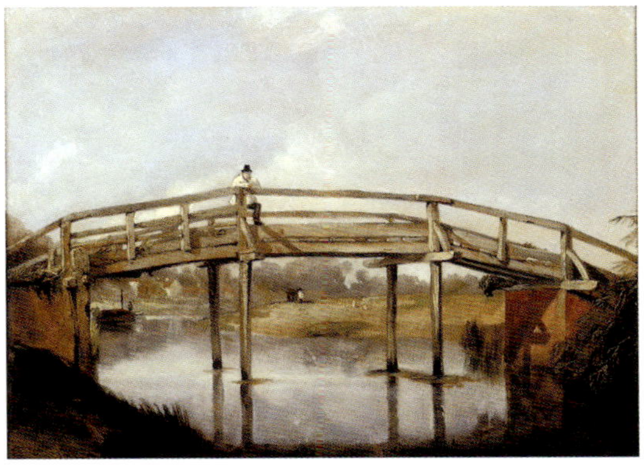

A488; oil on canvas, 30 × 39 cm
Weldon Bequest, 1937; WA1937.69

This crisply painted landscape has been variously attributed to Constable and to the artists of the Norwich School, Henry Bright (1814–1873) and Miles Edmund Cotman (1810–1858). None is completely convincing.

Anonymous British Artist
(*c.* 1815)

Alexander Hendras Sutherland

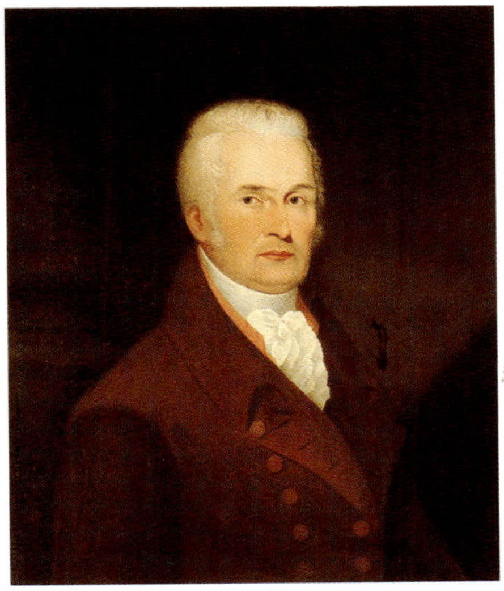

A797a; oil on canvas, 76 × 63 cm
(?)Presented by Mrs A.H. Sutherland, 1837; WA1951.226

Poole 1912, no. 282

Alexander Hendras Sutherland (1753–1820) was a wealthy merchant who devoted his considerable fortune to forming a remarkable collection of prints and drawings illustrative of the history of England in the 17th century, which he used to grangerize a number of titles, notably Clarendon's *History of the Rebellion*. His widow presented the collection to the University of Oxford in 1837. This portrait was presumably included in the gift.

Anonymous British Artist
(*c.* 1830)

Landscape with two Figures walking along a Track

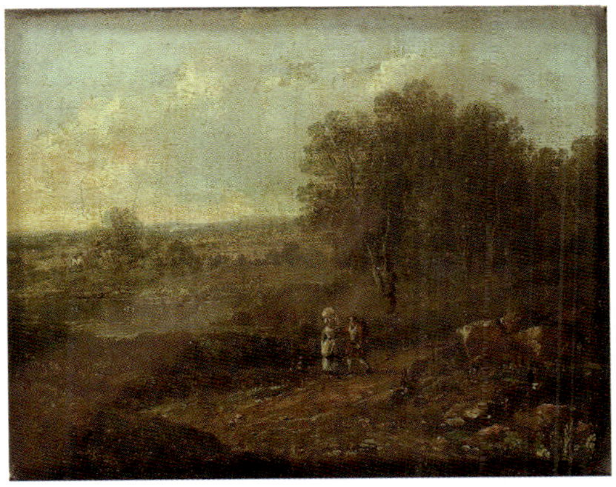

A419b; oil on canvas, 22 × 27 cm
Bequeathed by Miss I.A. Taylor, 1930; WA1932.216

Whilst this painting was traditionally attributed to Constable, its mediocre quality makes this impossible.

Anonymous British Artist
(*c.* 1830)

Landscape with a River Valley

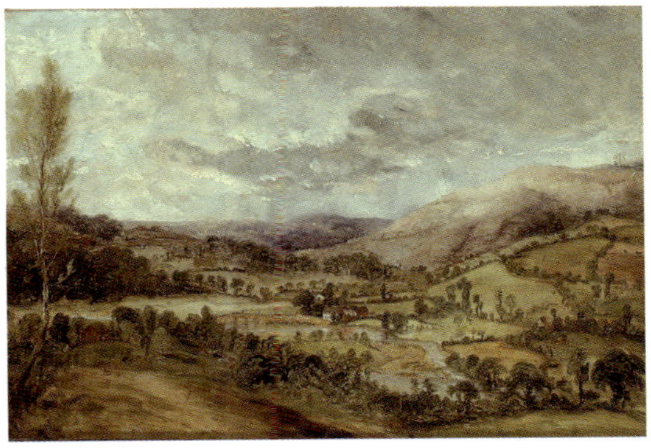

A646; oil on panel, 39 × 52 cm
Hindley Smith Bequest, 1939; WA1940.1.28

This rather crude sketch has been attributed to Constable and to Frederick Richard Lee (1798–1879), but is by a lesser artist who knew Constable's work.

Anonymous British Artist
(*c.* 1830)

Presumed Portrait of William Shakespeare

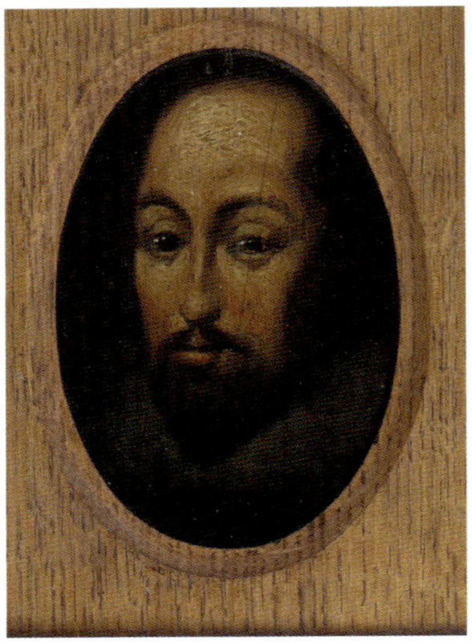

A736f; oil on oak panel, 13.5 × 9.5 cm
Prov.: Mrs Wright
Presented by the daughters of James Reddie Anderson, 1947; WA1947.201.4

If this is indeed intended to be Shakespeare, it was probably copied from a print by an amateur artist.

Elias van den Broeck
(1649/50 – 1708)

A Vase of Flowers

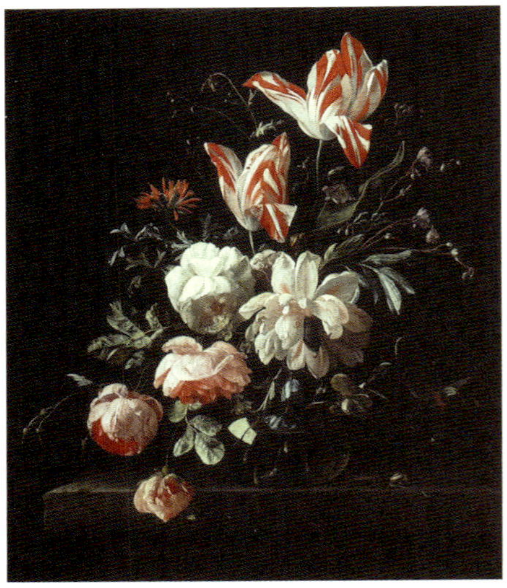

A610; oil on canvas, 62 × 53 cm
Daisy Linda Ward Bequest, 1939; WA1940.2.86

Meijer 2003, no. 18

Formerly attributed to Simon Verelst, now attributed to van den Broeck by comparison with a signed still life in the Statens Museum for Kunst, Copenhagen which includes an almost identical central rose and peony. Of all his known still-life paintings, this one is closest to the work of his first teacher, Cornelis Kick but there are also echoes of the work of Jan Davidsz. de Heem in the arrangement of small branches and flowers round the central motif. This indicates a fairly early date, about 1670, in the artist's career.

Elias van den Broeck
(1649/50 – 1708)

A Vase of Flowers

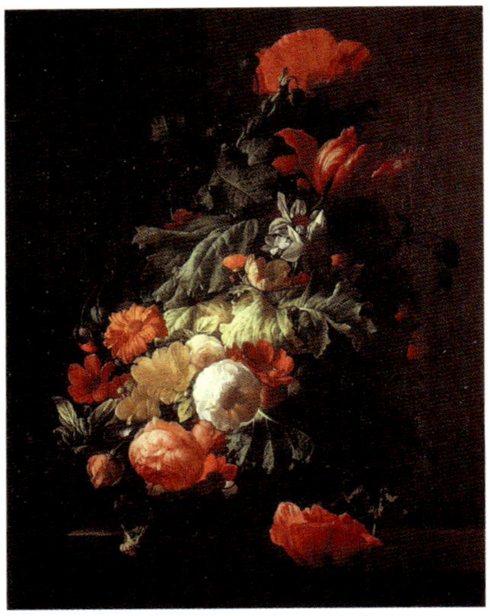

A540; oil on canvas, 90 × 71 cm
Signed: *VD.Broeck.f*
Daisy Linda Ward Bequest, 1939; WA1940.2.16

Meijer 2003, no. 19

It has been suggested that similarities between the radiant lighting used in this painting and similar effects in still-life paintings by Philip van Kouwenbergh indicate that this painting may date from the 1690s when van Kouwenbergh was in van den Broeck's studio. Like many of the artist's flower pieces, this one is arranged in a diagonal of overflowing blooms which partly conceal the glass vase.

Anonymous British Artist
(late 19th century)

The Descent from the Cross

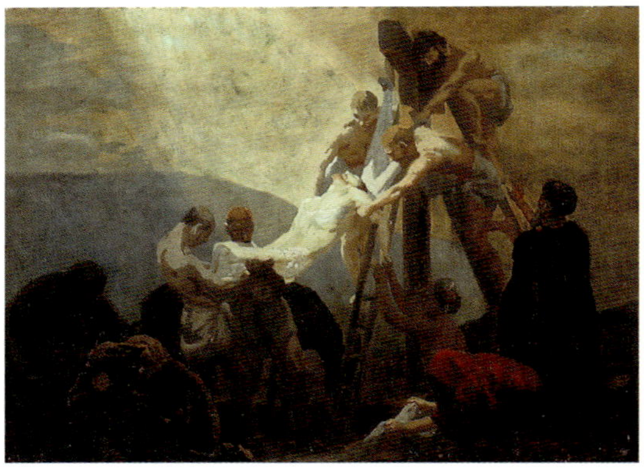

A806; oil on canvas laid on millboard, 71 × 92 cm
Signed indistinctly and dated: *R ...4*
Presented by Archibald G. B. Russell, 1951; WA1951.48

Formerly attributed to Ribot, probably on the basis of the illegible signature. This a work of the late 19th century, possibly by a British artist influenced by French art.

Elias van den Broeck
(1649/50 – 1708)

Still Life with a Snake

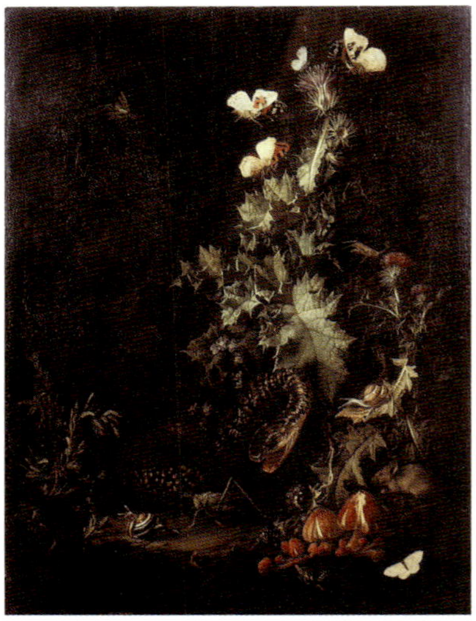

A587; oil on canvas, 62 × 53 cm
Inscribed: *R. Ruijsch*
Daisy Linda Ward Bequest, 1939; WA1940.2.63

Meijer 2003, no. 20

Formerly attributed to Rachel Ruysch, partly because of the false signature, this woodland scene is now attributed to van den Broeck by comparison with similar works like the *Bird's Nest at the Foot of a Tree* in the Museum Boijmans Van Beuningen, Rotterdam, or the signed woodland still life in the Staatliches Museum, Schwerin. As he did in other pictures, the artist has pasted down real butterflies into his composition, a time-saving device for which, it is said, he was reproached by his contemporaries in Antwerp.

Agnolo Bronzino
(1503 – 1572)

Giovanni de'Medici

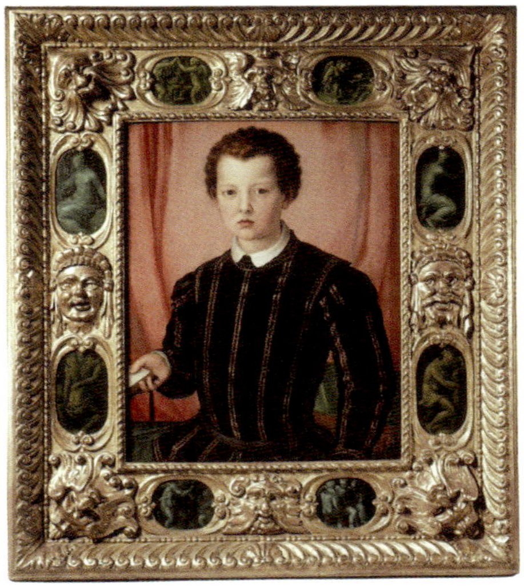

A105; oil on panel, 66.2 × 52.8 cm
Fox-Strangways Gift, 1850; WA1850.32

Lloyd 1977, pp. 39–43; McCorquodale 1981, pp. 131, 134

Giovanni de'Medici (1543–1562), the second son of Cosimo I and Eleanora of Toledo, was intended for a career in the Church: he was created deacon in 1550, Cardinal in 1560 and Archbishop of Pisa in 1561. A105 was painted *c.* 1550–51, when Bronzino, as court artist to Cosimo I, was working on a group of Medici family portraits. Although not original to this painting, the Florentine frame of *c.* 1580 is typical of Mannerist taste for the elaborate and the witty.

Copy after Agnolo Bronzino
(1503 – 1572)

Portrait of a Woman

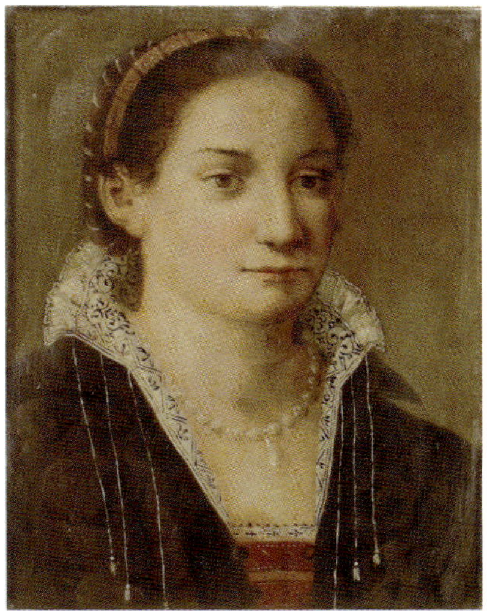

A672; oil on panel, 45.5 × 35.5 cm
Presented by Sir Arthur Evans, 1941; WA1941.5

Lloyd 1977, p. 43

Probably an 18th-century imitation, A672 may be copied from an engraving. No exact prototype for this portrait is known.

Peter Brook
(b. 1927)

Wytham, Oxford

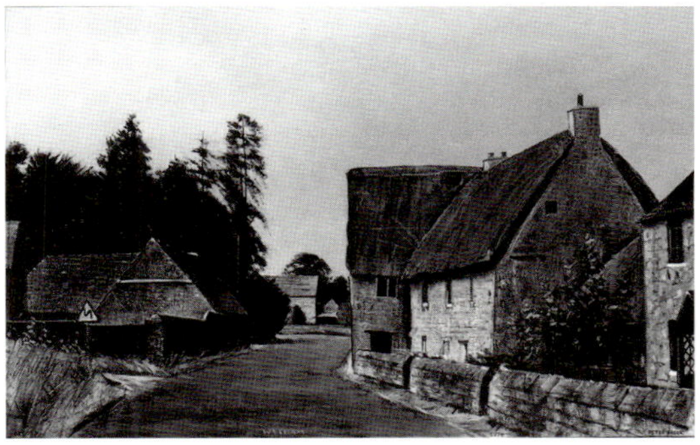

A1081; oil on canvas, 50.5 × 76.5 cm
Signed: *Peter Brook*; inscribed: *Oxford, Wytham*
Deposited by the Delegates of the Oxford University Press, 1976; WA1976.6

The Oxford Almanack, published annually by the University Press, always appears with a commissioned head-piece. The works on which these images have been based tend to be done in watercolour or bodycolour on paper. This view, painted in oil on canvas, represents a corner of Wytham, a village north-west of Oxford. It was reproduced as the Almanack for 1975.

Charles Brooking
(*c.* 1723 – 1759)

A Ship before a fresh Breeze and another to Leeward

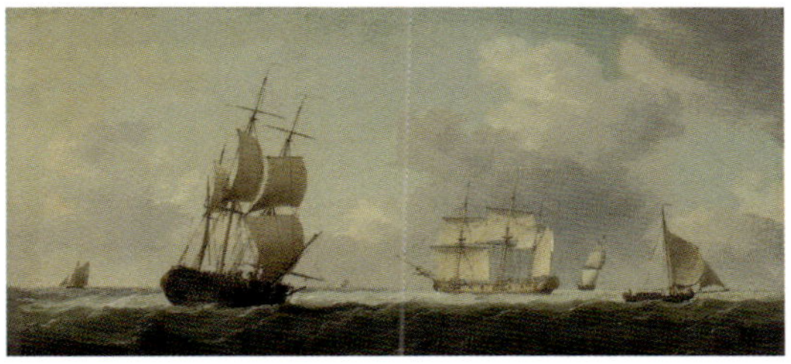

A965; oil on panel, 32 × 65 cm
Madan Bequest, 1962; WA1962.17.7

Aldeburgh and Bristol 1966, under no. 55

This is a reduced version of a painting in a private collection. It has not been established which was painted first.

Copy after Agnolo Bronzino
(1503 – 1572)

Eleanora of Toledo with a View of Florence behind

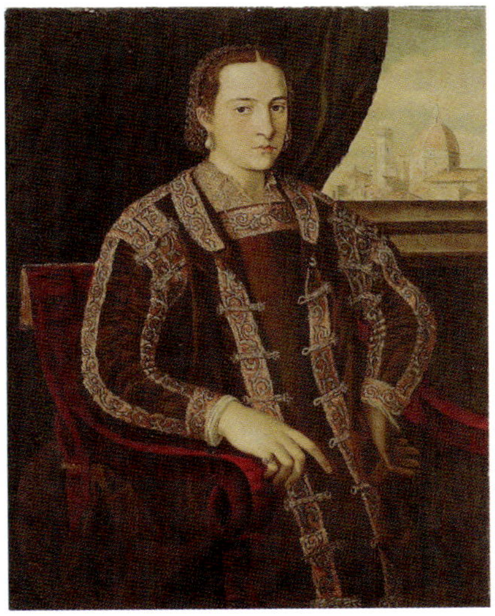

A520c; oil on panel, 104.2 × 85.2 cm
Prov.: C.J. Longman
Bequeathed by Mrs H.A. Longman, 1938; WA1938.125

Lloyd 1977, p. 43; Langedijk 1981, no. 35.8d

A pastiche of the 19th century, this picture is based on a celebrated portrait of Eleanora of Toledo by Bronzino, of which an important version is in the National Gallery of Art, Washington. A520c may derive from an engraving since the figure is in reverse with respect to Bronzino's design. The landscape background has been added and some details of the pose and costume changed.

Charles Brooking
(*c.* 1723 – 1759)

Shipping in a Breeze, with a Cutter close-hauled in the foreground

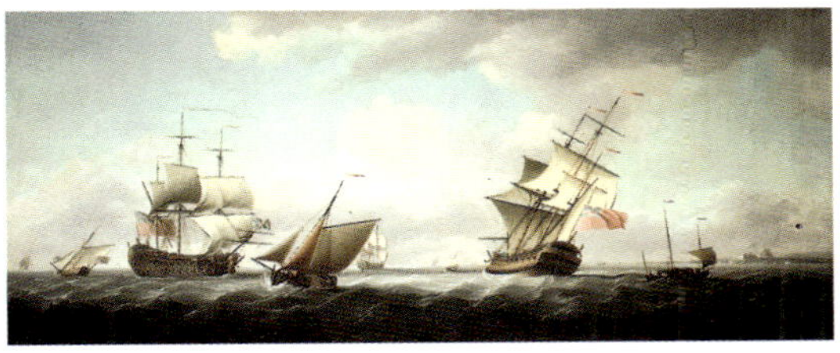

A1075; oil on canvas, 61.5 × 147.5 cm
Presented by Miss Norah M. Turner, 1975; WA1975.69

Aldeburgh and Bristol 1966, no. 10

Brooking's success dated from 1754, when he presented a huge sea piece to the Foundling Hospital in London and was elected a Governor and Guardian. He specialised in marine paintings, revealing in his detailed depictions his intimate knowledge of all aspects of ships and maritime life. His works are difficult to date, but this example may be comparatively early.

Adriaen Brouwer
(1605/6 – 1638)

Two Peasants

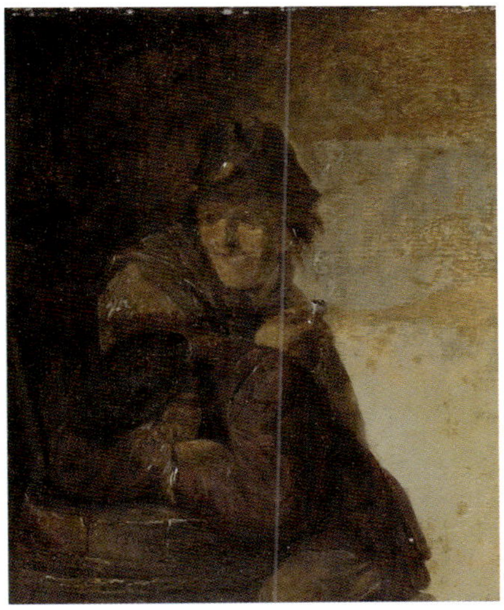

A966; oil on panel, 22 × 18 cm
Madan Bequest, 1962; WA1962.17.8

White 1999, p. 22

Brouwer is said to have been a pupil of Frans Hals in Haarlem. By *c.* 1632 he had settled in Antwerp, where he remained for the rest of his brief life. He is chiefly known as a painter of peasant subjects. This little picture may have been intended as a satire illustrating the evil effects of smoking and drinking.

Ford Madox Brown
(1821 – 1893)

Study for 'The Execution of Mary, Queen of Scots'

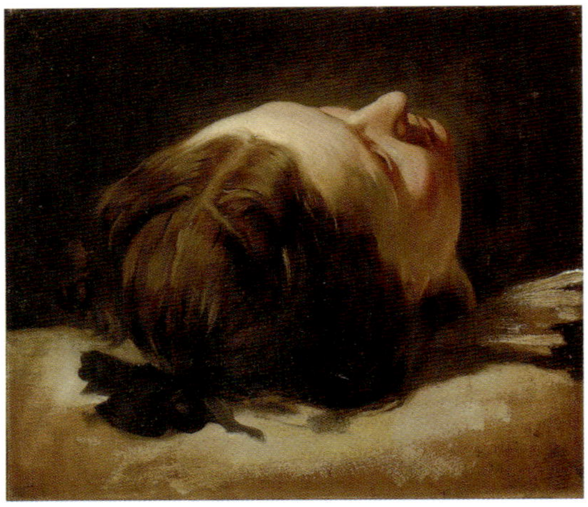

A1086; oil on paper on canvas, 39 × 44 cm
Prov.: by descent to Mrs Helen Rossetti Angeli
Bequeathed by John Bryson, 1977; WA1977.21

Newman and Watkinson 1991, pp. 13–14

The finished painting was begun in Antwerp 1840 and finished in Paris in 1841, where it was exhibited at the Salon (untraced); a smaller version is in the Whitworth Art Gallery, Manchester. The sitter for this study of a swooning attendant was the artist's cousin, Elisabeth Bromley, whom he married in 1841.

Ford Madox Brown
(1821 – 1893)

Mrs James Madox

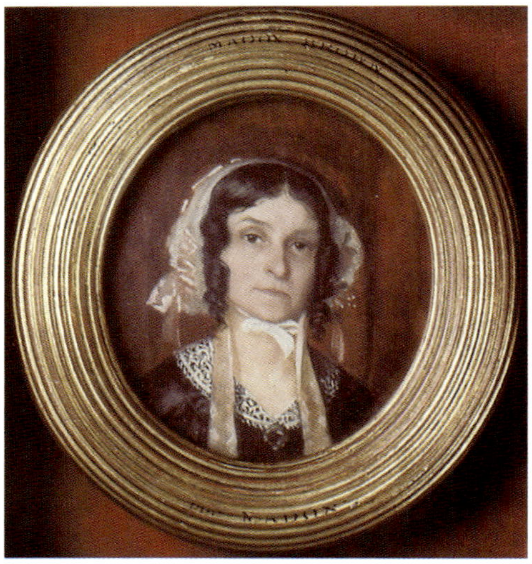

A936a; oil on panel, 10 × 8 cm
Prov.: William Michael Rossetti
Presented by Francis Falconer Madan, 1960; WA1960.53

This portrait of the artist's maternal aunt was painted at her home at Foot's Cray, Kent, towards the end of March 1840. It was one of a series of small family portraits made on this visit.

Ford Madox Brown
(1821 – 1893)

The Seeds and Fruits of English Poetry

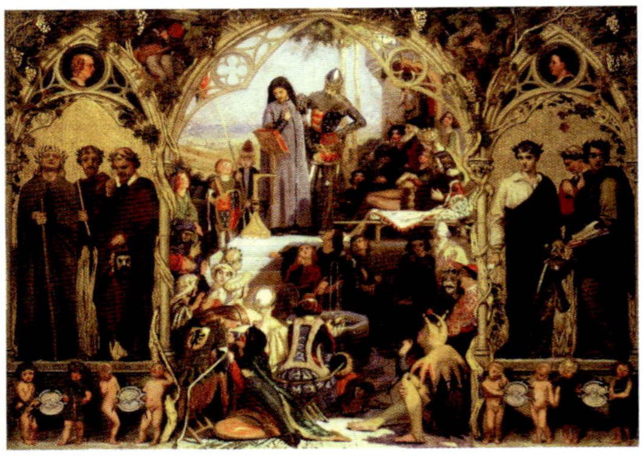

A360; oil on canvas, 36 × 46 cm
Inscribed: *FORD MADOX BROWN DEST IN ROMA. 1845. COLORAVIT IN HAMPSTEAD. 1853.*
Prov.: John Marshall
Presented by Mrs W.F.R. Weldon, 1920; WA1920.3

Parris 1984, no. 6; Brown 1987, no. 15; Newman and Watkinson 1991, pp. 29–36, 55

Devised to illustrate the ennobling of the English language by Chaucer, this painting was planned in London and composed in Rome in 1845 and completed after Brown's return to England. The central panel shows Geoffrey Chaucer reading at the court of Edward III, with his patron, the Black Prince, on his left. The 'fruits' of English poetry apppear in the wings: Milton, Spenser and Shakespeare on the left; Byron, Pope and Burns on the right; Goldsmith and Thomson in the roundels; and, inscribed in the cartouches beneath (held by the children), the names of Campbell, Moore, Shelley, Keats, Chatterton, Kirke White, Coleridge and Wordsworth. Although designed as a sketch for a larger work, Brown omitted the two wings and the Gothic details when he painted his monumental *Geoffrey Chaucer reading*, exhibited at the Royal Academy in 1851 (Sydney, Art Gallery of New South Wales).

Ford Madox Brown
(1821 – 1893)

The pretty Baa-Lambs

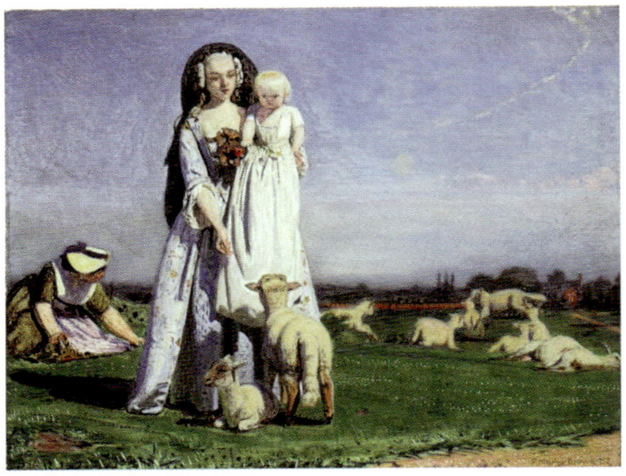

A327; oil on panel, 20 × 26 cm
Signed and dated: *F. Madox Brown, 52*
Prov.: D.T. White; Benjamin Godfrey Windus; William Connal
Purchased (Magdalen College Fund), 1909; WA1909.2

Newman and Watkinson 1991, pp. 59–61

Brown's second wife, Emma Hill and their daughter, Catherine, posed outdoors in 18th-century dress for the main group in 1851, at their home in Stockwell. The sheep were brought over each day from Clapham Common. This version is a small replica of the original in Birmingham City Art Gallery, and was painted in 1852 in Thomas Seddon's studio.

Ford Madox Brown
(1821 – 1893)

Lady Rivers and her Children

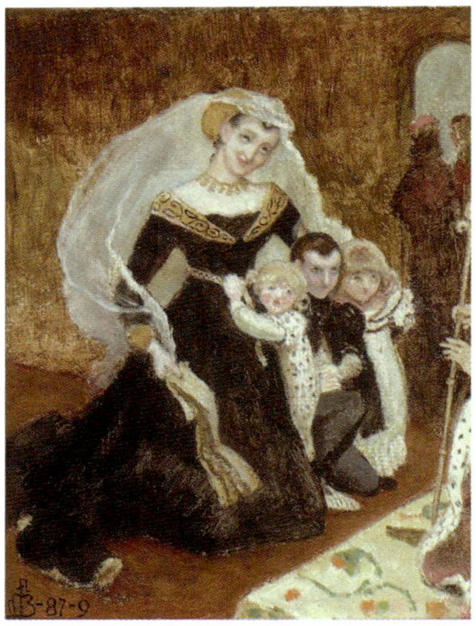

A1087; oil on canvas laid on panel, 21.4 × 17 cm
Signed and dated: *FMB – 87–9*
Prov.: Henry Boddington, Pownall Hall
Bequeathed by John Bryson, 1977; WA1977.22

Elizabeth Woodville, daughter of Earl Rivers and later wife of Edward IV, pleading before the king for the restitution of her dower.

Style of Jan Brueghel the Elder
(1568 – 1625)

Ferry-Boats by a wooded Riverbank

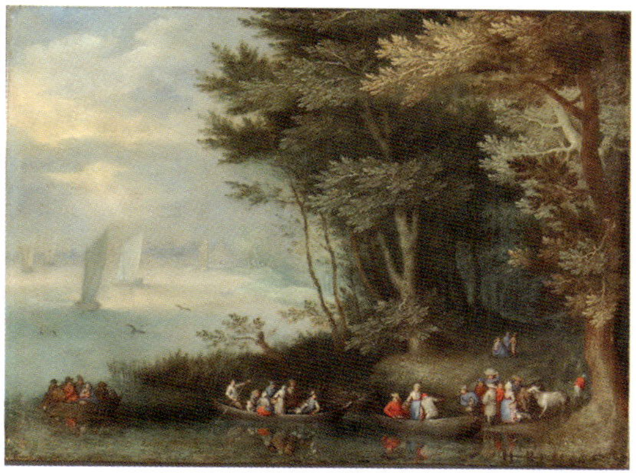

A812; oil on copper, 19 × 25 cm
Bequeathed by J. Reginald Jones, 1951; WA1951.51.6

White 1999, p. 22

A weak version of a painting by Jan Brueghel I, now in the Musée des Beaux-Arts, Nantes.

Hendrick ter Brugghen
(1588? – 1629)

Portrait of a Man playing the Bagpipes

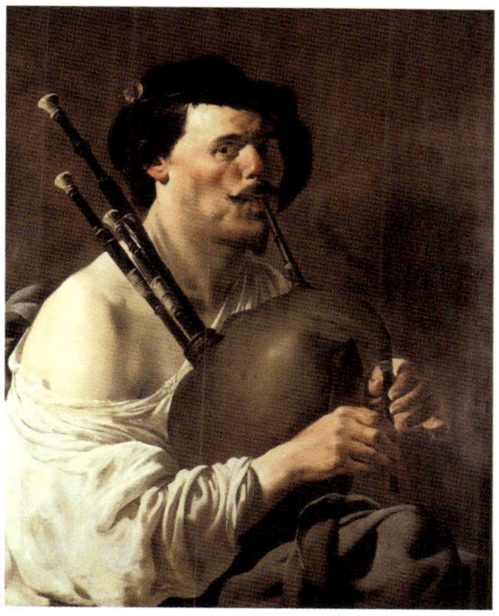

A710; oil on canvas, 94 × 75 cm
Signed and dated: *HTBrugghen fecit* 1624 (*HTB* in monogram)
Prov.: Harold Davis; W.W. Adams; Percy Moore Turner
Purchased, 1944; WA1944.101

White 1999, p. 24

The model in this painting seems to be the same as the bagpiper in a painting of the same year in the Wallraf-Richartz Museum, Cologne. Both belong to a group of similar half-length musicians which the artist started in 1621. The subject was popular among the followers of Caravaggio in Utrecht where ter Brugghen settled *c.* 1615 on his return from Rome.

Francesco Buoneri, called Cecco del Caravaggio
(active *c.* 1610 – 1621)

Interior with a young Man holding a Recorder

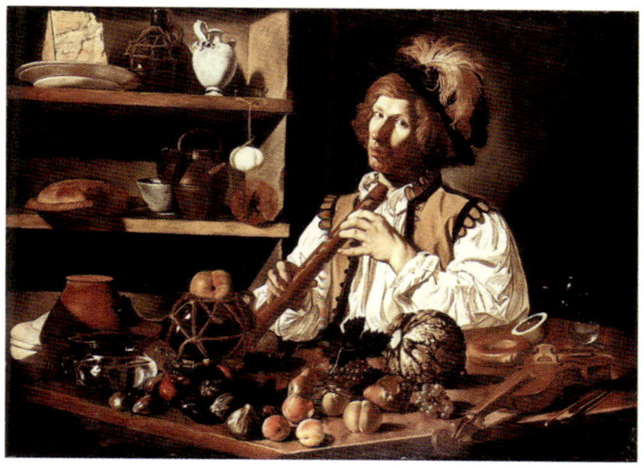

A451b; oil on canvas, 103 × 138 cm
Prov.: Mrs H. Shirlaw
Purchased, 1936; WA1936.222

Papi 2001, no. 13

Formerly attributed to Louis Finson, A451b was identified as by Cecco in 1943. Little documentary evidence exists for this distinctive follower of Caravaggio. Like his master, he favoured strongly-lit compositions often of enigmatic themes: here a young musician confronts the viewer with a challenging air, amidst an abundant assortment of still-life elements.

Attributed to Jan Brueghel the Younger
(1601 – 1678)

A Vase of Flowers

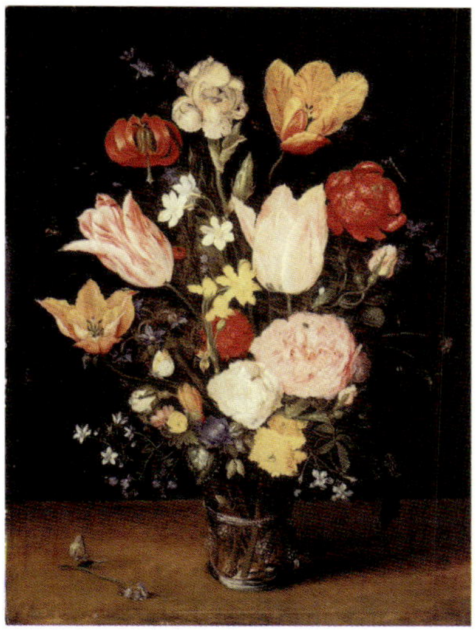

A541; oil on panel, 47 × 35 cm
Daisy Linda Ward Bequest, 1939; WA1940.2.17

Meijer 2003, no. 21

Although the design of this painting is clearly very close to the work of Jan Brueghel I, some weaknesses in the technique have led scholars to suggest that this might be the work of a follower, perhaps by his son, Jan Brueghel II, who took over his father's studio in Antwerp following the death of Jan I in 1625. There exists a close variant of the Oxford painting by Jan I (Sotheby Parke Bernet, 13 January 1978, lot 127).

Reginald Grange Brundrit
(1883 – 1960)

Yeoman Stock

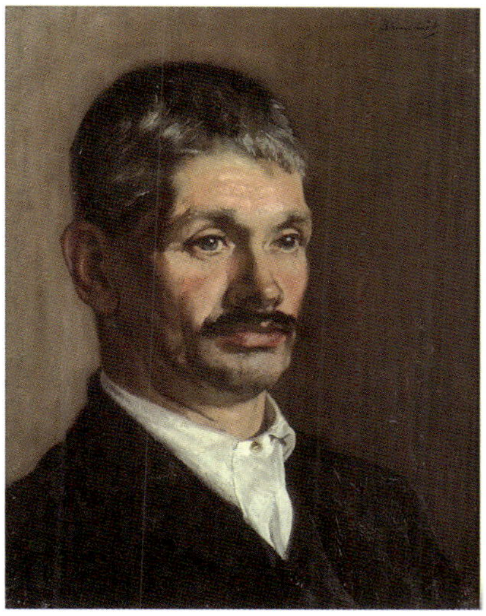

A1021; oil on canvas, 46.2 × 35.7 cm
Signed: *Brundrit*
Prov.: given by the artist to the donor
Presented by Stanley Anderson, 1965; WA1965.49.1

Exhibited at the Royal Academy in 1959. The subject was probably a farmer or farmworker from Yorkshire where Brundrit was based and where he found the inspiration for many of his works.

Attributed to Francesco Buonsignori
(*c.* 1460 – 1519)

The Lamentation with a Benedictine Donor

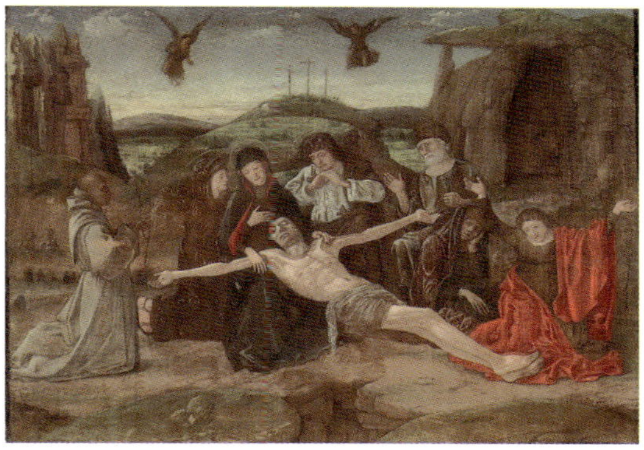

A347; oil on linen, 40.5 × 55.3 cm
Prov.: George Price Boyce
Bywater Bequest, 1915; WA1915.11

Lloyd 1977, pp. 46–47

In a harsh rocky landscape, the lamentation over the stiffened body of Christ is contemplated by a kneeling Benedictine. A347 is strongly influenced by Ferrarese and Mantuan art of the later 15th century, notably the art of Cosimo Tura and the late work of Andrea Mantegna, while there are also affinities with Caroto and Liberale da Verona. A plausible attribution to Buonsignori in his later career has recently been suggested.

Sir Edward Coley Burne-Jones, Bt
(1833 – 1898)

Danäe and the brazen Tower

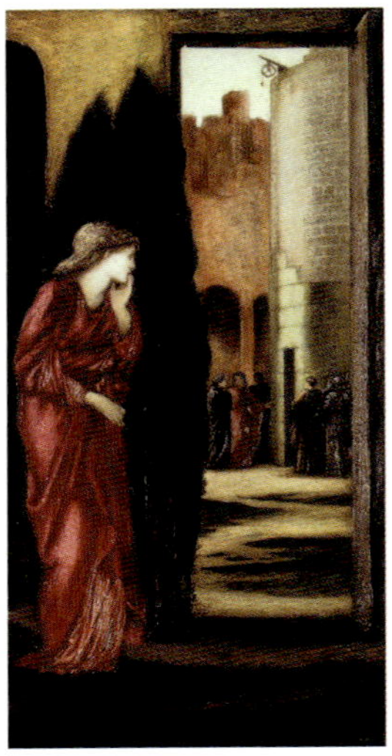

A757; oil on panel, 38 × 19 cm
Signed: *E.B.J.*
Prov.: John Graham; Mrs Joseph
Presented by F.J. Nettlefold, 1948; WA1948.32

Grundy 1933-8, III, p. 42

Burne-Jones probably used William Morris's *Earthly Paradise* as the source of this subject. Acrisius, King of Argos, having been warned by the oracle that he would be killed by his daughter's son, imprisoned her in a tower of brass. However, Danäe bore a son to Jove, who fulfilled the prophecy. Here, Danäe watches the construction of the tower with apprehension. This is one of two small versions of the subject painted by Burne-Jones for one of his strongest supporters, the Glasgow merchant, William Graham, in 1872; the second version, of 1876, is in the Fogg Art Museum. Burne-Jones's definitive treatment of the theme (Glasgow Museum and Art Gallery), was exhibited in 1888.

Philip Hermogenes Calderon
(1833 – 1898)

Broken Vows

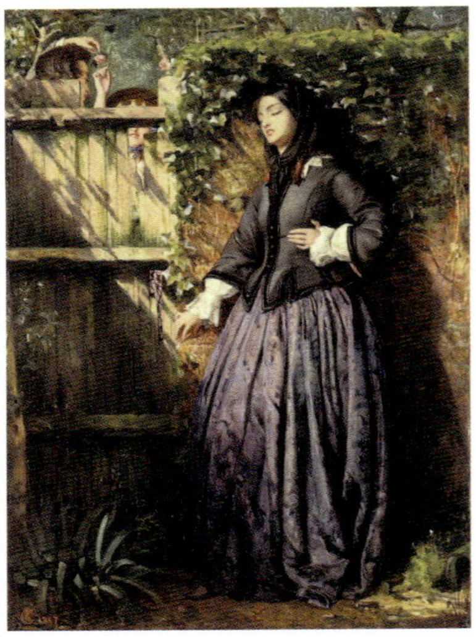

A967; oil on board, 29 × 22 cm
Signed in monogram and dated: *1857*
Prov.: Sir Jeremiah Colman
Madan Bequest, 1962; WA1962.17.9

Brown 1987, no. 40

A woman swoons against an ivy-clad wall, overhearing her lover flirting with a new friend. The sense of betrayal is reinforced by the initials carved on the gate. This is a smaller repetition of a painting exhibited at the Royal Academy in 1857, with a quotation from Longfellow's *The Spanish Student*, Act II, scene iv, spoken by Preciosa, 'More hearts are breaking in this world of ours' (Tate Britain).

Sir Augustus Wall Callcott
(1779 – 1844)

Southampton Castle

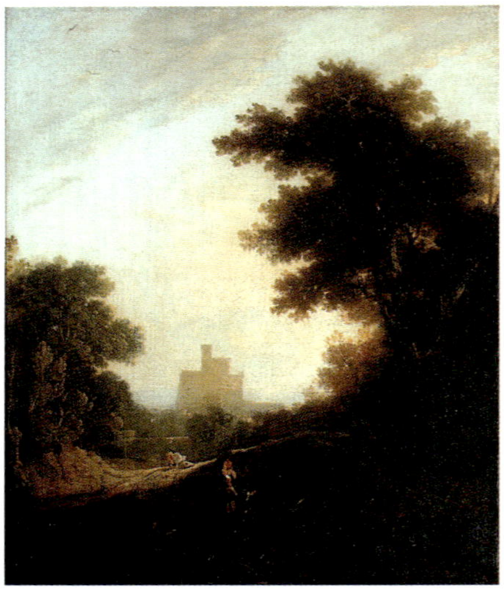

A135; oil on canvas, 77 × 64 cm
Bequeathed by the Revd Dr Thomas Penrose, 1851; WA1851.4

John Henry, 2nd Marquess Lansdowne, erected a whimsical tower on the site of the old Southampton Castle in 1804; it was demolished in 1818.

Sir Augustus Wall Callcott (1779 – 1844) after Joseph Mallord William Turner
(1775 – 1851)

The Junction of the Thames and the Medway

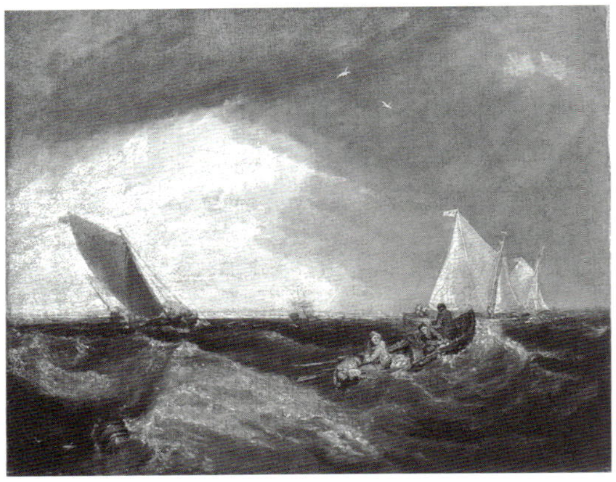

A132; oil on canvas, 36 × 46 cm
Bequeathed by the Revd Dr Thomas Penrose, 1851; WA1851.5

Brown 1975, pp. 721–2; Brown 1981, under no. 7

Turner's painting, *Sheerness and the Isle of Sheppey, with the Junction of the Thames and the Medway from the Nore*, (National Gallery of Art, Washington), was exhibited in 1807 and bought by Thomas Lister Parker. Callcott made two other copies: a life-size replica for Parker (private collection) and a smaller version (Tate Britain). This is the smallest and the most freely brushed of the three and was evidently the preliminary sketch.

Attributed to Abraham van Calraet
(1642 – 1722)

Still Life with Fruit

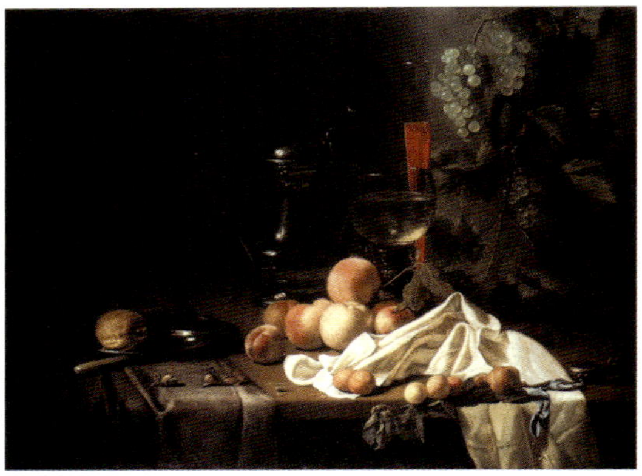

A547; oil on canvas, 72 × 96 cm
Inscribed: *A cuyp fecit*
Daisy Linda Ward Bequest, 1939; WA1940.2.23

Meijer 2003, no. 22

A group of thirty-two still-life paintings which are signed in monogram *AC* and were once attributed to Aelbert Cuyp are now attributed to Abraham van Calraet, including this painting which has been inscribed with a false signature. On the grounds of style, it may date from the 1670s or 80s. There is a comparable signed still life by Calraet in The Mauritshuis.

Edward Calvert
(1799 – 1883)
Classical Landscape with a Goatherd

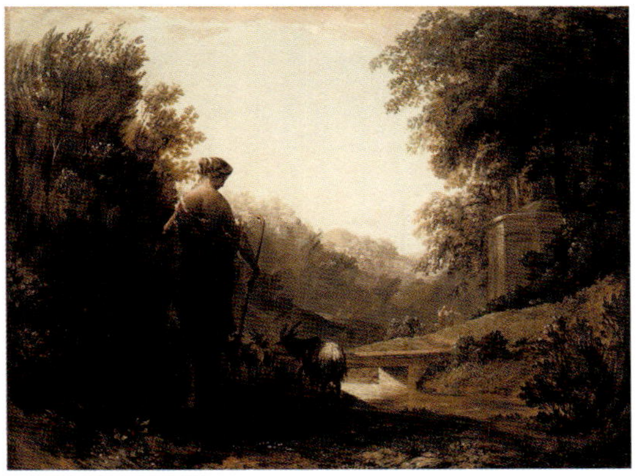

A417; oil on canvas, 71 × 92 cm
Prov.: from the artist by descent
Purchased, 1932; WA1932.196

This is Calvert's largest oil painting and has been dated to his first period, before 1827. He also painted a smaller version. The classical building and figure evoke a timeless ideal of pastoral simplicity.

Edward Calvert
(1799 – 1883)
In the Aegean Sea

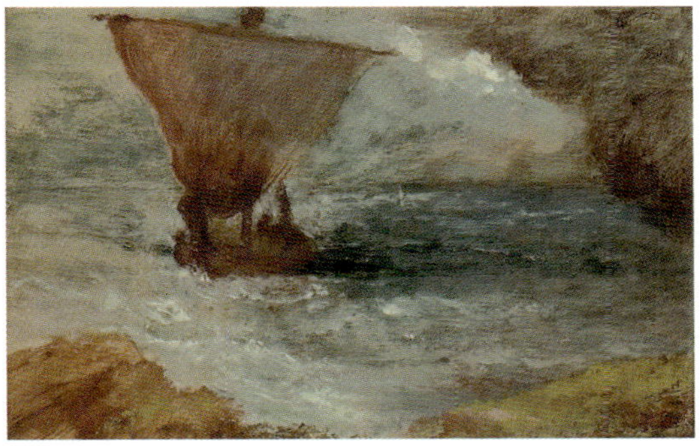

A490; oil on millboard, 24 × 36 cm
Weldon Bequest, 1937; WA1937.71

This unusually stormy sea and sky were presumably based on sketches made during Calvert's journey to Greece in 1844.

Edward Calvert
(1799 – 1883)
Mythological Scene

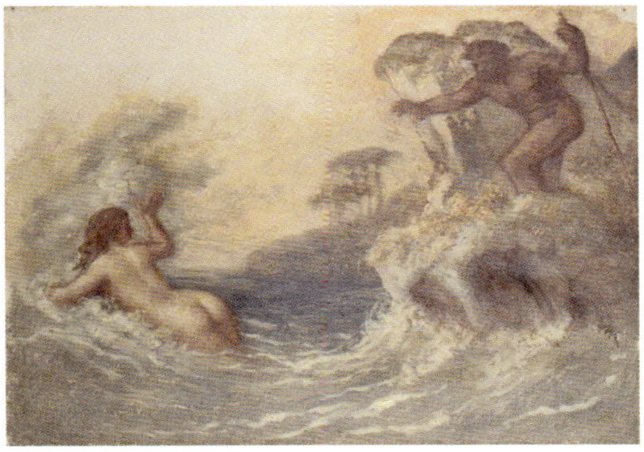

Oil on paper, mounted as a drawing, 19.2 × 26.6 cm
Prov.: from the artist by descent until 1932
Purchased, 1932; WA1932.198

Another late work, painted on a pink ground.

Edward Calvert
(1799 – 1883)
Psyche at the Stream

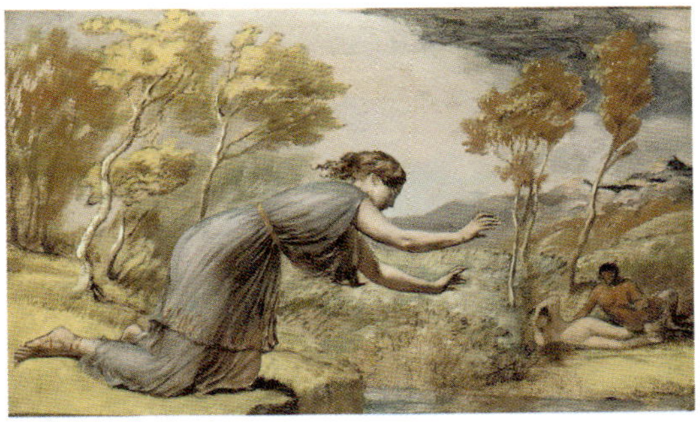

A1093; oil on board, 30 × 50.5 cm
Presented by Gerald Reitlinger, 1972; WA1978.34

Traditionally supposed to have been exhibited at the Royal Academy in 1836, though not listed in the catalogue.

Edward Calvert
(1799 – 1883)
Mars and Venus

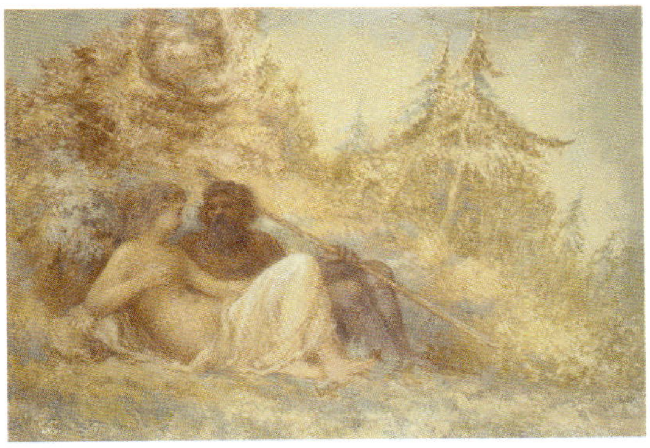

Oil on paper, 25.5 × 36.7 cm
Signed: *EC*
Weldon Bequest, 1937; WA1937.44

During his later years, Calvert produced many small works in thin oil colours on paper, the restrained colours and muted harmonies evocative of a dream world. They are generally peopled with figures from Greek mythology.

Edward Calvert
(1799 – 1883)
Psyche

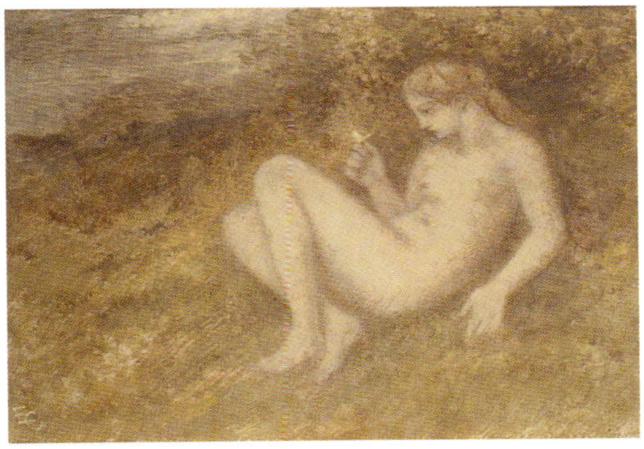

Oil on paper, mounted as a drawing, laid down, 18.8 × 26.3 cm (sight)
Signed: *EC*; and inscribed: *Simple*
Prov.: from the artist by descent until 1932
Purchased, 1932; WA1932.197

Edward Calvert, after Titian
(1799 – 1883)

Sleeping Nymph

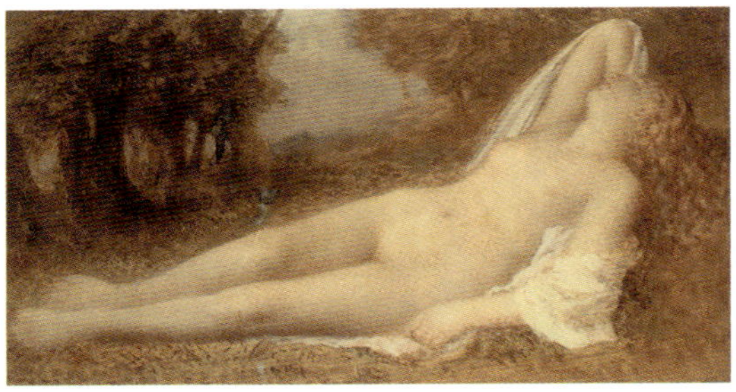

Oil on paper, mounted as a drawing, 19.8 × 37 cm
Weldon Bequest, 1937; WA1937.13

Based on the nymph in the foreground of Titian's *The Andrians* (Prado, Madrid), transposed into the timeless landscape Calvert invariably painted in later years.

Edward Calvert
(1799 – 1883)

Oak Trees in Summer

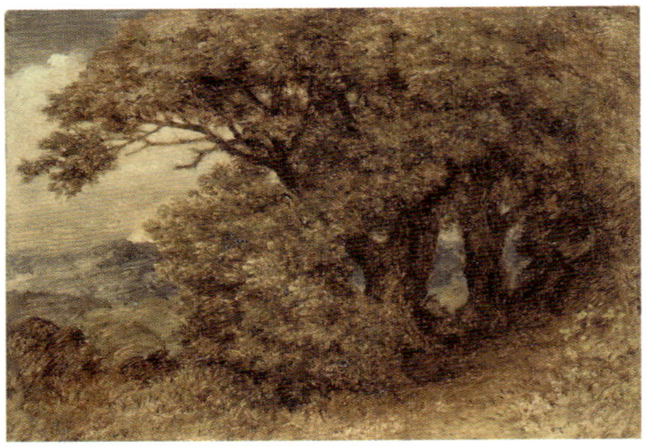

Oil on paper, mounted as a drawing, 15 × 21.1 cm
Prov.: Mrs Richmond; Eardley Knollys
Purchased (Madan Fund), 1976; WA1976.148

Binyon 1925, no. 70

One of only a handful of pure landscapes by Calvert, who preferred to people them with mythological figures.

Sir David Young Cameron
(1865 – 1945)

The Hills of Provence

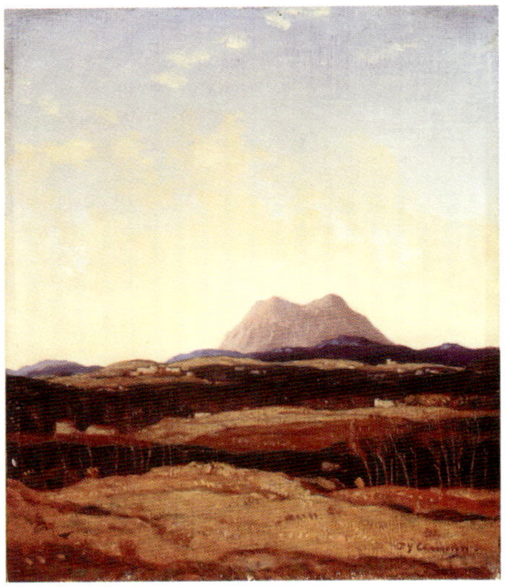

A478; oil on canvas, 36 × 30 cm
Signed: *D.Y. Cameron*
Weldon Bequest, 1937; WA1937.59

Stirling 1965, no. 43

After suffering a heart attack in August 1921, Cameron left for the South of France, where he remained for two years. He returned in 1926.

Edward Calvert
(1799 – 1883)

The Garden of Culture

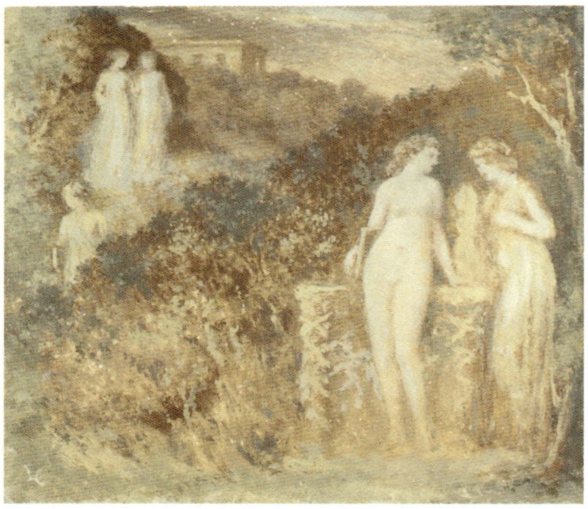

Oil on paper, mounted as a drawing, 24.5 × 27.3 cm
Signed: *EC*
Inscribed on back: *Votive Life Edw. Calvert*
Presented by Francis Falconer Madan, 1959; WA1959.48

One of Calvert's more complex figure subjects, evoking under a starlit sky the timeless ideal of Greek life devoted to culture.

Sir David Young Cameron
(1865 – 1945)

The Ruins of Ypres

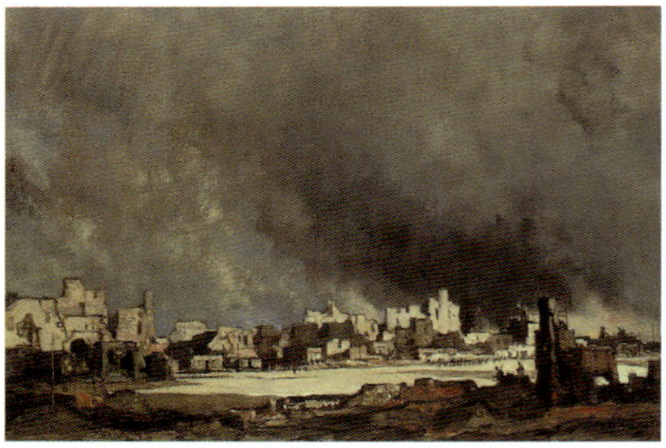

A394; oil on canvas, 50 × 74 cm
Signed: *D.Y. Cameron*
Presented by Mrs W.F.R. Weldon, 1929; WA1929.5

Stirling 1965, no. 34; Smith 1992, p. 84

Cameron had known Ypres from visits before the First World War and was shocked by the devastation he found in 1917–18, when he was making studies for paintings commissioned by Lord Beaverbrook. He returned in 1919 and based his major work, *The Battlefield of Ypres – After* (Imperial War Museum) on notes made on the road from Ypres to Menin. This view is substantially similar and was painted in 1919–20.

Giovanni Battista Camuccini
(1819 – 1904)

A Wayside Shrine

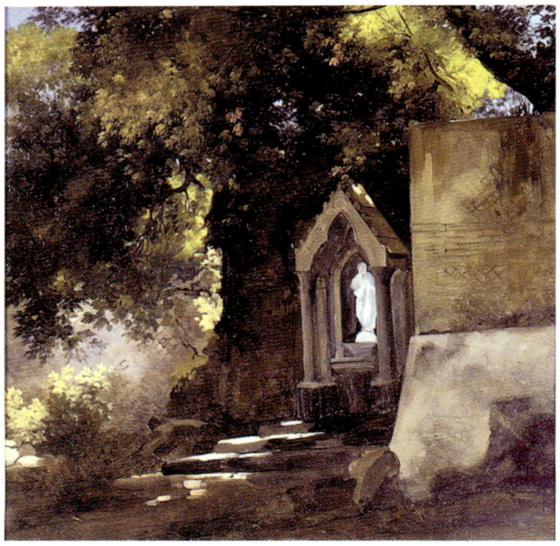

A1229; oil on card laid on canvas, 29.5 × 29.5 cm
Presented in memory of Michel Goldet by his wife Alice Goldet, 2001; WA2001.19

Moatti 2000, no. 7

The artist was the son of an important neo-classical painter and collector, Vincenzo Camuccini (1771–1844). Like many artists of his generation, he took up sketching out of doors in the 1840s. A1229 is chiefly a study of sunshine and shadow in which the textures of stone and foliage are rapidly evoked.

Giovanni Antonio da Canal, called Canaletto
(1697 – 1768)

A view of Dolo on the Brenta Canal

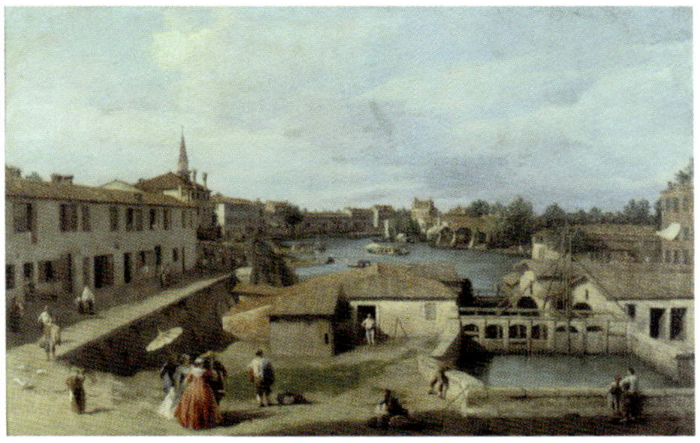

A146; oil on canvas, 63 × 96 cm
Chambers Hall Gift, 1855; WA1855.187

Constable and Links 1989, no. 371

The Brenta Canal, lined with elegant villas, was the gateway to Venice for visitors arriving from the north. Extensively damaged and restored, A146 was originally very similar in detail to the version in the Staatsgalerie, Stuttgart, datable to *c.* 1732–35. However, the far larger expanse of sky in that painting suggests that A146 was the prototype. Versions of the composition were painted by Bernardo Bellotto, Francesco Guardi and Giambattista Cimaroli.

Studio of Giovanni Antonio da Canal, called Canaletto
(1697 – 1768)

Entrance to the Grand Canal, looking west

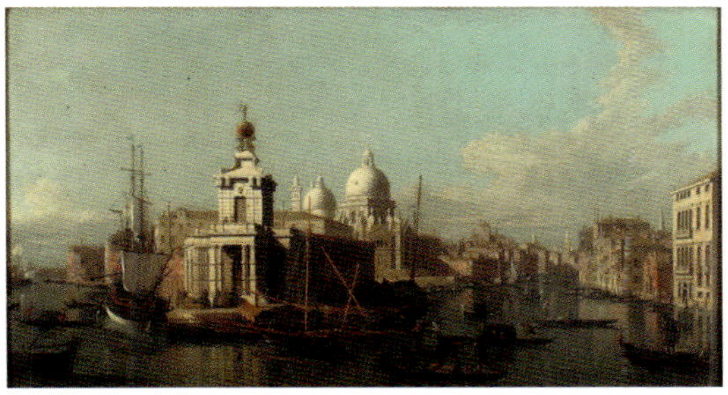

A296; oil on canvas, 52.7 × 96.5 cm
Bequeathed by John D. Chambers, 1897; WA1897.16

Constable and Links 1989, no. 161b.3

Canaletto's composition of the early 1730s in the Royal Collection was the model for a large number of copies and variations by the master, his studio and followers. A296 differs from the prototype in extending further to the left to include a view of the Zattere and Giudecca canal, with many differences in the details.

The Candlelight Master
(active *c.* 1620 – 1640)

A Physician with a Urine Sample

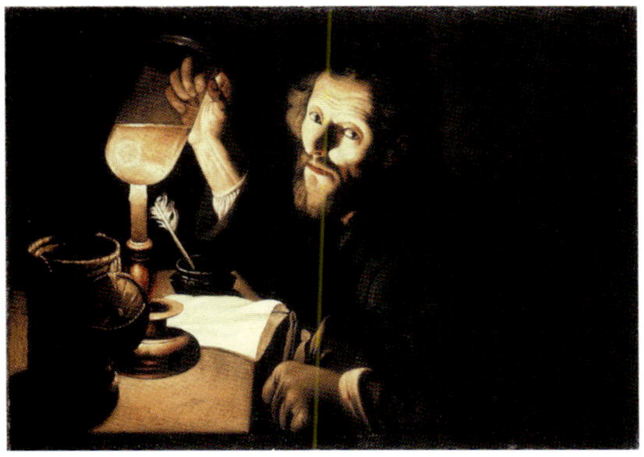

A693; oil on canvas, 72 × 99 cm
Inscribed on the stretcher: *Gherardo delle Notti – Chimico*
Presented by Percy Moore Turner, 1942; WA1942.18

Nicolson and Vertova 1990, p. 63, pl. 858

Physicians are characterised in early woodcuts by the attribute of a large glass container, which they hold up to the light to examine. In later genre painting, such doctors appear in a humorous light. A693 is unusual in that the physician is presented at work and looking directly at the spectator. Probably dating from *c.* 1630–33, it belongs to a group of works by the Candlelight Master, a follower of Caravaggio sometimes identified as Trophime Bigot (*c.* 1579–1650) who specialised in nocturnal scenes.

Giovanni Antonio da Canal, called Canaletto
(1697 – 1768)

A Puppet Show on the Piazzetta, Venice

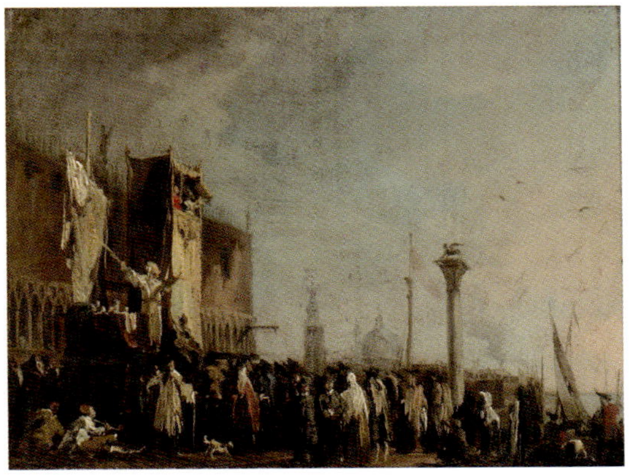

A147; oil on canvas, 24 × 31 cm
Chambers Hall Gift, 1855; WA1855.186

Constable and Links 1989, no. 363

Traditionally attributed to Canaletto and considered to be an early work, A147 with its ragged brushwork and anecdotal subject has been seen by some scholars as a later painting, perhaps from the end of the 18th century. Recent re-assessments of Canaletto's early career, when he painted freely-handled, theatrical views, suggest that A147 might well be by his hand.

Copy after Giovanni Antonio da Canal, called Canaletto
(1697 – 1768)

The Grand Canal, looking East from S. Vio

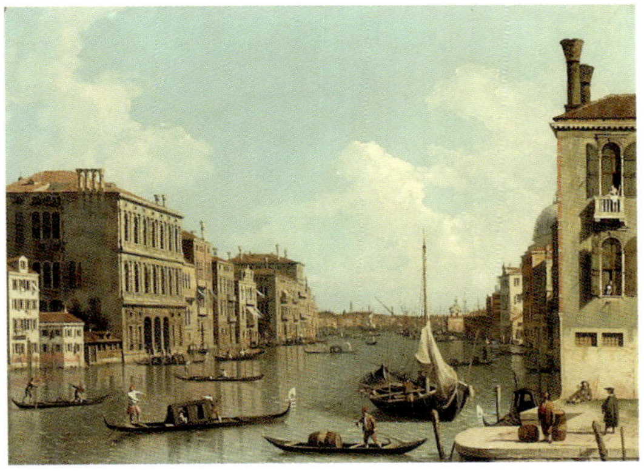

A1246; oil on canvas, 52.4 × 70.5 cm
Prov.: Elsestern collection, Berlin
Bequeathed by Thomas Melville Thompson, 2001; WA2001.183

Constable and Links 1989, no. 199aa

A1246 is an almost exact copy of Canaletto's painting in the Pinacoteca di Brera, Milan, one of a group of views of this part of the Grand Canal with only slight differences in viewpoint and detail.

Attributed to Bartolomeo Caporali
(active 1422 – *c.* 1503)

Christ as the Man of Sorrows

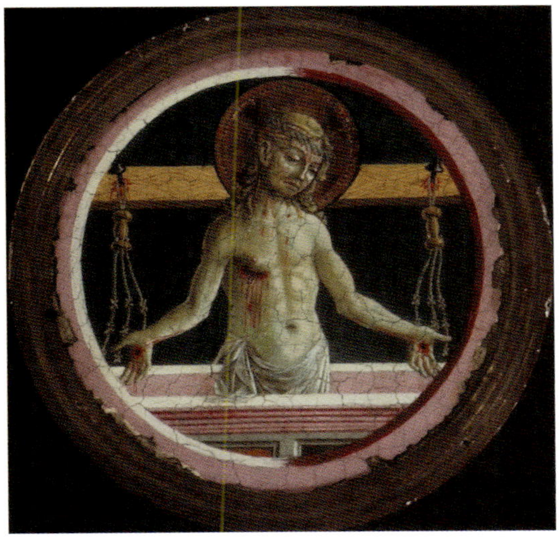

A803; tempera and gilding on panel, 16 cm in diameter
Bequeathed by Percy Moore Turner, 1951; WA1951.7

Lloyd 1977, pp. 43–5; Todini 1989, I, p. 51, II, pl. 812

The dead Christ is shown with many of the instruments of his Passion in a devotional image that has Eucharistic connotations. A803 comes from the central panel of a predella of which two other circular panels are known, showing St Peter and St Paul (Christie's, London, 10 July 1998, lot 53).

Luca Carlevaris
(1663 – 1730)

The Piazzetta, Venice

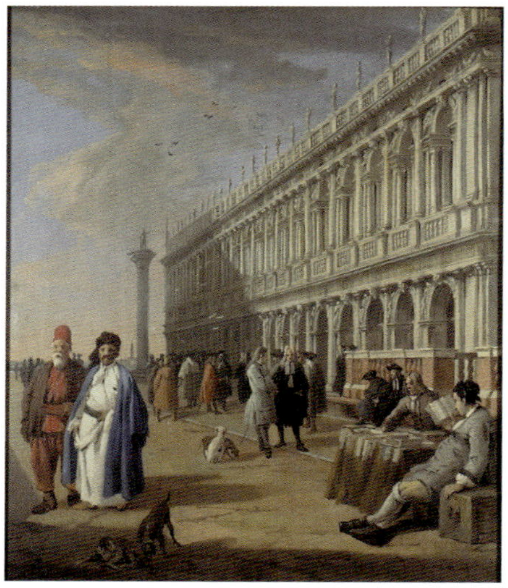

A772; oil on canvas, 48.5 × 41 cm
Prov.: Edward Cheney; Francis Capel Cure; Major Nigel Capel Cure
Presented by the National Art Collections Fund from the Robert Witt Fund, 1949; WA1949.6

Reale and Succi 1994, no. 69

Carlevarijs was an innovative painter whose pioneering publication of 104 etched views of Venice in 1703 was later used as a source by Canaletto and other view-painters. This informal view, perhaps of the 1720s, is one of a group depicting everyday life around the Piazza San Marco. A study for the figure of the man reading is in the V&A, London.

Richard Carline
(1896 – 1980)

The Artist's Mother

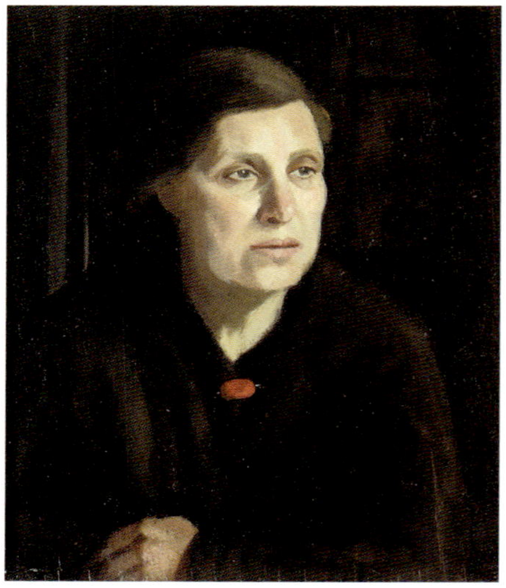

A1158; oil on panel, 43.1 × 35.6 cm
Presented by the artist's widow, Mrs Nancy Carline, 1988; WA1988.230

A study for *Family Group* of 1923 (destroyed), this shows the artist's mother, Anne Carline (1862–1945).

Carlo Innocenzo Carlone
(1686 – 1775)

The Triumph of Wisdom, or Learning

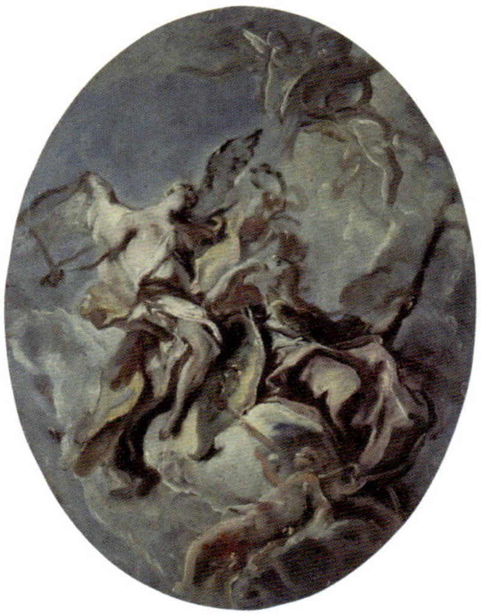

Oil on paper, mounted as a drawing, 43.2 × 32.5 cm
Purchased, 1939; WA1939.56

Parker 1956, no. 981; Krückmann 1990, no. 21

Minerva, goddess of wisdom, is accompanied by a winged genius with a palm (signifying victory or peace) and a wreath or crown. Possibly dating from *c.* 1760, when Carlone was working in northern Lombardy, this rapidly painted sketch has not been connected with any known ceiling. The design would have been suitable for the ceiling of a library. An oil-sketch of *Aurora attended by putti* of similar dimensions and style was on the art market in 1987.

George Carline
(1855 – 1920)

Scene on Otmoor

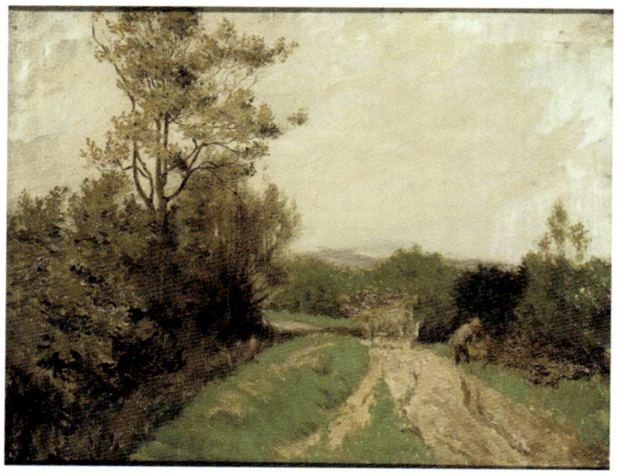

A1101; oil on canvas, 42.5 × 53 cm
Presented by Richard Carline, the artist's son, 1978; WA1978.76

A characteristic pastoral scene painted on Otmoor, a few miles north-east of Oxford, in 1912.

Sydney William Carline
(1888 – 1929)

Over the Hills of Kurdistan: Flying above Kirkuk

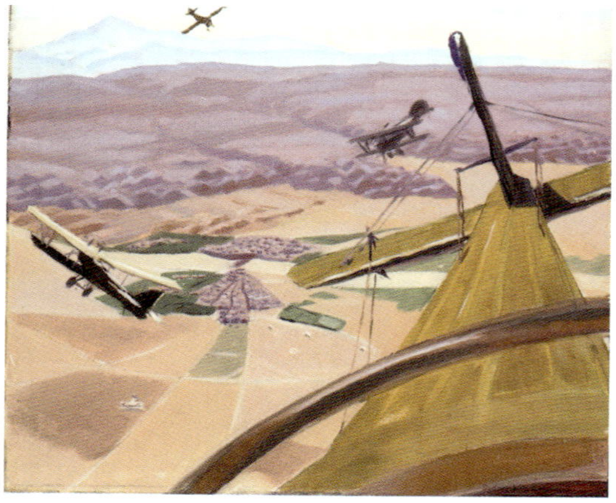

A398; oil on canvas, 38 × 45 cm
Signed and dated: *Sydney W. Carline 1919*
Presented by Gwendolyn Harter, the artist's widow, 1929; WA1929.30

Eustace 1999, no. 14

Carline joined the Royal Flying Corps in 1914. Later he was moved to the Department of Camouflage and sent to the Near East to record the war against the Turks. A drawing for this painting in the Imperial War Museum is dated 23 July 1919; they record a Bristol fighter plane returning to Mosul after a punitive expedition over Kurdistan.

Charles-Émile-Auguste Carolus-Duran
(1837 – 1917)

M. Berthon

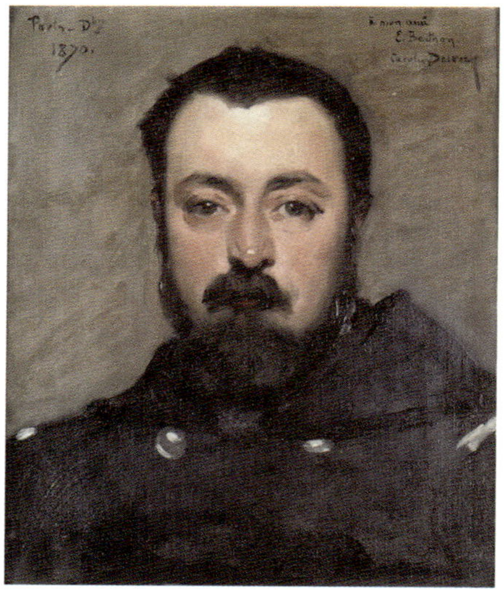

A764; oil on canvas, 45 × 37 cm
Dated: *Paris- Dbre 1870;* and dedicated: *à mon ami E Berthon Carolus-Duran*
Presented by Mrs H.E. Berthon, 1949; WA1948.102

The sitter wears a military uniform. The date implies that the portrait was made during the siege of Paris in the winter of 1870. The painter's taste for Spanish art of the 17th century, confirmed during a visit to Spain from 1866 to 1868, is evident in the broad application of dark paint on a greyish ground punctuated with sharp highlights.

Giovanni Francesco Caroto
(*c.* 1480 – *c.* 1555)

The Crucifixion with the Virgin Mary and St John

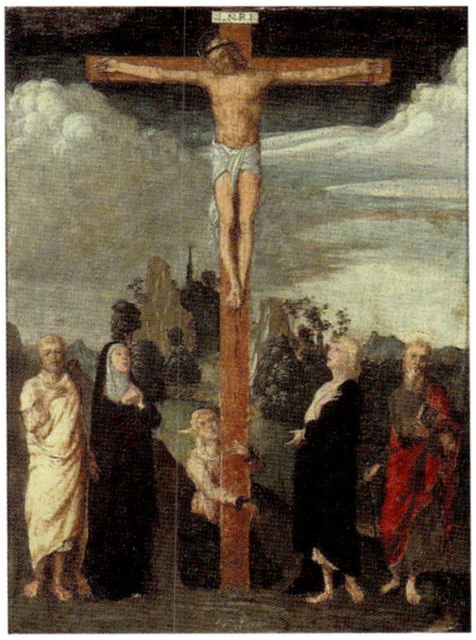

A783; oil on panel, 44 × 33 cm
Inscribed: *G.F. CHAROTUS PING.*
Prov.: George Richmond and by decent
Beqeathed by Mrs Hilda Fothergill Medlicott, 1950; WA1950.21

Lloyd 1977, pp. 45–6

The dramatic landscape and the intense emotion of the figures are characteristic of Caroto. In style A783 is close to a *Crucifixion* signed and dated 1545 (Museo Castelvecchio, Verona). Both paintings were probably inspired by a lost work by Jacopo Bellini for the Duomo at Verona.

Attributed to Naddo Ceccarelli
(documented 1347)

The Virgin and Child

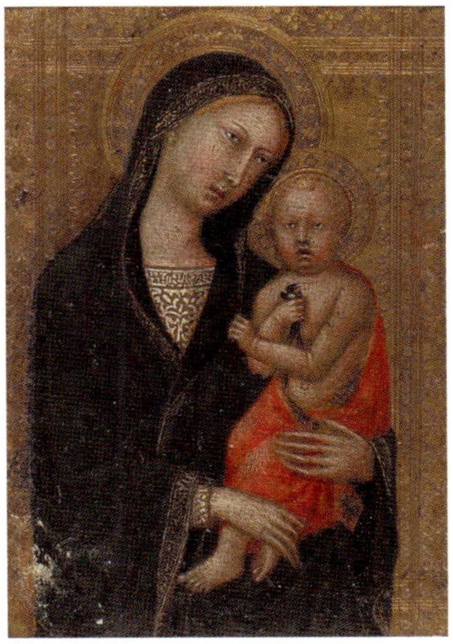

A1062; tempera and gilding on panel, integral frame, 10 × 10 cm
Bequeathed by Sir John Beazley, 1971; WA1971.258

Lloyd 1977, pp. 48–9; De Benedictis 1979, p. 82

Although few pictures are known by this Sienese pupil of Lippo Memmi, A1062 is comparable to the signed *Virgin and Child* of 1347 formerly in the Cook Collection. The Child clutches a goldfinch, a symbol of the Passion since according to legend the blood of Christ fell on the bird's feathers. A1062 could have formed part of a diptych, with a *Man of Sorrows* perhaps as its companion, although no hinge marks are now visible.

Anonymous Central Italian Artist
(late 18th or early 19th century)

The Virgin and Child with the young St John the Baptist and St Anne or St Elizabeth

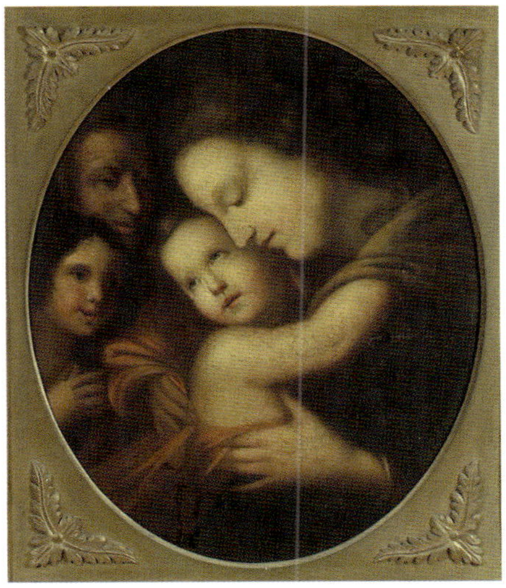

A304; oil on canvas, 61 × 49.5 cm
Fortnum Bequest, 1899; WA1899.CDEF.P2

The composition derives from Sienese 16th-century roundels made by Domenico Beccafumi and his circle. The elderly female saint could be either St Anne, mother of the Virgin, or St Elizabeth, mother of John the Baptist. The choice of colour and handling of paint, together with the painting's condition, suggest a far later date for A304, perhaps of the late 18th or early 19th century.

Andrea Casali
(1705 – 1784)

Sir Charles Frederick

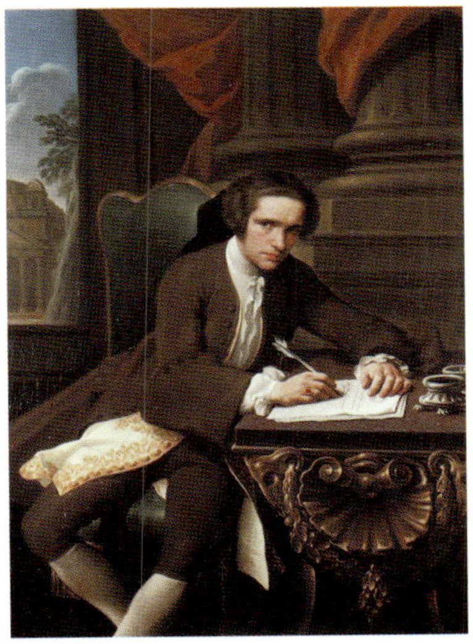

A1118; oil on canvas, 133.5 × 96.5 cm
Signed and dated: *Equ.s And.as Casali Pin.it Romae 1738*
Prov.: Sir Charles Frederick; by descent to Thomas Barker
Purchased with the assistance of the Victoria & Albert Museum Purchase Grant Fund, the National Art Collections Fund and other donors, 1980; WA1980.136

Sestieri 1994, I, pp. 43, 45; II, pl. 225

A1118 was painted while Frederick (1709–1785) was on the Grand Tour. His antiquarian and numismatic interests are emphasised. Frederick was MP for New Shoreham (1746–54) and Queenborough (1754–84) and was made Knight of the Bath in 1761. From 1741 to 1766 Casali worked for Frederick and other patrons in England.

Anonymous Central Italian Artist
(*c.* 1570 – 1590)

The Crucifixion with St Gregory and a Bishop Saint

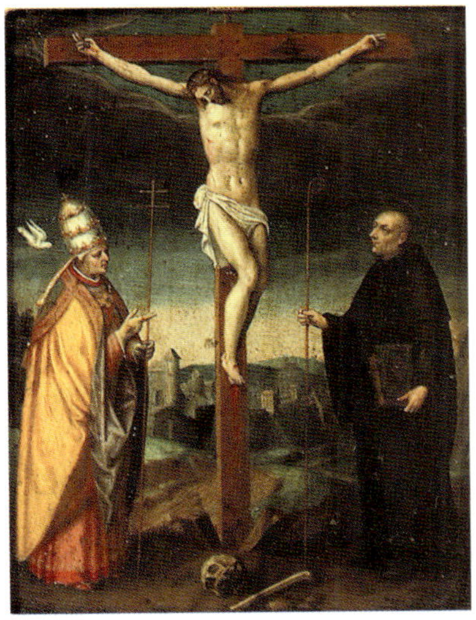

A259; oil on copper, 24.1 × 17.9 cm
Bequeathed by the Revd Greville John Chester, 1892; WA1892.4

Once considered to be Spanish, this is probably by an artist working in central Italy in the late 16th century. The elongated body of Christ is a motif disseminated in the work of various followers of Michelangelo; this motif also occurs in the later work of Pedro de Campana. St Gregory (*c.* 540–604) is traditionally shown with the dove of the Holy Spirit; the bishop saint may be St Augustine (354–430) in the robes of his Order.

Michelangelo Cerquozzi
(1602 – 1660)

Spring (Flora)

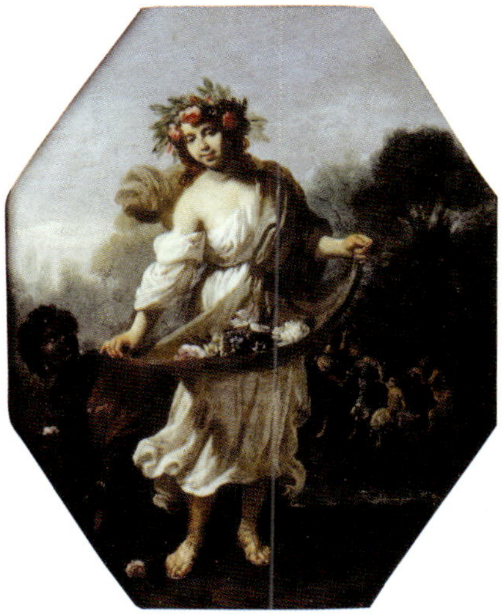

Oil on panel, 27.8 × 21.5 cm
Prov.: Carlo Sestieri, Rome
Mahon loan, 1999; WA.L.99.8

Finaldi and Kitson 1997, no. 12

Born and trained in Rome, Cerquozzi was closely associated with northern European artists there, who tended to specialise in landscape and scenes of everyday life. His paintings of battle scenes were particularly popular, but he painted a variety of subjects. These small octagons were part of a set of the four Seasons, dating perhaps from the 1630s. Flora, the goddess of flowers, personifies Spring and is shown against a background of a celebratory bacchic procession.

MICHELANGELO CERQUOZZI
(1602 – 1660)

Summer (Ceres)

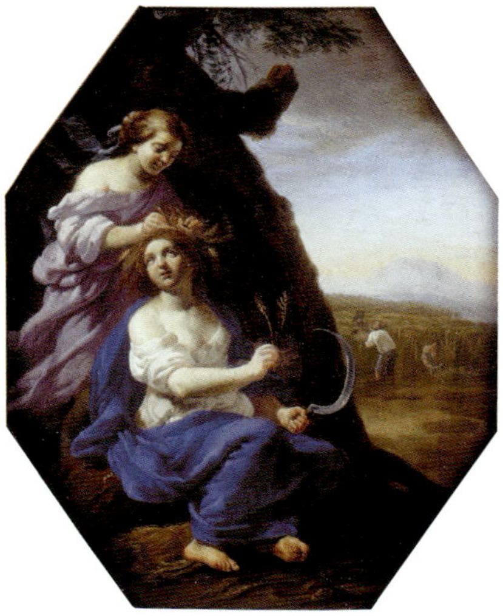

Oil on panel, 27.8 × 21.9 cm
Prov.: Carlo Sestieri, Rome
Mahon loan, 1999; WA.L.99.11

Finaldi and Kitson 1997, no. 13

Ceres, the goddess of agriculture, here personifies Summer. Ears of corn are being wound into her hair, while she holds a scythe and rests her foot on freshly-cut corn. Behind her labourers are gathering in the harvest.

PAUL CÉZANNE
(1839 – 1906)

Near Auvers-sur-Oise

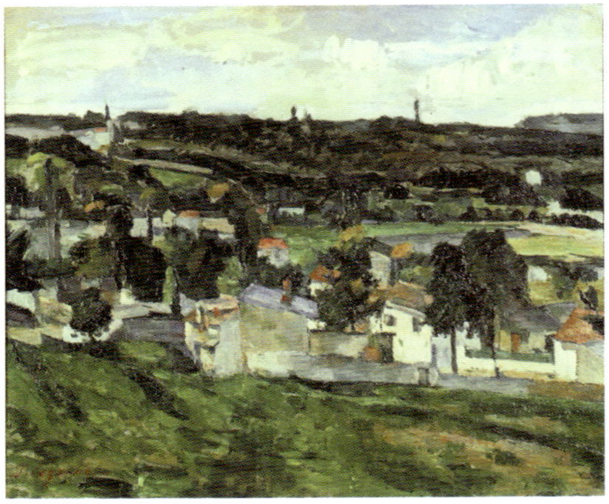

A1113; oil on canvas, 46 × 55 cm
Prov.: Victor Choquet; Thadée Natanson; Bruno Cassirer and by descent
Accepted in lieu of Inheritance Tax from the estate of Dr and Mrs Richard Walzer and allocated to the Ashmolean Museum, 1980; WA1980.79

Rewald 1996, no. 401

Painted with the distinct, touches of paint and strong colour which marked Cezanne's transition from Impressionism towards flatter and more compact effects in the 1880s. The precise site has not been located. This painting was stolen on 1 January 2000 and has not been recovered.

JEAN-SIMÉON CHARDIN
(1699 – 1779)

Still Life of Kitchen Utensils

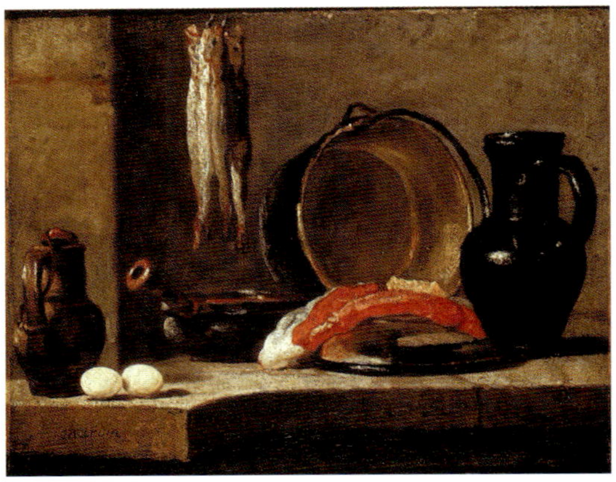

A388; oil on canvas, 32.5 × 40.3 cm
Signed: *Chardin*
Prov.: B.L. Dighton
Presented by Mrs W.F.R. Weldon, 1927; WA1927.3

Rosenberg 1979, no. 47; Paris 1999–2000, under no. 35

Chardin's studies of kitchen utensils fall roughly into the years 1728–34; before that, he concentrated on still life with game. He may have turned to kitchen subjects on his admission to the Academy in 1728 to distinguish himself from artists such as Desportes and Oudrey who specialised in game and hunting pieces. A388 was probably painted *c.* 1733–34 when Chardin was turning to genre scenes. Two other versions are known.

Copy after GIOVANNI DOMENICO CERRINI, called IL CAVALIER PERUGINO
(1609 – 1681)

The Head of St Catherine

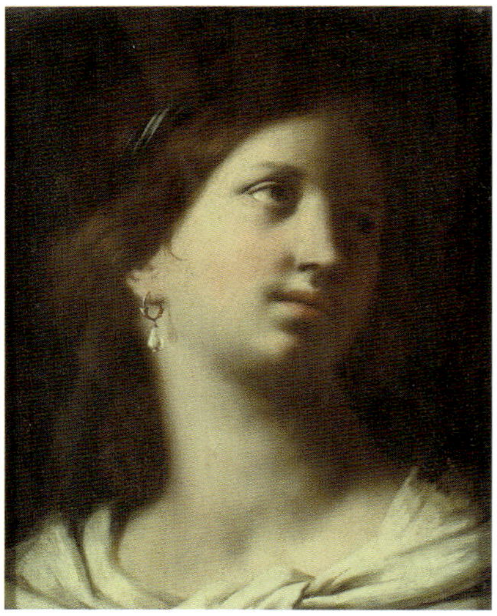

A383; oil on canvas, 42 × 34 cm
Bequeathed by Mrs Elizabeth Greenway, 1926; WA1926.9

Traditionally attributed to Guido Reni as the *Head of a Sibyl*, A383 was recently identified as a copy after Cerrini. The same expressive head appears in his altar-piece of *The Holy Family with Sts Catherine of Alexandria and Agnes* painted for San Carlo alle Quattro Fontane, Rome (consecrated in 1646) and now in the convent there.

Follower of PHILIPPE DE CHAMPAIGNE
(1602 – 1674)

Portrait of a Man

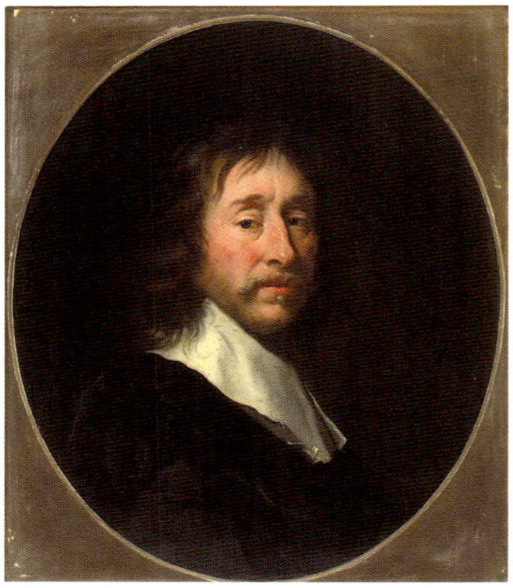

A118; oil on canvas, 66 × 54 cm
Bequeathed by the Revd Dr Thomas Penrose, 1851; WA1851.9

Wright 1985–6, p. 91

Traditionally attributed to Philippe de Champaigne, A118 displays some of the realism and sympathy with the sitter that made Champaigne's work so influential; it could be an early copy. A118 has also been attributed to Claude Lefevbre (1637–1675).

Copy after JEAN-SIMÉON CHARDIN
(1699 – 1779)

Auguste–Gabriel Godefroy (L'enfant au toton)

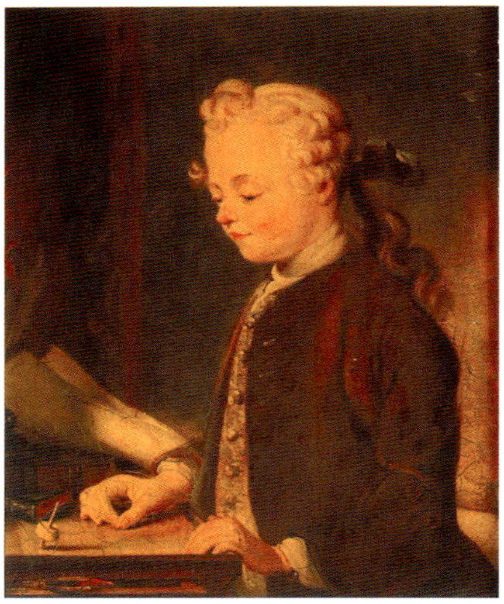

A907; oil on canvas, 58 × 50 cm
Bequeathed by Stephen Warner, 1957; WA1957.47

Auguste-Gabriel Godefroy (1728–1814), the future controller-general of the Navy, is depicted aged around ten playing with a spinning-top. A907 is a partial copy of the painting in the Musée du Louvre.

Antoine Chintreuil
(1814 – 1873)

Landscape: Morning Mist

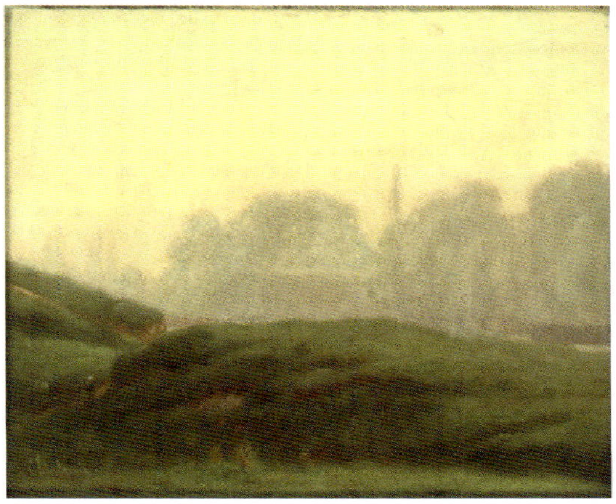

A645; oil on canvas, 26 × 31 cm
Signed: *Chintreuil*
Hindley Smith Bequest, 1939; WA1940.1.27

In 1857 Chintreuil settled at La Tournelle-Septeuil, near Mantes, and remained there until 1873. This small work is difficult to date but it probably belongs to this period when he painted a number of pictures of mist and autumnal effects.

Thomas Churchyard
(1798 – 1865)

Beach Scene

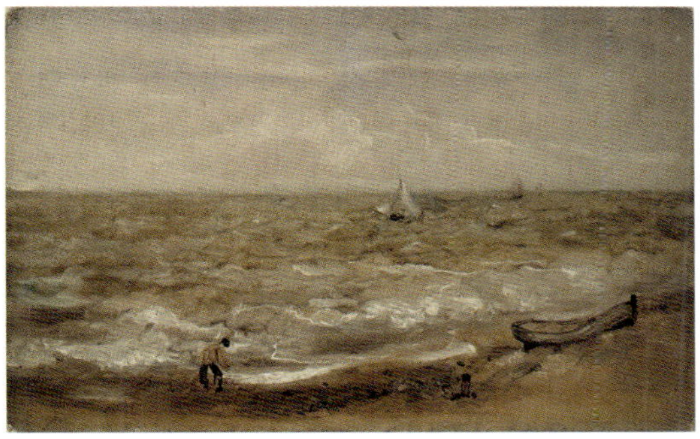

A520a; oil on board, mounted as a drawing, 14.1 × 22 cm
Presented by Victor Rienaecker, 1938; WA1938.64

Thomas Churchyard
(1798 – 1865)

Landscape with Haystack

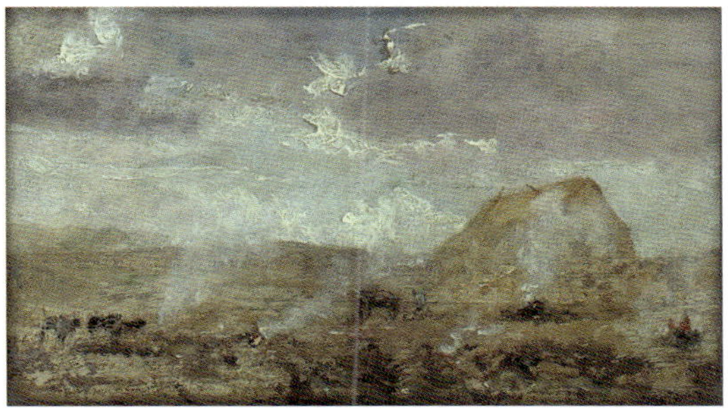

A494; oil on oak panel, 15 × 25 cm
Weldon Bequest, 1937; WA1937.75

Gerard Chowne
(1875 – 1916)

Still Life: A Bowl of mixed Flowers

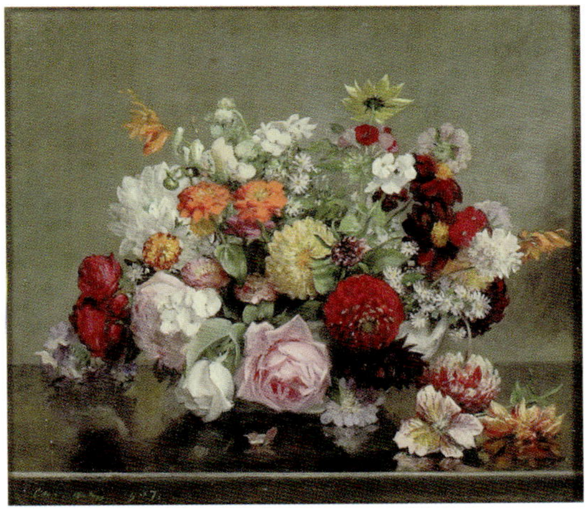

A473; oil on canvas, 45 × 41 cm
Signed and dated: *Chowne 1907*
Weldon Bequest, 1937; WA1937.53

On the back is a label inscribed by Mrs Weldon: 'Found in Chowne's bedroom after his death, so this he kept for himself.'.

Thomas Churchyard
(1798 – 1865)

A Fisherman's Hut by the Sea

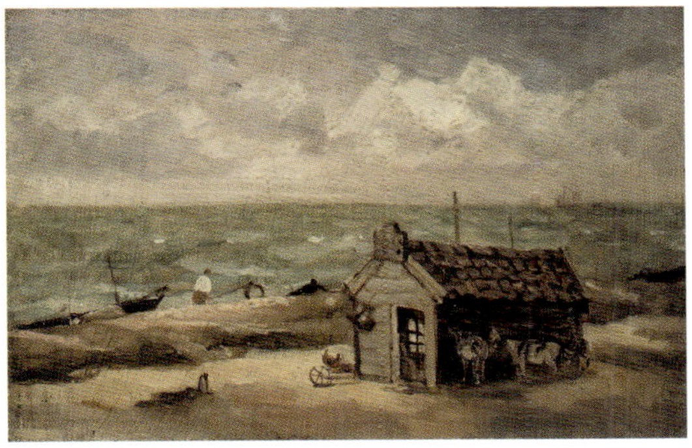

A520b; oil on board, mounted as a drawing 14 × 21.5 cm
Presented by Dr (later Sir) Karl Theodore Parker, 1938; WA1938.84

The attribution is retained in spite of the feeble draughtsmanship.

Follower of Carlo Cignani
(1628 – 1719)

A Putto with a Tambourine and an Infant Satyr with a Panpipe

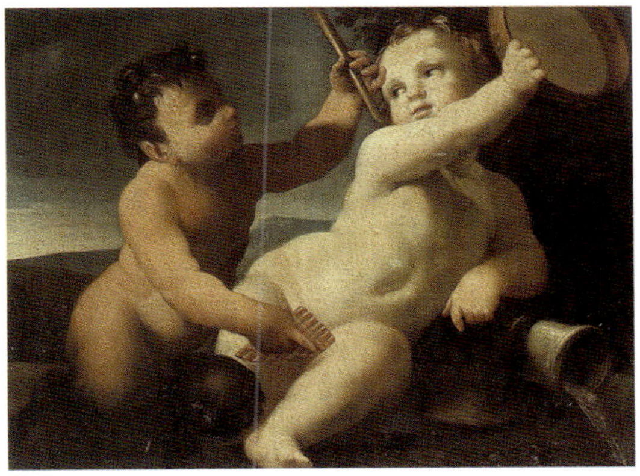

A257; oil on canvas, 68.5 × 91 cm
Bequeathed by the Revd Greville John Chester, 1892; WA1892.1

The subject derives from Guido Reni's pairs of playful *putti* in the Loggia of the Palazzo Pallavicini, Rome, *c.* 1611–12, which were engraved by Carlo Cesio. A convincing attribution has been suggested to a follower of Carlo Cignani, perhaps from Forlì where the artist worked from around 1685.

Attributed to Giacomo Francesco Cipper, Il Todeschini
(1664 – 1736)

Girl with a Dog and a Kitten

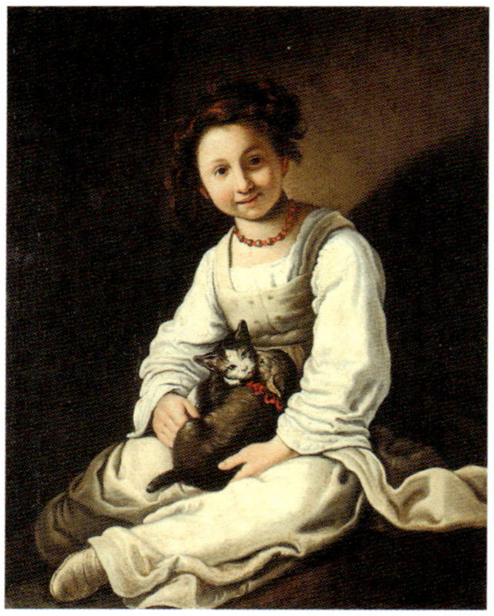

A671; oil on canvas, 94 × 75 cm
Bequeathed by Sir Arthur Evans, 1941; WA1941.4

A671 may be by Cipper, whose work bears similarities to that of Eberhard Keilhau, or by an artist working in Bologna or Bergamo in the later 17th century. Two other versions are known, one in the Museo Civico, Vicenza, attributed to Keilhau or a later follower; the other formerly at Althorp House, attributed in 1746 to 'Gobbo Carracci' (Pietro Paolo Bonzi, *c.* 1576–1636). The peaceful presence of the animals is a comment on the character of the young girl.

Pieter Claesz.
(*c.* 1597 – 1660)

Still Life with a Ham

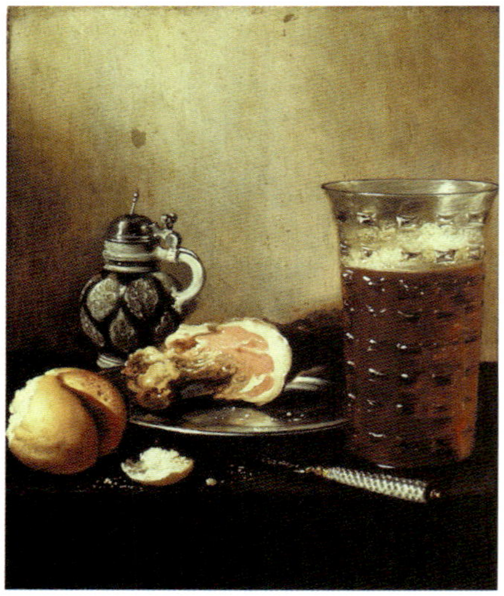

A543; oil on panel, 42 × 34 cm
Signed in monogram and dated: *PC 1642*
Daisy Linda Ward Bequest, 1939; WA1940.40.19

Meijer 2003, no. 24

In the 1640s Claesz.'s handling became freer and his colour range increased. This tendency, already evident in this painting of 1642, continued through the remainder of his life. The silver-handled knife first appeared in paintings of the early 1630s and seems to have disappeared shortly after this picture was painted. The glass beaker and mustard pot of Westerwald stoneware, on the other hand, had been recently added to his studio props and lasted in use until the early 1650s.

Jacques de Claeuw
(1623 – after 1694)

Vanitas Still Life with a Violin

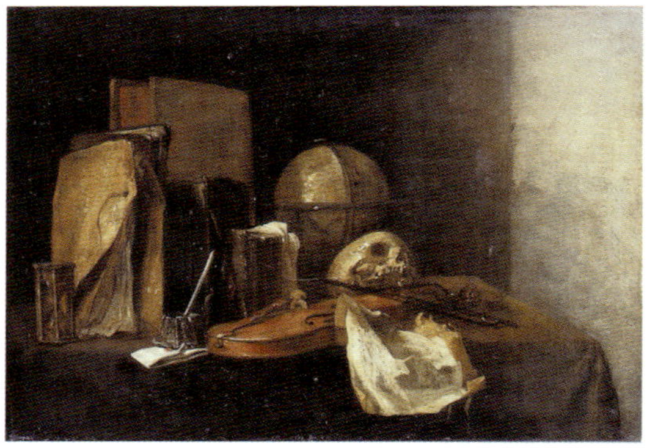

A544; oil on panel, 32 × 46 cm
Traces of signature and date: *2*
Daisy Linda Ward Bequest, 1939; WA1940.2.20

Meijer 2003, no. 25

Vanitas still-life paintings were de Claeuw's speciality. In this painting, explicit reminders of mortality and passing time, a skull and hourglass, are placed alongside a violin and bow, an ink-pot, a globe and books. The fragmentary date may have been 1652, to judge by dated paintings which are close in style and include a number of the same accessories.

Pieter Claesz.
(*c.* 1597 – 1660)

Still Life with a Gold Chain

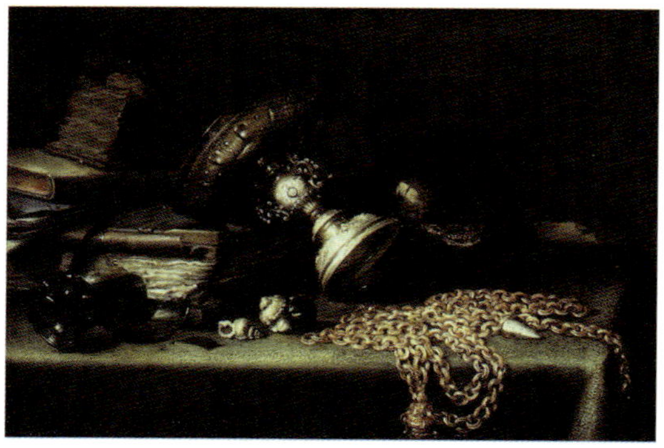

A542; oil on panel, 39 × 57 cm
Daisy Linda Ward Bequest, 1939; WA1940.2.18

Meijer 2003, no. 23

As Pieter Claesz. signed most of his large output and dated several, his development is easily followed. This painting can be dated to about 1636. It belongs to a group of *vanitas* still-life compositions, most of which he painted in the second half of the 1630s, although it does not include the more obvious attributes of a *vanitas* painting such as a skull or watch.

Style of Pieter Claesz.
(*c.* 1597 – 1660)

Still Life on a Table with Musical Instruments

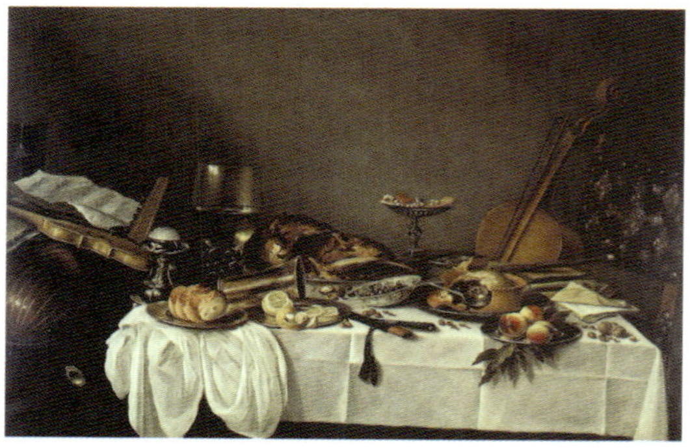

A11; oil on canvas, 106 × 162 cm
Bequeathed by the Revd Dr John King, 1737; WA1845.11

White 1999, p. 24

Pieter Claesz. came from Westphalia but was mainly active in Haarlem where his son, Nicolaes Berchem, was born in 1620. He specialised in painting still life. This painting has many elements which are found in his work but the style is wooden and it must be a copy or the work of a follower.

Claude Gellée (Le Lorrain)
(*c.* 1604/5 – 1682)

Landscape with a Goatherd

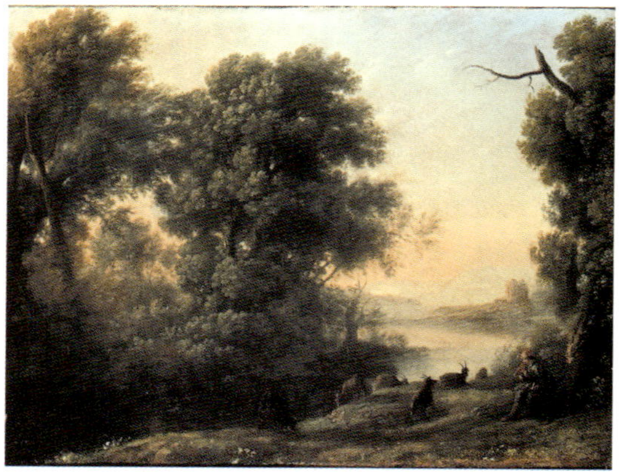

A969; oil on canvas, 38 × 49 cm
Prov.: Henry Pelham Fiennes Pelham-Clinton, 5th Duke of Newcastle and by descent until 1937
Madan Bequest, 1962; WA1962.17.11

Roethlisberger 1961, no. 215

A969 was probably painted around 1635–6, given its close affinity with a landscape in the Metropolitan Museum, New York, signed and dated 1636. Claude's early nature studies provided a basis for the luxuriant wooded landscape. A drawing of the early to mid 1640s in the Ashmolean (Roethlisberger 1968, no. 577) develops, in reverse, the composition and landscape type of A969 into a spatially more complex design.

Claude Gellée (Le Lorrain)
(*c.* 1604/5 – 1682)

Landscape with Ascanius Shooting the Stag of Sylvia

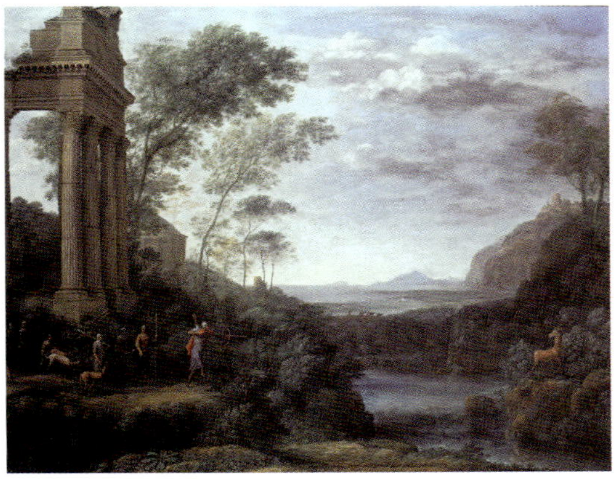

A376; oil on canvas, 120 × 150 cm
Signed and dated: *Clavdio .I.V.F.A Romae 1682*; and inscribed by the artist: *come. Ascanio. saetta il. Ceruo di Silvia figliuola di Tirro lib. 7. Vig.* Signed again below: *Clavdio Rom*
An inscription recorded on back of the original canvas was probably written by the artist: *Quadro per l'Ill.mo et excell.mo Sig. Contestablile Colonna questo di 5 Ottobre 1681.*
Prov.: Lorenzo Onofrio Colonna; Palazzo Colonna, Rome; bought by William Young Ottley; Sir Thomas Baring, Stratton Park, Hampshire, by 1837; by descent to the lords Northbrook; A.H. Buttery
Presented by Mrs W.F.R. Weldon, 1926; WA1926.1

Roethlisberger 1961, no. 222; Wine 1994, no. 60; Whiteley 2000, under no. 250

Painted for Lorenzo Onofrio Colonna in 1681–2 as a pendant to the *Dido and Aeneas before Carthage* of 1675–76 (now in the Kunsthalle, Hamburg), A376 is Claude's last picture. The subject is from Virgil's *Aeneid* VII, 483–99: Ascanius, hunting in Latium with his companions, becomes the instrument of the Fury Allecto who is sent by Juno to provoke war. Allecto, here evoked by the wind bending the trees in an impending storm, directs Ascanius's uncertain aim to wound mortally the tame stag of Silvia, the daughter of Tyrrheus, ranger to the King of the Latins; war ensues. The earlier pendant takes as its starting point Virgil's description of Dido and Aeneas leaving for the hunt (IV, 136–142) but the composition encapsulates other moments in the narrative, including Dido showing Carthage to Aeneas and Dido accusing Aeneas of betrayal. Both pictures explore moments of peacefulness and uncertainty before violence and sorrow and both are concerned with Aeneas's heir, Ascanius, for whose future Aeneas abandoned Dido. Each includes prominent reference to the Colonna family emblems of columns. The pendants remained together until 1801.

Imitator of Claude Gellée (Le Lorrain)
(*c.* 1604/5 – 1682)

Seaport with Buildings

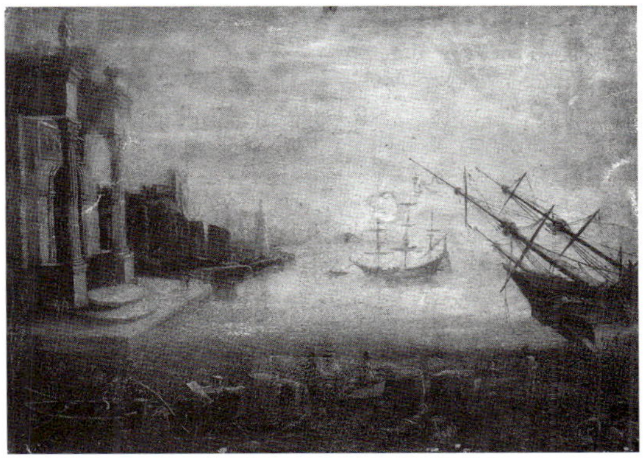

A47; oil on canvas, rolled, 56 × 76 cm
Presented by Richard Henry, 1805; WA1845.47

Considered to be by Claude Lorrain in the 19th century, A47 is a pastiche based on Claude's port scenes of the 1630s and may be by an 18th-century imitator.

Sir George Clausen
(1852 – 1944)

Farmer's Boy

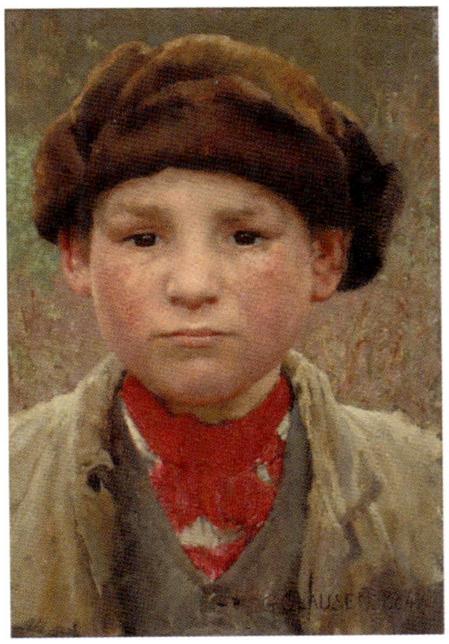

A885; oil on canvas, 36 × 25 cm
Signed and dated: *G CLAUSEN. 1884.*
Prov.: John Maddocks; Alfred Drury; Mrs Lucien Pissarro
Presented by Miss Orovida Pissarro, 1956; WA1956.18

McConkey 1980, no. 37

Clausen's large painting, *Labourers after Dinner* (1884; private collection), was the first sign that he was turning away from the sentimental peasant pictures popularised in England and France by Jules Bastien-Lepage, towards more naturalistic and brutal genre subjects. This is a study of the head of the boy at the centre of *Labourers after Dinner*.

Pieter Jacobsz. Codde
(1599 – 1678)

Portrait of a young Man standing

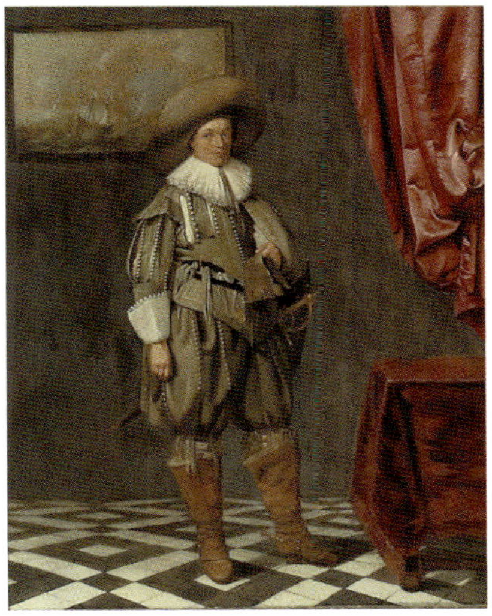

A21; oil on panel, 48 × 37 cm
Signed in monogram and dated: *CP* (P illegible) *ft 1625*
Bequeathed by the Revd Dr Richard Rawlinson, 1755; WA1845.21

White 1999, p. 26

Codde was a painter of small-scale portraits and genre scenes. This portrait of a fashionably dressed youth and a painting of a seated woman in the National Gallery, London, also dated 1625, are Codde's earliest known dated works.

Sir Egerton Bushe Coghill, Bt
(1853 – 1921)

Field of Rye, Barbizon

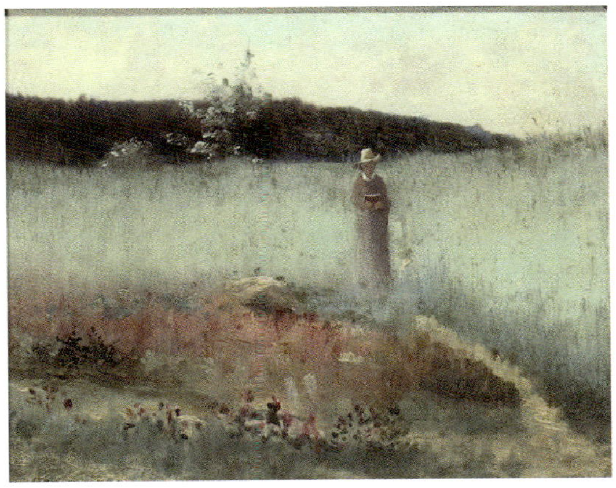

A958; oil on panel, 32 × 41 cm
Signed: *Coghill*
Presented by the artist's sons, Sir Patrick Coghill, Bt and Professor Nevill Coghill, 1962; WA1962.15

Oxford 1964, no. 10

Coghill studied at the Académie Julian in Paris from 1881 to 1884 and was greatly influenced by the Barbizon School and the Impressionists. He spent the remainder of his life at Castle Townshend, County Cork and succeeded to the baronetcy in 1905. This fresh and airy landscape was painted from nature during his years in Paris, around 1884.

Johannes Colaert
(?*c.* 1615 – after 1678)

A Stag Hunt in a Wood

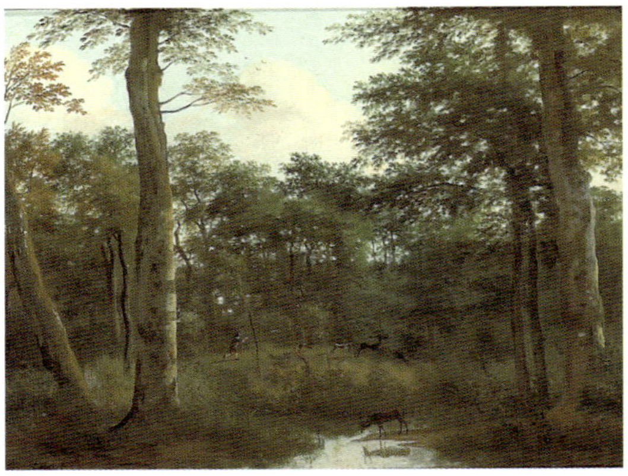

A281; oil on canvas, 45 × 57 cm
Signed: *JCollaert* (JC in monogram)
Presented by Thomas Humphry Ward, 1897; WA1897.4

White 1999, p. 28

Works by Collaert are very rare: only one other signed work, an Italianate *River Valley* in the Alte Pinakothek, Munich, is known today.

Sir William Menzies Coldstream
(1908 – 1987)

Freesias with a Skull

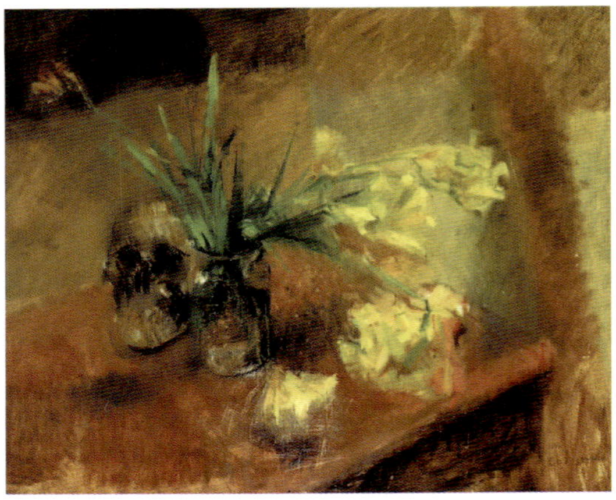

A1212; oil on canvas, 51.1 × 61.3 cm
Signed: *Coldstream*
Bequeathed by Alfred Leslie Rowse, C.H., F.B.A., 1998; WA1998.55

In 1939, Coldstream painted a portrait of the distinguished Cornish historian and Fellow of All Souls' College in Oxford, A.L. Rowse. Rowse bought this still life in the following year.

Charles Alston Collins
(1828 – 1873)

Convent Thoughts

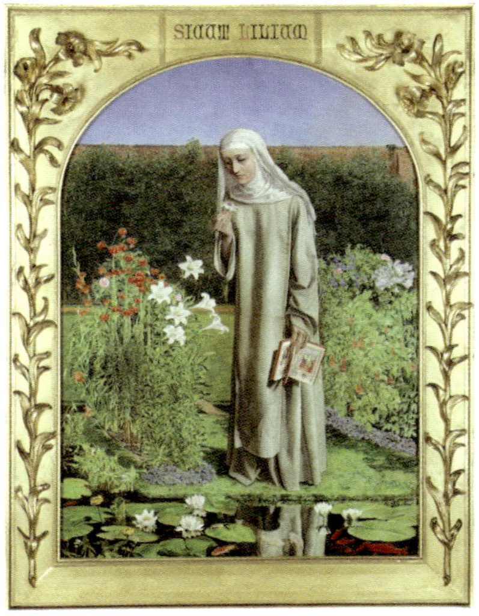

A273; oil on canvas, 84 × 59 cm
Signed with monogram and dated: *51*
Combe Bequest, 1893; WA1894.10

Parris 1974, no. 33; Brown 1987, no. 16; Staley 2001, pp. 15–16

A nun contemplates a passion flower, symbolising the crucifixion of Christ. In her left hand, she holds an illuminated missal open at an image of the Virgin Mary. The frame, designed by Millais, is inscribed: *SICUT LILIUM* ('As the lily among thorns') from the Song of Solomon. This was traditionally associated with the Virgin Mary, as was the enclosed garden. Collins painted the background while staying in Oxford and the flowers were painted in the garden of the Clarendon Press, where he was the guest of the Combes. The painting is executed in the minutely detailed style of the early Pre-Raphaelites, though Collins was never a member of the Brotherhood. It was exhibited at the Royal Academy in 1851 and was one of the works which provoked Ruskin's defence of the young artists.

Sir William Menzies Coldstream
(1908 – 1987)

Sleeping Cat

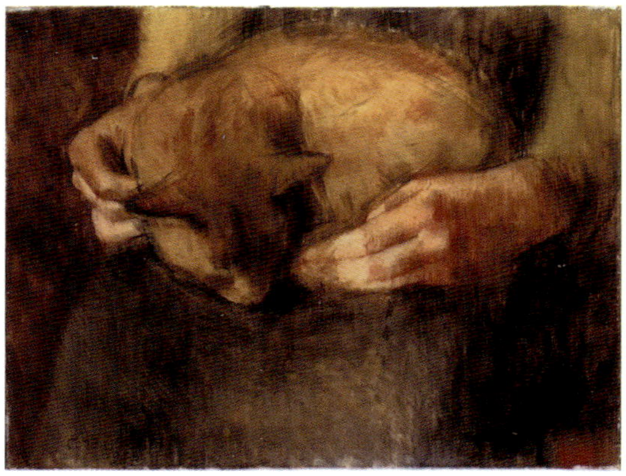

A751; oil on canvas, 35 × 45 cm
Signed and dated: *Coldstream / 1938*
Presented anonymously, 1948; WA1948.67

Gowing and Sylvester 1990, no. 15

The cat was sitting on the lap of the artist's wife, Nancy Sharp (1909–2001), whom he had married in 1931.

Cecil Collins
(1908 – 1989)

Landscape

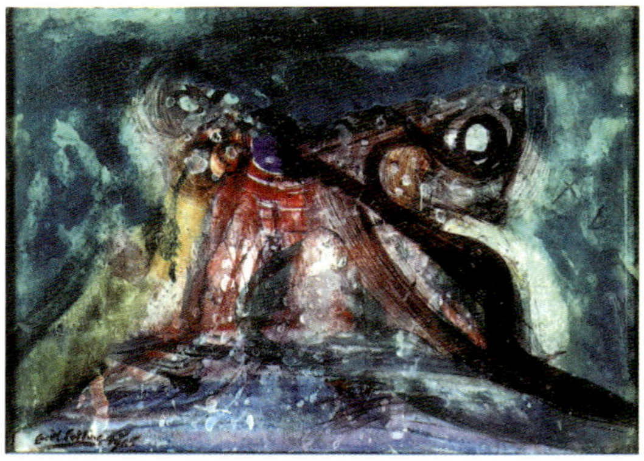

A1240; tempera and oil on hard-board, 15 × 20.3 cm
Signed and dated: *Cecil Collins 1965;* inscribed on back: *Landscape (1965) by Cecil Collins September 7 1965 35 Selwyn Gardens Cambridge England*
Bequeathed by Elizabeth Collins through the National Art Collections Fund, 2001; WA2001.54

After studying at the Plymouth School of Art and the Royal College of Art, Collins became one of the most prominent British painters of visionary and fantastic paintings with an inherent, deeply religious sense. This painting shows, as others of this time, his interest in representing an energetic life-force.

Charles Alston Collins
(1828 – 1873)

William Bennett

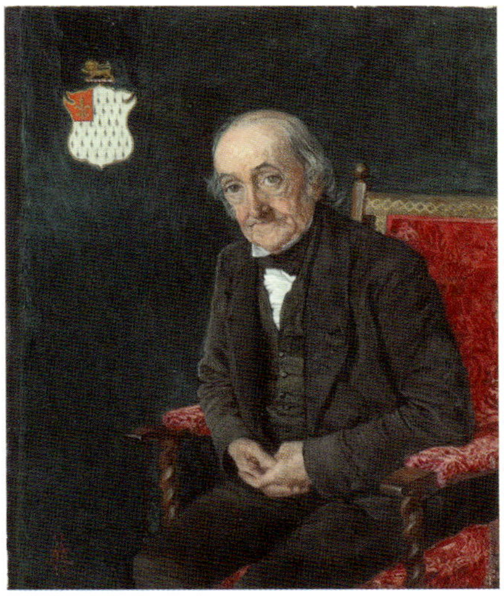

A274; oil on panel, 33 × 27 cm
Signed in monogram and dated: *1850*
Combe Bequest, 1893; WA1894.11

William Bennett was the uncle of Martha Combe on her mother's side. This portrait was painted at the same time as Collins's *Convent Thoughts*, as a pendant to Millais's portrait of Combe (see A272). The technique is even more meticulously detailed than in the companion portrait. It was exhibited at the Royal Academy in 1851.

Charles Conder
(1868 – 1909)

Apple Blossom at Dennemont

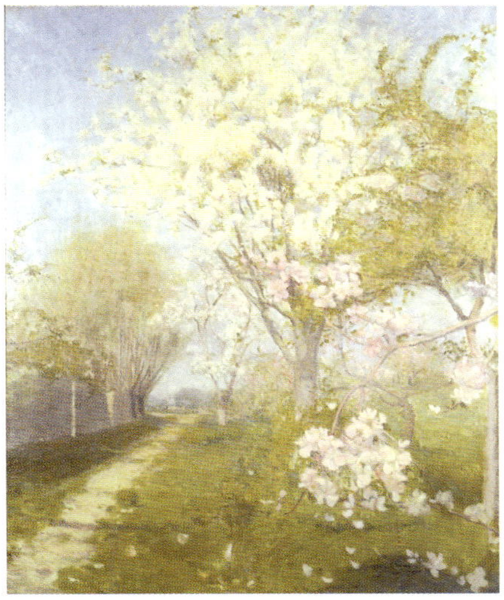

A658; oil on canvas, 73 × 60 cm
Signed and dated: *CHARLES CONDER / DENNEMONT 93*
Bequeathed by J.G. Legge through the National Art Collections Fund, 1940; WA1940.3

Gibson 1914, pl. X; Rothenstein 1938, p. 274

Conder first painted blossom in Australia, in the manner of Arthur Streeton. Even before he arrived in Paris in 1890, he had been interested in the paintings of Monet and in Japanese art. From 1892, he rented a house near Vetheuil and went on painting expeditions to nearby towns including Dennemont, where he painted this sumptuous, stylised evocation of apple blossom.

Philip Connard
(1875 – 1958)

Still Life with Crockery

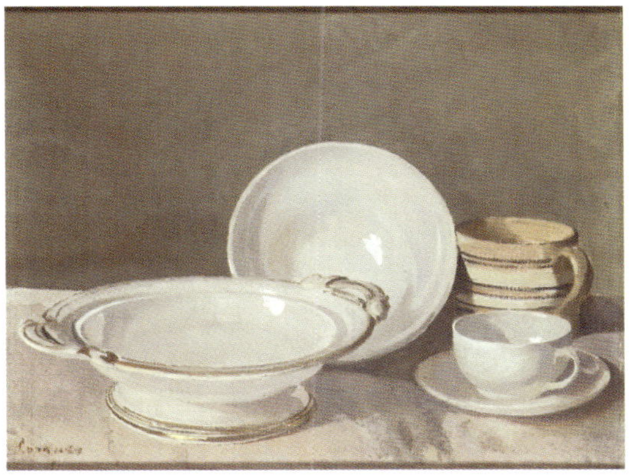

A495; oil on canvas, 35.6 × 45.8 cm
Signed: *Connard*
Weldon Bequest, 1937; WA1937.76

According to the artist, the date of the painting 'might be some time in the 1920s, perhaps the earlier part.'

Robert Collinson
(1832 – after 1889)

Ordered on foreign Service

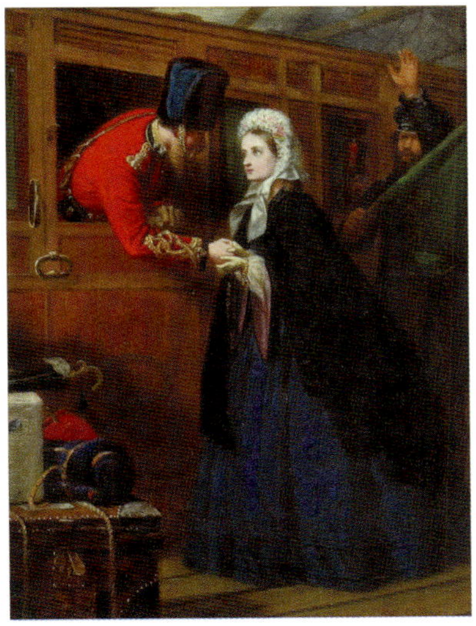

A910; oil on paper laid on canvas, 31 × 23 cm
Signed and dated: *Robt. Collinson / London 1863*
Russell Bequest, 1958; WA1958.57.4

It has been suggested that this shows an officer of either the 8th or 10th Hussars, probably leaving for the Crimea in 1854. He leans out of a railway carriage to say goodbye to his wife, while a porter signals that the train is ready to depart. This is probably the 'finished sketch' of the subject exhibited at the Royal Academy in 1864.

Charles Conder
(1868 – 1909)

Venetian Night

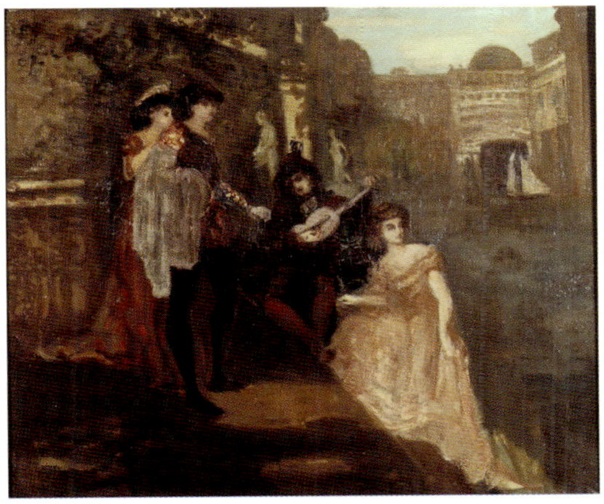

A911; oil on canvas, 68 × 80 cm
Russell Bequest, 1958; WA1958.57.5

Painted during the years when Conder was working in Paris, 1890–5. There is little sign in this painting of an influence from the Post-Impressionist painters with whom he was then associated and the colour and brushwork suggest, in keeping with the title, an evocation of the Rococo.

John Constable
(1776 – 1837)

West Lodge, East Bergholt

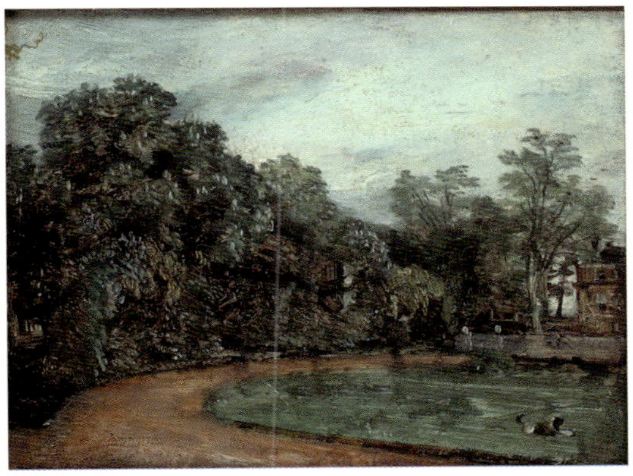

A375; oil on panel, 15 × 19 cm
Dated on back: *May 18*
Presented by Victor Rienaecker through the National Art Collections Fund, 1925; WA1925.1

Hoozee 1979, no. 131; Lyles 1999, p. 182

Constable was born at East Bergholt House and regarded the little Suffolk village as his home until the death of his parents and his marriage in 1817. From our knowledge of his movements, this panel dated *May 18* can be assigned to either 1811 or 1815. It shows the home of an elderly neighbour of the Constables, Mrs Roberts, and is one of the most freely painted and smallest of all Constable's oil-sketches.

John Constable
(1776 – 1837)

The Vale of Dedham from Langham

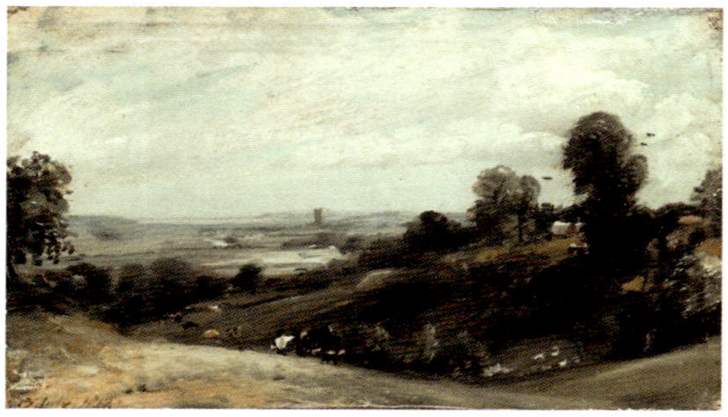

A399; oil on canvas, 19 × 32 cm
Dated: *13 July 1812*
Bequeathed by the Revd William Fothergill Robinson through the National Art Collections Fund, 1929; WA1929.32

Hoozee 1979, no. 155; Reynolds 1996, no. 12.27

Constable frequently drew and painted the view eastwards down the Stour valley from the hills between Langham church and Gun Hill. The focal point in all is the tower of Dedham church, which Constable described as 'a characteristic feature of the Vale'. He made a number of drawings and oil sketches of this particular view in 1812–13, perhaps intending to work them up into a larger exhibition picture, which, however, he never painted. One of these sketches (V&A, London) was the basis for David Lucas's mezzotint, *Summer Morning*, published in *English Landscape Scenery* in 1831.

John Constable
(1776 – 1837)

Study of Clouds

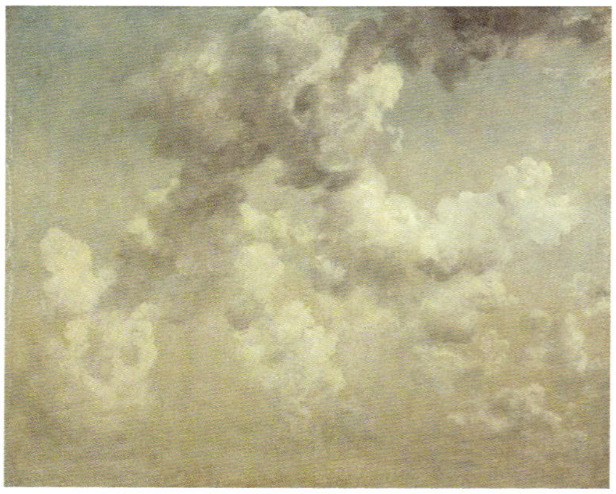

A423; oil on paper, 48 × 59 cm
Inscribed: *31 Sep.r 10-11 o'clock morning looking Eastward a gentle wind to East*
Presented by Sir E. Farquhar Buzzard, Bt, 1933; WA1933.7

Hoozee 1979, no. 349; Reynolds 1984, no. 22.30

One of a group of cloud studies from 1822, which are so accurate in their record of weather conditions that Constable's mistake in dating this example can be silently corrected to 1 October 1822.

Attributed to John Constable
(1776 – 1837)

Summer Sunset

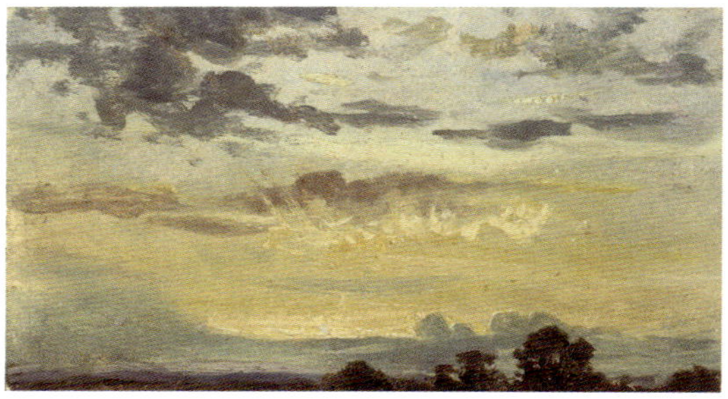

A493; oil on paper, 10 × 17.8 cm
Prov.: Isabel Constable; Capt. Charles Constable; Hugh Constable
Weldon Bequest, 1937; WA1937.74

Hoozee 1979, no. 625

The attribution to John Constable has been doubted and it has been suggested that this small painting is the work of one of his sons.

John Constable
(1776 – 1837)

Water Meadows near Salisbury

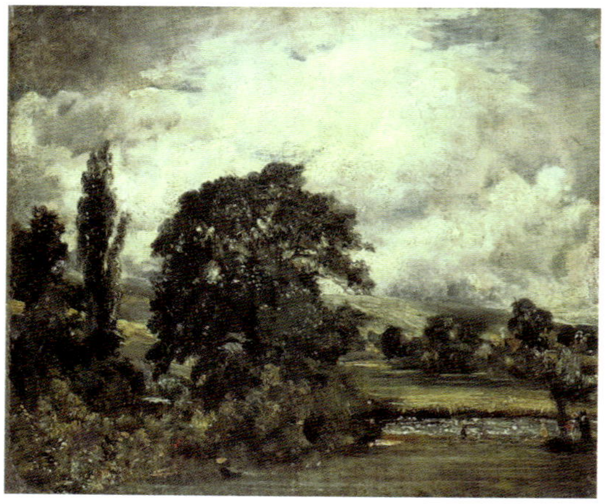

A202; oil on canvas, 32 × 38 cm
Chambers Hall Gift, 1855; WA1855.585

Hoozee 1979, no. 507; Reynolds 1984, no. 29.32

Archdeacon Fisher became Constable's closest friend and he made long visits to him in the Close at Salisbury in the summer of 1820 and in July 1829. Constable painted several sketches looking from the house towards the ridge running westwards from Harnham Hill. A202 corresponds to the left half of another sketch, dated 12 July 1829 (V&A, London), which is similarly painted with thick impasto and characteristic tiny dabs of red.

Style of John Constable
(1776 – 1837)

A Suffolk Landscape

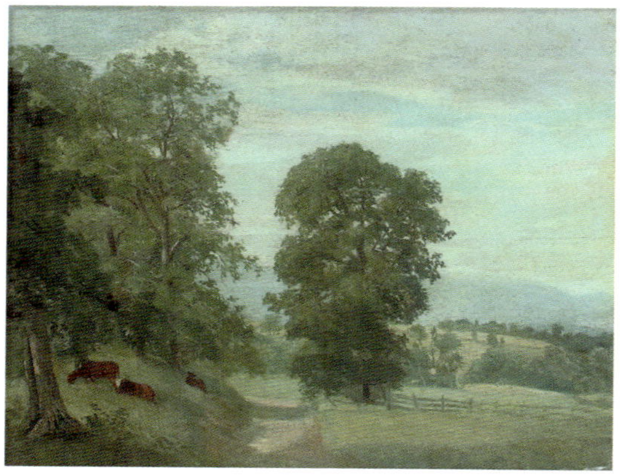

A968; oil on panel, 22 × 27 cm
Madan Bequest, 1962; WA1962.17.10

Accepted until recently as by Constable himself, this may be the work of one of his sons.

Style of John Constable
(1776 – 1837)

View across the Thames at Twickenham

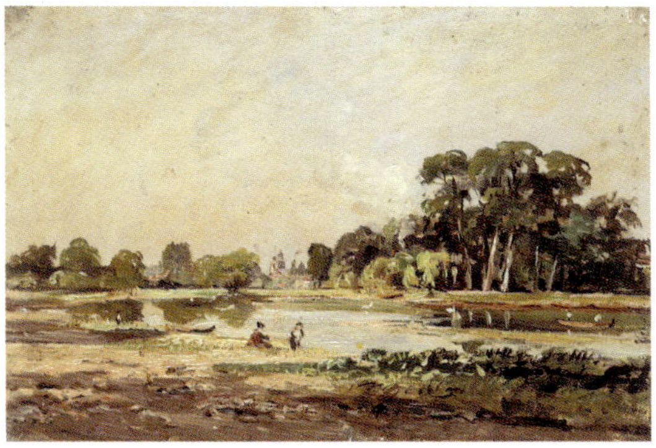

A469; oil on paper, mounted as a drawing, 17.4 × 25 cm
Prov.: Jacob G. Strutt; Robert G. Strutt; A.H. Buttery
Weldon Bequest, 1937; WA1937.49

Forgery of John Constable
(1776 – 1837)

A View in Suffolk

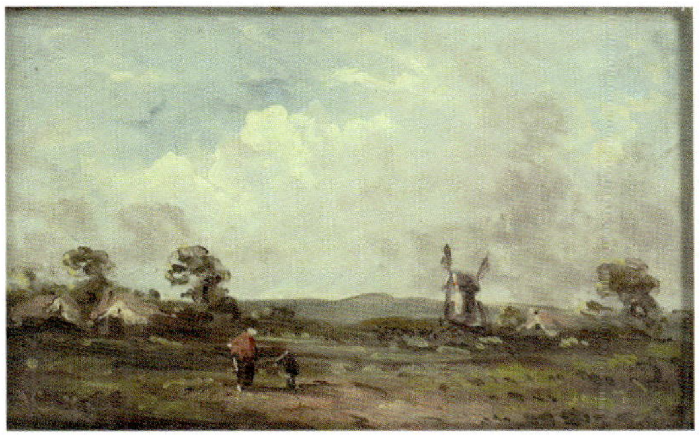

A765; oil on oak panel, 19 × 30 cm
Inscribed and dated: *JC 21*
Presented by L. V. Brandon, 1948; WA1948.178

The inscription and date indicate that this is a deliberate forgery of Constable's work, rather than an innocent imitation.

Lionel Constable
(1828 – 1887)

View of Hampstead looking towards Harrow

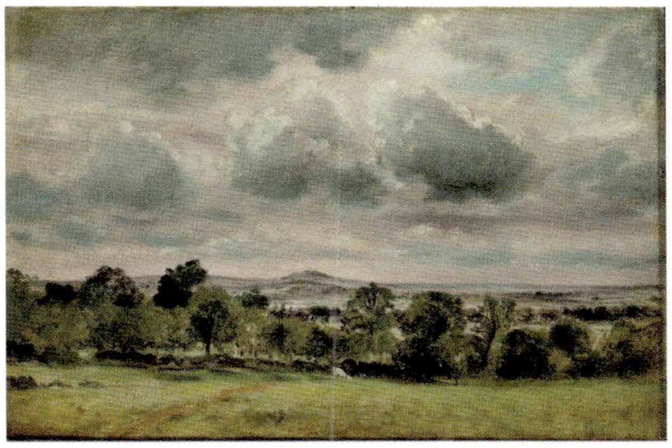

A487; oil on canvas, 24 × 36 cm
Prov.: Hugh Constable, 1899; A.H. Buttery
Weldon Bequest, 1937; WA1937.68

Hoozee 1979, no. 597; Parris and Fleming-Williams 1982, no. 27

The view looks from just below the Judges' Walk at Hampstead over the West Heath towards Harrow and the Wembley Hills. Although previously attributed to John Constable, this is the work of his son, working at one of his father's favourite subjects, but in his own distinctive colours.

Copy after John Constable
(1776 – 1837)

The Glebe Farm

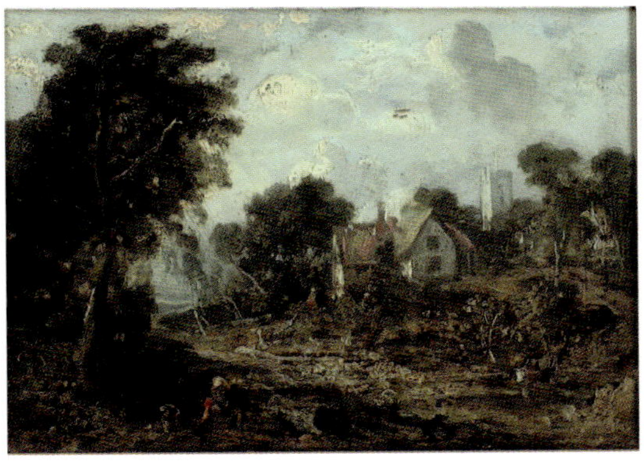

A484; oil on millboard, 18 × 25 cm
Prov.: (?)William James Muller; G.F. Williams; W. Butters
Weldon Bequest, 1937; WA1937.65

Formerly attributed to Constable himself, this is one of numerous copies of Constable's painting first exhibited in 1835 (Tate Britain). An alternative attribution to W.J. Muller cannot be sustained.

Lionel Constable
(1828 – 1887)

View towards Rame Head, Cornwall

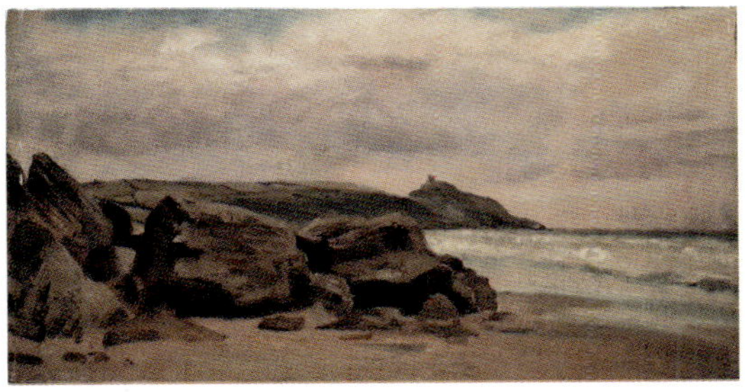

A405; oil on millboard, 18 × 33 cm
Prov.: Isabel Constable; Hugh Constable
Presented by Sir Michael Sadler in memory of Lady Sadler through the National Art Collections Fund, 1931; WA1931.3

Hoozee 1979, no. 592; Parris and Fleming-Williams, 1982, no. 4

The work of Lionel Constable has only recently been distinguished from that of his father, John. This sketch is one of several to survive from a visit to Cornwall in July 1850. Lionel exhibited two views of Cornwall at the Royal Academy in 1851 based on these sketches (untraced).

Edward William Cooke
(1811 – 1880)

Shipping on the Ij

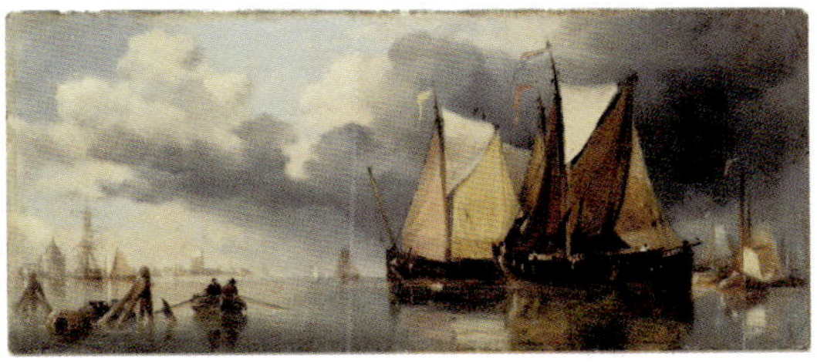

Oil on panel, mounted as a drawing, 10.9 × 24.8 cm
Inscribed: *Dutch boats on the Y, off Amsterdam. painted by E.W. Cooke. May 1848. purchased from E.W. Cooke 5.th April 1849 by EWC*
Prov.: Sir John Fiennes Twistleton Crampton and by descent ref. no. 0549
Bequeathed by Miss S.A.P. Boyle from the Crampton Collection, 1967; WA1967.52.5

Cooke first visited Holland in 1837 and the view of Dutch shipping on the Ij against the backdrop of the city of Amsterdam became a favourite.

Abraham Cooper
(1787 – 1868)

Study of a Cat

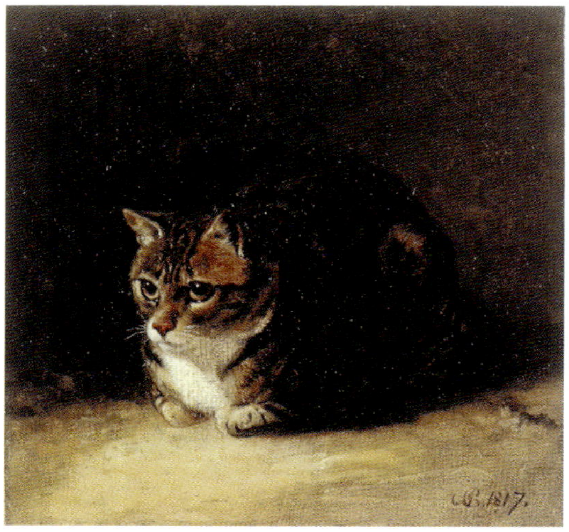

A1022b; oil on wooden panel, mounted as a drawing, 16.7 × 17.7 cm
Signed in monogram and dated: *1817*.
Prov.: Lord Ribblesdale
Presented by Miss Sylvia Gosse, 1966; WA1966.13.2

Although he later made his reputation as a battle painter, Cooper first gained popularity painting portraits of horses and pets. This is an early portrait of a tabby cat, relaxed but attentive.

Adriaen Coorte
(active 1683 – in or after 1707)

Still Life with Hazel-nuts

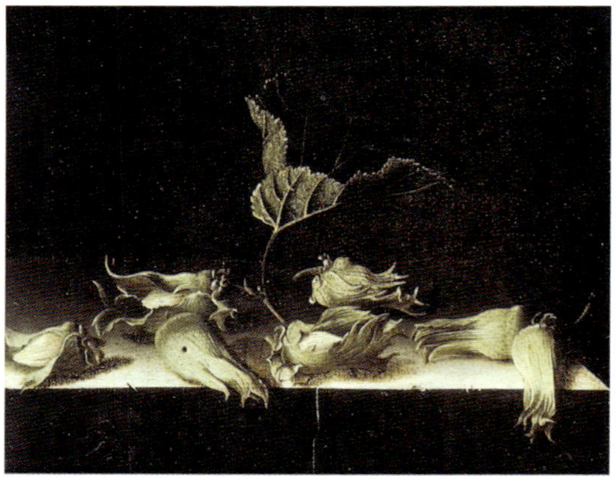

A545; oil on paper, 16.5 × 20 cm
Signed: *A. Coorte, 1696*
Daisy Linda Ward Bequest, 1939; WA1940.2.21

Meijer 2003, no. 26

Coorte frequently represents only one type of fruit or nut. This is the only recorded instance when he painted hazel-nuts. From about 1690, he painted on paper. These painted sheets were later laid down on stiffer backing. The simple presentation of these modest themes and the delicacy of his touch seem out of touch with the taste in Holland at this time for more elegant and decorative still-life compositions.

Edith Corbet
(*c.* 1850 – 1920)

Asolo

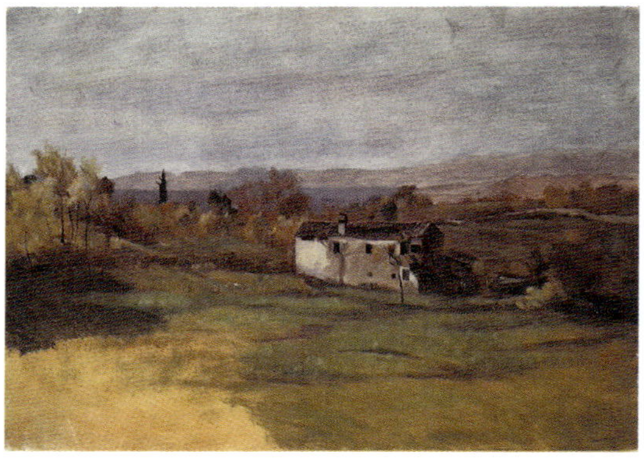

A1054; oil over graphite on plywood, mounted as a drawing, 23.6 × 32.6 cm
Presented by the Lady Berwick, 1969; WA1969.20

This American artist worked with Giovanni Costa in Rome in the 1870s and married Matthew Ridley Corbet (1850–1902) in 1891. This is a typical example of her work, thinly and quickly painted on a small panel. An inscription on the verso reads, *Asolo / Dec 2. 1899 / 10 to 12*. The painting was probably given or sold to W.S. Hulton or his wife.

Adriaen Coorte
(active 1683 – in or after 1707)

Oriental birds

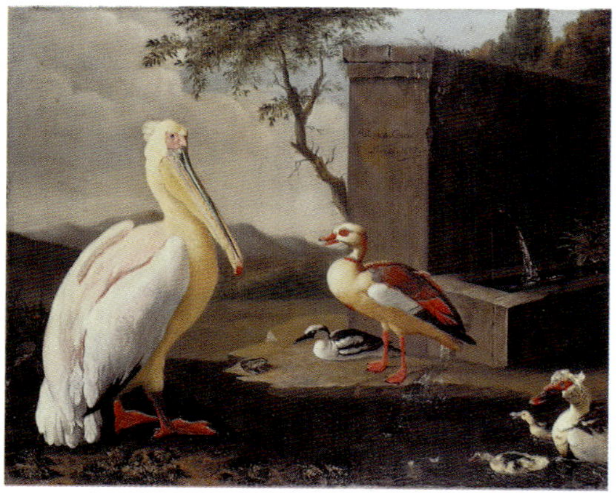

A813; oil on canvas, 39 × 48 cm
Signed and dated: *Adriaen Coorte / Anno. 1683*
Bequeathed by J. Reginald Jones, 1951; WA1951.51.7

White 1999, p. 29

Little is known about Coorte although from the record of a fine imposed on him in Middelburg in 1695/6 and from the number of his works in Middelburg collections, it seems likely that he was based in Middelburg. His speciality was small still-life paintings of fruit, vegetables, nuts and shells but he seems to have begun his career as a bird painter. This is his earliest known dated painting. The details are closely based on bird paintings by Melchior de Hondecoeter.

Adriaen Coorte
(active 1683 – in or after 1707)

Still Life of Asparagus

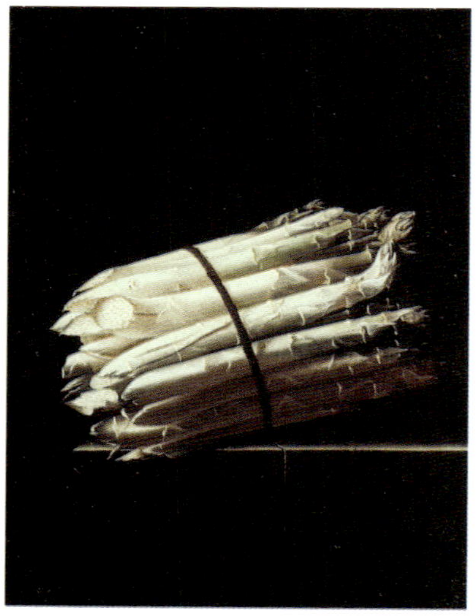

A546; oil on paper laid on panel, 30 × 22.5 cm
Signed: *A Coorte / 1699*
Daisy Linda Ward Bequest, 1939; WA1940.2.22

Meijer 2003, no. 27

Typically, the artist has isolated his motif and painted it with a refined touch and a subtle combination of soft green and purple. This was one of the artist's favourite themes. It appears in twelve known paintings, mostly in combination with other fruit. Only two of the series show the bundle of asparagus isolated on a ledge as here: one in the Rijksmuseum, Amsterdam, dated 1697, the other in the Fitzwilliam, Cambridge, dated 1703.

Cornelis Cornelisz. van Haarlem
(1562 – 1638)

A Scholar in his Study

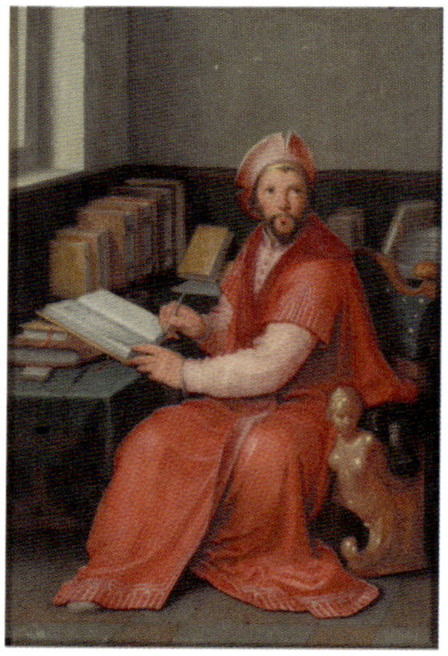

A883; oil on panel, 38.9 × 26 cm
Signed in monogram and dated: *CVH 1605* (or 1606)
Prov.: Willem Adriaan Tarée
Purchased, 1955; WA1955.28

White 1999, p. 30

In the early 1580s, Cornelis worked in his native Haarlem where he carried out a number of important commissions. This is an unusual subject for an artist better known for his larger mythological, religious and moralistic genre paintings. Some of the accessories – the chair, table and books – appear again in a drawing by Cornelis van Haarlem of *St Peter's Vision of Unclean Beasts* in the Prentenkabinet der Rijksuniversiteit, Leiden.

Jean-Baptiste-Camille Corot
(1796 – 1875)

Le Petit Chaville, near Ville-d'Avray

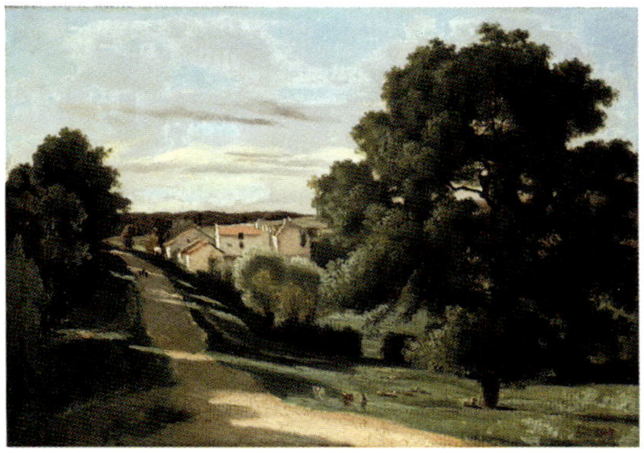

A642; oil on canvas, 24.8 × 34 cm
Stamped: *VENTE COROT*
Prov.: Gustave Tempelaere
Hindley Smith Bequest, 1939; WA1940.1.24

Robaut 1905, no. 16; Tinterow *et al.* 1996, no. 3

Dating from about 1823, this is one of the artist's earliest surviving works, painted out-of-doors in the village of Chaville near Ville d'Avray where Corot's parents had bought a house in 1817. The neat touches of paint, light colour and carefully structured view owe something to the example of Corot's master, Jean-Victor Bertin.

Jean-Baptiste-Camille Corot
(1796 – 1875)

M. Bison

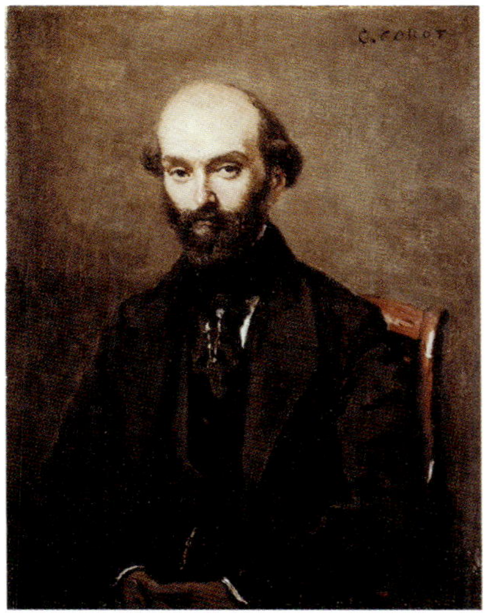

A631; oil on canvas, 32 × 25 cm
Signed: *C. Corot*
Prov.: James Staats Forbes
Hindley Smith Bequest, 1939; WA1940.1.13

Robaut 1905, no. 1055

This portrait forms a pair with the following. According to the early sources, they represent 'Monsieur Bison' and his wife painted in 1852. It has been plausibly suggested that this is a portrait of Louis-Auguste Bisson, a photographer known to the artist, although other candidates have been proposed.

Jean-Baptiste-Camille Corot
(1796 – 1875)

Montfermeuil, The Brook in the Wood

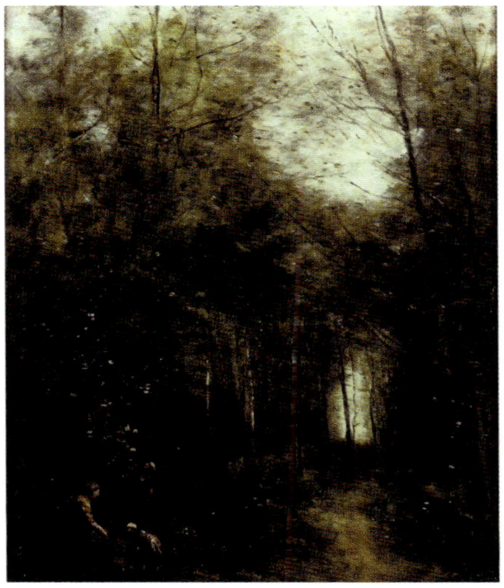

A1165; oil on canvas, 58 × 49 cm
Signed: *Corot*
Prov.: Tedesco; Sir Edward Cripps
Bequeathed by Mr and Mrs Francis Hock through the National Art Collections Fund, 1988; WA1988.293

Robaut 1905, no. 712

A characteristic work from Corot's later years when his colour became more monochromatic and his detail blurred. Corot stayed at Coubron, near Montfermeuil, from 30 June to 20 July 1867, when he probably painted this work.

Jean-Baptiste-Camille Corot
(1796 – 1875)

Lago di Piediluco, Umbria

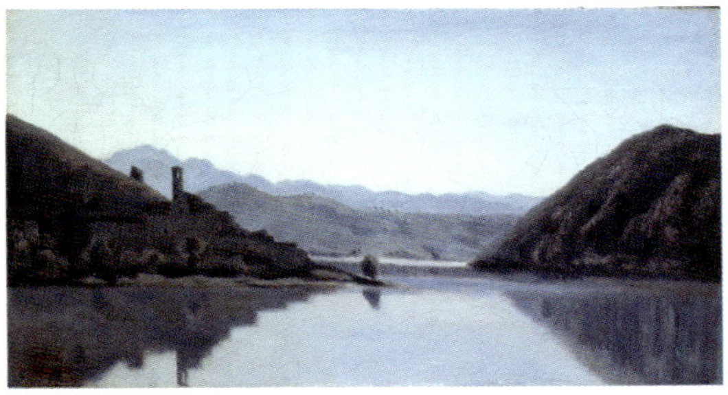

A403; oil on canvas, 22 × 41 cm
Stamped: *VENTE COROT*
Presented by Sir Michael Sadler in memory of Lady Sadler, through the National Art Collections Fund, 1931; WA1931.2

Robaut 1905, no. 123; Tinterow *et al.* 1996, no. 25

Painted on a warm summer's day in 1826 from a site overlooking the lake of Piediluco in the district of Terni, north of Rome. Corot used this sketch as a model for the background of two paintings of the 1860s, *Italian Landscape with Morning Sun* (J. Paul Getty Museum, Los Angeles) and *Souvenir of Italy* (Corcoran Gallery, Washington).

Jean-Baptiste-Camille Corot
(1796 – 1875)

Mme Bison

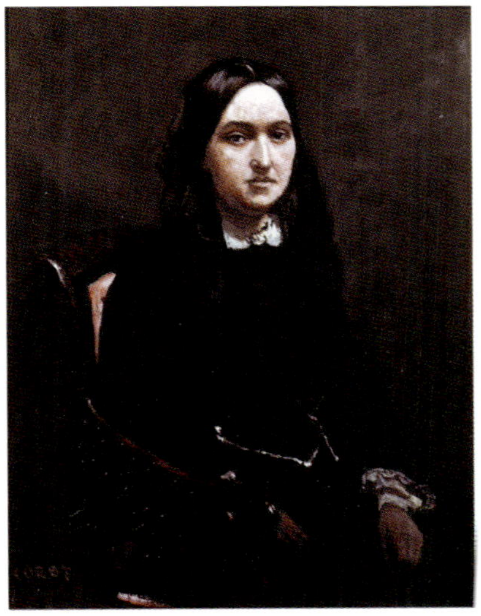

A632; oil on canvas, 32 × 25 cm
Signed: *Corot*
Prov.: James Staats Forbes
Hindley Smith Bequest, 1939; WA1940.1.14

Robaut 1905, no. 1056

A pair to the previous portrait. In common with several of Corot's sitters, Mme Bison has a modest air and is painted with a soft touch.

Copy after **Antonio Allegri**, called **Correggio**
(*c.* 1489 – 1534)

Head, in a circular frame

A110; dimensions unknown
Fox-Strangways Gift, 1850; WA1850.39

Recorded as missing by 1908.

Pietro da Cortona
(1596 – 1669)

The Oath of Semiramis

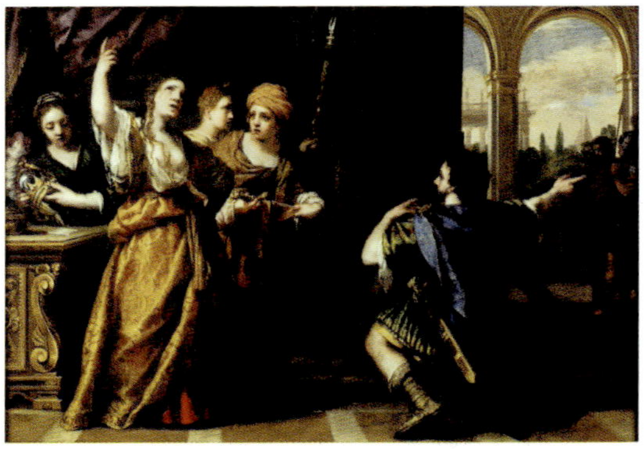

Oil on copper, 51.2 × 70.7 cm
Prov.: possibly Gerrit Uylenburg, Amsterdam 1675
Mahon loan, 1999; WA.L.99.7

Finaldi and Kitson 1997, no. 14

Semiramis, queen of Babylon, is interrupted while dressing by a messenger telling her of a rebellion; she takes a solemn oath to abandon her toilette until peace is restored (Valerius Maximus, *Facta et Dicta Memorabilia*). Her hair is undone and she prepares to take up weapons. Painted *c.* 1623–4, when he was in close contact with the erudite Cassiano dal Pozzo, Cortona used classical architecture to define a stage-like setting embellished with rich antiquarian detail.

Giovanni Costa, called Nino
(1826 – 1903)

View of Monte Amiata, Tuscany

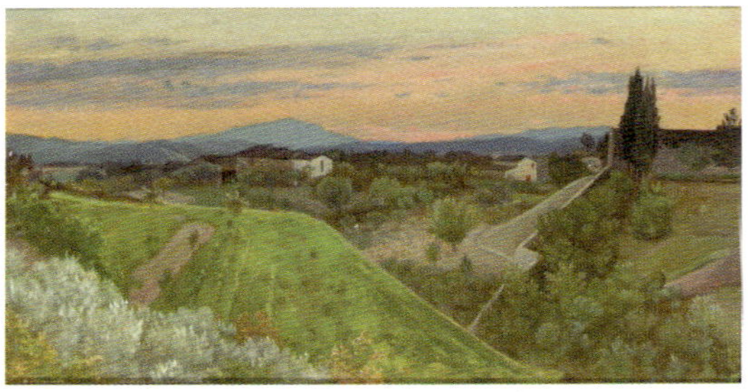

A410; oil on panel, 21 × 39 cm
Bequeathed by John Roscoe, 1931; WA1931.57

Newall 1989, no. 37

A political activist and landscape artist, Costa made plein-air studies in Tuscany, Umbria and Lazio and his Rome studio was a meeting-point for British artists and patrons. A410 may date from *c.* 1880. In 1883–4 he was at the head of a group of Italian and British artists ('The Etruscans') that favoured a type of naturalistic yet idyllic landscape imbued with sentiment.

Jean-Desire-Gustave Courbet
(1819 – 1877)

The Banks of a Stream

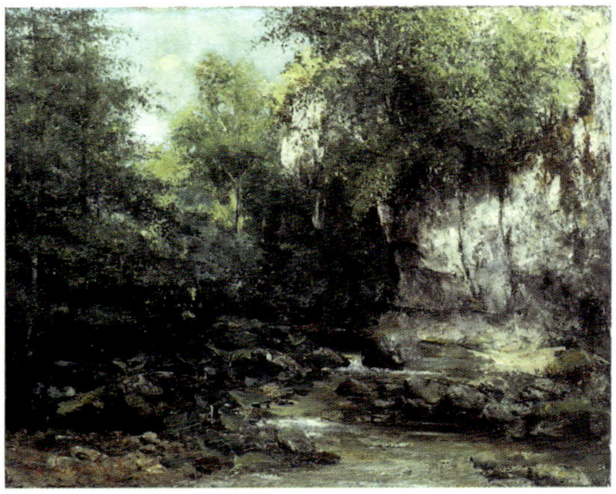

A470; oil on canvas, 60 × 73 cm
Signed and dated: *G. Courbet 1873*
Weldon Bequest 1937; WA1937.50

The view is typical of sites along the river valleys near Ornans, the artist's native town in the Franche-Comté. Courbet painted many similar views of streams in shaded, woodland gullies in the 1860s and 1870s. This picture, dated 1873, was painted in the studio but extensive use of the palette knife to spread and smudge the paint, gives it the rough spontenaity of a sketch done out-of-doors.

Giovanni Costa, called Nino
(1826 – 1903)

Ruins in the Colli Albani

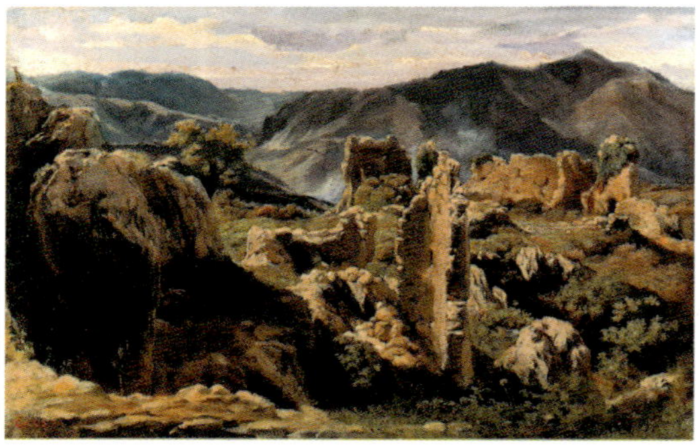

A1256; oil on paper, laid down on canvas, 28.5 × 43.5 cm
Signed: *G. COSTA*
Prov.: by descent from the artist
Purchased with the assistance of the National Art Collections Fund, the Friends of the Ashmolean and Alice Goldet, 2003; WA2003.139

Costa fought on the Republican side during the uprising in Rome in 1848 and fled to Ariccia following the return of pontifical rule in 1850. Over the next ten years he painted many oil sketches in the region including this sunlit view of Roman ruins seen against the background of the Alban hills.

Jean-Desire-Gustave Courbet
(1819 – 1877)

Winter Scene

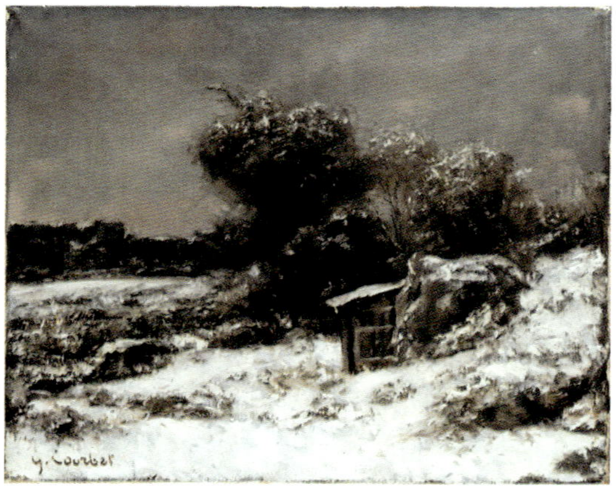

A447; oil on canvas, 32 × 40 cm
Signed: *G. Courbet*
Presented by Mrs W.F.R. Weldon, 1936; WA1936.48

From 1855 until his death, Courbet painted many landscapes under snow, inspired by the countryside of his native Franche-Comté. This atmospheric view, smaller and more refined than many, perhaps dates from the beginning of this period.

William Cowden
(active 1798 – 1820)

Scene on the Sea-coast with Fishermen

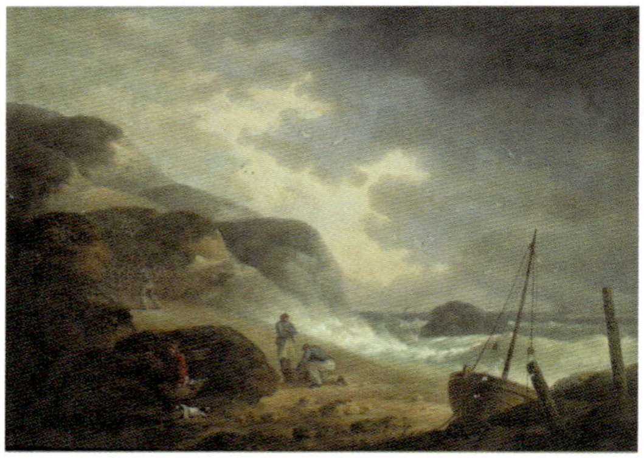

A50; oil on panel, 40 × 55 cm
Presented by the artist, 1806; WA1845.50

This seascape is reminiscent of those of George Morland.

David Cox
(1783 – 1859)

The Garden Terrace at Haddon Hall

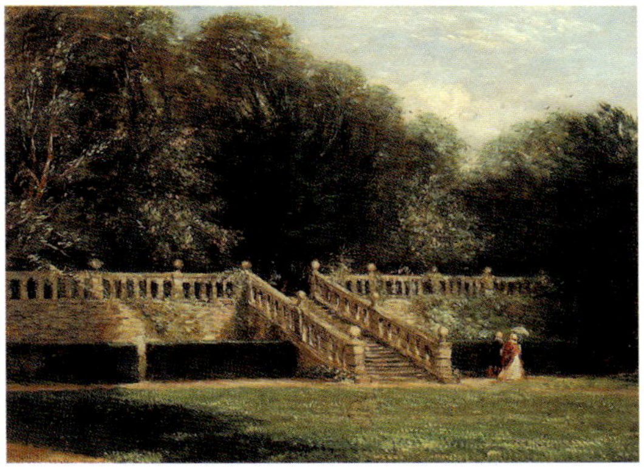

A412; oil on canvas, 45 × 60 cm
Signed and dated: *David Cox. / 1849.*
Prov.: W.J. Clement, sometime M.P. for Salisbury; Samuel H. Perks; Miss A. Bickham
Purchased, 1931; WA1931.62

Wildman 1983, p. 112

Haddon Hall, the Tudor seat of the Dukes of Rutland, was maintained but not inhabited during the 19th century. Cox visited it several times between 1831 and 1850, making numerous watercolours both of the interior and of the gardens and surroundings. This is the only oil and shares the same composition as the largest watercolour (Royal Albert Museum, Exeter).

Anonymous Cremonese Artist
(*c.* 1570 – 90)

Portrait of a Musician

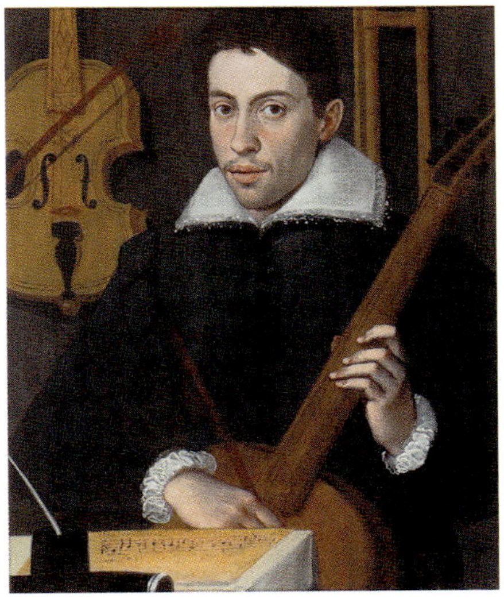

A863a; oil on canvas, 75 × 56 cm
Prov.: Giacomo Stradivari; J.B. Vuillaume; W.H., A.F. and A.E. Hill
Presented by W.E. Hill & Sons Ltd, 1952; WA1952.123

Lloyd 1977, pp. 49–50; Martineau 1981, no. 253

The sitter holds a viola da gamba, probably Brescian and an alto-viol with a bow is in the background. The musical notation and text on the sheet of paper in the foreground are illegible. Traditionally but wrongly said to be a portrait of Antonio Stradivari, A863a is a portrait of a musician or instrument-maker of the late 16th century and identifications of Claudio Monteverdi (1567–1643) and Gasparo da Salò (1540–1609) have been proposed.

Attributed to Giovanni Battista Crespi, Il Cerano
(*c.* 1575–6 – 1632)

The Rest on the Flight into Egypt

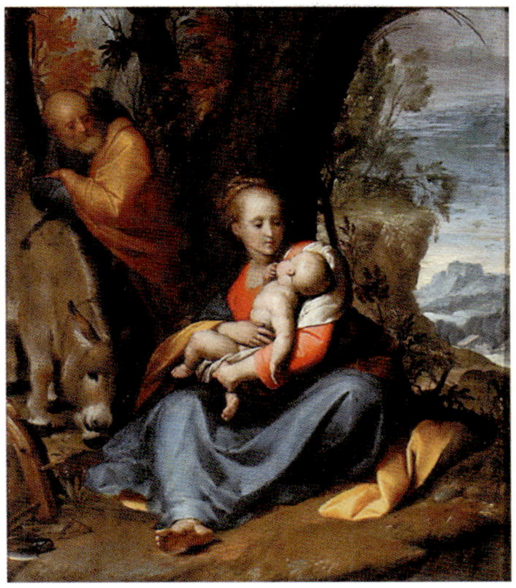

A887; oil on copper, 23.8 × 19.3 cm
Prov.: Franz Joseph I, Emperor of Austria; Artaria, Mannheim
Purchased, 1956; WA1956.13

Neilson 1979, no. 69; Rosci 2000, no. 11

A887 was traditionally attributed to Camillo Procaccini (1551/55–1629) and was engraved as such in 1805 by Giuseppe Longhi. It may well be a mature work by Procaccini because of its clear affinities with the graceful, tender religious art of Federico Barocci. Il Cerano by contrast was indebted to northern mannerist artists and treated religious subjects, with a disturbing intensity. If A887 is by Cerano, it must be a very early work. A small *Visitation* by Cerano (Musée des Beaux Arts, Dijon) also on copper, which is certainly close in the handling of draperies and physiognomy, may be a pendant and both pictures would date from *c.* 1598–1600.

Giuseppe Maria Crespi
(1665 – 1747)

Noli Me Tangere

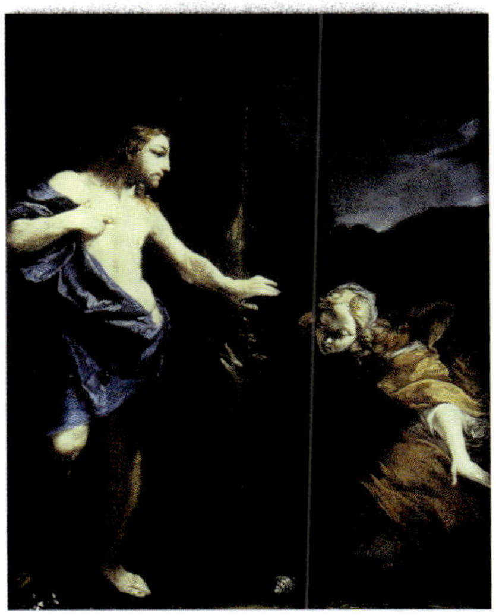

Oil on canvas, 52.8 × 41.3 cm
Prov.: probably Giovanni Ricci, Bologna before *c.* 1760; Luigi Grassi, Florence
Mahon loan, 1999; WA.L.99.10

Finaldi and Kitson 1997, no. 15

The risen Christ greets the sorrowful Mary Magdalen, who has found the tomb empty, saying 'Touch me not...' (John 20:15–17). In this early work of *c.* 1688, Crespi treated the story in an intensely concentrated way as a dramatically lit nocturnal encounter, recalling the work of artists such as Ludovico Carracci, Guercino and Reni. An important patron and friend of the artist, Giovanni Ricci was probably the first owner of this painting.

Attributed to Luigi Crespi
(1708 – 1779)

Portrait of a Young Man

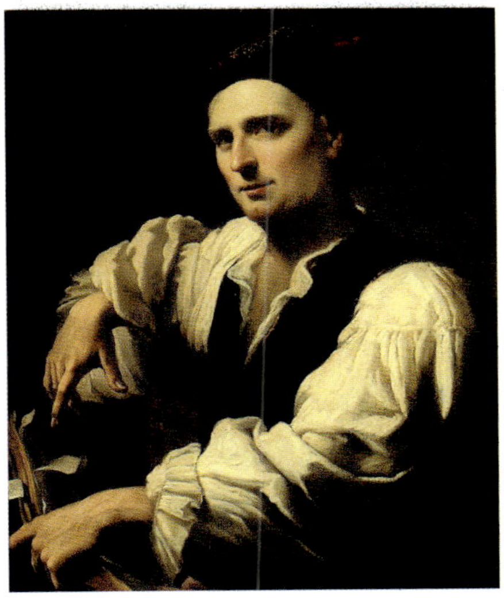

A389; oil on canvas, 79 × 63 cm
Presented by A.H. Buttery, 1927; WA1927.4

Roli 1977, pp. 171, 252 and fig. 324b

A painting of high quality, A389 is likely to be a portrait, although it also belongs to a popular type of 18th-century genre with half-length figures in mildly exotic dress. Formerly attributed to Piazzetta, A389 is probably by Luigi Crespi, painted in the mid-1740s at a time when he was establishing himself independently of his celebrated father.

Attributed to Emanuel de Critz
(1608 – 1665)

John Tradescant the Elder

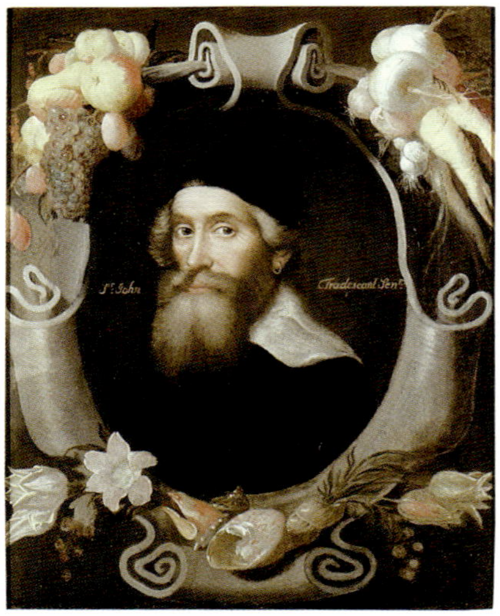

F659; oil on canvas, 79 × 62 cm
Inscribed: *Sr John Tradescant Senr:*
Prov.: Tradescant
Presented by Elias Ashmole, 1683; WA1898.8

Poole 1912, no. 414; MacGregor, 1983, no. 260

This portrait is assumed to be posthumous, based on the same source as F634. It has also been attributed to Cornelis de Neve. The surround, incorporating trophies of fruit and vegetables, with flowers and shells, alludes to Tradescant's interests in horticulture and conchology. The surround was probably painted by another artist, perhaps Alexander Marshal (*c.* 1610–1682), who painted flowers for the Tradescants.

Attributed to Emanuel de Critz
(1608 – 1665)

John Tradescant the Younger and Hester, his second Wife

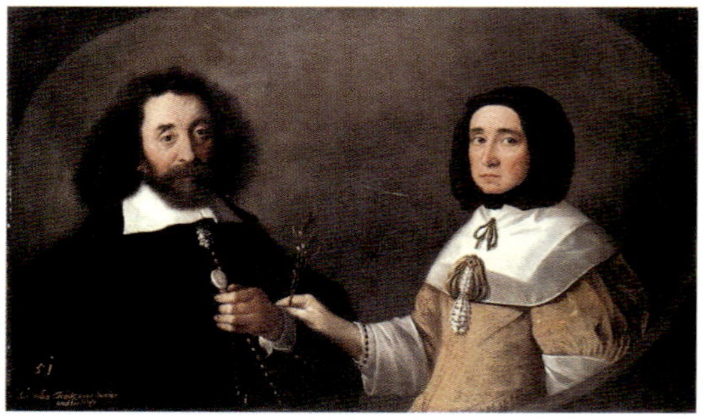

F663; oil on canvas, 72 × 118 cm
Inscribed: *50/1656*; and: *48/1656 Sir John Tradescant Junior and his Wife 51*
Presented by Elias Ashmole, 1683; WA1898.12

Poole 1912, no. 428; MacGregor 1983, no. 262

John Tradescant holds an open silver watch, while his wife presents a sprig of myrtle to her husband, symbolising her fidelity. The inscriptions in the spandrels refer to the numbers in the *Musaeum Tradescantianum*, published in 1656, and the portrait may have been commissioned to commemorate that publication.

Attributed to Thomas de Critz
(1607 – 1653)

John Tradescant the Younger as a Gardener

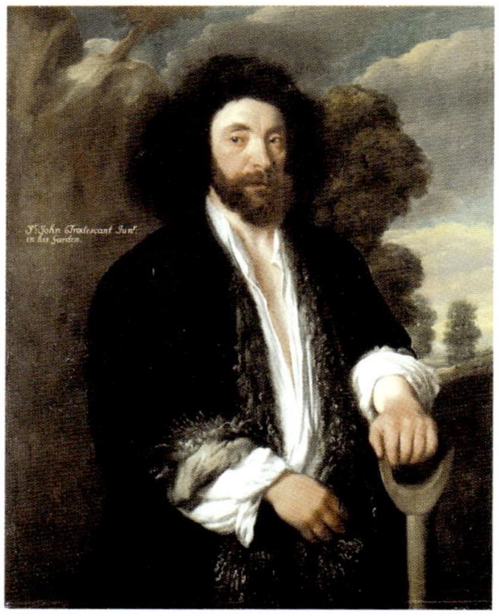

F684; oil on canvas, 107 × 86 cm
Inscribed: *Sr John Tradescant Junr in his Garden*
Presented by Elias Ashmole, 1683; WA1898.10

Poole 1912, no. 426; MacGregor 1983, no. 274

John Tradescant the Younger (1608–1662) lost his position as Keeper of the King's Gardens at Oatlands Palace in 1648; this painting may have been made soon afterwards. He is shown with the attributes of a gardener, holding a spade, with an extensive landscape behind him, probably not, as the inscription asserts, his own garden, but an imaginary park.

Attributed to Emanuel de Critz
(1608 – 1665)

John Tradescant the Elder

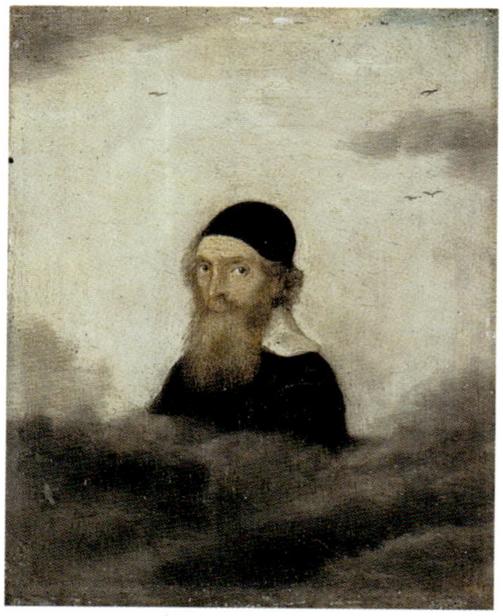

F634; oil on panel, 16 × 14 cm
Prov.: Tradescant
Presented by Elias Ashmole, 1683; WA1898.7

Poole, 1912, no. 413; MacGregor, 1983, no. 253

The disembodied head and shoulders in the clouds, with four birds, perhaps ravens, above, suggest that this portrait is posthumous and based on the same prototype as the more elaborate portrait, F659.

Attributed to Emanuel de Critz
(1608 – 1665)

Oliver de Critz

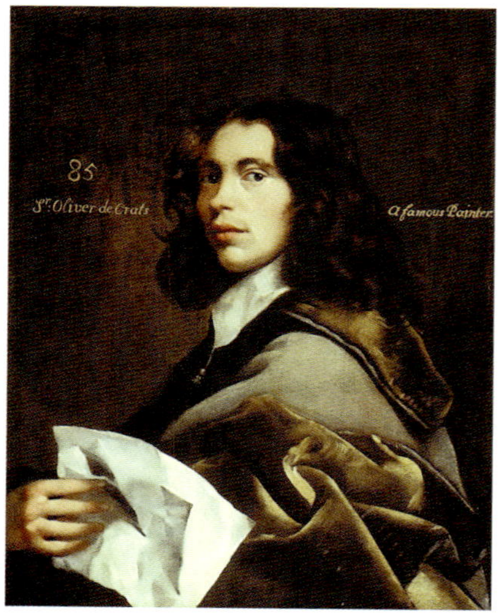

F658; oil on canvas, 67 × 52 cm
Inscribed: *85 S.r Oliver De Crats a famous Painter*
Presented by Elias Ashmole, 1683; WA1898.23

Poole 1912, no. 443; MacGregor 1983, no. 259

Oliver de Critz (*c.* 1626–1651) was the son of John de Critz (*c.* 1552–1642) by his third wife. This painting has generally been taken to be a self-portrait and on the basis of the inscription, attributed to Oliver de Critz, who, in 1646, inherited from his grandfather 'my greene Cloake', which he wears here. However, it has also been argued that it is a self-portrait by Oliver's half-brother, Thomas de Critz (1607–1653).

Attributed to Thomas de Critz
(1607 – 1653)

John Tradescant the Younger with Roger Friend and a Collection of Exotic Shells

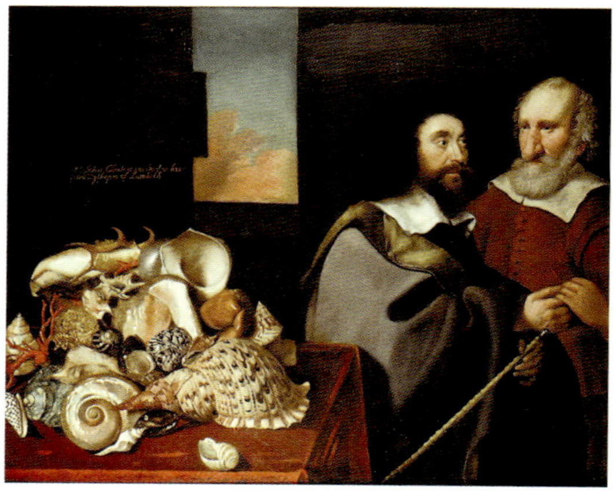

F667; oil on canvas, 107 × 132 cm
Inscribed: *Sr: John Tradescant Junr & his friend Zythepsa of Lambeth. 1645*
Presented by Elias Ashmole, 1683; WA1898.11

Poole 1912, no. 427; MacGregor 1983, no. 265

John Tradescant the Younger (1608–1662) succeeded his father as Keeper of the King's Gardens at Oatlands Palace and further enriched the family collection of specimens of natural and man-made curiosity. He is shown here with his friend, Roger Friend, a brewer (for which *Zythepsa* is the Greek) from Lambeth, who may have contributed the shells to Tradescant's museum.

Attributed to Thomas de Critz
(1607 – 1653)

Hester Tradescant and her stepson, John

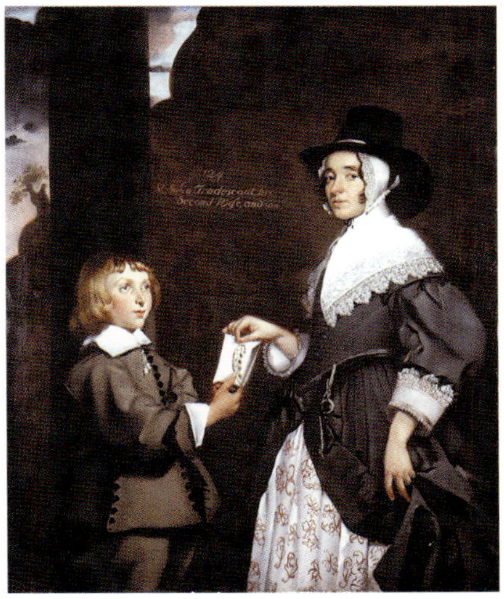

F707; oil on canvas, 136 × 111 cm
Inscribed: *Aetis: 37. Septbris Anno Domini 1645; Aetis 12 A.D. 1645;* and: *124 Sr John Tradescant his Second Wife, and Son*
Presented by Elias Ashmole, 1683; WA1898.14

Poole 1912, no. 439; MacGregor 1983, no. 280

Hester Pookes (*c.* 1608–1678) married John Tradescant the Younger as his second wife in 1638. His son by his first marriage was born in 1633 but died in 1652. In this portrait, he seems to be offering his step-mother a jewel. Dated 1645, it belongs to the group of contemporary portraits of the Tradescants presumably commissioned by John Tradescant the Younger.

Vittore Crivelli
(1444–9 – 1501–2)

St Catherine of Alexandria

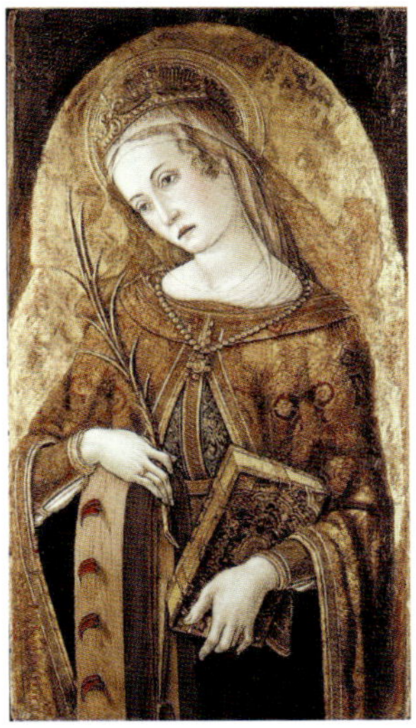

A301; tempera and gilding on panel, 73.7 × 41 cm
Prov.: Alessandro Castellani, Rome; Miss Mary Fortnum
Fortnum Bequest, 1899; WA1899.CDEF.P27

Lloyd 1977, pp. 52–4; Di Provvido 1997, no. 66

St Catherine, of royal birth, wears a crown and carries a book, recalling her erudition, and a martyr's palm. The wheel refers to earlier attempts at her martyrdom. Together with several panels in various collections, including a group in the Fitzwilliam Museum, Cambridge, A301 was part of a polyptych made for the church of San Francesco, Montesanto, in the early 1490s. Like his brother Carlo, Vittore aimed for expressiveness and richness of effect in his art.

Copy after John Crome
(1768 – 1821)

Bruges River, with Ostend in the distance; Moonlight

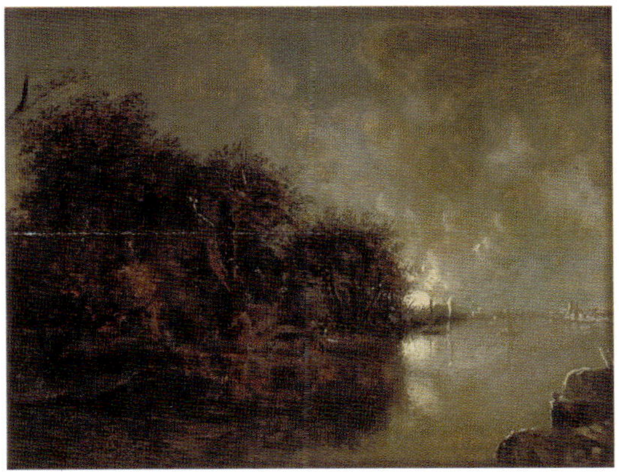

A892; oil on panel, 19 × 25 cm
Prov.: Norgate; J.P. Heseltine
Bequeathed by Percy Moore Turner, 1957; WA1957.59

Goldberg 1978, under no. 82

This is a contemporary copy after a painting exhibited in 1816 and based on studies made by Crome on his return from Paris in 1814 (now in Norwich Museum).

Carlo Crivelli
(*c.* 1430–5 – 1494–5)

St John the Baptist

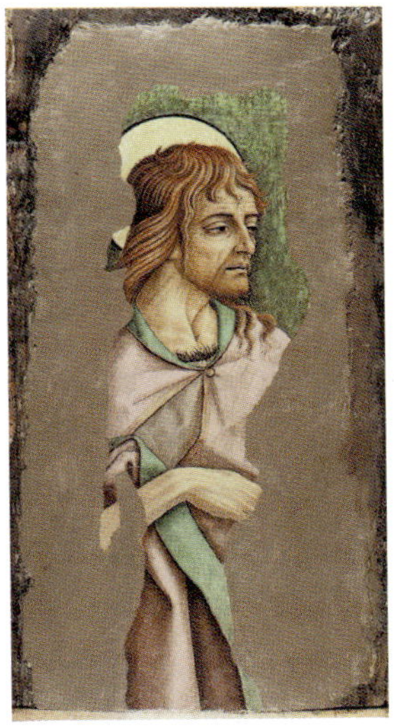

A314; tempera and gilding on panel, 73 × 39 cm
Presented by Henry Pfungst, 1903; WA1903.1

Lloyd 1977, pp. 51–2; Zampetti 1986, no. 120

A member of a Venetian family of artists, Crivelli was active mainly in the Marches from 1470. A314 was once part of a polyptych by Carlo and his studio of *c.* 1486–88, probably for the church of San Lorenzo in Castel San Pietro. Three other panels are known, *St Lawrence, St Augustine* and *A Bishop Saint*: the four would have been in pairs on either side of a *Virgin and Child*. Originally all four saints were full-length figures.

Attributed to John Crome (1768 – 1821), after Gainsborough

Old Orford Church and Mill, Suffolk

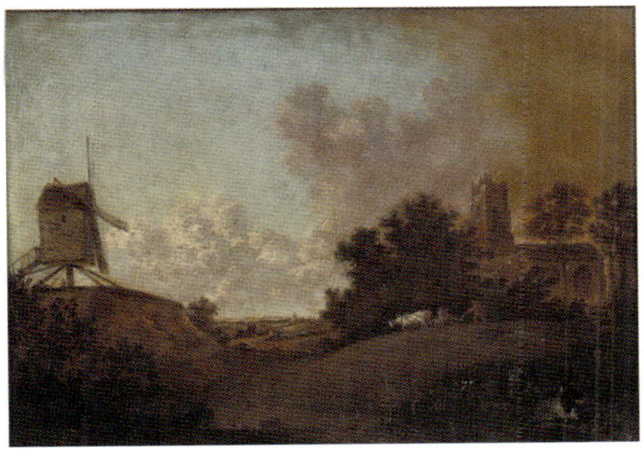

A760; oil on canvas, 54 × 76 cm
Prov.: Hamblin Smith
Presented by F.J. Nettlefold, 1948; WA1948.35

Grundy 1933–8, I, p. 182; Hayes 1982, I, pp. 256–7, II, under no. 46

A free copy after an early painting by Gainsborough, which was owned in 1782 by Panton Betew, when it was engraved. The attribution to Crome of this and other copies after Gainsborough landscapes has been made on the grounds of stylistic, rather than documentary, evidence.

Style of John Crome
(1768 – 1821)

Shepherds in a Grove; Moonlight

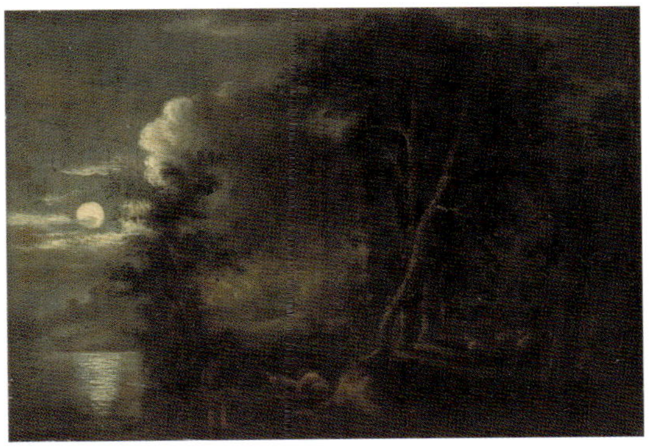

A942; oil on panel, 15 × 29 cm
Presented by G.W. Morris, in memory of Guy Wilfrid and Hilary Joliffe Morris, 1961; WA1961.1.3

Richard Dadd
(1817 – 1886)

Cupid and Psyche

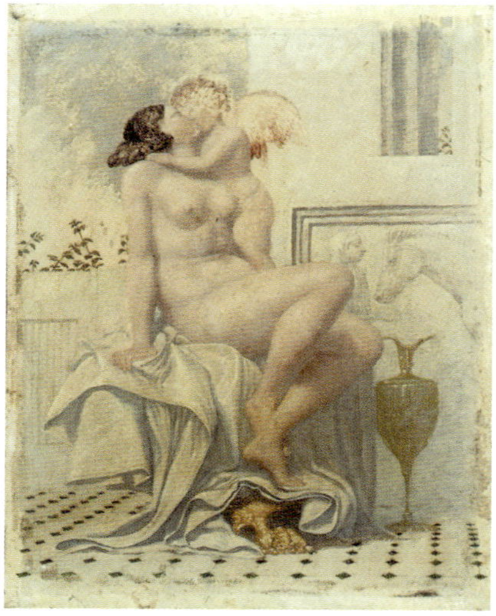

A657; oil on panel, mounted as a drawing, 16.2 × 12.5 cm
Presented by F.R. Meatyard, 1939; WA1939.54

Allderidge 1974, no. 180

Dadd's work after his confinement to Bethlem Hospital in 1844 shows little stylistic development and there is no agreement on the date of this panel. The small scale (Dadd probably trained as a miniature painter) and obsessive details are characteristic. In the background, the marble relief is apparently intended to represent Alexander and Bucephalus.

Adrian Maurice Daintrey
(1902 – 1988)

Portrait of a Woman

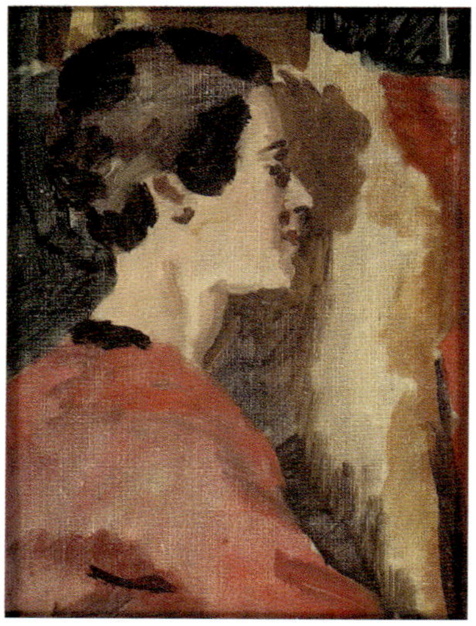

A1137; oil on canvas, 29.3 × 22.4 cm
Inscribed on wooden backboard: *A.M.Daintrey / 1927 / Portrait Woman*
Presented by Gerald Reitlinger, 1972; WA1985.198

The sitter of this portrait remains unknown. The inscription suggests, however, that it is no more than a head study. It dates from the year Daintrey was appointed art master at the Dean Close School, Cheltenham.

Charles-François Daubigny
(1817 – 1878)

Fisher Folk gathering Seaweed, Villerville

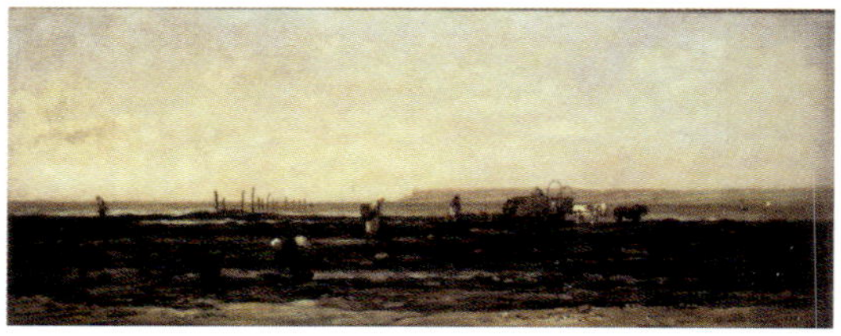

A1148; oil on canvas, 23.8 × 59.1 cm
Signed and dated: *Daubigny 1870*
Prov.: Day; MacArthur; Henry van den Bergh
Presented by the children of Mr and Mrs Henry van den Bergh (Mrs Dorrit Talbot, Mrs S. Roskill and Col Donald S. van den Bergh) through the National Art Collections Fund, in memory of Captain Seymour and Major James Van den Bergh, 1987; WA1987.44

Hellebranth 1976, no. 606

Daubigny painted many views of Villerville, situated near the Seine estuary, during the course of several visits spread across the years.

Adrian Maurice Daintrey
(1902 – 1988)

Beach Scene, Totland Bay

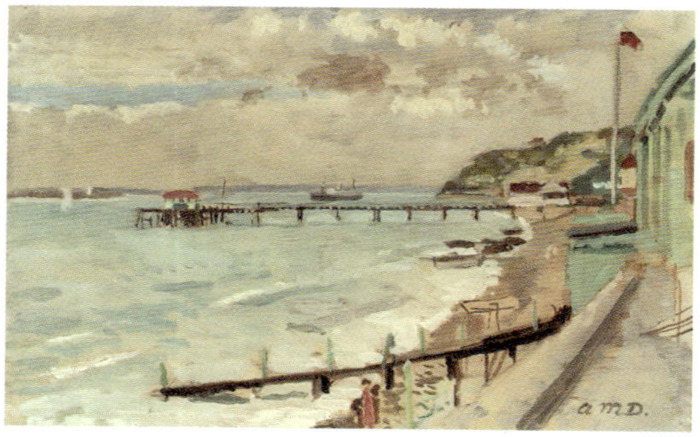

A1097; oil on canvas, 49.5 × 84 cm
Signed in monogram: *A M D.*
Presented by Gerald Reitlinger, 1972; WA1978.39

Daintrey was trained at the Slade School of Fine Art in London and attended the classes of Tonks and Steer. Later he introduced himself to Augustus John and went frequently to Paris between 1924 and 1927. In 1936 Gerald Reitlinger bought this vivid painting directly from the artist.

Anonymous Danish (?) Artist
(19th century)

Matilda Eiler

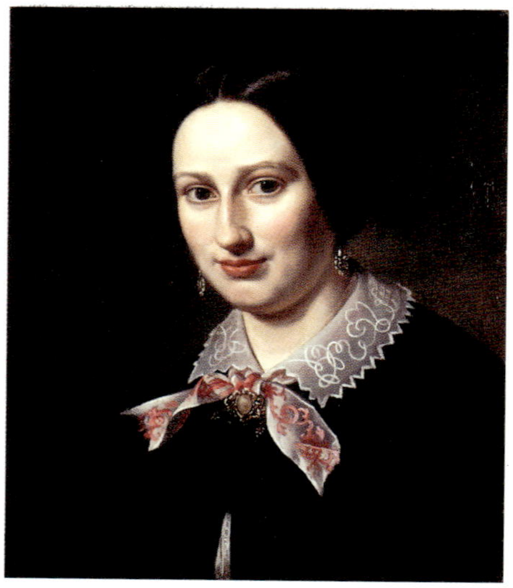

A1215; oil on canvas, 44.7 × 37.2 cm
Prov.: by descent from the sitter Mrs Jette Zerega
Purchased, 1998; WA1998.178

An attribution to Ary Scheffer (1795–1858) was passed down in the vendor's family but neither the choice of colour nor the brushwork are reminiscent of Scheffer's work and an attribution to a Danish artist should be considered.

Charles-François Daubigny
(1817 – 1878)

Evening at Bas Meudon

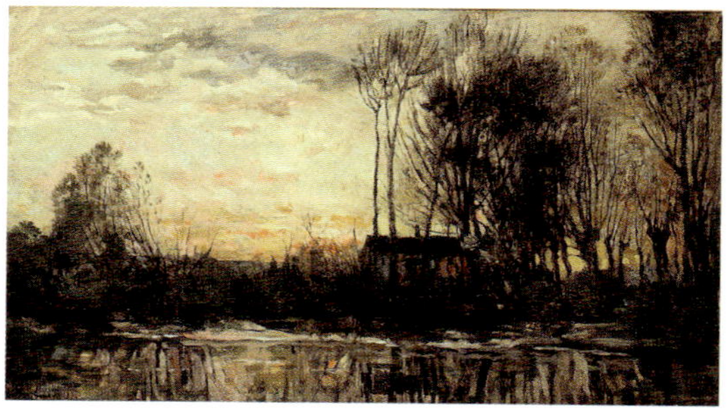

A1004; oil on panel, 38 × 67 cm
Signed and dated: *Daubigny 1874*
Prov.: Geoffroy-Dechaume; J. Crosmer
Bequeathed by Major Thomas Bouch, 1963; WA1963.150.1

Hellebranth 1976, no. 17

Painted at Bas Meudon near Paris in 1874. There is another painting, taken from the same spot, dated 1869, in the Louvre. The two paintings are very similar but as the trees are taller in the Oxford painting, it is unlikely to have been a copy of the other. River scenes, divided into bands of sky, water and dark banks, are very common in Daubigny's work.

Charles-François Daubigny
(1817 – 1878)

Landscape with Figures seated on a Bank

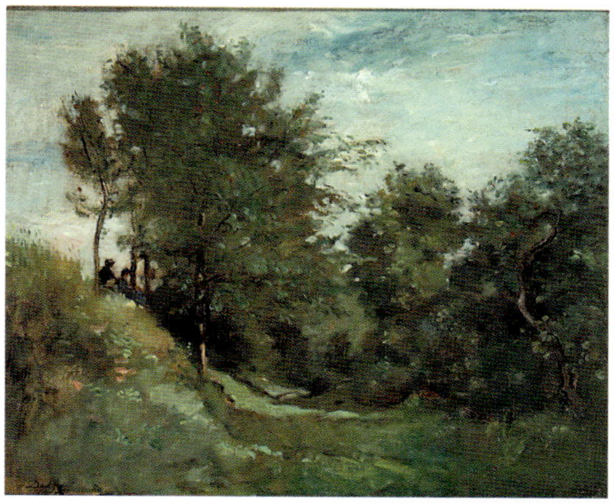

A655; oil on canvas, 63 × 77 cm
Signed: *Daubigny*
Presented by Mr and Mrs Julian G. Lousada through the National Art Collections Fund, 1939; WA1939.52

Hellebranth 1976, no. 199

The broad, fluent application of paint suggests a date in the late 1870s. The picture is said to represent a site in Valmondois in Val-d'Oise where Daubigny worked regularly from the 1840s to the 1870s.

Honoré Daumier
(1808 – 1879)

Landscape with a figure

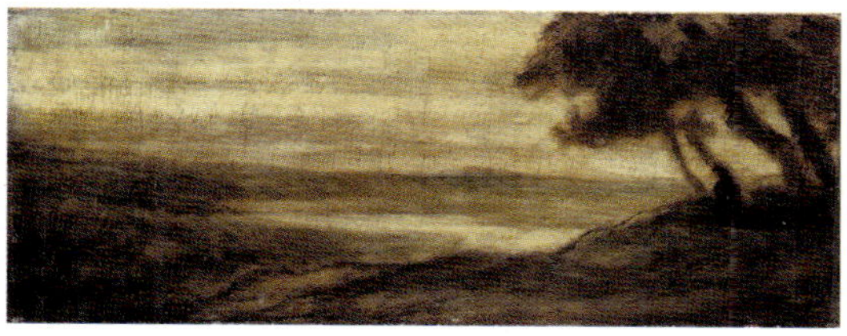

A1167; oil on panel, 13.5 × 36.5 cm
Bequeathed by Mr and Mrs Francis Hock through the National Art Collections Fund, 1988; WA1988.295

Daumier's paintings are difficult to date. The subject of this little atmospheric panel somewhat recalls a drawing by the artist dated *c.* 1860; the painting may be contemporary.

Pierre-Joseph Dedreux-Dorcy
(1789 – 1874)

Portrait of a Girl Holding a Rose

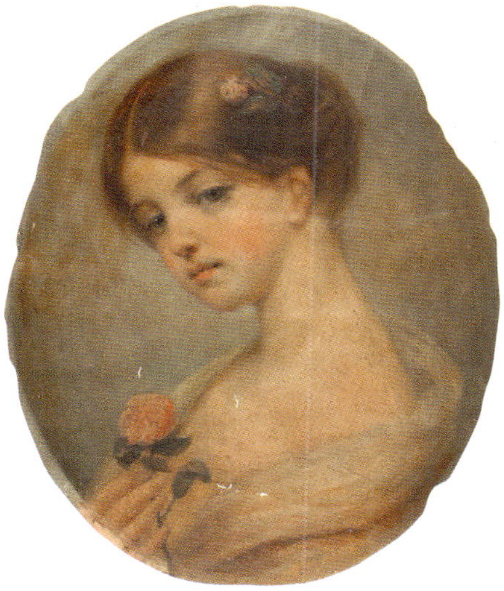

A137; oil on canvas, 46 × 38 cm
Bequeathed by the Revd Dr Thomas Penrose, 1851; WA1851.20

Dedreux-Dorcy, a close friend of Delacroix, was greatly impressed by Greuze, whose work he imitated. Recorded as painted in Paris in 1846, A137 was probably intended as a charming image of reverie rather than as a portrait. Dedreux-Dorcy exhibited various *têtes d'étude* of young girls at the Salon.

Charles-François Daubigny
(1817 – 1878)

Landscape: Sunset

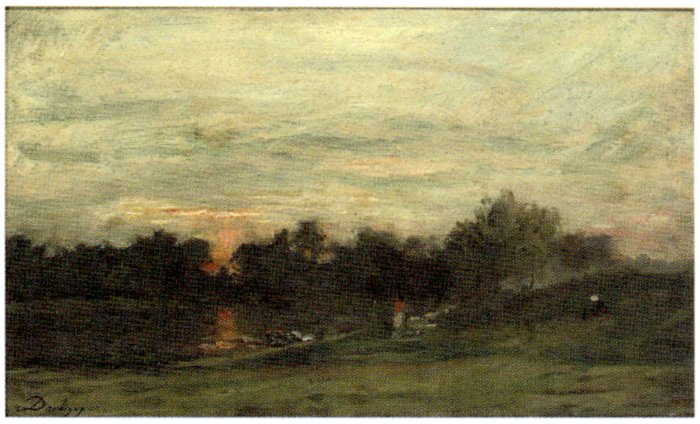

A462; oil on panel, 25 × 40 cm
Inscribed: *Daubigny*
Weldon Bequest, 1937; WA1937.57

Hellebranth 1976, no. 784

A fleeting, informal study of an effect of evening light of a kind which the artist used in many other works. The brush work is characteristically brisk but the signature has been added by another hand.

Cornelis Gerritsz. Decker
(before 1623 – 1678)

River Scene with a Cottage and Boat

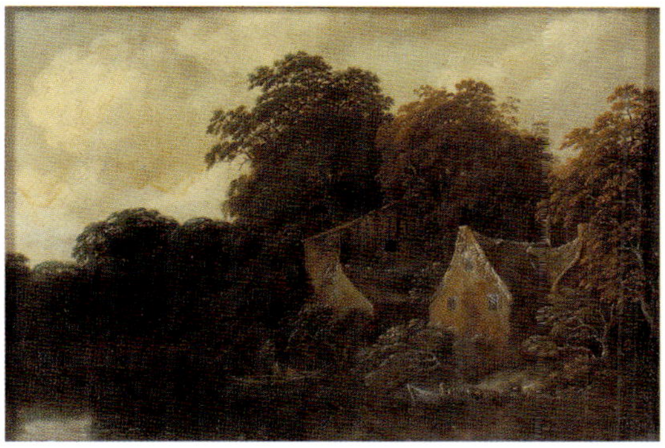

A284; oil on panel, 28 × 40 cm
Signed: *CD*
Presented by Thomas Humphry Ward, 1897; WA1897.7

White 1999, p. 31

Decker is first mentioned in Haarlem in 1643 and dated pictures are known from 1649 onwards. This rustic scene with a cottage and boat is a characteristic subject among Haarlem painters working in the circle of Jacob van Ruisdael.

William Alfred Delamotte
(1775 – 1863)

Lake Avernus

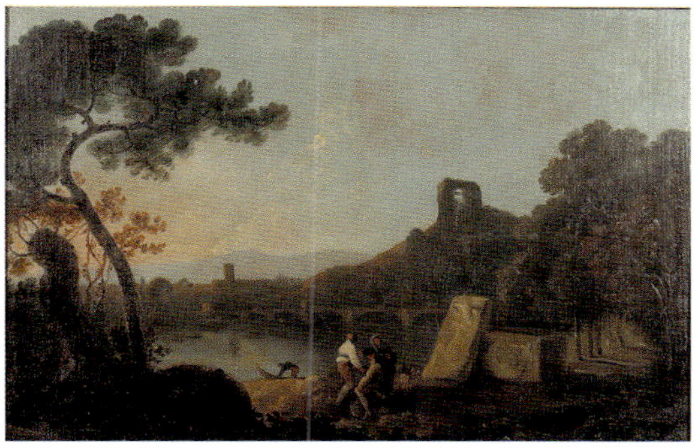

A953; oil on canvas, 55 × 84 cm
Signed: *Delamotte*
Prov.: Lady Gladstone
Presented by Lionel G. Duke, 1961; WA1961.36

Constable 1953, p. 195

Delamotte was primarily a painter in watercolours. He was active in Oxford in the 1790s and was appointed Drawing Master at the Royal Military College at Great Marlow in 1803. He made few oil paintings. This is adapted from two different paintings by Richard Wilson of Lake Avernus (Tate Britain and National Museum of Wales), the latter owned by Sir George Beaumont when Delamotte painted his adaptation.

Attributed to Jacques de l'Ange
(documented 1631–2 – 1642)

A Young Woman at her Toilet: 'Pride'

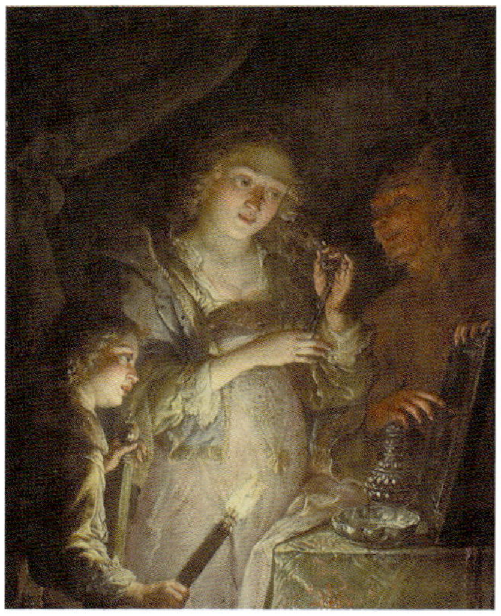

A22; oil on copper, 36 × 28 cm
Acquired before 1759; WA1845.22

White 1999, p. 182

This painting and the following six form a set representing The Seven Deadly Sins. They have been linked with a series of larger paintings on canvas, now divided between various collections which have been attributed to the author of a painting of *The Holy Family* in the Noordbrabants Museum in s'-Hertogenbosch, signed: *JAD*. These initials have been associated with Jacques de l'Ange, a little known Flemish painter. The painting which relates to *Avarice* (Gemäldegalerie, Kassel) is dated 1642.

Attributed to Jacques de l'Ange
(documented 1631–2 – 1642)

An Old Woman Holding a Heart: 'Envy'

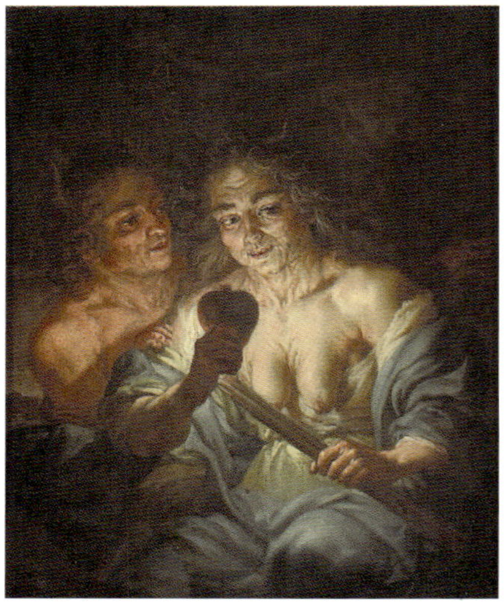

A24; oil on copper, 36 × 28 cm
Acquired before 1759; WA1845.24

White 1999, p. 182

Attributed to Jacques de l'Ange
(documented 1631–2 – 1642)

An Old Woman Weighing Gold: 'Avarice'

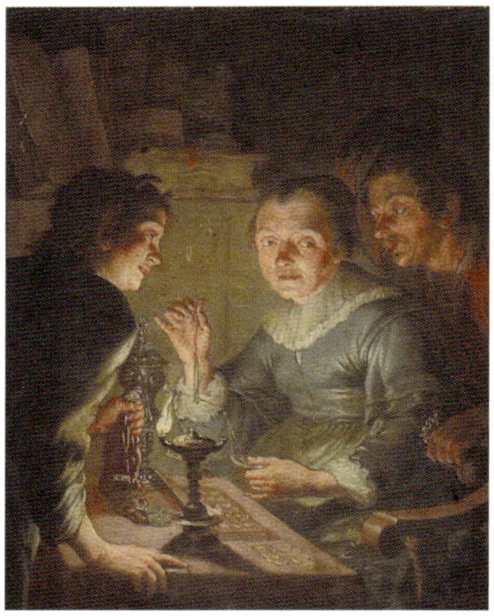

A26; oil on copper, 36 × 28 cm
Dated: *1642*
Acquired before 1759; WA1845.26

White 1999, p. 182

Attributed to Jacques de l'Ange
(documented 1631–2 – 1642)

A Loving Couple: 'Lust'

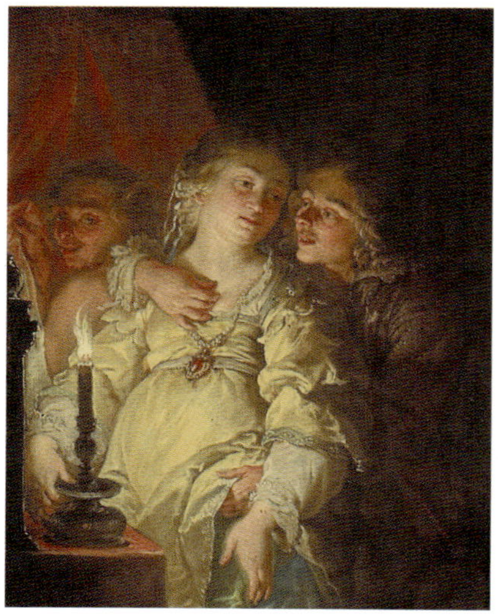

A23; oil on copper, 36 × 28 cm
Acquired before 1759; WA1845.23

White 1999, p. 182

Attributed to Jacques de l'Ange
(documented 1631–2 – 1642)

A Sleeping Man: 'Sloth'

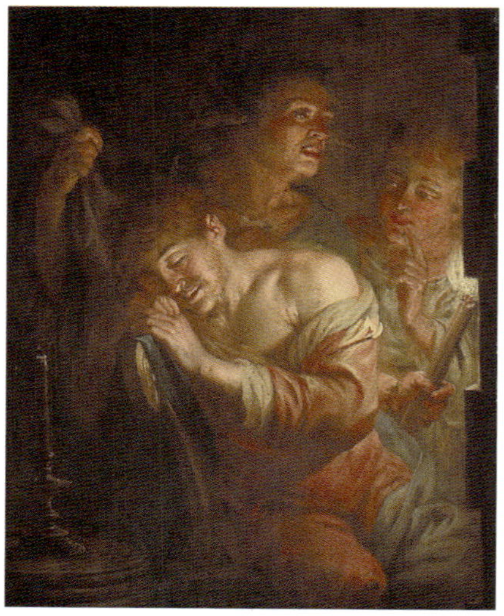

A25; oil on copper, 36 × 28 cm
Acquired before 1759; WA1845.25

White 1999, p. 182

Attributed to Jacques de l'Ange
(documented 1631–2 – 1642)

A Man Drinking: 'Gluttony'

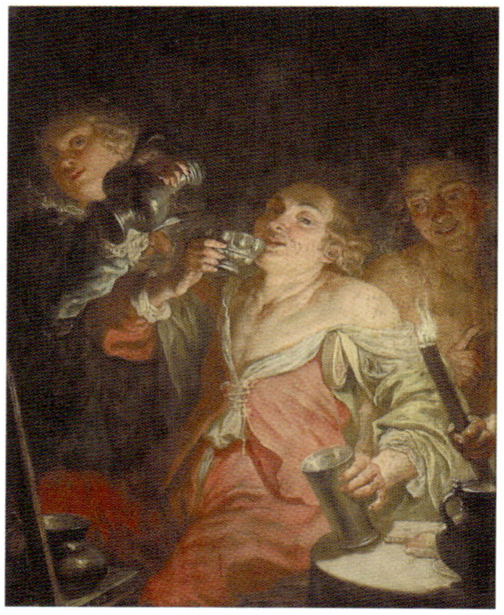

A27; oil on copper, 36 × 28 cm
Acquired before 1759; WA1845.27

White 1999, p. 182

Attributed to Jacques de l'Ange
(documented 1631–2 – 1642)

A Young Man with a Sword Restrained by a Young Woman: 'Anger'

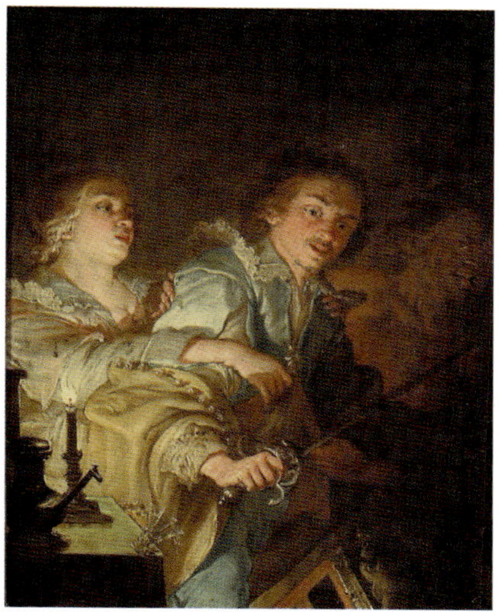

A28; oil on copper, 36 × 28 cm
Acquired before 1759; WA1845.28

White 1999, p. 182

Follower of Deodato Orlandi
(active 1284 – 1332)

Virgin and Child, with *St John the Evangelist* and *St Catherine of Alexandria*

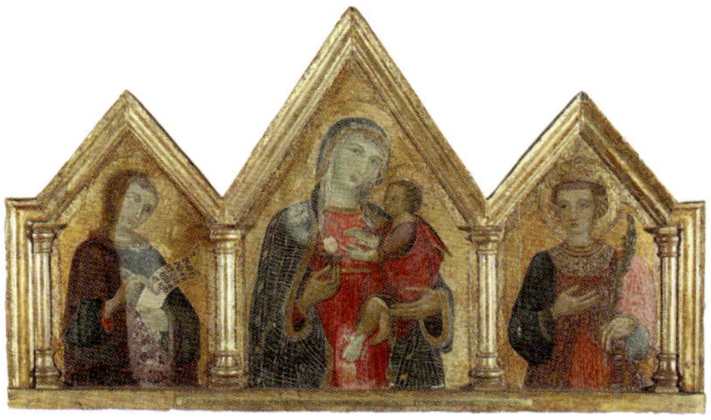

A365; tempera and gilding on panel,
58 × 33; 75 × 50; 58 × 33 cm
Inscribed on the scroll held by St John: *I / N / PRINCI / PIO.ER/AT.ÙBŪ / ZŪBŪ.ER / AT.APD. DEU (?)...*
(presumably intended for John I: 1)
Presented by G. Gidley Robinson, 1921; WA1921.2

Lloyd 1977, pp. 154–5; Tartuferi 1998, p. 44

The panels are heavily repainted: now shaped as a triptych, they may originally have been part of a larger ensemble. Deodato Orlandi was an eclectic artist working in Lucca and Pisa at a time of transition from a manner of painting deriving from Byzantine art to one based on the monumental naturalism of Giotto.

Walter Howell Deverell
(1828 – 1854)

Wykeham Deverell as a Child

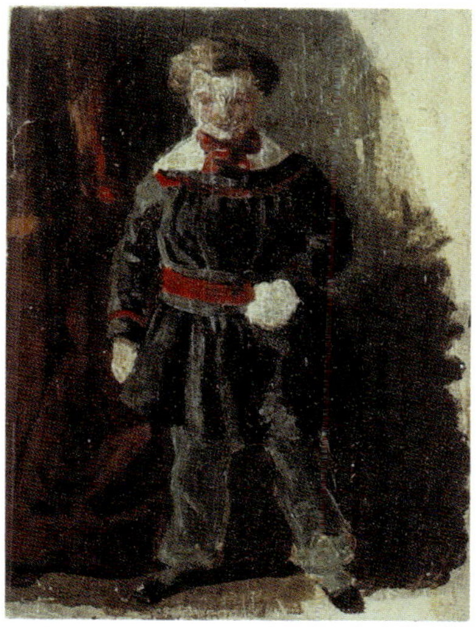

A687a; oil on card, mounted as a drawing, 19 × 14.2 cm
Prov.: the artist's family by descent
Purchased, 1941; WA1941.120

Lutyens 1984, pp. 95–6

Deverell was a disciple of Millais and Rossetti and although never formally elected a member of the Pre-Raphaelite Brotherhood, was one of their closest associates. This portrait of his younger brother, who was born in 1837, was probably made around 1846, when the artist was studying at the Royal Academy Schools.

Cornelis Jacobsz. Delff
(1570/1 – 1643)

Still Life of Kitchen Utensils

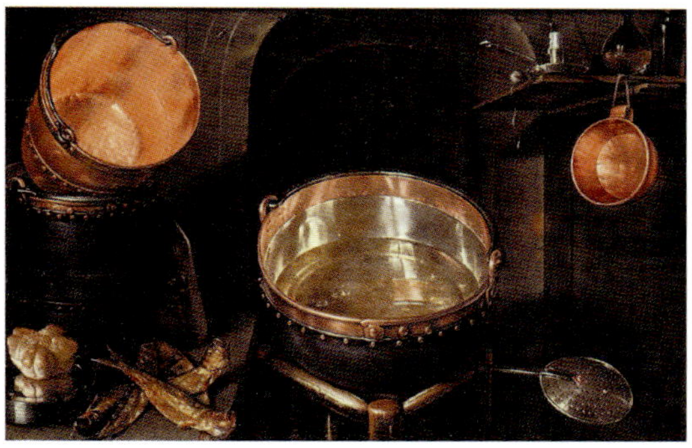

A548; oil on panel, 66 × 100 cm
Signed: *CJDelff.Fecit* (JD in monogram)
Ward Bequest, 1939; WA1940.2.24

Meier 2003, no. 28

Cornelis Delff trained with Cornelis Cornelisz. in Haarlem. By 1610, he had settled in Delft where he spent the rest of his life. He is one of the earliest painters of still life. A kitchen subject like this derives from the kitchen scenes of Joachim Beuckelaer and Pieter Aertsen but without the figures which feature in their work. The painting is chiefly an exercise in depicting metallic surfaces and effects of reflected light and was probably intended to hang in the kitchen of a substantial household.

André Derain
(1880 – 1954)

Still Life with Plums

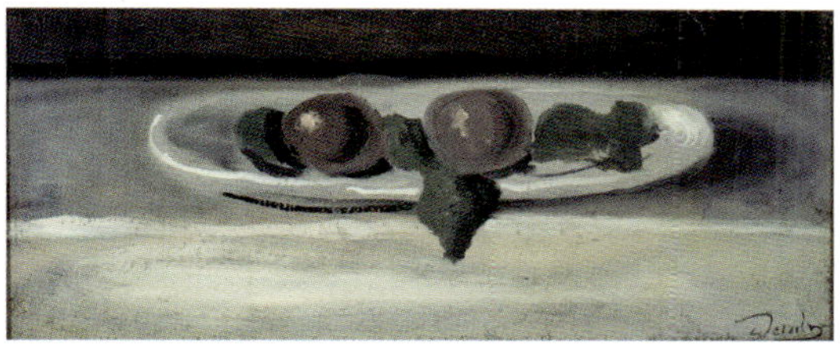

A638; oil on canvas, 18.4 × 42.2 cm
Signed: *Derain*
Hindley Smith Bequest, 1939; WA1940.1.20

Eustace 1999, no. 24

Derain and his colleagues earned the name Fauves (wild beasts) through their radical approach to fractured colour and form. From 1913 onwards, Derain painted many still lifes. In this painting from the mid 1920s, space is reduced to a single plane, the liquid paint is fluently applied, the composition is arranged like a frieze and the objects are clearly fixed in space.

Arthur B. Devis
(1711 – 1787)

Portrait of a Man

A502; oil, dimensions unknown
Weldon Bequest, 1937; WA1937.82.3

Missing since August 1965.

Arthur William Devis
(1762 – 1822)

Assayer at Work in the Mint, Calcutta

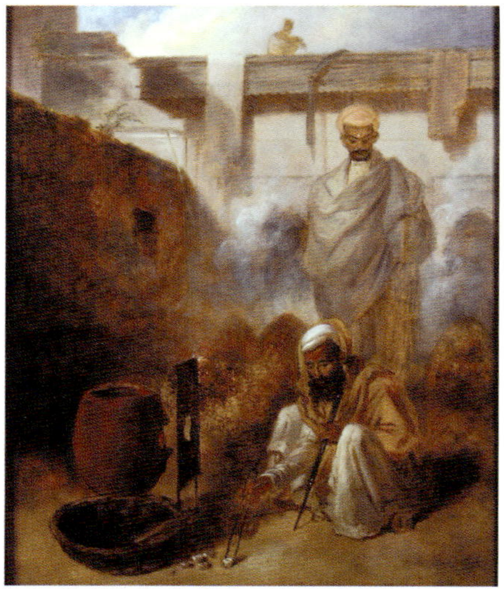

Oil on panel, 47 × 38.1 cm
Prov.: John Biddulph of Ledbury and by descent
Purchased, 1980; HCR1980.9.1

Pavière 1950, no. 104

Devis went to India in 1784 and specialised in portraiture. However, in 1792 he began a series of thirty paintings showing 'the arts, manufactures and agriculture of Bengal', to be engraved in England.

Samuel de Wilde
(1748 – 1832)

Mr Suett as Dicky Gossip in 'My Grandmother'

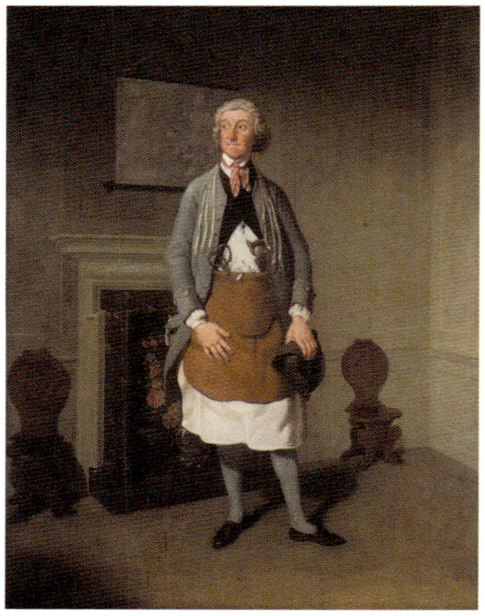

A374; oil on canvas, 74 × 58 cm
Signed and dated: *Samuel De Wilde f / 1797*
Presented by A.H. Buttery, 1924; WA1924.1

Mayes 1971, no. 11

Richard Suett (1755–1805) appeared at the Drury Lane theatre from 1780 until his death. He specialised in Shakespearian clowns and other comic parts. The role of Dicky Gossip in Prince Hoare's *My Grandmother*, which he created on 16 December 1793, became one of his most celebrated. This painting was exhibited at the Royal Academy in 1797.

Adriaen van Diest
(1655–6 – 1704)

Landscape with a Bull

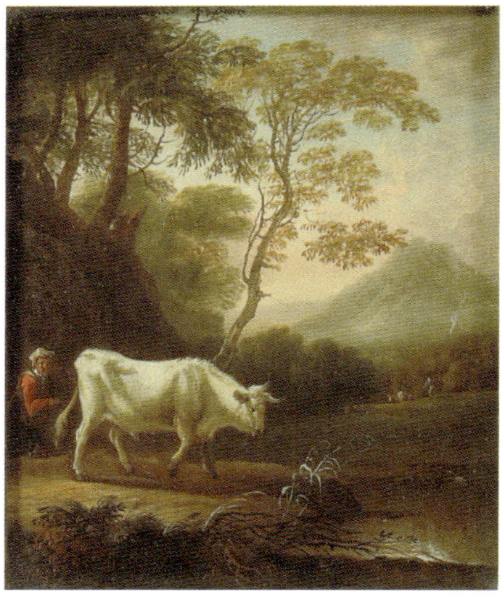

A385; oil on canvas, 37 × 30 cm
Signed in monogram: *AVD*
Bequeathed by Mrs E.C. Greenway, 1926; WA1926.11

White 1999, p. 32

The artist was a painter of landscapes and animals. By March 1638, he had moved to England where he became a specialist in painting landscapes for decorating interiors. A painting signed by Diest, very similar to this, was sold at Christie's, Amsterdam, 14 November 1991, lot 105.

Arthur William Devis
(1762 – 1822)

Stamping Coinage in the Mint, Calcutta

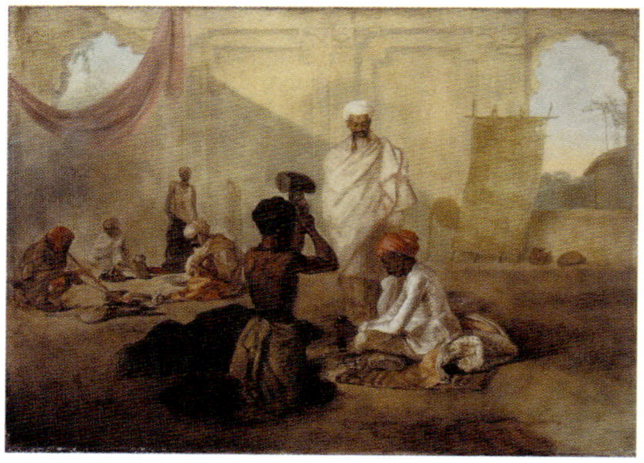

Oil on canvas, 44.5 × 60 cm
Prov.: John Biddulph of Ledbury and by descent
Purchased with the assistance of the National Art Collections Fund and the Victoria & Albert Museum Purchase Grant Fund, 1980; HCR1980.6.13

Pavière 1950, no. 103

Another painting from Devis's Bengal series, painted around 1792. It shows the last survival of the manual process of coining. In the foreground, a senior official holds the upper die about to be struck by a workman. The standing figure is the Superintendent of the Mint.

Peter de Wint
(1784 – 1849)

Still Life with a Basket between two Crocks

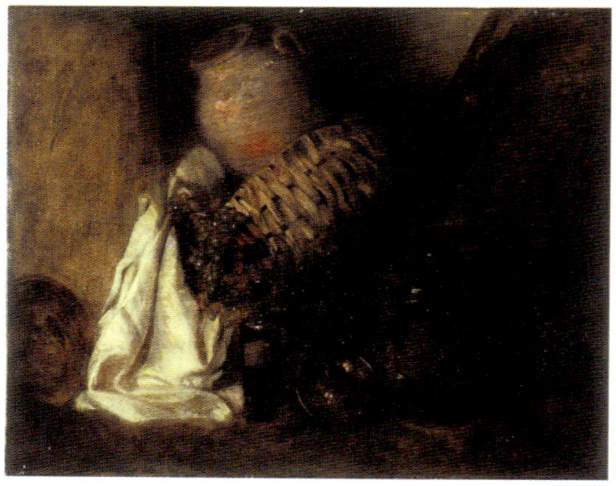

A664a; oil on canvas, 35 × 43 cm
Prov.: by descent to Miss H.H. Tatlock; Sydney D. Kitson
Presented by the Misses Kitson, 1940; WA1940.8.2.2

Smith 1982, p. 184

Although De Wint is best known as a watercolour artist, he exhibited a number of landscapes in oils at the Royal Academy until 1828. The majority remained in his studio until his death. Like his landscapes, his still lifes, which are uncommon, reflect his Dutch ancestry. In them, however, he was less concerned with the accurate depiction of different surfaces, than with tonal unity.

Eve Disher
(1894 – 1991)

Gerald Reitlinger

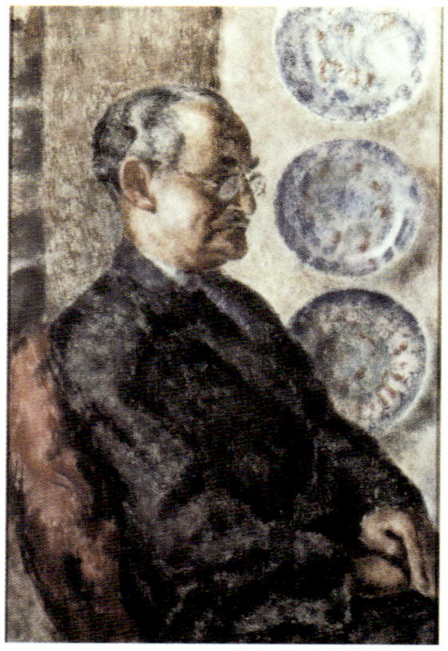

Oil on paper; mounted as a drawing, 75 × 50 cm
Signed: *Eve Disher*
Presented by Gerald Reitlinger, 1972; WA1978.33.1

Gerald Reitlinger (1900–1978) was an artist, traveller and writer, who presented his important collection of Far Eastern, European and Islamic ceramics to the Ashmolean in 1972.

Copy after William Dobson
(1611 – 1646)

Colonel Richard Neville

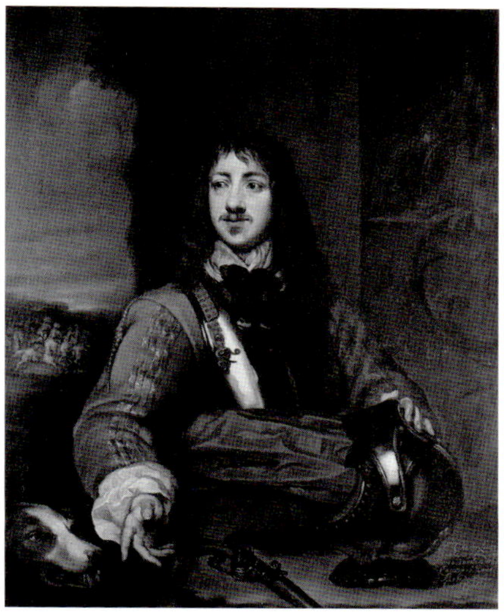

A1017; oil on canvas, 124 × 100 cm
Inscribed: *S.r Charles Lucas. / Brother to John Lord / Lucas and uncle to Mary / Countess of Kent / Shot to Death after / the Siege of Colchester / 1658*
Presented by Miss Orovida Pissarro, 1964; WA1964.60

Like other versions of this portrait, it is inscribed with the name of Sir Charles Lucas, who led the defence of Colchester against Cromwell's army in 1648. On the fall of the city, he was captured and executed. However, it has recently been proposed that it shows Colonel Richard Neville (1615–1676), another Royalist commander. Dobson's original is in the National Portrait Gallery.

John Dodgson
(1890 – 1969)

Lucchese

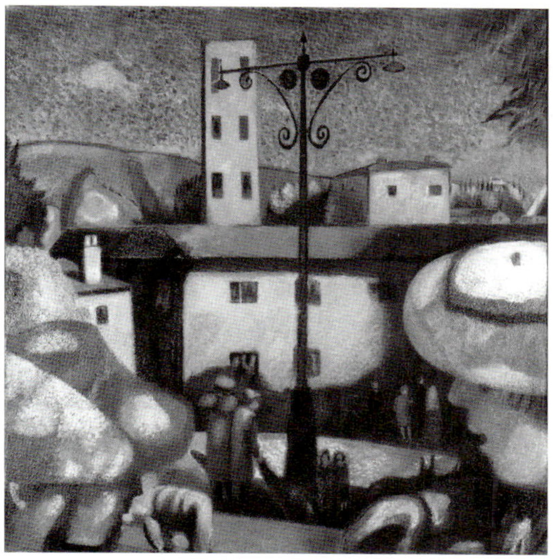

A1196; oil on canvas, 103 × 98 cm
Signed on back: *John Dodgson* and inscribed: *Summer Evening, Tuscany No 1*
Presented by Stephen, Sarah and Anne Dodgson, 1996; WA1996.385

Sudbury 1995, no. 29

Dodgson was active as printmaker, painter and collector. Although his work owes something to the Camden Town group and the Euston Road traditions, his manner retains a character of its own. In this painting, he constructs a sense of space by fairly simple means but the space and the figures are clearly defined and convey a sense of the Tuscan atmosphere of Lucca with bright colours

Copy after Carlo Dolci
(1616 – 1686)

Head of St Rosa

A107; oil on canvas, 38 × 28 cm
Fox-Strangways Gift, 1850; WA1850.36

Presumably this was a copy of Dolci's *St Rose of Lima* of 1668, in the Palazzo Pitti, Florence. Missing since 1917.

Mstislav Valerianovich Dobuzhinsky
(1875 – 1957)

New York Rooftops, my Window in New York

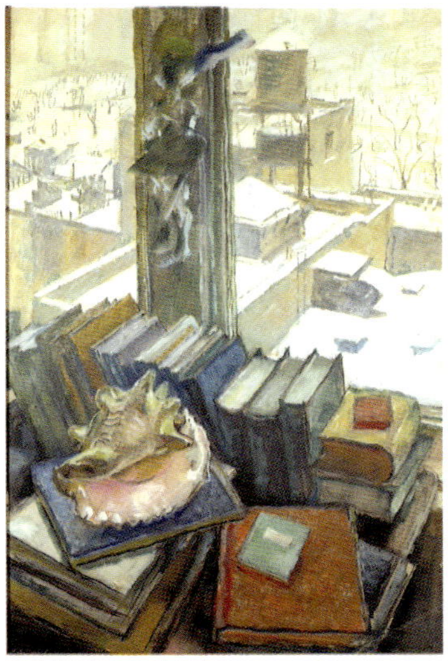

A1079; oil on cardboard, 76.5 × 50.5 cm
Dated: *1943*
Presented by Rostilov Dobuzhinsky, 1975; WA1975.125

Salmina-Haskell 1989, no. 41

Like a number of artists associated with the 'World of Art' movement, Dobuzhinsky designed sets and costumes for the theatre. His first work of this kind dates from 1907. In 1939, he went to New York and remained there for several years working for American theatres. This picture represents a corner of his studio in New York.

Copy after Carlo Dolci
(1616 – 1686)

Head of a young Saint (St Lucy?)

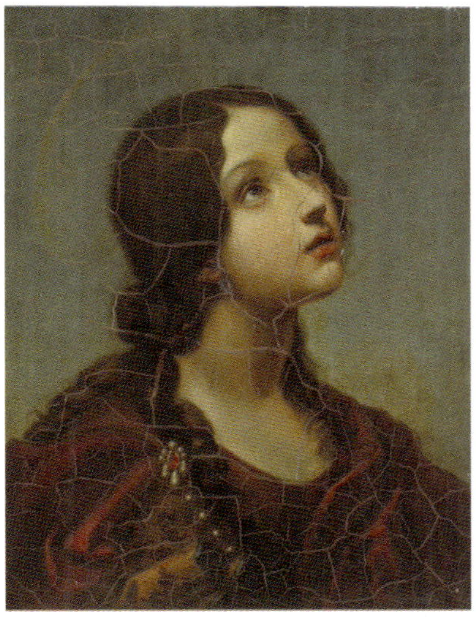

A321; oil on panel, 52 × 40 cm
Provenance unknown; WA.OA907

In a ruined condition, A321 was previously identified as a copy of Dolci's *St Mary Magdalen* (Uffizi, Florence). The prototype is the celebrated *St Lucy* of *c.* 1670 (Uffizi, now attributed to the studio of Dolci), a much-copied devotional image. A321 closely follows the costume, hair and expression, but omits the saint's attribute of a wound in her neck.

Domenico Zampieri, called Domenichino
(1581 – 1641)

The Vision of St Jerome

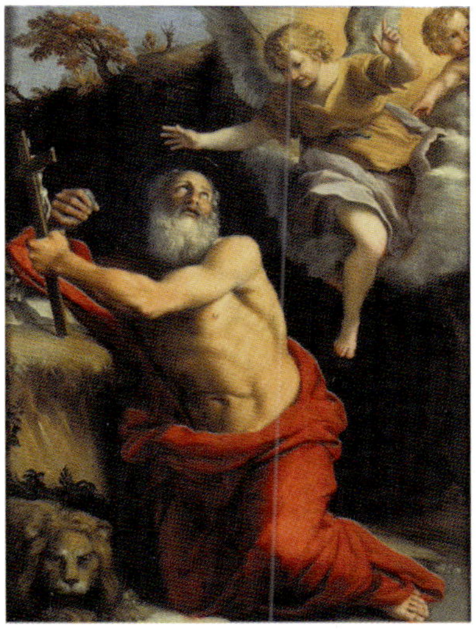

Oil on copper, 49.4 × 37.2 cm
Prov.: Monsieur Paillot; Duc d'Orléans; Henry Hope; George Watson Taylor; Mrs Whyte of Barron Hill, by descent to Captain Arthur Finch Dawson
Mahon loan, 1999; WA.L.99.12

Finaldi and Kitson 1997, no. 20; Schleier 2001, no. C6

St Jerome (*c.* 342–420), in prayer before a crucifix, is interrupted by a heavenly vision, signifying divine blessing and inspiration. Domenichino made several paintings of the saint when in Rome in 1602–10: this was apparently made *c.* 1606–8 when he was living in the household of Monsignor Giovanni Battista Agucchi and it had a companion of a St Francis in prayer.

Attributed to Dosso Dossi
(1486/7 – 1541/2)

Portrait of a young Man holding a Dog and a Cat

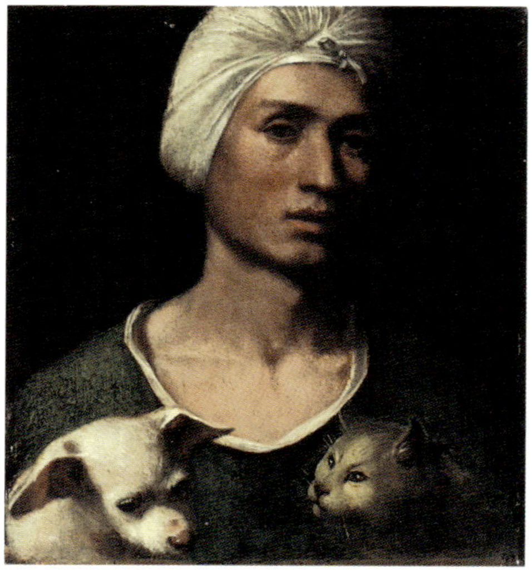

A886; oil on panel, 27.8 × 24.9 cm
Purchased, 1956; WA1956.15

Lloyd 1977, pp. 54–5; Ballarin 1994–5, I, no. 324

This kind of moody portrait, or image of a particular human type, was popularised by Giorgione: here the dog and cat may allude to conflicting sides of the man's personality. Dosso Dossi, who admired Giorgione, often painted unusual subjects. Other attributions have been suggested to Ortolano or his circle, or Moretto. The exotic sitter has also been described as a young woman.

John Downman
(1750 – 1824)

Portrait of a Lady seated under a Tree

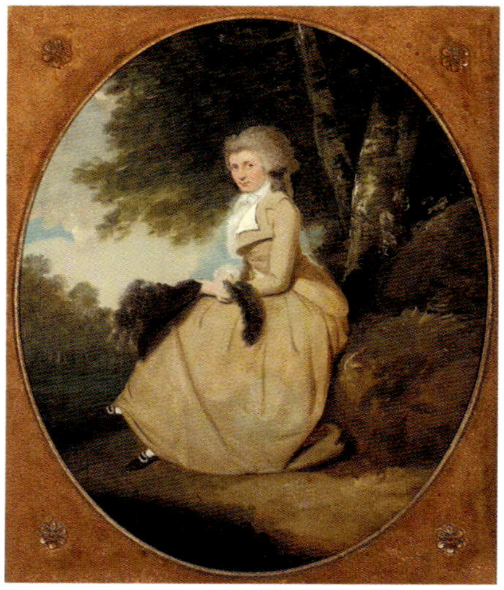

A1029a; oil on canvas, 71 × 58 cm
Bequeathed by Dr Eric George Millar in memory of his mother, Mrs Edith Millar, 1966; WA1966.87.1

The oval format is characteristic of Downman's portraits in oils.

John Downton
(1906 – 1991)

Frances Witts in Profile

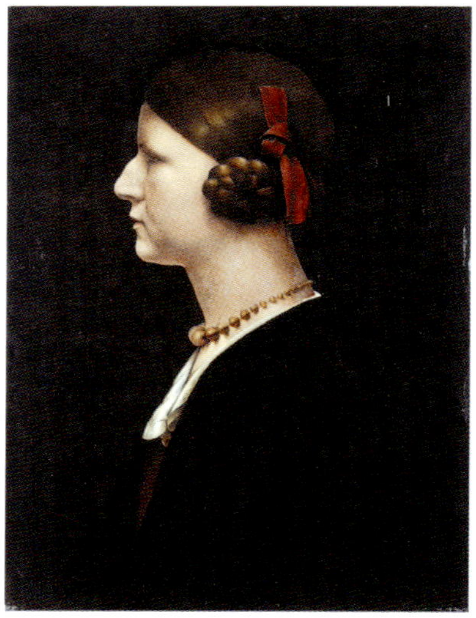

A1213; tempera on mahogany panel, 60.7 × 40.7 cm
Presented by The John Downton Trust, 1998; WA1998.83

Sheffield and elsewhere 1996–7, no. 83

Downton's cousin Frances Witts died of pneumonia in May 1935, at the age of twenty-six. Soon afterwards, Downton started painting portraits in her memory, using a photograph as his model. The composition is based on Ambrogio de Predis's so-called portrait of Beatrice d'Este. The technique and the neat manner of painting also relate directly to the Italian work.

John Downman
(1750 – 1824)

Mrs Thomas Pardoe

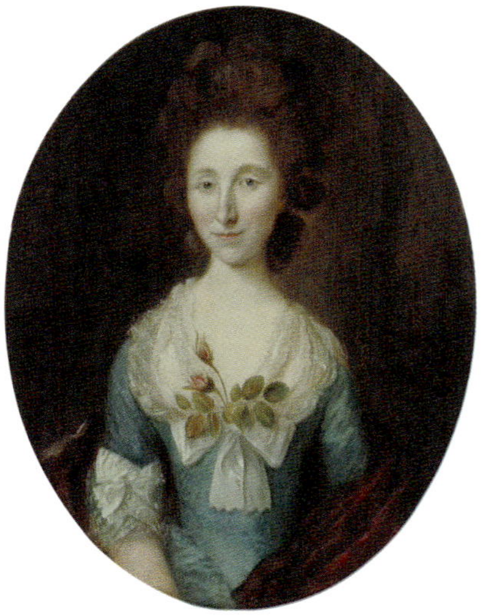

A993; oil on panel, 46 × 35 cm
Prov.: by descent to Mrs Ellis Morgan
Bequeathed by J. Reginald Jones, 1962; WA1962.35.2

Hester Bitterly (b. 1737) married Thomas Pardoe of Faintree (1731–1802), who served as High Sheriff of Shropshire in 1791. The portrait probably dates from *c.* 1780.

John Downman
(1750 – 1824)

Portrait of a Lady

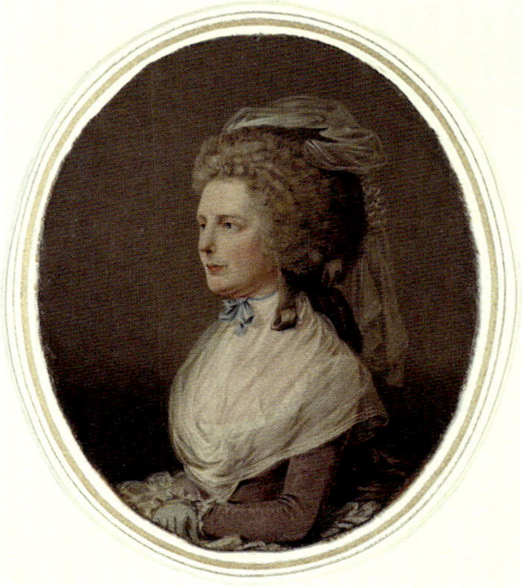

A1029b; oil on canvas, mounted as a drawing, 27.1 × 22.4 cm
Bequeathed by Dr Eric George Millar in memory of his mother, Mrs Edith Millar, 1966; WA1966.87.2

John Downton
(1906 – 1991)

Susan Saneon

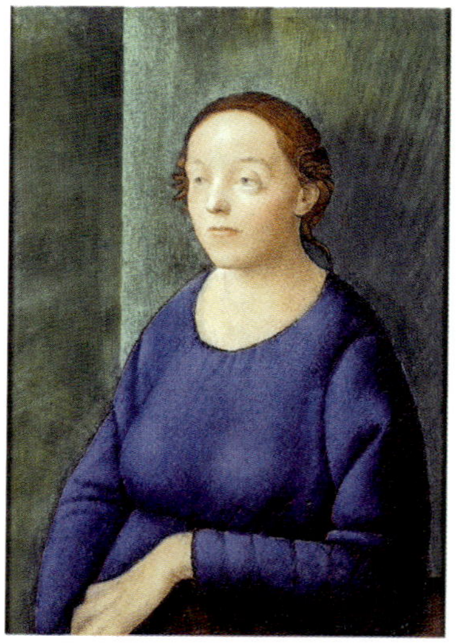

A1214; tempera on mahogany panel, 50.5 × 34.7 cm
Presented by The John Downton Trust, 1998; WA1998.84

Sheffield and elsewhere 1996–7, no. 128

The sitter remains unknown and the date unclear. It is thought that this painting dates from *c.* 1948. It appears to have been based, as Downton's pictures often are, on an earlier work of art. Here the specific painting he has used is difficult to identify, because the type is common among German portraits of the early 16th century, as well as in the work of Dod Proctor, who painted similar portraits in the 1930s.

Willem Drost
(*c.* 1630 – after 1680)

Ruth and Naomi

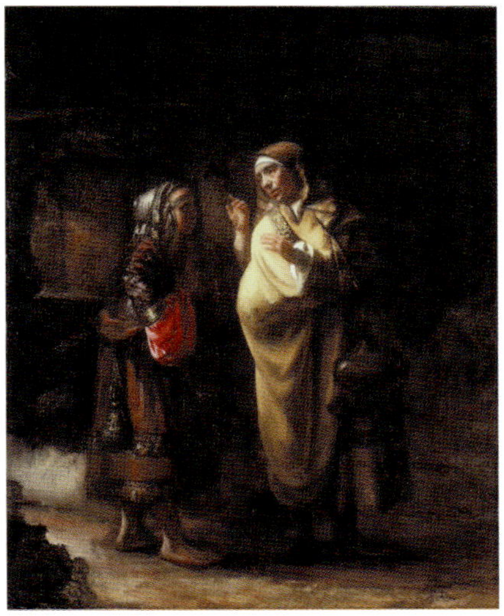

A390; oil on canvas, 89 × 71 cm
Prov.: C.D.T. Crews; A.H. Buttery; F.H. Schiller; Bamford
Presented by Mrs W.F.R. Weldon, 1929; WA1929.1

White 1999, p. 33

The subject illustrates the moment when Ruth declares her determination to accompany her mother-in-law, Naomi, back to Judah instead of remaining in her native Moabite country. The subject, taken from the Book of Ruth, was popular in Rembrandt's circle and Rembrandt's influence is evident in this painting. From the evidence of a preparatory drawing in Bremen, it seems likely that part of the canvas has been cut off on the right.

Guillam Dubois
(*c.* 1610 – 1680)

Wooded landscape: Figures by a Ford

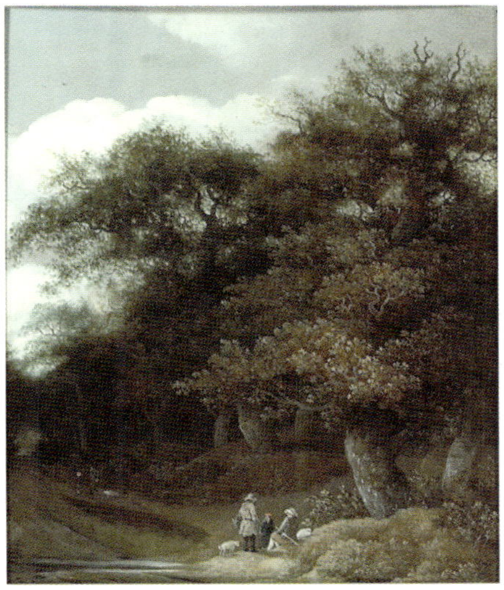

A280; oil on panel, 59.8 × 49.2 cm
Presented by Thomas Humphry Ward, 1897; WA1897.3

White 1999, p. 36

Dubois, like several other landscape painters working in Haarlem in the middle of the 17th century, was influenced by Jacob van Ruisdael. By comparison with a *Woodland Landscape*, signed and dated 1649 in the Herzog Anton Ulrich-Museum, Brunswick, this painting has been dated *c.* 1650.

Gaspard Dughet
(1615 – 1675)

View of Tivoli with Rome in the distance

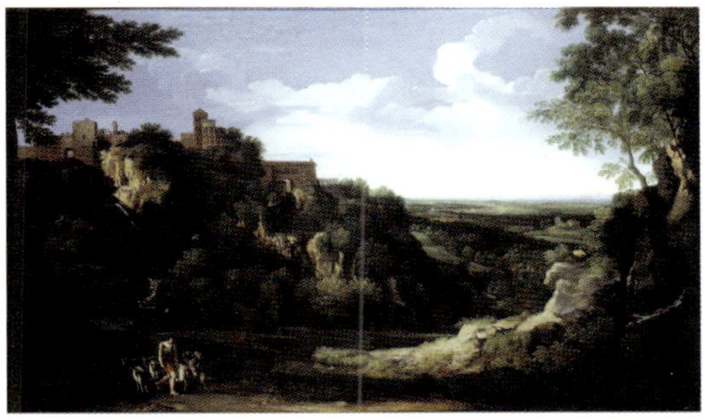

A295; oil on canvas, 76 × 126 cm
Bequeathed by John. D. Chambers, 1897; WA1897.15

Boisclair 1986, no. 186

The view is from the bank of the Anio and the Temple of Vesta (known as the Temple of the Sibyl) is amongst the buildings on the upper left; the Campagna recedes into the distance on the right, with the dome of St Peter's marking the city of Rome on the horizon. A brother-in-law and pupil of Nicolas Poussin, Dughet specialised in classical landscapes, which were particularly popular with English artists and collectors. The cool, clear tonality and high finish are characteristic of his work in the late 1650s.

Malcolm Drummond
(1880 – 1945)

A Chelsea Street

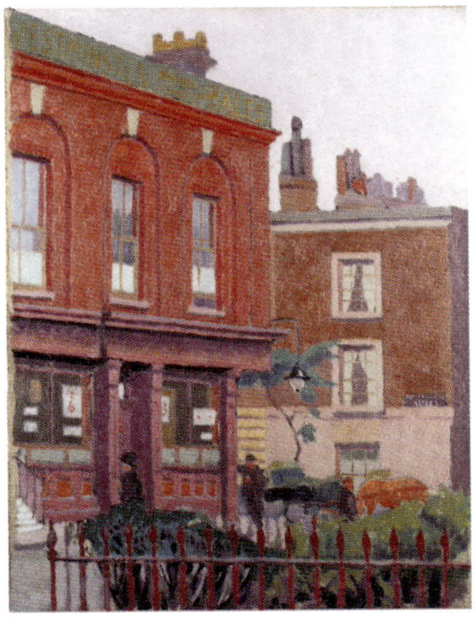

A899; oil on canvas, 60 × 45 cm
Presented by R.A. Bevan, 1957; WA1957.15

Baron 1979, p. 365; London 1988, no. 117

Drummond lived in Chelsea and frequently depicted the banality of his surroundings. Here, the subject is a corner shop. The use of railings in the foreground was a favourite compositional device of the Camden Town artists. There is a squared up drawing for this painting in the Ashmolean.

Attributed to Jacob Duck
(*c.* 1600 – 1667)

Merry Company in an Interior

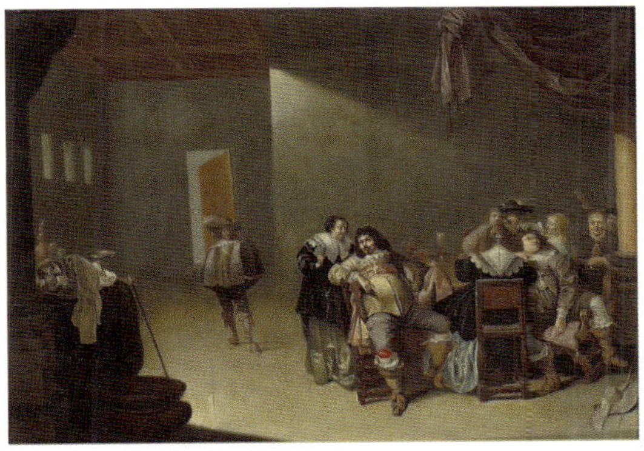

A992; oil on panel, 60 × 83 cm
Bequeathed by J. Reginald Jones, 1962; WA1962.35.1

White 1999, p. 37

Several elements in this painting correspond exactly to details of a painting by Jacob Duck in the Museum of Fine Art in Leipzig. This composition is either a variant by Duck or a painting by another artist based on his work. Jacob Duck worked mainly in Utrecht but spent shorter periods in Haarlem and in The Hague.

Gaspard Dughet
(1615 – 1675)

Landscape in the Roman Campagna

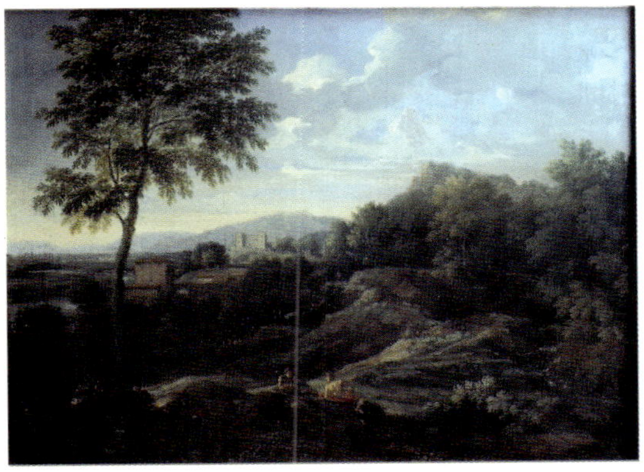

Oil on canvas, 50.7 × 67.4 cm
Prov.: Col R. Goff; Tomás Harris; George Pinney, Haywards Heath, Sussex
Mahon loan, 1999; WA.L.99.13

Boisclain 1986, no. 219; Finaldi and Kitson 1997, no. 23

It is difficult to date Dughet's works and this attractively-lit view is close stylistically to a landscape at Christ Church, Oxford, which may date from the early 1660s. The landscape is based on the countryside around Tivoli, with some narrative detail and classical context provided by the two figures in conversation in the foreground.

Karel Du Jardin
(1622 – 1678)

Farmyard with Animals

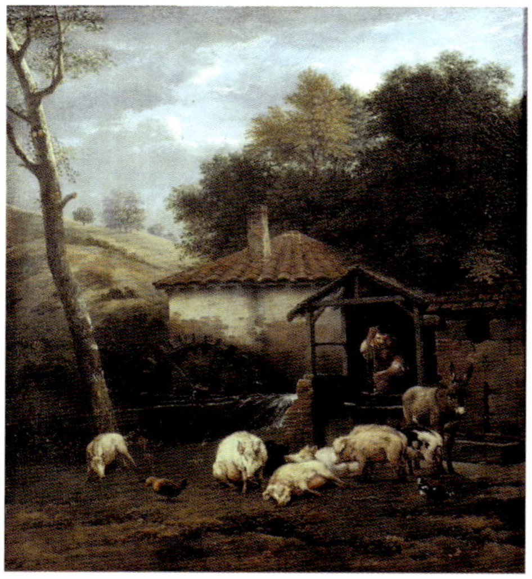

A665; oil on canvas, 45 × 40 cm
Signed: *K DV JARDIN*
Prov.: Leendert de Neufville; Niewenhoven; (?)Oudermoole; Bicker; Teengs; Gruyter, Alexander Baring; by descent to Lady Ashburton; Alfred de Rothschild; Countess of Carnarvon
Presented by T.W.H. Ward, 1940; WA1940.20

White 1999, p. 68

Du Jardin was principally a painter and etcher of landscapes but dealt with a wide range of subjects. By comparison with other paintings, this farmyard scene has been dated to the second half of the 1650s when he was living first in Amsterdam and then in The Hague.

Alfred Gainsborough Dupont
(1754 – 1797)

The Miser

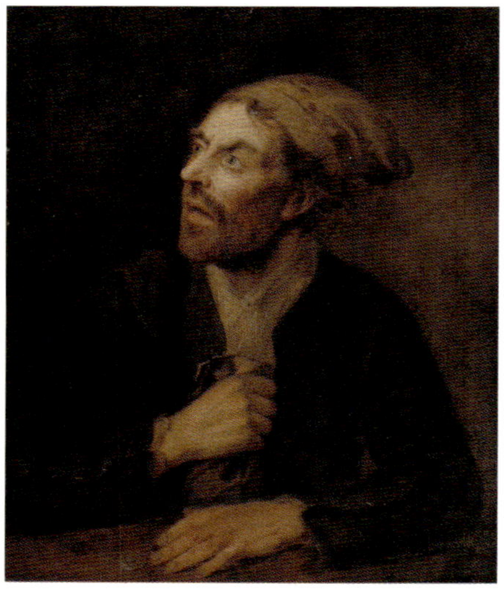

A392; oil on canvas, 75 × 63 cm
Presented by Mrs W.F.R. Weldon, 1929; WA1929.3

Waterhouse 1946, p. 40

Like his uncle, Thomas Gainsborough, Dupont specialised in portraits and landscapes, but also painted 'fancy pictures'. The figure of the miser had always been a stock character in literature, but was rarely represented in art before the 17th century. Dupont's boldly painted figure clutching his bag of gold coins probably dates from *c.* 1780. There is a second version of the painting in Hereford Art Gallery.

Anonymous Dutch Artist
(mid-17th century)

Portrait of a Man in a large black Hat

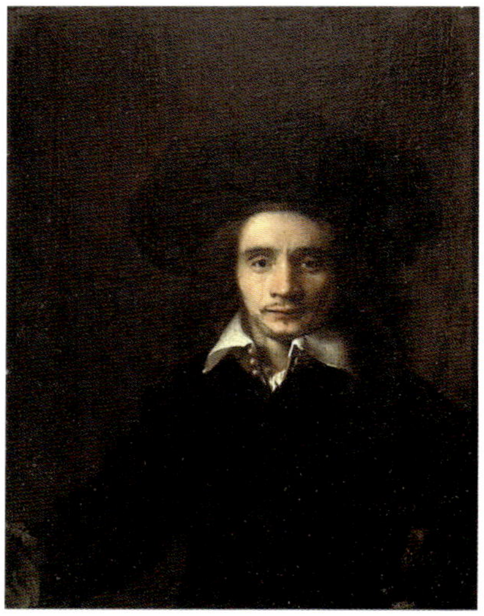

A891; oil on panel, 33 × 25 cm
Bequeathed by Percy Moore Turner, 1951; WA1957.59.3

White 1999, p. 175

Probably painted in the mid-17th century by a follower of Rembrandt.

Style of Karel Du Jardin
(1622 – 1678)

Portrait of a young Man

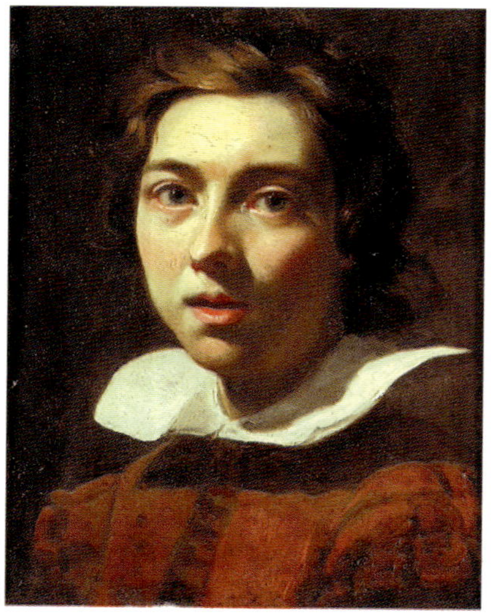

A974; oil on copper, 14 × 10 cm
Madan Bequest, 1962; WA1962.17.16

White 1999, p. 69

While there are similarities between this portrait and a self-portrait by Du Jardin, dated 1662, in the Rijksmuseum, Amsterdam, the difference in quality between the two suggests that this is no more than a work in his style by another artist.

François-Joseph Dupressoir
(1800 – 1859)

Landscape: Extensive View over a Vale

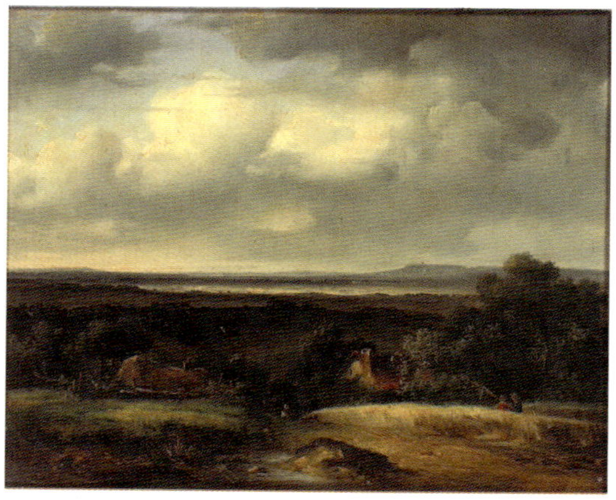

A763; oil on canvas, 46 × 56 cm
Signed and dated: *Dupressoir 1828*
Prov.: Charles Moyon
Presented by Mrs H.E. Berthon, 1948; WA1948.101

Dupressoir belonged to a group of French landscape artists who imitated the work of Constable and Bonington in the 1820s. The influence of English art in this panoramic rustic view is striking. The viewpoint, the overcast effect and sketchy brushwork recall the work of Paul Huet, which was also marked by English sources in this period.

Anonymous Dutch Artist
(*c.* 1690)

Adriaan Beverland

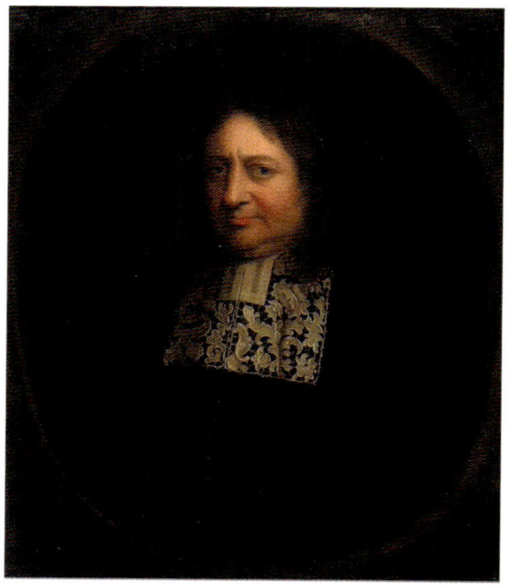

F643b; oil on canvas, 79 × 63 cm
Possibly presented by the sitter; WA1908.225

The gift of a portrait of Beverland to the Ashmolean by the sitter is recorded in 1692 but this may have been a miniature. Comparison with a contemporary portrait print of Beverland, however, suggests that the sitter has been correctly identified. Dr Adriaan Beverland (1650–1712) was a Dutch lawyer and free-thinker. He was in Leiden from 1673 to 1677 and then in Utrecht.

Anonymous Dutch Artist
(early 17th century)

The Prodigal Son returning to his Father

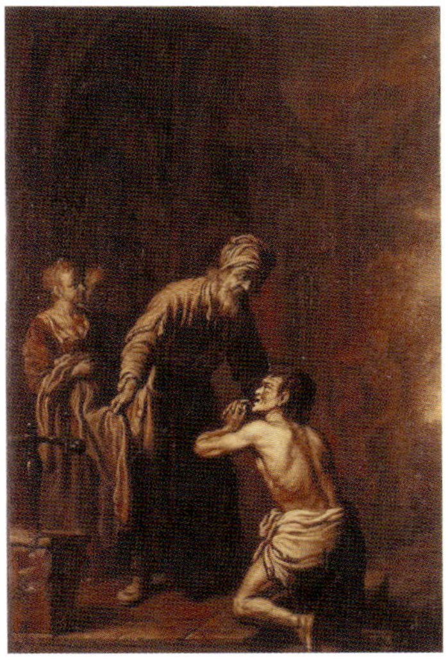

Monochrome oil pigment on paper, mounted as a drawing, 31.9 × 20.7 cm
Bequeathed by Francis Douce, 1834; WA1863.262

Parker 1938, no. 150

Formerly attributed to Pieter Lastman, Rembrandt's master. Apart from the difficulty in finding any preparatory oil-sketches of this kind in Lastman's work, the manner of painting is not his.

Anonymous Dutch Artist
(17th century)

Head of a Woman

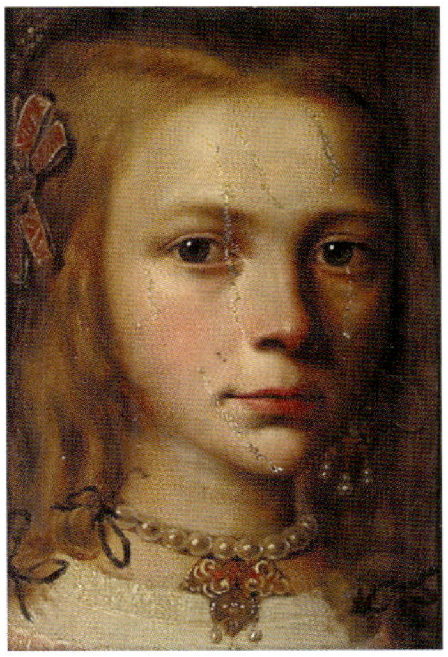

A1092; oil on canvas, 24.5 × 16 cm
Prov.: F. Wellesley
Presented by Gerald Reitlinger, 1972; WA1978.33

White 1999, p. 20

The head has been cut from a larger canvas, possibly from a group portrait. There are some similarities with the work of Jan de Bray (*c.* 1627–1697) to whom this painting was at one time attributed.

Anonymous Dutch Artist
(third quarter of 17th century)

Still Life with a Herring

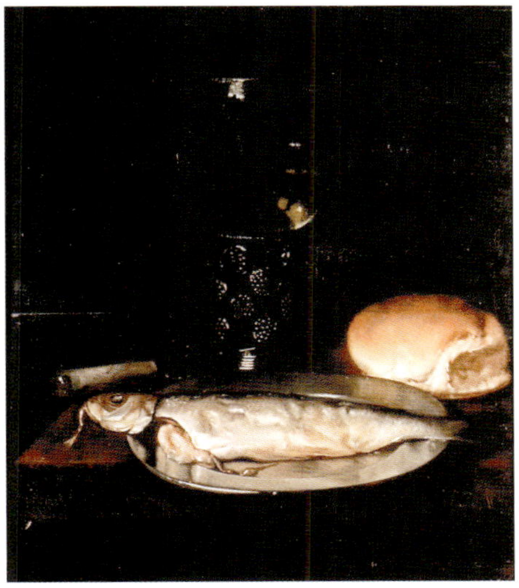

A579; oil on panel, 44 × 39 cm
Daisy Linda Ward Bequest, 1939; WA1940.2.55

Meijer 2003, no. 94

Most of the still-life paintings which were once attributed to Gabriel Metsu, including this painting of herrings, are no longer thought to be by him. No convincing attribution has been found but there are certain similarities with the work of Amsterdam artists like Metsu or Simon Luttichuys.

Anonymous Dutch Artist
(17th century)

A Moonlit Landscape

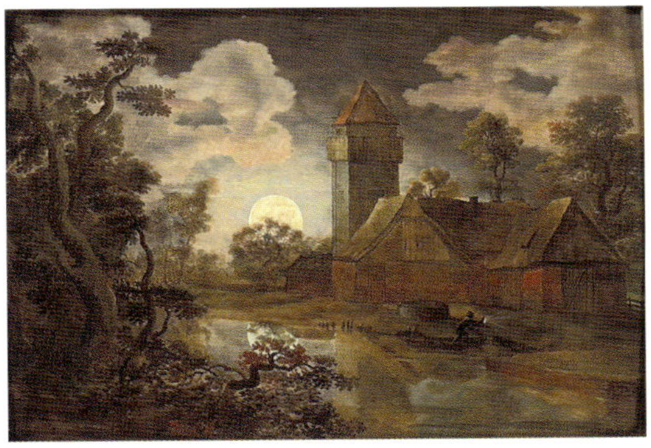

A168; oil on panel, 53 × 76 cm
Chambers Hall Gift, 1855; WA1855.165

White 1999, p. 189

This atmospheric landscape was at one time attributed to Rubens. The night effect may owe something to the landscapes of the German artist, Adam Elsheimer (1578–1610), whose paintings were widely popularised by the Utrecht engraver Hendrik Goudt.

Anonymous Dutch Artist
(mid-17th century?)

Portrait of a young Man

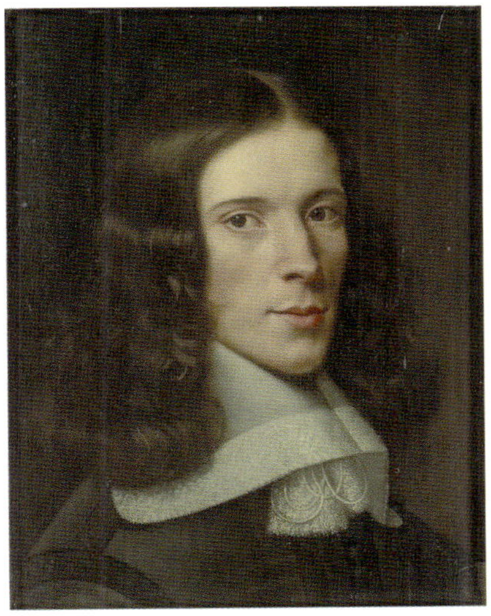

A674; oil on panel, 49 × 38 cm
Bequeathed by Sir Arthur Evans, 1941; WA1941.7

White 1999, p. 174

This appears to be the work of a mid- 17th-century Dutch artist. It is of indifferent quality and in poor condition.

Anonymous Dutch Artist
(19th century)

Winter Landscape with a Town or Village in the Distance

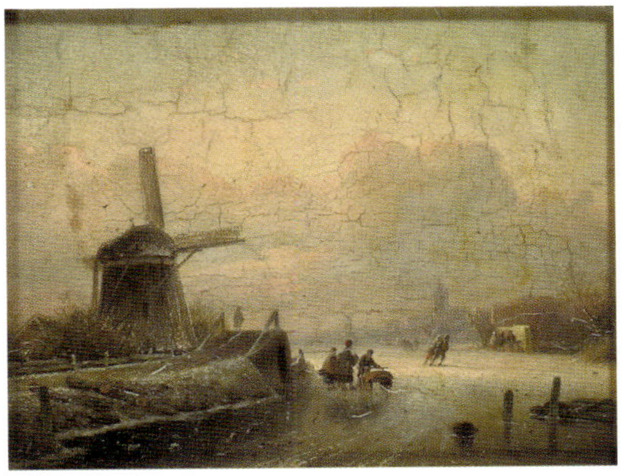

A235; oil on panel, 25 × 31 cm
Bequeathed by Mrs Wingfield of Kettel Hall, 1870; WA1870.1

White 1999, p. 176

A label formerly on the back mentions a sale of 1 July 1852 and identifies the artist as Theunissen. No such artist is recorded for this period but he may have had a family connection with Charles Theunissen, a painter from Liege, born in 1871.

Sir Anthony van Dyck
(1599 – 1641)

The Deposition

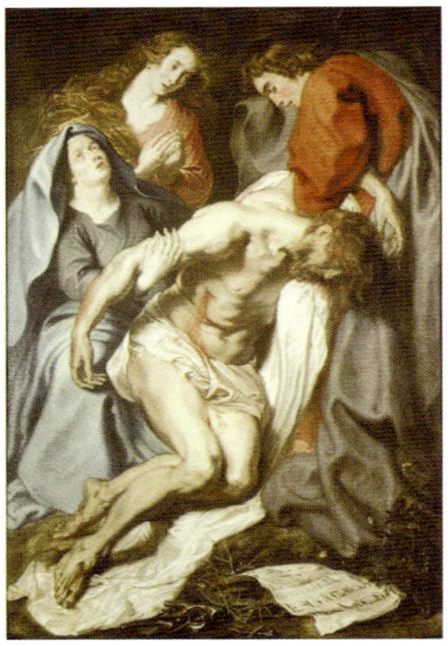

A232; oil on canvas, 207 × 137 cm
Prov.: P. Panné; Emerson
Presented by Charles T. Maude, 1869; WA1869.1

White 1999, p. 41

The composition is a reworking of an earlier painting of the *Deposition* by van Dyck (now in the Alte Pinakothek, Munich) which has been dated *c.* 1615. This painting is generally dated *c.* 1619 at about the time when he was working as an assistant to Rubens in Antwerp.

Sir Anthony van Dyck
(1599 – 1641)

Head of a bearded Man wearing a Falling Ruff

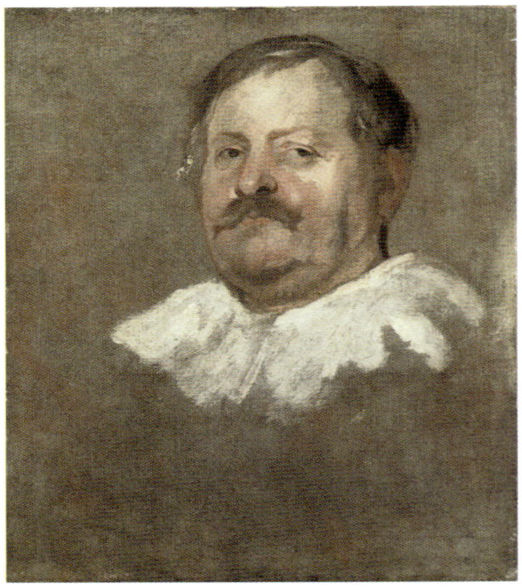

A176; oil on canvas, 52 × 46 cm
Chambers Hall Gift, 1855; WA1855.173

White 1999, p. 38

Sir Anthony van Dyck
(1599 – 1641)

Head of a bearded Man wearing a Wheel Ruff

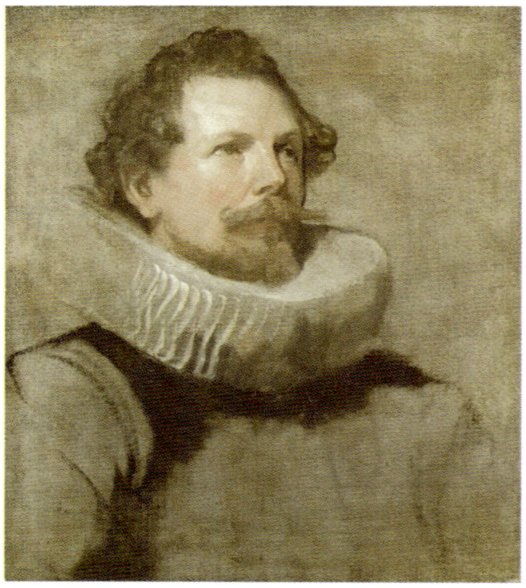

A175; oil on canvas, 52 × 46 cm
Chambers Hall Gift, 1855; WA1855.172

White 1999, p. 38

This sketch and the following are preparatory studies for two of the life-size figures in the large group portrait of the Aldermen of Brussels painted for the Town Hall in Brussels in 1634–5 and destroyed in the French bombardment in 1695.

Sir Anthony van Dyck
(1599 – 1641)

Charles I and the Knights of the Garter in Procession

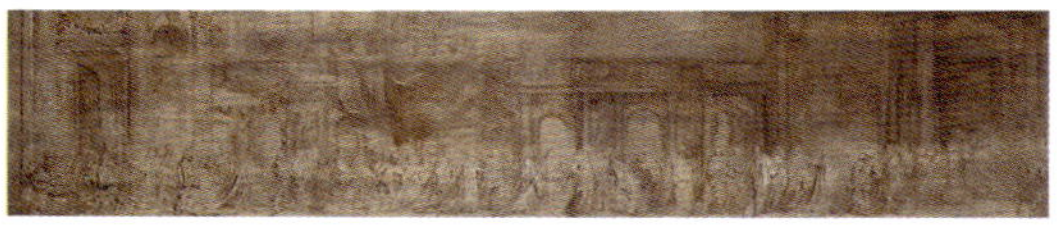

A1247; oil over silverpoint on panel, 29.2 × 130.8 cm
Prov.: Charles 1; Wagstaffe; Sir Peter Lely; Austin; Robert Henley; acquired by Sir Joshua Reynolds for the Duke of Rutland
Accepted by H.M. Government in lieu of Inheritance Tax from the estate of the 10th Duke of Rutland and allocated to the Ashmolean Museum, 2002; WA2002.55

This large, lightly painted oil-sketch was painted in about 1638 as a model for one of a set of tapestries to decorate the walls of the Banqueting Hall in Whitehall. It represents the procession of the Order of the Garter which took place annually on 23 April, the Feast of St George, and ended with a dinner in the Banqueting Hall. The Knights are followed by the officers, the Registrar, the Garter King of Arms and the Usher of the Black Rod; then the prelate, the chancellor and the sword. King Charles follows, carrying the orb and sceptre, walking beneath a canopy held by four attendants. There are over fifty figures in the procession. As the project for the tapestries was not taken any further, this sketch provides important evidence of what van Dyck intended. It was retained by the king and was sold for £5 in the sale of the Royal Collection in 1650.

Style of Sir Anthony van Dyck
(1599 – 1641)

The Supper at Emmaus

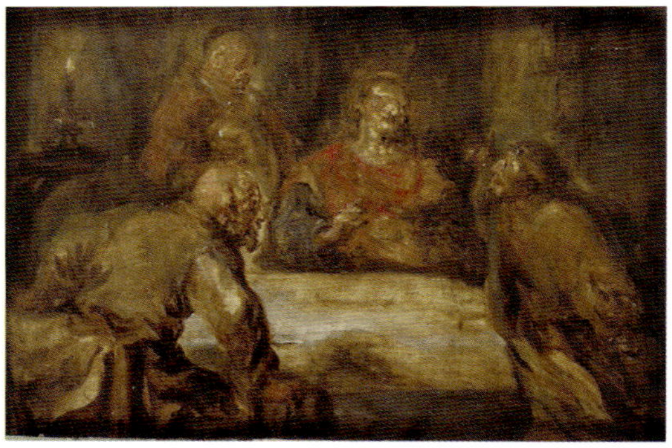

A173; oil on panel, 23 × 35 cm
Chambers Hall Gift, 1855; WA1855.225

White 1999, p. 43

Painted by an imitator of van Dyck, perhaps in the 18th century. The subject shows Christ, seated between St Peter on the right and Cleophas on the left, revealing himself to his disciples after his Resurrection (Luke 24: 13–32).

Copy after Sir Anthony van Dyck
(1599 – 1641)

Head of a Black Man

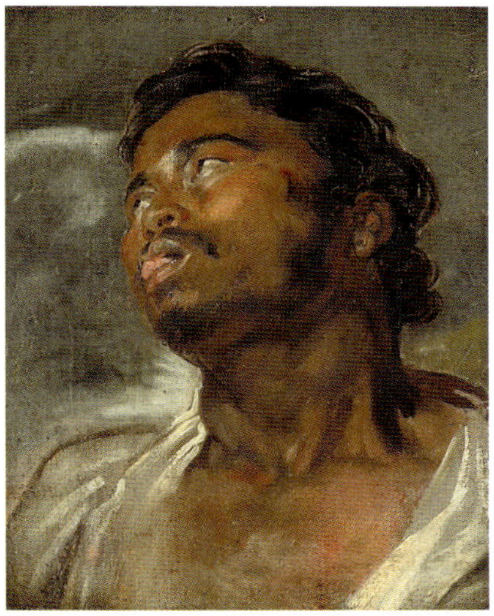

A177; oil on canvas, 47 × 37 cm
Chambers Hall Gift, 1855; WA1855.190

White 1999, p. 44

Connected with the head of a black man in the background of van Dyck's *Drunken Silenus* in the Gemäldegalerie, Dresden, but no more than a coarse copy or pastiche.

Copy after Sir Anthony van Dyck
(1599 – 1641)

St Augustine in Ecstasy

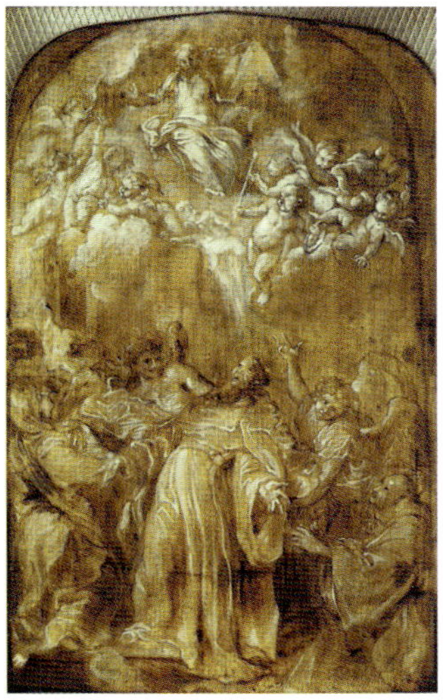

A172; oil on panel, 44 × 28 cm
Chambers Hall Gift, 1855; WA1855.228

White 1999, p. 45

Copied from a sketch in the Museum of Fine Arts, Antwerp, which van Dyck painted as the model for a large altar painting for the church of St Augustine in Antwerp.

Copy after Sir Anthony van Dyck
(1599 – 1641)

Charles I

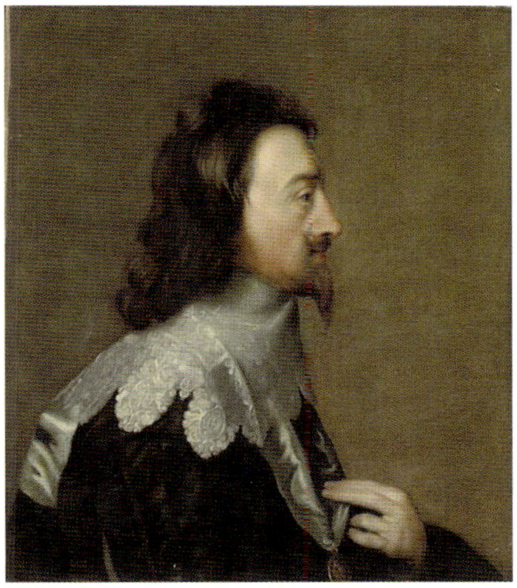

F670; oil on canvas, 75 × 63 cm
Presented by Elias Ashmole, 1683; WA1898.38

Poole 1912, no. 419; MacGregor 1983, no. 268

This painting is derived from the portrait on the left in the celebrated triple portrait by van Dyck in the Royal Collection. It has been suggested that, like the other copies after van Dyck in the Founder's Collection, it may have painted by Emanuel de Critz.

Copy after Sir Anthony van Dyck
(1599 – 1641)

Head of the Virgin mourning

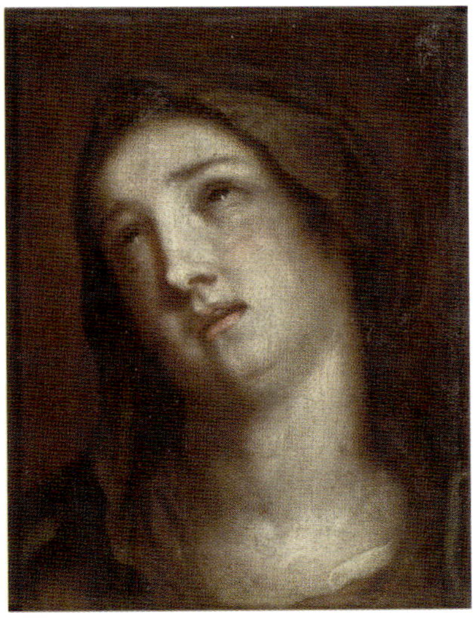

A179; oil on canvas, 37 × 28 cm
Chambers Hall Gift, 1855; WA1855.571

White 1999, p. 44

Possibly copied from the head of the Virgin in a composition of the Virgin and Child by van Dyck, known in several versions. As the head is in reverse direction to the paintings, the copyist's source may have been a print.

Copy after Sir Anthony van Dyck
(1599 – 1641)

Allegory of Charity

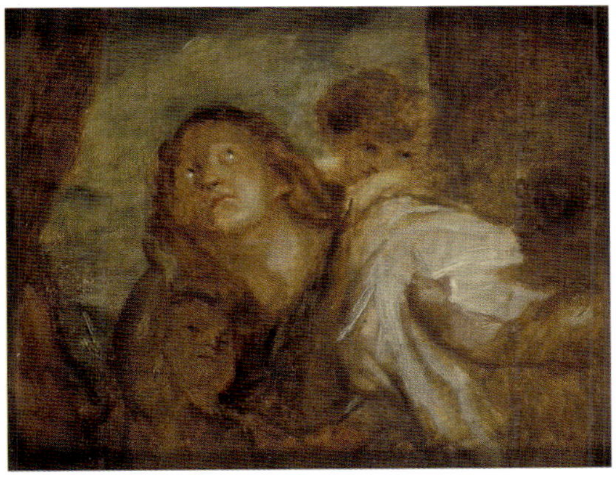

A174; oil on panel, 21 × 24 cm
Prov.: Sir Joshua Reynolds; Sir George Hayter
Chambers Hall Gift, 1855; WA1855.180

White 1999, p. 47

The subject relates to the central part of a lost painting by van Dyck, probably executed in Italy between 1622 and 1627. It has been suggested that the copyist might have been Sir Joshua Reynolds, who once owned this sketch.

Copy after Sir Anthony van Dyck
(1599 – 1641)

Thomas Howard, Second Earl of Arundel

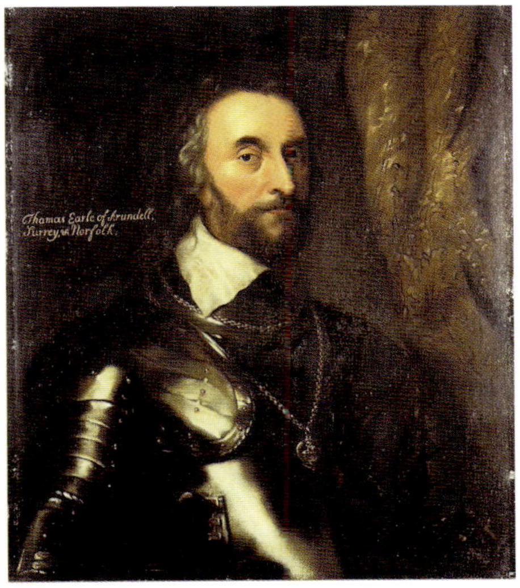

F668; oil on canvas, 78 × 68 cm
Inscribed: *Thomas Earle of Arundell, / Surrey, & Norfolk*
Presented by Elias Ashmole, 1683; WA1898.32

Poole 1912, no. 418; MacGregor 1983, no. 266

This is copied from one half of the painting of 1635–6 at Arundel Castle. See also the following.

Copy after Sir Anthony van Dyck
(1599 – 1641)

Thomas Howard, later Fifth Duke of Norfolk, when a Boy

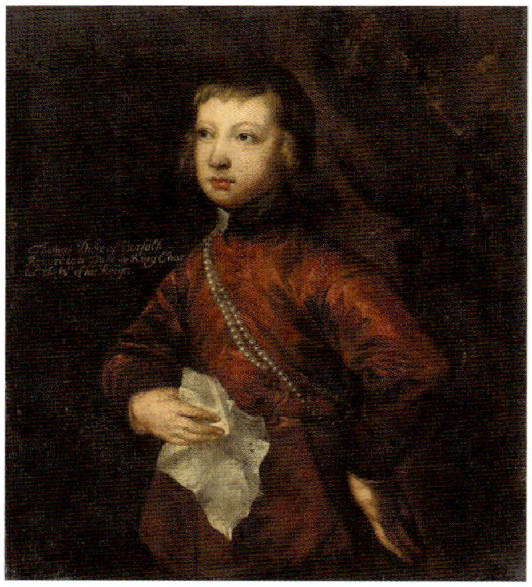

F669; oil on canvas, 79 × 69 cm
Inscribed: *Thomas Duke of Norfolkl, / Restord to be Duke, by King Char / les 2d, the 13th of his Reign*
Presented by Elias Ashmole, 1683; WA1898.33

Poole 1912, no. 438; MacGregor 1983, no. 267

Thomas Howard (1627–1677), eldest grandson of the second Earl of Arundel, spent the last decades of his life in Italy. This is copied from the other half of the painting of 1635–6 at Arundel Castle.

Chester Earles
(1821 – 1905)

Isabella

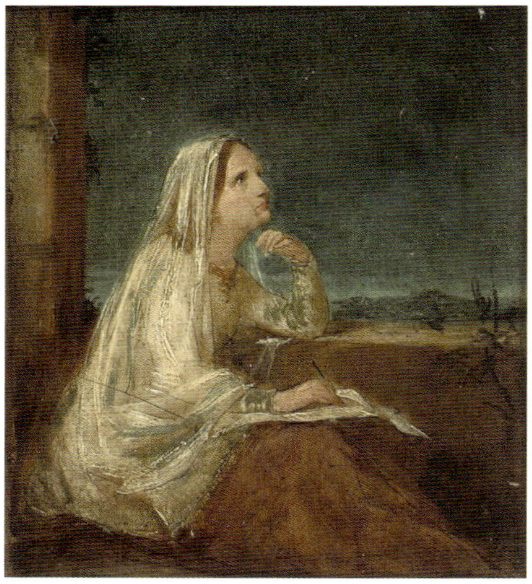

A933; oil on millboard, 21 × 18 cm
Dated: *12 Nov. 1852*; and inscribed:
She weeps alone for pleasures not to be; / Sorely she wept until the night came on, / And then, instead of love, O misery! / She brooded o'er the luxury alone: Keats
Presented by R.E. Alton, M.C., 1960; WA1960.6

This is a study for the painting exhibited at the Royal Academy in 1853 (untraced). The subject, taken from Keats's 'Isabella; or, The Pot of Basil', had already inspired a celebrated painting by Millais (R.A. 1849; Liverpool, Walker Art Gallery).

Augustus Leopold Egg
(1816 – 1863)

Outward Bound

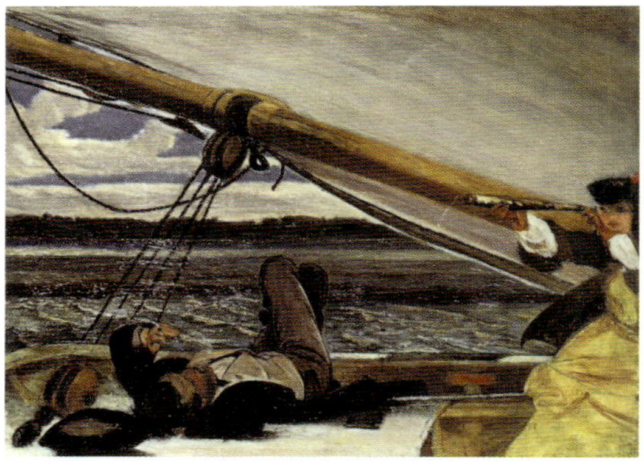

A689; oil on millboard, mounted as a drawing, 17.3 × 23.5 cm
Prov.: R.B. Martineau and by descent
Purchased, 1941; WA1941.158

Cummings and Staley 1968, no. 201

A small and sketchy picture which was apparently not developed into a full-size canvas. It was presumably painted in England before Egg left on his final travels on the Continent.

John Eagles
(1783 – 1855)

Landscape with Pan and the Nymphs

A225; oil on canvas, rolled, 125 × 173 cm
Prov.: John Kenyon
Presented by Miss Zoe King, 1857; WA1857.5

Eagles was an amateur painter who exhibited a varied range of subjects at the Royal Academy and British Institution from 1808 to 1852. According to the donor, this mythological scene was 'painted for his friend, John Kenyon'.

Gerbrand van den Eeckhout
(1621 – 1674)

The Infant Samuel brought by Hanna to Eli

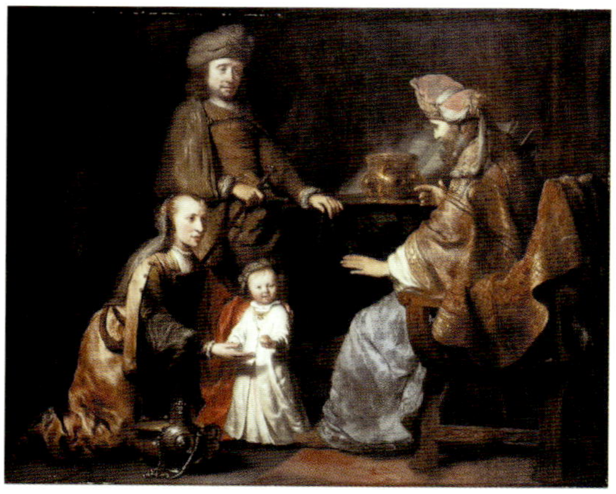

A714; oil on canvas, 110.8 × 137 cm
Presented by Sir George Leon, 1945; WA1945.73

White 1999, p. 48

The subject, illustrating a text in the Old Testament (I Samuel 1: 24–5), shows the moment when the infant Samuel is presented to the high priest by his parents so that he might serve in the Temple. Eeckhout appears to have been a pupil of Rembrandt in the later 1630s. This painting has been dated to the early 1660s, several years before Eeckhout painted a second version of this theme, now in the Louvre.

Augustus Leopold Egg
(1816 – 1863)

Desdemona

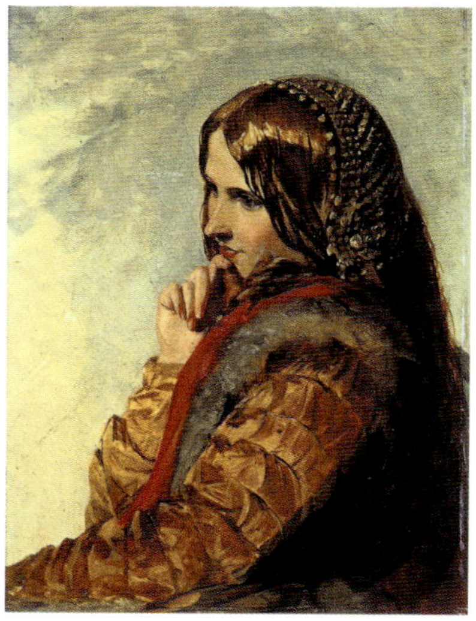

A697; oil on board, mounted as a drawing, 24.5 × 18.2 cm
Presented by the Leicester Galleries, 1942; WA1942.56

Throughout his career, Egg was concerned with literary and historical subjects. This study of Desdemona, heroine of Shakespeare's *Othello*, is one of a series of six half-length portraits of Shakespearian heroines, all apparently painted from the same model and engraved.

Augustus Leopold Egg
(1816 – 1863)

Preparatory Study for 'The Travelling Companions'

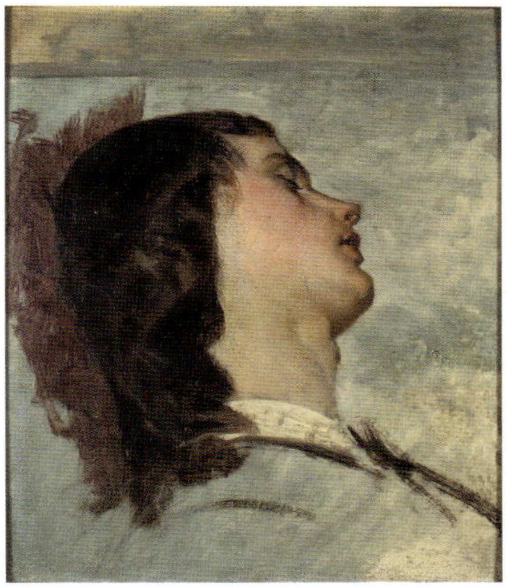

A1168; oil on panel, 19.5 × 16.2 cm
Prov.: James Coats, New York
Bequeathed by Rosalie, Lady Mander, 1988; WA1988.361

A study for the figure on the left of one of Egg's last works, *The Travelling Companions*, painted in 1862, which shows two sisters in a railway carriage on the outskirts of Mentone (City Museum and Art Gallery, Birmingham). Egg travelled to the Mediterranean for his asthma, but eventually died of it.

Pieter Janssens Elinga
(1623 – before 1682)

Still Life with Citrus Fruit

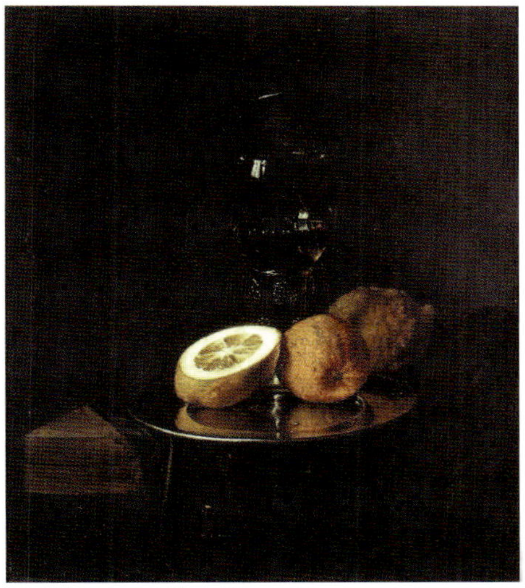

A562; oil on canvas, 55 × 47 cm
Daisy Linda Ward Bequest, 1939; WA1940.2.38

Meijer 2003, no. 39

Pieter Janssens Elinga's still-life paintings have been confused with the work of Willem Kalf. It is assumed that these paintings date from after his arrival in Amsterdam in 1653, the year in which Kalf also settled there. No dated works by Elinga have been found but this work and a group of similar works, one of which is in the Ferens Art Gallery in Hull, have been dated to the 1660s.

Hercules Enslin du Plessis
(1894 – 1978)

Cottage Garden

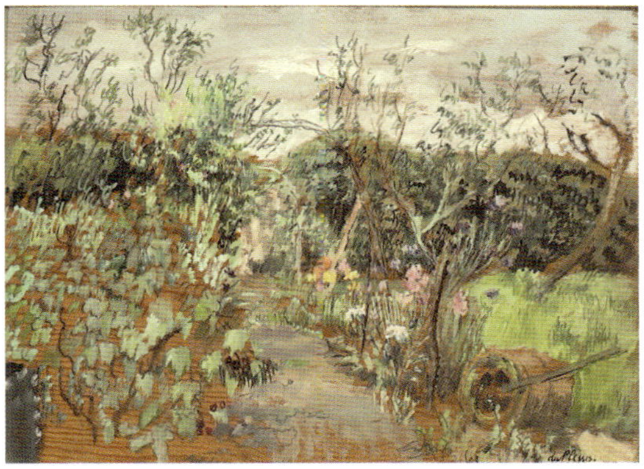

A752; oil on panel, 30 × 40 cm
Signed: *du Plessis.*
Presented by John Dodgson, 1948; WA1948.73

Born in South Africa, Enslin du Plessis became a journalist and self-taught artist before he settled in London shortly after the First World War. Although he is better known for his interior scenes he painted many landscapes.

Sir William Elford, Bt
(1747 – 1837)

A Landscape: The Approach of a Shower

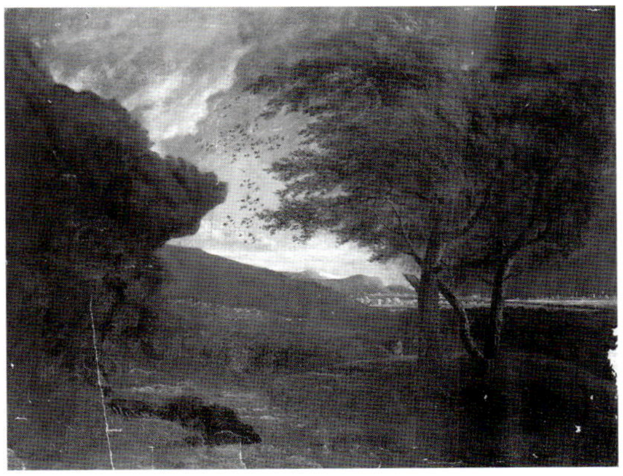

A48; oil on canvas, rolled, 86 × 111 cm
Presented by the artist, 1806; WA1845.48

Elford was a politician and amateur landscape painter who exhibited at the Royal Academy between 1774 and 1837, showing mostly views in his native Devonshire. This example was exhibited in 1801.

Ottmar Elliger
(1633 – 1679)

Still Life with Flowers

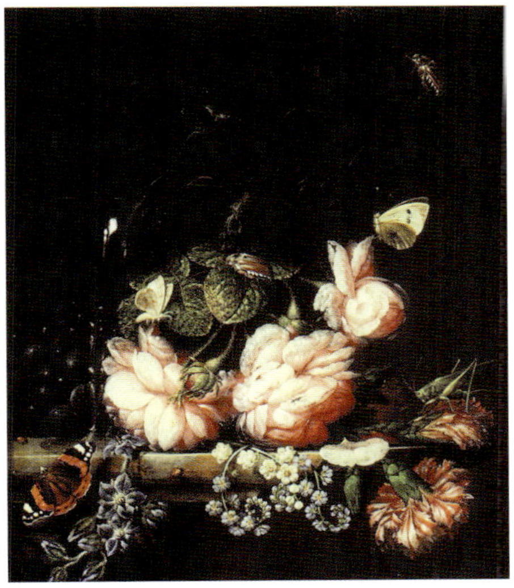

A549; oil on panel, 37 × 31 cm
Traces of an original signature and also of an added signature and date: ....*K / 16*[86?]
Daisy Linda Ward Bequest, 1939; WA1940.2.25

Meijer 2003, no. 29

Elliger seems to have spent his early days in Antwerp but his work from the period suggests he knew Jacob Marrel who was then working in Frankfurt. His still-life paintings are mostly of flowers and fruit. Comparison with dated works suggests that this arrangement of flowers dates from the period shortly after the artist had moved to Hamburg where he is first recorded in 1666.

Jacob Foppens van Es
(active *c.* 1616 – 1666)

Still Life with Oysters

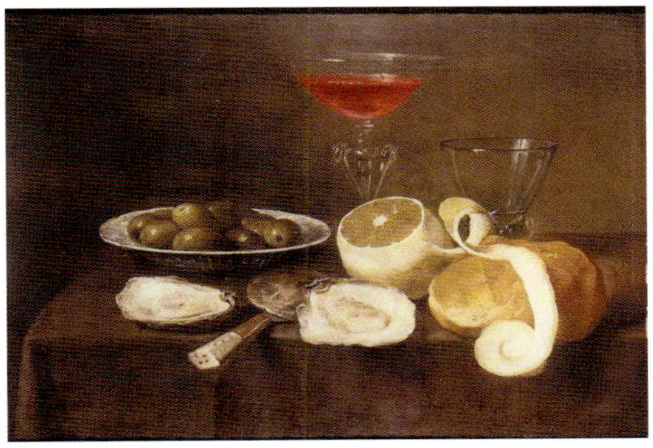

A550; oil on panel, 33 × 47 cm
Signed: ...*ESI*
Prov.: Edmonstone (?)
Daisy Linda Ward Bequest, 1939; WA1940.2.26

Meier 2003, no. 30

Van Es spent his entire life in Antwerp although he is said to have visited Rome in 1636. He seems to have worked exclusively as a painter of still life. Paintings of foodstuffs were his speciality. This shows a relatively modest meal with expensive accessories: a blue and white Wan-li porcelain plate from China, a Venetian-style drinking glass and an ivory-handled knife. The glass reappears in a number of van Es's paintings.

Jacob Esselens
(*c.* 1627 – 1687)

Lake Scene with a Fishing Party

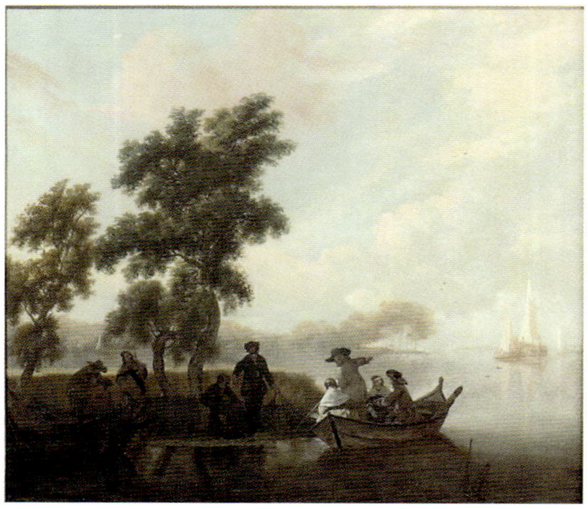

A279; oil on canvas, 59.1 × 67 cm
Prov.: William Angerstein; Eyre
Presented by Thomas Humphry Ward, 1897; WA1897.2

White 1999, p. 50

Esselens painted a number of similar scenes featuring elegant boaters mingling with fishermen. There are very similar figures in a painting signed by him in the Museum of Fine Art in Leipzig.

William Etty
(1787 – 1849)

The penitent Magdalen

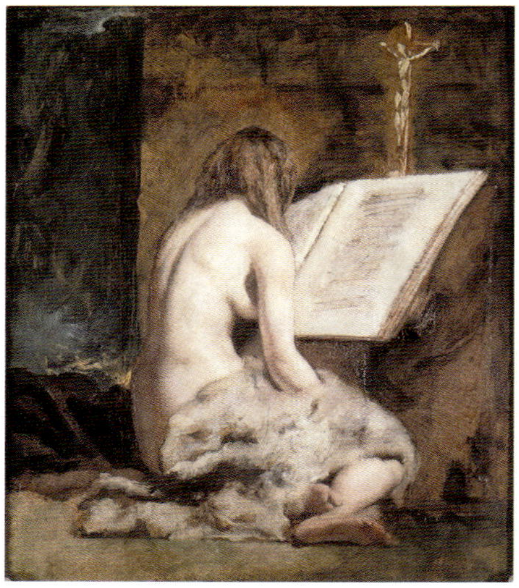

A422; oil on panel, 59 × 47 cm
Signed and dated: *W. Etty 1835*
Prov.: (?)C.W. Cass; William Wethered; Ernest J. Nathan; Mrs Bolton
Presented by Mrs W.F.R. Weldon, 1933; WA1933.4

Farr 1958, no. 30

Two other paintings of this subject by Etty are recorded.

William Etty
(1787 – 1849)

The Repentant Prodigal's Return to his Father

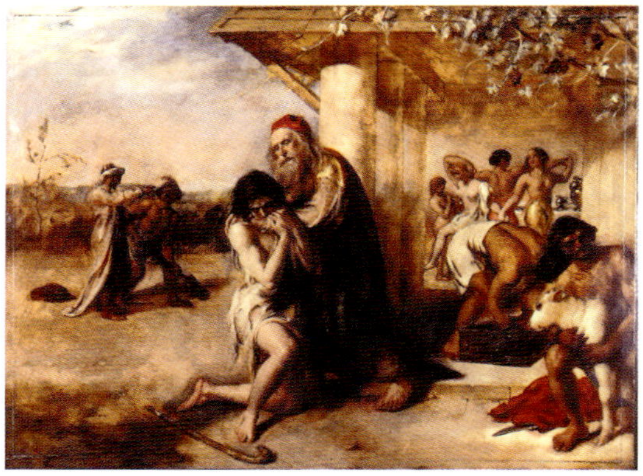

A458; oil on panel, 85 × 114 cm
Prov.: Lord Lansdowne; James Price
Weldon Bequest, 1937; WA1937.38

Farr 1958, no. 32

This painting was Etty's greatest success at the Royal Academy in 1841. It combines the homecoming of the prodigal son with the elder brother's return from the fields (Luke 15: 21). The central group was based on Murillo's *Return of the Prodigal* (1668; National Gallery of Art, Washington).

Frederick Etchells
(1886 – 1973)

On the Grass

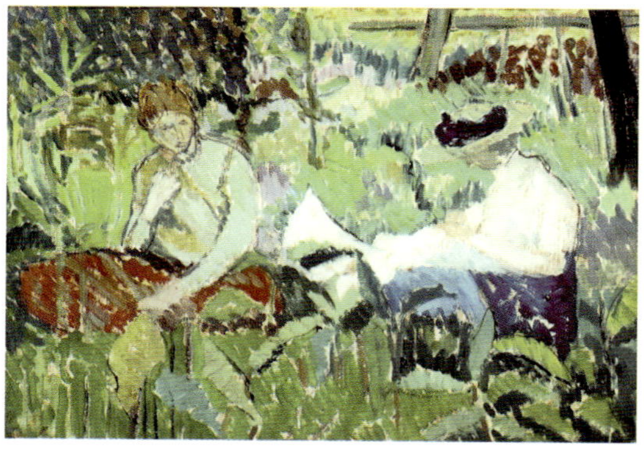

A730a; oil on panel, 35.9 × 50.6 cm
Prov.: Lord Henry Bentinck
Presented by the Contemporary Art Society, 1946; WA1946.376

Eustace 1999, no. 7

Etchells attended the Royal School of Art between 1908 and 1911 and was later one of the leading English modernist artists. Etchells himself described the picture as a sketch. It must date to *c.* 1911, probably from the time when he was finishing his studies. It shows the painter's sister, Jessie and a friend sitting in the garden of their house.

William Etty
(1787 – 1849)

Standing female Nude seen from behind

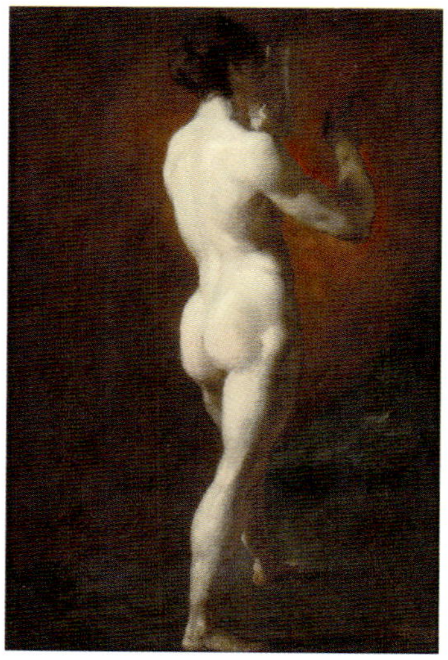

A692; oil on millboard, 55 × 37 cm
Bequeathed by Julian Gilbert Sampson, 1942; WA1942.16

Farr 1958, no. 220

This has been dated to *c.* 1835–40.

William Etty
(1787 – 1849)

Four Girls by a Stream

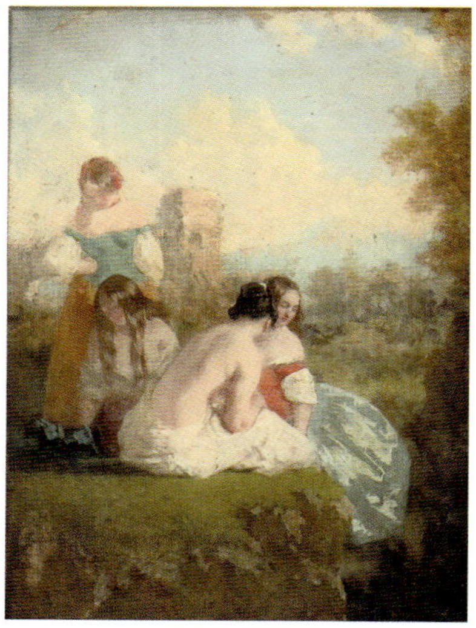

A971; oil on canvas, 43 × 31 cm
Madan Bequest, 1962; WA1962.17.13

Farr 1958, no. 255

William Etty
(1787 – 1849)

Nude Woman kneeling

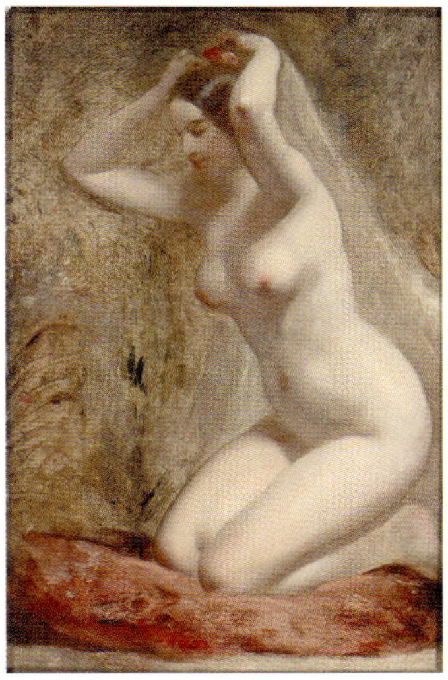

A1094; oil on board, 46.6 × 30 cm
Presented by Gerald Reitlinger, 1972; WA1978.35

William Etty
(1787 – 1849)

Venus, Cupid and Psyche

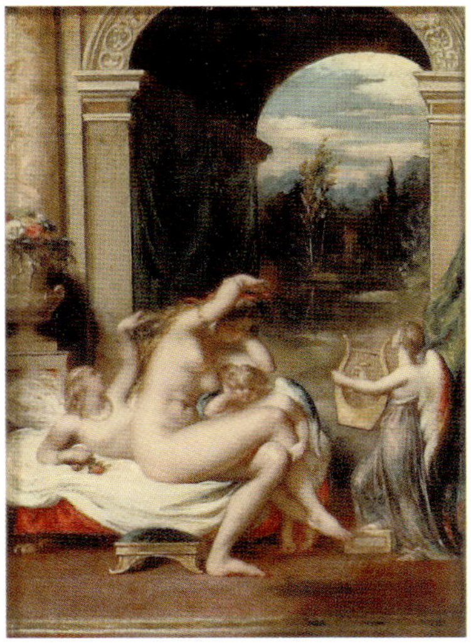

A502a; oil on canvas, 33 × 23 cm
Weldon Bequest, 1937; WA1937.82.2

Farr 1958, no. 101

One of many paintings on the theme of Venus by Etty.

Thomas Faed
(1826 – 1900)

A Peasant Family

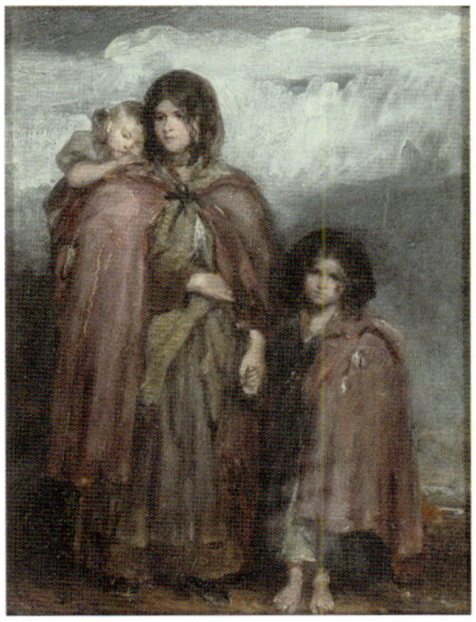

A517; oil on panel, 30 × 23 cm
Presented by Francis Falconer Madan, 1938; WA1938.3

McKerrow 1982, p. 99

Faed was deeply concerned by the continuing Highland clearances in his native Scotland, which left peasants and crofters unemployed and homeless. This painting probably depicts such a family, without a male breadwinner. Its sketchy quality may indicate that it was a study for a larger work.

William Etty
(1787 – 1849)

Nude Woman reclining

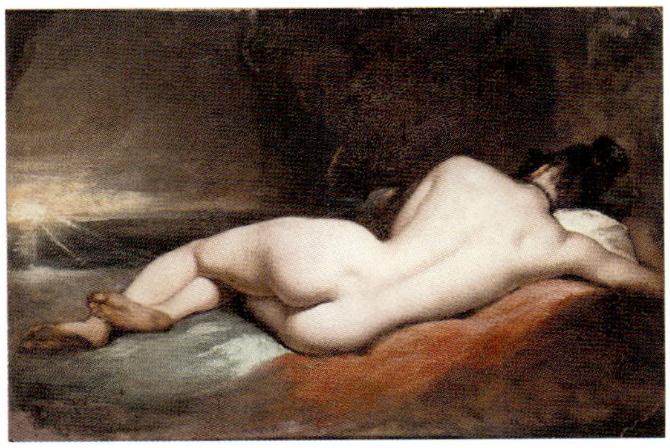

A497; oil on millboard, 37 × 55 cm
Weldon Bequest, 1937; WA1937.78

William Etty
(1787 – 1849)

Nude Woman kneeling

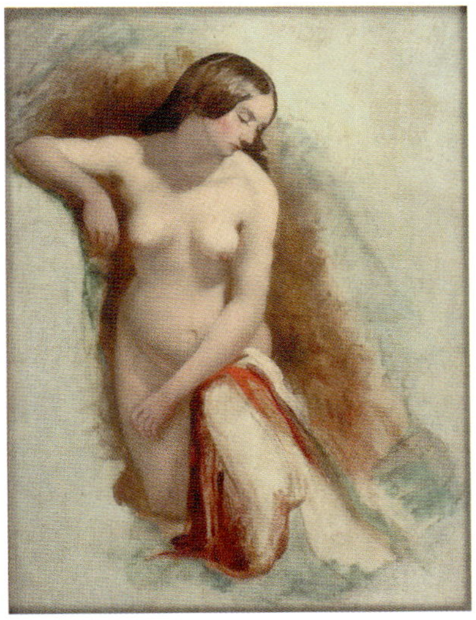

A917; oil on millboard, 34 × 26 cm
Russell Bequest, 1958; WA1958.57.6

Ignace-Henri-Jean-Théodore Fantin-Latour
(1836 – 1904)

A Basket of Plums

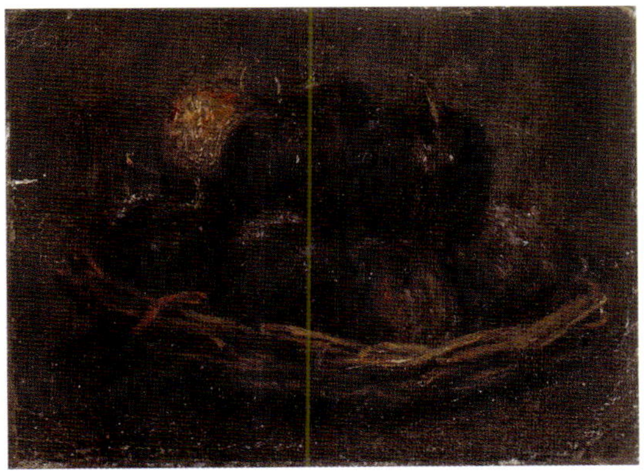

A461; oil on canvas, mounted as a drawing, 13.4 × 18 cm
Signed and dated: *Fantin 69*
Weldon Bequest, 1937; WA1937.41

Fantin-Latour specialised in portraits and flower pieces although, beginning in 1861, he also produced a series of paintings and lithographs on musical themes in an evocative style far removed from his carefully detailed paintings of still life. From the 1860s onwards, he painted studies of plums, of which this work of 1869 is one of the smallest and most informal.

Ignace-Henri-Jean-Théodore Fantin-Latour
(1836 – 1904)

Still Life: a yellow Rose

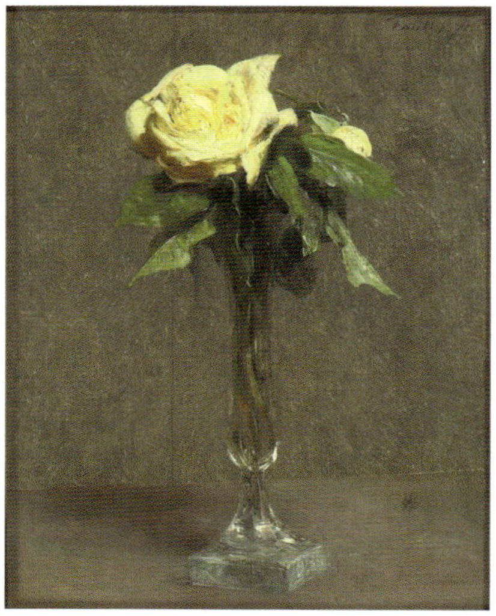

A463; oil on canvas, 30 × 24 cm
Signed and dated: *Fantin 71*
Prov.: given by the artist to Mrs Edwin Edwards
Weldon Bequest, 1937; WA1937.42

Fantin-Latour 1911, no. 545; Lucie-Smith 1977, p. 160

The same tall glass or similar glasses appear in other paintings of roses by Fantin-Latour, dated 1871 and 1872. He seems to have preferred stemmed and fluted glasses in the 1870s while bowls, baskets and wide-mouthed vases are more common in the 1880s. The Edwards, who met Fantin-Latour in 1861 and to whom he gave this painting, played an important role in finding English patrons for the artist.

Ignace-Henri-Jean-Théodore Fantin-Latour
(1836 – 1904)

Still Life: Pansies and Daisies

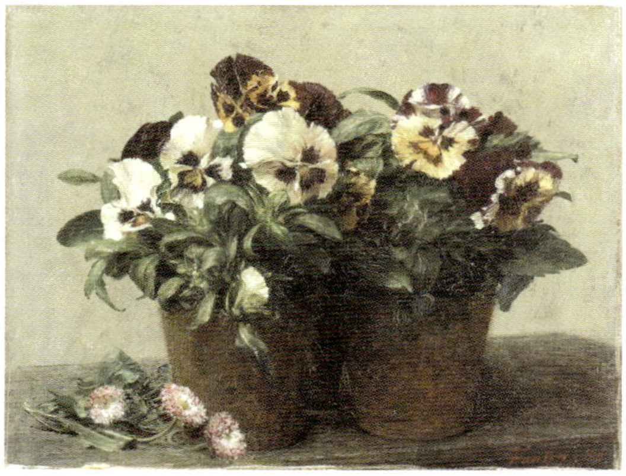

A485; oil on canvas, 29 × 38 cm
Signed and dated: *Fantin 80*
Weldon Bequest, 1937; WA1937.66

Fantin-Latour 1911, no. 992 ; Lucie-Smith 1977, pp. 152, 160

Ignace-Henri-Jean-Théodore Fantin-Latour
(1836 – 1904)

Still Life: pink, white and yellow Roses

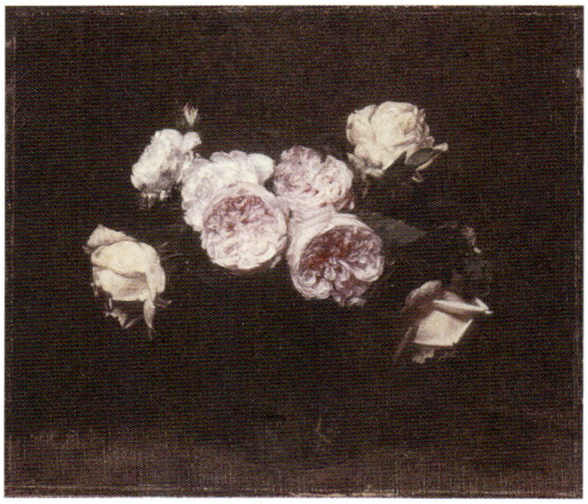

A506; oil on canvas, 35 × 40 cm
Prov.: Mrs Edwin Edwards
Presented by the executors of Miss Alice Squire in accordance with her wishes , 1937; WA1937.105

Fantin-Latour 1911, no. 1547; Lucie-Smith 1977, p. 160

Painted in 1894 and sold by the artist to Ruth Edwards on 4 October for £15.

Ignace-Henri-Jean-Théodore Fantin-Latour
(1836 – 1904)

Still Life: Malmaison Roses

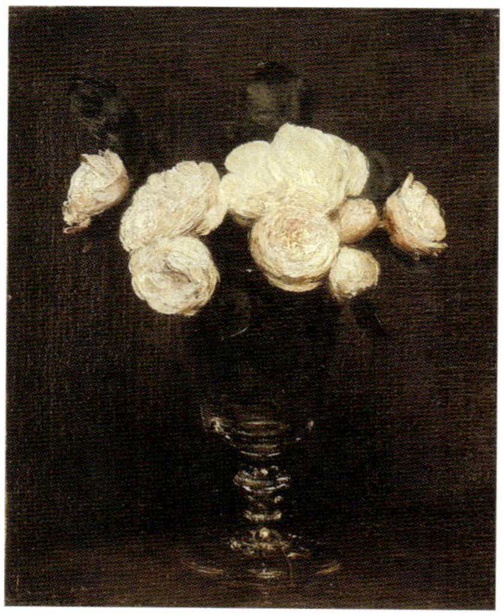

A474; oil on canvas, 30 × 24 cm
Signed and dated: *Fantin 72*
Prov.: Sir William Eden
Weldon Bequest, 1937; WA1937.54

Fantin-Latour 1911, no. 642; Lucie-Smith 1977, p. 160

Of the thirty or so species of flowers painted by Fantin-Latour, roses are by far the most common. He liked the combination of transparent glass and roses. English baluster-stemmed wine glasses of this kind appear elsewhere among his rose paintings of the early 1870s.

Ignace-Henri-Jean-Théodore Fantin-Latour
(1836 – 1904)

Still Life: pink and red Roses

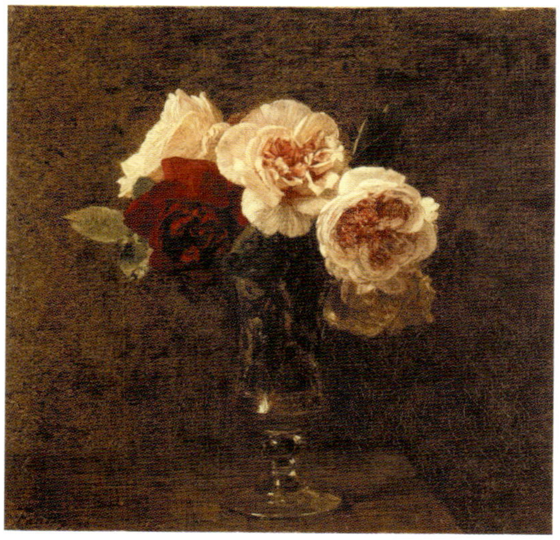

A486; oil on canvas, 39 × 40 cm
Signed and dated: *Fantin 86*
Weldon Bequest, 1937; WA1937.67

Fantin-Latour 1911, no. 1268; Lucie-Smith 1977, p. 160

Ignace-Henri-Jean-Théodore Fantin-Latour
(1836 – 1904)

Still Life: mixed Flowers

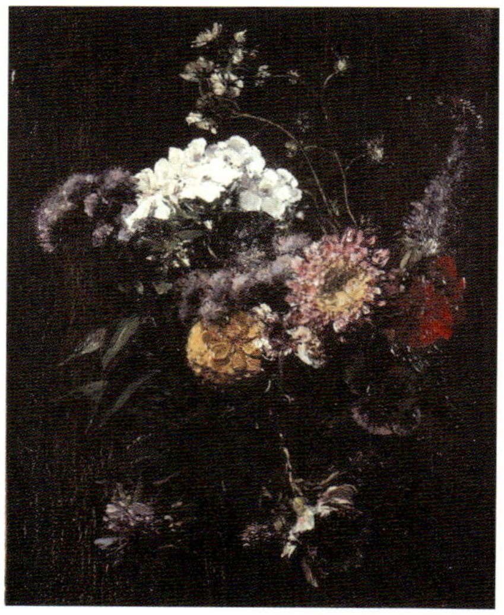

A430; oil on canvas, 23 × 19 cm
Presented by Mrs W.F.R. Weldon, 1934; WA1934.5

Fantin-Latour 1911, no. 846 (?)

Stephen Frederick Godfrey Farthing
(b. 1950)

The Last Day in the Old House

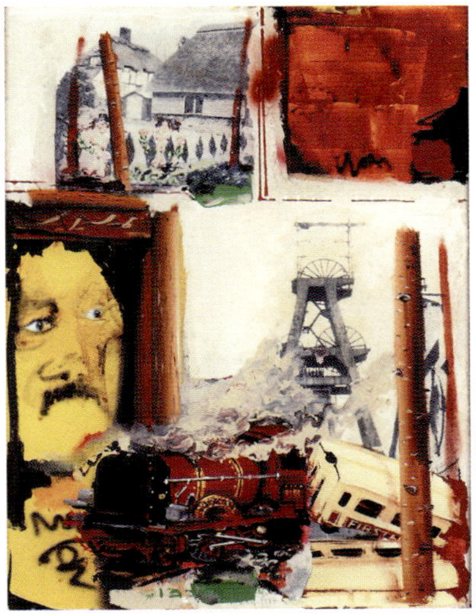

A1227; acrylic on cotton duck and paper, 79 × 59.5 cm
Signed and dated: *SF1987*
Purchased with the assistance of the Friends of the Ashmolean, 2000; WA2000.77

Farthing was Master at the Ruskin School of Drawing, Oxford, from 1990 until 2000. Mainly working as a painter, he also uses other media, such as printmaking, photography and drawing. Some of these are combined in this painting, reflecting his interest in urban landscape and portraiture.

Francesco Bianchi Ferrari
(active 1481 – d. 1510)

Arion riding on a Dolphin

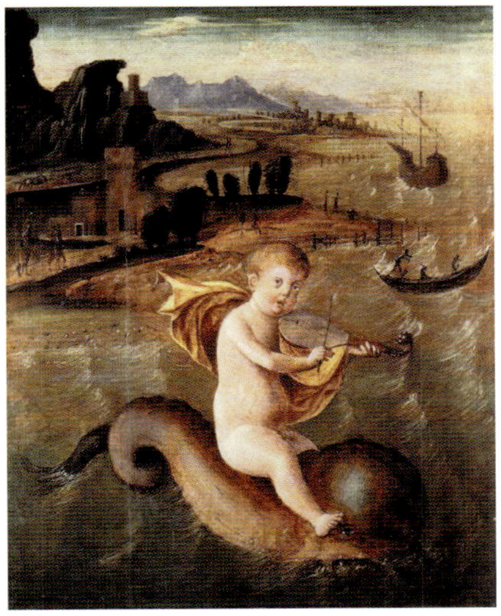

A733; tempera and oil (?) on panel, 68.1 × 53.7 cm
Presented by the daughters of James Reddie Anderson, 1947; WA1947.243

Lloyd 1977, pp. 57–8, Benati 1990, pp. 115, 152, 154

Painted *c.* 1509–10, A733 may have had some personal significance for its first owner. It is probably too large to have been the cover for a portrait. The poet Arion, having been thrown overboard by sailors in a storm, was carried to Corinth on the back of a dolphin, whom he charmed with his music (Ovid, *Fasti* 3, 83–118). Arion, unusually is shown as a child. However Amor (Love) appears in Renaissance art as a child holding or riding a dolphin.

Joseph Fisher
(1796 – 1890)

View in St Giles, Oxford, looking South

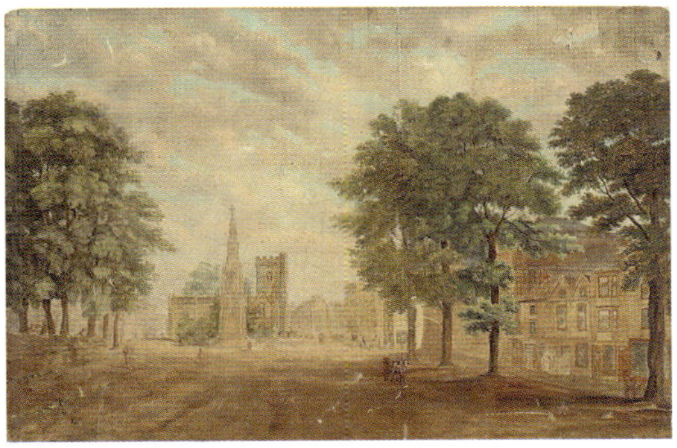

A323; oil on canvas, rolled, 40 × 60 cm
Provenance unknown; WA.OA910

Fisher was the first Keeper of the University Galleries at Oxford, between 1845 and 1886. This view looking south down St Giles includes the Martyrs' Memorial, built in 1841–3 to the design of George Gilbert Scott.

Anonymous Ferrarese Artist
(*c.* 1510 – 30)

The Holy Family with an Angel

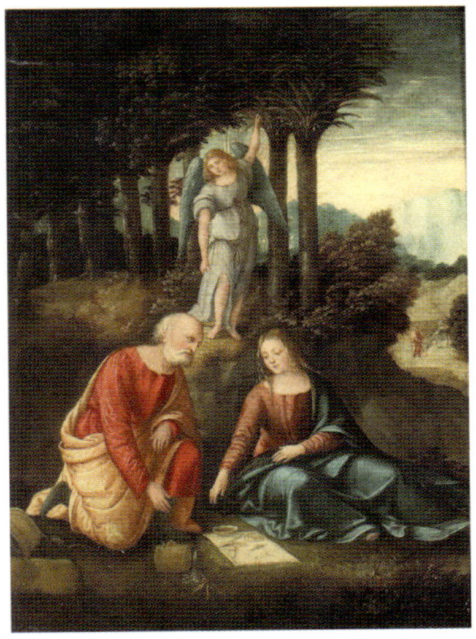

A335; oil on panel, 52 × 38 cm
Prov.: Melzi d'Eril Collection, Milan; Lochis Collection, Bergamo by 1858; Pinti
Presented by Mrs J. Reddie Anderson, 1913; WA1913.4

Lloyd 1977, pp. 55–7; Moro 1997, pp. 85, 107

Joseph and Mary take refreshment while an angel indicates a palm tree; in the background is the Flight into Egypt. Since the Christ Child is not present, the subject may be the Journey to Bethlehem. There are strong Ferrarese elements in this painting, although the Virgin is Leonardesque, reminiscent of Giovanni Agostino da Lodi. A335 may be by a follower of Ortolano; an attribution to Martino Piazza has recently been suggested.

Camillo Filippi
(*c.* 1500 – 1574)

The Adoration of the Shepherds

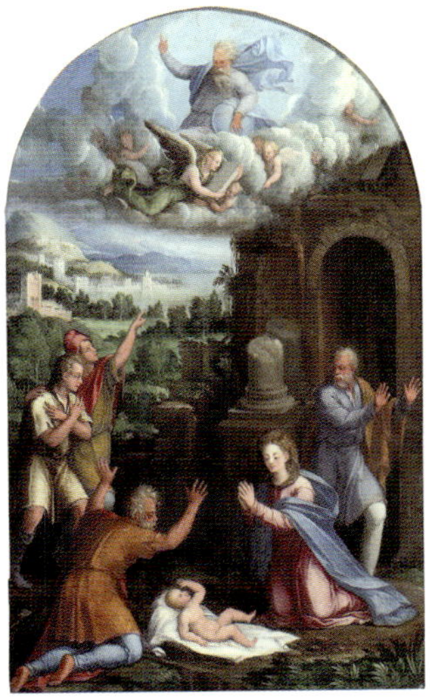

A678; oil on panel, 67.5 × 41 cm
Presented by Harold Bompas, 1941; WA1941.15

Lloyd 1977, pp. 59–60

While shepherds watched their flocks at night, an angel appeared to announce the birth of Christ and they brought gifts in honour of the new-born Child (Luke 2: 8–18). A678 is a characteristic richly-coloured, elegant painting by Filippi, who worked in the studio of the brothers Dosso and Battista Dossi. The composition is based on a painting by Battista of the 1520s (Residenzgalerie, Stuttgart), suggesting that A678 is an early work.

Joseph Fisher
(1796 – 1890)

View of Oxford from above Ferry Hinksey

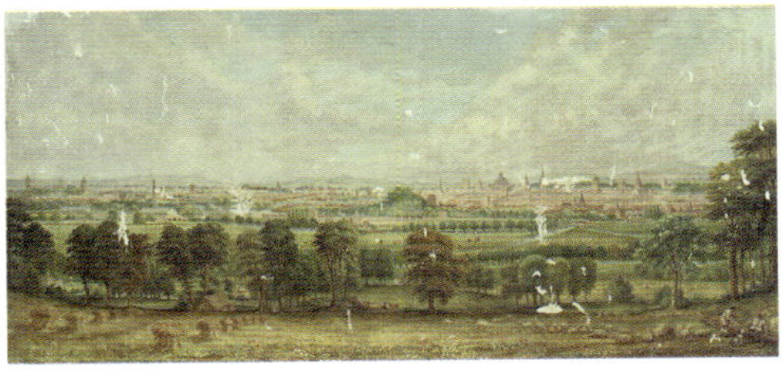

A324; oil on canvas, 41 × 84 cm
Provenance unknown; WA.OA911

A note on the back records that this was painted on the spot in 1872, during Fisher's period as Keeper of the University Galleries. It shows Oxford from almost the same vantage-point J.M.W. Turner had chosen for his watercolour of *Oxford from North Hinksey* (Manchester City Art Gallery), with the conduit house in the foreground. Unlike Turner, Fisher has included the railway line complete with train, and a chimney associated with the Clarendon Press in Jericho.

Joseph H. Vignoles Fisher
(1864 – 1945)

Summer Evening

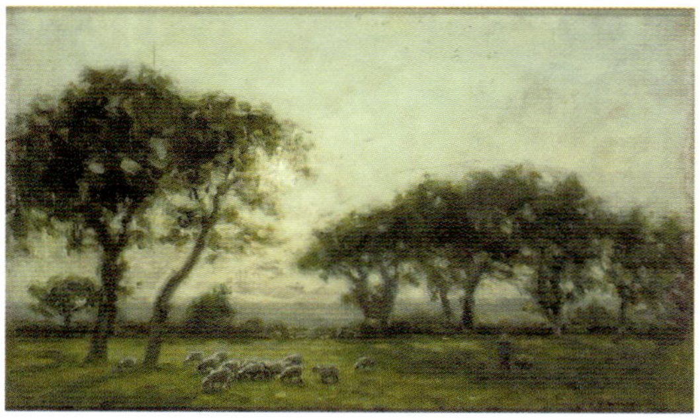

A737; oil on canvas, 23 × 38 cm
Signed: *J.H.V. Fisher*
Presented by Sir Wyndham Dunstan, K.C.M.G., F.R.S., 1947; WA1947.267

Hippolyte-Jean Flandrin
(1809 – 1864)

Head of a Young Woman

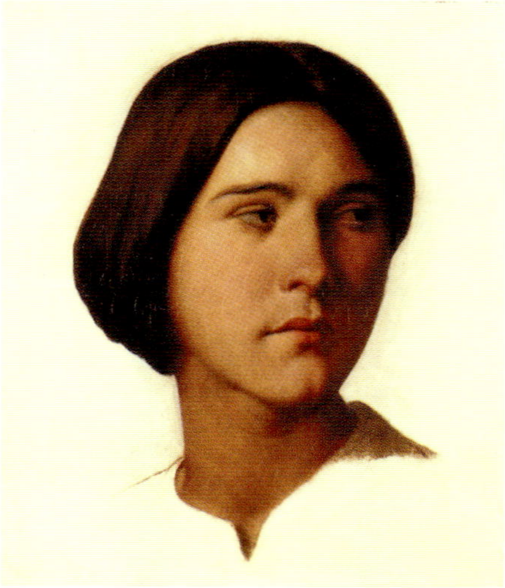

A1149; oil on canvas, 32.1 × 27 cm
Purchased with funds bequeathed by Dame Helen Gardner, 1987; WA1987.67

This head study, thinly painted on a white ground, probably dates from the 1840s. The delicacy of touch and the elegance of the contours recall the work of Flandrin's master, Ingres, to whom this study was at one time attributed. It is likely that these head studies were painted as exercises and do not link with any compositions.

Anonymous Flemish Artist
(*c.* 1500)

The Nativity

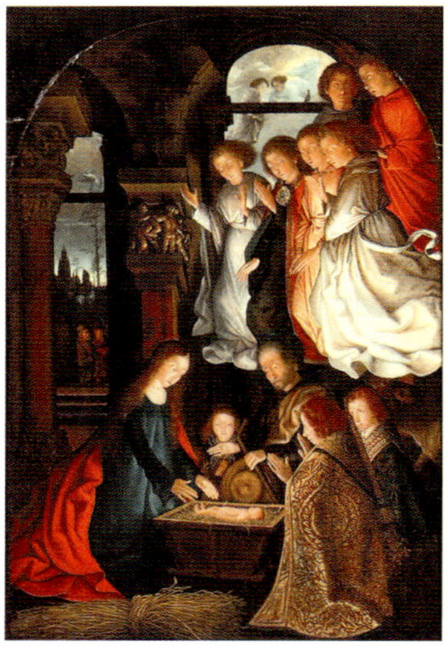

A427; oil on panel (arched top), 107 × 72 cm
Purchased, 1933; WA1933.23

White 1999, p. 176

One of several paintings by various artists dating from about 1500 which seem to have been based on a lost painting by the Flemish painter Hugo van der Goes.

Mark Fisher
(1841 – 1923)

A Normandy Lock

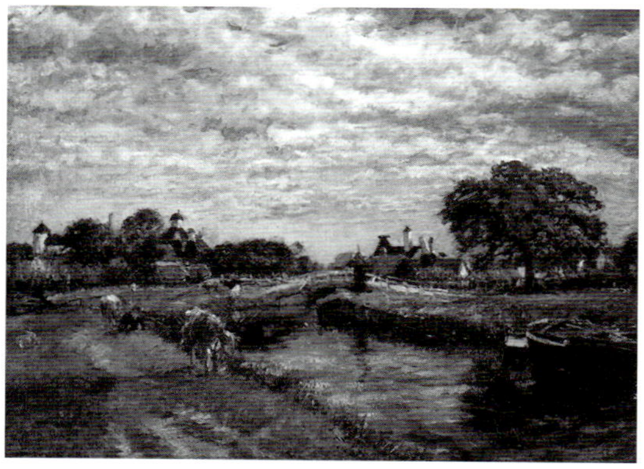

A950; oil on canvas, 52 × 69 cm
Signed: *Mark Fisher*
Bequeathed by J.E. Bullard, 1961; WA1961.31.1

Lines 1966, p. 21

Fisher was an American artist who studied with Charles Gleyre in Paris and returned to France in 1871, settling in England in the following year. He spent some time in Normandy, where this frankly Impressionist landscape was probably painted. It has also been titled, *The Lock, Sawbridgeworth*.

Jules Flandrin
(1871 – 1947)

Riders on the Corenc Road

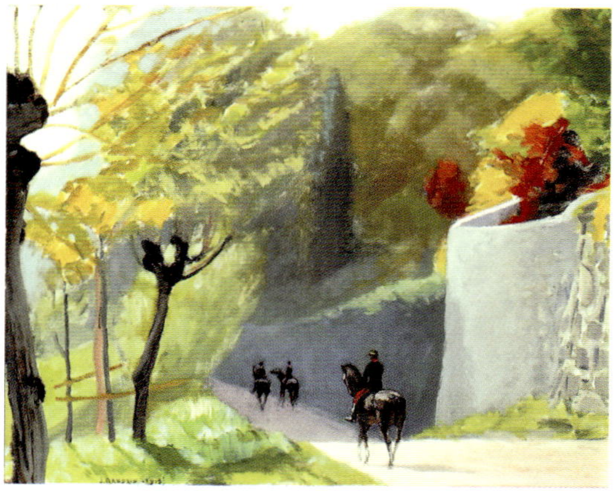

A1239; oil on canvas, 60 × 73 cm
Signed: *J. FLANDRIN-1913*
Presented by Georges and Monique Flandrin, 2001; WA2001.53

Simpson 2001, no. 61

Jules Flandrin began his career among a group of Gustave Moreau's pupils, later known as The Fauves on account of their interest in colour. By 1910, he had begun to incorporate more classical values of drawing and structure into his art. This painting, which combines elements of careful drawing with Fauve-like colour, marks the transition. The road is near Flandrin's native Corenc, in the Dauphiné.

Anonymous Flemish Artist
(*c.* 1500)

Balthazar, the African Magus

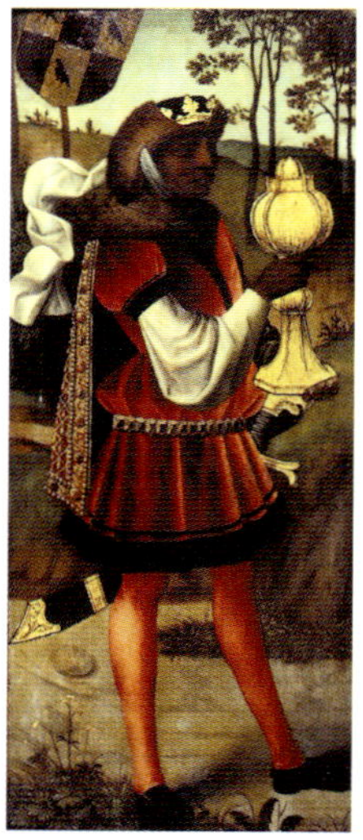

A519; oil on panel, 76 × 31 cm
Presented by Mrs Thomas Wood, 1938; WA1938.6

White 1999, p. 181

Balthazar, one of the three kings who came to Bethlehem to pay homage to the infant Christ, is traditionally supposed to have come from Africa. He is shown here carrying a vessel containing his gift of myrrh. This painting and the following must have formed side panels from an altar-piece.

Anonymous Flemish Artist
(*c.* 1500)

A Papal Saint

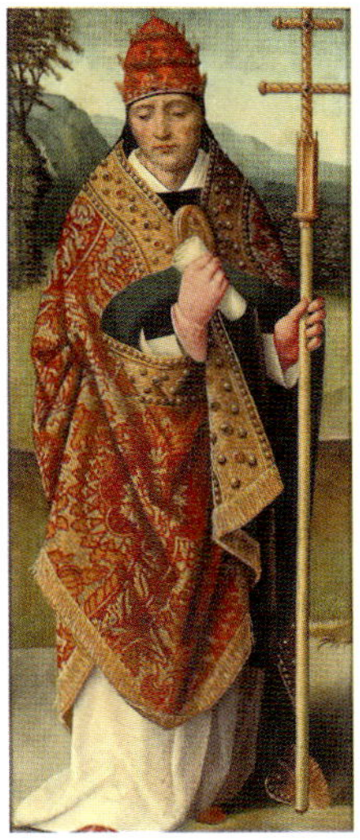

A520; oil on panel, 76 × 31 cm
Presented by Mrs Thomas Wood, 1938; WA1938.5

White 1999, p. 181

This saint was formerly identified as Gregory the Great, one of the four Fathers of the Church. He wears a Papal tiara but there are no attributes which would identify him with certainty. This painting, which forms a pair with the previous panel, might have been painted by the unidentified artist who painted a composition said to represent the marriage of Henry VI, now in the Museum of Art in Toledo, Ohio. The painting in Toledo has been dated between 1470 and 1500.

Anonymous Flemish Artist
(16th century)

The Annunciation

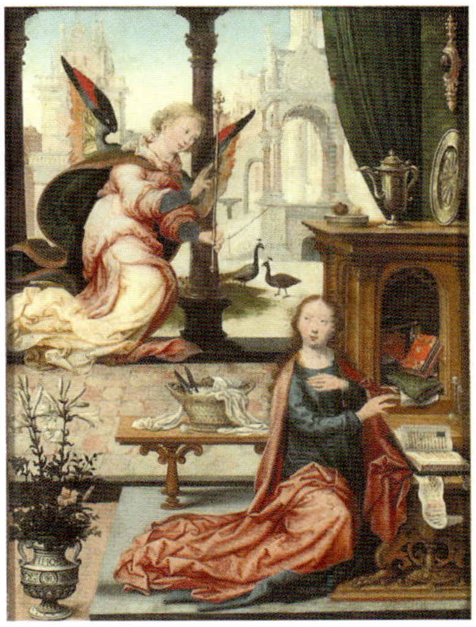

A513; oil on panel, 38 × 27 cm
Purchased by subscription, 1937; WA1937.123

White 1999, p. 178

Painted around 1520 by an artist who seems to have known the work of Barent van Orley: there is some similarity with paintings by van Orley of the same subject in the Nasjonalgalleriet, Oslo and the Fitzwilliam Museum, Cambridge.

Anonymous Flemish (?) Artist
(*c.* 1525 – 1530)

The Battle of Pavia

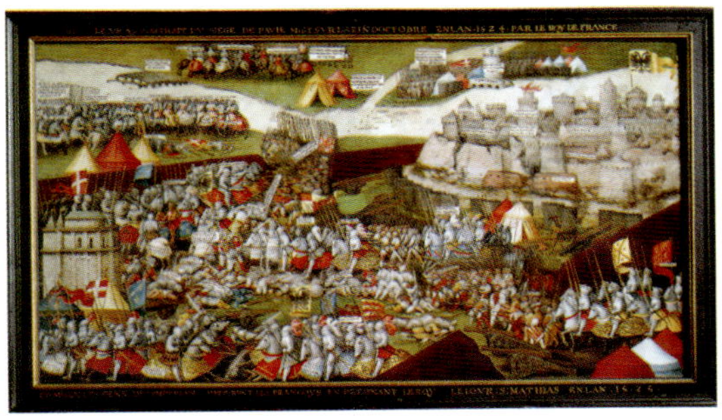

F664; oil on panel, 117 × 220 cm
For a full transcription of the inscriptions on the frame and painting, see Wilson 2003
Presented by Elias Ashmole, 1683; WA1908.226

MacGregor 1983, no. 263; Wilson 2003

The Battle of Pavia occurred at a crucial stage in the struggles between the French and Imperial forces in north Italy. The city of Pavia was besieged by the French army from October 1524; in February 1525, Imperial forces attacked the fortress of Mirabello, shown on the left, in order to relieve pressure on Pavia and divide the French forces. This decisive battle of 24 February involved the capture of King Francis I of France (left of centre) and led to the establishment of the Emperor Charles V in Lombardy. The complex panorama of the battle is ambitiously presented here, with inscriptions in French and a variety of flags and banners identifying the protagonists and locations. The noise and drama of battle is effectively conveyed, including realistic detail of dead and wounded. Painted on Baltic oak, F664 was probably made in the Burgundian Netherlands and remains one of the earliest images of the battle, which was to be commemorated in paintings, prints and tapestries in the 16th century. A painting from the same workshop, with variations in detail and inscriptions in Italian, is now in the collection of the Royal Armouries, Leeds and it is likely that the same cartoon was used for both pictures.

Anonymous Flemish Artist
(early 16th century)

St Catherine of Alexandria

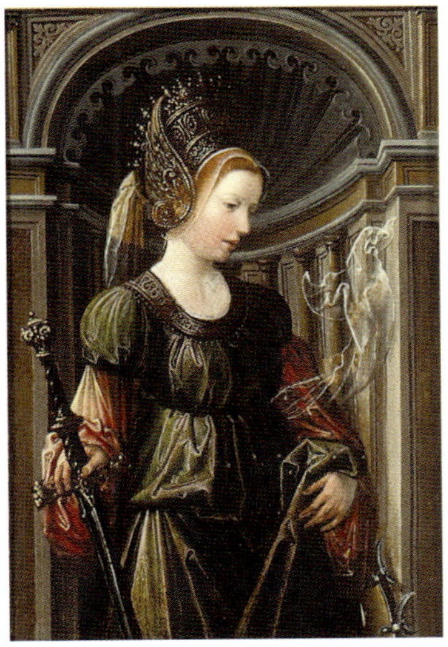

A868; oil on panel, 30 × 21 cm
Purchased (France Fund), 1953; WA1953.23

White 1999, p. 178

Possibly cut down from the wing of an altar-piece. The influence of Jan Gossaert (to whom it was once attributed) is evident in the facial type, architectural setting and rich, jewelled clothing but it is not of sufficient quality to be by Gossaert himself and must have been painted in the early 16th century by one of Gossaert's Antwerp followers.

Anonymous Flemish Artist
(16th century)

St Francis receiving the Stigmata

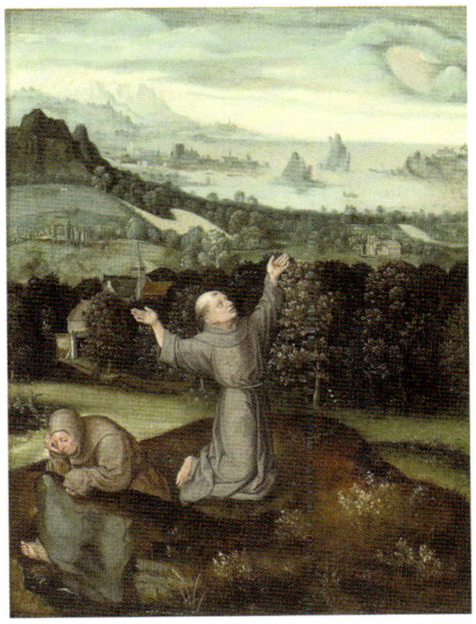

A959; oil on panel, 35 × 26 cm
Madan Bequest, 1962; WA1962.17.1

White 1999, p. 180

St Francis retreated to Mount Alverna in 1224 where he had a vision of the crucified Christ during which he was pierced with Christ's wounds. In this picture, his companion, Brother Leo, is seated on the left. The background of the painting is influenced by the work of Joachim Patenir and the painting was probably executed in Antwerp where Paternir was active in the early 16th century.

Anonymous Flemish Artist
(*c.* 1630)

Portrait of a Lady

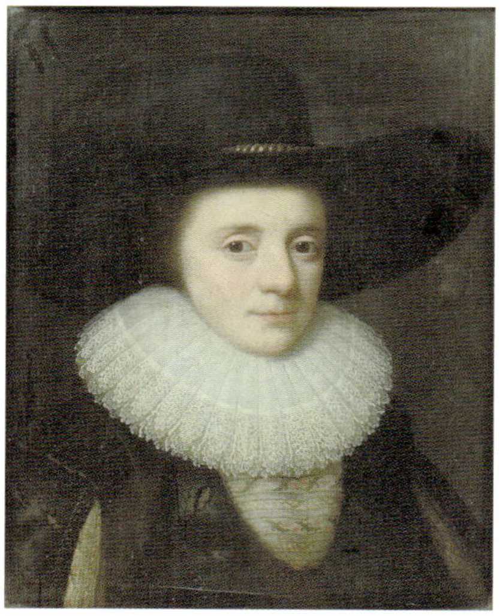

A66; oil on canvas, 56 × 45 cm
Presented by Philip Bury Duncan, Keeper of the Ashmolean Museum, 1846; WA1846.310

Poole 1912, no. 423

The sitter has been identified as Katherine Brydges (d. 1579), daughter and co-heiress of the 3rd Baron Chandos of Sudeley, who married Francis Russell, later 4th Earl of Bedford, in 1609. However, comparison with a full-length portrait of 1634 at Woburn Abbey does not support the identification. The style of the portrait is slightly reminscent of that of Cornelis Jonson.

Anonymous Flemish Artist
(17th century)

A Road through a Wood with a Lake

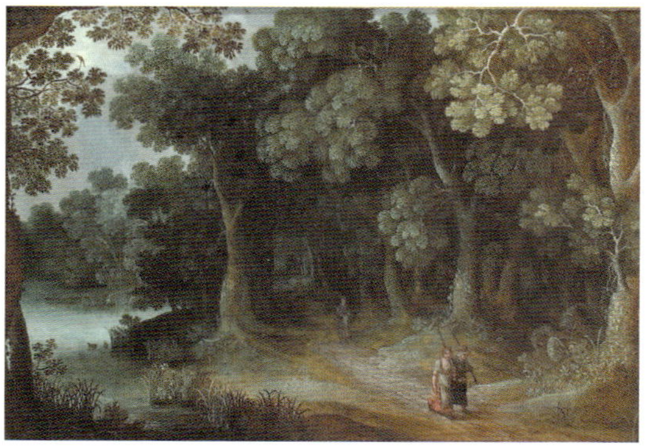

A705a; oil on panel, 22 × 35 cm
Presented by Percival H. Badcock, 1943; WA1943.117

White 1999, p. 188

Formerly attributed to Jan Brueghel the Younger but closer to the manner of the Brussels painter, Denis van Alsloot (born before 1570 – died before 1628), who combined landscape motifs from Jan Brueghel the Elder and Gillis van Coninxloo in the early 17th century.

Anonymous Flemish Artist
(17th century)

Portrait of an Ecclesiastic

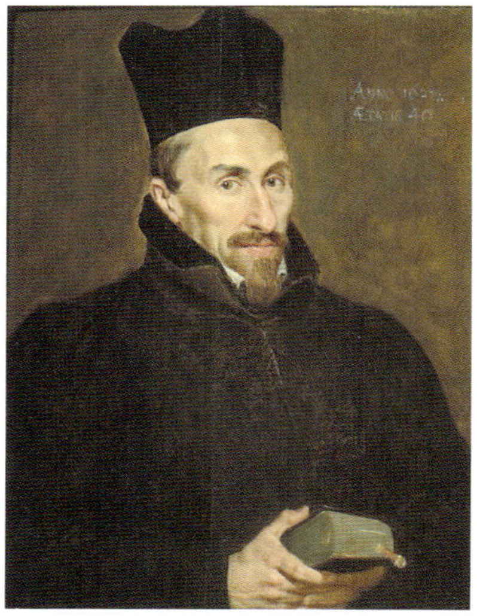

A960; oil on panel, 65 × 49 cm
Madan Bequest, 1962; WA1962.17.2

White 1999, p. 191

Painted by an anonymous Flemish artist working in the circle of Rubens.

Anonymous Flemish Artist
(17th century)

Portrait of a Man

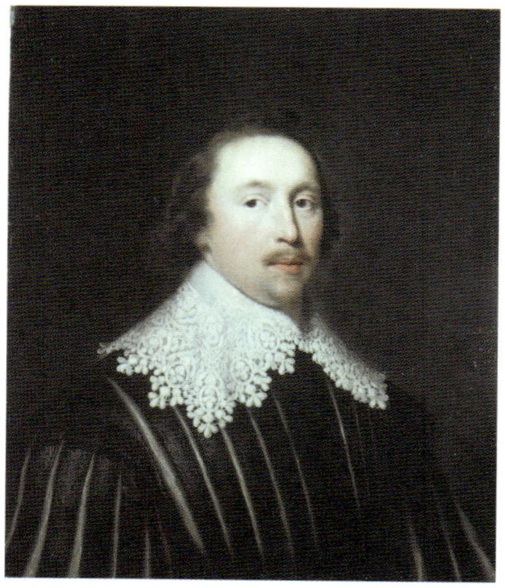

A182; oil on canvas, 67 × 56 cm
Chambers Hall Gift, 1855; WA1855.174

Formerly attributed to Joos van Craesbeeck. It has been suggested that this portrait might be by Cornelius Jonson (1593–1661) who was active in England in the early 17th century.

Anonymous Flemish Artist
(17th century)

The Temptation of St Anthony Abbot

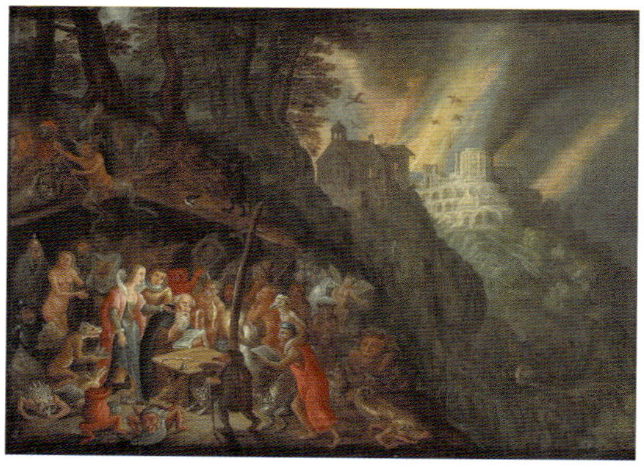

A894; oil on panel, 27 × 37 cm
Presented by Mrs Henry Rissik Marshall, 1957; WA1957.42

White 1999, p. 190

The scene represents St Anthony, tormented by demons in a mountainous landscape. He is accompanied by his traditional attributes, the bell and pig. The saint is said to have lived as a hermit in the Egyptian desert but European painters generally set the episode of his affliction by demons, as here, in a more familiar European setting.

Anonymous Flemish Artist
(early 17th century)

A young Man holding a jewel

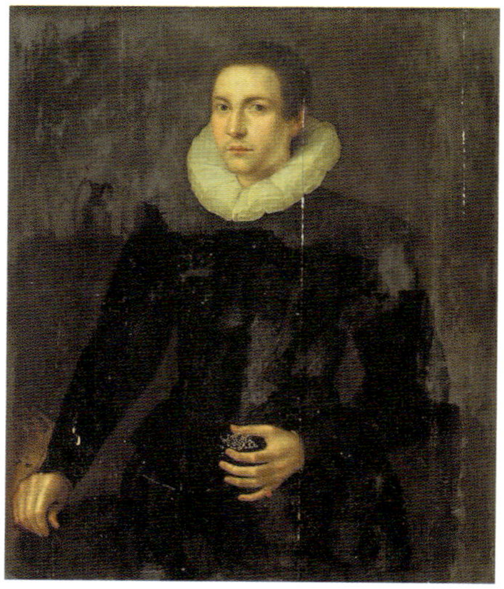

F661; oil on panel, 88 × 73 cm
Prov.: Tradescant
Presented by Elias Ashmole, 1683; WA1898.2

Poole 1912, no. 410; MacGregor 1983, no. 284

Possibly painted by a Flemish follower of Frans Pourbus. The pendant gem-set jewel which he holds in his left hand is of a common early 17th-century type. It is probably Flemish although it could also have been made in England. The jewel might indicate that the subject was a jeweller but it is more likely that it had a personal significance for him.

Anonymous Flemish Artist
(early 17th century)

Louis XIII on Horseback

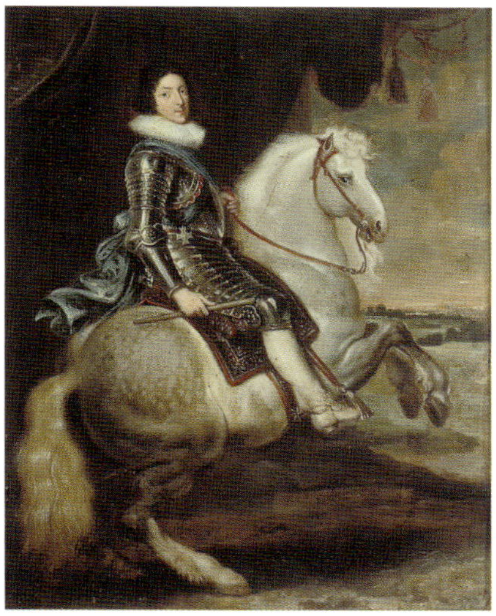

A18; oil on copper, 63 × 50 cm
Presented by the Revd Dr Richard Rawlinson, 1752; WA1845.18

The portrait corresponds generally to a number of paintings and prints of Louix XIII of France on a prancing horse. From the type and handling of the paint, it seems to be either by or after a Flemish painter. The appearance of the king suggests a date of about 1622.

Anonymous Florentine Artist
(*c.* 1470 – 1490)

The Crucifixion with Sts Bernardino of Siena and Lawrence

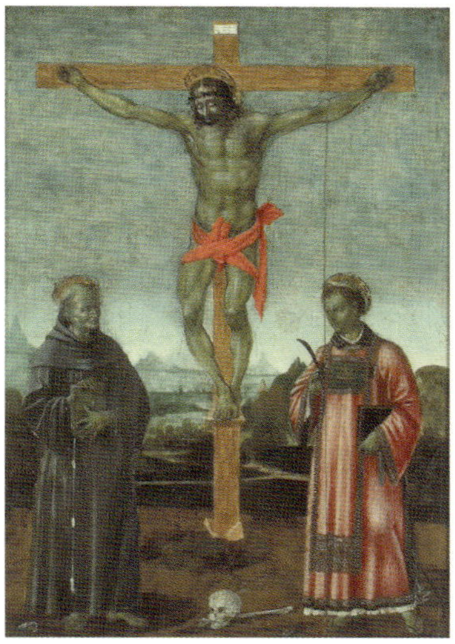

A734; tempera and gilding on wood, 38.2 × 26.8 cm
Presented by the daughters of James Reddie Anderson, 1947; WA1947.203

Lloyd 1977, pp. 11–12

St Lawrence (d. 258) appears with his attribute of a gridiron, the instrument of his martyrdom, while a gold crown and three palms form a prominent motif on his breast. St Bernardino (1380–1444), a famous Franciscan preacher and reformer, was a popular subject in Tuscan art. A plausible attribution has been recently suggested to Gherardo di Giovanni (di Miniato) del Fora (1445–1497), a painter and illuminator who maintained a workshop in Florence with his brothers.

Anonymous Florentine Artist
(*c.* 1580s – 1590)

Baccio Orlandini

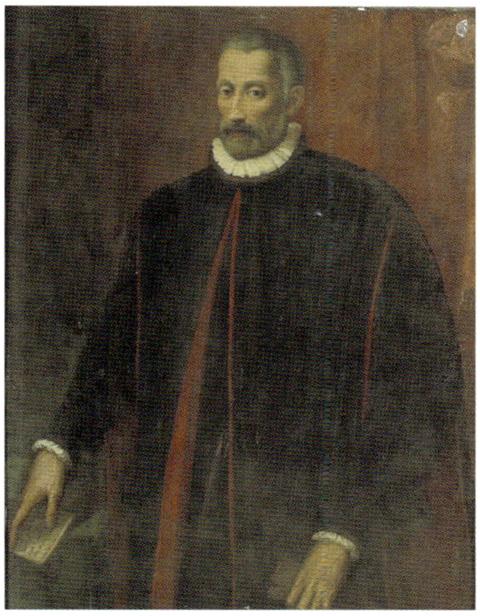

A70; oil on panel, 115 × 87.6 cm
The paper held in the sitter's right hand is inscribed: *Al Illr.e S.re Baccio Orlandini Am / Bas.te di Toschana Alle / Corte Catolicha e / Are di portogallo / Da lāno 1575 / Alāno 1580*
Presented by John Bayley, 1849; WA1849.2

Lloyd 1977, pp. 65–6

The son of Piero di Bartolommeo Orlandini, Baccio (1520–1598) was made senator in 1573 and was ambassador to the court of Philip II of Spain and Portugal from 1575 in addition to serving as commissioner for Cortona, Pistoia and Pisa. The present condition of the picture makes it difficult to suggest an attribution.

William Teulon Blandford Fletcher
(1858 – 1937)

The Farm Garden

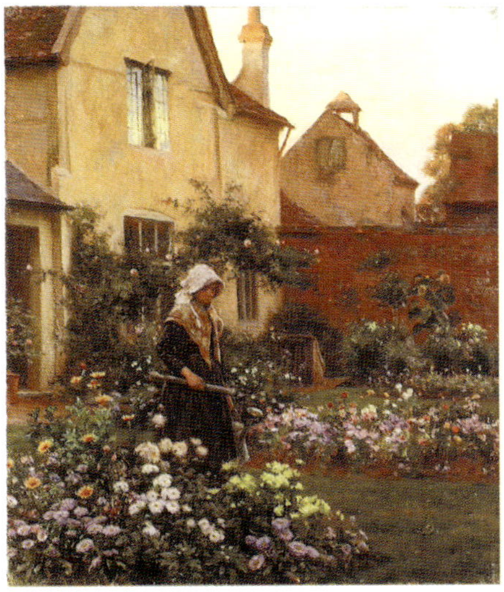

A1062a; oil on canvas, 61 × 51 cm
Signed: *BLANDFORD FLETCHER*
Presented by Miss Christina and Miss Rosamund Fletcher, daughters of the artist, 1971; WA1971.267

Painted in 1888 in Worcestershire. There exists an almost identical composition of *A Cottage Garden* by Walter Osborne with whom Fletcher was travelling and working at this time.

Anonymous Florentine Artist
(*c.* 1550 – 1570)

Portrait of an Artist

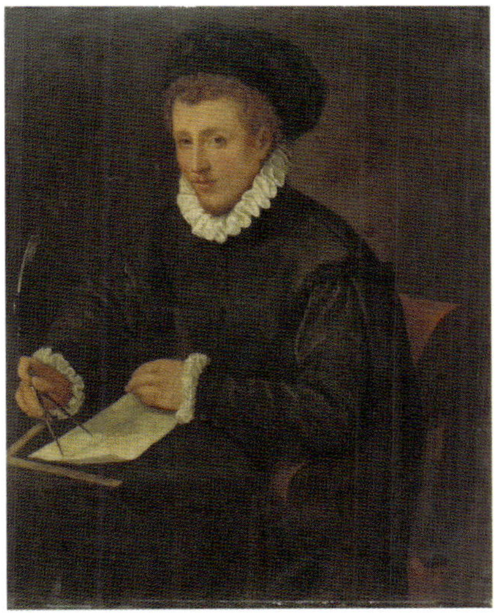

A20; oil on canvas, 100.5 × 78.8 cm
Prov.: Thomas Gibson
Presented by the Revd Dr Richard Rawlinson, 1752; WA1845.20

Lloyd 1977, pp. 89–90

The sitter's direct gaze and the fact that he is shown with drawing instruments, suggest that A20 might be a self-portrait. Traditionally A20 was known as a self-portrait by Federico Zuccaro, but his documented self-portraits do not portray the same person.

Anonymous Florentine Artist
(*c.* 1675 – 1695)

The Idolatry of Solomon

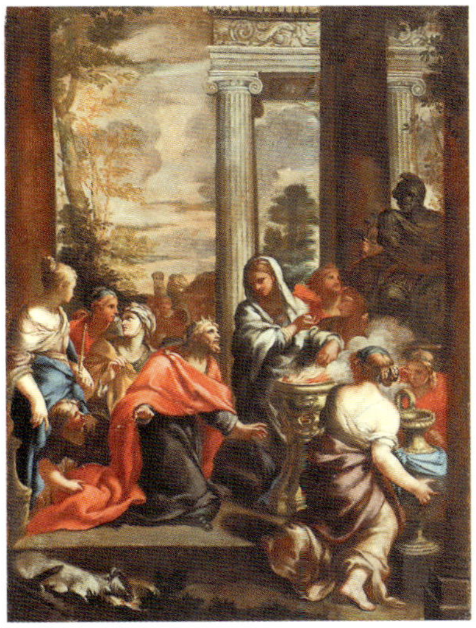

A675; oil on canvas, 90 × 66 cm
Prov.: acquired in Zante
Bequeathed by Sir Arthur Evans, 1941; WA1941.8

Solomon kneels in worship of false gods (I Kings 11: 7–8). The composition derives from Pietro da Cortona and was popular with his Roman and Florentine followers. A675 was painted in Florence in the late 17th century: a plausible attribution has been made to Antonio Domenico Gabbiani (1652–1726), datable to *c.* 1690–95, while another suggestion is Antonio Franchi (1634–1709) around 1675.

Attributed to Francesco Fontebasso
(1707 – 1769) after Veronese

The Feast in the House of Levi

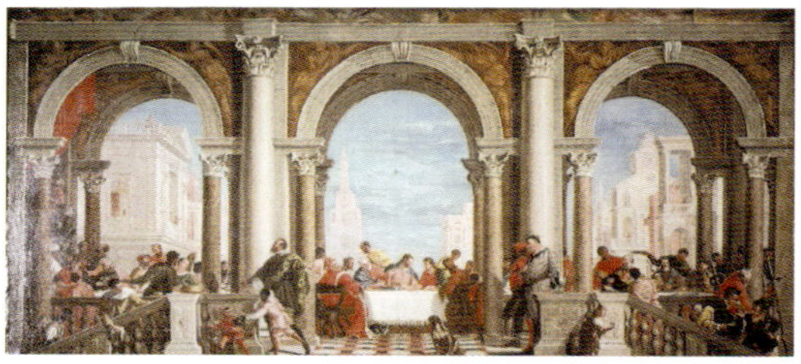

A142; oil on canvas, 107 × 228 cm
Chambers Hall Gift, 1855; WA1855.159

Lloyd 1977, pp. 190–1; Pignatti 1976, I, under no. 177

Veronese's celebrated *Last Supper* of 1573 for the refectory of SS Giovanni e Paolo, Venice, caused him to be examined by the Inquisition on the grounds of blasphemy; he changed the title to *The Feast in the House of Levi*, a subject which allowed for much colourful detail (Luke 6: 27–30). Numerous copies are known of this large painting, now in the Accademia, Venice. A142 is a reduced copy of fine quality by a mid-18th-century Venetian artist, probably Francesco Fontebasso.

Jean-Louis Forain
(1852 – 1931)

Seated Dancer

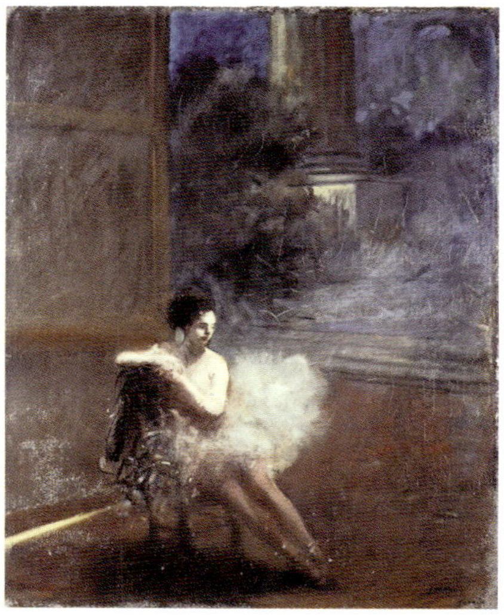

A1144; oil on canvas, 78.5 × 63 cm
Signed: *Forain* (twice)
Prov.: Mr and Mrs J. Kerrigan
Bequeathed by Mr and Mrs Francis Hock through the National Art Collections Fund, 1987; WA1987.17

Eleanor Fortescue-Brickdale
(1872 – 1945)

Time the Physician

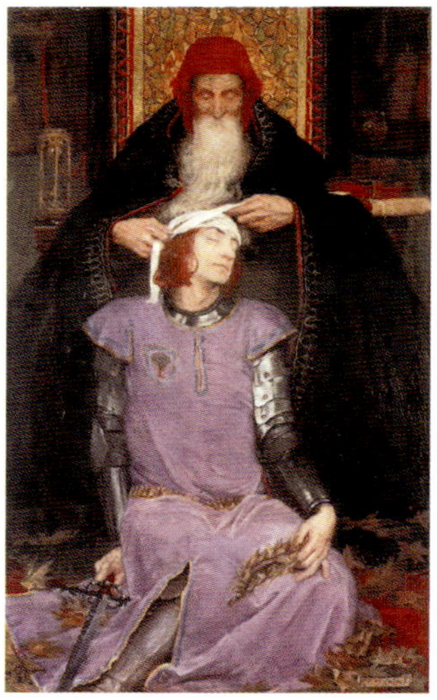

A1159; oil on panel, 45.6 × 27.7 cm
Signed: *E.F.BRICKDALE*
Bequeathed by the artist's nephew, Francis Fortescue-Brickdale, 1985; WA1988.231

Fortescue-Brickdale was described by her contemporaries as a 'Neo-Pre-Raphaelite' and in her oil paintings, she worked in the meticulous technique of the early Pre-Raphaelites. *Time the Physician*, one of her first oil paintings, was shown at the Royal Academy in 1900 and thus predates her greatest success, the exhibitions of drawings entitled 'Such Stuff as Dreams are made of', in 1901 and 1905, and her prolific activity as a book illustrator.

Jean-Louis Forain
(1852 – 1931)

Scene in the Wings of a Theatre

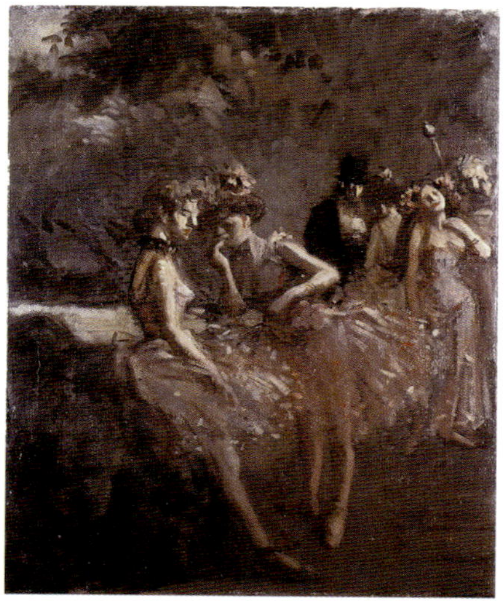

A498; oil on canvas, 74 × 60 cm
Prov.: William Marchant(?)
Weldon Bequest, 1937; WA1937.79

Forain's interest in themes from the ballet was formed through his friendship with Degas. His ballet pictures mostly date from between the late 1870s and 1900. He was a successful caricaturist and illustrator and he often introduced an illustrative or satirical note into his work. The scene probably takes place between the acts. An 'abonné' in top hat lurks in the background.

Jean-Louis Forain
(1852 – 1931)

Woman on a Chaise-longue

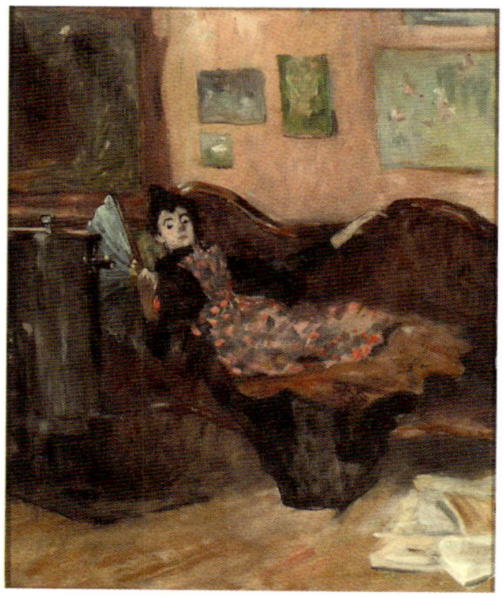

A1067; oil on panel, 41 × 34 cm
Bequeathed by Lt-Col G.E. Bouskell-Wade, 1972; WA1972.160

A colourful and spontaneous work probably dating from the 1880s. The influence of Manet, whose work Forain admired, is evident.

Francesco de' Franceschi
(active 1443 – 1468)

St Catherine of Alexandria

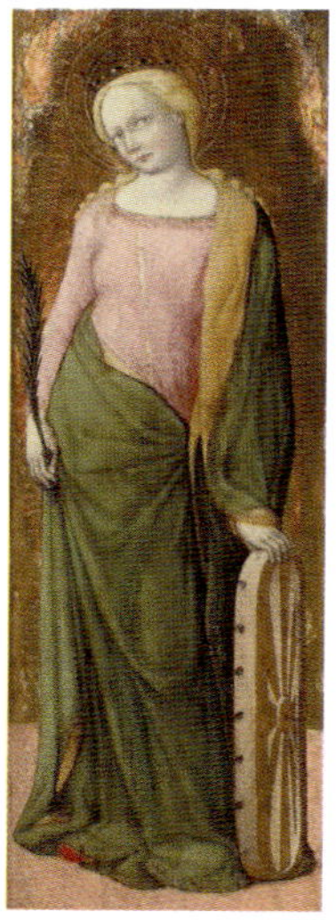

A86; tempera and gilding on panel, 92 × 35.5 cm
Fox-Strangways Gift, 1850; WA1850.11

Lloyd 1977, pp. 66–7

The only securely documented painting by the artist is an altar-piece of 1447 now in the Museo Civico, Padua.
A follower of Michele Giambono, Francesco may have collaborated with Antonio Vivarini in Venice.
St Catherine, of royal birth, wears a crown and carries her martyr's palm; the wheel refers to earlier attempts at her martyrdom.

Francesco de'Franceschi
(active 1443 – 1468)

St Mary Magdalen

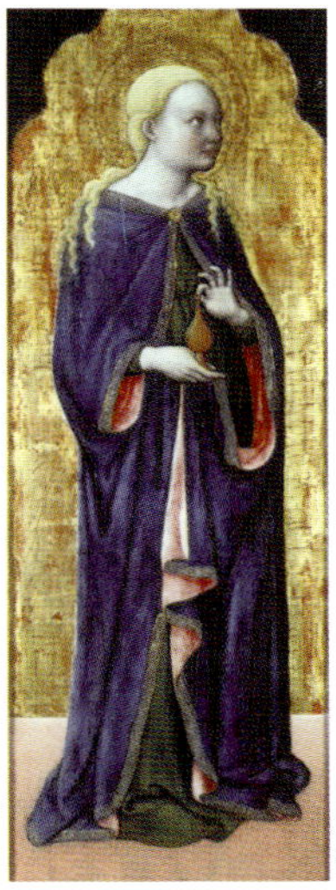

A87; tempera and gilding on panel, 92 × 35.5 cm
Fox-Strangways Gift, 1850; WA1850.10

Lloyd 1977, pp. 66–7

Together with A86, this panel was once part of an unknown altar-piece possibly for a church in Padua or Venice. St Mary Magdalen carries her attribute of a jar of ointment, as she is traditionally identified with the woman who anointed the feet of Christ in the house of Simon the Pharisee (Luke 7: 36).

Franciabigio
(1484 – 1525)

St Nicholas of Tolentino performing a Miracle

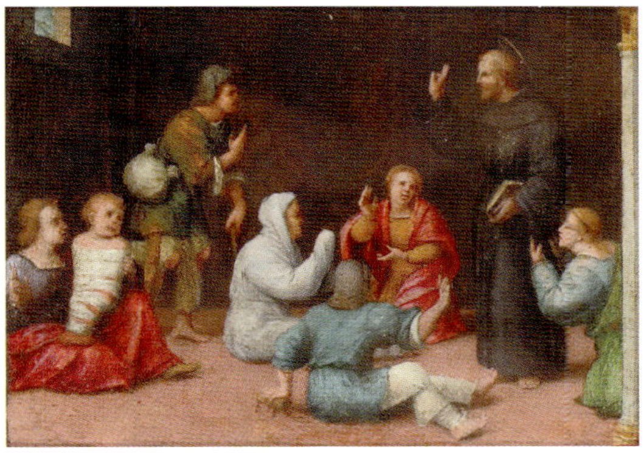

A342; oil on panel, 18.8 × 24.6 cm
Prov.: Tempi, Florence; Revd J. Sanford; T.W. Jackson
Presented by the legatees of T.W. Jackson, 1915; WA1915.1

Lloyd 1977, pp. 69–72; Pagnotta 1988, p. 721

Probably painted *c.* 1516–18, A342 was part of the predella of an altar-piece for the church of Santo Spirito, Florence, where the central image was a wooden statue of St Nicholas after a design by Jacopo Sansovino. The other predella panels show the *Canonization of St Nicholas*, *Two Miracles of the Saint* and *The Funeral of the Saint*.
St Nicholas of Tolentino (*c.* 1245–1306), an Augustinian friar, was canonised in 1446.

Anonymous Franco-Flemish Artist
(late 17th century)

Faith

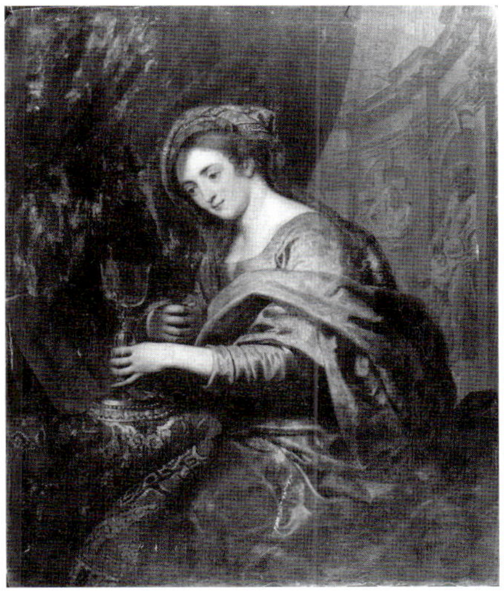

A32; oil on canvas, rolled, 122.5 × 101 cm
Presented by an unknown donor, 1762; WA1845.32

Faith is shown with her attributes of a veil and chalice, here elaborately and finely rendered. The setting is a baroque church interior; two statues in niches depict Christ with the cross and a figure with a sword, probably St Paul. Groups of Virtues, or of the Liberal Arts, were popular elements in the decoration of libraries.

Studio of Francesco Francia
(*c.* 1450 – 1517/18)

Virgin and Child with the young St John

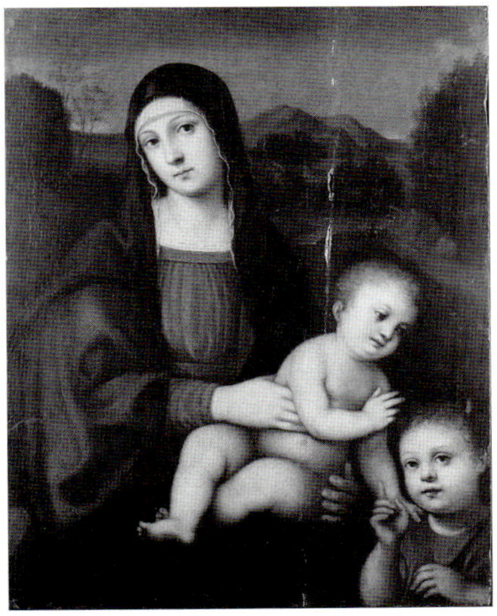

A419a; oil on panel, 47 × 37 cm
Prov.: Don Luis-Francisco de la Cerda y Aragón; Sir Henry Taylor and by descent
Bequeathed by Miss I.A. Taylor, 1930; WA1932.215

Lloyd 1977, pp. 68–9; Negro and Roio 1998, no. 140

Described on accession as a copy after Francia, A419a does not seem to have an exact prototype in the artist's work. However, the design is similar in reverse to a composition of *c.* 1510 known in two studio versions.

Anonymous Franco-Flemish Artist
(late 17th century)

Charity

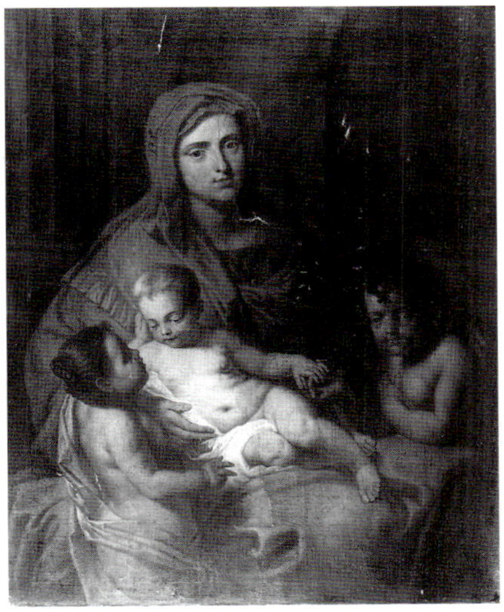

A31; oil on canvas, rolled, 123.5 × 101 cm
Presented by an unknown donor, 1762; WA1845.31

Charity, traditionally shown with the children she nurtures, is dressed as a Roman matron and is presented in an austere indoor setting with a giant fluted column suggesting antique grandeur. A31 to A36 are from a series of the seven Virtues (Hope is missing), probably painted by a North European artist working in England.

Anonymous Franco-Flemish Artist
(late 17th century)

Justice

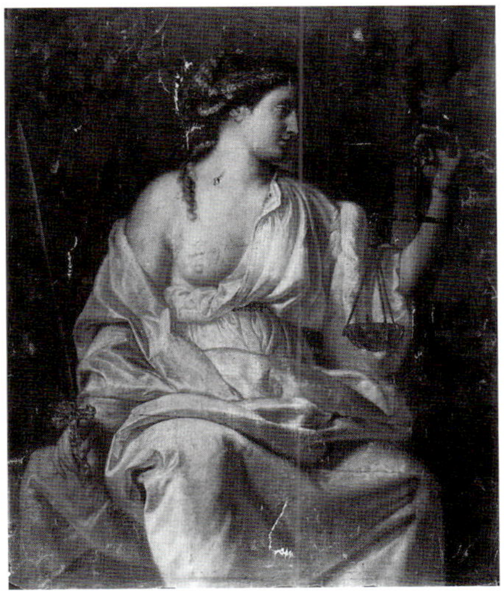

A33; oil on canvas, 123 × 102 cm
Presented 1762; WA1845.33

Traditionally depicted with a sword and scales, Justice appears here in an outdoor setting, before an archway with a sculptural decoration of a herm on the right. The decorative details (such as the jewels in her hair and the ornate sword hilt) are in marked contrast to the figure's severe profile.

Anonymous Franco-Flemish Artist
(late 17th century)

Fortitude

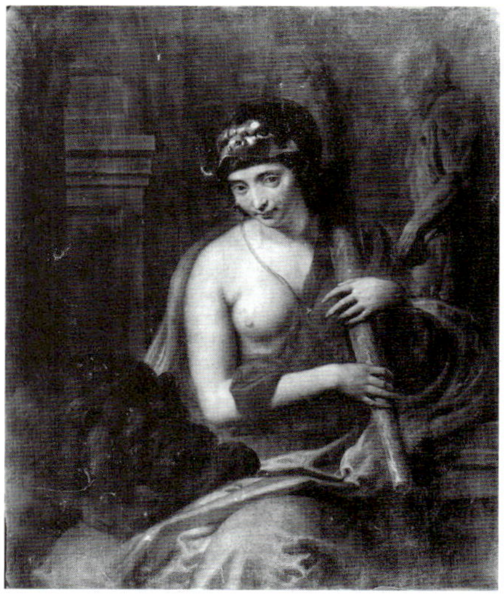

A34; oil on canvas, rolled, 123.5 × 105 cm
Presented by an unknown donor, 1762; WA1845.34

Fortitude in a helmet, accompanied by a lion, holds a long club, normally an attribute of Hercules, who is associated with this virtue. A statue of Hercules is visible on the right. As with others in the series, the allegorical figure derives from the *Iconologia* of Cesare Ripa with variations from other print sources.

Anonymous Franco-Flemish Artist
(late 17th century)

Prudence

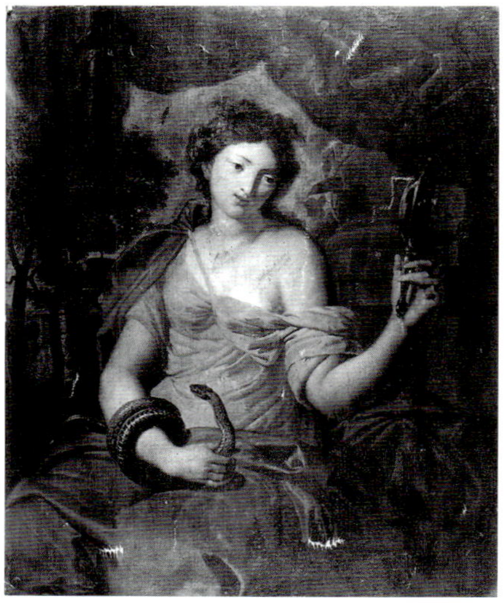

A36; oil on canvas, 122.5 × 100 cm
Presented by an unknown donor, 1762; WA1845.36

As with A35, Prudence appears in a lavish outdoor setting with antique references, including a temple with what appear to be two caryatids. Her traditional attributes are a mirror, symbolising truth, and a snake, the symbol of wisdom.

Anonymous French Artist
(*c.* 1620 – 1630)

Portrait of a young Man (Self-Portrait?)

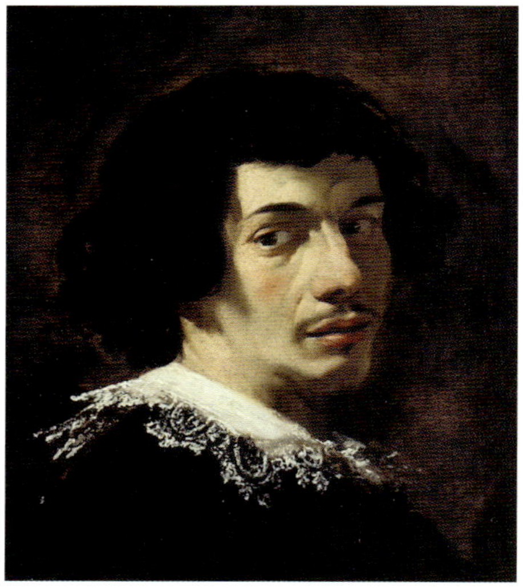

A781; oil on canvas, 43.8 × 38.7 cm
Prov.: Lord Belhaven and Stenton
Purchased, 1950; WA1950.10

Nicolson and Vertova 1990, p. 200; Baker 1998, no. 37

Formerly attributed to Bernini and often described as a self-portrait of *c.* 1625, A781 is more likely to be by a French artist in Rome, *c.* 1620–30. Such expressive, informal portraits were fashionable with French and northern European painters there. Attributions have been suggested to the young Simon Vouet and to Henry Traivoel, by whom, however, only one painting is known.

Anonymous Franco-Flemish Artist
(late 17th century)

Temperance

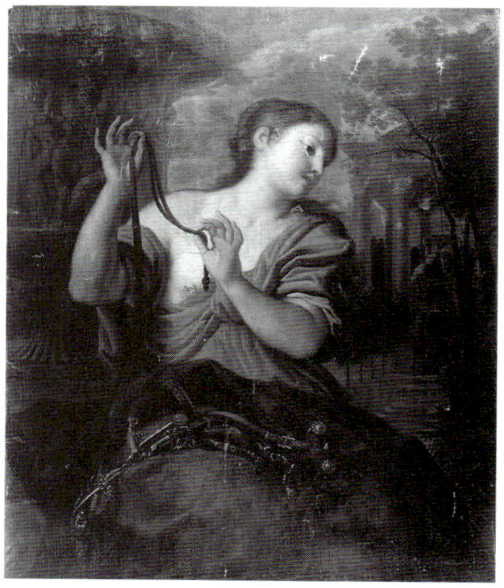

A35; oil on canvas, 122.5 × 102 cm
Presented by an unknown donor, 1762; WA1845.35

Temperance is shown as a woman with a bridle, in an elaborate garden setting including an antique vase and a fountain with river-gods. A35 and A36 are more Italianate in taste than the others in the series and may have been by a different artist in the same workshop.

Jean Frelaut
(1879 – 1954)

Apple Blossom

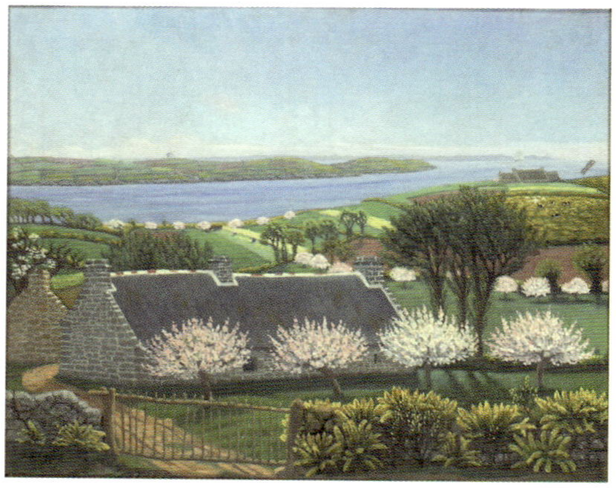

A648; oil on canvas, 60 × 74 cm
Hindley Smith Bequest, 1939; WA1940.1.30

Frelaut belonged to a group of French Post-Impressionist painters who were promoted by the English dealer, Percy Moore Turner. Turner admired Frelaut's naïve naturalism and must have introduced his work to his friend and client, Frank Hindley Smith.

Anonymous French or Italian Artist
(17th century)

Head Study of an Abbess

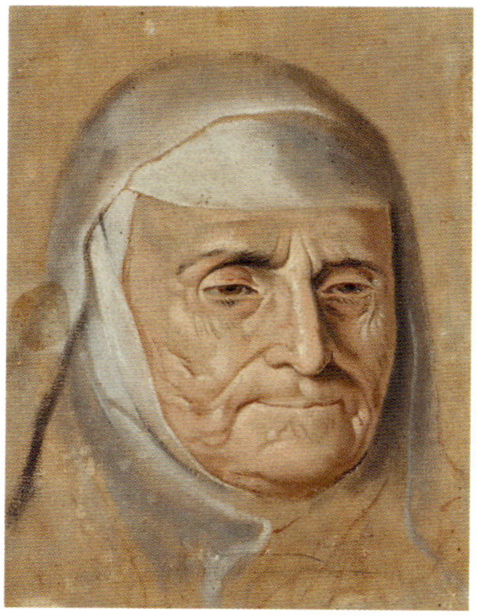

Oil on paper, mounted as a drawing, 29.8 × 22 cm
Prov.: Morosi, Florence
Presented by Mrs Burton, 1951; WA1951.40

Formerly attributed to the French artist, Nicolas Lagneau, who specialised in chalk drawings of this type but is not known as a painter.

Anonymous French Artist
(early 19th century)

A View of Olevano

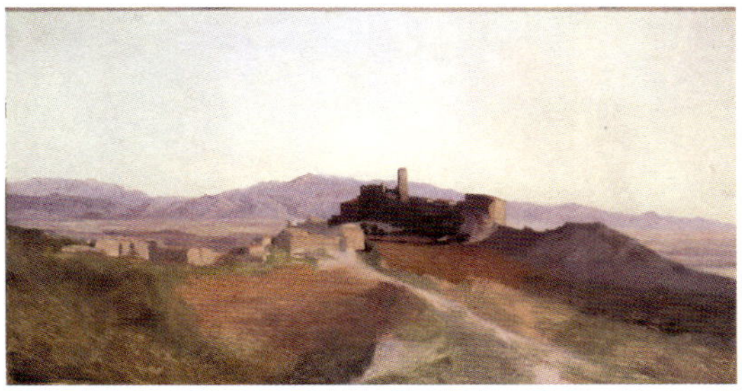

A393; oil on canvas, 24 × 44 cm
Presented by Mrs W.F.R. Weldon, 1929; WA1929.4

Robaut 1905, no. 162 or 163

Although this view of Olevano is of the same type as the sketches which Corot made in Italy in the mid 1820s, the thin, rubbed style of painting is uncharacteristic and the former attribution to Corot is not tenable. The sketch was probably made by one of Corot's French contemporaries working in Italy in the early 19th century. Olevano, a hill town east of Rome, was a popular site for foreign artists.

Anonymous French Artist
(*c.* 1800)

Still Life of a Plaster Head and Books

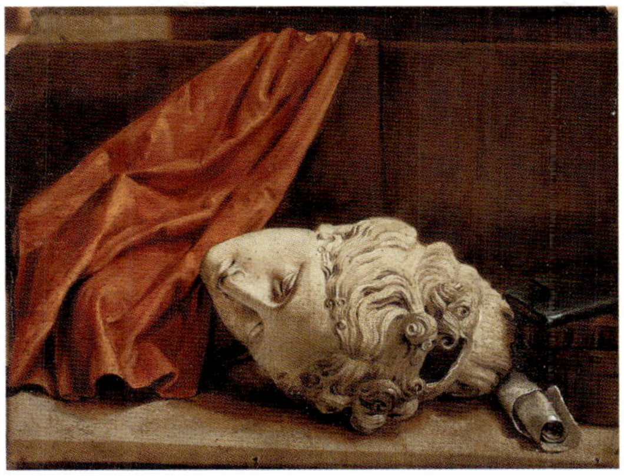

A1170; oil on paper, 45 × 52 cm
Presented by Dr Christopher Wright in memory of Steve Barraclough, 1990; WA1990.123

Probably a studio exercise. On the back of the paper are two classicizing heads, drawn in outline.

Emile-Othon Friesz
(1879 – 1949)

Les Vosges

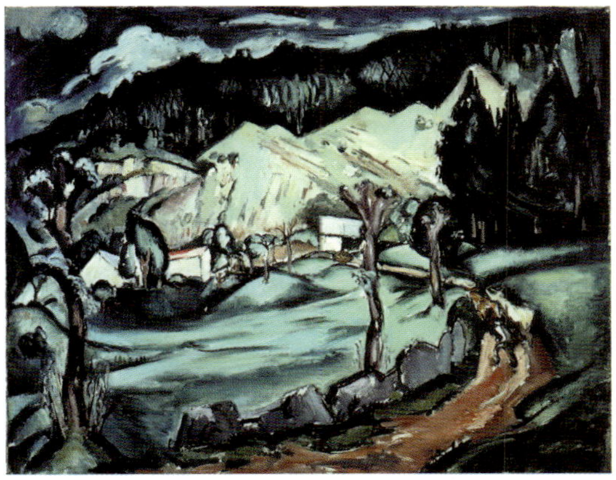

A625; oil on canvas, 65.5 × 81.2 cm
Signed: *Emile Othon Friesz*
Hindley Smith Bequest, 1939; WA1940.1.7

Eustace 1999, no. 16

Before the First World War, Friesz joined the Fauves and exhibited with Matisse and Braque in the Salon d'Automne. After his demobilization in March 1919, Friesz went to the Jura and the Vosges, where he painted this landscape.

Anonymous French or Italian Artist
(early 19th century)

The Dead Christ

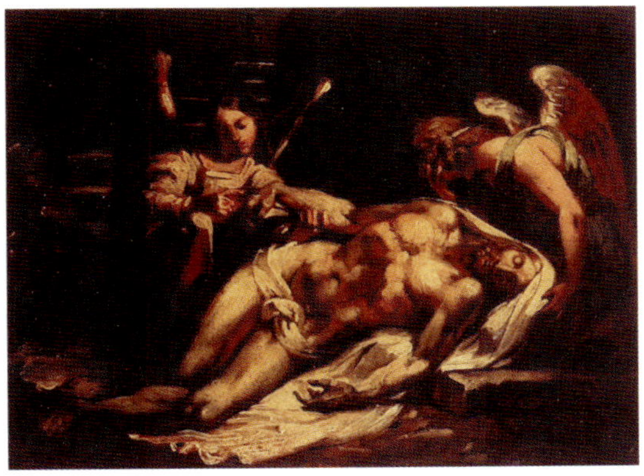

A511; oil on paper laid on canvas, mounted as a drawing, 23.5 × 31.5 cm
Presented by the Revd Dr S.H. Scott, 1937; WA1937.113

Formerly attributed to the French painter, Pierre-Paul Prud'hon (1758–1823). The idealisation in the features of the angels and the muscular figure of Christ suggests a French or Italian painter working in the 1820s.

Lucian Freud
(b. 1922)

Small Naked Portrait

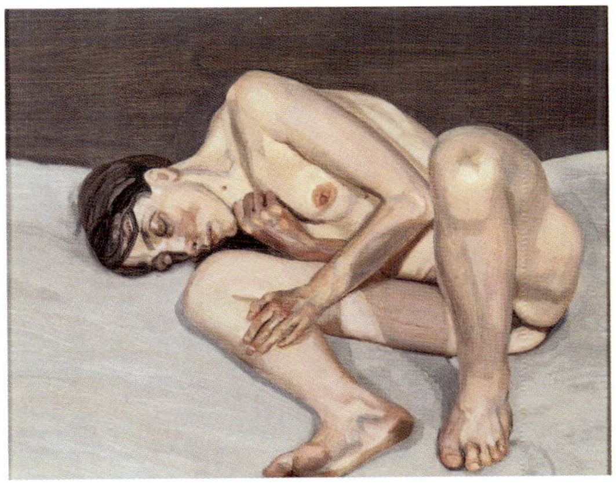

A1157; oil on canvas, 22.2 × 20 cm
Prov.: Lady Elliot; David Kelley
Purchased with the assistance of the Museums & Galleries Commission/Victoria & Albert Museum Purchase Grant Fund and the National Art Collections Fund, 1988; WA1988.229

Gowing 1982, p. 151; Eustace 1999, no. 34

Freud regularly returned to the motif of the reclining nude woman from the 1960s onwards. This painting, made in 1973–4, is one of a group of works which, by treating the figure with severe objectivity, create the effect of still life.

William Powell Frith
(1819 – 1909)

Before Dinner at Boswell's Lodging, 1769

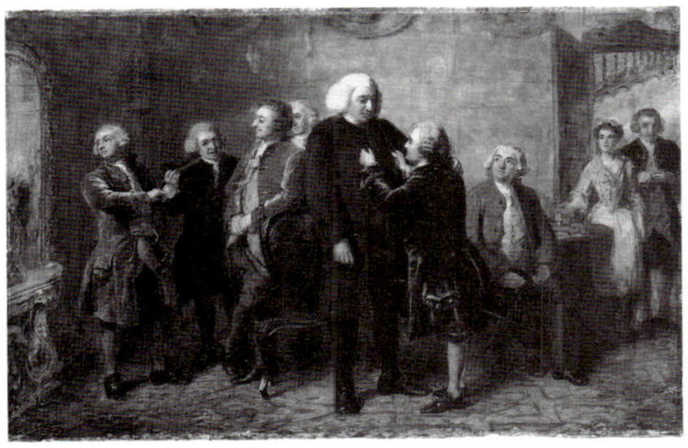

A508; oil on canvas, 41 × 63 cm
Inscribed: *1868*
Prov.: Snowdon Henry
Presented by the grandchildren of J. Snowdon Henry, 1937; WA1937.107

After the enormous success of *Ramsgate Sands*, exhibited at the Royal Academy in 1854 (Royal Collection), Frith added scenes from modern life to his repertoire. This is a reduced replica of a picture shown at the Royal Academy in 1868. It illustrates a party on 16 October 1769 recorded in Boswell's *Life of Johnson* the guests were Oliver Goldsmith, Sir Joshua Reynolds, Murphy, Bickerstaff, Thomas Davies, Dr Johnson and Boswell himself.

William Edward Frost
(1810 – 1887)

Self-portrait as a young Man

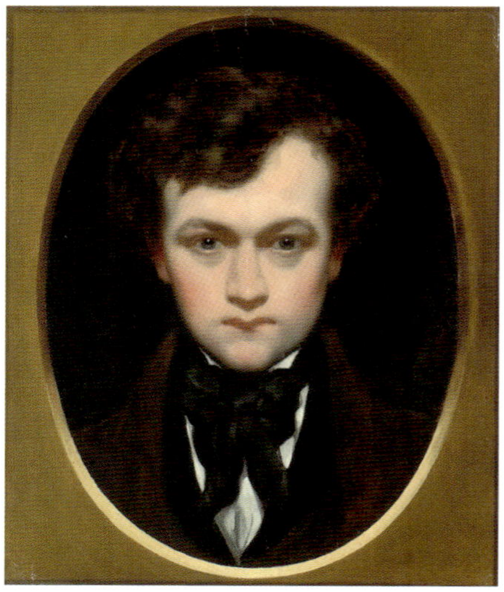

A687; oil on cardboard, 49 × 41 cm
Presented by G.T. Nicholson, 1941; WA1941.89

Frost was a protegé of William Etty and studied at the Royal Academy Schools. During his early years, he concentrated on portraiture, but eventually forsook it for mildly erotic subjects taken chiefly from Milton and Spenser. He is seen here at about the age of thirty.

Roger Fry
(1866 – 1934)

Frank Hindley Smith

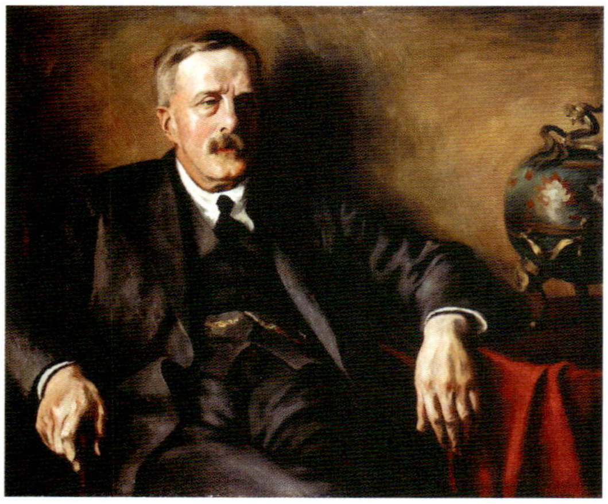

A1220; oil on canvas, 65.3 × 76.4 cm
Signed and dated: *Roger Fry 1923*
Purchased (Blakiston Fund), 1999; WA1999.21

Fry probably first met Frank Hindley Smith in 1920 and stayed with him at his house in Birkdale, Lancashire, on several occasions, when giving lecture tours in the North. He painted this portrait during a visit in 1923 .

Thomas Gainsborough, after Van Dyck
(1727 – 1788)

Two Monks reading

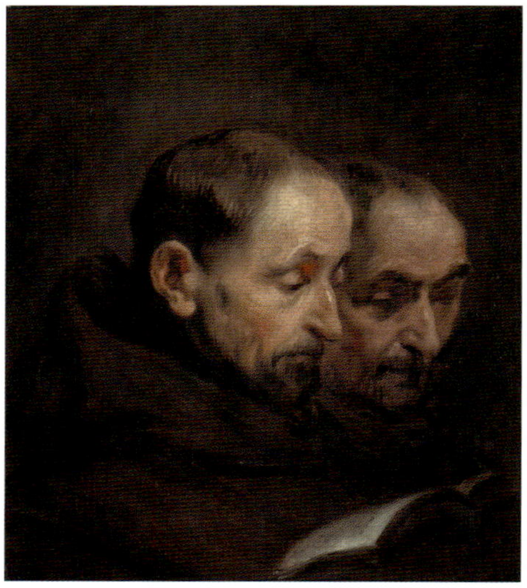

A482; oil on canvas, 54 × 47 cm
Prov.: Miss Gainsborough; Joseph Farington; Samuel Kilderbee; Hon. G. Agar Ellis, later Lord Dover; and by descent to Viscount Clifden; J.K. Stubbins
Weldon Bequest, 1937; WA1937.63

Waterhouse 1958, no. 1028

Copied from a painting by Rubens in Gainsborough's possession (Sotheby's, London, 13 July 1977, lot 46).

Roger Fry
(1866 – 1934)

La Salle des Caryatides in the Louvre

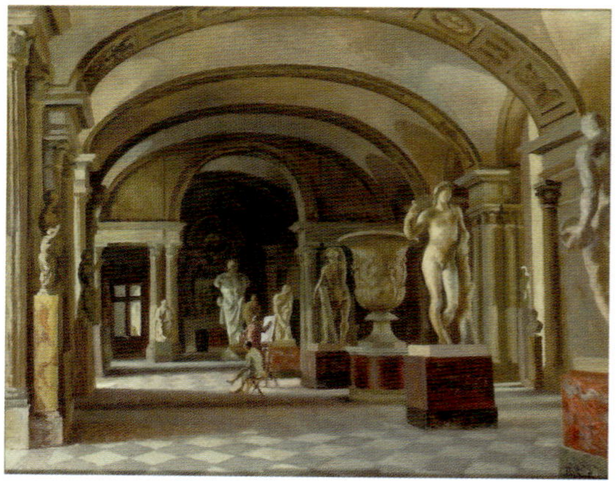

A424; oil on canvas, 65.5 × 82 cm
Signed: *Roger Fry*
Presented by the artist, 1933; WA1933.8

A view of the Salle des Caryatides in the Louvre, which owes its name to the four figures sculpted by Jean Goujon in 1550 to support the musicians' gallery, and which houses Roman statuary.

John Fulleylove
(1847 – 1908)

Cloisters at New College, Oxford

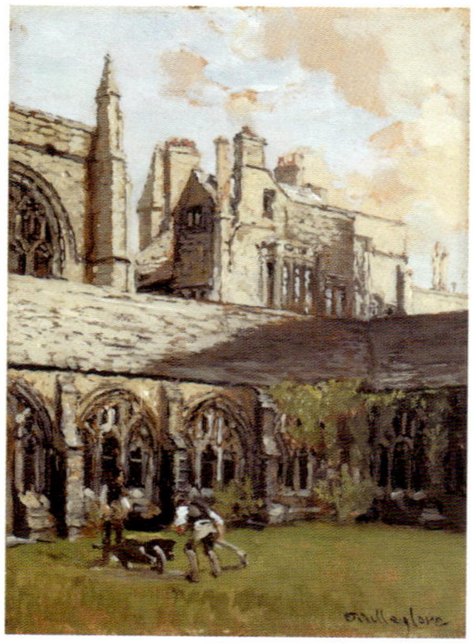

Oil on panel, mounted as a drawing, 19.1 × 13.8 cm
Signed: *Fulleylove*
Presented by Mrs W.S.S. Tyrwhitt, 1965; WA1965.44.9

Thomas Gainsborough
(1727 – 1788)

Portrait of an unknown Man

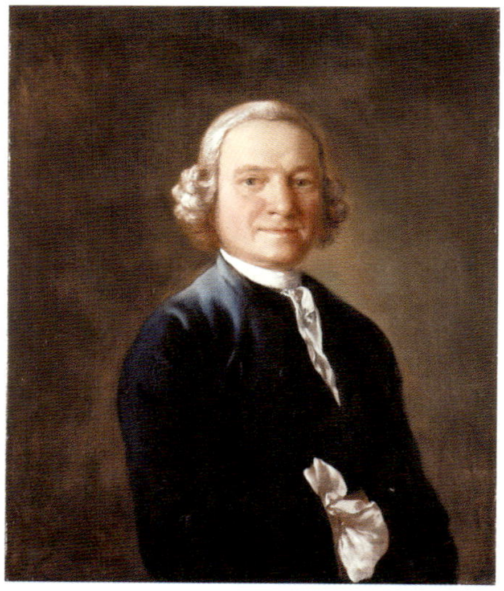

A1108; oil on canvas, 62.5 × 75 cm
Prov.: Henry Isherwood Kay
Bequeathed by Mrs Barbara Isherwood Kay, 1979; WA1979.49

Waterhouse 1958, no. 764

This portrait dates from the mid-1750s when Gainsborough was living in Ipswich. It may represent a member of the Gibbs family, though this cannot be confirmed.

Thomas Gainsborough
(1727 – 1788)

Margaret Gainsborough gleaning

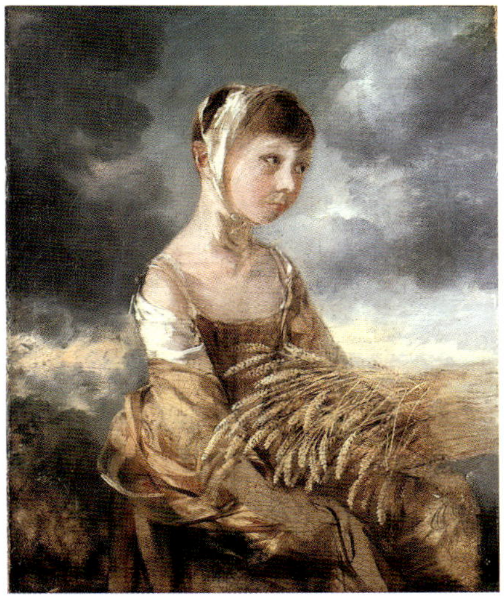

A1076; oil on canvas, 73 × 63 cm
Prov.: G. Strutt; Sir Hugh Lane; Louis Fleischmann and by descent
Purchased with the aid of a gift in memory of Helen, Henry and Marius Winslow and the assistance of the Victoria & Albert Museum Purchase Grant Fund, 1975; WA1975.72

Waterhouse, 1958, no. 283; Hayes 1981, no. 68

Margaret Gainsborough (1752–1820) is shown in peasant costume as a gleaner. This is the surviving half of a double portrait of Gainsborough's two daughters, probably painted in the late 1750s, which was intended as both portrait and 'fancy picture'.

Thomas Gainsborough
(1727 – 1788)

George Drummond

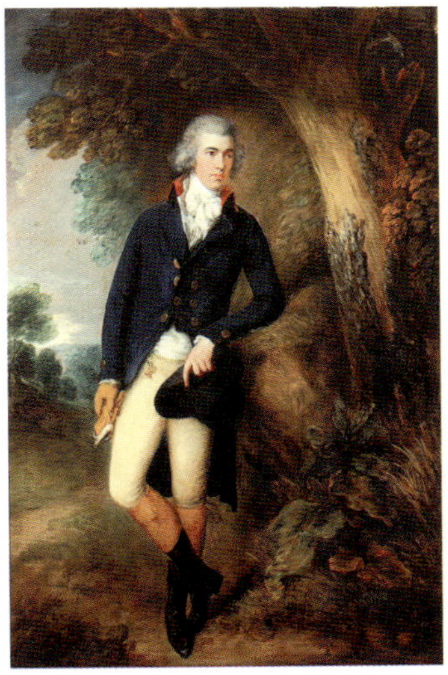

A878; oil on canvas, 233 × 151 cm
Prov.: commissioned by the Rt Hon. Thomas Harley; by descent to George, 7th Baron Rodney; Michael Bass, 1st Baron Burton and by descent
Presented by the National Art Collections Fund from the collection of Ernest E. Cook, 1955; WA1955.62

Waterhouse 1958, no. 210

George Drummond (1758–1789) of Stanmore, second son of Robert Hay Drummond, Archbishop of York, was a senior partner in Drummonds Bank. He married (secondly) Martha, the eldest daughter and heiress of Rt Hon. Thomas Harley on 30 November 1779. This portrait and its companion of Mrs Drummond (Montreal Museum of Fine Arts) were probably commissioned for Harley's new house, Berrington Hall, Herefordshire.

Style of Thomas Gainsborough
(1727 – 1788)

Landscape with Cattle and a Pond

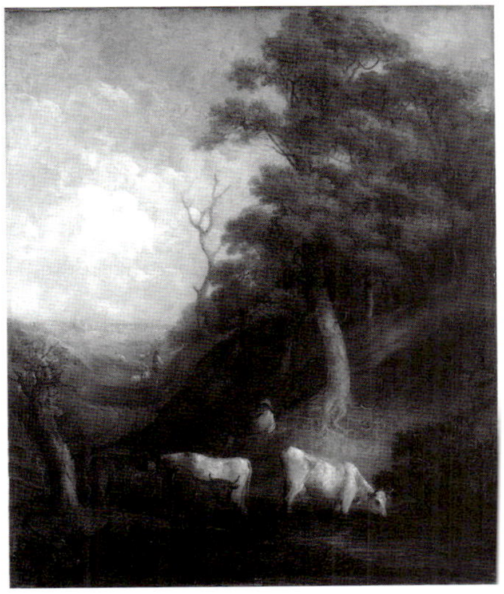

A130; oil on canvas, 74 × 62 cm
Bequeathed by the Revd Dr Thomas Penrose, 1851; WA1851.3

Waterhouse 1958, no. 892; Hayes 1982, II, p. 580

While the individual elements and general composition are reminiscent of Gainsborough's landscapes, this is by one of his many imitators.

Pieter Gallis
(1633 – 1687)

Still Life with a Lobster

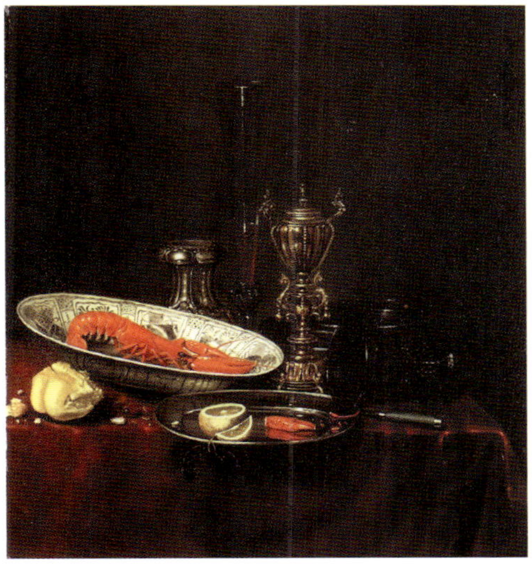

A552; oil on canvas, 73 × 67 cm
Indistinctly signed and perhaps dated
Prov.: James Brownlee Hunter
Daisy Linda Ward Bequest, 1939; WA1940.2.28

Meijer 2003, no. 31

Little is known about Gallis apart from his paintings, most of which are pictures of still life. This modest banquet includes a number of luxury items: a Wan-li blue and white porcelain dish, a knife with shagreen-covered handle, a silver standing salt and a cup-holder of a kind which would have been somewhat old-fashioned by the mid-1660s when this work was possibly executed.

Gaetano Gandolfi
(1734 – 1802)

The Adoration of the Shepherds

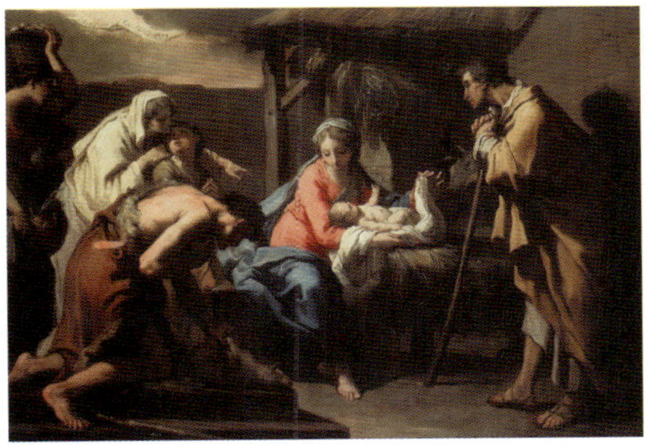

A784; oil on canvas, 48 × 70 cm
Prov.: Giovanni Battista Fornasari; George Richmond and by descent
Bequeathed by Mrs H.F. Medlicott, 1950; WA1950.22

Biagi Maino 1995, no. 245

An angel announces the birth of Christ to the shepherds, who hasten to worship the new-born saviour (Luke 2: 8–18). Two preparatory drawings for A784 and A785 were also in the Medlicott bequest (Parker 1956, nos. 999 and 1000): that for the *Adoration* is inscribed with details of the commission, including the fact that Gaetano's son Mauro made a copy in 1829 with the intention of engraving the composition.

Gaetano Gandolfi
(1734 – 1802)

The Flight into Egypt

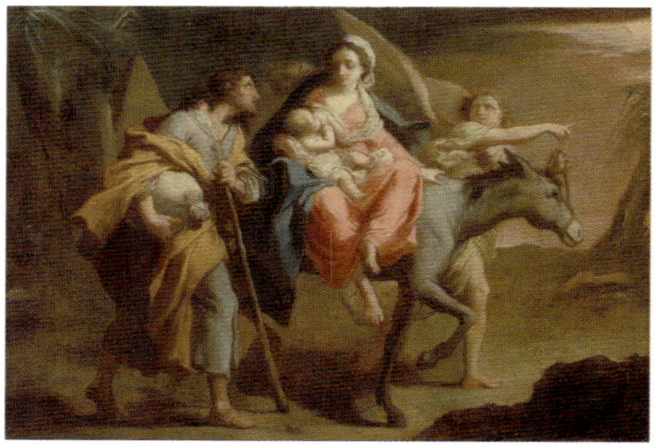

A785; oil on canvas, 76 × 63 cm
Prov.: Giovanni Battista Fornasari; George Richmond and by descent
Bequeathed by Mrs Hilda Fothergill Medlicott, 1950; WA1950.23

Biagi Maino 1995, no. 246

Having been warned by an angel that Herod has ordered the massacre of all new-born boys, Joseph takes Mary and the infant Christ to safety in Egypt (Matthew 2: 13–15). Together with A785, this was commissioned in 1798 by Giovanni Battista Fornasari, a pupil, friend and later patron of Gaetano.

Clive Gardiner
(1891 – 1960)

Wood Interior

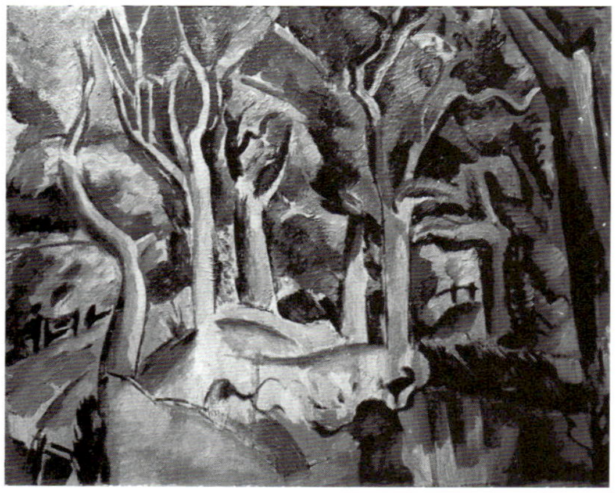

A924a; oil on canvas; 51 × 61 cm
Signed: *Clive Gardiner*
Presented by A.H. Smith, Warden of New College, 1959; WA1959.43.2

Beside his role as painter, Gardiner was active as director of the Goldsmith's College of Art in London. During this period many etchers, the so-called 'Goldsmith's school', had been trained at the College, often specialising in landscapes. The treatment of this landscape recalls paintings by Friesz, in which strong outlines and a patchy application of paint create a sense of space and atmosphere.

Norman Garstin
(1847 – 1926)

Across the River, St Paul's

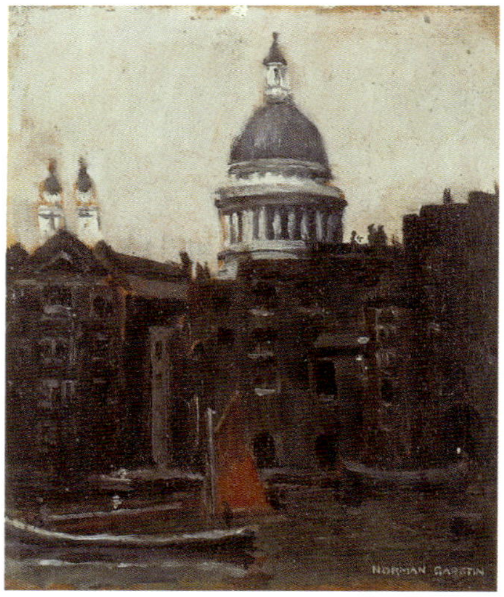

Oil on board, mounted as a drawing, 15 × 12.2 cm
Signed: *NORMAN GARSTIN*
Presented by the Contemporary Art Society, 1980; WA1980.120

St Ives 1978, no. 33

The dome of St Paul's Cathedral, seen from the south. The body of the church is masked by riverside warehouses.

Ubaldo Gandolfi
(1728 – 1781)

Head of a young Woman

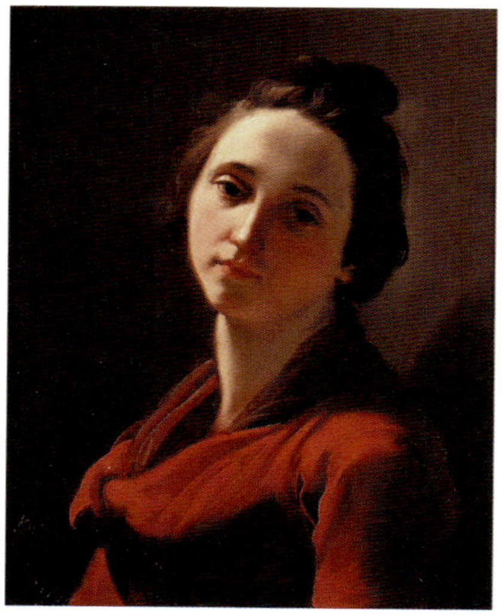

A1122; oil on canvas, 48.5 × 39 cm
Prov.: Giuliano Briganti
Purchased with the assistance of the Victoria & Albert Museum Purchase Grant Fund, the National Art Collections Fund and other donors, 1982; WA1982.36

Whistler 2002

Rosa Spisani, the artist's wife, may have been the model for a type of female beauty that recurs in Ubaldo's art. This tender expressive study forms part of a large group of *teste di carattere* or studies of character and emotion dating probably from 1775–78. Many of these were owned by Gregorio Casale, a leading Bolognese intellectual who was a friend and patron of the artist.

Norman Garstin
(1847 – 1926)

Ludgate Hill

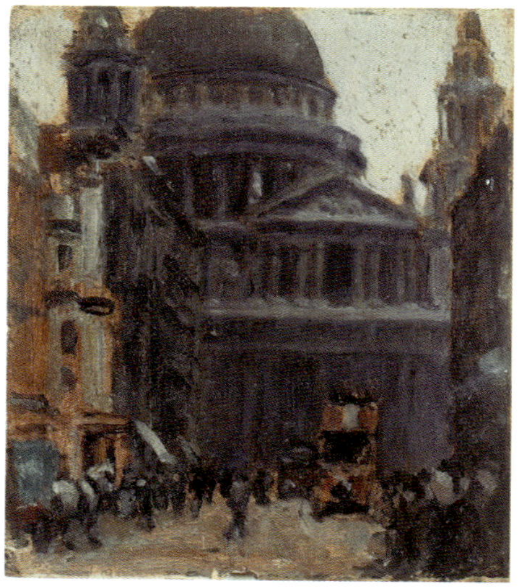

Oil on board, mounted as a drawing, 14.9 × 12.7 cm
Presented by the Contemporary Art Society, 1980; WA1980.121

St Ives 1978, no. 30

The west front of St Paul's Cathedral, seen from Ludgate Hill, with an omnibus approaching on the right. This sketch and the two following may date from 1919. Garstin spent most of his working life as the father of the Newlyn School. He settled in Newlyn in 1886, but made frequent visits to London.

Norman Garstin
(1847 – 1926)

St Mary-le-Strand

Oil on board, mounted as a drawing, 15 × 12.8 cm
Presented by the Contemporary Art Society, 1980; WA1980.122

St Ives 1978, no. 39

St Mary-le-Strand was designed by James Gibbs (1682–1754) and erected between 1714 and 1717. During Garstin's lifetime, it was threatened with demolition because it obstructed the traffic in the Strand.

Circle of Luigi Garzi
(1638 – 1721)

Vigilance and Love's Oblivion

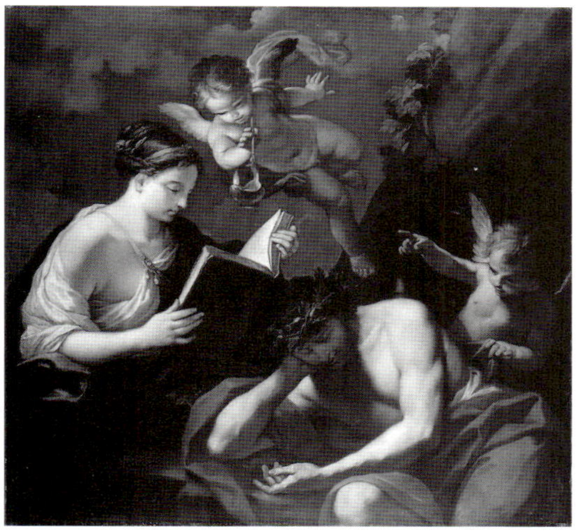

A396; oil on canvas, 139 × 147 cm
Presented by Sir Arthur Evans, 1929; WA1929.8

Formerly attributed to Guido Reni and to Claudio Francesco Beaumont, A396 is clearly by a follower of Carlo Maratta and has affinities with the art of Luigi Garzi. It may have formed part of a decorative scheme with other pairs of allegorical figures: here, Cesare Ripa's descriptions of *Vigilanza* and *Oblivione d'Amore* are quite closely followed.

Anonymous German Artist
(c. 1500 – 1525)

St Anne between St John the Baptist and St Anthony Abbot

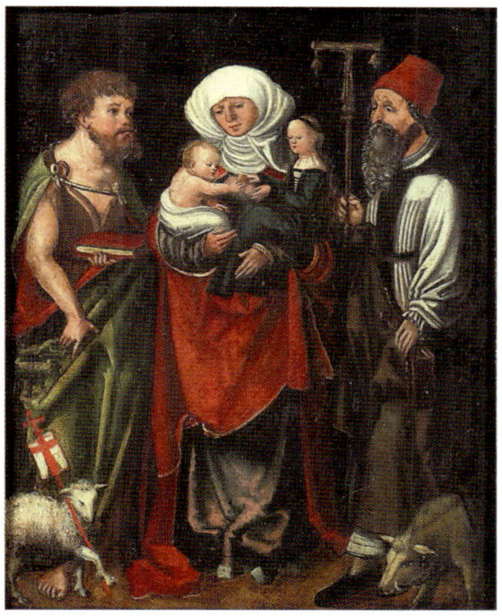

A908; oil on panel, 26 × 21 cm
Purchased, 1957; WA1957.44

White 1999, p. 192

St Anne holds the Virgin Mary and the Christ Child in her arms with St John on the left and St Anthony accompanied by his pig on the right. Images representing three generations of the Holy Family were popular in 16th-century German art. This painting is by an artist of the Saxon School.

Gerolamo da Santacroce
(c. 1485 – 1556)

The Annunciation

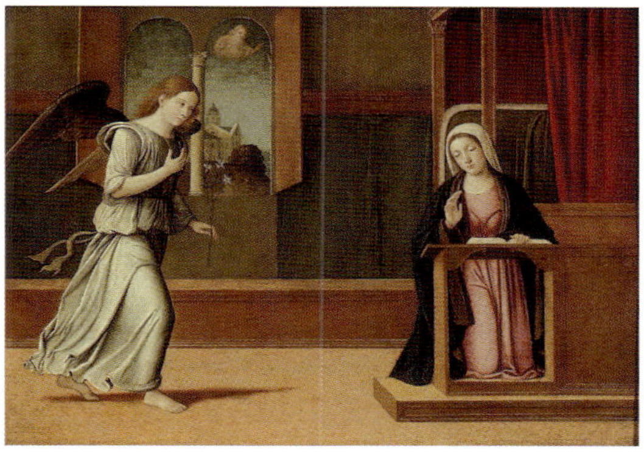

A292; oil on panel, 51 × 70 cm
Bequeathed by John D. Chambers, 1897; WA1897.21

Della Chiesa and Baccheschi 1976, no. 63; Lloyd 1977, p. 72

The Angel Gabriel announces to the Virgin Mary that she will bear the son of God (Luke 1: 26–8). A simplified version of *the Annunciation* by Cima da Conegliano of 1495, now in the Hermitage, St Petersburg, A292 is a characteristic work. Gerolamo da Santacroce was one of a family of artists who painted in a conservative, eclectic manner for a range of patrons in Venice and the Veneto.

Anonymous Genoese Artist (?)
(c. 1650 – 1680)

A Dog lying on a Ledge

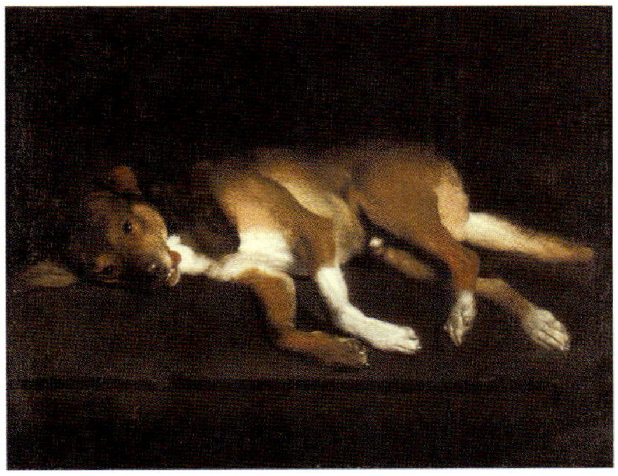

A890; oil on canvas, 49 × 63 cm
Prov.: Galerie Espagnole of Louis-Philippe, Paris; P.L. Hind; J.F. Austen, Horsmonden
Bequeathed by Percy Moore Turner, 1951; WA1957.59.2

Baticle and Marinas 1981, pp. 255, 410

In the mid-19th century, A890 was attributed to Zurbarán and then to Velázquez: it is a portrait of a plebeian dog, rather than the more common type of image of hunting dogs or courtly lapdogs. The artist may have been Genoese and an attribution has been suggested to Giovanni Agostino Cassana (post 1659–1720).

Anonymous German Artist
(c. 1770 – 1780)

The Artist and his Family in a Park

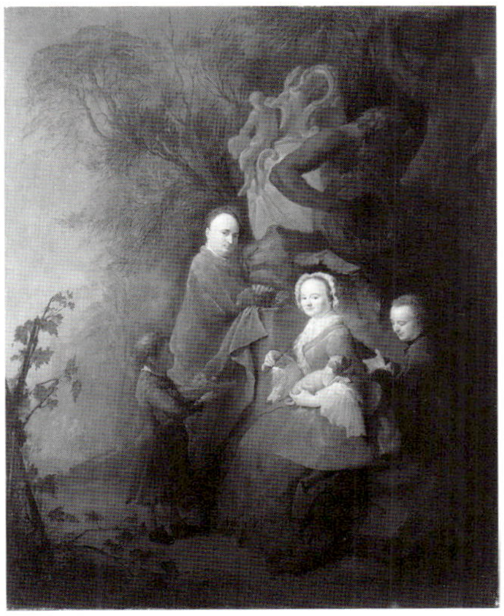

A428; oil on canvas, 135 × 107 cm
Prov.: Friedrich von Amerling; Antiquités au Vieux Cluny, Beaulieu, 1933
Purchased, 1933; WA1933.24

Roland Michel 1984, no. PP.11

Against the background of an elaborate fountain, the man (identified as an artist by his cap) and his wife and son are offered a basket of fruit by a young boy. Perhaps the artist wished to portray his family in a sophisticated setting, or he may have been a theatrical designer or a sculptor. A428 was formerly attributed to Jacques de Lajoue (1687–1761).

Jean-Léon Gérôme
(1824 – 1904)

View of the Nile at Luxor

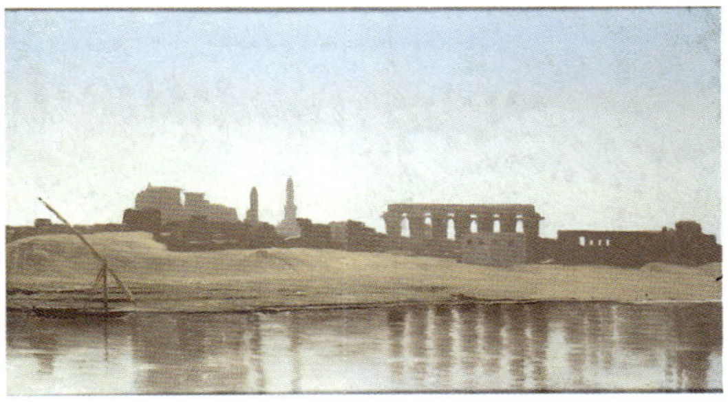

A1238; oil on canvas laid on board, 16.5 × 28.7 cm
Prov.: Count Charles de Salis
Purchased (Miller Fund), 2001; WA2001.45

Painted during the artist's first visit to Egypt in 1857. It is unusual to find a work by Gérome without a figure or an animal. The sketch was used as a model for the background of one of the artist's most famous paintings, *The Prisoner*, painted in 1861, now in the Musée des Beaux-Arts, Nantes. Following the trip to Egypt in 1857, the artist became one of the best known and most successful painters of near-eastern subjects in France.

Mark Gertler
(1891 – 1939)

Gilbert Cannan and his Mill

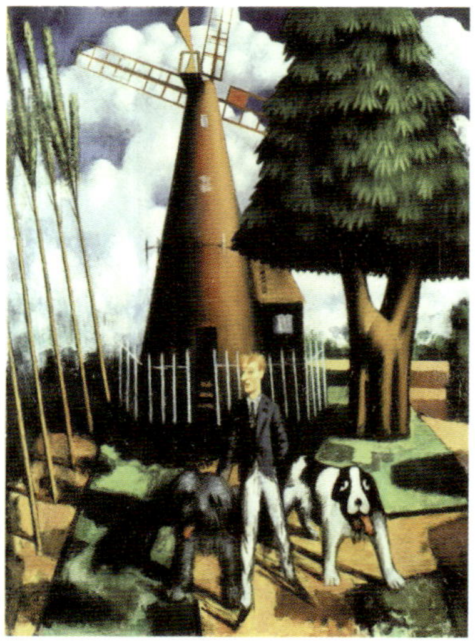

A1041; oil on canvas, 99.5 × 70 cm
Signed and dated: *THE MILL. / By. Mark Gertler. / april. 1916*
Bequeathed by Thomas Balston through the National Art Collections Fund, 1968; WA1968.24

London 1992, no. 49; Eustace 1999, no. 11

In 1914 Gertler went to stay with the writer Gilbert Cannan (1884–1955) and his wife in a converted windmill at Cholesbury, Hertfordshire. Over the next two years, he became a regular visitor and introduced Cannan to the music-hall life of the East End, where he had been brought up. He must have begun this painting during his first visit. It is one of his most radical pictures and reflects his interests in contemporary art.

Mark Gertler
(1891 – 1939)

Thomas Balston

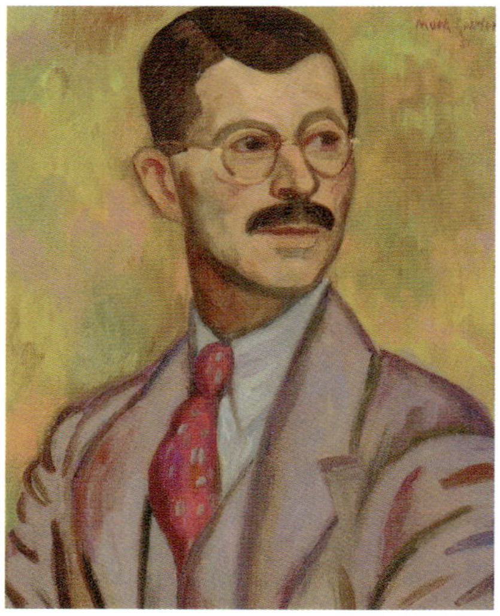

A1038; oil on canvas, 51 × 41 cm
Signed and dated: *Mark Gertler 21*
Bequeathed by Thomas Balston through the National Art Collections Fund, 1968; WA1968.21

Oxford 1971

Thomas Balston (1883–1967), a member of the Whatman paper-making dynasty, worked from 1921 to 1934 for the publishing house Duckworth & Co, where he employed many wood engravers as illustrators. In the same period he was a keen supporter of Gertler. This portrait, made in 1921, shows Balston in a close-up view. His jacket is painted with with powerful, broad outlines and is modelled with a pattern of dynamic brush-strokes.

Mark Gertler
(1891 – 1939)

Apples in a Bag

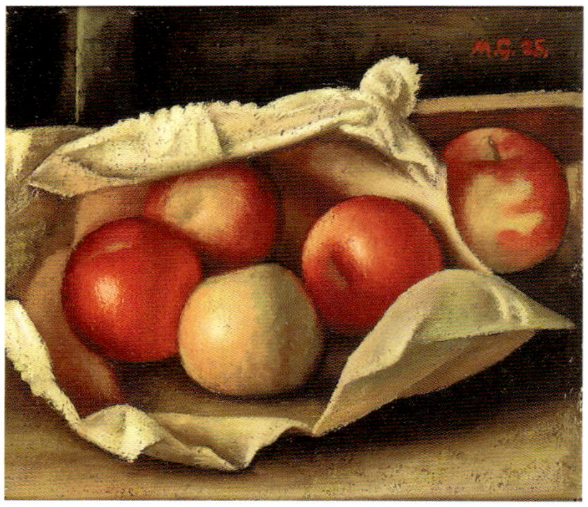

A1040; oil on cardboard, 26.7 × 29.9 cm
Signed in monogram and dated: *M.G. 25.*
Bequeathed by Thomas Balston through the National Art Collections Fund 1968; WA1968.23

Oxford 1971, no. 37

Mark Gertler
(1891 – 1939)

Young Girlhood, No.2

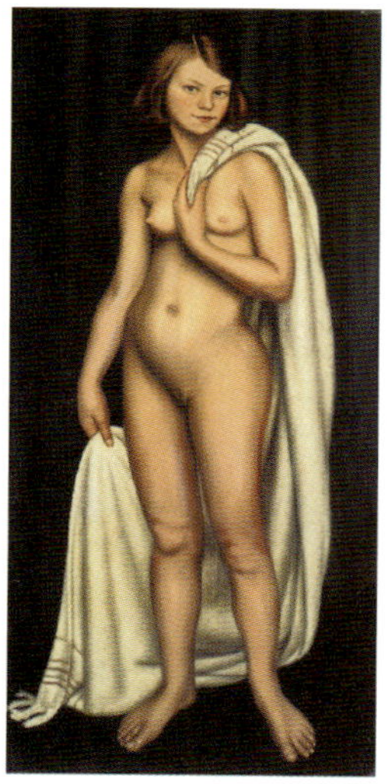

A925; oil on canvas, 13.5 × 64 cm
Signed and dated: *Mark Gertler 25*
Presented by Thomas Balston, 1959; WA1959.54.2

London 1991, no. 48; MacDougall 2002, fig. 8

In the 1920s, Gertler used Alice Edwards as the model for a series of portraits. In these voyeuristic paintings, he aimed to capture the charm of young girlhood, here using the traditional motif of a standing nude.

Mark Gertler
(1891 – 1939)

Staffordshire Group

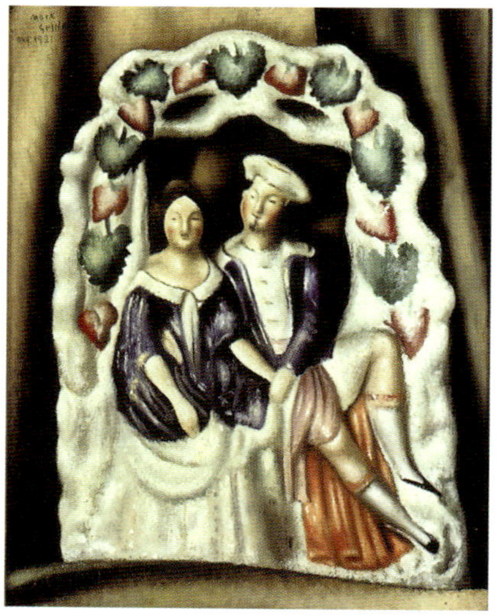

A1039; oil on canvas, 56.2 × 43.6 cm
Signed and dated: *Mark Gertler Aug. 1921*
Bequeathed by Thomas Balston through the National Art Collections Fund, 1968; WA1968.22

Thomas Balston, who first owned this work, was a collector of Staffordshire figures and author of a standard work on this subject, *Staffordshire Portrait Figures of the Victorian Age* (1958).

Davide Ghirlandaio
(1452 – 1512)

Sts Nicholas of Bari and Dominic

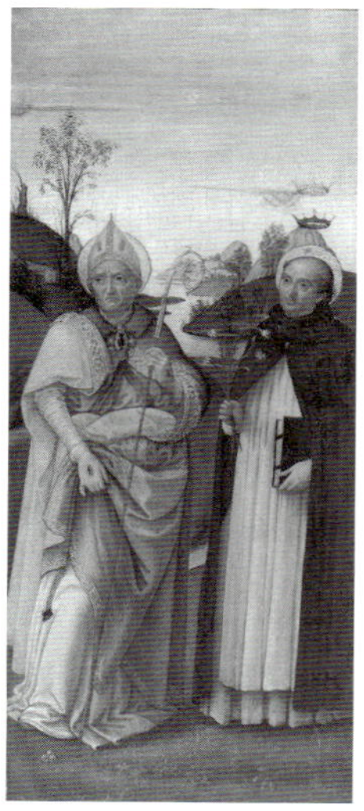

A84; oil and gilding on panel, 69 × 31 cm
Fox-Strangways Gift, 1850; WA1850.12

Lloyd, 1977, pp. 109–11; Cadogan 2000, pp. 322–3

A companion piece showing *The Crucifixion with St Thomas Aquinas and St Augustine* was formerly with Colnaghi, London. Dating from the mid-1480s, the two panels could have formed the wings of a small altar-piece, or part of the lower register of a larger one. St Dominic has a double crown, a reference to his status as a doctor of the Church and a virgin saint. The artist formerly known as the Master of the St Louis Altar-piece has been convincingly identified as Davide Ghirlandaio, who collaborated with his brother, Domenico.

Domenico Ghirlandaio
(1449 – 1494)

Portrait of a young Man

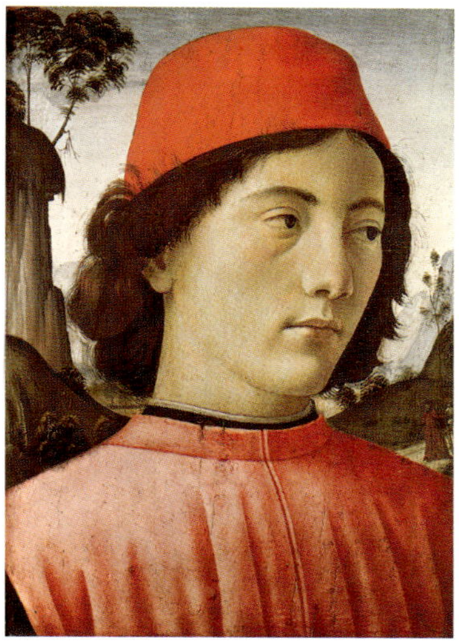

A83; tempera on panel, 43 × 32.3 cm
Fox-Strangways Gift, 1850; WA1850.15

Lloyd 1977, pp. 73–4

Initially trained as a goldsmith, Ghirlandaio was one of the leading artists of late 15th-century Florence, counting the young Michelangelo amongst his pupils. A83 is an early work, datable to *c.* 1477–8; the portrait type was stimulated by developments in Flemish portraiture.

Follower of Corrado Giaquinto
(1703 – 1766)

The Immaculate Conception

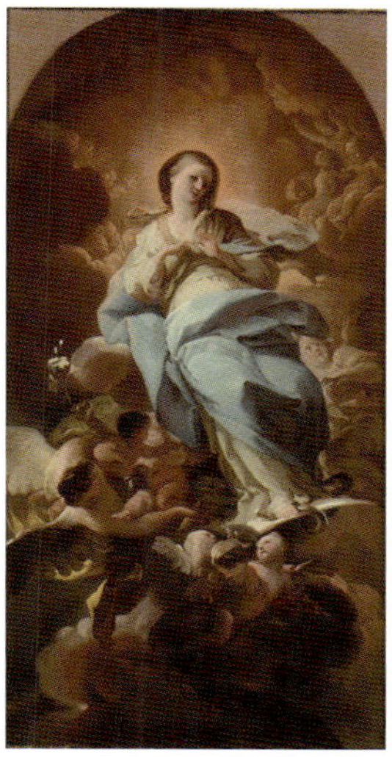

A934; oil on canvas, 61 × 31 cm
Purchased, 1960; WA1960.32

The Virgin is borne through clouds by angels, one of whom holds a lily, symbol of purity; she stands on a crescent moon, a symbol of chastity and crushes the serpent beneath her feet (Genesis 4: 14–15). While A934 was thought to be a model for a larger picture, perhaps from *c.* 1740–42, it is probably an independent work by one of Giaquinto's many followers in Puglia.

Harold Gilman
(1876 – 1919)

Cave Dwellers, Dieppe

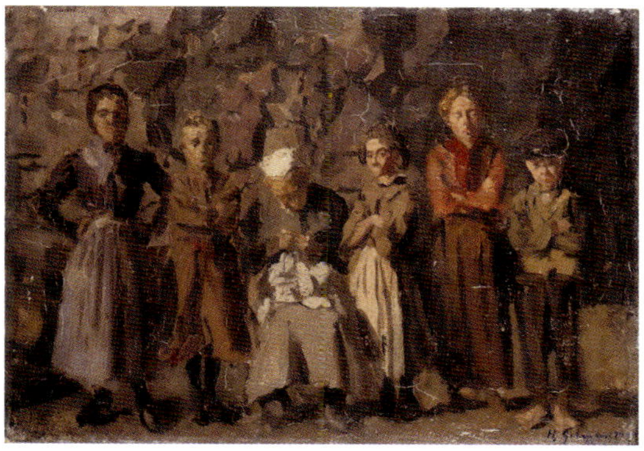

A900; oil on canvas, 25 × 36 cm
Signed and dated: *H. Gilman 1907*
Prov.: Sir Louis F. Fergusson; Rex Nan Kivell
Presented by R.A. Bevan, 1957; WA1957.16

Baron 1979, no. 45

This scene, apparently painted from life, was painted while Gilman was staying with Sickert at Neuville, near Dieppe. The subjects are posed as for a group photograph, hostile and uncommunicative. The painting was much admired by Sickert and Lucien Pissarro.

Michele Giovanni Boni, called Giambono
(*c.* 1400 – 1462)

A Bishop Saint

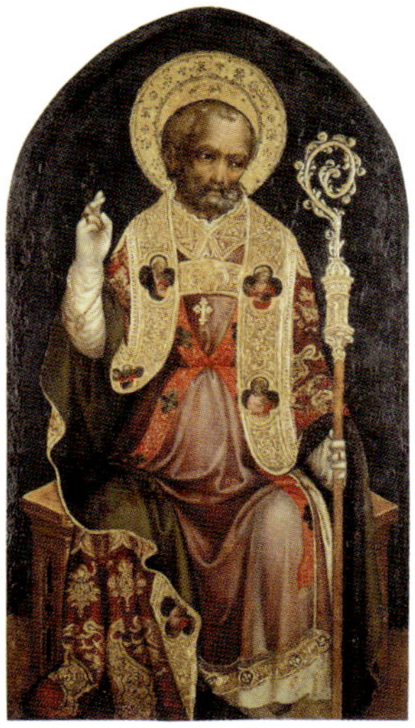

A1133; tempera and gilding on panel, 84.5 × 47.7 cm
Purchased with the assistance of the National Art Collections Fund, 1984; WA1984.149

Franco 1998, pp. 107, 109

A1130 was probably part of a large altar-piece of *c.* 1440, such as that recorded in Sant' Alvise, Venice in 1581. The bishop saint, who has no identifying attributes, is possibly St Louis of Toulouse, or alternatively St Prosdocimo, the first bishop of Padua. Giambono was a leading artist who worked extensively in Venice and Padua.

Jacob Gillig
(*c.* 1636 – 1701)

Still Life of Fish

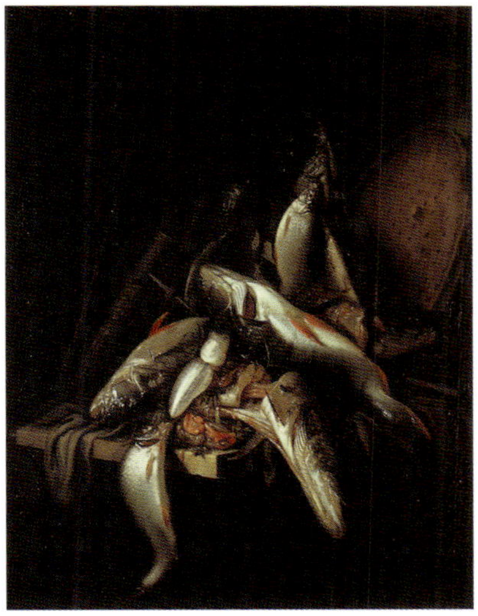

A553; oil on canvas, 71 × 56 cm
Signed: *Jacobus Gillig 1670*
Daisy Linda Ward Bequest, 1939; WA1940.2.29

Meijer 2003, no. 32

Gillig spent his life in Utrecht, specializing in painting still-life compositions of fish. In this characteristically pyramidal composition, he paints two perch, a gutted pike, several roach and other fresh-water fish. In his early works, he sometimes painted sea-water fish but fresh-water fish became his main interest.

Harold Gilman
(1876 – 1919)

Dieppe from the East

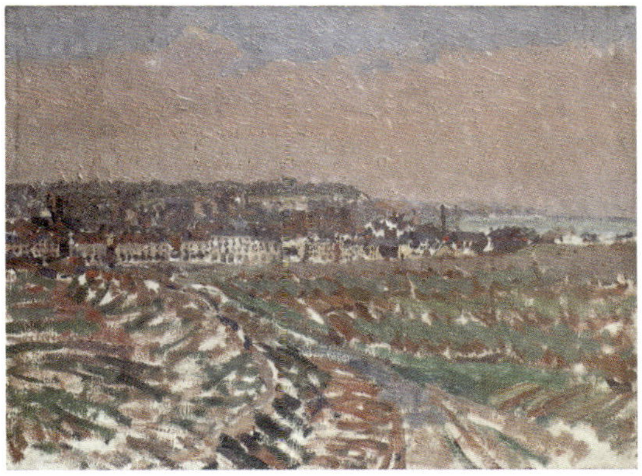

A954; oil on canvas, 45 × 60 cm
Prov.: L.H. Gilman, the artist's brother
Purchased (Bevan Fund), 1961; WA1961.46

Baron 1979, p. 368

In late 1910 or early 1911, Gilman visited Paris with Charles Ginner. The wealth of Impressionist and Post-Impressionist paintings he saw at the dealers marked him deeply. On the return journey, he stayed with Sickert at Neuville, near Dieppe. This unfinished view shows Dieppe, looking east from west of the harbour, with the towers of the harbour slightly to the left of centre.

Harold Gilman
(1876 – 1919)

Interior with Mrs Mounter

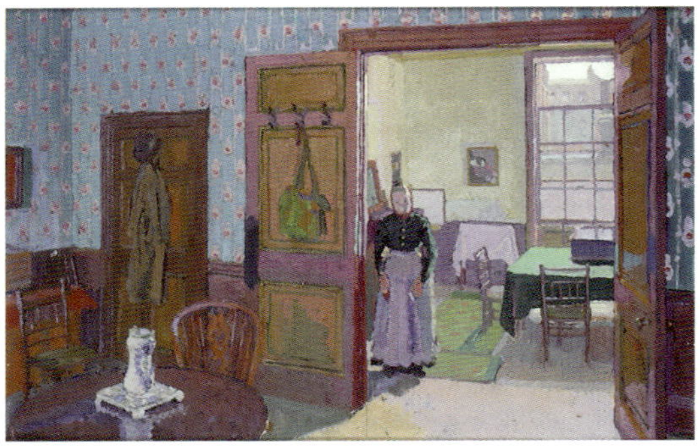

A1037; oil on canvas, 51 × 76 cm
Prov.: Hugh Blaker; Edward Le Bas
Presented by Brian Fairfax Hall in memory of Edward Le Bas, 1968; WA1968.20

London 1988, no. 176; Eustace 1999, no. 12

Mrs Mounter was Gilman's landlady at 47 Maple Street, off the Tottenham Court Road, where he lodged between the failure of his first marriage and his second to Sylvia Hardy in 1917. He was apparently fond of the garish blue wallpaper and included it in several interiors of 1916–17.

Charles Isaac Ginner
(1878 – 1952)

Cornish Cliffs

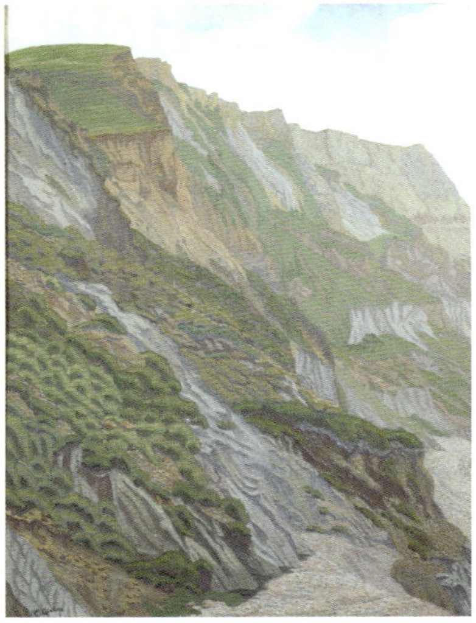

A901; oil on canvas, 69 × 51 cm
Signed: *C. GINNER*
Prov.: David Croal Thomson; Hugh Blaker
Presented by R.A. Bevan, 1957; WA1957.17

Eustace 1999, no. 21

After working as an official war artist during the First World War, Ginner turned exclusively to landscapes. After the deaths of his close friends, Gore and Gilman, his style developed little and he continued to paint in the decorative geometric manner of his early years. This landscape probably dates from the 1920s, when he exhibited a number of Cornish subjects.

Circle of Giorgione
(*c.* 1477/78 – 1510)

Virgin and Child with a View of Venice (The Tallard Madonna)

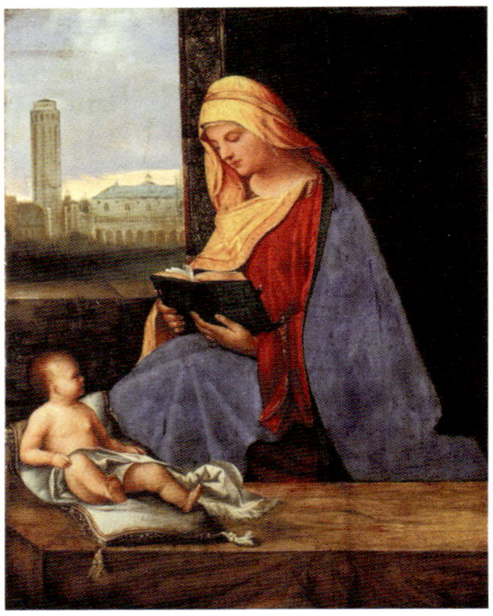

A777; oil on panel, 76.7 × 60.2 cm
Prov.: 13th Duc de Tallard; 6th Earl Cathcart
Purchased, 1949; WA1949.222

Lloyd 1977, pp. 75–9; Anderson 1997, pp. 332, 334; Pignatti and Pedrocco 1999, no. 23

Although Giorgione was celebrated in his lifetime, few pictures can be securely attributed to him. While some scholars attribute A777 to Giorgione, it is more likely to be by a pupil in Venice such as Sebastiano del Piombo, or an artist close to Giorgione such as Giovanni Cariani. The hazy view of the Piazza San Marco from the bacino shows the campanile with a temporary flat-roofed bell-chamber, which was in place from 1489 to 1511.

Charles Isaac Ginner
(1878 – 1952)

Hampstead Heath – Spring

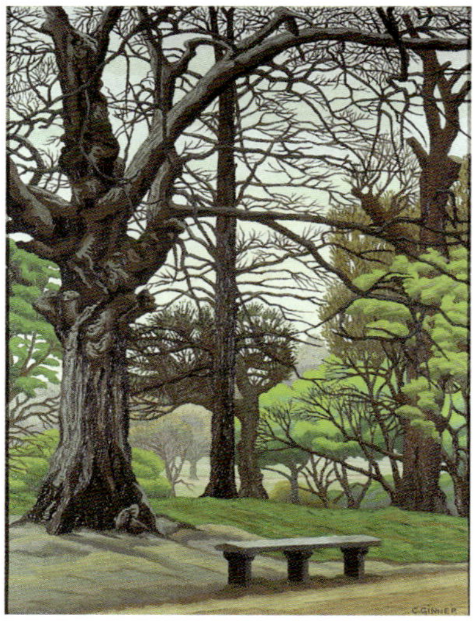

A1042; oil on canvas, 69 × 51 cm
Bequeathed by Thomas Balston through the National Art Collections Fund, 1968; WA1968.25

Painted in the spring of 1932 when Ginner was living at Hampstead.

Luca Giordano
(1632 – 1706)

The Crucifixion

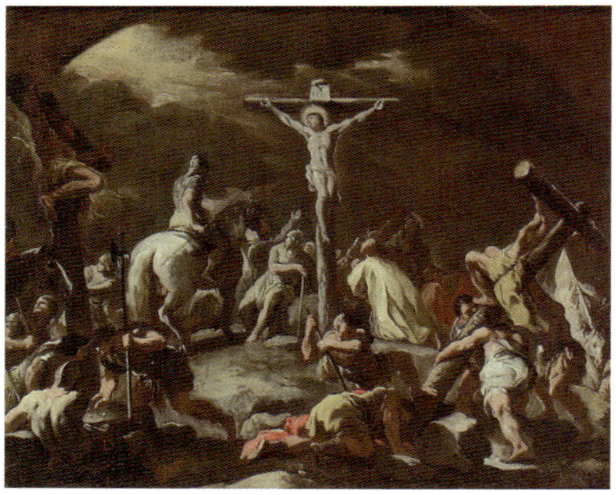

A1058; oil on canvas, 63 × 77 cm
Purchased with the assistance of the National Art Collections Fund, 1970; WA1970.78

Ferrari and Scavizzi 1992, no. A726

After his return from Spain in 1702, Giordano made some oil-sketches for the commission of the sacristy of S. Brigida, Naples. The frescoes were completed by his pupil Giuseppe Simonelli. For *The Crucifixion*, in a lunette over the altar, Giordano looked back to Tintoretto's painting in the Scuola Grande di S. Rocco, Venice and Lanfranco's fresco in S. Martino, Naples. A similar oil-sketch is in the Kurt Rossacher collection, Salzburg.

Studio of Giotto di Bondone
(1266/67? – 1337)

The Virgin and Child

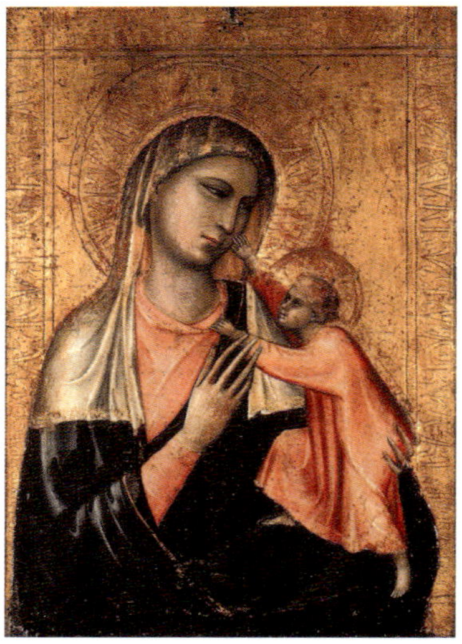

A332; tempera and gilding on panel, integral frame, 28.5 × 19.7 cm
Presented by Mrs James Reddie Anderson, 1913; WA1913.1

Lloyd 1977, pp. 79–82; Flores d'Arcais 1995, pp. 124–5; Volpe 2002, pp. 52, 53, 70

Giotto was admired by contemporaries as a highly original artist and an important teacher. A332 was probably painted *c.* 1310 by an assistant who worked closely with him. The traditional severe types of the Virgin and Child as venerable figures have been endowed with a new naturalism. The lettering in the border seems to be ornamental rather than meaningful.

GIOVANNI ANTONIO DA PESARO
(documented 1461 – 1511)

St Mark

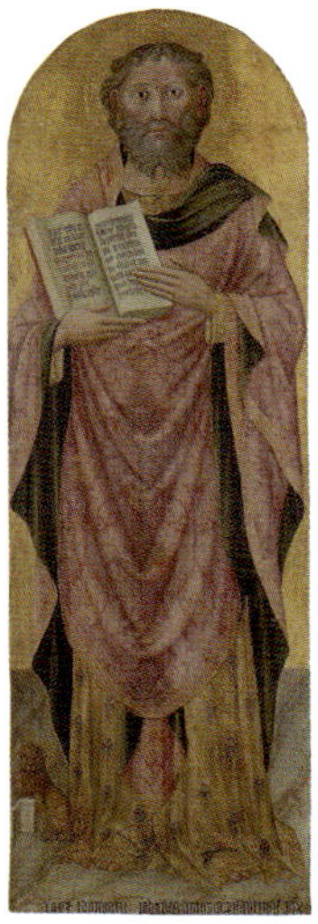

A882; tempera and gilding on panel, 170 × 55 cm
Inscribed: *1463 IANNUARII IOHAÑES ANTONIUS PISAURENSIS PIX.*
For inscriptions on the book held by St Mark see Lloyd 1977, p. 82
Prov.: Nicolò Paglieri, Pesaro; Monte di Pietà, Rome until 1875; K.J. Hewett, Ashford, Kent
Purchased with the assistance of the National Art Collections Fund, 1955; WA1955.78

Lloyd 1977, pp. 82–4; Berardi 1988, pp. 114–19

St Mark the evangelist, patron of Venice, is shown with his attributes of a lion and a book, open at the words of comfort (*Pax tibi marce*) spoken by Christ in a vision to the imprisoned saint. A882 was once flanked by panels with two pairs of saints each: left, Sts Blaise and John the Baptist above Sts Sebastian and Jerome and right, Sts James Major and Anthony Abbot above Sts Peter and Paul. The complex was probably painted for Santa Maria di San Marco, Pesaro, demolished *c.* 1501. Giovanni Antonio looked to Venetian paintings of the early 14th century in Pesaro as a source for his figures.

GIOVANNI DI PAOLO
(*c.* 1399 – 1482)

The Baptism of Christ

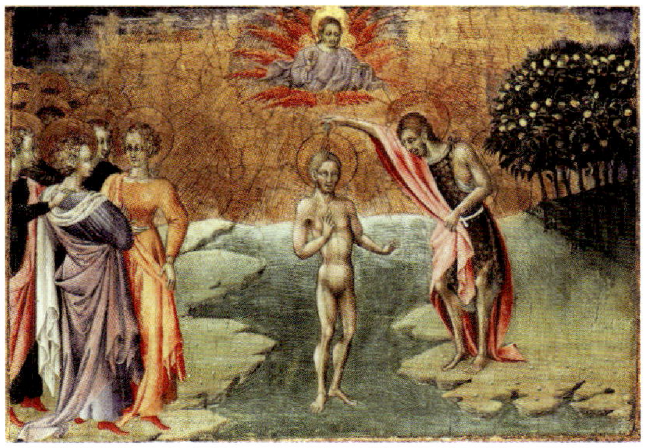

A333; tempera and gilding on panel, 25.7 × 35.7 cm
Presented by Mrs James Reddie Anderson, 1913; WA1913.2

Lloyd 1977, pp. 84–6; Christiansen *et al.* 1988, under no. 51

Christ was baptised by St John in the River Jordan when the Holy Spirit descended in the form of a dove and the voice of God proclaimed his Son (Matthew 3: 13–17). A333 formed part of the predella of an altar-piece painted *c.* 1460 which was once in the Silvestrine church at Montepulciano. Giovanni often reused his own compositions and A333 is similar to a predella panel in the National Gallery dating from *c.* 1454.

GIOVANNI DI PAOLO
(*c.* 1399 – 1482)

The Virgin and Child

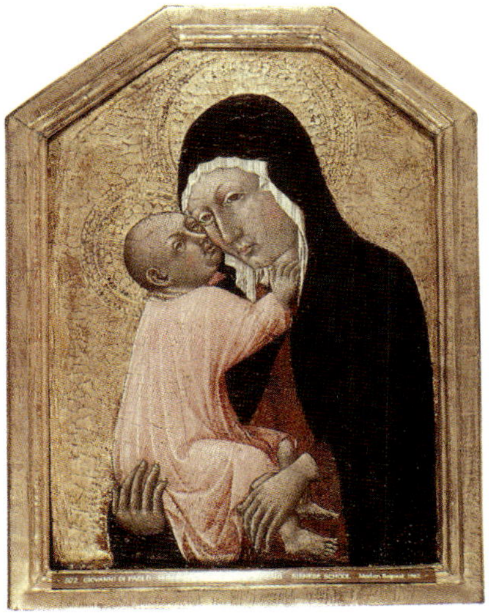

A972; tempera and gilding on panel, 35 × 25.5 cm
Prov.: Ferretti, Perugia (?); Dan Fellows Platt; E A. Silbermann
Madan Bequest, 1962; WA1962.17.14

Lloyd 1977, pp. 86–7

Giovanni worked mainly in Siena, developing a sophisticated, expressive manner that deliberately recalls the art of the great Sienese masters of the previous century. Although rather worn, this small devotional work is of fine quality. A relatively late work, it perhaps dates from the early 1460s.

VINCENT VAN GOGH
(1853 – 1890)

Restaurant de la Sirène, Asnières

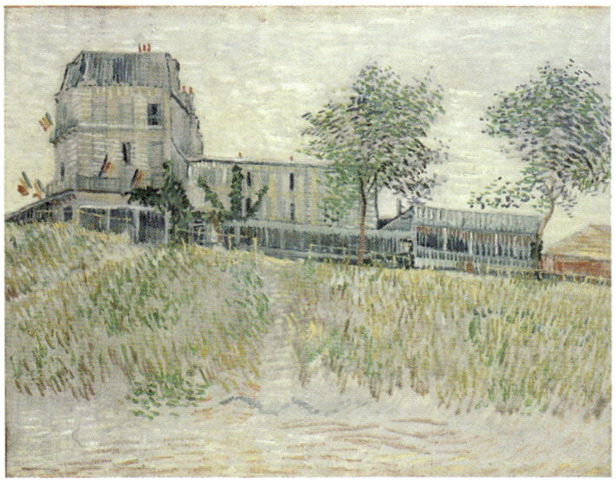

A1066; oil on canvas, 52 × 64.4 cm
Prov.: Tetzen-Lund; Mme Paret; Mrs Alport
Bequeathed by Dr Erich Alport, 1972; WA1972.18

White 1999, p. 51

Painted in 1887, a year after van Gogh had moved to Paris from his native Holland. The artist's response to the work of the Impressionists is evident in the short, straw-like strokes of paint and bright colour. Asnières, a district on the river Seine near Paris, was popular with the Impressionists and the site of several paintings by van Gogh, dating from his first period in Paris.

SPENCER FREDERICK GORE
(1878 – 1914)

The Cinder Path

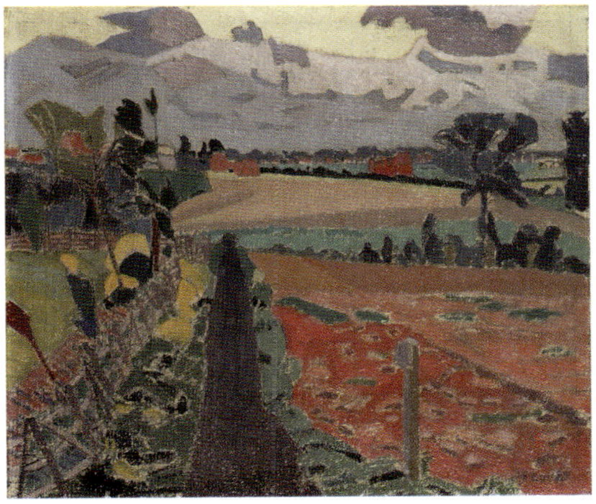

A903; oil on canvas, 35 × 40 cm
Signed: *SF GORE*
Prov.: Mrs R.P. Bevan
Presented by R.A. Bevan, 1957; WA1957.18.2

Baron 1979, under no. 113; Eustace 1999, no. 8

The Gore family spent August and September 1912 in Harold Gilman's house at Letchworth, the fashionable garden city begun in 1903. The cinder path linked the old market town of Baldock to the end of Works Road in Letchworth, about a mile from where he stayed. This is one of three versions of the subject painted by Gore. The bold juxtaposition of bright patches of unmodulated colours reflects his interest in modern French painting.

Spencer Frederick Gore
(1878 – 1914)

Richmond Park

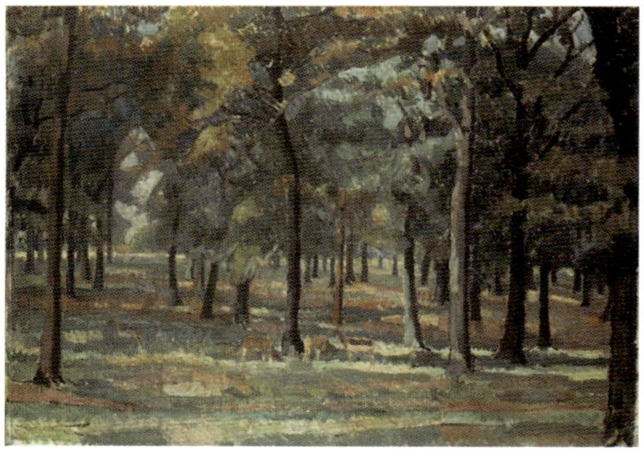

A902; oil on canvas, 55 × 75 cm
Presented by R.A. Bevan, 1957; WA1957.18.1

Baron 1979, p. 375; Richmond 1996, pp. 30–31

One of a series of thirty-two landscapes painted in Richmond Park during the last months of Gore's life. While painting them, he caught a cold which degenerated into pneumonia and pleurisy and resulted in his death. This example demonstrates his understanding of Cézanne's technique.

Sylvia Gosse
(1881 – 1965)

Versailles

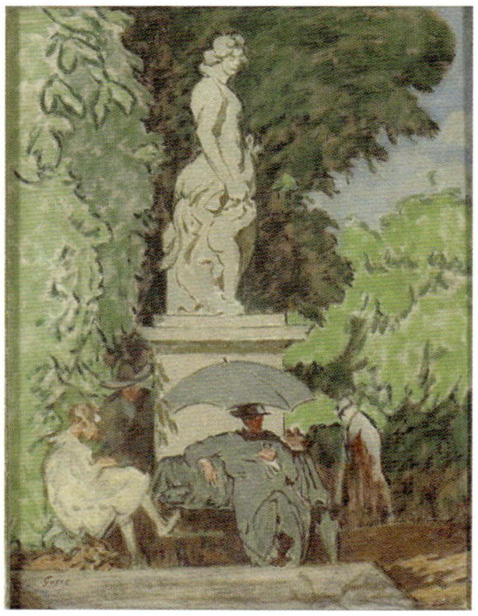

A1028; oil on canvas, 69 × 51 cm
Signed: *Gosse*
Prov.: Dr R.D. Fox
Purchased, 1966; WA1966.60

This view of the gardens at Versailles, seen on a warm summer's day, includes the statue of *Noon*, commissioned from Gaspard and Balthazar Marsy in 1674 for the *Parterre d'Eau*.

Sir Lawrence Burnett Gowing
(1918 – 1994)

Lady with Book

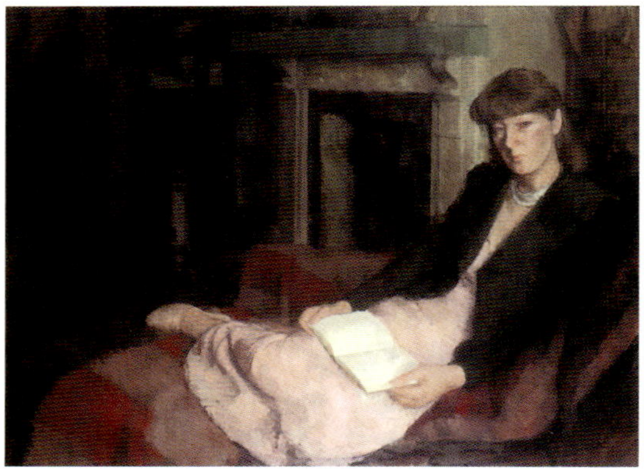

A718a; oil on canvas, 91.5 × 122.1 cm
Purchased (Gavin Bone Bequest Fund), 1945; WA1945.101

The portrait, made *c.* 1942, shows Julia Strachey, later Gowing's wife, reclining on a chaise-longue, dressed in a white robe, apparently reading a book but momentarily looking at the viewer. The picture, like other paintings by Gowing, aims to capture the atmosphere of the moment, reflecting with its warm reddish tones, the hospitality of the room, without concentrating unduly on the details of the sitter.

Attributed to Spencer Frederick Gore
(1878 – 1914)

Harbour Scene

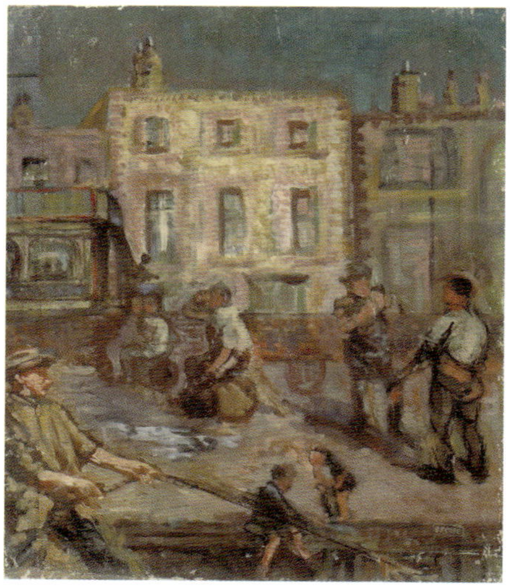

A1096; oil on canvas, 60 × 50.5 cm
Signed: (?)*S.F. GORE*
Presented by Gerald Reitlinger, 1972; WA1978.38

Perhaps made while Gore was staying in Sickert's house at Neuville, near Dieppe, in the summer of 1906. The quality of the painting is unusually coarse and the attribution questionable.

Henryk Gotlib
(1890 – 1966)

Fela, the Artist's Cousin

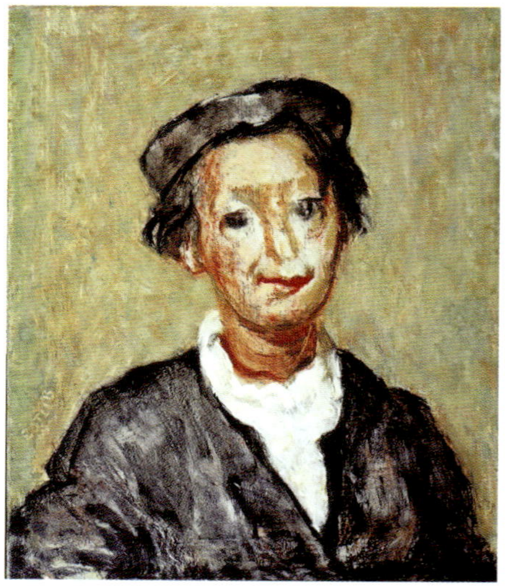

A1176; oil on canvas, 61 × 50.5 cm
Signed: *Gotlib*
Presented by Mrs Janet Gotlib, the artist's widow, 1991; WA1991.437

This portrait of the artist's cousin Fela shows not only Gotlib's predilection for Rembrandt, but also a deep sense of humanity. The colour is applied in extremely dry, quick, broad touches. The effect is not naturalistic but captures the personality of the sitter.

Follower of Francisco de Goya y Lucientes
(1746 – 1828)

Scene at a Bullfight: Dibersión de España

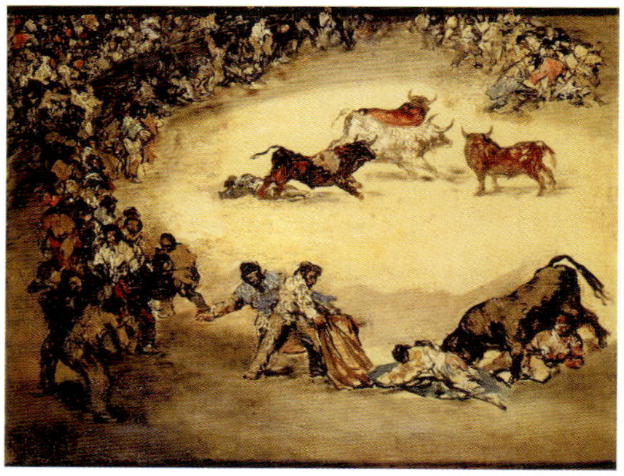

A433; oil on canvas, 45 × 57 cm
Incised: *C107*
Prov.: Mrs Davis
Presented by Mr and Mrs J.G. Lousada through the National Art Collections Fund, 1934; WA1934.9

Arnáiz 1981, no. 344; Whistler 2003, pp.127–41

A433 and A434 are by a follower of Goya who was influenced by Goya's late technique. They are related in reverse to the set of four Bordeaux lithographs published by Goya in December 1825. He made one painting of a bullfight in Paris in 1824 for his friend Joaquín María Ferrer, now in the J. Paul Getty Museum.

Follower of Francisco de Goya y Lucientes
(1746 – 1828)

Scene at a Bullfight: División de place

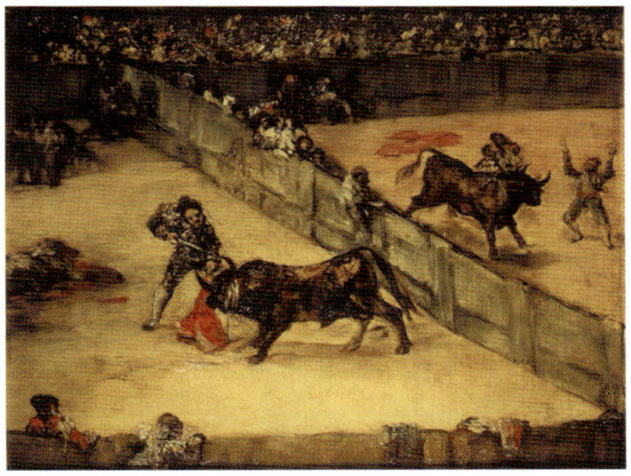

A434; oil on canvas, 46 × 58 cm
Incised: *C106*
Prov.: Mrs Davis
Presented by Mr and Mrs J.G. Lousada through the National Art Collections Fund, 1934; WA1934.10

Arnaiz 1981, no. 345; Whistler 2003, pp.127–41

While Eugenio Lucas y Velázquez also painted variations on the Bordeaux lithographs, they are different in approach and handling. A similar unidentified collector's mark appears on *The Forge* (Frick Collection, New York) and *Les Jeunes* (Musée des Beaux Arts, Lille), both by Goya.

Jan van Goyen
(1596 – 1656)

A Castle by a River

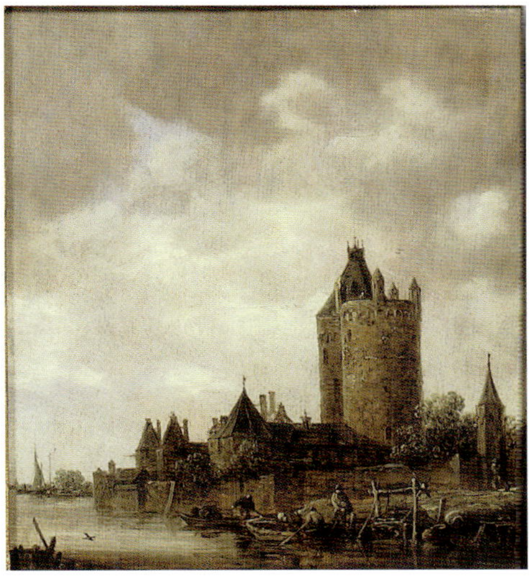

A973; oil on oak panel, 36 × 30 cm
Signed in monogram and dated: *VG 1647*
Prov.: Sir Georges Donaldson; Hans Koenig
Madan Bequest, 1962; WA1962.17.15

White 1999, p. 53

The same castle appears in a number of works by van Goyen, several with dates in the 1640s. The castle has been tentatively identified as the castle of Culemborg, near Tiel, on the Waal in Gelderland.

Francesco Granacci
(1469/70 – 1543)

St Anthony of Padua

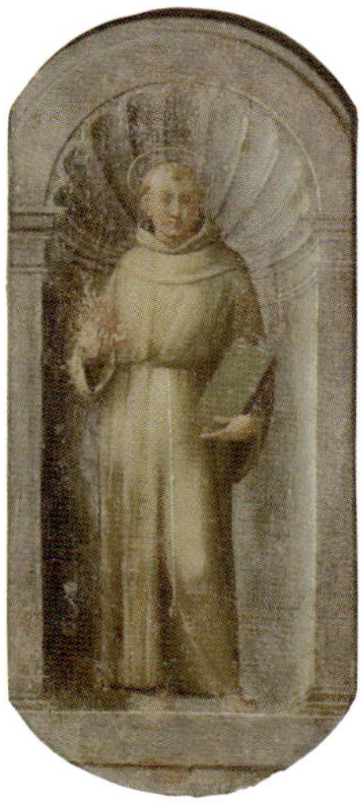

A100; oil on panel, transferred to canvas, 33 × 14 cm
Fox-Strangways Gift, 1850; WA1850.13

Lloyd 1977, pp. 87–9

A Franciscan saint, Anthony (1195–1231) carries his attributes of a book, recalling his erudition, and a flaming heart, a reference to his spiritual fervour. A100 is a companion piece to A101. Granacci was a follower of Ghirlandaio who was particularly interested in the art of Fra Bartolomeo and Raphael.

Jan van Goyen
(1596 – 1656)

Skating Scene before the Noordenpoort, Hoorn

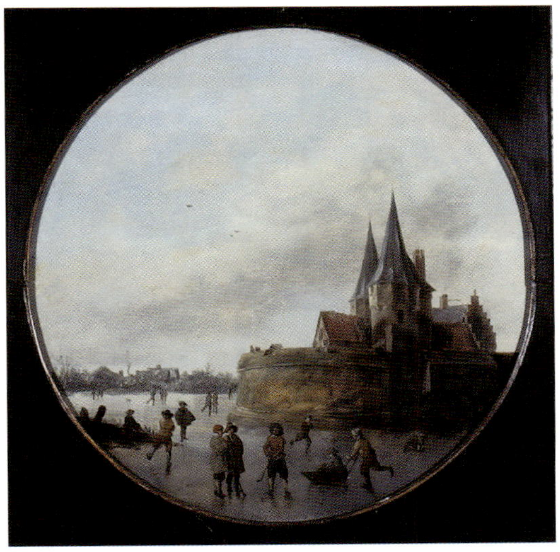

A811; oil on panel, 34 × 34 cm
Bequeathed by J. Reginald Jones, 1951; WA1951.51.5

White 1999, p. 52

In his early years van Goyen produced a number of landscape roundels. These follow a format established in Flemish art in the 16th century. The setting in this work features one of the gateways, the Noorderpoort, of the town of Hoorn on the west bank of the Zuiderzee.

Attributed to Thomas Alexander Ferguson Graham
(1840 – 1906)

Two Women seated on Deck

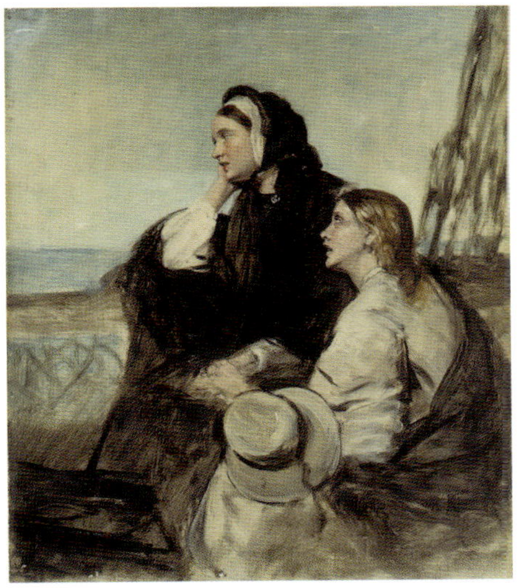

A520f; oil on canvas, mounted as a drawing, 35 × 30 cm
Presented by Dr K.T. Parker, 1938; WA1938.85

The subject of two women on the deck of a ship leaving home is reminiscent of Ford Madox Brown's *The Last of England* of 1852–4 (Birmingham City Art Gallery). The attribution to Graham is tentative.

Francesco Granacci
(1469/70 – 1543)

An Angel

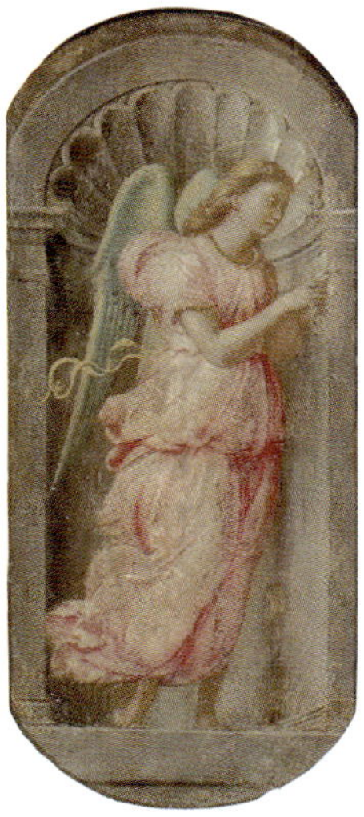

A101; oil on panel, transferred to canvas, 33 × 14 cm
Fox-Strangways Gift, 1850; WA1850.13.1

Lloyd 1977, pp. 87–9

Together with a *St Francis* (Christ Church, Oxford) and a *Risen Christ* (National Gallery of Wales), A100 and A101 come from a lost altar-piece by Granacci, painted around 1520. The four panels may have been placed in the pilasters.

Attributed to Francesco Granacci
(1469/70 – 1543)

Christ in the Tomb supported by the Virgin

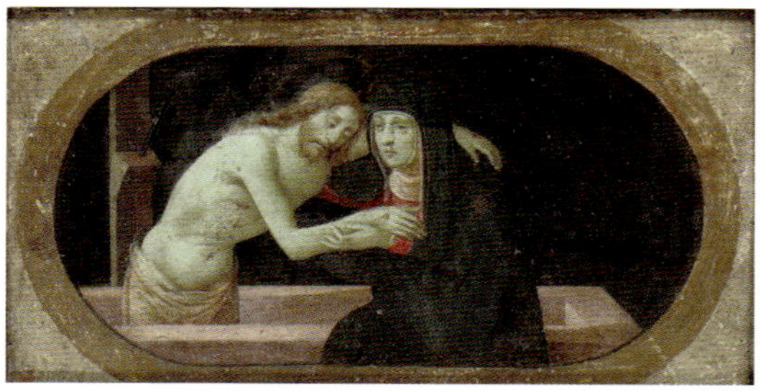

A338; tempera and oil (?) and gilding on panel, 27 × 50 cm
Presented by Bernard Berenson, 1913; WA1913.7

Lloyd 1977, pp. 64–5

A predella panel from an unknown altar-piece, A338 may date from the early 1490s. Images of the dead Christ have a Eucharistic significance and here the cross and nail on the left recall the Passion. Unusually, the Virgin is given equal prominence with her son, being placed in front of the tomb. The expressiveness and gracefulness of A338 is typical of Granacci's work.

Duncan Grant
(1885 – 1978)

Landscape in Provence: Cassis

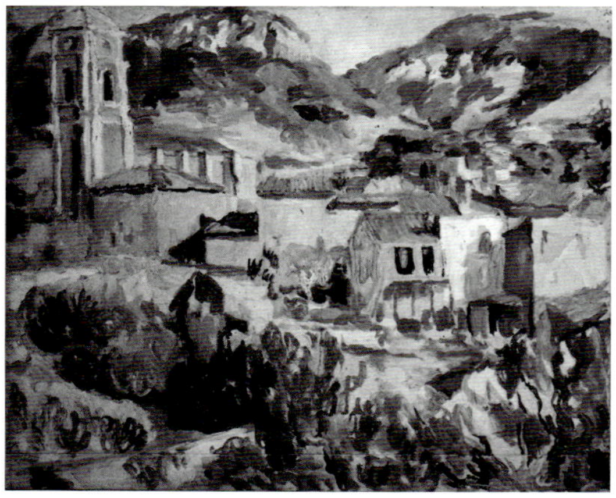

A623; oil on paper, 54 × 65.2 cm
Hindley Smith Bequest, 1939; WA1940.1.5

Between 1927 and 1938, Grant travelled several times to Provence, especially to Cassis near Marseille. Being trained partly in Paris, he had strong links to French Post-Impressionism and the paintings he made during these visits show his response to the movement, with the bright colours loosely applied.

Duncan Grant
(1885 – 1978)

Dancing Figure

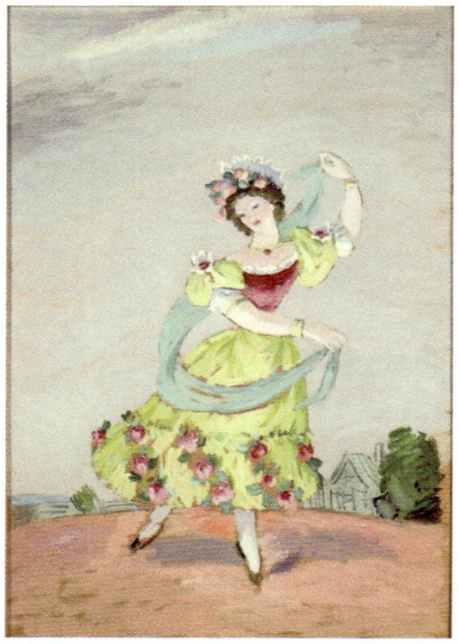

A650; oil on cardboard, 81 × 56 cm
Hindley Smith Bequest, 1939; WA1940.1.32

This relates directly to the stage-designs work, which Grant produced from the early 1910s onwards. He was deeply interested in the whole field of decorative art and design.

François-Marius Granet
(1775 – 1849)

A View of a Garden, seen from within a Roman Vault

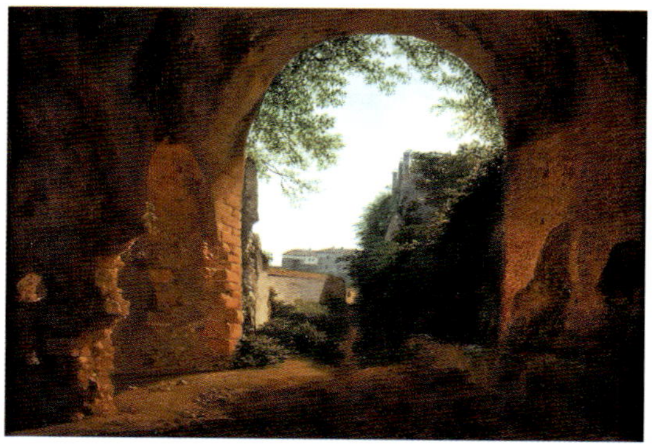

A1206; oil on canvas, 47.3 × 60.9 cm
Purchased in commemoration of the Directorship of Professor Sir Christopher White (1985–1997), with the assistance of the National Art Collections Fund, the Pilgrim Trust and the Friends of the Ashmolean, 1997; WA1997.26

This luminous view framed within an ancient Roman vault is one of a number of scenes painted in and around Rome by Granet between 1802 and 1824. He made many outdoor oil-sketches of the Roman landscape during this period but this view is likely to have been painted largely or entirely in the studio using a pen and ink drawing (which is also in the Ashmolean) as his model.

Duncan Grant
(1885 – 1978)

Interior

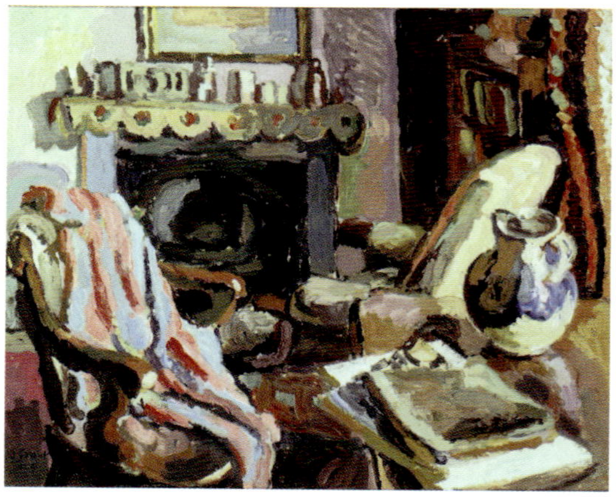

A649; oil on canvas, 60.5 × 73.5 cm
Signed and dated: *Grant 1929*
Hindley Smith Bequest, 1939; WA1940.1.31

Many of Grant's works from the 1920s show a manner of painting which partly derives from the style of Cézanne and Derain, with broad brush-strokes and thickly applied paint.

Attributed to Walter Greaves
(1846 – 1930)

Symphony in Silver and Grey

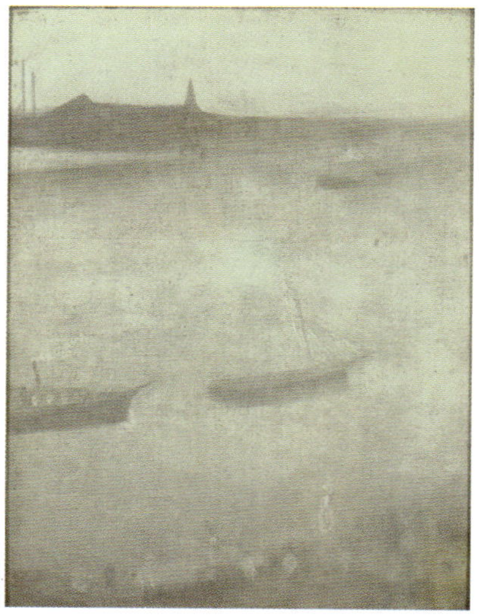

A916; oil on canvas, 61 × 45 cm
Inscribed with butterfly
Prov.: E. Ellis
Russell Bequest, 1958; WA1958.57.10

It has recently been suggested that this work, formerly attributed to Whistler, is by his studio assistant and imitator, Walter Greaves, perhaps reworking one of the many unfinished canvases sold after Whistler's bankruptcy in 1879. In the background is Battersea power station, which Whistler included in several of his views of the Thames.

Peter Greenham
(1909 – 1992)

Interior of St Paul's Cathedral

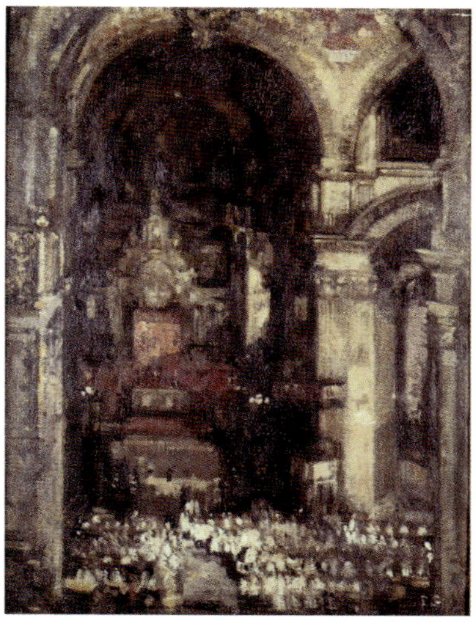

A1142; oil on canvas, 41 × 31 cm
Signed in monogram: *PG*
Bequeathed by Dame Helen Gardner, 1986; WA1986.97

Greenham, who graduated with a degree in English, was one of the most prolific British portraitists in the second half of the 20th century, but he also painted landscapes and other subjects. In this interior view of St Paul's Cathedral, he tried to give an impression of the huge choir of the church during a service. Although the people attending the event are painted in an extremely summary manner, the painting itself aims to evoke the colourful scene and powerful interior.

Peter Greenham
(1909 – 1992)

The Pool of London

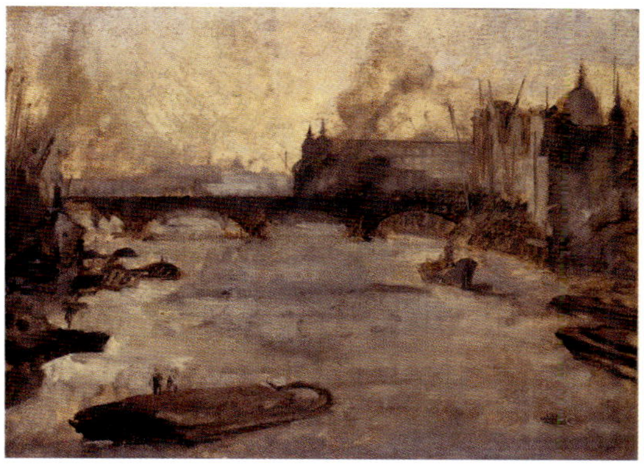

A1141; oil on canvas laid on board, 36.5 × 49.5 cm
Signed in monogram: *PG*
Bequeathed by Dame Helen Gardner, 1986; WA1986.96

This is a later version of the view of London painted from Tower Bridge (see A1174). The atmosphere is much lighter and less dramatic, the paint applied more thinly and the view itself seems to be much closer. The buildings in the background appear only as light distant shadows.

Peter Greenham
(1909 – 1992)

Mrs Lia Ralli

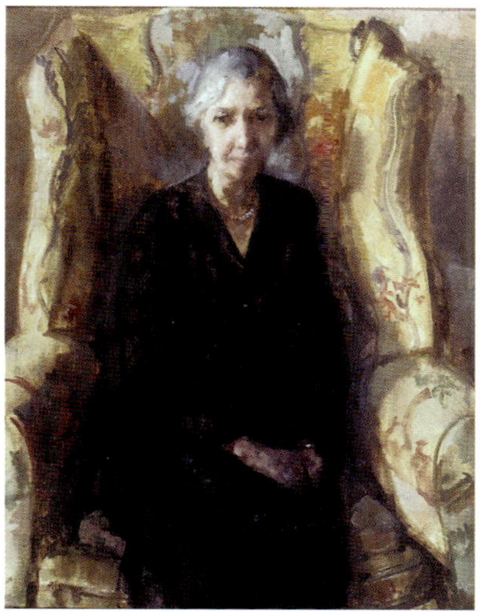

A1200; oil on canvas, 43 × 32.5 cm
Signed in monogram: *PG*
Bequeathed by Miss Anna Hornby, 1996; WA1996.37

Greenham was best known for his portraits, which were painted over many sittings in subtle colours and with remarkable sensitivity.

Peter Greenham
(1909 – 1992)

The Pool of London

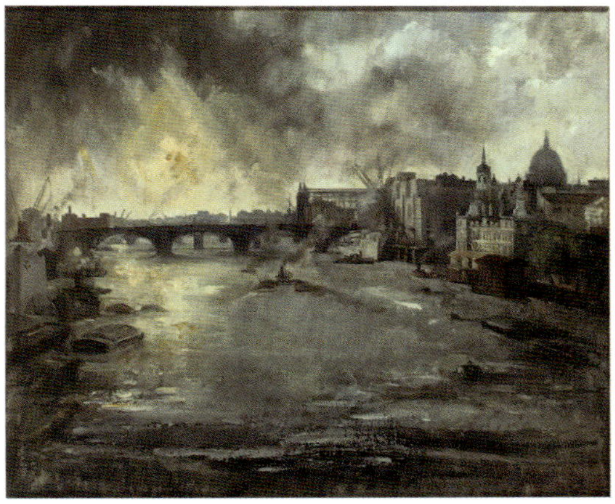

A1174; oil on canvas, 63.7 × 76.4 cm
Signed in monogram: *PG*
Bequeathed by Dr Muriel Tomlinson, 1991; WA1991.345

This painting, exhibited in 1951 in the Guildhall in London, is one of several versions of this view. This painting represents the dramatic view from London Bridge. In this version, there are no boats on the river; all of them are moored at the banks. The river itself and the prominent buildings occupy the space.

Peter Greenham
(1909 – 1992)

Jane and Mary

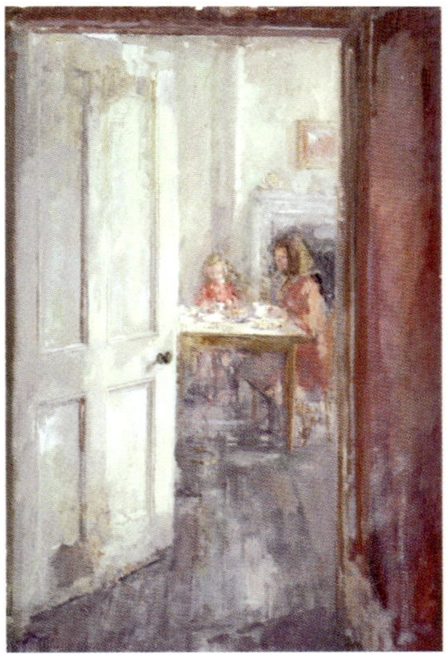

A1199; oil on canvas, 61.2 × 40.8 cm
Bequeathed by Miss Anna Hornby, 1996; WA1996.36

This painting, made in 1969, represents a view into a bright and sunny room through an open door. The artist's wife and their daughter are shown sitting at a table, drinking tea and talking. The work was exhibited at the Royal Academy in 1970.

Attributed to Giovanni Francesco Grimaldi
(1606 – 1680)

Landscape with Tobias and the Angel

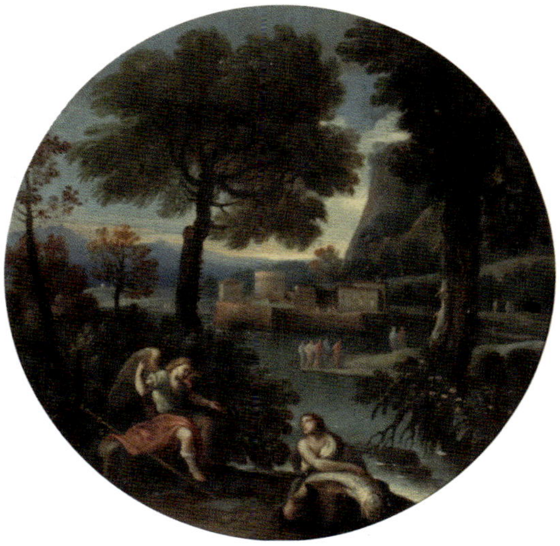

A970; oil on copper, 23 × 23 cm
Prov.: Percy Moore Turner
Madan Bequest, 1962; WA1962.17.12

The story is from the apocryphal Book of Tobit: Tobias, instructed by the angel, catches a fish so as to make an ointment to cure Tobit's blindness. The scene is set in a classical landscape. An attribution to Grimaldi has generally been accepted, as there are similarities with his paintings of the 1650s, although another suggestion is an artist in the circle of Giovanni Battista Viola. The tonality and decorative quality might also suggest a later date.

Adriaen de Gryeff
(*c.* 1670 – 1715)

Dogs with dead Game

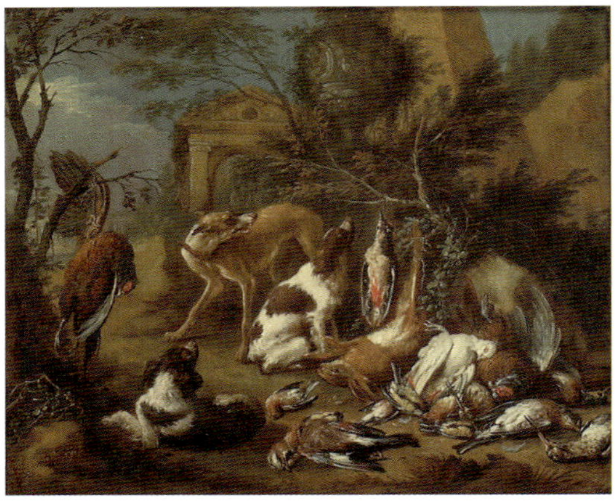

A384; oil on canvas, 38 × 41 cm
Signed: *AGrijef*
Bequeathed by Mrs E.C. Greenway, 1926; WA1926.10

White 1999, p. 55

A characteristic example of the artist's compositions of dogs with dead game. Gryeff worked mainly in Antwerp and Brussels. The antique arch and pyramid add a decorative, classicizing element to this popular theme.

Francesco Guardi
(1712 – 1793)

A Night Procession in the Piazza San Marco

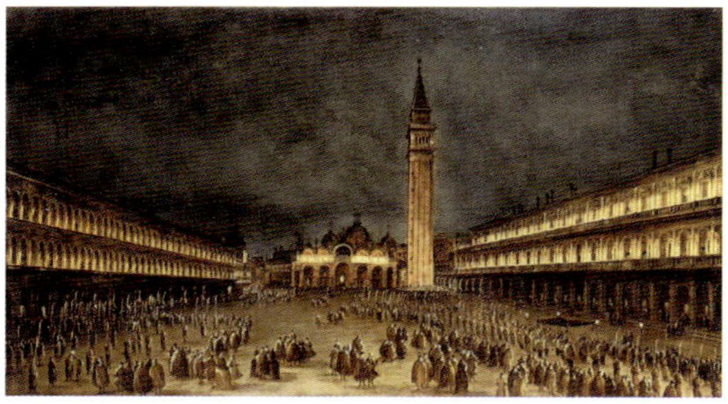

A386; oil on canvas, 48 × 84.5 cm
Prov.: Henry Francis Pelham-Clinton-Hope, 8th Duke of Newcastle, Deepdene
Presented by Mrs W.F.R. Weldon, 1927; WA1927.1

Morassi 1973, no. 337

Part of the celebrations to mark Good Friday, this nocturnal procession winds its way back to the Basilica of San Marco. A386 is now considered to be an early work of *c.* 1755.

Francesco Guardi
(1712 – 1793)

Pope Pius VI blessing the Crowd at Campo SS Giovanni e Paolo, Venice

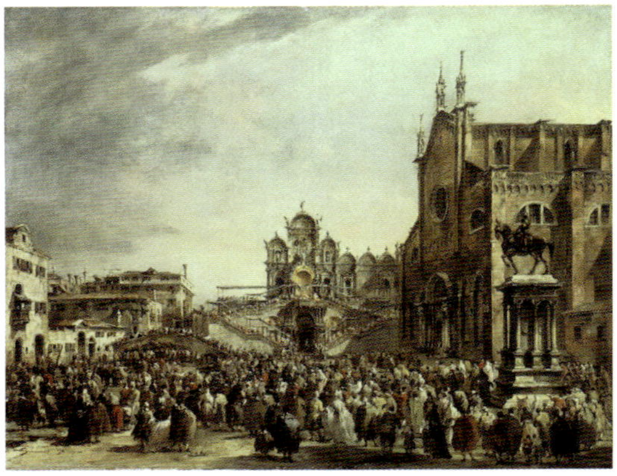

A149; oil on canvas, 64 × 81 cm
Chambers Hall Gift, 1855; WA1855.183

Morassi 1973, no. 269; De Grazia and Garberson 1996, p. 126

Guardi painted four scenes to celebrate the historic visit of Pius VI to Venice from 15–19 May 1782: *The Pope met by the Doge* (Philadelphia Museum of Art); *The Te Deum at SS Giovanni e Paolo* (private collection, Paris); the *Audience of the Senate* (Sotheby's, Florence, 24 September 1985, lot 19); and the *Papal Blessing* (A149). Commissioned by the Venetian state through the agency of Pietro Edwards on 21 May 1782, they were completed by 24 December 1782. A number of preparatory drawings for A149 are known, while Guardi and his studio made other versions, of which the most important is that at Upton House (National Trust). An elaborate temporary staircase and balcony was erected in front of the Scuola Grande di San Marco to accommodate the Pope, the Doge, the Patriarch of Venice and other dignitaries. Guardi elongated the proportions of the buildings and of the Colleoni statue to give greater verve and dramatic effect to the scene.

Francesco Guardi
(1712 – 1793)

Two Vessels in a Storm

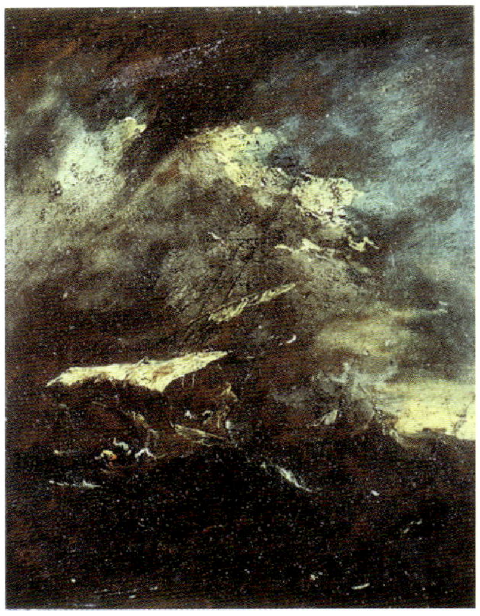

A151; oil on panel, mounted as a drawing, 19.6 × 15.1 cm
Chambers Hall Gift, 1855; WA1855.185

This tiny, rapid sketch was probably made as an independent work. Guardi treated this subject in several paintings and drawings and the same scene appears on the left side of a painting in a private collection, Bergamo (Morassi 1973, no. 695).

Francesco Guardi
(1712 – 1793)

Capriccio Landscape

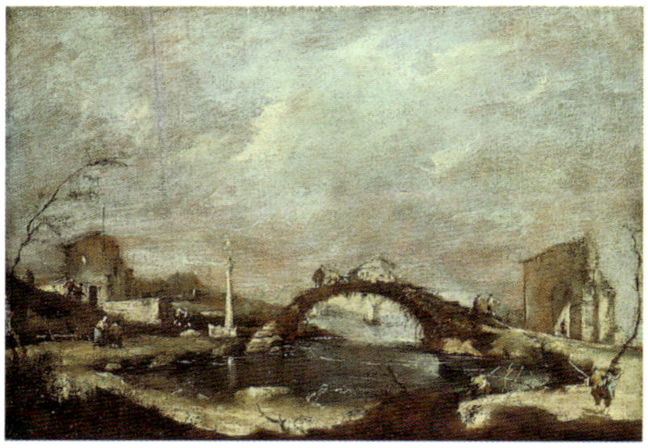

A1166; oil on panel, 29 × 38 cm
Prov.: Dr Einar Perman, Stockholm; Dr W. Katz, London
Bequeathed by Mr and Mrs Francis Hock through the National Art Collections Fund, 1987; WA1988.294

Morassi 1973, I, under no. 863

One of a large number of hastily painted *capricci* made for sale, A1166 seems characteristic of Guardi's hand.

Circle of Francesco Guardi
(1712 – 1793)

Capriccio: Ruins and a Bridge

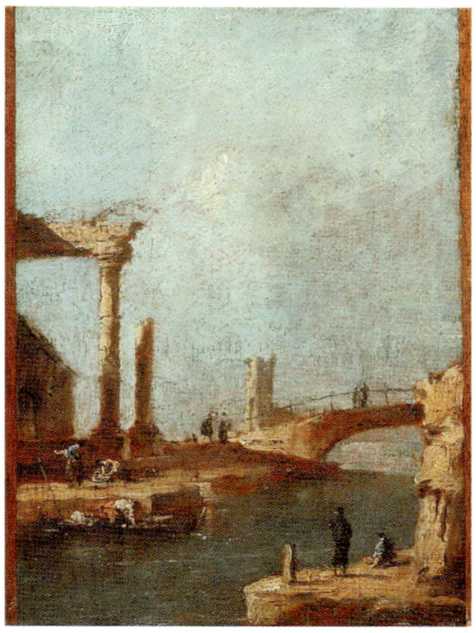

A1033; oil on canvas, 23.5 × 16.2 cm
Prov.: John Henderson; Sir John Fiennes Twistleton Crampton and by descent
Bequeathed by Miss S.A.P. Boyle, 1967; WA1967.52.1

Numerous quick, sketchy scenes of this type were produced by Guardi and his studio. Similar compositions occur in drawings and paintings by Francesco.

Follower of Francesco Guardi
(1712 – 1793)

The Grand Canal with the Palazzo Corner della Ca' Grande

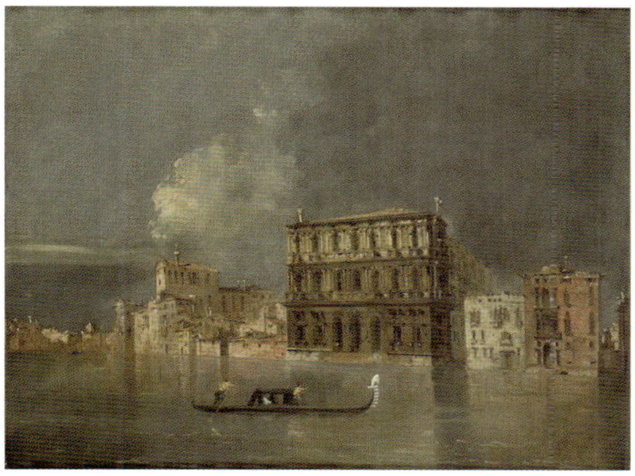

A148; oil on canvas, 48.8 × 63.1 cm
Chambers Hall Gift, 1855; WA1855.182

Morassi 1973, no. 516

The view is taken from the Palazzo Venier; to the right the Palazzo Minotto and the Palazzo Barbarigo can be seen. A similar composition by Guardi was formerly in the Treccani collection, Milan (Morassi 1973, no. 515). A148 is not of sufficient quality to be by Guardi himself.

Follower of Francesco Guardi
(1712 – 1793)

The Venetian lagoon at sunset

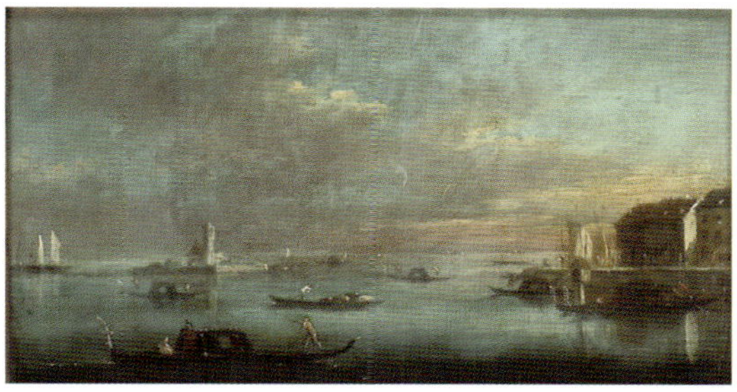

A1035; oil on canvas, 23.1 × 41.6 cm
Prov.: John Henderson; Sir John Fiennes Twistleton Crampton and by descent
Bequeathed by Miss S.A.P. Boyle, 1967; WA1967.52.3

This picturesque scene was probably painted in the early 19th century for the tourist market.

Circle of Francesco Guardi
(1712 – 1793)

Capriccio: an Archway

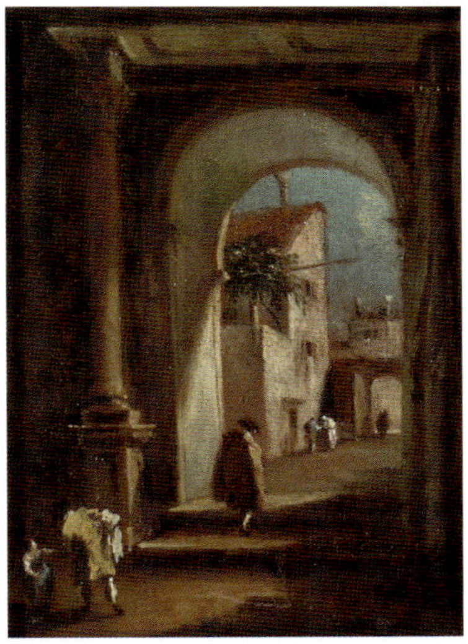

A1034; oil on canvas, 24 × 17.8 cm
Prov.: John Henderson; Sir John Fiennes Twistleton Crampton and by descent
Bequeathed by Miss S.A.P. Boyle, 1967; WA1967.52.2

A companion to A1033.

Follower of Francesco Guardi
(1712 – 1793)

A Venetian squero or Boatyard

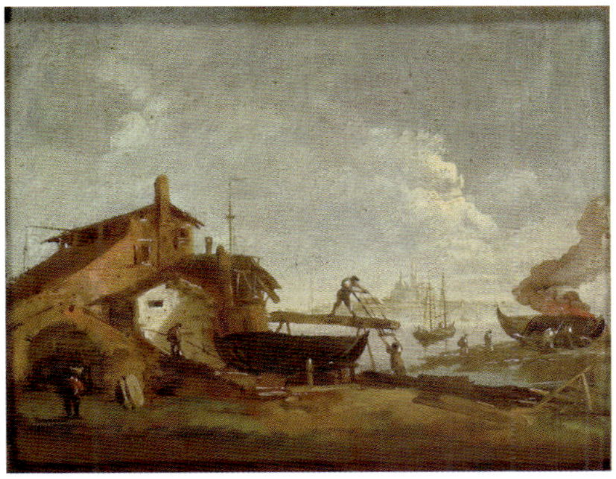

A150; oil on canvas, 22.2 × 27.9 cm
Chambers Hall Gift, 1855; WA1855.184

The island and church of San Giorgio Maggiore are visible in the distance. A150 is not close to Guardi in either handling or quality, but may be an early 19th-century copy by an artist such as Giovanni Migliara after a lost painting.

Giovanni Francesco Barbieri, called Guercino
(1591 – 1666)

Head of an old Man

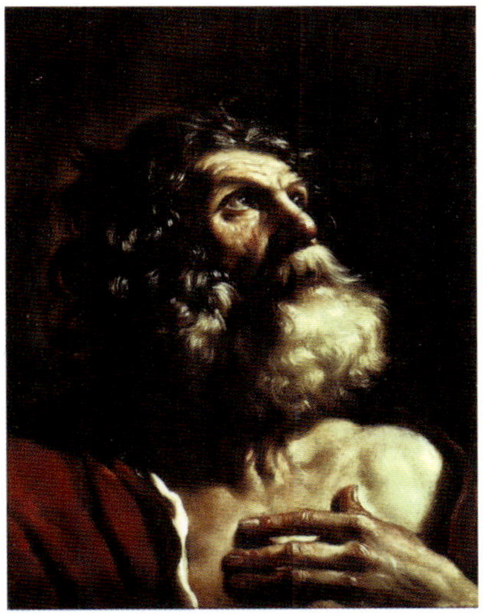

Oil on canvas, 63 × 48.3 cm
Prov.: Lt-Col R.W. Barclay, Bury Hill House, Dorking
Mahon loan, 1999; WA.L.99.14

Finaldi and Kitson 1997, no. 41

This boldly executed painting is probably an oil-sketch made from the life as a study of physiognomy and expression. Although the man's gaze and the warm lighting suggest that Guercino had in mind a figure of a saint or a prophet, it is not connected with a final painting, nor is it a fragment of a finished work. The freedom of handling suggests a dating of *c.* 1619–20. A copy is in the Hermitage, St Petersburg.

Copy after Giovanni Francesco Barbieri, called il Guercino
(1591 – 1666)

The Vision of St Jerome

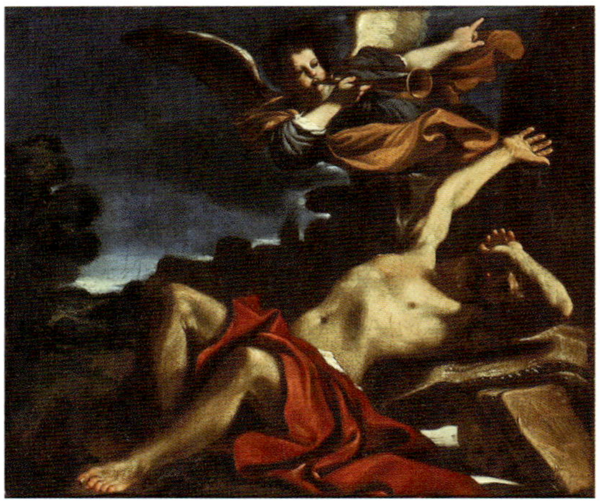

A654; oil on canvas, 44 × 50 cm
Prov.: Philippe, duc d'Orléans and by descent to 1792; 2nd Baron Northwick; 5th Duke of Newcastle; by descent to 16th Earl of Lincoln; H.M. Calmann
Purchased, 1939; WA1939.51

Loire 1996, p. 245

The saint has a vision of an angel blowing the trumpet of the Last Judgement a popular subject in the 17th century. The original from which A654 was copied, was probably made for Alessandro Ludovisi in 1619–20 and was purchased for Louis XIV in 1685. A654 is a slightly larger but otherwise exact copy, which may have been painted in France.

Jean-Baptiste-Armand Guillaumin
(1841 – 1927)

Landscape: Harvest-time in the Somme Valley

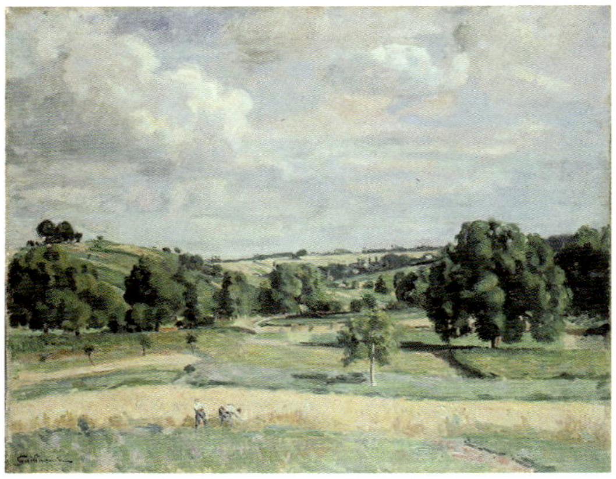

A1005; oil on canvas, 65 × 81 cm
Signed: *Guillaumin*
Bequeathed by Major Thomas Bouch, 1963; WA1963.150.2

Neither the brushwork nor the colouring are entirely consistent with Guillaumin's mature work. It is not inconceivable that this is a work by Guillaumin's son, whose signature is very similar to his father's.

Christopher Hall
(b. 1930)

Garden of St Hugh's College, Oxford

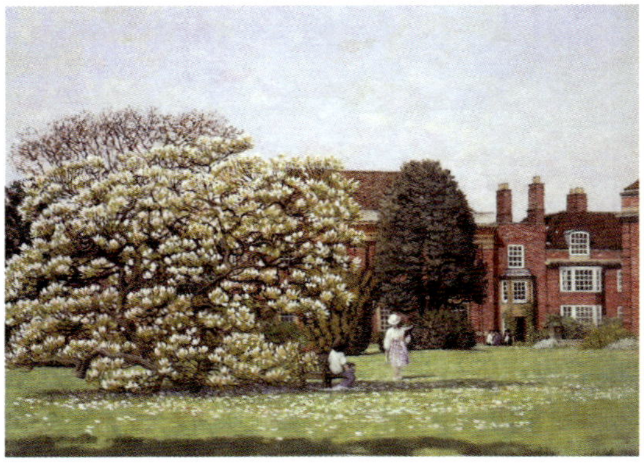

A1143a; oil on board, mounted on cardboard, 33 × 45 cm
Signed and dated: *C. C. Hall –1985*
Deposited by the Delegates of the Oxford University Press, 1987; WA1987.3

This landscape was commissioned for the Oxford Almanack and shows a scene during the spring in the gardens of St Hugh's College, concentrating on the magnolia tree in full blossom and the buildings in the background.

Paul Guigou
(1834 – 1871)

Village in Vaucluse on the Banks of the River Durance

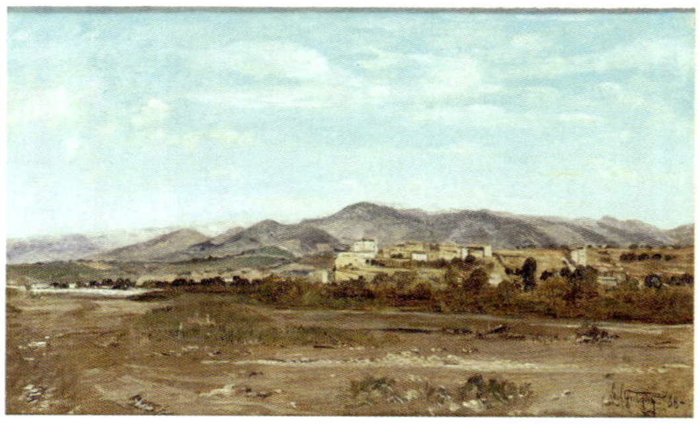

A1242; oil on canvas, 25 × 40.1 cm
Signed and dated: *Paul Guigou 68*
Presented by Artemis Fine Arts Ltd, 2001; WA2001.151

Bonnici 1989, no. 218

In 1862, Guigou abandoned a career in law and devoted himself to painting landscape. He moved to Paris and took up painting as a career, specialising in small, spirited views of his native Provence.

Allan Gwynne-Jones
(1872 – 1982)

Still Life

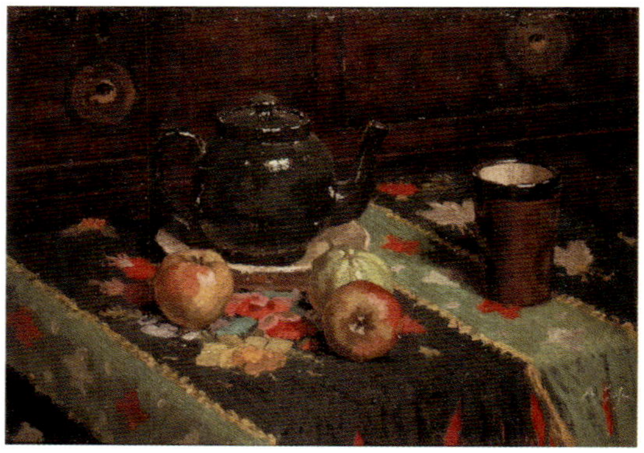

A1117; oil on canvas, 40.6 × 56 cm
Signed: *A.G.J.*
Presented by the National Art Collections Fund, 1980; WA1980.93

Painted in Fitzroy Street, Soho, *c.* 1935. The artist seems to have turned to painting still-life compositions as a relaxation from portraits. He always used the most commonplace kitchen utensils as well as plants and fruit from his garden.

Dirck Hals
(1591 – 1656)

Merry Company in an Interior

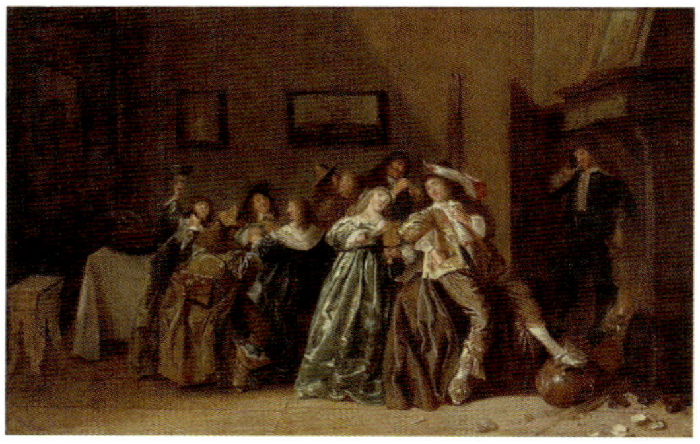

A815; oil on panel, 38 × 58 cm
Signed in monogram and dated: *DHALS / 1640* (the DH in monogram)
Bequeathed by J. Reginald Jones, 1951; WA1951.51.9

White 1999, p. 55

A characteristic late work by this artist from Haarlem who made a speciality of painting merry companies. He was the brother of Frans Hals who may have been his master.

Nicolaes (Claes) Hals
(1628 – 1686)

A Village Street with a Church Tower

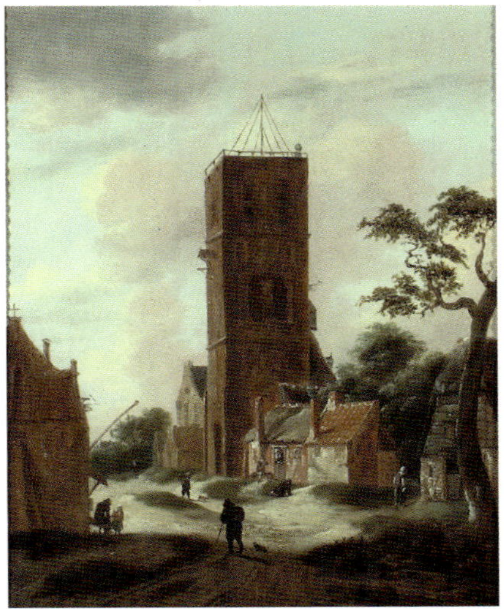

A364; oil on panel, 56 × 44
Signed: *Claes Hals* and again with monogram: *CH*
Presented by Sir Robert Witt through the National Art Collections Fund, 1921; WA1921.1

White 1999, p. 56

Claes Hals was the son of Frans Hals in Haarlem. He was possibly his pupil although works like this have more in common with the Haarlem followers of Jacob van Ruisdael. The view is probably imaginary.

Maggi Hambling
(b. 1945)

Francis Bacon

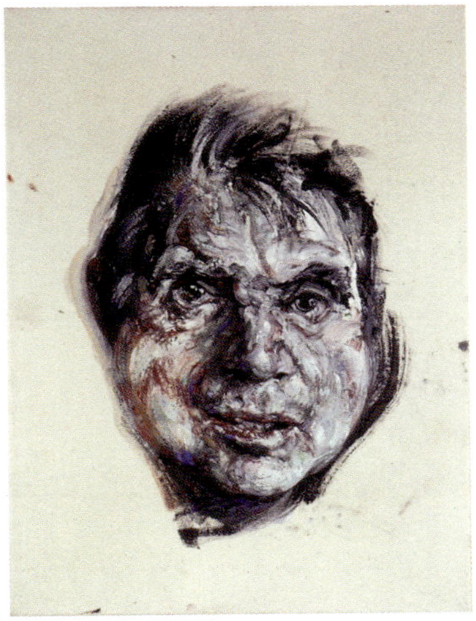

A1248; oil on canvas, 38 × 28.2 cm
Signed and dated: *Hambling 1985*
Presented anonymously through the National Art Collections Fund, 2002; WA2002.65

Hambling was the first Artist in Residence at the National Gallery in London in 1980–81, during which period she painted a celebrated series of portraits of the comedian, Max Wall. Her admiration for Francis Bacon (1909–1992), the greatest English painter of the human figure in the 20th century, is evident in this portrait.

Edward Hamilton
(documented 1805–6)

Landscape

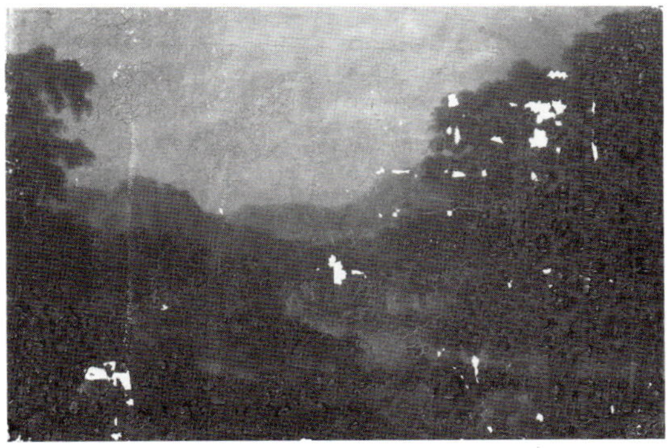

A49; oil on canvas, rolled, 35 × 51 cm
Presented by the artist, 1806; WA1845.49

One of a number of paintings by amateur British artists presented to the Bodleian Library in the early 19th century.

Attributed to Gawen Hamilton
(*c.* 1697 – 1737)

An Assembly of 'Virtuosi'

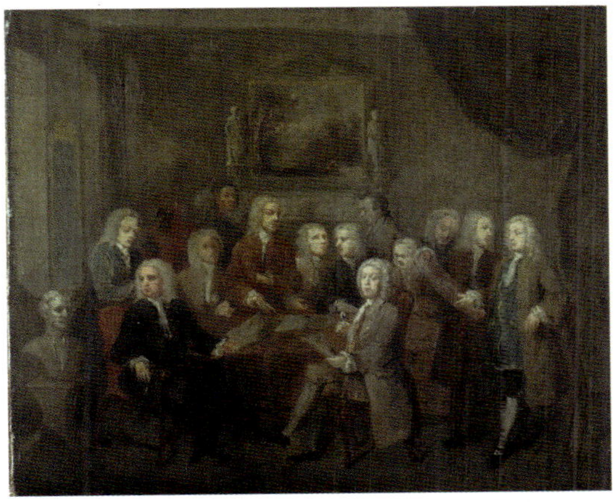

A188; oil on canvas, 61 × 72 cm
Prov.: Alderman Boydell; W.B. Tiffin
Chambers Hall Gift, 1855; WA1855.194

Poole 1912, no. 454

This unfinished work may be related to Gawen Hamilton's celebrated *Assembly of Virtuosi* of 1735 (National Portrait Gallery). It was etched by Richard Sawyer and published by W.B. Tiffin, on 1 May 1829. The etching identifies eight of the fifteen sitters, including the painters Dahl, Laroon, Hamilton himself and Vanderbank; the architect William Kent; the sculptor Rysbrack; the gardener, Charles Bridgeman, and an unknown 'Gibbons'. Although the etching calls the group simply 'A Society of Artists', it has been suggested that they may be 'Rosacoronians', members of the Rose and Crown Club. The names from the print have been copied out at the top left corner of the painting. The list may have been invented.

Studio of Adriaen Hanneman
(?1604 – 1671)

Charles II as Prince of Wales

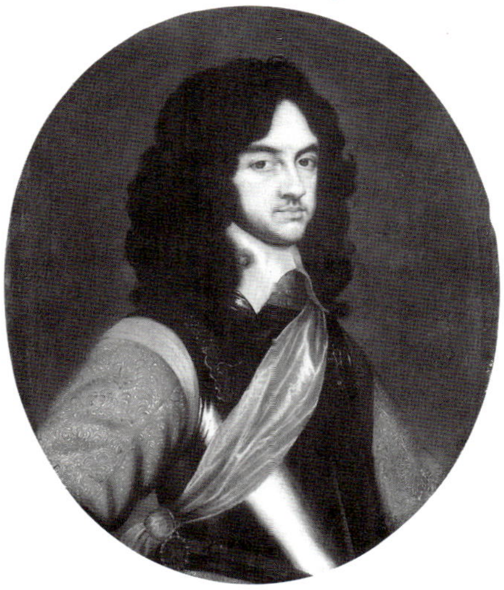

A1050e; oil on canvas, 79 × 65 cm
Bequeathed by Miss Orovida Pissarro, 1968; WA1968.474.3

Ter Kuile 1976, no. 14k; White 1999, p. 57

Copied from a lost original by Hanneman which was probably painted in The Hague in 1648 when Charles was eighteen and staying with his sister, Elizabeth of Bohemia. At least thirty versions are known, of varying quality.

Johannes Hannot
(1633 – 1684)

Still Life with Fruit

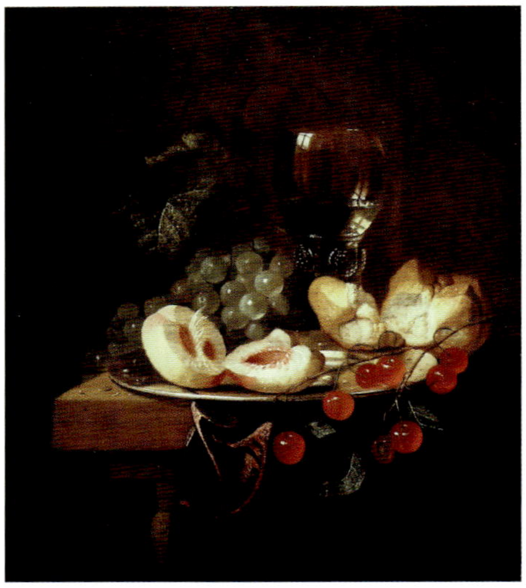

A554; oil on panel, 41 × 37 cm
Signed in monogram: *j.h.fe*
Daisy Linda Ward Bequest, 1939; WA1940.2.30

Meijer 2003, no. 33

Hannot worked in Leiden. Only fifteen paintings have been attributed to him. He was a painter of still life, primarily of fruit. He was also a wine merchant and most of his paintings include one or more glasses of wine. His work shows an awareness of the work of Jan Davidsz. de Heem. It has been suggested that this painting might date from before 1654 – the earliest date found on his work – and, as such, is probably the earliest work by him which can be identified with certainty.

Fairle Harmar, Viscountess Harberton
(1876 – 1945)

The Laurel Walk

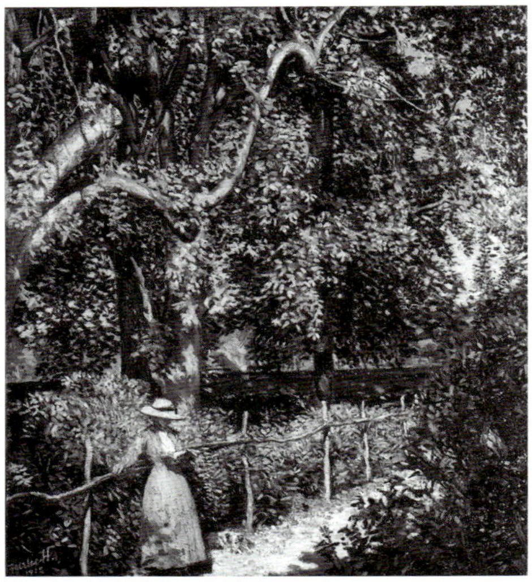

A1024; oil on canvas, 68 × 58 cm
Signed and dated: *Fairlie H 1912*
Bequeathed by Mrs W.S.S. Tyrwhitt, 1966; WA1966.42.1

According to a label on the back of the frame, this represents a site at Ramsridge near Andover. The figure is that of the donor.

Joan Hassall
(1906 – 1988)

Mrs Charles Blakeman

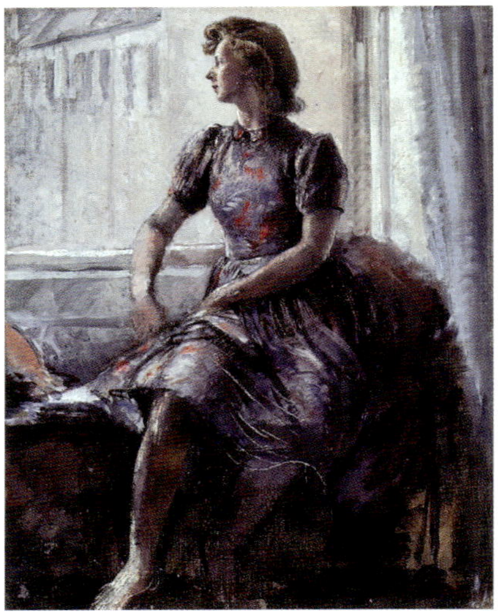

A1223; oil on canvas on board; 38 × 33.3 cm
Inscribed on a label on back: *Mrs Charles Blakeman (Sketch) / Oil / £ 10 s 10 / No. 2*
Presented by Mr and Mrs Charles Blakeman, 1981; WA2000.20

Although she was a painter and typographer, Joan Hassall is best known as book-illustrator and wood-engraver. The sitter in this portrait, May Blakeman (d. 2000), served as Secretary of the Friends of the Ashmolean from 1975 to 1989.

George Simon, Second Earl Harcourt
(1736 – 1809)

Landscape: Cottages in Nuneham Park

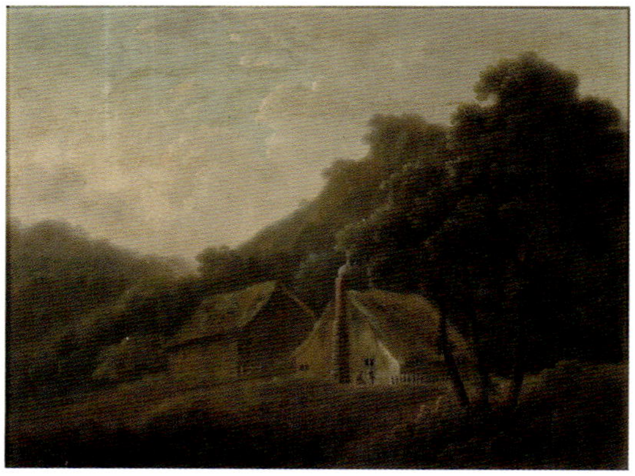

A41; oil on panel, 49 × 64 cm
Presented by the artist, 1797; WA1845.41

In addition to creating at Nuneham one of the most celebrated gardens and parks in England, Lord Harcourt was a keen amateur artist, a friend and patron of Paul Sandby, Sir Joshua Reynolds and others. The cottages in this landscape were erected as part of the improvements to the estate begun by his father in the 1760s.

Henri-Joseph Harpignies
(1819 – 1916)

Valley Landscape

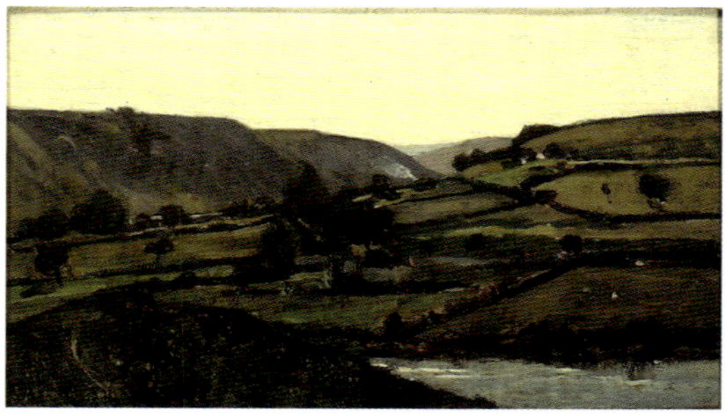

A460; oil on canvas, 18 × 31 cm
Signed: *H.J.Harpignies*
Weldon Bequest, 1937; WA1937.40

The concise form, strong contours and broad handling of paint are found commonly in Harpignies's work. This sketch was probably painted in the open air in one of the many valleys in central France where he painted regularly.

William Havell
(1782 – 1857)

Tintern Abbey

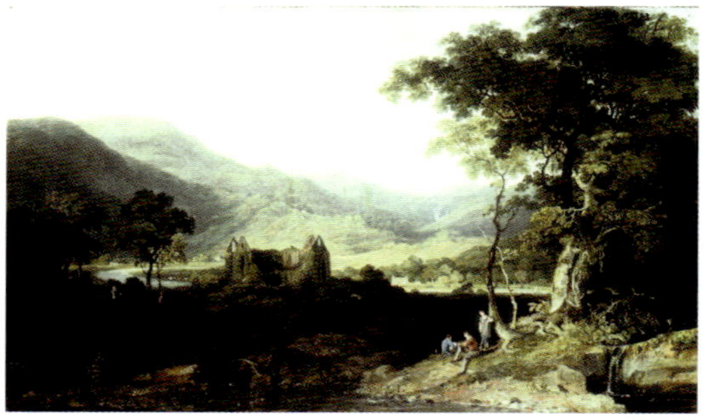

A663; oil on canvas, 67 × 110 cm
Signed and dated: *W. HAVELL 1804*
Prov.: Sydney D. Kitson and by descent
Presented by the Misses Kitson, 1940; WA1940.8.1

Owen and Stanford 1981–2, no. 7

Havell made tours of Wales in 1802 and 1803 and included paintings worked up from sketches made on those tours in his first Royal Academy in 1804. *Tintern Abbey* dates from that year and takes up a subject popularised by Turner and Girtin in the 1790s.

William Havell
(1782 – 1857)

Wooded Landscape with Sheep

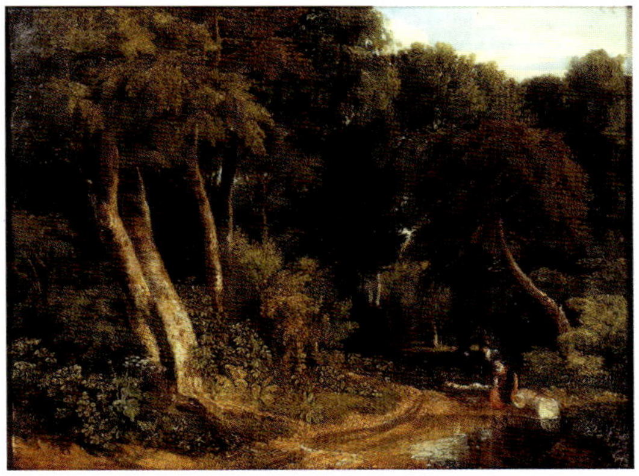

A664; oil on canvas, 51 × 66 cm
Prov.: Sydney D. Kitson and by descent
Presented by the Misses Kitson, 1940; WA1940.8.2

This may be the *Scene in Windsor Forest* exhibited at the British Institution in 1809 and the Liverpool Academy in 1811. The landscape certainly resembles the Thames Valley. Havell was born at Reading and lived there for most of his life.

Benjamin Robert Haydon
(1786 – 1846)

Portrait of a Man

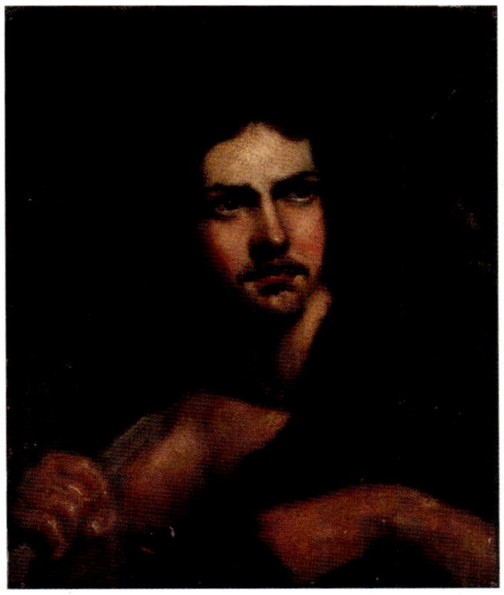

A448a; oil on canvas, 53 × 43 cm
Presented by Edmund Blunden, 1936; WA1936.31

Identified by the donor as a portrait of Leigh Hunt (1784–1859), but the features do not correspond with authenticated portraits of this author.

Sir George Hayter
(1792 – 1871)

Thomas Babington Macaulay

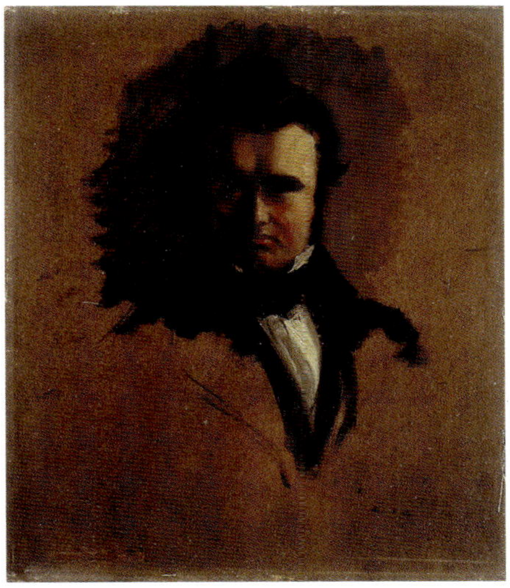

A990; oil on board, mounted as a drawing, 35.2 × 29.6 cm
Inscribed: *Thomas Babington Macaulay / M.P. for Leeds / Study for my great picture of the / House of Commons. in 1833. / No 311 / George Hayter / 1838.*
Presented in memory of Professor David Nichol Smith, by his widow, 1962; WA1962.18.1

A study for Hayter's *The House of Commons, 1833* (National Portrait Gallery), which contains nearly 400 portraits. Thomas Babington Macaulay (1800–1859), the author of a *History of England* (1848–55) and of *Lays of Ancient Rome* (1842), sat as Liberal M.P. for Leeds in 1832–4.

William Havell
(1782 – 1857)

Sheep and Horses grazing under Trees

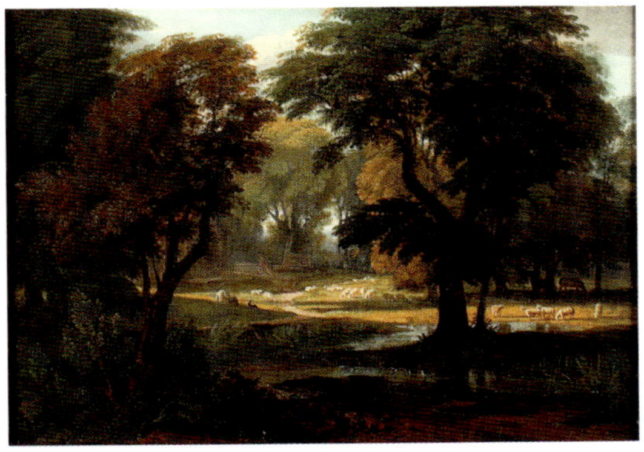

A1008; oil on canvas, 51 × 66 cm
Signed and dated: *W. HAVELL 1810*
Bequeathed by Major Thomas Bouch, 1963; WA1963.150.5

Louis Hayet
(1864 – 1940)

Landscape

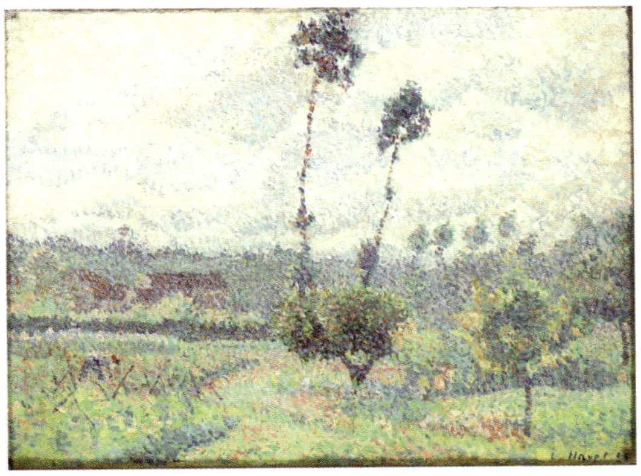

A866; oil on canvas, 24 × 32 cm
Signed and dated: *L. Hayet 89*
Prov.: probably Camille Pissarro and by descent
Presented by Miss Orovida Pissarro, 1953; WA1953.84

Camille Pissarro met Hayet in Pontoise where Pissarro lived from 1872 to 1883. Hayet was already keenly interested in colour theory when Pissarro introduced him to the neo-Impressionists in the mid-1880s. This little landscape, painted with comma-like spots of colour, is an exercise in the neo-Impressionist manner. It was probably given by the artist to Pissarro.

Sir George Hayter
(1792 – 1871)

Anna Feodorovna, Princess Hohenlohe-Langenburg

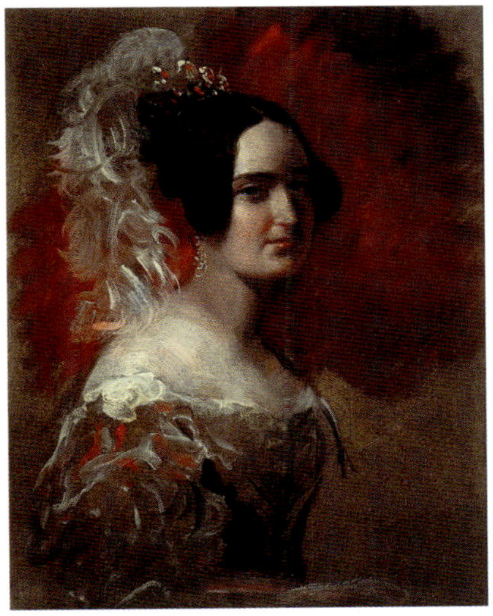

A690a; oil on millboard, mounted as a drawing, laid down, 29.3 × 22.6 cm (sight)
Inscribed on back: *Her Serene Highness. The / Princess Hohenlohe – / study for my great picture of the coronation of her Majesty / Queen Victoria. June 28 1838.*
Purchased (Hope Fund), 1941; WA1941.162

Millar 1992, under no. 305

A study for Hayter's *The Coronation of Queen Victoria*. The sitter (1807–1872) was a half-sister of the Queen. She sat to Hayter on 4, 13, 14, 18 August 1838 and this sketch was presumably made at the first sitting.

Style of Willem Claesz. Heda
(1594 – 1682)

Breakfast-piece with a Flagon and an overturned Wine-cup

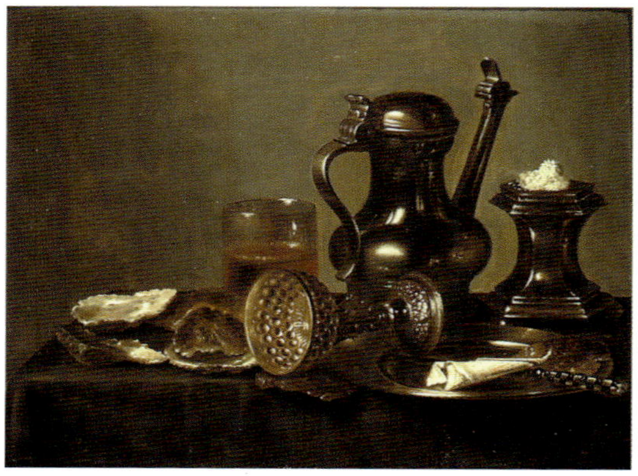

A994; oil on panel, 38 × 49 cm
Bequeathed by J. Reginald Jones, 1962; WA1962.35

White 1999, p. 58

Heda worked in Haarlem where he specialized in painting still life and the occasional historical composition. While showing several features of Heda's work of the 1630s – e.g. the overturned tazza which appears in numerous examples – the poor quality of this painting suggests it is the work of a follower.

David Cornelisz. de Heem
(1663 – 1701/14)

Still Life of Fruit

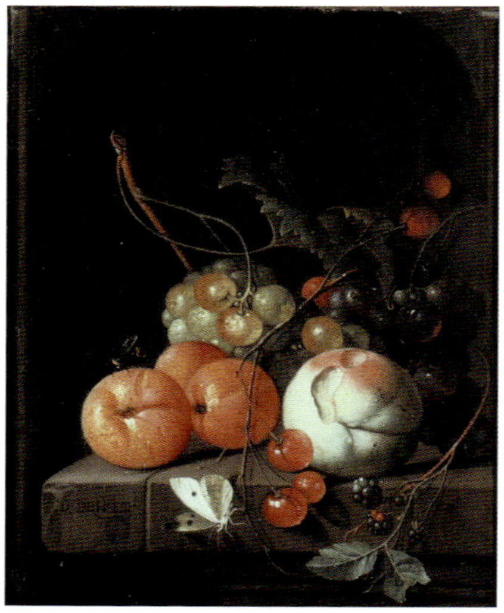

A557; oil on canvas, 28 × 23 cm
Signed: *D. DE HEEM*
Daisy Linda Ward Bequest 1939; WA1940.2.33

Meijer 2003, no. 35

David de Heem was the son of Cornelis de Heem and grandson of Jan Davidsz. de Heem. He was probably trained by his father in The Hague. Confusion between the work and signatures of the different members of the family has caused the work of the grandson to become submerged in misattributions. This signed work closely relates to a number of his father's late, modest still-life paintings and may date from the time David was in his father's studio.

Jan Davidsz. de Heem
(1606 – 1684)

Still Life with Fruit and Oysters

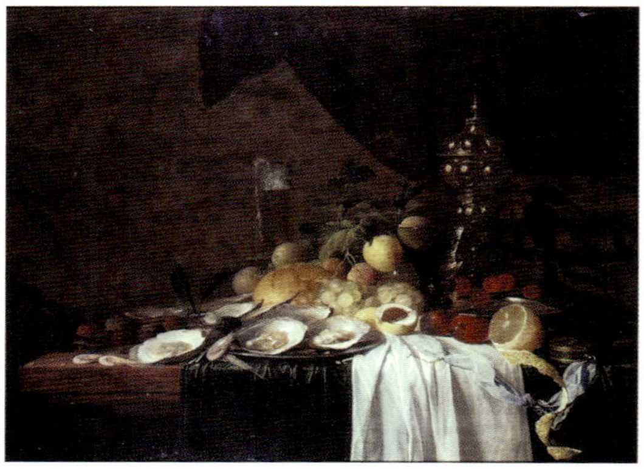

A559; oil on panel, 65 × 87 cm
Signed and dated: *j.De heem F.Ao. 1643*
Prov.: Earl Howe until 1918
Daisy Linda Ward Bequest, 1939; WA1940.2.35

Meijer 2003, no. 37

Characteristic of the more sumptuous manner which de Heem adopted in the later 1630s when he enlarged his format and included draperies and columns in the background. The accessories in this painting appear elsewhere in his work. The cup-and-cover, with minor variations in the detail, was a favourite motif. The watch appears in a number of paintings dated between 1642 and 1645.

Cornelis de Heem
(1631 – 1695)

Still Life with Fruit and Oysters

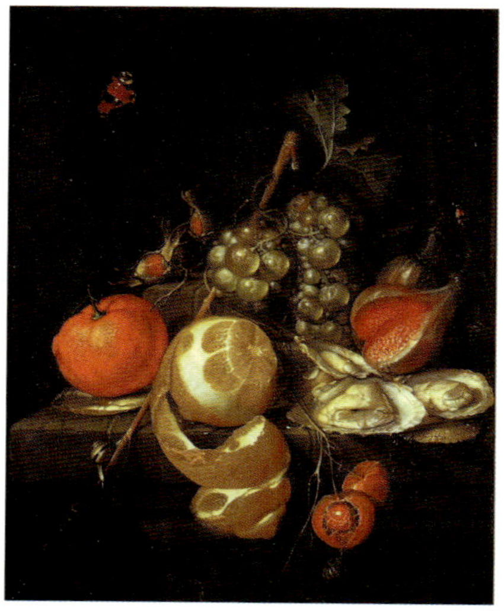

A556; oil on panel, 42 × 34 cm
Signed: *C. De Heem f*
Daisy Linda Ward Bequest, 1939; WA1940.2.32

Meijer 2003, no. 34

The early work of Cornelis de Heem from the mid-1650s, when he was still working in the studio of his father in Antwerp, includes a number of large, luxury still-life paintings. Later, he showed a preference for smaller compositions in a more independent style. This has many characteristics of his late work and was probably painted in the 1680s in The Hague.

Jan Davidsz. de Heem
(1606 – 1684)

Interior of a Room with a young Man seated at a Table

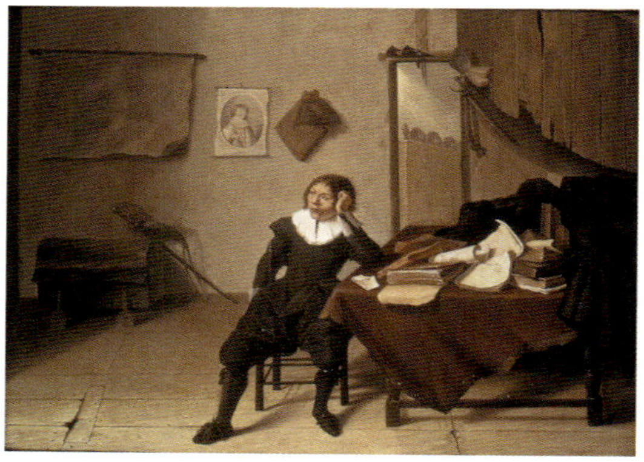

A558; oil on panel, 60 × 82 cm
Signed and dated: *johannis. De / Heem. Fecit / Anno.i628*
Daisy Linda Ward Bequest, 1939; WA1940.2.34

Meijer 2003, no. 36

The pose of the young man, the discarded books and other items suggest that the painting is intended to express the state of melancholy. The engraving on the wall is based on W.J. Delff's engraving of Michiel Jansz. van Miereveldt's portrait of Christian of Brunswick, now at Hampton Court. The subject is exceptional for de Heem. This theme has obvious links with the *vanitas* subjects which he painted on occasion in the late 1620s. It may be a self-portrait.

Copy after Jan Davidsz. de Heem
(1606 – 1684)

A Vase of Flowers

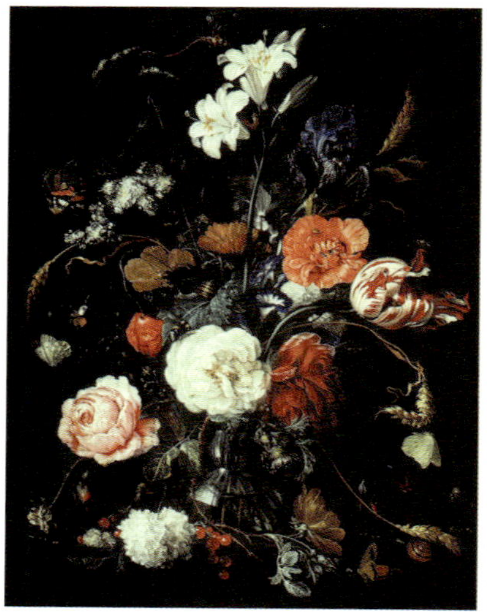

A560; oil on canvas, 54 × 42 cm
Daisy Linda Ward Bequest, 1939; WA1940.2.36

Meijer 2003, no. 38

Copied by a skilled hand from an original now in a private collection in America. The original is one of the more lavish bouquets which de Heem began to paint in the second half of the 1650s. It has been dated to about 1660, shortly before the artist moved to Utrecht.

Copy after Egbert van Heemskerk
(1634/5 – 1704)

A Quaker Meeting

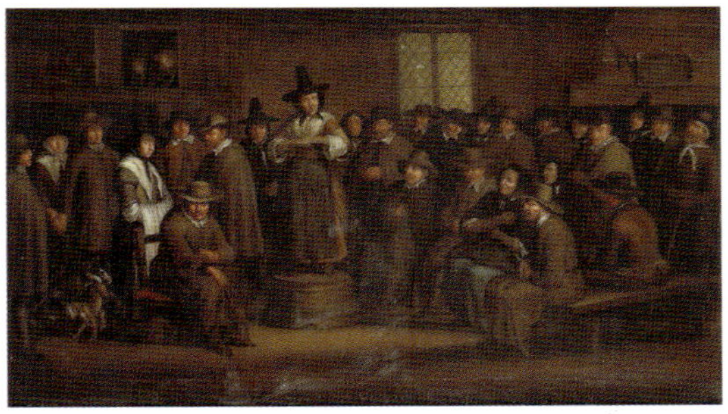

A776; oil on canvas, 42 × 72 cm
Presented by Miss Helen Cam, 1949; WA1949.202

White 1999, p. 59

This satirical view of a Quaker Meeting is known in many painted and printed versions. Only four of these are thought to be the work of Heemskerk himself, one of which, in the Powisland Museum in Welshpool, is signed and dated 1678 and inscribed 'London'. It has been suggested that A776 is an anonymous copy after one of the prints.

Sir Hubert von Herkomer
(1849 – 1914)

Study of Sir Henry Wentworth Acland

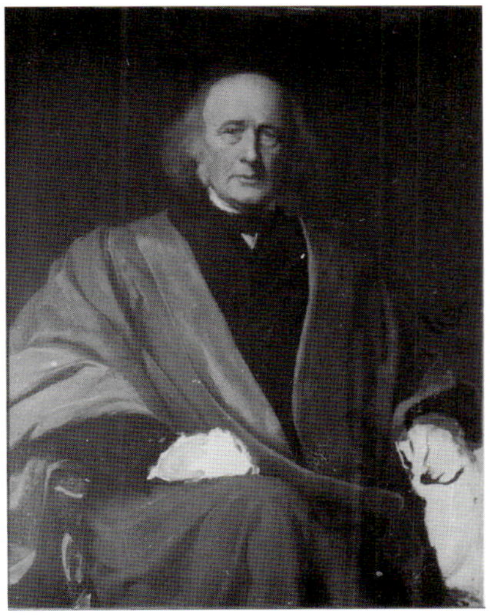

A249; oil on canvas, 110 × 84 cm
Signed and dated: *H.H. 88*
Presented by the artist, 1891; WA1891.3

Poole 1912, no. 503; Hewison 1996, no. 3

Sir Henry Acland (1815–1900) was educated at Christ Church, Oxford, trained as a doctor and culminated his University career as Regius Professor of Medicine. He was instrumental in establishing the University Museum and a close friend of John Ruskin. This portrait and three of the following were made as demonstrations while Herkomer was Slade Professor, between 1885 and 1895. The portraits were painted in six sittings of one hour each, and were not necessarily completed.

Sir Hubert von Herkomer
(1849 – 1914)

Study of the Revd Henry George Woods, D.D.

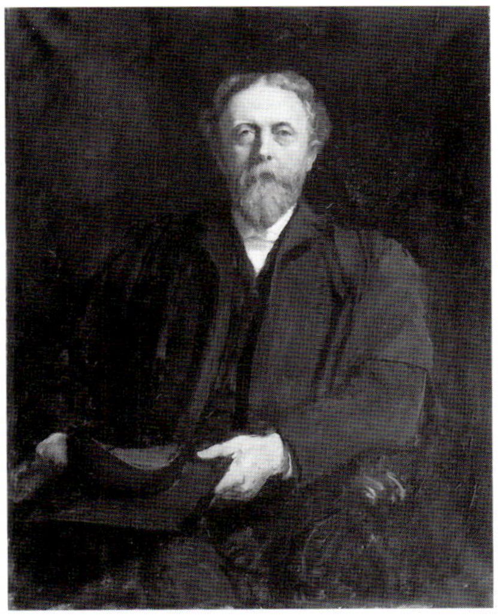

A251; oil on canvas, 112 × 86 cm
Signed and dated: *H.H. 90*
Presented by the artist, 1891; WA1891.5

Poole 1912, no. 508

Henry George Woods (1842–1915) was elected a Fellow of Trinity College, Oxford in 1865 and served as President of Trinity between 1887 and 1897. A further example of Herkomer's demonstration portraits.

Paulus Hennekyn
(*c.* 1611 – 1672)

Portrait of a young Man

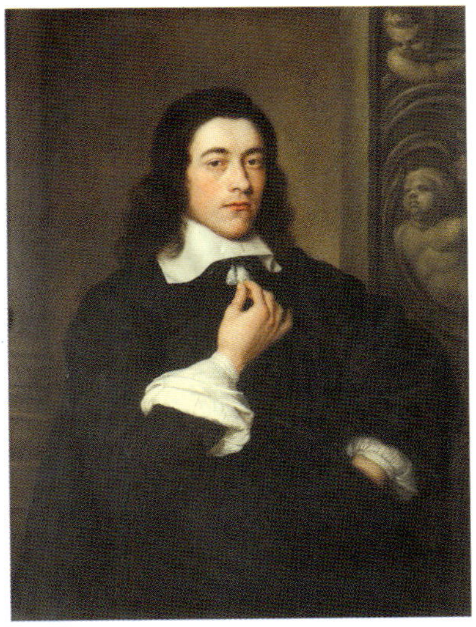

A361; oil on canvas, 100 × 74 cm
Signed and dated: *Paulus Hennekyn / 1655*
Presented by A.H. Buttery, 1920; WA1920.4

White 1999, p. 60

Hennekyn's work is not common. A small number of half or three-quarter length portraits are know, dated between 1645 and 1665. These show a debt to the work of the fashionable Amsterdam portrait painter, Bartholomeus van der Helst (*c.* 1613–1670).

Sir Hubert von Herkomer
(1849 – 1914)

Study of Alexander Macdonald

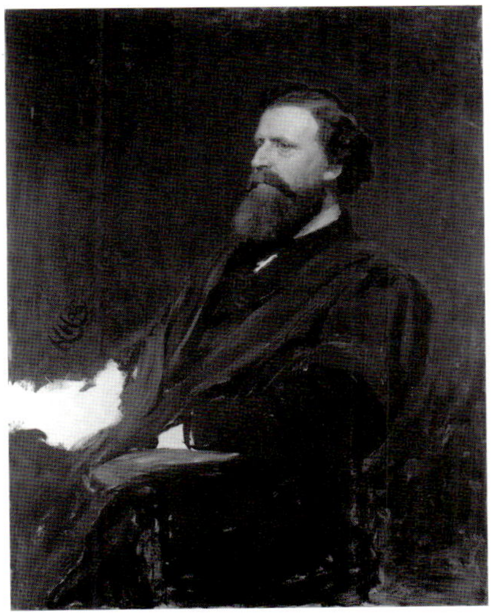

A250; oil on canvas, 111 × 86 cm
Signed and dated: *H.H. '88*
Presented by the artist, 1891; WA1891.4

Poole 1912, no. 507; Hewison 1996, no. 5

After training as an art master at the South Kensington Schools, Alexander Macdonald (1839–1921) ran the Oxford Art School from 1865. He was appointed first Ruskin Master at the Ruskin School of Drawing in 1871 and served as Keeper of the University Galleries between 1890 and 1908. This is another example of the portraits painted by Herkomer as demonstrations during his classes as Slade Professor.

Sir Hubert von Herkomer
(1849 – 1914)

Professor John Obadiah Westwood

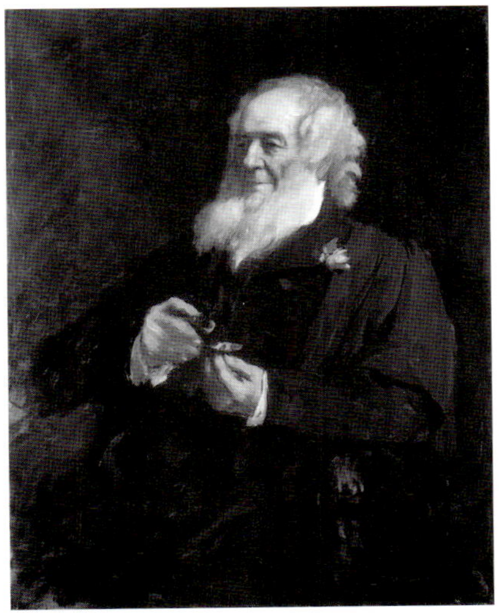

A252; oil on canvas, 112 × 86 cm
Signed and dated: *H.H. 1890*
Presented by the artist, 1891; WA1891.6

Poole 1912, no. 492

John Obadiah Westwood (1805–1893) was an eminent entomologist and palaeographer. He was the first Hope Professor of Zoology in the University of Oxford from 1861 until 1893. This portrait was not made during a demonstration, but as a finished work.

Sir Hubert von Herkomer
(1849 – 1914)

The Very Revd Henry George Lidell, D.D.

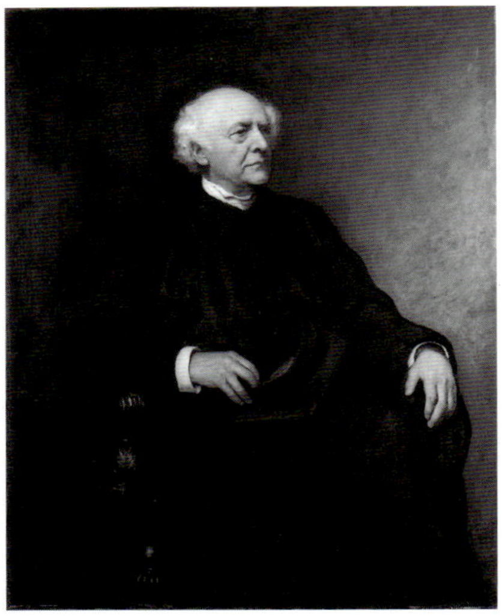

A248; oil on canvas, 142.5 × 112.4 cm
Signed and dated: *H.H. 91*
Presented by the artist, 1891; WA1891.2

Poole 1912, no. 496; Hewison 1996, no. 4

Liddell (1811–1898) was successively Student of Christ Church, Head Master of Westminster School (1846) and long-serving Dean of Christ Church between 1855 and 1892. He was the father of Alice 'in Wonderland' and author, with Robert Scott, of the celebrated *Greek-English Lexicon*, published in 1843. This portrait, exhibited at the Royal Academy in 1891, shows him in academic robes shortly before his retirement.

Louis-Adolphe Hervier
(1818 – 1879)

The Outskirts of a Village

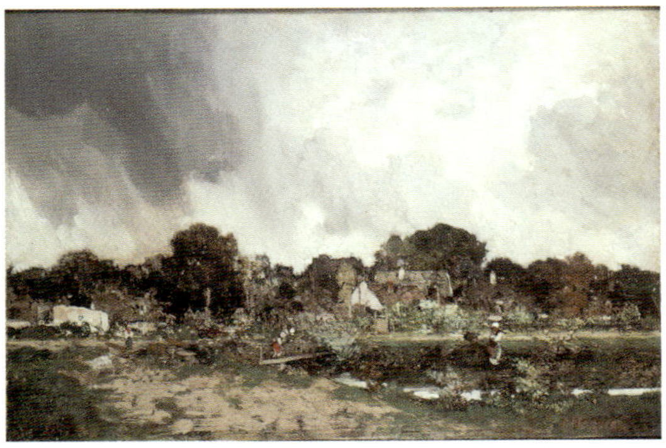

A651; oil on canvas, 23 × 33 cm
Signed and dated: *A Hervier 1852*
Hindley Smith Bequest, 1939; WA1940.1.33

Hervier worked extensively as a landscape painter and printmaker in northern France. The spotted, lively handling of paint and choice of subject in this little painting are marked by the influence of Eugène Isabey with whom Hervier studied. Hervier's manner is, however, crisper than Isabey's. He handled paint and watercolour with an easy virtuosity and attracted notable support from Gautier, Corot and the Goncourt brothers among others, but had little commercial success.

Tristram Paul Hillier
(1905 – 1983)

A Rose

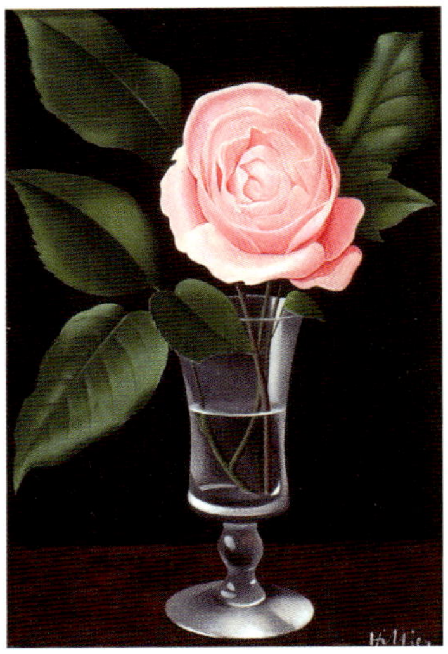

A1036a; oil on panel, 23 × 15 cm
Signed: *Hillier*
Bequeathed by A.G. Gooch through the National Art Collections Fund, 1967; WA1967.60.2

Hillier studied at the Slade School of Fine Art in London and later lived mostly in France. Many of his paintings, including this still life of *c.* 1944, are meticulously and carefully arranged. The composition and the extremely finished surface evoke an appearance which suggests a cautious link to surrealist, French tendencies.

Sir Hubert von Herkomer
(1849 – 1914)

Study of the Revd Robert H. Charsley

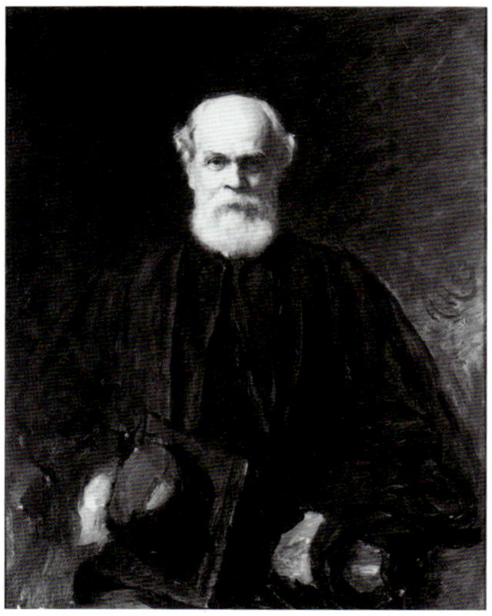

A331; oil on canvas, 112 × 86 cm
Signed and dated: *H.H. '93*
Presented by the artist, 1912; WA1912.1

This demonstration portrait depicts the Revd Robert Charsley (b. *c.* 1836), who was appointed Chaplain to the Radcliffe Hospital in 1855.

Arthur Derek Hill
(1916 – 2000)

Snow over Rome

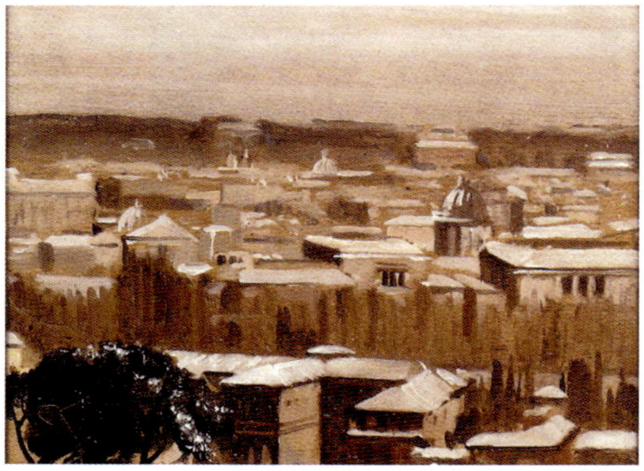

A1209; oil on hardboard, 19 × 26.5 cm
Presented by Mrs Virginia Surtees in memory of John Gere, 1998; WA1998.10

Hill, who first trained and worked as a stage designer, later became an independent painter. Between 1952 and 1955 and 1957 and 1959 he was art director at the British School in Rome. This enabled him to see the city in many different aspects. In this case, he painted Rome in winter, the roofs covered with snow. The city is represented in a style somewhere between the Italian postwar Neo-Realists and the 'pittura metafisica', combining naturalistic elements with a strong geometric structure.

Tristram Paul Hillier
(1905 – 1983)

Trott's Lane

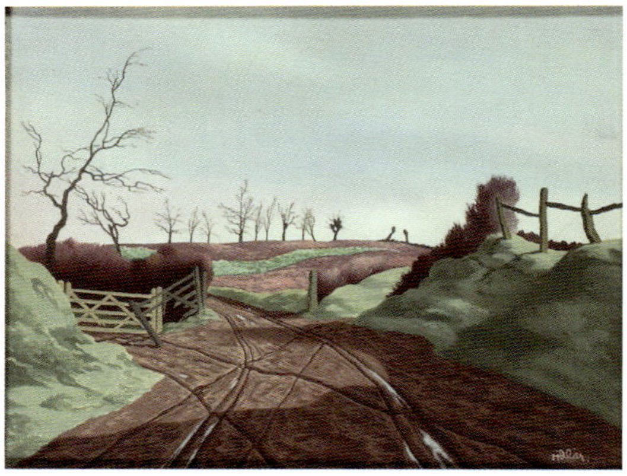

A1036b; oil on panel, 20 × 25 cm
Signed: *Hillier*
Bequeathed by A.G. Gooch through the National Art Collections Fund, 1967; WA1967.60.3

In this landscape, painted in the same year as A1036a, the empty terrain and the absence of people who have left their traces in the ground, create an unreal atmosphere. The leafless trees are combined with very sparse vegetation. The horizon is nearly in the centre of the painting and contrasts sharply with the sombre foreground.

Anonymous Hispano-Flemish Artist
(*c.* 1500)

The Virgin and Child

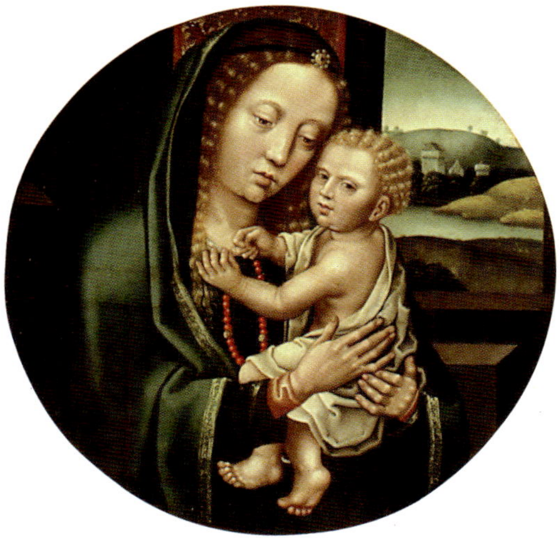

A336; oil (?) on panel, integral frame, 32.4 cm in diameter
Inscribed on the frame: *Quien rezare la manifica o la salve regina a nra senora gana treinta mil anos de perdon oto[rga]dos por el papa clemente*
Presented by Mrs James Reddie Anderson, 1913; WA1913.5

Gaya Nuño 1958, no. 63

This devotional image, probably painted in northern Spain, may derive from a composition by Gerard David or Ambrosius Benson. The inscription, which asserts that whoever recites the Magnificat or the Salve Regina to Our Lady will gain 30,000 years of pardon authorised by Pope Clement, may refer to Clement VI (1342–52).

Ivon Hitchens
(1893 – 1979)

A Border Day (Morning, Bankshead)

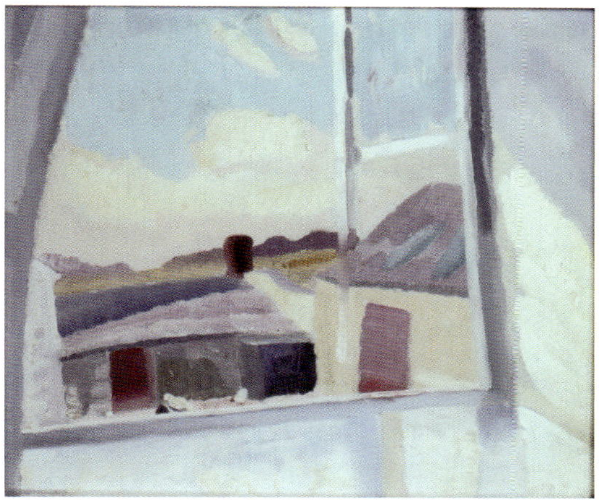

A1146; oil on canvas, 56.4 × 61 cm
Signed: *Ivon Hitchens*
Prov.: Mrs Dudley Short and by descent
Bequeathed by Mrs Mary Freeman, 1986; WA1987.37

Bowness 1973, no. 129; Eustace 1999, no. 23

Hitchens spent the summer of 1925 with Ben and Winifred Nicholson. He painted a serives of views from a window, a device common in the work of the Nicholsons. This allowed him to combine a small part of an interior with a view into the courtyard of a farm. It can also be seen as a step towards abstraction, reducing natural forms and architecture to their basic geometric elements.

Eliot Hodgkin
(1905 – 1987)

Study of Asparagus

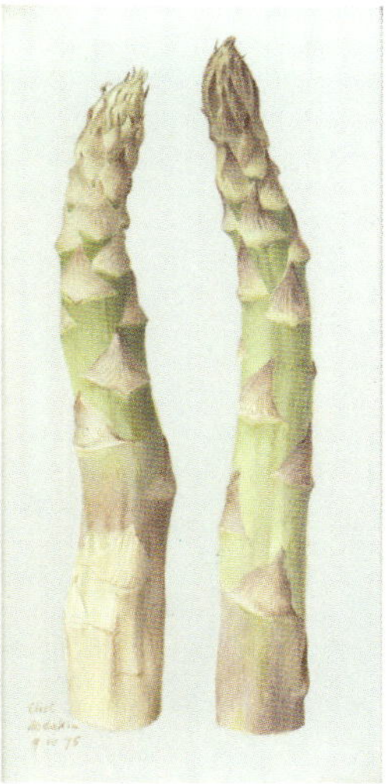

Tempera on wood mounted on cardboard, mounted as a drawing, 25.7 × 12.8 cm
Signed and dated: *Eliot Hodgkin 9iv75*
Purchased from the artist, 1976; WA1976.23

Throughout his career Hodgkin was deeply interested in still-life painting. He painted many pictures in which fruit and vegetables, often exotic or unexpected, are depicted in meticulous detail.

Ivon Hitchens
(1893 – 1979)

Chestnut Waters

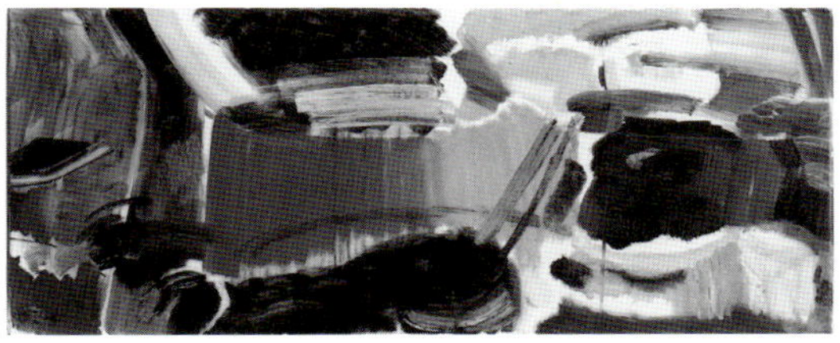

A1015; oil on canvas, 53 × 132 cm
Signed: *Hitchens*
Presented by Patrons of the Oxfam Art Exhibition, 1964; WA1964.46

Hitchens attempted to find a particular and contemporary approach to landscape, based on an inner harmony of colour and form, which he developed in conjunction with the Nicholsons (see A1146). Later he reduced landscape to a rich abstraction. In this large canvas, no figurative element remains and the landscape is reconfigured in large patterns created with quick, broad brush-strokes.

William Hoare
(*c.* 1707 – 1792)

Portrait Study of the Countess of Ashburnham

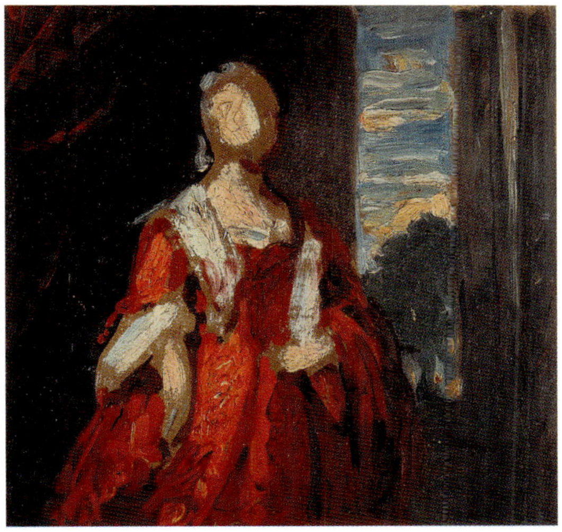

Oil on canvas, mounted as a drawing, 13.5 × 14 cm
Purchased (Hope Fund), 1978; WA1978.107

Brown 1982, no. 855

Hoare studied in Rome and built up a lucrative practice as a fashionable portrait painter in Bath. This freely handled oil-sketch is a preparatory study for his portrait of Elizabeth Crowley, who married John, 2nd Earl of Ashburnham, in 1756. She died in 1787. As the face has been left blank, the sketch is probably a record of her pose and Hoare would have made other drawings or sketches of her features.

Carl Hoffmann the Younger
(1838 – after 1890)

Head of a Girl

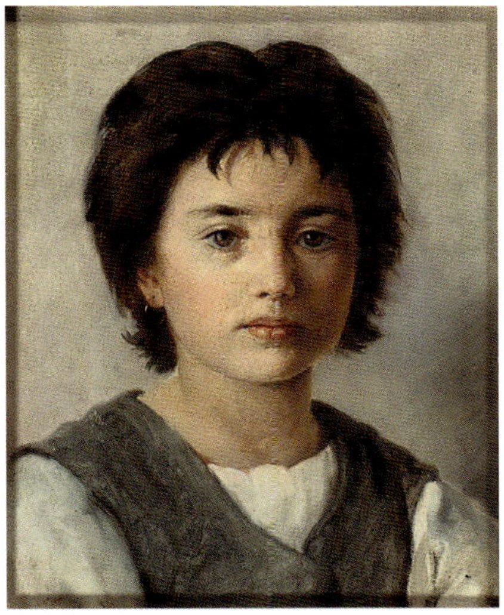

A262; oil on canvas, 26 × 21 cm
Inscribed on back of canvas: *C.Hoffman 23 / 3. 1872 / of Dusseldorf*
Bequeathed by the Revd Greville John Chester, 1892; WA1892.7

White 1999, p. 61

Hoffmann grew up in Rome but studied in Düsseldorf from 1863 until 1866. He returned to Rome in 1866 and remained there until 1877. According to an inscription on the stretcher, this head study was painted at Ischia in 1871.

William Hogarth
(1697 – 1764)

The Marriage Contract

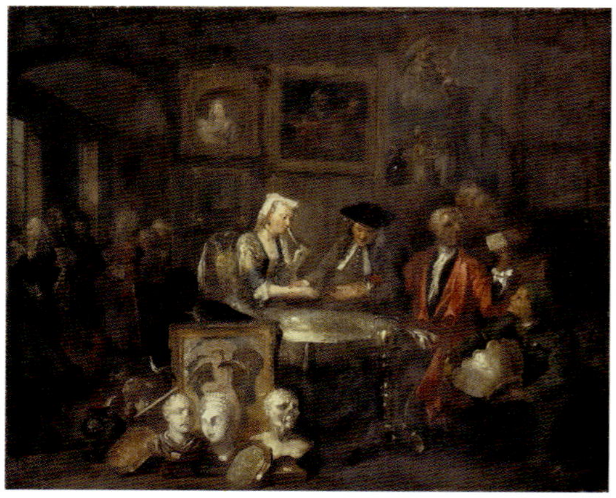

A858; oil on canvas, 62 × 75 cm
Inscribed: *Willm Hogarth*
Prov.: Mrs Hogarth; Samuel Ireland; J. Hawkins
Bequeathed by Sir Robert Witt through the National Art Collections Fund, 1952; WA1952.63

Gowing 1971–2, no. 63; Paulson 1989, p. 89; Woodward 1998

This enigmatic painting of the early 1730s contains elements later incorporated into three of the series, *A Rake's Progress*, for which the paintings (Sir John Soane's Museum, London) were completed in 1734 and the engravings published in June 1735. The scene takes place in a prosperous household. The father, seated in the centre, is joining his daughter's hand to that of the young man on the right, who turns away to read a letter. A jockey indicates other distractions for the young man. The marriage is clearly doomed. The painting has suffered a disastrous cleaning in the 19th century and many parts of it are repainted.

William Hogarth
(1697 – 1764)

The Enraged Musician

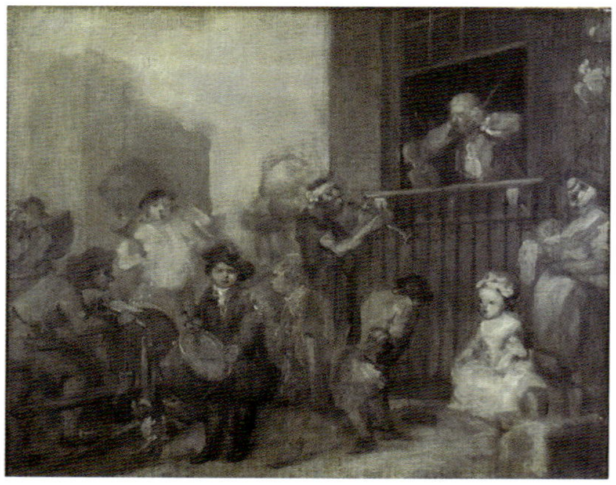

A189; oil on canvas, 38 × 48 cm
Prov.: Mrs Hogarth; Samuel Ireland
Chambers Hall Gift, 1855; WA1855.193

Beckett 1949, p. 65; Gowing 1971–2, no. 76; Paulson 1989, under no. 152

A study with minor differences for Hogarth's print of *The Enraged Musician*, published in November 1741 and advertised as a companion piece to *The Distressed Poet* (1736), for which the preparatory painting is in Birmingham City Art Gallery. A third composition on the troubles of a painter was projected but never completed. The musician stopping his ears in the window has been interrupted by the sounds from the street: a knife grinder, a dustman, a drummer, an itinerant oboe player, a mother holding a screaming baby and singing, while a child waves a rattle. The scene probably took place in St Martin's Lane, London, on a feast day, when the peal of the bells of St Martin's in the Fields would have added to the cacophony.

William Hogarth
(1697 – 1764)

The Suicide of the Countess

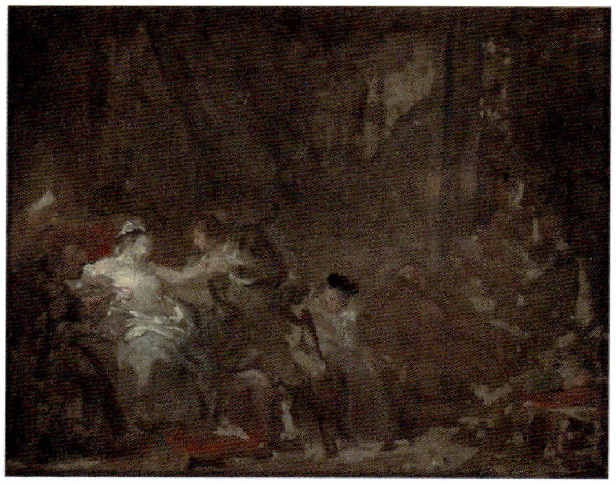

A190; oil on canvas, 30.3 × 37.5 cm
Inscribed: *Willm Hogarth*
Prov.: Mrs Hogarth; Samuel Ireland
Chambers Hall Gift, 1855; WA1855.583

Beckett 1949, p. 68; Gowing 1971–2, no. 128

It is generally accepted that this very lively oil-sketch is related to the final episode in the series *Marriage à la Mode*, for which the paintings (National Gallery, London) were completed in 1743 and the prints published in June 1745. The relationship between the sketch and the final version is not close.

William Hogarth
(1697 – 1764)

Sir James Thornhill

A187; dimensions unknown
Chambers Hall Gift, 1855; WA1855.195

Missing since February 1907.

Attributed to William Hogarth
(1697 – 1764)

The Stage Coach or The Country Inn Yard

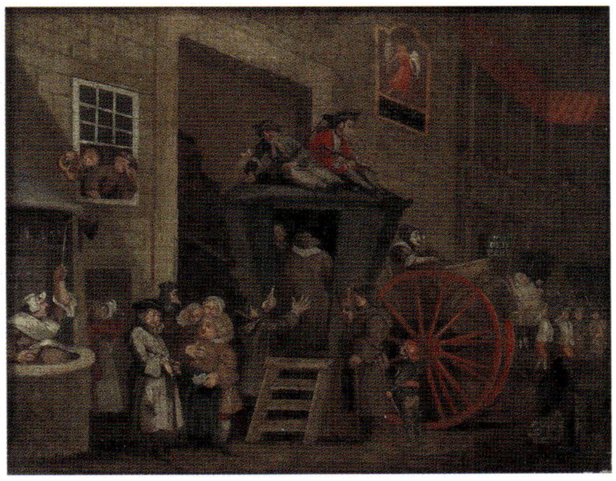

A186; oil on canvas, 32 × 40 cm
Chambers Hall Gift, 1855; WA1855.192

Paulson 1989, under no. 167

The relationship of this sketch to the print of the same title published in 1747 is problematic. Unlike other studies for prints, the image is not in reverse, suggesting that it may have been copied from the print. However, it is stylistically comparable with other sketches. The scene shows an inn, The Old Angle In (i.e. Old England), at the time of the General Election. The banner in the background, inscribed *No Old Baby*, refers to the Old Pretender, who was said to have been introduced into his mother's bed in a warming-pan.

Copy after Hans Holbein the Younger
(*c.* 1497 – 1543)

Desiderius Erasmus

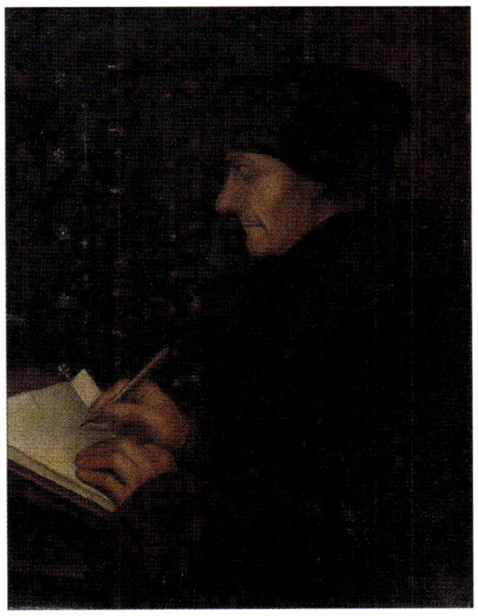

F737 or 674; oil on canvas, 43.8 × 32.3 cm
Presented by John Aubrey; WA1898.42

Desiderius Erasmus (1466/9–1536) was among the greatest of Humanist scholars. He sat to Holbein on several occasions. The original of this portrait is probably that in the Louvre, which was owned for some years by Charles I.

Francis Montague Holl
(1845 – 1888)

Faces in the Fire

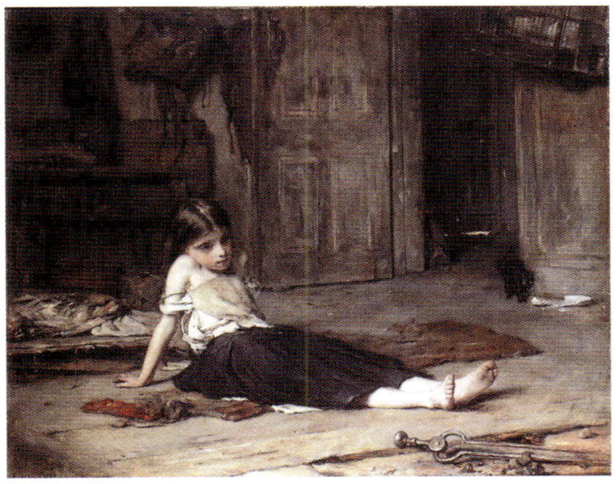

A1173; oil on canvas, 46.5 × 67.5 cm
Signed and dated: *F.Holl 1867*
Prov.: Sir David Piper
Presented by the Friends of the Ashmolean, 1991; WA1991.184

Whiteley 1991, p. 15

Holl made his name as a painter of genre subjects, before turning to portraits. *Faces in the Fire* was one of his earliest successes when exhibited at the Royal Academy in 1867. A young girl gazes into the fire, oblivious of the cat whose saucer is broken. The birdcage, a common attribute of servitude, indicates that she is a servant or a hard-worked daughter of the house.

Attributed to William Hogarth
(1697 – 1764)

The Theft of the Watch

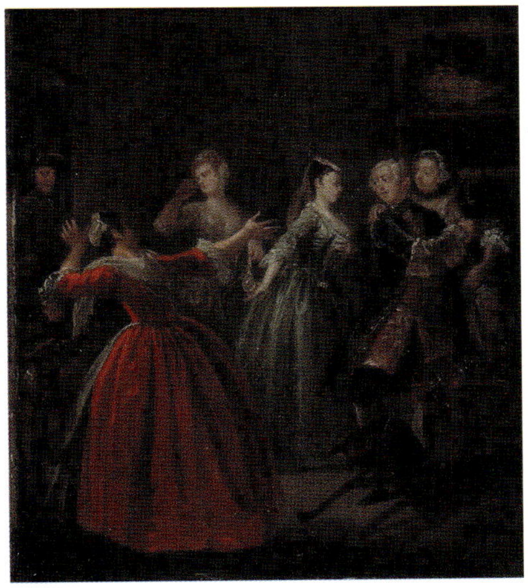

A127; oil on canvas, 36 × 31 cm
Bequeathed by the Revd Dr Thomas Penrose, 1851; WA1851.25

Gowing 1971–2, no. 20

The attribution to Hogarth is traditional. A more convincing recent suggestion links the painting to the circle of Flemish artists working in London in the 1730s, such as J.F. Nollekens.

Copy after Hans Holbein the Younger
(*c.* 1497 – 1543)

Desiderius Erasmus

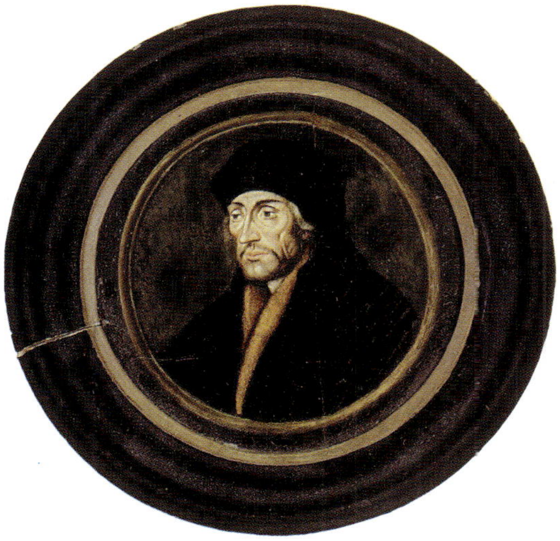

F637; oil on oak panel, 14 cm in diameter
Presented by Elias Ashmole, 1683; WA1898.4

MacGregor 1983, no. 255

Rather loosely based on the portrait of Erasmus sent by Holbein to Archbishop Warham in 1524 (on loan to the National Gallery, London).

James Holland
(1799 – 1870)

A View of Venice

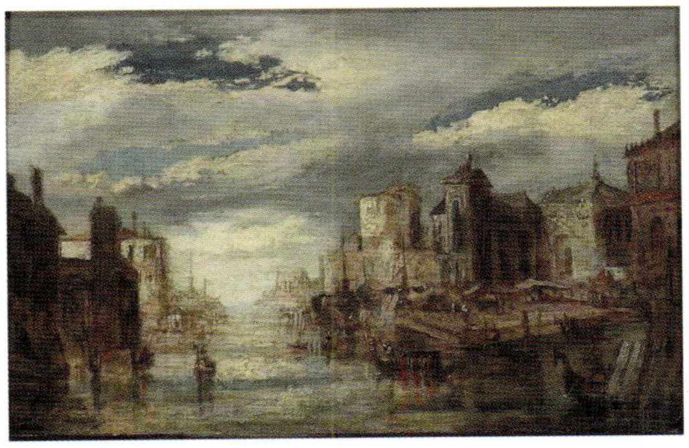

A275; oil on panel, 29 × 45 cm
Combe Bequest, 1893; WA1894.12.1

The specific view has not been identified and the attribution is not certain. Holland first visited Venice in 1835 and the city provided him with material for the remainder of his career.

Sir Charles John Holmes
(1868 – 1936)

Coniston Old Man from Levens Water

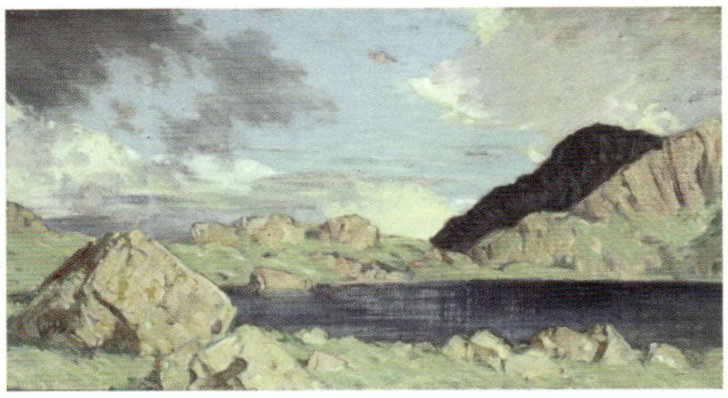

A328; oil on canvas, 46 × 81 cm
Signed and dated: *C.J.H.10*
Presented by the artist, 1911; WA1911.1

Sir Charles Holroyd
(1861 – 1917)

The Rialto, Venice

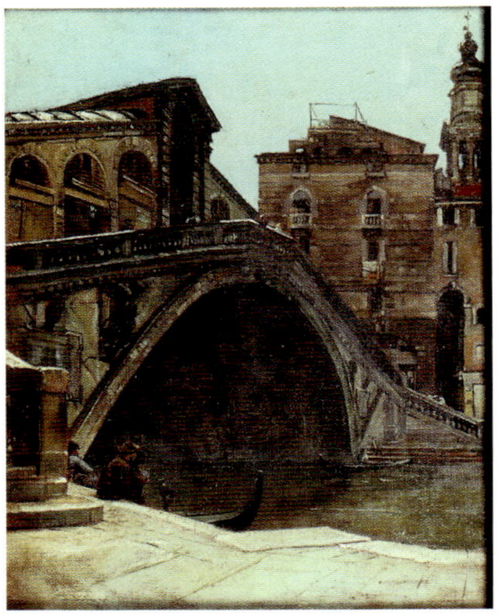

Oil on canvas, 41 × 33 cm
Presented by Mrs Michael Holroyd, 1954; WA1954.80.8

Holroyd travelled extensively in Italy between 1888 and his appointment as Keeper of the Tate Gallery ten years later. This bridge over the Rialto was a favourite subject for painters from the 18th century onwards.

Percy Frederick Horton
(1897 – 1970)

Self-portrait

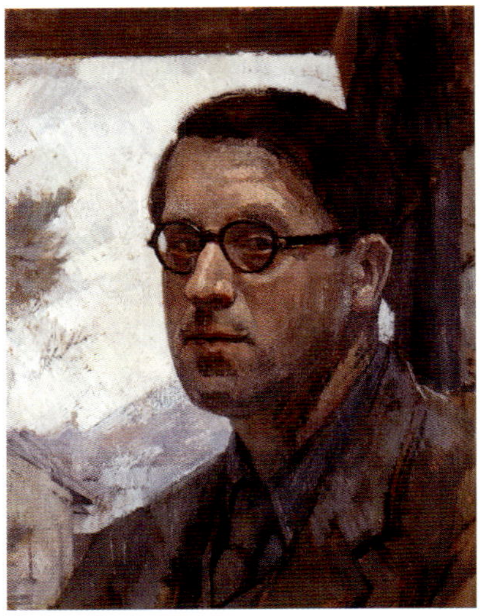

A909; oil on paper, 34 × 26 cm
Presented by the artist, 1957; WA1957.85.1

Oxford 1964, no. 31

Between 1930 and 1949, Horton taught painting at the Royal College of Art. He was Ruskin Master of Drawing at Oxford between 1949 and 1964.

Sir Charles John Holmes
(1868 – 1936)

Saddleback from the South-west

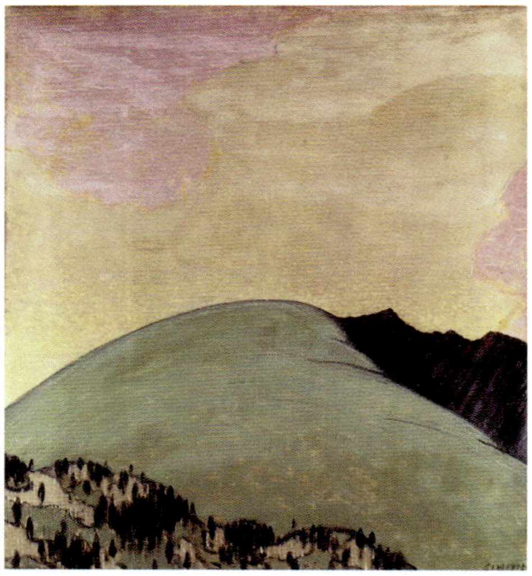

A775; oil on canvas, 76 × 68 cm
Signed and dated: *CJH 1911*
Bequeathed by Reginald Cripps, 1949; WA1949.186

According to Holmes, the present work was 'an experiment inspired by the example of Korin' which 'shocked Claude Phillips and others by its violence, but really interested Ricketts and so pleased my friend Cripps that when it remained unsold I made him a present of it'. In addition to the influence of the Japanese artist Korin, the painting is indebted to Gauguin and the Post-Impressionists.

Percy Frederick Horton
(1897 – 1970)

Flowerpiece

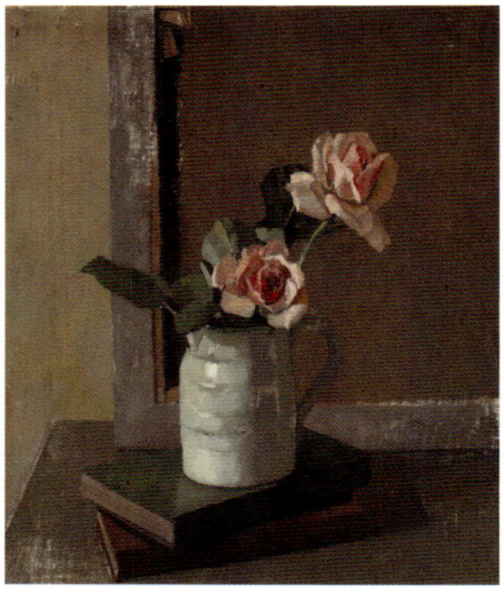

A1254; oil on canvas board, 44 × 33.9 cm
Bequeathed by Miss Philippa Hesketh-Williams, 1999; WA2003.94

Oxford 1964, no. 9

One of a number of still lifes painted early in Horton's career, this probably dates from *c.* 1929, when he was teaching at the Working Men's College.

Percy Frederick Horton
(1897 – 1970)

The Rugmaker

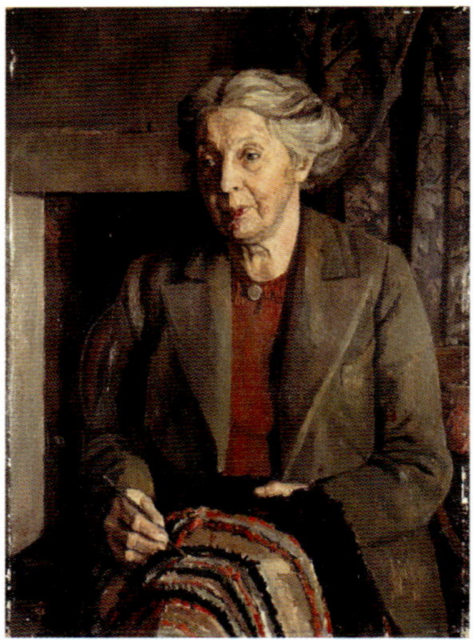

A906; oil on canvas on board, 55 × 39 cm
Presented by Mrs J.H. Walmsley, 1957; WA1957.84

Oxford 1964, no. 34

A portrait of the donor, exhibited at the Royal Academy in 1946.

After René-Antoine Houasse
(1644/5 – 1710)

The Opening of the Tomb of Nitocris by Darius (?)

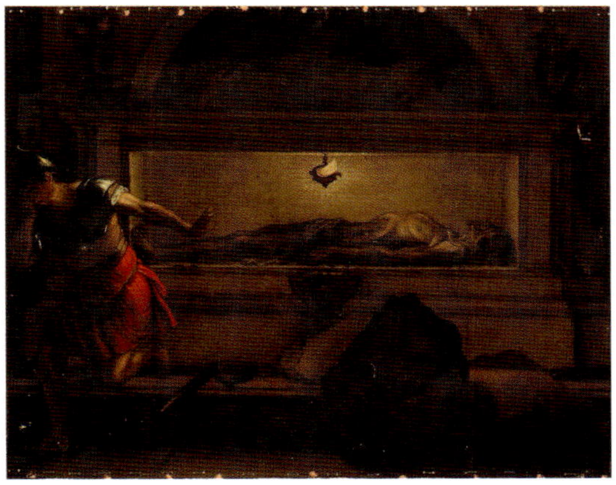

A63; oil on canvas, 56 × 71 cm
Presented by the Revd Bulkeley Bandinel, *c.* 1830; WA1845.63

O'Neill 1981, under no. 82

A63 derives from a lost painting by Houasse, known in an engraving by Etienne Baudet (1686). It may represent King Darius opening the tomb of Queen Nitocris of Babylon in search of hidden treasure (Herodotus, *Histories*, I, 187). Equally, it may be an invention, designed to convey an emotion, or to act as a *memento mori*. The original appears in Jouvenet's portrait of Houasse, now in Grenoble.

Albert Houthuesen
(1903 – 1978)

Night Sea, Autumn

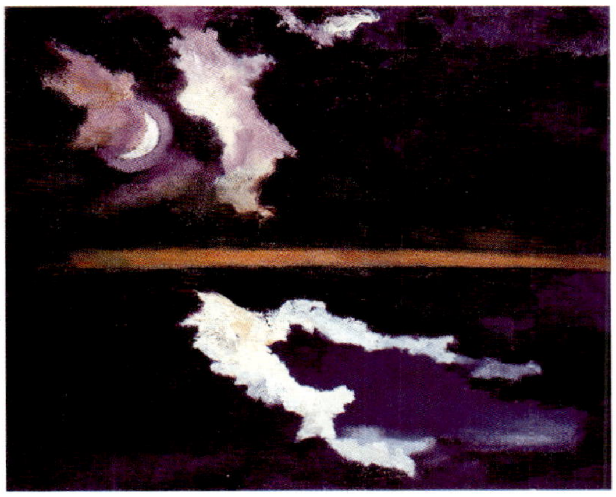

A1104; acrylic on canvas, 62.5 × 74.5 cm
Signed: *Houthuesen*; inscribed on back: *Acrylic 1968 Varnished with Rowneys No. 800 Mar. 1969 NIGHT SEA, AUTUMN, II*
Presented by Sir John Rothenstein, 1978; WA1978.122

Houthuesen often painted religious and visionary subjects. This romantic, moonlight scene at sea, precisely titled, brings to mind a number of landscapes and marine paintings by early 19th-century German artists who shared Houthuesen's deeply-felt response to the spirituality of the natural world.

Arthur Hughes
(1832 – 1915)

The Eve of St Agnes

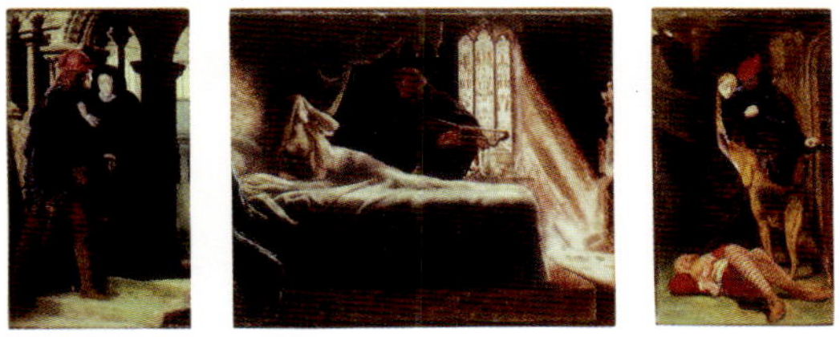

A708; oil on paper on panel, 26 × 16, 27 × 31, 26 × 16 cm
Signed: *A.HUGHES*
Prov.: Alexander Munro and by descent
Bequeathed by John Arthur Ruskin Munro, 1944; WA1944.13

Roberts and Wildman 1997, no. 30.8

Hughes painted a large triptych of *The Eve of St Agnes* in 1855–6 (Tate Britain). This reduced version, on paper rather than canvas, was perhaps begun around the same time, but completed and exhibited in 1858. The triptych illustrates three episodes of Keats's poem of the same title. On the left, Porphyro is shown into Madeline's chamber by her nurse; in the centre, Madeline wakes from her dream and finds her imaginary lover is real; on the right, the pair escape from the castle. The panels are arranged like a medieval altar-piece. Holman Hunt had illustrated the last episode in a painting of 1848 (Guildhall Art Gallery), but Hughes's version shows a sensitivity to the text that is lacking in Hunt's.

Arthur Boyd Houghton
(1836 – 1875)

Playmates

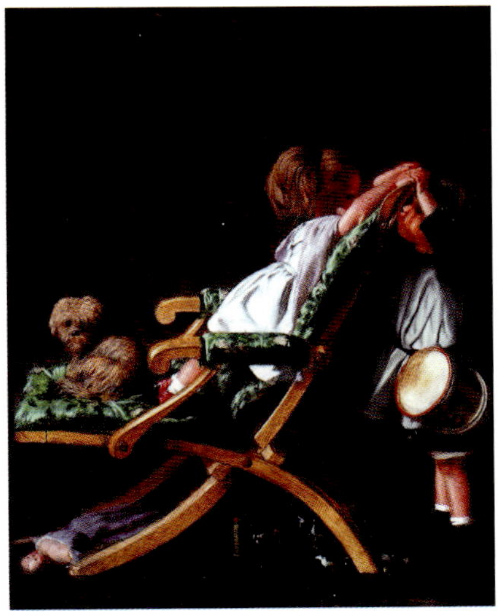

A715; oil on canvas, mounted as a drawing, 25 × 20 cm
Presented by Francis Falconer Madan, 1945; WA1945.74

Hogarth 1975, no. 52; Hogarth 1981, pp. 28–9

The composition was based on the wood engraving, *Kiss me*, reproduced in *Good Words* in 1863. The models were the artist's children, Georgina and Arthur. This painting was begun in 1866 and completed in early 1869.

George James Howard, 9th Earl of Carlisle
(1843 – 1911)

Tennyson reading aloud in a Glade

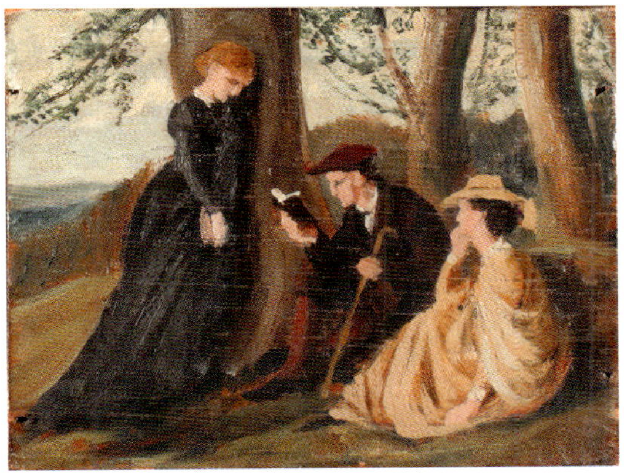

A680a; oil on panel, 9 × 11 cm
Prov.: presumably Francis Turner Palgrave and by descent
Presented by the Revd F.M.T. Palgrave and Miss Annora Palgrave, 1941; WA1941.21.1

F.T. Palgrave (1824–1897), who compiled the *Golden Treasury*, was a close friend of the Poet Laureate, Alfred Lord Tennyson. This sketch was presumably painted for Palgrave.

Arthur Hughes
(1832 – 1915)

Home from Sea

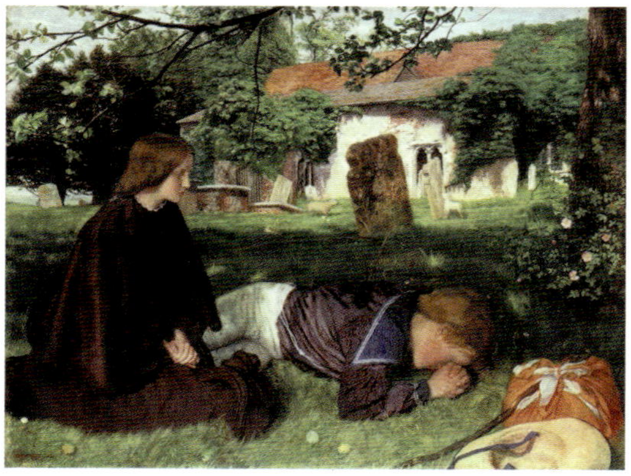

A316; oil on panel, 50 × 65 cm
Signed and dated: *ARTHUR HUGHES 1862*
Prov.: John Hamilton Trist; James Macandrew
Presented by Vernon Watney, 1907; WA1907.3

Roberts and Wildman 1997, no. 33

The genesis of this painting began in 1857, when it was exhibited as *The Mother's Grave*. The original composition, known from a drawing in the Ashmolean, showed the boy desolate over the grave of his mother. The landscape was begun in the summer of 1856 in the old churchyard at Chingford, Essex. Around 1862, Hughes altered the background and added the figure of the sister, for which the artist's daughter, Tryphena, posed. The detail is used to reinforce the pathos of the subject, so that the ephemeral nature of spider's webs, dew drops, dog roses and dandelion seeds all emphasise the theme of transience. The boy's loss is retold in the lamb separated from its mother by the barrier of the tomb.

Arthur Hughes
(1832 – 1915)

Pansies

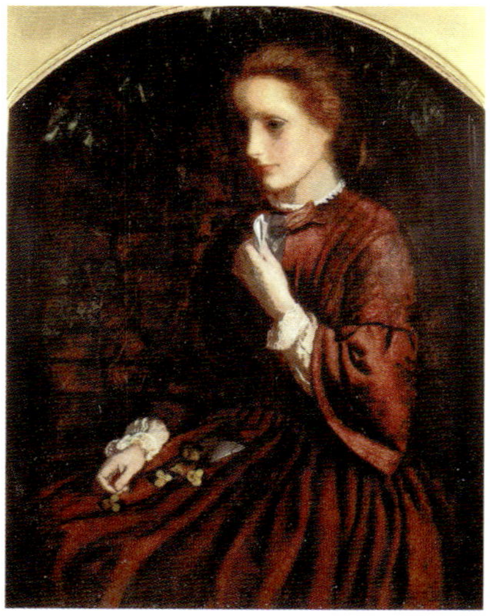

A995; oil on canvas, 38 × 29 cm
Prov.: Benjamin Godfrey Windus; William Graham; J.R. Thomas
Russell Bequest, 1962; WA1962.58.1

Brown 1987, no. 54; Roberts and Wildman 1997, no. 47

The girl clutches a letter that has moved her deeply. She holds on her lap yellow pansies, the flower of memory. The scene is characteristically suggestive and affecting and recalls the theme of Hughes's *April Love* of 1856 (Tate Britain). *Pansies* was probably painted around 1860.

Arthur Hughes
(1832 – 1915)

Cecily Ursula, aged three years

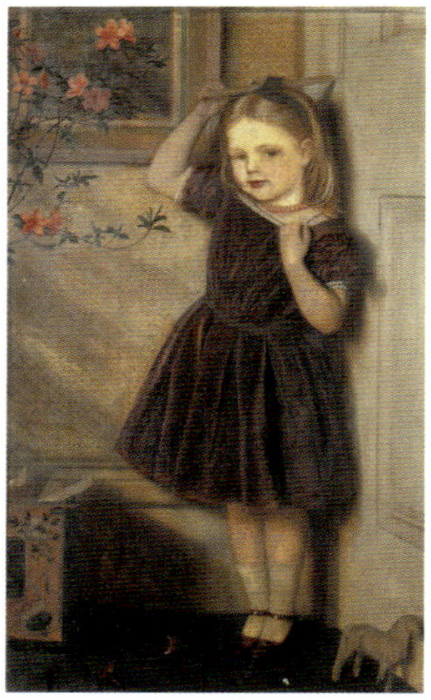

A679; oil on canvas, 70 × 43 cm
Prov.: by descent
Presented by the Revd F.M.T. Palgrave and Miss Annora Palgrave, 1941; WA1941.28

Roberts and Wildman 1997, no. 90

Cecily Ursula Palgrave was the daughter of the critic, Francis Turner Palgrave. She is seen measuring her height against a door. This work was exhibited at the Royal Academy in 1867.

Arthur Hughes
(1832 – 1915)

Ophelia

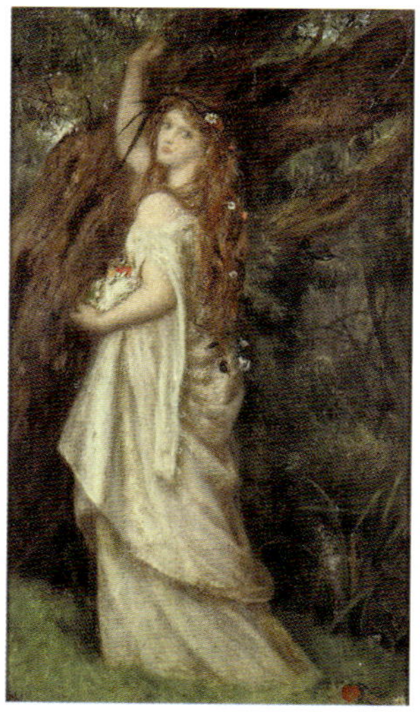

A1088; oil on panel, 33.3 × 21.1 cm
Bequeathed by John Bryson, 1977; WA1977.23

Roberts and Wildman 1997, no. 67.2

A sketch of *c.* 1863 for the painting completed in 1871 (Toledo Museum of Art). It illustrates the scene in Shakespeare's *Hamlet* (Act IV, scene 7) in which Ophelia picks flowers to make garlands shortly before she is drowned.

Malcolm Hughes
(1920 – 1997)

Painting/Moquette (Mixed Media)

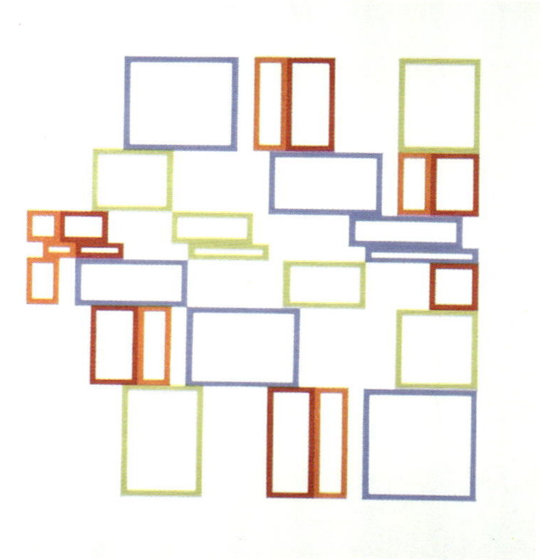

Mixed media on paper, mounted on cardboard, mounted as a drawing, 35.8 × 35.8 cm
Presented by the Contemporary Art Society, 1979; WA1979.86

For much of his career, Hughes was a constructivist painter and draughtsman. This kind of constructivism was very important during the 1960s in Britain and elsewhere. Here, Hughes explores not only the arrangement of rectangles of different sizes, but also the harmony of colours applied on a white ground in carefully arranged areas of different density and dimensions.

WILLIAM HUGHES
(1842 – 1901)

Still Life of Kitchen Utensils and Vegetables

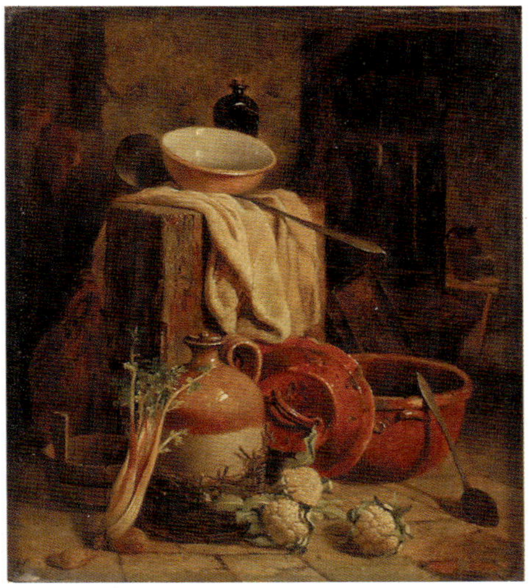

A451d; oil on panel, 24 × 20 cm
Signed and dated: *W Hughes 1868*
Presented by Mrs Leslie Milne, 1936; WA1936.6

An early work by Hughes, who exhibited at the Royal Academy from 1866 to 1901, specializing in still lifes.

WILLIAM STOKES HULTON
(1851 – 1921)

Interior of the Church of Sta Maria in Porto Fuori, Ravenna

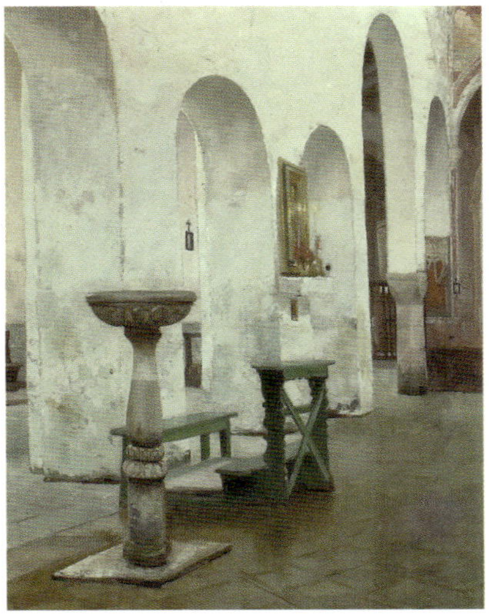

A1071; oil on canvas, 105 × 80 cm
Prov.: by descent from the artist
Bequeathed by the Lady Berwick, the artist's daughter, 1973; WA1973.4

The nave and left aisle of the medieval church of Sta Maria in Porto Fuori, about two miles outside Ravenna, which was entirely destroyed in 1944. This view was painted in 1887.

ALFRED WILLIAM HUNT
(1830 – 1896)

View of Nantlle, Caernarvonshire

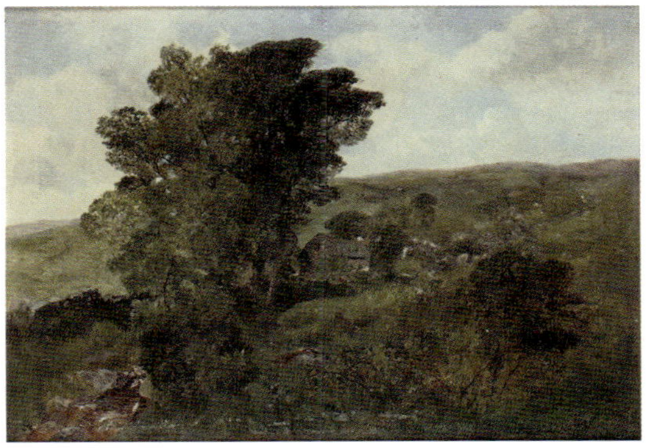

A340; oil on canvas, 26 × 36 cm
Signed and dated: *A.W. Hunt 1855*
Bequeathed by Charles J. Moss, 1914; WA1914.2

Hunt was elected a Fellow of Corpus Christi College, Oxford in 1853, but resigned in 1861. He became best known for his watercolours, which combine a Pre-Raphaelite preoccupation with detail with Turner's love of atmospheric effects. This early oil painting was probably made during the Oxford long vacation; Hunt made tours of North Wales in 1854 and 1855.

Attributed to FRANS DE HULST
(*c.* 1610 – 1661)

Cottages beside a River

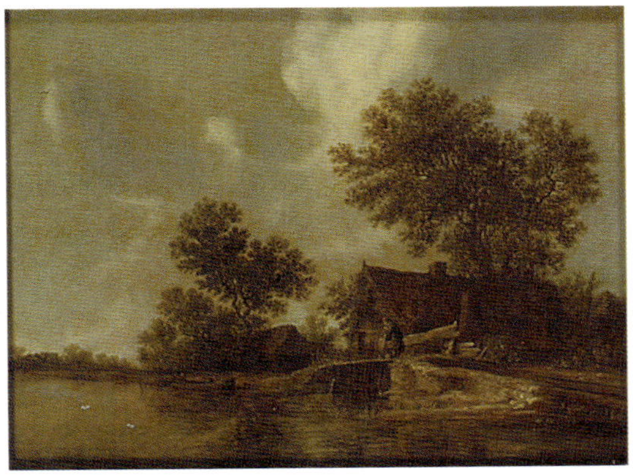

A350; oil on panel, 34 × 44 cm
Signed in monogram: *FDH*
Presented by A.H. Buttery, 1915; WA1915.61

White 1999, p. 62

The monogram FDH may belong to Frans de Hulst but the painting is not particularly close to works which are fully signed.

WILLIAM STOKES HULTON
(1851 – 1921)

Reginald Barratt

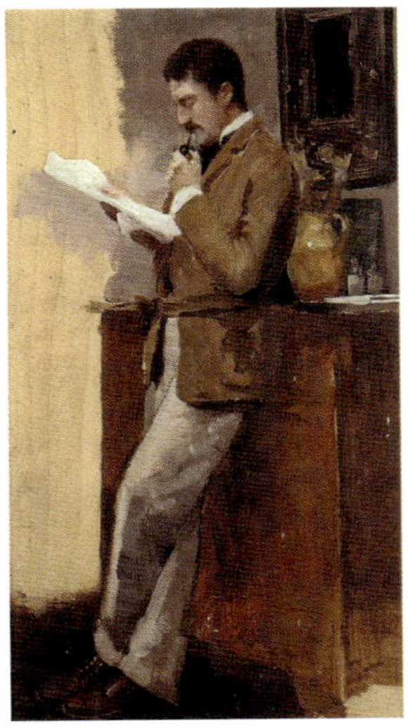

A1059a; oil on panel, mounted as a drawing, 30.8 × 17.2 cm
Prov.: by descent from the artist
Presented by the Lady Berwick, the artist's daughter, 1970; WA1970.128

Reginald Barratt (1861–1917) was a painter of landscapes and architectural subjects. He had been articled to Norman Shaw and then studied in Paris under Lefebvre and Bouguereau. He worked for a time as an illustrator for the *Graphic* and the *Daily Graphic* and was commissioned by Queen Victoria to paint her favourite view of Florence.

ALFRED WILLIAM HUNT
(1830 – 1896)

Dunstanborough

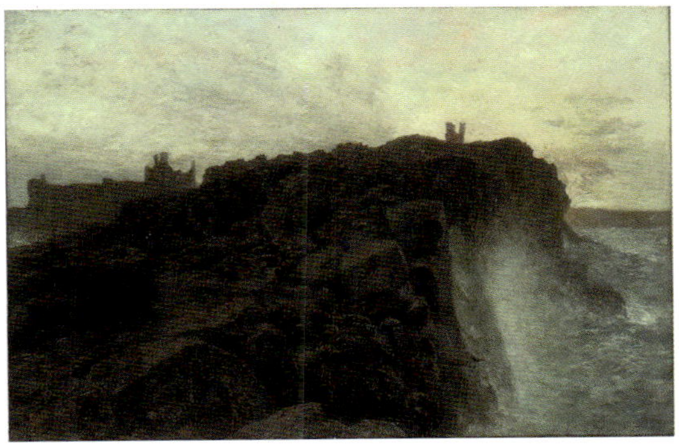

A358; oil on canvas, 81 × 121 cm
Signed and dated: *A.W.H. 1886*
Presented by Mrs W.A.S. Benson and Mrs Fogg-Elliot, the artist's daughters, 1918; WA1919.2

Dunstanborough Castle, on the north-east coast of Northumberland, was painted by several 19th-century artists, including J.M.W. Turner. Hunt, whose wife came from neighbouring Durham and who lived there for a time in the 1860s, had easy access to the site and painted it on more than one occasion. This unusually large example was probably exhibited at the Royal Academy in 1886.

Alfred William Hunt
(1830 – 1896)

Glen Lyon by Moonlight, Snowdon

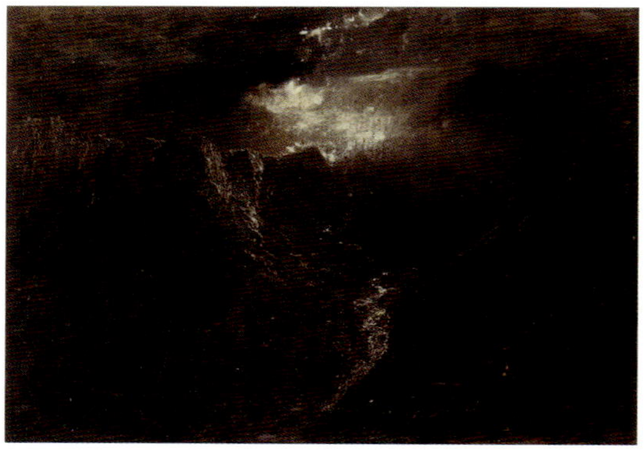

Oil on canvas, mounted as a drawing, 27.1 × 37.5 cm
Presented by Mrs W.A.S. Benson and Mrs Fogg-Elliott, the artist's daughters, 1918; WA1918.7.1

Hunt visited Wales frequently throughout his career as an artist and exhibited numerous paintings and watercolours worked up from his sketches on the spot. This painting, which has darkened with age, has not been dated.

William Holman Hunt
(1827 – 1910)

Self-portrait at the Age of 14

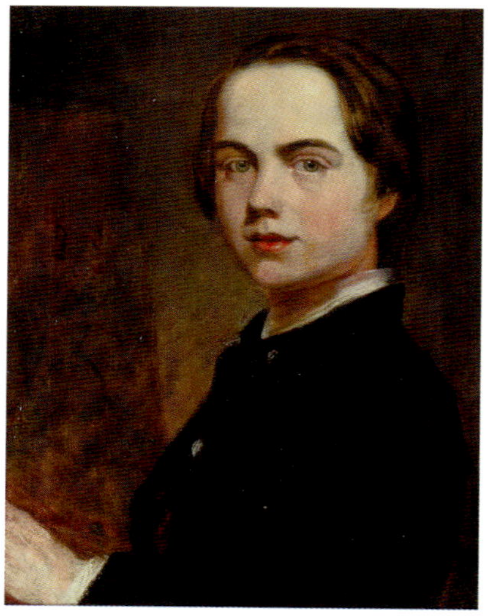

A947; oil on canvas, 46 × 36 cm
Prov.: by descent from the artist to Mrs Burt
Purchased (Virtue-Tebbs Bequest Fund), 1961; WA1961.23

One of Hunt's earliest paintings, dating from 1841, when he was working as an office clerk by day, attending drawing classes by night, and taking weekly lessons with the portrait painter, Henry Rogers. He adopted a similar pose in a *Self-portrait at the Age of 17* (Birmingham City Art Gallery).

William Holman Hunt
(1827 – 1910)

A converted British Family sheltering a Christian Missionary from the Persecution of the Druids

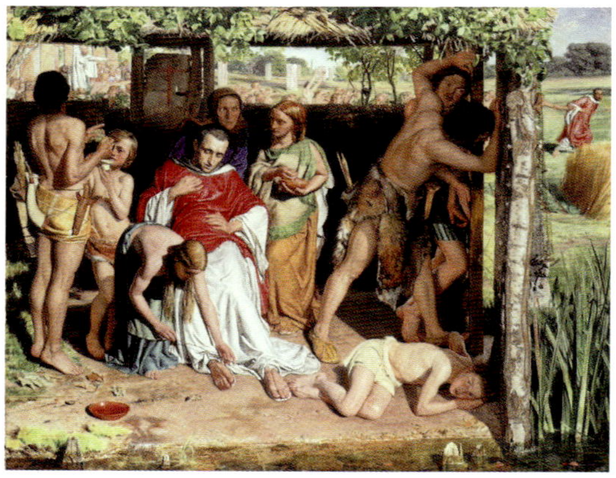

A265; oil on canvas, 111 × 141 cm
Signed and dated: *W. HOLMAN HUNT 1850*
Prov.: purchased by William Bennett as a gift for Thomas Combe
Combe Bequest, 1893; WA1894.1

Parris 1984, no. 25; Brown 1987, no. 18

Originally conceived as an entry on the theme 'An Act of Mercy' for a Gold Medal competition at the Royal Academy in 1849, this painting depicts an early incident in the history of the English church. A Christian family is hiding a priest from a crowd of heathens and Druids, who have already caught another priest in the background. The painting is full of symbolic allusions, in keeping with contemporary High Anglican thinking: the priest recalls Christ and his disciples, the child with the fur loincloth John the Baptist and the older youth squeezing grapes evokes the Eucharist. It was one of Hunt's earliest Pre-Raphaelite paintings and caused controversy when exhibited at the Royal Academy in 1850.

William Holman Hunt
(1827 – 1910)

The School-Girl's Hymn

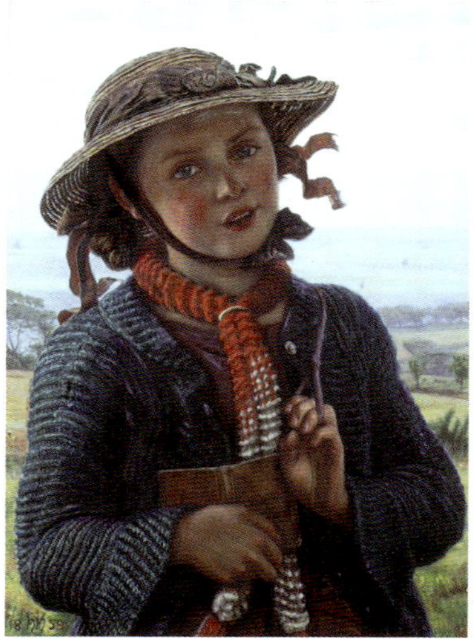

A266; oil on panel, 35 × 25 cm
Signed and dated: *18 WHH 59*
Combe Bequest, 1893; WA1894.2

Parris 1984, no. 102

This is a 'pot-boiler' and shows 'a girl going to school in a smiling summer Sunday morning, singing her hymn as she walks along'. The model was Miriam Wilkinson, a labourer's daughter Hunt met while staying with Thomas Combe at a farmhouse near Hastings in Kent in 1858. The painting was completed in October 1859 and bought by Combe before the opening of an exhibition at Gambart's gallery.

William Holman Hunt
(1827 – 1910)

The Afterglow in Egypt

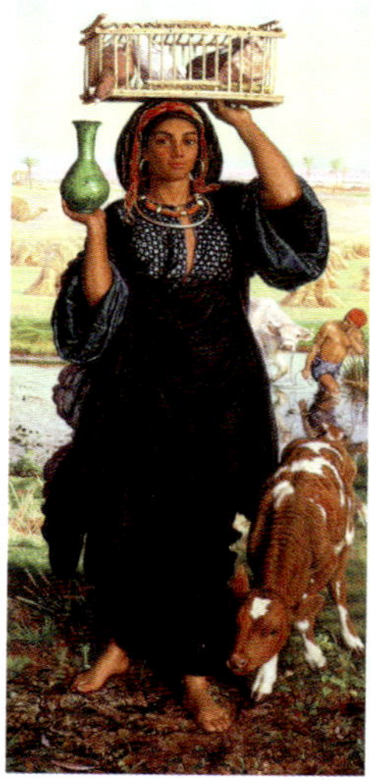

A267; oil on canvas, 82 × 37 cm
Signed with monogram: *WHH*
Combe Bequest, 1893; WA1894.3

Brown 1987, no. 44

Financed by the sale of his paintings, Holman Hunt left England on 13 January 1854, hoping to rediscover the biblical lands in Egypt and Palestine. He wrote to Combe in 1854 that he had begun a life-sized study of an Egyptian girl, but that the trials of heat and dust and the difficulty of persuading the model to pose, caused him to abandon the painting. He returned to it back in England in 1861 (Southampton Art Gallery) and at the same time painted this smaller version.

William Holman Hunt
(1827 – 1910)

London Bridge on the Night of the Marriage of the Prince and Princess of Wales

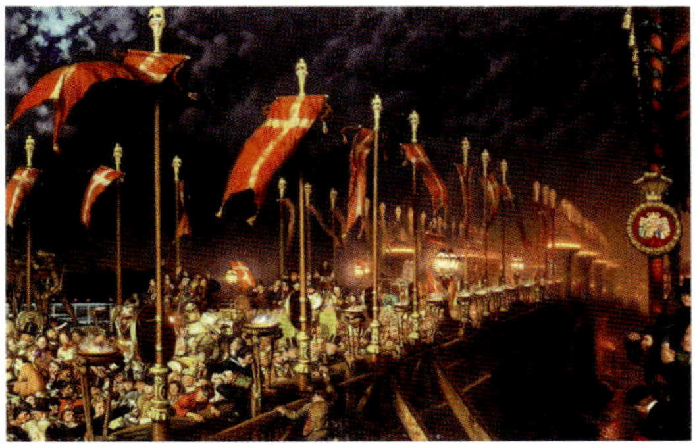

A268; oil on canvas, 65 × 98 cm
Signed with monogram and dated: *1863.6 Whh*
Combe Bequest, 1893; WA1894.4

Parris 1984, no. 124; Brown 1987, no. 41

Holman Hunt was among the crowd on London Bridge on the night of 10 March 1863, celebrating the marriage of Princess Alexandra of Denmark to the future Edward VII. He made sketches of it, but did not complete this painting until 16 May 1864, retouching it in 1866. He was fascinated by the contrasts of natural and artificial light and by the 'Hogarthian humour' of the crowds. He introduced portraits of several friends and acquaintances, including Thomas Combe in a top hat on the extreme left, arm in arm with the artist himself; and Mrs Combe with Millais's father and brother and the artist Robert Braithwaite Martineau. The frame was designed by Hunt to combine emblems appropriate to a wedding and the arms of the royal families of Denmark and England.

William Holman Hunt
(1827 – 1910)

Plain of Esdraelon from the Heights above Nazareth

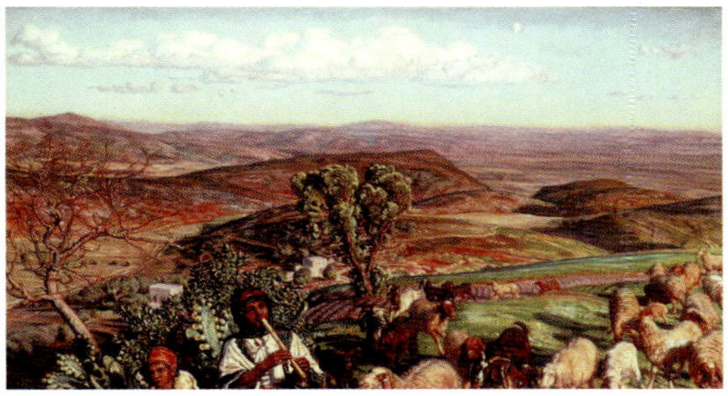

A270; oil on canvas, 41 × 75 cm
Signed in monogram
Combe Bequest, 1893; WA1894.6

Parris 1984, no. 148; Brown 1987, no. 17

Hunt first made studies of this landscape at Nazareth in 1870, intending to incorporate it as the background for the *Shadow of Death* (Manchester City Art Galleries). He later made several versions of the composition, of which this is the last. It was painted during his third visit to Jerusalem and intended for the inaugural exhibition at the Grosvenor Galleries in 1877. Hunt later described the view down the valley and of the 'flanking hills reaching to 'Gebel el Cowis', the Hill of Precipitation.... On the great lower plain stretched the patchwork slope of Tabor, continuing to the hills of Gilboa and Dothan and these branched out into the swelling heights of Samaria, as well as the extended range of Carmel, bounding on south Jezreel, Megiddo and the lowland'.

William Holman Hunt
(1827 – 1910)

The Festival of St Swithin (The Dovecot)

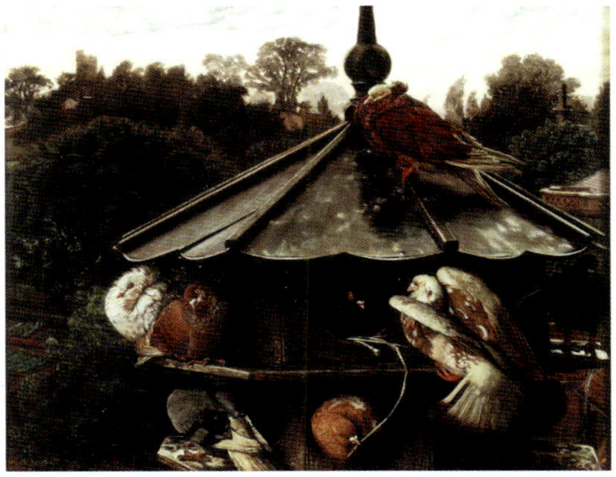

A269; oil on canvas, 73 × 91 cm
Signed with monogram and dated: *Whh 66-75*
Prov.: John Heugh of Holmewood
Combe Bequest, 1893; WA1894.5

Parris 1984, no. 134; Brown 1987, no. 42

The composition was designed by Holman Hunt for his sister Emily to paint. They began work in 1865, but she gave up and Hunt completed it himself in the following year. In his own view, it was the most highly finished picture he had ever painted: he had even bought the pigeons, all different, and the dovecot.

John William Inchbold
(1830 – 1888)

A Study, in March

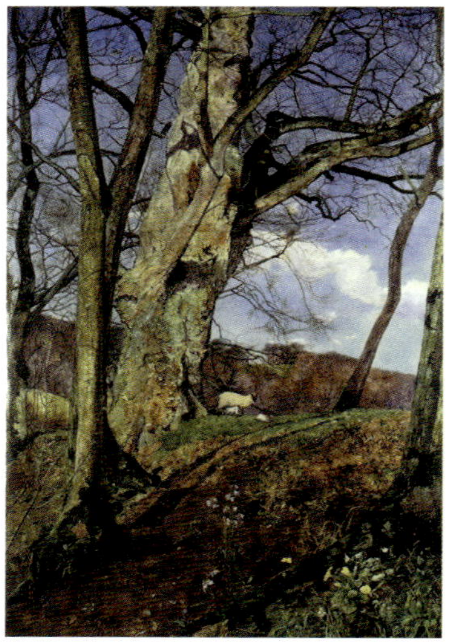

A957; oil on canvas, 53 × 35 cm
Signed: *J. W. I.*
Prov.: Sir Henry Thompson, Bt and by descent
Bequeathed by Miss G.E.G. Watkins in memory of Sir Henry Thompson, Bt, 1961; WA1962.4.2

Parris 1974, no. 66; Brown 1987, no. 45; Newall 1993, p. 12; Staley 2001, pp. 152–4

It is generally agreed that this was the painting exhibited as *A Study, in March* at the Royal Academy in 1855 and inspired by lines from Wordsworth's *Excursion*, book 1: 'When the primrose flower peeped forth to give an earnest of the spring.' The primrose and harebells in the foreground and the ewe and two lambs on the ridge, herald the arrival of spring, though the trees are still bare, their branches picked out in sharp detail against the blue sky. The microscopic detail epitomises the Pre-Raphaelite approach to landscape painting, which sacrificed perspective to careful finish. Inchbold exhibited a companion work, *Mid-Spring*, in 1856 (private collection).

John William Inchbold
(1830 – 1888)

Cuillin Ridge, Skye, from Sligachan

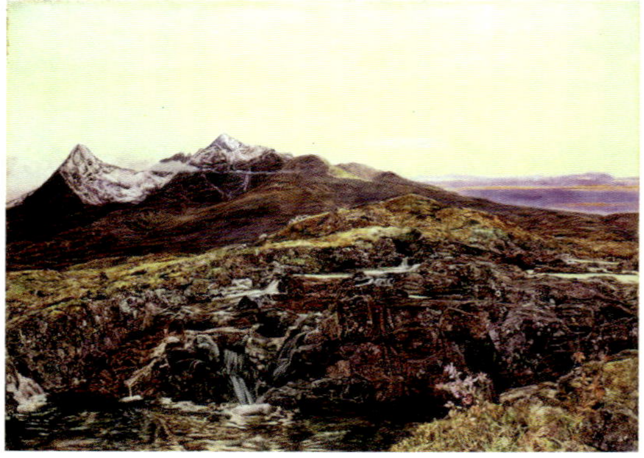

A326; oil on canvas, 51 × 69 cm
Prov.: Alfred Morrison
Presented by Sir Arthur Church, K.C.V.O., 1909; WA1909.1

Newall 1993, under no. 7; Staley 2001, pp. 156–8

Probably the painting entitled *The Burn, November – the Cucullen Hills*, exhibited at the Royal Academy in 1856. The view is taken from Sligachan, looking southwards over the Sligachan Burn towards the Cuillin Hills. It was painted in true Pre-Raphaelite manner, on a visit to Skye in the autumn of 1855. Ruskin praised the 'exquisite painting of withered heather and rock' and commissioned four drawings from the artist.

William Ingalton
(1794 – 1866)

View of the Thames near Eton

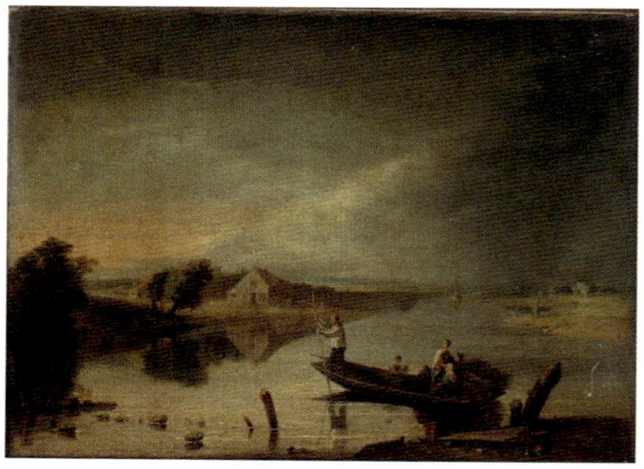

A312; oil on canvas, 46 × 61 cm
Signed and dated: *W. Ingalton 1816*
Fortnum Bequest, 1899; WA1899.CDEF.P6

Before he took up a career as an architect, Ingalton lived at Eton and exhibited views of the College in 1818 and 1819.

Louis-Eugène-Gabriel Isabey
(1803 – 1886)

The Preacher

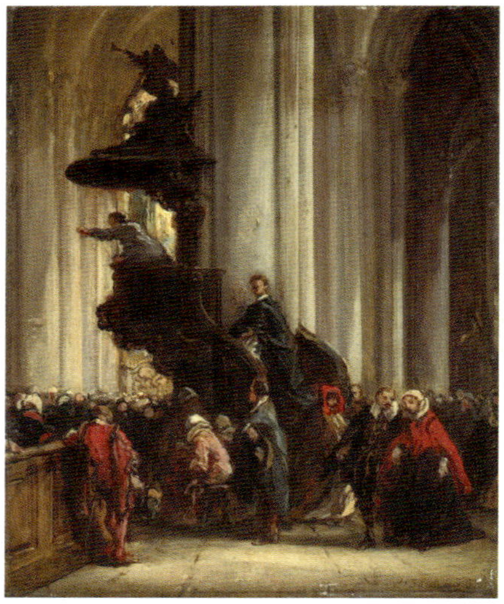

A481; oil on panel, 28 × 22 cm
Signed and dated: *E. Isabey 63*
Prov.: James Staats Forbes
Weldon Bequest, 1937; WA1937.62

A late example of a type of small, historical scene first painted by Delacroix and Bonington in the 1820s. It exemplifies the freer technique which Isabey used in many of his historical pictures of the 1860s. The flame-like curve of the composition and the virtuosity of his brush convey the charged atmosphere of the subject set in the 16th century, probably during the wars of religion.

Adriaen Isenbrandt
(active 1510 – d. 1551)

The Deposition

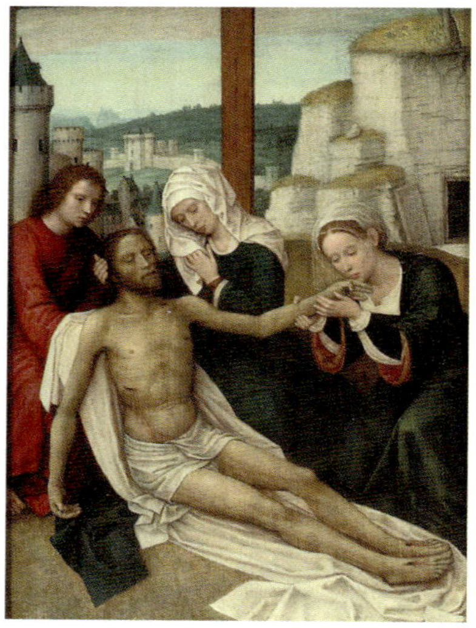

A440; oil on panel, 37 × 28 cm
Prov.: C.G. Hare; A.H. Buttery
Presented by Mrs W.F.R. Weldon, 1935; WA1935.60

White 1999, p. 63

Isenbrandt's work shows a debt to Gerard David who may have been his master. The composition and landscape background of this painting are both influenced by the example of David and the attribution of this work to Isenbrandt has been generally accepted.

Isaac Israels
(1865 – 1934)

Barrack Yard in Winter

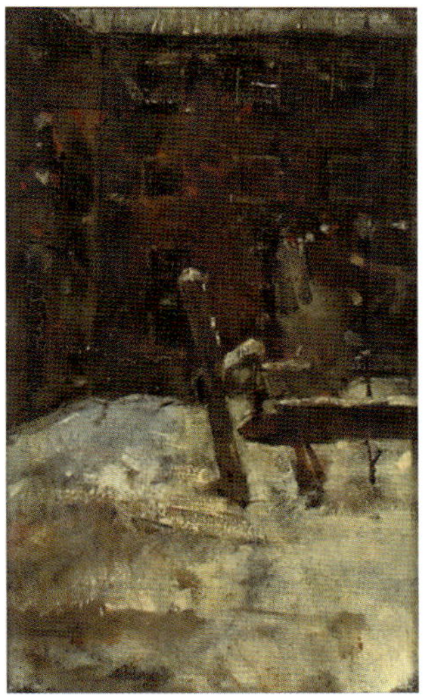

A1181; oil on mahogany panel, 27.8 × 16.5 cm
Bequeathed by Professor Edith Bulbring, 1993; WA1993.418

White 1999, p. 65

Possibly painted in Amsterdam in the 1890s. The subject and subdued colour suggest the influence of Israels's friend, George Breitner, with whom he studied from 1878 until 1880 at The Hague Academy. Isaac Israels was Jozef Israels's son.

Jozef Israels
(1824 – 1911)

A Fishergirl on a Dune, knitting

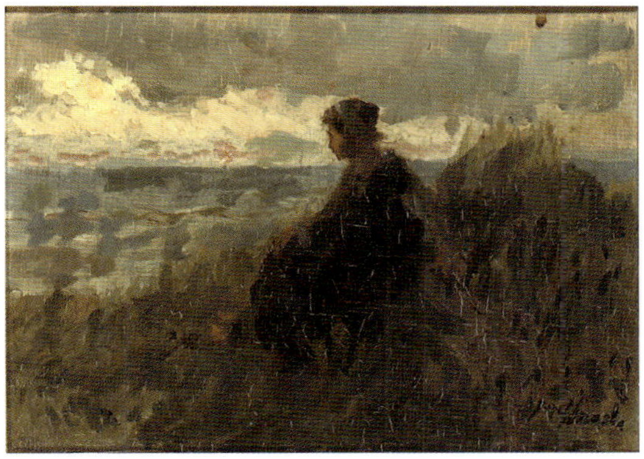

A1183; oil on panel, 23.5 × 34 cm
Bequeathed by Professor Edith Bulbring, 1993; WA1993.420

White 1999, p. 65

A late sketch by Israels of a favourite theme.

Anonymous Italian Artist
(*c.* 1600)

The Man of Sorrows

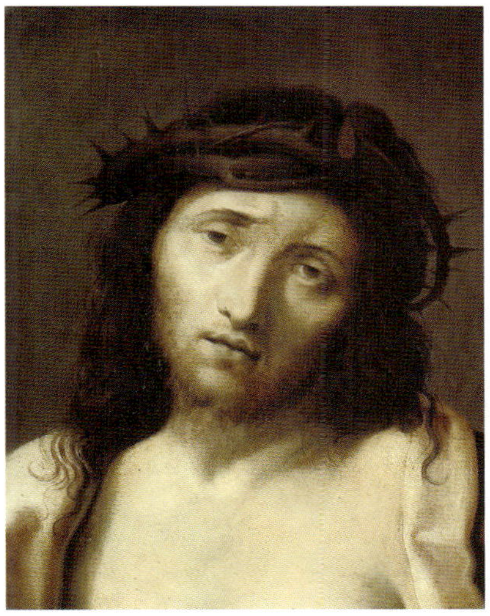

A695; oil on copper, 47 × 36 cm
Prov.: Rufford Abbey, Nottingham; George Halifax Lumley Savile, 3rd Baron Savile
Presented by Percy Moore Turner, 1942; WA1942.20

Traditionally thought to be a Spanish painting and attributed to Luis de Morales, A695 is by an Italian artist of the early 17th century, possibly Florentine, who looked back to the art of Correggio in particular. This type of devotional image, with a direct emotional appeal, was developed in the north of Italy early in the previous century and was popularised in Counter-Reformation art.

Jozef Israels
(1824 – 1911)

Girl on a Dune

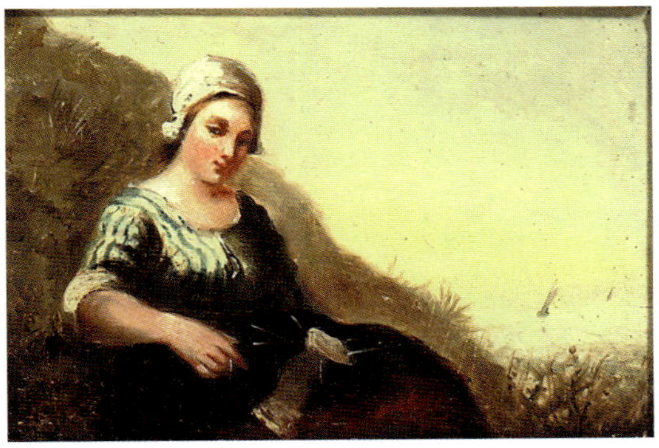

A1182; oil on panel, 11 × 16.5 cm
Bequeathed by Professor Edith Bulbring, 1993; WA1993.419

White 1999, p. 65

This painting has been dated to the first half of the 1890s. It is characteristic of the subjects which the artist found among the fishing people on the Dutch coast. Israels was the great-uncle of Edith Bulbring who bequeathed this painting and several other Hague School pictures to the Ashmolean.

Anonymous Italian Artist
(perhaps 16th century)

St John the Baptist, a Bishop Saint and St Anthony of Padua (?)

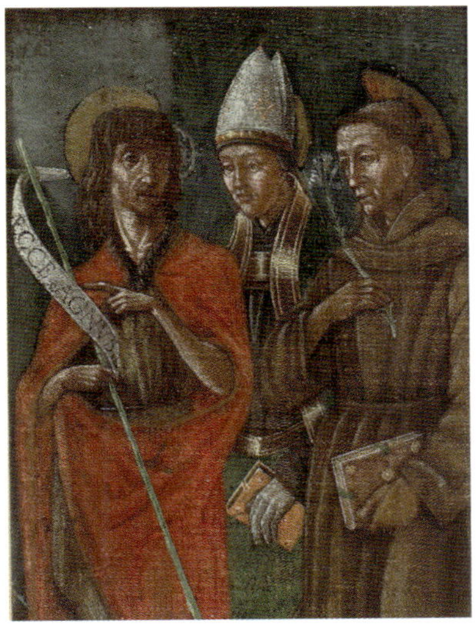

A736a; oil on canvas, laid on panel, 31.3 × 24.5 cm
Inscribed: *ECCE AGNUS D[EI]* on the scroll held by St John
Presented by the daughters of James Reddie Anderson, 1947; WA1947.244

Lloyd 1977, p. 201

Painted in imitation of late 15th-century Paduan painting, A736a is of uncertain date. The Franciscan saint with a book and lily may be St Anthony, although he is usually shown as a younger man.

Anonymous Italian Artist
(17th century)

Portrait of St Thomas Aquinas

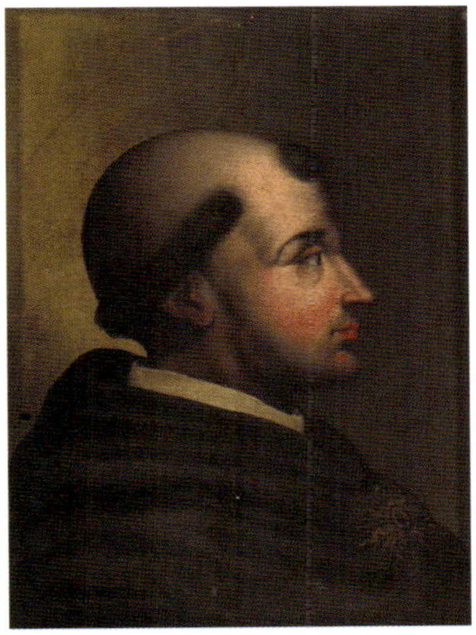

A106; oil on panel, 27 × 20.1 cm
Fox-Strangways Gift, 1850; WA1850.35

Lloyd 1977, p. 200

Fox-Strangways may have acquired this painting as a work by or after Fra Bartolommeo, judging by an old label on the back. St Thomas Aquinas (*c.* 1225–1274), Dominican philosopher and theologian, was declared a Doctor of the Church in 1567.

Anonymous Italian artist
(early 18th century)

Boy with Cattle in a Landscape

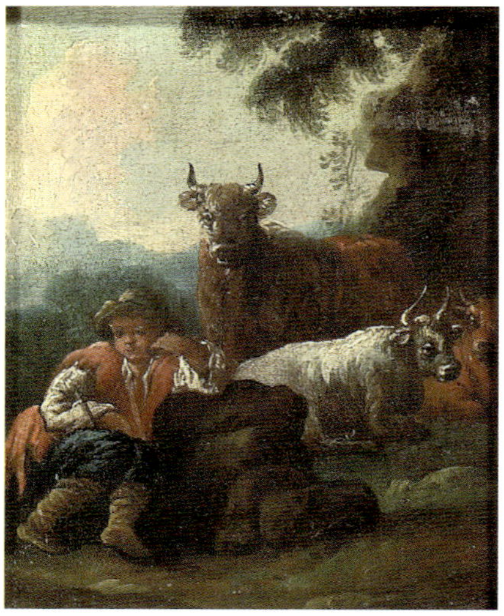

A261; oil on canvas, 20 × 16 cm
Bequeathed by the Revd Greville John Chester, 1892; WA1892.6

A painting with some generic links with the work of Johann Melchior Roos.

Anonymous Italian(?) Artist
(19th century)

Panoramic View of a Valley and distant Mountains

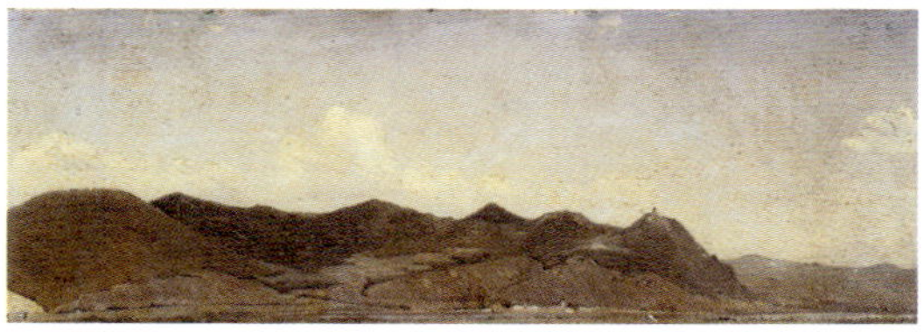

Oil on canvas, mounted as a drawing, 12 × 31.2 cm
Provenance unknown; WA.OA411

The view may have been made in the north of Italy and could have been sketched out of doors.

Anonymous Italian(?) Artist
(19th century)

Courtyard Scene

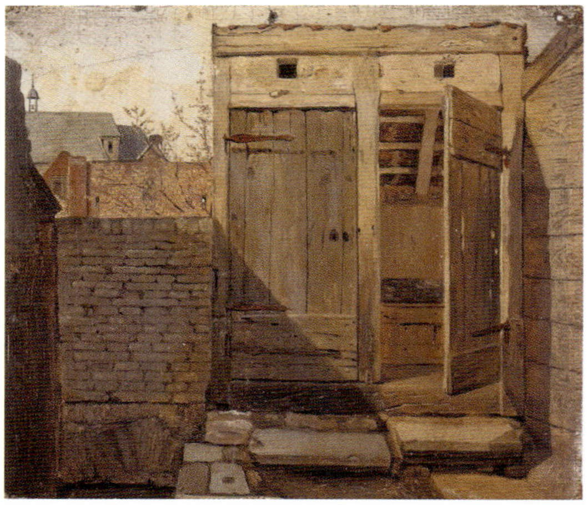

Oil on canvas, mounted as a drawing, 12.2 × 13.8 cm
Provenance unknown; WA.OA413

The scene is inspired by Dutch 17th-century painting.

Anonymous Italian Artist
(*c.* 1800 – 1820)

St Dominic

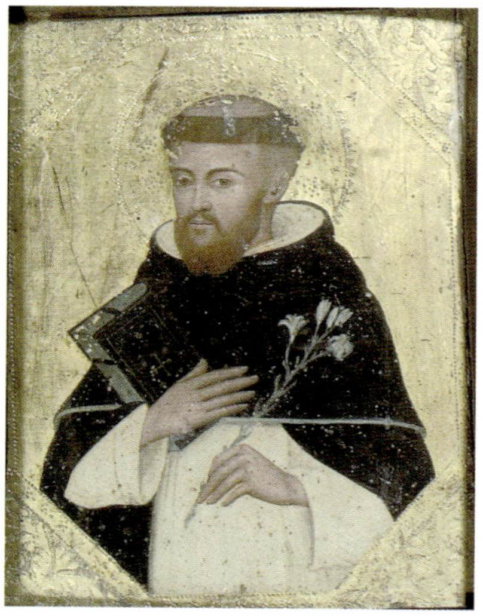

A254; tempera (?) and gilding on panel, 25 × 18 cm
Presented by the Revd Greville John Chester, 1892; WA1892.9

Lloyd 1977, p. 200

Made in emulation of mid 14th-century devotional images, A254 was probably painted towards the beginning of the 19th century. St Dominic (1170–1221) founded the Order of Friars Preachers or Dominican order and was canonised in 1234; the lily refers to his purity.

Anonymous Italian(?) Artist
(19th century)

View of Mountains and a Lake

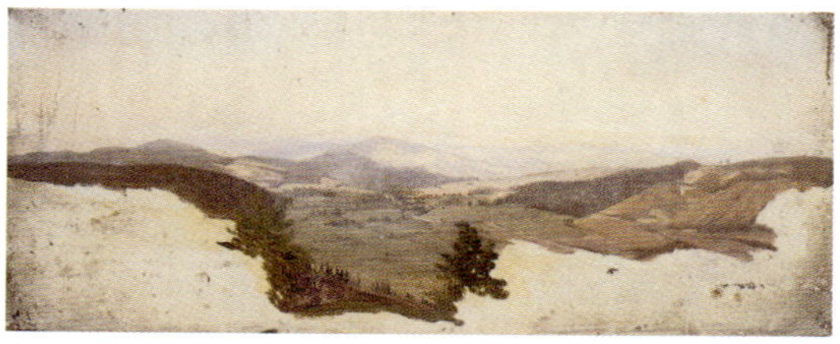

Oil on canvas, mounted as a drawing, 9.9 × 27 cm
Provenance unknown; WA.OA412

This small oil-sketch is unfinished, perhaps deliberately. It was probably made out of doors, perhaps around the mid-century.

Anonymous Italo-Flemish Artist
(*c.* 1560 – 1570)

The Adoration of the Shepherds

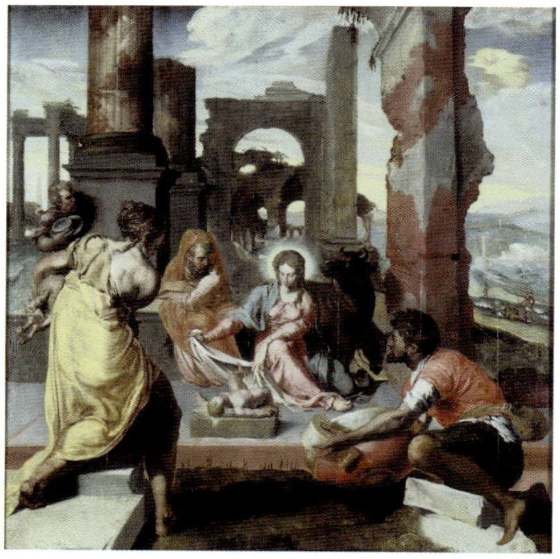

A512; oil on panel, 119 × 111.3 cm
Prov.: William Young Ottley; Warner Ottley; Lt-Col Warner Ottley; Captain R. Langton Douglas
Presented by the National Art Collections Fund, 1937; WA1937.122

Lloyd 1977, pp. 185–7

Three shepherds bring gifts to the new-born Christ while the earlier Annunciation to the shepherds can be seen on the right (Luke 2: 8–18). The extensive classical ruins refer to the passing of the old pagan order. Painted on oak, A512 is by a northern artist who had worked in Venice and central Italy. Various attributions have been suggested, including Hermann Posthumous, Dirk

Barendsz or the anonymous Flemish follower of Tintoretto who painted a *Last Judgement* fresco in the abbey of Farfa in 1565, tentatively identified as Pieter Vlerick, or as Hendrick van der Broeck. The handsome aedicular frame, bearing a dedicatory inscription and the date of 1578, was adapted for the painting in 1955.

Francis Ernest Jackson
(1872 – 1945)

Dorothy Hutton

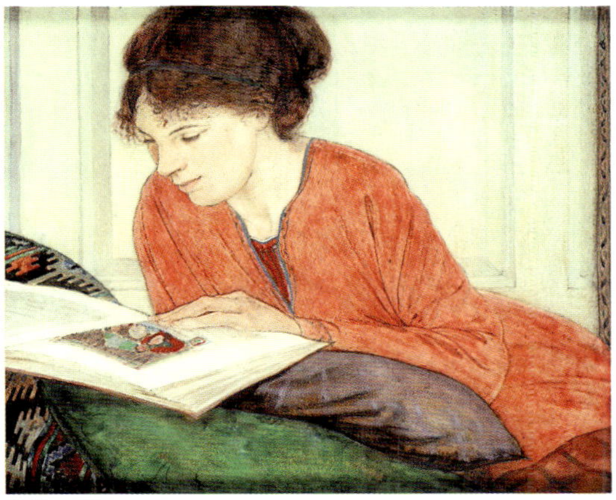

A1197; egg tempera on panel, 28 × 31.7 cm
Prov.: C.H. St. J. Hornby
Bequeathed by Miss Anna Hornby, 1996; WA1996.34

Dorothy Hutton (1889–1984) studied at the Central School of Arts and Crafts under Jackson. She painted flowers but was also an illustrator and scribe and is shown here studying a manuscript. Jackson was a pioneer in the revival of tempera painting, the technique used here. The painting dates from *c.* 1921. In 1922, Jackson became President of the Tempera Society.

John Jackson
(1778 – 1831)

Sir William Beechey

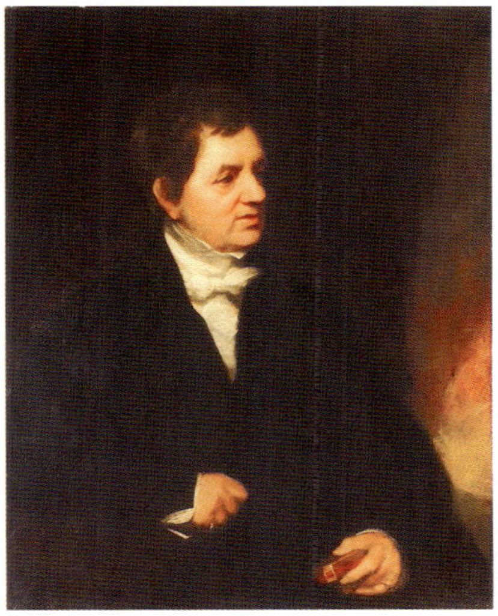

A419; oil on canvas, 90 × 70 cm
Prov.: Warland Andrew, Abingdon
Purchased, 1932; WA1932.200

Sir William Beechey (1753–1839) was appointed portrait painter to Queen Charlotte in 1793 and was knighted in 1798. He continued to receive royal patronage into the 1830s but his reputation as a portrait painter was eclipsed by the lustre of Sir Thomas Lawrence.

Alexander Andreyevich Ivanov
(1806 – 1858)

Study of Heads

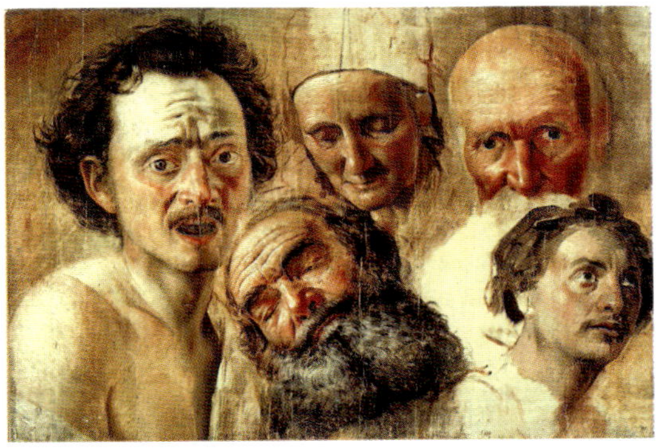

A1171; oil on board, 42 × 61 cm
Prov.: Sergei Ivanov; Mikhail Petrovich Botkin
Purchased, 1990: WA1991.12

Although an inscription on the back suggests this is a preparatory study for Ivanov's masterpiece, *Christ Appearing to the People*, completed in Rome in 1858, no corresponding heads appear in the painting. It is typical of his many studies after the Old Masters but, while clearly suggesting heads from a composition or compositions, no source has been identified. The technique, mixing sketchy passages with more detailed work, is characteristic of his early work. It was probably painted soon after his arrival in Italy in 1830.

Francis Ernest Jackson
(1872 – 1945)

Lindsay M. Gladstone

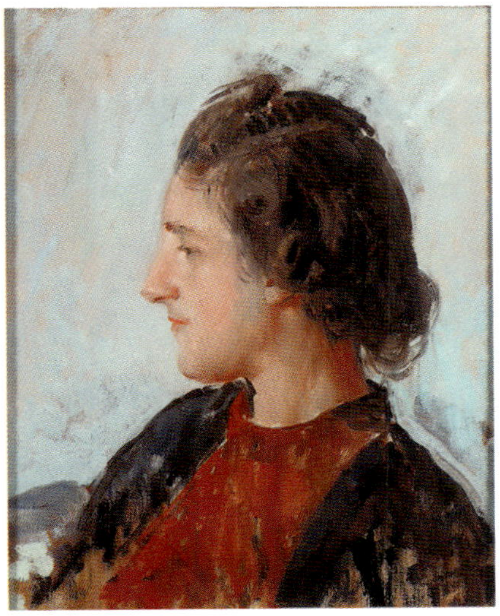

A1198; oil on canvas, 51.5 × 41 cm
Bequeathed by Miss Anna Hornby, 1996; WA1996.35

Painted in about 1940. Lindsay Gladstone (d. 1963) studied at the Byam Shaw School under Jackson in the late 1930s.

George Percy Jacomb-Hood
(1857 – 1929)

A Summer's Day

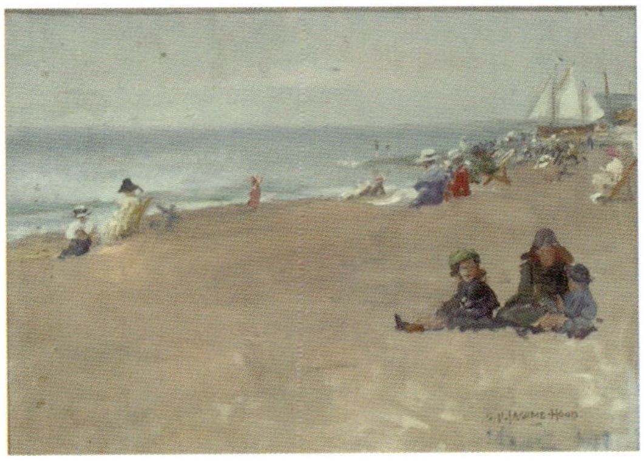

A401a; oil on canvas on board, 25 × 33 cm
Signed: *G.P. JACOMB-HOOD*
Presented by the artist's widow, 1930; WA1930.9

This is indebted to the beach scenes of the Impressionists, notably Manet and Degas.

Charles-Émile Jacque
(1813 – 1894)

Shepherdess watering her Flocks

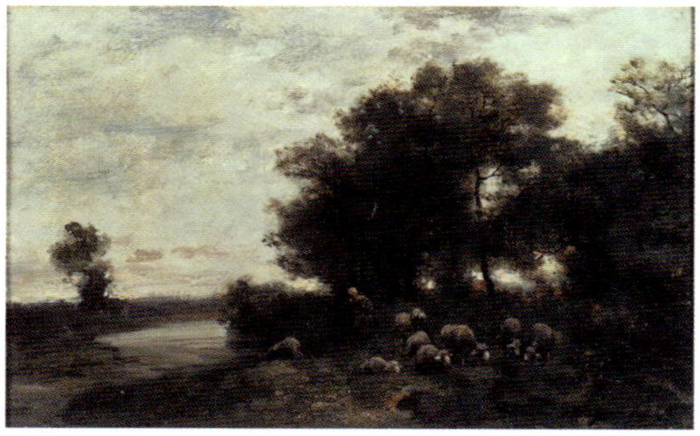

A809; oil on canvas, 25 × 38 cm
Signed: *Ch. Jacque*
Bequeathed by J. Reginald Jones, 1951; WA1951.51.3

In 1849, Jacque set up studio in the village of Barbizon in company with Millet. The works of the first decade of his Barbizon period include many scenes of shepherds and shepherdesses, painted on small panels and canvases. This is probably a work of the 1850s.

Alexander Jamieson
(1873 – 1939)

Place des Pyramides, Paris

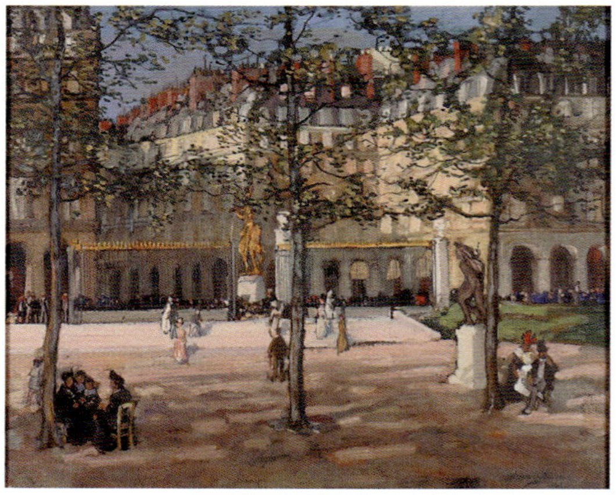

A511b; oil on canvas, 50 × 61 cm
Signed and dated: *Alexander Jamieson 1906*
Presented by Mrs Richard Shute, 1937; WA1937.119

The colonnaded Place des Pyramides lies at the juncture of the rue de Rivoli and the rue des Pyramides in one of the most fashionable quarters of Paris. Frémiet's statue of Joan of Arc is near the centre.

Alexander Jamieson
(1873 – 1939)

The Wedding Procession

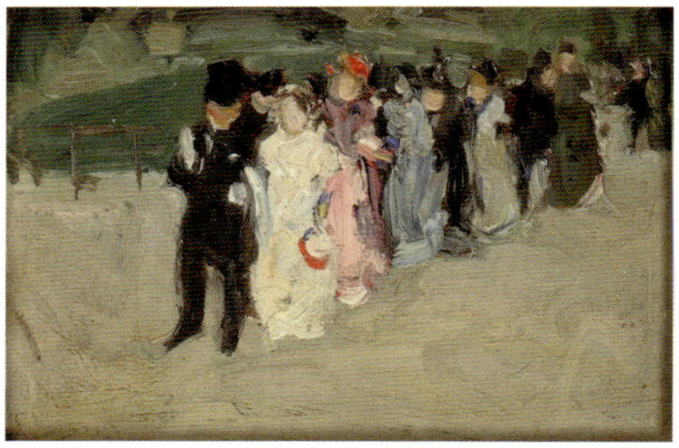

A924; oil on panel, 160 × 220 cm
Bequeathed by Mrs H.H. Turner, 1959; WA1959.4.2

Style of Charles-Émile Jacque
(1813 – 1894)

Interior of a Sheepfold by Night

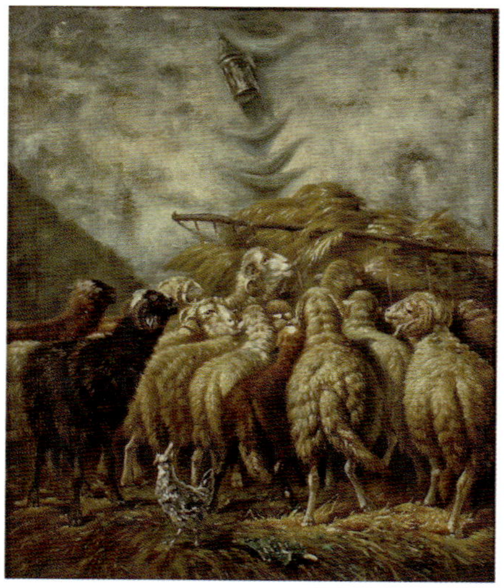

A1030; oil on canvas, 64 × 53 cm
Inscribed: *C.Jacque / C. Beranger*
Purchased, 1966; WA1966.96

A copy or a bad pastiche of Jacque's work. The subject is one which Jacque treated on many occasions but the quality of the brushwork is very coarse. The artist may have been the C. Beranger named in the inscription but this can hardly be Charles Béranger (1816–1853), the genre and animal painter, whose style is different and far superior.

Alexander Jamieson
(1873 – 1939)

Cloister of the Dominican Monastery, Dubrovnik

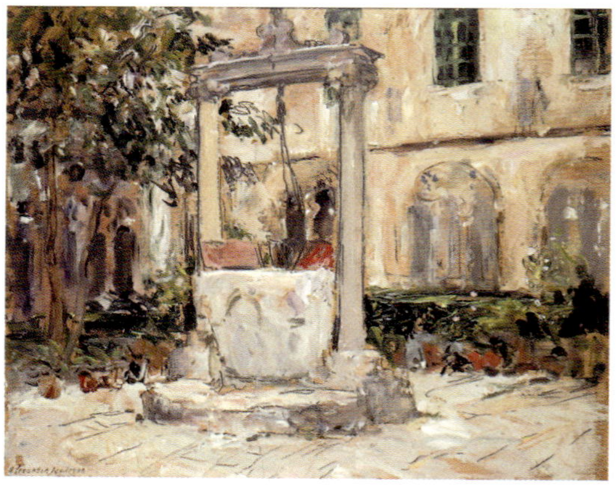

A923; oil on panel, 16 × 22 cm
Bequeathed by Mrs H.H. Turner, 1959; WA1959.4.1

This small sketch and the following were presumably made from the life during an otherwise unrecorded visit to Croatia.

Attributed to Étienne Jeaurat
(1699 – 1789)

Interior with two Women

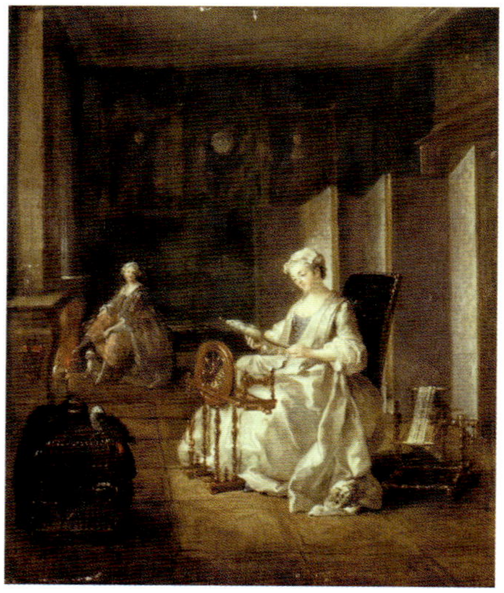

A299; oil on canvas, 61 × 51 cm
Bequeathed by John D. Chambers, 1897; WA1897.18

A299 was formerly known as *Industry and Idleness* because one woman spins while another warms her feet by the fire. A dog lies curled at the spinner's feet and a cat looks into the fire: traditionally the dog and cat are seen as incorporating opposing personality traits. Jeaurat's attractive figure groups in elegant interiors were very popular and A299 may date from the late 1730s or early 1740s.

Augustus Edwin John
(1878 – 1961)

The Emir Feisal

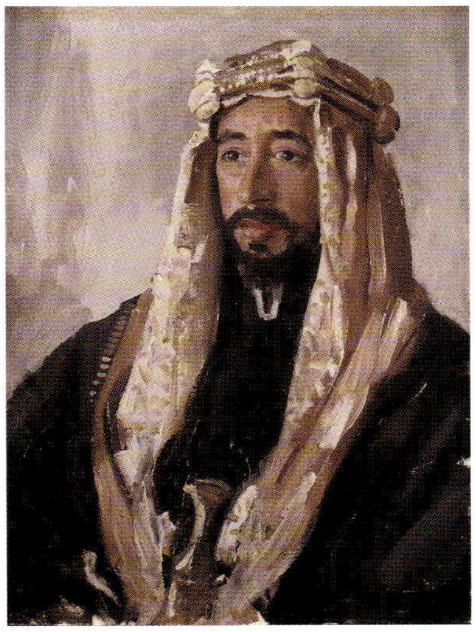

A449; oil on canvas, 72 × 53 cm
Signed and dated on back: *Feisal, 16.4.19 by A.E.J.*
Prov.: T.E. Lawrence
Presented by Mr and Mrs Eric Kennington in accordance with the wishes of Col T.E. Lawrence, 1936; WA1936.30

Wilson 1988–9, no. 98

Emir Feisal (1883–1933) was a younger son of Hussein, Sherif and Emir of Mecca (*c.* 1854–1931), who represented his father at the Paris Peace Conference in 1919. He was one of the delegates who sat to John on that occasion. He later became King of Syria (1920) and the first King of Iraq (1921–1933).

Augustus Edwin John
(1878 – 1961)

Villiers David

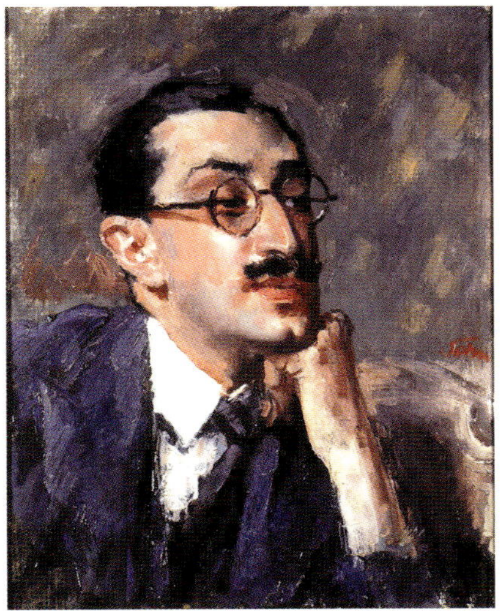

A1192; oil on canvas, 51 × 40 cm
Presented by the Executors of Gérard Schlup in accordance with his wishes, 1994; WA1994.141

Eustace 1999, no. 26

Villiers David (1906–1985), was an aesthete. He was self-taught as a painter and had several exhibitions of his work. He travelled extensively in the Near and Far East as well as Europe. He collected sculpture from India and Europe, Picasso prints and Japanese woodcuts and drawings and paintings by Old Masters and contemporary artists. This portrait was completed in June 1932 and is in John's most fluid and flashy vein.

George Jones
(1786 – 1869)

H.R.H. the Prince Regent received by the University and City of Oxford, June 14, 1814

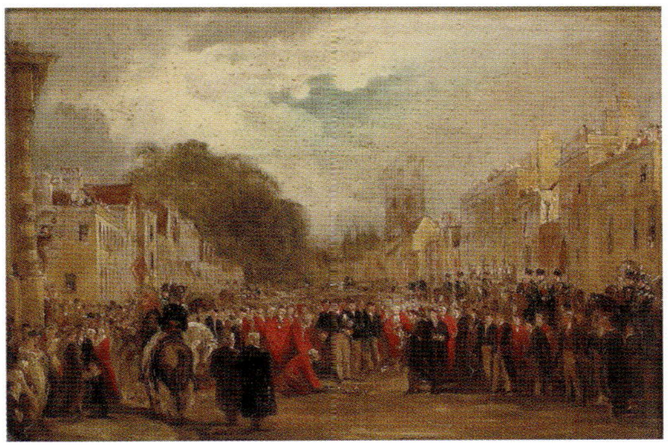

A861; oil on panel, 18 × 25 cm
Prov.: J.C.B. Gamlen
Presented by Mrs A.T. Waterhouse, 1952; WA1952.116

A sketch for the painting exhibited at the Royal Academy in 1815 (Magdalen College, Oxford), which shows the Chancellor, Mayor and other dignitaries paying homage to the Prince of Wales, accompanied by the Duke of York and the Prince of Orange in the High Street, Oxford.

Augustus Edwin John
(1878 – 1961)

T.E. Lawrence

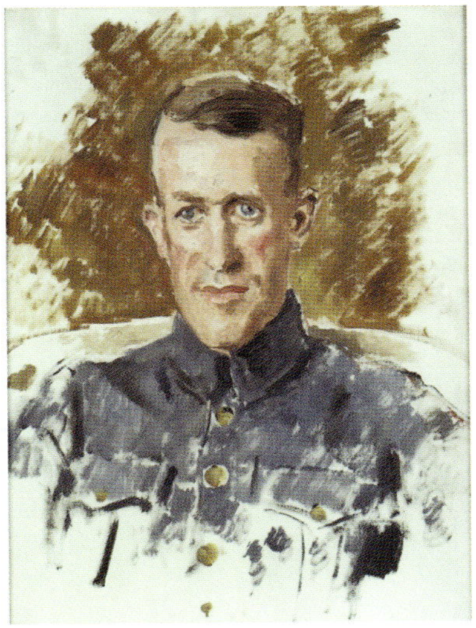

A726; oil on canvas, 66 × 50 cm
Presented by Professor A.W. Lawrence, 1946; WA1946.266

Wilson 1988–9, no. 293

An inscription on the reverse reads, *Painted in the morning and afternoon of an August day in 1929 at Freiern, Fordingbridge, while I was going to Solent, for the Schneider Cup. TES.* The Schneider Cup was for seaplanes and took place in September 1929. John had made several paintings and drawings of Lawrence at the Paris Peace Conference in 1919 and was eager to record his changing features.

Ernest Yarrow Jones
(1870 – 1951)

Landscape with Trees

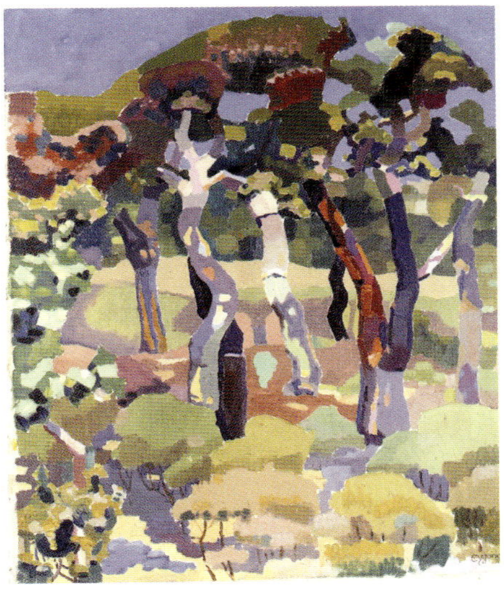

A1130; oil on canvas, mounted as a drawing, 54.5 × 45.5 cm
Signed: *E.Y. Jones*
Presented by Miss Yvonne Yarrow-Jones, the artist's daughter, 1983; WA1983.168

George Jones
(1786 – 1869)

The Conferment of Honorary Degrees on the Allied Sovereigns in the Sheldonian Theatre

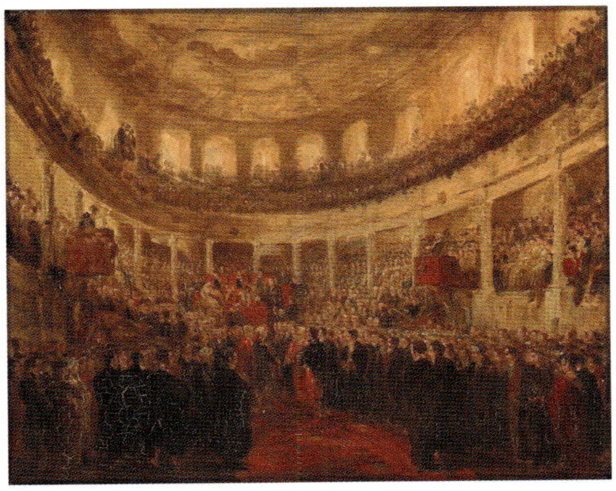

A862; oil on panel, 35 × 43 cm
Prov.: J.C.B. Gamlen
Presented by Mrs A.T. Waterhouse, 1952; WA1952.117

A companion to the preceding and presumably also a sketch for a larger painting, though none is known. Following the official reception of the Prince Regent and his party, the allied sovereigns (the Emperor of Russia and the King of Prussia) arrived at Oxford and proceeded to the Sheldonian Theatre to receive honorary degrees.

George Jones
(1786 – 1869)

Commodore Nelson boarding the San Joseph in the Battle of St Vincent

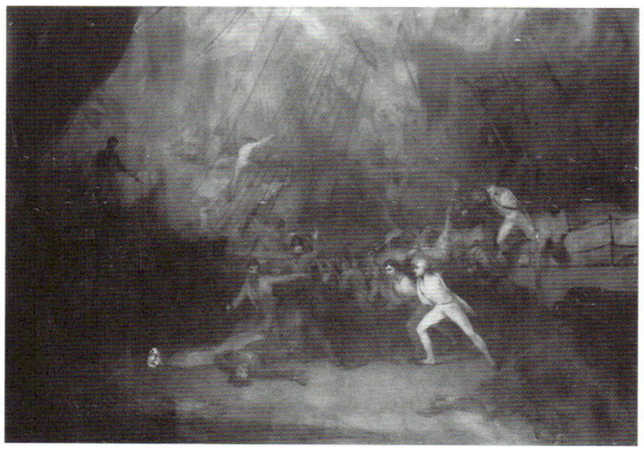

A240; oil on canvas, rolled, 122 × 168 cm
Signed: *G.Jones R.A.*
Presented by the artist's widow, 1881; WA1881.347

This sketch, exhibited at the Royal Academy in 1832, is for a large picture, commissioned for the British Institution and shown there in 1829 (National Maritime Museum). It depicts the moment of capitulation of the Spanish fleet at Cape St Vincent on 14 November 1797: Commodore Nelson and Captain Berry lead the boarders onto the deck of the San Joseph, having taken the San Nicholas, which lies between the San Joseph and Nelson's own ship, H.M.S. Captain. A Spanish officer presents his sword in surrender.

George Jones
(1786 – 1869)

An Archway at Bologna, with the Piazza Maggiore beyond

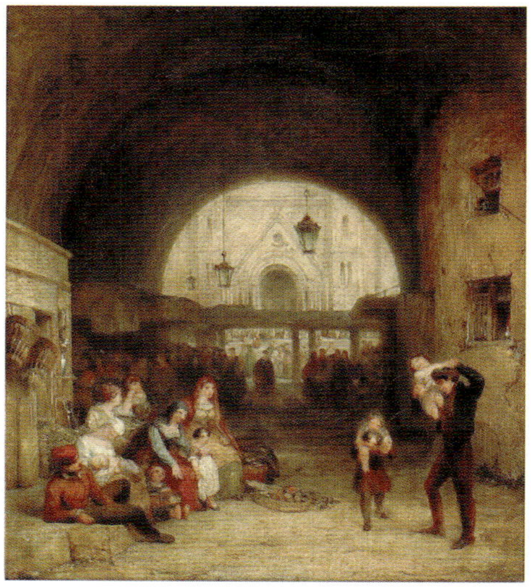

A237; oil on canvas, 47 × 41 cm
Presented by the artist's widow, 1873; WA1873.19

Jones made many tours of the continent during the 1820s and 1830s, travelling extensively in France, Switzerland, Northern Italy and the Low Countries. Here, the Piazza Maggiore at Bologna is seen through an archway, with the church of S. Petronio in the background.

George Jones
(1786 – 1869)

Turner's Body lying in State, 29 December 1851

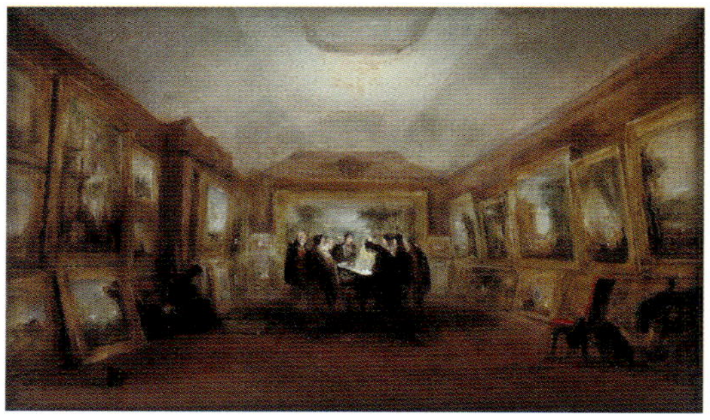

A242; oil on millboard, 14 × 23 cm
Presented by the artist's widow, 1873/1881; WA1881.349

Royal Academy 1974–5, no. B.75

Turner died at his cottage in Cheyne Walk, Chelsea, on 19 December 1851 and soon afterwards, his body was transferred to his house in Queen Anne Street, where it was placed in the centre of the gallery. The funeral took place on 30 December.

George Jones
(1786 – 1869)

Market Place at Péronne

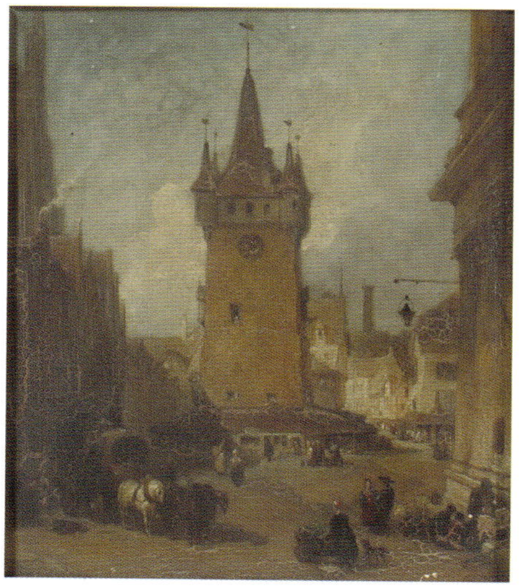

A238; oil on panel, 35 × 30 cm
Presented by the artist's widow, 1873; WA1873.18

Péronne, on the River Somme about twenty miles south of Arras in Picardie, has a 16th-century town hall with clock tower. This painting was executed in 1836, but probably based on sketches made during the 1820s.

George Jones
(1786 – 1869)

Interior of Turner's Gallery: the Artist showing his Works

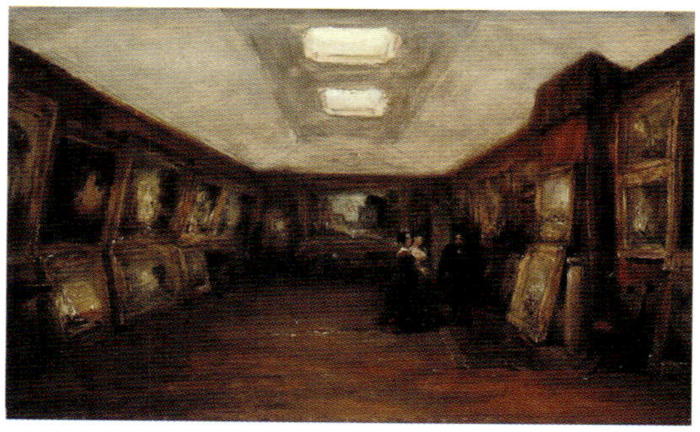

A241; oil on millboard, 14 × 23 cm
Presented by the artist's widow, 1873 or 1881; WA1881.348

Jones was a close friend of Turner and one of his executors. He probably painted this from memory, shortly after Turner's death. With its companion, it forms the only visual record of Turner's last gallery, an extension of his house in Queen Anne Street West, where he exhibited unsold works. Among the paintings which can be identified here are *Hannibal crossing the Alps* (1812; Tate Britain), *Dido building Carthage* (1815; National Gallery, London) and *Frosty Morning* (1813; Tate Britain).

George Jones
(1786 – 1869)

Turner's Burial in the Crypt of St Paul's

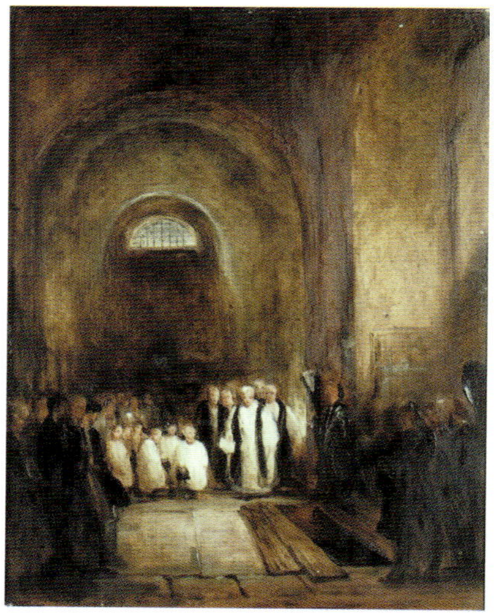

A243; oil on millboard, 23 × 18 cm
Presented by the artist's widow, 1873/1881; WA1881.350

Turner's funeral took place on 30 December 1851, in St Paul's Cathedral. He had stipulated in his will that he wished to be buried 'among my Brothers in Art' in the crypt and his body was placed close to the tombs of Sir Joshua Reynolds, Sir Thomas Lawrence and other artists. George Jones was present as an executor and painted this evocation soon afterwards.

George Jones
(1786 – 1869)

The Battle of the Alma

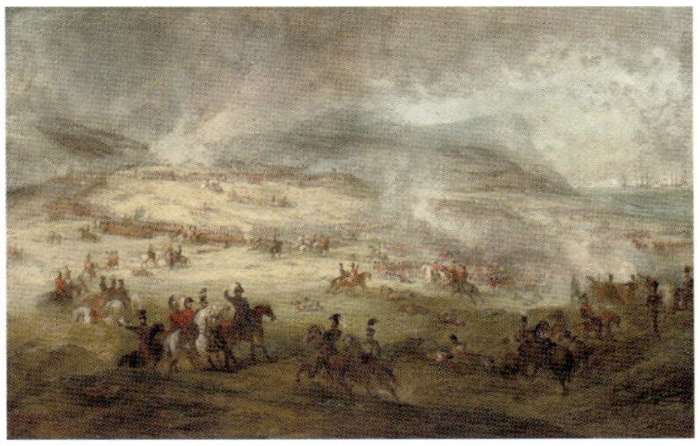

A236; oil on canvas, 61 × 91 cm
Presented by the artist's widow, 1873; WA1873.17

This battle in the Crimean War took place on 20 September 1854, between British, French and Turkish forces on one side and Russian on the other. This painting was shown at the Royal Academy in 1855: 'The army, having passed the river Alma, is ascending the hill. The Light Division, supported by the First division, Guards and Highlanders, attacks the battery. The Second and Third divisions are following in support. Lord Raglan and staff in the foreground. Columns of Russians are descending the hill in support of their battery... The French army, with the Zouaves, are advancing from the sea.'

Thomas Jones
(1742 – 1803)

Rooftops in Naples

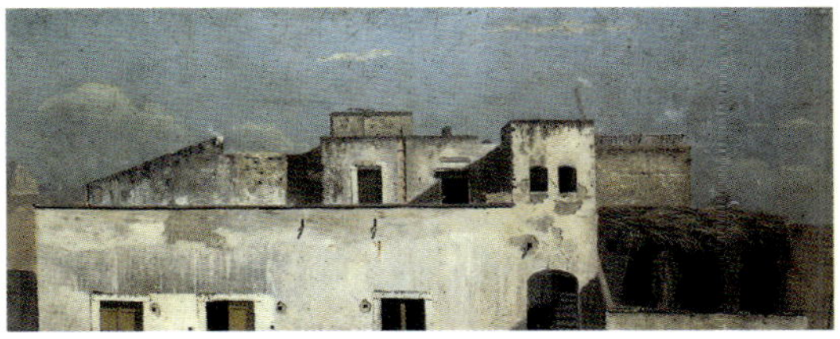

A872b; oil on paper, mounted as a drawing, 14.3 × 35 cm
Signed and dated: *T.J. Naples Aprile 1782*
Prov.: by descent from the artist
Purchased, 1954; WA1954.81

Brown 1982, no. 869; Sumner and Smith 2003, no. 111

This study and a similar study in the National Museum of Wales are dated April 1782, the month before the lease on Jones's apartment near the Castel Nuovo ran out. Both were painted from a window in his lodgings.

Cornelius Jonson (Cornelis Janssens van Ceulen)
(1593 – 1661)

Portrait of a Woman in a Dress worked with Flowers

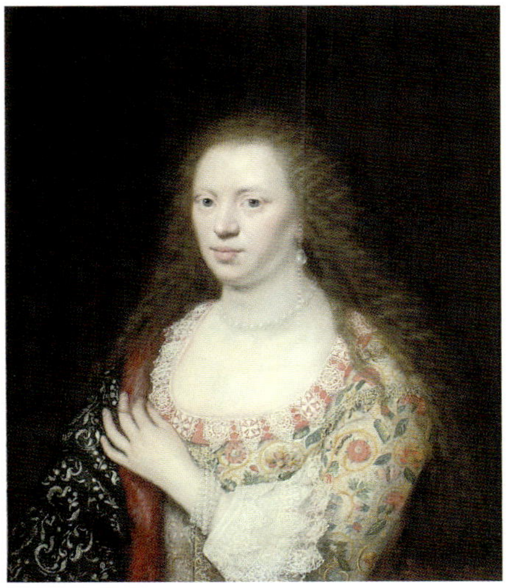

A975; oil on panel, 70 × 58 cm
Madan Bequest, 1962; WA1962.17.17

After training in the Netherlands, Jonson returned to England in *c.* 1618 and painted a large number of portraits over the next twenty-five years. He was especially noted for his delicate painting of flesh and hair. This is probably an early work.

George Jones
(1786 – 1869)

Wollenberg: Entrance to a Courtyard

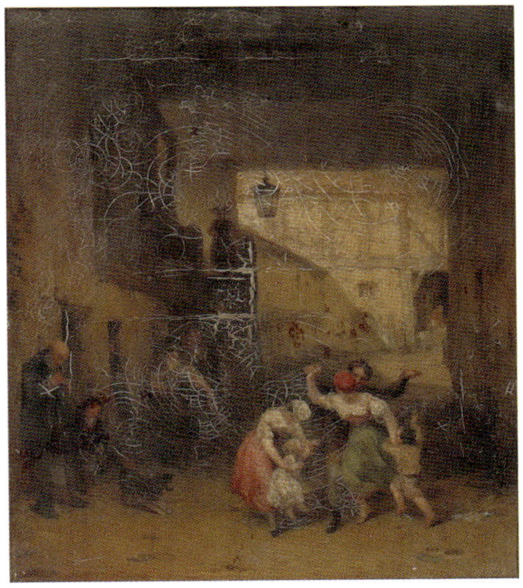

A239; oil on canvas, 49 × 42 cm
Presented by the artist's widow, 1873; WA1873.20

Jones exhibited posthumously a view of *Vollenberg, Switzerland* at the Royal Academy in 1870, which may be the present picture.

Jean-Berthold Jongkind
(1819 – 1891)

View of Notre-Dame, Paris

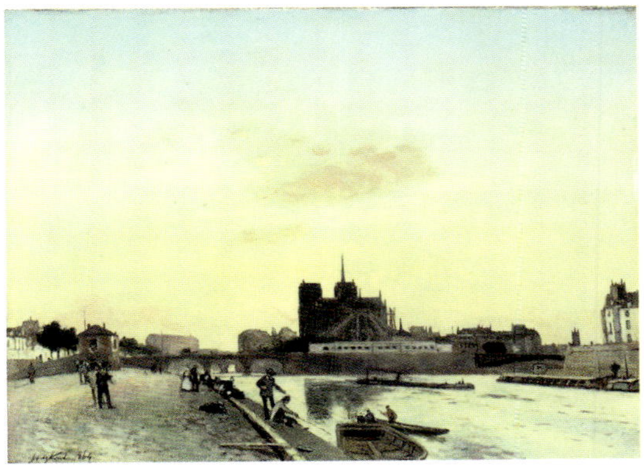

A489; oil on canvas, 42.5 × 56.5 cm
Signed and dated: *Jongkind 1864*
Prov.: Théophile Bascle; James Staats Forbes
Weldon Bequest, 1937; WA1937.70

White 1999, p. 70; Stein *et al.* 2003, no. 330

Jongkind's precise, light-filled, atmospheric landscapes were admired by the Impressionists but, unlike them, he tended to work in the studio from drawings and watercolours made on the spot. This painting, showing the effect of the setting sun over the cathedral of Notre-Dame in Paris, was painted for the Bordeaux collector, Théophile Bascle, in 1864.

Copy after Cornelius Jonson (Cornelis Janssens van Ceulen)
(1593 – 1661)

Prince William of Orange, later King William III

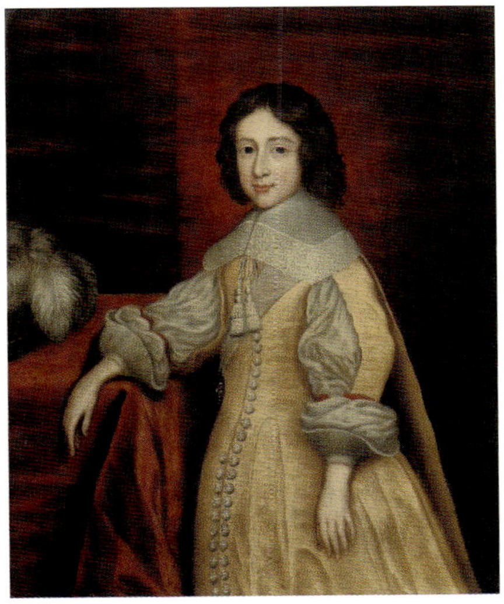

F706; oil on canvas, 90 × 73 cm
Presented by Elias Ashmole, 1683; WA1898.14

Poole 1912, no. 452; MacGregor 1983, no. 279

Prince William (1650–1702) was created a Knight of the Garter in 1653 and here wears the ribbon and George of that order. This is one of numerous copies after an original dated 1657 at Knole.

Studio of Jacob Jordaens
(1593 – 1678)

The Virgin and Child in a Cartouche Decorated with Flowers

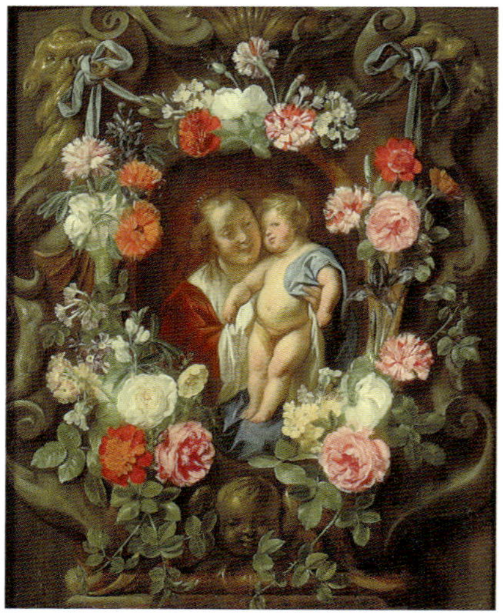

A976; oil on panel, 68 × 54 cm
Madan Bequest, 1962; WA1962.17.18

White 1999, p. 71

This type of painting was usually a collaboration between two artists, one painting flowers, the other supplying figures. The flowers may have been painted by an artist such as Daniel Seghers or his pupil, Jan Philip van Thielen. The Virgin and Child are in Jordaens's style but he is not known to have done shared work of this kind and the figures are probably by one of his studio assistants.

Wassily Kandinsky
(1866 – 1944)

Murnau-Staffelsee I

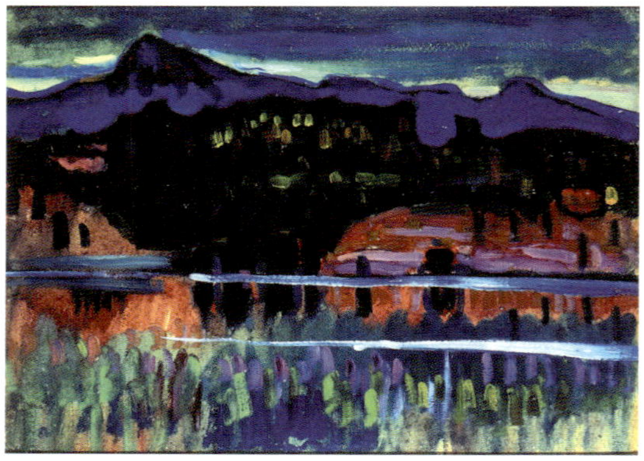

A1207; oil on paper laid on board, 33 × 44.5 cm
Dated: *1908*
Prov.: Gabriele Münter; Sir Antony Hornby
Accepted by H.M. Government in lieu of inheritance tax and allocated to the Ashmolean Museum, 1997; WA1997.33

Roethel-Benjamin 1982, I, no. 237; Eustace 1999, no. 5

In 1908 Kandinsky and his pupil and companion Gabriele Münter (1877–1962) moved to Murnau in Bavaria, where he begun to paint a series of landscapes inspired by the nearby Staffelsee and its surrounding mountains in fluid brush-strokes and dark colours.

Stanislawa de Karlowska
(1876 – 1952)

The Quay at Binic, Brittany

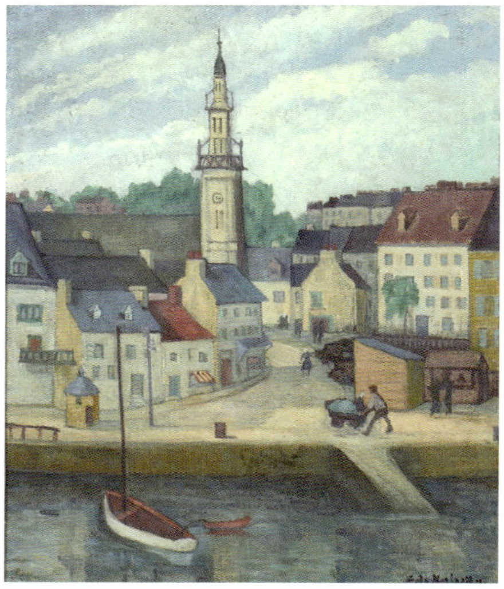

A1001; oil on canvas, 60 × 50 cm
Prov.: Mrs L.M. Owen; Mrs Iona Thrupp
Presented by R.A. Bevan, the artist's son, 1963; WA1963.56

This may have been painted during a summer holiday in 1935.

Willem Kalf
(1619 – 1693)

Still Life with an Oriental Rug

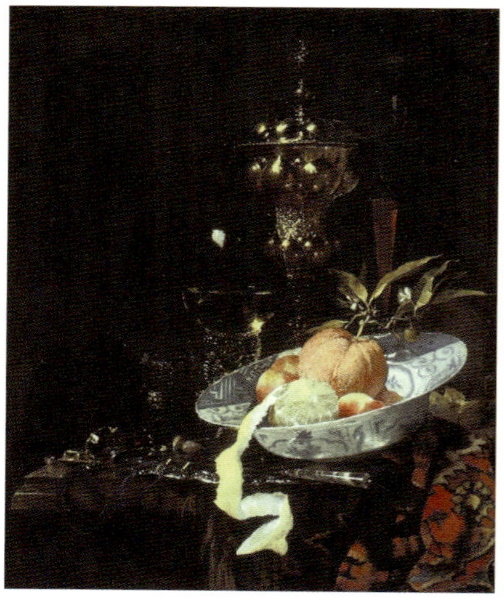

A563; oil on canvas, 65 × 54 cm
Daisy Linda Ward Bequest, 1939; WA1940.2.39

Meijer 2003, no. 40

After painting a number of barn interiors in the early 1640s, Kalf devoted himself to painting luxury still-life compositions, filled with precious objects which he rendered with a notable sense of light and texture. The silver dish and knife with a cornelian handle, the watch, standing cup-and-cover, oriental rug, Wan-li porcelain bowl and various glasses are placed in the dark and lit with romantic and varied effects of light. As several of these items are found in paintings of the early 1660s, it is supposed that this composition is of the same date.

Stanislawa de Karlowska
(1876 – 1952)

A Wealden Farm

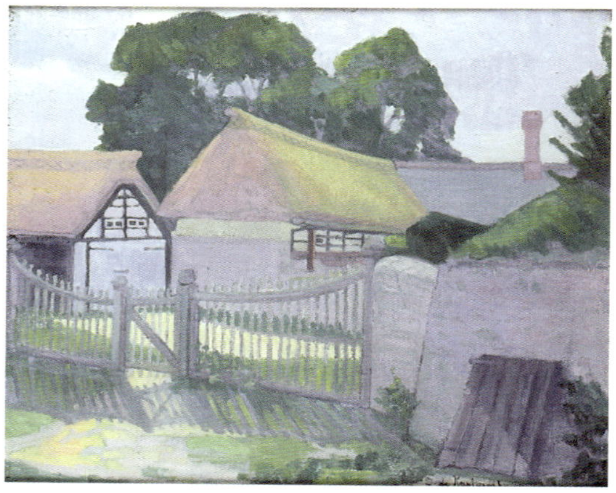

A1049; oil on canvas, 38 × 48 cm
Signed: *S de Karlowska*
Presented by the artist's children, R.A. Bevan and Mrs C.W. Baty, 1968; WA1968.139

One of several landscapes painted by Karlowska in Kent and Sussex *c.* 1927.

Bernhard Keilhau, known as Monsù Bernardo
(1624 – 1687)

The Lacemaker

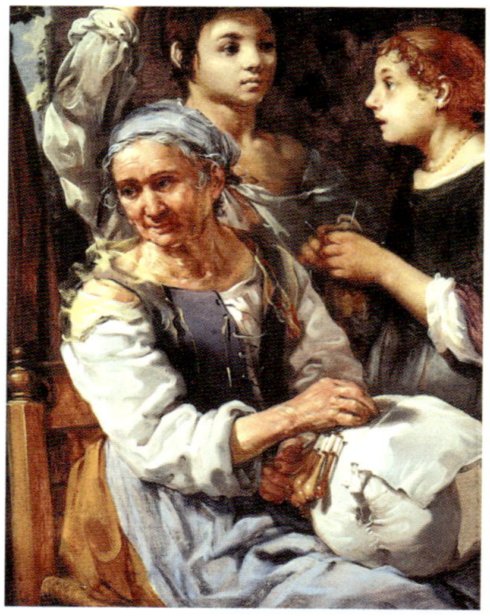

A1029; oil on canvas, 91 × 71 cm
Prov.: Arnold Haskell
Purchased with the aid of the Victoria & Albert Museum Purchase Grant Fund, 1966; WA1966.65

Heimbürger 1988, no. 175; White 1999, pp. 72–3

This is perhaps a fragment of a larger composition. It has sometimes been called an allegory of sight, implying that it formed part of a group of genre scenes epitomising the five senses. Keilhau settled in Rome from 1656, having worked in Amsterdam and northern Italy, and developed this type of genre scene from 1660 onwards. It was to be immensely influential.

Jan van Kessel I
(1626 – 1679)

A Cockchafer, Beetle, Woodlice and *other Insects, with a Sprig of Auricula*

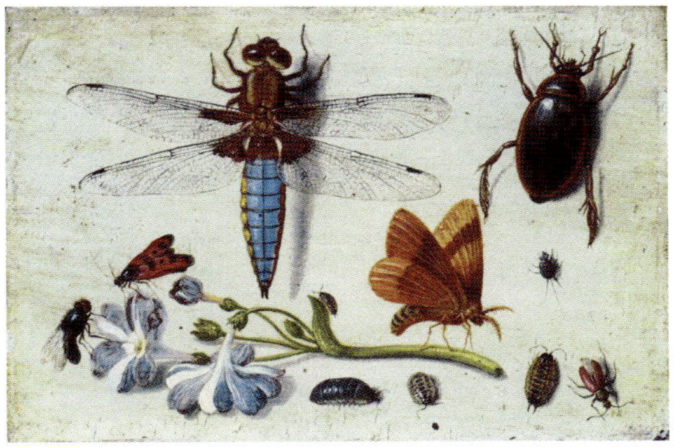

A564; oil on copper, 8.3 × 12.1 cm
Daisy Linda Ward Bequest, 1939; WA1940.2.40

Meijer 2003. no. 41

Jan van Kessel was a versatile painter of still life in Antwerp, best known for his small paintings on copper on which he painted insects, shells and flowers similar to the works in Oxford. This little picture and the three which follow may have formed part of a larger set of painted fronts for small drawers in a cabinet. As his early work of this kind tends to be more meticulous than his later work and as these works are very neatly finished, they may date from the early 1650s when he seems to have begun painting panels of this type.

Jan van Kessel I
(1626 – 1679)

Three Butterfiles, a Beetle and *other Insects, with a Cutting of Ragwort*

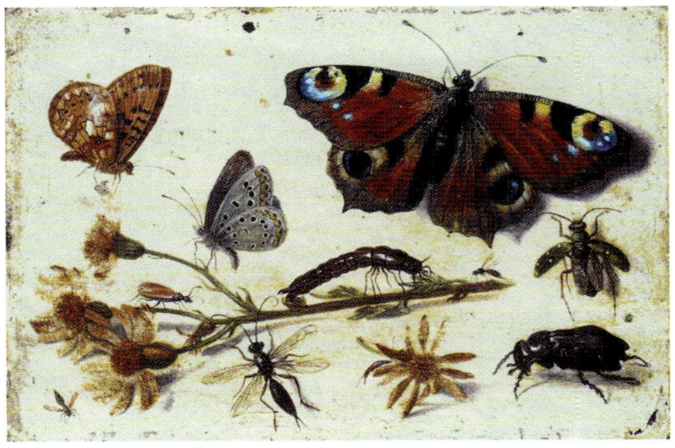

A566; oil on copper, 9 × 13 cm
Daisy Linda Ward Bequest 1939; WA1940.2.42

Meijer 2003, no. 43

Jan van Kessel I
(1626 – 1679)

Flowers and Insects

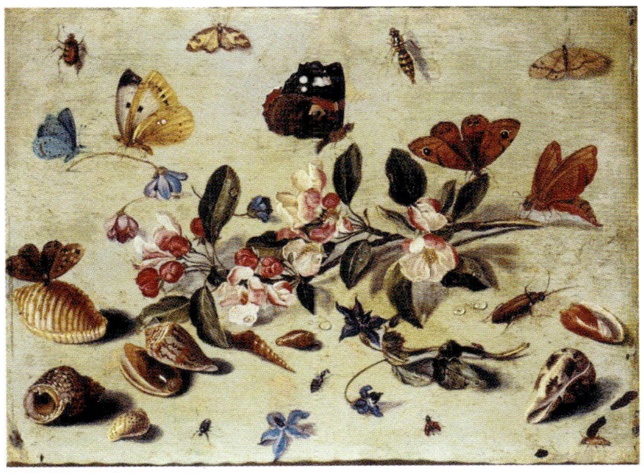

A568; oil on copper, 28.7 × 22 cm
Prov.: Richard Warner
Daisy Linda Ward Bequest, 1939; WA1940.2.44

Meijer 2003, no. 45

This is one of the larger examples of van Kessel's small pictures showing specimens of plant and animal life. It is possible that it may have formed the centre-piece in a set of smaller panels. By comparison with the other panels in Oxford, the handling is rougher, suggesting a later date, probably in the late 1650s or early 1660s.

Jan van Kessel I
(1626 – 1679)

Various Spiders and Caterpillars, with a Sprig of Gooseberry

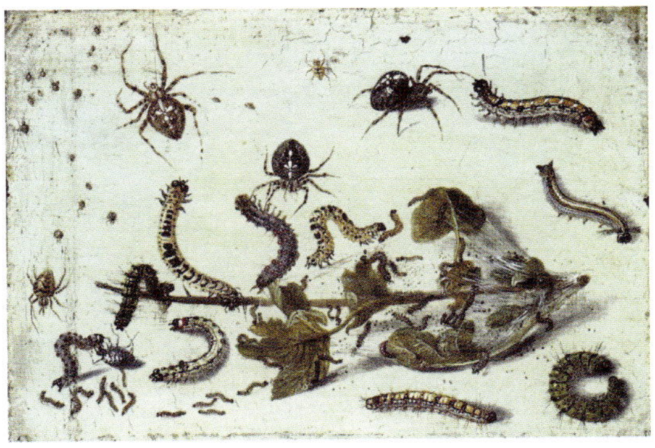

A565; oil on copper, 9 × 13 cm
Daisy Linda Ward Bequest 1939; WA1940.2.41

Meijer 2003, no. 42

Jan van Kessel I
(1626 – 1679)

A Dragon-fly, two Moths, a Spider and some Beetles, with wild Strawberries

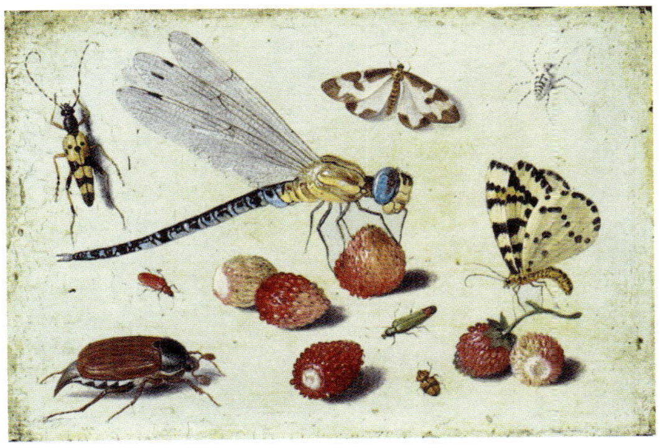

A567; oil on copper, 9 × 13 cm
Daisy Linda Ward Bequest 1939; WA1940.2.43

Meijer 2003, no. 44

Jan van Kessel I
(1626 – 1679)

Decorative Still-Life Composition with a Basket of Fruit

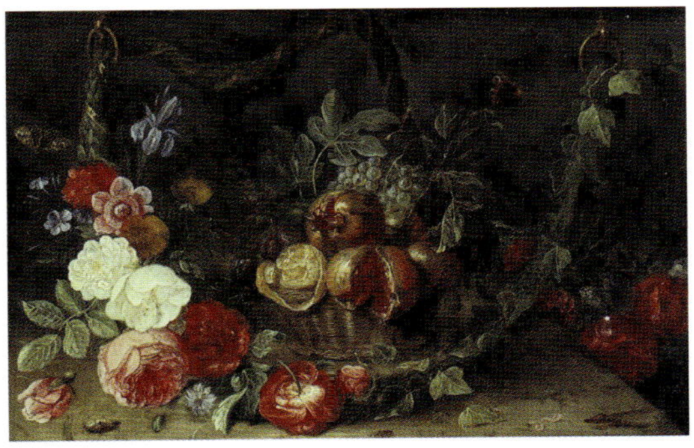

A569; oil on copper, 14 × 20 cm
Prov.: E.J.Spicer
Daisy Linda Ward Bequest, 1939; WA1940.2.45

Meijer 2003, no. 46

This panel and the three following were at one time attributed to a German painter, Peter van Kessel, on the grounds that they are somewhat coarser in texture than works by his Dutch namesake. All four are now firmly reattributed to Jan van Kessel whose later work tends to be rougher than his early work of this kind. They must form a set with some emblematic significance but the sense of this is not obvious.

Jan van Kessel I
(1626 – 1679)

Decorative Still-Life Composition with a Garland of Flowers

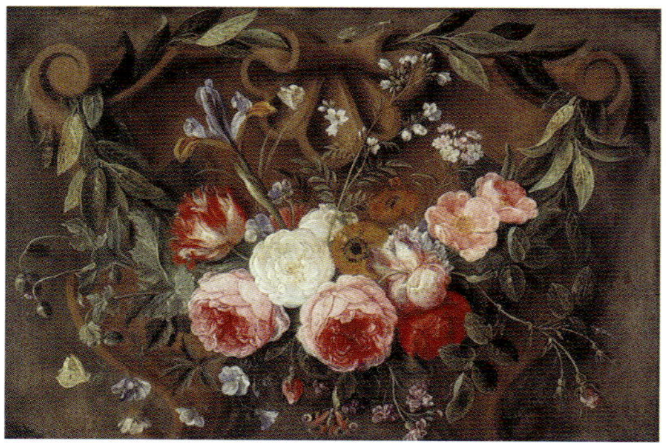

A570; oil on copper, 14 × 20 cm
Prov.: E.J.Spicer
Daisy Linda Ward Bequest, 1939; WA1940.2.46

Meijer 2003, no. 47

Jan van Kessel I
(1626 – 1679)

Decorative Still-Life Composition with a Porcelain Bowl, Fruit and Insects

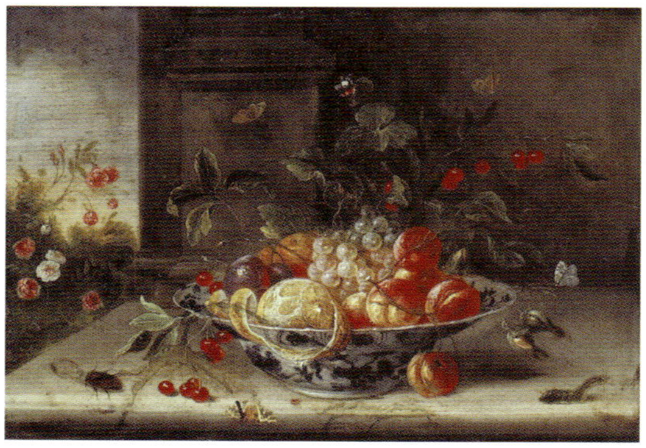

A572; oil on copper, 14 × 20 cm
Prov.: E.J.Spicer
Ward Bequest 1939; WA1940.2.48

Meijer 2003, no. 49

Style of Willem Key
(*c.* 1515 – 1568)

Half-length Portrait of a bearded Man

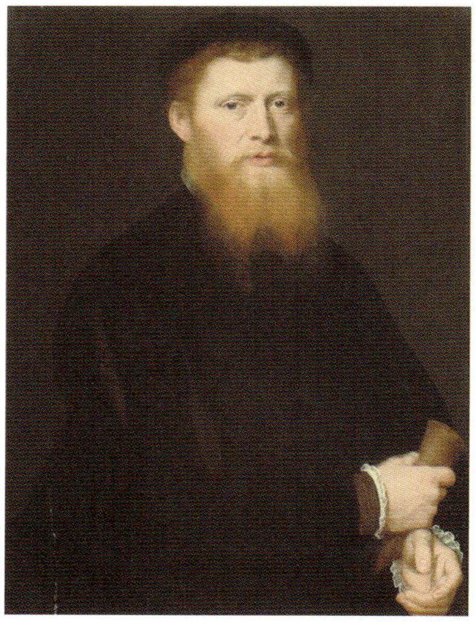

A1073; oil on panel, 65 × 48 cm
Prov.: (?)Francis Seymour-Conway, 1st Marquess of Hertford; Dr A.B. Bett
Bequeathed by Alan Pilkington in memory of his wife Mary, 1973; WA1973.104

White 1999, p. 73

The attribution to the Antwep painter, Willem Key, is based on a comparison with other portraits by Key, including one in the Musei Civici in Verona, dated 1556, and another in the Philadelphia Museum of Art in which the face is handled with a similar softness of touch.

Jan van Kessel I
(1626 – 1679)

Decorative Still-Life Composition with Birds and Two Bats

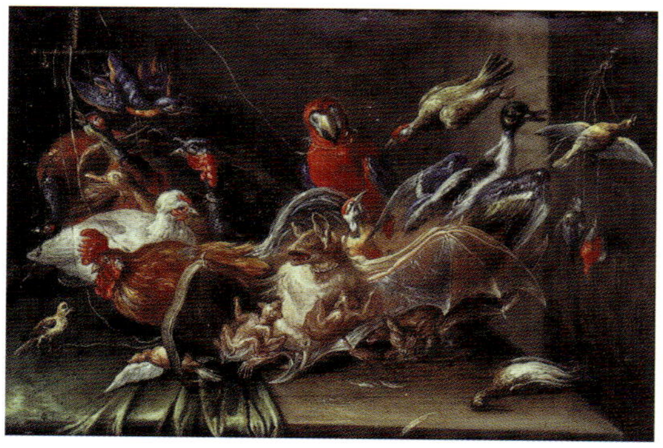

A571; oil on copper, 14 × 20 cm
Prov.: E.J.Spicer
Daisy Linda Ward Bequest, 1939; WA1940.2.47

Meijer 2003, no. 48

Tilly Kettle
(1735 – 1786)

Mrs Drewry Ottley

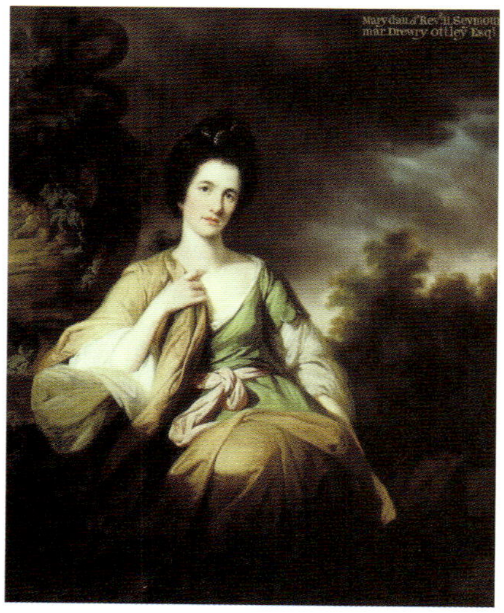

A308; oil on canvas, 126 × 103 cm
Signed and dated: *1768*; and inscribed: *Mary dau. of Revd H. Seymour mar. Drewry Ottley Esqr.*
Fortnum Bequest, 1899; WA1899.CDEF.P26

Milner 1926–7, p. 88

Drewry occurs as the forename of several generations of the Ottley family, landowners in St Christopher's, West Indies. It may be assumed that Mary Seymour's husband was the grandson and heir of the original Drewry Ottley of St Christopher's and died at Teddington in 1794. Mrs Ottley's portrait was painted shortly before Tilly Kettle left for India in 1768, where he enjoyed considerable success.

Style of Thomas de Keyser
(1596 – 1667)

Portrait of a bearded Man aged 72

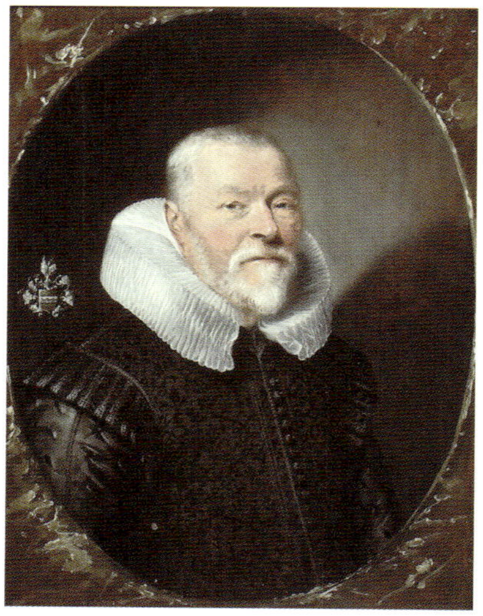

A305; oil on panel, 77.4 × 58.7 cm
Inscribed: *Aetatis sue 72 / Anno 1634*
Fortnum Bequest, 1899; WA1899.CDEF.P4

White 1999, p. 74

Perhaps painted by an artist in Amsterdam with some knowledge of the work of Thomas de Keyser who was the city's leading painter before Rembrandt's arrival in 1631. The coat of arms resembles that of the Boelens-Meertens family of Amsterdam.

Cornelis Kick
(1631/4 – 1681)

A Vase of Flowers

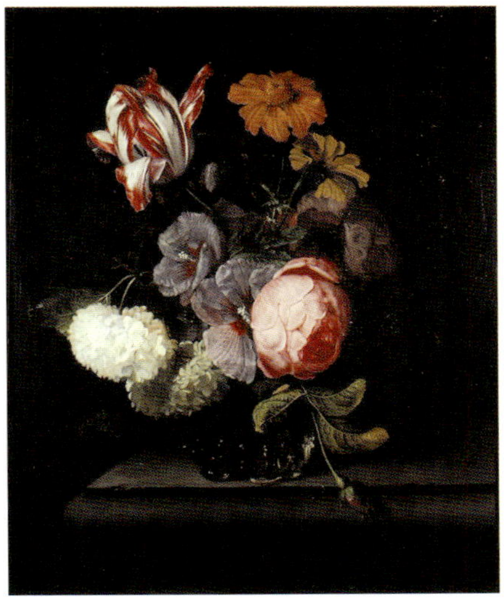

A573; oil on panel, 46 × 36 cm
Signed: *C Kick*
Daisy Linda Ward Bequest, 1939; WA1940.2.49

Meijer 2003, no. 50

Cornelis Kick was trained by his father, Simon Kick, in Amsterdam. It is said that the fame of Jan Davidsz. de Heem inspired him to turn to painting flowers and fruit. This still life is less ambitious than some of his flower pieces which tend to be more crowded and less well arranged. Signed flower pieces by him are rare and only one example with a date – 1670 – is known.

Attributed to Simon Kick
(1603 – 1652)

A Woman seated beside a Table

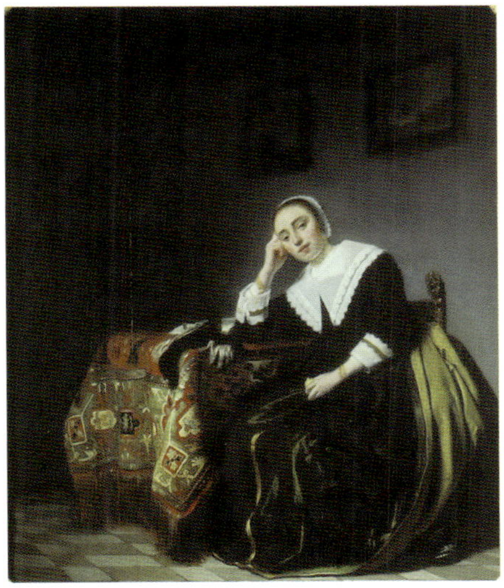

A124; oil on panel, 61 × 50 cm
Bequeathed by the Revd Dr Thomas Penrose, 1851; WA1851.21

White 1999, p. 74

Perhaps a study in melancholy. The attribution to Kick, which is based on a general kinship with the languorous figures found in several of Kick's paintings, is very uncertain.

Thomas Kirkby
(active 1796 – 1847)

John Shute Duncan

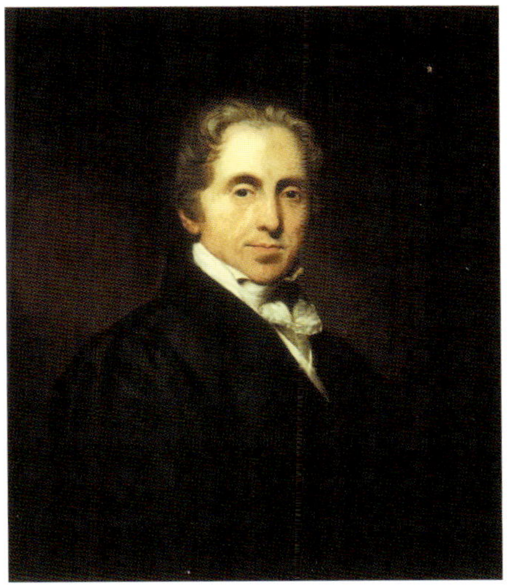

A66a; oil on canvas, 76 × 64 cm
Acquired after 1836; WA1845.66

Poole 1912, no. 477

John Shute Duncan (?1769–1844) was the brother of P.B. Duncan (see A66b). He was elected a Fellow of New College in 1791 and was Keeper of the Ashmolean Museum between 1823 and 1826.

Cornelis Kick
(1631/4 – 1681)

Still Life with a Lemon and pink Roses

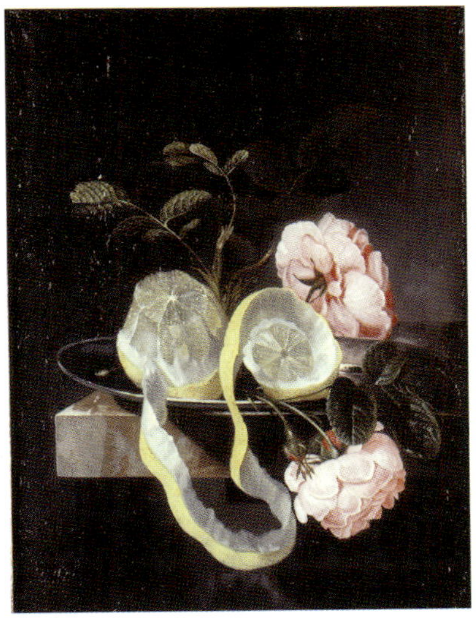

A616; oil on panel, 37 × 29 cm
Daisy Linda Ward Bequest, 1939; WA1940.2.92

Meijer 2003, no. 51

Formerly attributed to Walscapelle and then to Ottmar Elliger, this modest still life is now given to Walscapelle's teacher, Cornelis Kick. The rose drooping on lower right reappears in a painting attributed to Kick, now in a private collection. The somewhat careless handling of the paint also points in his direction.

Peter Kinley
(1926 – 1988)

Grey Cow

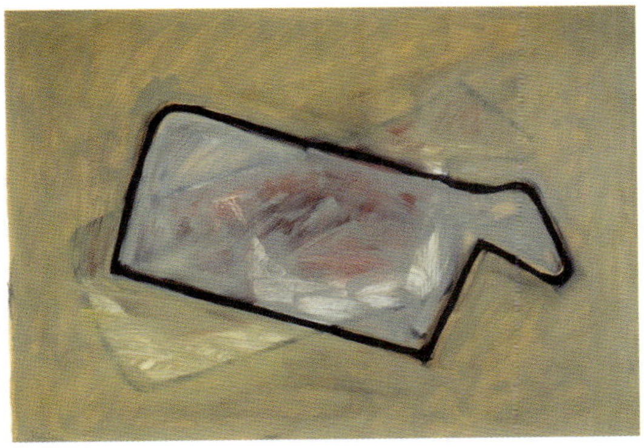

A1121; oil on paper, 55 × 75.5 cm
Signed: *Kinley*
Purchased with funds donated by Sir Rex Richards, 1982; WA1982.35

Wouter Knijff
(*c.* 1607 – after 1693)

A Canal Scene

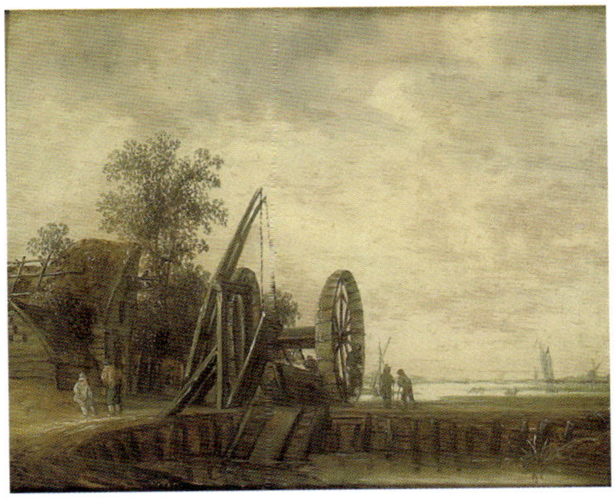

A287; oil on panel, 27 × 33 cm
Signed in monogram and dated: *WK 1648*
Presented by Thomas Humphry Ward, 1897; WA1897.10

White 1999, p. 76

The subject and composition of this picture shows the influence of Jan van Goyen and Salomon van Ruysdael who, like Knijff, worked in Haarlem in the first half of the 17th century.

Johann Koenig
(1586 – 1642)

The Toilet of Bathsheba

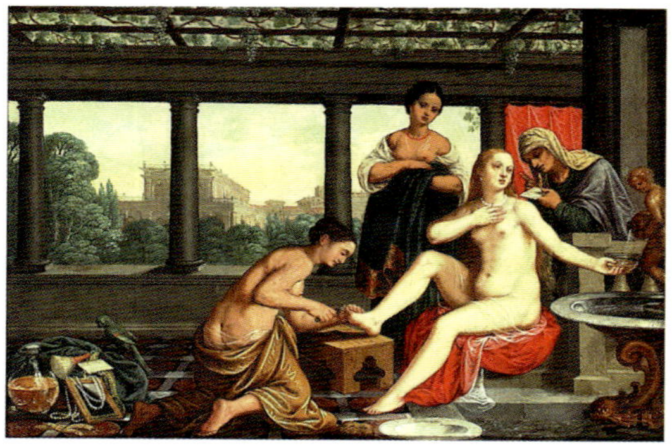

A718; oil on copper, 23 × 33 cm
Signed: *Johannes* (?) *König fecit*
Purchased, 1945; WA1945.100

White 1999, p. 76

Following his arrival in Rome in 1610, Koenig joined the circle of his fellow German, Adam Elsheimer, who specialised in painting small, precisely detailed compositions on copper. The influence of Elsheimer and the Italianate setting of this work indicate that it may date from Koenig's Roman years (1610–16). The subject, showing Bathsheba, wife of Uriah the Hittite, bathing in sight of King David's palace (I Samuel, 13: 11–17), was popular with 16th- and 17th-century painters.

Konstantin Alekseevich Korovin
(1861 – 1939)

Winter Landscape with two wooden Huts

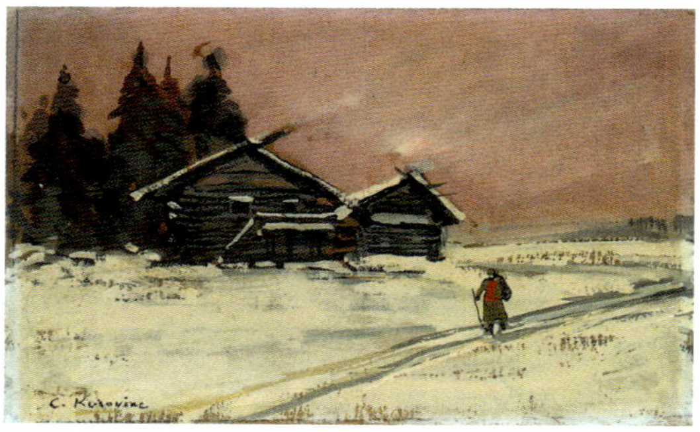

Bodycolours and oil on cardboard, mounted as a drawing, 11.8 × 18.6 cm
Bequeathed by Dr Tatiana Gourlande, 1960; WA1960.36.5

Salmina-Haskell 1989, no. 66

Korovin was a member of the 'World of Art' movement in late 19th-century St Petersburg. He worked in an Impressionist style, devoting himself mainly to landscape. He also designed sets and costumes for the opera. The set of four winter landscapes in the Ashmolean all represent Russian scenes, painted with the same thin, flat, fluent touch and were probably painted at the same time.

Konstantin Alekseevich Korovin
(1861 – 1939)

Winter Landscape

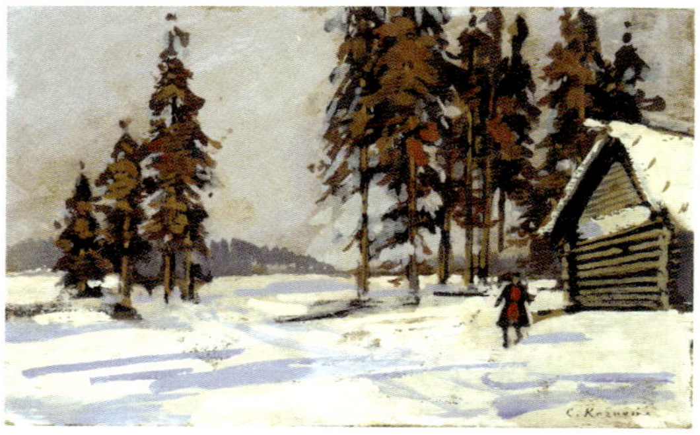

Bodycolours and oil on paper, mounted as a drawing, 11.5 × 18.4 cm
Bequeathed by Dr Tatiana Gourlande, 1960; WA1960.36.4

Salmina-Haskell 1989, no. 65

Philips Koninck
(1619 – 1688)

A View over flat Country

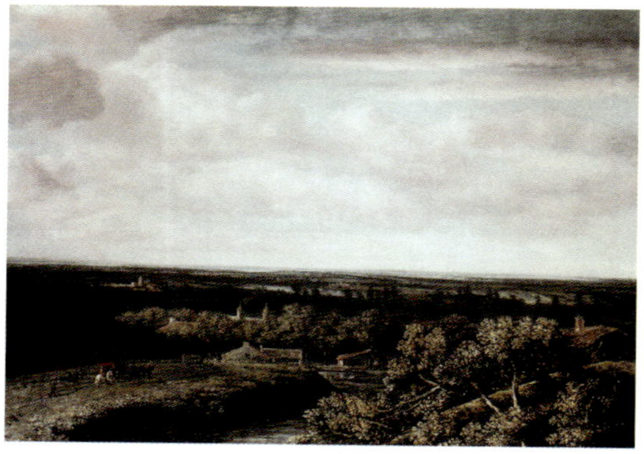

A719; oil on canvas, 118 × 166 cm
Prov.: R. Napier; J. Bell; Sir William Farrer
Bequeathed by Gaspard O. Farrer through the National Art Collections Fund, 1946; WA1946.197

White 1999, p. 77–8

Koninck painted genre subjects and portraits but is now best known for his large, panoramic views of the coastal plains of Holland. This landscape has been dated between 1655 and 1660. The broad handling of paint supports the supposition that the artist had studied with Rembrandt. There is a similarly extensive view in the National Gallery in London, dated 1655.

Konstantin Alekseevich Korovin
(1861 – 1939)

Winter Landscape with a small Church

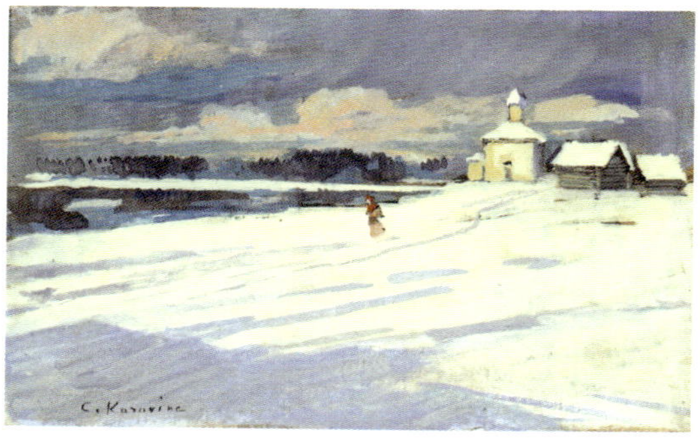

Oil on paper, mounted as a drawing, 11.5 × 18.4 cm
Bequeathed by Dr Tatiana Gourlande, 1960; WA1960.36.3

Salmina-Haskell 1989, no. 64

Konstantin Alekseevich Korovin
(1861 – 1939)

Winter Landscape with a Hunter

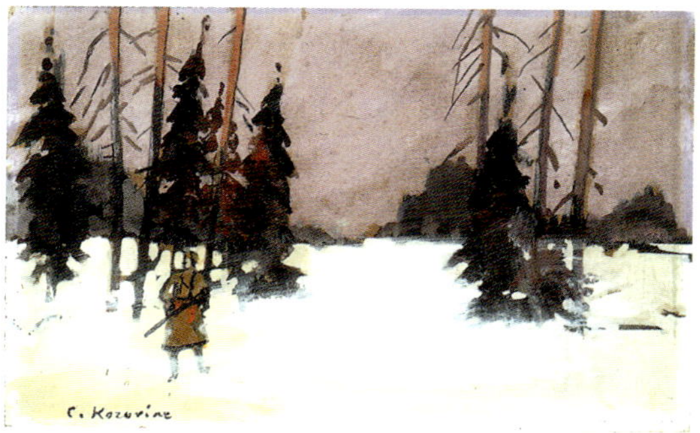

Bodycolours and oil on cardboard, mounted as a drawing, 12 × 18.5 cm
Inscribed in Russian on the back: *hunters Vladimir district*
Bequeathed by Dr Tatiana Gourlande, 1960; WA1960.36.6

Salmina-Haskell 1989, no. 67

Konstantin Alekseevich Korovin
(1861 – 1939)

Design for a Ballet

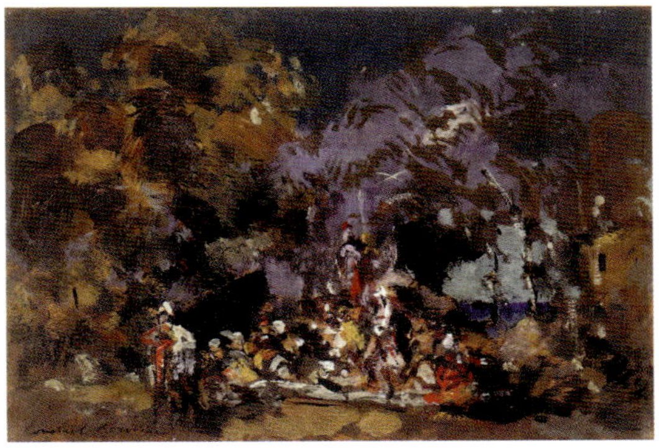

Oil on thin panel, mounted as a drawing, 15 × 21.5 cm
Bequeathed by Dr Tatiana Gourlande, 1960; WA1960.36.10

Salmina-Haskell 1989, no. 58

Korovin worked for Savva Mamontov's private opera from 1885 to 1891. In 1898, he designed sets and costumes for the Imperial Opera in Moscow and St Petersburg and later for many theatres in Western Europe and America. It is not possible to identify the production for which this study of a stage set was made.

Konstantin Alekseevich Korovin
(1861 – 1939)

Sketch of a Russian Village

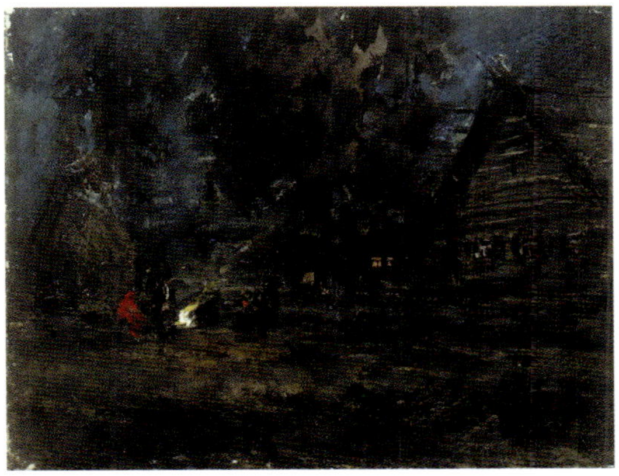

Oil on cardboard, mounted as a drawing, 14 × 18 cm
Inscribed in Russian on the back: *Russia village night*
Bequeathed by Dr Tatiana Gourlande, 1960; WA1960.36.7

Salmina-Haskell 1989, no. 62

Konstantin Alekseevich Korovin
(1861 – 1939)

View of Paris by Night

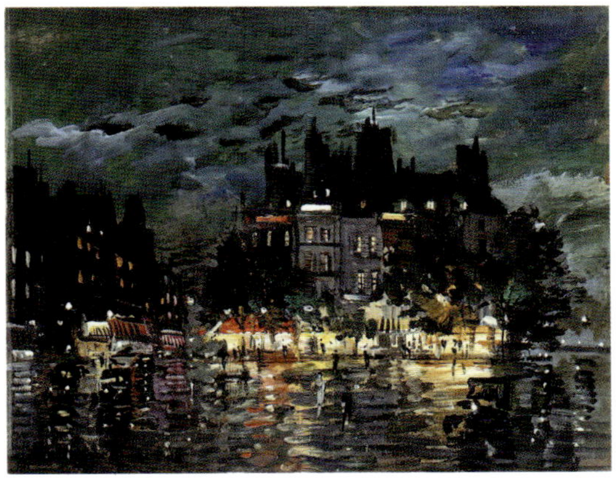

Oil on cardboard, mounted as a drawing, 33 × 41 cm
Bequeathed by Dr Tatiana Gourlande, 1960; WA1960.36.9

Salmina-Haskell 1989, no. 61

In 1923, Korovin settled in Paris. This painting was made from a viewpoint looking across the Seine to the houses on the Ile de la Cité. The effect of noctural light and the loose manner in which it is painted recall the work of late Impressionists working in Paris in this period.

Konstantin Alekseevich Korovin
(1861 – 1939)

Nocturnal Landscape with a Group round a Fire

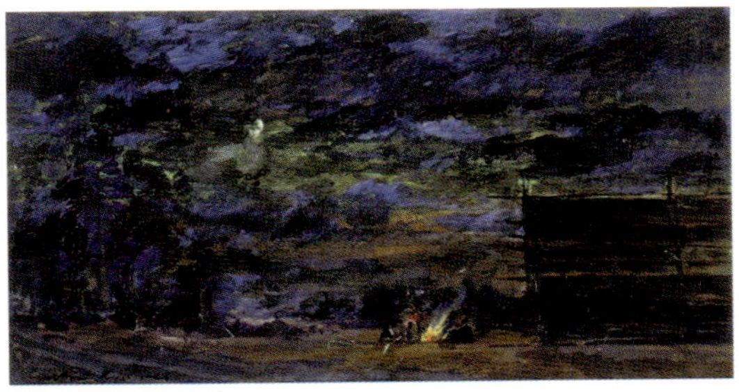

Oil on cardboard, mounted as a drawing, 20 × 37 cm
Bequeathed by Dr Tatiana Gourlande, 1960; WA1960.36.8

Salmina-Haskell 1989, no. 63

This sketch and the following appear to be views of the same site seen from different angles.

Konstantin Alekseevich Korovin
(1861 – 1939)

Design for the Ballet ('The Corsair')

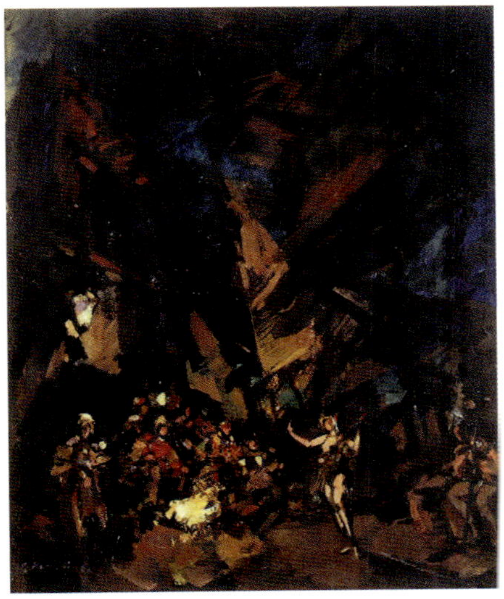

Oil on cardboard, mounted as a drawing, 39.3 × 32.1 cm
Bequeathed by Dr Tatiana Gourlande, 1960; WA1960.36.11

Salmina-Haskell 1989, no. 56

Korovin designed the sets and costumes for a production of *The Corsair* at the Moscow Bolshoi Theatre in 1915.

George Lance
(1802 – 1864)

Still Life of Fruits with the Figure of a young Man

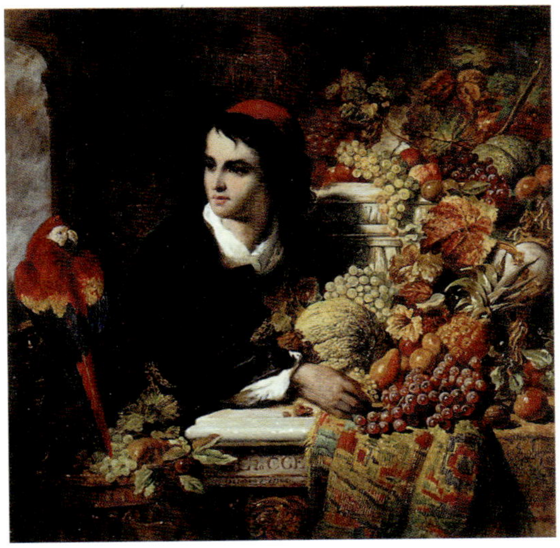

A698; oil on paper, mounted as a drawing, 31 × 30 cm
Inscribed: *GL to CGE / October 8th 1854*
Purchased, 1942; WA1942.57

Lance specialised in painting still lifes of abundance – fruit, vegetables and game. His most popular composition was shown at the Royal Academy in 1854 as *Fruits* (untraced) and numerous versions exist. This autograph replica dates from the same year and was probably made as a commission or gift for the unidentified *CGE* of the inscription.

Attributed to Willem van de Lande
(c. 1610 – after 1650)

Two Huntsmen and Peasants beside a Pond

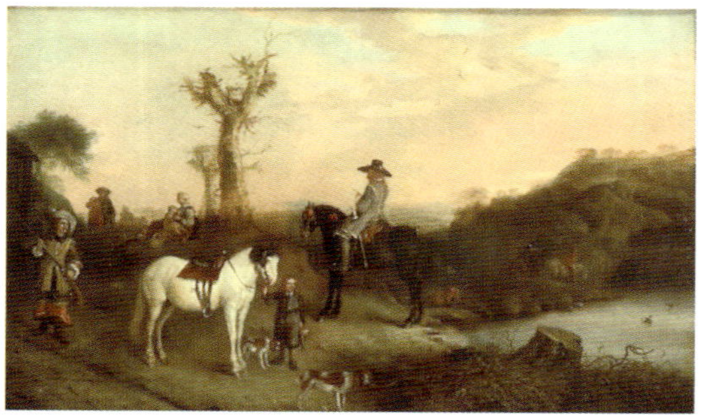

A285; oil on panel, 37 × 61 cm
Signed with initials: *WL*
Presented by Thomas Humphry Ward, 1897; WA1897.8

White 1999, p. 78

The artist is very little known. He is recorded in Delft in 1635 and seems to have been active in Amsterdam in the mid-century. The attribution rests mainly on the initials and to some extent on a signed painting which was sold at Sotheby's on 2 July 1952, lot 64.

Sir Edwin Henry Landseer
(1802 – 1873)

Study of a Ruff

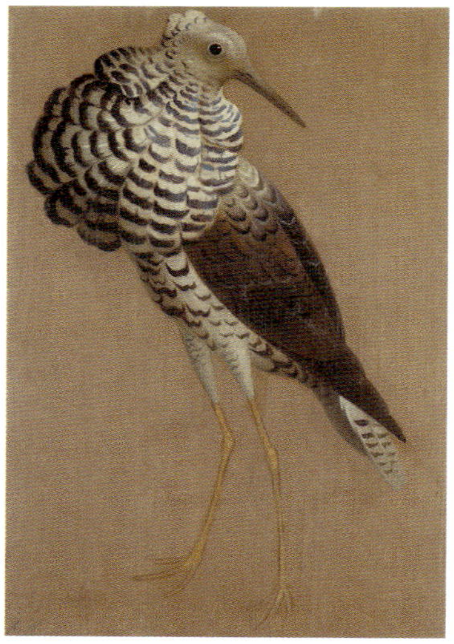

A1002a; oil on canvas, mounted as a drawing, 33.1 × 24 cm
Signed and dated on original mount: *E.L. 1845* and inscribed: *Ruff.*
Prov.: Sir Bruce Ingram
Purchased (Virtue-Tebbs Bequest Fund), 1963; WA1963.89.48

London 1961, no. 167

One of numerous studies of single birds or mammals, drawn or painted, executed by Landseer throughout his career and reflecting his interest in the characteristics of different species.

Giovanni Lanfranco
(1582 – 1647)

Christ and the Woman of Samaria

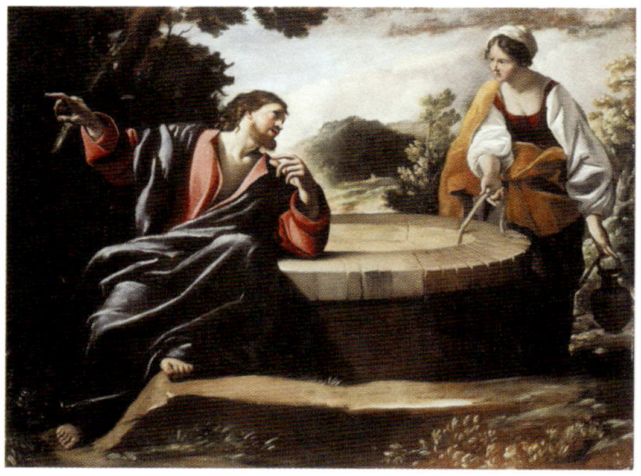

A1134; oil on canvas, 66 × 86.5 cm
Prov.: probably Filippo II Colonna, Rome, by 1706
Purchased to mark the Keepership of Dr Kenneth Garlick (1968–84) with the assistance of the Victoria & Albert Museum Purchase Grant Fund, the National Art Collections Fund and other donors, 1985; WA1985.29

Schleier 2001, under no. 72

Resting at Jacob's well in Samaria, Christ asked a woman for water; she recognized him as the Messiah (John 4: 5–30). This painting dates from c. 1625–8. Another version is in a private collection and a derivation is at Capodimonte, Naples. Lanfranco looked back to Annibale Carracci's well-known composition of the 1590s, now in the Brera, Milan.

Sir Edwin Henry Landseer
(1802 – 1873)

Queen Victoria on a highland Pony

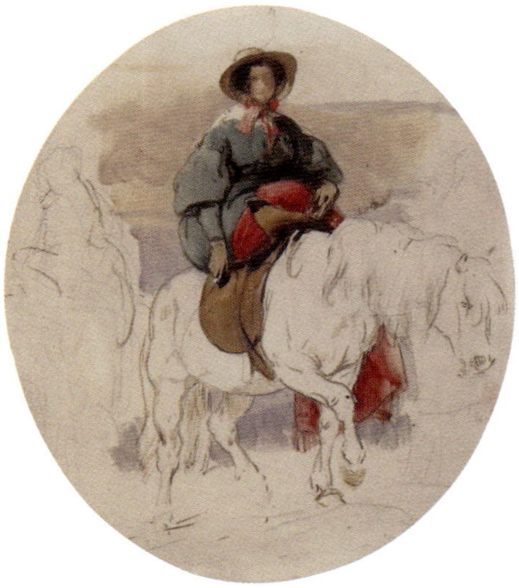

A1083; oil on board, mounted as a drawing, 22 × 20 cm
Prov.: James Patrick (of Hull); Lord Plunkett
Purchased (Bouch Fund), 1976; WA1976.70

Landseer's first major royal commission was a full-size portrait of Queen Victoria seated on her white horse, Leopold. Begun in January 1838, it was never completed (Lord Fairhaven). Many related sketches attest to the difficulty Landseer had in painting a picture worthy of hanging with the van Dycks at Windsor Castle. This unfinished oil-sketch may be related to the larger portrait; or simply be a sketch made during one of the artist's visits to the Highlands.

Sir Edwin Henry Landseer
(1802 – 1873)

Two Studies of a Stag's Head

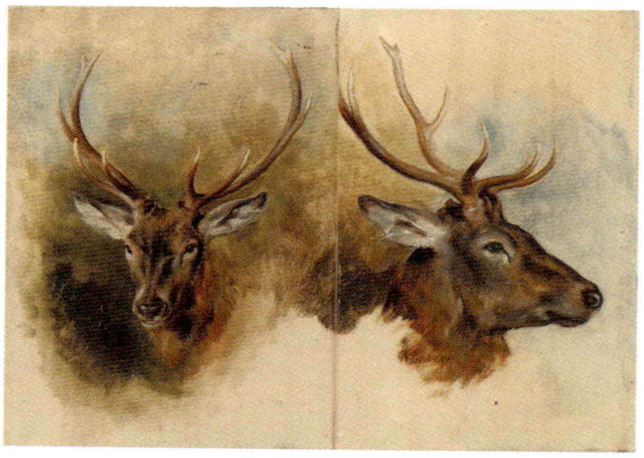

A443; oil on canvas, 65 × 47 cm
Presented by Mrs E.W. Creed, 1935; WA1935.65

From his childhood onwards, Landseer had a remarkable facility for drawing animals, based on an intimate knowledge of their anatomy. Even before his first visit to the Highlands in 1824, he had drawn deer and hunting scenes, but his discovery of Scotland stimulated his interest in deer, which culminated in his most celebrated picture, *The Monarch of the Glen* (1851; Dewars). These studies probably date from the later part of Landseer's career.

Peter Lanyon
(1918 – 1964)

Greystone

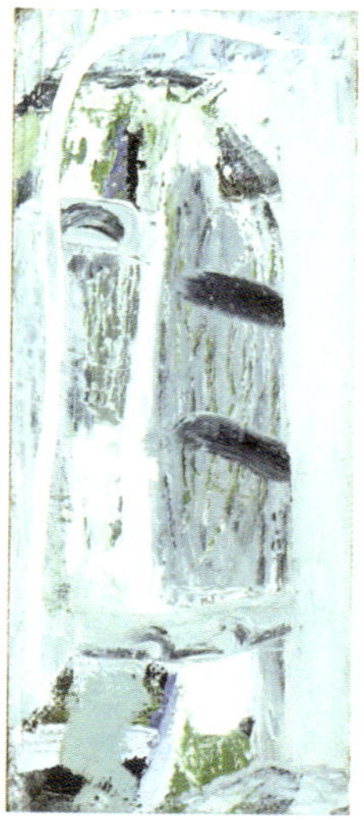

A1245; oil on board attached to a painted backboard, 54.3 × 36 cm
Signed: *Lanyon*; inscribed on back of the backboard: *Greystone / Peter Lanyon 53*
Purchased (Blakiston and Molly Freeman Bequest Funds) with the assistance of the National Art Collections Fund and the Friends of the Ashmolean, 2001; WA2001.176

As one of the leading members of post-war generation of St Ives artists, Lanyon was primarily interested in the representation of landscape. This work epitomises the tension between abstraction and figuration in an otherwise carefully descriptive work.

Philip Alexius de László
(1869 – 1937)

William Richard Morris, Viscount Nuffield

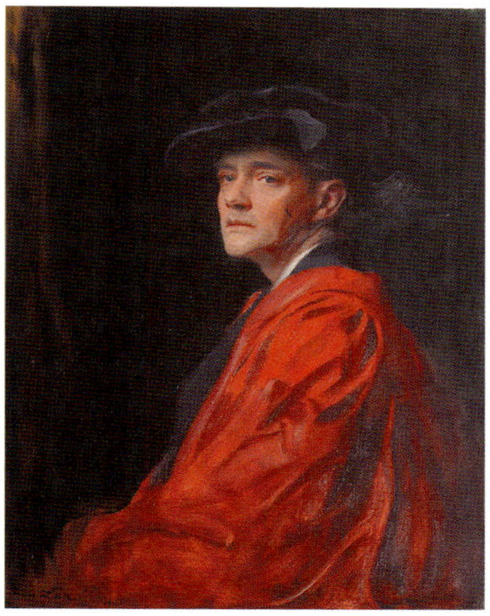

A509; oil on canvas, 91 × 71 cm
Presented by the artist, 1937; WA1937.108

A portrait of the manufacturer and philanthropist, William R. Morris (1877–1963), wearing the red gown and flat cap of a doctor of civil law at Oxford. There is another painting of the same sitter by de László in St Peter's College, Oxford. The stretcher brace is inscribed: 'painted / during / four hours / P.A.de L. / offered to the / Ashmolean / Oxford'.

Marie Laurencin
(1883 – 1956)

The Artist's Mother

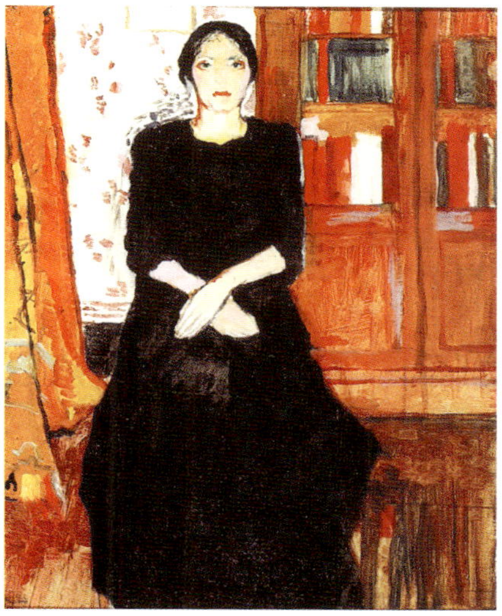

A1098; oil on canvas, 41.7 × 33.7 cm
Signed: *M.L.*
Prov.: Marie Sterner, New York
Purchased with the assistance of the Friends of the Ashmolean, 1978; WA1978.64

Eustace 1999, no.3; Sendai/Tateshima/Utsunomia 2003, no. 5

Laurencin turned herself into an independent artist after being trained as porcelain painter. She painted her mother *c.* 1906 using a bold combination of bright red and deep black which – even in her early paintings – is difficult to match in her other works.

Cecil Gordon Lawson
(1851 – 1882)

Sunset

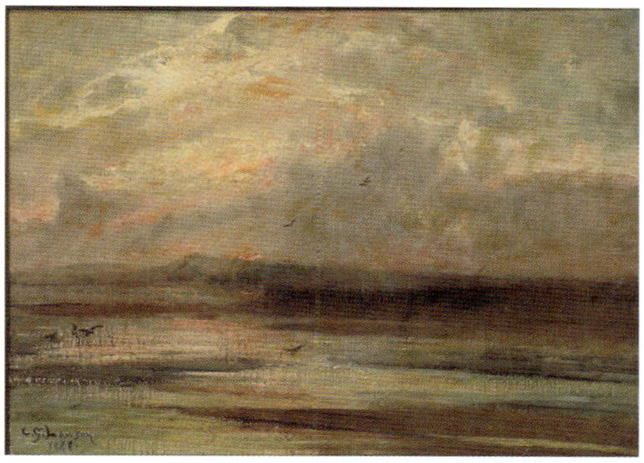

A1009; oil on canvas, 43 × 58 cm
Signed and dated: *C.G. LAWSON 1877*
Bequeathed by Major Thomas Bouch, 1963; WA1963.150.6

Lawson was widely considered one of the greatest Scottish landscape painters before his early death. He was especially fond of twilight scenes.

Samuel Laurence
(1812 – 1884)

Self-portrait

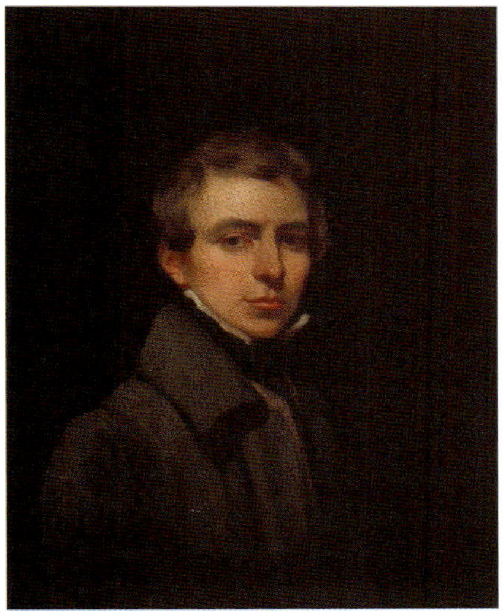

A932; oil on canvas, 33 × 26 cm
Presented by W.B. Laurence, the artist's grandson, 1959; WA1959.20.1

Miles 1982

Laurence exhibited portraits at the Royal Academy between 1836 and 1882, working mostly in coloured chalks. This self-portrait has been dated to 1836, when the artist was twenty-four.

Jean-Paul Laurens
(1838 – 1921)

The Judgement of Chilperic

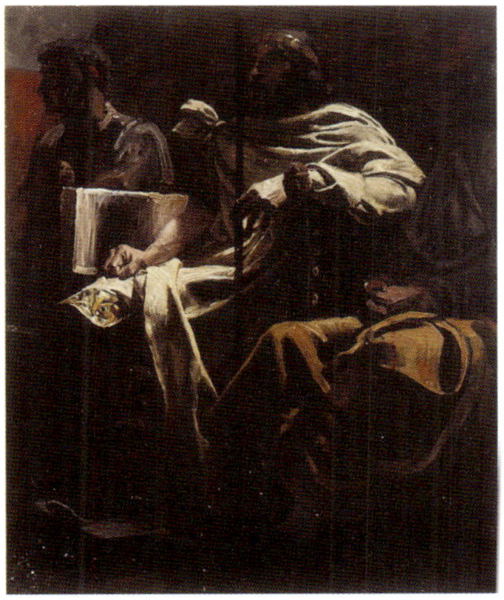

Oil on canvas, mounted as a drawing, 45.2 × 36.9 cm
Purchased, 1965; WA1965.30.1

A study for the right-hand side of one of Laurens's illustrations for Augustin Thierry's *Premier récit des temps Mérovingiens*, published by Hachette in 1881. Laurens was a prolific and ingenious painter of historical subjects of all periods.

Edward Lear
(1812 – 1888)

Thermopylae

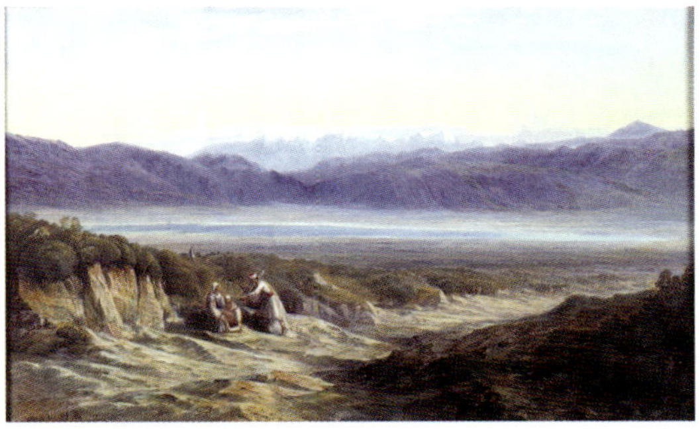

A1205; oil on canvas, 33.6 × 53.8 cm (sight)
Signed in monogram
Prov.: Augustus George Vernon Harcourt and by descent
Presented by Pamela Schiele in memory of Isabel Olivier, 1997; WA1997.14

Strachey 1907, no. 243; Noakes 1985, under no. 50

Lear arrived at the pass of Thermopylae during his visit to Greece in the summer of 1848. As was his habit, he made a number of pencil sketches which he later redrew in ink. He used these as the basis for a painting of *The Mountains of Thermopylae* dated 1852 (Bristol City Art Gallery), one of a group of four landscapes painted according to the Pre-Raphaelite precepts of Holman

Hunt. They were painted in translucent colours on a white ground. The view is taken looking southwards across the plain of the Spercheios; the deep gorge in the centre is the pass of Thermopylae itself. This smaller version was completed twenty years later according to the same principles.

William Lee
(1809 – 1865)

Gaslight

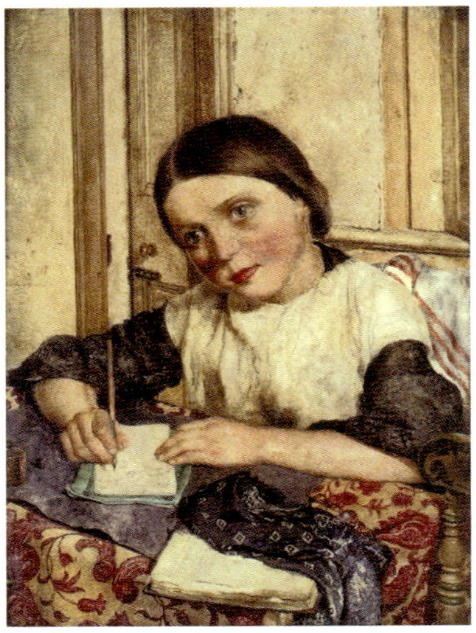

A884; oil over pencil on panel, mounted as a drawing, 20 × 14.7 cm (sight)
Purchased, 1955; WA1955.68

Lee worked mainly in watercolours and exhibited sporadically at the Royal Academy between 1844 and 1854. This portrait of a child dates from 1854.

Alphonse Legros
(1837 – 1911)

Interior with an Organist and a Procession

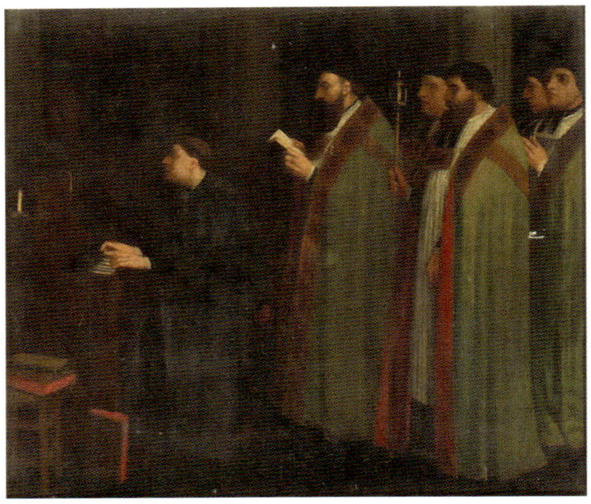

A661; oil on paper laid on canvas, 51 × 59 cm
Signed and dated: *Legros 1865*
Bequeathed by Miss Emily G. Kemp, 1940; WA1940.5.1

Legros's interest in Spanish art in the 1860s is evident in this painting. The composition is close to a painting exhibited at the Salon of 1863 (private collection, Paris), which Legros modified before sending it to the Royal Academy in London in 1865. Similar compositions of monks and worshippers are common in his paintings and prints of the 1860s.

Edward Lear
(1812 – 1888)

The Plains of Lombardy from Monte Generoso

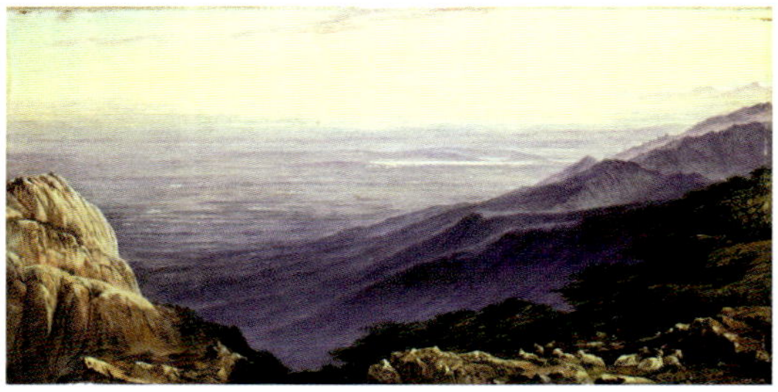

A353; oil on canvas, 24 × 47 cm
Signed in monogram
Bequeathed by the Revd Henry Fanshawe Tozer, 1916; WA1916.39

Lear moved into the Villa Emily at San Remo in 1871 and spent the summers from 1878 to 1883 at Monte Generoso, to the west of Como on the Italian-Swiss border. From near his hotel, he had stunning views over the plains and lakes of Italy and he drew them frequently. This oil painting, based on such sketches, was made in 1880 and bought by Tozer, a geographer who also bequeathed a fine collection of Lear's watercolours to the Ashmolean.

Derwent Lees
(1885 – 1931)

Trees, Provence

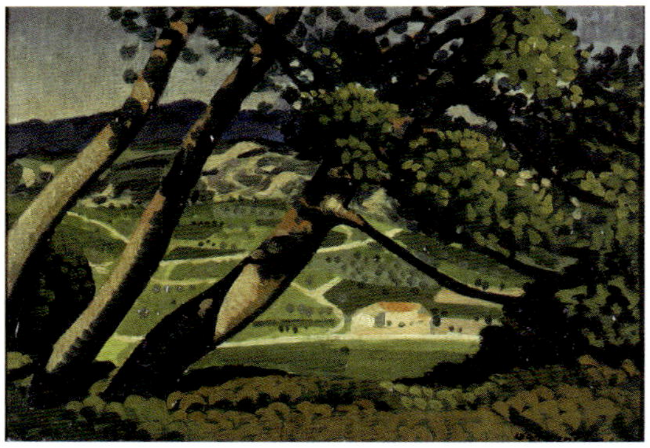

A926; oil on board, 25 × 35.5 cm
Signed and dated: *Derwent Lees 1912*
Presented by Thomas Balston, 1959; WA1959.54.1

One of a number of landscapes painted during a stay in Provence in 1912.

Alphonse Legros
(1837 – 1911)

Interior with an Organist and Three Figures

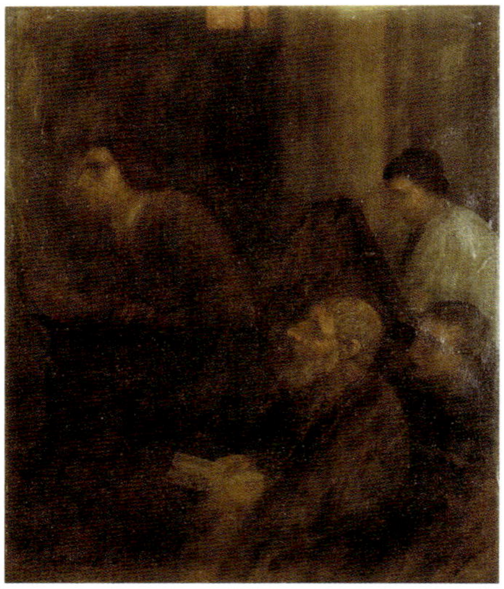

A662; oil on paper laid on canvas, mounted as a drawing, 36. 4 × 30.5 cm
Bequeathed by Miss Emily G. Kemp, 1940; WA1940.5.2

A variation on the same theme as the previous painting.

Alphonse Legros
(1837 – 1911)

Interior of a Church with kneeling Figures

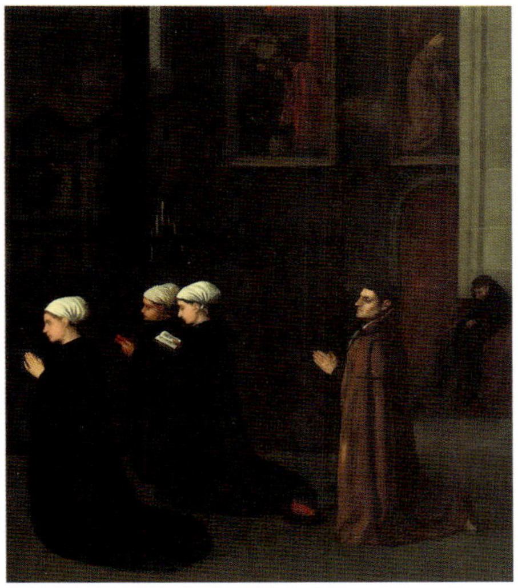

A865; oil on canvas, 84 × 71 cm; a large insert, lower right quarter
Signed: *Legros*
Presented by Guy Knowles, 1953; WA1953.67

Dating from the second half of the 1860s when Legros painted several church interiors. These were popular with his English patrons. The painting in the background has been identified as a free version of Zurbaran's *St Bonaventura* in the Louvre, a tribute from the artist to one of the Spanish painters to whom he turned for inspiration in the 1860s.

Frederic Lord Leighton
(1830 – 1896)

Acme and Septimius

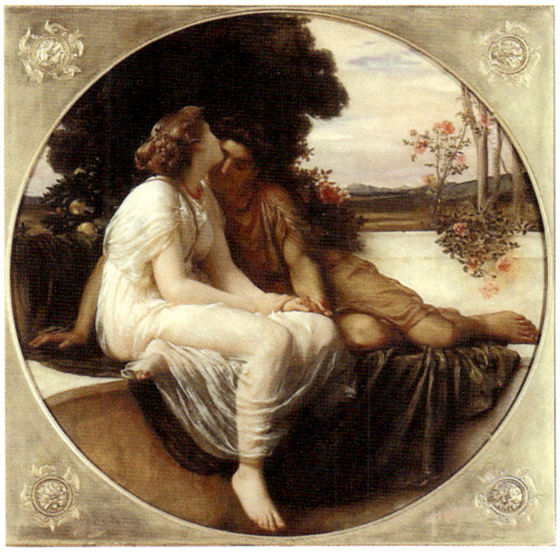

A1089; oil on canvas, 99 × 99 cm
Prov.: Robert Stirling Newall, F.R.S. and by descent
Bequeathed by Robert Stirling Newall, F.S.A., 1978; WA1978.7

Ormond 1975, no. 181; London 1996, no. 55

The subject of this scene of idyllic love is taken from Catullus, *Carmine* XV. Both the round shape and composition are indebted to Raphael's Madonnas. The background includes the rose, traditionally the symbol of love, and orange trees. When it was exhibited at the Royal Academy in 1868, it was praised by critics, who noted with approval Leighton's chaste treatment of the scene.

Copy after Sir Peter Lely
(1618 – 1680)

King Charles I

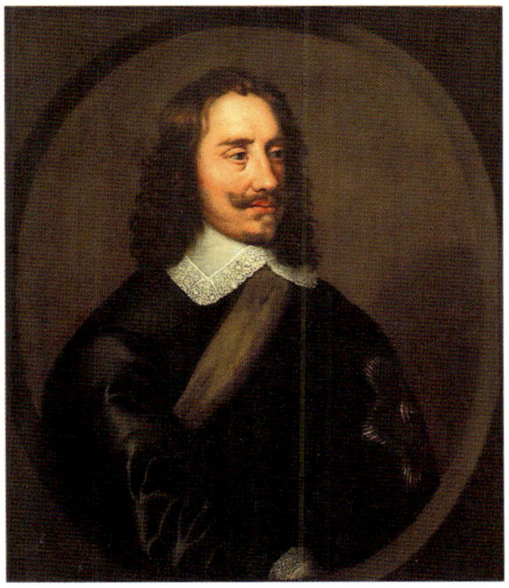

F739 or 670; oil on canvas, 75 × 62 cm
Probably bequeathed by Elias Ashmole, 1692 (or presented, 1683); WA1898.37

Poole 1912, no. 420; MacGregor 1983, no. 287

Copied from one half of the celebrated double portrait of King Charles I and the Duke of York painted in 1647 for the 10th Earl of Northumberland and known as the 'Clouded Majesty' picture (Syon House).

Frederic Lord Leighton
(1830 – 1896)

Monte Croce

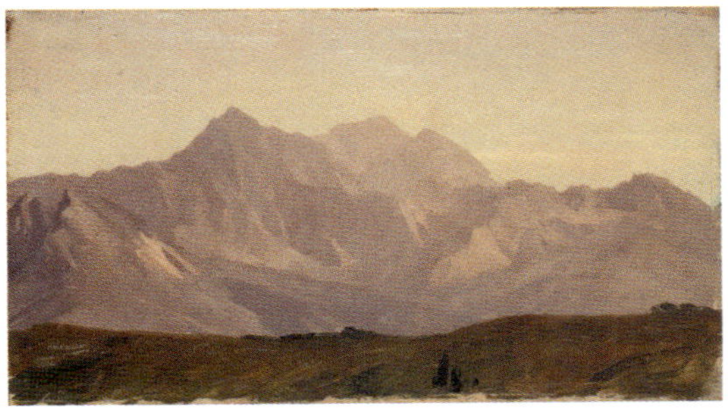

Oil on panel, mounted as a drawing, 10 × 17.7 cm
Presented by Charles Emanuel, 1950; WA1950.178.442

One of Leighton's smallest landscape oil-sketches. Inscriptions on the back identify the view as the *Pizzo dell'uccello* and *Monte alle croce*, in the Apuan Alps in Northern Tuscany. Leighton made frequent visits to Tuscany and no date for this sketch has been proposed.

Studio of Sir Peter Lely
(1618 – 1680)

John Selden

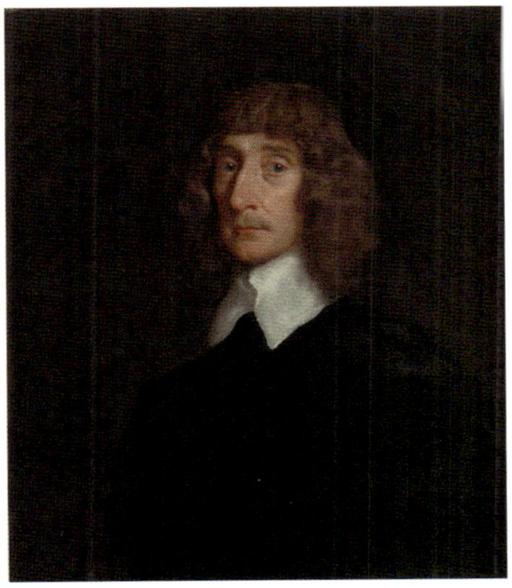

F655 or 745; oil on canvas, 74 × 62 cm
Bequeathed by Elias Ashmole, 1692; WA1898.28

Poole 1912, no. 434; Beckett 1951, under no. 472; MacGregor 1983, no. 256

John Selden (1584–1654) was a celebrated jurist and antiquary, who was also a benefactor to the Bodleian Library. The prime version of this portrait is in Yale Law Library and numerous others are recorded.

Copy after Sir Peter Lely
(1618 – 1680)

Prince Rupert of the Rhine in Garter Robes

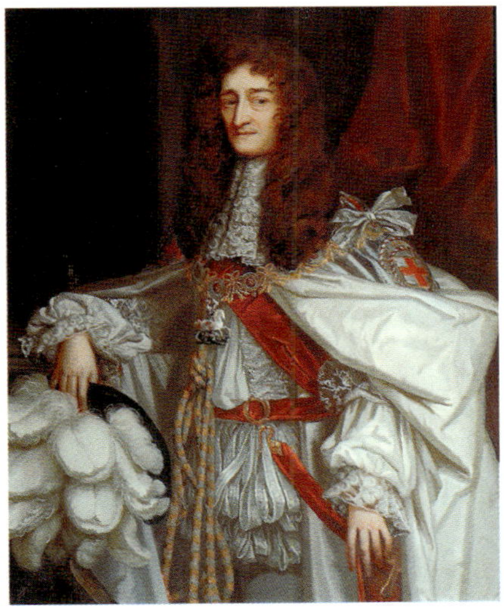

A1050c; oil on canvas, 127 × 102 cm
Bequeathed by Miss Orovida Pissarro, 1968; WA1968.474.1

Rupert (1619–1682) was the third son of Elector Frederick V of the Palatinate, elder cousin of Charles II. This is one of many versions and copies after a painting of *c.* 1672, showing Rupert in the stock pose and attire for Knights of the Garter.

Arthur Lemon
(1850 – 1912)

Landscape with silver Birch and distant Mountains

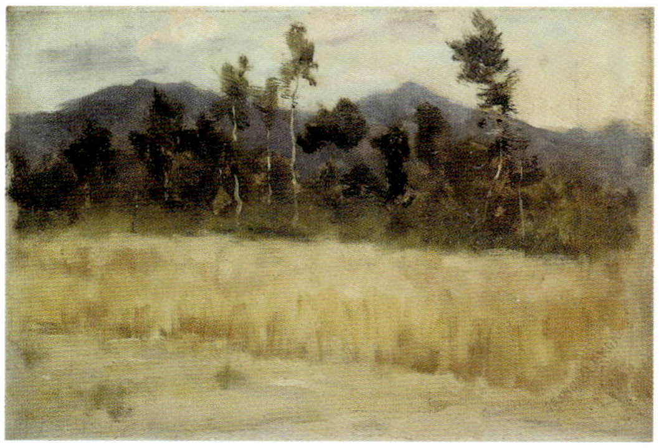

A1053; oil on paper, mounted as a drawing, 24.2 × 34.3 cm
Signed: *ARTHUR LEMON*
Prov.: Mrs William Hulton and by descent
Presented by the Lady Berwick, 1969; WA1969.19

Lemon studied in Rome and in Paris with Carolus-Duran, but spent his early years in California. He exhibited at the Royal Academy from 1880 and came into contact with Giovanni Costa and his circle of Etruscans in Italy. This slight sketch from nature probably dates from the last years of the 19th century.

Studio of Leonardo da Vinci
(1452 – 1519)

St John the Baptist

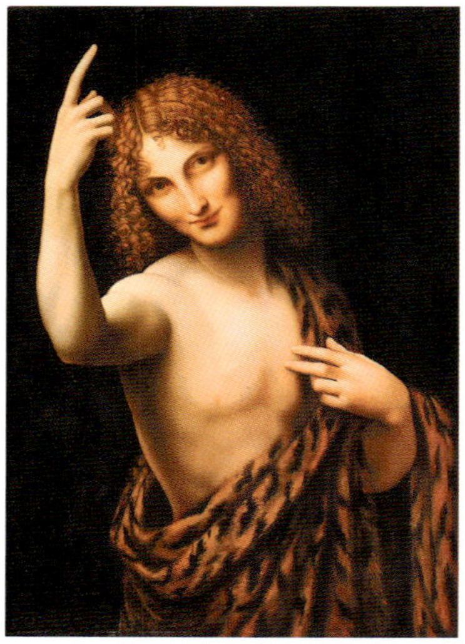

A503; oil on panel, 75 × 53.4 cm
Prov.: F.R. Leyland; W.G. Waters
Presented by Dr Arthur Waters, 1937; WA1937.102

Lloyd 1977, pp. 91–3; Marani 1989, under no. 12A

The idea of an angel pointing upwards indicating the Incarnation of Christ, originates with Leonardo *c.* 1506–8 and appears in paintings by his studio and followers. While A503 is close in design to a version at Basle, the figure here is not an angel, but St John, identifiable by his animal skin robe. Leonardo also painted *St John the Baptist* *c.* 1509 with a soft, atmospheric chiaroscuro (Louvre, Paris). A503 may be an adaptation by a Milanese follower of both motifs into a composite image.

Henri-Eugène-Augustin Le Sidaner
(1862 – 1939)

A Canal in Bruges at Dusk

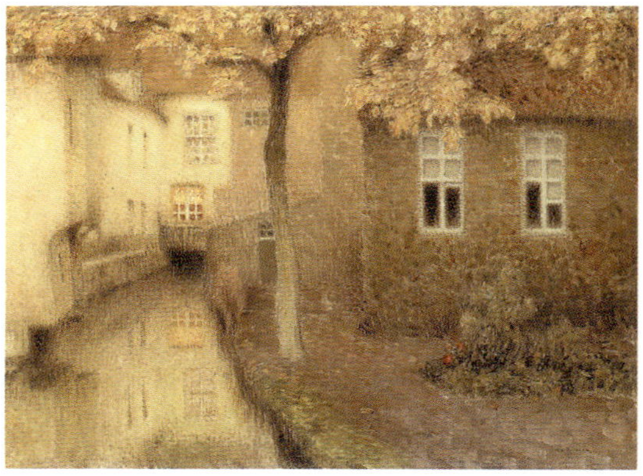

A471; oil on canvas, 49 × 65 cm
Signed: *Le Sidaner*
Weldon Bequest, 1937; WA1937.51

On the advice of Camille Mauclair, Le Sidaner visited Bruges in 1898, finding among the canals a theme which he varied constantly over the years. Evening and night effects on deserted canals became a favourite motif. His second visit to Bruges in 1899 to 1900 lasted over a year. A label from the Goupil Gallery on the back suggests that Mrs Weldon might have bought this from the proprietor, William Marchant, who promoted Le Sidaner's work on the London market.

Studio of Leonardo da Vinci
(1452 – 1519)

Virgin and Child with the young St John

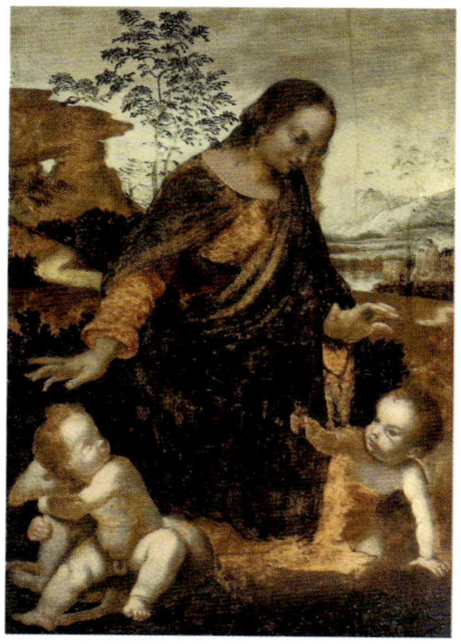

A790; oil on panel, 72.2 × 50.5 cm
Prov.: Walter Landor; Walter Savage Landor
Bequeathed by Henry Harris, 1950; WA1950.166

Lloyd 1977, pp. 93–6; Dalli Regoli *et al.* 2001, under no. 11.8

St John hugs his attribute of a lamb and the Child holds a goldfinch (traditionally associated with Christ's Passion). A drawing by Leonardo of *c.* 1480–5 in the Metropolitan Museum, New York, reveals an earlier stage of this design. The concept was developed in drawings for a composition of Leda with her twin sons. A790 (in ruined condition) is closely related to a painting in the Uffizi, Florence and derives from the same lost prototype by Leonardo which may have been a drawing or cartoon.

Stanislas-Victor-Edouard Lépine
(1835 – 1892)

The Seine at La Garenne Saint-Denis

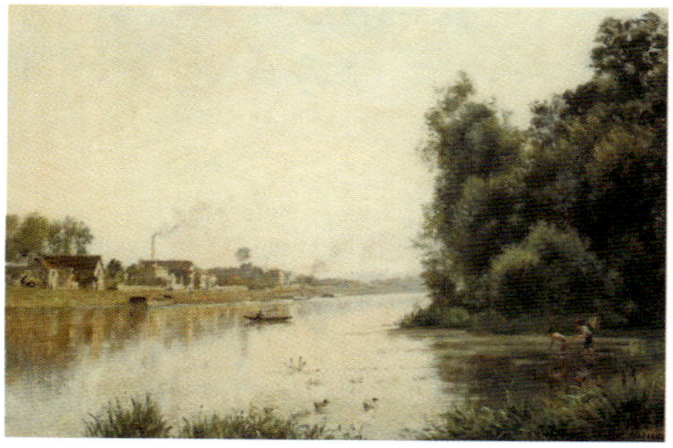

A496; oil on canvas, 38 × 55 cm
Signed: *S. Lepine*
Weldon Bequest, 1937; WA1937.77

Schmit 1993, no. 396

Lépine's tranquil river views derive from the example of Corot. Like Corot, he painted mostly in the studio using studies made in the open air. This view of a turning on the river Seine at La Garenne was painted by him on several occasions. The factory chimneys which had become a feature of the rivers in the vicinity of Paris by the 1870s appear often in his art.

Isaak Il'ich Levitan
(1860 – 1900)

Copse by a Lake (Autumn)

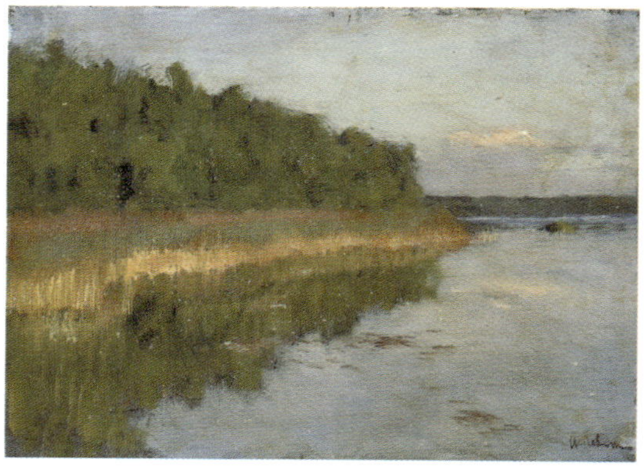

A779; oil on paper, mounted as a drawing, 11.1 × 15.1 cm
Bequeathed by Mikhail Vasil'evich Braikevitch, 1949; WA1949.313

Salmina-Haskell 1989, no. 72

Levitan is regarded as Russia's foremost painter of landscape. He studied at the Moscow School of Painting and became a teacher at the school from 1898. On stylistic grounds this study can be placed late in Levitan's career. It probably dates from the autumn of 1898 when Levitan was staying on Lake Senezh in Central Russia.

Bernardino Licinio
(c. 1490 – after 1549)

Portrait of a young Man with a Skull

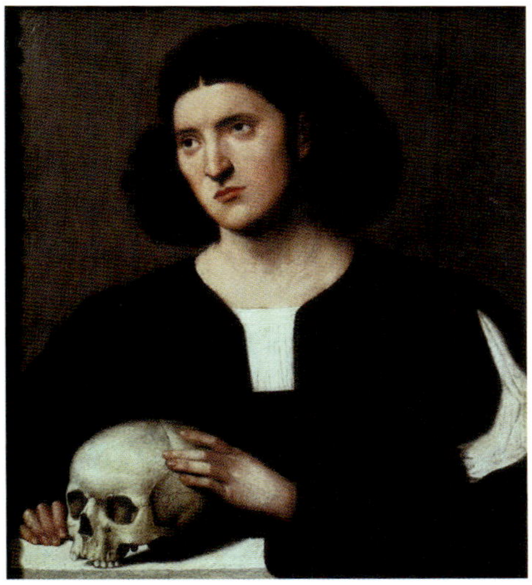

A721; oil on canvas, 75.7 × 63.3 cm
Prov.: Cardinal Ludovico Ludovisi (?); Thomas Howard, Earl of Arundel (?); Louisa, Lady Ashburton; by descent to 5th Marquess of Northampton; Sir William Farrer
Bequeathed by Gaspard O. Farrer through the National Art Collections Fund, 1946; WA1946.199

Lloyd 1977, pp. 98–100

Licinio was impressed by the art of Giorgione, exploring the type of poetic portrait that he and artists in his circle had developed. Youth and beauty are contrasted with death and decay in this expressive portrait of c. 1510–5. The sitter was traditionally thought to be a woman, due to overpainting which was removed in 1956.

John Linnell
(1792 – 1882)

The Assumption of the Virgin

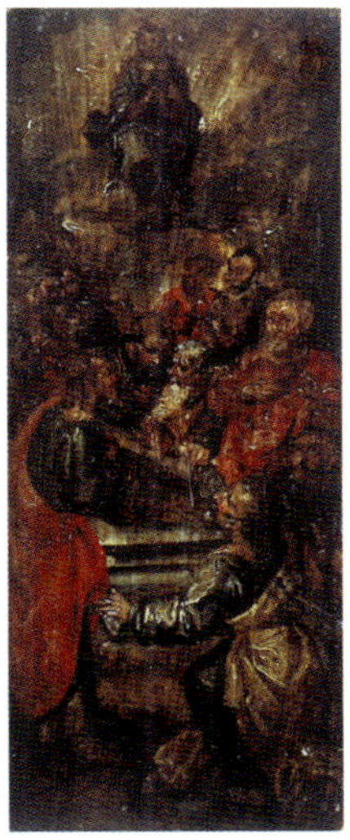

A204; oil on panel, 25 × 10 cm
Chambers Hall Gift, 1855; WA1855.223

Apparently copied from an Old Master painting and probably dating from the late 1820s.

John Linnell
(1792 – 1882)

Sketch for 'Christ's Appearance to the Two Disciples journeying to Emmaus'

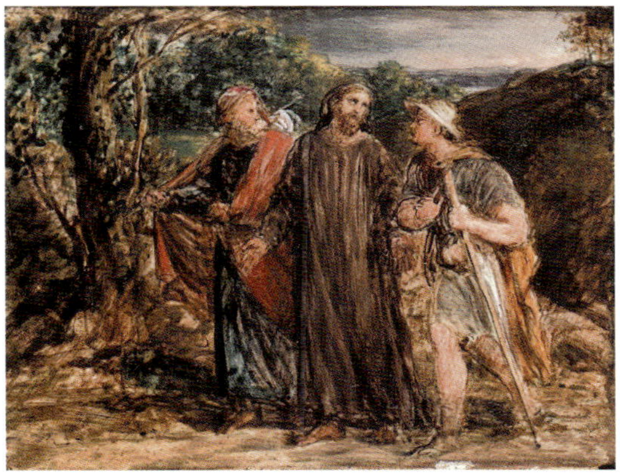

A401; tempera on panel, 17 × 21 cm
Bequeathed by the Revd William Fothergill Robinson through the National Art Collections Fund, 1929; WA1929.34

A study for the following. It was executed in the experimental medium Linnell and the 'Ancients' were trying in the late 1820s.

John Linnell
(1792 – 1882)

View of Southampton

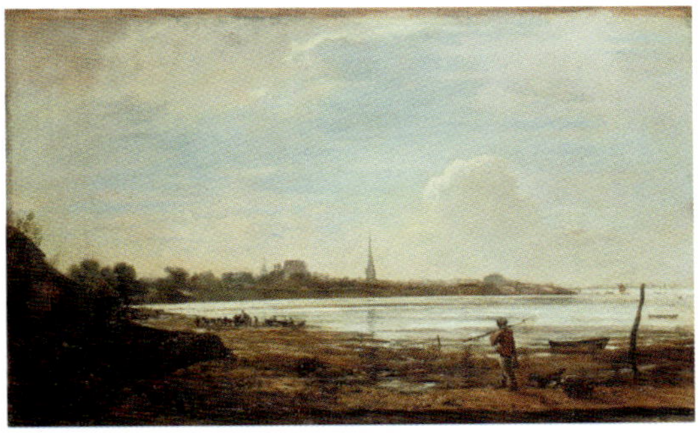

A203; oil on canvas, 46 × 79 cm
Prov.: given to David Charles Read
Chambers Hall Gift, 1855; WA1855.205

Linnell travelled to Southampton in August 1819 at the invitation of D.C. Read and remained until October. This view of Southampton was probably made during this visit; several related drawings survive. Read later sold it to his patron, Chambers Hall.

John Linnell
(1792 – 1882)

The Supper at Emmaus

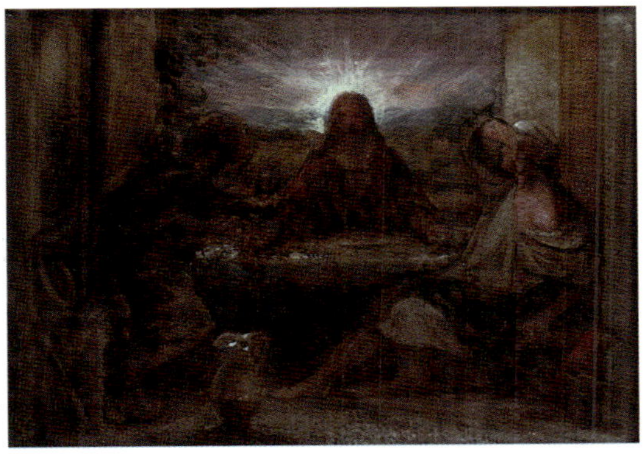

A1138; oil and watercolours on panel, 20.5 × 30.4 cm
Presented by David Gammer, 1986; WA1986.73

Presumably dating from the late 1820s and painted in a similar experimental medium to the following.

John Linnell
(1792 – 1882)

Christ's Appearance to the Two Disciples journeying to Emmaus

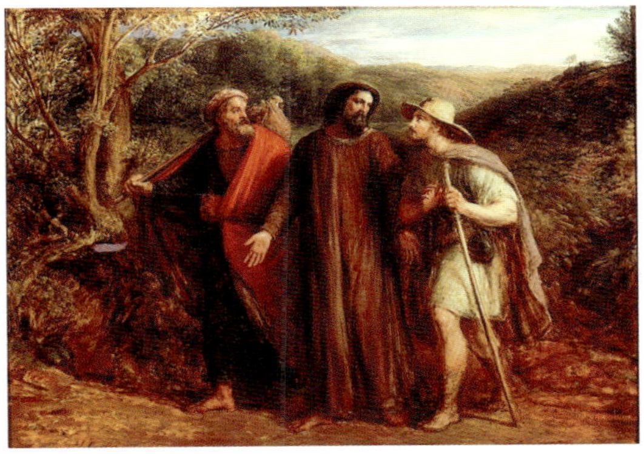

A1003; oil on panel, 56 × 78 cm
Signed and dated: *J. Linnell f. 1835*
Prov.: Art Union; Revd Edward Daniell and by descent
Bequeathed by Mrs Ruby Lambe, 1963; WA1963.122

One of Linnell's most important religious paintings, this was exhibited at the Royal Academy in 1835 and sold to the Art Union for the purposes of engraving in 1838. It was based on sketches made in 1829, when Linnell was closely associated with the 'Ancients' at Shoreham. Samuel Palmer was the model for the disciple on the right. The source is Luke 25: 13–35.

John Linnell
(1792 – 1882)

John Varley

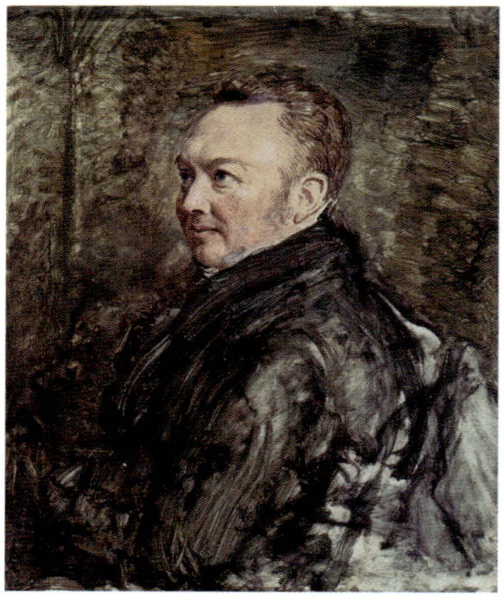

Oil on board, mounted as a drawing, 23.6 × 18.5 cm
Purchased (Hope Fund), 1963; WA1963.54

John Linnell became a pupil of John Varley (1778–1842) in 1804 and was close to him for the rest of his life. Varley introduced him to many artists, including William Mulready, who was to have a formative influence on his art. In a celebrated drawing of 1821 (Fitzwilliam Museum, Cambridge), Linnell drew William Blake and Varley together in animated discussion. This portrait of his master, in very thin oil paint and pencil, probably dates from *c.* 1830.

Lorenzo Lippi
(1606 – 1665)

An Allegory of Innocence

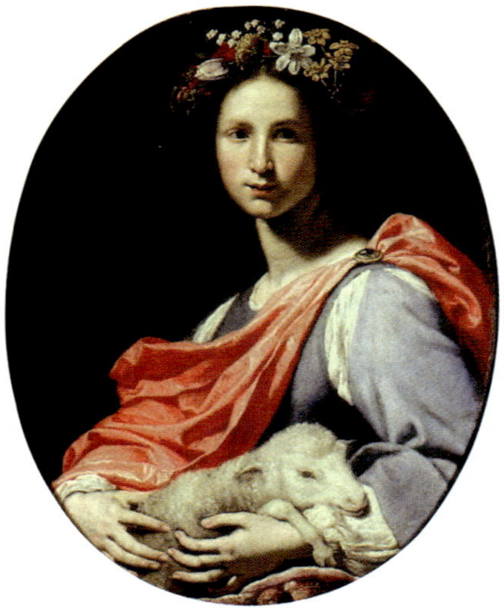

A667; oil on canvas, 74.5 × 59.6 cm
Prov.: E. Trevelyan Turner; H.M. Calmann
Purchased with the assistance of Francis Falconer Madan, 1940; WA1940.22

McCorquodale 1979, no. 32

Innocence as described by Cesare Ripa (*Iconologia* 1611, p. 255) is shown as a young girl, dressed in white, with a garland of flowers and holding a lamb. According to Filippo Baldinucci, Lippi painted portraits of six of the twelve daughters of Agnolo Galli . The same sitter appears in the *Triumph of David*, a group portrait of the Galli family commissioned from Lippi in 1656.

Andrea Locatelli
(1695 – 1741)

Landscape with a wounded Bandit and other Figures

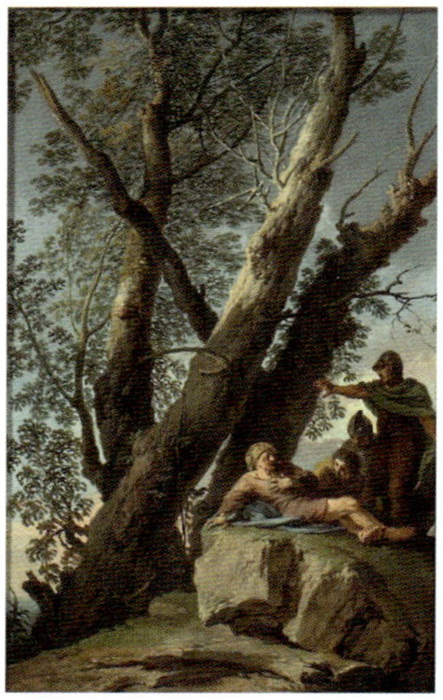

A117; oil on canvas, 48.5 × 30.5 cm
Inscribed with monogram: *AL*
Bequeathed by the Revd Dr Thomas Penrose, 1851
WA1851.14

Busiri Vici 1976, no. 151

See under A117. By 1724, as reported by Nicola Pio, cabinet paintings by Locatelli were in great demand from both Romans and foreign visitors to Rome. A specialist in picturesque or classical landscape, Locatelli briefly rivalled Panini in reputation.

Fra Filippo Lippi
(*c.* 1406 – 1469)

The Meeting at the Golden Gate

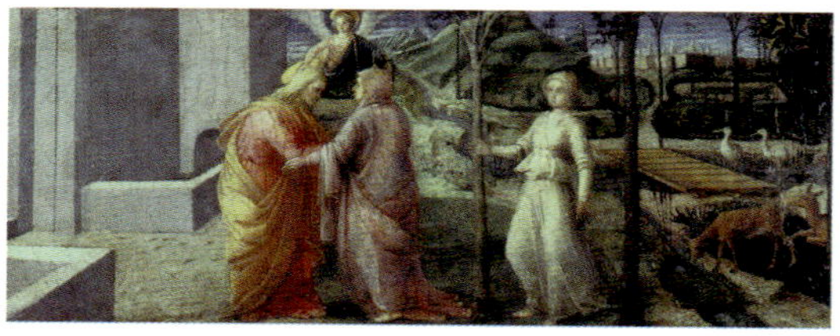

A81; tempera and gilding on panel, 21.9 × 49.7 cm
Fox-Strangways Gift, 1850; WA1850.8

Lloyd 1997, pp. 100–2; Ruda 1999, no. 28

The apocryphal subject of the reunion of Joachim and Anna, with the help of the Angel Gabriel, signifies the miraculous conception of the Virgin Mary. The iconography is unusual, since normally Anna emerges from the Golden Gate of Jerusalem to meet Joachim on his return from the mountains. The animals and birds may incorporate references to Psalm 42. A81 was probably painted *c.* 1440–45 as part of the predella of an altar-piece and it has been conjecturally associated with *The Annunciation*, now in the Alte Pinakothek, Munich.

Andrea Locatelli
(1695 – 1741)

Landscape with Bandits and a Dog

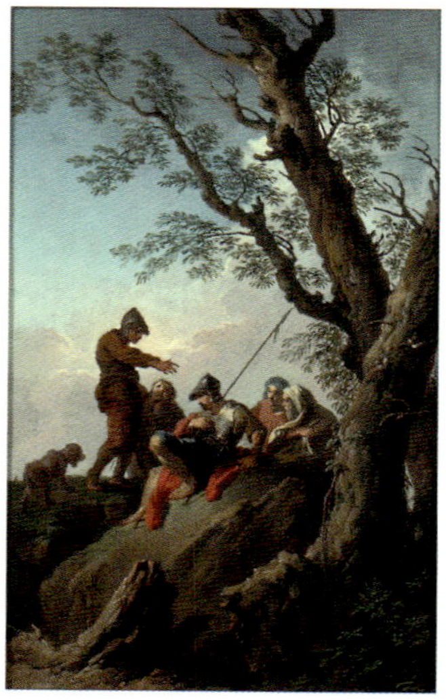

A116; oil on canvas, 48.5 × 30.5 cm
Bequeathed by the Revd Dr Thomas Penrose, 1851; WA1851.13

Busiri Vici 1976, no. 150

Although originally accessioned as Locatelli, the paintings were attributed to Panini until cleaning in 1946 revealed the monogram on A117. Dating from *c.* 1725–30, these companion pieces show Locatelli working in the picturesque manner of Salvator Rosa.

Gustave Loiseau
(1865 – 1935)

Landscape at Incarville

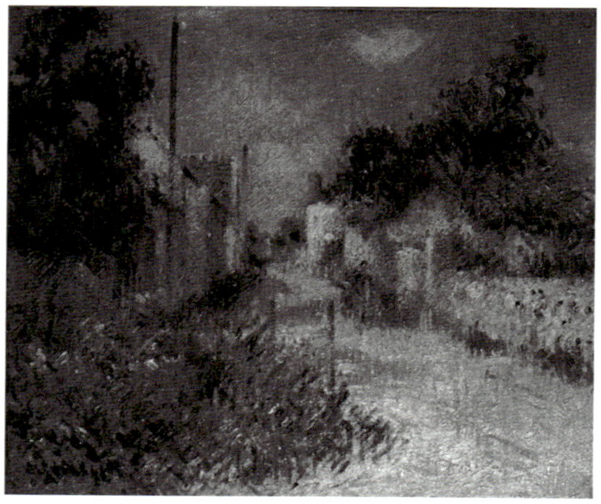

A1006; oil on canvas, 45 × 55 cm
Signed: *Loiseau*
Bequeathed by Major Thomas Bouch, 1963; WA1963.150.3

The splintered, cross-hatched touches of paint are characteristic of Loiseau's brushwork from the early 1920s onwards. This view perhaps dates from *c.* 1923 when he was working in the area of Incarville, a village located in the Eure.

ANONYMOUS LOMBARD ARTIST
(*c.* 1520 – 30)

Three Putti with musical Instruments

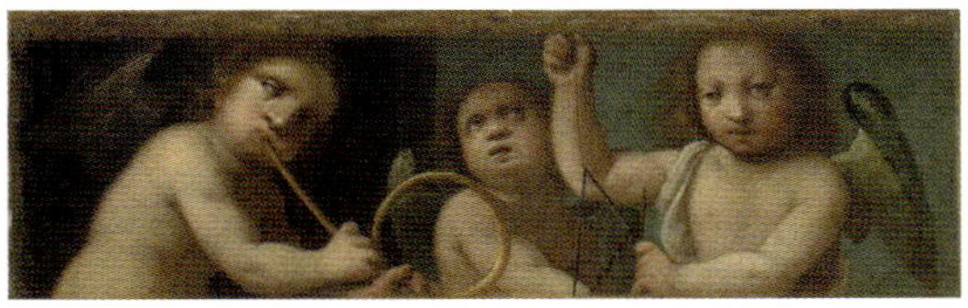

A141; oil on canvas laid on panel, 14.5 × 44 cm
Chambers Hall Gift, 1855; WA1855.582

Lloyd 1977, pp. 102–3

Acquired by Chambers Hall as Bernardino Luini, A141 is closer in style to Gaudenzio Ferrari, while also displaying affinities with Zenale. Presumably it formed part of a larger decorative scheme.

Follower of PIETRO LONGHI
(1702 – 1785)

A Procurator of San Marco receiving a Petition

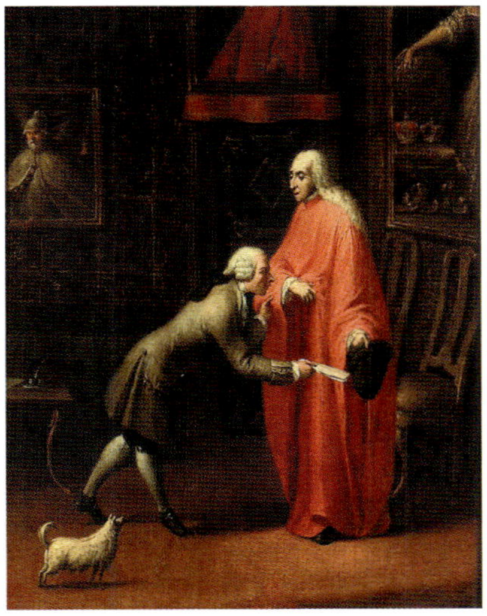

A329; oil on canvas, 59 × 46 cm
Purchased, 1911; WA1911.2

Pignatti 1974, no. 381

Presiding over this scene of diplomacy is an imperial portrait, perhaps of the Empress Elizabeth Petrovna of Russia. While the artist is close to the Maestro del Ridotto, a follower of Longhi whose work is characterised by thin, elongated figures and an uncertain grasp of perspective, A329 is of better quality.

PHILIP JAMES DE LOUTHERBOURG
(1740 – 1812)

The Angel appearing to the Shepherds

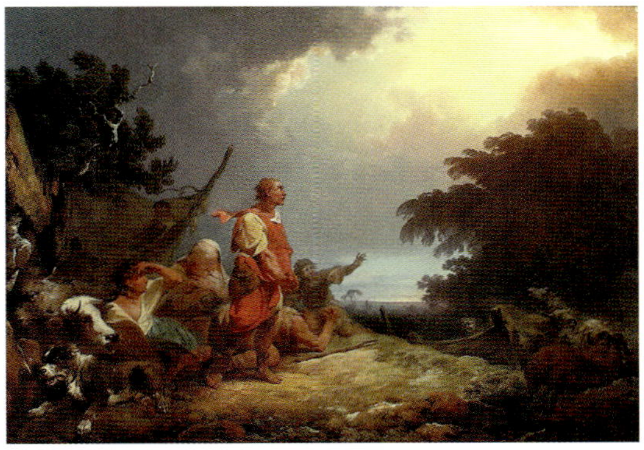

A136; oil on canvas, 40 × 56 cm
Prov.: Hubert Robert
Bequeathed by the Revd Dr Thomas Penrose, 1851; WA1851.19

This is one of a number of religious subjects painted in France in the 1760s. The domestic treatment of the theme suggests the artist's liking for Dutch 17th-century art.

EDWIN LONGSDEN LONG
(1829 – 1891)

Study for the Portrait of Ernest Renan

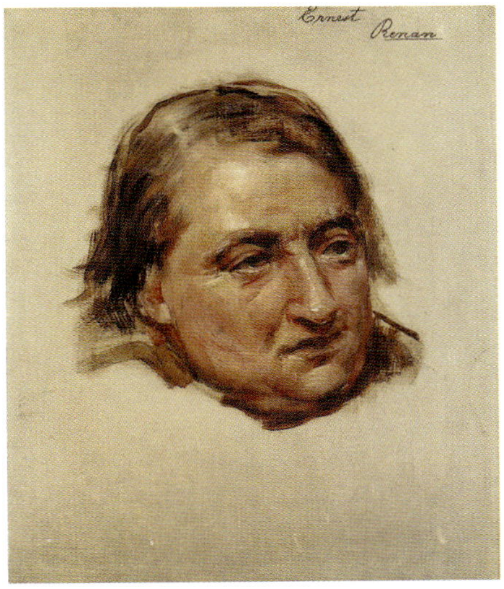

A1027a; oil over black chalk on canvas, mounted as a drawing, 36.4 × 30.6 cm
Inscribed: *Ernest Renan*
Prov.: A. Lucas; Mrs Seymour Lucas
Presented by K.E.G. Bonfiglioli; WA1966.51

Bills 1998, no. 168.1

An inscription on the old mount records that this study of the French author Ernest Renan (1823–1892) was painted in 1880, when Renan was delivering the Hobbert Lectures in London. There is no evidence that the full-size painting was ever completed.

LORENZO DI CREDI
(*c.* 1457 – 1536)

The Virgin and Child

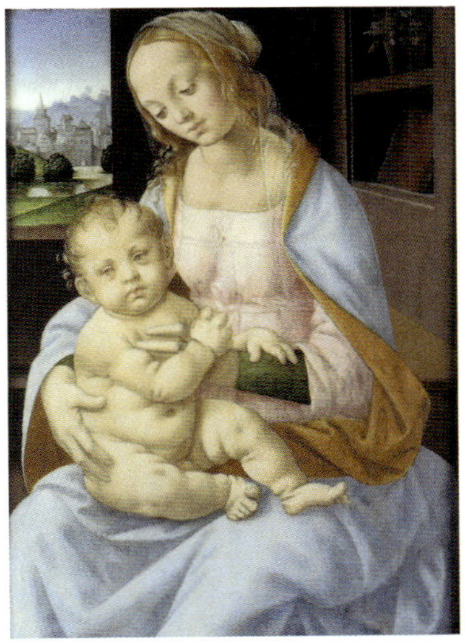

A103; oil and tempera on panel, 57.2 × 39.3 cm
Fox-Strangways Gift, 1850; WA1850.4

Lloyd 1977, pp. 103–4

A pupil of Verrocchio, Lorenzo looked to Florentine marble relief sculpture as a source for the composition of this devotional picture, while the detailed landscape reflects his interest in Flemish art. The painting appears to be unfinished. Two other panels of *The Virgin and Child*, in the Musée des Beaux-Arts, Strasbourg and the Musée Fesch, Ajaccio, are similar in design and the same cartoon may have been used for the figures.

Attributed to PHILIP JAMES DE LOUTHERBOURG
(1740 – 1812)

Landscape with a fortified Gateway

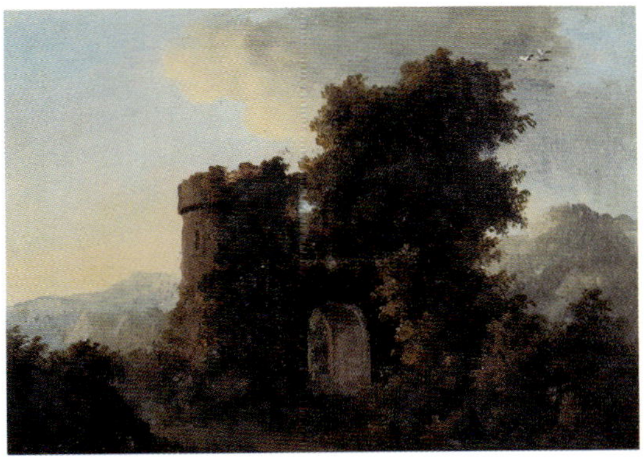

A940; oil on cartridge paper, mounted as a drawing, 12.5 × 17.3 cm
Presented by Mrs G.W. Morris, in memory of Guy Wilfrid and Hilary Jolliffe Morris, 1961; WA1961.1.1

The attribution of this sketch and the following is traditional but difficult to support by comparison with Loutherbourg's known landscapes.

Attributed to PHILIP JAMES DE LOUTHERBOURG
(1740 – 1812)

Landscape with a Waterfall

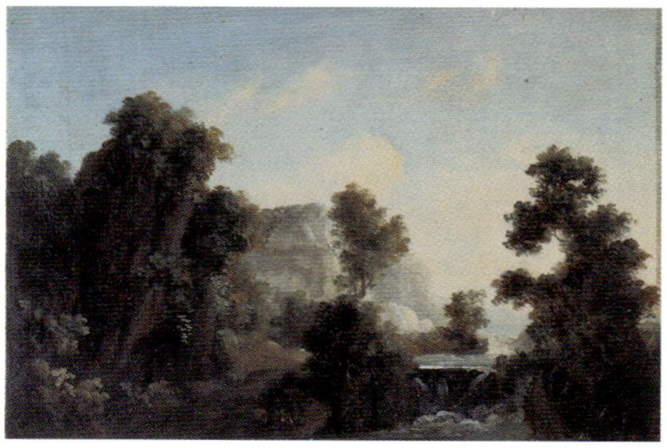

A941; oil on cartridge paper, mounted as a drawing, 12.1 × 17.6 cm
Presented by Mrs G.W. Morris, in memory of Guy Wilfrid and Hilary Jolliffe Morris, 1961; WA1961.1.2

A companion to the preceding.

THOMAS LUNY
(1759 – 1837)

The Engagement between H.M.S. Phoenix and the French Frigate Didon, 10 August 1805

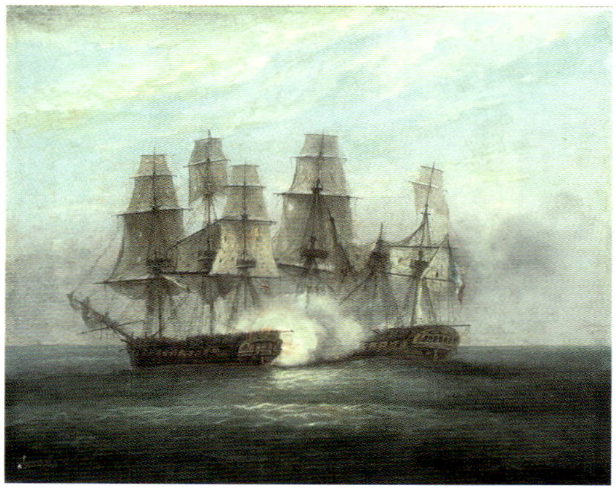

A353a; oil on canvas, 46 × 56 cm
Signed and dated: *Luny 1829*
Bequeathed by the Revd Henry Fanshawe Tozer, 1916; ANT1916.23

Luny served in the Royal Navy during the Napoleonic Wars and retired to Teignemouth in 1807. From that date until his death, he painted over 2,200 pictures, many of engagements he had experienced at first hand. H.M.S. Phoenix defeated the French ship Didon off Cape Finistère on 10 August 1805. The French flag was afterwards presented to Aaron Tozer who was wounded in the engagement, and is now in the Ashmolean.

NEVIL OLIVER LUPTON
(1828 – after 1877)

The Harvest Field

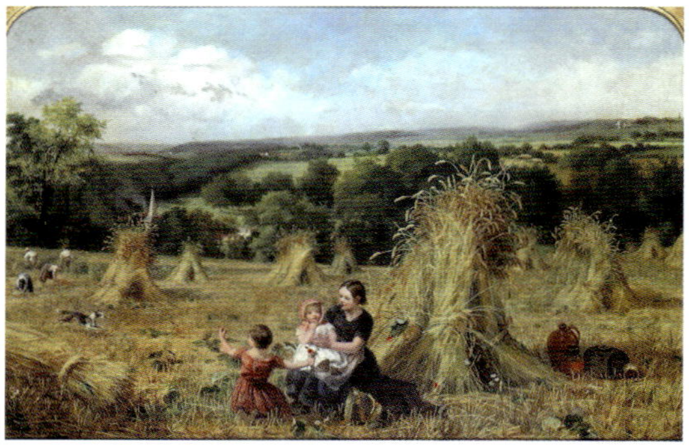

A706; oil on canvas, 41 × 61 cm
Signed and dated: *Nevil O. Lupton. 1857–8*; and initialled on the cask: *NOL 58*
Prov.: George Ruddall
Purchased, 1943; WA1943.3

Payne 1993, no. 31

A characteristic work by Lupton, who specialised in landscapes and genre paintings, depicting in bright colours a dream of pastoral happiness in the Victorian countryside. This painting was exhibited at the Royal Academy in 1858.

THOMAS ESMOND LOWINSKY
(1892 – 1947)

Miss Avril Turner

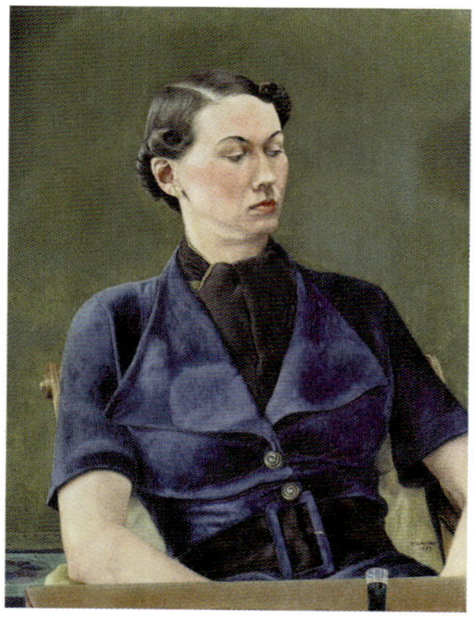

A766; oil on canvas, 43.5 × 32.8 cm
Signed and dated: *T.Lowinsky 1937*
Presented by Mrs Ruth Lowinsky, 1948; WA1948.80

Eustace 1999, no. 28

A series of portraits, begun in the early 1930s, marks the point where Lowinsky turned from his previous imaginative figure compositions to portraiture. All the sitters in the series have pursed, closed lips and a rather bored attitude. The sitter, Avril Constance Turner, was born in 1916 and must have been twenty or twenty-one at the date of her portrait.

THOMAS LUNY
(1759 – 1837)

H.M.S. Victorious taking the Rivoli, 22 February 1812

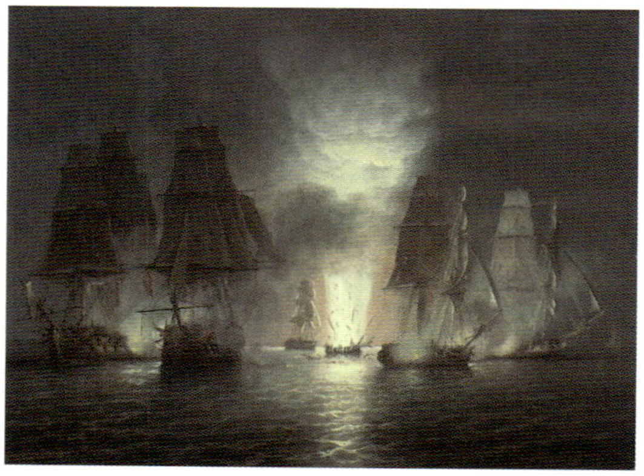

A353b; oil on canvas, 38 × 51 cm
Signed and dated: *Luny 1833*
Bequeathed by the Revd Henry Fanshawe Tozer, 1916; ANT1916.24

Another painting by Luny of this engagement is in the National Maritime Museum.

ABRAHAM DE LUST
(active *c.* 1650 – after 1659)

Still Life of a Peach and Grapes

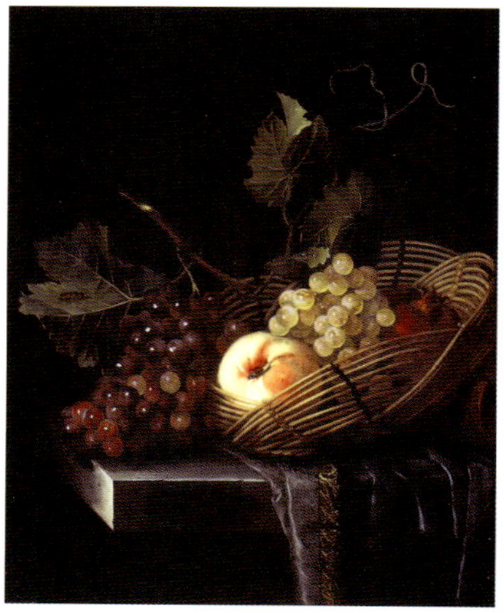

A575; oil on canvas, 56 × 45 cm
Signed: *a.d.lust*
Daisy Linda Ward Bequest, 1939; WA1940.2.51

Meijer 2003, no. 52

The painter who signed his name *a. d. lust* in gothic script is probably the painter, Abraham de Lust, who is recorded in Leeuwarden in 1659 and later in Germany. He may also be the same de Lust who was in Lyon in 1656. This is one of his few still-life paintings of fruit. The use of a gold-fringed blue table cloth, folded to reveal the underside, is a characteristic of French still-life paintings. It has been dated to the mid 1650s.

Abraham de Lust
(active c.1650 – after 1659)

A Vase of Flowers

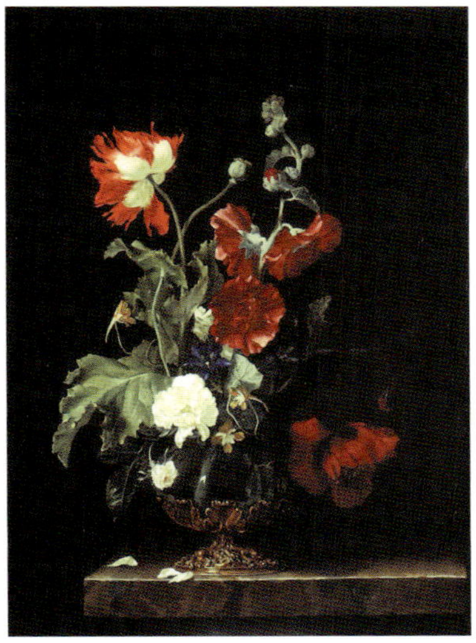

A574; oil on canvas, 66.5 × 53.5 cm
Inscribed: *R. Ruysch 166..*
Daisy Linda Ward Bequest, 1939; WA1940.2.50

Meijer 2003, no. 53

The rich vase, centrally placed, recalls the work of Jean Michel Picart, a Flemish painter of flowers who had worked in France since 1632. Several similar vases appear in de Lust's paintings. The 'signature' is clearly wrong. The date is too early for Rachel Ruysch who was born in 1664 but would fit plausibly with the little that is known about de Lust.

Dugald Sutherland MacColl
(1859 – 1948)

Self-portrait

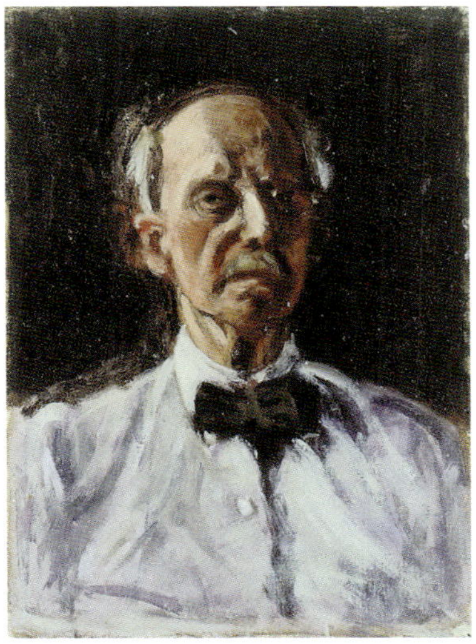

A1050; oil on canvas board, mounted on board, 35.2 × 25.3 cm
Purchased (Hope Fund), 1968; WA1968.457

MacColl is better known as art critic, writer and founding member of the National Art Collections Fund, than as a painter. He was also Keeper of the Tate Gallery (1906–11) and of the Wallace Collection (1911–24). Despite his other commitments, he exhibited with the English Art Club and continued painting throughout his life. He was one of the most important advocates of Impressionist painting in Britain. His own self-portrait illustrates his view that technique and painting method are more important that representational content.

Nicolaes Maes
(1634 – 1693)

Still Life of Fruit in a Formal Garden

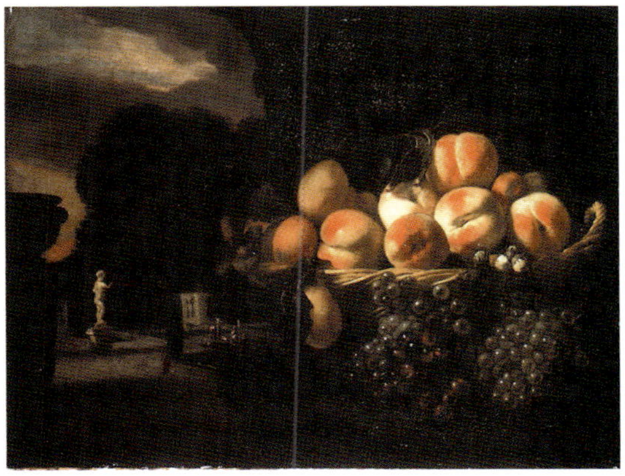

A577; oil on canvas, 56 × 72 cm
Inscribed: *A. Cuyp. f*
Prov.: Pieter Quinting; A. van Strij; P. Norton; Mrs A. Mitchell
Daisy Linda Ward Bequest, 1939; WA1940.2.53

Meijer 2003, no. 55

Apart from an early painting of a branch of peaches, this is the only still life which is generally attributed to Maes. The addition of Cuyp's name was probably inspired by similarities between this painting and works by Abraham Calraet which were, at one time, attributed to Cuyp.

Simon Luttichuys
(1610 – 1661)

Still Life with Fruit and Roses

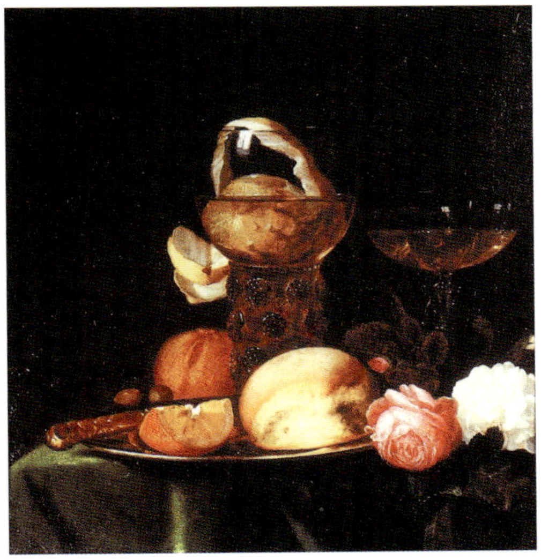

A576; oil on canvas, 42 × 40 cm
Signed in monogram: *S.Lf*
Daisy Linda Ward Bequest, 1939; WA1940.2.52

Meijer 2003, no. 54

Luttichuys is known to have painted portraits but all his identified surviving works are still-life compositions. Around the mid-1640s he painted a number of *vanitas* subjects in a somewhat monochromatic manner but in the late 1640s turned suddenly to works like this still life which are often placed against a dark background with a few strong colour accents.

Nicolaes Maes
(1634 – 1693)

A Man holding a Carnation to a Woman's Nose: An Allegory of the Sense of Smell

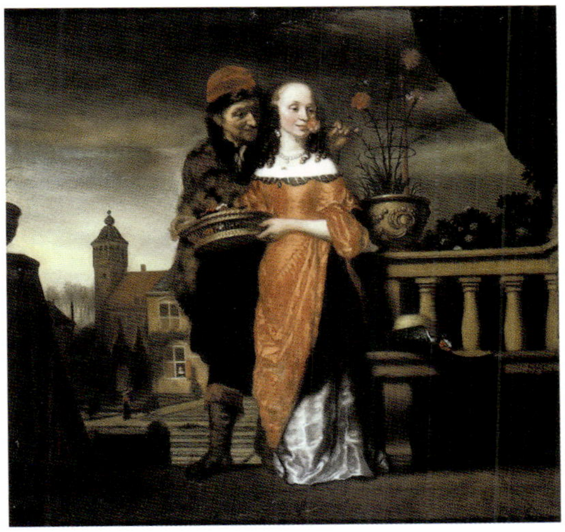

A355; oil on canvas, 59 × 62 cm
Presented by Mrs W.F.R. Weldon, 1917; WA1917.1

White 1999, p. 79

This painting must date from before *c.* 1660 when Maes abandoned his early career as a painter of genre scenes and religious works and devoted himself to painting portraits. The dark, rich colour and heavy brushwork indicate a debt to Rembrandt, with whom Maes is said to have studied in the late 1640s.

Francesco Maffei
(*c.* 1605 – 1660)

The Adoration of the Shepherds

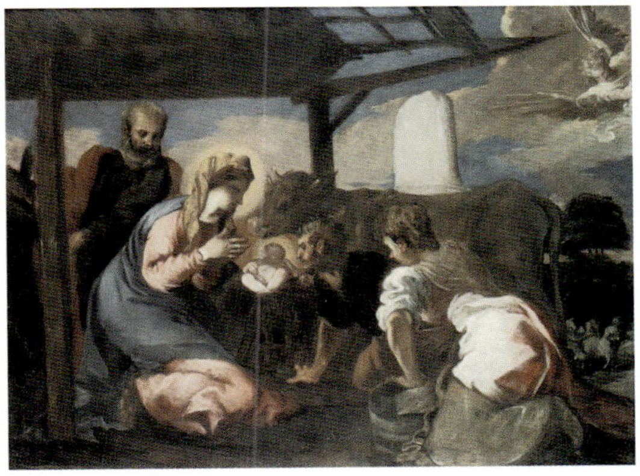

A922; oil on canvas, 72 × 95 cm
Purchased, 1958; WA1958.22

Rossi 1991, no. 51

Bassano, Tintoretto and Veronese were important influences on Maffei's art, while his mature work is rich in drama, brilliant colour and imaginative innovations. A922, with its characteristically sketchy handling, probably dates from the 1650s, with the artist paying homage to Bassano both in the design and figure types.

Alessandro Magnasco (1667 – 1749) and Antonio Francesco Peruzzini (c. 1668 – 1724)

Landscape with two hermits in meditation

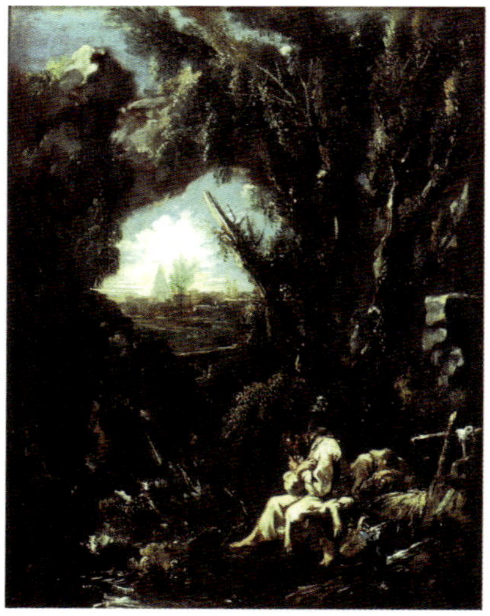

A359; oil on canvas, 94 × 73 cm
Prov.: Tancred Borenius
Purchased (Magdalen College Fund), 1919; WA1919.30

Muti and De Sarno Prignano 1994, no. R 350

While monks and hermits were no more than picturesque figures in later 17th-century landscapes, Magnasco often treated these intense ascetic figures more seriously. Here, the nervous handling of paint and the vivid description of detail in the two figures is characteristic of Magnasco. It is likely that the landscape is by Peruzzini and the figures are by Magnasco, painted c. 1700–10.

Aristide-Joseph-Bonaventure Maillol (1861 – 1944)

In the western Pyrenées

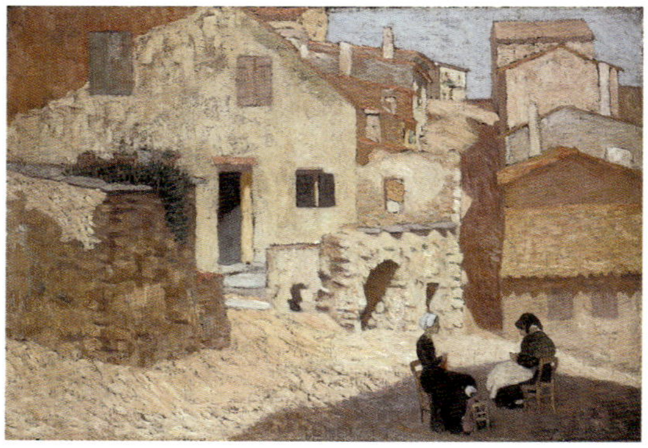

A1068; oil on canvas, 46 × 65 cm
Signed and inscribed: *a Maillol pyrenées / orientales*
Bequeathed by Lt-Col G.E. Bouskell-Wade, 1972; WA1972.161

Lorquin 2001, no. 14

Maillol was born at Banyuls-sur-Mer in south-east France near the Spanish border. He moved to Paris in 1881 to study painting but retained links with his locality. This is one of a number of views painted in strong sunlight by Mailliol in the western Pyrenees in the mid-1880s.

Attributed to Mair von Landshut (active 1485 – d. 1510)

Portrait of a young Woman holding a Flower

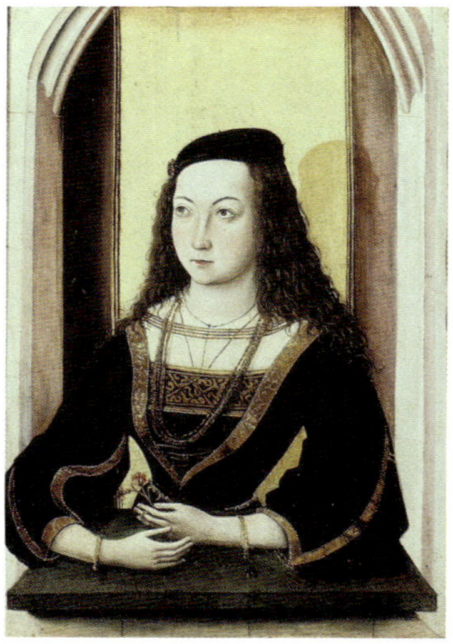

A1046; oil on panel, 61 × 41 cm
Prov.: Jacob Goldschmidt; Walter Rappolt
Bequeathed by William W. Spooner, 1968; WA1968.136

White 1999, p. 81

This painting is the work of an accomplished late 15th-century artist from South Germany but the attribution to the engraver, Mair von Landshut, is far from certain. Very few paintings by Mair have been identified and there is little to compare. It was possibly paired at one time with a portrait of a husband or fiancé.

Charles Cyril Mahoney (1903 – 1968)

Yellow Ox-eye Daisies

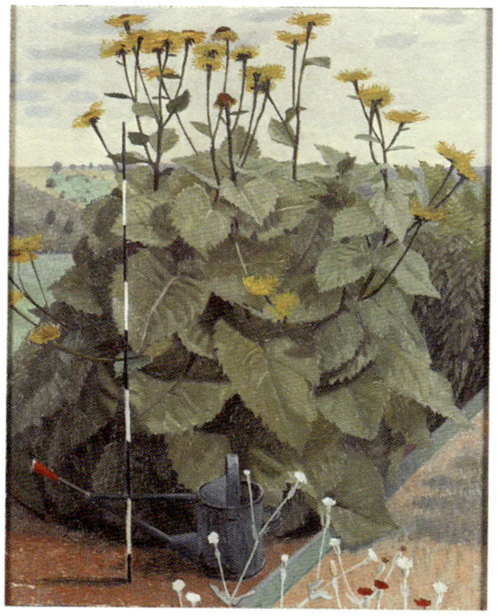

A1082; oil on board, 47 × 36.9 cm
Presented by Mrs Dorothy Mahoney, the artist's widow, 1976; WA1976.63

Mahoney, who taught at the Royal Academy Schools, endows a naturalistically painted plant with an air of magic. This painting, executed in quick but controlled brush-strokes, represents a clump of ox-eye daisies in a garden, but with an outlook into a rural landscape behind, including a surveyor's wooden rod to mark the exact height of the plant.

Juan Bautista Maino (1581 – 1641)

Portrait of a Monk

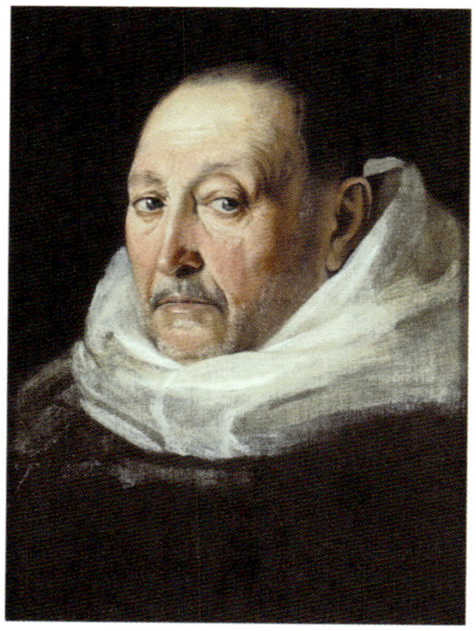

A802; oil on canvas, 47 × 33.3 cm
Prov.: Tomás Harris, London
Bequeathed by Percy Moore Turner, 1951; WA1951.161

Angulo Iñiguez and Pérez Sánchez 1969, no. 53

Formerly attributed to Hals, Rubens, Velázquez and Zurbarán, this striking picture was identified as a rare portrait by Maino in 1933. It has been suggested that it is a self-portrait, since Maino became a Dominican friar in 1613. However, the sitter may be a Camaldolese monk.

Roy de Maistre (1894 – 1968)

Christ falling under the Weight of the Cross

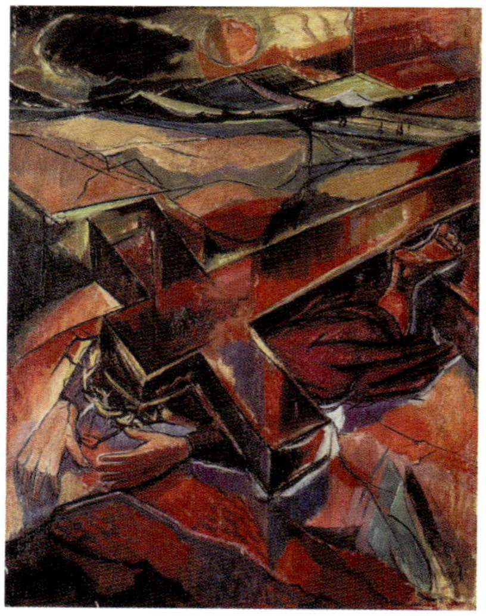

A1131; oil on canvas, 80 × 61 cm
Signed: *R. de M*
Presented by Sir John Rothenstein through the Friends of the Ashmolean, 1984; WA1984.61.1

The subject is not common in modern religious paintings. Christ fell several times on the road to Calvary, but De Maistre does not represent the moment of the actual fall or the surrounding crowd. Christ unusually appears in an apparently deserted landscape.

Paul Fordyce Maitland
(1863 – 1909)

Kensington Gardens

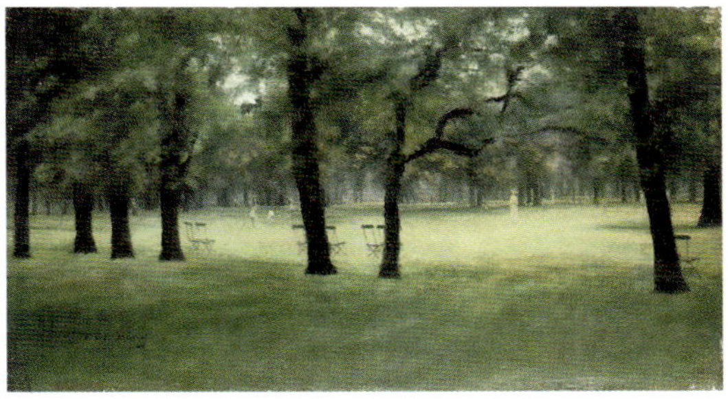

A978; oil on canvas, 26 × 46 cm
Signed: *Maitland*
Madan Bequest, 1962; WA1962.17.20

McConkey 1995, no. 129

Maitland was a disciple of both Whistler and Theodore Roussel and spent most of his short working life painting the streets of Chelsea and views in Kensington Gardens. This work has been dated *c.* 1890 and typically shows the park almost empty save for some diminutive figures in the distance.

Paul Fordyce Maitland
(1863 – 1909)

A House seen through Trees

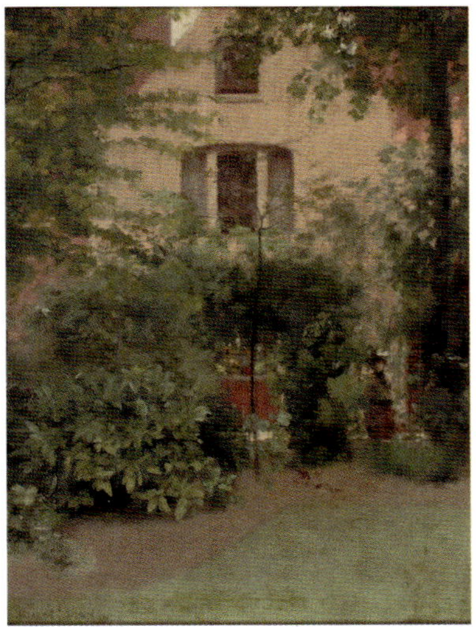

A977; oil on canvas, 41 × 31 cm
Signed: *Maitland*
Madan Bequest, 1962; WA1962.17.19

The woman, half-concealed by the trees, is the artist's mother.

Édouard Manet
(1832 – 1883)

A Garden Urn

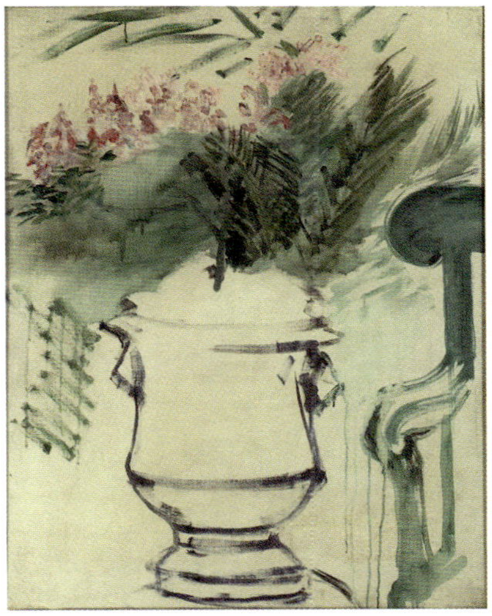

A1118a; oil on canvas, 78 × 60 cm
Prov.: Mme Manet; Hermann Paechter; Max Liebermann
Accepted by H.M. Government in lieu of Inheritance Tax from the estate of Dr and Mrs Richard Walzer and allocated to the Ashmolean Museum, 1980; WA1981.11.1

Rouart and Wildenstein 1975, no. 402

This seems to be a large study for the left side of *In the Conservatory* (Nationalgalerie, Berlin), painted in the studio of the Swedish painter, Otto Rosen, which Manet occupied in 1878–9.

Paul Fordyce Maitland
(1863 – 1909)

Beech Trees at Sunset, Kensington Gardens

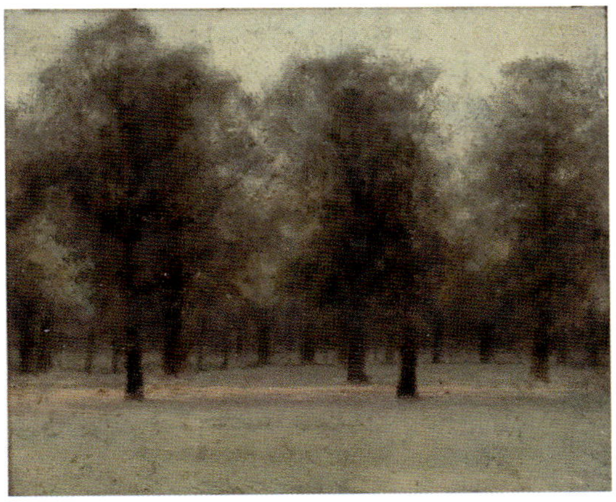

A952; oil on panel, 15 × 19 cm
Painted in 1905.
Bequeathed by J.E. Bullard, 1961; WA1961.31

Édouard Manet
(1832 – 1883)

Landscape with a Village Church

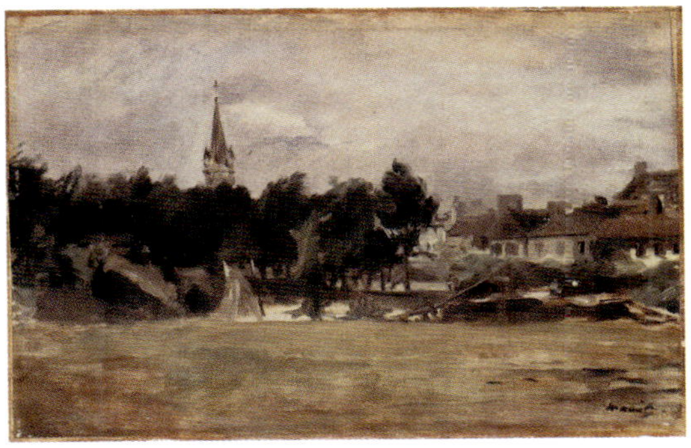

A624; oil on canvas, 30 × 44 cm
Signed: *Manet*
Hindley Smith Bequest, 1939; WA1940.1.6

Pure landscape is not common in Manet's work despite his friendship with the Impressionists. The subdued colour and light, thin brushwork suggests that this view of an unidentified town dates from the early 1870s.

Édouard Manet
(1832 – 1883)

A Basket of Pears

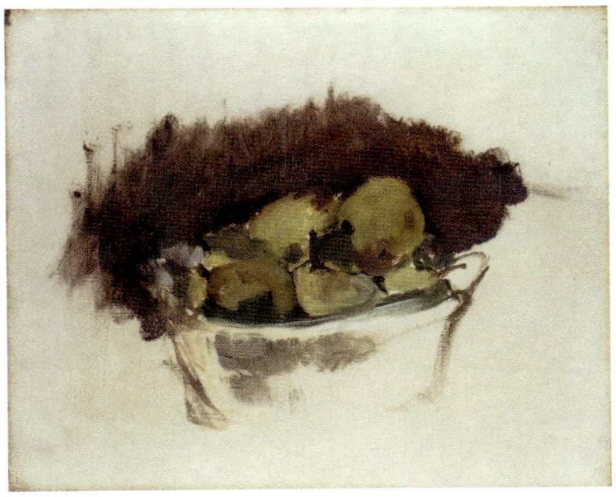

A1114; oil on canvas, 42.2 × 51.1 cm
Prov.: Hermann Paechter; Max Liebermann, Berlin; Bruno Cassirer, Berlin
Accepted by H.M. Government from the estate of Dr and Mrs Richard Walzer in lieu of Inheritance Tax and allocated to the Ashmolean Museum, 1980; WA1980.80

Rouart and Wildenstein 1975, no. 412

The same basket of pears appears in a more finished painting in the Ordrupgaard Museum, Denmark.

James Bolivar Manson
(1879 – 1945)

Lucien Pissarro reading

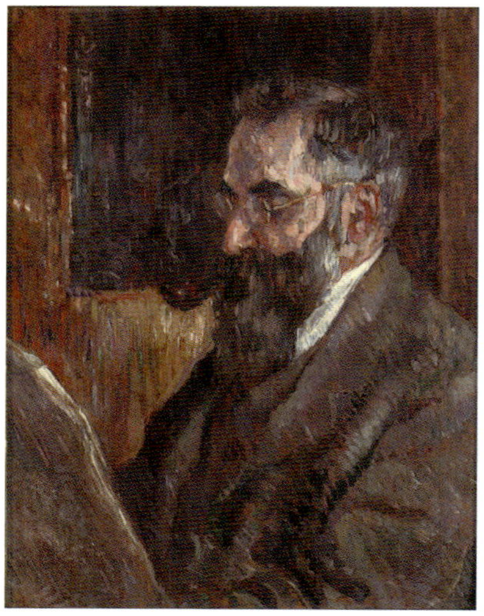

A1000; oil on panel, 45 × 35 cm
Prov.: Lucien Pissarro
Presented by Miss Mary Manson and Mrs Jean Goullett, the artist's daughters, 1963; WA1963.44

Manson met Lucien Pissarro in 1910 and they became good friends. They later went on painting expeditions together and, as a member of staff of the Tate Gallery from 1912 to 1938, Manson was influential in promoting Pissarro's interests. This informal portrait of Pissarro reading and smoking a pipe may date from August 1913, when they rented Western House, near Rye and painted in the vicinity. Manson painted another portrait of Lucien in 1939.

James Bolivar Manson
(1879 – 1945)

Miss I. Aylward Lord

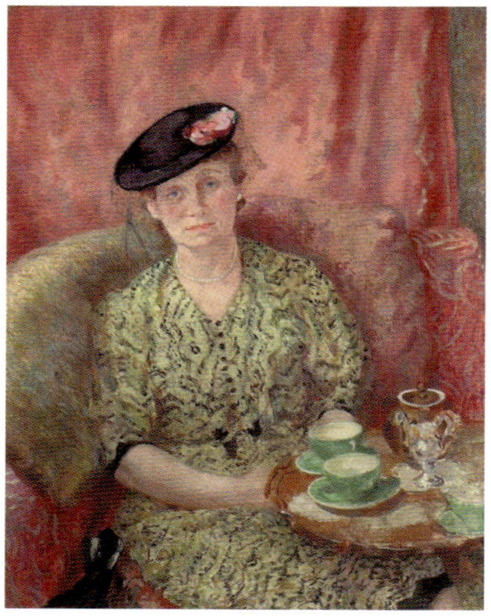

A1016; oil on canvas, 90 × 70 cm
Presented by the sitter, 1964; WA1964.59

The sitter was the owner of the family business of Isaac Lord, Maltsters, Colchester. This portrait was painted in 1939.

Carlo Maratta
(1625 – 1713)

The Visitation

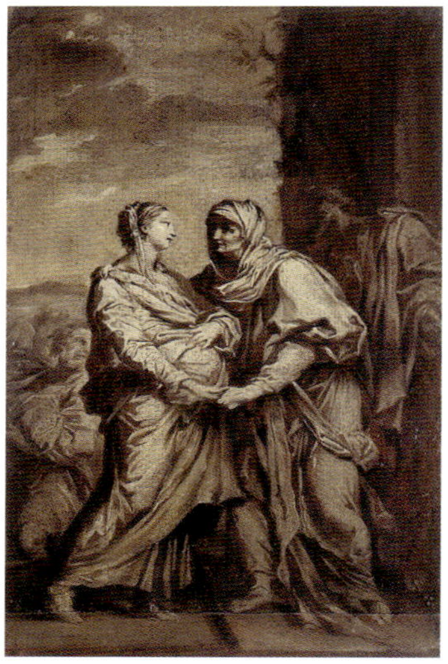

Oil on paper, mounted as a drawing, 30.5 × 19.9 cm
Prov.: Ercole Lelli; R. Udney; Sir Thomas Lawrence; Samuel Woodburn
Purchased, 1940; WA1940.109

Parker 1956, no. 900; Macandrew 1980, p. 302

After the Annunciation, Mary visits her cousin Elizabeth who will soon give birth to John the Baptist (Luke 1: 36–56). This is a preparatory oil-sketch for a composition which first appears in an etching by Maratta and then, with some changes, in his painting of *c.* 1656 in S. Maria della Pace, Rome.

James Bolivar Manson
(1879 – 1945)

Mrs Crump's Garden

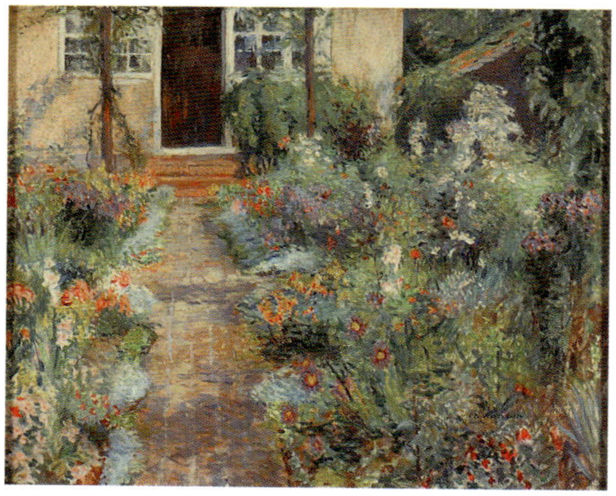

A903a; oil on canvas, 50 × 60 cm
Signed: *J B Manson*
Presented by R.A. Bevan, 1957; WA1957.105

Buckman 1973, p. 27

Charles Crump was an official in the Public Record Office, who lived with his wife near Manson in Hampstead Garden Suburb. He painted a portrait of Crump in 1925 and this view of his wife in their garden at about the same time.

Attributed to Giovanni Mansueti
(active 1484 – d. 1526/7)

The Virgin and Child

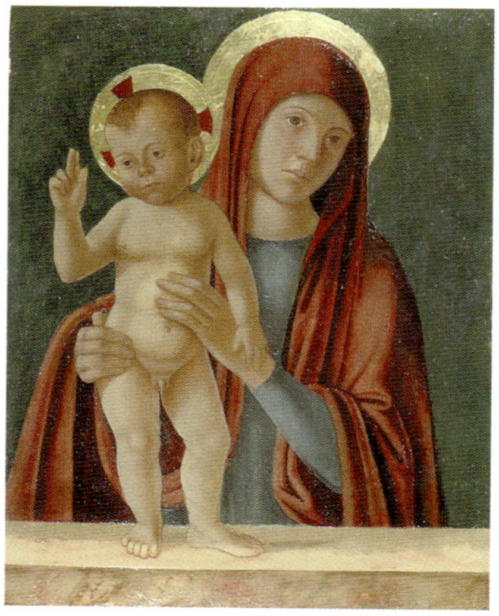

A736b; oil (?) and gilding on panel, 53 × 42 cm
Presented by the daughters of James Reddie Anderson, 1947; WA1947.201

Lloyd 1977, p. 105

The design derives from Giovanni Bellini while the stiff, polished effect, recalling polychrome sculpture, is typical of Venetian devotional paintings of the 1470s and 1480s. The attribution to Mansueti is tentative.

Follower of Carlo Maratta
(1625 – 1713)

The Sacrifice of Noah

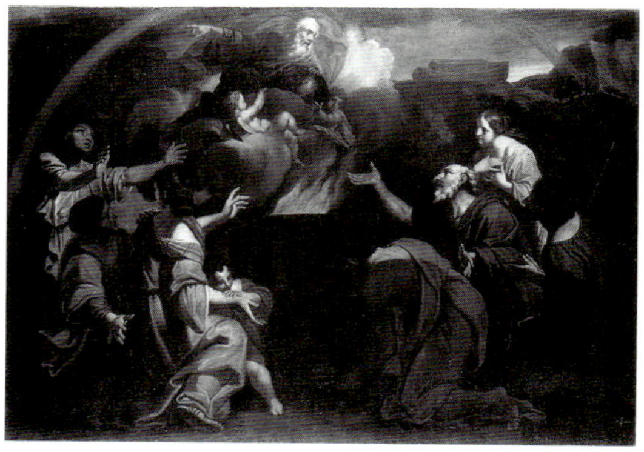

A29; oil on canvas, 118 × 166 cm
Presented by John Cornish, 1759; WA1845.29

Wright 1985–6, p. 161

Noah gives thanks to God for having saved him and his family from the destruction of mankind by flood (Genesis 9: 20–21). On accession, A29 was attributed to Sébastien Bourdon. It has been heavily restored. The composition is based on a popular mid-17th-century design, deriving from Poussin (with numerous variations by Genoese, Neapolitan and French artists) and developed by Carlo Maratta. A29 may date from the 1670s or 1680s by an artist who knew the work of Maratta.

Jean Hippolyte Marchand
(1882 – 1941)

Les Terrasses

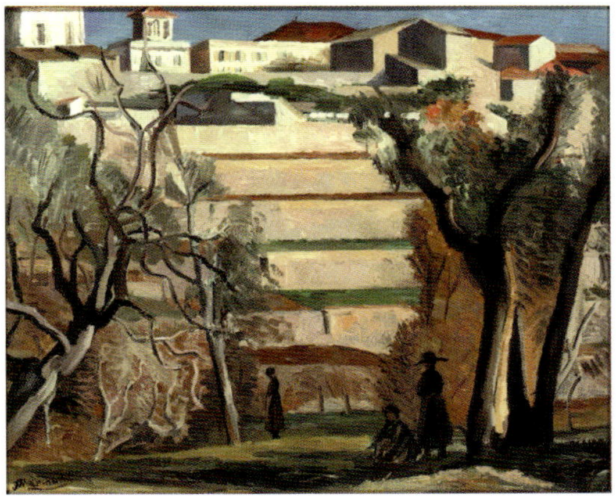

A652; oil on canvas, 55 × 66 cm
Signed: *JHMarchand*
Hindley Smith Bequest, 1939; WA1940.1.34

Marchand was trained at the Ecole des Beaux-Arts in Paris. His landscapes recall the work of Cézanne and Gauguin. At an early stage, he became known as a painter who was able to give his compositions a clear structure, create forms and evoke emotions through shape and colour. In this case, as in other landscapes painted shortly after the First World War, he confined the architecture to the background, drawing a sharp contrast with the trees and abbreviated figures in the foreground.

Willem Maris
(1844 – 1910)

Ducks, Spring

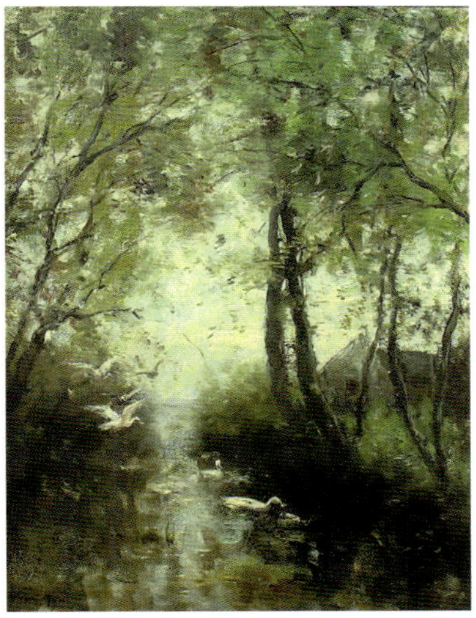

A1185; oil on canvas, 53 × 40 cm
Bequeathed by Professor Edith Bulbring, 1991; WA1993.423

White 1999, p. 83

Willem Maris and his two brothers, Jacob and Matthijs, were prominent members of the Hague School. They were chiefly painters of rustic life. The subject of this painting is characteristic of Willem's interest in scenes with ducks and farmyard animals.

Charles Marq
(b. 1923)

Antichambre

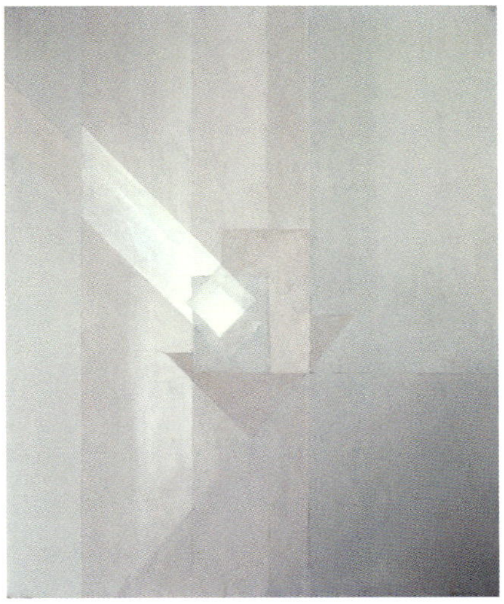

A1153; oil on canvas, 81 × 65 cm
Signed: *Charles Marq*
Presented by the Family of Christopher Hewett, 1987; WA1987.138

Oxford 1987, no. 69; Eustace 1999, no. 32

Marq, who first trained as philosopher, was later involved in the restoration and design of stained glass, through his wife, the painter Brigitte Simon. While his early works owed much to works by Giacometti, he reduced the figurative element in favour of a purer spatial concept, created through a monochromatic palette and simple geometric forms.

Jacob Maris
(1837 – 1899)

Stormy Landscape, Autumn

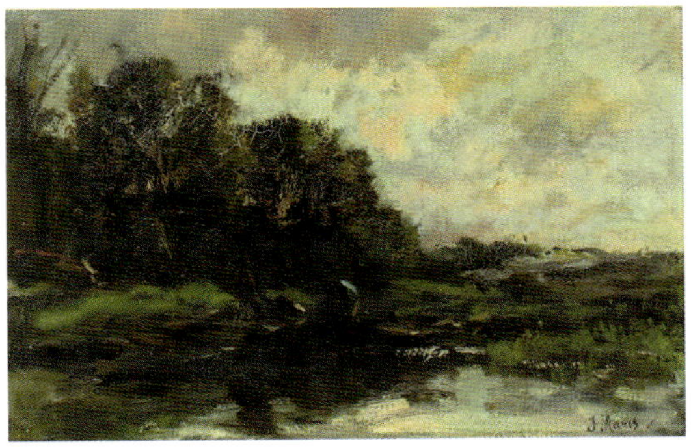

A1184; oil on canvas, 40.5 × 60 cm
Signed: *J Maris*
Bequeathed by Professor Edith Bulbring, 1991; WA1993.422

White 1999, p. 82

This landscape is marked by Jacob's interest in the painters of Barbizon whose work he studied in Paris in the 1860s. A date after 1880 has been suggested. The paint is applied with the broad brush-strokes typical of the artist's mature style.

Follower of Simon Marmion
(*c.* 1425 – 1489)

Pietà

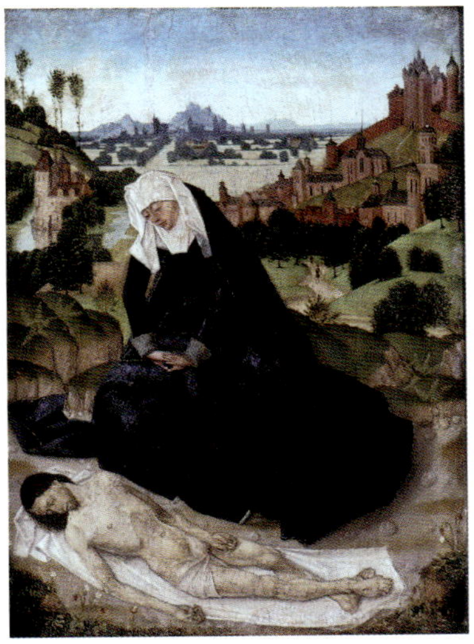

A297; tempera on panel, 30 × 22 cm
Bequeathed by John D. Chambers, 1897; WA1897.19

Ainsworth 1992, p. 254

The Virgin mourns over the body of Christ in an extensive landscape of a mid-15th-century Flemish type. Traditionally attributed to Marmion, A297 is by an artist who may have known his work, but was not in his immediate circle. Recently an attribution has been suggested to Lieven van Laetham (d. 1493), who was active in Ghent and Antwerp.

Charles Marq
(b. 1923)

Double Composition

A1154; oil on board, 23.9 × 32.8 cm
Signed: *CM*
Presented by the Family of Christopher Hewett, 1987; WA1987.139

Oxford 1987, no. 70

As in other paintings Marq concentrated entirely on the representation of space, light and the relation of forms within a linear composition. Built with mainly vertical and horizontal blocks, the diagonal lines mark another element and include a movement, which runs counter to the other rectilinear forms. The three-dimensional quality of the paint adds an important element to the appearance of the work.

JACOB MARREL
(1614 – 1681)

A Vase of Flowers

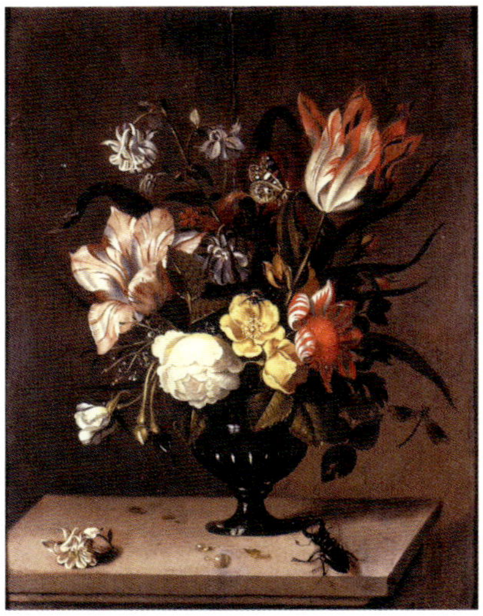

A578; oil on panel, 42.5 × 32 cm
Daisy Linda Ward Bequest, 1939; WA1940.2.54

Meijer 2003, no. 56

By the end of 1632 Marrel had settled in Utrecht but returned at intervals to his native Frankfurt where he died. This flower piece was painted a little over a year after he arrived in Utrecht. The central vase of flowers shows his response to the Bosschaert school which was active in the city. The large beetle, however, is a detail found more readily in the work of Georg Flegel with whom he had worked in Frankfurt.

JOHN MARTIN
(1789 – 1854)

The Isle of Man

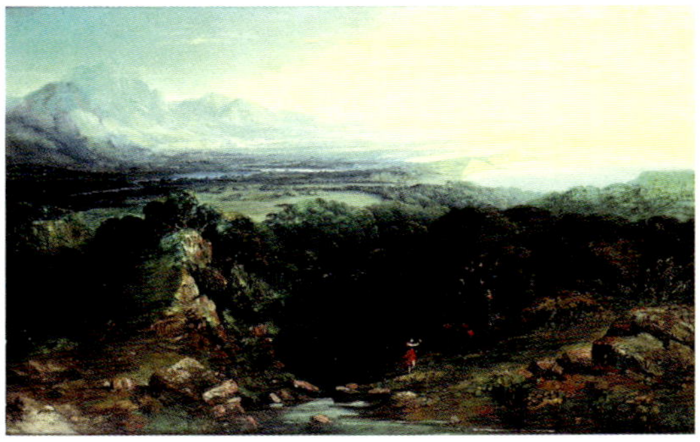

A1211; oil on mahogany panel, 30.3 × 46.5 cm
Bequeathed by Alfred Leslie Rowse, C.H., F.B.A., 1998; WA1998.54

Between 1848 and 1854, Martin made annual visits to the Isle of Man to stay with his brother-in-law. They provided him with holidays and a change of scenery from London and from his imaginary landscapes.

ROBERT BRAITHWAITE MARTINEAU
(1826 – 1869)

Katherine and Petruchio

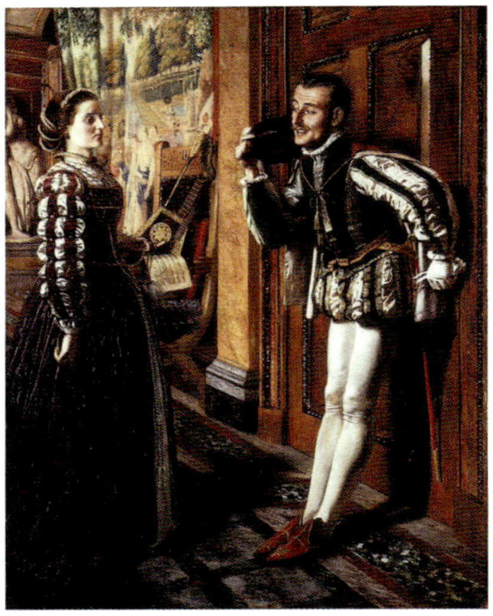

A798; oil on canvas, 92 × 71 cm
Signed with monogram and dated: *1855*
Prov.: James Leathart
Bequeathed by Miss Helen Martineau, 1951; WA1951.197

Martineau 1924, p. 208; Brown 1987, no. 20

This is an illustration to Shakespeare's *The Taming of the Shrew* (Act II, scene 1), in which Petruchio begins his wooing of Katherine ('the shrew'). It was probably begun under the supervision of Holman Hunt in 1852 and exhibited at the Royal Academy in 1855.

JOHN MARTIN
(1789 – 1854)

Joshua commanding the Sun to stand still

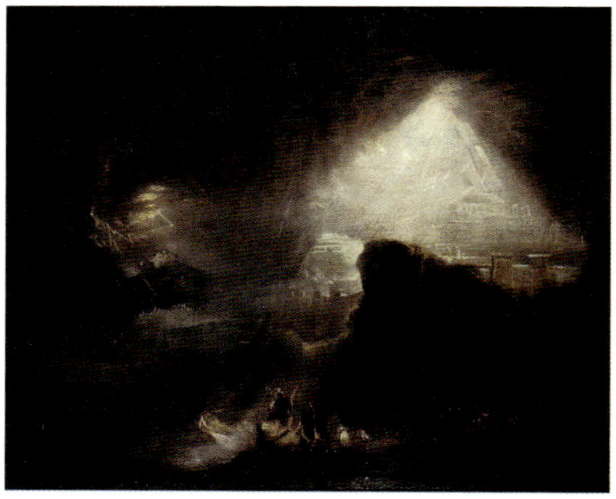

A448b; oil on canvas, 63 × 76 cm
Presented by Edmund Blunden, 1936; WA1936.229

Martin's first attempt at an epic and densely populated composition was his large painting of *Joshua commanding the Sun to stand still*, shown to great acclaim at the Royal Academy in 1816 (now owned by the United Grand Lodge). The subject is taken from Joshua 10: 12–14. Martin later published a large mezzotint of the painting in 1827. This is probably a preparatory sketch, as dramatically lit as the final painting but far less detailed.

WILLIAM MARTIN
(active 1765 – 1831)

Cardinal Langton and the Barons at St Edmundsbury

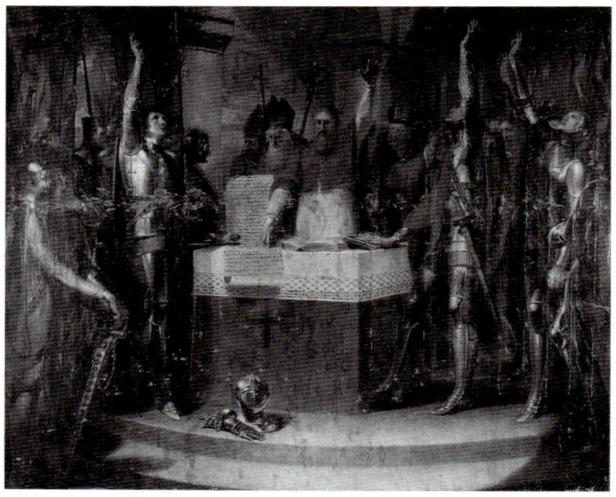

A40; oil on canvas, rolled, 32 × 38.1 cm
Presented by the artist, 1796; WA1845.40

Martin painted history paintings and presented two to his native Norwich in 1787. The subject is recorded in Roger of Wendover's *Flores historiarum*: on St Edmund's Day, 20 November 1214, the nobles and barons of England met at St Edmund's Abbey to swear that, if King John refused to uphold the liberties and laws granted to the church under the Cardinal-Archbishop of Canterbury, Stephen Langton (d. 1228), they would withdraw their allegiance to the crown. The scene probably never took place.

ROBERT BRAITHWAITE MARTINEAU
(1826 – 1869)

The poor Actress's Christmas Dinner

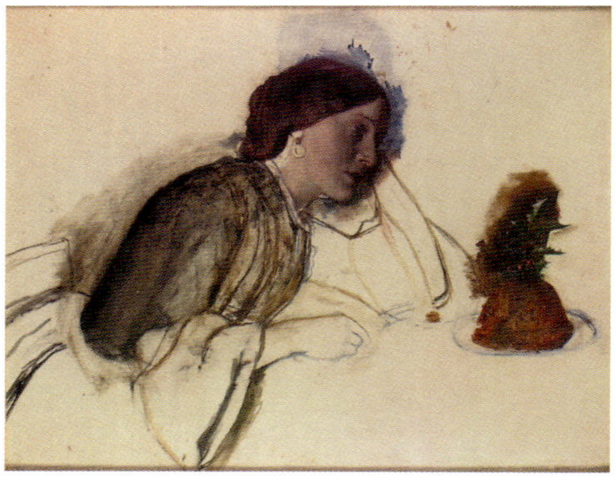

A685; oil on canvas, 36 × 47 cm
Presented by Miss Helen Martineau, 1941; WA1941.61

Martineau 1924, p. 208; Brown 1987, no. 46

An unfinished and poignant example of mid-Victorian pathos, painted in sharp detail on a white ground.

Robert Braithwaite Martineau
(1826 – 1869)

The Knight's Guerdon

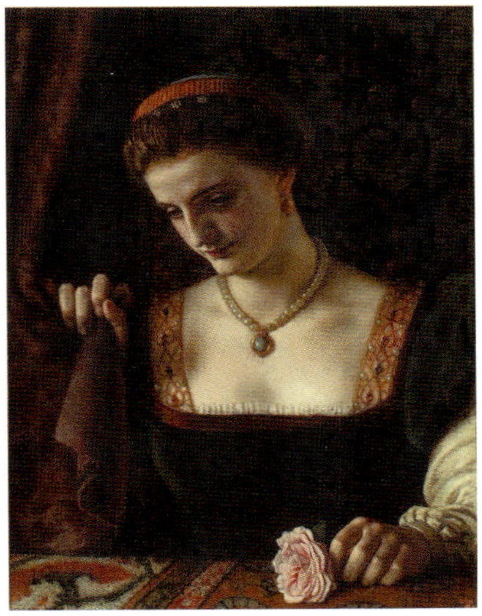

A799; oil on panel, 42 × 32 cm
Signed and dated: *RBM / 1864*
Prov.: Sir Thomas Fairbairn
Bequeathed by Miss Helen Martineau, 1951; WA1951.198

Martineau 1947, p. 78

On the frame is a label in the painter's hand recording lines from Tennyson's *Sir Galahad*: *How sweet are looks that ladies bend / On whom their favours fall*. This painting was exhibited at the Royal Academy in 1864.

Robert Braithwaite Martineau
(1826 – 1869)

Girl with a Hoop

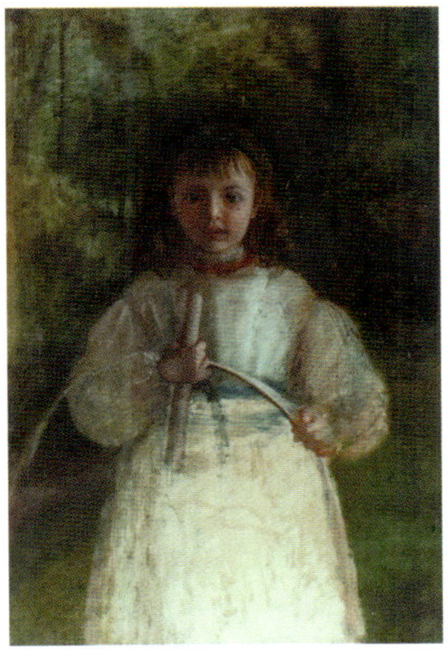

A801; oil on millboard, 72 × 48 cm
Bequeathed by Miss Helen Martineau, 1951; WA1951.200

According to an inscription on the back, this is an unfinished portrait of Miss Alice Holdsworth, painted in June 1868.

Tommaso d'Antonio Manzuoli, called Maso da San Friano
(1531 – 1571)

The Holy Family with St John the Baptist

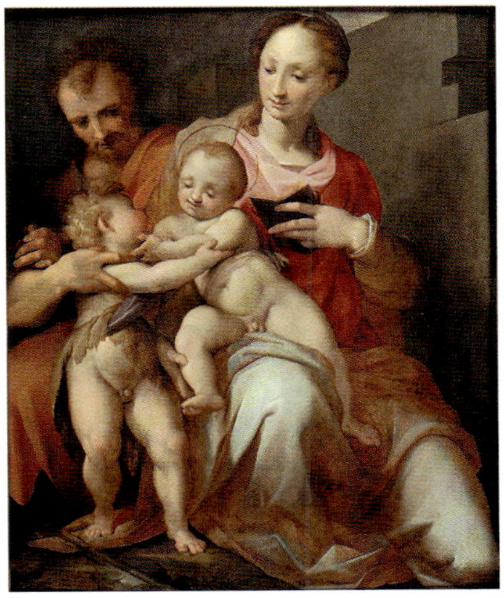

A793; oil on panel, 102.9 × 83.4 cm
Prov.: 2nd Baron Northwick; Sir Thomas Phillips and by descent to Phillips Fenwick; A.G. Fenwick
Purchased, 1950; WA1950.179

Lloyd 1977, pp. 106–7

This tightly-knit composition of *c.* 1569 looks back to the work of Andrea del Sarto and his pupil Pontormo; two other versions are known. A793 appears to be unfinished and may have been intended as a small altar-piece for a private patron. Maso enjoyed Medici patronage and was a founder member of the Accademia del Disegno in Florence.

Robert Braithwaite Martineau
(1826 – 1869)

The Artist's Wife

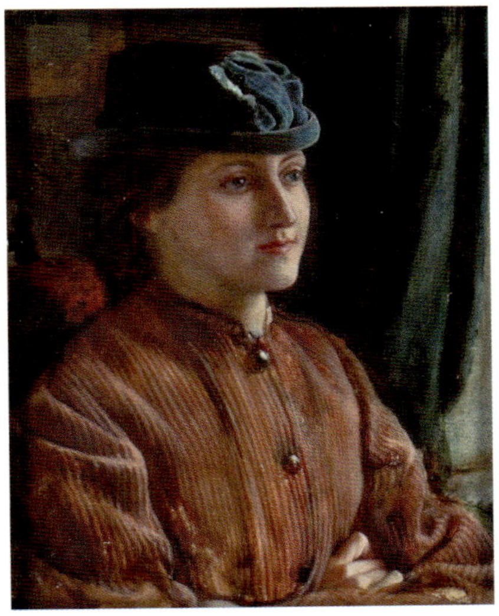

A800; oil on canvas, 35 × 29 cm
Bequeathed by Miss Helen Martineau, 1951; WA1951.199

Martineau married Maria Wheeler in 1865. This unfinished portrait was probably painted around that time.

Attributed to Martino da Verona
(documented 1396 – 1410)

The Consecration of St Eligius

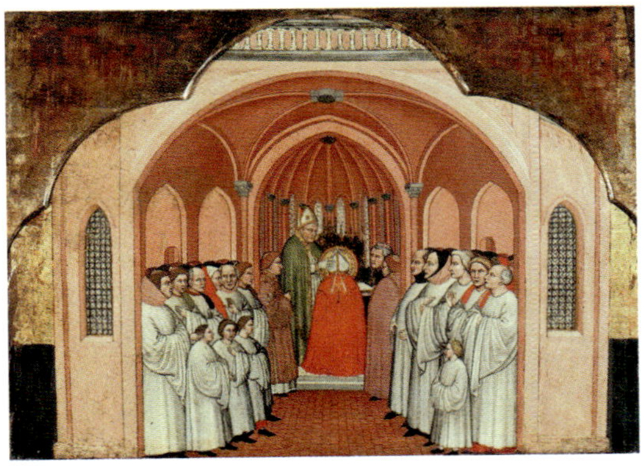

A732; tempera and gilding on panel, 49 × 59 cm
Presented by the daughters of James Reddie Anderson, 1947; WA1947.246

Lloyd 1977, pp. 1–2

St Eligius, bishop of Noyon, is the patron saint of goldsmiths. Together with three other surviving panels of a similar shape, this may have formed part of the predella of an altar-piece, perhaps of the 1390s. The other panels illustrate the saint's birth; his mother foretelling her son's future fame; and a miracle of the saint. Martino based his style on that of his celebrated master Altichiero, who favoured architecturally complex settings and lively narrative detail.

Master of the Ashmolean Predella
(active mid to late 14th century)

The Birth of the Virgin Mary

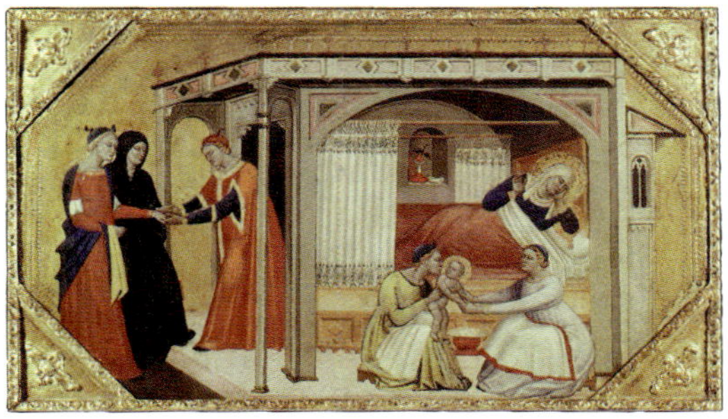

A74; tempera and gilding on panel, 37.4 × 65.2 cm
Fox-Strangways Gift, 1850; WA1850.6

Lloyd 1977, pp. 136–9; Wilson 1996, under no. 7

This popular apocryphal subject allows for attractive domestic detail. Perhaps painted *c.* 1365–70, A74 is from the predella of an unknown altar-piece together with other panels of *The Presentation of Christ*, the *Annunciation to Joachim* and the *Flight into Egypt*. The anonymous master worked with both Andrea di Cione (Orcagna) and his younger brother Jacopo, collaborating with Jacopo on the *Crucifixion* altar-piece in the National Gallery. Owing to its superb quality, A74 has also been attributed to Orcagna, or has been seen as an early work by Jacopo.

Attributed to THE MASTER OF BALDRACCANI
(active *c.* 1480 – 1510)

Portrait of an unknown Lady

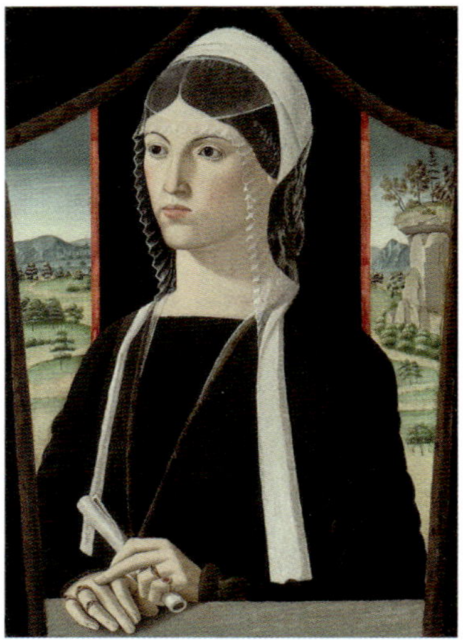

A711; oil on panel, 50.4 × 35.2 cm
Bequeathed by Miss Emily G. Kemp, 1940; WA1945.61

Lloyd 1977, pp. 47–8; Zeri 1986, p. 25

The sitter is expensively dressed and holds a document, displaying her fine rings. The artist's name derives from an altar-piece formerly in the Muti-Bussi collection, Rome, which carries the coat of arms of the Baldraccani family from Forlì. A711 is close in handling and in the details of the landscape to this painting.

MASTER OF THE BIELEFELD ALTAR
(active *c.* 1400 – *c.* 1435)

Christ before Pilate

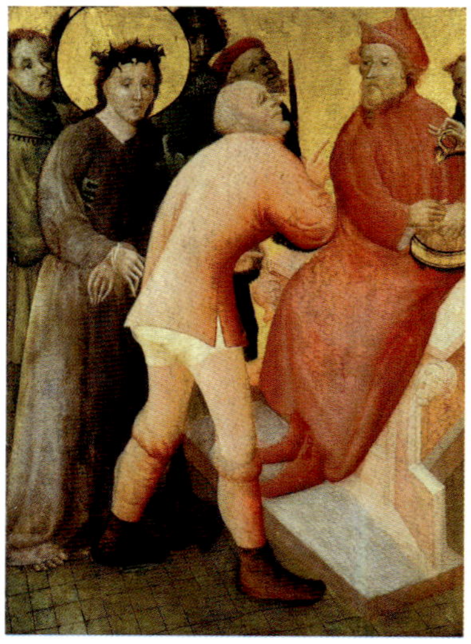

A337; oil on panel, 57.5 × 42 cm
Prov.: Geheimrat Krüger; National Gallery, London
Presented by Mrs James Reddie Anderson, 1913; WA1913.6

White 1999, p. 83

This panel was originally inserted into the left shutter of an altar-piece in the Neustädter Marienkirche in Bielefeld, Westphalia. In 1840, the altar-piece, which consisted of eighteen panels, was dismembered. Twelve panels have since been identified in a number of museums, including the Fitzwilliam Museum in Cambridge and the Metropolitan Museum in New York. The artist appears to have worked in the circle of Conrad von Soest.

MASTER OF CHARLES III OF DURAZZO
(active *c.* 1390)

Tarquin and Lucretia

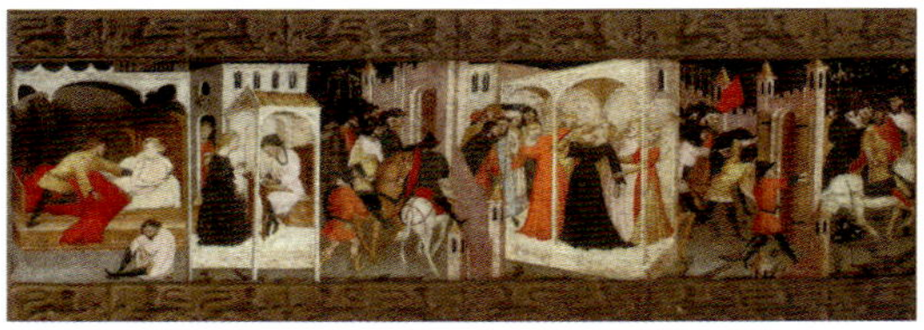

A231; tempera and gilding on panel, 29 × 115 cm
Presented by the Revd Greville John Chester, 1864; WA1864.1

Lloyd 1977, pp. 132–3; Fahy 1994, p. 239; Miziolek 1996

The narrative, from left to right, follows the sequence in Livy, *Ab urbe condita* I, 58–60: Tarquin enters Lucretia's bedroom in order to rape her; she dictates a letter to her husband asking him to return; after his arrival, she commits suicide; the Tarquins are expelled from Rome. Although considerably worn, A231 is an important early *cassone* panel whose subject celebrates the honour of married women. The pastiglia decoration of fleur-de-lys and lions or leopards refers to the Angevin kings of Naples, suggesting that A231 had a Neapolitan patron or destination. The same composition occurs, with variations, on three other *cassone* panels from the same workshop. These panels may all have been painted around 1400 in the workshop of the Master of Charles III of Durazzo, the Florentine artist whose name-piece is in the Metropolitan Museum, New York.

MASTER OF THE DOMINICAN EFFIGIES
(active 1336 – 1345)

The Crucifixion

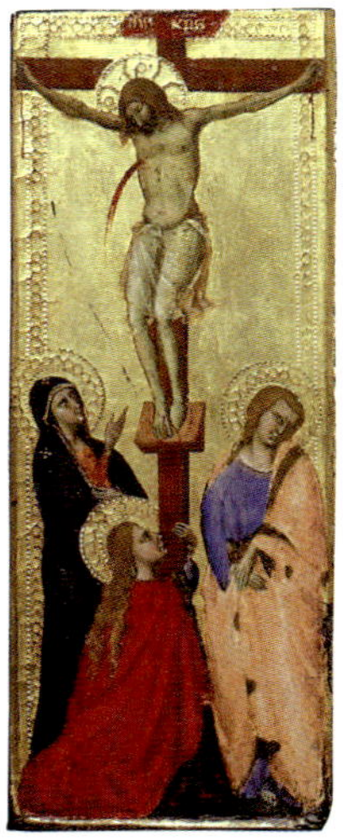

A676; tempera and gilding on panel, 29.5 × 12.1 cm
Presented by Harold Bompas, 1941; WA1941.14

Lloyd 1977, pp. 107–9

A676 and A677 were painted by the same anonymous artist who painted a *Christ and the Virgin attended by seventeen Dominican Blessed and Friars* in the sacristy of Santa Maria Novella, Florence. Originally the panels served as the shutters of a small altar-piece, probably with a *Virgin and Child* in the centre and the *Angel* and *Virgin of the Annunciation* above each side panel. Traditionally, the Virgin, St John the Evangelist and Mary Magdalen are depicted at the Crucifixion.

MASTER OF THE DOMINICAN EFFIGIES
(active 1336 – 1345)

The Lamentation

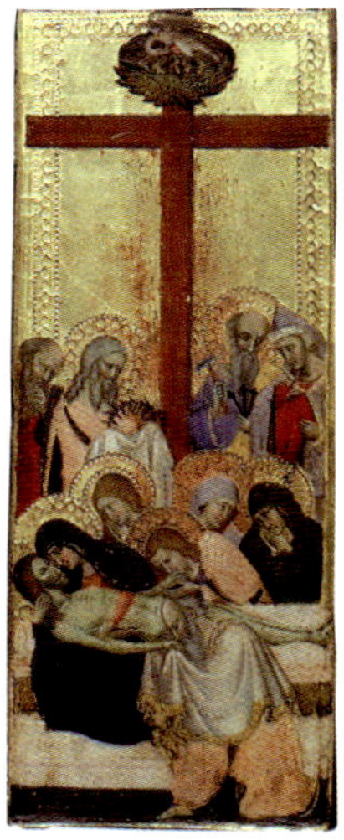

A677; tempera and gilding on panel, 29.8 × 12.1 cm
Presented by Harold Bompas, 1941; WA1941.14

Lloyd 1977, pp. 107–9

The same figures as in A676 appear lamenting over the body of Christ, together with other mourners mentioned in the Gospels. The figures without halos may be included in the scene to represent humanity in general with whom the viewer, meditating on the Lamentation, could identify. Above the cross, the scene of the pelican feeding its young with its own blood is a traditional symbol of the Crucifixion.

Master of Marradi
(active *c.* 1500)

The Virgin and Child with the young St John and an Angel

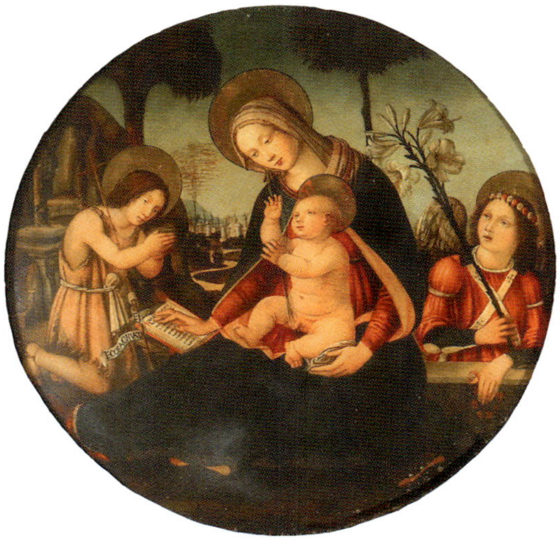

A520d; oil on panel, 88 cm in diameter
Inscribed: *ECCE AGNUS DEI*
Prov.: C.J. Longman
Bequeathed by Mrs H.A. Longman, 1938; WA1938.126

Lloyd 1977, p. 109; Olson 2000, pp. 237–8

The Virgin is depicted as the Madonna of Humility, seated on the ground. Her finger rests on a book open at Luke 1: 28, a reference to the Annunciation, while an angel bears a garland of roses and a lily, references to the purity of the Virgin. The unknown, conservative artist was close to Domenico Ghirlandaio.

Henri Matisse
(1869 – 1954)

Nude on a Sofa

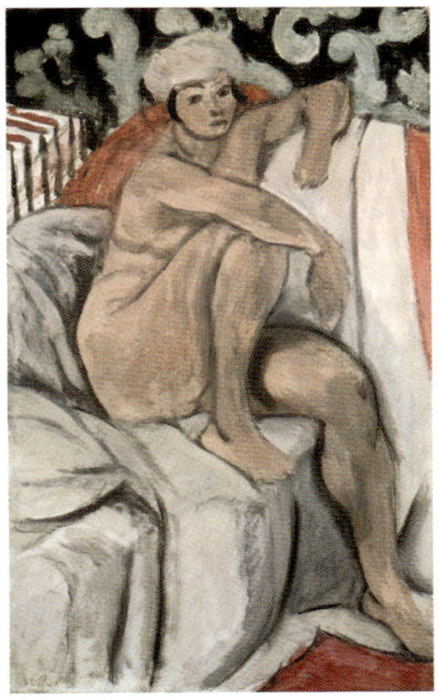

A629; oil on canvas, 55.7 × 33.3 cm
Signed: *Henri Matisse*
Hindley Smith Bequest, 1939; WA1940.1.11

Eustace 1999, no. 17

In 1919, when this painting was made, Matisse was staying in Nice. In reaction to the pre-war aesthetics of Cubism, Futurism and Vorticism, Matisse concentrated on sketch-like studies of the female form. As in other pictures, he abandoned strong and intense colours and used a reduced palette of greens, greys and pinks, leading to a softening of forms and a new sense of space and atmosphere.

Master of San Martino alla Palma
(active *c.* 1310 – *c.* 1335)

The Entombment

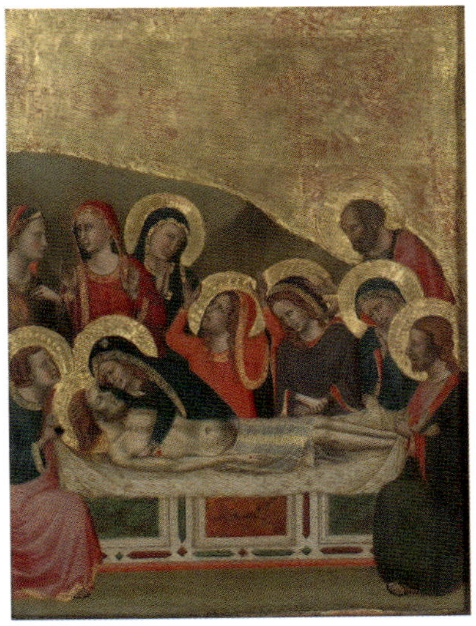

A300; tempera and gilding on panel, 31.5 × 23.7 cm
Prov.: purchased, Florence, 1864
Fortnum Bequest, 1899; WA1899.CDEF.P3

Lloyd 1977, pp. 111–2; Boskovits and Schleier 1988, under no. 50

The mourning figures include the Virgin, St John the Evangelist, Mary Magdalen, Joseph of Arimathea and Nicodemus. Together with a similarly-sized panel of a *Last Judgement* (Musée Fesch, Ajaccio) A300 might have been part of a larger complex, perhaps the shutters of an elaborate tabernacle, made *c.* 1320. The gold background and the top of the mountain were reconstructed in a restoration of 1957.

Paolo de' Matteis
(1662 – 1728)

The Choice of Hercules

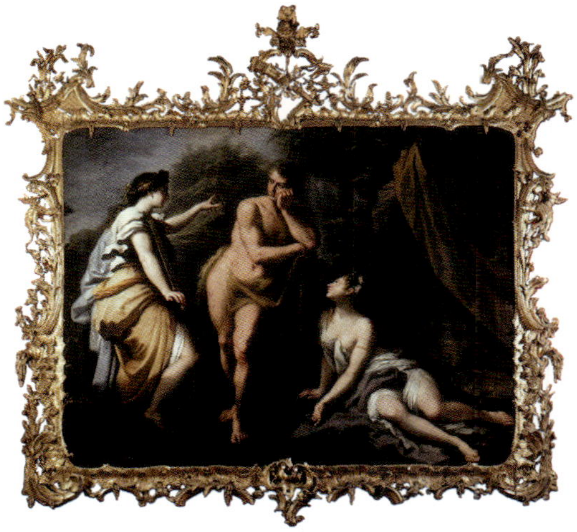

A1116; oil on canvas, 198.2 × 256.5 cm
Faintly inscribed: *Shaftesbury*
Prov.: Anthony Ashley-Cooper, 3rd Earl of Shaftesbury and by descent
Purchased (Blakiston, France, Bouch, Russell, Madan Funds) with the assistance of the Victoria & Albert Museum Purchase Grant Fund, the National Art Collections Fund, the Pilgrim Trust and the National Heritage Memorial Fund, 1980; WA1980.92

O'Connell 1988; Pestelli 1990

Anthony Ashley-Cooper, 3rd Earl of Shaftesbury, retired to Naples in 1711 due to ill-health and planned a second, illustrated edition of his philosophical works, *Characteristicks*. For his treatise on the advantages of Virtue over Pleasure he commissioned an allegory of *The Choice of Hercules* from Paolo de' Matteis. A talented pupil of Luca Giordano, de Matteis had studied in Rome and worked in France: his graceful classicism earned him high-ranking patronage. Annibale Carracci's *Choice of Hercules* in the Palazzo Farnese was a source for the composition. Shaftesbury provided detailed instructions for the attitudes and expressions of the figures. Hercules must choose between the hedonistic life exemplified by Pleasure, or Vice, and the rocky path of Virtue. Completed by March 1712, the picture was probably framed in a plain dark moulding; the fine mid 18th-century rococo frame, perhaps designed by the architect Henry Flitcroft (1697–1769), was given to A1116 by the fourth Earl. An oil-sketch is now in Munich; a smaller, autograph version was commissioned for Shaftesbury's friend, Sir John Cropley (now Leeds City Art Gallery). A1116 was engraved by Simon Gribelin.

Style of Matteo di Giovanni
(active 1452 – d. 1495)

The Virgin and Child

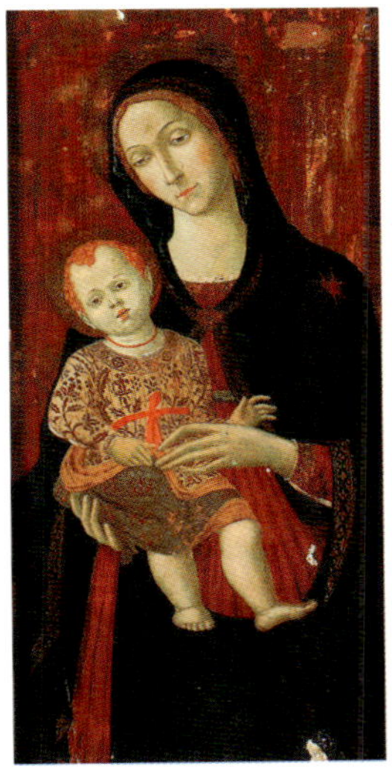

A873; tempera and gilding on panel, 99 × 49 cm
Bequeathed by Mrs R.M. Muriello-Langton, 1955; WA1955.93

Lloyd 1977, p. 201; Mazzoni 2001, pp. 44, 375

Acquired as a painting by Matteo di Giovanni, A873 is probably a 20th-century fake by Bruno Marzi who specialised in the production of fake 15th-century Sienese paintings. It has also been suggested that A873 is a completely repainted fragment by Matteo di Giovanni.

Style of ANTON MAUVE
(1838 – 1888)

Shepherd and Sheep, Evening

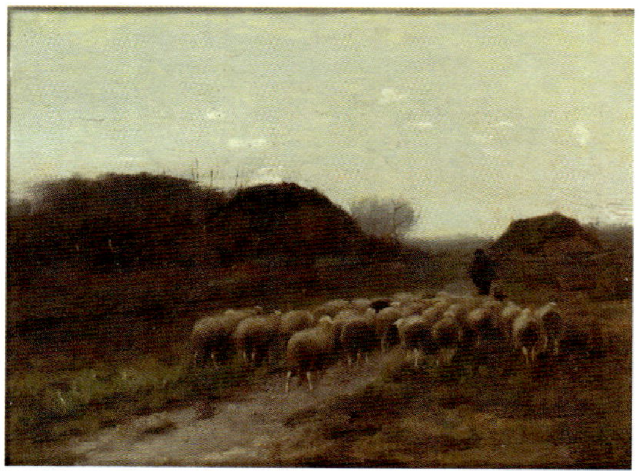

A1186; oil on canvas, 29 × 40.5 cm
Inscribed: *Mauve*
Bequeathed by Professor Edith Bulbring, 1993; WA1993.423

White 1999, p. 86

The pastoral subject of this painting is typical of Mauve's work but the weak execution makes it difficult to attribute it to him. The signature may have been added to an unsigned work by another artist or it may have been painted as a forgery of the work of an artist who was very sought after in his lifetime.

ROBERT MEDLEY
(1905 – 1994)

Maggi Hambling

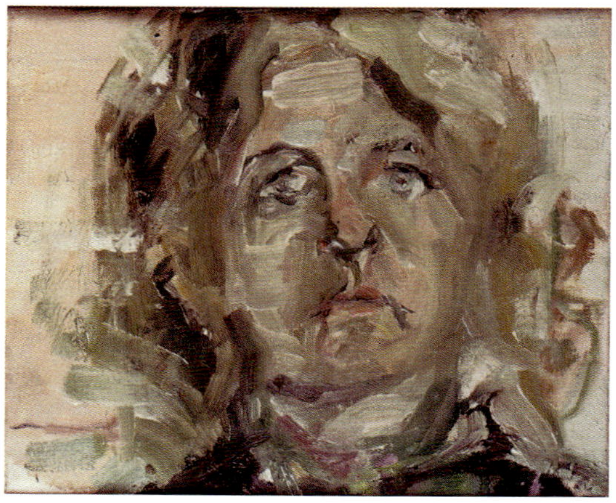

A1250; oil on canvas, 25.5 × 30.5 cm
Signed on back: *Robert Medley*
Presented anonymously through the National Art Collections Fund, 2002; WA2002.67

Robert Medley practised a sort of figurative painting, sometimes even comparatively realistic. In this late painting of Maggi Hambling (see A1248), however, he tried to represent the much younger painter with a reduced palette, based on a few greens and modelled in broad, rapid brush-strokes.

ERNEST MEISSONIER
(1815 – 1891)

An Abbé

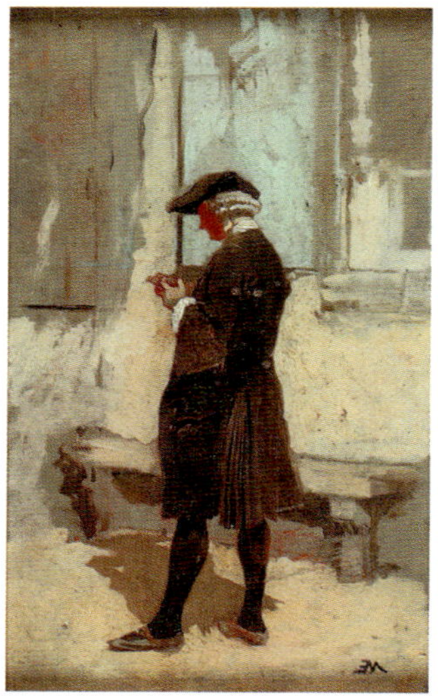

A956; oil on panel, 15 × 9 cm
Signed with monogram: *EM*
Bequeathed by Miss G.E.G. Watkins in memory of Sir Henry Thompson, Bt, 1962; WA1962.4.1

Meissonier is known chiefly for painting small pictures, executed with a detailed but delicate touch. He seems to have based his style on the fine manner of the 17th-century Leiden painters but, as here, often took his subjects from 18th-century everyday life. There are a number of similar single figures in Meissonier's work, dating from the 1850s.

JOCK MCFADYEN
(b. 1950)

Limehouse Basin

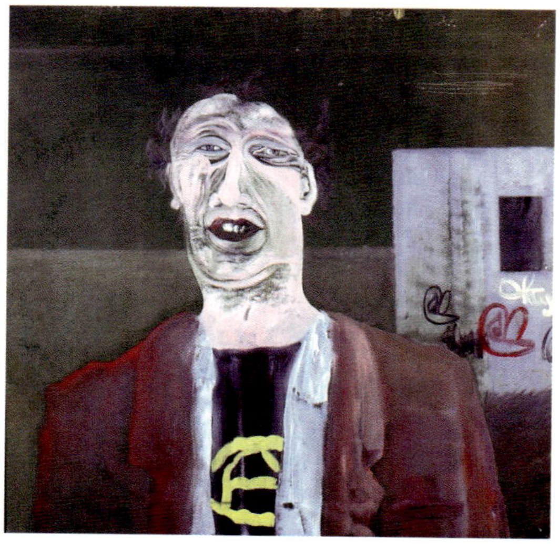

A1249; oil on canvas, 92 × 92.5 cm
Presented anonymously through the National Art Collections Fund, 2002; WA2002.66

Cohen 2001, p. 30

In the late 1980s, McFadyen made a group of close-up views of men, apparently half-length portraits. He used a pared-down style he had developed some years earlier, but now more realistic and detailed and executed with thin paint. This painting of 1990 is typical of this group. The figure shown is not really a portrait, but represents a generic type.

HAN VAN MEEGEREN
(1889 – 1947)

Theodore W.H. Ward

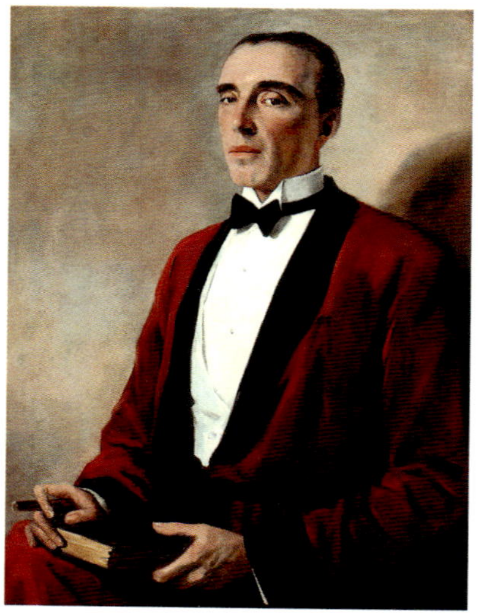

A1204; oil on canvas, 101.5 × 76.5 cm
Signed: *Han v Meegeren / 1928*
Presented by Mr and Mrs Theodore A.T. Ward, 1997; WA1997.3

Theodore William Holzapfel Ward (1889–1955), who donated the Ward collection of Dutch and Flemish still-life paintings to the Ashmolean, derived his fortune from the family paint company, The International Paint and Composition Company, which had thirteen factories in several countries. He is shown here in evening dress.

ALTOBELLO MELONE
(*c.* 1490 – d. before May 1543)

Tobias and the Angel

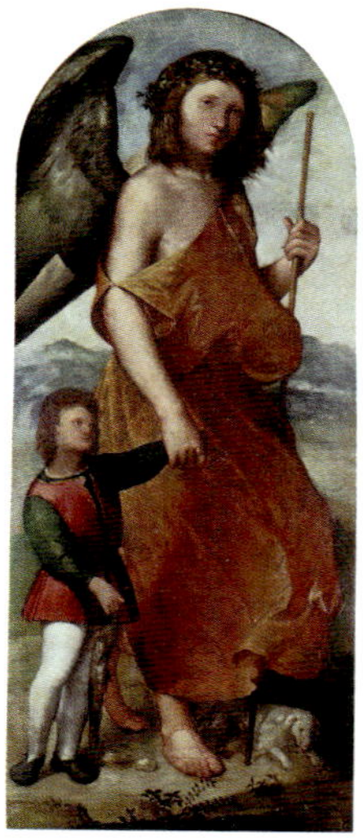

A290; oil on panel, 112 × 48 cm
Prov.: Sommi-Picenardi collection, Cremona; Araldi-Erizzo
Bequeathed by John D. Chambers, 1897; WA1897.14

Lloyd 1977, pp. 113–5; Land 1999, under no. 8

Together with A290, this shaped panel was part of a large altar-piece, probably made for a church in Cremona in the early 1520s, of which the centre panel with *The Virgin and Child* and the predella with scenes from the life of St Helena are known. From the apocryphal Book of Tobit, the story of Tobias concerns the miraculous cure of Tobit's blindness, thanks to the instructions of the Archangel Raphael who is invoked as a guardian or protector.

Altobello Melone
(*c.* 1490 – d. before May 1543)

St Helena

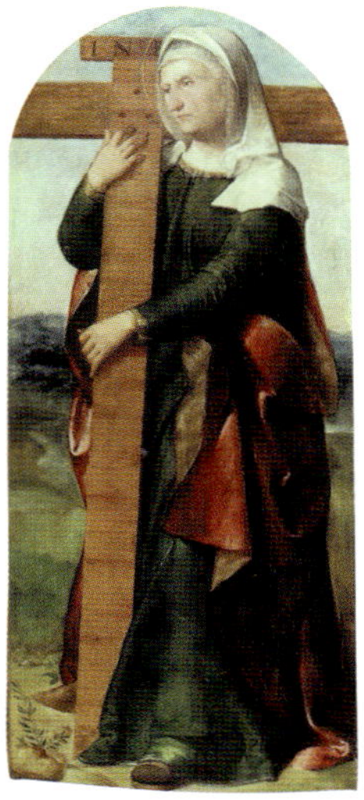

A291; oil on panel, 112 × 48 cm
Prov. and lit.: as for A290; WA1897.14.1

According to legend, Helena (*c.* 255–*c.* 330), the mother of the emperor Constantine, discovered the True Cross in Jerusalem and she is depicted as a regal figure holding a cross. The predella scenes show *St Helena questioning Judas; The Finding of the True Cross* and *The Proving of the True Cross.* Altobello was interested in the painterly qualities of Giorgione and Titian and in the strong expressive forms of Gerolamo Romanino and Dürer.

Anton Raphael Mengs
(1728 – 1779)

William Fermor

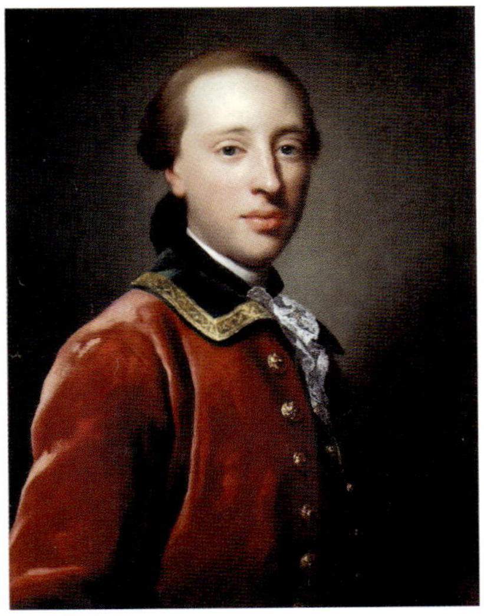

A1100; oil on canvas, 61 × 47 cm
Inscribed on the stretcher: *Wm Fermor in a Masque dress / Anton Raphael Mengs pinxit / Rome 1757 / Price 10 guineas*
Purchased with the assistance of the National Art Collections Fund and the Victoria & Albert Museum Purchase Grant Fund, 1978; WA1978.75

Roettgen 1999, no. 207; White 1999, pp. 87–8

The eldest son of Henry Fermor of Tusmore, Oxfordshire, William Fermor (1737–1806) went on the Grand Tour in 1757–8. Like other English visitors to Rome, he had his portrait painted by both Mengs and Pompeo Batoni: the latter portrait (1758) is now in the Kress Collection, Museum of Fine Arts, Houston. His elegant costume is not masquerade dress, despite the old inscription. Mengs's portraits are sober and frank in approach, with a polished finish.

Bernard Meninsky
(1891 – 1950)

Bathers

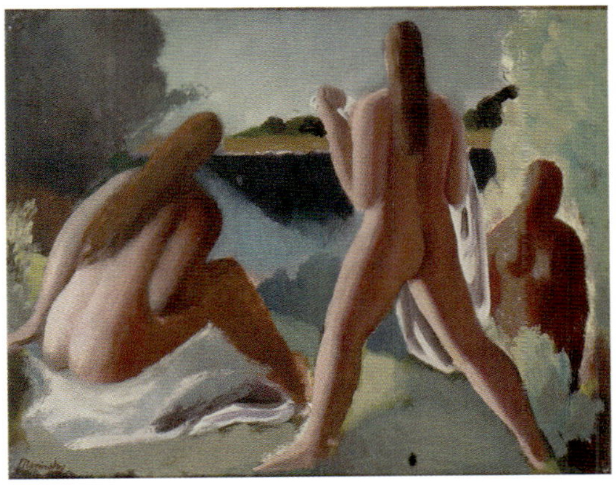

A1124a; oil on canvas, 40.5 × 51 cm
Signed: *Meninsky*
Purchased, 1981; WA1981.623

Meninsky was trained at the Slade School of Fine Arts, London and was official War Artist during the First World War. During his lifetime he had a high reputation as an excellent draughtsman and a skilful painter with an exquisite sense of colour and space, as is evident in the manner in which these figures have been placed within a landscape, somewhat recalling paintings by Cézanne of the same subject.

Adam Frans van der Meulen
(1632 – 1690)

Landscape with Bandits attacking a Convoy of Travellers

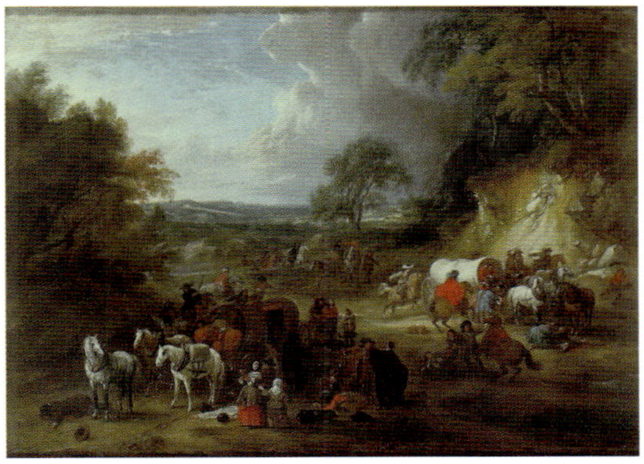

A768; oil on canvas, 89 × 121 cm
Signed: *A. FV. MEULEN*
Bequeathed by Mrs Arthur J. Mathews, 1948; WA1948.116

White 1999, p. 88

Van der Meulen was born in Brussels but lived from 1664 until his death in Paris He painted topographical views and battle pictures and designed tapestries for the Gobelins factory. There is a similar picture of bandits at Petworth House, Sussex, signed and dated 1657.

Georges Michel
(1763 – 1843)

Landscape with Fishermen at the Mouth of a River

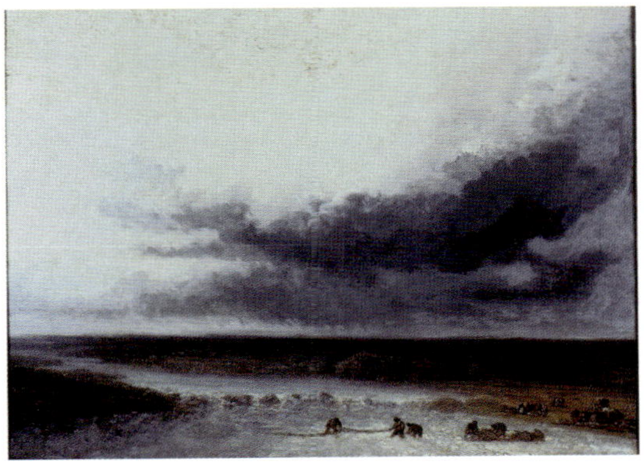

A466; oil on canvas, 51 × 67 cm
Weldon Bequest, 1937; WA1937.46

With its lavish handling of paint, A466 is comparable with *The Old Château* in the Metropolitan Museum, New York, and probably dates from late in the artist's career. Called 'The Ruisdael of Montmartre' by an early biographer, Michel was poor and unsuccessful in his own lifetime, but his art was greatly appreciated by Rousseau, Millet and other realist landscape painters of the mid-19th century.

Attributed to Georges Michel
(1763 – 1843)

Landscape with Goatherds

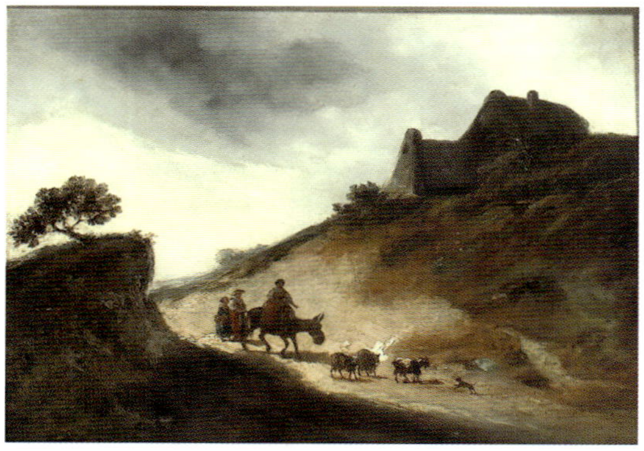

A431; oil on panel, 42 × 59 cm
Presented by Mrs W.F.R. Weldon, 1934; WA1934.6

Although displaying in some parts the handling of paint associated with Michel, A431 is more conventional in design and flatly executed than is usual in his work. There were already pastiches of his work on the art market in Paris by the 1870s.

Abraham Mignon
(1640 – 1679)

A Carafe of Flowers with Blackberries

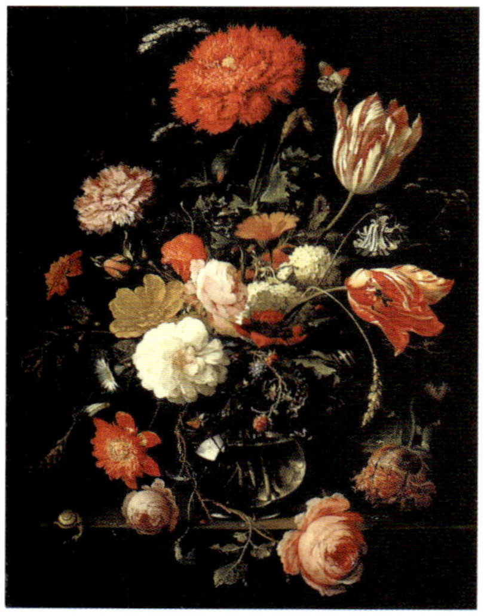

A583; oil on panel, 50.8 × 37.5 cm
Signed: *A. Mignon. fe.*
Daisy Linda Ward Bequest, 1939; WA1940.2.59

Meijer 2003, no. 57

Mignon followed his first master, Jacob Marrel, from Frankfurt to Utrecht and settled there, entering the studio of Jan Davidsz. de Heem whose influence now dominated his art. This painting, dated to the 1660s, includes a number of flowers found elsewhere in paintings by both de Heen and Mignon. The composition, topped by a red poppy, is also a type found in de Heem's work.

Abraham Mignon
(1640 – 1679)

A Vase of Flowers with two Carnations

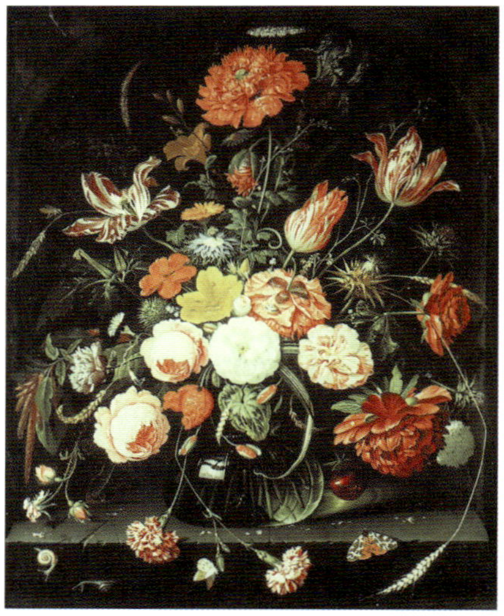

A581; oil on canvas, 78 × 62 cm
Inscribed: *AM*
Daisy Linda Ward Bequest, 1939; WA1940.2.57

Meijer 2003, no. 59

A characteristic example of Mignon's tendency to compose his larger bouquets in a dense pyramid of blooms, including round cabbage roses, a peony and a slender central tulip, encircled with smaller flowers and drooping stalks of wheat and grass. None of Mignon's paintings are dated but it is generally accepted that his art became harder and his pigment more opaque in the years after he left de Heem's studio. By this test, this painting seems to occupy a point in his mid-career.

Attributed to Michelangelo Buonarroti
(1475 – 1564)

The Holy Family with St John the Baptist

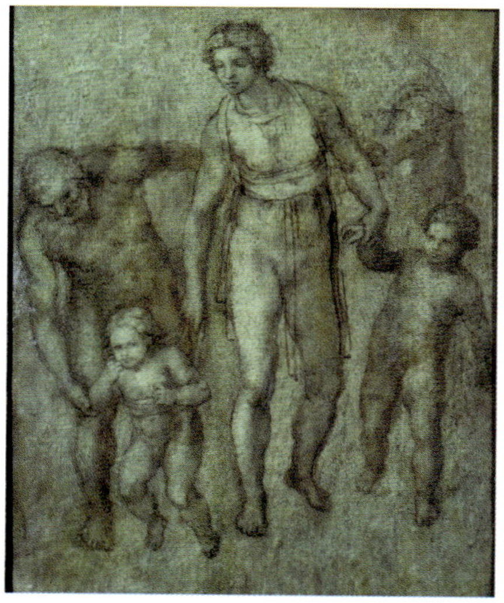

A66c; brush and brown wash on panel, 62 × 49.5 cm
Prov.: Royal Collection, Naples; William Young Ottley; Sir Thomas Lawrence
Presented by a Body of Subscribers, 1846; WA1846.309

Lloyd 1977, pp. 115–9

The panel reflects an unfinished design by Michelangelo perhaps *c.* 1540. While it could be a copy or variant of a lost design, the unusual qualities of A66c suggest an attribution to his hand. The poplar panel does not have the initial preparation of *gesso* that would be normal in planning a painting. The subject may be *The Return of the Holy Family from Egypt*: Michelangelo was interested in such apocryphal religious subjects.

Abraham Mignon
(1640 – 1679)

Interior with a Still Life

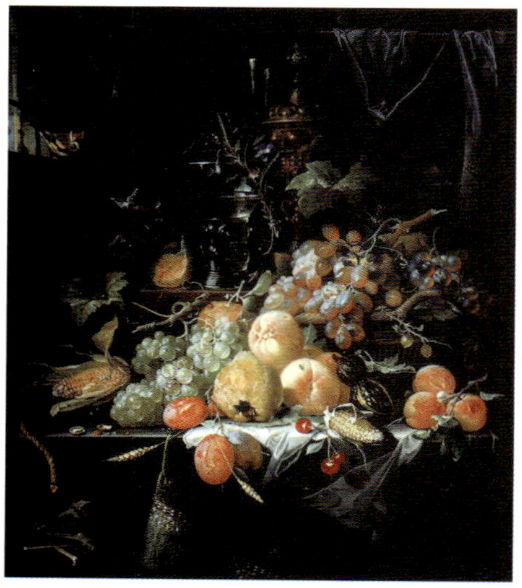

A580; oil on canvas, 80 × 70 cm
Signed: *AB.Mignon fe.* (AB in monogram)
Daisy Linda Ward Bequest, 1939; WA1940.2.56

Meijer 2003, no. 58

The general composition, style and several details of this painting are heavily indebted to the example of de Heem. The nearest comparisons are with works of the 1660s. The laurel wreath, decorating the rummer of white wine, is a motif common to both Mignon and de Heem. A page of an almanac, holding tobacco, may have been inserted at lower left as an allusion to passing time.

Copy after Abraham Mignon
(1640 – 1679)

Flowers in an Ornamental Vase

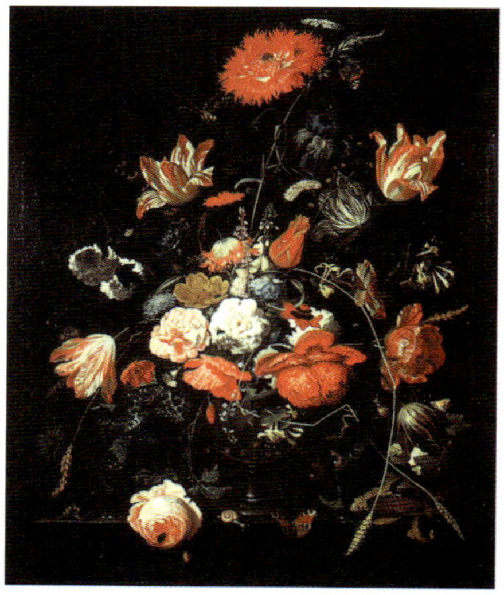

A582; oil on canvas, 90 × 78 cm
Daisy Linda Ward Bequest, 1939; WA1940.2.58

Meijer 2003, no. 59

A complex arrangement of many flowers with butterflies, insects and snails which seems to have been copied from an original in the Mauritshuis by a skilled hand. The two paintings are very close but there are empty margins round the painting in Oxford which are not characteristic of Mignon's work and are not found in the Mauritshuis picture.

Sir John Everett Millais, Bt
(1829 – 1896)

Thomas Combe

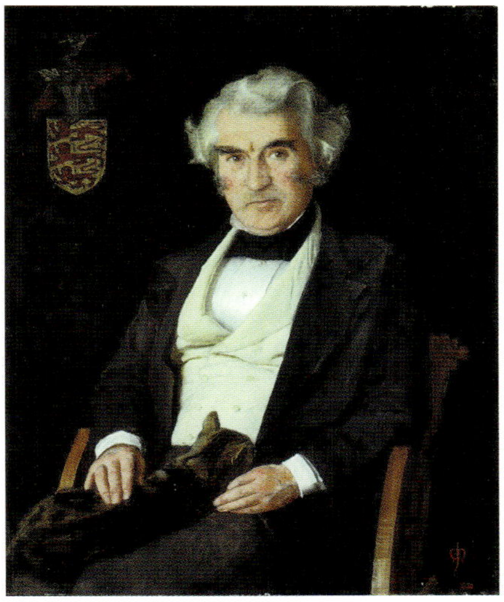

A272; oil on panel, 33 × 27 cm
Signed in monogram and dated: *1850*
Combe Bequest, 1893; WA1894.9

Poole 1912, no. 487; Funnell and Warner 1999, no. 6

Thomas Combe was printer to the University of Oxford from 1838 until 1872. He met Millais and Charles Collins in 1850 while they were painting at Botley. His wife presided over a salon at her home in Walton Street and it was there that this portrait and the companion by Collins of William Bennett, were painted. This painting was made in four sittings of two hours each. The coat of arms is that granted to Shakespeare's friend, John Combe in 1584. He was no relation of Thomas Combe.

Sir John Everett Millais, Bt
(1829 – 1896)

The Return of the Dove to the Ark

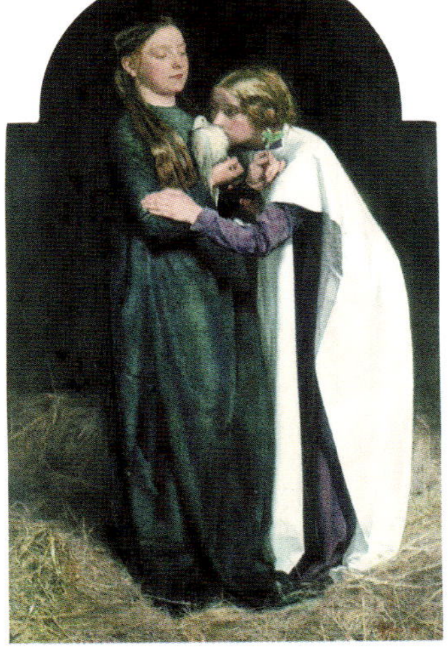

A271; oil on canvas, 88.2 × 54.9 cm
Signed and dated: *J Millais 1851*
Combe Bequest, 1893; WA1894.8

Parris 1984, no. 34; Brown 1987, no. 21

In 1850, Millais began work on an ambitious painting of *The Deluge*, known from descriptions in letters to Combe and from a drawing in the British Museum. His eventual painting, which is not the sermon he had at first envisaged, is much less rhetorical. The subject is from Genesis, 8: 11: in order to ascertain whether the flood had abated, Noah sent out a dove, which returned with a sprig of olive. Here, the daughters of Noah hold the dove and the olive sprig. Although the background is untypically dark, the details are painted with astonishing fidelity and Ruskin so admired the work that he tried to buy it when it was exhibited at the Royal Academy in 1851. It had already been sold to Combe in March. Its new owner hung it on one side of Holman Hunt's *The Converted British Family*, with Collins's *Convent Thoughts* on the other. The frame is original and includes elements appropriate to the painting: olive leaves and fruit.

Attributed to Sir John Everett Millais, Bt
(1829 – 1896)

Portrait of a young Girl

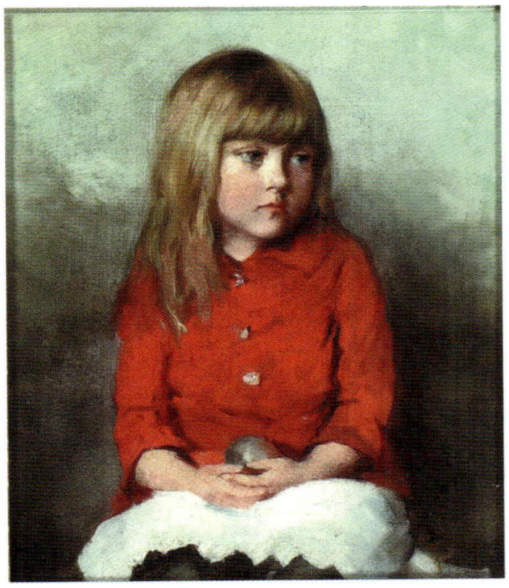

A500; oil on canvas, 36 × 31 cm
Weldon Bequest, 1937; WA1937.81

Until recently, the attribution to Millais was accepted without question and the sitter identified as Mary Millais, the artist's daughter. Both artist and sitter are now doubtful, though no convincing alternatives have been proposed.

Jean-François (called Francisque) Millet
(1642 – 1679)

Mountainous Landscape with a Citadel

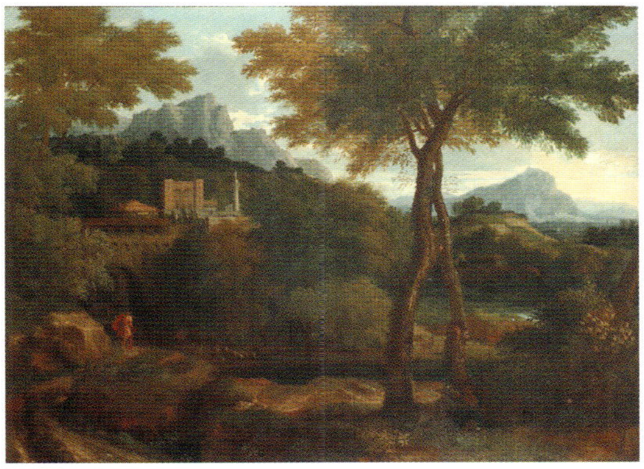

A416; oil on canvas, 76 × 99 cm
Purchased, 1932; WA1932.195

Biard 2003, no. 30

Millet, who trained in France and travelled to England and Holland, studied the work of Poussin and made his reputation with austere classical landscapes in his manner. Some were engraved at an early date, providing virtually the only documentation for his work. The chronology of his paintings is difficult to establish. A416 depicts a richly varied, extensive landscape, with a solitary traveller on the left providing a romantic note.

Jean-François Millet
(1814 – 1875)

Recalling the Flock

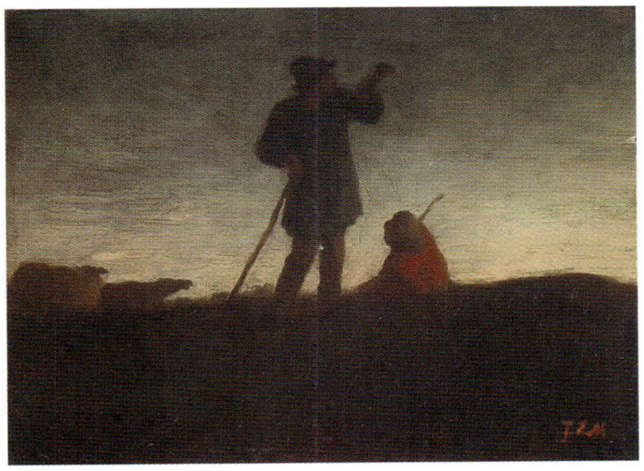

A888; oil on panel, 11.5 × 15.5 cm
Signed: *J.F.M*
Prov.: Alfred Sensier; Miss L. Coats
Purchased, 1956; WA1956.44

Moreau-Nélaton 1921, III, p. 86

Closely related to a drawing of about 1866 and to a larger painting of 1872.

Hilda Lucy Milne
(*c.* 1870 – 1960)

Study of a Man on Horseback

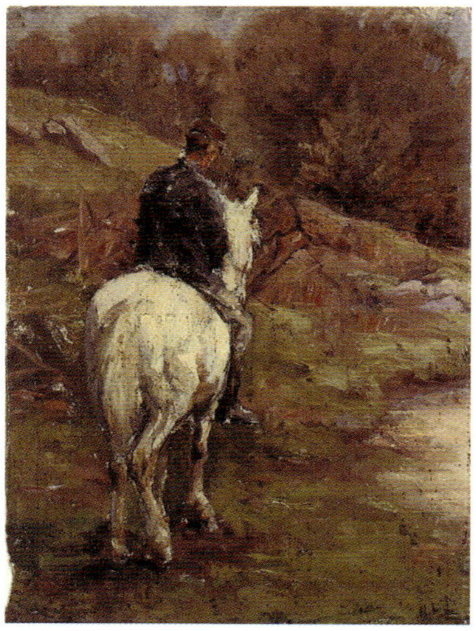

A1061a; oil on canvas, mounted as a drawing, 27.6 × 20 cm
Signed: *H.L.M.*
Presented by L.M. Angus-Butterworth in memory of his father, 1971; WA1971.107

Hendrick van Minderhout
(1632 – 1696)

View of the Roads of Antwerp from the West Bank

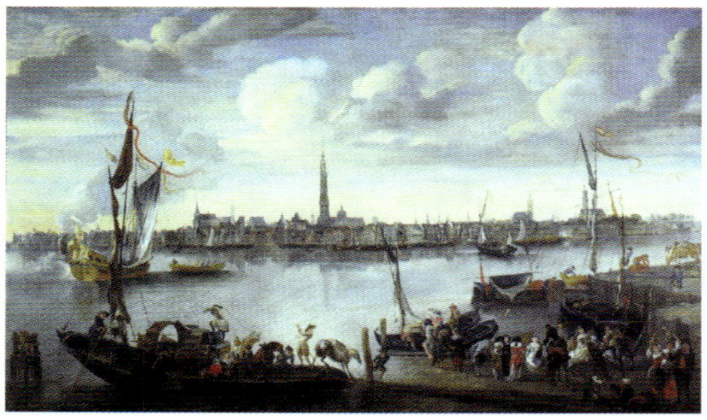

A19; oil on canvas, 121 × 201 cm
Presented by the Revd Dr Richard Rawlinson before 1755; WA1845.19

White 1999, p. 88

Minderhout was born in Amsterdam but moved to Antwerp in 1672. He specialised in painting marines and may have been commissioned to paint this view of Antwerp for a civic building in the city. Four other variants of the painting are known.

Pier Francesco Mola
(1612 – 1666)

Echo and Narcissus

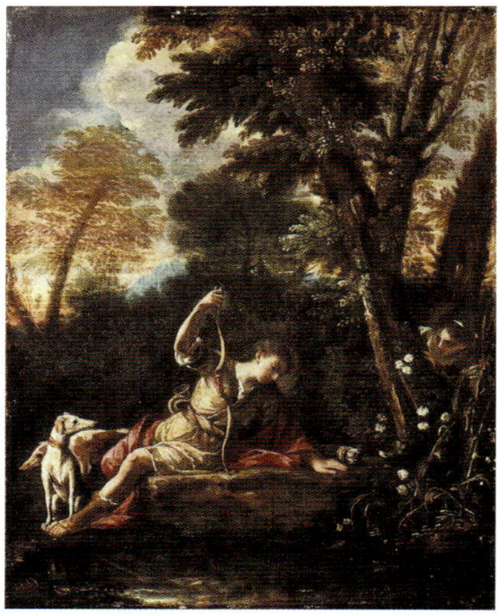

A872; oil on canvas, 50 × 39 cm
Prov.: probably George Frederick Handel
Purchased, 1954; WA1954.84

Genty 1979, pp. 90–1

According to Ovid, *Metamorphoses*, III, 339–510, the talkative nymph Echo, now only an echoing voice, vainly pursued the self-absorbed Narcissus, who fell in love with his own beauty as reflected in a pool and was transformed into a flower. A872 is clearly an early work, from 1633–41, a time when Mola supported himself by painting small scenes with attractive landscapes, often as here in a neo-Venetian manner.

Malcolm Midwood Milne
(1887 – 1954)

View near Lancing from the South Downs

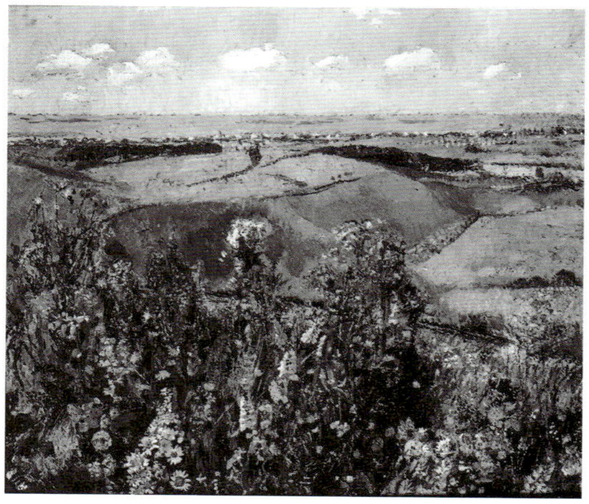

A1051; oil on blockboard, 75 × 86 cm
Signed: *MALCOLM MILNE*
Bequeathed by Mrs C.W. Dyson Perrins, the artist's sister, 1969; WA1969.7

Lowe 1966, no. 17

In 1926, Milne went to live at The Dykes, Henfield, Sussex, where he constructed a studio and where much of his work was painted. This view was commissioned by the donor for her drawing room, perhaps around 1930.

Attributed to Claes Cornelisz. Moeyaert
(*c.* 1590 – 1655)

Two Children stealing an Apple from a Man with a Basket

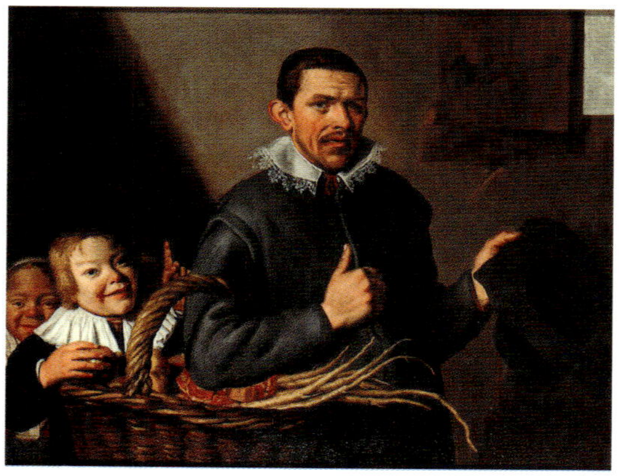

A782; oil on canvas, 82.4 × 106.3 cm
Bequeathed by the Revd Dr John King, 1739; WA1950.20

White 1999, p. 90

In the 18th century, this picture was attributed to Frans Hals. A more plausible attribution to the Amsterdam painter, Moeyaert, has been made on the basis of a comparison with a painting in the Rijksmuseum, Amsterdam, *The Choice between Young and Old.*

Pier Francesco Mola
(baptized 1612 – 1666)

An Oriental Figure

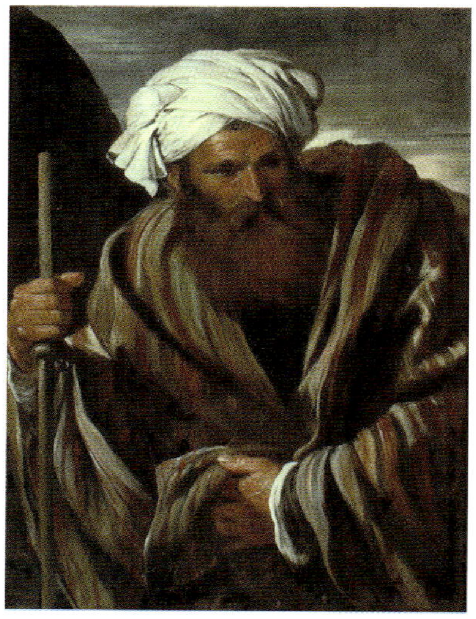

A937; oil on canvas, 99 × 74 cm
Purchased with the assistance of the Victoria & Albert Museum Purchase Grant Fund, 1960; WA1960.73

Cocke 1972, no. R 33

The figure carries no identifying attributes, but his turban, staff and striped robe suggest a Biblical context. A937 forms part of a group of paintings of single figures of the early 1650s, for which the splendid *Barbary Pirate* (Louvre, Paris), signed and dated 1650, is a point of reference.

Style of Jan Miense Molenaer
(*c.* 1610 – 1668)

Interior with three Peasants

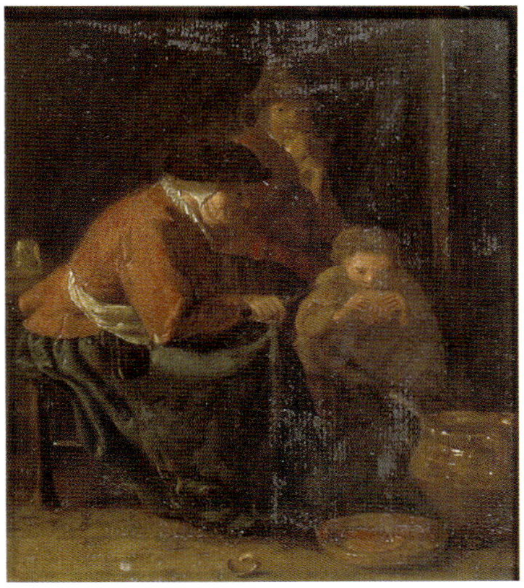

A306; oil on panel, 23 × 20 cm
Fortnum Bequest, 1899; WA1899.CDEF.P24

White 1999, p. 91

This painting is badly damaged and difficult to assess. It seems to have been painted in Molenaer's style. The artist was a genre painter from Haarlem to whom a number of similar peasant subjects have been attributed.

Claude Monet
(1840 – 1926)

A Mill near Zaandam

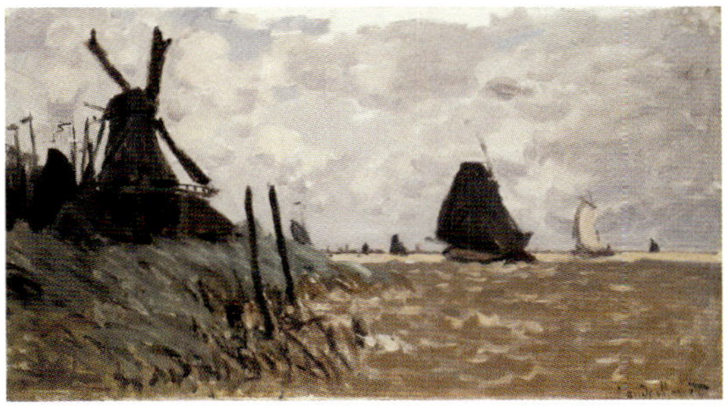

A1115; oil on canvas, 42 × 73.5 cm
Signed: *Claude Monet*
Prov.: Durand-Ruel; Cassirer
Accepted by H. M. Government in lieu of Inheritance Tax from the estate of Dr and Mrs Richard Walzer and allocated to the Ashmolean Museum, 1980; WA1980.81

Wildenstein 1974, no. 178

Painted during a visit to Holland in 1871. The colour is subdued and the sky overcast but the white ground on which it is painted gives a natural luminosity to the scene and the varied brush-strokes create a fresh, windswept effect. It was painted near Zaandam, about twelve miles from Amsterdam.

Bartolomeo Montagna
(*c.* 1450 – 1523)

The Marriage of Antiochus and Stratonice

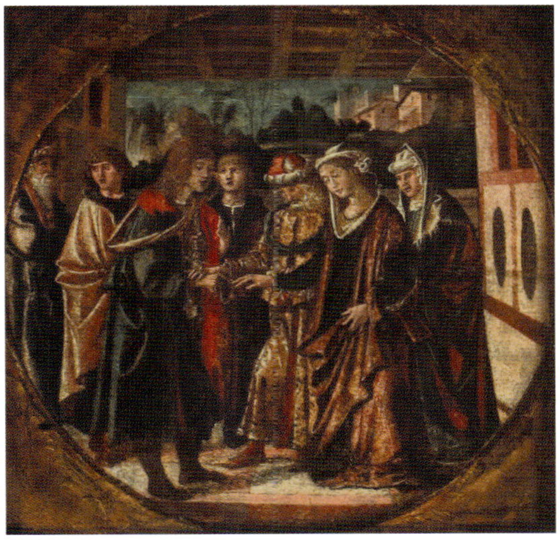

A722; tempera and oil (?) on panel, 29 cm in diameter
Prov.: H. Merritt; Sir William Farrer
Bequeathed by Gaspard O. Farrer through the National Art Collections Fund, 1946; WA1946.200

Lloyd 1977, pp. 122–4; Balboni Brizza 1995, p. 26

Together with A723, this roundel was inserted into the front of a *cassone*. A *cassone* in Milan has two similar roundels by Montagna with scenes from ancient history. Both chests would have been commissioned to celebrate a wedding in the early 1490s. Antiochus was ill with love for his stepmother, Stratonice: realising this, Seleucus handed over both his wife and his kingdom to his son (Plutarch, *Lives*, 43: 38).

Joos de Momper
(1564 – 1635)

Wintry Landscape with the Flight into Egypt

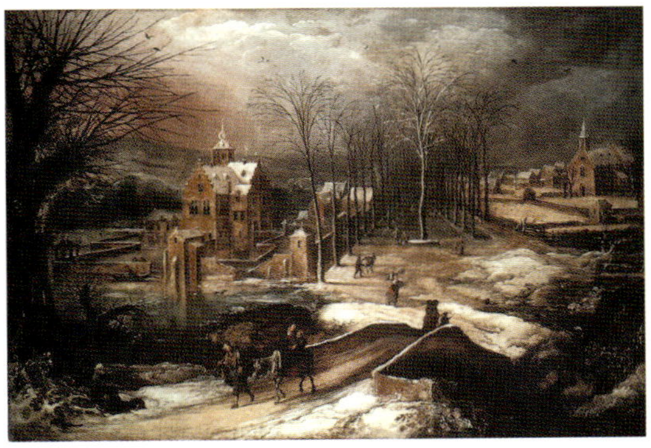

A407; oil on canvas, 114 × 164 cm
Signed in monogram: *IDM*
Presented by Sir Arthur Evans, 1931; WA1931.16

White 1999, p. 92

One of a large group of winter landscapes painted by de Momper. He repeated this particular landscape at least twice but with different figures. It may be that the figures in this picture were painted by a collaborator. Although the landscape is plainly North European, the setting is intended to represent the route from the Holy Land into Egypt where the Holy Family took refuge from Herod's persecution (Matthew 2: 13–15).

Bartolomeo Montagna
(*c.* 1450 – 1523)

The Virgin and Child

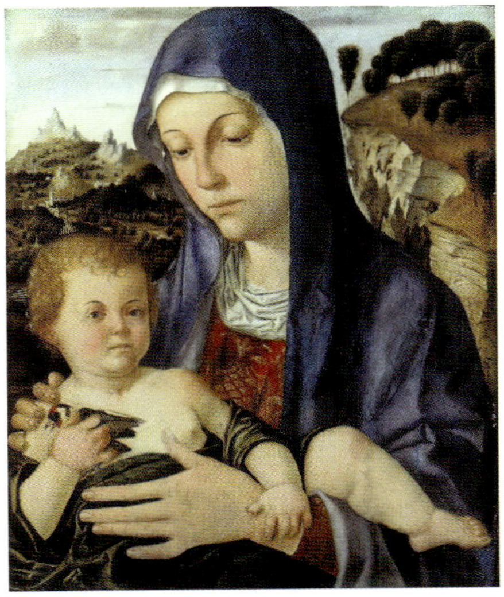

A724; tempera and oil (?) on panel, 34 × 28 cm
Prov.: Bonomi-Cereda, Milan; Sir William Farrer
Bequeathed by Gaspard O. Farrer through the National Art Collections Fund, 1946; WA1946.202

Lloyd 1977, pp. 120–2

Probably dating from the 1480s, A724 is a fine example of a type of intimate devotional image popularised by Giovanni Bellini. Montagna, a leading painter in Vicenza, may have worked in Bellini's studio in Venice in the 1470s. The Child holds a goldfinch, a symbol of the Passion since the blood of Christ was said to have fallen on the bird's feathers on the way to Calvary.

Bartolomeo Montagna
(*c.* 1450 – 1523)

An Incident in the Story of the Vestal Claudia

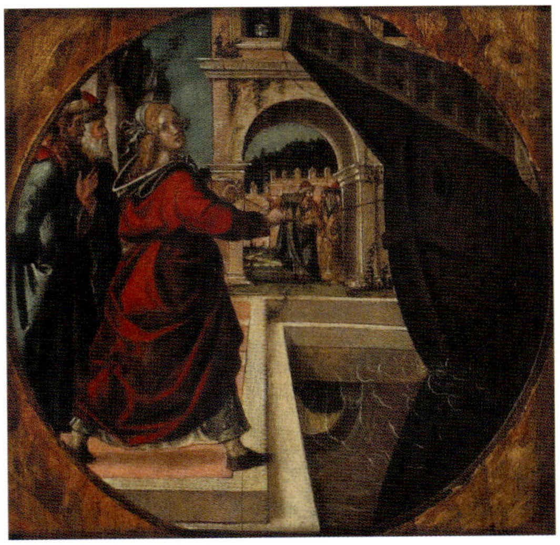

A723; tempera and oil (?) on panel, 29 cm in diameter
Prov.: H. Merritt; Sir William Farrer
Bequeathed by Gaspard O. Farrer through the National Art Collections Fund, 1946; WA1946.201

Lloyd 1977, pp. 122–4; Balboni Brizza 1995, p. 26

As with A723, the narrative illustrates the theme of chastity. The Vestal Virgin Claudia proved her chastity by a feat of miraculous strength, pulling a loaded boat free from the shallows of the Tiber (Ovid, *Fasti*, IV, 305–28).

Bartolomeo Montagna
(c. 1450 – 1523)

Christ carrying the Cross

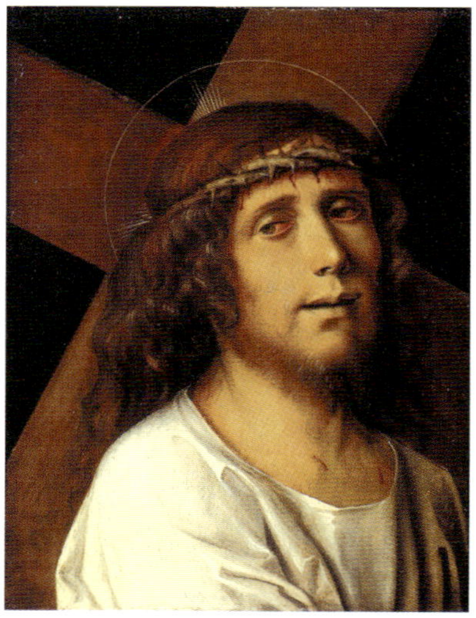

A874; oil and tempera (?) on panel, 28.4 × 21.6 cm
Prov.: Lady Cheetham; Sir Thomas Barlow
Presented by the National Art Collections Fund, 1955; WA1955.3

Lloyd 1977, pp. 124–5; Humfrey 1983, no. 110

This type of image of the suffering Christ was highly popular in Venetian art of the early 16th century, particularly in the circle of Bellini. It may derive from the work of Leonardo da Vinci. A874 probably dates from c. 1503.

Henry Moore
(1831 – 1896)

On the Seine near Les Andelys

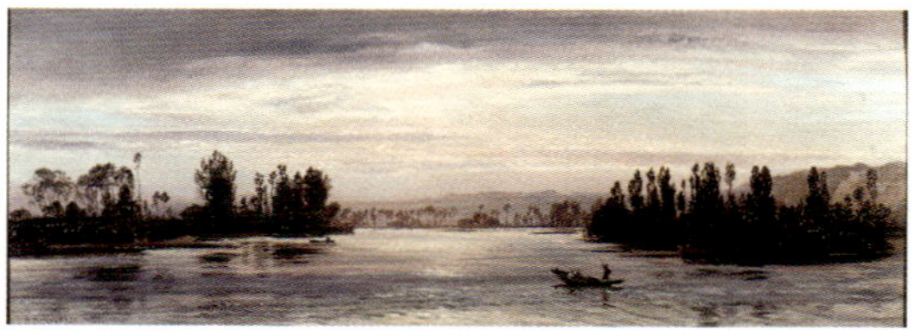

A373; oil on canvas, 30 × 81 cm
Bequeathed by Mrs A.V. Dicey, 1923; WA1923.3

Moore came from a family of artists and in later life, was regarded as one of the most important painters in England. He specialised in marine painting. This view of the Seine near Les Andelys, the birthplace of Nicolas Poussin in Normandy, probably dates from his years of success in the 1880s.

Domenico Morelli
(1826 – 1901)

Self-portrait

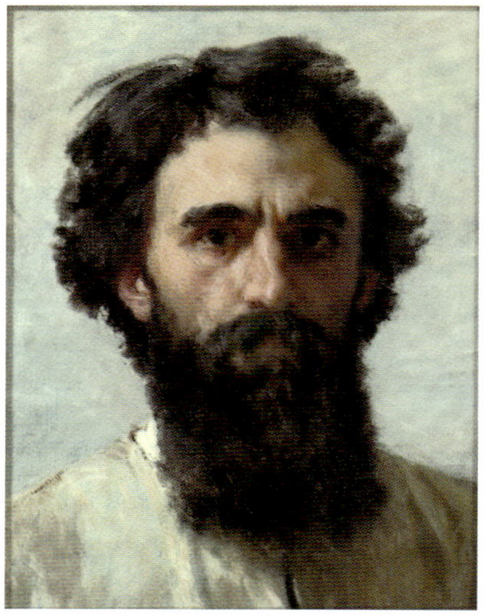

A1072; oil on canvas, 43 × 33.5 cm
Prov.: Professor Pasquale Villari, brother-in-law of the artist, and by descent
Bequeathed by the Lady Berwick, 1973; WA1973.5

Spalletti 1979, under no. A618

Judging by the artist's appearance, the portrait may date from the early 1860s. Three other self-portraits are known: Accademia di Belle Arti, Naples, painted in 1852; Uffizi, Florence, c. 1870–80; and Galleria Nazionale d'Arte Moderna, Rome, 1886. A pupil of Costanzo Angelini and Camillo Guerra in Naples, Morelli painted many subjects with Christian or patriotic allusions.

Attributed to Carel de Moor the Younger
(1655 – 1738)

Portrait of a young Man

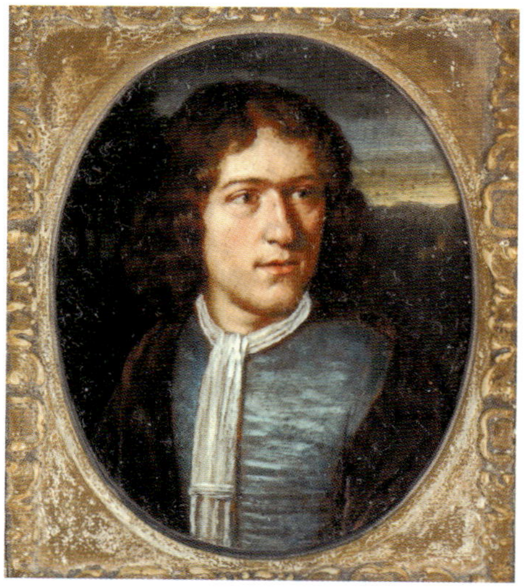

A979; oil on panel, 11 × 9 cm
Madan Bequest, 1962; WA1962.17.21

White 1999, p. 93

The attribution to de Moor is somewhat supported by a small oval *Self-portrait* in the Rijksmuseum, Amsterdam, but A979 is more coarsely executed.

Luis de Morales
(c. 1520 – after 1585)

Virgin and Child

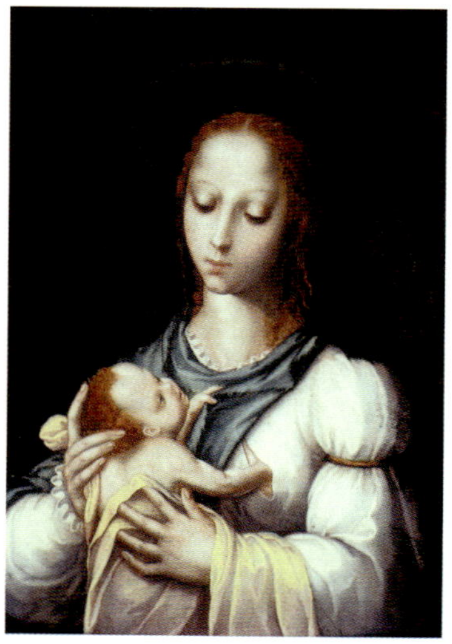

A871; oil and tempera (?) on panel, 43.5 × 29.5 cm
Prov.: Benito Garriga, Madrid; Sir Augustus M. Daniel
Purchased, 1954; WA1954.52

Solís Rodríguez 1999, no. 61

Morales spent his career in Badajoz; the majority of his pictures are small devotional works. A similar composition is in the National Gallery and other versions are in the Museo del Prado, Madrid. Unlike these and unusually, A871 combines the idea of the Virgin feeding the Child with that of the Virgin as a traveller, wearing a straw hat or sombrero (a reference to the Flight into Egypt). A871 may date from c. 1567.

Alessandro Bonvicino, called Moretto da Brescia
(c. 1498 – 1554)

The Virgin and Child with St Jerome

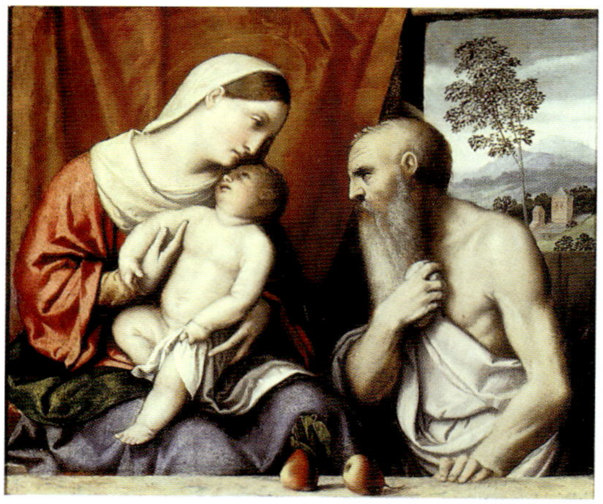

A980; oil on panel, 50.4 × 58.7 cm
Prov.: Henry Manfield
Madan Bequest, 1962; WA1962.17.22

Lloyd 1977, pp. 125–7; Begni Redona 1988, no. 48

Moretto was keenly interested in Venetian art: in this expressive devotional painting of c. 1530–5 the landscape and figure types reveal his study of Titian. St Jerome (c. 342–420) holds a stone to his breast, a reference to his acts of penitence. A variant is in the Accademia Carrara, Bergamo and a copy is in a private collection.

George Morland
(1763 – 1804)

Farmyard Scene: a Donkey and Goats

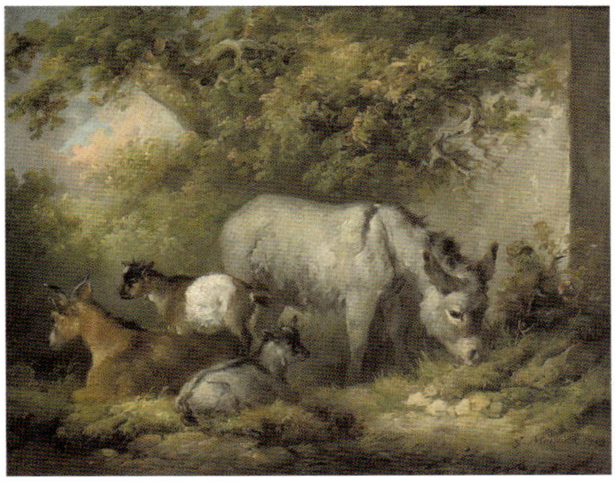

A688; oil on canvas, 32 × 39 cm
Signed and dated: *G. Morland. 1792*
Purchased, 1941; WA1941.157

A characteristically sentimental work and one of many with the same date.

Giovanni Battista Moroni
(*c.* 1520 – 1578)

The Mystic Marriage of St Catherine

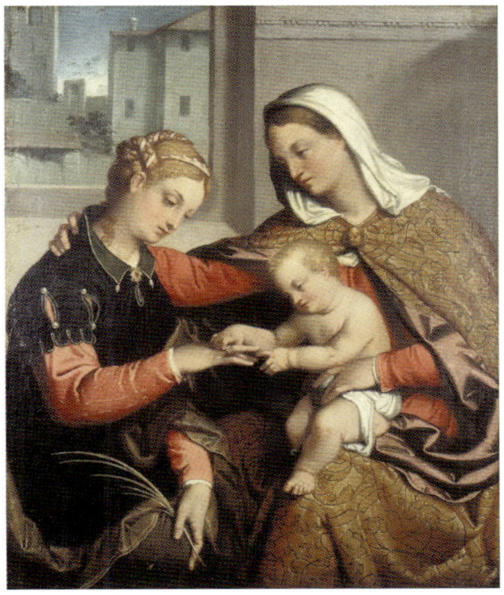

A446; oil on canvas, 82.6 × 67.5 cm
Prov.: Sampieri, Bologna; Sir Robert Gordon; Samuel Rogers; M.A. Whyte; Captain Arthur Finch Dawson
Purchased, 1935; WA1935.160

Lloyd 1977, pp. 127; Gregori 1979, no. 169

An early Christian martyr of royal birth, St Catherine is shown receiving a wedding-ring from Christ, symbolising her spiritual closeness to God. A pupil of Moretto, Moroni worked mainly in Bergamo. This devotional painting, an early work of *c.* 1550, is close in style to the mature paintings of Moretto. The Torre del Comune, which later appears in two of his portraits, is shown on the left.

Jan Mortel
(*c.* 1650 – 1719)

Still Life of Fruit

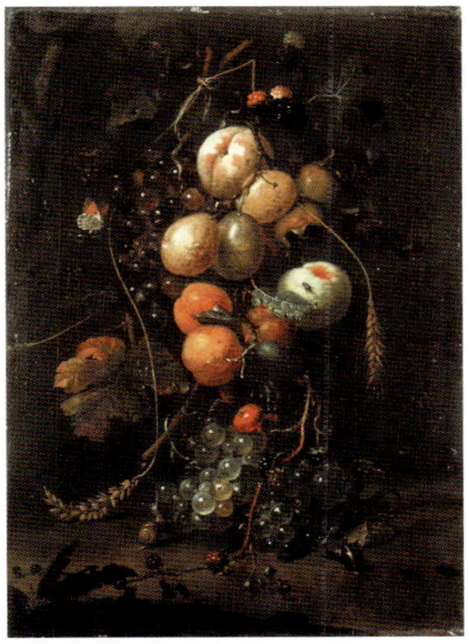

A584; oil on canvas, 54 × 38 cm
Signed: *JMortel fecit. / 1708* (JM in monogram)
Prov.: Earl of Camperdown until 1919
Daisy Linda Ward Bequest, 1939; WA1940.2.60

Meijer 2003, no. 61

Mortel worked in Leiden, painting fruit and flowers in a manner that shows an early interest in the work of Jan Davidsz. de Heem. His later work shows a debt to Abraham Mignon whose work seems to have provided the model for this painting. Many of the details are copied from a painting by Mignon now in the Gemäldegalerie, Dresden.

George Morland
(1763 – 1804)

Landscape with Huntsmen and Hounds

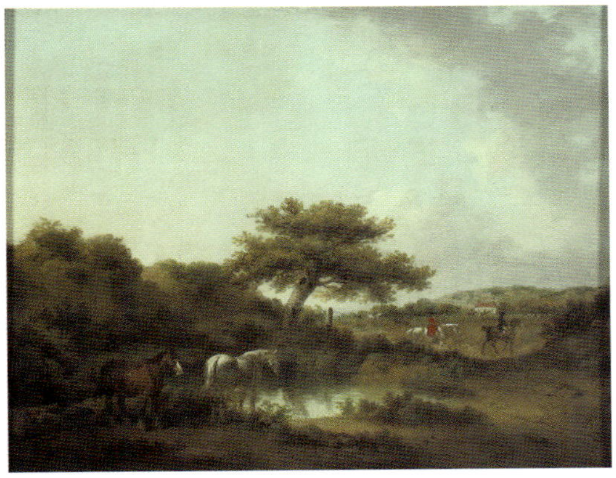

A134; oil on canvas, 43 × 56 cm
Signed: *G. Morland pinx.*
Prov.: Auckland
Bequeathed by the Revd Dr Thomas Penrose, 1851; WA1851.6

Philip Morsberger
(b. 1933)

The White Background

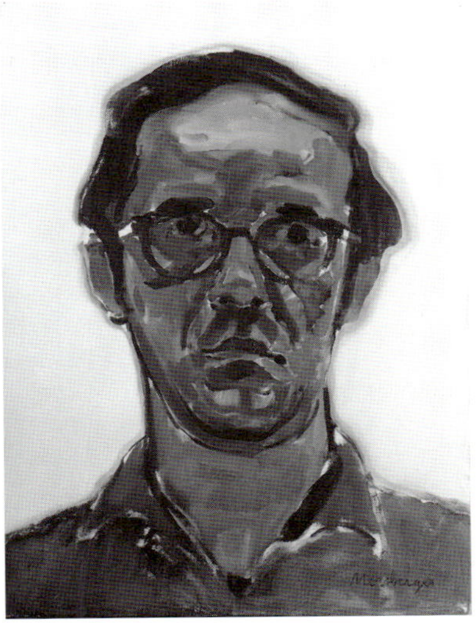

A1132; oil on canvas, 64.5 × 48 cm
Signed: *Morsberger*; inscribed with title on back: *The White Background Morsberger Oxford 1972*
Purchased (Hope Fund) to mark the artist's years as Ruskin Master, 1984; WA1984.148

Philip Morsberger studied at the Ruskin School of Drawing in Oxford in the 1950s and became the Master at the School in 1971, a position he held until 1984. At the beginning of his time as Ruskin Master he painted this self-portrait in a semi-realistic style, a straight frontal image reduced to a pattern of large brush-strokes.

Rodrigo Moynihan
(1910 – 1990)

The Orchard in Autumn

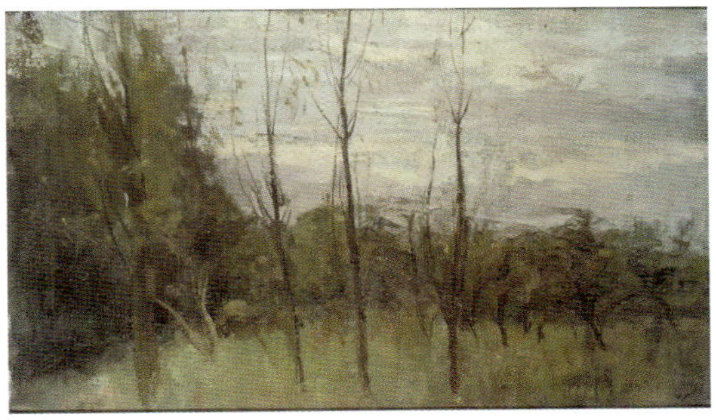

A753; oil on canvas, 30.9 × 51 cm
Presented by John Dodgson, 1948; WA1948.70

Moynihan was associated with the Euston Road School, although he was not an official member. In common with the artists of this School, he concentrated on the figurative tradition but his manner of painting differs from theirs in its much freer use of paint and gesture. His art was not so closely bound to the close representation of nature, but, as here, by the sense of delight felt by the observer before the spectacle of a light-filled landscape.

David Muirhead
(1867 – 1930)

Chepstow Castle

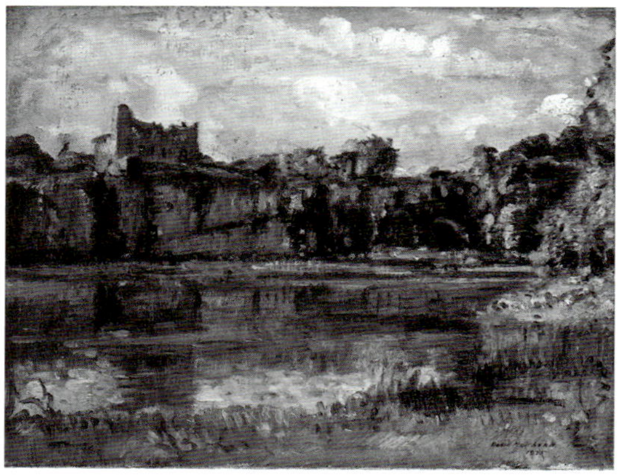

A472; oil on canvas, 36 × 46 cm
Signed and dated: *David Muirhead / 1925*
Weldon Bequest, 1937; WA1937.52

This view, taken from the bank of the River Wye, is painted with the lively brushwork much seen at the exhibitions of the New English Art Club.

George Mullins
(active 1763 – 1775)

Landscape with a fishing Party by a Waterfall

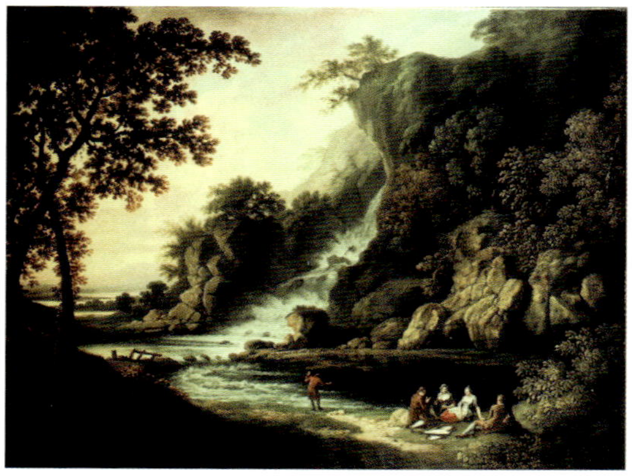

A339; oil on canvas, 117 × 151 cm
Signed and dated: *George Mullins Pinx Anno 1772*
Bequeathed by Charles J. Moss, 1914; WA1914.1

Crookshank and Glin 2002, pp. 143–4

Mullins worked in Dublin and exhibited at the Royal Academy between 1770 and 1775. This painting is typical of the decorative landscapes he produced in the manner of Joseph Vernet. It has recently been proposed that it was the painting, *A Cataract; a rude scene*, illustrating a passage from Thomson's *Seasons – Summer*, shown at the Royal Academy in 1772.

Sir Alfred James Munnings
(1878 – 1959)

Tombland Fair

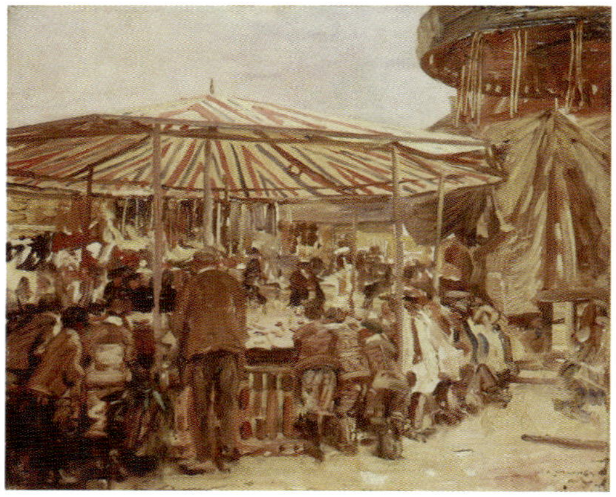

A1010; oil on canvas, 51 × 62 cm
Signed and dated: *A.J.Munnings / 1911*
Bequeathed by Major Thomas Bouch, 1963; WA1963.150.7

Tombland is an area in the centre of Norwich, where an annual fair was held from medieval times.

William James Müller
(1812 – 1845)

Keynsham, near Bristol

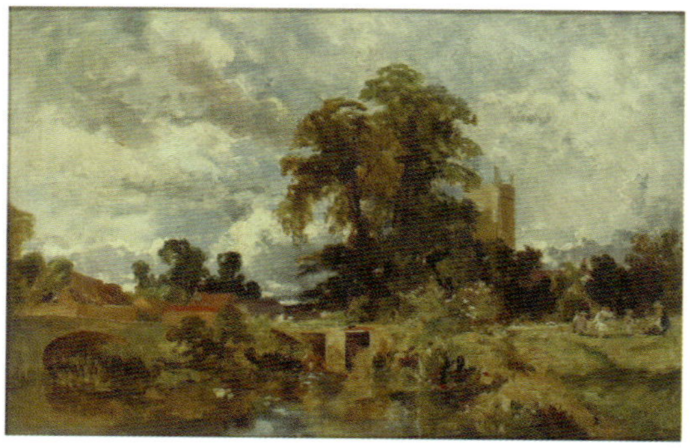

A1052; oil on canvas, 54 × 80 cm
Bequeathed by Mrs C.W. Dyson Perrins, 1969; WA1969.8

For most of his life, Müller was based in his native Bristol, although he travelled on the Continent in 1834–5, Egypt in 1838–9 and France in 1840. This view of Keynsham, a few miles south-east of Bristol, probably dates from the late 1830s.

Sir Alfred James Munnings
(1878 – 1959)

Two Calves grazing by a Hedge

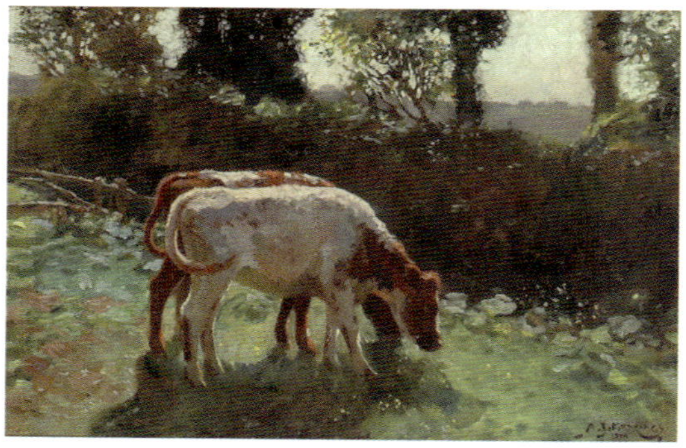

A1011; oil on canvas, 52 × 78 cm
Signed and dated: *A.J.Munnings / 1904*
Bequeathed by Major Thomas Bouch, 1963; WA1963.150.8

Attributed to Francesco de Mura
(1696 – 1782)

Tobias and the Angel

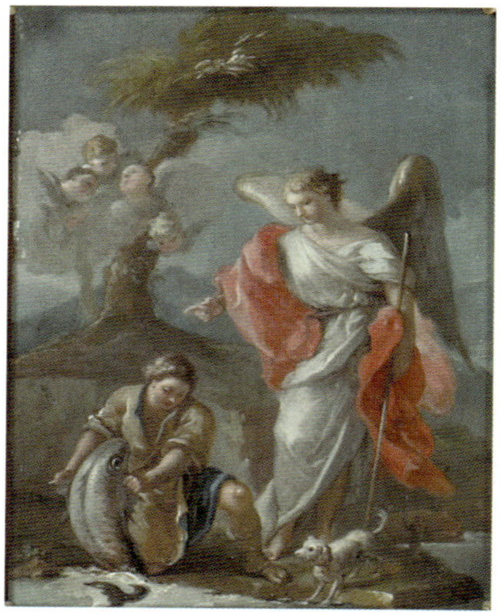

A1090; oil on panel, 21 × 17.3 cm
Inscribed on back: *Francesco La Mura Pittore di Napoli fect 17[35?]*
Bequeathed by the Revd W.H. Simmons, 1977; WA1978.25

Guided by an angel, Tobias cured Tobit's blindness with an ointment made from a fish. The subject occurs a number of times in the work of de Mura and his pupils. The silvery tonality, delicate handling and figure types have affinities with paintings of the 1740s by the master. Attributions to Pietro Bardellino and Francesco Celebrano have also been suggested.

Richard Arthur Crosthwaite Murry
(1902 – 1984)

Still Life with Lemons and Lettuces

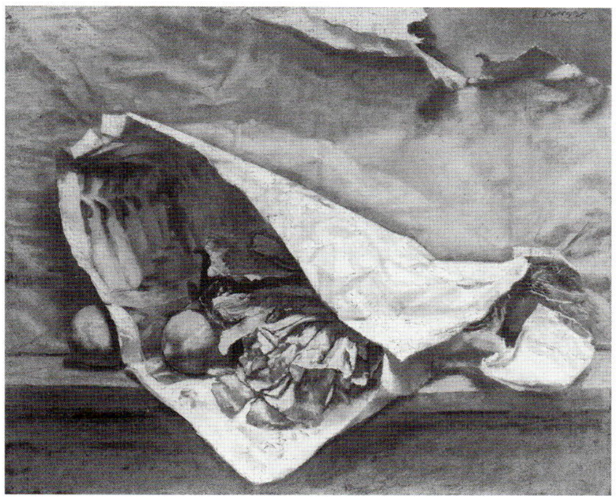

A453; oil on canvas, 51 × 61 cm
Signed and dated: *R Murry 25*
Weldon Bequest, 1937; WA1937.33

Murry, who later painted the portrait of Mrs Weldon, is also represented in her collection with this small still life.

Richard Arthur Crosthwaite Murry
(1902 – 1984)

Mrs W.F.R. Weldon

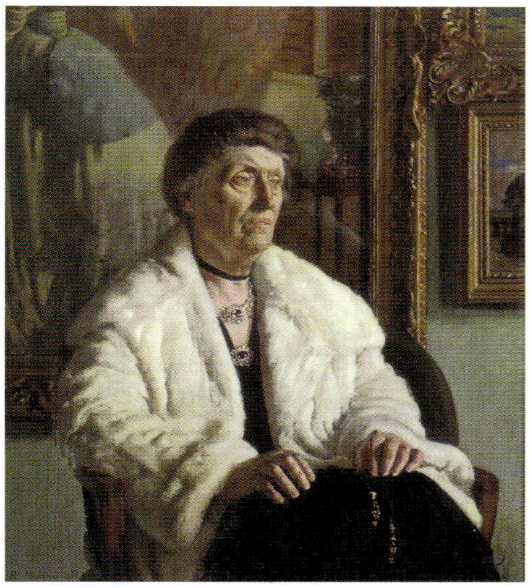

A501; oil on canvas, 89 × 76 cm
Signed and dated: *R. Murry 28*
Weldon Bequest, 1937; WA1937.82.1

In 1928 Florence Weldon commissioned Murry to paint her portrait, which he prepared in an oil-sketch (see A929). The light in the finished portrait is sharper and sometimes merciless, the posture of the right hand tenser and the whole appearance is more representional. Behind her is part of the collection of paintings she gave to the Ashmolean. In the sketch were paintings by Tonks (A439), Steer (A467) and Corot (A393). In the definitive version the Corot was replaced with a painting by Bonington (A421).

Giovanni Battista Naldini
(1537 – 1591)

Christ in Glory with Sts Agnes and Helena

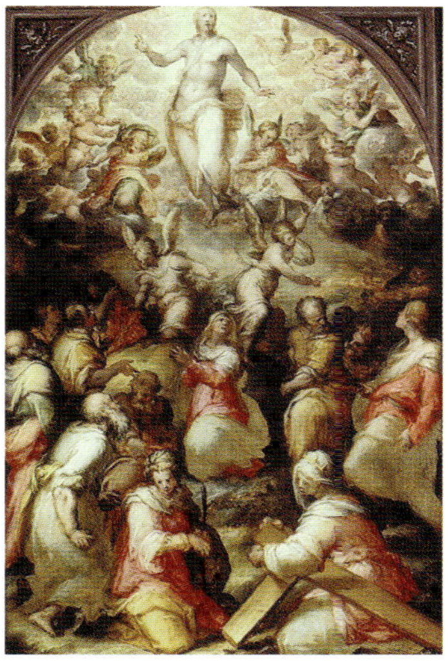

A1014; oil on panel, 49 × 32 cm
Prov.: Palazzo Riccardi, Florence
Purchased, 1964; WA1964.41.1

Lloyd 1977, pp. 129–32; Clover 1999

Helena (*c.* 255–*c.* 330), mother of the emperor Constantine, carries a cross because of her discovery of the True Cross, while the attribute of Agnes is a lamb (*agnus*). Lena Ottinelli commissioned an altar-piece from Maso da San Friano in 1563 for the chapel of the confraternity of St Agnes at S. Maria del Carmine, Florence. After Maso's death in 1571 the commission passed to Naldini and this colourful compositional sketch was part of his preparatory process; the altar-piece was destroyed by fire in 1771.

Richard Arthur Crosthwaite Murry
(1902 – 1984)

Sketch for the Portrait of Mrs W.F.R. Weldon

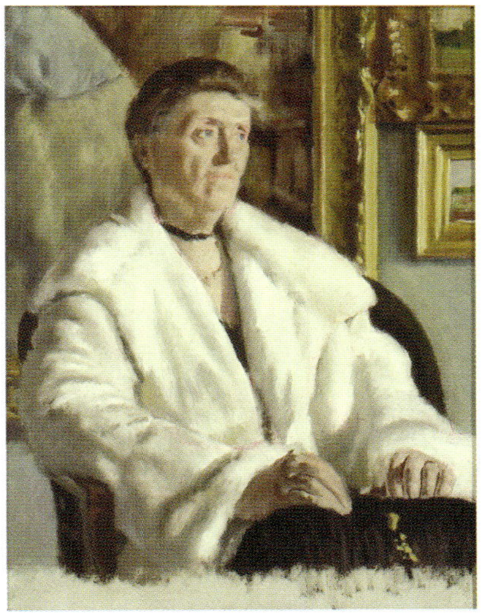

A929; oil on canvas, 46 × 35.5 cm
Presented by I.G. Robertson, 1959; WA1959.3

This canvas was a preparatory sketch for the much larger finished portrait (see A501) and must have been painted *c.* 1928.

Richard Ellis Naish
(1912 – 1988)

Self-portrait

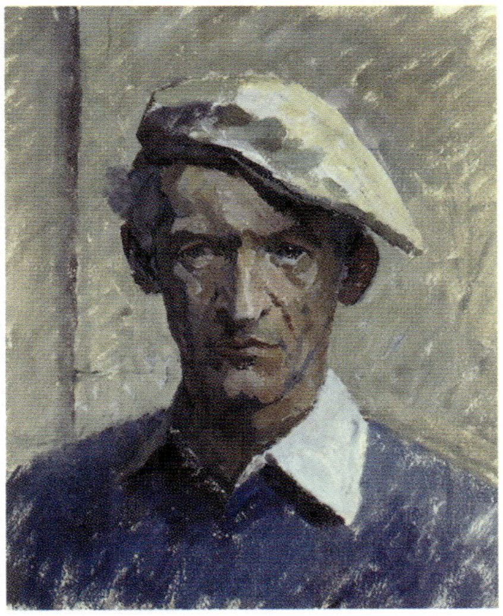

Oil on paper, mounted on cardboard, mounted as a drawing, 31.8 × 25 cm
Purchased (Hope Fund), 1965; WA1965.31

Naish was primarly a portrait and still-life painter. In this painting he showed himself in a frontal pose, wearing a French beret in the tradition of self-portraits of artists wearing hats or berets.

John Northcote Nash
(1893 – 1977)

A Gloucestershire Landscape

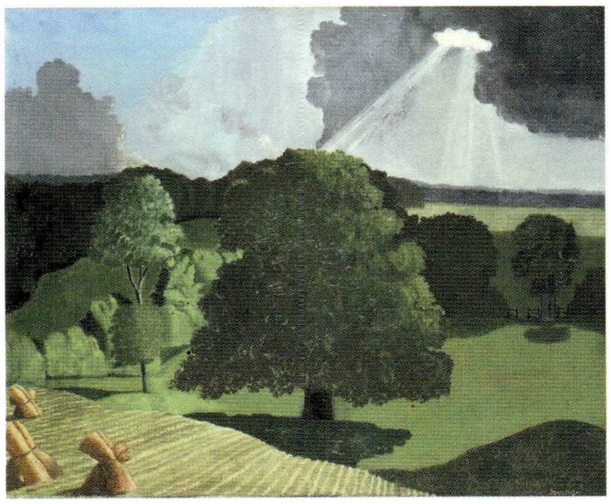

A1099; oil on canvas, 51.2 × 61.5 cm
Signed and dated: *John Nash 1914*
Presented by the New Grafton Gallery and the Trustees of the John Nash Estate, 1978; WA1978.67

Eustace 1999, no. 10

Despite his lack of formal art training, John Nash participated in exhibitions of the Camden Town Group. This scene is deserted, although human activity is evident in sheaves at the left and the well-cultivated countryside. With its reduced palette, based on greens, yellow, blue and black, it captures the atmosphere of a late summer day, shortly before a thunderstorm.

John Northcote Nash
(1893 – 1977)

Skye

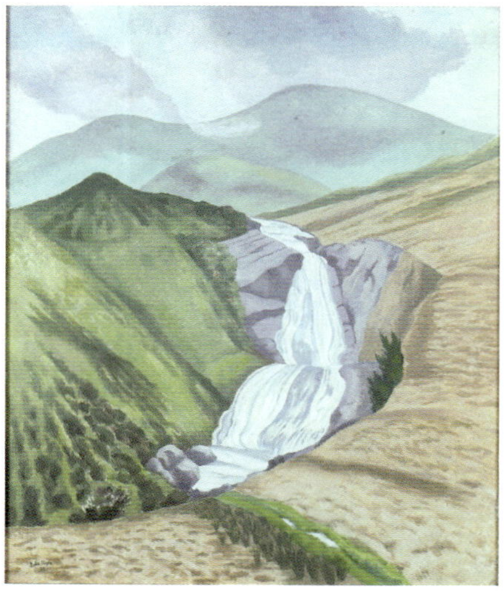

A1253; oil on canvas, 76 × 63.5 cm
Signed and dated: *John Nash / 74*
Bequeathed by Miss G. Dickinson through the National Art Collections Fund, 2002; WA2002.288

John Nash became well known for his landscapes painted in watercolour during the First World War. In the 1920s he started painting in oil. His work owed much to French landscape painting, combining an evocative style with a sense of tight construction. This is evident in this very late painting of a scene in the hills on the Isle of Skye, painted in 1974.

Thomas Saunders Nash
(1891 – 1968)

In the Orchard (The Apple Pickers)

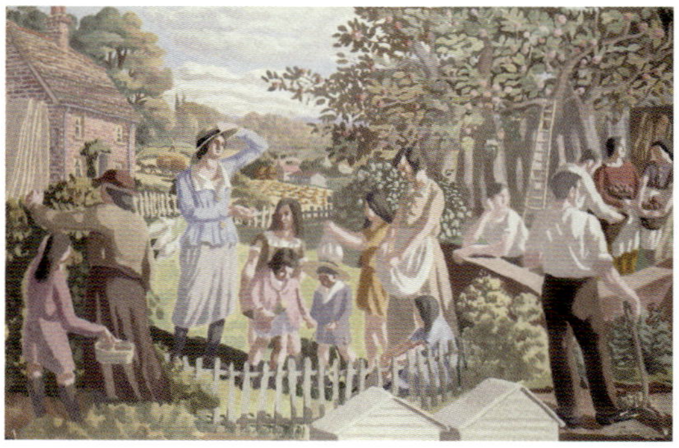

Oil on paper, mounted on cardboard, mounted as a drawing, 37.7 × 56 cm
Signed and dated: *Tom Nash 1927*
Bequeathed by Thomas Balston through the National Art Collections Fund, 1968; WA1968.37

As in other paintings, Nash depicts an arcadian world of social harmony, with people working effortlessly. Although the harvest of apples is under way, nobody seems to be working. It might be a picture of a game or a scene of leisure than real work. The dappled light and the patched application of paint, which Nash normally used in his paintings, reinforce the effect of unreality.

Patrick Nasmyth
(1787 – 1831)

Old Cottages on the Brent, looking towards Harrow

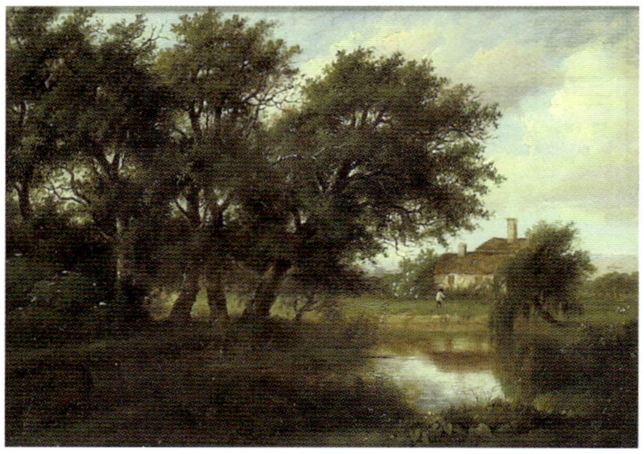

A761; oil on canvas, 26 × 37 cm
Signed and dated: *Patrick Nasmyth 1830*
Presented by F.J. Nettlefold, 1948; WA1948.37

Grundy 1933–8, III, p. 142

A very late work, painted in the year before the artist's death, but reflecting the influence of Hobbema and other Dutch masters of the 17th century.

Thomas Saunders Nash
(1891 – 1968)

In a Wood

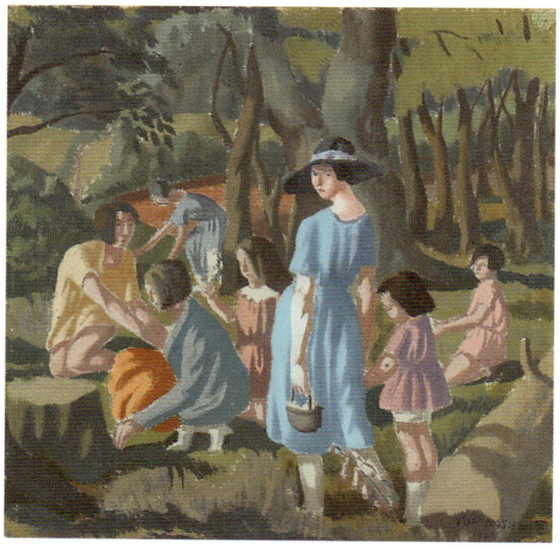

A927; oil on paper, mounted on cardboard, 28.4 × 27.8 cm
Signed and dated: *Tom Nash 1928*
Presented by Thomas Balston, 1959; WA1959.54.3

Tom Nash studied from 1908 to 1911 at the Slade School of Fine Art in London and followed in a British tradition of figurative painting. In his paintings he often represented scenes of peaceful and innoocent life in the countryside, using broad brush-strokes to evoke the forms in a reduced palette. In this case, he concentrates on some well-dressed middle-class women and children in a light and sunny wood, preparing a picnic.

Patrick Nasmyth
(1787 – 1831)

Woody Landscape

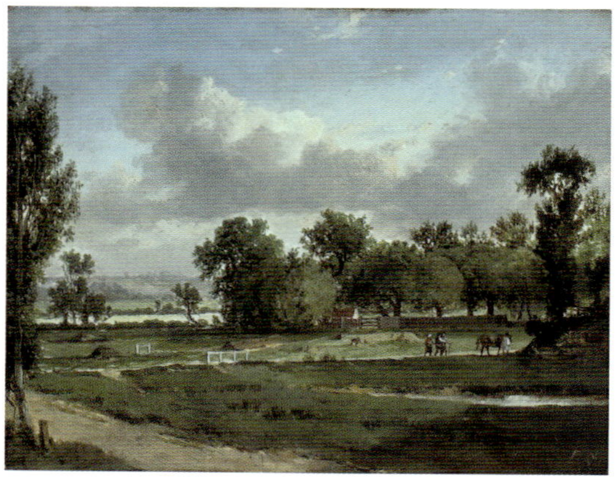

A707; oil on panel, 16 × 20 cm
Signed: *P.N.*
Prov.: Sir George Knight
Presented by Francis Falconer Madan, 1944; WA1944.11

A freely painted sketch from nature.

Pieter Nason
(1612 – 1688–90)

John Maurice, Count of Nassau Siegen

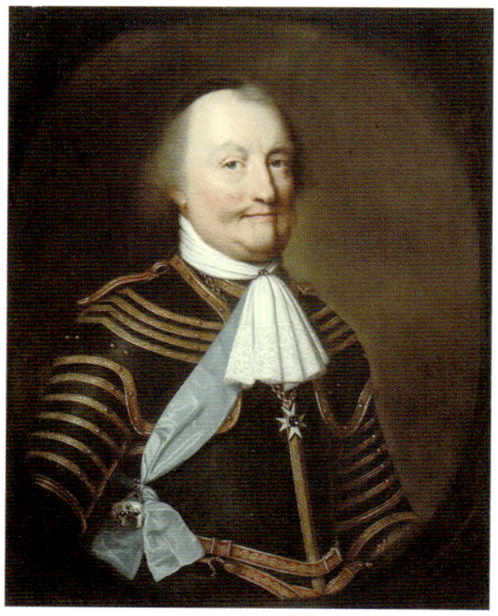

A6; oil on canvas, 86 × 88 cm
Prov.: Thomas Rawlinson and Lord Craven sale, London 4 April 1734, lot 20
Presented by Revd Dr Richard Rawlinson, 1734; WA1845.6

White 1999, p. 93

Nason painted several portraits of Johan Maurits (1604–1679) who was Governor of Brazil from 1636 to 1644. There is a three-quarter length version of this portrait, signed and dated 1663, in the Museum Mazurskie, Olsztyn, in Poland.

Bartolomeo Nazari
(1693 – 1758)

Luca Carlevarijs

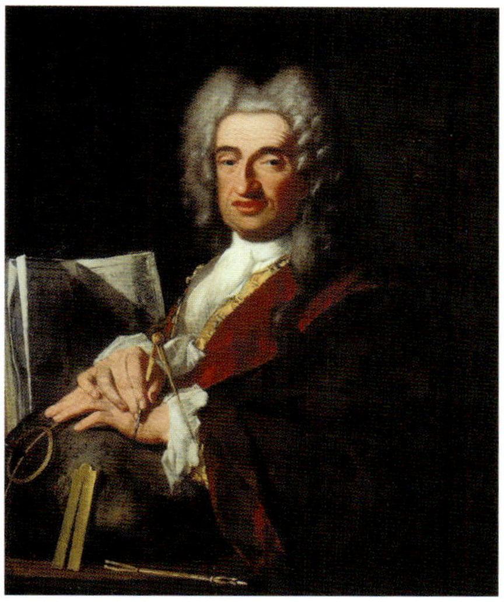

A409; oil on canvas, 97 × 79.5 cm
Presented by friends of C.F. Bell, first Keeper of the Department of Fine Art, 1931; WA1931.18

Noris 1982, no. 30

Luca Carlevarijs (1663–1731) is elegantly portrayed with the tools of the mathematician and cartographer; a palette indicates his profession. A409 was engraved by G.A. Faldoni. Nazari made his reputation as a portraitist in Venice from 1724 to 1736, before returning to his native Bergamo. A409 dates from *c.* 1724, when Canaletto was emerging as a rival in the field of view painting.

Aert van der Neer
(1603–4(?) – 1677)

Winter Landscape

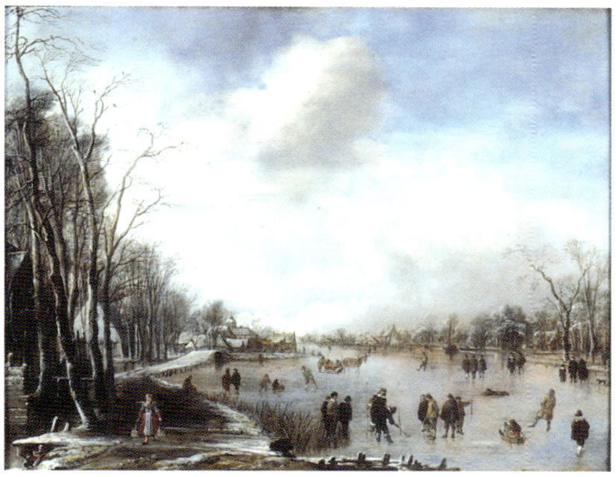

A1210; oil on panel, 56 × 71 cm
Signed in monogram and dated: *AVDN 1645*
Accepted by H.M. Government in lieu of Inheritance Tax from the estate of Elizabeth Alys Sandars and allocated to the Ashmolean Museum, 1998; WA1998.52

White 1999, p. 96

Aert van der Neer spent most of his life in Amsterdam where he specialized in moonlit and winter landscapes, painted with a subtle feeling for atmosphere and light effects. A variant of A1210, also dated 1645, is in the Corcoran Gallery, Washington.

Cornelis de Neve
(before 1609 – 1678)

Portrait of a Man, called Nicholas Fiske

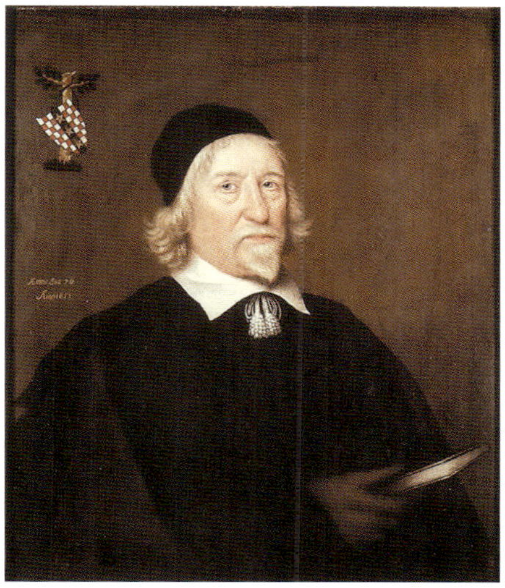

F740; oil on canvas, 76 × 64.3 cm
Signed: *CDN fecit* and inscribed: *AEatis Suae 76 Anno 1651*
Bequeathed by Elias Ashmole, 1692; WA1898.24

Poole 1912, no. 435; MacGregor 1983, no. 288

The sitter was identified from the coat of arms and the inscription as Nicholas Fiske (1575–1659), who practised as an astrologer in Colchester and London and, with Elias Ashmole's help, published Sir Christopher Heydon's *Astrological Discourse* in 1650. He was also a friend of William Lilly (see p. 27).

Copy(?) after Pieter Neefs the Elder
(1578 – 1656/61)

Interior of Antwerp Cathedral

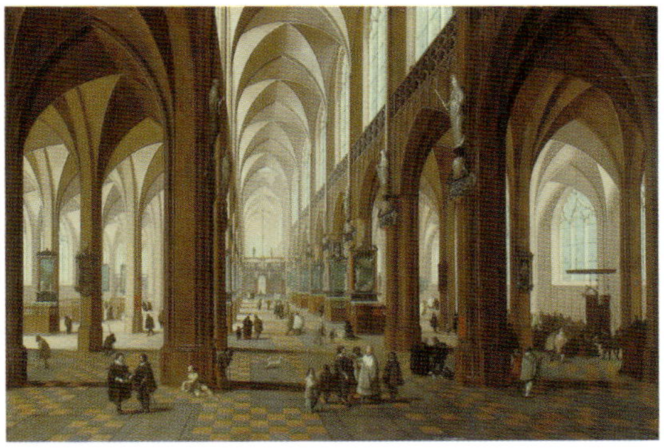

A371; oil on panel, 64 × 94 cm
inscribed: *P.NEFS*
Bequeathed by the Revd George Francis Lovell, 1923; WA1923.1

White 1999, p. 95

Neefs and his sons, Lodewijck and Pieter II, specialised in painting church interiors of this type. Neefs's studio produced a large number of views of the interior of Antwerp cathedral and it is not always easy to distinguish between the different hands. In view of the poor quality of A371, it may be no more than a copy.

Attributed to Neri di Bicci
(1419 – 1492)

The Virgin and Child with two Angels

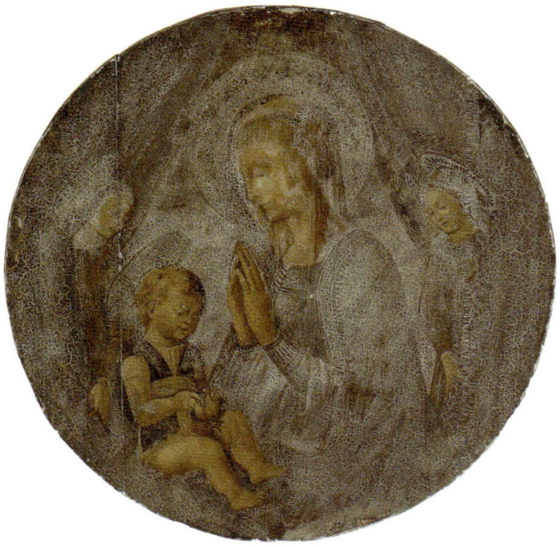

A348; tempera on panel, 45 cm in diameter
Bywater Bequest, 1915; WA1915.12

Lloyd 1977, pp. 146–7

A plausible attribution to Neri di Bicci has recently been suggested for this ruined painting. Many of Neri's devotional images were based on Florentine relief sculpture. His refined, conservative manner was extremely popular.

Cornelis de Neve
(before 1609 – 1678)

Self-portrait

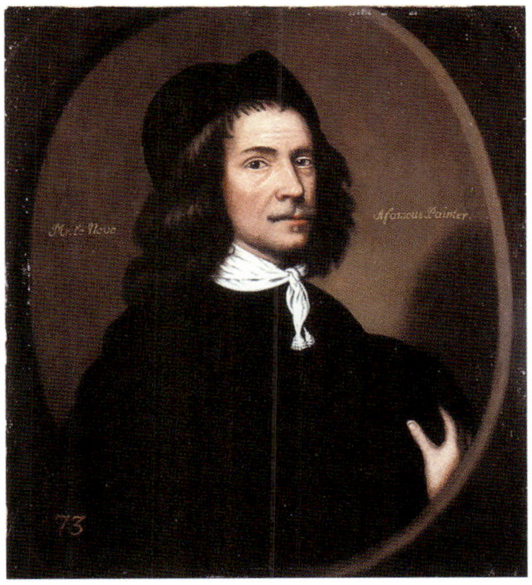

F657; oil on canvas, 67 × 57 cm
Inscribed: *Mr: le Neve A famous Painter. 73*
Prov.: Tradescant
Presented by Elias Ashmole, 1683; WA1898.24

Poole 1912, no. 432; MacGregor 1983, no. 258

De Neve was first recorded as a portrait painter in 1627 and seems to have enjoyed some success. He was related by marriage to the de Critz family and was also a kinsman of Hester Tradescant. Among other surviving paintings by de Neve is a portrait of Elias Ashmole of 1664, wearing the uniform of Herald (private collection). A date of *c.* 1645 has been proposed for this portrait.

Cornelis de Neve
(before 1609 – 1678)

Captain Nicholas Burgh

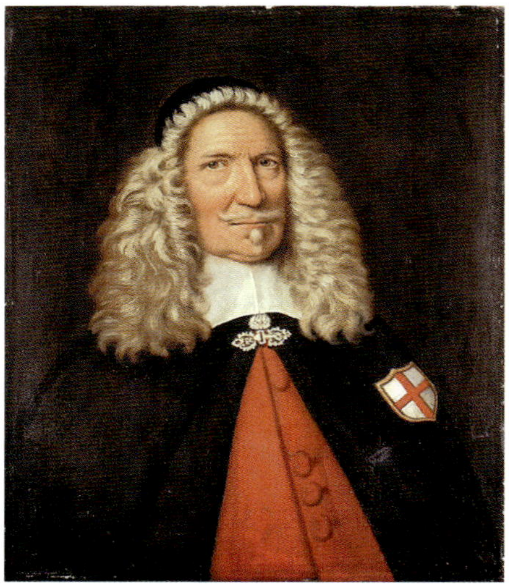

F743; oil on canvas, 69 × 59 cm
Bequeathed by Elias Ashmole, 1692; WA1898.25

Poole 1912, no. 433; MacGregor 1983, no. 290

The sitter has been identified as Captain Nicholas Burgh and wears the uniform of a 'Poor Knight of Windsor', a position he occupied from 1661 until his death in 1670. The portrait is apparently the only record of the uniform of the Poor Knight before it was changed in 1833. Burgh may have trained as a goldsmith and was certainly a virtuoso carver: he gave examples of cherry stone carvings of St George and other subjects to the Tradescants for their museum.

Ben Nicholson
(1894 – 1982)

Still Life with Flag

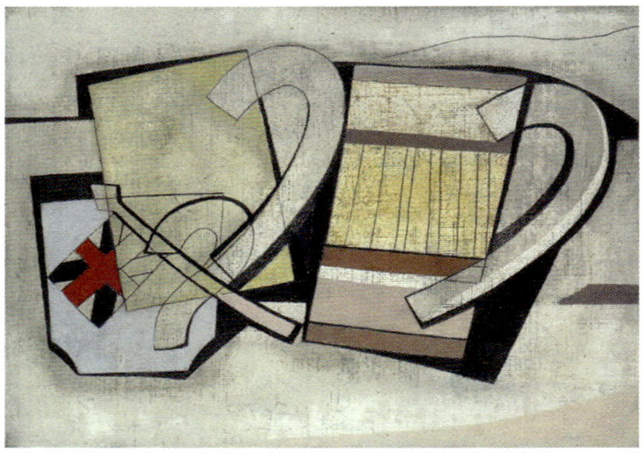

A1202; oil on canvas laid on board, 17.3 × 24 cm
Inscribed on the back of the frame: *Still life / Ben Nicholson 1945; Nicholson / 3 Mall Studios / Parkhill Rd / London NW£*
Bequeathed by Professor Stuart Piggott, 1996; WA1996.459

Eustace 1999, no. 30

As in his plaster reliefs, Nicholson explored in his still lifes the effect of shadows in the creation of space. He preferred objects of everyday life. Although placed in the same plane, they evoke a spatial quality.

Nicola di Maestro Antonio d'Ancona
(active 1472 – 1510)

St Mary Magdalen

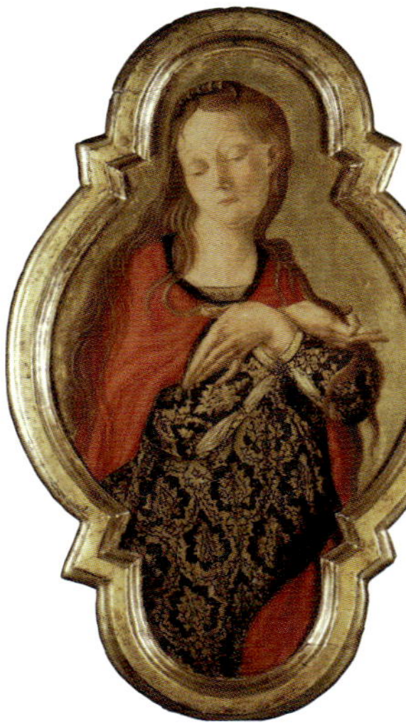

A96; tempera and gilding on panel, 67.5 × 41 cm
Fox-Strangways Gift, 1850; WA1850.20

Lloyd 1977, pp. 134–5; Hedberg 1975

A96 and A97 are fragments of a large altar-piece of which two other similarly-shaped panels survive. The artist's name and style are known from a signed and dated work of 1472, which displays affinities with the art of Carlo Crivelli who worked extensively in the Marches. The Magdalen is recognisable by her long flowing hair, a reference to her traditional identification with the woman who anointed Christ's feet and dried them with her hair (Luke 7: 36–50).

Christopher Richard Wynne Nevinson
(1889 – 1946)

The Towpath

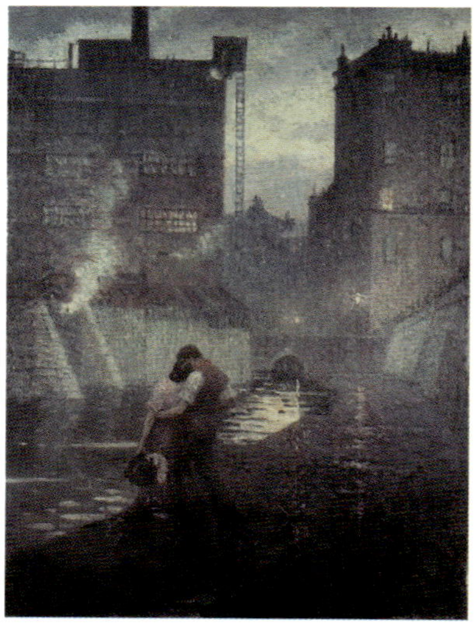

A499; oil on canvas, 76.5 × 56 cm
Weldon Bequest, 1937; WA1937.499

Eustace 1999, no. 6

In 1912, shortly before Nevinson had broken with the use of traditional narrative elements to turn towards Futurism, he painted this episode of urban life. The technique is characteristic of the post-Impressionist style Nevinson used at this time, creating an unsettling, intensely romantic atmosphere. He accurately records Regent's Canal at Marylebone, where the canal enters the Maida Hill tunnel.

Sir William Nicholson
(1872 – 1949)

The Rose-crested Cockatoo

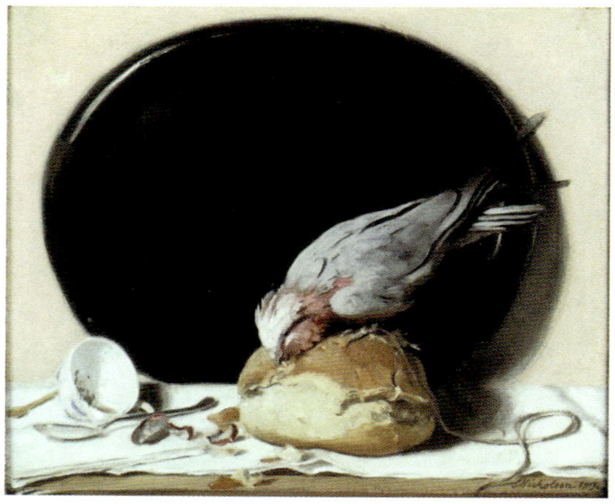

A728; oil on canvas, 49 × 58 cm
Signed and dated: *Nicholson. 1917*
Prov.: Mrs R.A. Workman
Presented by Mrs T.W.H. Ward, 1946; WA1946.268

Browse 1956, no. 223

One of Nicholson's more idiosyncratic still lifes, showing a cockatoo tethered with a string round its leg, perched on a loaf of bread and pecking at it. The other elements of the composition are equally exotic: a black Japan tray and an overturned cup with tea leaves and a spoon.

Nicola di Maestro Antonio d'Ancona
(active 1472 – 1510)

St James of the Marches

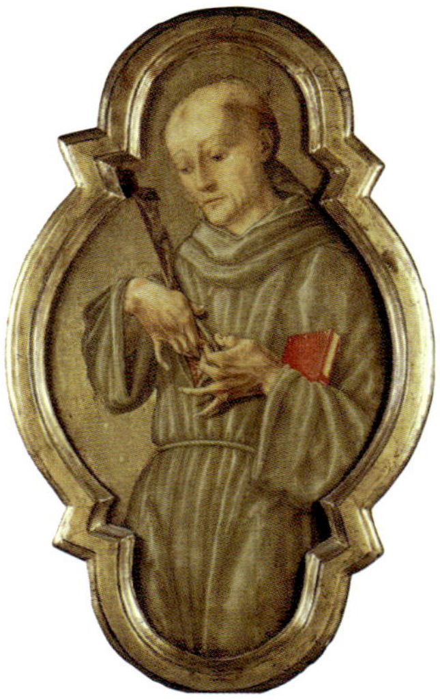

A97; tempera and gilding on panel, 68 × 42 cm
Fox-Strangways Gift, 1850; WA1850.21

Lloyd 1977, pp. 134–5; Hedberg 1975

See under A96. The ascetic Franciscan saint, sometimes called St Francis, is likely to be the miracle-working James of the Marches (1391–1476) who is depicted with a wound in his side, a reference to his casting out of devils. Many devotional images were commissioned after his death.

Joseph Francis Nollekens
(1702 – 1748)

Fête galante

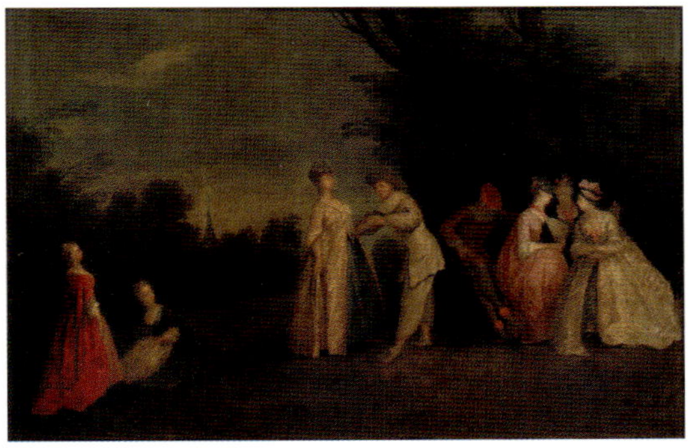

A444; oil on canvas, 54 × 81 cm
Presented by Miss E.R. Price, 1935; WA1935.40

Nollekens was best known for his pastiches of Watteau's *fêtes galantes*, which generally include figures from the *Commedia dell'arte* in landscape settings.

Anonymous North Italian Artist
(*c.* 1530)

The Adoration of the Magi

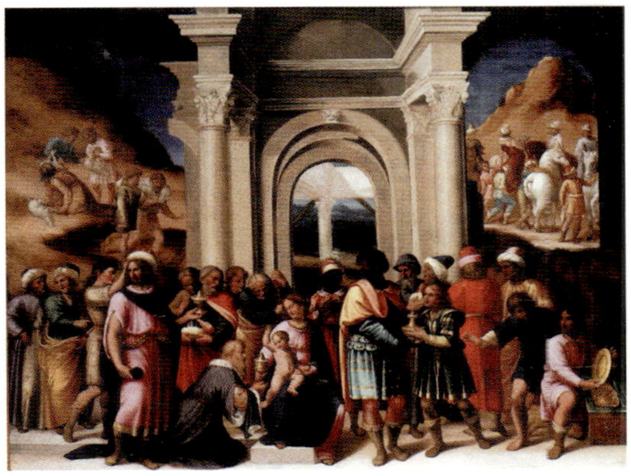

A1107; oil on panel, 42.3 × 53 cm
Prov.: Orléans Collection, Paris; 3rd Duke of Bridgewater and by descent until 1946
Presented by M.V.B. Hill, 1979; WA1979.8

The three Magi, with their exotic entourage worship the new-born Christ (Matthew 2: 1–12). Traditionally attributed to Baldassare Peruzzi, this composition derives from Peruzzi's cartoon of 1522–3 now in the National Gallery and from a lost design from Raphael's studio for the Scuola Nuova tapestry. The artist, who may have been Emilian, also refers to Andrea del Sarto. Two drawings in the Uffizi and in Berlin relate to A1107 or a lost prototype.

Anonymous North Italian Artist
(*c.* 1600)

St Mary Magdalen

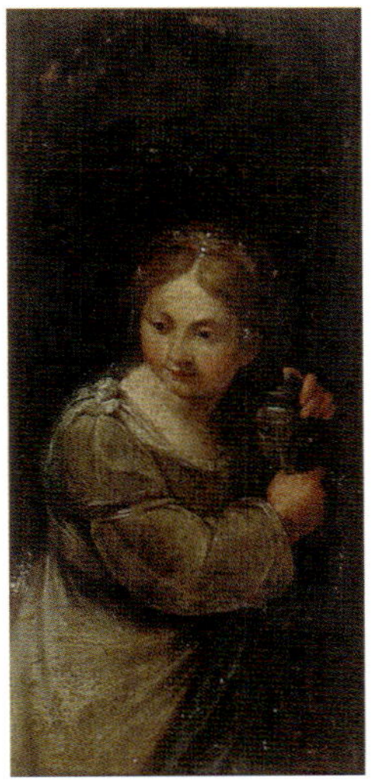

A109; oil on panel, 31.2 × 15 cm
Fox-Strangways Gift, 1850; WA1850.38

The Magdalen is recognisable by her jar of ointment, a reference to her traditional identification with the woman who anointed the feet of Christ and dried them with her hair (Luke 7: 36–50). Possibly cut from a larger composition, this small panel has been enlarged by being fitted into another and the figure extended. The artist may have worked in Parma in the early 17th century in the circle of Bartolomeo Schedoni.

François de Nomé
(*c.* 1593 – after 1644)

The Martyrdom of a Female Saint

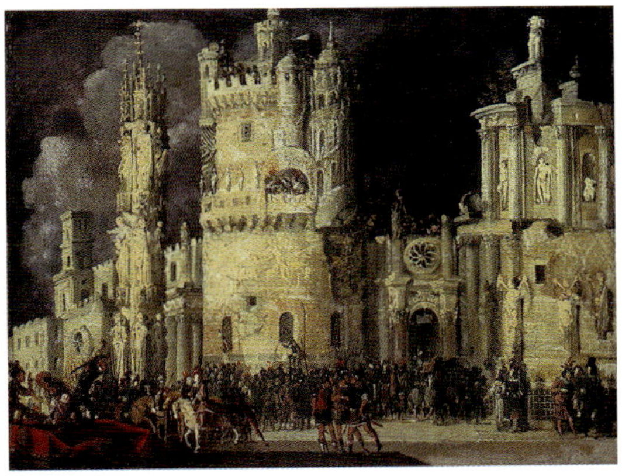

A981; oil on canvas, 25.4 × 32.8 cm
Prov.: E. Kersley
Madan Bequest, 1962; WA1962.17.23

Nappi 1991, no. A18

Born in Metz, de Nomé travelled to Rome in 1602 and settled in Naples from 1610. He specialised in religious and historical subjects with imaginative, even bizarre, settings, often inspired by the antique and medieval monuments of Naples. His sensuous handling of paint is seen in A981 in the thick impasto which gives a relief-like effect, while his inventive details include vegetation growing from the ancient buildings.

Anonymous North Italian Artist
(*c.* 1600)

The Head of St John the Baptist on a Charger

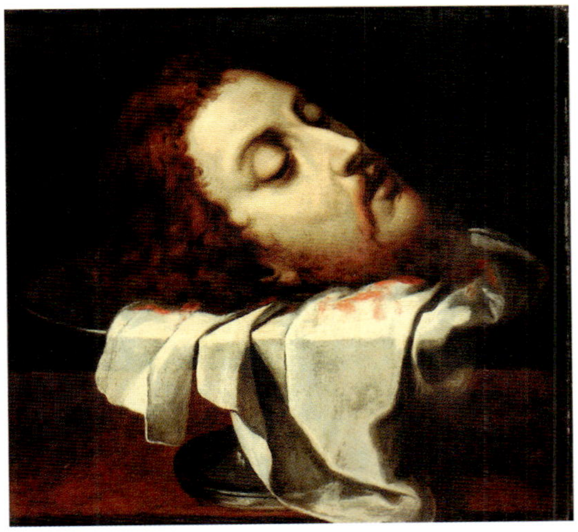

A450; oil on panel, 40.8 × 43.3 cm
Presented by Percy Moore Turner, 1936; WA1936.39

Formerly attributed to Luis de Morales, this is a late 16th- or early 17th-century variation on a famous composition by Andrea Solario of 1507 (Louvre, Paris) which was widely disseminated in northern Italy and France. The head of the martyred saint was associated with the Eucharistic symbolism of the sacrificial Lamb of God.

Anonymous North Italian Artist
(*c.* 1650)

Boy with a Flageolet

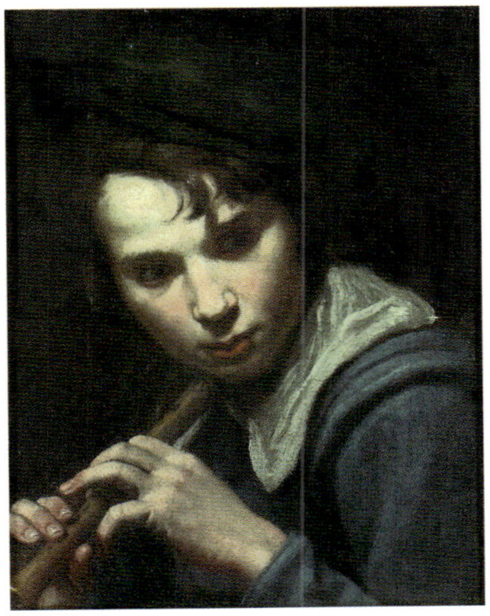

A113; oil on canvas, 45 × 35 cm
Bequeathed by the Revd Dr Thomas Penrose, 1851; WA1851.12

Until 1912 this moody genre scene had an attribution to Caravaggio. Attributions have since been proposed to Piazzetta; to Neapolitan or Spanish 17th-century artists; to Louis Finson; or to different French or Flemish followers of Caravaggio. The subject of pensive musicians was especially popular in the circles of Angelo Caroselli and of Michelangelo Cerquozzi. However, A113 appears to be northern Italian.

Anonymous North Italian Artist (?)
(*c.* 1750)

Venus and Cupid with a Putto in the clouds

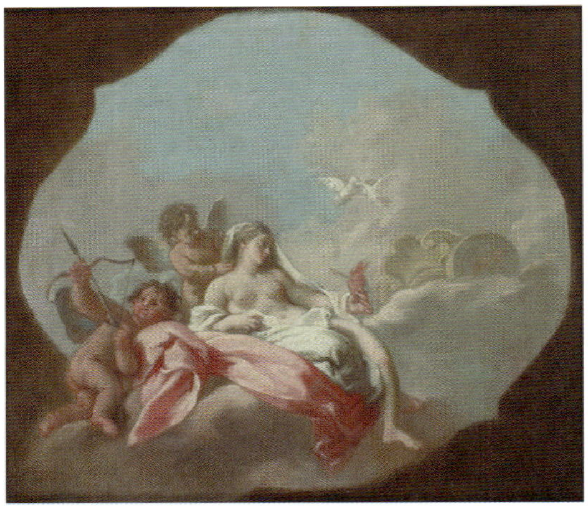

A1216; oil on canvas, 312 × 395 cm
Bequeathed by Walter Ison through the National Art Collections Fund, 1998; WA1998.185

This small sketch may be an idea for a ceiling decoration, or a copy of an oil-sketch or of a painted ceiling. The figure types derive from Carlo Carlone who worked extensively in the north of Italy, Germany and Austria.

John Opie
(1761 – 1807)

Sebastian Grandi

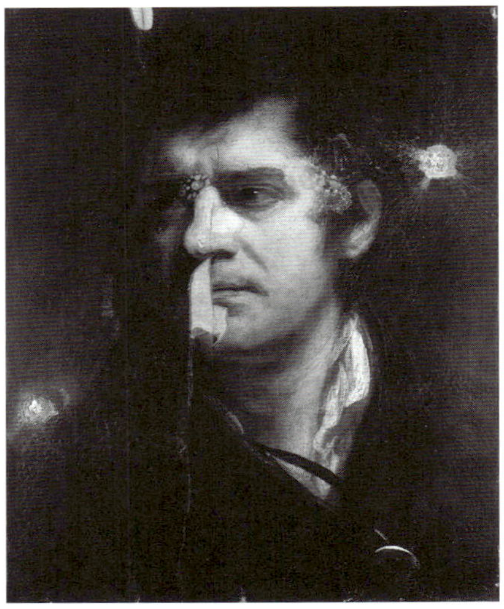

A133; oil on panel, 45 × 36 cm
Bequeathed by the Revd Dr Thomas Penrose, 1851; WA1851.1

Rogers 1878, p. 100

Grandi was an Italian colour grinder who sat to Reynolds for King Henry VI in *The Death of Cardinal Beaufort* (National Trust, Petworth) and obtained a silver medal from the Society of Arts and Sciences for the discovery of an absorbent ground. This portrait was apparently painted on an experimental ground, which resulted in a rapid deterioration in its condition.

John Opie
(1761 – 1807)

Sarah, Mrs Francis Smith

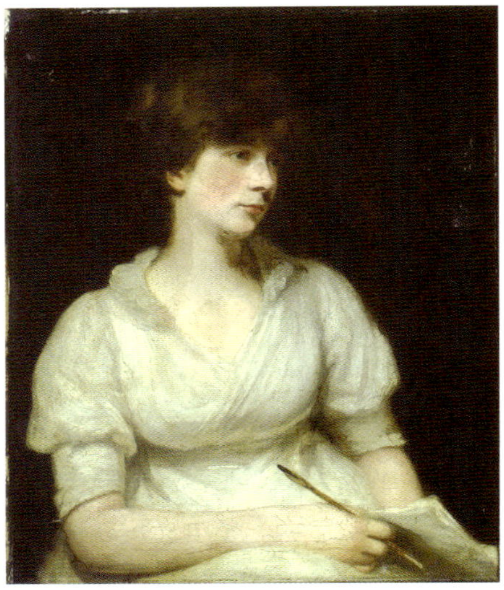

A438f; oil on canvas, 77 × 63 cm
Prov.: by descent from the sitter
Pierrepont Barnard Bequest, 1934; WA1934. 423

A companion to the preceding.

Anonymous Northern European Artist
(*c.* 1620 – 1630)

Truth presenting a Mirror to the Vanities of the World

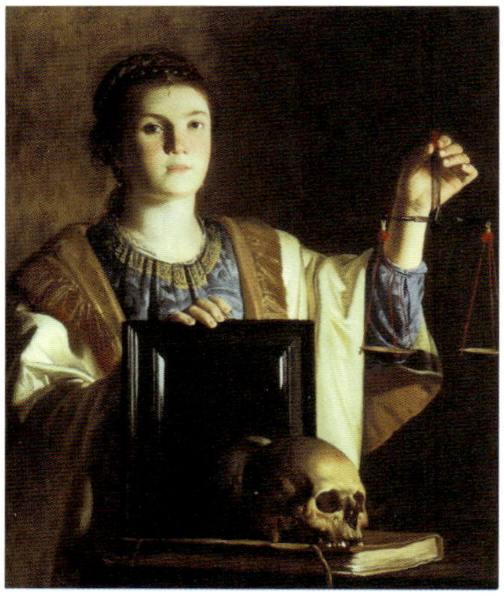

A653; oil on canvas, 104 × 84 cm
Prov.: private collection, Berlin; J. Block; N.S. Trivas
Purchased with the assistance of the National Art Collections Fund, 1939; WA1939.50

Gaskell 1984, pp. 558–9; Nicolson and Vertova 1990, p. 128

One of the traditional personifications of Truth is a female figure with scales and a mirror. The mirror may be set with precious stones, but here the stones are in Truth's headband and earrings. The subject was popular in the 1620s and 1630s with Northern followers of Caravaggio. Some scholars consider A653 to be French, *c.* 1630.

John Opie
(1761 – 1807)

Francis Smith

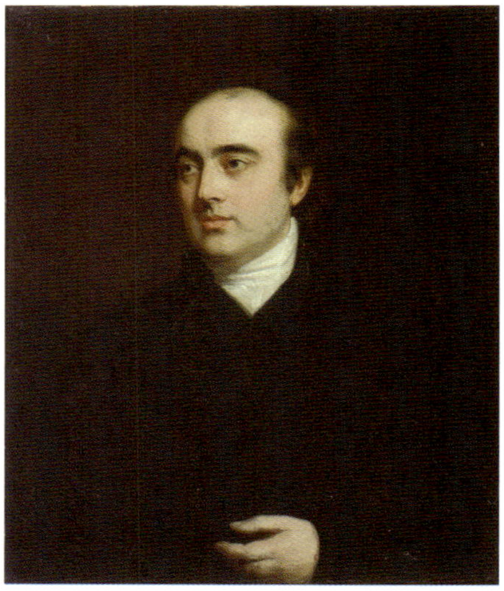

A438e; oil on canvas, 76 × 64 cm
Prov.: by descent from the sitter
Pierrepont Barnard Bequest, 1934; WA1934.422

Francis Smith (1764–1815) was the uncle of Sir James Smith (see Worlidge, A438c). This portrait and its pendant were exhibited at the Royal Academy in 1800.

John Opie
(1761 – 1807)

The blind Beggar of Bethnal Green and his Daughter

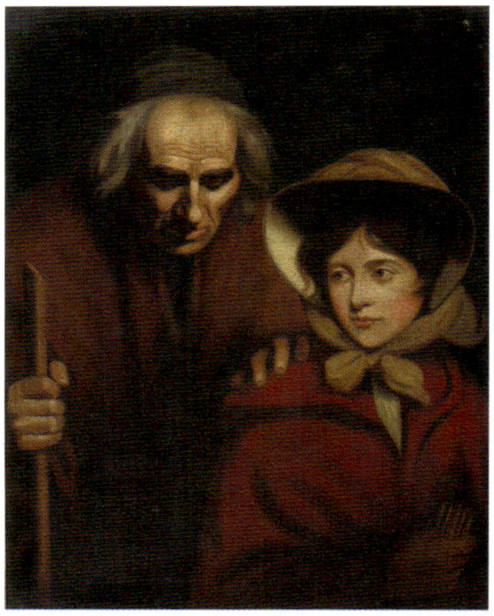

A309; oil on canvas, 90 × 70 cm
Prov.: (?)Charles Fortnum
Fortnum Bequest, 1899; WA 1899.CDEF.P9

Rogers 1878, p. 201; Earland 1911, p. 339

One of a number of versions of the painting. The subject is reminiscent of the Roman hero, Belisarius. The model for Opie's painting is said to have been George White, Reynolds's model for *The Captive* (see A128).

John Opie
(1761 – 1807)

Thomas Girtin

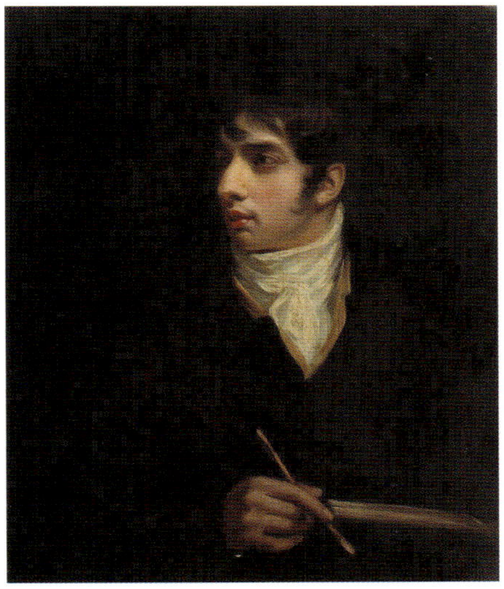

A438a; oil on canvas, 75 × 63 cm
Prov.: by descent from the sitter
Pierrepont Barnard Bequest, 1934; WA1934.418

Earland 1903, p. 278; Girtin and Loshak 1954, p. 219

Thomas Girtin (1775–1802) was one of the leading watercolour artists of the 1790s and a close friend of J.M.W. Turner. This is one of at least six versions of the celebrated portrait of *c.* 1800 (Whitworth Art Gallery). It was probably made for a member of Girtin's family, perhaps after his early death.

Studio of Andrea Orcagna
(*c.* 1315/20 – 1368)

The Angel of the Annunciation
The Virgin of the Annunciation

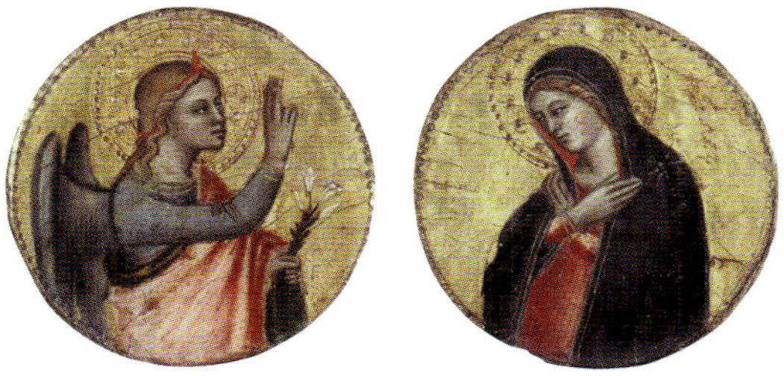

A300a and b; both tempera and gilding on panel, 6.5 cm in diameter
Fortnum Bequest, 1899; WA1899.5 & 6

Lloyd 1977, pp. 139–40; Wilson 1996, under no. 7

These delicately executed roundels probably come from the gables of a small altar-piece. They appear to be by the Master of the Golden Gate (whose name-piece is at Houston), an artist close to both Orcagna and Jacopo di Cione. Some art-historians would see this master as identical with the Master of the Ashmolean predella, or with Jacopo di Cione, but neither argument is conclusive.

Pietro Orioli
(1458 – 1496)

The Virgin and Child with Four Saints

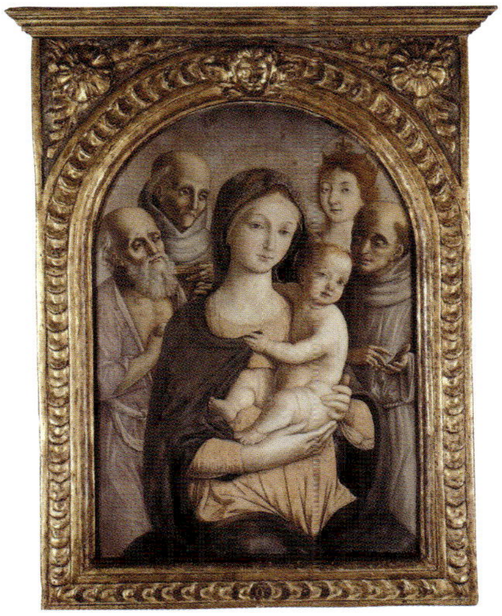

A930; tempera and gold on panel, 74.6 × 52.7 cm
Prov.: S. Matteo, Ortignano di Raggiolo; Richard Fisher; Gunhilda Fisher
Purchased, 1959; WA1959.6

Lloyd 1977, pp. 143–5

Renowned for his religious devotion as well as his artistic skill, Orioli painted almost exclusively sacred subjects. He was probably a pupil of Matteo di Giovanni. Sts Jerome, Catherine and Francis are identified by their attributes, St Bernardino by his distinctive features. The frame was made in Lombardy *c.* 1580 with pastiglia decoration.

John Opie
(1761 – 1807)

Amelia Alderson, the Artist's Second Wife

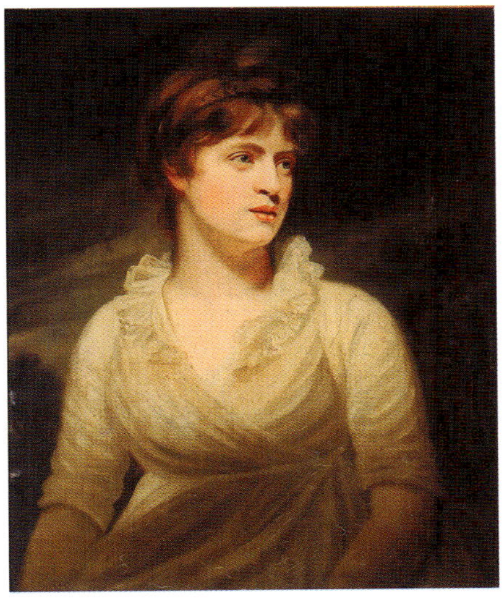

A785a; oil on canvas, 76 × 63 cm
Prov.: by descent to Nevil Vincent Sidgwick, Fellow of Lincoln College
Presented by N.V. Sidgwick, 1935 (?); WA.OA881

Rogers 1878, p. 6; Earland 1911, p. 261

Amelia Alderson (1769–1853) was the only child of a Norfolk doctor. She married Opie as his second wife in 1798 and this portrait probably dates from this period. She later published novels and poetry. There is another portrait of her of a similar date in the National Portrait Gallery.

Studio of Andrea Orcagna
(*c.* 1315/20 – 1368)

The Crucifixion with the Virgin Mary and St John

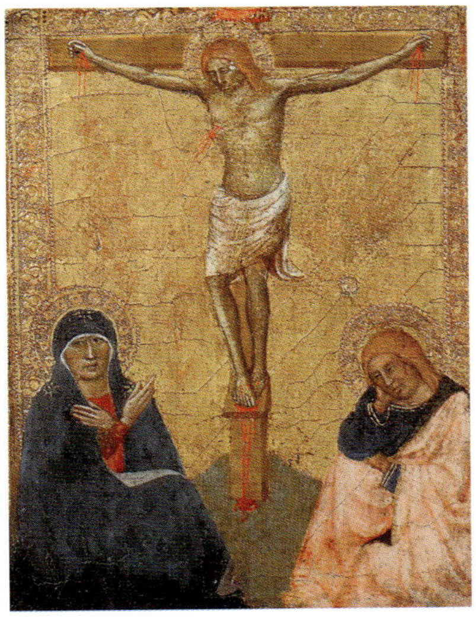

A366; tempera and gilding on panel, 24 × 18 cm
Presented by G. Ridley Robinson, 1921; WA1921.3

Lloyd 1977, pp. 140–1; Offner 1981, p. 29

The grief-stricken figures of the Virgin and St John the Evangelist make this small panel a powerful devotional image; it may have been the right wing of a portable diptych, although no hinge-marks are now visible. The anonymous artist was very close to Jacopo di Cione (to whom A366 has also been attributed) and would have trained in the large workshop of Orcagna, the leading artist in mid 14th-century Florence.

Sir William Orpen
(1878 – 1931)

The Chess Players

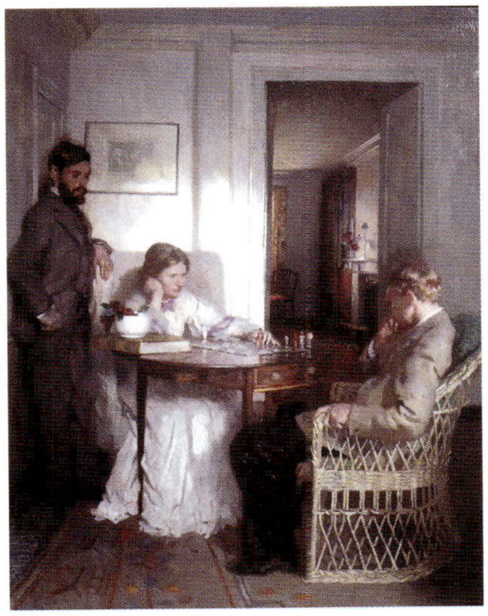

A465; oil on canvas, 92 × 71 cm
Prov.: James Staats Forbes
Weldon Bequest, 1937; WA1937.45

Dublin 1978, no. 22

First exhibited at the New English Art Club in 1902, this is one of Orpen's most sophisticated early works. It includes portraits of the artist's wife (centre) and of Sir Francis Meynell (1891–1975) or his elder brother Everard Meynell (1885–1956) (left); it has been suggested that the third figure is the artist himself.

Attributed to Sir William Orpen
(1878 – 1931)

Portrait of a Boy

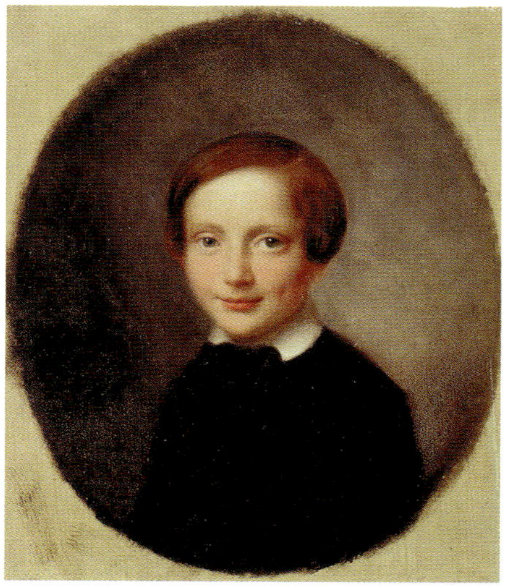

A997; oil on canvas, mounted as a drawing, 25.1 × 21.2 cm
Signed and dated: *W. Orpen. 1891.*
Prov.: Miss Olivia E. Russell
Purchased, 1963; WA1963.1

This is apparently Orpen's first surviving oil painting. It has been identified as a self-portrait at the age of thirteen, but the costume suggests it may have been copied from a work of thirty or forty years earlier. There is nothing comparable at so early a date in Orpen's career and the attribution cannot be confirmed.

Jan van Os
(1744 – 1808)

Still Life of Flowers and Fruit

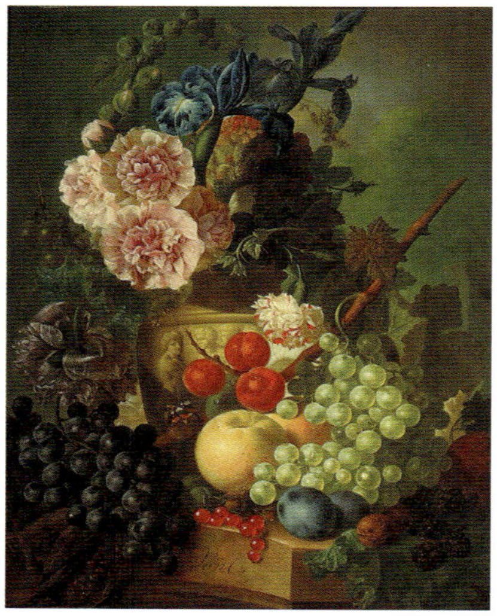

A758; oil on panel, 56 × 43 cm
Signed: *J. Van Os fecit*
Prov.: Thomas Humphry Ward
Presented by F.J. Nettlefold, 1948; WA1948.33

White 1999, p. 97

Van Os spent his career in The Hague painting fruit and flowers in the tradition of his predecessors. The classical urn and sinuous arrangement of fruit and flowers which feature in this painting and are common in his work derive from a formula developed by Jan van Aelst a century earlier. Van Huysum, in particular, was his model for works of this kind.

Attributed to Rodrigo de Osona
(active 1463 – 1513)

The Dead Christ supported by an Angel

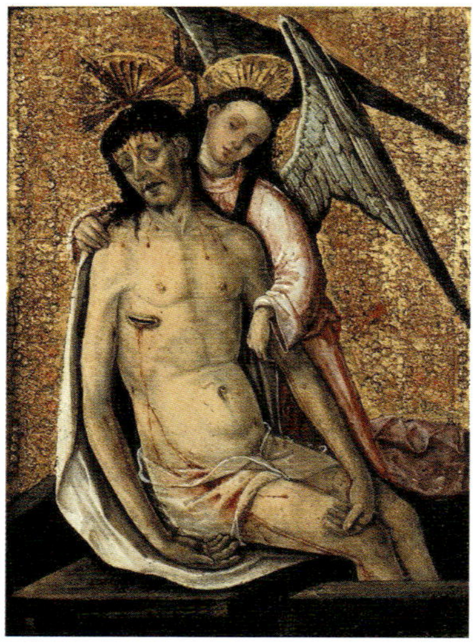

A921; tempera (?) and gilding on panel, 21 × 15 cm
Purchased with the assistance of the National Art Collections Fund, 1958; WA1958.10

Company i Climent and Berg Sobre 1995, p. 56

Possibly the central part of a *banco* of a retable, where traditionally in Valencian art the Dead Christ or Pietà was shown. The Eucharistic links are given added emphasis by the clothing of the angel, who is dressed as a deacon. Of fine quality, A921 is comparable with the *S Miguel Arcangel* of *c.* 1485–90 by Rodrigo in Valencia Cathedral.

Attributed to Lelio Orsi
(1508/11 – 1587)

St Michael subduing Satan and weighing the Souls of the Dead

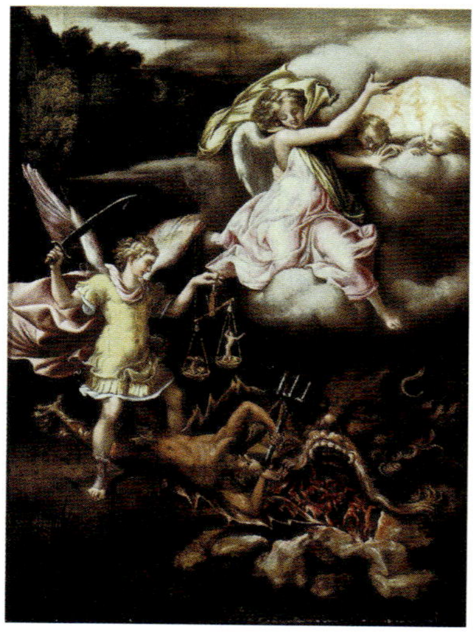

A938; oil on panel, 54 × 40 cm
Prov.: Cowper, Panshanger: John Harinden, Lechlade
Purchased, 1960; WA1960.70

Lloyd 1977, pp. 142–3; Romani 1984, pp. 21–3; Reggio Emilia 1987, no. 39

The Archangel Michael who defeated Satan is shown in medieval art weighing the souls of the dead; here another angel reveals a vision of the blessed in heaven (Revelation 12: 7–9). Influenced by the sinuous elegance of Correggio, Orsi developed a distinctive style, with an idiosyncratic approach to religious subjects. Painted in the 1540s, A938 has affinities with Flemish art. The mouth of hell, however, derives from Giulio Romano.

Style of Jan van Os
(1744 – 1808)

Still Life of Flowers

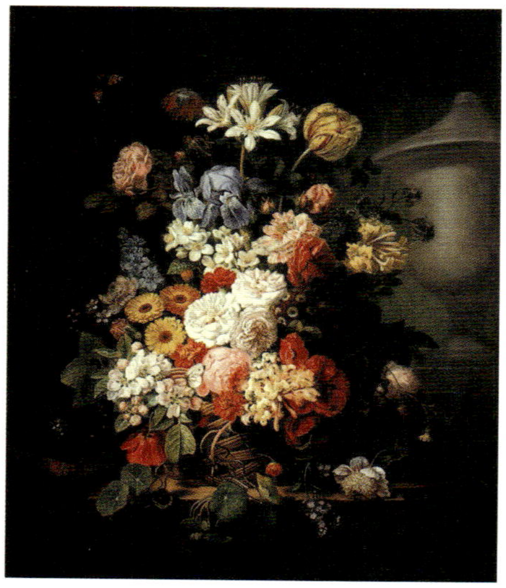

A759; oil on canvas, 87 × 72.5
Presented by F.J. Nettlefold, 1948; WA1948.34

White 1999, p. 98

The elaborate arrangement of flowers and other accessories recalls the work of van Os to whom the painting was at one time attributed. It must be the work of a contemporary or follower.

Adriaen van Ostade
(1610 – 1684)

A Peasant Family eating in an Interior

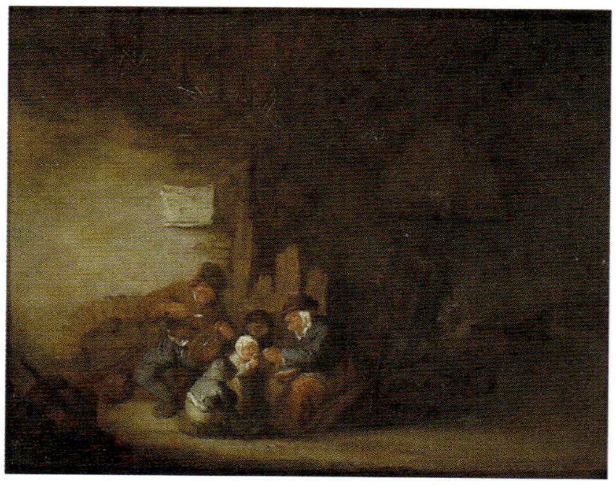

A123; oil on panel, 20 × 24 cm
Signed and dated: *Ostade 1637*
Bequeathed by the Revd Dr Thomas Penrose, 1851; WA1851.24

White 1999, p. 98

A good, early work by Ostade who worked mainly in Haarlem where he is said to have been a pupil of Frans Hals and of Adriaen Brouwer. He followed Brouwer in painting subjects of peasant life.

Isack van Ostade
(1621 – 1649)

Landscape with Cottages and Peasants

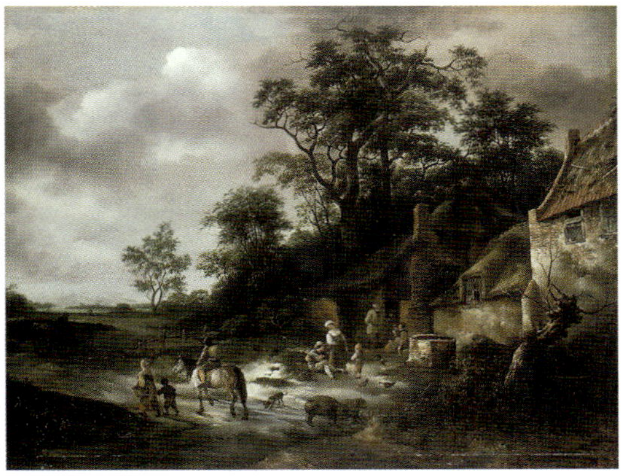

A1064; oil on canvas, 107 × 137 cm
Signed and dated: *I. Ostade f 1644*.
Prov.: Henry Hope; George Vivian and by descent; Asher Wertheimer and by descent
Presented by Mrs J.C. Conway, 1972; WA1972.7

White 1999, p. 99

Isack Osade lived in Haarlem where he is said to have been trained by his brother, Adriaen. Like Adriaen, Isack specialised in painting peasant subjects.

Jacopo Negretti (Palma Vecchio)
(*c.* 1480 – 1528)

The Holy Family with Mary Magdalen

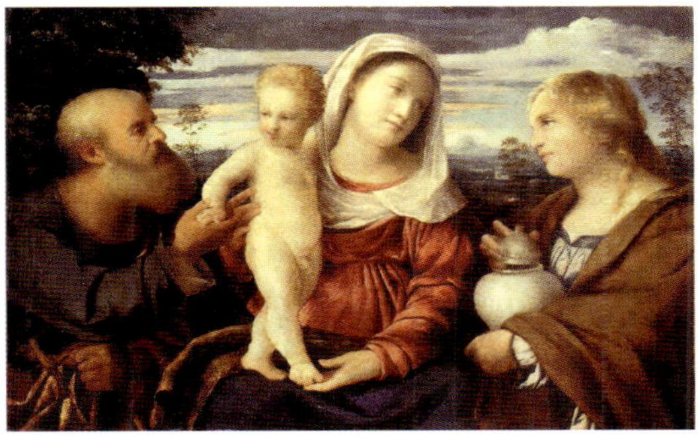

A504; oil on panel, 61 × 99 cm
Presented by Dr Arthur Waters, 1937; WA1937.103

Lloyd 1977, p. 145; Rylands 1988, no. A48

Datable to *c.* 1513–14, A504 is extensively damaged and repainted but was once of fine quality. A copy attributed to Jacopo Pisbolica is in the Museo Civico, Padua. The Magdalen is recognisable by her long hair and jar of ointment, a reference to her traditional identification with the woman who anointed Christ's feet and dried them with her hair (Luke 7: 36 ff.).

Samuel Palmer
(1805 – 1881)

Pastoral Scene

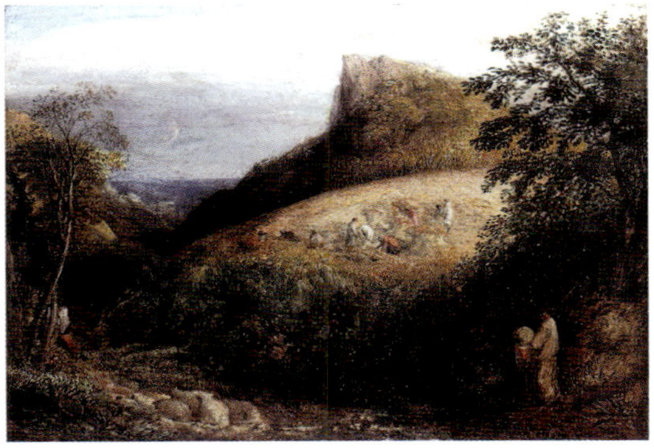

A666; oil on panel, 30 × 40 cm
Prov.: William Fothergill Robinson, Q.C.; Mrs Abbott; Mrs Hilda Fothergill Medlicott
Purchased, 1940; WA1940.21

Brown 1982, no. 22; Lister 1988, no. 215

The most complex and resolved of Palmer's small panels of the early 1830s, this landscape combines elements from the landscape around Shoreham and the swelling hills of North Devon, which Palmer visited in early 1833. It may have been exhibited at the Royal Academy in 1835.

Attributed to Gerolamo del Pacchia
(1477 – after 1533)

The Holy Family with the young St John

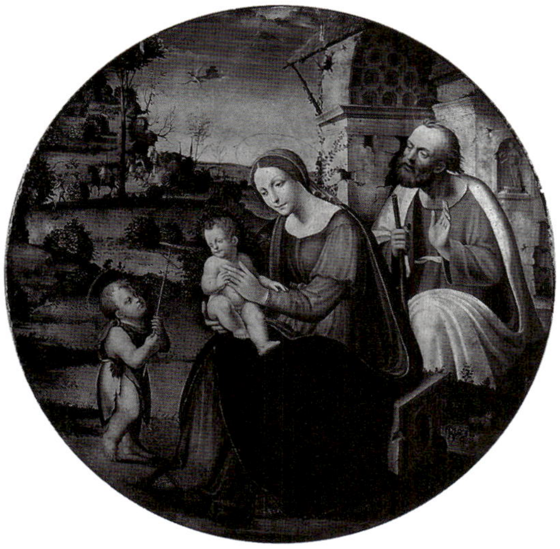

A88; oil on panel, 102 cm in diameter
Fox-Strangways Gift, 1850; WA1850.2

Lloyd 1977, p. 143; Olson 2000, p. 280

The background is enlivened with narrative scenes referring to the Nativity: the Annunciation to the Shepherds and an entourage of horsemen, presumably the arrival of the three Magi. Painted by a Sienese artist close to Sodoma *c.* 1510, A88 has generally been attributed to del Pacchia. An attribution to Vincenzo Tamagni, after Sodoma, *c.* 1507–8, has also been suggested.

Samuel Palmer
(1805 – 1881)

Landscape with the Repose of the Holy Family

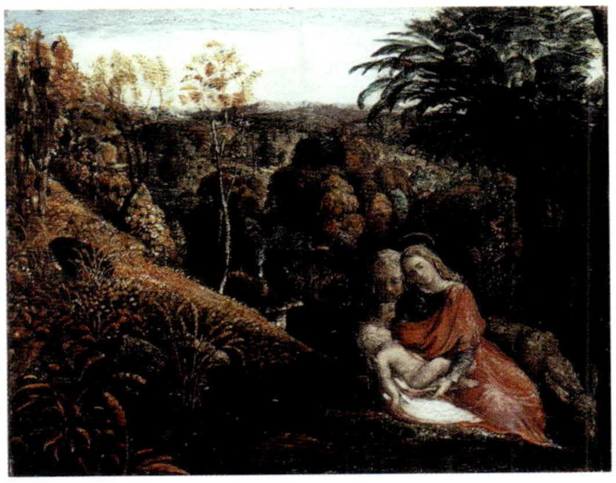

A414; oil on panel, 31 × 39 cm
Prov.: John Giles; John Richmond
Presented by the National Art Collections Fund, 1932; WA1932.2

Brown 1982, no. 4; Lister 1988, no. 46

Palmer's earliest surviving oil painting and the first manifestation of his visionary period. It was executed during the winter of 1824–5. The landscape was based on that at Shoreham. The palm tree is adapted from Dürer's woodcut of the same subject and the donkey from Blake's print of *Hecate*. The technique is experimental and was intended to revive that of the Old Masters whom Palmer and his fellow 'Ancients' admired.

Samuel Palmer
(1805 – 1881)

The white Cloud

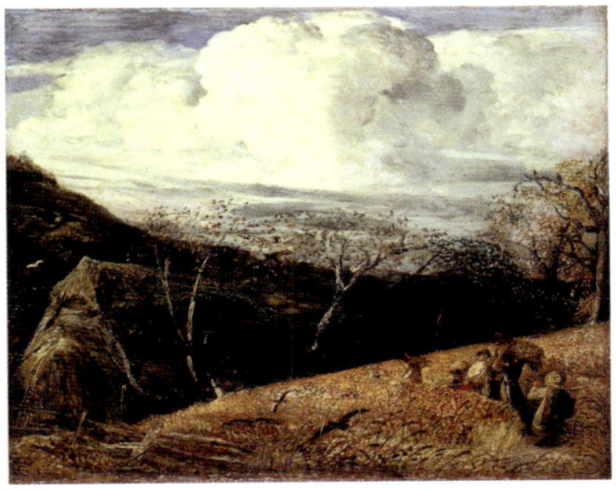

A1150; oil on canvas, 22.3 × 27.4 cm
Prov.: George Richmond; given as a 25th wedding anniversary present to the parents of the Hon. Mrs Arthur Davey, 1894, and by descent
Bequeathed by Ian Lawrence Phillips, 1987; WA1987.68

Lister 1988, no. 175

Based on a drawing of *c.* 1831–2, this landscape was painted a year or two later. The composition reverses the general lines of *The Bright Cloud* (Manchester City Art Gallery), painted at about the same period. The atmosphere is altogether lighter, with animated figures returning home to the cottage under a huge white cloud.

Samuel Palmer
(1805 – 1881)

A Cornfield bordered by Trees

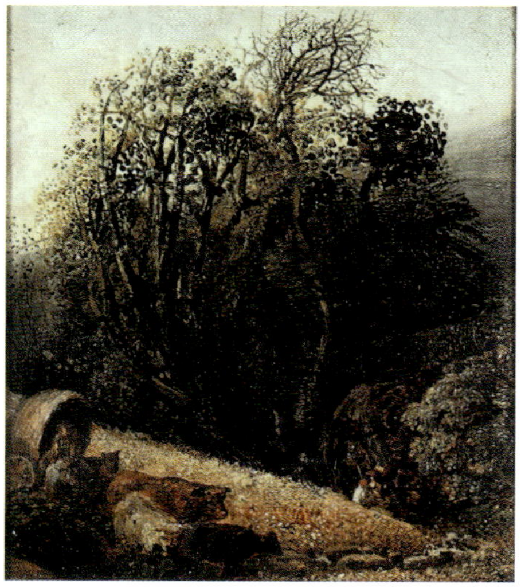

A743; oil on panel, mounted as a drawing, 17.5 × 14.9 cm
Prov.: Miss May Wright
Purchased, 1947; WA1947.168

Brown 1982, no. 21; Lister 1988, no. 171

This is the smallest of a number of panels of *c.* 1833–4. Many elements of the composition can be found in other works of the period: the waggon drawn by a horse, the path winding down the hillside and the timeless figures. The scene evokes Palmer's vision of a pastoral paradise in the English countryside and was one of the last paintings he made at Shoreham.

Giovanni Paolo Panini
(1691 – 1765)

Ruins with a Sibyl and other Figures

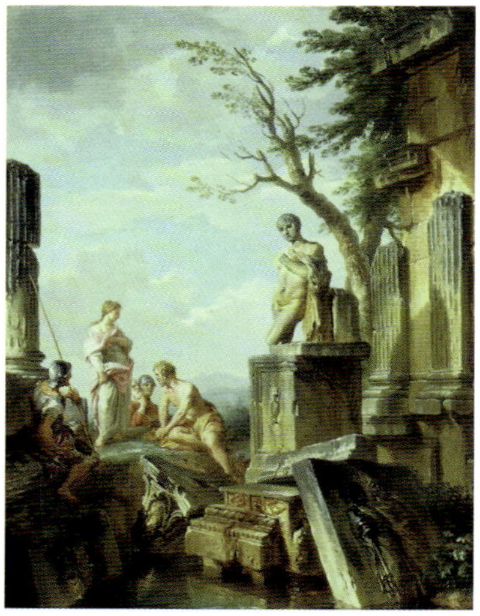

A114; oil on canvas, 64 × 49 cm
Bequeathed by the Revd Dr Thomas Penrose, 1851; WA1851.10

Arisi 1986, no. 130; Marshall 1997

A114 and A115, datable to *c.* 1720, are amongst Panini's earliest exercises in this genre. The artist returned often to pendants with sibyls and prophets. The statue of the elegant young man is found, with variations, in several other works, while the relief with standing male figures is close to that in the *Ruins with a Soldier and Philosopher* in the Fitzwilliam Museum, Cambridge.

Giovanni Paolo Panini
(1691 – 1765)

Roman Capriccio

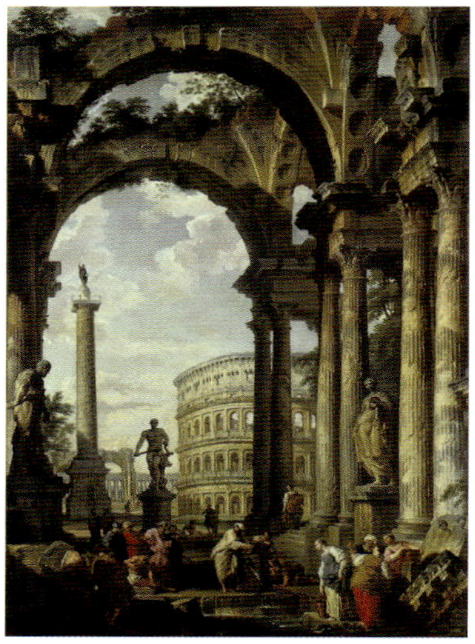

A725; oil on canvas, 176 × 126 cm
Signed: *G. PAVL PANINI [...] Romae*
Presented by Richard Walter John Hely-Hutchinson, 6th Earl of Donoughmore, 1946; WA1946.265

Arisi 1986, no. 369

Foreign visitors to Rome enjoyed Panini's fantasy views, where famous ancient remains are assembled in a picturesque setting – here, the Farnese Hercules, Trajan's Column, *Hercules and the Hydra* and the Flora Farnese. The seated beggar may be Diogenes, the philosopher who threw away his cup when he saw a man drinking water from his hands. A725 probably dates from the 1740s.

Pan (Jacqueline Regina Ward)
(b. 1923)

Neige Joyeuse

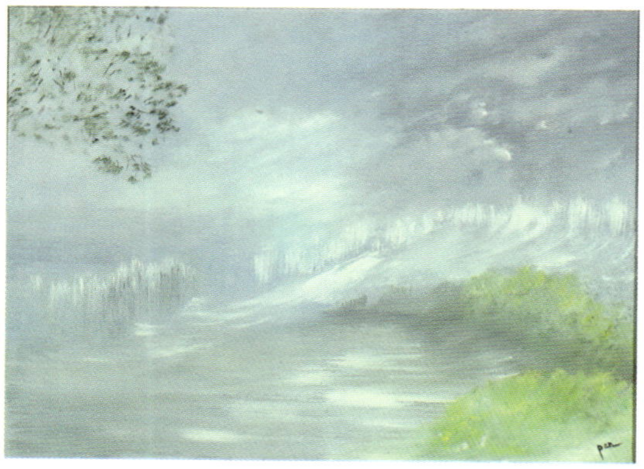

A1077; oil on canvas, 60.4 × 81.5 cm
Signed: *Pan*; signed and dated on back: *PAN Nov 73*; titled on back: *Neige Joyeuse*
Presented by Mrs T.A.J. Ward (the artist), 1975; WA1975.73

Giovanni Paolo Panini
(1691 – 1765)

Ruins with a Prophet and other Figures

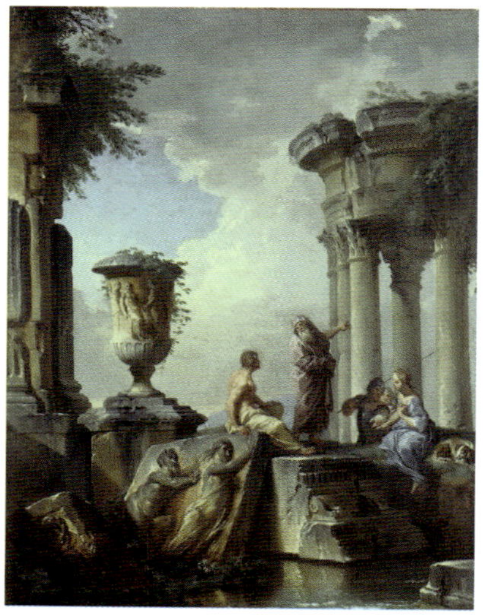

A115; oil on canvas, 64 × 49.5 cm
Bequeathed by the Revd Dr Thomas Penrose, 1851; WA1851.11

Arisi 1986, no. 129; Marshall 1997

See under A114. The vase in A115 is based on a celebrated antiquity, the Borghese Vase, while the temple evokes that of the Sibyl at Tivoli, popular with tourists. The combination of antique vase and relief with *Pan and Syrinx* or a satyr chasing a nymph appears elsewhere in Panini's work.

Studio of Giovanni Paolo Panini
(1691 – 1765)

The Piazza del Popolo, Rome

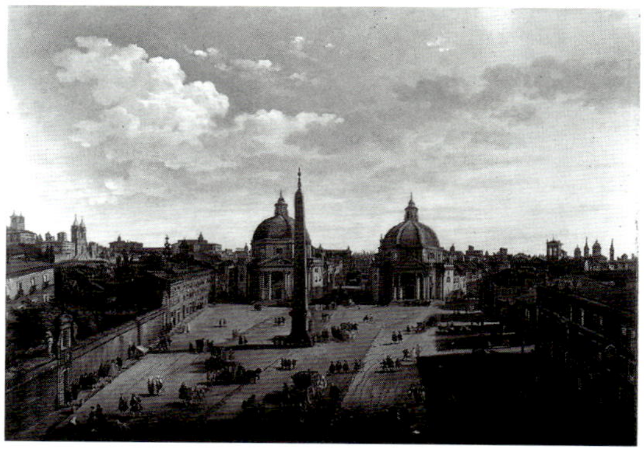

A69; oil on canvas, 97 × 133 cm
Bequeathed by the Revd J.W. Mackie, 1847; WA1847.1

The Piazza del Popolo, with its red granite Egyptian obelisk, fountain and twin churches of S. Maria di Montesanto on the left and S. Maria dei Miracoli, was the gateway to Rome for the pilgrim or Grand Tourist. The view is roughly from the top of the Porto del Popolo itself. The prototype is a small composition by Gaspar van Wittel (1652/3–1736) signed and dated 1683, of which several versions are known. This served as a source for Panini, Antonio Joli, Pietro Favris and Hendrick Frans van Lint. A69 is very close to Vanvitelli's prototype in the architecture, but there are considerable variations in the placing of the figures and their costumes, which are later in date and similar to those in Panini's views of the piazza. One of these, in the Nelson-Atkins Museum of Art, Kansas City, is identical in every detail to A69 except for the clouds and sky. Panini and his studio produced pictures of the piazza at different times of the day for the tourist market.

Alfred William Parsons
(1847 – 1920)

River Landscape

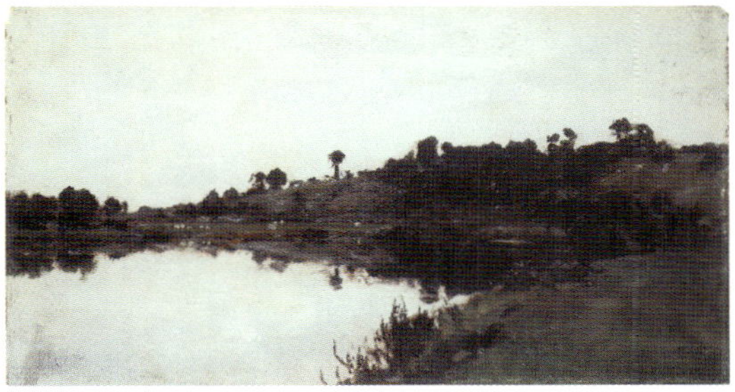

Oil on paper, mounted as a drawing, 19.6 × 35.8 cm
Signed: *ALFRED PARSONS*
Presented by Charles Emanuel, 1949; WA1949.164

Parsons exhibited landscapes and still lifes at the Royal Academy and other institutions from 1871. He travelled widely and the subject of this modest oil sketch has not been identified.

Victor Pasmore
(1908 – 1998)

Snow Scene

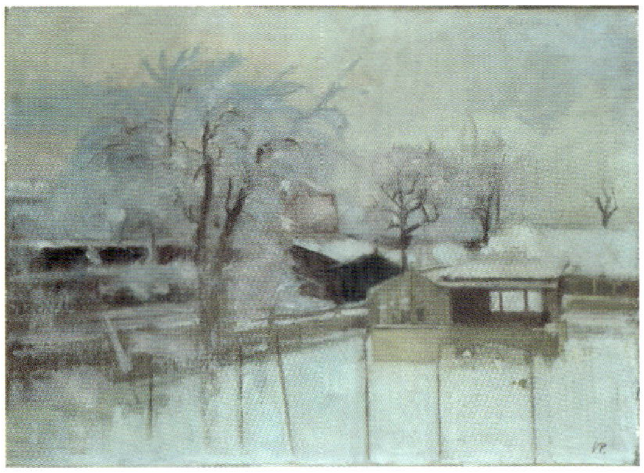

A755; oil on canvas, 45.8 × 61.2 cm
Signed in monogram: *VP.*
Presented by John Dodgson, 1948; WA1948.69

Eustace 1999, no. 29

This landscape, painted in 1944 at his home in Hammersmith Terrace, was part of a series in which Pasmore studied the structure of things. He recorded the clutter of sheds, trees and hedges during a snowfall, exploring the patterns they created. The palette is reduced to grey, white and a few colours. The image already suggests the interest in abstraction, which began to preoccupy him four years later.

Attributed to Pietro Paolini
(1603 – 1681)

St Catherine of Alexandria

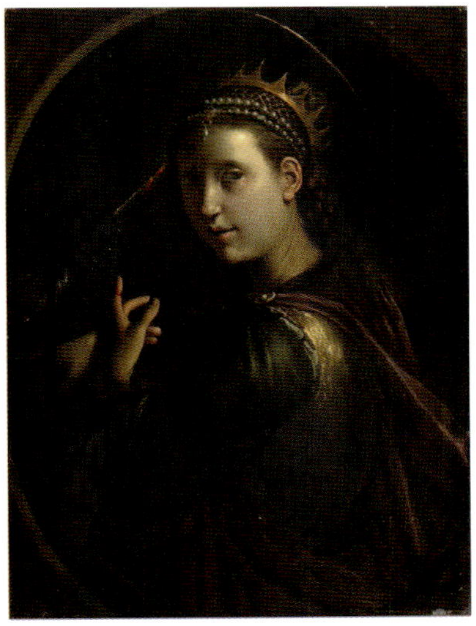

A673; oil on canvas, 74.5 × 55.3 cm
Prov.: private collection, Zakinthos, Hellas
Bequeathed by Sir Arthur Evans, 1941; WA1941.6

Wearing an elaborate jewelled headdress and crown, the saint points towards a bloodstained sword with an ornate hilt, the instrument of her martyrdom, while she holds a martyr's palm in her right hand and her attribute of a broken wheel is on the left. The figure is set within a painted oval and may have been one of a series of half-length saints. A673 has recently been convincingly attributed to Paolini, a pupil of Angelo Caroselli, with a dating in the late 1630s.

Victor Pasmore
(1908 – 1998)

Woman in a red Hat

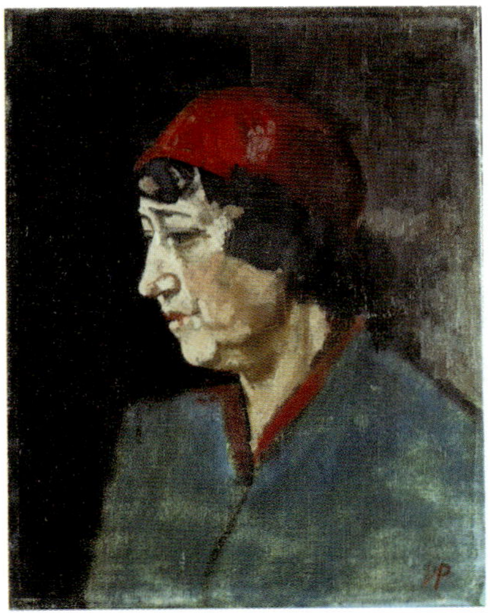

A754; oil on canvas, 40.6 × 31.3 cm
Signed: *VP*
Presented by John Dodgson, 1948; WA1948.68

Pasmore painted this portrait of a woman who worked for the Redfern Gallery in 1944. Except for the face, the paint is applied rather thinly and summarily, in a manner which is also found in Pasmore's landscapes in this period. There is another portrait of the same model in Tate Britain.

Pierre Patel the Elder
(*c.* 1605 – 1676)

Landscape in the Roman Campagna

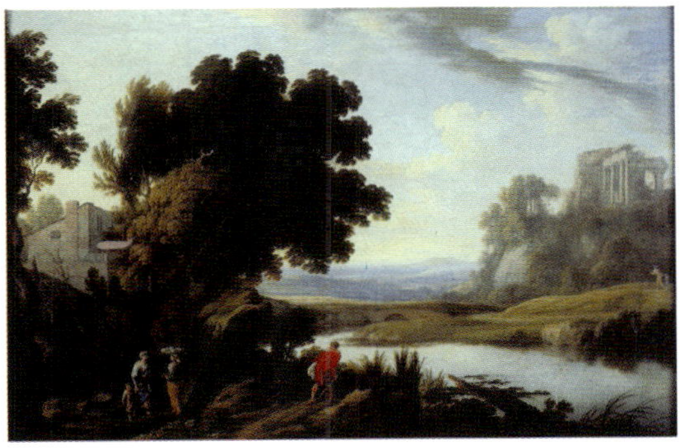

Oil on canvas, 40.7 × 60.6 cm
Prov.: Richard Boyle, 3rd Earl of Burlington; by descent to the Dukes of Devonshire, 1748
Mahon loan, 1999; WA.L.99.15

Finaldi and Kitson 1997, no. 58; Coural 2001, no. PP4

Probably dating from *c.* 1635–8, this carefully structured classical landscape reveals the artist's interest in the atmospheric landscapes of Claude Lorrain. Patel is not known to have visited Rome, but he could have seen contemporary Italian landscape paintings and particularly works by Claude in Parisian collections.

Copy(?) after Joachim Patenir
(active 1515 – before 1524)

Landscape with the Destruction of Sodom and Gomorrah

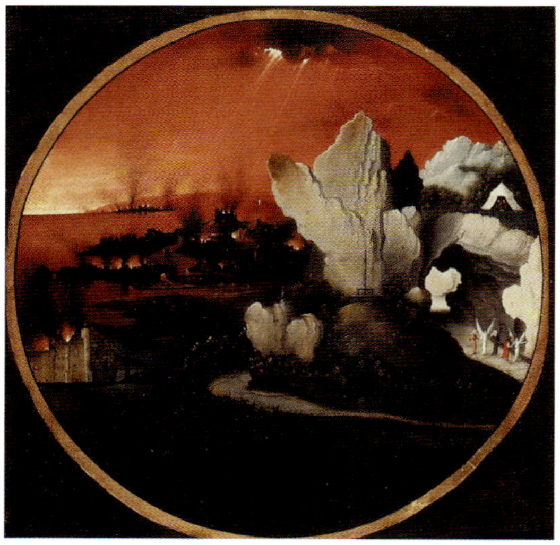

A451; oil on panel, 34 × 33 cm
Presented by the National Art Collections Fund, 1936; WA1936.36

White 1999, p. 100

The scene illustrates the escape of Lot and his two daughters from the burning cities (Genesis 19: 9). The tiny figure of Lot's wife, turned to salt, is visible in the centre. A similar composition is found in the centre of a painting by Patenir belonging to the Dienst voor's Rijksverspreide Kunstvoorwerpen in The Hague. The Oxford painting may be a copy by Patenir himself or by a close associate. There is an old attribution on the back to Patenir's nephew, Herri de Patenir, written in Italian.

J. Patrick (first half of 19th century) after François-Marius Granet

Interior of the Capuchin Monastery in Rome

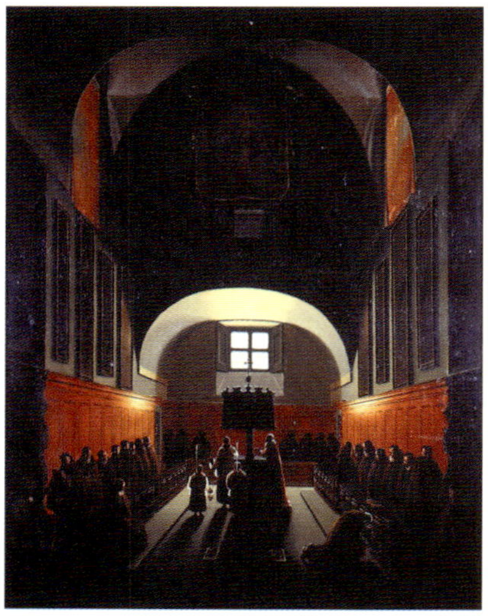

A1208; oil on canvas, 910 × 710 cm
Inscribed: *J. Patrick / 1830*
Presented anonymously in memory of Steven Kerkez, 1997; WA1997.38

Wright 1974, pp. 209–13

Copied from Granet's painting *The Choir of the Capuchin Church in Rome* exhibited at the Salon of 1819, of which there are numerous versions by the artist (e.g. in the National Museum and Gallery of Wales, Cardiff) and copies by other hands. The name inscribed on this copy may indicate an artist, J. Patrick, who exhibited portraits at the Royal Academy in 1808 and 1813 but is otherwise unrecorded.

Gianantonio Pellegrini
(1675 – 1741)

An Allegory of Dawn

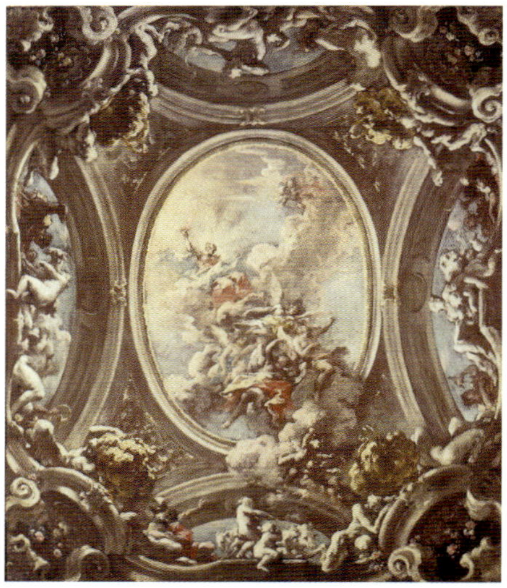

A515; oil on canvas, 82 × 70 cm
Prov.: M. Guggenheim; Mrs F. Perry
Presented by the National Art Collections Fund, 1938; WA1938.1

Knox 1995, pp. 205, 250

Formerly attributed to Sebastiano Ricci, A515 is a sketch for the lost ceiling of the Roter Saal at Mannheim Castle (destroyed in 1945), the first of four ceilings Pellegrini designed and painted in 1736–7 for Karl Philipp von der Pfalz. The central oval of the Roter Saal showed Aurora in her chariot with its ribbon-like reins held by four Hours, while the surrounding architectural and figurative elements seem to have followed A515 closely.

Jean-Baptiste Pater
(1695 – 1736)

The Departure of the Troops

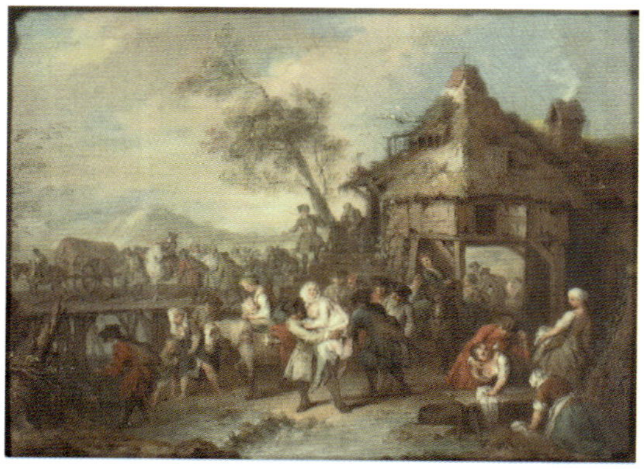

A744; oil on canvas, 29 × 39 cm
Prov.: Princess Souwarow; Henri Bischoffsheim; his daughter, Lady Fitzgerald; Samuels; H. Winterfield; Vicars
Bequeathed by Sir Bernard Eckstein, 1948; WA1948.155

Ingersoll-Smouse 1928, no. 459

Pater's essays in military genre derive from a group of similar subjects painted by his master Watteau *c.* 1709. He treated these subjects light-heartedly, depicting troops on the move with an entourage of women, babies, animals and baggage and companion pieces with soldiers at rest in their encampment. A pendant to A744, *Halte de Troupes*, was also in the Souwarow collection.

Clara Peeters
(active 1607 – after 1621)

Still Life of Fruit and Flowers

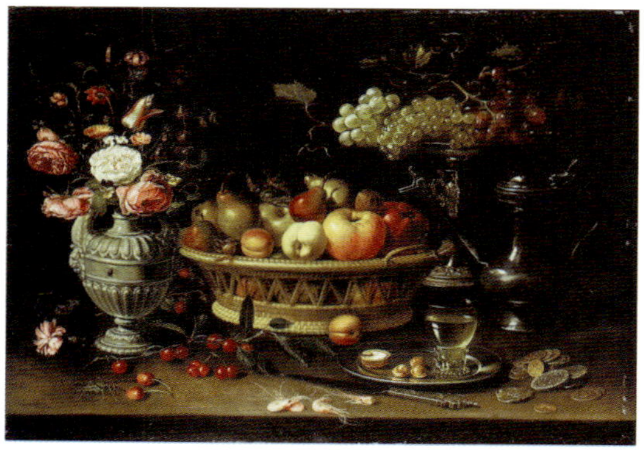

A585; oil on copper, 64 × 89 cm
Signed: *CLARA.PETERS*
Prov.: Ralph Warner
Daisy Linda Ward Bequest,1939; WA1940.2.61

Meijer 2003, no. 62

The presence of a coin of the United Provinces issued in 1608–9 provides the earliest possible date for this painting. The white stoneware vase does not appear elsewhere in Peeters's art but most of the other accessories appear in several of her compositions. The knife, in particular, appears in another five of her paintings.

Edward Penny (1714 – 1791) after Van Dyck

Cardinal Guido Bentivoglio

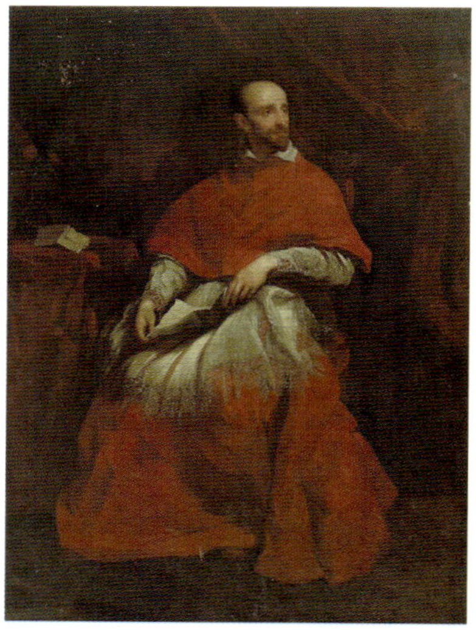

A37; oil on canvas, 196 × 145 cm
Signed and dated: *E. Penny pinx Florence / 1741*
Presented by the artist, 1787; WA1845.37

Penny studied in London with Thomas Hudson and with Marco Benefial in Rome. He is recorded in Florence from July 1741, where he made this copy after the painting of 1623 in the Palazzo Pitti. It is his earliest surviving work.

Edward Penny
(1714 – 1791)

The Death of General Wolfe

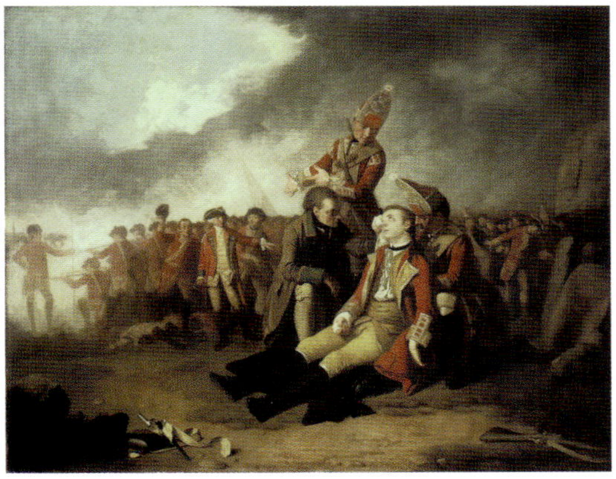

A38; oil on canvas, 102 × 127 cm
Signed and dated: *E.Penny Pinx^{t} 1763*
Presented by the artist, 1787; WA1845.38

Mitchell 1944, p. 30; McNairn 1997, pp. 102–5

James Wolfe (1727–1759), a professional soldier who rose to be Major-General, commanded the force sent up the Saint Lawrence River against Quebec in 1759. He was shot during the battle on the Plains of Abraham and died on 13 September 1759 after hearing that his attack had been successful. Penny's work, arguably the first heroic history painting in modern dress, shows the death of General Wolfe surrounded by his officers, while a messenger runs in to announce the news of victory.

Edward Penny
(1714 – 1791)

The Marquis of Granby giving Alms to a sick Soldier and his Family

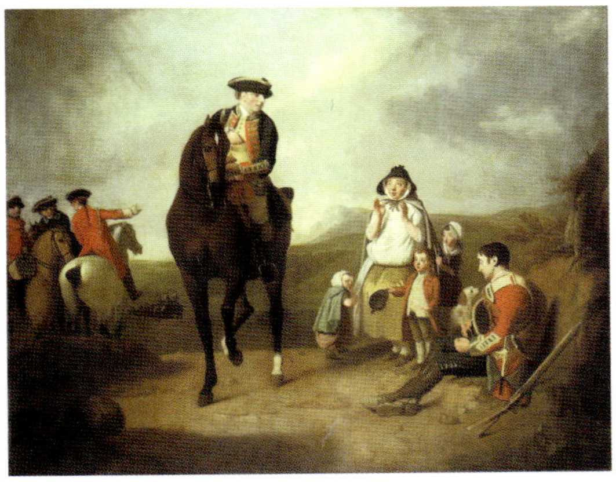

A39; oil on canvas, 101 × 127 cm
Signed and dated: *E.Penny pinx 1764*
Presented by the artist, 1787; WA1845.39

Mitchell 1944, p. 33; Solkin 1986

John Manners, Marquis of Granby (1721–1770) was a career soldier who performed brilliantly during the Seven Years War (1756–63) and rose to be commander-in-chief in 1766. Penny exhibited this work as *An Officer relieving a sick Soldier (Lord Granby – Walpole)* at the Society of Artists in 1765 and, like his *Death of General Wolfe* of the previous year, intended it as a history painting in modern dress.

Copy after Pietro Perugino
(documented 1469 – 1523)

The Head of the Virgin

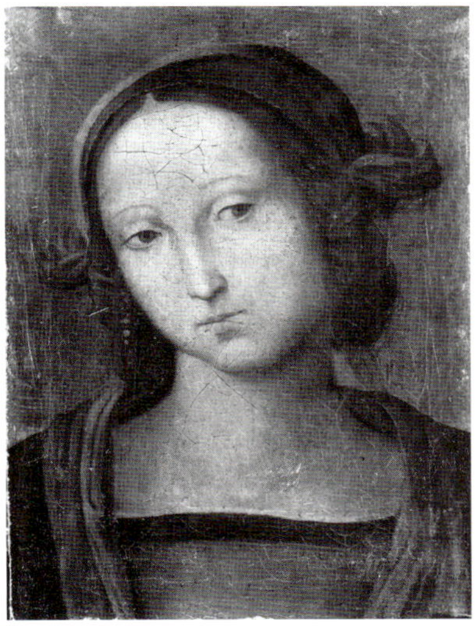

A108; oil on canvas, rolled, 31.7 × 24.1 cm
Fox-Strangways Gift, 1850; WA1850.37

Lloyd 1977, pp. 145–6

A108 is a free copy, or a pastiche, perhaps of the 18th century, based on Perugino's altar-piece of the *Madonna della Consolazione* of 1498, now in the Galleria Nazionale, Perugia.

Attributed to Antonio Francesco Peruzzini
(*c.* 1668 – 1724)

Landscape with a waterfall

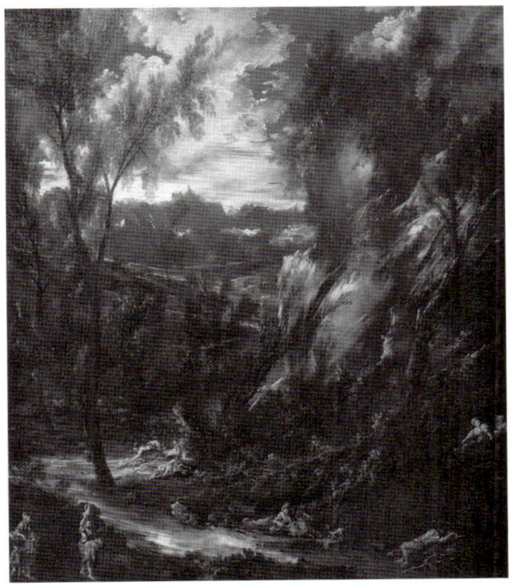

A717a; oil on canvas, 163 × 137 cm
Purchased, 1945; WA1945.99

Formerly attributed to Alessandro Magnasco and a collaborator, this is more likely to be by Peruzzini and his workshop. This type of romantic landscape, deriving from Salvator Rosa, was very popular in the late 17th century. The landscape is of better quality than the figures and is perhaps by Peruzzini's hand.

John Pettie
(1839 – 1893)

Study of the Head of the old Lieutenant

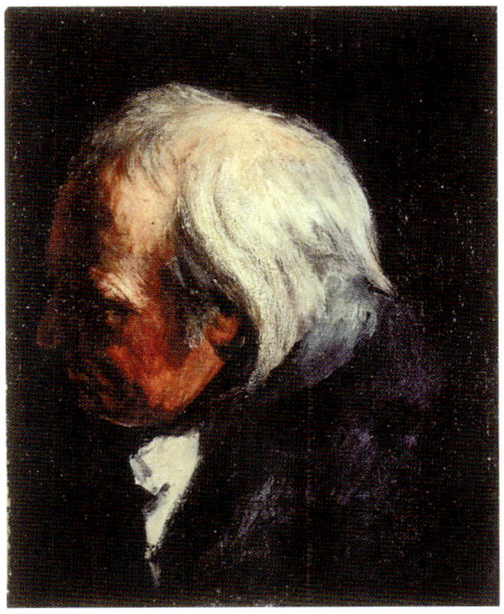

A1023b; oil on canvas, mounted as a drawing, 20 × 15.8 cm
Prov.: C.M. Hardie, R.S.A.
Presented by Mrs Martin Hardie, 1966; WA1966.37

Pettie's first painting in his mature style, *The Old Lieutenant and his Son*, was commissioned by Alexander Strahan, founder and publisher of *Household Words*, as an illustration to Dr Norman Macleod's 'Ned's Return'; it was exhibited at the Royal Scottish Academy in 1862. This head study and another of the head of the son were cut from an earlier version of the painting.

John Pettie
(1839 – 1893)

Portrait of the Artist's Wife

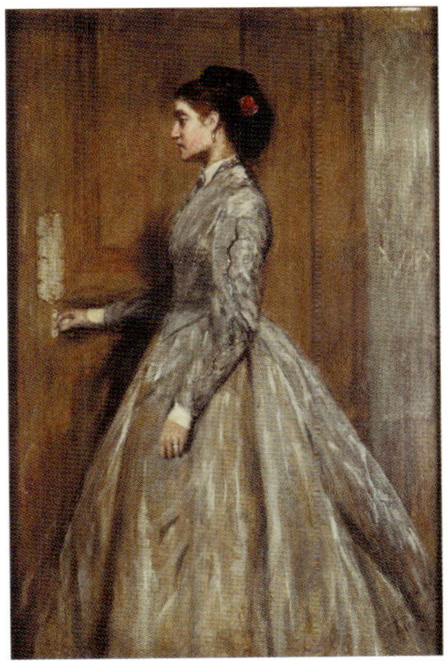

A684b; oil on canvas, 78 × 54 cm
Signed and dated: *J Pettie 1865*
Prov.: C.E. Johnson, R.I.
Presented by Francis Howard, 1941; WA1941.58.2

Hardie 1908, p. 220

Pettie met Miss Elizabeth Ann Bossom at Hastings during the summer of 1864 and they were married on 25 August 1865. This portrait perhaps commemorates that event.

John Pettie
(1839 – 1893)

Study of two Flowers

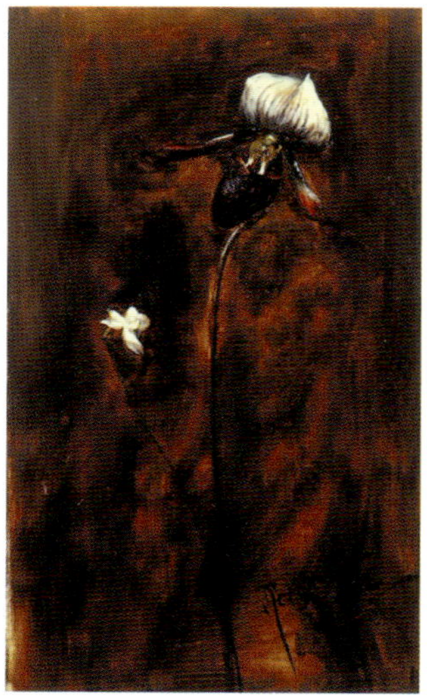

Oil on canvas, mounted as a drawing, laid down,
41 × 24 cm (sight)
Signed and dated: *J Pettie 82*
Prov.: Sir Harry Veitch
Purchased, 1967; WA1967.39.1

Pettie is not otherwise known to have painted botanical specimens, although flowers are included in a number of his compositions. Those depicted here are the lady's slipper orchid (*Cypripedium*) and a narcissus.

Attributed to Thomas Phillips
(1770 – 1845)

Revd James Douglas

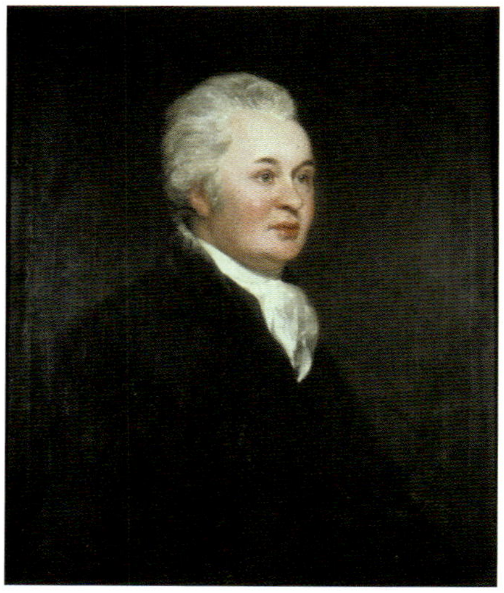

A63a; oil on canvas, 75 × 57 cm
Probably presented by Sir Richard Colt Hoare, 1825; WA1845.69

Poole 1912, no. 469

The Revd James Douglas (1753–1819) was an antiquary and painter and the author of *A Sepulchral History of Great Britain* (1803). After his death, his widow sold his collection of Anglo-Saxon antiquities to Sir Richard Colt Hoare of Stourhead, who presented them to the Ashmolean Museum in 1825.

Glyn Warren Philpot
(1884 – 1937)

Italian Soldier

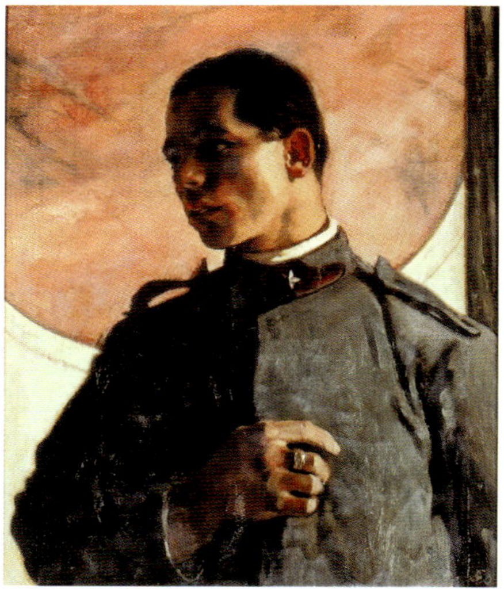

A684a; oil on canvas, 66.5 × 55 cm
Presented by Francis Howard, 1941; WA1941.58.1

Eustace 1999, no. 19

This is one of three paintings entitled *Italian Soldier* which Philpot exhibited at the Grosvenor Galleries in 1923; another is in the Courtauld Institute Galleries. They were painted in Italy in the previous year.

Thomas Phillips
(1770 – 1845)

Portrait of an Oxford Undergraduate, perhaps Sir Henry Delves Broughton, Bt

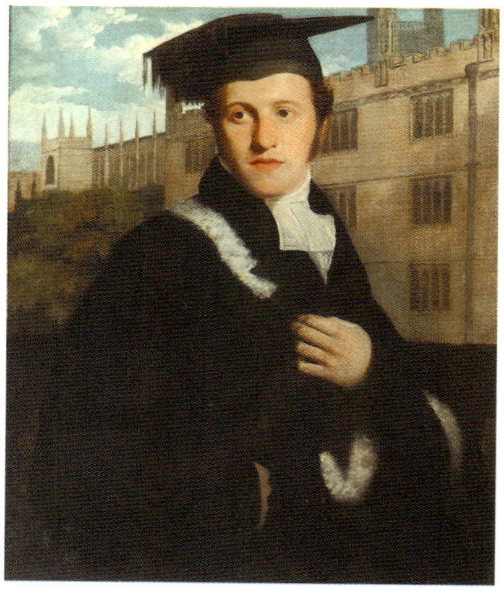

A912; oil on canvas, 76 × 61 cm
Russell Bequest, 1958; WA1958.57.7

The sitter was identified by the donor as Sir Henry Delves Broughton, 9th Baronet (1808–1899), but this cannot be confirmed. The background represents the Divinity Schools and the Bodleian Library.

Tom Phillips
(b. 1937)

The Artist's Mother at 18 and 88

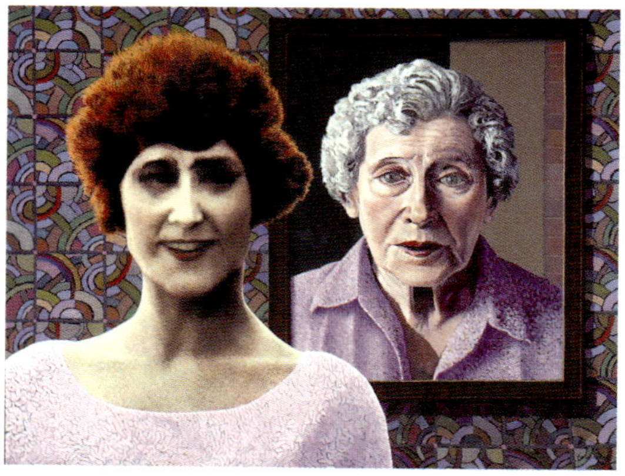

A1222; acrylic on canvas, 71.4 × 91.8 cm
Purchased from the artist (Blakiston Fund), with the assistance of Lloyds TSB, Sir Nicholas Goodison and the Friends of the Ashmolean, 2000; WA2000.19

Phillips 2000

In this double portrait Phillips represented his mother twice, once as a young woman based on a blurred photograph taken in 1919 and secondly from life at the age of 88. Instead of presenting the old photograph as a framed memory on the wall, he used it as a symbol of the still youthful soul of his mother, while her actual appearance in the background is older and much changed.

Glyn Warren Philpot
(1884 – 1937)

Gabrielle and Rosemary

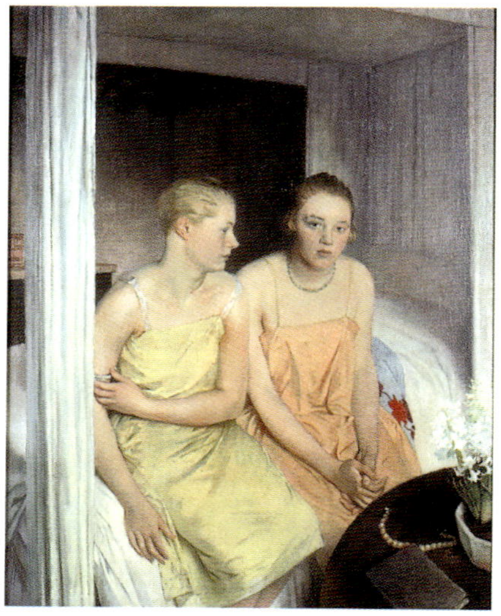

A1023a; oil on canvas, 143 × 112 cm
Signed and dated: *Glyn / Philpot / 1928*
Prov.: Mrs Clement Cross, the artist's sister
Presented by Miss Gabrielle Cross, 1966; WA1966.28

Sewter 1951, pl. 4

Philpot's sister Gertrude (1879–1957) married Clement Cross in 1907. Their daughters, Gabrielle (b. 1910) and Rosemary, became favourite models for their uncle. This double portrait, which has echoes of Philpot's portrait of his own two sisters (1922; private collection), was painted at the artist's home, Baynards Manor, near Horsham, and exhibited at the Royal Academy in 1928.

Glyn Warren Philpot
(1884 – 1937)

Man with a Gun

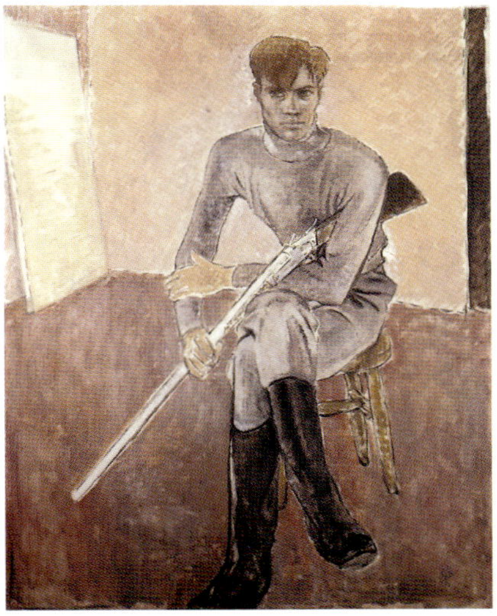

A1140; oil on canvas, 114.5 × 92 cm
Signed in monogram: *GP*
Bequeathed by Jeffrey Daniels, 1986; WA1986.80

Sewter 1951, p. 8; Gibson 1984–5, no. 53

Painted at Baynards Manor during the latter half of 1933 in preparation for Philpot's one-man show at the Leicester Galleries in February 1934, this is a portrait of a young Norwegian friend, Jan Erland, who also appeared in other paintings of this period. The portrait is carefully and rigidly posed: the gun was borrowed from the local station master. The work is painted in Philpot's newly broken style which gained him favour among progressive patrons.

Pablo Picasso
(1881 – 1974)

Blue Roofs, Paris

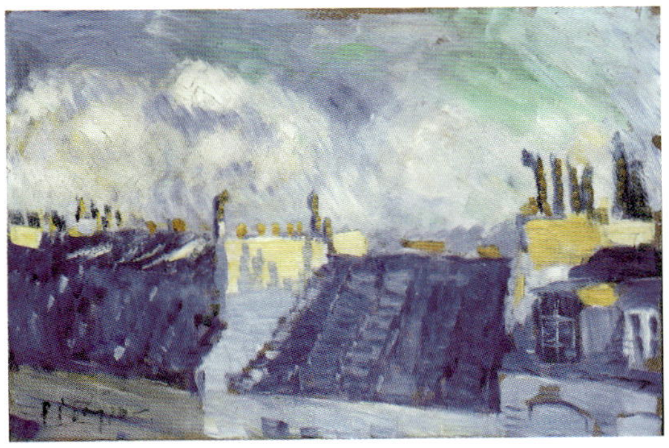

A634; oil on millboard, 39 × 57.7 cm
Signed: *Picasso*
Hindley Smith Bequest, 1939; WA1940.1.16

Eustace 1999, no. 1

In 1901, during his second visit to Paris, Picasso painted sixty-four paintings and made a number of drawings for an exhibition at Vollard's gallery. His palette at that time was restricted to blue, yellow and white, using mainly bright and clear tones. This work was painted in May–June 1901, looking out of his lodgings at 130, boulevard de Clichy.

Piero di Cosimo
(1461 – 1522)

The Forest Fire

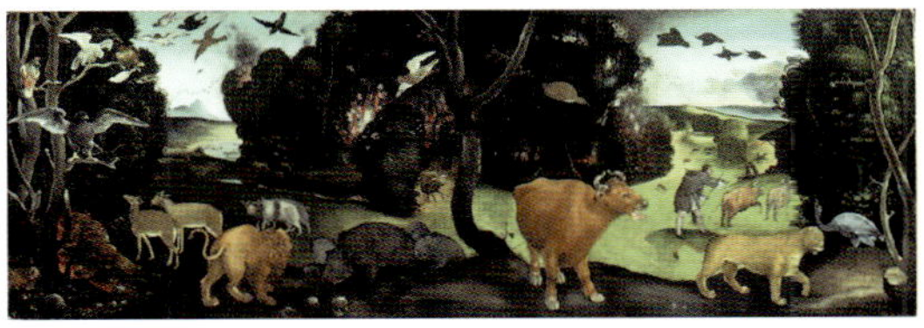

A420; oil on panel, 71.2 × 202 cm
Prov.: Count Giulio Rucellai, Florence; Prince Paul of Yugoslavia
Presented by the National Art Collections Fund, 1933; WA1933.2

Lloyd 1977, pp. 147–51; Whistler and Bomford 1999; Franklin 2001, pp. 49–50

Renowned for his originality and inventiveness, Piero di Cosimo painted many *spalliera* panels with themes from classical literature. Dating from *c.* 1505, A420 may have been one of a series described by Vasari as painted for Francesco del Pugliese. Two other panels of *The Hunt* and *The Return from the Hunt*, now in the Metropolitan Museum, New York, are thematically related but seem to have been painted in the 1490s. All three are concerned with the history of early man, inspired by passages from Book 5 of *De Rerum Natura* by Lucretius (98–*c.* 55 BC), who traces the origins of life on earth and the birth of community life, emphasising the role of fire as a catalyst for change. The New York pendants vividly depict a primitive world, while A420 could have been made for a different patron, taking up particular themes relating to more advanced stages of human life. Piero painted a poetic interpretation of the classical source, with idiosyncratic details of hybrid beasts added at a late stage. The masterly rendition of the fire and distant landscape place him in the forefront of the development of landscape painting.

Attributed to Pietro degli Ingannati
(active 1529 – 1547)

The Virgin and Child with St Peter and three unidentified saints

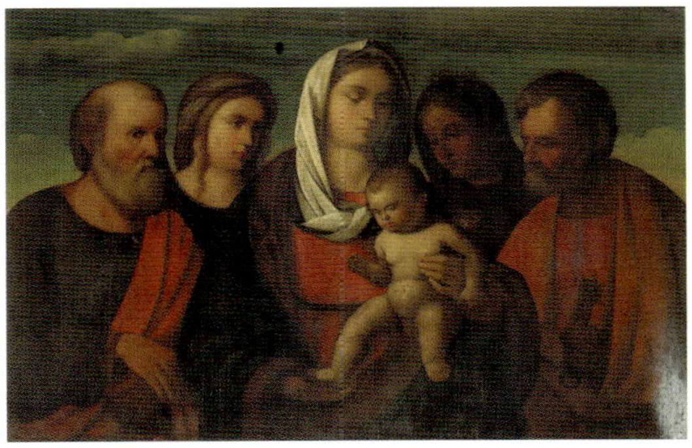

A400a; oil on canvas, 70.7 × 109.5 cm
Provenance unknown; WA.OA281

Lloyd 1977, pp. 151–2

The condition of A400a makes judgement of its style and quality difficult. The attribution is based on comparison with signed works by Pietro. The composition may derive from Giovanni Bellini and such groupings of saintly figures absorbed in meditation around the Virgin and Child are common in the work of his followers. St Peter carries his attributes of a key, but the other saints have no visible attributes.

Bernardino Pintoricchio
(*c.* 1452 – 1513)

The Virgin and Child

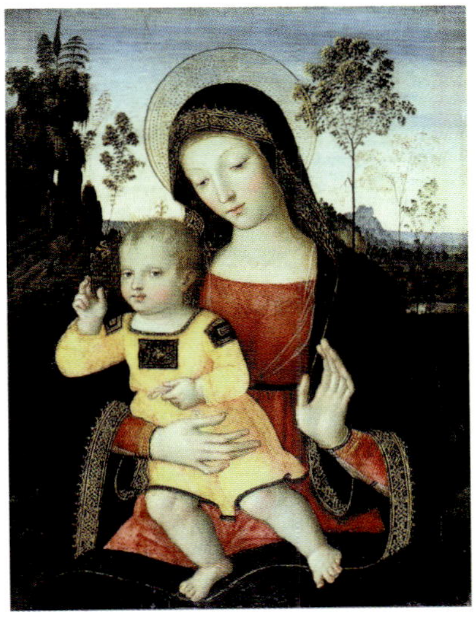

A303; tempera (?) and gold on panel, 41.3 × 30.2 cm
Fortnum Bequest, 1899; WA1899.CDEF.P10

Lloyd 1977, pp. 152–3; Todini 1989, I, p. 292

A prolific artist and a miniaturist, Pintoricchio worked in Rome, Siena and in Umbria and was one of the most influential painters in central Italy. His taste was for the delicate and refined, as this jewel-like painting attests. A303 is one of a group of small devotional images painted in a similar manner which are difficult to date: dates from the 1470s to the 1490s have been proposed.

John Piper
(1903 – 1992)

June Landscape

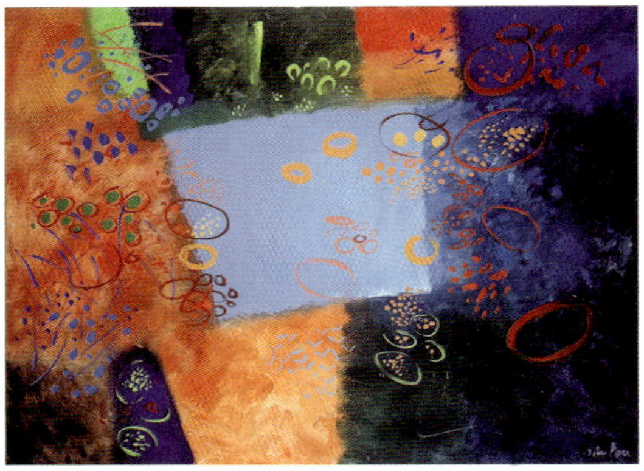

A1056; oil on canvas, 92.2 × 121.8 cm
Signed: *John Piper*
Presented by Lord and Lady Franks, 1969; WA1969.138

Eustace 1999, no. 31

Piper committed himself to Constructivism in the 1930s, developing a very strong topographical sense and sensitivity for space. Later he explored the relationship of architecture to landscape. He used these qualities from the 1950s onwards for many of his designs for stained glass. These concerns can be found in this painting which, with its bright colours, is typical of his work in the mid-1960s.

Camille Pissarro
(1830 – 1903)

Landscape at Pontoise

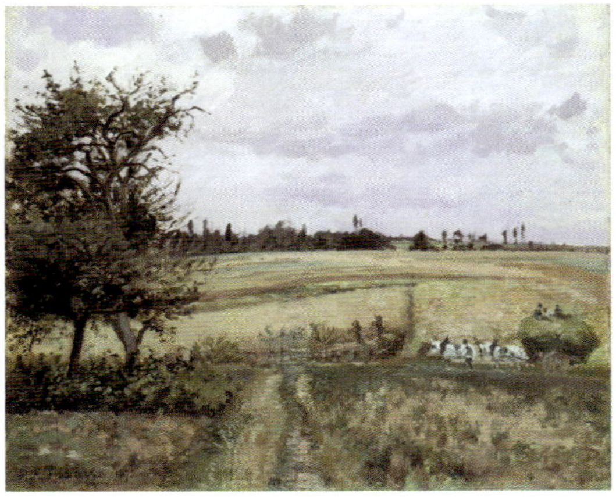

A659; oil on canvas, 46 × 55 cm
Signed and dated: *C. Pissarro 1872*
Prov.: Edgar Degas
Bequeathed by Montague Shearman through the Contemporary Art Society, 1940; WA1940.4.1

Pissarro and Venturi 1939, no. 163; Thorold and Erickson 1993, no. 3

Pissarro moved to Pontoise in 1866 and began the intensive study of the rural landscape which was to remain the backbone of his art. Here, the thin lively brush-strokes and light tonality reflect the influence of Monet, who was especially close to Pissarro at this period.

Camille Pissarro
(1830 – 1903)

Jeanne holding a Fan

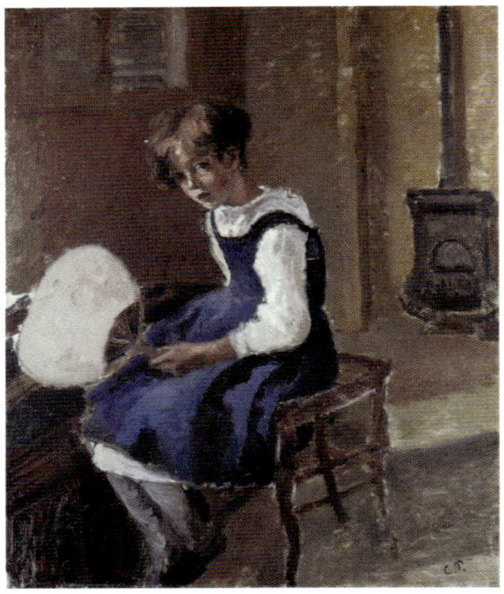

A821; oil on canvas, 56 × 46.5 cm
Signed with initials: *C.P.*
Pissarro Family Gift, 1952; WA1952.6.2

Pissarro and Venturi 1939, no. 232; London, Paris, Boston 1980–81, no. 34; Thorold and Erickson 1993, no. 5

The artist's daughter Jeanne-Rachel, known as Minette, was born in 1865 and died at Pontoise on 6 April 1874. She was a sickly child and treated by Dr Paul Gachet. In this portrait, painted when she was eight, the subdued colouring and tentative handling give an added intimacy to the scene. She holds a Japanese fan, reflecting her father's increasing interest in Japanese art.

Camille Pissarro
(1830 – 1903)

Mme Pissarro sewing

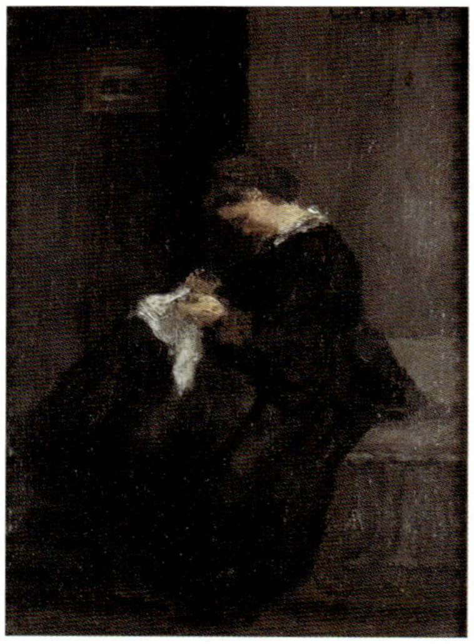

A819; oil on panel, 16 × 11 cm
Signed: *C.Pissarro*
Pissarro Family Gift, 1952; WA1952.6.1

Pissarro and Venturi 1939, no. 14; Thorold and Erickson 1993, no. 2

Julie Vellay (1839–1926) was a servant in Pissarro's parents' home in Paris. She was neither Jewish nor educated and therefore Pissarro's parents refused him permission to marry her, although she was already pregnant in 1860. This tiny portrait was painted in 1860 and reflects the intimate tone and sombre colouring of Corot's portraits. The couple were eventually married in London in 1871.

Camille Pissarro
(1830 – 1903)

Bouquet of pink Peonies

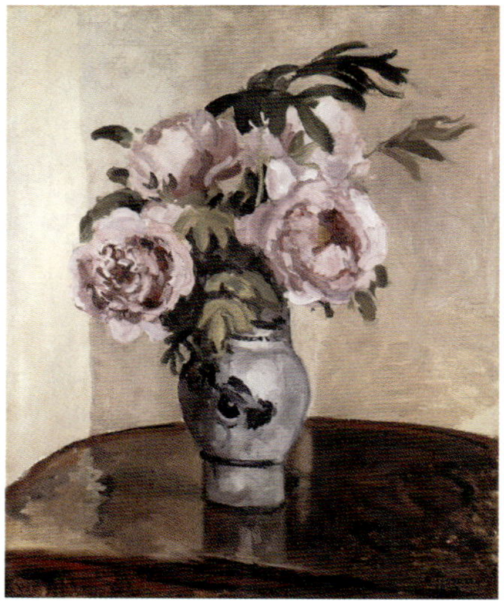

A820; oil on canvas, 73 × 60 cm
Signed and dated: *C. Pissarro 1873*
Pissarro Family Gift, 1951; WA1951.225.1

Pissarro and Venturi 1939, no. 199; Thorold and Erickson 1993, no. 4

Pissarro painted relatively few still lifes, including only thirteen flower pieces in his whole career. This example, dating from May–June 1873, is fluently painted in his most freely Impressionist style.

Camille Pissarro
(1830 – 1903)

Farm at Montfoucault: Snow Effect

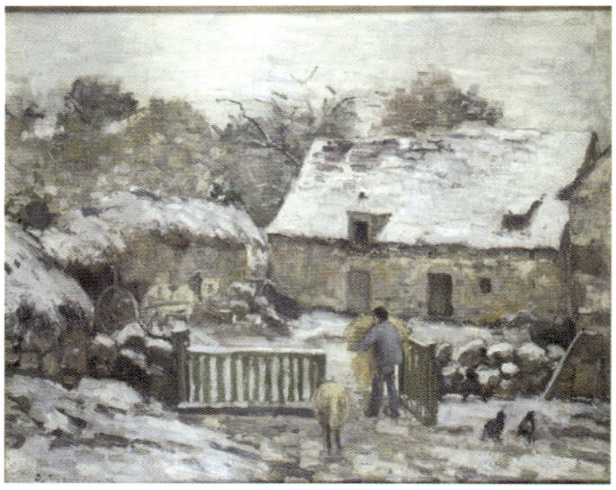

A822; oil on canvas, 54 × 65 cm
Signed and dated: *C. Pissarro 1876*
Pissarro Family Gift, 1951; WA1951.225.2

Pissarro and Venturi 1939, no. 283; Thorold and Erickson 1993, no. 6

Montfoucault was one of the farms owned by the Piette family in Mayenne, where Pissarro spent long periods between 1874 and 1876. The landscape was different from that at Pontoise, made up of small fields enclosed by hedgerows and the horizons blocked. Pissarro's style became more rustic, with shorter brush-strokes in thicker paint creating a more rugged surface and expressive texture in keeping with the landscape.

Camille Pissarro
(1830 – 1903)

Mme Pissarro sewing beside a Window

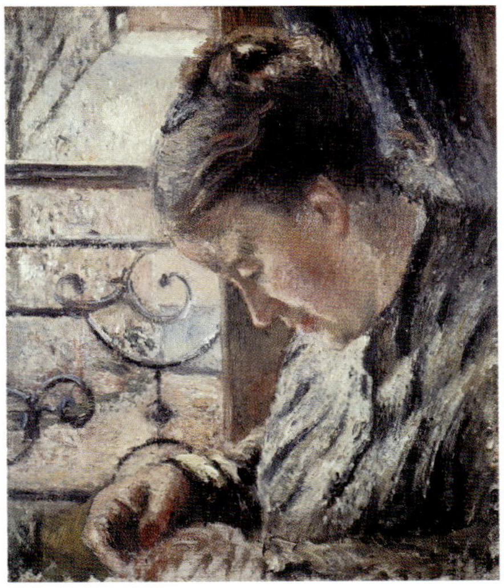

A823; oil on canvas, 54 × 45 cm
Stamped with initials: *C.P.*
Pissarro Family Gift, 1951; WA1951.225.3

Pissarro and Venturi 1939, no. 423; London, Paris, Boston 1980–81, no. 49; Thorold and Erickson 1993, no. 7

This oil, painted in 1878 shortly after the death of Minette and before the birth of Ludovic-Rodo, shows Mme Pissarro sewing in front of a window in their home at Pontoise. She is absorbed in her task, calm and detached. Pissarro has concentrated on her face and the curling ironwork of the balcony, in heavily worked strokes of gentle colours, to create a mood of intimacy and hard work.

Camille Pissarro
(1830 – 1903)

The Village of Éragny

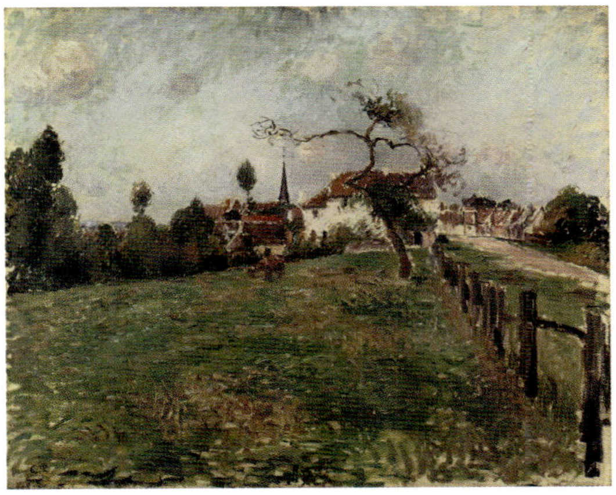

A824; oil on canvas, 55 × 35 cm
Stamped with initials: *C.P.*
Pissarro Family Gift, 1952; WA1952.6.3

Pissarro and Venturi 1939, no. 666; Thorold and Erickson 1993, no. 12

From the same year as the preceding.

Camille Pissarro
(1830 – 1903)

Bath Road, London

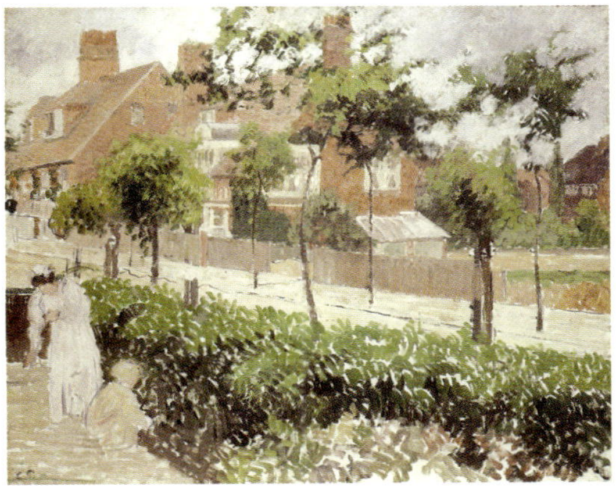

A825; oil on canvas, 54 × 65 cm
Stamped with initials: *C.P.*
Pissarro Family Gift, 1952; WA1951.225.4

Pissarro and Venturi 1939, no. 1009; Thorold and Erickson 1993, no. 19

Lucien Pissarro settled in London in 1893 and in 1896 moved with his wife and daughter to 62, Bath Road, Bedford Park, a newly completed garden suburb. Between 7 May and 20 July 1897, Camille stayed there while Lucien was convalescing from a stroke. He made several paintings of the front and the back of the house. Here, Esther and Orovida play in the front garden. The painting is unfinished, especially in the foreground.

Camille Pissarro
(1830 – 1903)

Brick Kiln at Éragny

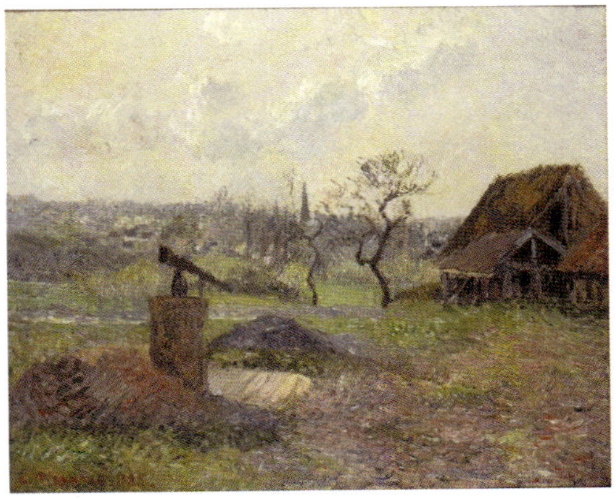

A630; oil on canvas, 38 × 46 cm
Signed and dated: *C. Pissarro 1885*
Hindley Smith Bequest, 1939; WA1940.1.12

Pissarro and Venturi 1939, no. 661; Thorold and Erickson 1993, no. 11

Pissarro moved from Pontoise to Éragny-sur-Epte in 1884 and remained there for the rest of his life. The village was smaller and less modernised than Pontoise. The brick kiln, owned by M. Delafolie, could be seen from the Pissarros' home. It had almost fallen into disuse. The water pump stands forlorn in the foreground and the buildings in the background are overgrown. The short brush-strokes anticipate Pissarro's interest in Pointillism.

Camille Pissarro
(1830 – 1903)

View from my Window, Éragny-sur-Epte

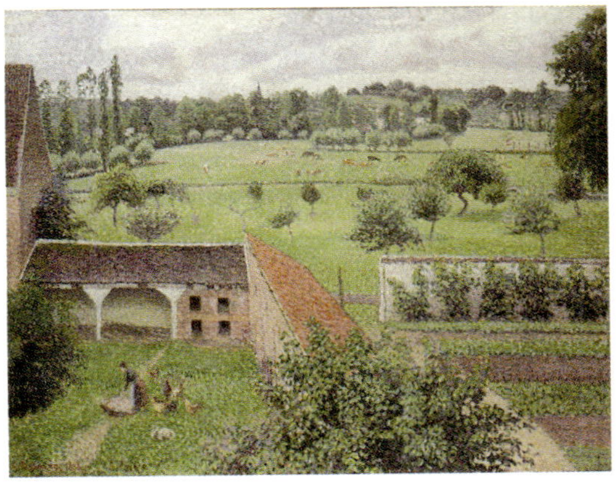

A794; oil on canvas, 65 × 81 cm
Signed and dated: *C. Pissarro 1888*
Presented by Mrs Lucien Pissarro, 1950; WA1950.184

Pissarro and Venturi 1939, no. 721; Thorold and Erickson 1993, no. 13

The painting shows a view from the Pissarros' house at Éragny, looking towards the village of Bazincourt. The tall building on the left was converted into Pissarro's studio when he bought the property in 1892. The composition, which the artist referred to as 'modern primitive', was begun in 1886 but not completed until two years later, in the painstaking Pointillist technique Pissarro used for only a few years.

Camille Pissarro
(1830 – 1903)

The Tuileries Gardens, Rainy Weather

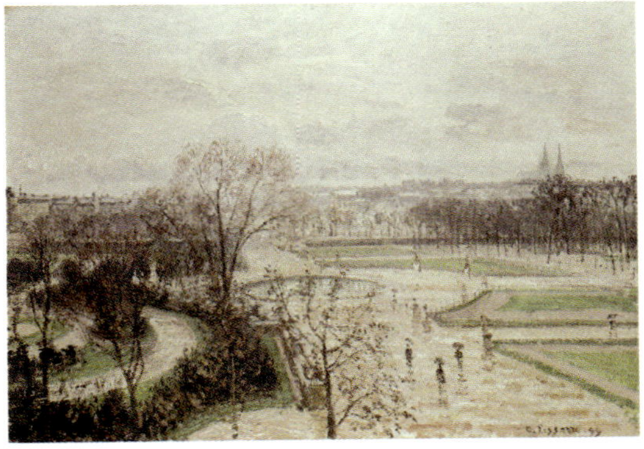

A492; oil on canvas, 65 × 92 cm
Signed and dated: *C. Pissarro. 1899*
Prov.: Lucien Pissarro
Weldon Bequest, 1937; WA1937.73

Pissarro and Venturi 1939, no. 1102; Thorold and Erickson 1993, no. 20

This is one of sixteen canvases painted from the windows of the apartment Pissarro rented at 204 rue de Rivoli, Paris, from January 1899. The view looks over the Tuileries towards the Seine, with the spires of the church of Sainte-Clotilde on the right. The weather was wet and cold, but appropriate for the pearly light and subdued effects Pissarro wished to convey.

Camille Pissarro
(1830 – 1903)

Autumn, Morning Mist, Éragny-sur-Epte

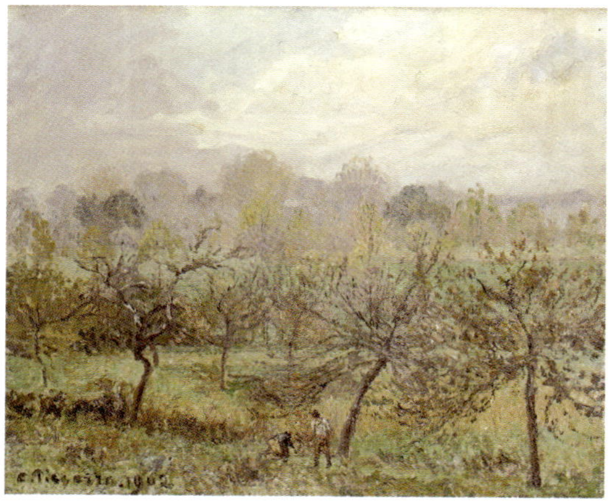

A826; oil on canvas, 46 × 55 cm
Signed and dated: *C. Pissarro. 1902*
Pissarro Family Gift, 1951; WA1951.225.5

Pissarro and Venturi 1939, no. 1265; Thorold and Erickson 1993, no. 21

Pissarro grew to dislike the bright, clear light of summer, preferring the gentler, more elusive tones of the other seasons. He was especially fond of autumn. He painted this view of the orchard repeatedly, altering the viewpoint and even the size and shapes of trees and seeking to convey the interaction of season, air and space within a limited subject matter. Here, the green and brown vegetation dissolves into a hazy grey horizon.

Camille Pissarro
(1830 – 1903)

Quayside at Le Havre

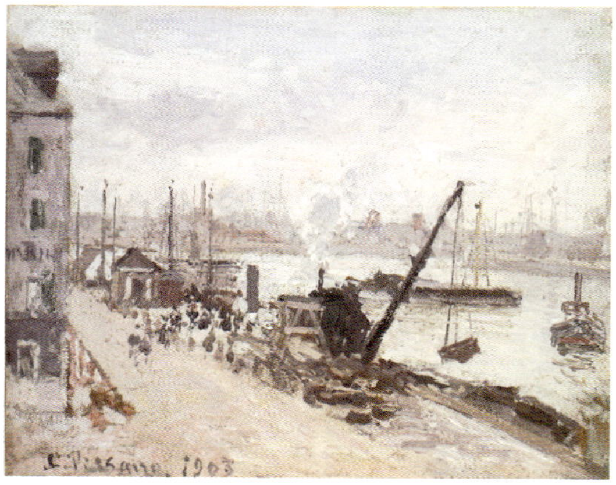

A827; gouache on silk, 24 × 29.5 cm
Signed and dated: *C. Pissarro 1903*
Pissarro Family Gift, 1952; WA1952.6.4

Pissarro and Venturi 1939, no. 1303; Brettell & Lloyd 1980, no. 279; Thorold and Erickson 1993, no. 23

Pissarro painted his last works at Le Havre between July and September 1903. They generally show the port, full of bustle and activity, in bold, geometric compositions. This is the smallest, painted on 'batiste', a form of cambric, and shows the view from his room at the Hôtel Continental on the main quay of the inner harbour. It was painted during poor weather at the end of July.

Félix Pissarro
(1874 – 1897)

View at Hemiksem

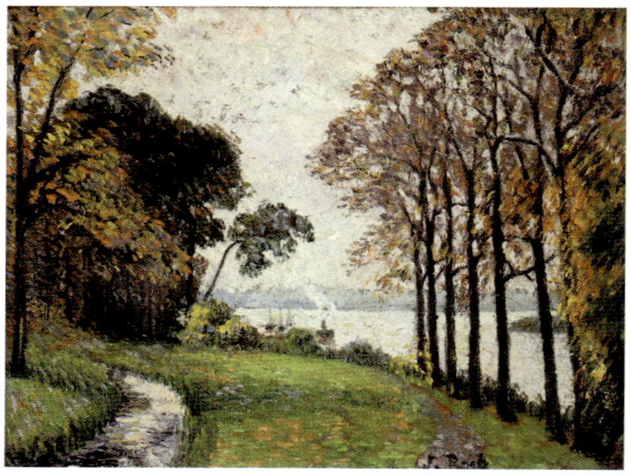

A831; oil on canvas, 31.5 × 40.5 cm
Signed: *J.Roch*
Pissarro Family Gift, 1951; WA1951.225.9

Like his brothers, Félix tried to distance himself from his Pissarro heritage and adopted the pseudonym 'J. Roch', with which this painting is signed. Hemiksem is a small village south of Antwerp and this view probably dates from the same visit to Belgium as A828.

Camille Pissarro
(1830 – 1903)

Sunset at Éragny-sur-Epte, Autumn

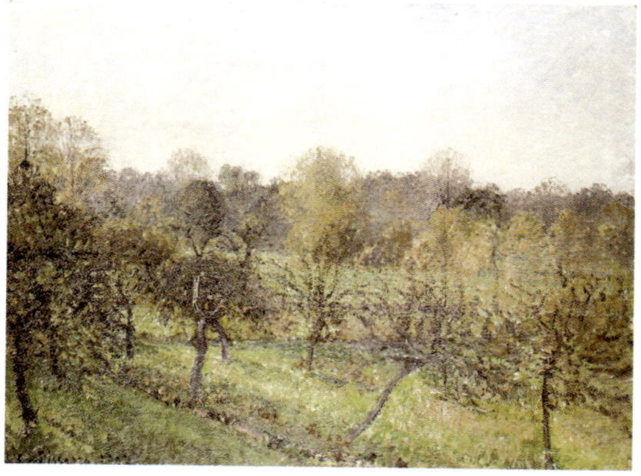

A795; oil on canvas, 73 × 92 cm
Signed and dated: *C. Pissarro 1902*
Presented by Mrs Lucien Pissarro, 1950; WA1950.186

Pissarro and Venturi 1939, no. 1268; London, Paris, Boston 1980–81, no. 89

Like the preceding work, this was painted in October 1902, looking from the studio window at Éragny and concentrating on the effects of light and atmosphere and the delicate tones of autumn.

Félix Pissarro
(1874 – 1897)

Sand Dunes at Knokke

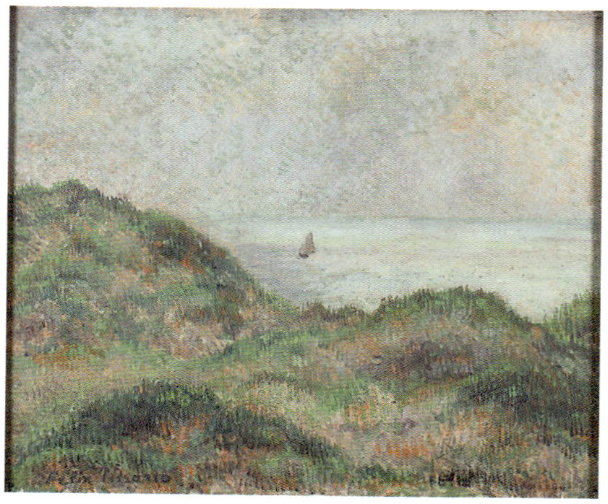

A828; oil on canvas, 46 × 54 cm
Signed: *Felix Pissarro*
Pissarro Family Gift, 1951; WA1951.225.6

The third son of Camille Pissarro, Félix studied with his father and was especially close to his elder brother, Georges, called Manzana. Following political unrest in France, Camille and Félix spent the summer of 1894 in Belgium, in the company of Theo van Gogh and Van Rysselberghe. They stopped at the coastal resort of Knokke-sur-Mer during July and August, when this painting was executed.

Félix Pissarro
(1874 – 1897)

Wooded Landscape: a Woman walking with a Dog

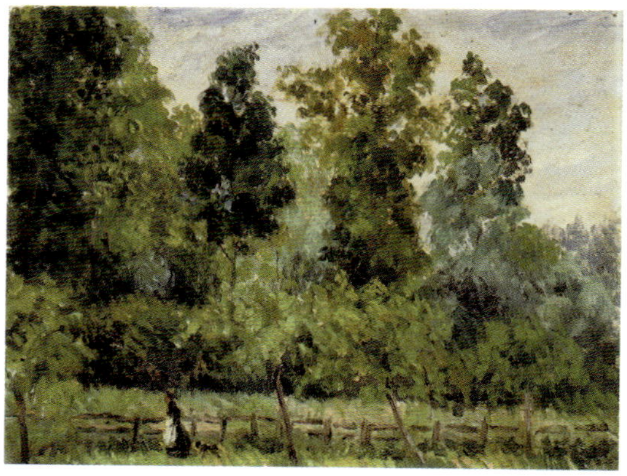

A832; oil on canvas, 27 × 35.5 cm
Pissarro Family Gift, 1951; WA1951.225.10

Although Félix's style varied within the broadly Impressionist language of his father, it did not develop much in his short life and his works are impossible to date.

Félix Pissarro
(1874 – 1897)

Landscape with Riders

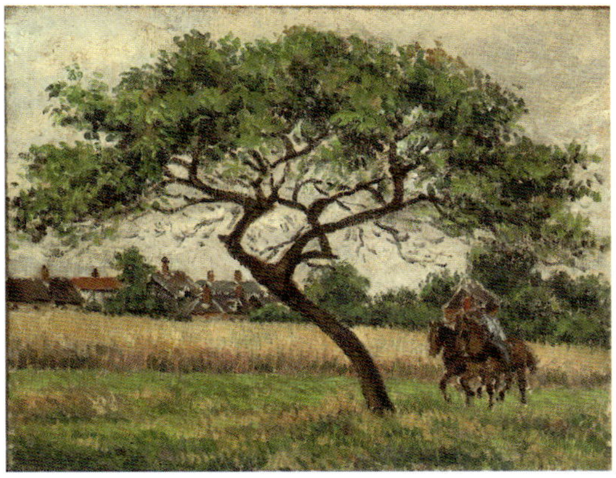

A834; oil on canvas, 32 × 41 cm
Pissarro Family Gift, 1952; WA1952.6.5

Félix was fascinated by the horse and included it as a subject in his prints, drawings and paintings from his childhood onwards. This work was probably painted in the orchard at Éragny.

Félix Pissarro
(1874 – 1897)

The River

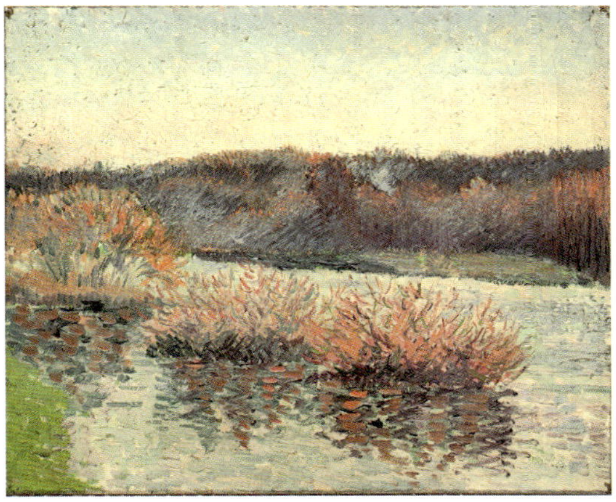

A833; oil on canvas, 37.7 × 46 cm
Pissarro Family Gift, 1951; WA1951.225.11

Lucien Pissarro
(1863 – 1944)

La Maison de la Sourde, Éragny

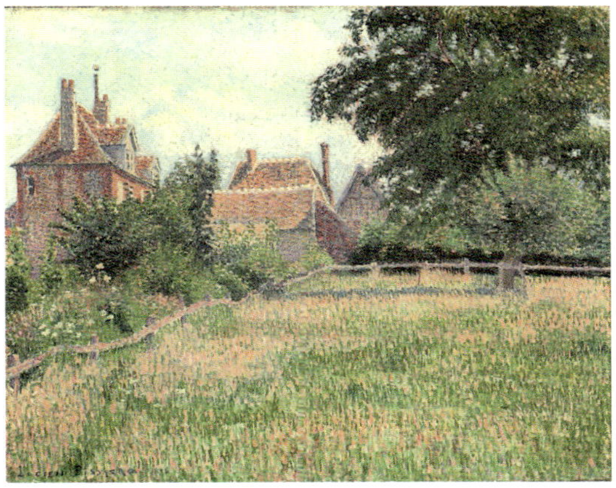

A835; oil on canvas, 58 × 72 cm
Signed and dated: *Lucien Pissarro 1886*
Pissarro Family Gift, 1952; WA1952.6.6

Thorold 1983, no. 9; Thorold and Erickson 1993, no. 25

The house of the deaf woman, also known as the house of the Englishman, was next to that of the Pissarro family at Éragny and painted from various angles by both Camille and Lucien in 1886. This painting, which was shown at the Salon des Independants in autumn 1886, was painted in a modified pointillist technique, using a variety of brush-strokes, from the short dabs in the background to the long upright strokes of the side of the brush in the field.

Félix Pissarro
(1874 – 1897)

Poplar Trees

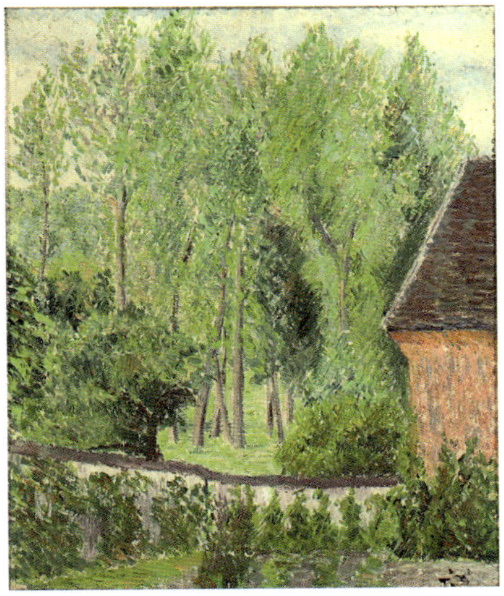

A830; oil on canvas, 46 × 38 cm
Signed: *TiTi*
Pissarro Family Gift, 1951; WA1951.225.8

'Titi' was a family nickname for Félix.

Félix Pissarro
(1874 – 1897)

The Rat

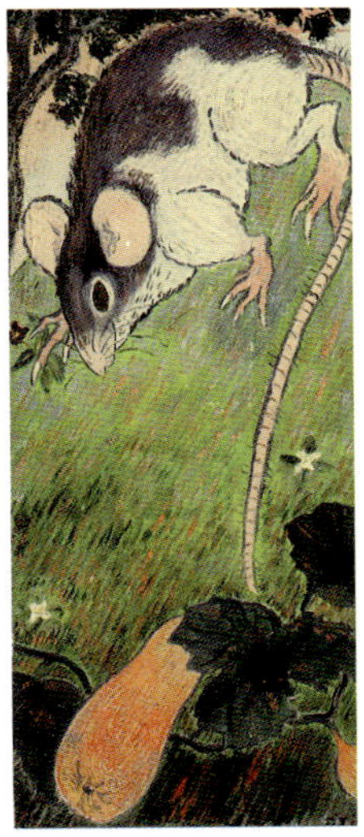

A829; oil on panel, 81 × 34 cm
Signed: *TiTi*
Pissarro Family Gift, 1951; WA1951.225.7

This was painted on a panel of a bedroom door.

Lucien Pissarro
(1863 – 1944)

Éragny Church

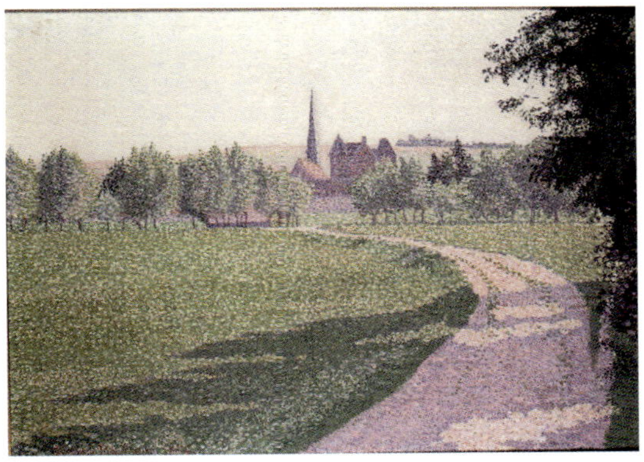

A836; oil on canvas, 53.2 × 72.2 cm
Signed and dated: *LUCIEN PISSARRO 1886*
Pissarro Family Gift, 1952; WA1952.6.7

Thorold 1983, no. 10

Following his father's example, Lucien experimented with Pointillism during the summer of 1886. This was his first oil in the new technique, in a strongly stylised composition. The road curves gracefully from the foreground towards the distant village of Éragny, with its prominent church spire.

Lucien Pissarro
(1863 – 1944)

The Thierceville Road, Early Spring

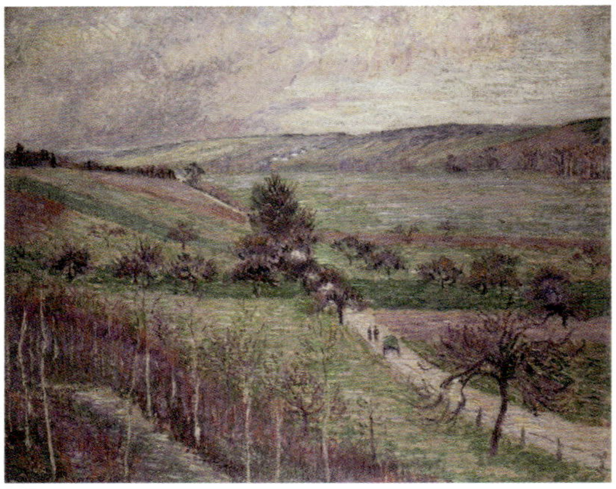

A837; oil on canvas, 60 × 73 cm
Signed and dated: *Lucien Pissarro 1893*
Pissarro Family Gift, 1952; WA1952.6.8

Thorold 1983, no. 61

By 1893, Pissarro had abandoned Pointillism and reverted to his own version of the more fluid Impressionist technique practised by his father. This painting, presumably completed in March or April 1893, shows the road from Éragny to the neighbouring village of Thierceville.

Lucien Pissarro
(1863 – 1944)

The Garden Gate, Epping

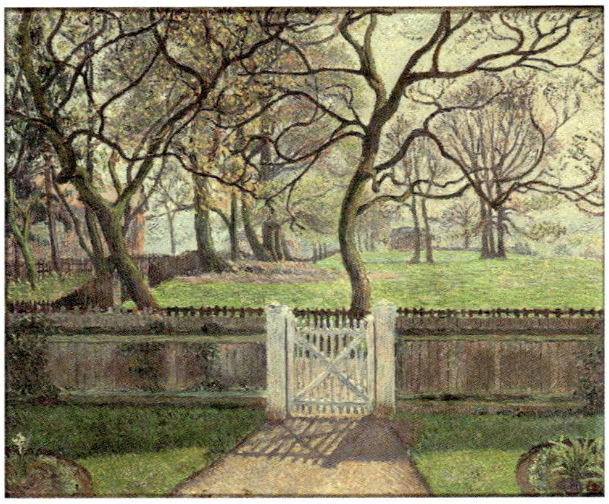

A840; oil on canvas, 54 × 65 cm
Signed in monogram and dated: *1894*
Presented by Mrs Lucien Pissarro, 1951; WA1951.225.13

Thorold 1983, no. 79

A view from the front door of Lucien's cottage, Eragny House, at Hemnall Street, Epping. The use of a fence was one of Lucien's favourite compositional devices, which he used throughout his career. Here, it is combined with complicated patterns formed by the trees receding into the distance.

Lucien Pissarro
(1863 – 1944)

November Morning, Epping

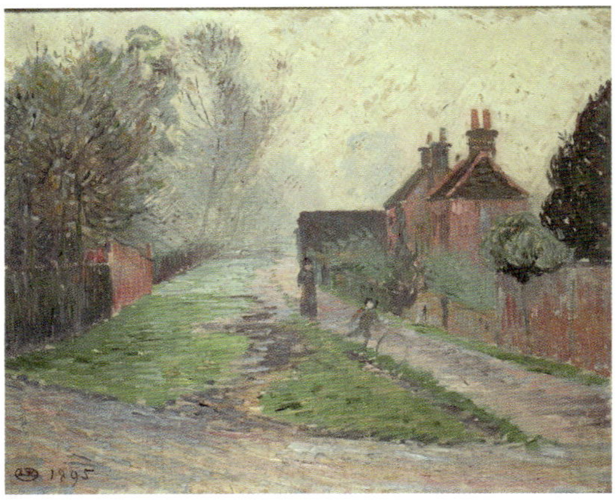

A1255; oil on canvas, 45 × 55 cm
Signed in monogram and dated: *1895*
Bequeathed by John Bensusan-Butt, 1997; WA2003.96

Thorold 1983, no. 87

During his later years at Eragny House, Hemnall Street, Epping, Lucien concentrated his energies on his work for the Eragny Press. This is the last surviving painting from this period and one of the most boldly executed. It shows the road in front of Eragny House (cf. A840), with Esther and Orovida playing with a hoop.

Lucien Pissarro
(1863 – 1944)

Landscape at Epping

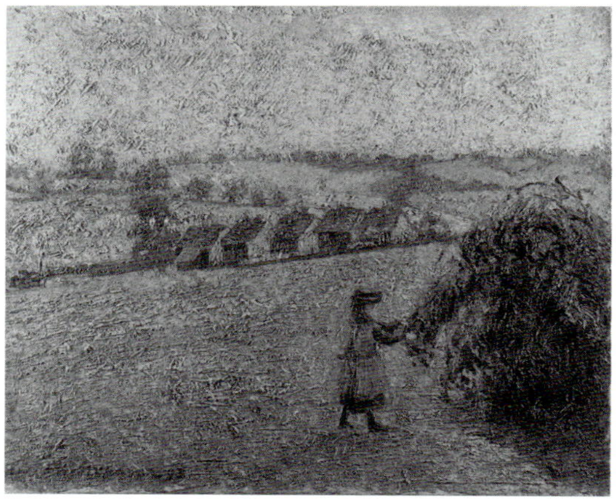

A838; oil on canvas, 59.7 × 73.2 cm
Signed and dated: *Lucien Pissarro 1893*
Pissarro Family Gift, 1952; WA1952.6.9

Thorold 1983, no. 72

Lucien returned to England in May 1893 and leased a cottage he christened Eragny House at Hemnall Street, Epping. He lived there until 1897 and the village and surrounding countryside provided numerous subjects for his brush. Here, the landscape is enlivened by the figure of a girl blackberrying, which suggests the work was completed in August or September 1893.

Lucien Pissarro
(1863 – 1944)

The Fairy

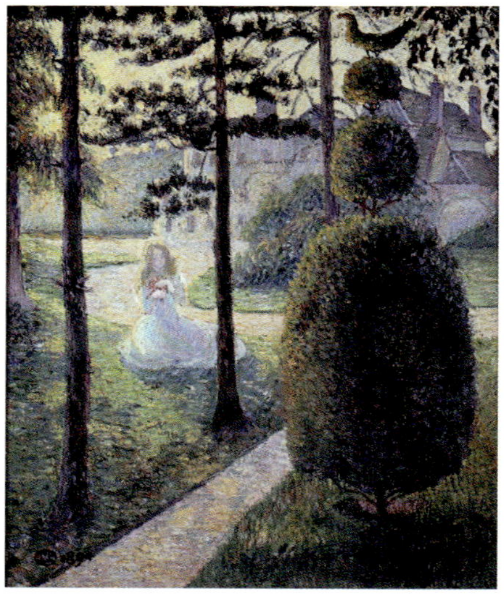

A839; oil on canvas, 73 × 60 cm
Signed in monogram and dated: *1894*
Pissarro Family Gift, 1952; WA1951.225.12

Thorold 1983, no. 81

The second of two paintings of Coopersale Hall, Essex; the first, *An Essex Hall* (private collection), dates from the previous year. In *The Fairy*, the strange shape of topiary lends a magical atmosphere to the scene and the brightly lit girl seen between two straight tree trunks appears as unreal as a fairy.

Lucien Pissarro
(1863 – 1944)

View over the Estuary, Harfleur

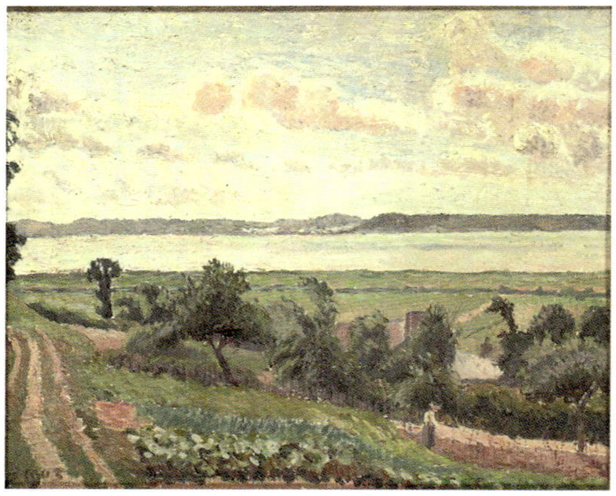

A841; oil on canvas, 45 × 55 cm
Signed in monogram and dated: *1903*
Pissarro Family Gift, 1952; WA1952.6.10

Thorold 1983, no. 96

Lucien spent July 1903 painting with his father at Le Havre. While Camille concentrated on the bustling port at Le Havre, Lucien preferred the landscape around the nearby town of Harfleur. Lucien made four paintings at Harfleur, two of scenes in the town and two of the surroundings. In this view, the sun sets over the estuary.

Lucien Pissarro
(1863 – 1944)

Hoar Frost, Chiswick

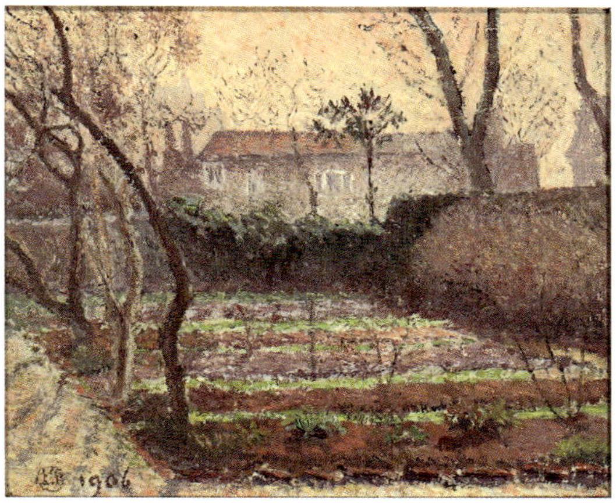

A842; oil on canvas, 39 × 46 cm
Signed in monogram and dated: *1906*
Pissarro Family Gift, 1952; WA1952.6.11

Thorold 1983, no. 107; Thorold & Erickson 1993, no. 26

Lucien moved to 'The Brook', Stamford Brook Road, Chiswick, in 1902 and lived there for the rest of his life. Like his father, he painted the simple garden scene outside his house on numerous occasions. This painting, of January 1906, shows frost on the lines of recently turned earth in the garden, the trees thickly painted and standing proud of the surface.

Lucien Pissarro
(1863 – 1944)

The Cottage Garden, Fishpond

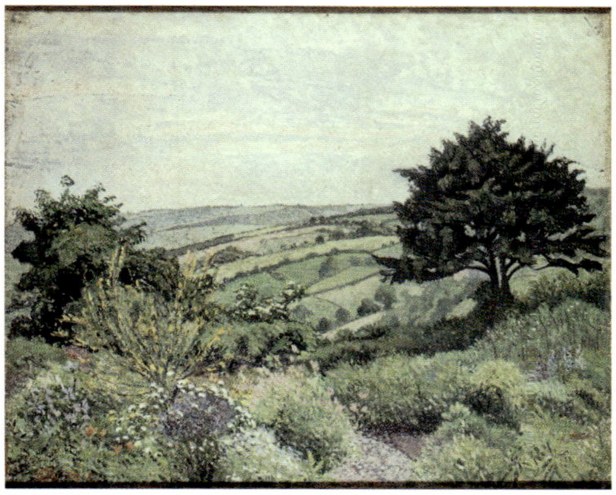

A844; oil on canvas, 53 × 65 cm
Signed in monogram and dated: *1915*
Pissarro Family Gift, 1951; WA1951.225.15

Thorold 1983, no. 211

From the end of May until November 1915, Lucien stayed at Sea View Cottage, Fishpond, near Charmouth in Dorset. There, he explored motifs offered by the rolling hills and distant sea and, as here, by the luxuriant vegetation of the cottage gardens.

Lucien Pissarro
(1863 – 1944)

Hastings: Mist, Sun and Smoke

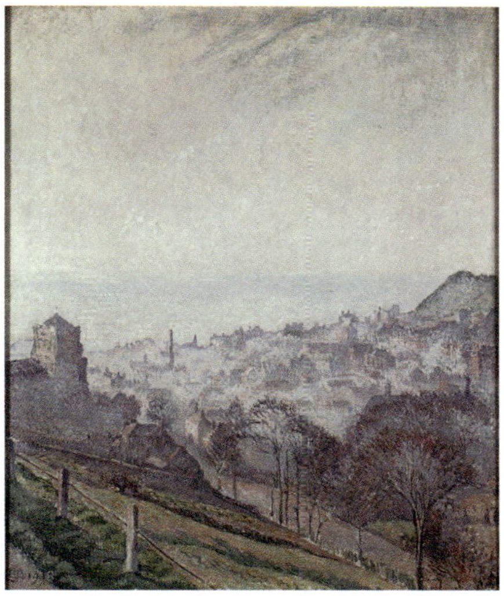

A845; oil on canvas, 65 × 53 cm
Signed in monogram and dated: *1918*
Pissarro Family Gift, 1951; WA1951.225.16

Thorold 1983, no. 270

During the first half of 1918, Lucien painted at Hastings in Sussex, producing eight landscapes, in several of which the ancient town is seen under grey sky and through the sea mist common during the winter months.

Lucien Pissarro
(1863 – 1944)

Poulfenc à Riec

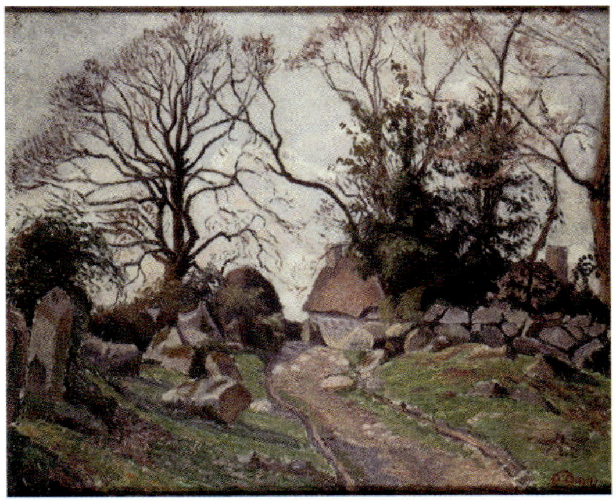

A843; oil on canvas, 54 × 65 cm
Signed in monogram and dated: *1910*
Pissarro Family Gift, 1952; WA1951.225.14

Thorold 1983, no. 134; London 1988, no. 70

From the end of January to 10 April 1910, Lucien stayed at the Hôtel Cadoret, Riec-sur-Belon, Brittany, where his mother and brother, Ludovic-Rodo visited him. The countryside delighted him, but he found painting difficult, suffering one of his numerous crises of confidence in the shadow of his father. Nevertheless, he completed ten paintings, including three of boulders and trees in the nearby quarry.

Lucien Pissarro
(1863 – 1944)

East Knoyle Church: Snow

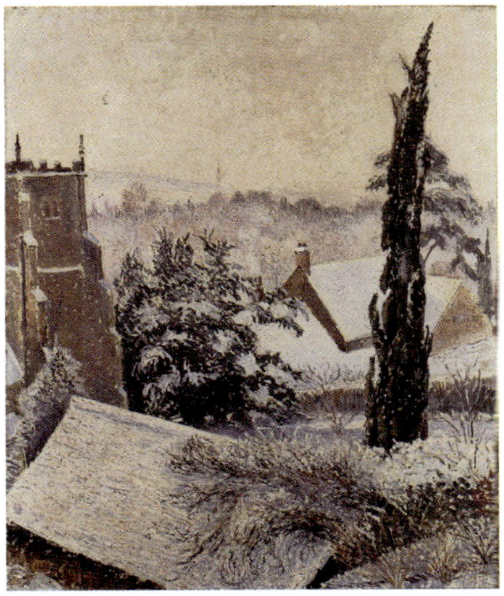

A797; oil on canvas, 73 × 60 cm
Signed in monogram and dated: *1917*
Presented by S.L. Bensusan, 1950; WA1950.189

Thorold 1983, no. 254

Lucien spent the winter of 1916–17 at 'Enterprise', East Knoyle, about five miles north of Shaftesbury in Wiltshire. St Mary's Church, with its distinctive tower, provided him with the motif for seven paintings, all but one in the snow.

Lucien Pissarro
(1863 – 1944)

Mme Camille Pissarro

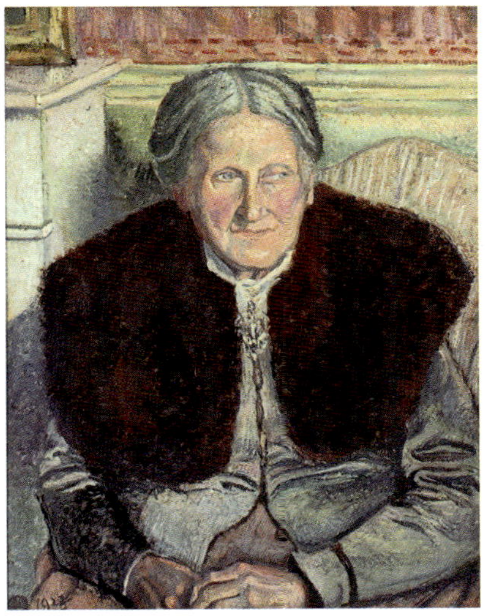

A796; oil on canvas, 65 × 49 cm
Signed in monogram and dated: *1923*
Presented by Dr Ruth Bensusan-Butt, 1950; WA1950.188

Thorold 1983, no. 363

Lucien's mother, who had been painted by her husband all their married life (see A819 & A823) and by their sons, remained in the house at Éragny after Camille's death in 1903. This portrait was completed in March 1923.

Lucien Pissarro
(1863 – 1944)

La Pointe de Cougoussa, Sunset

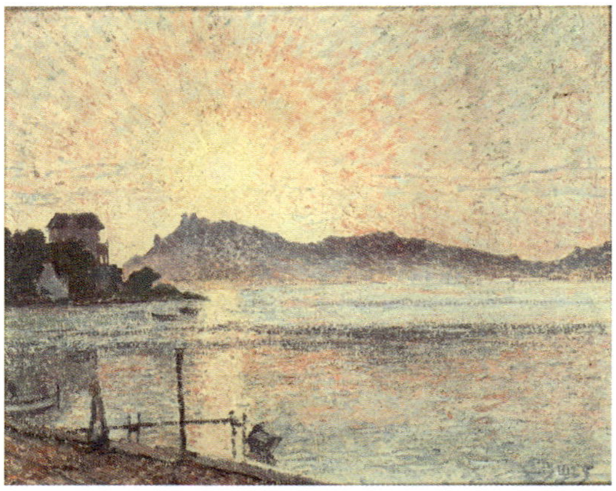

A847; oil on canvas, 38 × 46 cm
Signed in monogram and dated: *1925*
Presented by Mrs Lucien Pissarro, 1951; WA1951.225.18

Thorold 1983, no. 403

Lucien first visited the Var, in southern France, in 1922 and returned there frequently, eventually buying a small house in 1929, after his mother's death. He spent the first five months of 1925 at Le Brusq, during which time he completed twenty-five oil paintings. He painted this study of the sun setting over the Pointe de Cougoussa during a windy month of March.

Lucien Pissarro
(1863 – 1944)

Le Mistral, le Brusq

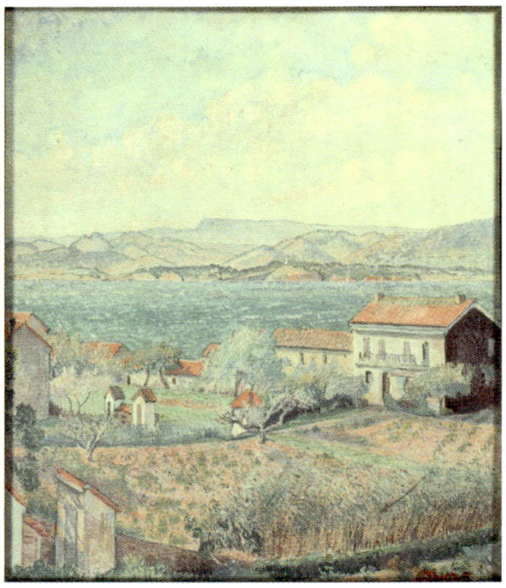

A846; oil on canvas, 64 × 54 cm
Signed in monogram and dated: *1925*
Presented by Mrs Lucien Pissarro, 1951; WA1951.225.17

Thorold 1983, no. 414

Like the preceding, completed in May 1925. The middle distance evokes the effect of the wind on the sea.

Lucien Pissarro
(1863 – 1944)

Six-Fours from Chemin de L'Hubac

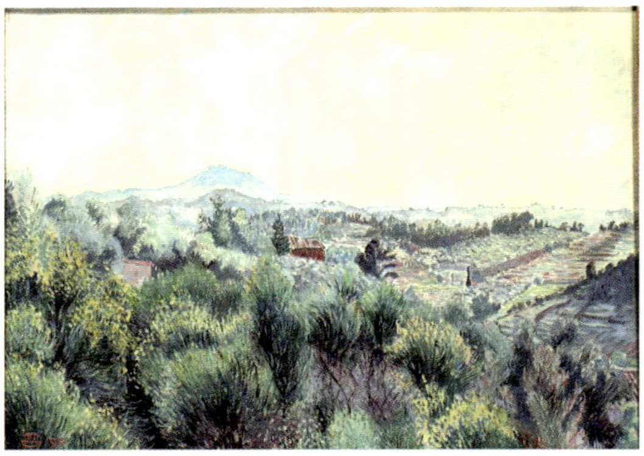

A849; oil on canvas, 54.5 × 73 cm
Signed in monogram and dated: *1931*
Pissarro Family Gift, 1952; WA1952.6.13

Thorold 1983, no. 487

From his house in the Var, renamed Camapgne Orovida, Lucien made numerous paintings of the surrounding countryside. This work, executed in May 1931, shows the village of Six-Fours-les-Plages, a few miles north-east of Le Brusq.

Lucien Pissarro
(1863 – 1944)

Thistles, Le Brusq

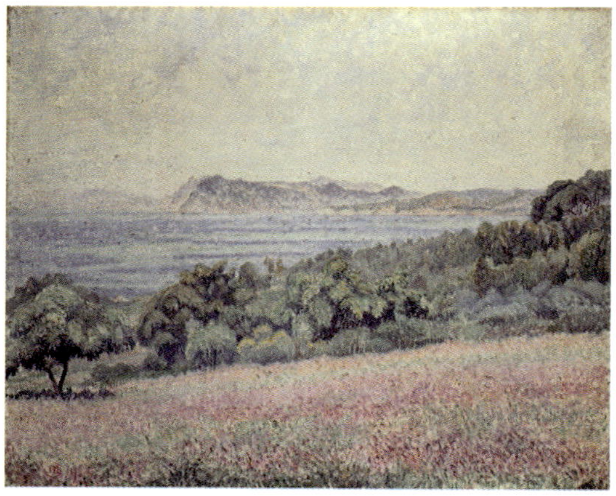

A848; oil on canvas, 60 × 73 cm
Signed in monogram and dated: *1925*
Pissarro Family Gift, 1952; WA1952.6.12

Thorold 1983, no. 413

This atmospheric painting of a field of thistles at Le Brusq was completed in May 1925.

Lucien Pissarro
(1863 – 1944)

Broom, Le Brusq

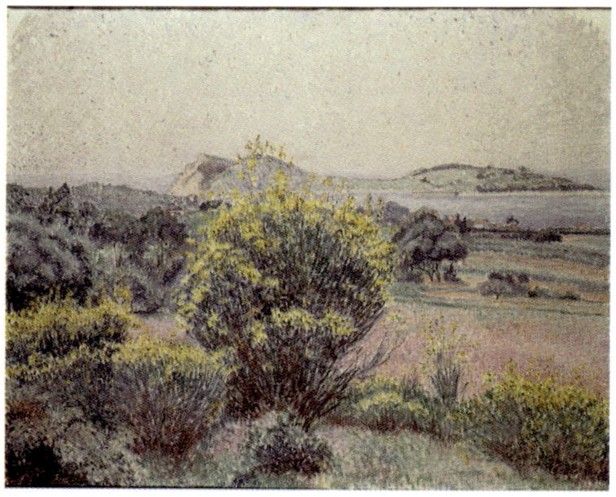

A491; oil on canvas, 60.1 × 73 cm
Signed in monogram and dated: *1925*
Weldon Bequest, 1937; WA1937.72

Thorold 1983, no. 416; Thorold and Erickson 1993, no. 28

One of Lucien's most extrovert works, painted in June 1925 and illustrating the broom in full flower at Le Brusq.

Lucien Pissarro
(1863 – 1944)

Bookcase and Flowers

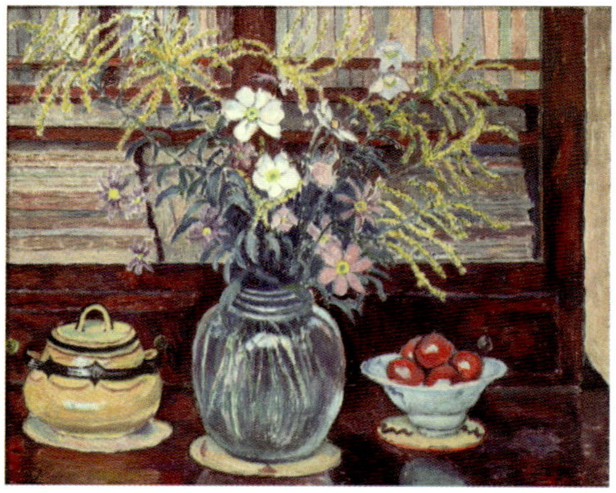

A851; oil on canvas, 46 × 55 cm
Signed in monogram and dated: *1935*
Pissarro Family Gift, 1952; WA1952.6.14

Thorold 1983, no. 521

Painted in early autumn, 1935, probably at The Minories, Colchester, where Lucien was visiting his sister-in-law, Dr Ruth Bensusan-Butt, this is one of the artist's last still lifes.

Lucien Pissarro
(1863 – 1944)

Still Life: Eucalyptus and Chrysanthemums

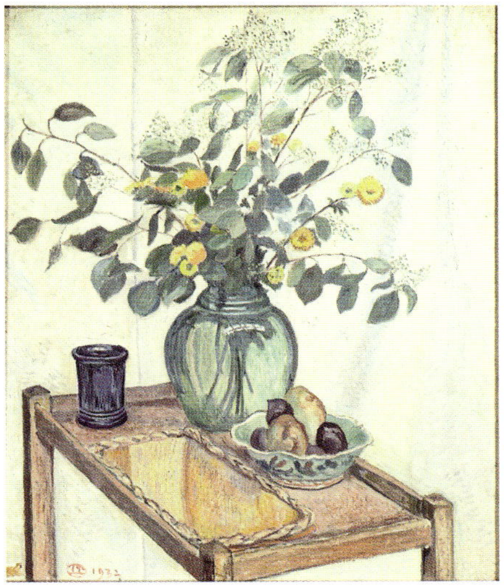

A850; oil on canvas, 65 × 55 cm
Signed in monogram and dated: *1935*
Presented by Mrs Lucien Pissarro, 1951; WA1951.225.19

Thorold 1983, no. 496

A simple arrangement of flowers and foliage from the garden at The Brook, painted in November 1935.

Lucien Pissarro
(1863 – 1944)

My Studio Garden

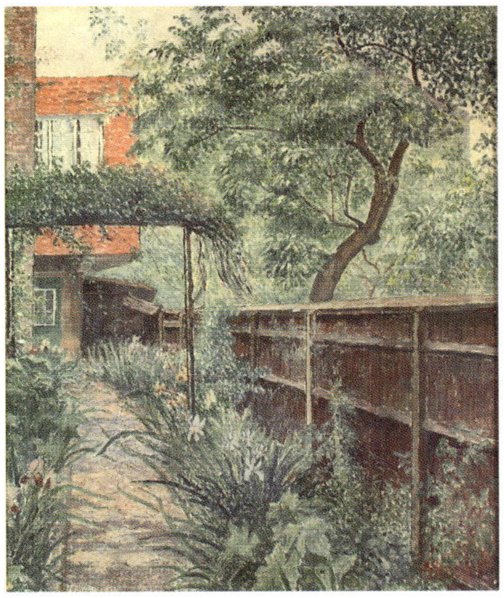

A853; oil on canvas, 65 × 55 cm
Signed in monogram and dated: *1938*
Presented by Mrs Lucien Pissarro, 1951; WA1951.225.20

Thorold 1983, no. 540

A view from the studio at The Brook, painted in June 1938.

Orovida Pissarro
(1893 – 1968)

Self-portrait

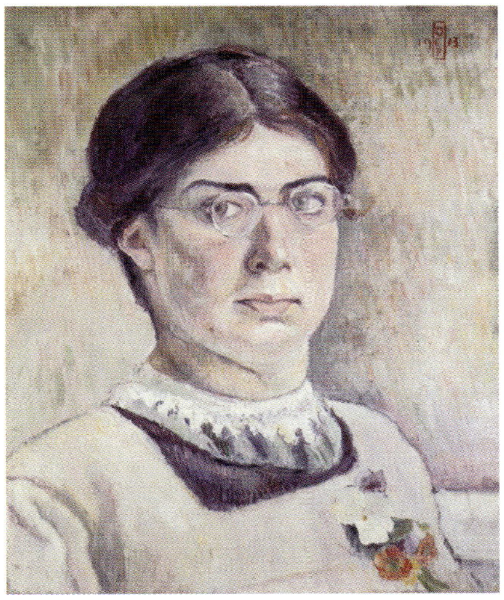

A855; oil on canvas, 39.5 × 32 cm
Signed and dated: *OCP 1913*
Pissarro Family Gift, 1952; WA1952.6.17

Erickson 1992, no. 5

Painted at the age of twenty and the first of only two painted self-portraits (for the other, see A1019), this shows the strong influence on Orovida's technique of her father, Lucien, who restricted her palette to five colours. It was completed at Blackpool and may have been prompted by Lucien's *Portrait of Orovida* (private collection) of the same year.

Lucien Pissarro
(1863 – 1944)

La Nouvelle Route, Cotignac

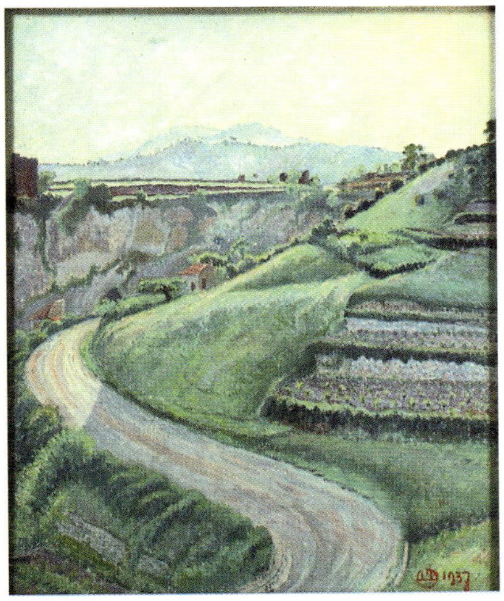

A852; oil on canvas, 65 × 55 cm
Signed in monogram and dated: *1937*
Pissarro Family Gift, 1952; WA1952.6.15

Thorold 1983, no. 530

Lucien stayed at the Hôtel du Cours, Cotignac (Var) from March to 9 July 1937, where he painted six landscapes.

Ludovic-Rodolphe Pissarro
(1878 – 1952)

Still Life with a Green Jar

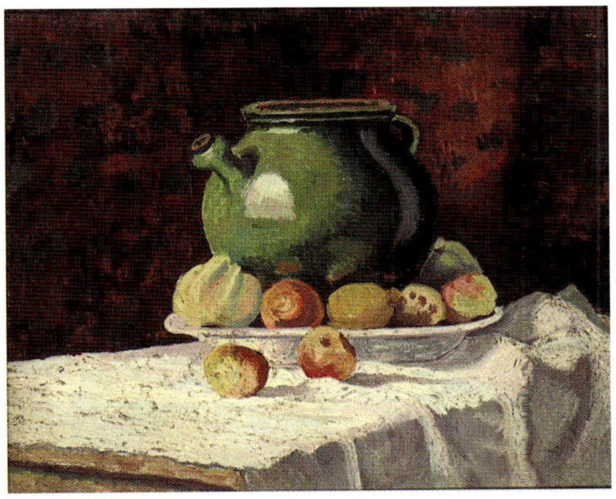

A854; oil on canvas, 46 × 55 cm
Pissarro Family Gift, 1952; WA1952.6.16

Like his elder brother Lucien, Rodo occasionally painted still lifes, though he was primarily interested in landscape. This example probably dates from before the First World War.

Orovida Pissarro
(1893 – 1968)

The Archer's Return

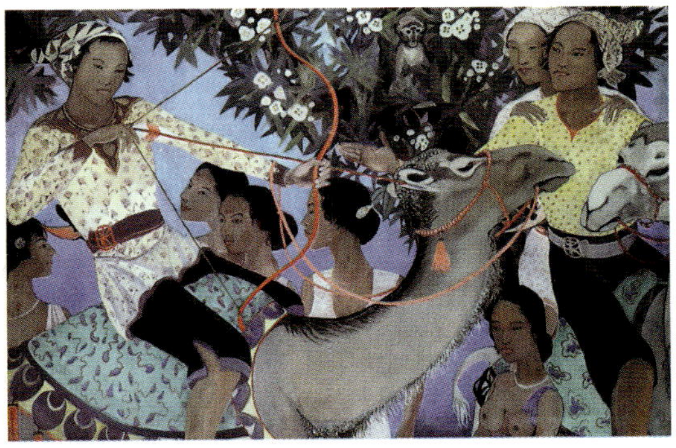

A1050a; tempera on linen, 112 × 160 cm
Signed and dated: *Orovida 1931*
Bequeathed by the artist, 1968; WA1968.471

Erickson 1992, no. 37; Thorold and Erickson 1993, no. 34

Although she travelled widely in Europe, Orovida never visited the Far East and the orientalist vein which was prevalent in her work in the 1920s and 1930s was based entirely on works of art seen in museums and in reproductions. *The Archer's Return* is specifically indebted to Assyrian bas-reliefs.

OROVIDA PISSARRO
(1893 – 1968)

The Tiger Hunt

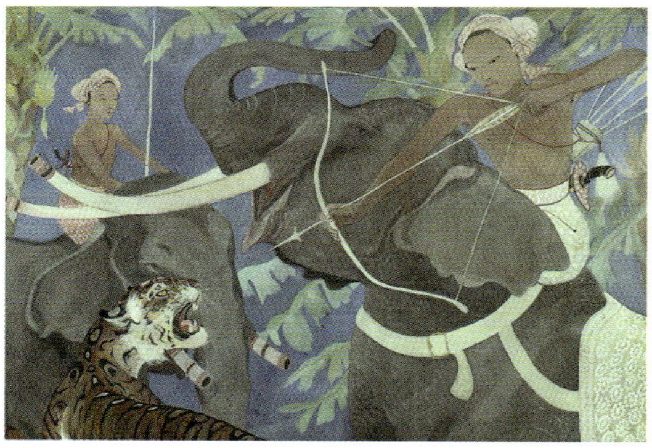

A1050b; tempera on fine lawn, 99 × 142 cm
Signed and dated: *1932 Orovida*
Bequeathed by the artist, 1968; WA1968.472

Erickson 1992, no. 39

The composition is a reversed and much modified version of *The Archer's Return*, for which it was designed as a companion.

OROVIDA PISSARRO
(1893 – 1968)

Spring

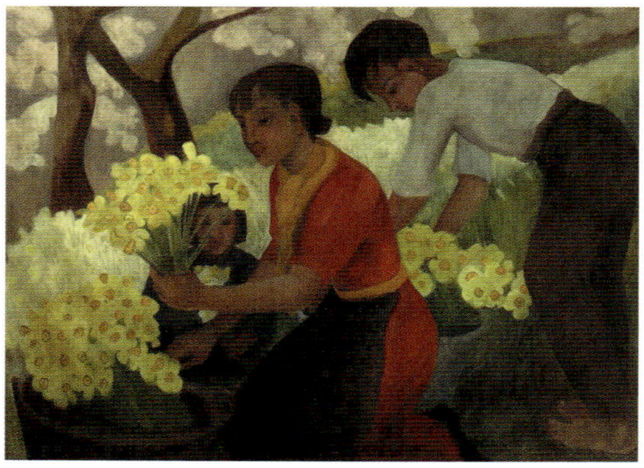

A856; egg tempera, wax varnish on linen, 86.5 × 114.5 cm
Signed and dated: *Orovida 1938*
Pissarro Family Gift, 1952; WA1952.6.18

Erickson 1992, no. 81

Orovida painted three sets of Seasons, the first between 1936 and 1938. They were apparently never exhibited as a set and their original destination is not known. In them, she emphasised the decorative nature of her work, rather than the subject-matter, which was conventional.

OROVIDA PISSARRO
(1893 – 1968)

Little Girl with a Cat

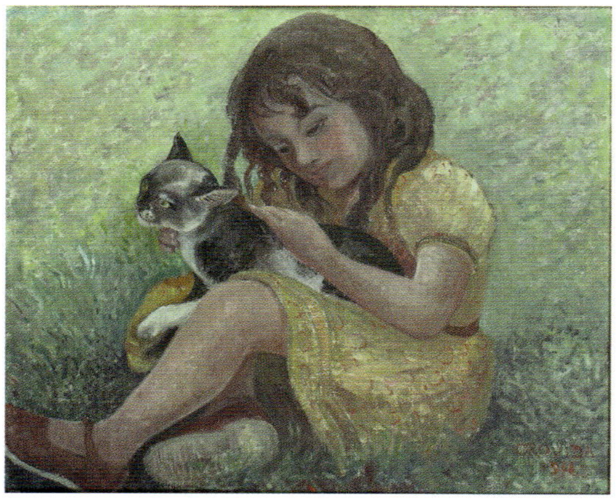

A857; oil on canvas, 54 × 65 cm
Signed and dated: *Orovida 1948*
Presented by Mrs Lucien Pissarro, 1951; WA1951.225.21

Erickson 1992, no. 117

Big cats and domestic cats appear in Orovida's work in all media throughout her life. This is one of a number of depictions of children with cats which began during the Second World War.

OROVIDA PISSARRO
(1893 – 1968)

Dora Clarke

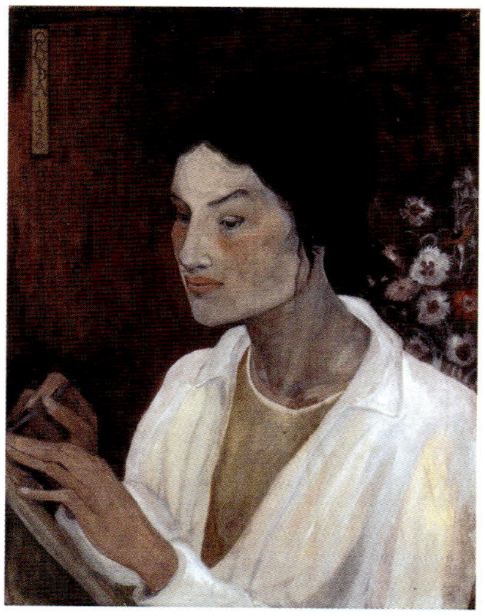

A1172; tempera on linen, mounted on gold brocade and linen, 74.4 × 58.8 cm
Signed and dated: *Orovida 1936*
Bequeathed by Mrs Dora Middleton, 1991; WA1991.27

Erickson 1992, no. 64

Dora Thacker Clarke (1895–1989) exhibited sculptures at the Royal Academy between 1923 and 1959. Orovida painted her portrait in 1935 (destroyed) and this second portrait in the following year. Orovida also bequeathed Clarke's *Coloured Girl from Massachusetts* (1962) to the Ashmolean.

OROVIDA PISSARRO
(1893 – 1968)

Winter

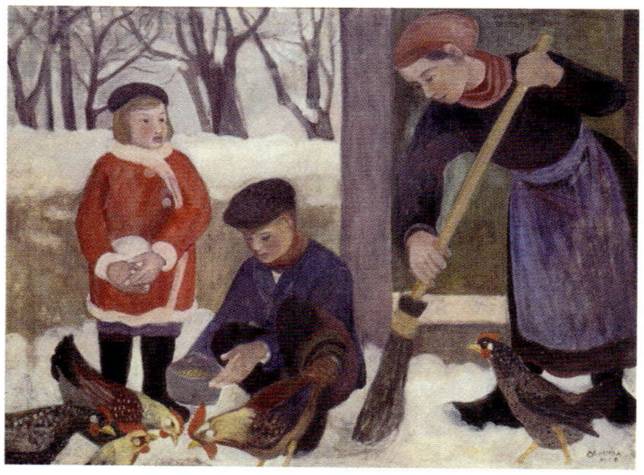

A856a; linen, 86.7 × 114.5 cm
Signed and dated: *Orovida 1940*
Pissarro Family Gift, 1952; WA1952.6.9

Erickson 1992, no. 88

In her first set of Seasons, Orovida included as *Winter* a skating scene (private collection). However, the present work, although not completed until 1940, may have been originally conceived as part of the set, since it has the same dimensions.

OROVIDA PISSARRO
(1893 – 1968)

Self-portrait

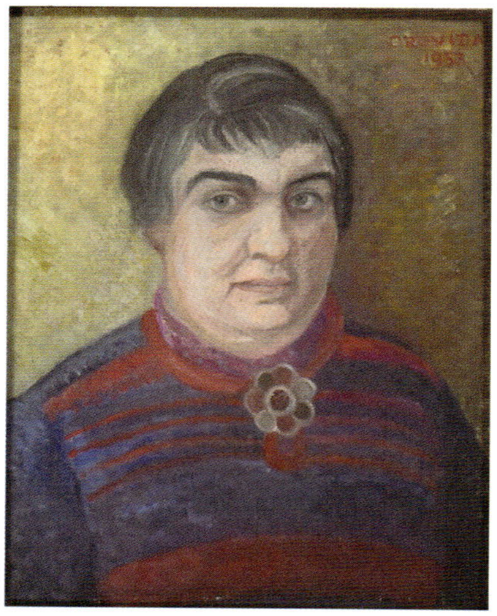

A1019; oil on canvas, 51 × 41 cm
Signed and dated: *Orovida 1953*
Purchased (Hope Fund), 1965; WA1965.22.1

Erickson 1992, no. 160

Orovida at the age of sixty portrayed herself in the same serious manner she had used when she was twenty. In the later portrait, she has broken away from Lucien's colours and Impressionist technique and instead turned to a conventional form of realism, the sombre atmosphere relieved only by the red and green brooch.

Barry Pittar
(1880 – 1948)

Interior of St Paul's Cathedral

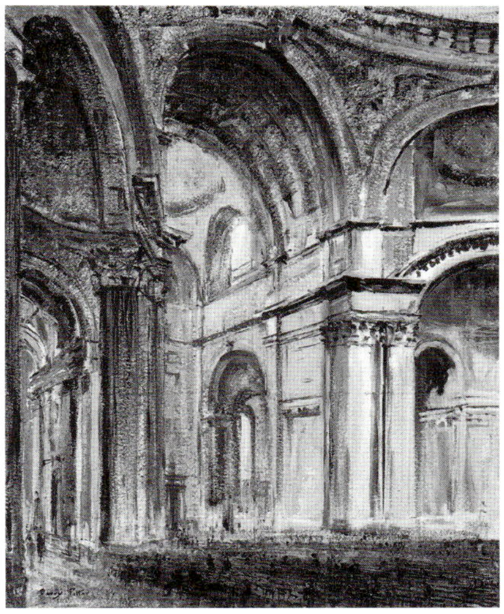

A455; oil on canvas laid on board, 60 × 48 cm
Signed: *Barry Pittar*
Weldon Bequest, 1937; WA1937.35

Douglas Frederick Pittuck
(1911 – 1993)

Bust of John Ruskin after the Marble Bust by J.E. Boehm in the Ruskin School of Drawing

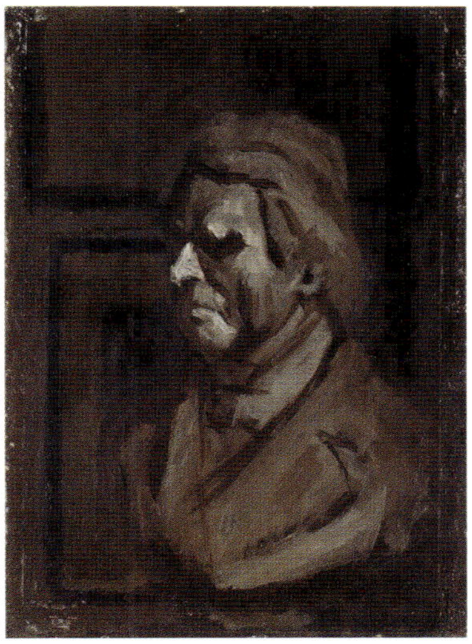

Oil on cardboard, mounted as a drawing, 17.8 × 12.5 cm
Prov.: presented by the artist to Albert Rutherston, 1948
Presented by Dr H.C. Ezra, 1981; WA1981.562

Joseph Edgar Boehm, born and trained in Austria, was one the most highly regarded portrait sculptors in Britain between 1862 and 1890. His bust of John Ruskin was commissioned in 1880 to stand in the Drawing School in Oxford. It remained there until it was transferred to the Ashmolean in 2000.

Jan Porcellis
(*c.* 1584 – 1632)

Three 'Damloopers' in a fresh Breeze

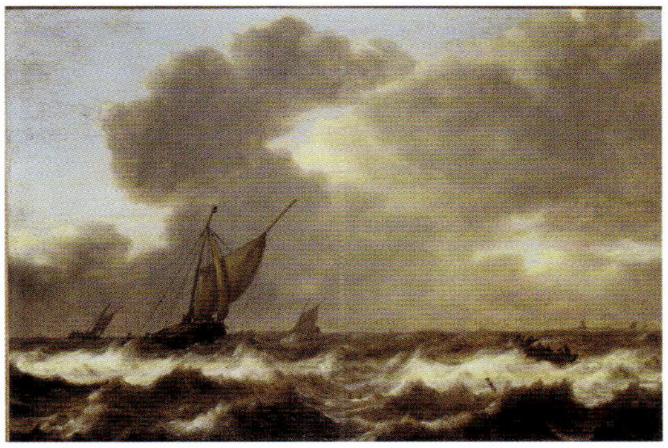

A354; oil on panel, 39 × 55 cm
Signed with initials: *IP F*
Presented by A.H. Buttery, 1917
WA1917.2

White 1999, p. 102

Porcellis introduced a taste for small-scale, naturalistic marine paintings into early 17th-century Dutch art. This atmospheric view of ships on a boisterous sea, punctuated with patches of light and shadow, was probably painted towards the end of his life.

Giambattista Pittoni
(1687 – 1767)

Christ's Charge to Peter

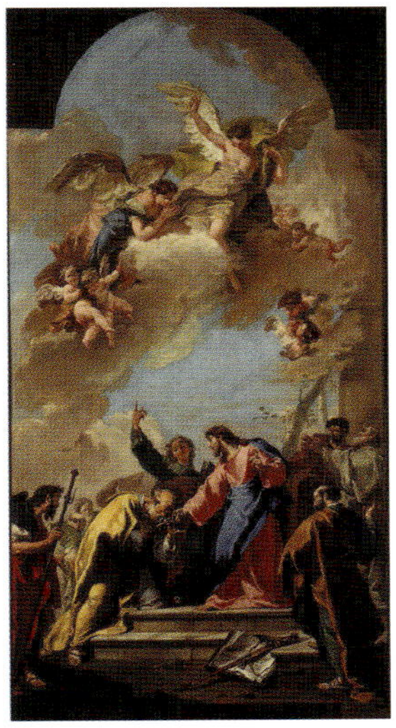

A769; oil on canvas, 80 × 42 cm
Prov.: Cyril Flower, 1st Baron Battersea; Lady Battersea; Mrs G. Denis Berry
Purchased, 1948; WA1948.76

Zava Bocazzi 1979, no. 136 and under no. 146

Christ hands the keys of the kingdom of heaven to St Peter (Matthew 16: 18–19), while St John the Evangelist gestures upwards. St Paul with a sword and book is on the right and St James the Great with his pilgrim's staff is on the left. A769 may be an autograph replica of a lost altar-piece made for an Austrian patron *c.* 1740 (since numerous derivations are known in central Europe) for which an oil-sketch in the Louvre, Paris, was the *modello*.

Vera Ellen Poole
(1890 – 1965)

The Artist's Mother and her Brother Jack

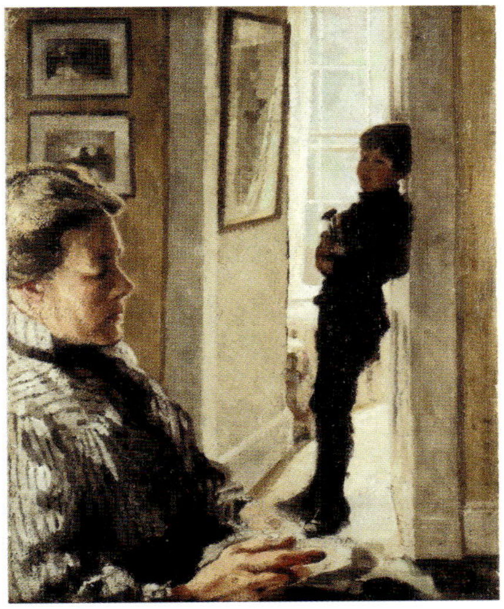

A1136; oil on canvas, 38.2 × 30.8 cm
Presented by Mrs Catherine Dupre, the artist's daughter, 1985; WA1985.192

A portrait of Ada Margaret Courtauld, who married Arthur Dendy, Professor of Zoology at King's College London. It was probably painted during the First World War.

Copy after Giovanni Antonio de Sacchis, called Pordenone
(1483 – 1539)

Head of Francesco Tiezzo

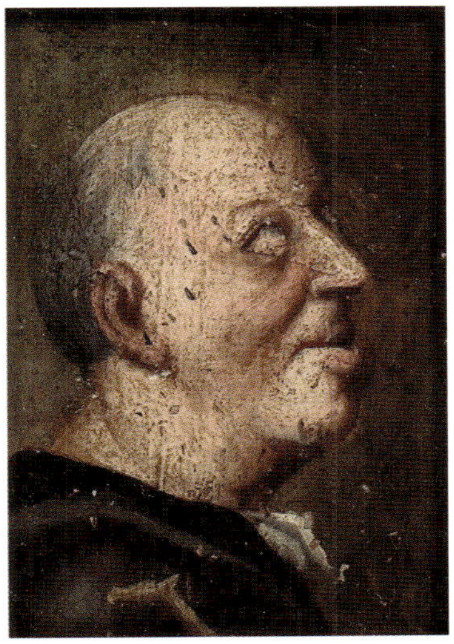

A144; oil on panel, 17.3 × 12.2 cm
Prov.: Count Pietro Montereale, Pordenone (1823); Montereale-Mantica, Pordenone (1837)
Chambers Hall Gift, 1855; WA1855.219

Lloyd 1977, pp. 154–5; Cohen 1996, II, under no. 17

The donor, Francesco detto Cargnelutto di Tiezzo, is portrayed with his wife in the foreground of the *Madonna della Misericordia with Sts Christopher, Joseph and Donors*, painted by Pordenone in 1515–6 for the Duomo at Pordenone. A144 is a partial copy of the figure of Tiezzo; its companion, a bust of the donor's wife, is in the Montereale Collection in Pordenone. Traditionally both copies were said to be preparatory oil-sketches.

Frederick James Porter
(1883 – 1944)

Peonies in a yellow Vase

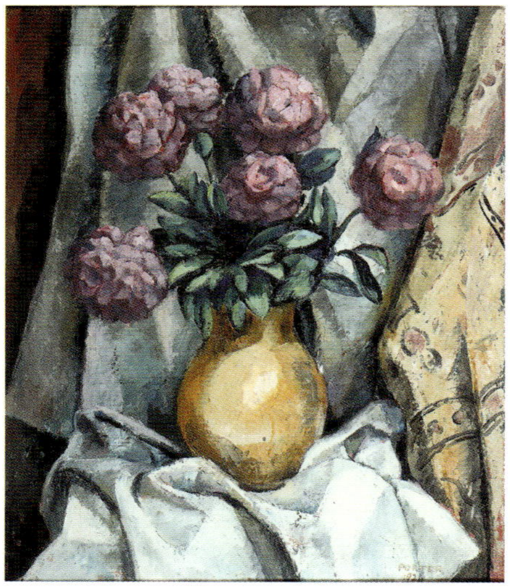

A620; oil on canvas, 65 × 54 cm
Signed and dated: *PORTER 1921*
Hindley Smith Bequest, 1939; WA1940.1.2

The subject and manner of painting recall the work of Duncan Grant, with whom Porter shared a study at 8 Fitzroy Street at the time he painted this still life.

Nicolas Poussin
(1594 – 1665)

The Exposition of Moses

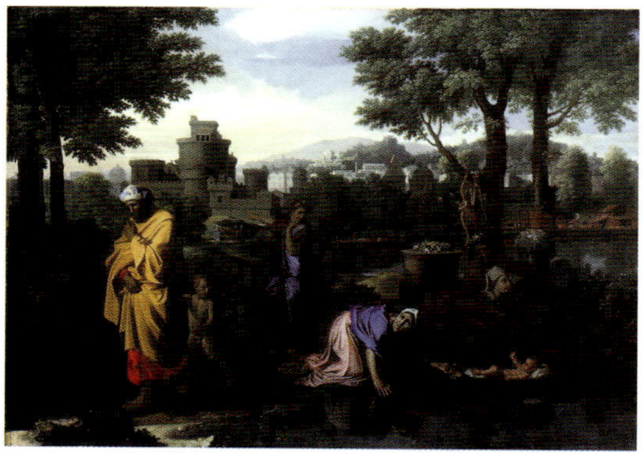

A791; oil on canvas, 149.5 × 204.5 cm
Prov.: Jacques Stella and by descent; Philippe, duc d'Orléans by 1717; Edouard de Walkuers; Richard, Earl Temple (later 1st Duke of Buckingham and Chandos); by descent until 1848; Francis Gibson of Saffron Walden, Essex; his son-in-law, Lewis Fry; by descent to the Misses Joan, Agnes, Isabel, Margery and Ruth Fry
Purchased through the generosity of the daughters of the Rt Hon. Sir Edward Fry, G.C.B. with the assistance of the National Art Collections Fund, 1950; WA1950.169

Blunt 1966, no. 11; Mérot 1990, no. 8; Colantuono 1996; Bull 1999

When Pharaoh ordered all new-born Hebrew sons to be killed, Moses's mother put him in an ark of bulrushes in the Nile. His sister stayed to watch while Pharaoh's daughter came to the river with her maidens and found the child (Exodus 2: 2–4). A791 is striking for its emotional intensity, with the focus on Moses's grief-stricken parents. The joyful scene of the finding of Moses was a popular one, whereas this subject is far less common (Poussin earlier treated it *c.* 1627). Painted in 1654 for Jacques Stella, A791 was greatly admired by contemporaries for the artist's learned treatment of the subject, his skill in painting reflections and the beauty of the landscape. Pharaoh's city is based on Pirro Ligorio's reconstruction of some of the most famous buildings of ancient Rome. A sphinx accompanied by a river-god and cornucopia identifies the Nile. Different explanations, based on Poussin's antiquarian interests and wide-ranging visual references, have been proposed for the significance of the pipes of Pan that hang from a tree behind this group. Two painted copies are recorded in the 17th century; other copies and variations are known (including a tapestry version of the right side) and three engraved versions were made, the first by Stella's niece, Claudine Bouzonnet Stella, in 1672.

Copy after Giovanni Ambrogio de' Predis
(*c.* 1455 – after 1508)

Portrait of an unknown Woman

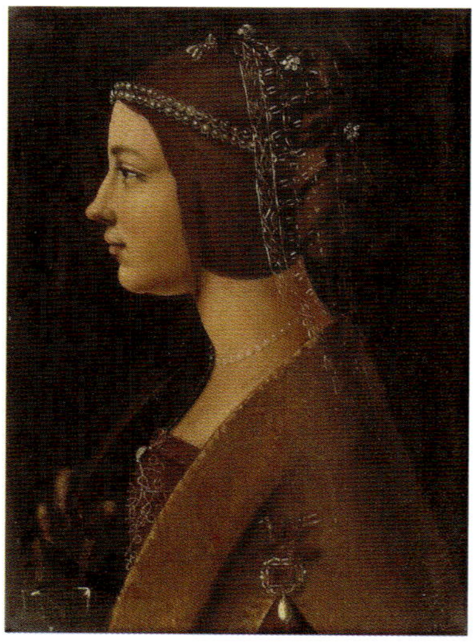

A713; oil on canvas, 46 × 33.7 cm
Prov.: George Salting
Bequeathed by Miss Emily G. Kemp, 1940; WA1945.63

Lloyd 1977, pp. 96–8

This is a variation on a Leonardesque portrait of an unknown woman in the Pinacoteca Ambrosiana, Milan, now generally attributed to Giovanni Ambrogio de' Predis. Apart from some changes to details of the costume and jewellery, the figure has been given a hand holding a spiked wheel, the attribute of St Catherine of Alexandria.

Mattia Preti
(1613 – 1699)

The Game of Draughts

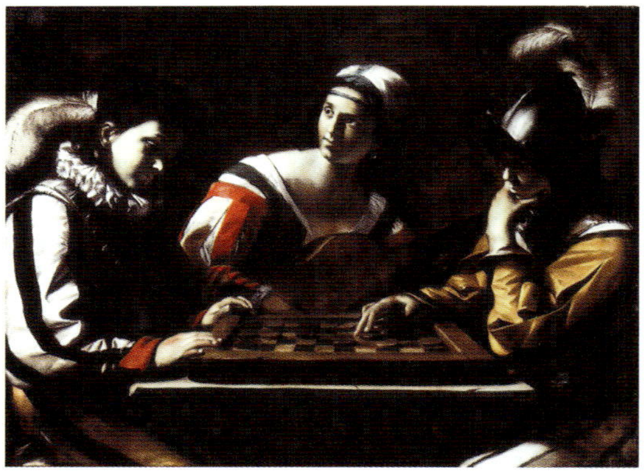

A1105; oil on canvas, 109 × 144 cm
Prov.: Mrs Robert Frank, from whom purchased by Benedict Nicolson, 1953
Presented by the Friends of Benedict Nicolson with the assistance of the National Art Collections Fund, 1978; WA1978.123

Spike 1999, no. 148

A1105 is an early work by Preti, probably of the mid-1630s, after a period of close study of Caravaggio. Ostensibly a scene of everyday life, this strongly-lit gathering of richly costumed players is highly theatrical. The boy with the feathered hat reappears in Preti's *Concert* (Hermitage, St Petersburg).

Attributed to Valentine Cameron Prinsep
(1836 – 1904)

John Ruskin

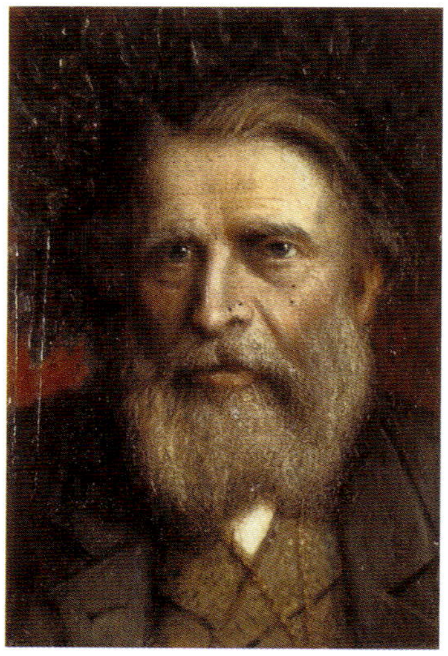

A438k; oil on ivory, 15 × 10 cm
Purchased (Hope Fund), 1934; WA1934.414

Brown 1987, no. 14; Dearden 1999, no. 170

John Ruskin (1817–1900), one of the most influential thinkers in Victorian Britain, was Slade Professor of Fine Art at Oxford, 1870–9 and 1883–4. This portrait can be dated by comparison with others to *c.* 1882, when Ruskin was sixty-three. The attribution is based on a larger version, now lost, which was apparently signed in monogram. Prinsep was a member of the Pre-Raphaelite circle and would have first met Ruskin when he submitted a decoration for the Oxford Union in 1857.

Margaret Millicent Fisher Prout
(1875 – 1963)

Summer Flowers by a Window

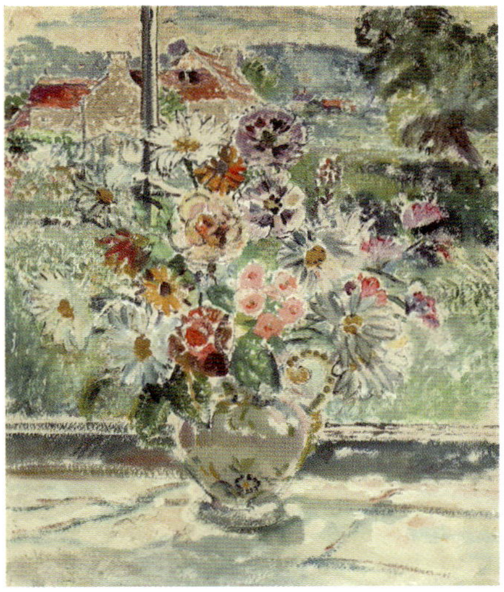

A1025; oil on board, 60 × 56 cm
Signed: *Fisher Prout*
Bequeathed by Mrs W.S.S. Tyrwhitt, 1966; WA1966.42.2

Mrs Prout painted several variations on this theme during the 1930s. The landscape may be the view from her house at Ashurst Wood, East Grinstead.

Copy after Scipione Pulzone
(1544 – 1598)

Portrait of a young Man

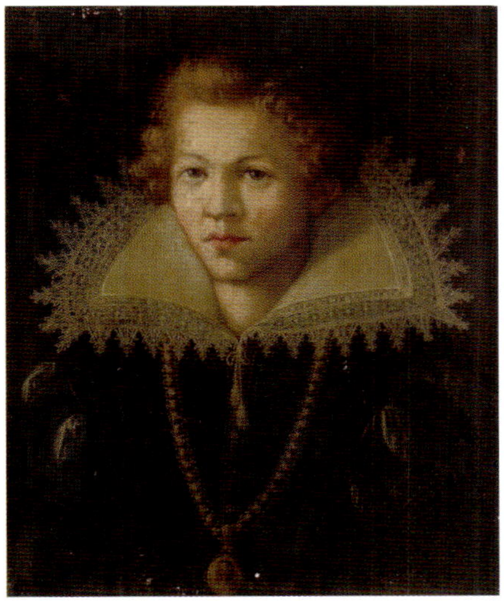

A256; oil on canvas, 64.7 × 52.8 cm
Prov.: acquired in Florence, 1875
Presented by the Revd Greville John Chester, 1892; WA1892.2

Lloyd 1977, pp. 155–156

The sitter wears a Medici collar and pendant. A256 may be a copy after Scipione Pulzone, although the prototype has not been identified.

Sir Henry Raeburn
(1756 – 1823)

Mrs John Brown of Lanfine and Waterhaughs

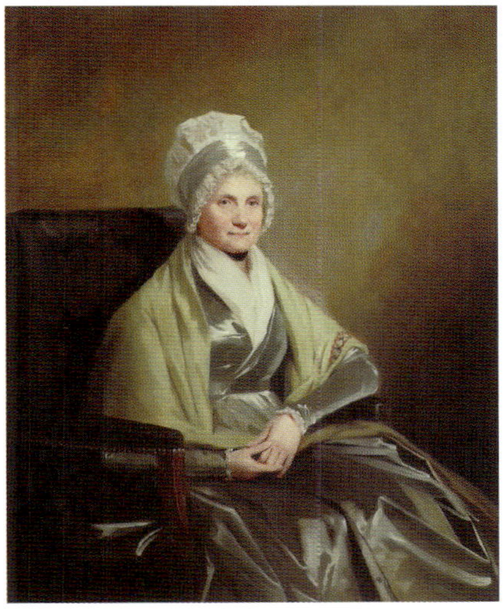

A946; oil on canvas, 100 × 127 cm
Prov.: by descent from the sitter until 1898
Bequeathed by Mary, Viscountess Harcourt, 1961; WA1961.20

Armstrong, 1901, p. 97; Greig 1911, p. 39

John Brown (1729–1802) was a successful textile merchant and banker, who bought the estates of Waterhaughs and Lanfine in Ayrshire. In 1798–9, he commissioned from Raeburn portraits of himself and of his wife (the companion is in a private collection). She was ill at the time and died before the painting was completed. The restrained and harmonious colouring is typical of Raeburn's work at this period.

James Ferrier Pryde
(1866 – 1941)

The Slum

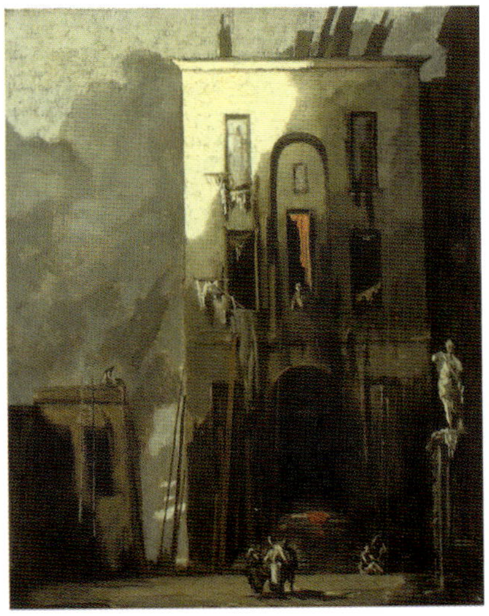

A943; oil on canvas, 91 × 71 cm
Signed: *Pryde*
Bequeathed by Donald Bradley, Baron Somervell of Harrow, 1961; WA1961.2

Hudson 1949, pp. 64, 98; Edinburgh 1992, no. 89

In addition to designs for theatrical sets and posters, Pryde's principal achievement was a series of highly personal paintings of architectural subjects. During the First World War, these became increasingly sombre, dwelling on the theme of ruin and decay. *The Slum*, completed by February 1916, is one of the most monumental and evokes the grim tenement buildings of the Edinburgh of Pryde's childhood.

Edmond Jean de Pury
(1845 – 1911)

Boats in the Lagoon at Venice

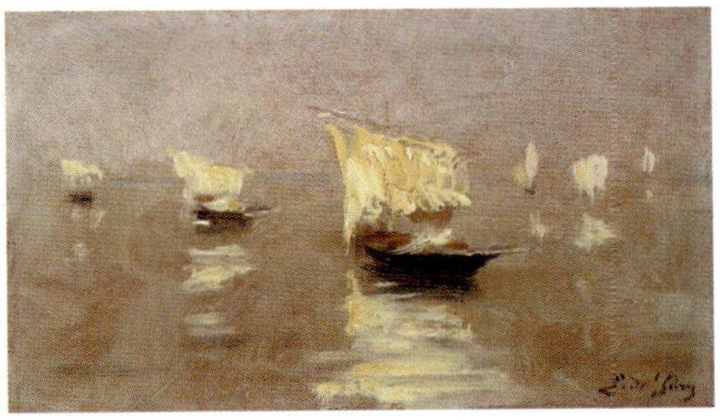

A1055; oil on wooden panel; 12.1 × 20.8 cm
Signed: *E. de Pury* and inscribed on back: *Souvenir du Jour de l'An 1901 Venise*
Presented by the Lady Berwick, 1969; WA1969.21

Presumably a gift to Mr and Mrs W.S. Hulton, the donor's parents.

Copy after Sir Henry Raeburn
(1756 – 1823)

James Wardrop

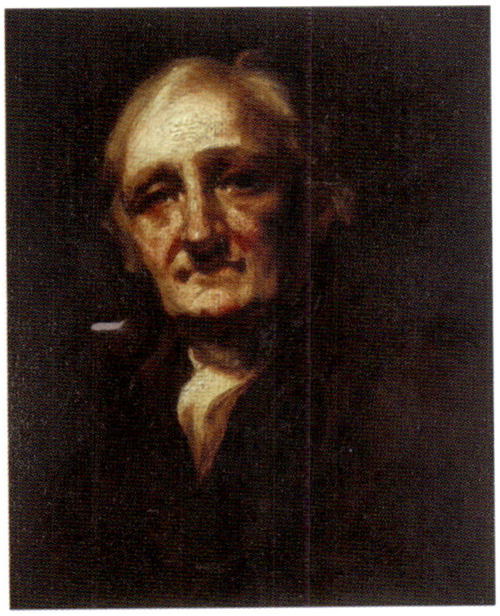

Oil on board, mounted as a drawing, 18.1 × 14.7 cm
Bequeathed by W.R.B. Young, 1971; WA1971.384

A reduced copy of indifferent quality of Raeburn's portrait of James Wardrop of Torbane Hill (1738–1830), of which the prime version was painted around 1820 (National Gallery of Victoria, Melbourne).

Allan Ramsay
(1713 – 1784)

Flora Macdonald

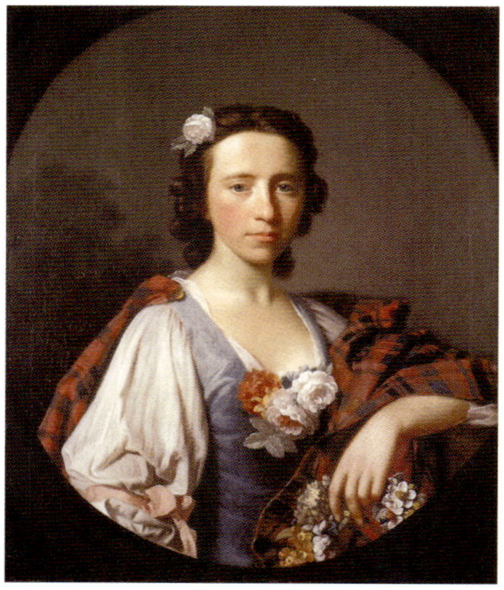

A438l; oil on canvas, 74 × 61 cm
Signed and dated on back: *Ramsay pinxit anno 1749.*
Prov.: Dr Richard Mead; The Revd Dr Richard Rawlinson
Acquired before 1840; WA1960.76

Poole 1912, no. 271; Smart 1999, no. 337

Flora Macdonald (1722–1790), daughter of a farmer of South Uist, assisted Prince Charles Edward Stuart to escape to Skye after his defeat at Culloden in 1746. In this portrait, painted after she had been released from the Tower of London and before her marriage to Allan Macdonald of Kingsburgh in 1750, she wears in her hair the white rose, a Jacobite emblem; the flowers in her hand no doubt allude to her Christian name.

Copy after Raphael
(1483 – 1520)

The miraculous Draught of Fishes

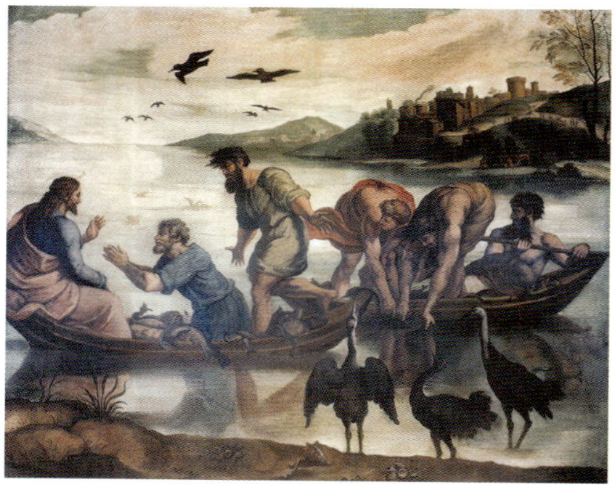

A52; oil on canvas, 352 × 427 cm
Presented by George, 3rd Duke of Marlborough, 1807; WA1845.52

A52–58 are full-size copies of seven of ten cartoons made by Raphael and his assistants in 1515–16 for a set of tapestries to hang in the Sistine Chapel. The subject illustrates episodes from the Acts of the Apostles. The originals (V&A, London, on loan from the Royal Collection) were brought to England in the 1620s and were installed in a gallery in Hampton Court Palace in 1699. The copies were attributed in the 19th century to the minor painter, Henry Cooke (1642–1700), probably on account of a passage in Walpole's *Anecdotes*, which describes a set of copies made by Cooke when he was hired by William III to repair the original cartoons in the 1690s. The text in the *Anecedotes*, however, describes these as paintings 'in the Manner of Distemper' which does not seem to apply to the Oxford copies. They have also been attributed to the French painter, Christophe Le Blon (1640–1741) who is known to have opened a subscription for the purpose of making copies of the cartoons. It seems unlikely, however, that Le Blon completed this project. Since 1992, the Oxford copies have hung in the Cartoon Gallery at Hampton Court Palace in place of the originals.

Copy after Raphael
(1483 – 1520)

Sts Peter and John at the beautiful Gate

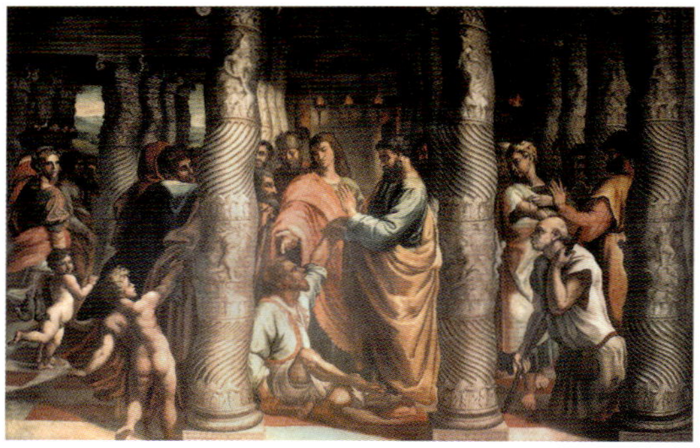

A54; oil on canvas, 355 × 548.5 cm
Presented by George, 3rd Duke of Marlborough, 1807; WA1845.54

Copy after Raphael
(1483 – 1520)

St Paul preaching at Athens

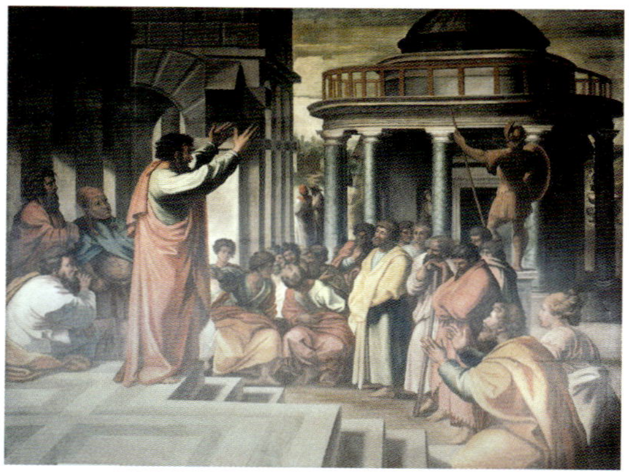

A53; oil on canvas, 352 × 457.20 cm
Presented by George, 3rd Duke of Marlborough, 1807; WA1845.53

Copy after Raphael
(1483 – 1520)

Elymas

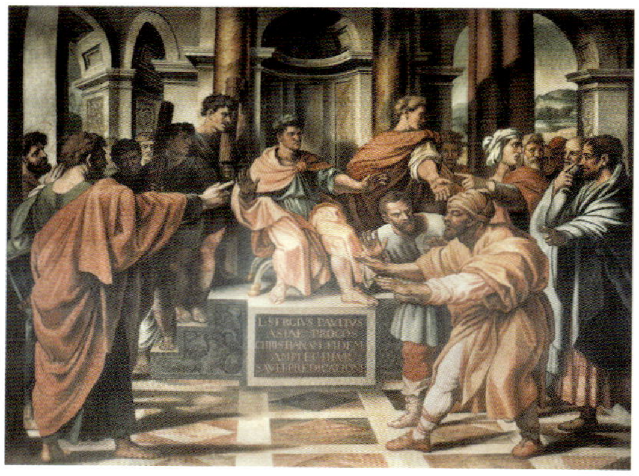

A55; oil on canvas, 352 × 458 cm
Presented by George, 3rd Duke of Marlborough, 1807; WA1845.55

Copy after RAPHAEL
(1483 – 1520)

Sts Paul and Barnabas at Lystra

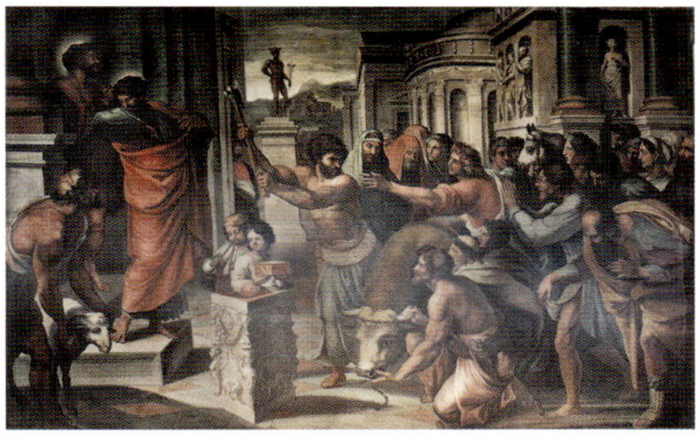

A56; oil on canvas, 352 × 555.32 cm
Presented by George, 3rd Duke of Marlborough, 1807; WA1845.56

Copy after RAPHAEL
(1483 – 1520)

The Death of Ananias

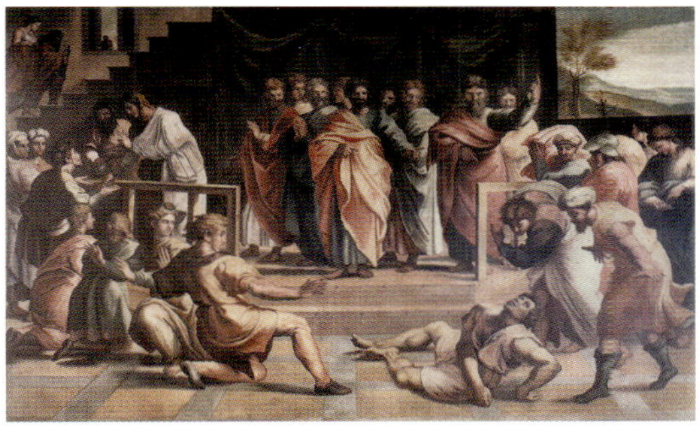

A58; oil on canvas, 352 × 550.5 cm
Presented by George, 3rd Duke of Marlborough, 1807; WA1845.58

Copy after RAPHAEL
(1483 – 1520)

The School of Athens

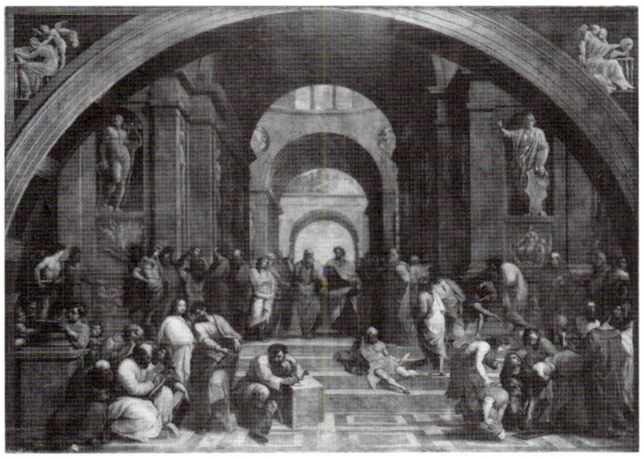

A45; oil on canvas, 170.4 × 234 cm
Presented by Sir Francis Page, 1804; WA1845.45

Lloyd 1977, pp. 156–7

Traditionally attributed to Giulio Romano, A45 is a fine early 17th-century copy of Raphael's fresco in the Stanza della Segnatura in the Vatican, Rome. The copyist has improvised an area lower left where a door cuts through the fresco. Raphael's lunette-shaped composition is embellished by allegorical figures in the spandrels of A45 which are based on the Sibyls painted by Michelangelo on the Sistine ceiling.

Copy after RAPHAEL
(1483 – 1520)

Christ's Charge to St Peter

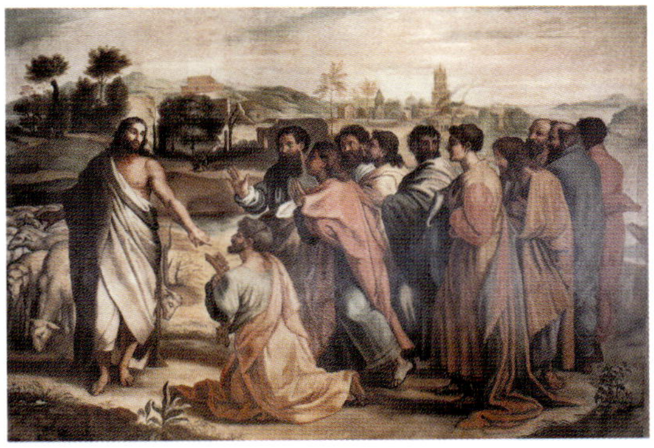

A57; oil on canvas, 352 × 500 cm
Presented by George, 3rd Duke of Marlborough, 1807; WA1845.57

Copy after RAPHAEL
(1483 – 1520)

The Virgin and Child with the young St John

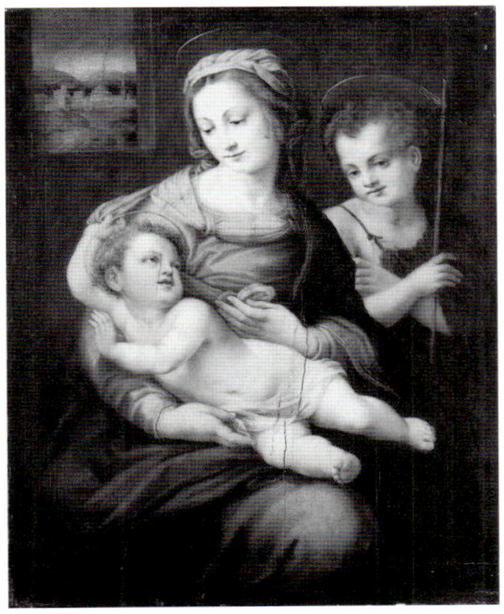

A505; oil on panel, 87 × 69.5 cm
Prov.: W.G. Waters
Presented by Dr Arthur Waters, 1937; WA1937.299

Lloyd 1977, pp. 119–120

A derivation of Raphael's *Bridgewater Madonna* (Sutherland Collection, on loan to the National Gallery of Scotland), A505 may date from mid 16th-century Florence. The variations include the addition of a landscape background and the figure of St John, while the Child has been given some decorous drapery and the facial expressions are sweeter. A505 has been attributed to Michele di Ridolfo.

Copy after RAPHAEL
(1483 – 1520)

Bindo Altoviti

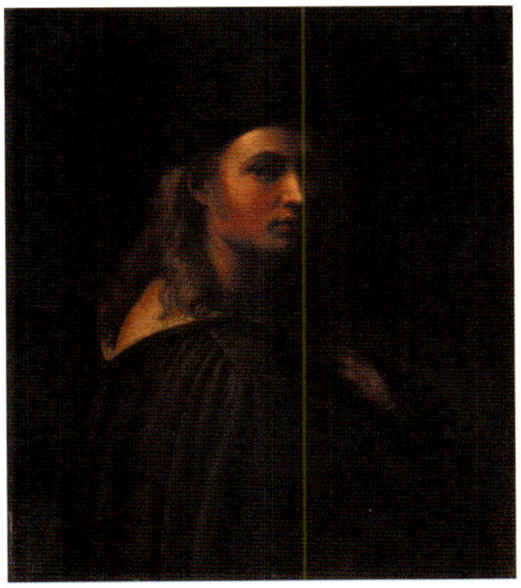

A59; oil on canvas, 65.6 × 56 cm
Acquired before 1845; WA1845.59

Lloyd 1977, p. 157

A59 is a late 17th- or early 18th-century copy of the portrait by Raphael now in the National Gallery of Art, Washington, which was in the Palazzo Altoviti, Rome, until shortly before 1790. From around the mid 18th century it was thought to be a self-portrait by Raphael.

Copy after Raphael
(1483 – 1520)

Jupiter and Cupid

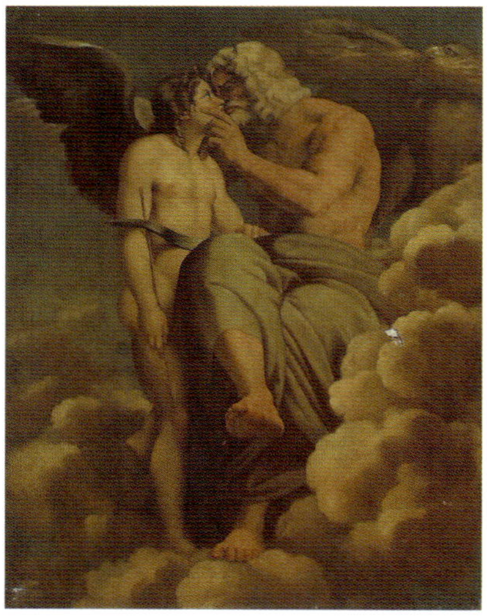

A228; oil on canvas, 195.7 × 152.3 cm
Presented by John Bayley, 1859; WA1859.1.

Lloyd 1977, pp. 157–8

A free copy, dating from the late 17th or early 18th century, of the fresco in one of the spandrels of the painted Loggia di Psiche in the Villa Farnesina, Rome. Raphael and his studio decorated this space in 1518–19 with scenes from the story of Cupid and Psyche. The spandrel from which A228 was copied may have been painted by Raphael's senior assistant, Giulio Romano. The copyist has altered the format to a square shape.

David Charles Read
(1790 – 1851)

Britford Vale, near Salisbury

A213; oil on millboard, 21 × 35 cm
Inscribed on back: *This Study I painted in the Field in the Year of our Lord and Saviour Jesus Christ 1830. David C. Read.*
Chambers Hall Gift, 1855; WA1855.220

Recorded missing in 1965.

David Charles Read
(1790 – 1851)

View near Elmfield Lodge, Southampton

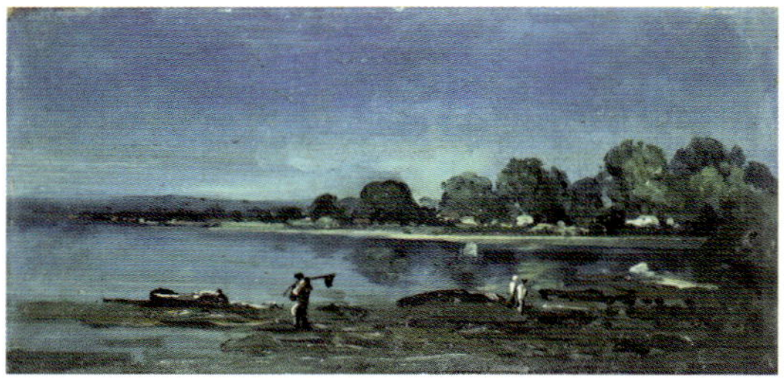

A210; oil on millboard, mounted as a drawing, 17.5 × 35.3 cm
Chambers Hall Gift, 1855; WA1855.216

A view looking towards Redbridge from the bottom of Chambers Hall's garden at Millbrook, near Southampton, painted in 1835.

David Charles Read
(1790 – 1851)

View in the New Forest near Southampton

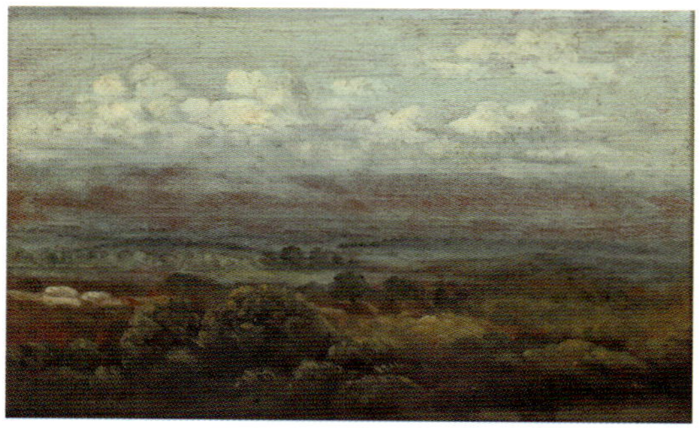

A221; oil on paper on panel, 15.2 × 24.3 cm
Chambers Hall Gift, 1855; WA1855.578

Painted in 1823.

David Charles Read
(1790 – 1851)

Britford Vale and Church

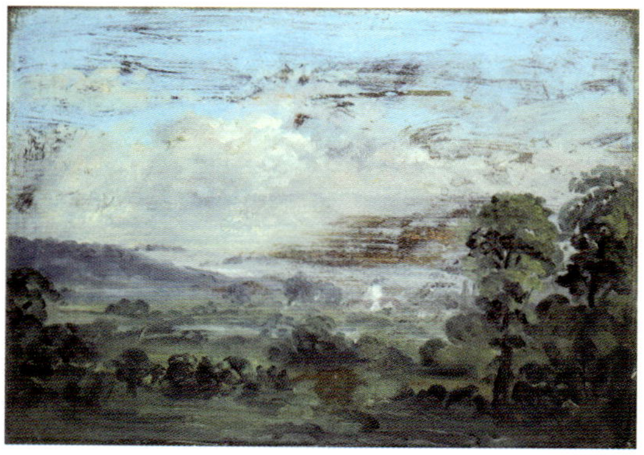

A215; oil on panel, mounted as a drawing, 28 × 39 cm
Inscribed: *This is the last sketch / I made up 1831 / D.C. Read*
Chambers Hall Gift, 1855; WA1855.226

David Charles Read
(1790 – 1851)

Morning Effect at Elmfield Lodge

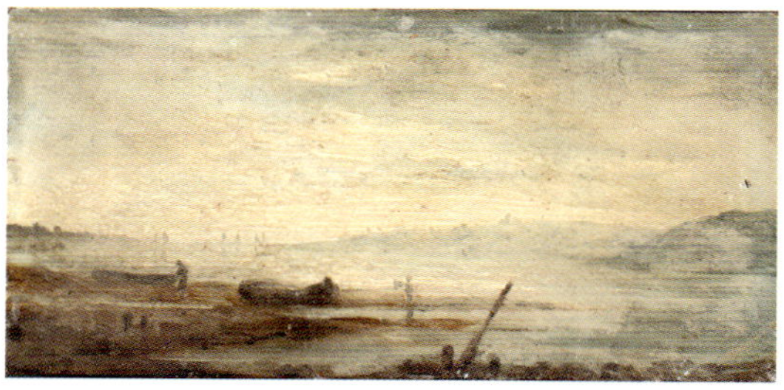

A211; oil on panel, 7 × 14.2 cm
Chambers Hall Gift, 1855; WA1855.217

David Charles Read
(1790 – 1851)

View from Pugin's House near Salisbury

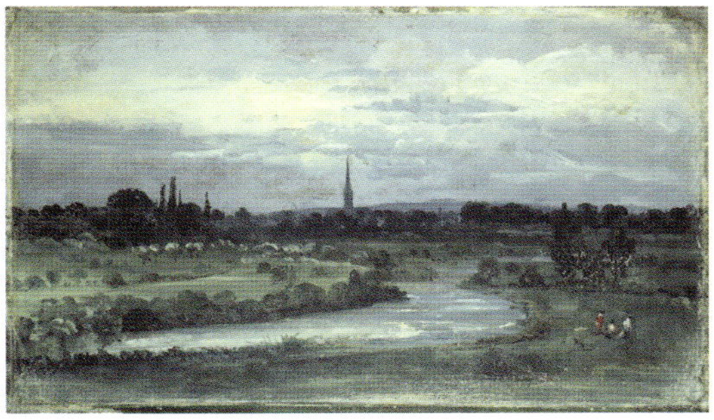

A205; oil on millboard, mounted as a drawing, 28.3 × 47.3 cm
Chambers Hall Gift, 1855; WA1855.206

Painted in 1835.

David Charles Read
(1790 – 1851)

Coniston Water

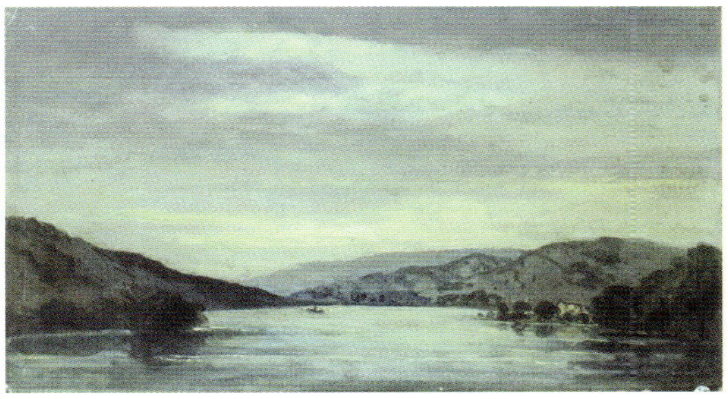

A218; oil on millboard, mounted as a drawing, 14.7 × 26.4 cm
Inscribed: *Coniston Water. Sketched on the spot. D.C. Read. 1838.*
Chambers Hall Gift, 1855; WA1855.575

David Charles Read
(1790 – 1851)

A Barley Rick: Storm

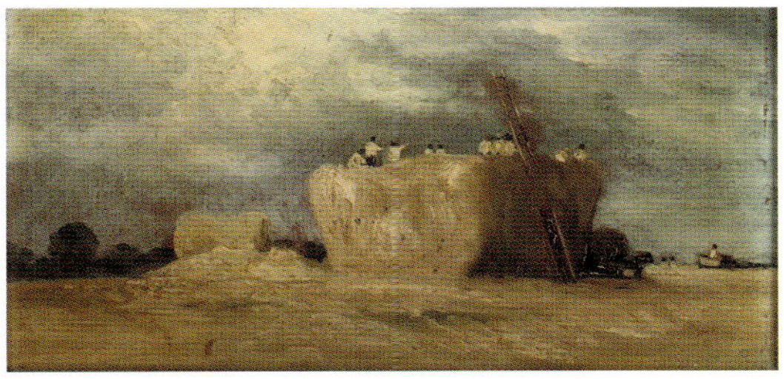

A207; oil on paper on board, 16.8 × 34.2 cm
Chambers Hall Gift, 1855; WA1855.213

David Charles Read
(1790 – 1851)

Britford Vale: Water Meadows

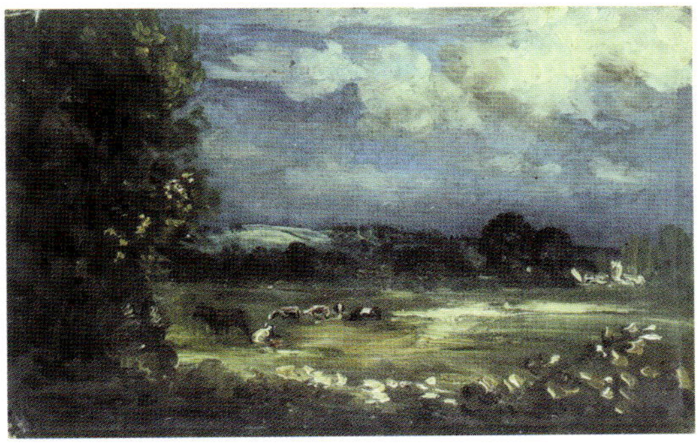

A206; oil on millboard, mounted as a drawing, 21.7 × 33.8 cm
Chambers Hall Gift, 1855; WA1855.207

Painted in 1835.

David Charles Read
(1790 – 1851)

Woodcock from Nature

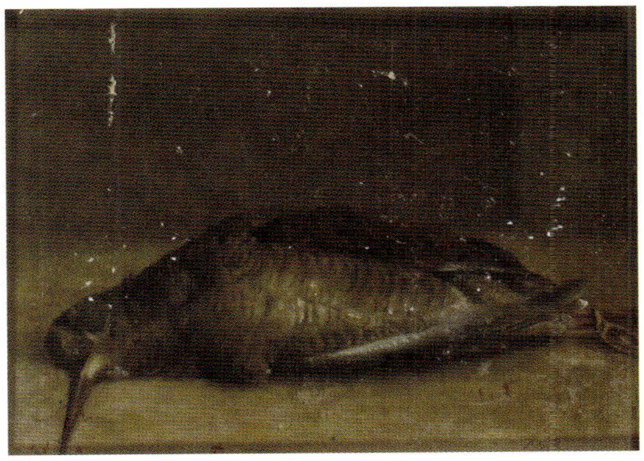

A216; oil on cardboard, 23 × 33 cm
Signed and dated: *D.C.R. 1851.*
Chambers Hall Gift, 1855; WA1855.227

David Charles Read
(1790 – 1851)

Southampton Water

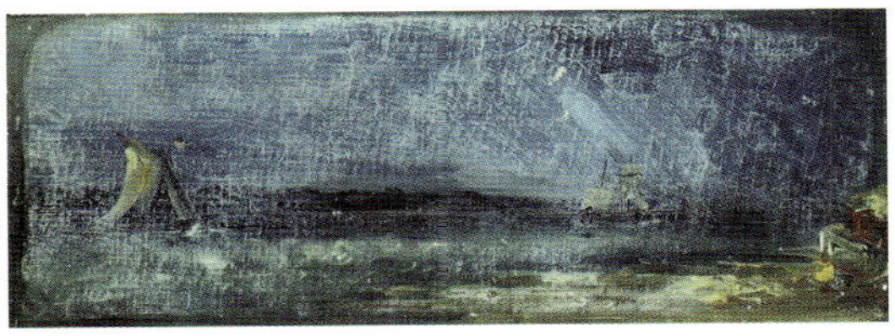

A208; oil on panel, mounted as a drawing, 12.3 × 32.5 cm
Chambers Hall Gift, 1855; WA1855.214

David Charles Read
(1790 – 1851)

The Pass of Llanberis

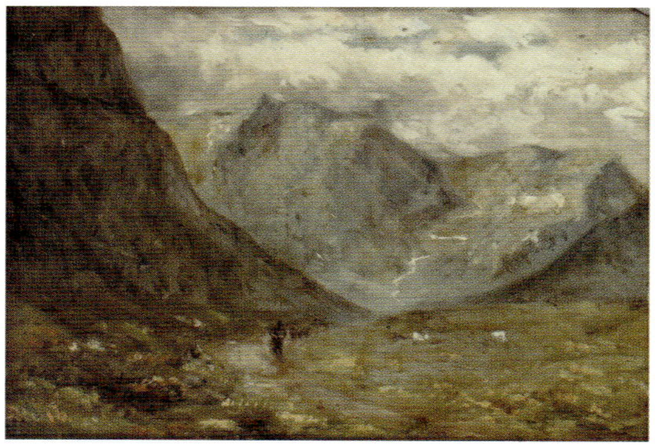

A209; oil on panel, 26.2 × 36.1 cm
Chambers Hall Gift, 1855; WA1855.215

David Charles Read
(1790 – 1851)

Evening – Antwerp

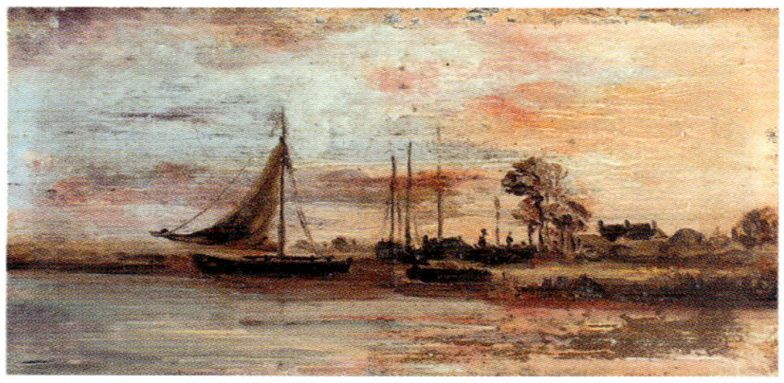

A212; oil on panel, 7.1 × 14.3 cm
Chambers Hall Gift, 1855; WA1855.218

Apparently worked up in his Salisbury studio from sketches made on the spot.

David Charles Read
(1790 – 1851)

Meadow Scene

A217; oil on panel, 24 × 36 cm
Chambers Hall Gift, 1855; WA1855.574

Recorded missing in 1965.

David Charles Read
(1790 – 1851)

The Top of Snowdon

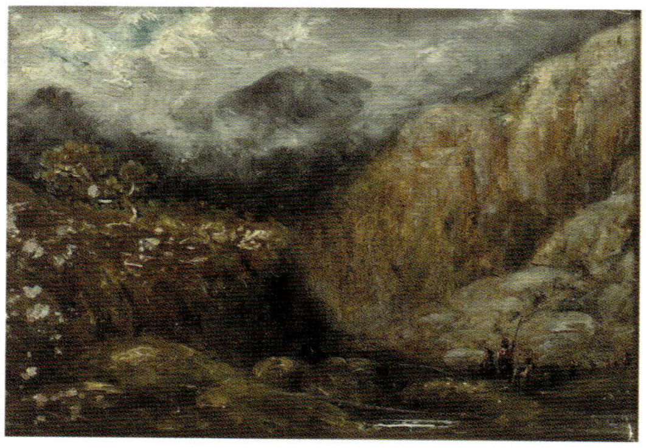

A219; oil on wooden panel, 18.1 × 25.8 cm
Signed: *D. Read*
Chambers Hall Gift, 1855; WA1855.576

David Charles Read
(1790 – 1851)

Moonlight

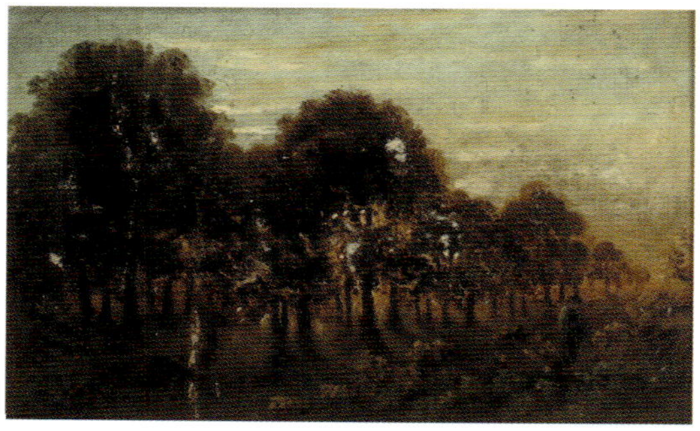

A214; oil on millboard, 19.1 × 30.1 cm
Chambers Hall Gift, 1855; WA1855.224

David Charles Read
(1790 – 1851)

Group of Trees near a Pond

A220; oil on panel, 20 × 21 cm
Chambers Hall Gift, 1855; WA1855.577

Recorded missing in 1965.

David Charles Read
(1790 – 1851)

Harnham, near Salisbury

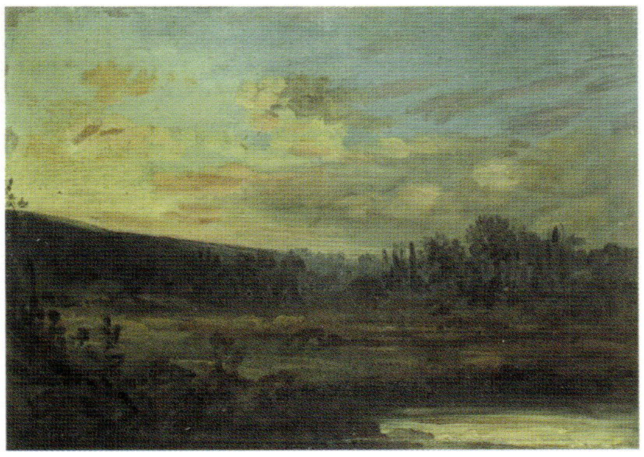

A222; oil on panel, mounted as a drawing, 25 × 34.4 cm
Chambers Hall Gift, 1855; WA1855.579

David Charles Read
(1790 – 1851)

Landscape

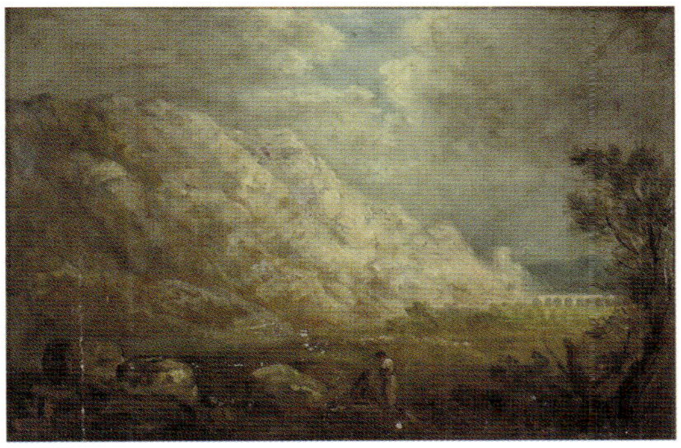

A224; oil on panel, 41.3 × 60.5 cm
Chambers Hall Gift, 1855; WA1855.581

Style of Rembrandt Harmensz. van Rijn
(1606 – 1669)

Head of a Bearded Man

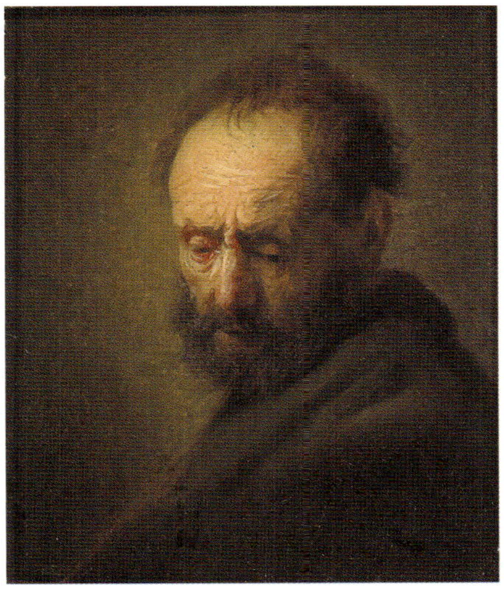

A804; oil on panel, 16 × 13 cm
Prov.: Paul Cailleux
Bequeathed by Percy Moore Turner, 1951; WA1951.8

White 1999, p. 102

The same head appears in two other paintings and an etching, none of which are now believed to be by Rembrandt. Although painted with a spirited touch, this little study can only be loosely associated with Rembrandt's style in about 1630.

David Charles Read
(1790 – 1851)

Southampton Estuary – Low Water showing the Effect of Mud, Evening

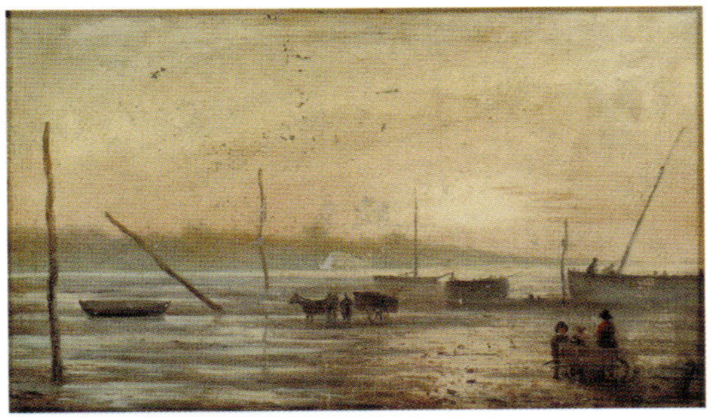

A223; oil on paper on board, 32 × 53.3 cm
Chambers Hall Gift, 1855; WA1855.580

William Reader
(active 1672 – 1680)

Robert Plot

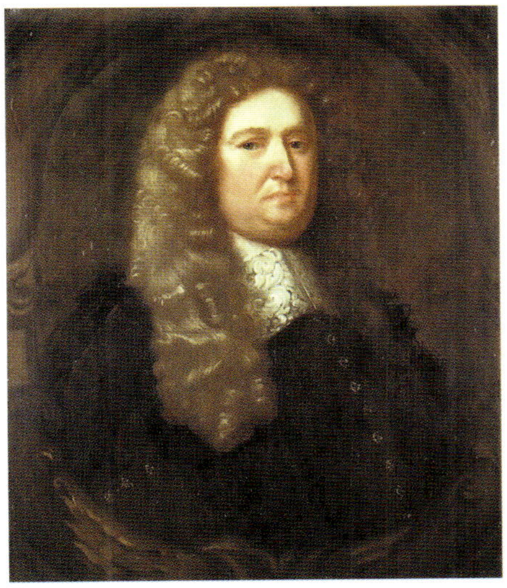

F476; oil on canvas, 75 × 63 cm
Acquired before 1756; WA1898.31

Poole 1912, no. 449

Robert Plot (1640–1696) published the *Natural History of Oxfordshire* in 1677 and was appointed the first Keeper of the Ashmolean Museum and Professor of Chemistry at Oxford, 1683–90. He also served as Fellow and Secretary of the Royal Society, 1682–4.

Copy after Rembrandt Harmensz. van Rijn
(1606 – 1669)

Self-portrait

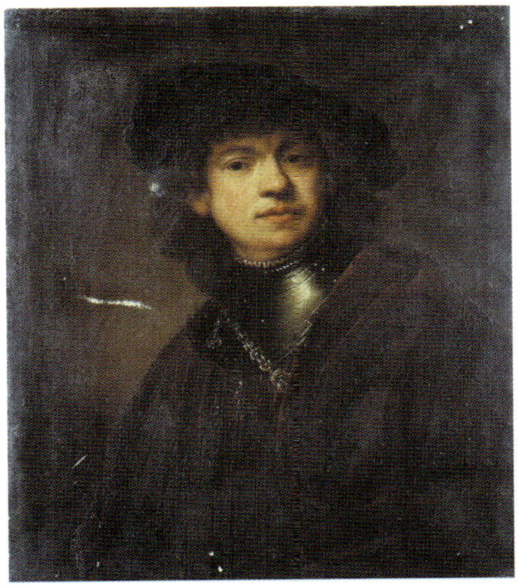

A60; oil on canvas, 65 × 56 cm
Provenance unknown; WA1845.60

White 1999, p. 104

One of several known old copies of Rembrandt's *Self-portrait* in the Uffizi, Florence.

Copy after GUIDO RENI
(1575 – 1642)

The Holy Trinity Adored by Angels

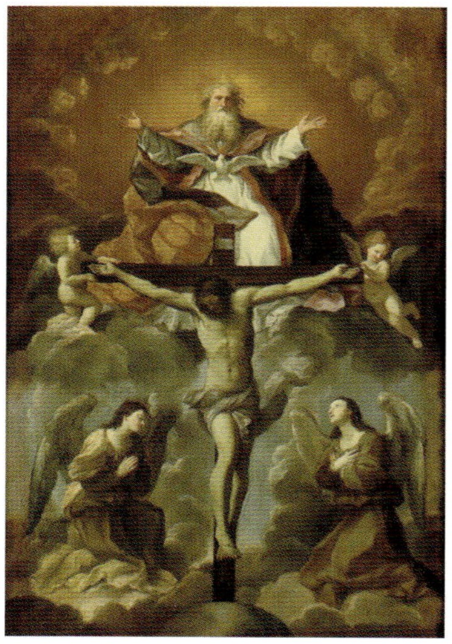

A652a; oil on canvas, 67.1 × 46 cm
Hindley Smith Bequest, 1939; WA1940.1.35

Pepper 1984, p. 251, under no. 100

This traditional subject was revitalized in the Counter-Reformation period. God the Father is enthroned in the heavens and surrounded by cherubim and the dove of the Holy Spirit is poised above the crucified Christ. A652a is a small, freely-handled copy, dating from the mid or late 17th century, of Reni's painting for the high altar of S. Trinità dei Pellegrini, Rome, commissioned by Cardinal Lodovico Ludovisi in 1624 and completed in July 1626.

PIERRE–AUGUSTE RENOIR
(1841 – 1919)

Nude Figure of a Girl

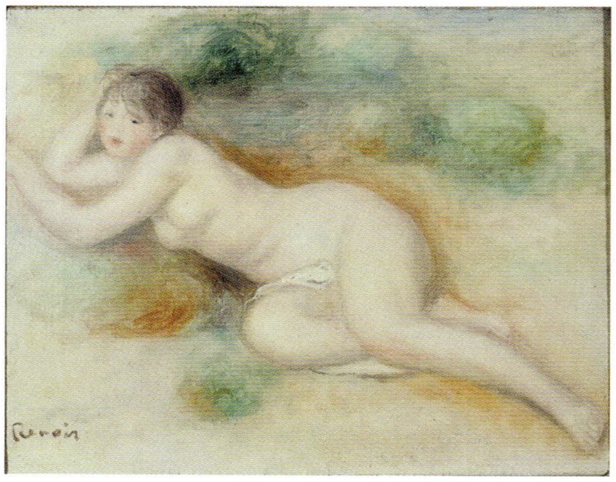

A643; oil on canvas, 32 × 40 cm
Signed: *Renoir*
Hindley Smith Bequest, 1939; WA1940.1.25

Probably dating from the 1880s when Renoir painted several variations on the traditional theme of the nude model.

PIERRE-AUGUSTE RENOIR
(1841 – 1919)

A Garden in Montmartre

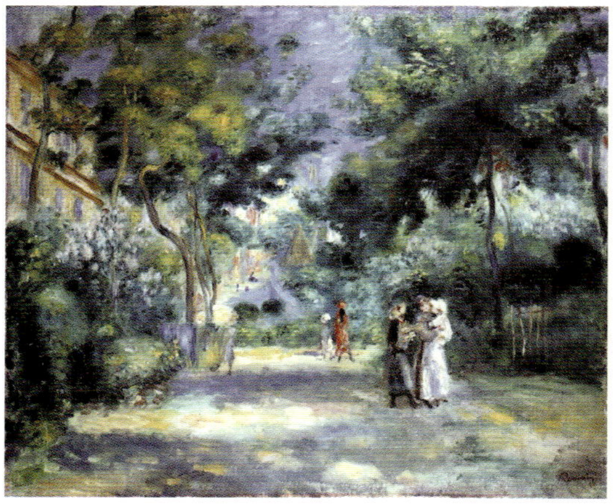

A622; oil on canvas, 46 × 55 cm
Signed: *Renoir*
Hindley Smith Bequest, 1939; WA1940.1.4

A late painting, perhaps dating from the 1890s.

Copy after GUIDO RENI
(1575 – 1642)

Salome with the Head of St John the Baptist

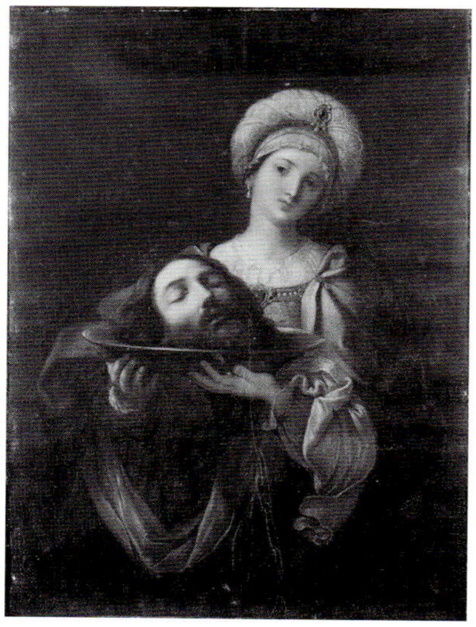

A227; oil on canvas, rolled, 140 × 102 cm
Prov.: Corsini collection; Miss Grove
Presented by Mrs Jenkyns before 1859; WA.OA904

Having danced before Herod, Salome requested the head of John the Baptist on a charger (Matthew 14: 6–11). Reni's painting, now in the Galleria Nazionale, Palazzo Corsini, Rome, was executed in 1638–9 and acquired by Urban VIII Barberini in December 1639. A227 is similar in size and closely corresponds except that the copyist has slightly prettified Salome. Various copies are known, although none are recorded in the Corsini inventories.

PIERRE-AUGUSTE RENOIR
(1841 – 1919)

Still Life with a faience Figure

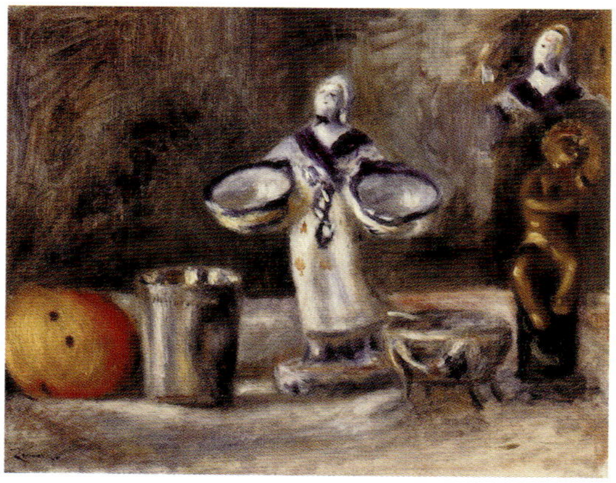

A1160; oil on canvas, 33 × 41.3 cm
Signed: *Renoir*
Prov.: Alphonse Kann; W.R. Kent
Bequeathed by Mr and Mrs Francis Hock through the National Art Collections Fund, 1988; WA1988.288

PIERRE-AUGUSTE RENOIR
(1841 – 1919)

Still Life of Roses in a Vase

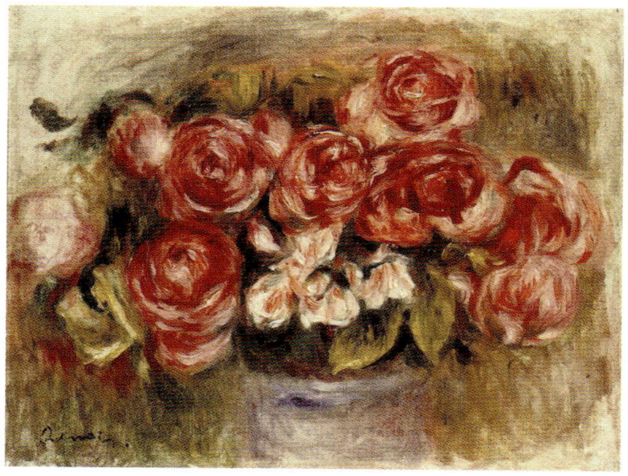

A1161; oil on canvas, 29 × 37 cm
Signed: *Renoir*
Prov.: Simon Kuesnacht, Zurich; Dr W. Katz
Bequeathed by Mr and Mrs Francis Hock through the National Art Collections Fund, 1988; WA1988.289

Renoir painted a large number of still-life paintings in the last decade of his life. These include a series of paintings of roses in round bowls. The motif is somewhat similar to a number of still-life paintings by Fantin-Latour of the 1880s and 1890s.

Pierre-Auguste Renoir
(1841 – 1919)

Landscape with Trees

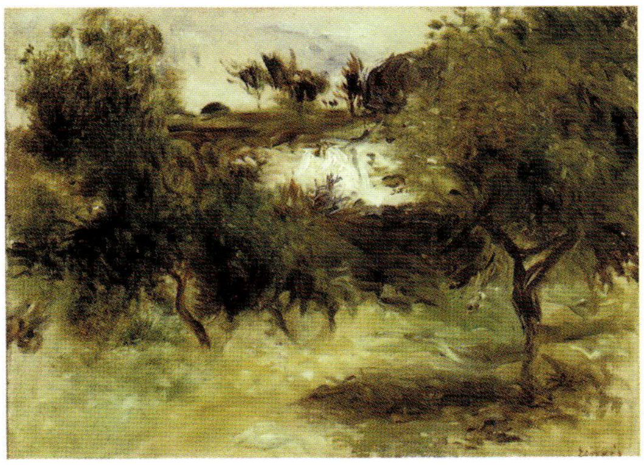

A1162; oil on canvas, 27.5 × 31.5 cm
Signed: *Renoir*
Prov.: Dr W. Katz
Bequeathed by Mr and Mrs Francis Hock through the National Art Collections Fund, 1988; WA1988.290

A late sketch of a meadow with bushes, woodland and a lake in the background.

Sir Joshua Reynolds
(1723 – 1792)

James Paine, Architect and his Son, James

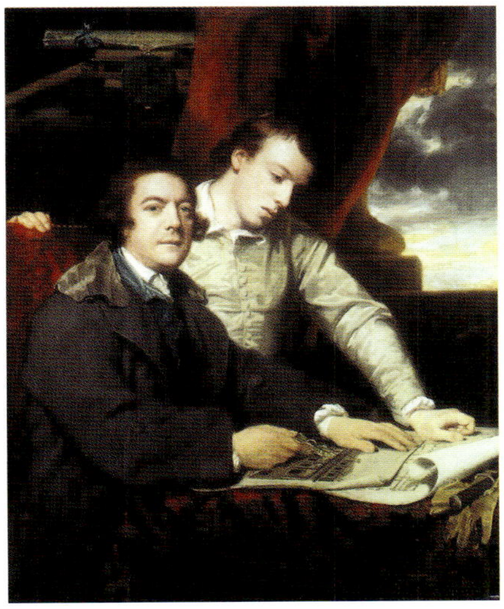

A64; oil on canvas, 127 × 101 cm
Inscribed: *JAMES PAINE. ARCH.T – AND JA.S PAINE JUN.R 1764 REYNOLDS. EQUES*
Bequeathed by James Paine, Jr, 1834; WA1845.64

Poole 1912, no. 464; Mannings 2000, no. 1376

James Paine (1725–1789) was the architect of many country houses. His son followed in his profession. Reynolds painted a companion portrait in 1764, showing Mrs Paine and her two daughters, (Lady Lever Art Gallery, Port Sunlight). Here, Paine shows his plans for a pavilion for the 9th Duke of Norfolk at Worksop Manor. The seal of the charter of the Society of Artists, of which James Paine was President, can be seen above the sitters.

Sir Joshua Reynolds
(1723 – 1792)

Charity

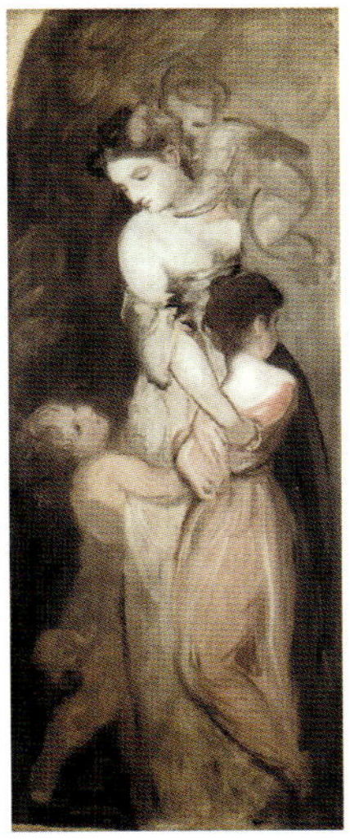

A191; oil on canvas, 173 × 69 cm
Chambers Hall Gift, 1855; WA1855.158

Postle 1995, pp. 168–85; Mannings 2000, no. 2117

Through the intervention of Joseph Warton, Reynolds was commissioned in 1777 to provide designs for new glass in the chapel of New College, Oxford. The upper register contains the Nativity, with figures of the seven Virtues below. He made preliminary drawings, full-size oil-sketches and cartoons, from which Thomas Jervais (d. 1799) painted the glass. This is the sketch for the figure of *Charity*, which was based on an engraving of the antique statue of Niobe and for which the actress, Mrs Sheridan, served as the model.

Sir Joshua Reynolds
(1723 – 1792)

Sketch for a Portrait of Captain Philemon Pownall, R.N.

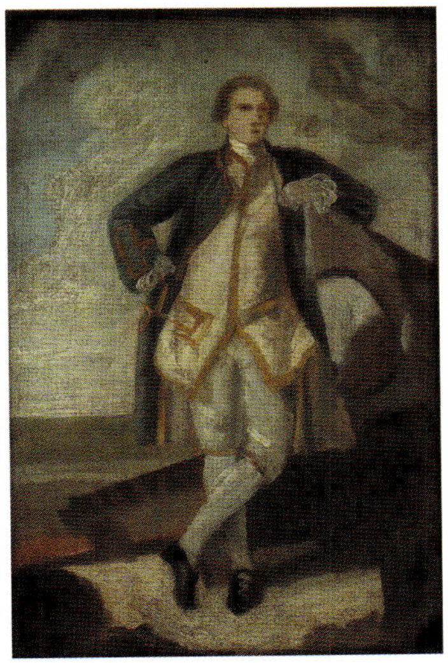

A193; oil on canvas, 50 × 33 cm
Chambers Hall Gift, 1855; WA1855.191

Poole 1912, no. 462; Mannings 2000, no. 1470

A sketch for a full-sized painting of 1762 (Mannings 2000, no. 1471, untraced). Pownall was born at Plymouth. He served as a Lieutenant under Admiral Boscawen in 1750 and was involved in the capture of the Spanish frigate Hermione off St Vincent. He was killed in action on 15 June 1780. He married at Gibraltar, Jane Majendie of Exeter on 16 May 1762. Six sittings are recorded for Captain and Mrs Pownall in December 1762. This sketch presumably dates from this period.

Sir Joshua Reynolds
(1723 – 1792)

Dr Joseph Warton

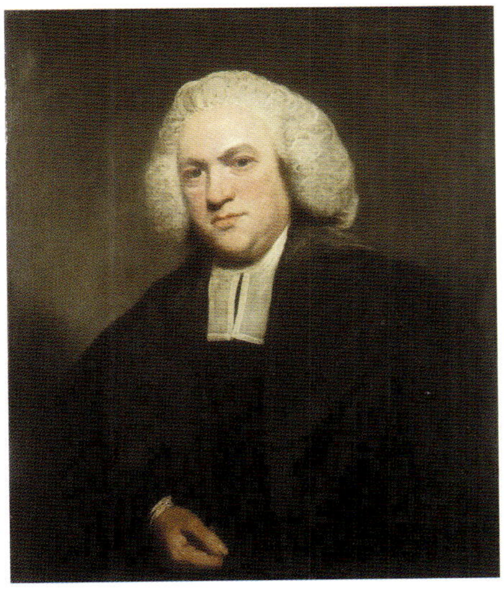

A129; oil on canvas, 75 × 63 cm
Bequeathed by the Revd Dr Thomas Penrose, 1851; WA1851.8

Poole 1912, no. 466; Mannings 2000, no. 1837

Joseph Warton (1722–1800) was educated at Oriel College, Oxford, before entering the church. He was Headmaster of Winchester College between 1766 and 1793 and an accomplished poet. This portrait was painted and exhibited at the Royal Academy in 1777, the year in which Warton was also elected to 'The Club'. He was the brother of Thomas Warton, the Poet Laureate, whose portrait Reynolds also painted (Trinity College, Oxford; Mannings 2000, no. 1838).

Sir Joshua Reynolds
(1723 – 1792)

Miss Elizabeth Keppel, later Mrs Thomas Meyrick

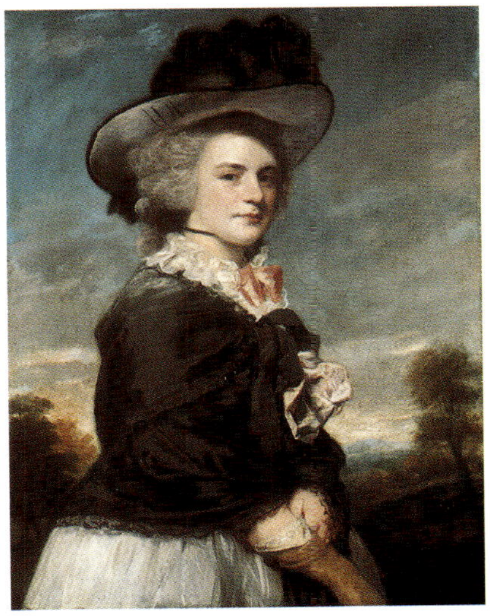

A192; oil on canvas, 91 × 70 cm
Chambers Hall Gift, 1855; WA1855.157

Mannings 2000, no. 1057

Miss Keppel (d. 1821) was the natural daughter of Admiral Augustus Keppel (1725–1786), who was appointed First Lord of the Admiralty and created Viscount Keppel in 1782. She married Captain Thomas Meyrick in 1787. This portrait, completed in 1782, was probably commissioned at the same time as one of her father (Tate Britain), who was a friend of the artist. Fifteen appointments for Miss Keppel are recorded in Reynolds's sitter books between 22 May and 12 December 1782. The portrait cost 50 guineas.

Sir Joshua Reynolds
(1723 – 1792)

Charles Fitzroy, 2nd Duke of Grafton

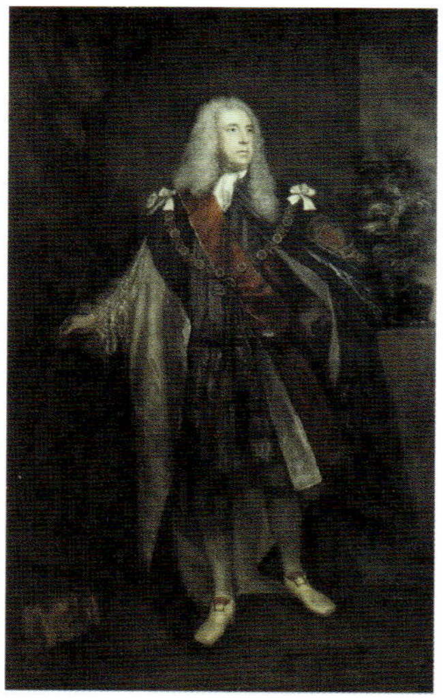

A46; oil on canvas, 236 × 145 cm
Presented by R.H. Beaumont, 1805; WA1845.46

Poole 1912, no. 459; Mannings 2000, no. 640

Charles Fitzroy, second Duke of Grafton (1683–1757) wears the robes of the Order of the Garter, to which he was appointed in 1721, and carries the wand of Lord Chamberlain, in which office he served from 1724 to 1757. Reynolds painted two full-length portraits of Grafton and two others of smaller format. This example was probably completed shortly before the sitter's death.

Copy after Sir Joshua Reynolds
(1723 – 1792)

Sketch of Sir Abraham Hume

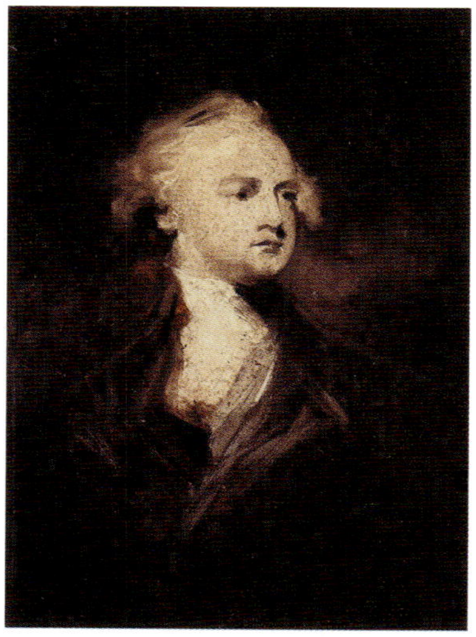

A918; oil on paper, mounted as a drawing, 39.6 × 21.3 cm
Russell Bequest, 1958; WA1958.57.3

Sir Abraham Hume, 2nd Bt (1749–1838), was a keen collector and patron. He sat to Reynolds in 1783 (National Trust, Belton House). There are numerous copies after Reynolds's original. This example has been described as a sketch for the painting but is more probably a copy after it, perhaps made when the original was exhibited at the British Institution in 1813 or 1833.

Style of Sir Joshua Reynolds
(1723 – 1792)

Head of a Girl

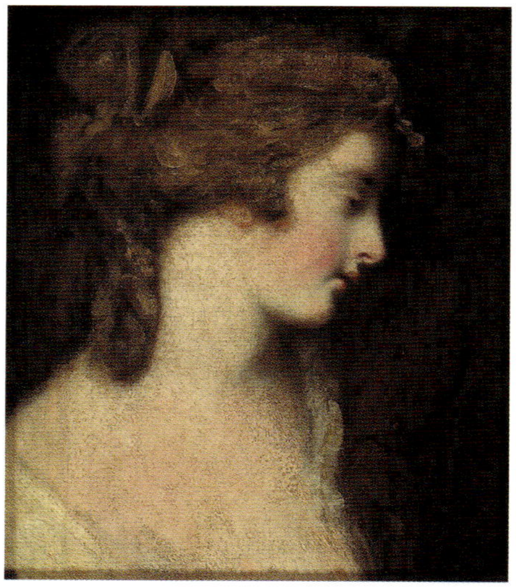

A437; oil on canvas, 50 × 40 cm
Purchased by subscription, 1934; WA1934.13

Attributions to Daniel Gardner (1750–1805) and the Revd Matthew William Peters (1742–1814) have been proposed, but neither is convincing.

Sir Joshua Reynolds
(1723 – 1792)

The Captive

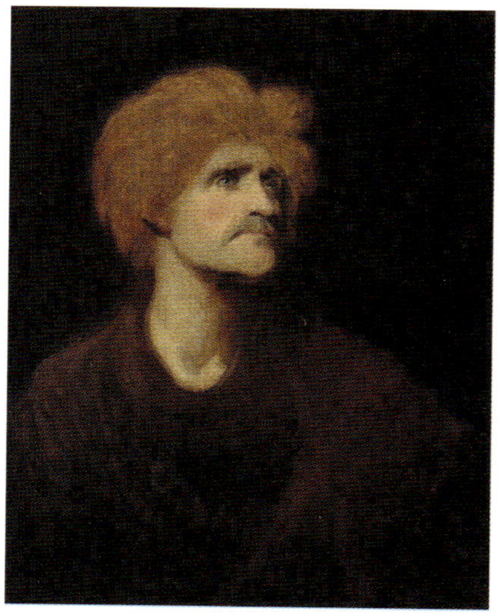

A128; oil on canvas, 75 × 59 cm
Bequeathed by the Revd Dr Thomas Penrose, 1851; WA1851.7

Mannings 2000, no. 2032

The identification as a portrait of Reynolds's model, George White, has recently been doubted. The painting was engraved by J.R. Smith as *A Study from Nature – Beggar Man*. Its present title refers to a scene in Laurence Sterne's *Sentimental Journey* (1768). The status of the painting, which is in poor condition, is also in doubt and it may be a studio version rather than a straightforward copy of the original (Lambton collection).

Copy after Sir Joshua Reynolds
(1723 – 1792)

The Holy Family with the Infant St John

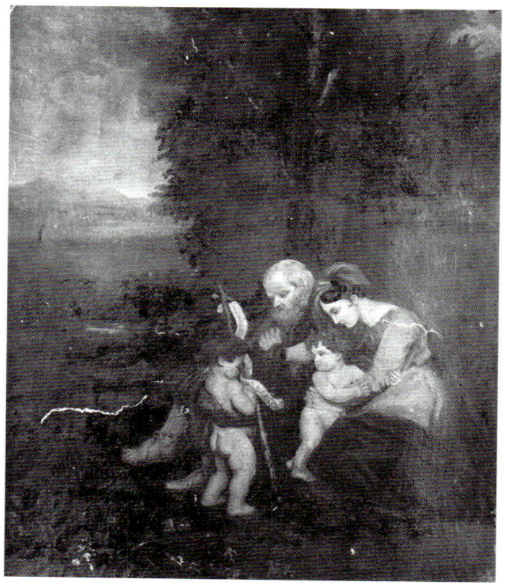

A324a; oil on canvas, rolled, 75 × 62 cm
Provenance unrecorded; WA.OA282

A copy of poor quality and uncertain date after Reynolds's *Holy Family*, which was exhibited at the British Institution in 1829, acquired by the National Gallery in 1830 and transferred to the Tate Gallery in 1949 (Mannings 2000, no. 2089). Numerous other copies exist.

Samuel William Reynolds the Younger
(1794 – 1872)

The Death of Addison

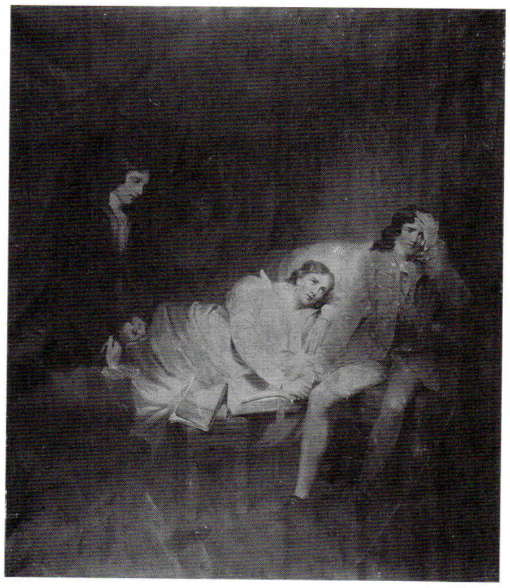

A62; oil on canvas, rolled, 290 × 259 cm
Presented by Charles N. Palmer, M.P., 1827; WA1845.62

Joseph Addison (1672–1719) was a statesman, poet and wrote essays in the *Tatler* and the *Spectator*. He was a friend of Swift and other writers. He married the Dowager Countess of Warwick in 1713. He is said to have died in the presence of John Gay and of his stepson, the Earl of Warwick, to whom he said, 'See in what peace a Christian can die'. S.W. Reynolds was the son of the celebrated mezzotint engraver of the same name and exhibited mostly portraits.

Geoffrey Hamilton Rhoades
(1898 – 1980)

Landscape at Charlbury

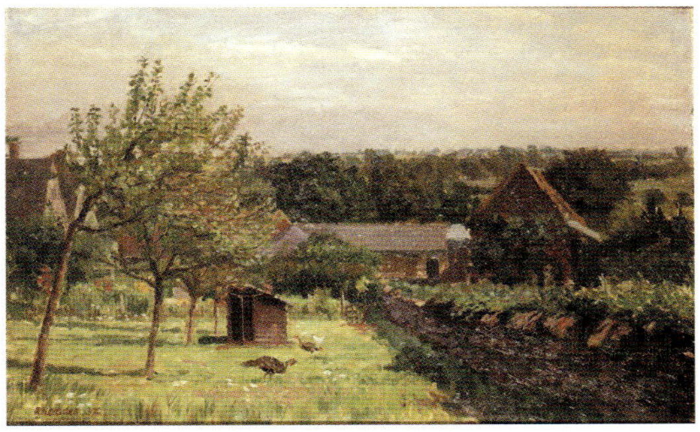

A1112; oil on canvas, 35.5 × 56 cm
Signed and dated: *Rhoades 32*
Presented by the artist, 1980; WA1980.2

From 1954 to 1972 Rhoades taught at the Ruskin School of Drawing in Oxford. His entire art was devoted to landscape, sometimes populated with figures but often without. The flickering brush-strokes, evoking light and shadow or creating forms and structures, represent a peaceful, sunny and idyllic countryside, far removed from the concerns of contemporary art.

Augustin-Théodule Ribot
(1823 – 1891)

Kitchen Scene

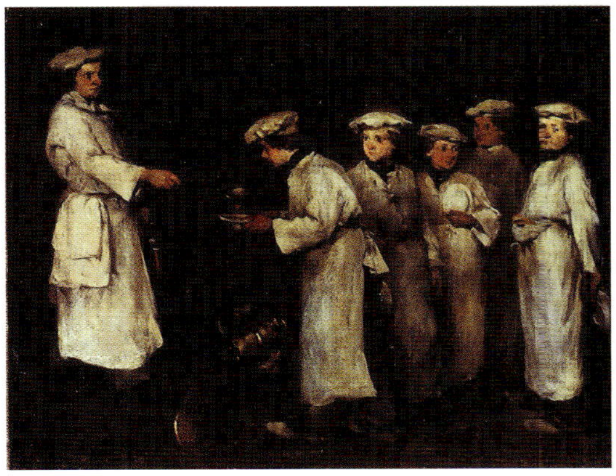

A477; oil on panel, 33 × 41 cm
Signed: *t. Ribot*
Weldon Bequest,1937; WA1937.58

The theme of cooks at work or at rest is often found in Ribot's paintings of the early 1860s. He used his son, Germain Théodore, as a model. The artist's liking for dark colour and subjects from everyday life, set against dark, generalised backgrounds, was affected by his taste for 17th-century Spanish art.

Attributed to Sebastiano (1659 – 1734) or Marco Ricci (1676 – 1730) and a Collaborator

Mountainous Landscape with Groups of Monks

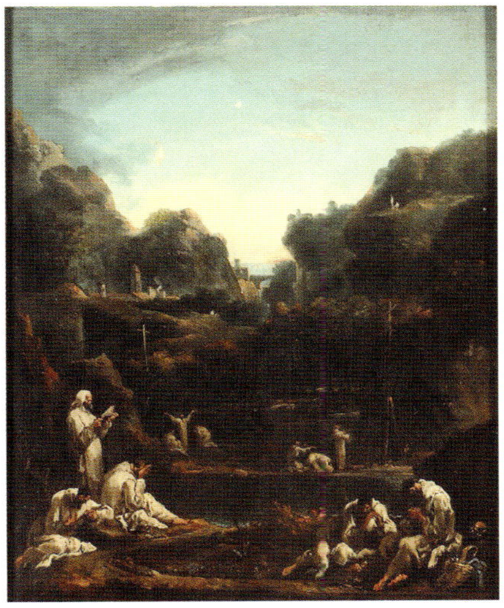

A516; oil on canvas, 51 × 41 cm
Presented in memory of Blanche Rathbone by her children, Major Rathbone and Lady Richmond, 1938; WA1938.2

Muti and de Sarno Prignano 1994, no. R 349

This type of landscape with monks is associated with Alessandro Magnasco; the genre was taken up by Sebastiano Ricci, who worked with his nephew Marco at the court in Florence in 1706–7, with Magnasco and Peruzzini. A516 is one of a group of paintings which have been seen as collaborative works by two or more of these artists. The figures here are close to Sebastiano, while the landscape is in a central Italian rather than Venetian taste.

Augustin-Théodule Ribot
(1823 – 1891)

A Woman at the Piano

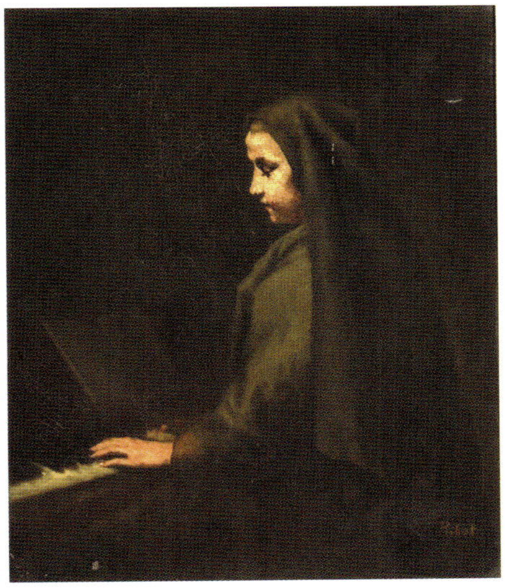

A464; oil on canvas, 54.2 × 45 cm
Signed: *Ribot*
Weldon Bequest, 1937; WA1937.43

One of a number of paintings of musicians painted by Ribot.

Louis-Gustave Ricard
(1823 – 1873)

Portrait of a young Girl

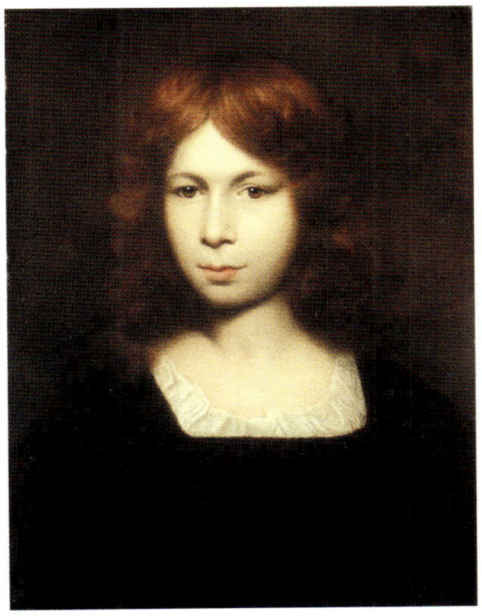

A640; oil on canvas, 45 × 35 cm
Hindley Smith Bequest, 1939; WA1940.1.22

The restricted colours of russet and black and the antique costume look back to Venetian 16th-century art although the technique is generally smoother. Head studies of this kind are not uncommon in Ricard's art and indicate an interest in the art of 16th-century Florence and Venice.

George Richmond
(1809 – 1896)

On the Eve of Separation

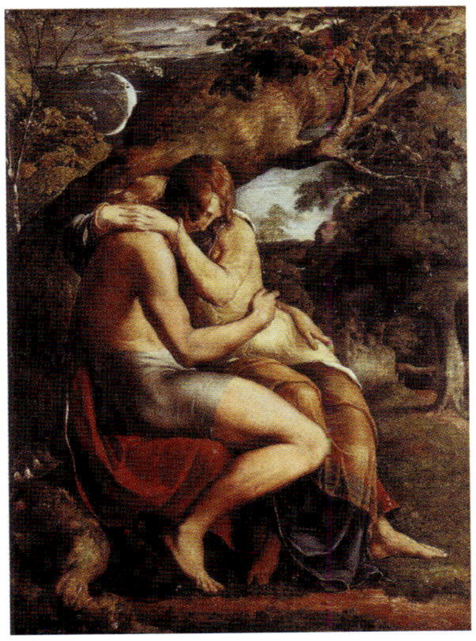

A400; oil and watercolours on panel, 49 × 36 cm
Signed and dated: *G Richmond pin. 1830*
Bequeathed by the Revd William Fothergill Robinson through the National Art Collections Fund, 1929; WA1929.33

Lister 1981, pp. 128–9

This is one of a number of works painted by Palmer, Richmond and Linnell at this period in the same experimental technique of oil over watercolour, attempting to recreate the effect of early oil paintings. According to a note by the artist, it was begun in watercolour and finished with colours ground in turpentine used with copal varnish. The subject was developed through a series of preparatory drawings and reached its final form in this painting, one of Richmond's most successful subject paintings before he turned exclusively to portraiture. It was exhibited at the Royal Academy in 1830.

Sir William Blake Richmond
(1842 – 1921)

The Sea, Bocca d'Arno

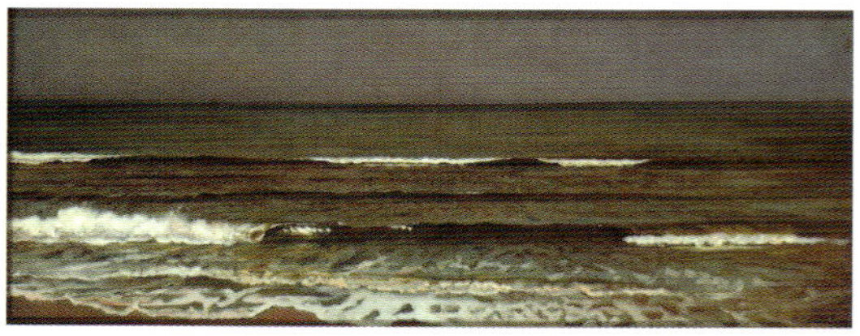

A788; oil on panel, 25 × 62 cm
Prov.: from the artist by descent
Bequeathed by Mrs Hilda Fothergill Medlicott, 1950; WA1950.47

Reynolds 1995, pp. 68–9

After the birth of his son, Francis, at Assisi on 6 August 1868, Richmond took his family to Bocca d'Arno, on the Tuscan coast. The village consisted only of a customs house and a fisherman's hut, and Richmond lodged in the latter for two weeks, in order to witness the dawn coming up over the sea. This small panel shows the influence of Giovanni Costa, whom Richmond had met in Rome in 1866, and is one of Richmond's few seascapes.

Charles de Sousy Ricketts
(1866 – 1931)

Jephthah's Daughter

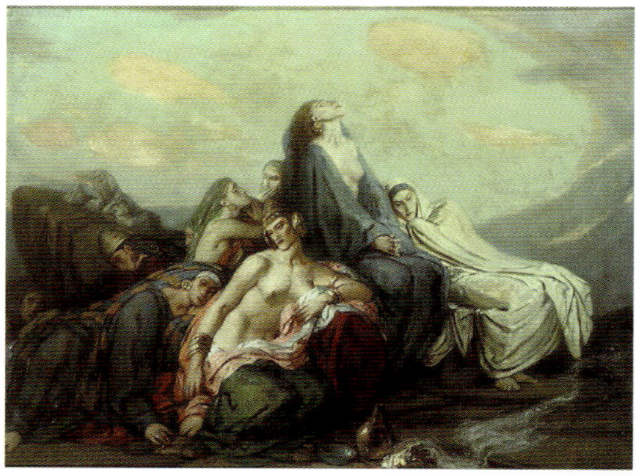

A729; oil on canvas, 94 × 120 cm
Signed in monogram
Presented by Mr and Mrs Henry Winslow, 1946; WA1946.269

Darracott 1980, pp. 72–3

Most of Ricketts's early paintings were illustrations of biblical or classical subjects. In this work, from *c.* 1905–7, the subject is taken from Judges 11: 30–40: Jephthah vowed to God that if he was granted victory against Ammon, he would sacrifice the first thing he saw on returning home. This was his daughter running to greet him. She therefore went with her companions for two months to the mountains to bewail her virginity.

George Richmond after Raphael
(1809 – 1896)

The Archimedes Group from 'The School of Athens'

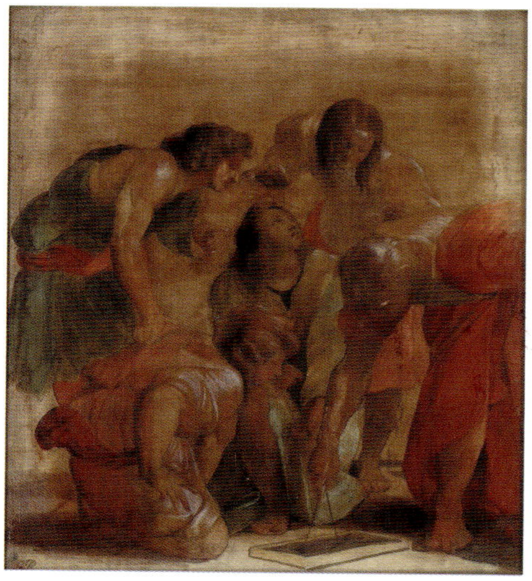

A680; oil on canvas, 69 × 61 cm
Signed: *G.R.*: and inscribed on back: *Group from / The School of Athens / Rome, 1839 / Geo. Richmond*
Presented by the Revd F.M.T. Palgrave and Miss Annora Palgrave, 1941; WA1941.29

Richmond was in Italy from 1837 to 1839 spending part of the time with Samuel Palmer on his honeymoon. He made an intensive study of the Old Masters, hoping to incorporate their lessons into his art much as Sir Joshua Reynolds had done. This painting shows Archimedes with his pupils, copied from Raphael's fresco of *The School of Athens* in Vatican.

Sir William Blake Richmond
(1842 – 1921)

Sir Arthur Evans among the Ruins of the Palace of Knossos

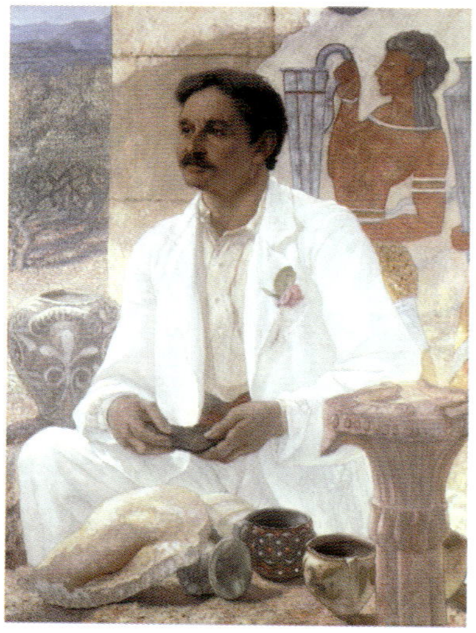

A316a; oil on canvas, 124 × 90 cm
Presented by an International Body of Subscribers, 1907; WA1907.2

Reynolds 1995, pp. 299–300

Sir Arthur Evans (1851–1941) was the Keeper of the Ashmolean Museum between 1884 and 1908. He is best known for his excavation of the palace of Minos at Knossos and his work on Minoan civilisation. This portrait, painted in the year before his retirement from the Ashmolean, depicts him against a background of Minoan stonework and hills covered in olive trees, under the strong sunlight of Crete. It was entirely executed in Richmond's studio in London.

Charles de Sousy Ricketts
(1866 – 1931)

Tobias being comforted by the Angel

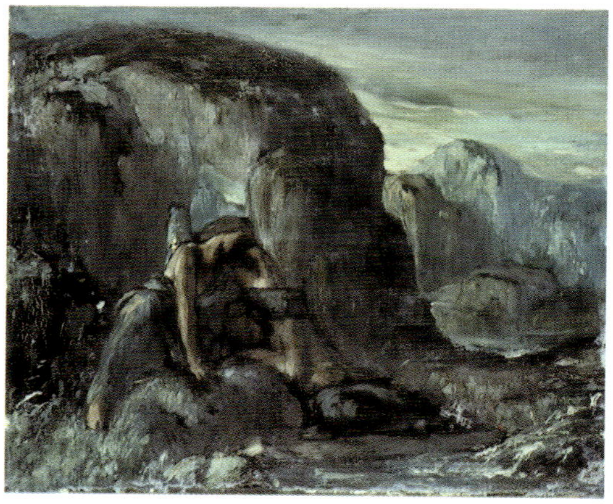

A913; oil on canvas, 46 × 55 cm
Russell Bequest, 1958; WA1958.57.8

Delaney 1990, p. 145

This is a replica of a larger painting, commissioned by Katherine Bradley and Edith Cooper, who wrote under the pseudonym 'Michael Field'. Like many of Ricketts's paintings, its condition has deteriorated owing to his poor technique: he was taught oil painting by Charles Shannon, who learnt from books.

Charles de Sousy Ricketts
(1866 – 1931)

Jacob wrestling with the Angel

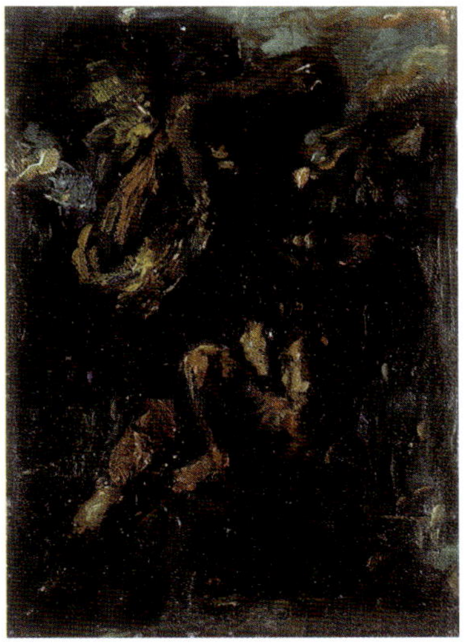

A341; oil on canvas stuck on panel, mounted as a drawing, 20 × 14 cm
Presented by Miss Katherine Harris Bradley, 1914; WA1914.3

Jacob wrestled all night with the angel and at daybreak the angel blessed him and called him Israel (Genesis 32: 24–32). This sketchy work is difficult to read, having darkened considerably due to Ricketts's faulty technique.

Charles de Sousy Ricketts
(1866 – 1931)

The Deposition

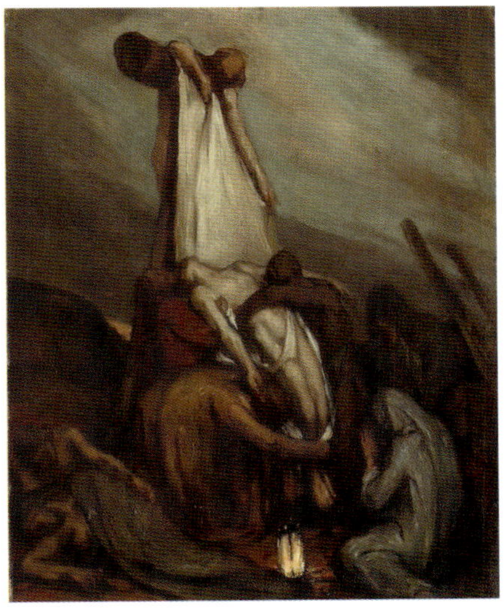

A1175; oil on canvas, 71.5 × 57 cm
Prov.: Mrs Winslow and by descent until 1973
Presented by Charles Stewart, 1991; WA1991.433

Ricketts made a number of paintings of Christ's Passion. He was fascinated by the tragedy and pathos of Christ's suffering, rather than any more overtly religious significance. This *Deposition* probably dates from *c.* 1910.

James Rielly
(b. 1956)

Trainerspotting

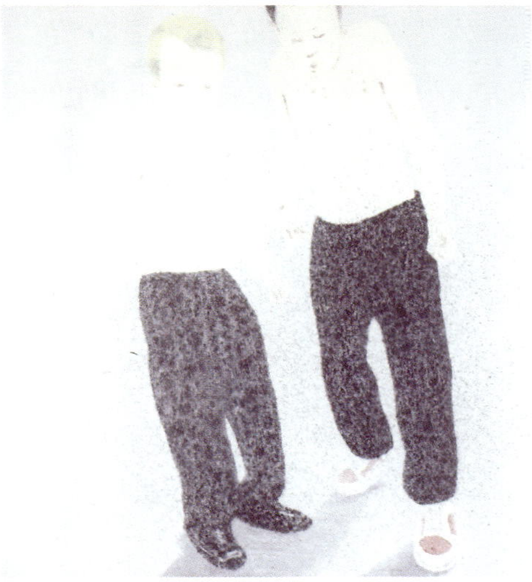

A1251; oil on canvas, 50.8 × 46 cm
Signed, dated and inscribed on back
Presented anonymously through the National Art Collections Fund, 2002; WA2002.68

From early in his career, Rielly concentrated on the human figure. He often showed figures from a slightly unconventional angle or subtly deformed, as here in this painting of two young boys, wearing track-suit trousers, seen from a somewhat sloping viewpoint. The angle at which they are seen tends to shorten their bodies, while the posture of their arms adds to the appearance of deformation.

John Francis Rigaud
(1742 – 1810)

Stephen Peter Rigaud and Mary Anne Rigaud

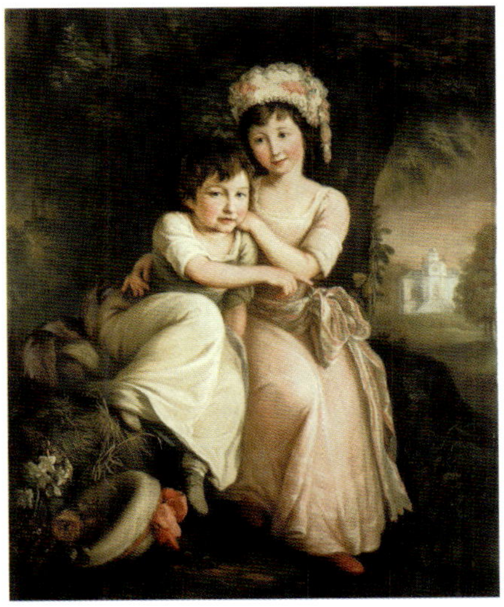

A246; oil on canvas, 126 × 100 cm
Presented by Miss Rigaud, 1889; WA1889.1

Pressly 1984, p. 62

This portrait, exhibited at the Royal Academy in 1778, shows the children of the artist's brother, James Stephen Rigaud, Astronomer Royal: Stephen Peter Rigaud (1774–1839), who was four, and his elder sister, who was seven. They are seen playfully embracing each other in Richmond Park; the building in the background is Kew Observatory, where their father was employed.
S.P. Rigaud spent his later years at Oxford, where he was Savilian Professor of Geometry, 1810–27 and of Astronomy, 1827–39.

John Riley
(1646 – 1691)

Elias Ashmole

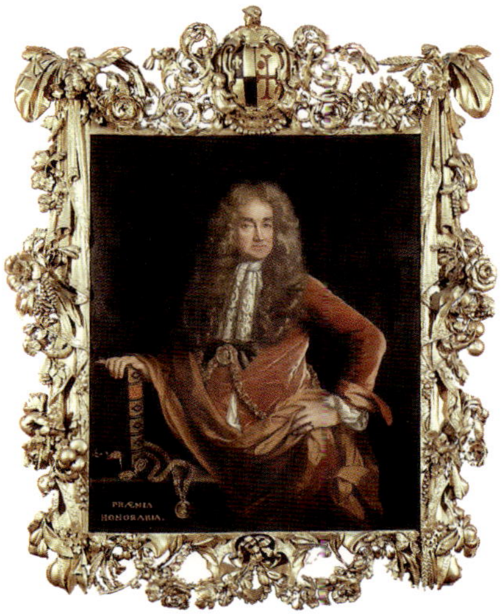

F730; oil on canvas, 124 × 101 cm
Presented by the sitter, 1683; WA1898.36

Poole 1912, no. 447; MacGregor 1983 no. 281

Elias Ashmole (1617–1692), whose gift to the University of Oxford in 1683 formed the basis of the Ashmolean Museum in Broad Street (now the Museum of the History of Science), is portrayed with objects reflecting his scholarly interests as an antiquary and herald. The book, *Ashmole of the Garter*, represents his *Institution, Laws* and *Ceremonies of the most Noble Order of the Garter* (1672). The medals (*Praemia honoraria*), carefully depicted, no doubt at Ashmole's request, are a filigree chain and portrait medallion of Frederick William, Elector of Brandenburg (worn by the sitter); a portrait medal of Karl Ludwig of Bavaria; the George of the Order of the Garter which had belonged to Thomas Howard, 2nd Earl of Arundel and which was given to Ashmole by the Earl Marshal; and another chain and medal, given by the King of Denmark. It is likely that the portrait was painted in 1681–2 for presentation to the new museum in Oxford. The spectacular frame was carved by Grinling Gibbons (1648–1720), for whom Ashmole cast a horoscope in 1682. It is surmounted by Ashmole's arms and his motto, *EX UNO OMNIA* ('all things come from one').

John Riley
(1646 – 1691)

Elias Ashmole

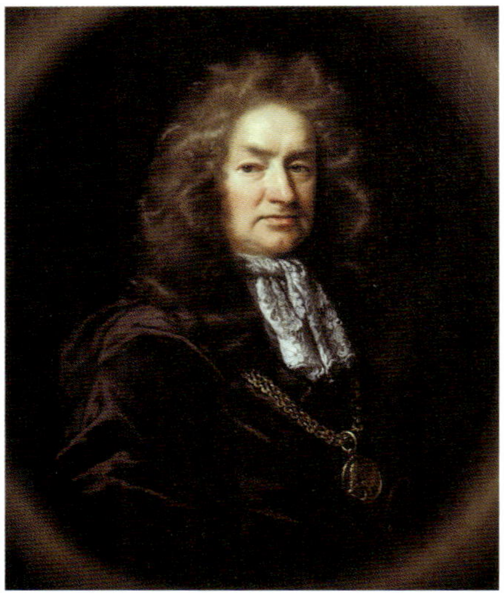

A316b; oil on canvas, 74 × 60 cm
Inscribed: *AETA. 73 1689*
Presented by T. Whitcombe Greene, 1907; WA1907.1

Poole 1912, no. 448

This is generally presumed to be Riley's 'second portrait' of Ashmole, for which a sitting is recorded in Ashmole's diary for 14 September 1687. The inscription was probably added for an early owner, but the provenance of the painting before 1907 is unknown.

John Riley
(1646 – 1691)

James, Duke of York, later King James II

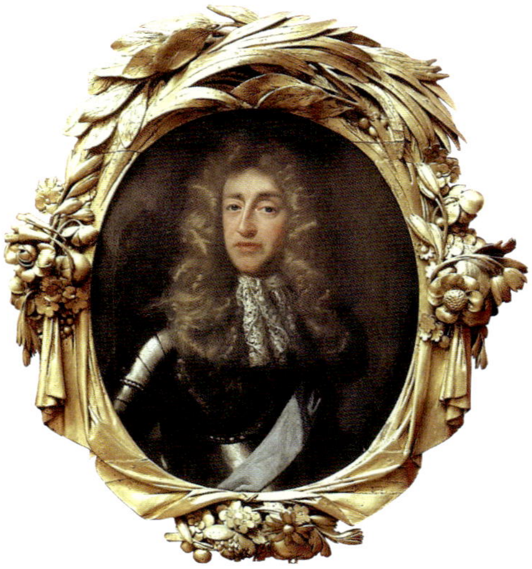

F732; oil on canvas, 76 × 61 cm
Presented by Elias Ashmole, 1686–7; WA1898.40

Poole 1912, no. 451; MacGregor 1983, no. 283

James, Duke of York (1633–1701), ascended to the throne on the death of his brother in 1685. He also wears the blue sash of the Order of the Garter. This painting, designed as a pendant to that of *King Charles II*, has a matching frame made in the studio of Grinling Gibbons.

William Rivière
(1806 – 1876)

William Young Ottley

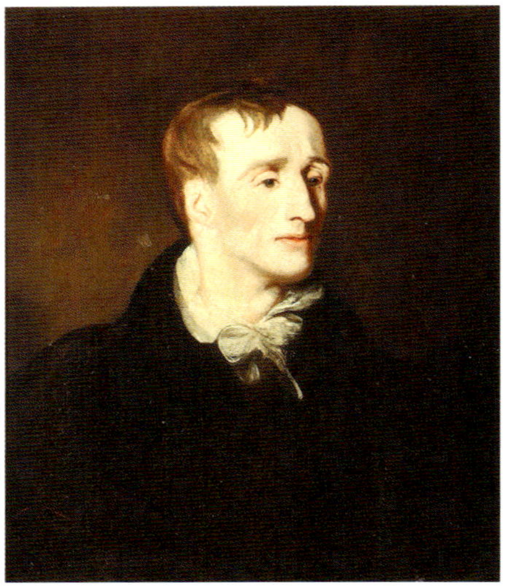

A507; oil on canvas, 76 × 64 cm
Prov.: by descent from the sitter
Presented by A.G.B. Atkinson, 1937; WA1937.106

Gere 1953, p. 44

William Young Ottley (1771–1836) was an amateur artist who amassed an important collection of Old Master drawings and published several books, including *The Italian School of Design* (1808–23), a pioneering work with outstanding facsimiles of drawings. He later became Keeper of Prints at the British Museum (1833–6). This portrait, which was engraved by F.C. Lewis, is attributed to William Rivière, the father of Briton, who painted portraits in Oxford and elsewhere.

John Riley
(1646 – 1691)

King Charles II

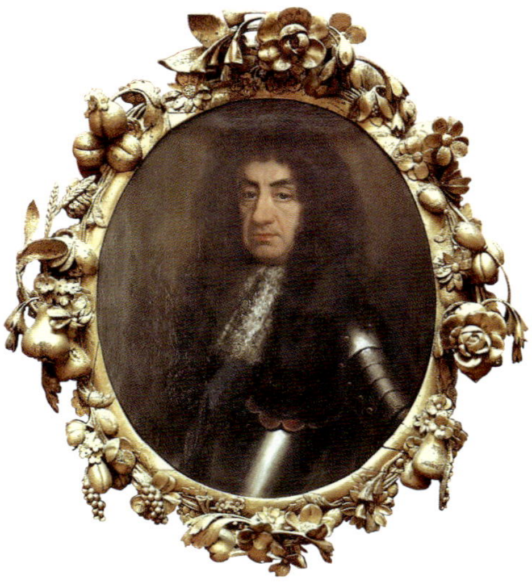

F731; oil on canvas, 76 × 61 cm
Presented by Elias Ashmole, 1686–7; WA1898.39

Poole 1912, no. 445; MacGregor 1983, no. 282

Charles II (1630–1685) was restored to the throne in 1660. He wears the blue sash of the Order of the Garter. The elaborate frame of carved limewood was probably made by Grinling Gibbons or in his studio.

Briton Rivière
(1840 – 1920)

Prometheus

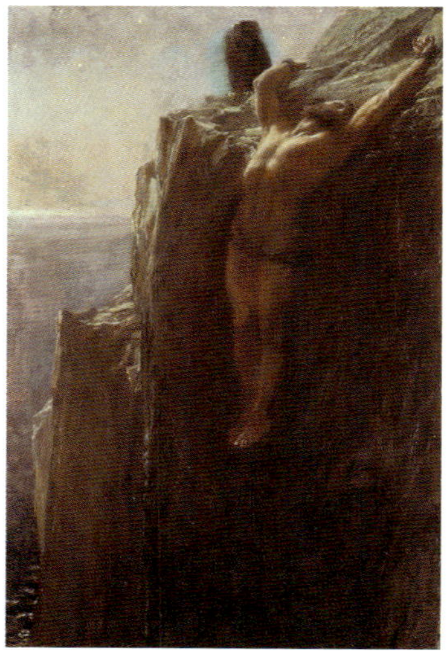

A363; oil on canvas, 89.5 × 58.7 cm
Signed and dated: *B.R. 1889*
Presented by the artist's family, 1920; WA1920.5

Newall 1995, p. 119

In Greek mythology, Zeus banished Prometheus for several acts of defiance, by ordering him to be tied to Mount Caucasus, where every day an eagle devoured his liver, which was restored during the night. This depiction of the fall of night, and the coming of relief, was exhibited at the Grosvenor Gallery in 1889 with a quotation from Elizabeth Barrett Browning's translation of Aeschylus: 'Night shall come up with garniture of stars to comfort thee with shadow.'

Clare Roberts
(second half of 20th century)

The Botanic Gardens, Oxford

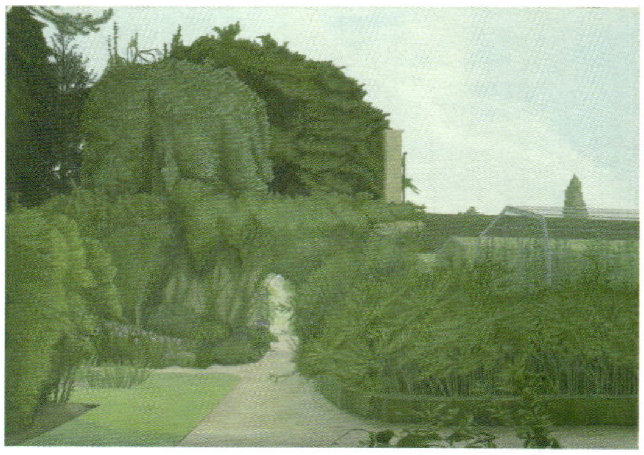

A1106; oil on canvas laid on board, 29 × 40.7 cm
Deposited by the Delegates of Oxford University Press, 1979; WA1979.3.1

This painting served as the head-piece for the Oxford Almanack in 1979.

William Roberts
(1895 – 1980)

T.E. Lawrence as Aircraftman Shaw

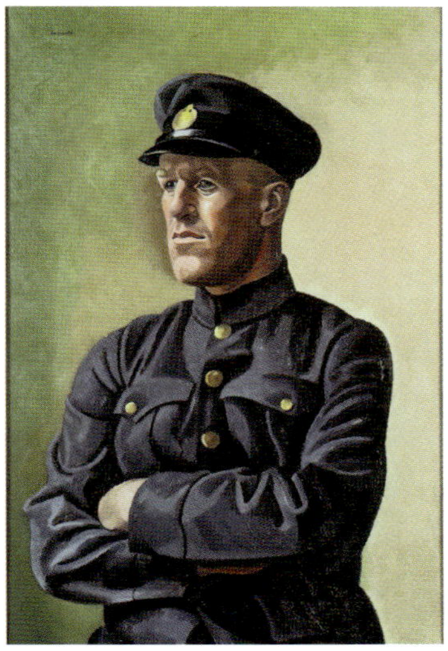

A727; oil on canvas, 91.5 × 61 cm
Signed: *Roberts.*
Presented by Professor A.W. Lawrence, the sitter's brother, 1946; WA1946.267

Wilson 1988-9, no. 257; Eustace 1999, no. 20

Lawrence joined up as J.H. Ross in June 1922 and rejoined in 1923 as T.E. Shaw. Roberts illustrated Lawrence's *Seven Pillars of Wisdom*, for which the drawings and a portrait were exhibited in 1923. This portrait was painted in a rented room in Coleherne Terrace, Earl's Court.

Anonymous Roman Artist
(*c.* 1690 – 1740)

Ecce Homo

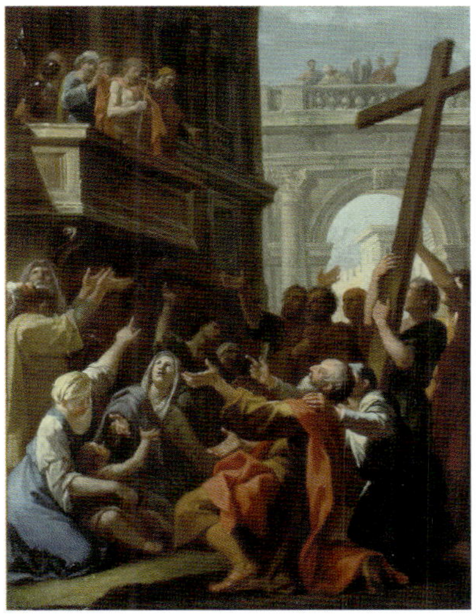

A869; oil on canvas, 65 × 49 cm
Purchased, 1953; WA1953.148

Having been scourged and crowned with thorns, Christ is presented to the people with Pontius Pilate's words, 'Behold the Man' (John 19: 4–5). The inclusion of a cross is more common in northern European paintings. Formerly attributed to Simon Vouet and then to various French artists, A869 is by an artist working in Rome, perhaps in the circle of Luigi Garzi. Recently an attribution has been suggested to Niccolò Ricciolini (1687–1772), whose early work displays the same crowded compositions and over-emphatic gestures.

Giovanni Francesco Romanelli
(*c.* 1610 – 1662)

Angelica encountering the wounded Medoro

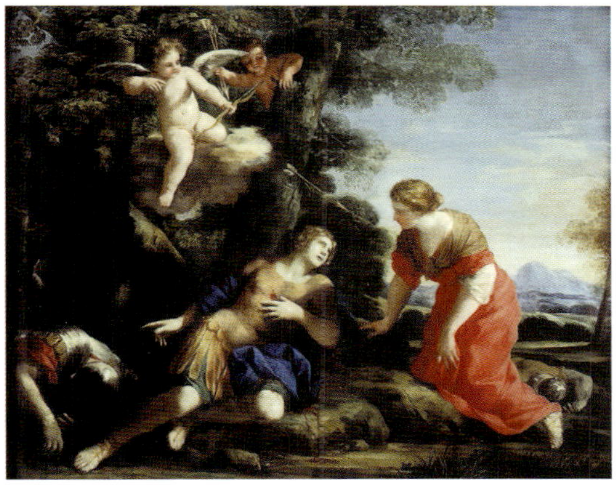

Oil on canvas, 61.6 × 76.3 cm
Prov.: Cardinal Jules Mazarin by 1653; (?)Marquis of Stafford; Earls of Ellesmere until 1946
Mahon loan, 1999; WA.L.99.16

Finaldi and Kitson 1997, no. 65

The wounded Medoro is tended by Angelica, while Cupid ensures she will fall in love with him (Ariosto, *Orlando Furioso*, XIX, 19). A pentimento is visible, where the arrow was placed further to the right. The painting may have been made for Mazarin during Romanelli's first visit to France in 1646–8, although there are arguments for a dating of a decade earlier. It was engraved by Jean Charles Le Vasseur as *Tancred and Erminia*.

Claude Maurice Rogers
(1907 – 1979)

Snow in Bloomsbury

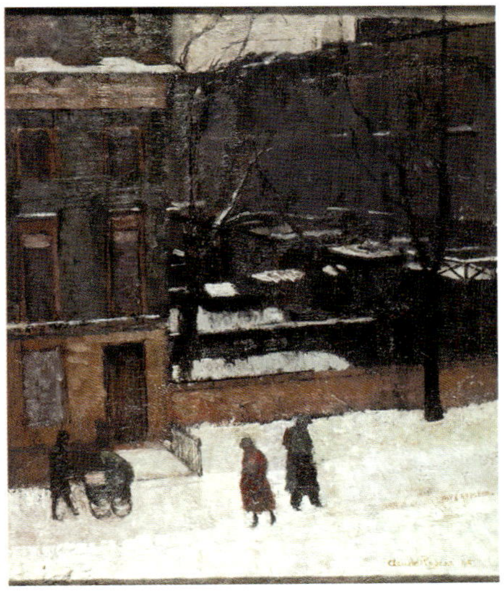

A756; oil on canvas, 60.7 × 50.7 cm
Signed and dated: *Claude Rogers 45*
Presented by John Dodgson, 1948; WA1948.71

Along with Victor Pasmore and William Coldstream, Rogers was a founding member of the Euston Road School in 1937. The School aimed to inject new realism and craftsmanship into painting. Unlike Pasmore, who later converted to abstract painting, Rogers's style remained figurative as in this atmospheric winter scene.

Anonymous Roman Artist
(*c.* 1700 – 1720)

The Creation of Eve

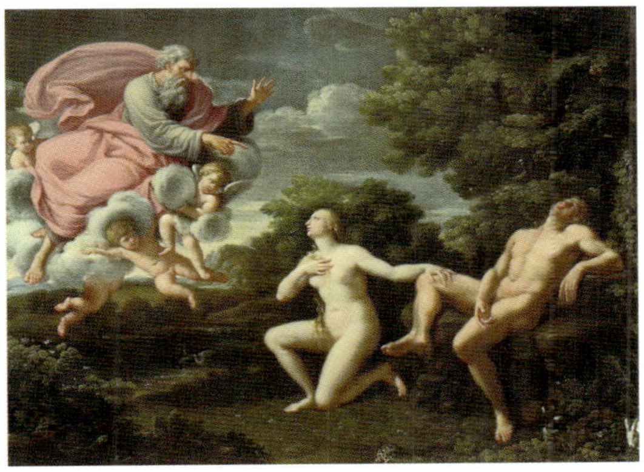

A944; oil on canvas, 72 × 97 cm
Prov.: P.E. Bromley Martin
Bequeathed by Major Guy Cassie through the National Art Collections Fund, 1961; WA1961.8

God created Eve from the rib of the sleeping Adam (Genesis 2: 21–23). The composition is inspired by Domenichino's *Rebuke of Adam and Eve*, a much-copied painting in the Palazzo Colonna, Rome and displays some similarities with Francesco Albani's treatments of the *Creation of Eve*. Given the revival of interest in Bolognese classicism in early 18th-century Rome and the implausible old attribution of A944 to Angelo Trevisani, it might well be an early work by Francesco Trevisani.

George Romney
(1734 – 1802)

Mrs Siddons

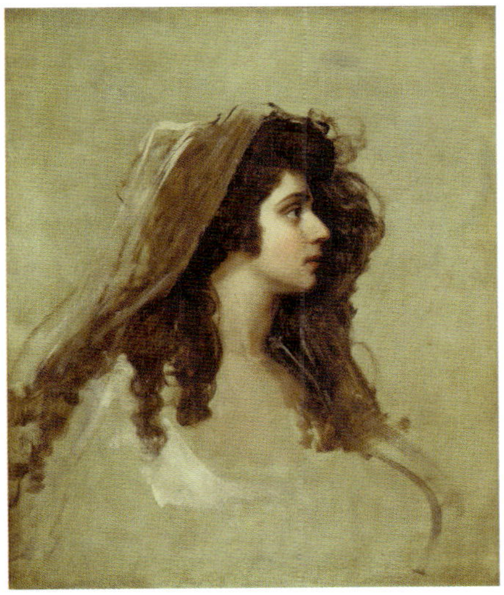

A391; oil on canvas, 75 × 65 cm
Prov.: James H. Worthington
Presented by Mrs W.F.R. Weldon, 1929; WA1929.2

Kidson 2002, no. 105

Sarah Kemble (1755–1831), who married William Siddons in 1773, was the most celebrated tragic actress of her time. She sat to many artists and was portrayed as the Tragic Muse by Sir Joshua Reynolds (Huntington Art Gallery). This sketch dates from *c.* 1784 and was lent out to other artists to copy.

Thomas Matthews Rooke
(1842 – 1942)

The Dancing Girls

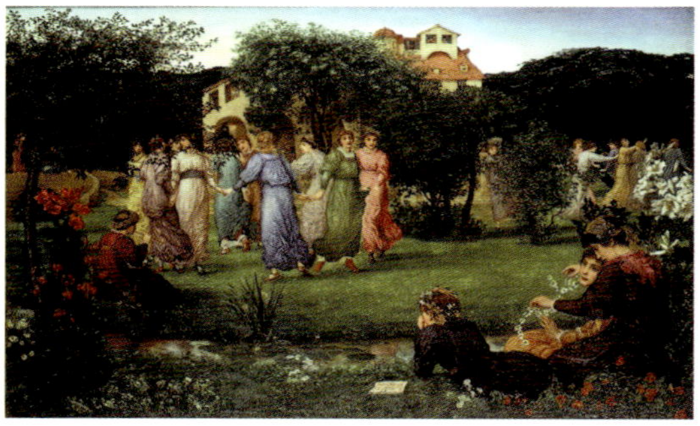

A686; oil on canvas, 61 × 97 cm
Signed and dated: *TMR 1882*
Presented by Mrs Maud Rolleston, 1941; WA1941.65

Christian 1989, no. 27

Rooke became Burne-Jones's studio assistant around 1869 and continued devotedly in this role until his master's death in 1898. He was also active in the Arts and Crafts movement and a skilled topographical draughtsman. This oil shows the strong influence of Burne-Jones in the classicising figures, who dance in a timeless landscape with eclectic architecture in the background.

Follower of Salvator Rosa
(1615 – 1673)

Landscape with a cleft Tree

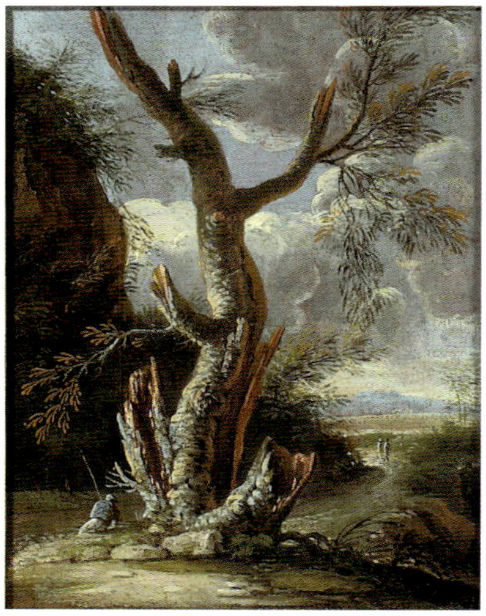

A998; oil on canvas, 30 × 23 cm
Inscribed on back: *SIL.o CARD VALE(N)TI / JOL.*
Prov.: Cardinal Silvio Valenti Gonzaga; Winter; 7th Duke of Leinster; Professor Thomas Bodkin; Dr Alfred Scharf, London
Purchased, 1963; WA1963.27

Pietrangeli 1961, nos. 100–1

One of a pair of paintings from the Valenti Gonzaga collection, A998 seems likely to be by an early imitator of Rosa. Its companion, showing a fisherman at a pool under a rocky archway, is now in a private collection.

Formerley attributed to Salvator Rosa
(1615 – 1673)

Battle Scene

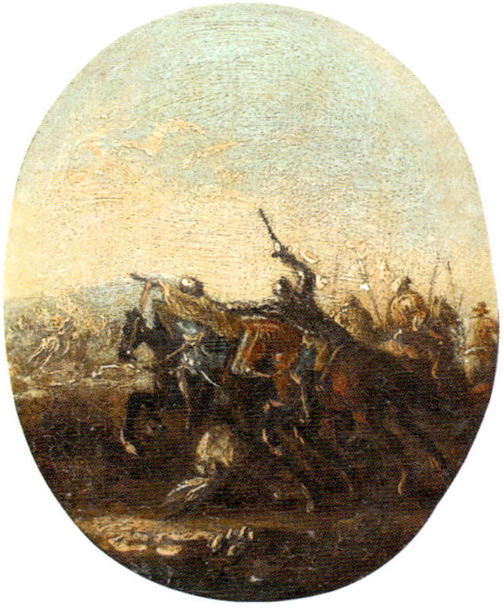

A368; oil on panel, 17.3 × 13 cm
Presented by Mrs G. Sollas, 1921; WA1921.5

See under A367.

Style of Johann Melchior Roos (Rosa da Tivoli)
(1659 – 1731)

Landscape with Cattle

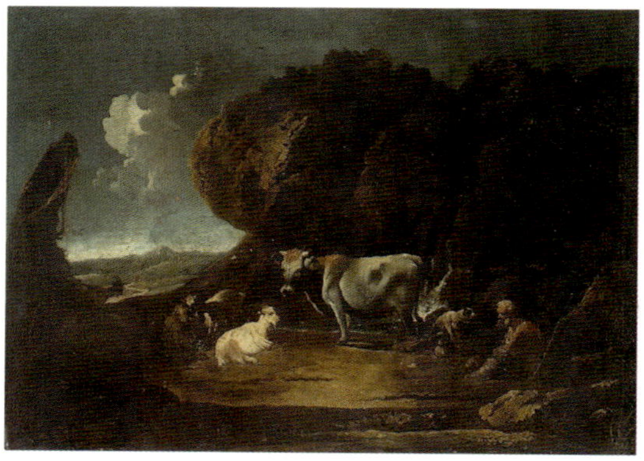

A111; oil on canvas, 91 × 124 cm
Fox-Strangways Gift, 1850; WA1850.40

An early 18th-century painting, somewhat in the style of Roos.

Formerley attributed to Salvator Rosa
(1615 – 1673)

Battle Scene

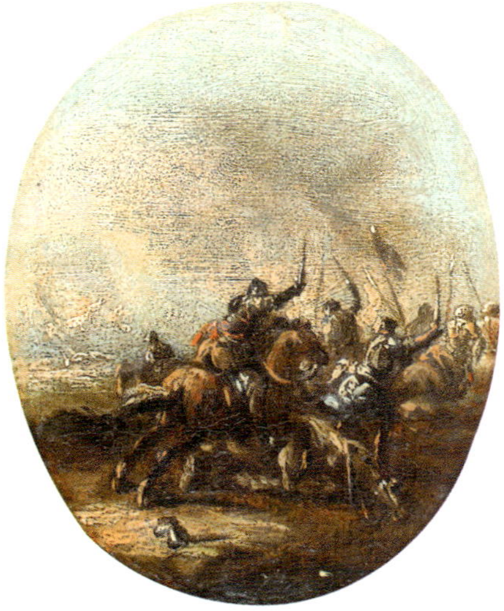

A367; oil on panel, 17.4 × 13 cm
Presented by Mrs G. Sollas, 1921; WA1921.4

A367 and A368 are pendants, dating from the late 17th century and perhaps by a Neapolitan artist.

Sir William Rothenstein
(1872 – 1945)

South-west Wind

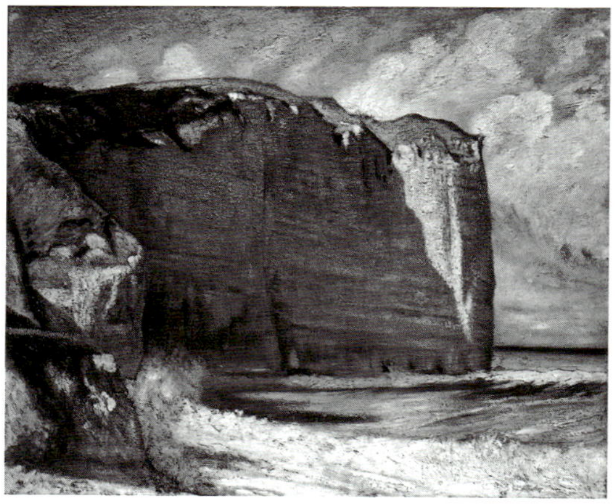

A483; oil on canvas, 62 × 75 cm
Weldon Bequest, 1937; WA1937.64

Between 1899 and 1910, Rothenstein usually spent his summer holidays on the Normandy coast. The cove at Vaucottes was a favouite bathing place and its cliffs a frequent subject in his paintings. This work reflects Rothenstein's admiration for similar compositions by Courbet.

Sir William Rothenstein
(1872 – 1945)

Night

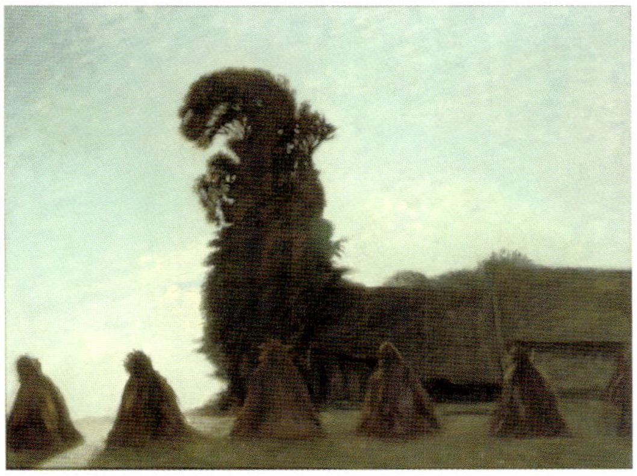

A716; oil on canvas, 86 × 112 cm
Presented by the Contemporary Art Society, 1945; WA1945.75

First exhibited in 1910, this landscape relects Rothenstein's interest in symbolism. The formation of the tree and buildings recall the prow of a Viking ship, while the hayricks are reminiscent of mourners at a funeral.

Sir Peter Paul Rubens
(1577 – 1640)

The Conversion of St Paul

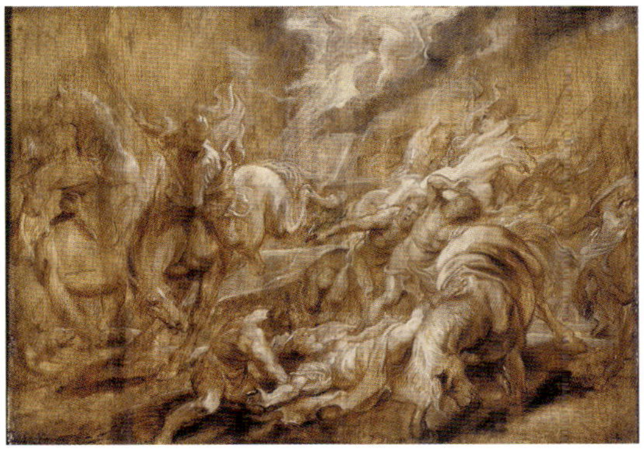

A889; oil on panel, 32.8 × 45.8 cm
Prov.: Sir William Hamilton; John B.S. Morritt and by descent
Bequeathed by Percy Moore Turner, 1957; WA1957.59.1

White 1999, p. 116

This sketch, painted almost entirely in brown monochrome with some white and a few touches of colour, is a study for a large canvas, formerly in Berlin (destroyed, 1945). The circumstances of the commission are unknown. It has been variously dated between 1616 and 1620. The subject shows St Paul cast off his horse by divine intervention (Acts 9: 3–5).

Sir Peter Paul Rubens
(1577 – 1640)

St Clare of Assisi

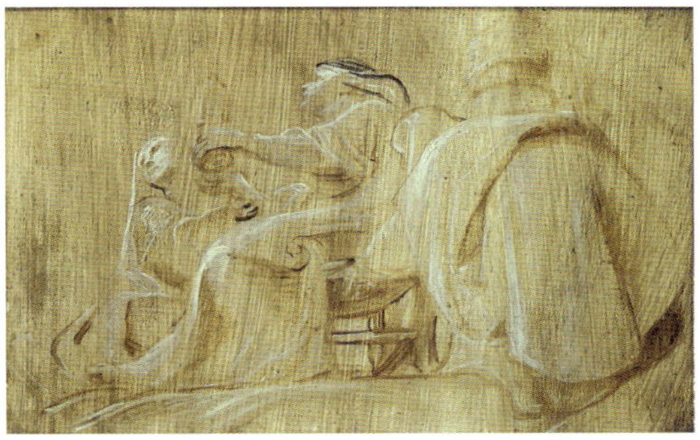

A156; oil on panel, 14.6 × 22 cm
Prov.: (?)Maximilien de Hase and Cuypers de Reymenam; (?)Charles Spruyt; Thomas Loridon de Ghellinck
Chambers Hall Gift, 1855; WA1855.179

White 1999, pp. 108

In March 1620, Rubens agreed to produce thirty-nine paintings for the ceilings of the galleries in the Jesuit Church in Antwerp. These were executed by assistants from models supplied by the artist. Rubens also painted a number of summary monochrome sketches of which this is one. St Clare is shown holding up the host with which she is said to have put the Saracens to flight. In 1718, the ceilings were destroyed by fire.

Willem Frederiksz. van Royen
(*c.* 1645 – probably 1723)

Still Life of Peaches and Grapes

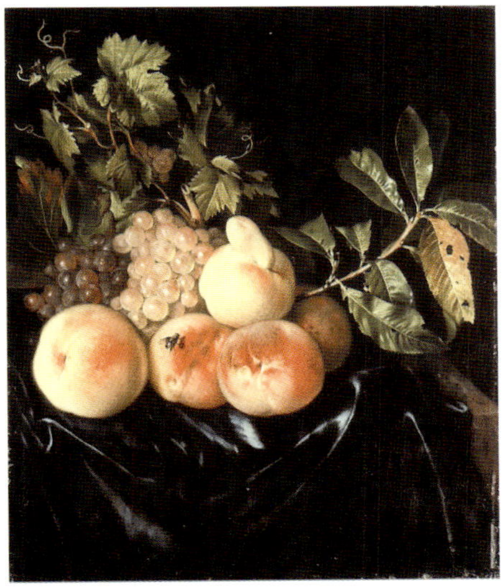

A586; oil on canvas, 46 × 39 cm
Signed and dated: *W.F. / van Roye / Ao 1705 / fecit.*
Daisy Linda Ward Bequest, 1939; WA1940.2.62

Meijer 2003, no. 63

Van Royen spent most of his life in Germany but his art is rooted in the Dutch tradition. His fruit pieces show an awareness of the work of Willem van Aelst. Like van Aelst, he occasionally signed his Christian name in its Italian form. The choice of the misshapen peach, however, is idiosyncratic.

Sir Peter Paul Rubens
(1577 – 1640)

A Satyr pressing Grapes with a Tiger and Leopard

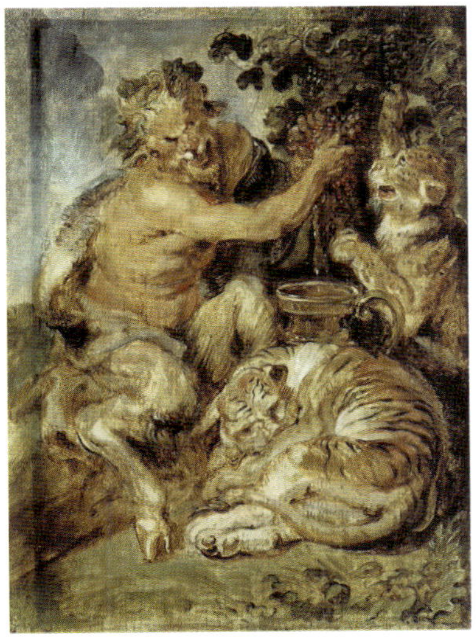

A153; oil on panel, 33.4 × 24.2 cm
Chambers Hall Gift, 1855; WA1855.170

White 1999, pp. 104–6

The pose of the satyr is based on a figure in an antique group of *Pan and Daphnis* which Rubens saw in Rome during his early years in Italy (1600–8). This sketch probably dates from about ten years after his return. The subject, combining tigers, leopards and satyrs, appears elsewhere in his art, e.g. in the *Allegory of War and Peace* in the National Gallery, London.

Sir Peter Paul Rubens
(1577 – 1640)

St Barbara pursued by her Father

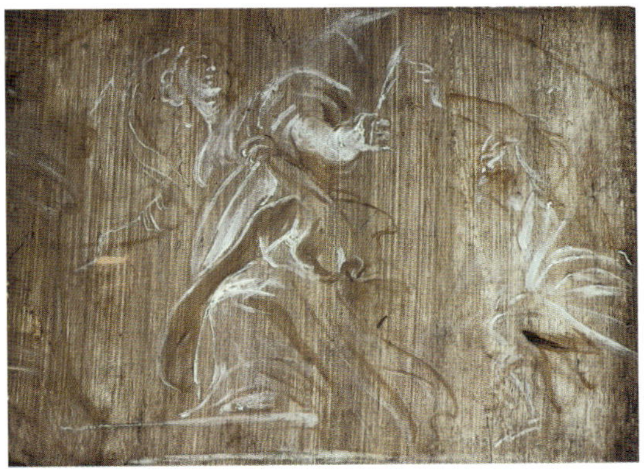

A157; oil on panel, 15.5 × 20.7 cm
Prov.: (?)Maximilien de Hase and Cuypers de Reymenam; Charles Spruyt; Thomas Loridon de Ghellinck
Chambers Hall Gift, 1855; WA1855.178.

White 1999, p. 110

A preliminary sketch for a ceiling panel in the left-hand aisle of the Jesuit Church in Antwerp. St Barbara is shown in flight from her father who persecuted her for converting to Christianity. The finished painted model to which this lively sketch relates is in Dulwich Picture Gallery.

Sir Peter Paul Rubens
(1577 – 1640)

The Sacrifice of Noah

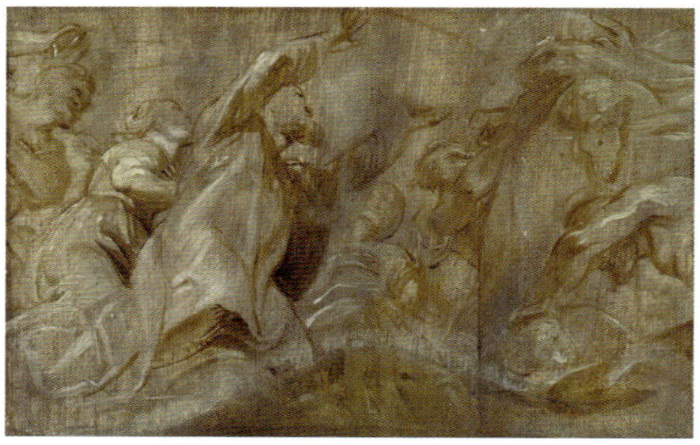

A158; oil on panel, 18.7 × 28.8 cm
Prov.: (?)Maximilien de Hase and Cuypers de Reymenam; Charles Spruyt; Thomas Loridon de Ghellinck
Chambers Hall Gift, 1855; WA1855.176

White 1999, p. 111–3

The ceiling panels in the Jesuit Church in Antwerp included both Old and New Testament subjects. This scene from the Book of Genesis, illustrating Noah's sacrifice after the Flood, was not included in the final commission. The lower part of the panel has been damaged and repaired with the insertion of a section of new wood.

Sir Peter Paul Rubens
(1577 – 1640)

The Annunciation

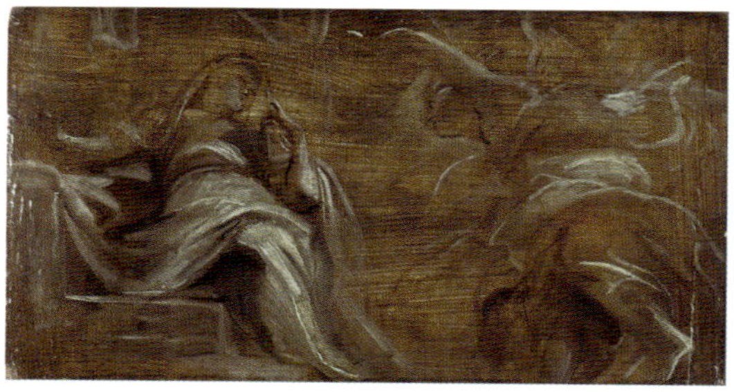

A159; oil on panel, 14.2 × 26.4 cm
Prov.: (?)Maximilien de Hase and Cuypers de Reymenam; Charles Spruyt; Thomas Loridon de Ghellinck
Chambers Hall Gift, 1855; WA1855.171

White 1999, p. 113

This was one of the subjects commissioned for the aisle ceilings in the Jesuit Church in 1620 but not included in the final scheme. The coloured model is in the Gemäldegalerie der Akademie der bildenden Künste in Vienna.

Sir Peter Paul Rubens
(1577 – 1640)

The Emperor Maximilian I

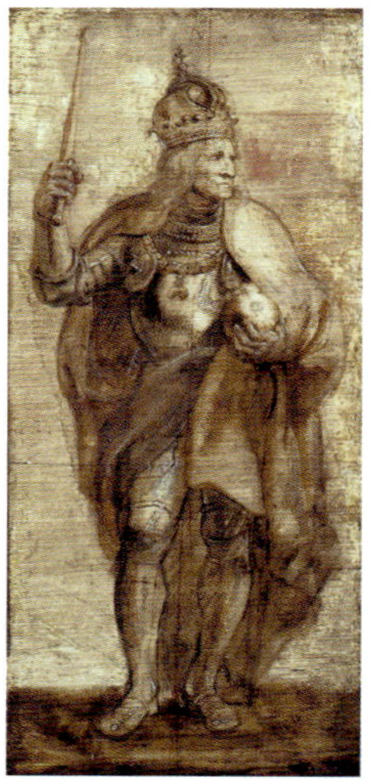

A155; oil on panel, 38.7 × 18.8 cm
Chambers Hall Gift, 1855; WA1855.161

White 1999, p. 106

In 1634 Rubens was commissioned to design a series of street decorations for the 'Joyous Entry' into Antwerp of the newly appointed Governor of the Spanish Netherlands, the Cardinal-Infante Ferdinand. Rubens produced a large number of oil-sketches as models for the artists and craftsmen who realised his designs. The most elaborate structure was the Portico of the Emperors, which included twelve over-life-size gilded stone statues of the Habsburg emperors. This sketch is a study for the statue of Maximilian I (1459–1519).

Sir Peter Paul Rubens
(1577 – 1640)

The Annunciation

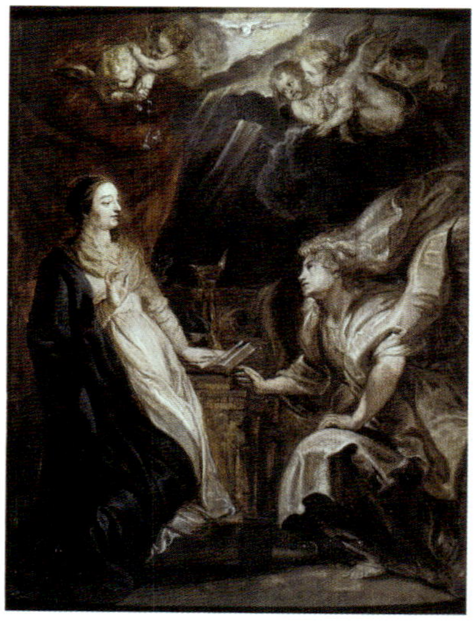

A171; oil on panel, 44 × 33 cm
Chambers Hall Gift, 1855; WA1855.222

White 1999, p. 114

Shortly after the Jesuits had founded a Fraternity in Antwerp in 1609, Rubens painted an altar-piece of *The Annunciation* for their chapel, now in the Kunsthistorisches Museum, Vienna. This was reproduced in an engraving by Schelte à Bolswert with some changes of detail and format. The sketch in the Ashmolean, which corresponds closely to the print, must be the model painted by Rubens for the engraver. As the print seems to have been made some years after the altar-piece, the painting, too, must be later in date.

Sir Peter Paul Rubens
(1577 – 1640)

The 'Apotheosis of Germanicus': copy after an Antique Cameo (The 'Gemma Tiberiana')

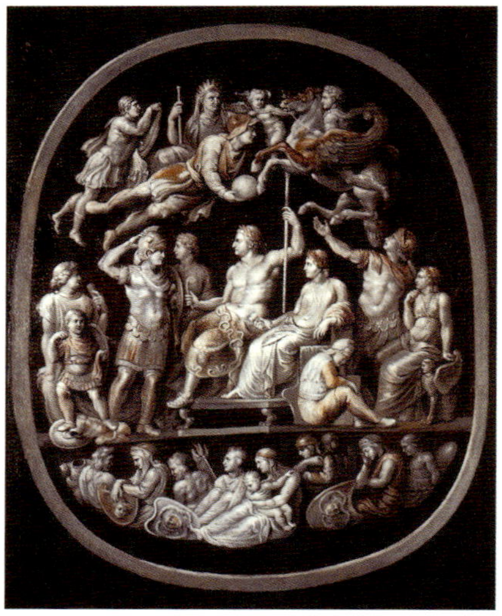

A1169; oil on canvas, 100.7 × 78 cm (enlarged on all sides)
Prov.: Nicolas-Claude Fabri de Peiresc; Jacques and Pierre Dupuy; bequeathed by former to President Jacques-Auguste de Thou II; De Buscher; Charles Philippe Campion de Tersan; possibly M. Maurice; Shorting
Accepted by H.M. Government in part settlement of Inheritance Tax from the estate of Christopher Norris and purchased with the assistance of the Museums & Galleries Commission/Victoria & Albert Purchase Grant Fund, the National Art Collections Fund, National Heritage Memorial Fund, the Friends of the Ashmolean and other funds, 1989; WA1989.74

White 1999, p. 117

In 1620, the French antiquary, Nicolas-Claude Fabri de Peiresc discovered a large Roman cameo in the Treasury of the Sainte-Chapelle in Paris. He was intrigued by the subject in which he recognised a number of Roman Imperial portraits. It is now generally thought to represent Germanicus taking leave of his parents, the Emperor Tiberius and his mother, Livia, with other members of the Julio-Claudian family, past and present. In 1621, Peiresc suggested to Rubens that he might care to publish the discovery. This led to a project to compile an illustrated *Gem Book* which came to nothing. Rubens also promised to make an enlarged copy of the cameo for Peiresc as a companion to a copy of another famous cameo painted by Niccolò dell'Abbate which was in Peiresc's collection. This copy, now in Oxford, was based on the drawing made by Rubens for the book and delivered to Peiresc in 1626. While remaining generally true to the appearance of the cameo, Rubens added a life-like warmth to the cold stone and restored two heads where they are missing in the original.

Sir Peter Paul Rubens
(1577 – 1640)

The Coronation of Henri IV

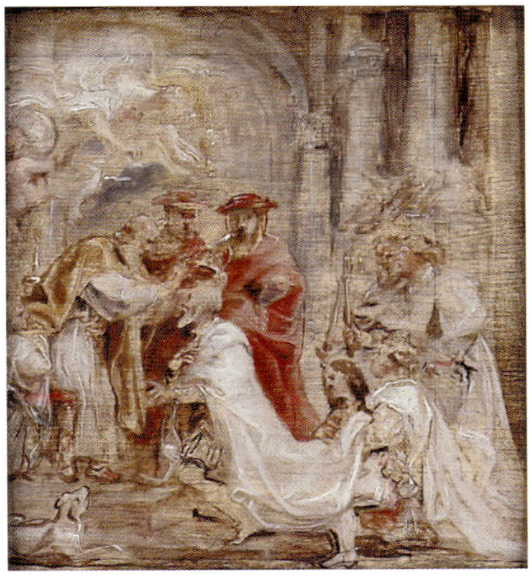

A1243; oil on panel, 23.3 × 21 cm
Purchased (Miller Fund) with the assistance of the National Art Collections Fund, 2002; WA2002.43

Held 1980, no. 87

A preparatory oil sketch for one of a series of paintings celebrating the reign of Henri IV of France commissioned by his widow, Maria de' Medici in 1627 along with a similar series (now in the Louvre) illustrating events in her own life. The paintings of Henri IV were abandoned about the time Maria de' Medici was exiled from the French court in 1631, and the artist's intentions for the series are only known from a number of surviving sketches like this.

Attributed to Sir Peter Paul Rubens
(1577 – 1640)

A Dead Child carried to Heaven by Angels

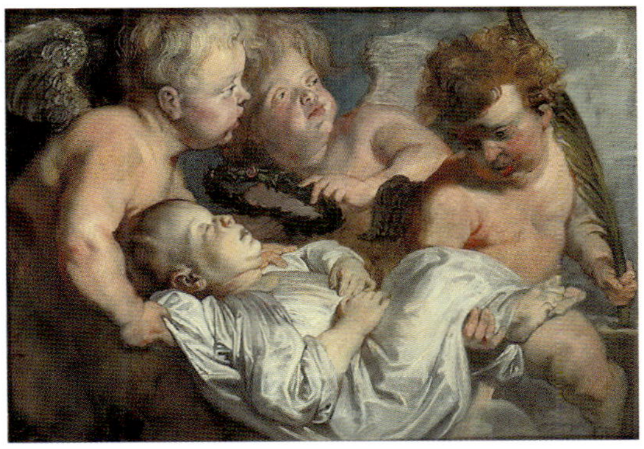

A167; oil on panel, 44 × 60 cm
Prov.: Jacob Loys; Jan van der Hulk; Pompe van Meerdervoort; Hoetvoordt; Johan van der Linden van Slingeland; Abraham Delfos; Alexis Delahante; Edward Gray
Chambers Hall Gift, 1855; WA1855.162

White 1999, p. 125

The uneven execution of this picture has encouraged doubts about the attribution to Rubens. It is possible that it was begun by Rubens and finished by another artist.

Style of Sir Peter Paul Rubens
(1577 – 1640)

Head of a Huntress (?Diana)

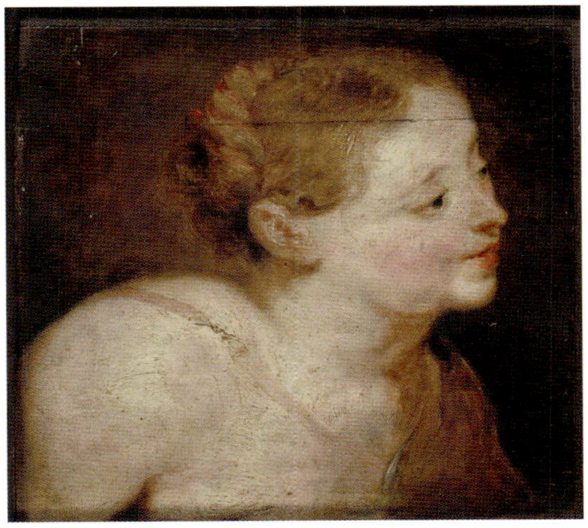

A163; oil on panel, 29 × 31 cm
Chambers Hall Gift, 1855; WA1855.189

White 1999, p. 128

A damaged and indifferent head study in the style of Rubens.

Attributed to Sir Peter Paul Rubens
(1577 – 1640)

Landscape with Farm Buildings at Sunset

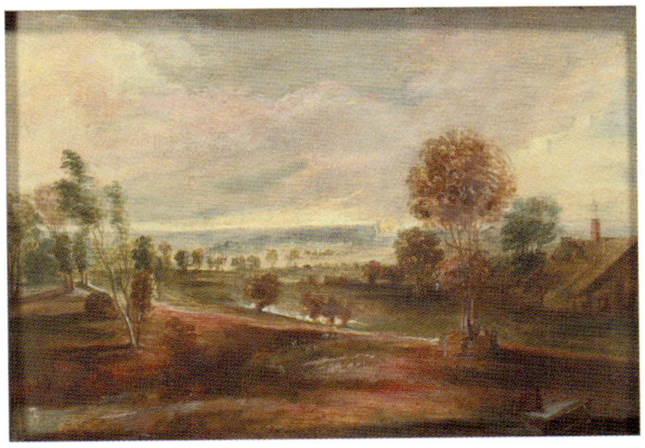

A161; oil on panel, 27 × 39 cm
Chambers Hall Gift, 1855; WA1855.163

White 1999, p. 123

It has been suggested that Rubens may have painted this sketch out of doors in the vicinity of Het Steen and used it as a study for his *Landscape with a Tower at Het Steen at Sunset* in the National Gallery in London. It has also been affirmed that the sketch may not have been painted by Rubens but copied with variations by another artist from the work in London. There are arguments for both views.

Style of Sir Peter Paul Rubens
(1577 – 1640)

St Augustine

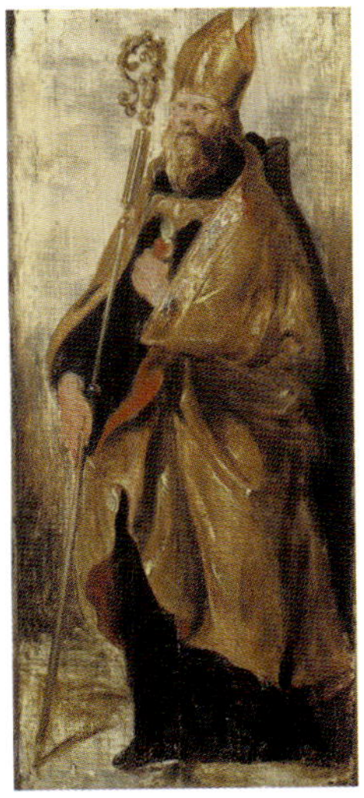

A154; oil on panel, 38 × 17 cm
Chambers Hall Gift, 1855; WA1855.177

White 1999, pp. 127–8

This appears to be a preparatory sketch. It has been attributed to Rubens (whose work it closely resembles) but no related work by Rubens is known. This, combined with an uncharacteristically thin touch, tends to cast doubt on the former attribution. Augustine (354–430) was Bishop of Hippo in North Africa. The burning heart which he holds in his left hand alludes to the words of his Confessions: 'thou hast pierced our heart with the arrow of thy love'.

Style of Sir Peter Paul Rubens
(1577 – 1640)

Landscape: a Storm

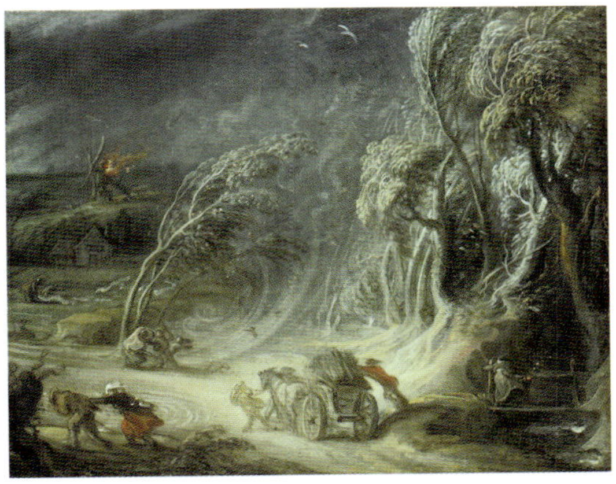

A164; oil on canvas, 54 × 69 cm
Chambers Hall Gift, 1855; WA1855.164

White 1999, p. 129

This freely sketched composition has been attributed to Rubens himself although it seems more likely that it is a painting by another artist, somewhat in his manner, perhaps dating from the 18th century.

Style of Sir Peter Paul Rubens
(1577 – 1640)

Christ on the Cross

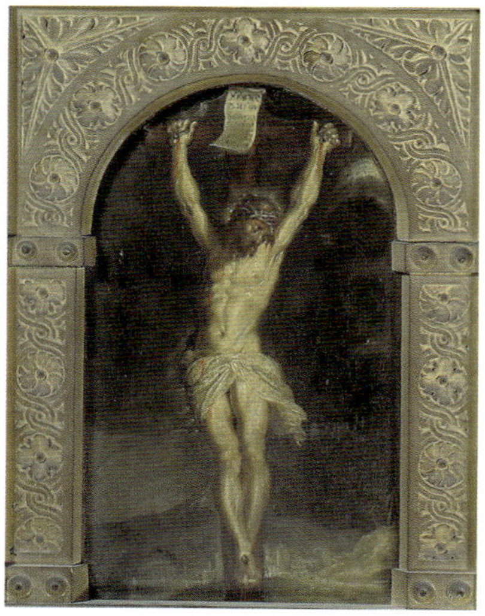

A165; oil on panel, 45 × 27 cm
Chambers Hall Gift, 1855; WA1855.168

White 1999, p. 129

A poor quality copy or imitation of Rubens. It is similar to a painting of the *Crucifixion* in the Courtauld Institute Galleries in London, but in reverse direction and by a different hand.

Copy after Sir Peter Paul Rubens
(1577 – 1640)

Archduke Albert of Austria

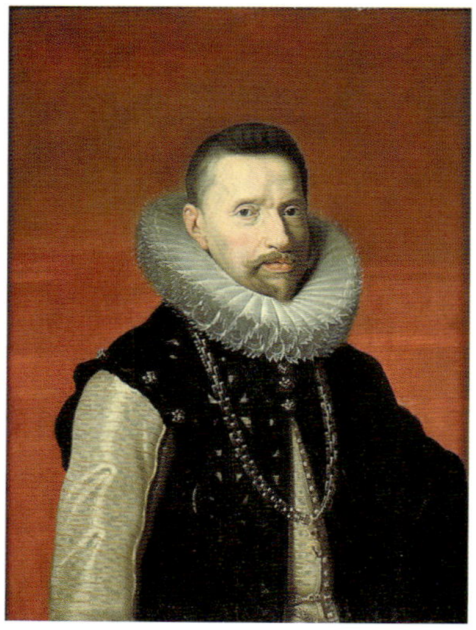

A805; oil on canvas, 78 × 57 cm
Prov.: Ralph Bernal; Cecil Dunn-Gardener; Martin Colnaghi
Bequeathed by Percy Moore Turner, 1951; WA1951.9

White 1999, p. 134

A copy with some variations of a lost portrait of the Archduke by Rubens, known in an engraving by Jan Muller and in other copies. Albert (1559–1621), sixth son of the Emperor Maxmilian II, became Governor of the Netherlands in 1595 and ruled jointly with the Infanta Isabella following their marriage in 1598.

Copy after Sir Peter Paul Rubens
(1577 – 1640)

Self-portrait

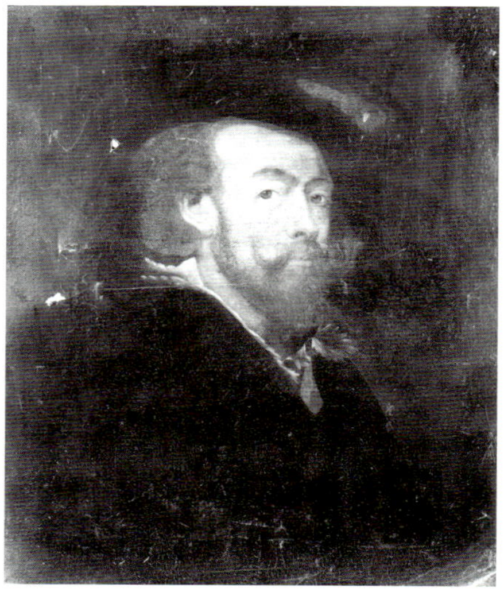

A322; oil on canvas, rolled, 68 × 58 cm
Provenance unknown; WA.OA909

White 1999, p. 133

A copy of poor quality after a painting at Windsor, signed and dated 1623, possibly based on a print.

Style of Sir Peter Paul Rubens
(1577 – 1640)

A Child Angel

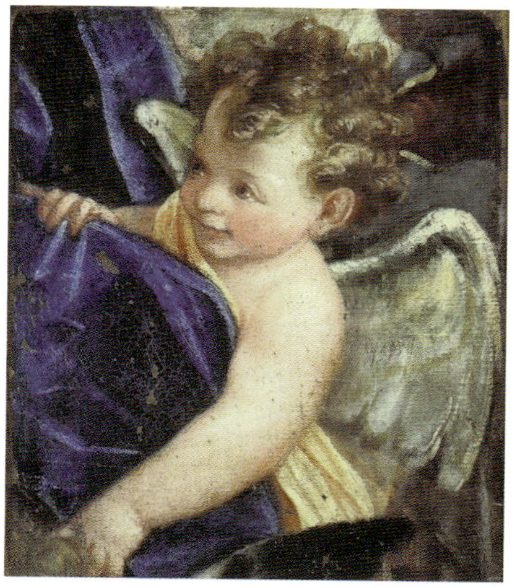

A170; oil on canvas, 76.4 × 63.5 cm
Chambers Hall Gift, 1855; WA1855.573

White 1999, p. 130

An inscription in English on the back suggests that this is a copy by Rubens from an Italian original. The painting is damaged and in poor condition but seems to be no more than a work with some affinities to Rubens's style.

Copy after Sir Peter Paul Rubens
(1577 – 1640)

The Hunting of the Calydonian Boar

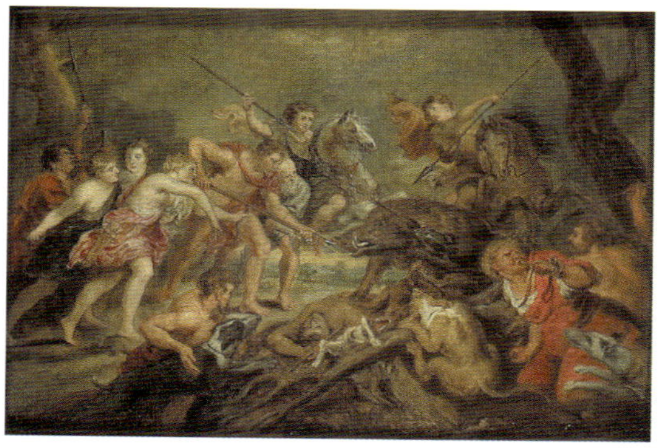

A162; oil on panel, 38 × 54 cm
Chambers Hall Gift, 1855; WA1855.175

White 1999, p. 132

This is a greatly reduced copy after a painting of about 1620 from Rubens's workshop, now in the Kunsthistorisches Museum, Vienna. The inscription *SDPAPE* on the back of the panel suggests it may have been painted by or belonged to Simon de Pape II (1623–1677). The subject, taken from Ovid's *Metamorphoses*, shows Meleager on the left about to strike the boar with his lance.

Copy after Sir Peter Paul Rubens
(1577 – 1640)

The Apotheosis of James I

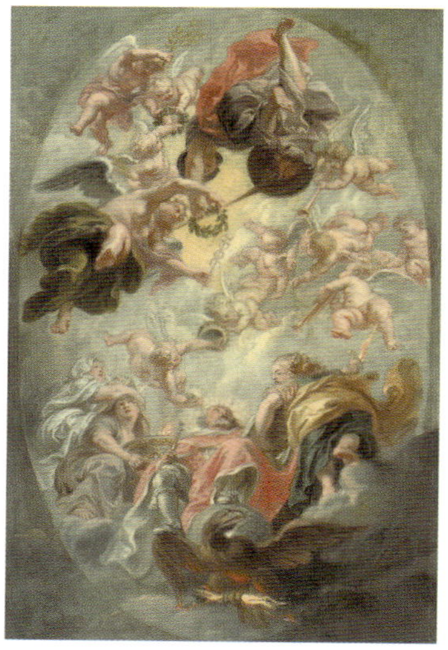

A169; oil on canvas, 80 × 53 cm
Chambers Hall Gift, 1855; WA1855.169

White 1999, p. 132

Copied from a sketch by Rubens for the painting in the central oval in the ceiling of the Banqueting House in Whitehall. This sketch, which is now in the Hermitage Museum in St Petersburg, remained in England until it was sold to Catherine the Great and sent to Russia. The copyist may, therefore, have been an English painter although not one of high merit.

Copy after Sir Peter Paul Rubens
(1577 – 1640)

Landscape with a Tower at Het Steen at Sunset

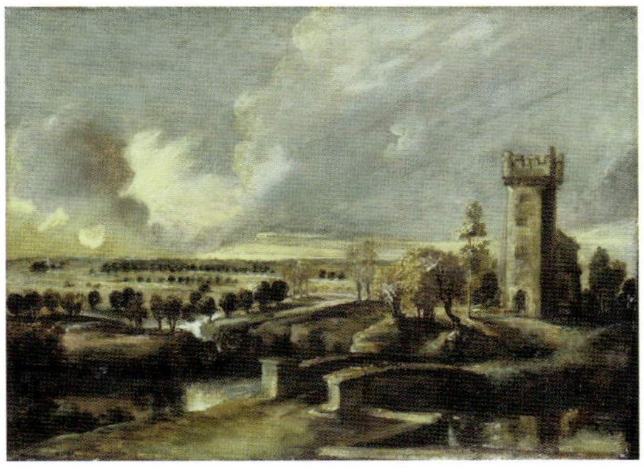

A160; oil on panel, 28 × 37 cm
Chambers Hall Gift, 1855; WA1855.166

White 1999, p. 130

In May 1635 Rubens purchased the Castle of Steen near Malines. This view shows the medieval tower situated at the back of the house. There is a second version of this composition in the Gemäldegalerie in Berlin which seems to have been used as a study for a large composition of a *Tournament in Front of a Castle* (Louvre, Paris). A160 is probably a copy by another hand.

Copy(?) after Sir Peter Paul Rubens
(1577 – 1640)

Madonna and Child in a Niche

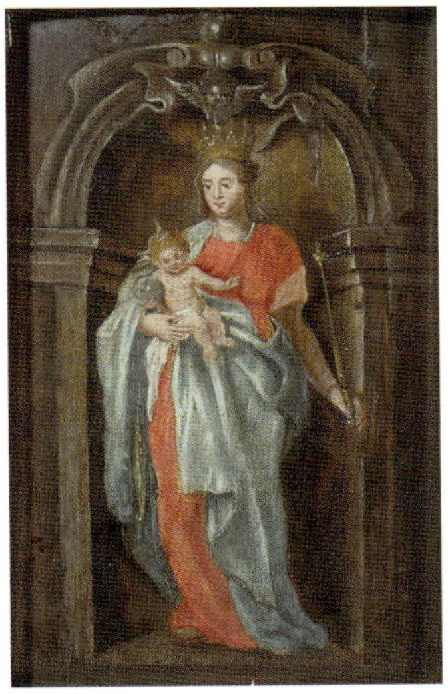

A181; oil on panel, 34 × 22 cm
Chambers Hall Gift, 1855; WA1855.221

White 1999, p. 134

Copied after a sketch on panel in a private collection in London, attributed to Rubens. The sketch in London appears to have been the model for an engraving after a composition by Rubens.

Jacob van Ruisdael
(1628/9 – *c.* 1682)

Landscape near Muiderberg

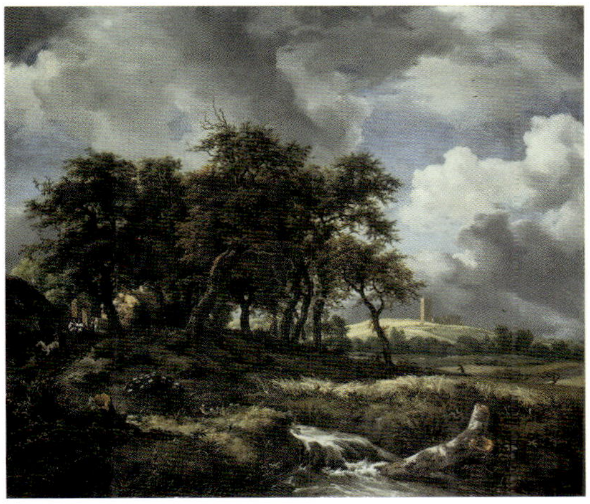

A875; oil on canvas, 66 × 75 cm
Signed in monogram: *JvR*
Prov.: Danoot; Hennessy; Buchanan (?); Edward Loyd and by descent to Edward N.F. Loyd
Presented by the National Art Collections Fund from the bequest of Ernest E. Cook, 1955; WA1955.66

White 1999, p. 135 pl. 13

The ruined church of Muiderberg (seen on the hill in the distance) is situated near Naarden, south-east of Amsterdam on the Zuider Zee, where Ruisdael's father was born. Probably painted in the early 1650s, when the artist was still living in Haarlam, it is based on drawings made in the locality. There is a compositional study for the painting in the Albertina, Vienna, which corresponds closely but does not include the carriage and riders on the right. It may be that this group has been added by another hand but at an early date as it appears almost unaltered in a landscape in the Szépmüvészeti Múzeum, Budapest, attributed to Ruisdael's contemporary, Jan van Kessel.

Jacob van Ruisdael
(1628/9 – *c.* 1682)

Landscape with a Waterfall

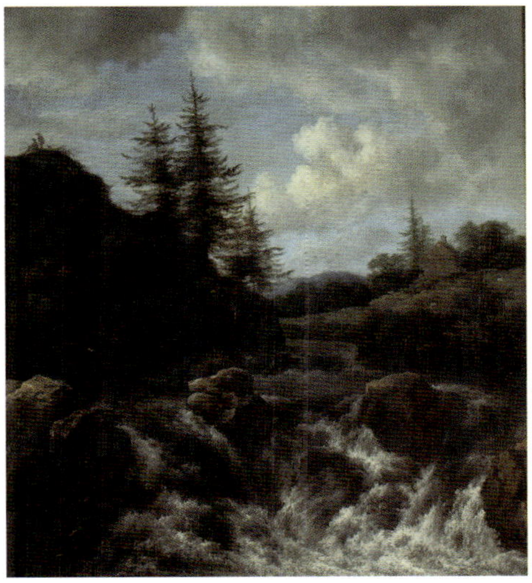

A982; oil on canvas, 49 × 42 cm
Signed: *JvRuisdael* (JvR in monogram)
Prov.: Willem II; Nieuwenhuys; Sir Thomas Baring and by descent to the 2nd Earl of Northbrook
Madan Bequest, 1962; WA1962.17.24

White 1999, p. 137

One of a group of paintings of waterfalls in mountainous scenery with fir trees painted by Ruisdael in the early 1660s. The details are based on the artist's recollections of the countryside along the Dutch-German border which he visited in about 1650.

Giovanni Battista Ruoppolo
(1629 – 1693)

Still Life of Flowers and Vegetables

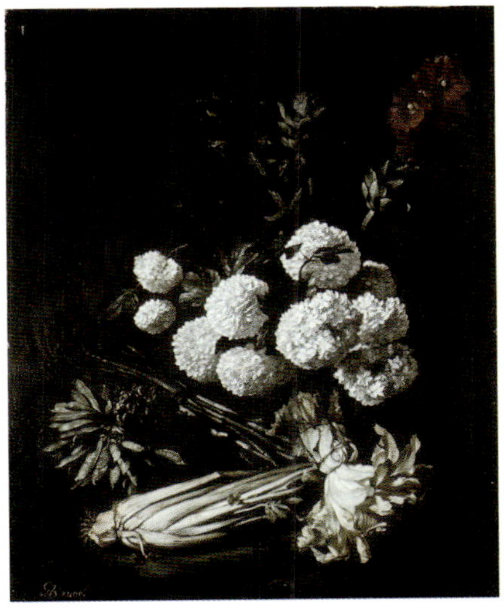

A432; oil on canvas, 108 × 87 cm
Signed *GB ruop.lo*
Prov.: Tomás Harris; Hans Mackowsky
Presented by the National Art Collections Fund, 1934; WA1934.8

Confalone 2002, pp. 204, 475

In the foreground are Florentine fennel, sea-kale, green peas, a leaf artichoke and asparagus; behind, guelder roses, leaf artichokes and a dark red hollyhock. Ruoppolo painted still lifes for wealthy Neapolitans and Flemish bankers. The restrained composition and austere palette suggest A432 is an early work of the 1650s.

Rachel Ruysch
(1664 – 1750)

A 'Forest Floor' Still Life of Flowers

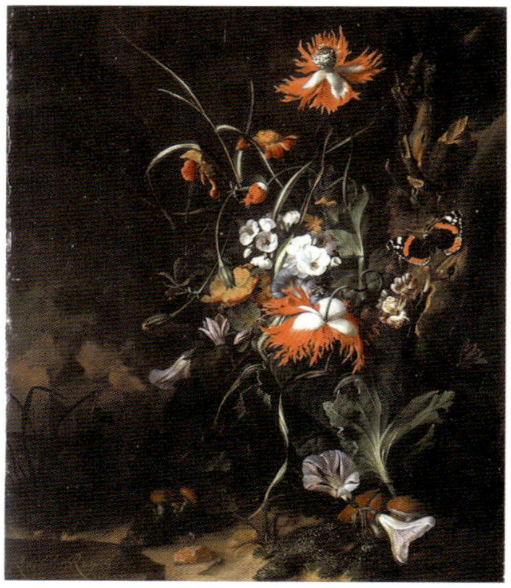

A588; oil on canvas, 47 × 40 cm
Signed and dated: *Rachel.Ruysch. / MDCLXXXVII*
Daisy Linda Ward Bequest, 1939; WA1940.2.64

Meijer 2003, no. 64

Rachel Ruysch, according to the artist, was taught by Willem van Aelst. From her studio in Amsterdam, she painted a long succession of flower paintings, several fruit pieces and a number of 'forest floors' of which this is a relatively early example. The type was invented by Otto Marseus van Shrieck in about 1650 and imitated by Ruysch. A number of details in the composition have been inspired by pictures of this kind by de Heem, Mignon and Willem van Aelst.

Copy after Rachel Ruysch
(1664 – 1750)

A Vase of Flowers

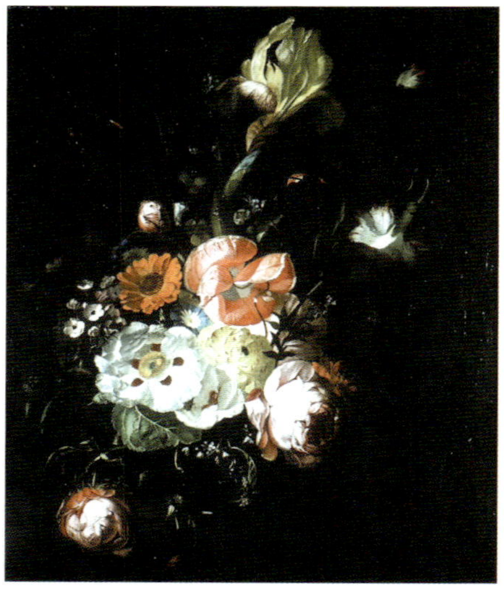

A589; oil on canvas, 48 × 40.5 cm
Daisy Linda Ward Bequest,1939; WA1940.2.65

Meijer 2003, no. 66

Closely copied with a few minor alterations from a painting by Ruysch, dated 1716, in the Rijksmusum, Amsterdam.

Salomon van Ruysdael
(1600/3? – 1670)

Scene before a Maypole with Alkmaar Church in the Background

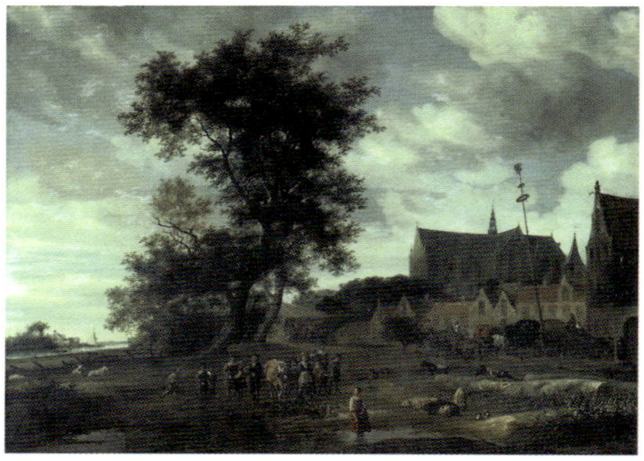

A1164; oil on canvas, 76 × 104 cm
Signed and dated: *SvRuysdael 1669* (SvR in monogram)
Bequeathed by Mr and Mrs Francis Hock through the National Art Collections Fund, 1988; WA1988.292

White 1999, p. 140

The church at Alkmaar in North Holland appears in at least three other paintings by Ruysdael. This painting, which dates from the end of the artist's life, is a variant of an earlier work in the Szépmüvészeti Múzeum, Budapest, signed and dated 1644, which includes the musicians but omits the girl standing in the pond, guarding pigs.

Rachel Ruysch
(1664 – 1750)

Vase of Flowers

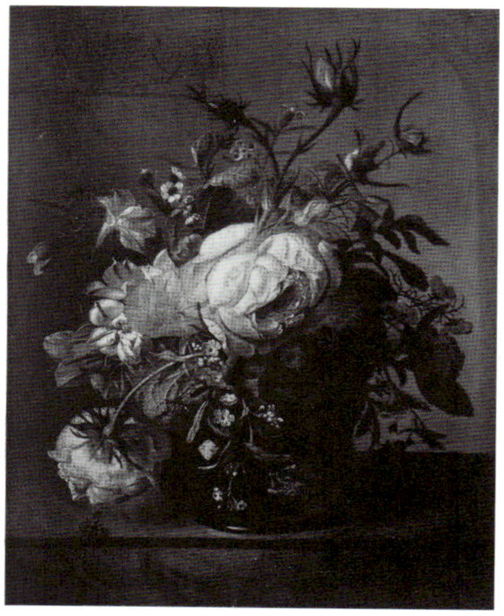

A590; oil on canvas, 26 × 24 cm
Signed and dated: *Rachel Ruysch / AE 78 1741*
Prov.: Robert White
Daisy Linda Ward Bequest, 1939; WA1940.2.66

Meijer 2003, no. 65

After 1739, Ruysch painted mainly small-scale paintings of bouquets and posies, inscribed with her age, as here. The arrangement of curving stems, full, rounded roses and a number of smaller flowers looks back to the work of Willem van Aelst. This painting was stolen from the Museum in March 1949 and has not been recovered.

Salomon van Ruysdael
(1600/3? – 1670)

A Draw-Well with Cattle before Beverwijck Church

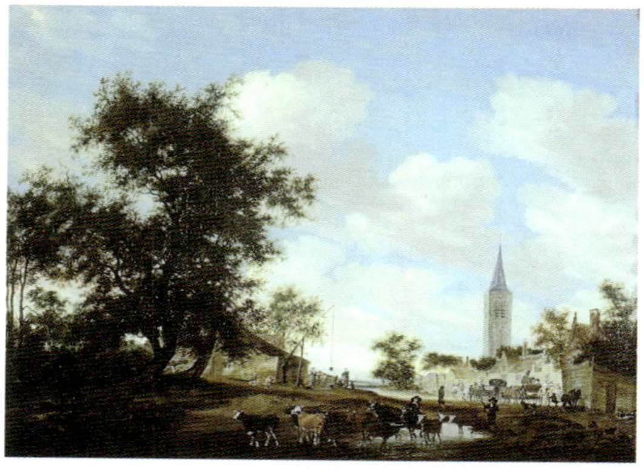

A1065; oil on canvas, 112 × 150 cm
Signed in monogram and dated: *SVR 1657*
Prov.: Richard Fort; Asher Wertheimer and by descent
Presented by Mrs J.C. Conway, 1972; WA1972.8

White 1999, p. 137

Salomon van Ruysdael worked mainly in Haarlem where he influenced the fashion for tonal landscape painting. He appears to have travelled extensively in the Netherlands and incorporated details of the places he visited into his paintings. The village of Beverwijck which appears in this painting is situated on the road to Alkmaar, north of Haarlem.

Gyula Sajó
(1918 – 1989)

On the Balcony

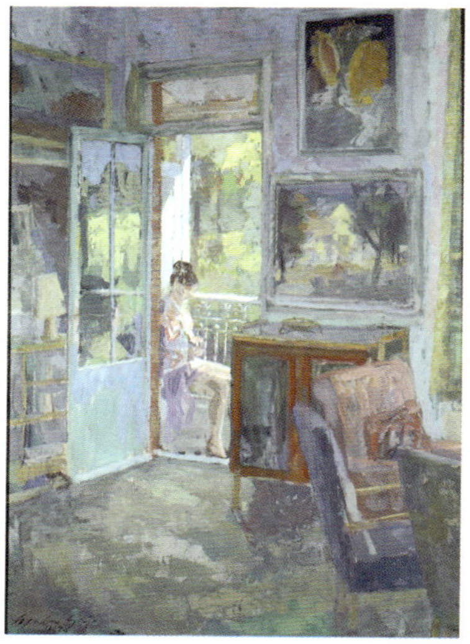

A1177; tempera on hardboard, 76 × 107 cm
Signed and dated: *Gyula Sajo 1967*
Presented by Mrs Erzsèbet Sajó, the artist's widow, 1993; WA1993.333

London 1989

Sajó trained in Hungary and worked first in Austria before he moved in 1957 to Britain, where he settled in Worthing, Sussex. The view represents a part of the sitting-room in his house-cum-atelier, showing his wife Erzsèbet sitting on the balcony. This arrangement allowed Sajó to show various effects of light and shadow using several manners of applying the paint.

Paul Sandby
(1731 – 1809)

The Old Rectory Barn, Denton

A245; oil on canvas, 35 × 43 cm
Presented by the Revd Greville John Chester, 1887; WA1887.3

Sandby 1892, p. 223

Sandby's brother, the Revd George Sandby, D.D., was Rector of Denton, Norfolk, from 1751 to 1807. A watercolour of the same subject is in the Ashmolean. The painting was accidentally destroyed in 1965.

Frederick Sandys
(1829 – 1904)

Gentle Spring

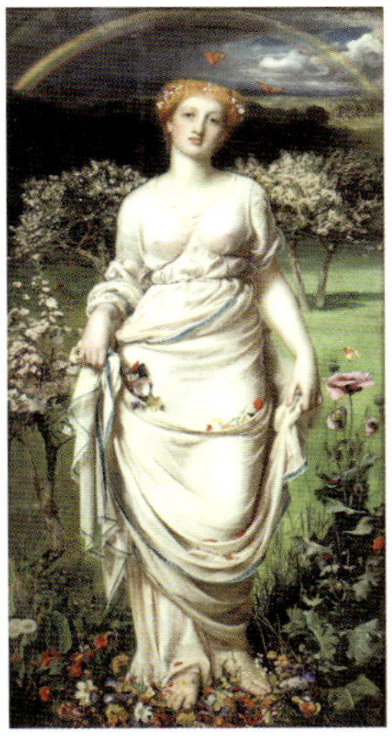

A372; oil on canvas, 121 × 64 cm
Prov.: Ernest Gambart; A.A. Ionides and by descent
Presented by Captain R. Langton Douglas in memory of his son, Lt Archibald Douglas, killed in action, 1916, 1923; WA1923.2

Brown 1987, no. 93; Elzea 2001, no. 2.A.70

Exhibited at the Royal Academy in 1865 accompanied in the catalogue by a sonnet by the artist's friend, Charles Algernon Swinburne. The figure was painted in the garden of the poet and novelist, George Meredith. She represents Proserpina returning from the land of the dead. Sandys joined Rossetti's circle in 1857 and lived with him in Cheyne Walk for most of 1866.

John Singer Sargent
(1856 – 1925)

A Balustrade

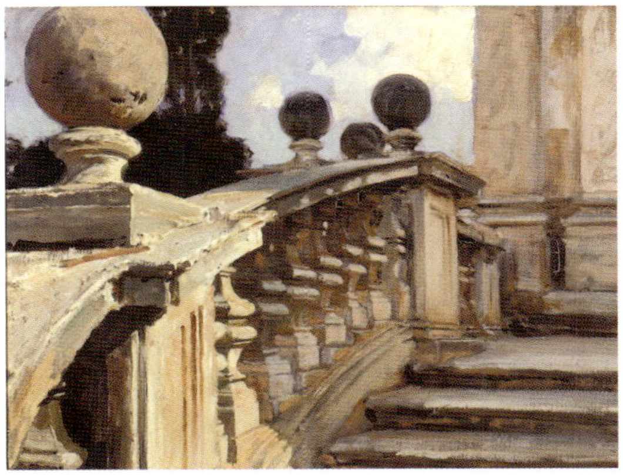

A395; oil on canvas, 55 × 71 cm
Presented by the artist's sisters, Mrs Ormond and Miss Emily Sargent, 1929; WA1929.7

Eustace 1999, no. 4; Robertson 2003, pp. 184–5

The balustrade leads to the front door of the church of SS Domenico e Sisto in Rome. During his visits to Italy, Sargent sought relief from painting portraits and turned to landscapes, both in oils and watercolours. The artist described this as 'a study of a magnificent curved staircase and balustrade, leading to a grand façade that would reduce a millionaire to a worm'. He later used the study for the background to a portrait of Charles E. Eliot, President of Harvard University (Harvard).

Ethel Sands
(1873 – 1962)

A dressing Room

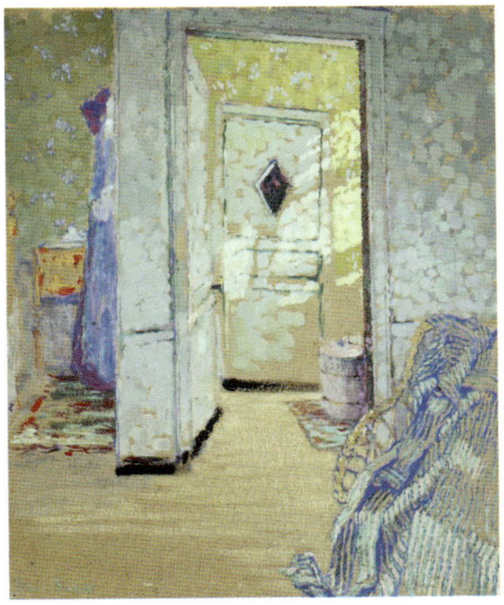

A767; oil on millboard, 46 × 38 cm
Signed: *Ethel Sands*
Prov.: Logan Pearsall Smith
Presented by the artist, 1948; WA1948.81

The influence of Vuillard is strongly marked. There is a less finished version of the same composition on the verso.

Sano di Pietro
(1405/6 – 1481)

The Virgin and Child with St Jerome, St Catherine of Alexandria and two Angels

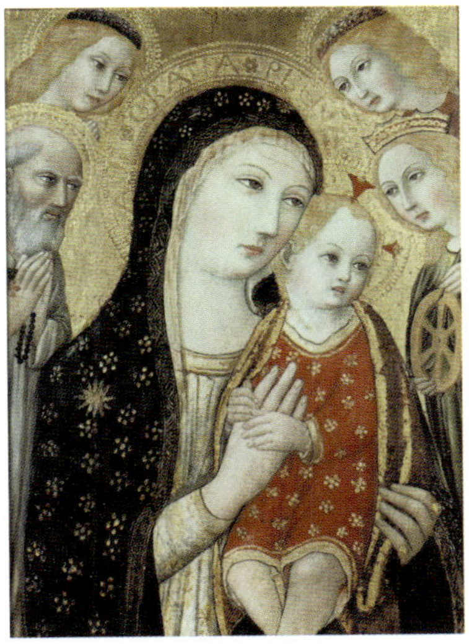

A76; tempera and gilding on panel, 49.7 × 35.4 cm
Inscribed: *AVE GRATIA PLENA* on the Virgin's halo
Fox-Strangways Gift, 1850; WA1850.22

Lloyd 1977, pp. 158–9

Sano di Pietro was a refined craftsman who produced a large number of devotional works for private homes and for monastic cells. A76 is a characteristic type of composition from his later career, around 1470. The star on the Virgin's robe refers to her evocation as Stella Maris (Star of the Sea) in litanies. St Jerome (*c* 342–420) is identifiable by his penitential stance; St Catherine wears a crown and holds a wheel, referring to her attempted martyrdom.

Copy after Andrea del Sarto
(1486 – 1530)

The Last Supper

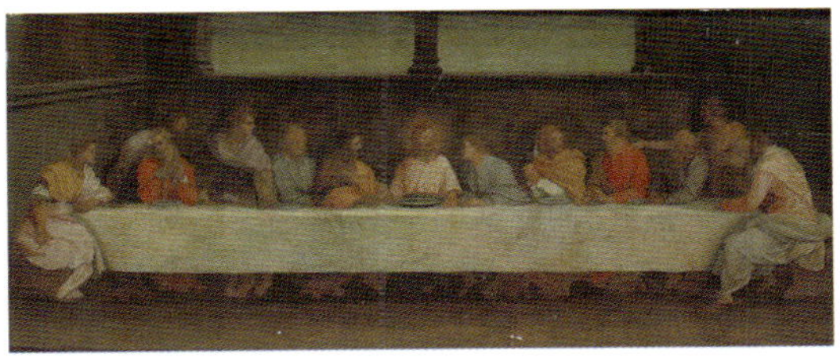

A102; oil on panel, 74 × 179 cm
Fox-Strangways Gift, 1850; WA1850.33

Lloyd 1977, pp. 159–60

A102 is a free copy of the fresco in the refectory of the Vallombrosan monastery of San Salvi, Florence, painted by Sarto probably *c.* 1526–7: a notable variation is with the background, where an expanse of open sky replaces the indoor setting, while there are other differences in detail. Traditionally but erroneously referred to as a preparatory sketch for the fresco, A102 is probably by an artist of the late 16th century when there was a revival of interest in Florence in the art of Sarto.

Studio of Giovanni Battista Salvi, called Sassoferrato
(1609 – 1685)

Mater Dolorosa

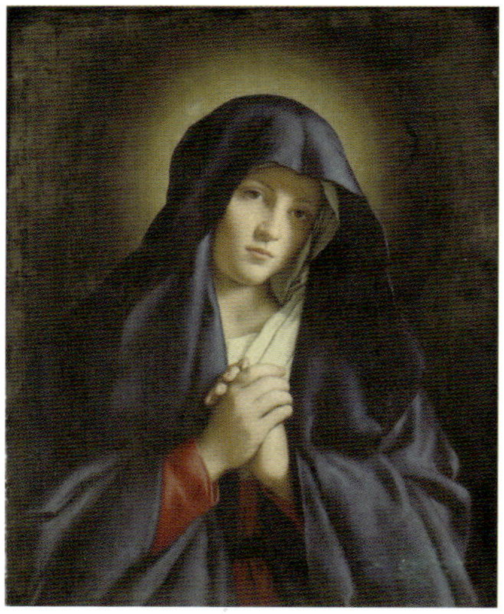

A294; oil on canvas, 75 × 60 cm
Bequeathed by John D. Chambers, 1897; WA1897.20

Images of the veiled Madonna, hands clasped in prayer and gazing directly at the viewer, were popular in the Counter-Reformation period: she is perceived as a bereaved figure, contemplating the sacrifice of her Son. Sassoferrato painted many versions of this subject and the number of early copies and variations testify to its success. A294 is of fine quality and may be from his studio.

Ippolito Scarsella, called Lo Scarsellino
(*c.* 1550 – 1620)

The Holy Family with the young St John the Baptist

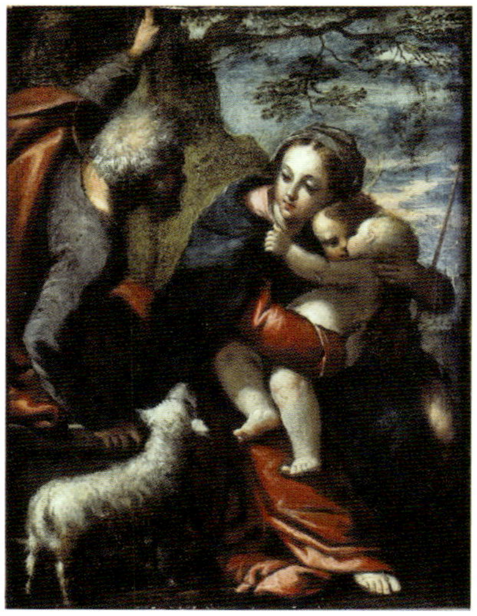

Oil on panel, 28 × 20.8 cm
Prov.: Earls of Pembroke, Wilton House, before 1731 and by descent until 1951
Mahon loan, 1999; WA.L.99.17

Finaldi and Kitson 1997, no. 72

The Ferrara-born artist apparently studied in Venice with Veronese from *c.* 1570 and was deeply interested in the art of the Carracci. His rich handling of paint and tender approach to devotional subjects is seen in this small painting of *c.* 1590.

Godfried Schalcken
(1643 – 1706)

A Vase of Flowers

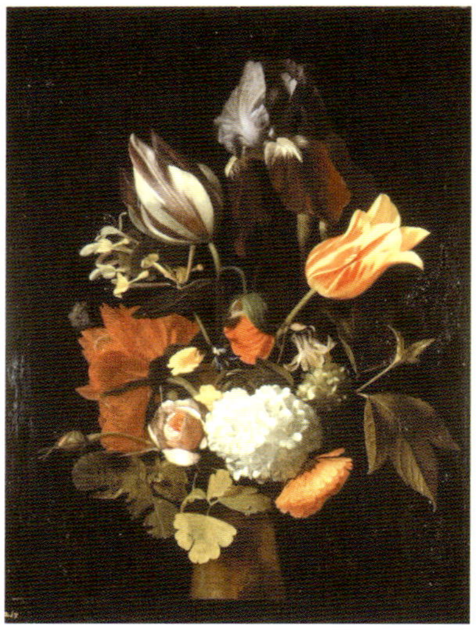

A592; oil on panel, 44 × 32 cm
Prov.: J. Herbrand
Daisy Linda Ward Bequest, 1939; WA1940.2.68

Meijer 2003, no. 67

Trained by Hoogstraaten in Dordrecht and by Gerard Dou in Leiden, Schalcken became a figure painter, treating still life only occasionally. Apart from this bouquet, only two other still-life paintings by him are known. The details of the flowers are realistically painted in the smooth 'fine manner' of Dou. The *trompe-l'oeil* frame adds an additional element of illusionism to the effect. The smooth handling suggests a relatively early date, perhaps in the 1670s.

Style of Roelandt Savery
(1576 – 1639)

Elijah at the Brook Kerith

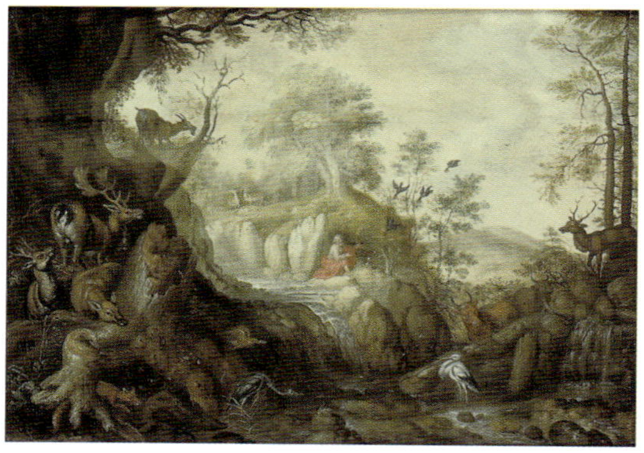

A408; oil on panel, 37 × 51 cm
Presented by Francis Falconer Madan through the National Art Collections Fund, 1931; WA1931.17

White 1999, p. 141

The quality suggests this is a repetition by another hand of a painting on copper, signed by Savery and dated 1634, in the Rijksmuseum, Amsterdam. It has been suggested that it might be a late work by Roelandt's nephew, Hans II Savery (1589–1654), who lived and worked with his uncle in Utrecht from about 1619. Elijah is shown as he is described in the Old Testament (1 Kings 17: 5–6), sustained by ravens who brought bread and meat to his retreat in the ravine of Kerith.

Ippolito Scarsella, called Lo Scarsellino
(*c.* 1550 – 1620)

The Infant Christ blessing the Virgin

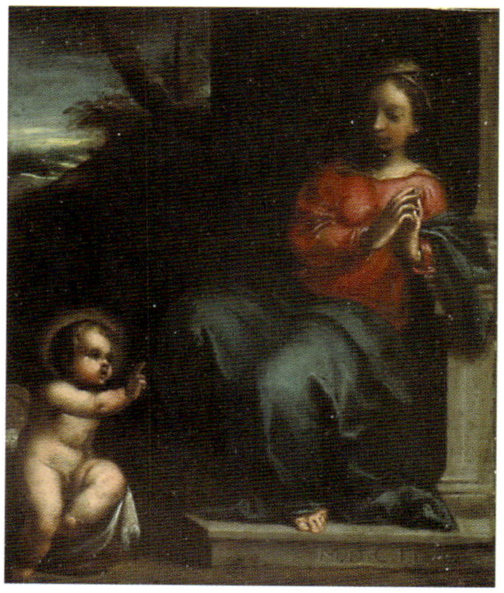

A867; oil on copper (glued to a larger panel), 15 × 12 cm
Inscribed: *MDCII*
Purchased, 1953; WA1953.77

Scarsellino made numerous small devotional works characterised by their intimacy and by the appearance of domestic detail – here, the Child is seated on the edge of a cradle. Dated works are unusual, but some importance may have been attached to the date of 1602 perhaps by the patron. In A867 Scarsellino recalls the art of Parmigianino while retaining affinities with the religious art of the Carracci.

Bartolomeo Schedoni
(1578 – 1615)

The Holy Family with the young St John the Baptist

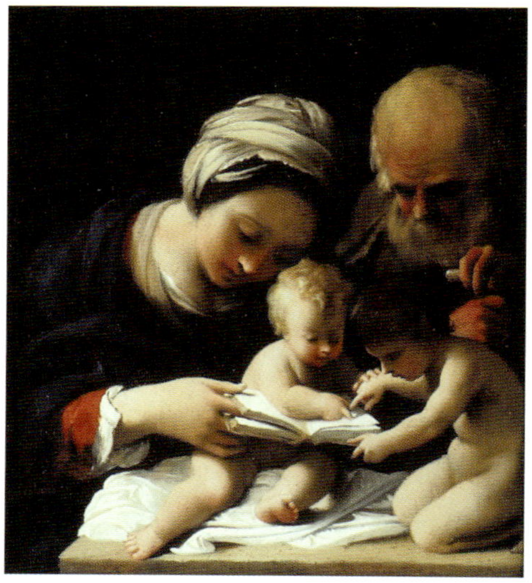

A789; oil on panel, 23 × 21 cm
Prov.: Alfred de Rothschild; Sir Arthur Ellis
Purchased, 1950; WA1950.74

Negro and Roio 2000, no. 42

The Child guides the hand of St John in a tender domestic scene that also contains a clear religious message. Schedoni made a speciality of this type of intimate devotional picture for private clients: here his interest in the art of Ludovico Carracci is apparent. A variation of similar size is in the Uffizi; a similar composition of the Holy Family, with a landscape background, is in the Mahon Collection.

Attributed to Giovanni di Ser Giovanni, called Lo Scheggia
(1407 – 1486)

A Tournament

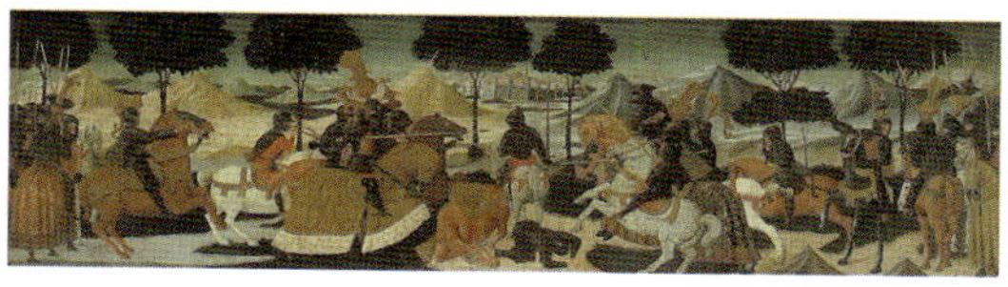

A91; tempera and gilding on panel, 44 × 164 cm
Fox-Strangways Gift, 1850; WA1850.29

Lloyd 1977, pp. 63–4; Bellosi and Haines 1999, pp. 86, 90

The brother of Masaccio, Lo Scheggia was an eclectic artist who painted numerous works for domestic settings. This type of decorative, ceremonial subject is often found on *cassone* panels. Although the picture is much abraded, it has sufficient affinities with the mature work of Lo Scheggia to make the attribution convincing.

Cornelis Schut
(1597 – 1655)

The Nativity

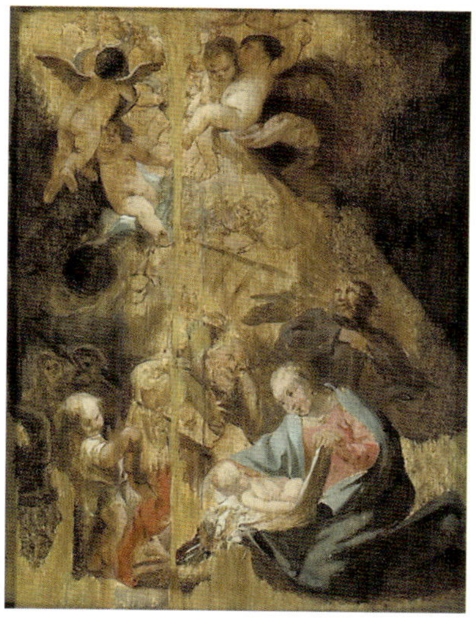

A178; oil on panel, 31 × 23 cm
Chambers Hall Gift, 1855; WA1855.570

White 1999, p. 141

Cornelis Shut was an engraver and painter of historical, religious and allegorical subjects from Antwerp. This is evidently a sketch for an otherwise unknown composition.

Style of Samuel Scott
(*c.* 1702 – 1772)

The Thames at Greenwich

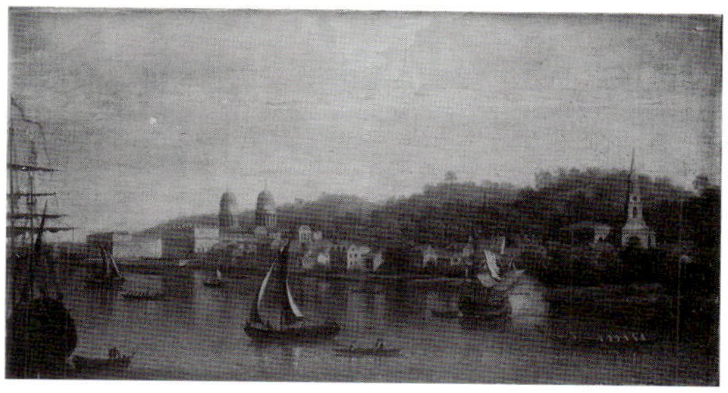

A229; oil on canvas, 60 × 103 cm
Bequeathed by the Revd Noel Thomas Ellison, 1861; WA1861.2

Samuel Scott had studios in Covent Garden and Twickenham, from which came a flood of views of London, inspired by the vogue for Canaletto. This work and the following have been attributed to William James (active 1761–1771), on no convincing grounds.
This is a view of Greenwich Hospital with St Alphege's Church on the right. Related paintings of similar views are in the Royal Collection, the Athenaeum and elsewhere.

Attributed to Paolo Schiavo
(1397 – 1478)

David reproved by Nathan

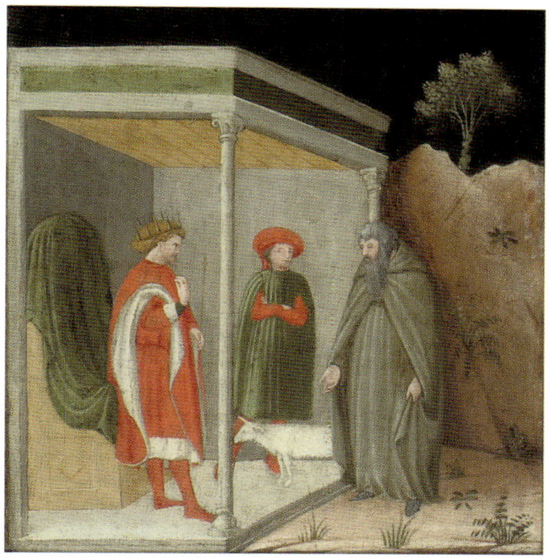

A334; tempera on panel, 36.6 × 38.7 cm
Presented by Mrs James Reddie Anderson, 1913; WA1913.3

Lloyd 1977, pp. 62–3

David displeased God by commanding the death of Uriah and Nathan was sent to rebuke him and prophesy his punishment (II Samuel 2: 1–25). A334 was probably one of a series of related narratives. According to Vasari, Schiavo took pains to imitate the style of his master Masolino, but his figures are often weakly drawn. The work of this obscure artist is becoming more clearly defined and an attribution to Schiavo himself has recently been suggested.

Cornelis Schut
(1597 – 1655)

Allegory on the Death of Thomas Howard, Earl of Arundel

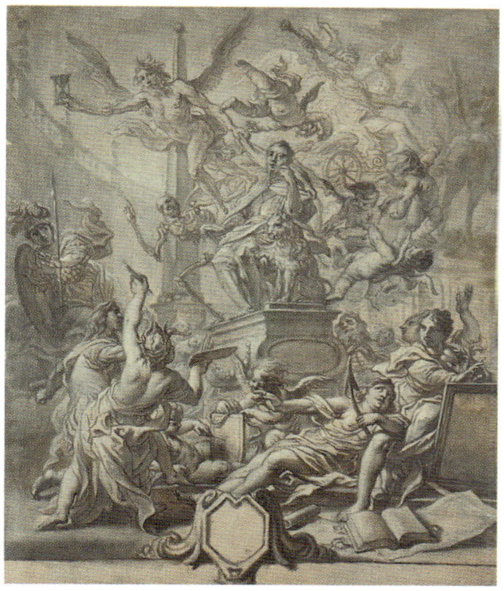

Oil, wash, bodycolour and ink on paper, mounted as a drawing, 38.7 × 31.6 cm
Presented by Mrs A.H. Sutherland, 1837; WA.C.I.44

Brown 1982, no. 207

This monochrome sketch was prepared for a print etched by Wencelaus Hollar in memory of Thomas Howard, 2nd Earl of Arundel, who died in Padua in 1646. The composition is based on a design by the Italian sculptor, Fanelli, for the Earl's tomb. The agitated figures represent the Virtues and the Arts.

Style of Samuel Scott
(*c.* 1702 – 1772)

The Thames at Chelsea Hospital

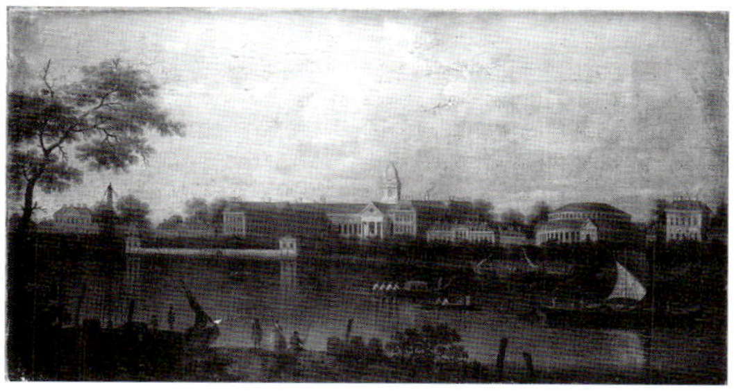

A230; oil on canvas, 60 × 112 cm
Bequeathed by the Revd Noel Thomas Ellison, 1861; WA1861.1

Chelsea Hospital, built by Charles II to the designs of Sir Christopher Wren, is seen from the south bank of the Thames. To the right stands Ranelagh Gardens and the Rotunda which was opened in 1742.

Style of Samuel Scott
(*c.* 1702 – 1772)

The Thames at Lambeth

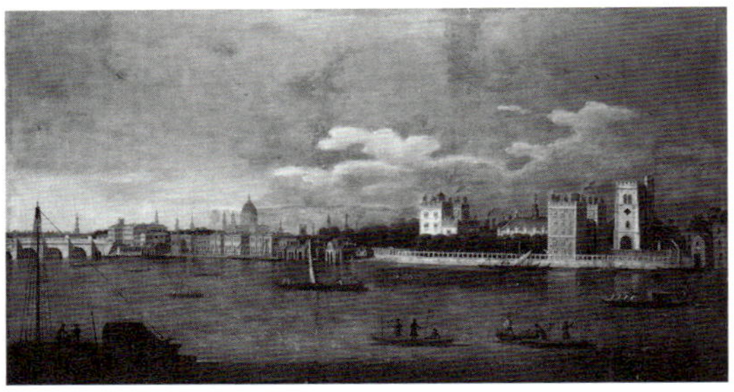

A233; oil on canvas, 62 × 117 cm
Prov.: Dr Cyril Jackson, Dean of Christ Church; Canon Pett and by descent
Bequeathed by Mrs Anne Hind, 1870; WA1870.2

A view looking from Millbank towards Lambeth Palace and Lambeth Church, with Westminster Bridge and St Paul's Cathedral beyond.

William Bell Scott
(1811 – 1890)

Keats's Grave

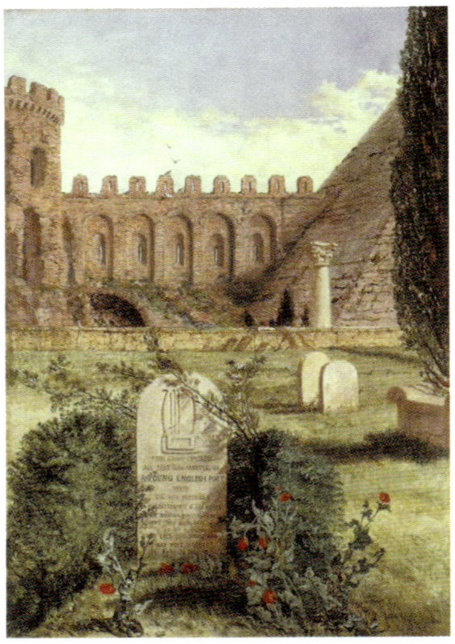

A263; oil on canvas, 48.8 × 33.4 cm
Signed and dated: *W.B.S. Rome June 1873*
Presented by Miss Alice Boyd, 1893; WA1893.3

Brown 1987, no. 94

The poet John Keats (1795–1821) was buried in the New Protestant Cemetery in Rome on 26 February 1821. Arthur Severn arranged the tombstone, which bears the epitaph: *THIS GRAVE CONTAINS ALL THAT WAS MORTAL OF A YOUNG ENGLISH POET WHO ON HIS DEATH-BED In the BITTERNESS of his HEART* [at] *the malicious power of his* [enemies] *desired these words to be engrav[ed] on his tombstone "HERE LIES ONE WHOSE NAME WAS WRIT IN WATER" Feby 24 1821.*

Attributed to Sebastiano Secante
(active 1518 – 1576)

The Virgin and Child with Sts Stephen, Augustine, Jude and Jerome

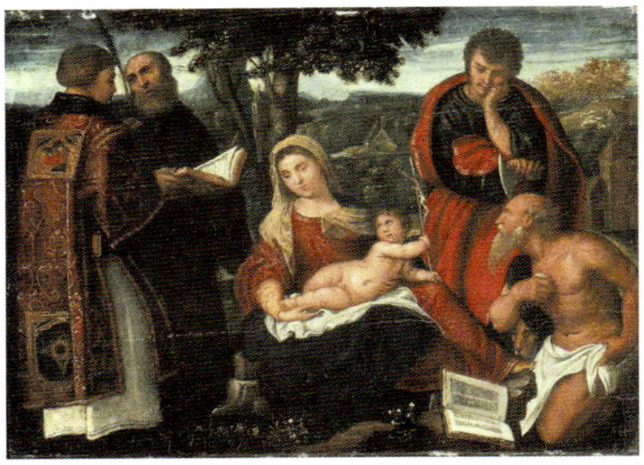

A939; oil on panel, 24 × 38 cm
Prov.: Palazzo Porto, Vicenza; F.E. Sotheby
Purchased, 1960; WA1960.56

Lloyd 1977, pp. 160–2

St Stephen, clothed as a deacon, carries a martyr's palm, while Augustine wears the robes of his Order: both he and Jerome, as Doctors of the Church, are shown with books. The Apostle Jude carries an axe, the instrument of his martyrdom. Prototypes for the group on the left and for the figure of St Jerome, are found in Titian's work of *c.* 1509–10 and *c.* 1530, while the strongly characterized Child derives in reverse from Raphael's *Bridgewater Madonna* of *c.* 1507–8. A939 may date from *c.* 1540–50.

Style of Samuel Scott
(*c.* 1702 – 1772)

The Thames at the Savoy

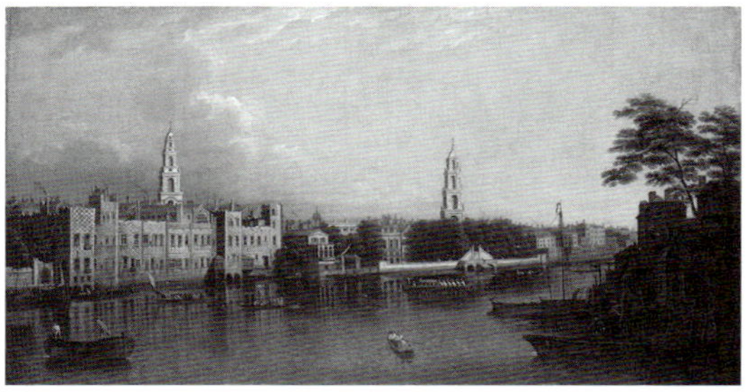

A234; oil on canvas, 56 × 111 cm
Prov.: Dr Cyril Jackson; Canon Pett and by descent
Bequeathed by Mrs Anne Hind, 1870; WA1870.3

A view of the Savoy Palace, with Somerset House beyond. The prominent spires are of the churches of St Mary-le-Strand (left) and St Clement Danes (right). A number of versions of this view exist, including one in the Royal Collection.

William Bell Scott
(1811 – 1890)

Shelley's Grave

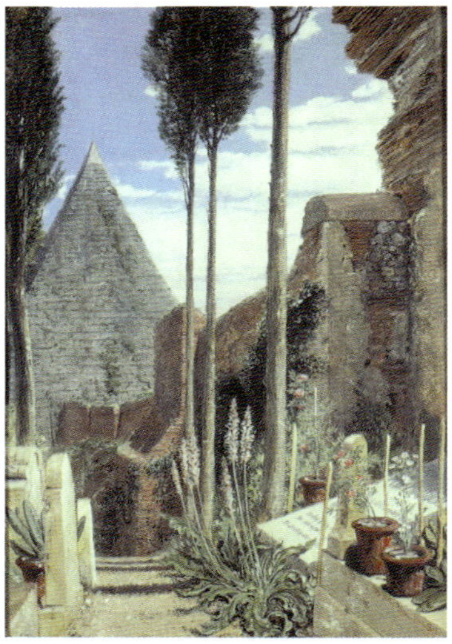

A264; oil on canvas, 48.2 × 33 cm
Signed and dated: *WB. Scott. Rome. June. 1873*
Presented by Miss Alice Boyd, 1893; WA1893.2

Percy Bysshe Shelley (1792–1822) was buried close to the Pyramid of Caius Cestius in the Old Protestant Cemetery, Rome on 7 December 1822. The Latin epitaph partly visible in this picture was composed by Leigh Hunt.

Thomas Seddon
(1821 – 1856)

View on the Nile

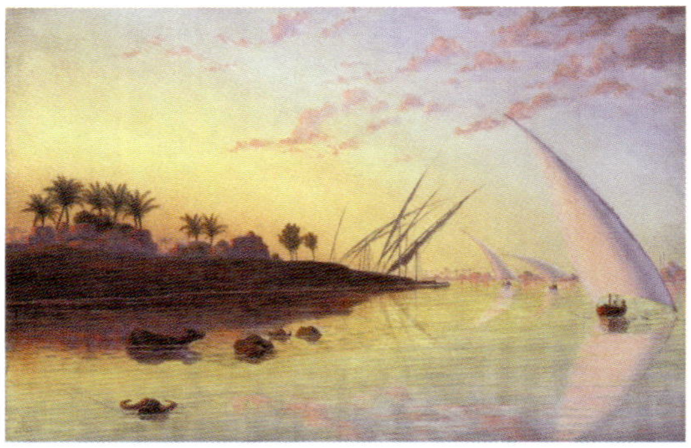

A708a; oil on canvas, 20 × 31 cm
Signed in monogram and dated: *TS 1855*
Presented by Miss H.M. Virtue-Tebbs, 1944; WA1944.31

Brown 1987, no. 47; Staley 2001, pp. 137–8

Following a serious illness, Seddon travelled to Egypt in the winter of 1853–4, where he met Holman Hunt. He made two trips up the Nile, in December 1853 and May 1854, and found the scenery more beautiful than he expected. This painting was executed in London. It recalls his description of 'the picturesque palm trees and long sloping yards of the boats, looking black as night against the red golden sky'.

André Dunoyer de Segonzac
(1884 – 1974)

The Lockgate

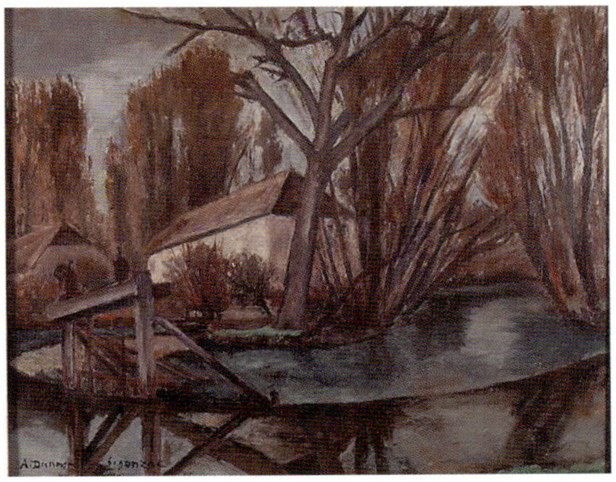

A637; oil on canvas, 81 × 100 cm
Signed: *Segonzac*
Hindley Smith Bequest, 1939; WA1940.1.19

Segonzac's work was brought to England in the years after the First World War chiefly by the dealer, Percy Moore Turner, from whom Hindley Smith bought many of the works in his collection. It is probable that this painting came from the same source and dates from shortly after 1918.

Gioacchino Serangeli
(1768 – 1852)

Portrait of a young Woman

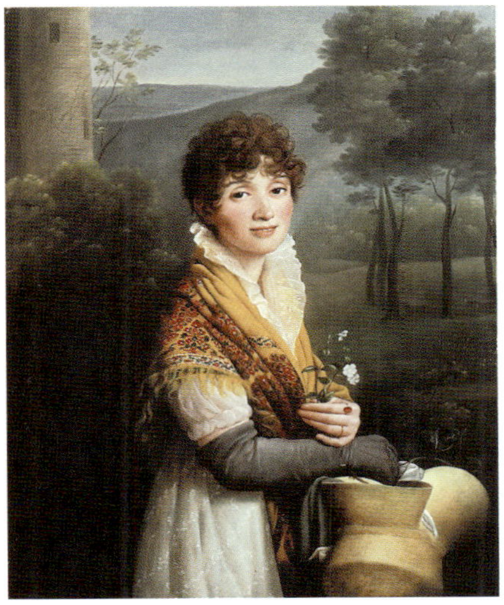

A1063; oil on canvas, 91.7 × 73.6 cm
Prov.: Herner Wengraf
Purchased, 1971; WA1971.387

Judging by the costume, the portrait probably dates from *c.* 1807–10. Serangeli, a pupil of David, exhibited some portraits at the Salon in addition to history paintings, but none are identifiable with A1063. The outdoor setting suggests the influence of English portraiture. Serangeli returned to Italy in 1812, working first in Milan and then as court painter in Turin.

Charles Haslewood Shannon
(1863 – 1937)

The Apple Gatherers

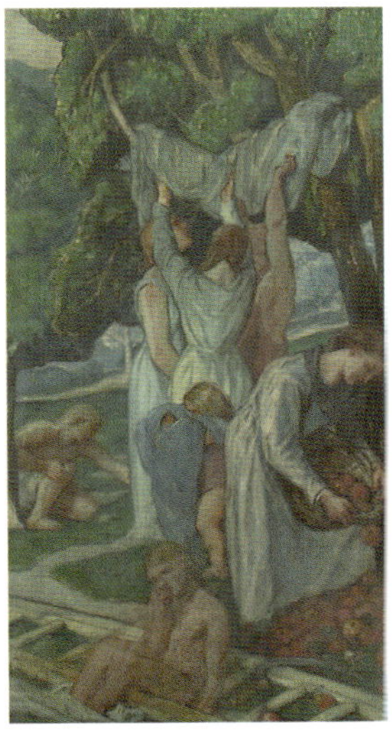

A683; oil on canvas, 175 × 92 cm
Presented by Francis Howard, 1941; WA1941.57

Christian 1989, no. 254

The subject, the flat and dry handling and the monumental quality of the figures show Shannon's debt to Puvis de Chavannes. The painting has been dated to *c.* 1910 and is a variation on one of the artist's favourite themes.

Domingos António de Sequeira
(1768 – 1837)

Adriao Ribeiro Neves

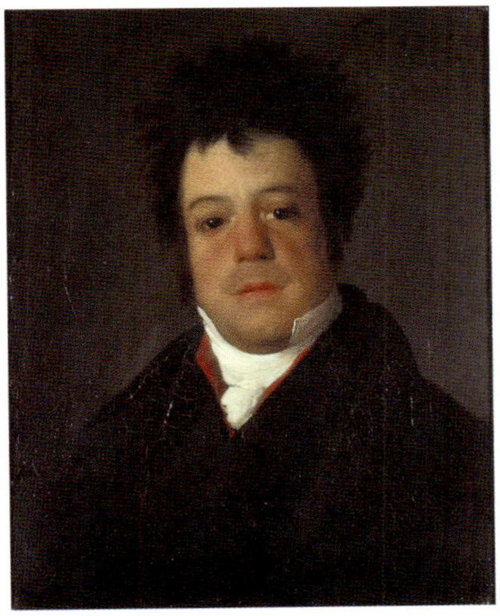

A741; oil on canvas, 40 × 32 cm
Inscribed on the stretcher: *Adriao Ribeiro Neves, adude 43 por Domingos Antonio da Sequeira, pintou em Paris 1825*
Prov.: Tomás Harris; Percy Moore Turner
Purchased, 1947; WA1947.270

Carvalho 1996, no. 65

Trained in Lisbon and Rome, Sequeira was court painter in Lisbon from 1802. He left Portugal for France in 1823, exhibiting at the Paris Salon in 1824. The sitter was apparently an intimate friend of the artist and they were reunited in Paris as expatriate Portuguese liberals.

Joseph Severn
(1793 – 1879)

Ariel riding on a Bat

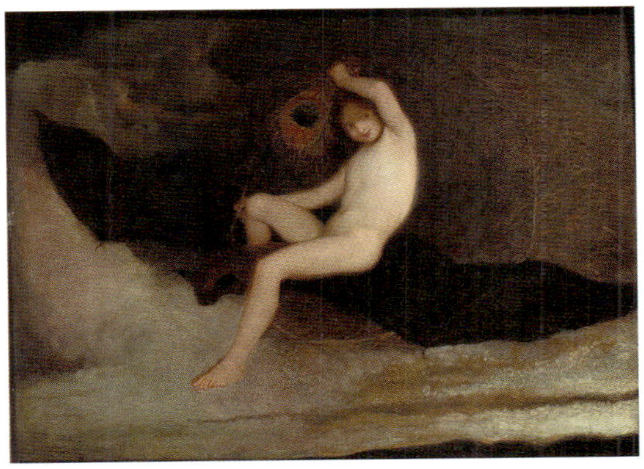

A369; oil on panel, 53 × 39 cm
Bequeathed by the Revd Robert Finch, 1830; WA1921.6

Sharp 1892, p. 273

This painting, in ruinous condition owing to the bitumen with which it was painted, represents Ariel flying on a bat's back, holding a peacock's feather. The subject occupied Severn for over ten years: the first painting is dated 1826 (Victoria and Albert Museum, London) and he exhibited others in 1830, 1836 and 1838. This version was shown to enthusiastic reviews in 1830, when it was bought by Finch, who had already bought the preparatory sketch.

Joshua Shaw of Bath
(1776 – 1861)

Figure by a wooded Stream

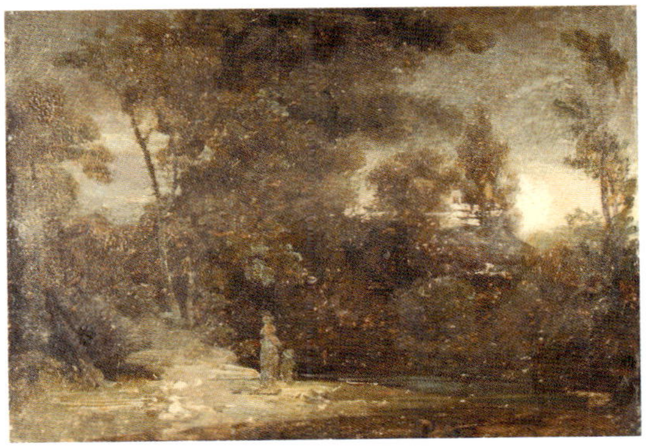

A1095; oil on board, 25 × 36 cm
Inscribed on the reverse: *Nov 30 1810 / Painted by J. Shaw of Bath in half an hour.*
Presented by Gerald Reitlinger, 1972; WA1978.36

Shaw lived at Bath between 1802 and 1817 and exhibited views of places popular with artists in search of the picturesque, including Derbyshire and Wales.

Richard Shirley Smith
(b. 1935)

Still Life with Marble Foot

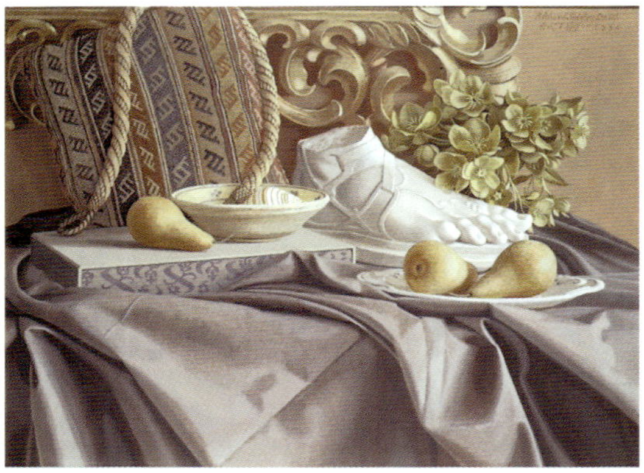

A1203; acrylic on board, varnished, 45.2 × 58.7 cm
Signed, dated and dedicated: *Richard Shirley Smith / for A.W.S. ~ 1996*
Presented by friends of Anne Stevens to commemorate her voluntary work for the Museum (1976–1995), 1996; WA1996.482

Many of Richard Shirley Smith's subjects occupy a setting which seems somewhat unreal. By comparison with others, this painting is untypically straightforward, combining the foot of a sculpture set on a table or sofa with a book, some pears and a bunch of flowers. The surface, as is usual in his work, has a smooth sophistication, undisturbed by any trace of brushwork.

Walter Richard Sickert
(1860 – 1942)

St Mark's, Venice: The West Front

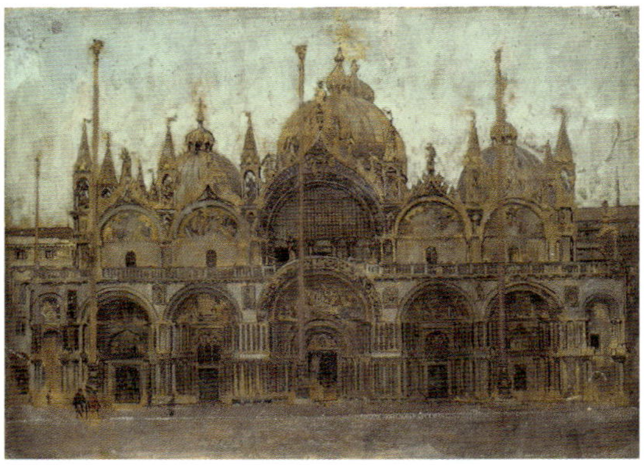

A660; oil on paper on panel, mounted as a drawing, 22 × 31 cm
Signed: *Sickert.*
Bequeathed by Montague Shearman through the Contemporary Art Society, 1940; WA1940.4.2

Browse 1960, no. 1; Baron 1973, no. 81

This study was painted during Sickert's visit to Venice in 1895, together with numerous other sketches. These served as the basis for a series of larger paintings made in Venice in 1895–6 and in London, 1896–8.

Walter Richard Sickert
(1860 – 1942)

Venetian Woman

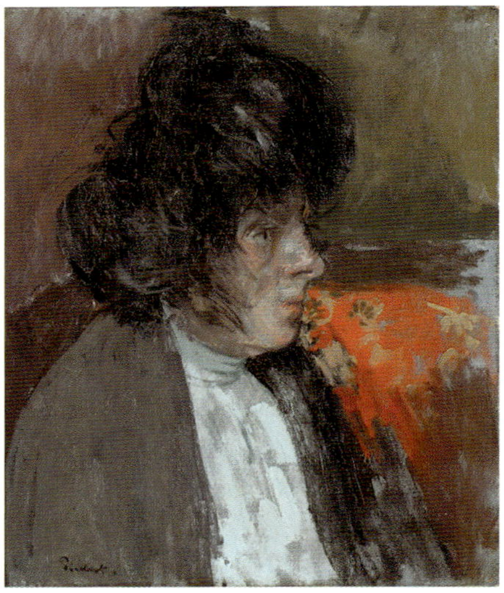

A1236; oil on canvas, 53.3 × 63.5 cm
Signed: *Sickert*
Presented by the Christopher Sands Trust, 2001; WA2001.34

Sickert painted a number of portraits of Venetian characters in 1903–4, notably La Giuseppina and her elderly mother, and Carolina dell'Aqua. This portrait probably dates from this period; the model has not been identified.

Style of Jan Siberechts
(1627 – 1703)

Landscape with Cattle and a Couple under a Tree

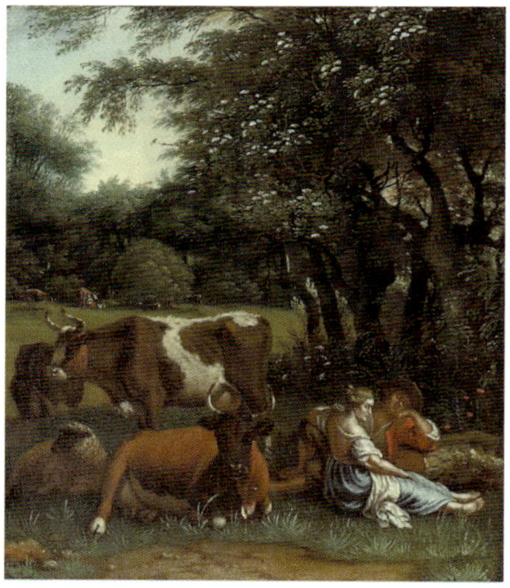

A983; oil on canvas, 36 × 30 cm
Inscribed: *J sibrechts / 1694*
Prov.: the Revd J.C. Uppleby
Madan Bequest, 1962; WA1962.17.25

White 1999, p. 143

The painting is characteristic of Siberechts's work in Antwerp where he lived until 1672. After moving to England in the 1670s, he began to paint more extensive landscapes with smaller figures. The date inscribed on this painting, which is too late for a work of this type, and the hard manner in which it is painted, suggest it is not by Siberechts himself.

Walter Richard Sickert
(1860 – 1942)

The Bridge of Sighs, Venice

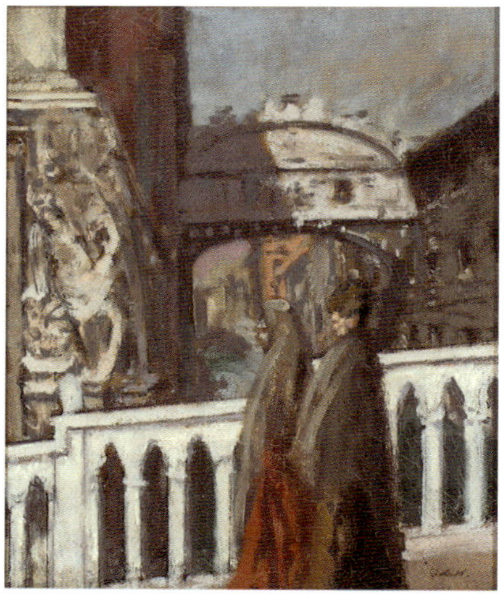

A1234; oil on canvas, 35.6 × 30.5 cm
Signed: *Sickert*
Prov.: Morton Sands and by descent
Presented by the Christopher Sands Trust, 2001; WA2001.32

Browse 1960, under no. 28; Baron 1973, no. 136

One of the most popular tourist attractions in Venice, the Bridge of Sighs joins the ducal palace to the prison. This work was probably painted around 1901.

Walter Richard Sickert
(1860 – 1942)

The Lady in the Gondola

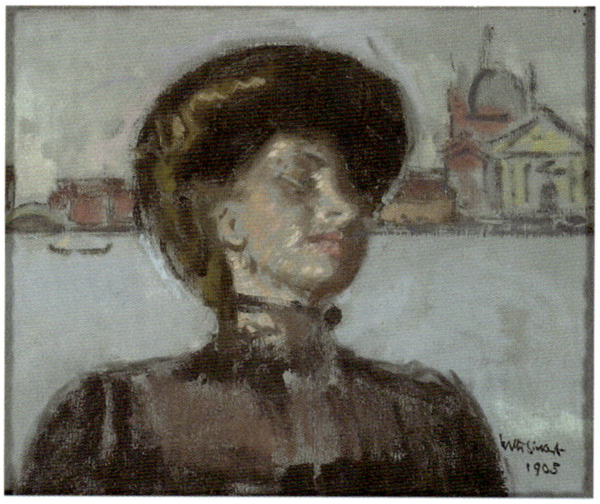

A635; oil on canvas, 30 × 35 cm
Signed and dated: *Sickert. 1905*
Hindley Smith Bequest, 1939; WA1940.1.17

Browse 1960, no. 2; Baron 1973, no. 203

Elsie Ebsworth, Mrs George Swinton (1874–1966), was a society beauty who enjoyed a successful career as a singer. She sat to a number of artists, including Sargent, and became a close friend of Sickert, whom she met at a party given to enable Rodin to meet the most beautiful women in London. She had never been to Venice and this portrait was based on photographs and studies and painted in Sickert's studio in Fitzroy Street.

Walter Richard Sickert
(1860 – 1942)

Gaieté Montparnasse, dernière galerie de gauche

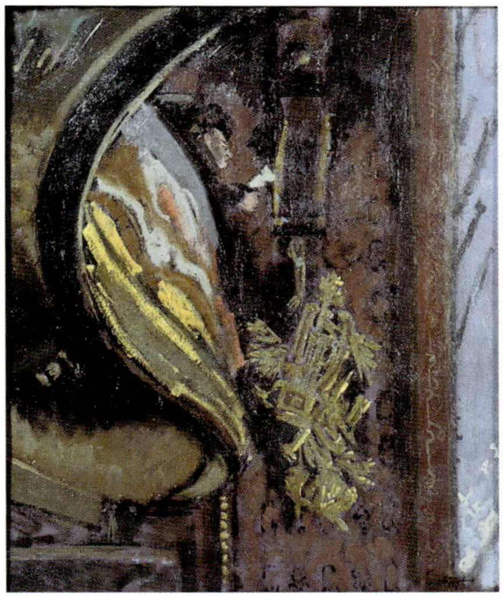

A1230; oil on canvas, 61 × 50 cm
Signed: *Sickert*
Prov.: Morton Sands and by descent
Presented by the Christopher Sands Trust, 2001; WA2001.28

Baron 1973, no. 237

Sickert went to Paris in the autumn of 1906 and began a new series of music-hall subjects. This is one of his most daring paintings of music-halls, the vibrant colours accentuating the vertiginous sweep of the balcony and the contrasting rectangular severity of the stage.

Walter Richard Sickert
(1860 – 1942)

Rue Aguado, Dieppe

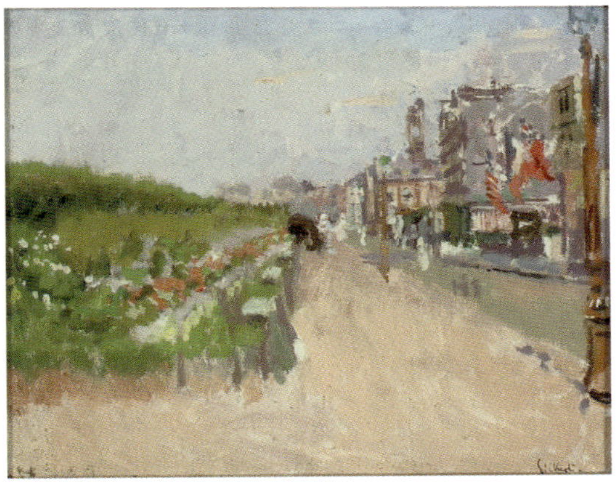

A948; oil on canvas, 33 × 41 cm
Signed: *Sickert.*
Bequeathed by J.E. Bullard, 1961; WA1961.28.1

On the outbreak of war in August 1914, Sickert moved to Dieppe and was able to concentrate on subjects he had first considered in the 1890s. He painted a number of views of the *Rue Aguado, Dieppe* in 1914, fascinated by the contrast of the flower beds edged with wire on the sea front and the street with the Hôtel Royal and flags on the right.

Walter Richard Sickert
(1860 – 1942)

Ennui

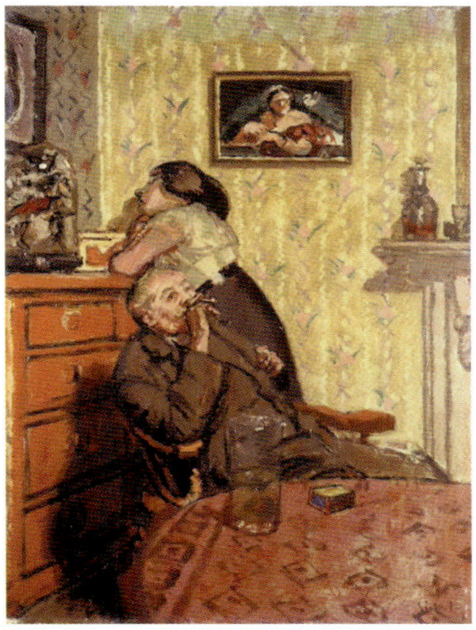

A618a; oil on canvas, 76 × 56 cm
Signed: *Sickert.*
Hindley Smith Bequest, 1939; WA1940.1.92

Browse 1960, no. 71 and p. 107, no. 3; Baron 1973, no. 313; Eustace 1999, no. 13

Generally dated 1917–18, this is the last of Sickert's four paintings on this theme. The first (Tate Britain), exhibited in 1914, was painted at 15 Fitzroy Street, London, W1, but inspired by 'a decayed first floor' on the corner of Granby Street and Mornington Square. Hubby, the model, was an old school friend of Sickert's fallen on hard times, whom he kept in beer. Numerous preparatory drawings survive, including several in the Ashmolean. It was this version of *Ennui*, exhibited at Agnew's gallery in 1933, which inspired Virginia Woolf's well-known account of the work published in her pamphlet on Sickert in 1934.

Walter Richard Sickert
(1860 – 1942)

The Brighton Pierrots

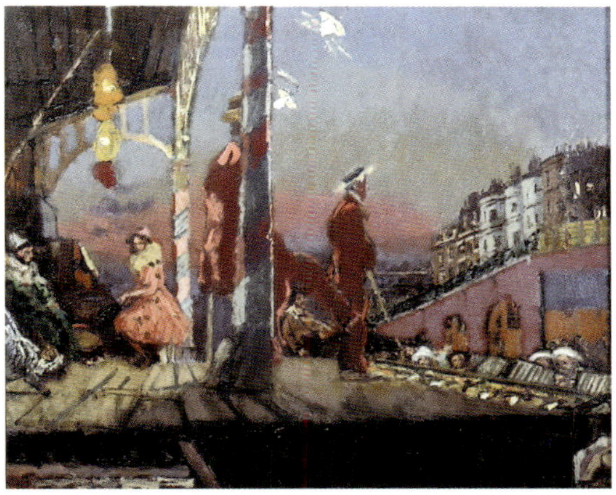

A1231; oil on canvas, 64 × 76.8 cm
Signed: *Sickert*
Prov.: Morton Sands and by descent
Presented by the Christopher Sands Trust, 2001; WA2001. 29

Browse 1960, under no. 69; Baron 1973, no. 364

Sickert stayed with his friend Walter Taylor at Brighton in August and September 1915 where he had access to the pierrots on the Promenade. He told Ethel Sands that he went every night for five weeks to the Pierrot Theatre. He painted A1231 on his return to London and sold it to Morton Sands. Sir William and Lady Jowett immediately commissioned a replica (Tate Britain).

Walter Richard Sickert
(1860 – 1942)

Santa Maria del Carmelo

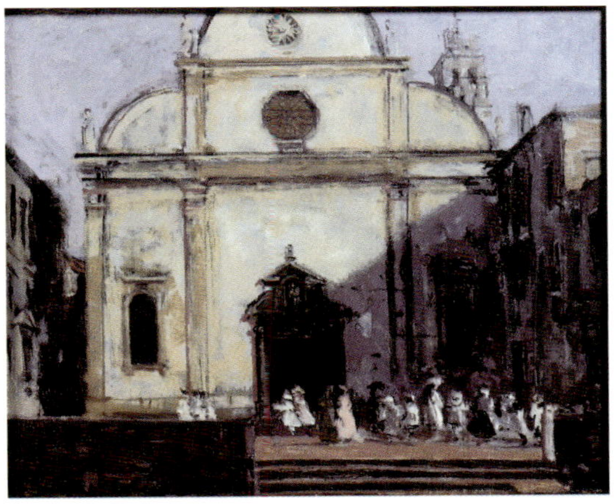

A1232; oil on canvas, 38.5 × 45.5 cm
Signed: *Sickert*
Prov.: Morton Sands and by descent
Presented by the Christopher Sands Trust, 2001; WA2001.30

The church of the Carmelites, popularly known as the Carmini, was essentially built in the early 16th century and stands near the Palazzo Zenobio. This painting probably dates from one of Sickert's visits to Venice in the late 1890s.

Walter Richard Sickert
(1860 – 1942)

The rue Notre-Dame des Champs, Paris: the Entrance to Sargent's Studio

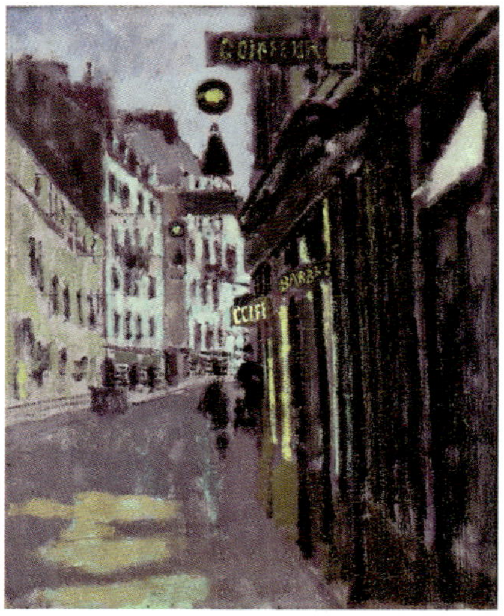

A1233; oil on canvas, 61.2 × 50.8 cm
Signed: *Sickert*
Prov.: Morton Sands and by descent
Presented by the Christopher Sands Trust, 2001: WA2001.31

Baron 1973, no. 286

This painting was probably exhibited in January 1907. It shows the entrance to John Singer Sargent's studio at 73 bis, rue Notre-Dame des Champs.

Walter Richard Sickert
(1860 – 1942)

The Bust of Tom Sayers; a Self-portrait

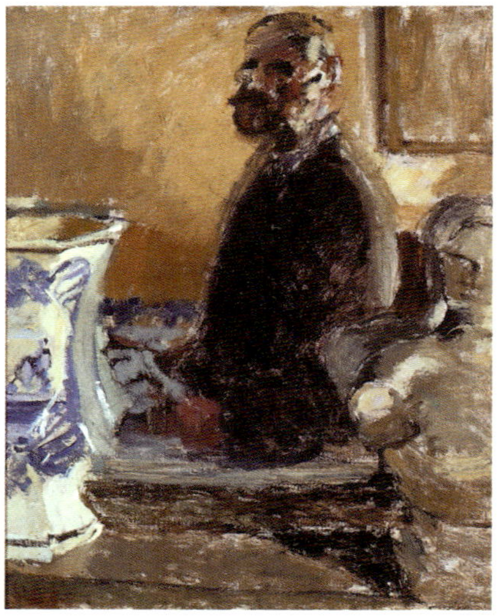

A1237; oil on canvas, 61 × 50.3 cm
Signed: *Sickert*
Prov.: Morton Sands and by descent
Presented by the Christopher Sands Trust, 2001; WA2001.35

Browse 1960, pl. 75; Baron 1973, no. 354

Sickert included the marble bust of the boxer Tom Sayers (1826–1865) in several works executed during the First World War. This is the earliest of Sickert's self-portraits to show him wearing a beard and was probably painted *c.* 1913–15.

Brigitte Simon
(b. 1926)

Au Delà

A1155; oil on canvas, 27 × 35 cm
Signed: *Brigitte Simon*: signed and inscribed twice on the back: *Brigitte Simon Au Delà*; and dated: *1977*
Prov.: Christopher Hewett
Presented by the Family of Christopher Hewett, 1987; WA1987.182

Oxford 1987, no. 114

Simon explores ways of creating a sense of space through effects of colour. In this case her palette is monochrome and the paint acts as the form and as a symbol of content.

Walter Richard Sickert
(1860 – 1942)

The rue Notre-Dame and the Quai Duquesne, Dieppe

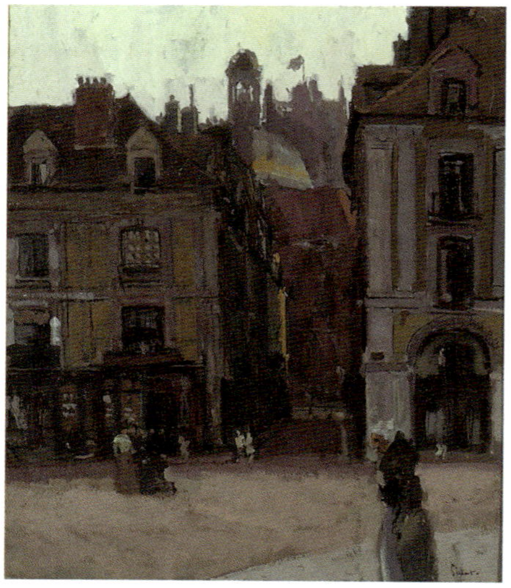

A1235; oil on canvas, 61.2 × 50.8 cm
Signed: *Sickert*
Prov.: Judge William Evans; Morton Sands and by descent
Presented by the Christopher Sands Trust, 2001; WA2001.33

Browse 1960, pl. 20; Baron 1973, no. 112

Sickert painted this subject many times in 1899–1900. This example shows a wide expanse of the Quai Duquesne in the foreground, with the rue Notre-Dame running at right angles towards the church of Notre Dame.

Walter Richard Sickert
(1860 – 1942)

Her Majesty's

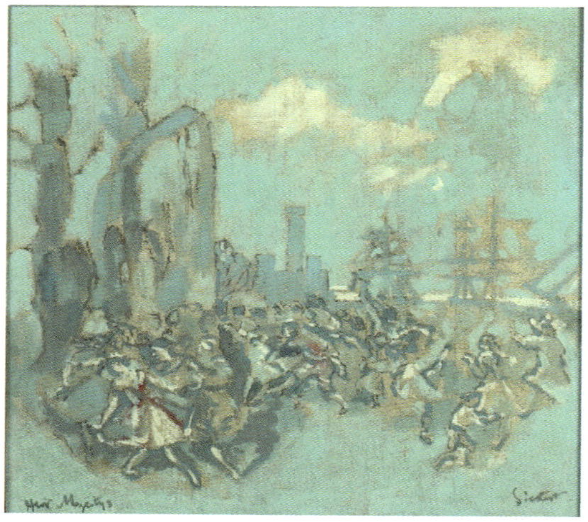

A870; oil on canvas, 60 × 65 cm
Inscribed: *Her Majestys*; and signed: *Sickert*
Presented by the Contemporary Art Society from the Bequest of Sir Edward Marsh, 1954; WA1954.85

Browse 1960, no. 4

One of Sickert's latest treatments of the music-hall theme he began exploring in the 1890s, this very diffuse painting has been dated to *c.* 1934.

Brigitte Simon
(b. 1926)

Tryptique: Tombeau de Charchoune

A1156; oil on canvas, 46 × 65 cm
Signed: *brigitte simon*
Prov.: Christopher Hewett
Presented by the Family of Christopher Hewett, 1987; WA1987.183

Oxford 1987, no. 115

The title, *Triptych: Charchoune's Tomb*, refers to the death of the Russian abstract painter, Serge Charchoune (1888–1975).

Simone dei Crocifissi
(active 1355 – 1399)

The Crucifixion (centre); *The Angel Gabriel and a Saint* (left); *The Virgin and St James* (right)

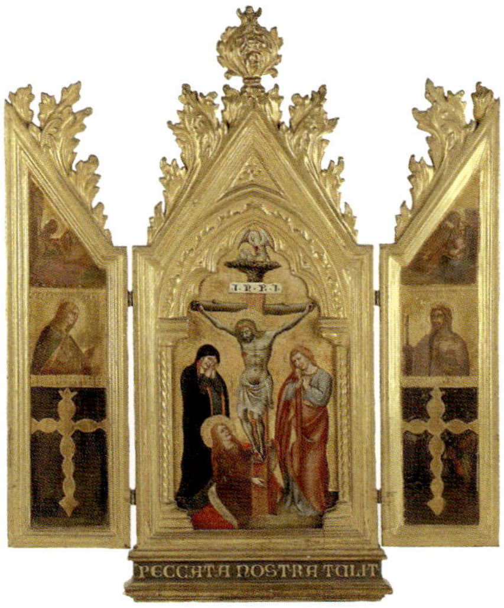

A255; tempera and gilding on panel, 39.5 × 20.5 cm (centre); 45.5 × 9.5 cm (left wing); 45.5 × 9.3 cm (right wing)
Bequeathed by the Revd Greville John Chester, 1892; WA1892.8

Lloyd 1977, pp. 162–3

A triptych or portable altar, A255 has a 19th-century frame. The Virgin Mary, St John and St Mary Magdalen are shown in the central panel, while on the lower right panel a male donor is depicted. Simone dei Crocefissi, a leading artist in Bologna, ran an important workshop that produced a large number of devotional works for private clients. This may date from late in his career, *c.* 1380.

Alfred Sisley
(1839 – 1899)

A Bend in the River Loing

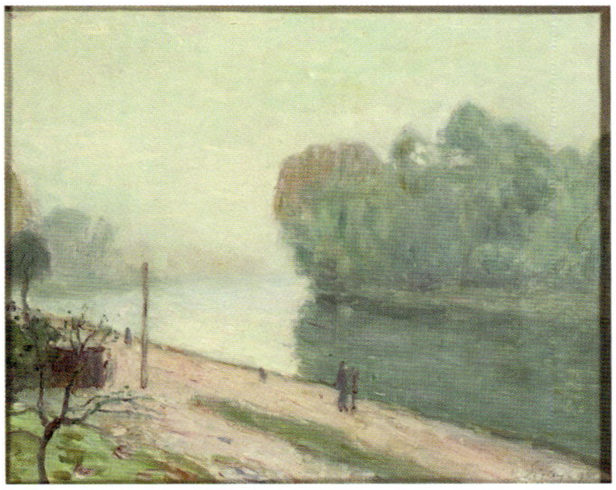

A479; oil on canvas, 38 × 46 cm
Signed and dated: *Sisley. 96*
Weldon Bequest,1937; WA1937.60

In 1880, Sisley settled at Veneux-Nadon, near Moret, at the confluence of the Loing and the Seine, where he remained for the rest of his life. This view of a bend in the Loing is one which he painted on many occasions in the course of 1896 in all conditions of weather and in all seasons. This is one of the smallest and most summary of the series, rapidly painted with a full brush and signed in pencil.

John Skippe
(1742 – 1811)

The Birth of Erichthonius

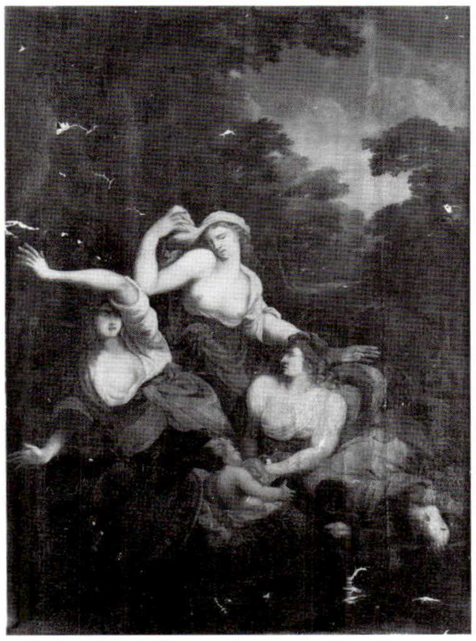

A44; oil on canvas, rolled, 164 × 114 cm
Presented by the artist, 1801; WA1845.44

The subject is found in Ovid's *Metamorphoses*, II, 553–63: Vulcan, in an effort to ravish Minerva, accidentally spilt his semen on the ground and Mother Earth, thus fertilised, gave birth to Erichthonius. Minerva shut the infant in a basket and entrusted it to the three daughters of Cecrops, king of Attica, but they opened it and discovered that the infant had a serpent's tail for legs. They then threw themselves off the Acropolis. The child later became King of Athens. Mother Earth is represented by the many-breasted Diana of Ephesus. Ovid says the scene was witnessed by a crow.

Kevin Sinnott
(b. 1947)

Wrestlers II

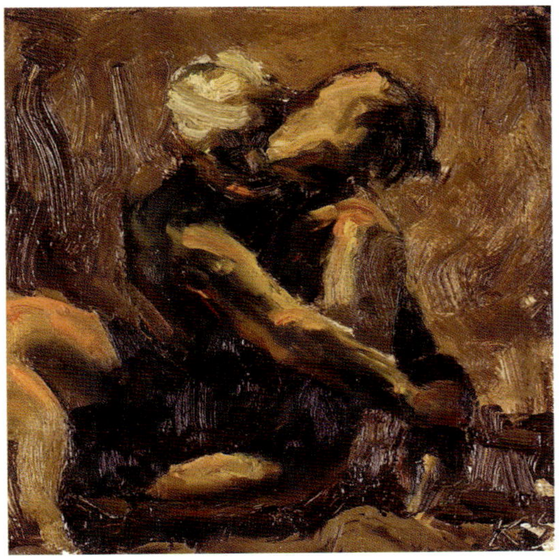

A1252; oil on cardboard on plywood, 18.8 × 18.5 cm
Initialled: *KS*; inscribed with title, initialled and numbered on the back: *Wrestlers II KSP 89*
Presented anonymously through the National Art Collections Fund, 2002; WA2002.69

Sinnott is well known for his complex figurative compositions. He often deals with the human figure in a context. Although the same fluid brush-strokes can be seen in the background and in the figures, the two wrestling men can be distinguished by a lighter touch and a slight variation in the use of paint. The underpainting, in places, appears through the upper layers, accentuating the sense of speed in the painting process.

John Skippe
(1742 – 1811)

The Calling of St Matthew

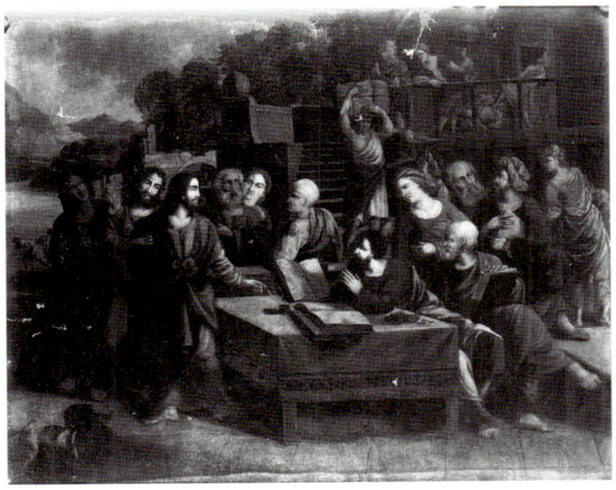

A43; oil on canvas, rolled, 102 × 125 cm
Presented by the artist, 1801; WA1845.43

The subject is taken from Matthew 9: 9: Matthew was seated in the customs house when Jesus called him to follow Him.

J. van Slechtenhorst
(active before 1662 – after 1669)

A Vase of Flowers

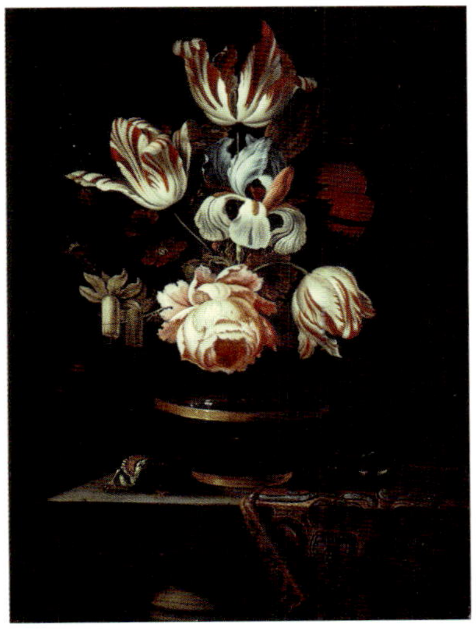

A561; oil on panel, 48 × 36 cm
Signed and dated: *SLHorst / 1670*
Daisy Linda Ward Bequest, 1939; WA1940.2.37

Meijer 2003, no. 68

One of six known flower paintings which were formerly attributed to an otherwise unknown artist 'S.L. Horst' on account of the signature. The discovery of a painting of flowers by the same hand, fully signed by J. van Slechtenhorst, has provided the key to their true authorship. The paintings suggest a debt to Jacob Marrel who worked in Utrecht but no artist with the name of Slechtenhorst has been found in the Utrecht archives.

JAMES SMETHAM
(1821 – 1889)

Twilight

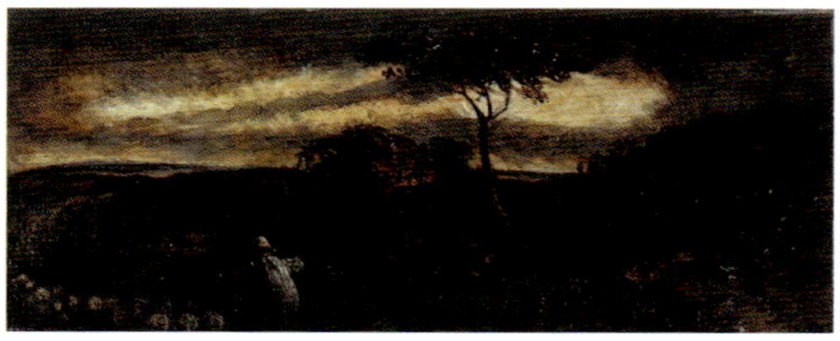

A738b; oil on panel, mounted as a drawing, 12.3 × 30.4 cm
Signed: *J. Smetham*
Prov.: by descent from the artist
Presented by S.W. Hutton, 1947; WA1947.315

This panel of 1871 resumes a subject frequently painted by Samuel Palmer.

JAMES SMETHAM
(1821 – 1889)

Beachy Head

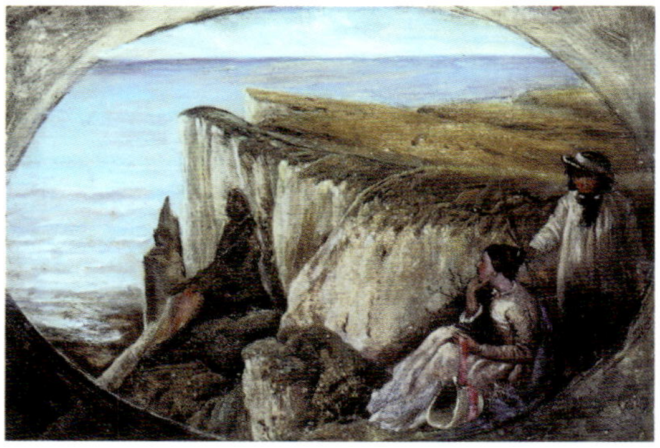

A740; oil on paper, mounted as a drawing, 17.7 × 25.5 cm
Prov.: by descent from the artist
Presented by Denis Smetham, 1947; WA1947.318

The artist spent his honeymoon at Eastbourne in 1854 and was there again in 1855 and 1860.

SIR MATTHEW SMITH
(1879 – 1959)

Still Life of Flowers

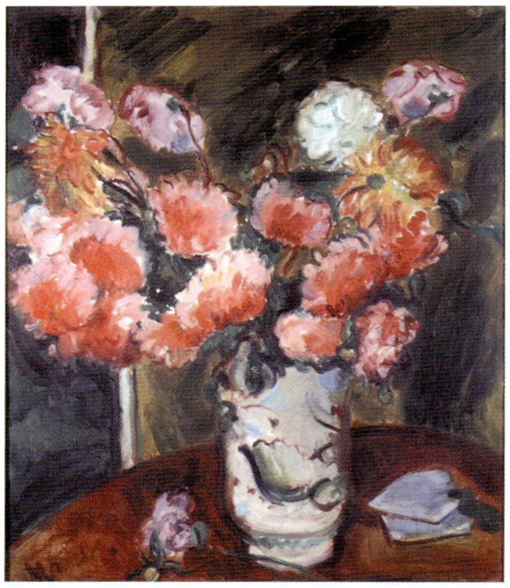

A626; oil on canvas, 66 × 57 cm
Signed in monogram: *MS*
Hindley Smith Bequest, 1939; WA1940.1.8

Eustace 1999, no. 22

After studying at the Slade School from 1905 to 1908, Smith spent a year in Pont Aven and later joined Matisse's class. After the First World War he returned to France and in the mid-1920s, the date of A626, he painted a series of nudes and still lifes with a new bravura. He painted directly from the subject without any preliminary studies.

JAMES SMETHAM
(1821 – 1889)

'Thoughts too deep for tears'

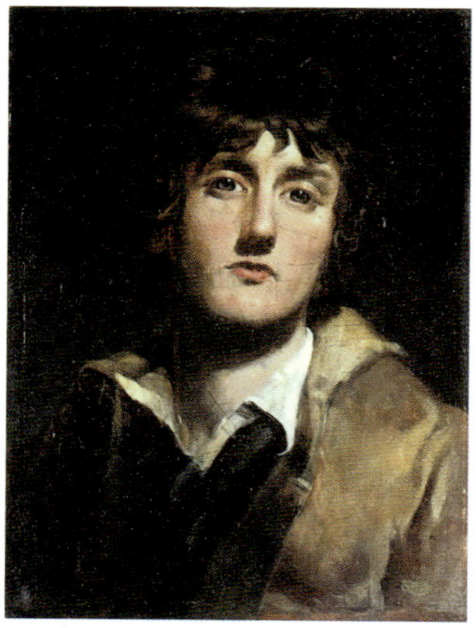

A738a; oil on panel, mounted as a drawing, 20.3 × 14.9 cm
Prov.: by descent from the artist
Presented by S.W. Hutton, 1947; WA1947.314

Casteras 1995, pp. 11–13

This romanticised self-portrait of the artist when a young man was painted in 1844 at his house at 1 Park Lane, Paradise Square, Stoke Newington. The title is adapted from the last lines of Wordsworth's 'Intimations of Immortality'.

COLVIN SMITH
(1795 – 1875)

Sir Walter Scott

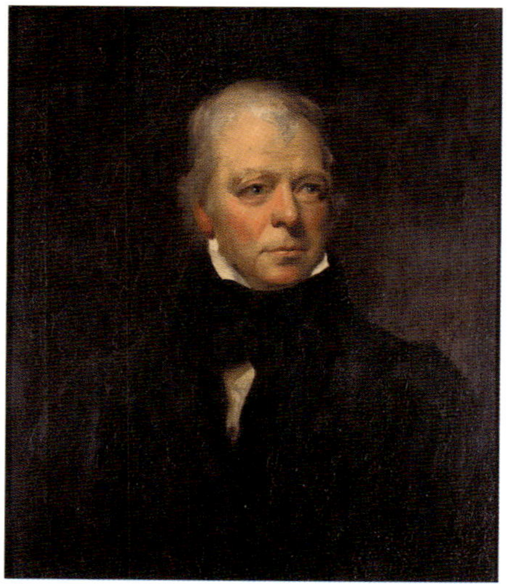

A139; oil on canvas, 75 × 62 cm
Prov.: Dr Thomas Hughes; Very Revd Edward Copleston, Bishop of Llandaff and by descent
Presented by the Revd J. Treherne, 1854; WA1854.1

Poole 1912, no. 474; Russell 1987, no. 188

Sir Walter Scott, the most celebrated Scots author of the 19th century, sat to Colvin Smith in 1828. The artist himself made at least fifteen replicas of his painting. This version was made for Dr Thomas Hughes, Canon of St Paul's, to be presented to Dr Edward Copleston, Bishop of Llandaff and was delivered before 16 July 1829.

WILLIAM SMITH
(active 1815 – 1859)

Philip Bury Duncan

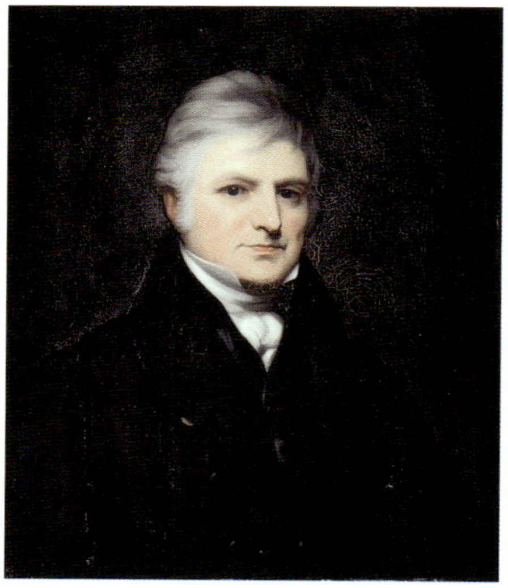

A518; oil on canvas, 33 × 28 cm
Inscribed on the reverse: *P.B. Duncan Esq. / Wm Smith Pinxt. 1837*
Presented by Dr Henry Donner, 1938; WA1938.4

Philip Bury Duncan (1772–1862) was elected a Fellow of New College in 1792 and served as Keeper of the Ashmolean Museum, 1826–1855.

William Smith
(active 1815 – 1859)

Philip Bury Duncan

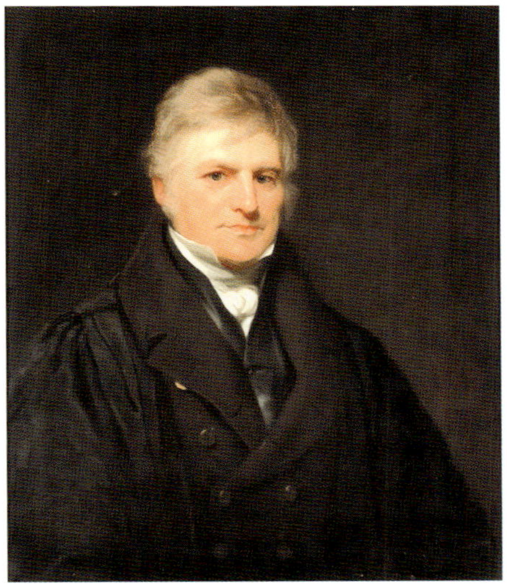

A66b; oil on canvas, 76 × 63 cm
Provenance unknown; WA1845.67

Poole 1912, no. 483

A replica, of very similar quality, of the preceding.

Pieter Snijers
(1681 – 1752)

Still Life with Fruit and Flowers

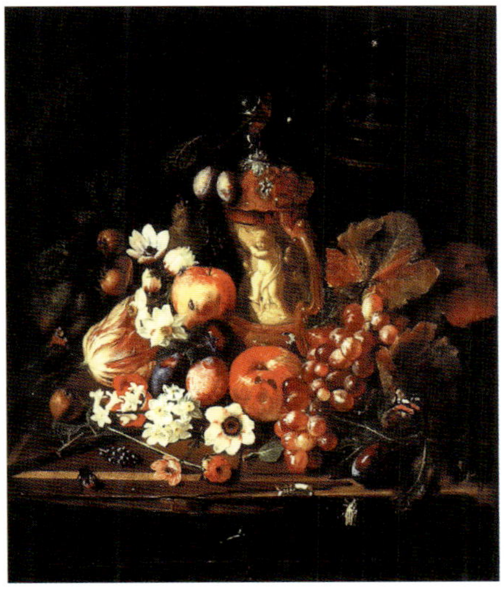

A593; oil on canvas, 58.8 × 49 cm
Signed (?): *P.Snÿers. f*
Daisy Linda Ward Bequest, 1939; WA1940.2.69

Meijer 2003, no. 70

Pieter Snijers spent most of his life in Antwerp painting genre scenes, portraits, landscapes and still life. His still-life paintings include subjects of dead game and forest floors, set out of doors and profuse compositions of small objects, fruit, single blossoms, nuts and other objects scattered across a surface in an interior. Two other paintings by him are known which include the ivory tankard featured here.

Francesco Solimena
(1657 – 1747)

Study of a female Figure

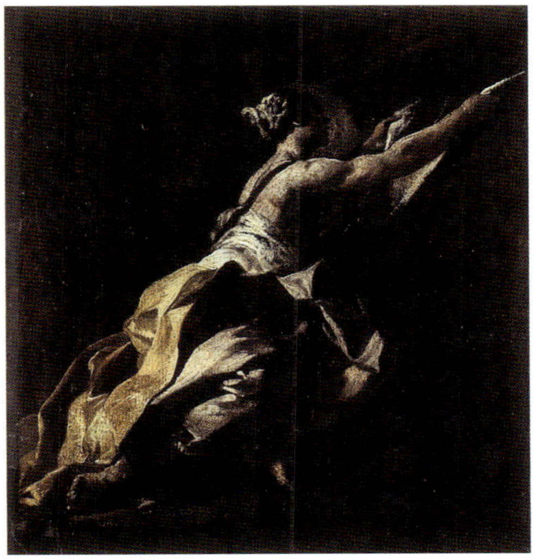

Oil on paper, mounted as a drawing, 26.4 × 24.5 cm
Purchased, 1937; WA1937.128

Parker 1956, no. 955; Spinosa 1986, under no. 18

Boreas, the icy North Wind, carried off the beautiful Orithya to be his wife (Ovid, *Metamorphoses* VI, 692–715). This oil-sketch is a study for one of the handmaids in Solimena's composition of *The Rape of Orithyia*. He made two versions of the subject and the figure is identical in both: the first, of 1700–1 for Fabrizio Spada Veralli (Galleria Spada, Rome), and the second of 1728–9, an Imperial commission (Kunsthistorisches Museum, Vienna).

Theodoor Smits
(active before 1657 – after 1658)

Still Life with Shell-fish

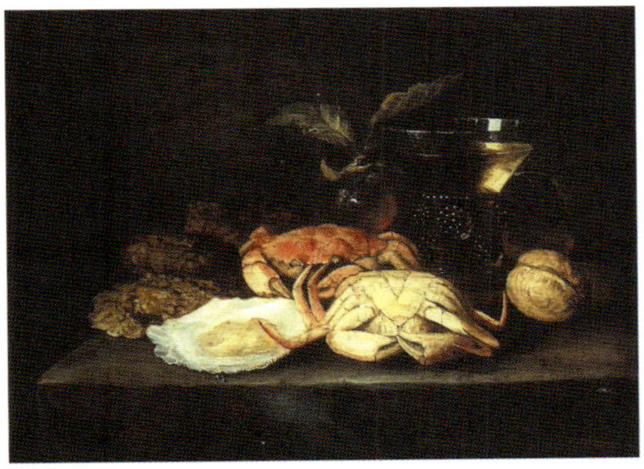

A591; oil on panel, 24 × 33 cm
Signed: *TD.S* (TD in monogram)
Daisy Linda Ward Bequest,1939; WA1940.2.67

Meijer 2003, no. 69

Smits is recorded in the books of the Antwerp guild when he was entered as a master in 1658–9. He usually signed with his initials or with his name T. Smits. On two occasions his signature has been misread (or misrestored) as T. Sauts: hence the former attribution of this painting to Sauts. Most of the dozen still-life paintings by Smits are modest pictures of subjects like this, often including crabs.

Andrea Solario
(*c.* 1465 – before 1524)

Ecce Homo

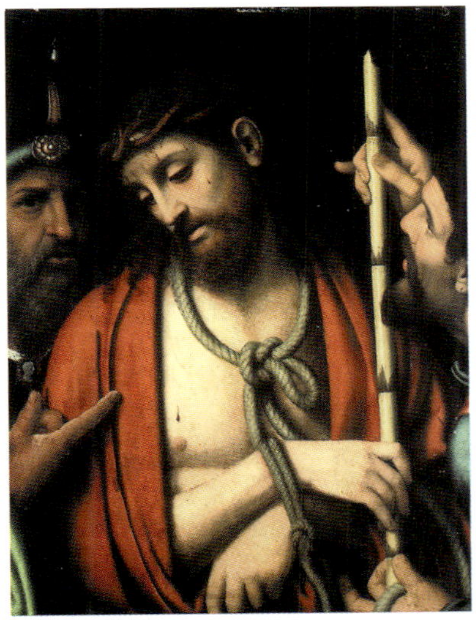

A817; oil and tempera (?) on panel, 57 × 44 cm
Prov.: Lord Conway of Allington; the Hon. Mrs A.E. Horsfield
Purchased, 1951; WA1951.49

Lloyd 1977, pp. 163–4; Brown 1987, pp. 110, 113 and no. 31

A close follower of Leonardo da Vinci, Solario was also interested in northern prints and in the work of Andrea Mantegna. A817 is datable to *c.* 1505–7. Unusually, the subject combines the scenes of Pilate presenting Christ to the people with the words 'Ecce Homo' or 'Behold the man' (John 19: 5) and the mocking of Christ (Matthew 27: 28–31). A variation is in the Musée des Beaux-Arts, Abbeville.

Francesco Solimena
(1657 – 1747)

The Holy Trinity with St Philip Neri in Glory

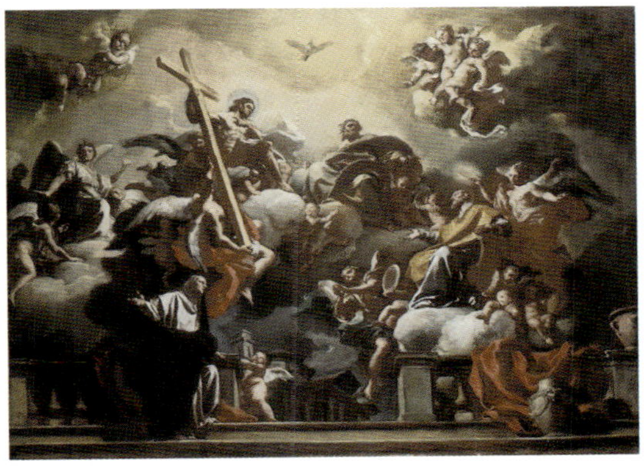

A514; oil on canvas, 75.5 × 102.5 cm
Prov.: J. Brandon
Purchased by subscription, 1937; WA1937.124

Bologna 1958, pp. 116, 260 and 271

A514 served as a model for the fresco in the cupola of the chapel of S. Filippo Neri in the church of the Oratorians, Naples, which was painted by Solimena in 1727–30. St Philip Neri (1515–1595), the founder of the Oratorian order, receives a crown or halo from an angel, while a female religious, probably St Francesca Romana (1384–1440), looks on. The leading Neapolitan artist of the late baroque period, Solimena was a rapid and versatile painter who worked for an international clientele.

Konstantin Andreevich Somov
(1869 – 1939)

Evgenii Sergheevich Mikhailov, the Artist's Nephew

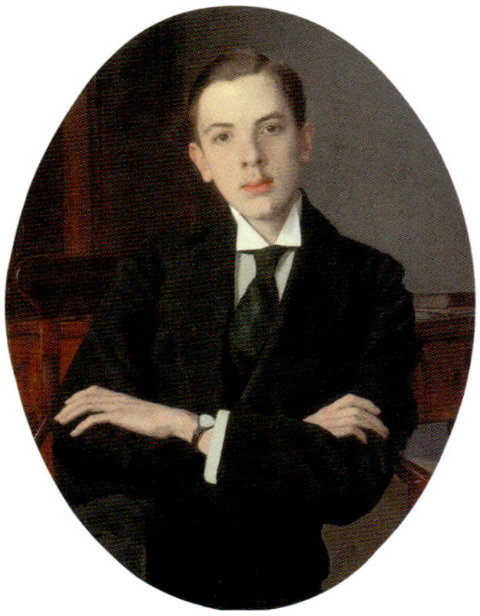

A1084; oil on canvas, 76 × 57 cm
Signed in Cyrillic and dated: *K. Somov 1916*
Presented by M. Braikevitch, 1976; WA1976.260

Salmina-Haskell 1989, no. 112

Somov was a member of the 'World of Art' group and a prolific book illustrator. Braikevitch collected drawings and watercolours by Somov in abundance. According to the artist's diary, he sold this painting to Braikevitch in 1938.

Isaak Soreau
(1604 – after 1645)

Still Life of Fruit and Flowers

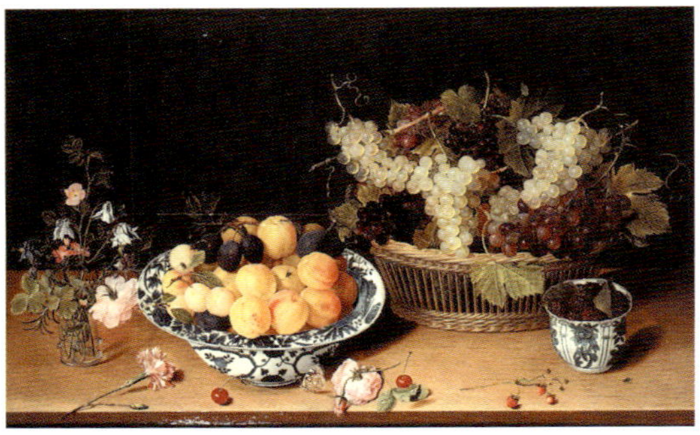

A594; oil on panel, 57 × 89 cm
Prov.: Robert White
Daisy Linda Ward Bequest, 1939; WA1940.2.70

Meijer 2003, no. 71

Soreau was born near Frankfurt. He may have spent some time in Antwerp as his work seems to depend on the example of the Antwerp artist, Jacob van Hulsdonck and as two of his works are painted on Antwerp panels. He occasionally repeated a composition and often reused the same objects in a new arrangement. The larger bowl and the basket of fruit in this painting reappear in works in the Hamburger Kunsthalle and in the Musée du Petit Palais, Paris.

Anonymous Spanish Artist (?)
(*c.* 1620)

St Teresa of Avila in Ecstasy

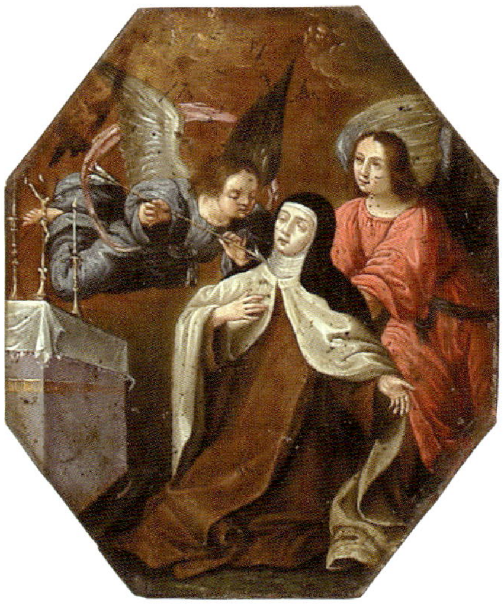

A908a; oil on copper, 25 × 20.5 cm
Bequeathed by Dr W.L. Hildburgh, 1957; WA1957.80.18

St Teresa (1515–1582), Spanish reformer and mystic, wrote of the stages of spiritual and mystical contemplation leading to ecstasy. This devotional image is based on her description of a state of ecstasy in which an angel appeared to pierce her with a spear; Bernini treated the same moment in his celebrated sculpture at S. Maria della Vittoria, Rome. Images of the saint were very popular in the period leading to her canonisation in 1622. This one may be by an artist working in Italy rather than in Spain.

Konstantin Andreevich Somov
(1869 – 1939)

Copy of the so-called Portrait of Simonetta Vespucci

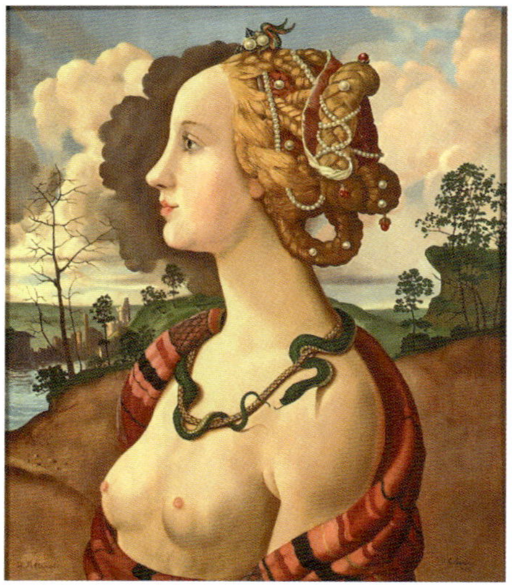

A1085; oil on canvas, 55 × 46 cm
Presented by M. Braikevitch, 1976; WA1976.261

Salmina-Haskell 1989, no. 142

Copied from the painting in the Musée Condé in Chantilly, thought at one time to be a portrait of Simonetta Vespucci by Pollaiuolo. It is now thought to be by Piero di Cosimo and the idea that it represents Simonetta Vespucci has been discarded.

Anonymous South German Artist
(15th century)

St Sebastian

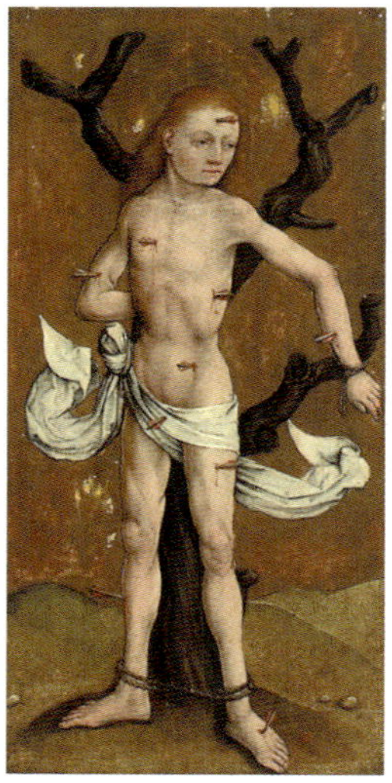

A426; oil on panel, 37 × 18 cm
Prov.: Alexander Haas, Frankfurt
Purchased, 1933; WA1933.22

White 1999, p. 191

This appears to have been the right-hand shutter from a small triptych. Sebastian was a third-century Roman Christian soldier who survived when he was tied to a tree and shot with arrows but was later martyred. He was commonly invoked as a protection against the plague. His cult was particularly wide-spread in late 15th-century Germany.

Anonymous Spanish Artist (?)
(?19th century)

St Catherine of Alexandria

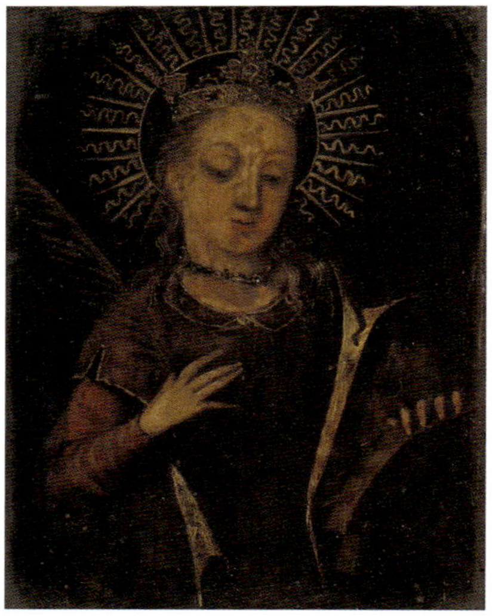

A1191; oil on copper, 20.7 × 14.5 cm
Bywater Bequest, 1915; WA1994.43

St Catherine, of royal birth, wears a crown and carries her attributes of a martyr's palm and spiked wheel, a reference to her attempted martyrdom. The saint's halo is unusual and recalls medieval Spanish types, yet copper was rarely used as a support in Spain until the 17th century. Possibly A1191 is by a Mexican or Latin American artist.

Anonymous Spanish Artist
(17th century)

Landscape with a Boar-hunt

A260; dimensions unknown
Bequeathed by the Revd Greville John Chester, 1892; WA1892.5

A description on file reads: 'The scene is laid in a wooded landscape. In the extreme foreground on the left, is seen a man in yellow on a white horse, next to him a boy in rose purple jacket, armed with a spear, holding a dog. Further, men on horseback and on foot and some dogs are attacking the boar.' This painting was recorded as missing in 1968.

Gilbert Spencer
(1892 – 1979)

Elm Trees at Garsington

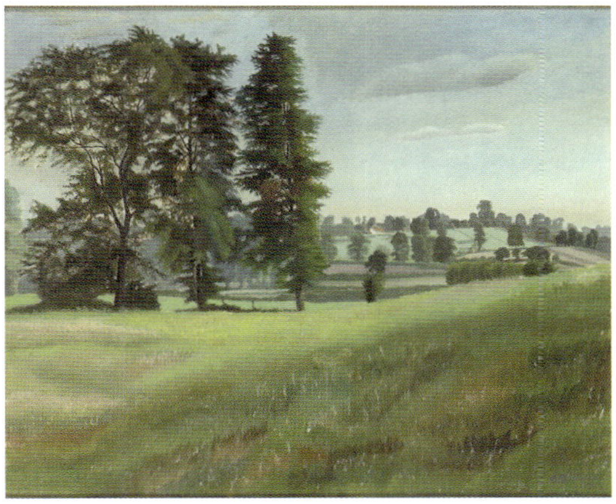

A457; oil on canvas, 51 × 61 cm
Signed and dated: *Gilbert Spencer 1925*
Weldon Bequest, 1937; WA1937.37

Garsington Manor, a few miles east of Oxford, was the home between 1913 and 1924 of the celebrated society hostess and patron of the arts, Lady Ottoline Morrell (1873–1938). Gilbert Spencer was among her visitors. This landscape, painted shortly after she had left Garsington for London, is symbolically empty of all human presence.

Gilbert Spencer
(1892 – 1979)

Cottage Garden at Compton Abbas

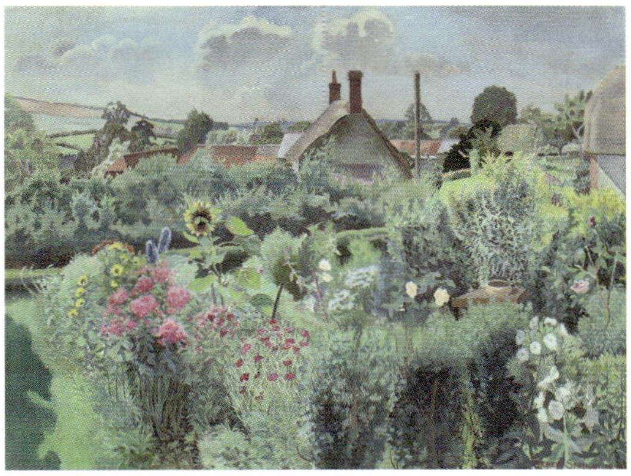

A521; oil on canvas, 71.4 × 91.7 cm
Signed and dated: *Gilbert Spencer 1939*
Purchased by subscription, with the assistance of the Contemporary Art Society, 1939; WA1939.1

Spencer's style did not change dramatically during his career. He specialized in landscapes, This is not a distant view, but a detailed glimpse into a cottage garden on a sunny summer day. The colourful flowers in the foreground dominate the picture, with the village of Compton Abbas in the middleground and the landscape in the far background.

Gilbert Spencer
(1892 – 1979)

Pegwell Bay, Kent

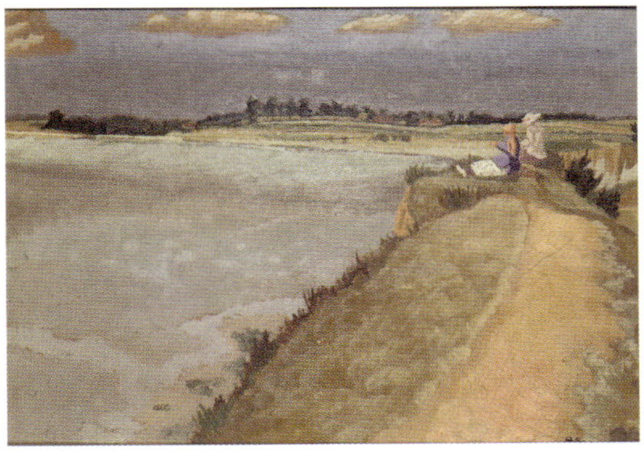

A441; oil on panel, 25.2 × 35.7 cm
Signed: *G Spencer*; signed and dated on the back: *Gilbert Spencer 1921*
Presented by Mr and Mrs Julian G. Lousada through the National Art Collections Fund, 1935; WA1935.76

Gilbert Spencer, the brother of Stanley Spencer, attended the Camberwell School of Arts and later the Slade School of Fine Arts. After the First World War he made his name for his landscapes, mainly painted in the South of England. This early painting from 1921 shows a view of Pegwell Bay, looking down from the high dunes. The viewpoint raises the horizon and gives an outlook across the bay, which dominates this tranquil composition.

Gilbert Spencer
(1892 – 1979)

Mill Pond, Durweston

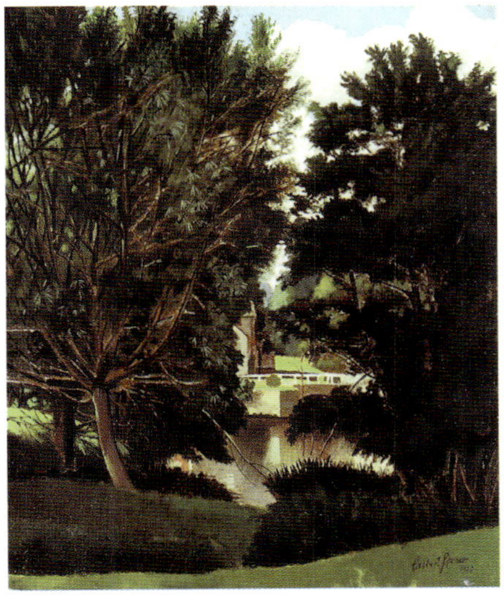

A1043; oil on canvas, 61.2 × 51.3 cm
Signed and dated: *Gilbert Spencer 1927*
Bequeathed by Thomas Balston, through the National Art Collections Fund, 1968; WA1968.26

As is common in Spencer's landscapes, this painting from 1927 concentrates on a detail seen here within an upright format, which is less usually found in landscape painting than the standard 'landscape' format. He was probably influenced by the verticality of the trees on the bank of the river Stour, which crosses Durweston in Dorset. The mill, the main subject of the painting, is shown as a small bright green detail in the centre of the painting, framed by the dark green trees in the foreground.

Stanley Spencer
(1891 – 1959)

Cows at Cookham

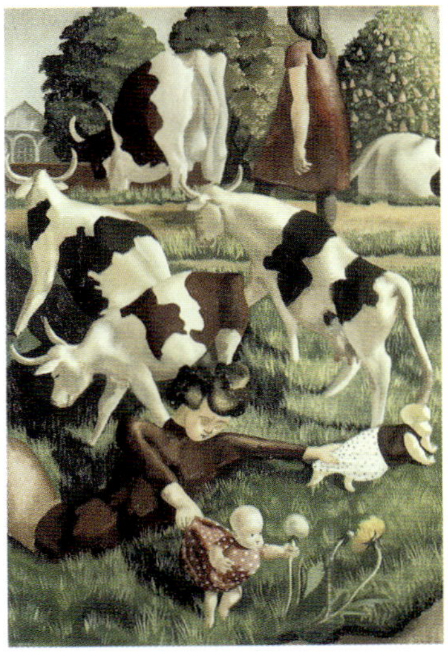

A1044; oil on canvas, 76.3 × 50.8 cm
Initialled and dated: *SS 36*
Bequeathed by Thomas Balston through the National Art Collections Fund, 1968; WA1968.27

Eustace 1999, no. 27

Spencer identifed himself throughout his life with the area round Cookham in Berkshire. He attempted to recover his sense of inner equilibrium lost during the First World War by creating a chapel – finally unrealised – which would encapsulate the tranquility of Cookham. In a semi-realistic manner he recreates an ideal, rural harmony in a sun-filled landscape.

Karl Spitzweg
(1808 – 1885)

Mountain Landscape

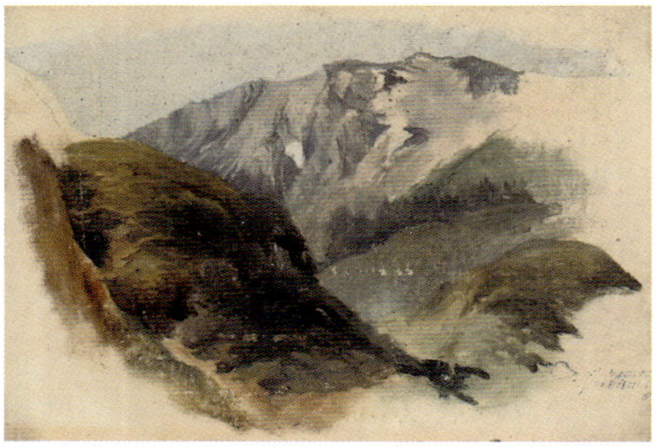

A872a; oil on paper, mounted as a drawing, 17.3 × 24.6 cm
Bequeathed by Dr Grete Ring, 1954; WA1954.70.164

Bailey 1987, no. 152

Spitzweg chiefly painted figure subects usually of a wry, humourous nature. Following a visit to Paris in 1851, he discovered the painters of the Barbizon School and became interested in landscape as a subject in its own right. This sketch was probably painted in the Bavarian Alps in the late 1850s or early 1860s. Altenatively, it might have been painted in the Tyrol in 1874.

William Clarkson Stanfield
(1793 – 1867)

A View of Vietri in the Gulf of Salerno

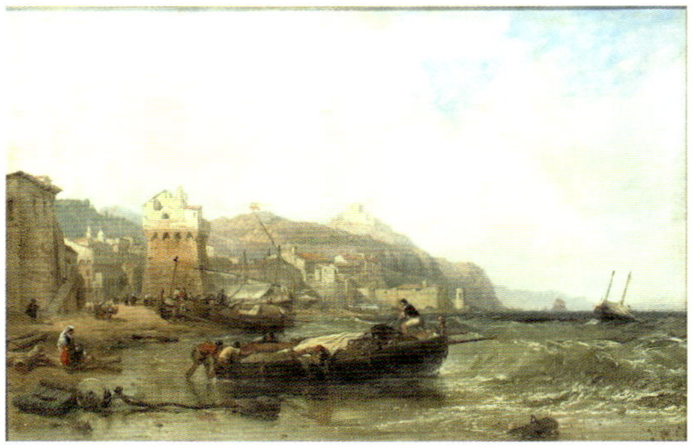

A1221; oil on canvas, 41 × 61.2 cm
Signed and dated: *Clarkson Stanfield 1855*
Prov.: James Dugdale, Wroxall Abbey, Warwicks.; Sir Francis d'Arcy Cooper
Bequeathed by Dr Courtenay Arthur Ralegh Radford, 1998; WA1999.54

Stanfield sketched in the Gulf of Salerno during his stay of twelve days at Amalfi in November 1838. He painted this view in 1840 (Royal Collection) and this is evidently a later version based on the same sketches: the landscape is substantially the same, though the staffage is entirely different.

Harmen van Steenwyck
(1612 – after 1656)

Still Life with Fruit

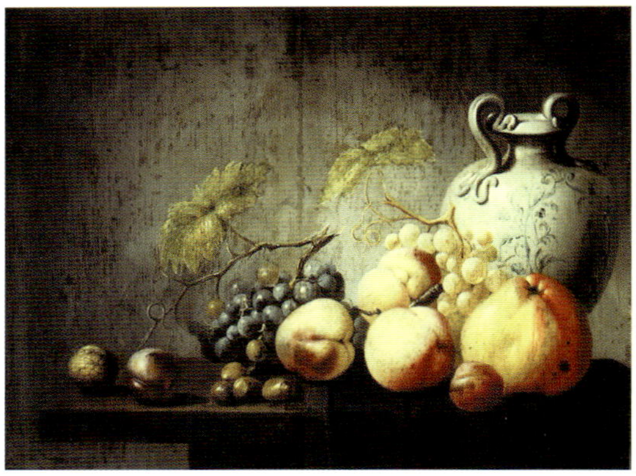

A596; oil on panel, 41 × 52 cm
Signed in monogram: *HS*
Prov.: J.J. Chappuis; Mrs B. Inggs
Daisy Linda Ward Bequest, 1939; WA1940.2.72

Meijer 2003, no. 76

The elaborate blue and white vase is an unusual item in the work of Steenwyck who, as a rule, used commonplace earthenwares in his still-life compositions. It has been dated on grounds of style to the 1640s, perhaps towards the end of the decade.

Johannes Spruyt
(*c.* 1627 – 1671)

A Pair of Ducks in a Landscape

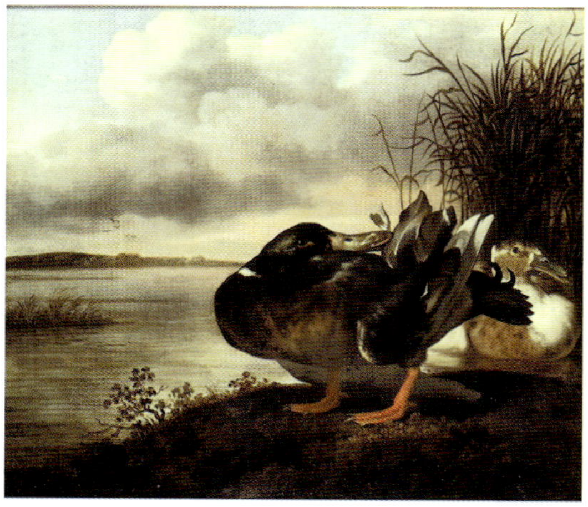

A595; oil on canvas, 62 × 71 cm
Signed and dated: *J Spruÿt / Fecit. 1659.*
Daisy Linda Ward Bequest, 1939; WA1940.2.71

Meijer 2003, no. 72

Scenes with ducks on the edge of a lake were Spruyt's favourite subject but he also painted still-life pictures of dead birds. History pictures are mentioned in the documents although no history paintings by him have been identified. He worked in Amsterdam.

James Stark
(1794 – 1859)

The Willow Stream

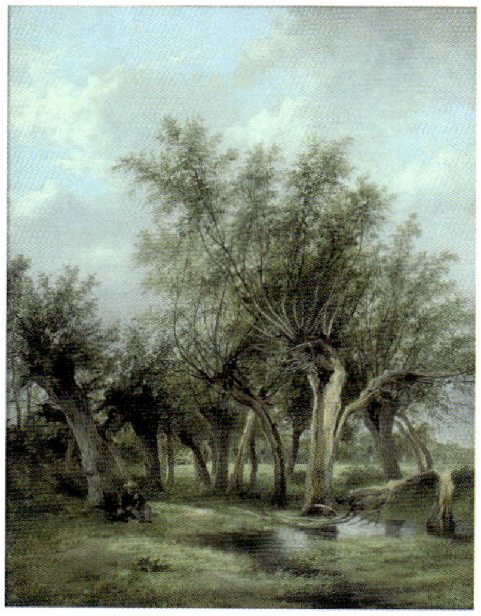

A762; oil on panel, 53 × 41 cm
Presented by F.J. Nettlefold, 1948; WA1948.36

Grundy 1933–8, III, p. 244

Stark was a pupil of John Crome at Norwich, but painted more detailed, less atmospheric landscapes. A companion painting of similar dimensions was entitled *A Lane near Norwich*, suggesting that both were painted in Stark's native town, perhaps between 1819 and 1840.

Harmen van Steenwyck
(1612 – after 1656)

Still Life of Kitchen Utensils with Fruit and Game

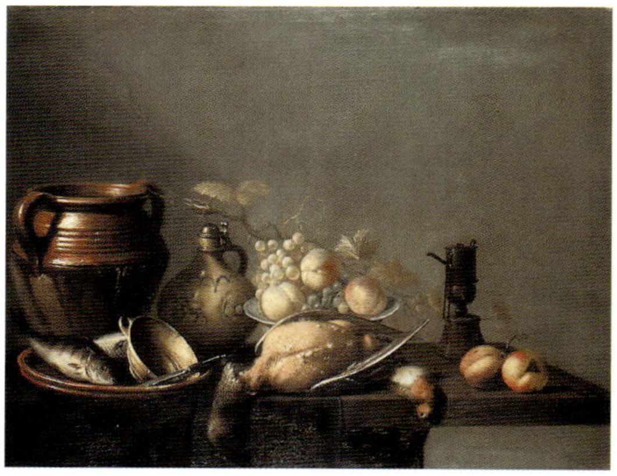

A597; oil on panel, 28 × 35 cm
Signed: *H. Steenwyck*
Daisy Linda Ward Bequest, 1939; WA1940.2.73

Meijer 2003, no. 75

Steenwyck's accessories are typically commonplace utensils. Red earthenware like the crock and platter were humble articles while the stoneware jar was a mass produced type, imported from Westerwald near Cologne.

Harmen van Steenwyck
(1612 – after 1656)

Still Life of Fruit on a Ledge

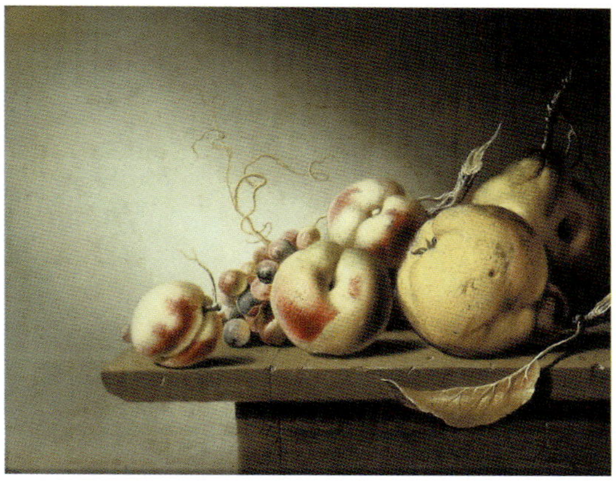

A598; oil on panel, 28.8 × 35.1 cm
Signed: *H. Steenwyck*
Daisy Linda Ward Bequest, 1939; WA1940.2.74

Meijer 2003, no. 73

All Steenwyck's known paintings are still lifes or include still-life elements. His dated work ranges from 1644 to 1652. This simple group of fruit, set on a ledge and softly lit, has marked similarities with the dated paintings of the mid-1640s.

Harmen van Steenwyck
(1612 – after 1656)

Still Life of Game, Fish, Fruit and Kitchen Utensils

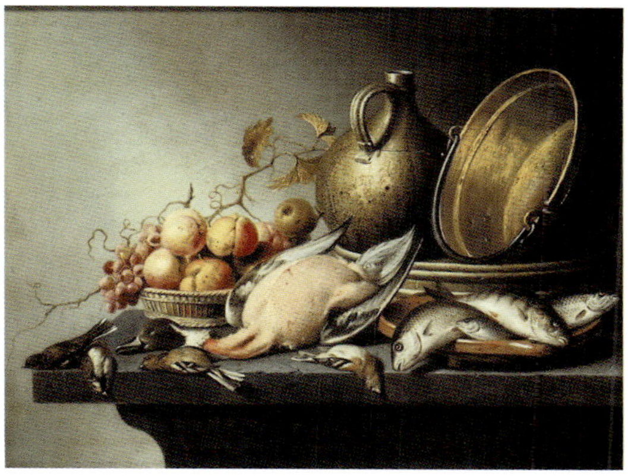

A600; oil on panel, 36 × 46 cm
Signed: *H. Steenwyck*
Daisy Linda Ward Bequest, 1939; WA1940.2.76

Meijer 2003, no. 74

The majority of Steenwyck's still-life paintings represent kitchen tables with foodstuffs and ustensils arranged with a marked diagonal emphasis. This painting is close in technique and composition to a pair of kitchen still-life paintings in the Heinz Family Collection in Washington, dated 1646.

Philip Wilson Steer
(1860 – 1942)

Evening, Ludlow

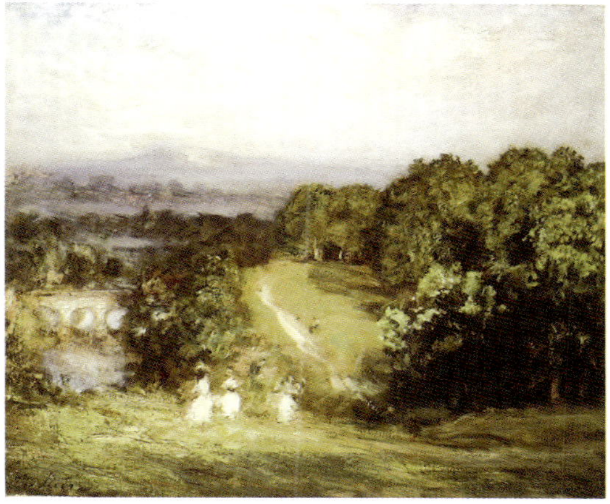

A467; oil on canvas, 41 × 49 cm
Signed: *P.W. Steer*
Weldon Bequest, 1937; WA1937.47

Laughton 1971, no. 236

Steer first visited Ludlow in Shropshire in 1898 and returned there in 1906. He painted a number of views of the town seen from the surrounding hills. The vantage point in this painting is the same as that in another, *Ludlow Walks* (Southampton Art Gallery). It was probably exhibited at the New English Art Club in 1899.

Harmen van Steenwyck
(1612 – after 1656)

Still Life of Fish, a Pear, Game and Kitchen Utensils

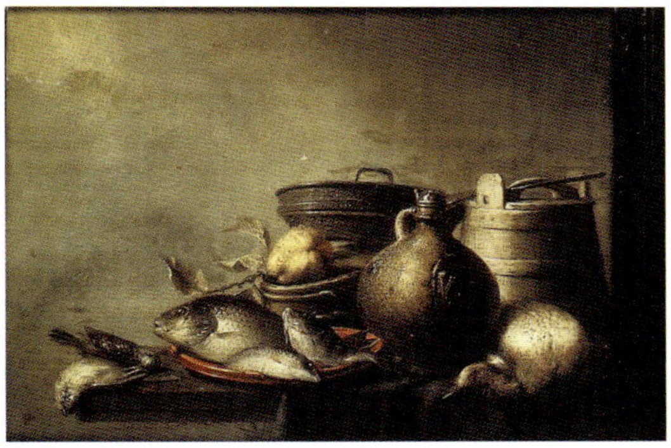

A599; oil on panel, 23 × 30 cm
Signed: *H Steenwyck*
Prov.: Sir Bruce Seton; Cohen
Daisy Linda Ward Bequest, 1939; WA1940.2.75

Meijer 2003, no. 77

Steenwyck's work seems to have coarsened between the early 1640s and the early 1650s. Similarities between this little still-life painting and two in the Rijksmuseum, dated 1652, suggest a similar date or somewhat later, as the handling of the Oxford painting is coarser than it is in the paintings in Amsterdam.

Philip Wilson Steer
(1860 – 1942)

The Worktable

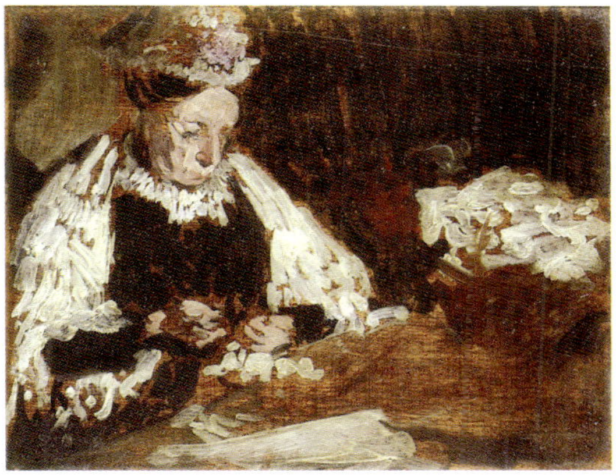

A1060; oil on panel, mounted as a drawing, 21 × 26 cm
Inscribed on back: *Portrait of my mother, Emma Steer / P.W. Steer*
Prov.: Mrs Charles E. Hamilton and by descent
Presented by Miss D.E. Hamilton, the artist's niece, 1971; WA1971.46

Laughton 1971, no. 153

This study of Steer's elderly mother was exhibited at the New English Art Club in 1894. It is one of the most intimate of a number of portraits he painted in his early years and is rapidly painted in the broken brush-strokes he had begun to employ in 1888–9. Mrs Steer died on 6 March 1898, aged 80.

Philip Wilson Steer
(1860 – 1942)

Stroud: View over the Plain

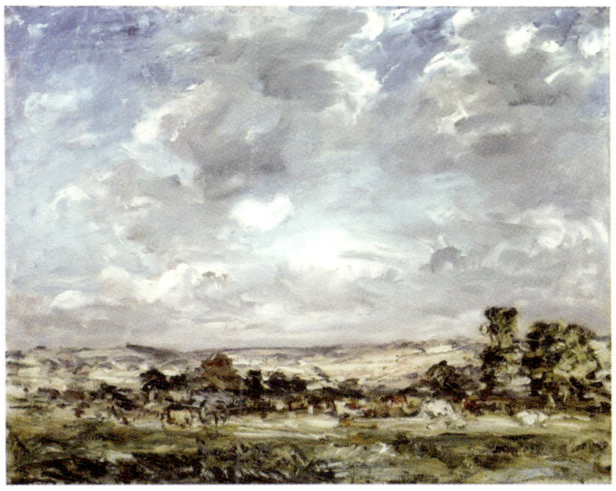

A935; oil on canvas, 56 × 69 cm
Bequeathed by C.H. Collins Baker, 1960; WA1960.37

Laughton 1971, no. 301

Steer was especially prolific during his stay at Stroud, Gloucestershire, in 1902. Once again, he preferred views looking down into the valley, which he named 'The Golden Valley' in tribute to Samuel Palmer's views of Shoreham.

Philip Wilson Steer
(1860 – 1942)

Richmond, Yorkshire

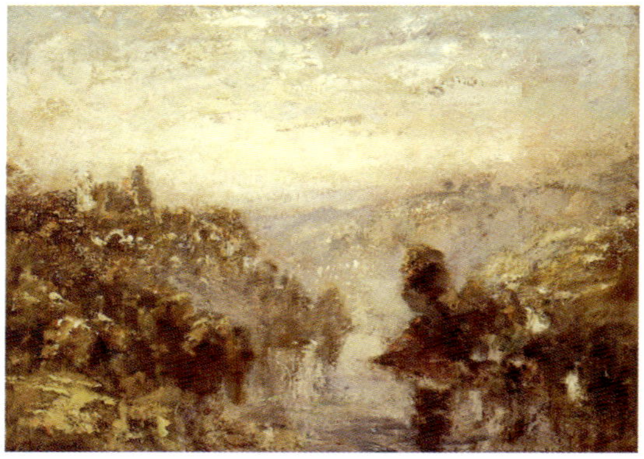

A406; oil on canvas, 46 × 61 cm
Signed: *P.W. Steer*
Presented by Sir Michael Sadler in memory of Lady Sadler through the National Art Collections Fund, 1931; WA1931.4

Laughton 1971, no. 326

This view of Richmond is atmospheric, rather than topographical. The heavy impasto suggests that it was painted in Steer's studio.

Philip Wilson Steer
(1860 – 1942)

Outskirts of a Town (Montreuil from the Ramparts)

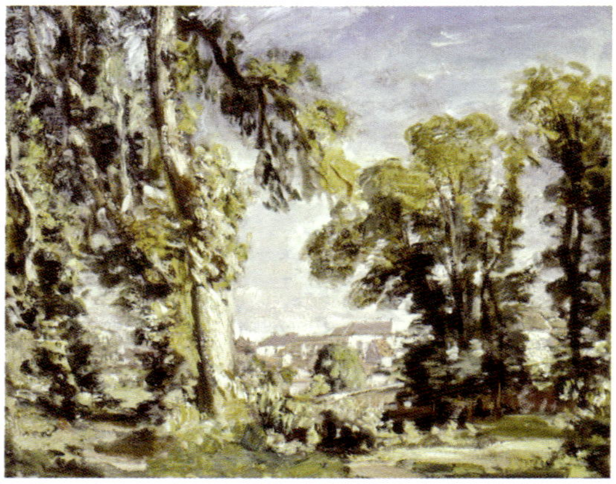

A619; oil on canvas, 50 × 61 cm
Prov.: Mrs Fisher
Hindley Smith Bequest, 1939; WA1940.1.1

Laughton 1971, no. 401

This is a smaller version of a painting in Tate Britain; another is in the Fitzwilliam Museum. Both appear to have been painted on the spot, whereas the larger work, very heavily worked, was no doubt completed in the studio.

William Strang
(1859 – 1921)

The Fisherman's Home

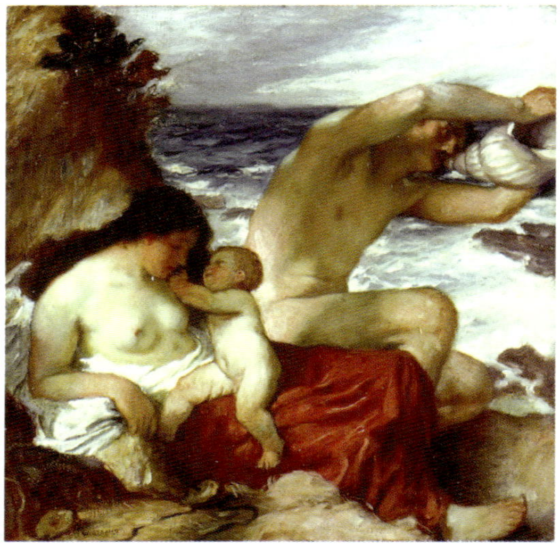

A684; oil on canvas, 61 × 61 cm
Signed: *W. Strang*
Presented by Francis Howard, 1941; WA1941.58

Athill and Goodchild 1980–81, no. 13; Christian 1989, no. 219

Painted in 1905, this is reminiscent of the work of Puvis de Chavannes, whom Strang admired, tempering his severity with the warm colouring of 16th-century Venetian paintings. The subject is related to Puvis's *Poor Fisherman* (Musée d'Orsay). It is also heavily indebted to the paintings of Charles Shannon, who himself admired Puvis.

Philip Wilson Steer
(1860 – 1942)

La Grande Place, Montreuil

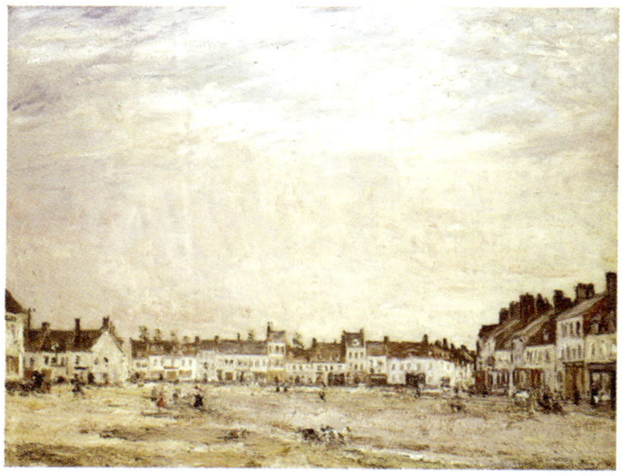

A468; oil on canvas, 96 × 123 cm
Signed and dated: *P.W. Steer 1907*
Prov.: Mrs Wills
Weldon Bequest, 1937; WA1937.48

Laughton 1971, no. 395

Based on a watercolour and an oil study, this painting is one of a series depicting the town of Montreuil in northern France. The dramatic composition shows the square bordered by houses and shops underneath a vast expanse of sky, described by the critic Roger Fry as 'one of those discoveries of proportion that only very real artists make and the colour and handling altogether exceptional'.

Jan Jacobsz. van der Stoffe
(*c.* 1611 – 1682)

Huntsmen in a Landscape

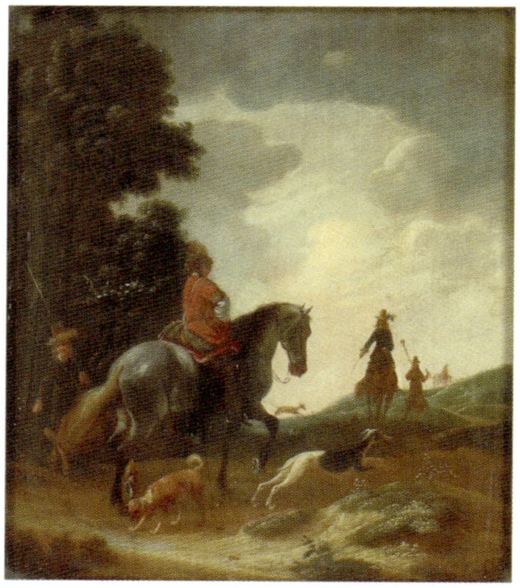

A282; oil on panel, 41 × 35 cm
Signed: *JJStoffe f*
Presented by Thomas Humphry Ward, 1897; WA1897.5

White 1999, p. 143

Stoffe worked in Leiden, painting cavalry engagements and hunting scenes. The earliest record of this painting mentions a date of 1659 in the inscription. In later records, this is given as 1650. No trace of a date is now visible.

Juriaen van Streek
(1632 – 1687)

Still Life with Fruit

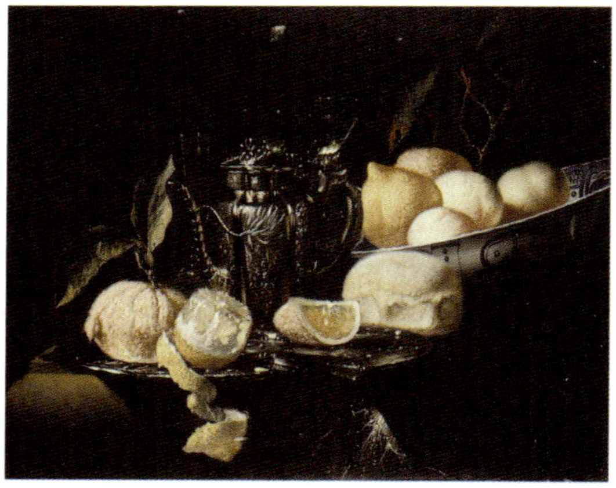

A602; oil on canvas, 45 × 56 cm
Signed: *J. v. Streek*
Prov.: W.E. Duits; Ralph Warner
Daisy Linda Ward Bequest, 1939; WA1940.2.78

Meijer 2003, no. 78

Streek seems to have been based in Amsterdam and is said to have given up painting in about 1680. No dated paintings by him are known. The wine jar in this composition, however, is of a type which dates from the 1670s, suggesting that the painting is a relatively late work. The influence of Willem Kalf is evident in his liking for dark backgrounds against which rich objects and glittering fruit are picked out in spots of light.

Christian Jansz. Striep
(1634 – 1673)

Still Life with a Silver-gilt Cup

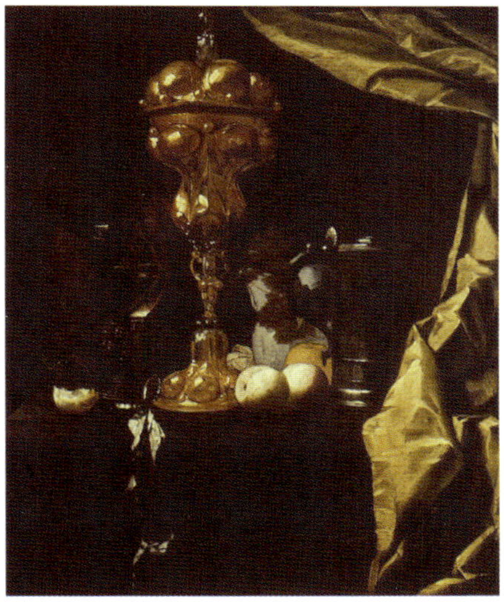

A603; oil on canvas, 99 × 81 cm
Daisy Linda Ward Bequest, 1939; WA1940.2.79

Meijer 2003, no. 79

Very few works by Striep have been identified. Most show a debt to Willem Kalf although the influence is less obvious here than it is elsewhere. The arrangement is top-heavy by comparison with Kalf's harmonious compositions. The tankard is too plain an object to have interested Kalf and the curtain pulled back to reveal the still life is a device which is not found in Kalf's work.

Jacob van Strij
(1756 – 1815)

Landscape with Figures, Cattle and Sheep

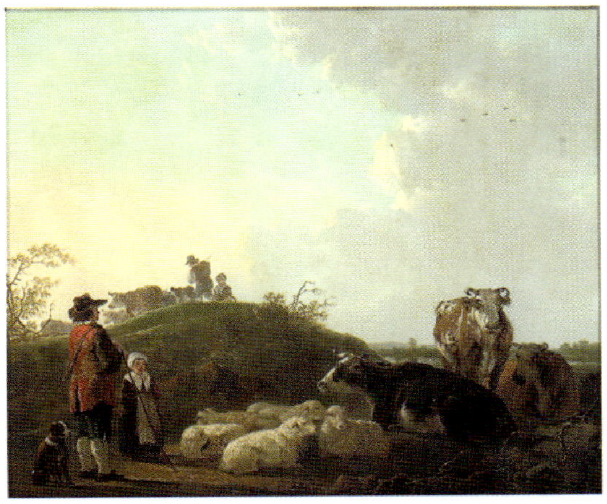

A126; oil on panel, 36 × 42 cm
Inscribed: *A. Cuyp*
Bequeathed by the Revd Dr Thomas Penrose, 1851; WA1851.23

White 1999, p. 144

Van Strij worked in Dordrecht. He specialised in painting scenes with animals, often in the style of Aelbert Cuyp, whose name has fraudulently been added to this painting.

Ermanno Stroiffi
(1616 – 1693)

The Virgin and Child with Sts John the Baptist, Francis and James the Great

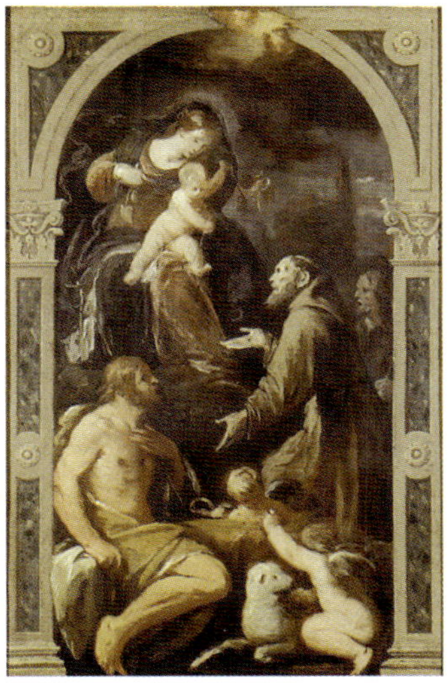

A1002; oil on canvas, 106 × 67.5 cm
Purchased with the assistance of the Victoria & Albert Museum Purchase Grant Fund, 1963; WA1963.63

Ferrari 1990, pp. 235, 238

A preparatory oil-sketch for an altar-piece of 1652 in S. Maria dei Derelitti (the Ospedaletto), Venice, A1002 represents the Virgin of Mount Carmel with St John the Baptist in the foreground, St Francis in his distinctive habit to the right, together with the pilgrim saint, James the Great. The altar-piece, with considerable variations in the figures, is in a different architectural surround from that envisaged here; it was commissioned from Stroiffi, a pupil of Bernardo Strozzi, by the heirs of Giovanni Battista Gariboldi (d. 1651), who is buried nearby. A variant oil-sketch, with the same architectural design, is in the Fondazione Longhi, Florence.

Charles Edward Strong
(exhibited 1851 – 56)

Sea-piece: off Calshot Castle

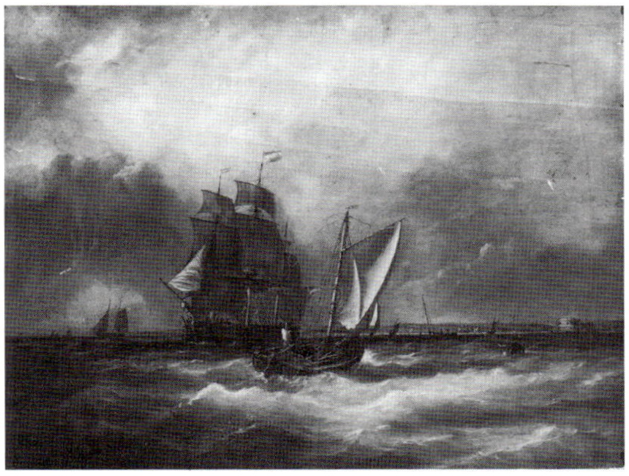

A112; oil on canvas, rolled, 70 × 90 cm
Presented by the Revd Charles Strong, the artist's father, 1850; WA1850.41

This obscure artist is recorded as an exhibitor at the Royal Academy between 1851 and 1856, but is otherwise unknown and probably died young. Calshot Castle dominates the entrance to Southampton Water and was constructed in 1530 as part of Henry VIII's defence of England.

Bernardo Strozzi
(1581/2 – 1644)

A Betrothal

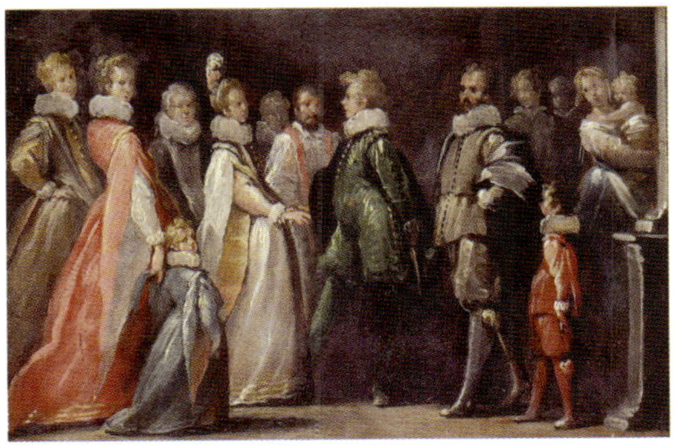

Oil on paper, mounted as a drawing, 18.5 × 28 cm
Prov.: Sir Abraham Hume; Lord Brownlow
Purchased, 1946; WA1946.338

Parker 1956, no. 215 (as Jacopo da Empoli); Newcome 1993, p. 15

Datable to the 1620s, this oil-sketch resembles, in reverse, a scene of betrothal in a silver plaquette from a silver box made for the Spinola family in 1636 by Mattheus Melijn (1589–1653) now in the Rikjsmuseum. It has been suggested that the betrothal scene refers to the marriage of Giambattista Spinola and Maria Spinola in 1625. The oil-sketch is close in style to that of *Horatius Cocles* (see following) A1057 above.

Bernardo Strozzi
(1581/2 – 1644)

Design for a silver Basin

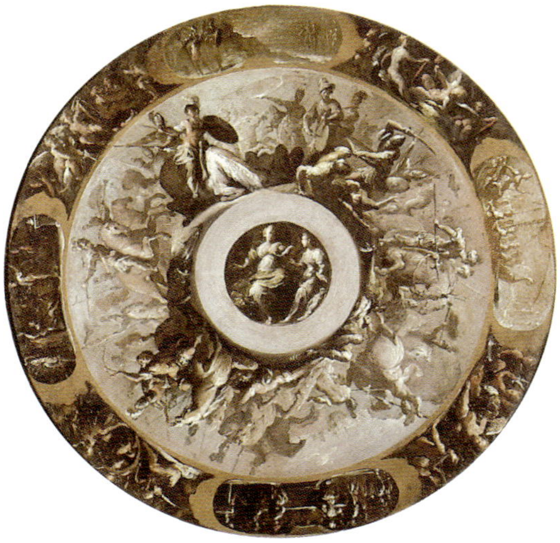

A1057; oil on canvas, 57 × 74 cm
Prov.: Sir George Donaldson; H.M. Calmann
Purchased with the assistance of the Victoria & Albert Museum Purchase Grant Fund, 1969; WA1969.139

Mortari 1995, no. I.333

A1057 is a design for the chased decoration of a silver basin, now in the J.Paul Getty Museum, formerly owned by the Giustiniani Longo family in Genoa and possibly dating from the 1620s. Pliny's *Historia Naturalis* and Plutarch's *Lives* are the sources for the narrative scenes: the central roundel shows *The Death of Cleopatra*, surrounded by a battle scene of cavalry and footsoldiers with distant ships, while the four ovals at the rim show *The Formation of the Triumvirate* (Antony, Octavian and Lepidus); *The Arrival of Cleopatra* (her barge is on the river Cydnus); *The Banquet of Cleopatra* and *The Death of Antony*. There are considerable variations between *modello* and silver basin. Suggestions for the dating of A1057 range from *c.* 1613–15 to *c.* 1623–4.

Bernardo Strozzi
(1581/2 – 1644)

Horatius Cocles Defending the Bridge

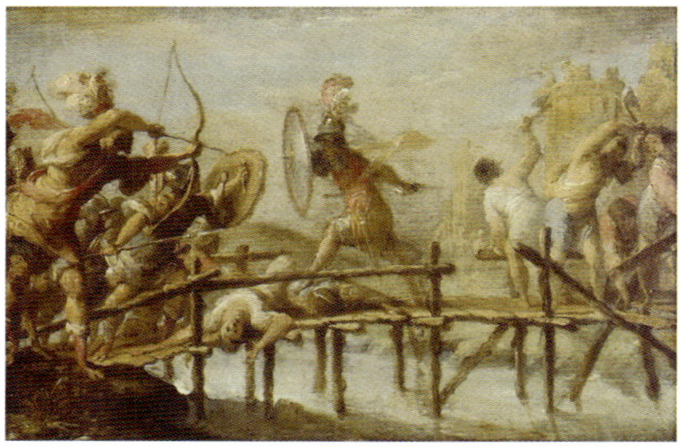

Oil on paper laid down on canvas, 24 × 35.5 cm
Mahon loan, 1999; WA.L.99.18

Finaldi and Kitson 1997, no. 78

Horatius Cocles kept the Etruscan army at bay while his companions destroyed the bridge behind him (Livy, *Ab Urbe Condita*, II, Ch. X). This is a preparatory oil-sketch for a ceiling fresco in the Villa Centurione-Carpaneto in Sampierdarena, commissioned with other frescoes on subjects of Roman history by Filippo Centurione, perhaps *c.* 1623–5. Strozzi studied both the design and the colouring in this free, rapid sketch.

Bernardo Strozzi
(1581/2 – 1644)

The Adoration of the Shepherds

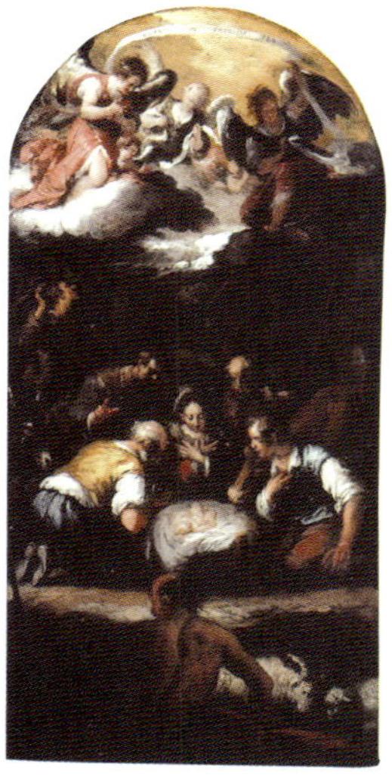

A780; oil on copper, 79.2 × 42.3 cm
Prov.: Ponte (?Lorenzo da Ponte); John Strange by 1785; Dr Grete Ring
Purchased, 1950; WA1950.6

Mortari 1995, no. I.506

Deriving from Jacopo Bassano, A870 is unique in Strozzi's oeuvre as a picture closely based on the work of another master. Strozzi lived in Venice from 1633 and became strongly interested in the art of Veronese, but Jacopo's rich handling of paint and dramatic chiaroscuro also impressed him.

Copy after Bernardo Strozzi
(1581/2 – 1644)

Giulio Strozzi

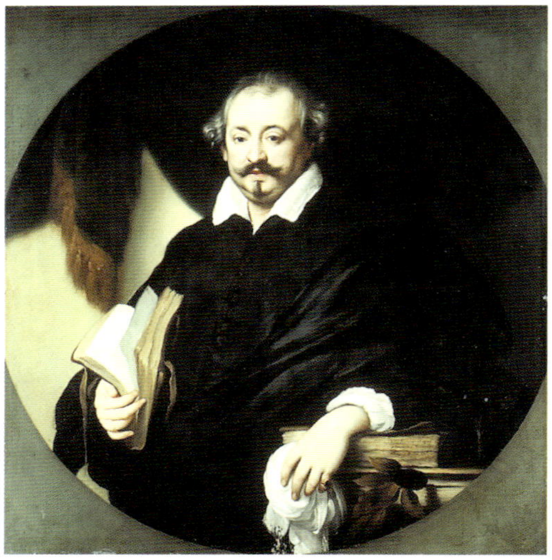

A1031; oil on canvas, 119.3 × 114.8 cm
Inscribed on the book: *Julij Strozzi Effigies / a Presbytero Bernardo / Strozzio Picta an.o / 1635.*
Prov.: Major J.S. A'Deane Coke; J. Pollak
Purchased, 1967; WA1967.24

Macandrew 1967; Erbentraut 1999, under no. 13

A poet and librettist, Giulio Strozzi (1583–1660) worked with Monteverdi and was a leading member of the Venetian Accademia degli Incogniti. Bernardo portrayed him in 1635; the prototype is probably the portrait now in the Staatliches Museum, Schwerin. Purchased as a portrait by Vouet, A1031 is an early copy, perhaps that recorded in the collection of the sitter's nephew in 1678.

Thomas Sully
(1783 – 1872)

The Love Letter

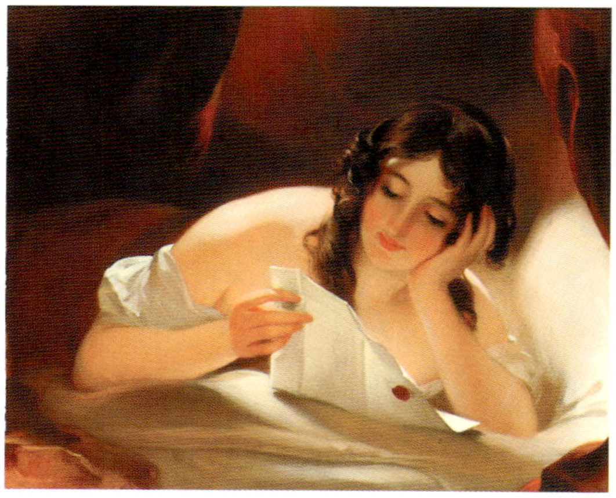

A313; oil on canvas, 64 × 76 cm
Signed in monogram and dated on verso: *TS 1834*
Prov.: Joseph Wood of Woolley Moor, Yorks. and by descent
Presented by Robert Henry Wood, 1902; WA1902.3

One of Sully's most popular compositions, of which he painted numerous replicas (Biddle and Fielding 1921, nos. 2396–2403). This version was presumably bought by the tenor Joseph Wood and his wife, the soprano Mary Ann Paton, during their American tour in 1836 when Sully painted Mary Ann's portrait (National Portrait Gallery), or perhaps when Sully visited England to paint Queen Victoria in 1837.

Maud Sumner
(1902 – 1985)

Land of Light

A1078; oil on canvas, 88.7 × 114.8 cm
Signed: *Sumner*
Presented by the artist, 1975; WA1975.108

After reading English Literature and Language in Oxford Sumner went to London and in 1926 to Paris to study art, mainly under Maurice Denis. At first she used a descriptive style but her later work is less clearly defined. Although her oil paintings remain essentially figurative, they often concentrate on atmospheric effects of light, shadow and space. *Land of Light* is typical of her later work.

Abraham Susenier
(*c.* 1620 – between 1666 and 1672)

Still Life with Oysters

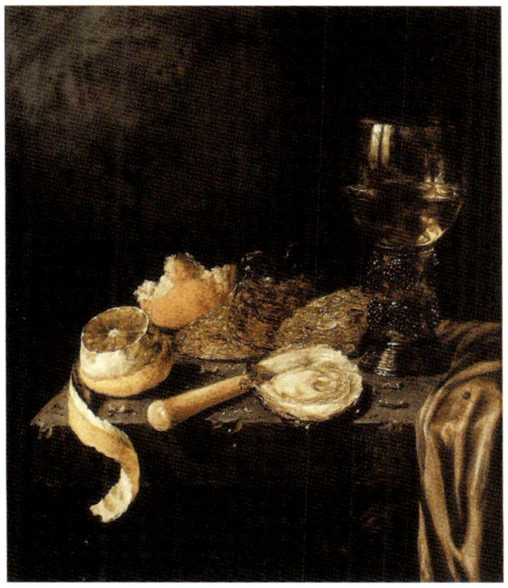

A604; oil on canvas, 41 × 34 cm
Signed and dated: *AB:S:1666* (AB in monogram)
Daisy Linda Ward Bequest, 1939; WA1940.2.80

Meijer 2003, no. 80

On account of the AB monogram, several of Susenier's paintings, including this example, have been misattributed to Abraham van Beyeren.There is not much kinship otherwise with van Beyeren. Susenier's fruit pieces show more affinities with the work of the Haarlem artists, Roelof Koets and Hans Bollongier. Similar humble, domestic glass rummers appear in most of his still lifes. There are no paintings dated later than 1666 and he may have died shortly after this.

Justus Suttermans (Sustermans)
(1597 – 1681)

The Senators of Florence swearing Allegiance to Ferdinando II de' Medici

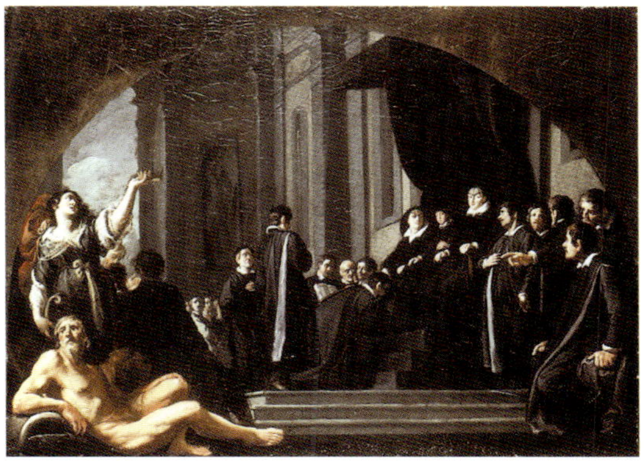

A1074; oil on canvas, 61 × 82 cm
Purchased with the assistance of the Museums & Galleries Commission/Victoria & Albert Museum Purchase Grant Fund and the Friends of the Ashmolean, 1974; WA1974.3

White 1999, p. 145

This is one of three known preparatory paintings for a large overdoor commissioned from Suttermans to celebrate the accession of the young Ferdinando as Grand Duke in 1621. The reclining nude represents the river Arno. The Grand Duke is seated between his mother, Maria Maddalena of Austria on his right and his grandmother, Christine of Lorraine, on his left.

Maud Sumner
(1902 – 1985)

Misty Evening

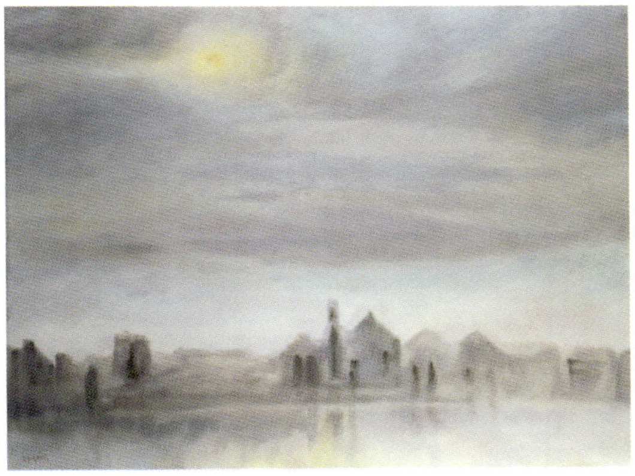

A1124; oil on canvas, 90 × 116 cm
Signed: *Sumner*
Presented by the artist, 1982; WA1982.40

In many landscapes of the 1960s and 1970s Sumner explored the effect of silence, the luminosity of space and the relation of the desert and the coast. These qualities are represented in this landscape. It remains unclear if the houses and the trees visible are at the coast or near a lake. This is chiefly a study of atmosphere, charged with light, which evokes a sense of space without any identifiable detail.

Attributed to Lambert Sustris
(*c.* 1510–15 – after 1560)

St Jerome in the Wilderness

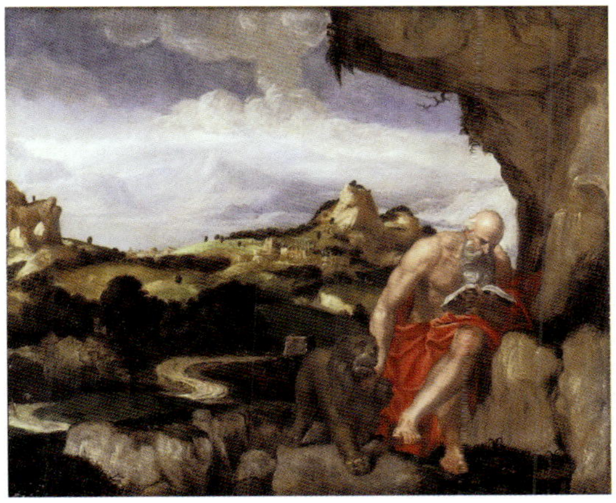

A717; oil on canvas, 95 × 112 cm
Prov.: William Angerstein; D.W. Freshfield; G. Fenwick Owen
Purchased, 1945; WA1945.98

Lloyd 1977, pp. 164–6

St Jerome (*c.* 342–420) is shown as a penitent hermit, accompanied by his attribute of a lion, against a backdrop of a panoramic, atmospheric landscape. A717 has had a variety of attributions to Venetian and Veronese artists: it is by a northern European artist who knew the art of Tintoretto and may have worked in his studio. The attribution to Lambert Sustris remains very tentative.

Style of Michiel Sweerts
(1618 – 1664)

Portrait of a Sculptor (?)

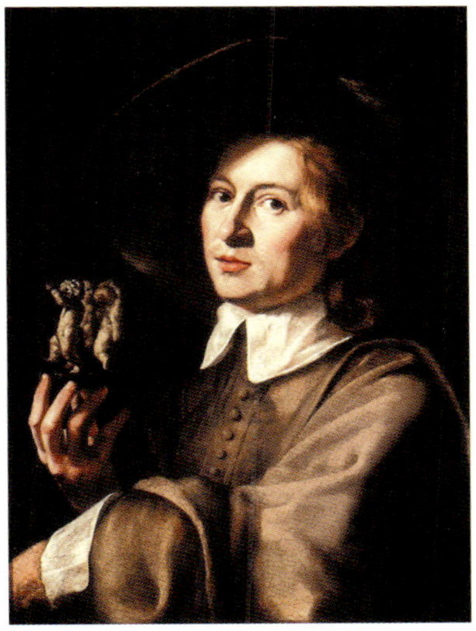

A859; oil on canvas, 64 × 47 cm
Prov.: Thomas Hudson
Presented by Sir Robert Witt through the National Art Collections Fund, 1952; WA1952.64

White 1999, p. 147

The group of dancing *putti* corresponds to an ivory in Braunschweig attributed to Frans Duquesnoy but this is not a portrait of Duquesnoy.

Anna Louisa Swynnerton
(1844 – 1933)

Head of a Bacchante

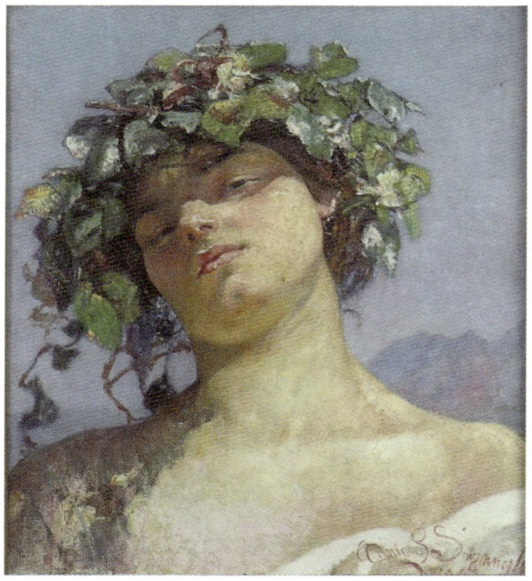

A511a; oil on canvas, 46 × 41 cm
Signed and dated: *Annie L Swynnerton 1903*
Presented by Mrs Richard Shute, 1937; WA1937.118

Anna Robinson married the sculptor, Joseph Swynnerton, in Rome in 1883 and remained there until his death in 1910. This painting was probably made from a local model, the garland added to raise the subject from a simple portrait.

David Teniers the Younger
(1610 – 1690)

A Distillery with an elderly Man buying Gin from a Woman

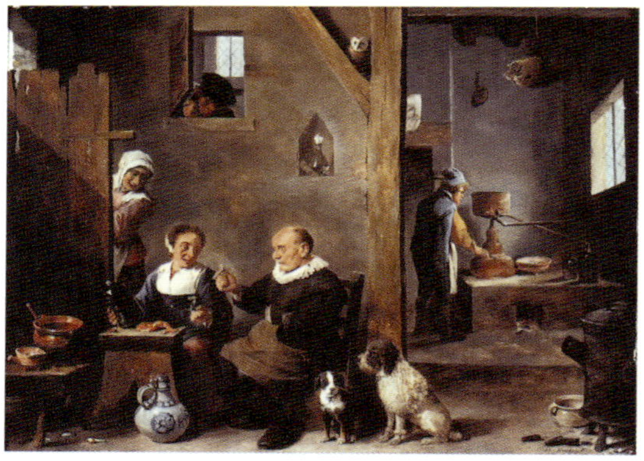

A1218; oil on panel, 48.4 × 65.4 cm
Prov.: Jean-Antoine Gros; Vicomte de Choiseul-Praslin; Wauter; Philippe; Solirène; J.-B. Lebrun; Prince de Talleyrand; Buchanan; John Webb; Alexander Baring; Asher Wertheimer and by descent
Accepted by H.M. Government in lieu of Inheritance Tax from the estate of Mrs Joan Cecily Conway and allocated to the Ashmolean, 1998; WA1999.9

White 1999, p. 194

Teniers was a prolific painter in several genres, including peasant subjects in the manner of Brouwer which were widely known through engravings. This painting has been dated to the 1640s. It was known in 18th-century France as 'Le Manchot' – 'The One Armed Man' – on account of the seated figure whose left hand is concealed below his apron. He holds up a coin to buy a glass of gin from the woman seated opposite. The distillery – probably an illegal still – appears in the background in another room. The owl may have been included as an allusion to human folly.

David Teniers the Younger
(1610 – 1690)

The Mocking of Christ

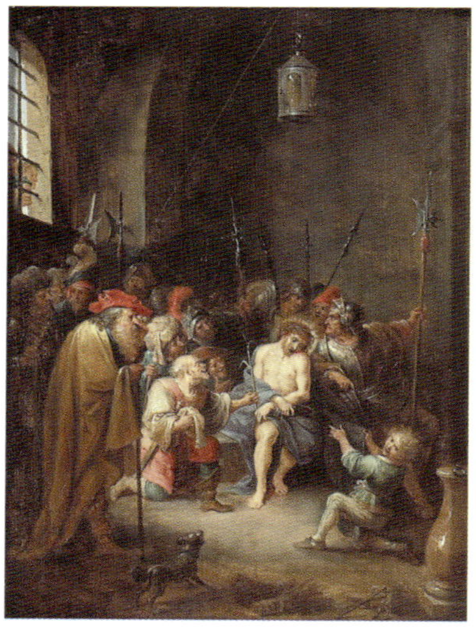

A119; oil on panel, 49 × 36 cm
Bequeathed by the Revd Dr Thomas Penrose, 1851; WA1851.15

White 1999, p. 148

Teniers made reduced copies of a number of paintings in the collection of the Archduke Leopold Wilhelm for whom he worked as court painter. This work is typical of the series although the original cannot be identified in the Archduke's collection. It appears to have been copied from an otherwise unknown painting by Frans Francken I (1542–1616).

David Teniers the Younger
(1610 – 1690)

The Foot Doctor

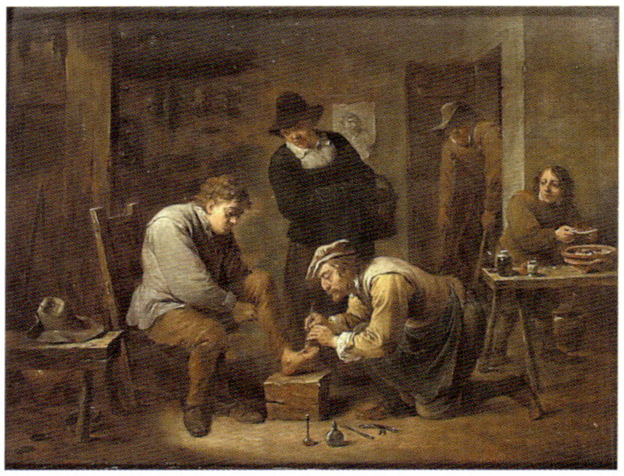

A120; oil on panel, 26 × 34 cm
Prov.: Richard Artis
Bequeathed by the Revd Dr Thomas Penrose, 1851; WA1851.16

White 1999, p. 148

Probably painted in the 1650s. The treatment of the theme derives from the work of Adriaen Brouwer. Teniers repeated the theme frequently throughout his career.

David Teniers the Younger
(1610 – 1690)

A young Peasant seated in an Interior

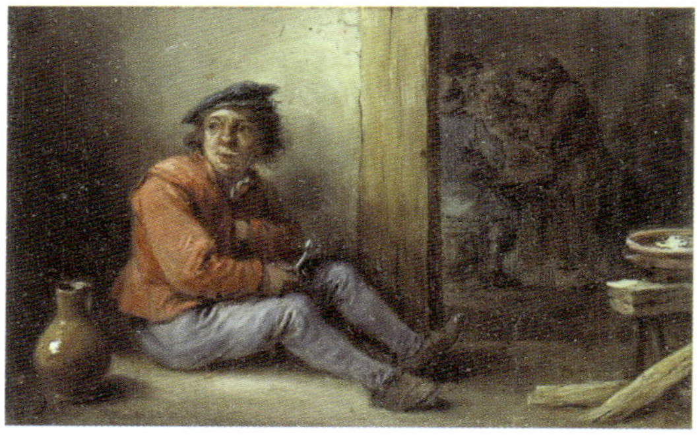

A184; oil on copper, mounted as a drawing, 7 × 11.2 cm
Signed in monogram: *DT*
Chambers Hall Gift, 1855; WA1855.212

White 1999, p. 151

The same model appears in two other paintings by Teniers, one of which is in the Wallraf-Richartz Museum, Cologne.

David Teniers the Younger
(1610 – 1690)

A Peasant carrying a Rod over his Shoulder

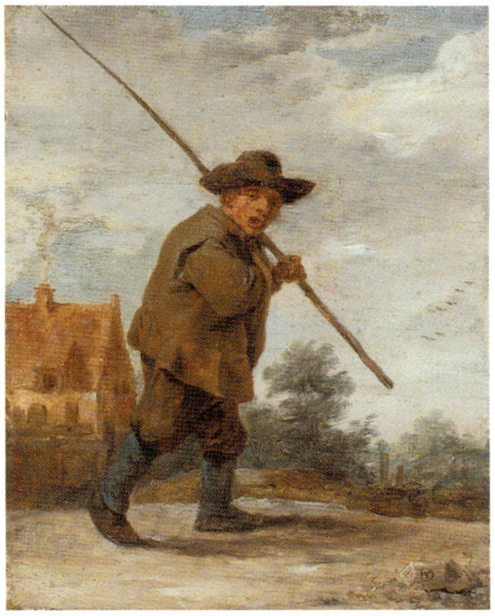

A1035a; oil on panel, mounted as a drawing, 16 × 12 cm
Prov.: Sir John Fiennes Twistleton Crampton and by descent
Bequeathed by Miss S.A.P. Boyle, 1967; WA1967.52.40

White 1999, p. 152

One of a number of similar studies by Teniers, sometimes made in sets and pairs.

David Teniers the Younger
(1610 – 1690)

Landscape with a Farmhouse and Figures

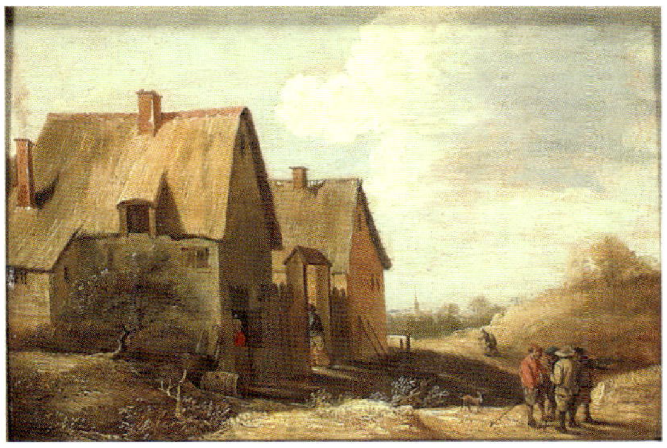

A121; oil on panel, 24 × 34 cm
Signed in monogram: *DT*
Bequeathed by the Revd Dr Thomas Penrose, 1851
WA1851.17

White 1999, p. 151

A pair to the following painting. Both panels are marked on the back with the monogram of Lambrechts I Steen, a 17th-century panel-maker.

Pietro Testa
(1611 – 1650)

The Dead Christ mourned by Angels

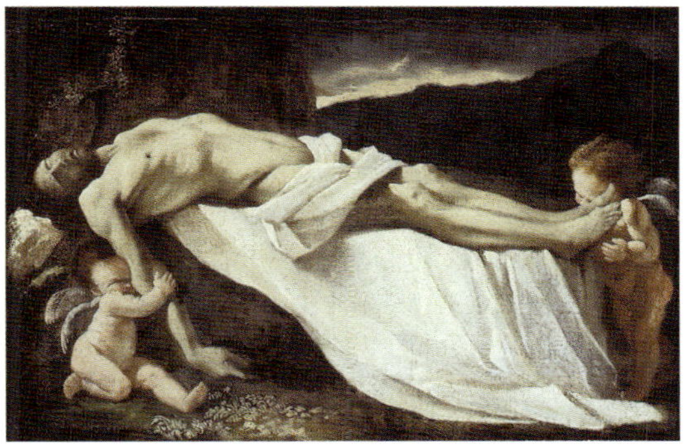

A436; oil on canvas, 31 × 46 cm
Prov.: Major George St John Mildmay
Presented by Sydney D. Kitson, 1934; WA1934.12

Cropper 1984, pp. 60–1

This small image, emphasising the suffering of Christ and the anguish of the cherubs, may have been made for a clerical patron in the mid-1640s. It closely relates to *The Prophecy of Basildes* (Capodimonte, Naples), a Carmelite commission. A prolific draughtsman and printmaker, Testa painted relatively little and his intellectual approach often resulted in unusual images. A version of A436 is in the Musée des Beaux-Arts, Tours.

David Teniers the Younger
(1610 – 1690)

An Old Beggar

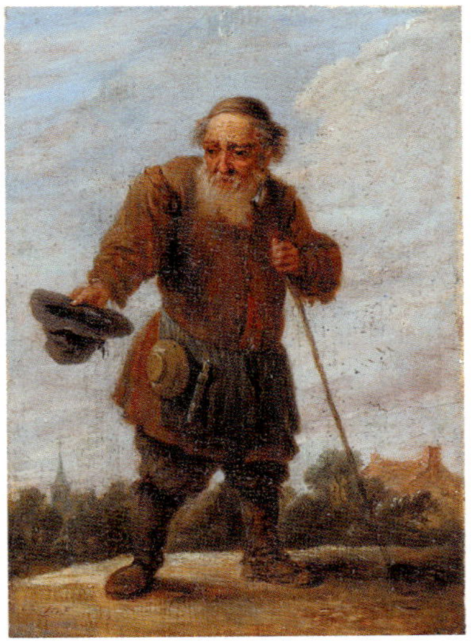

A1035b; oil on canvas, mounted as a drawing, 16 × 11.3 cm
Prov.: Sir John Fiennes Twistleton Crampton and by descent
Bequeathed by Miss S.A.P. Boyle, 1967; WA1967.52.41

White 1999, p. 154

Probably painted as a pair with the previous painting of a youth. It was originally painted on panel, like its companion, but was transferred to canvas by the restorer, Bauquin, in 1785.

David Teniers the Younger
(1610 – 1690)

Landscape with a Farmhouse and Figures on the Bank of a River

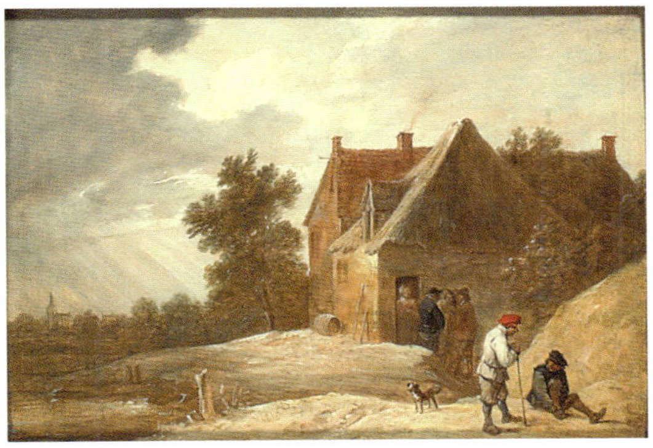

A122; oil on panel, 24 × 34 cm
Bequeathed by the Revd Dr Thomas Penrose, 1851; WA1851.18

White 1999, p. 151

A pair to the previous painting.

Style of Jan Philip van Thielen
(1618 – 1667)

Still Life of Flowers

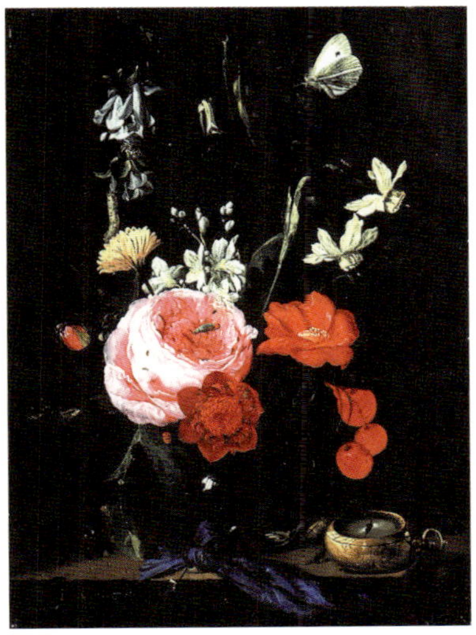

A605; oil on panel, 33 × 22 cm
Inscribed: *i.Pvan ThiLE*
Daisy Linda Ward Bequest, 1939; WA1940.2.81

Meijer 2003, no. 81

As a flower painter, Van Thielen tended to follow Seghers, composing his blooms in tall, footed vessels and leaving the shelf bare. This painting does not conform to the type and the handling of paint is heavier than usual. There are two other known versions of this painting, one of which is signed by Jan Pauwel Gillemans (1618–after 1675). It seems likely that the Oxford painting and the other copy both originated in Gillemans's studio.

Johannes Thomas
(1617 – 1678)

St Sebastian succoured by St Irene

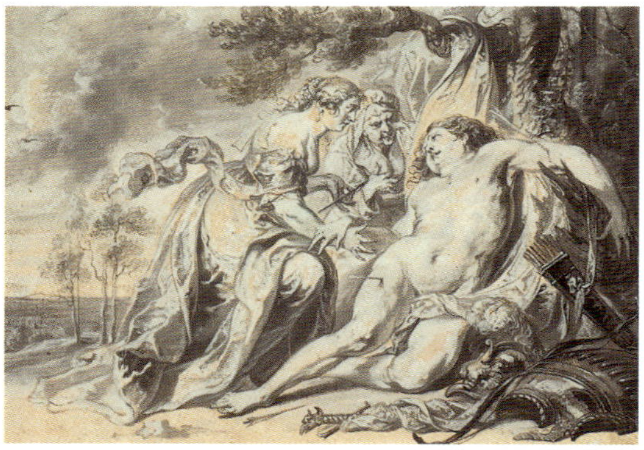

Oil pigments on paper, mounted as a drawing, 27.7 × 38.8 cm
Bequeathed by Francis Douce, 1834; WA1863.287

Parker 1938, no. 220

Thomas was a painter, etcher and mezzotint engraver who studied with Rubens in Antwerp. He moved to Vienna in 1661 to work at the court of Leopold I. This Rubensian sketch is a study (in reverse) for an etching of the same subject.

Sir James Thornhill
(1676 – 1734)

Sketch for a Ceiling Design

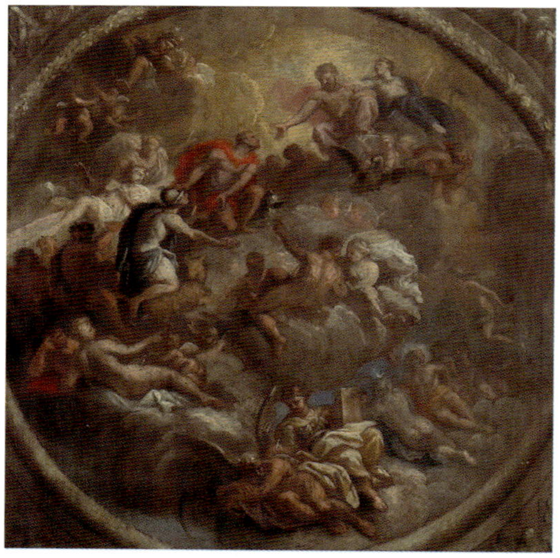

A510; oil on canvas, 62 × 58 cm
Presented by G. McN. Rushforth, 1937; WA1937.110

London 1958, no. 9

The subject is obscure. It seems to represent Mars (in the red cloak) presenting a warrior to Vulcan, who stretches out his right hand in welcome, while Venus attempts to distract him. Below, History is writing on the back of Time (with wings and a scythe). It has been suggested that the sketch shows Mars pleading with Jupiter for the deification of Romulus (Ovid, *Metamorphoses*, XIV). No related mural is known.

Giovanni Battista Tiepolo
(1696 – 1770)

A young Woman with a Macaw

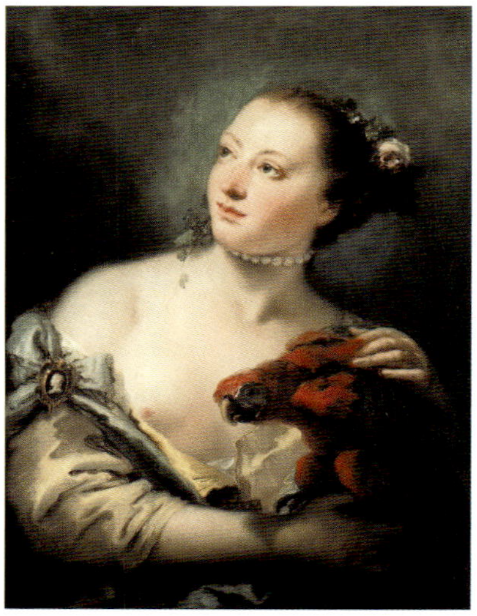

A876; oil on canvas, 71 × 53.4 cm
Prov.: (?)Charles, Marquis de la Rochelambert; George L. Durlacher
Presented by the National Art Collections Fund from the collection of Ernest E. Cook, 1955; WA1955.67

Gemin and Pedrocco 1993, no. 502; De Grazia 1996, pp. 254, 256, 268

A876 probably belongs to a series of half-length *capriccio* portraits of women for Elizabeth Petrovna, Empress of Russia on which Tiepolo was working in late 1760. This distinctive Venetian genre of poetic or fantasy portraits derives from Giorgione, and Tiepolo (celebrated as a latter-day Veronese) often looked to 16th-century Venetian art. Such images of beautiful women are often categorised as courtesans. Exotic birds are common in Tiepolo's work and here the macaw provides a colourful and witty motif. The cameo portrait shows one of the Caesars, possibly Augustus. Lorenzo Tiepolo made a pastel copy of A876 (National Gallery of Art, Washington), together with a pendant showing a woman in a fur wrap (*Allegory of Winter*, Kress Collection, El Paso Museum) which may record a lost oil painting. A drawing with variations after A876 probably by Lorenzo is in the Ashmolean (Parker 1956, no. 1082).

Copy after Giovanni Battista Tiepolo
(1696 – 1770)

The Gathering of Manna

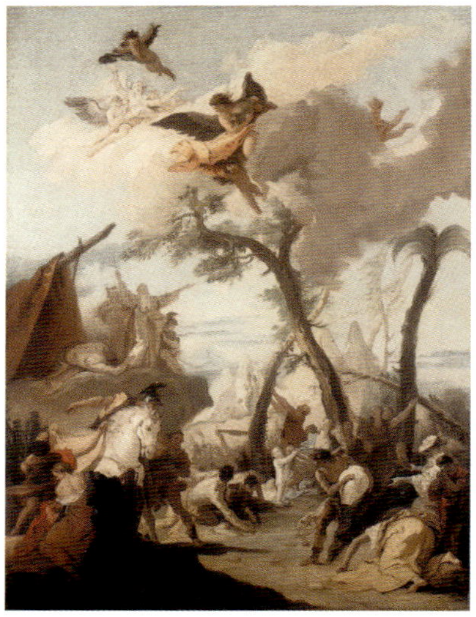

A362; oil on canvas, 96 × 71.5 cm
Prov.: Von Goldammer; Tancred Borenius
Presented by Sir Herbert Cook through the National Art Collections Fund, 1920; WA1920.1

Gemin and Pedrocco 1993, under no. 251

The hungry Israelites gather bread from heaven (Exodus 16: 4–36). A362 is connected with two vast canvases painted for the Confraternity of the Holy Sacrament at S. Lorenzo, Verolanuova (Brescia), *The Sacrifice of Melchisedek* and *The Gathering of the Manna*, painted 1740–42 and still *in situ*. Five small-scale versions of the latter composition are known, including A362, which is a studio copy of Tiepolo's *modello*, now in Buenos Aires.

David Tindle
(b. 1932)

Head Study

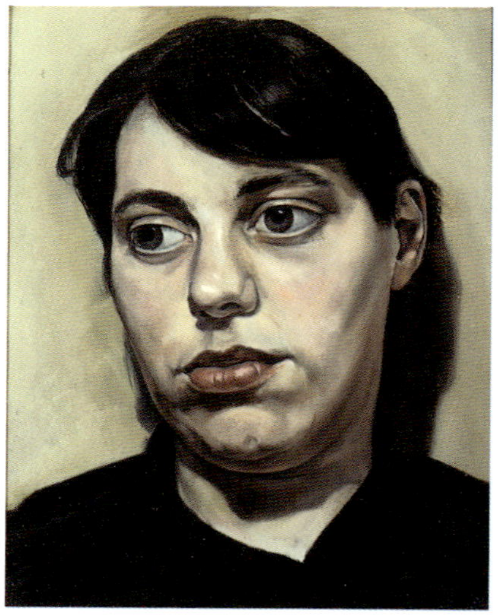

A1188; oil on canvas, 24.5 × 14.5 cm
Inscribed on the back: *David Tindle 1955 Address: Old Chapel, East Haddon, Northamptonshire.*
Presented by the artist, 1993; WA1993.541

Eustace 1999, no. 33

This close-up view of a female model belongs to a group of contemporary British paintings, such as those by John Minton or Lucian Freud. The claustrophobic intensity of observation is a result of the tight borders and reduced palette, using only black and various tones of a greyish brown. It is a remarkable example of a specific sort of British realistic painting.

David Tindle
(b. 1932)

Portrait

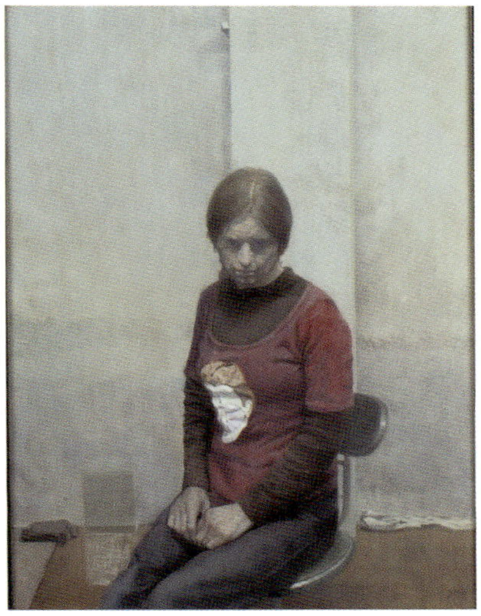

A1189; egg tempera on canvas, 40.5 × 30.5 cm
Signed with monogram and dated: *DT 75*; inscribed on back: *David Tindle 75 / Portrait / Egg tempera / [...] Egg yolk and distilled water only*
Presented by the artist, 1993; WA1993.542

In the 1950s Tindle and other British painters adopted an extremely close-up stance to the people he painted. Tindle retained this sharp realism in his later work. In this painting, for example, he shows a girl sitting in a nearly empty room, apparently vulnerable and looking desperately down to the floor. Tindle used the rare technique of egg tempera, which is partly responsible for the sharpness of the lines and the differentiation of the colours.

Jacopo Robusti, called Tintoretto
(1519 – 1594)

Head of a bearded Man

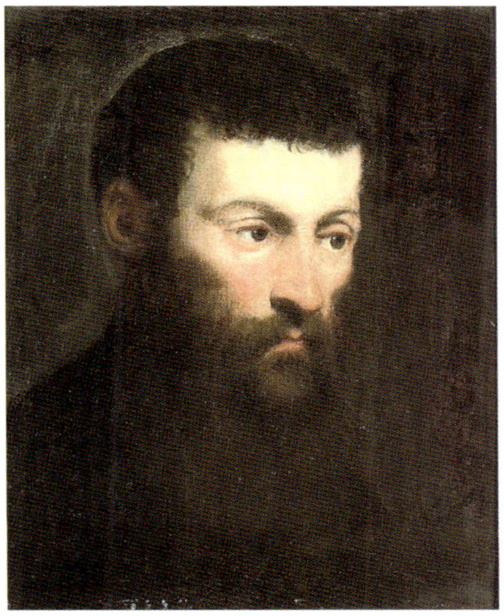

A678a; oil on canvas, 42 × 35 cm
Prov.: Frederic Lord Leighton
Presented by Harold Bompas, 1941; WA1941.18

Lloyd 1977, pp. 167–8

A678a may be a fragment from a larger painting, but the top and bottom edges have been extended. It has suffered much damage in the past but was once a painting of fine quality, probably made *c.* 1550.

Copy after Jacopo Tintoretto
(1519 – 1594)

The Annunciation

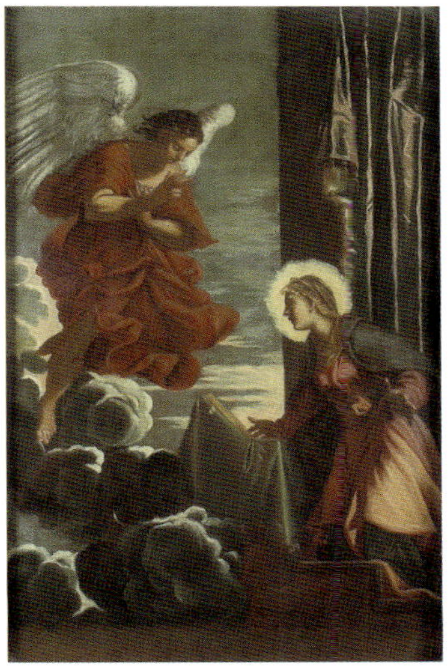

A397; oil on canvas, 88.8 × 56.8 cm
Presented by Sir Arthur Evans, 1929; WA1929.9

Lloyd 1977, pp. 170–71; Palluchini and Rossi 1982, under nos 433–4

Possibly dating from the late 17th century, this is a reduced copy of the right-hand organ shutter in the church of S. Rocco, Venice, painted by Tintoretto and his workshop between 1582 and 1586. The copyist has omitted the dove of the Holy Spirit in a ray of heavenly light: the painted shutter was taller in shape.

Domenico Robusti, called Tintoretto
(1560 – 1635)

Portrait of a Man

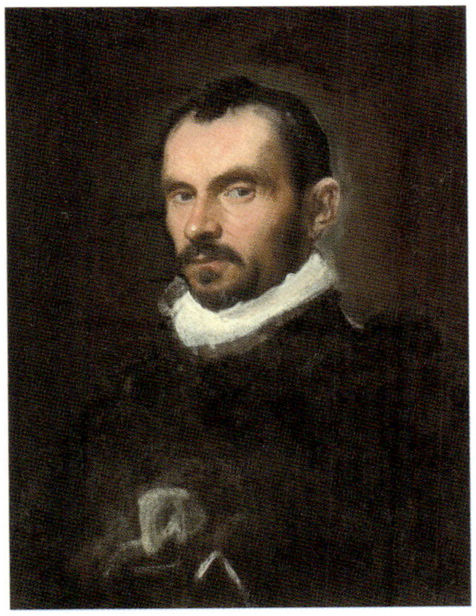

A731; oil on canvas, 63 × 48 cm
Purchased, 1946; WA1946.271

Lloyd 1977, pp. 166–7

Formerly attributed to Jacopo Bassano, this is an early work by Domenico of *c.* 1589, which reveals his great strength as a portraitist. The very sketchy treatment of the collar and costume suggests that A731 may be unfinished.

Jacopo Robusti, called Tintoretto
(1519 – 1594)

The Resurrection of Christ

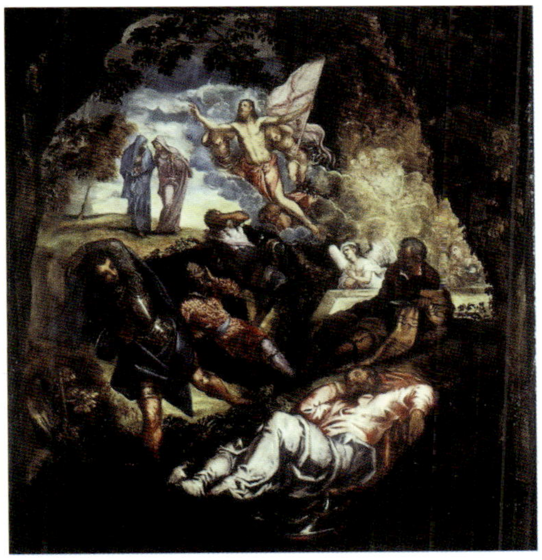

A720; oil on canvas, 161 × 153 cm
Prov.: William Douglas-Hamilton, 12th Duke of Hamilton; Sir William Farrer
Bequeathed by Gaspard O. Farrer through the National Art Collections Fund, 1946; WA1946.198

Lloyd 1977, pp. 168–71; Palluchini and Rossi 1982, no. 199

Originally shaped as an octagon (the additions may date from the 17th century), this composition was intended to hang high, perhaps as a prominent element in a wall or ceiling decoration in a carved and gilded surround. Suggestions for the dating have varied from the mid-1550s to the early 1570s. Domenico Tintoretto painted a variation of A720, now in the Staatsgalerie, Stuttgart.

Tiziano Vecellio, called Titian
(*c.* ?1485–90 – 1576)

Giacomo Doria

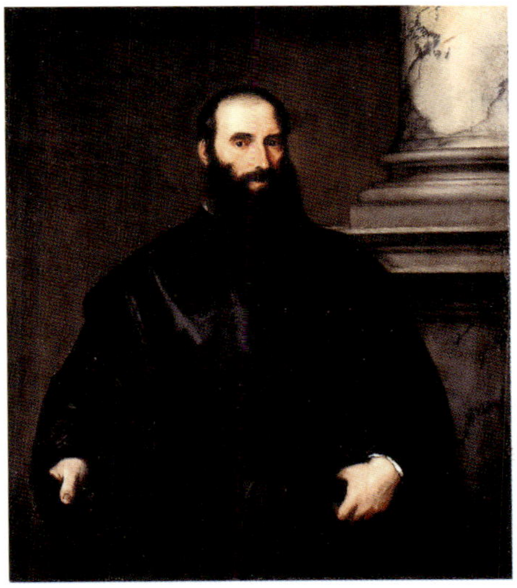

A1228; oil on canvas, 115.5 × 97.7 cm
Prov.: Giacomo Doria; by descent to the Doria Principi d'Angri; Giovanna Lancellotti; Ferdinando Colonna, Principe d'Agliano; Sir Julius Wernher and by descent to Sir Harold Wernher
Purchased in memory of Professor Francis Haskell with the assistance of the Heritage Lottery Fund, the National Art Collections Fund and other donors, 2000; WA2000.85

Wethey 1971, no. 25; Pedrocco 2001, no. 115; Jaffé 2003, no. 21

Giacomo Doria, a Genoese merchant resident in Venice from 1529–41, commissioned this dignified, restrained portrait around 1533–5. Doria acted as diplomat for the Genoese state and had connections with the Hapsburg court; two of his sons were to become Doge of Genoa. A1228 displays Titian's keen psychological sensitivity and his painterly skills in orchestrating a near-monochrome composition. He used possibly for the first time in his portraiture the device of a grand, polished marble column, thereby expanding the picture space and denoting the sitter as a person of wealth and authority.

Copy after Tiziano Vecellio, called Titian
(*c.* ?1485/90 – 1576)

Venus blindfolding Cupid

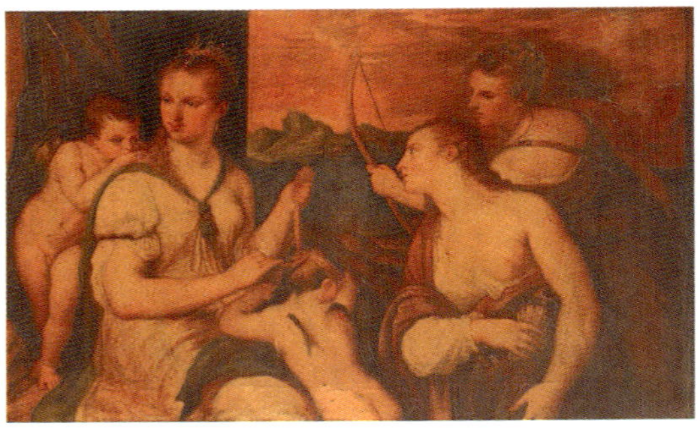

A226; oil on canvas, 45.1 × 72 cm
Provenance unknown; WA.OA903

Lloyd 1977, p. 171

A226 is a reduced, careful copy of the painting by Titian in the Galleria Borghese, Rome, dating from *c.* 1565, which was in the Borghese collection by 1613. The subject has been variously interpreted as the Education or the Punishment of Love and may be an allegory of Love in its different guises. Titian altered the appearance of the figure of Venus as he painted.

Henry Tonks
(1862 – 1937)

Adam and Eve

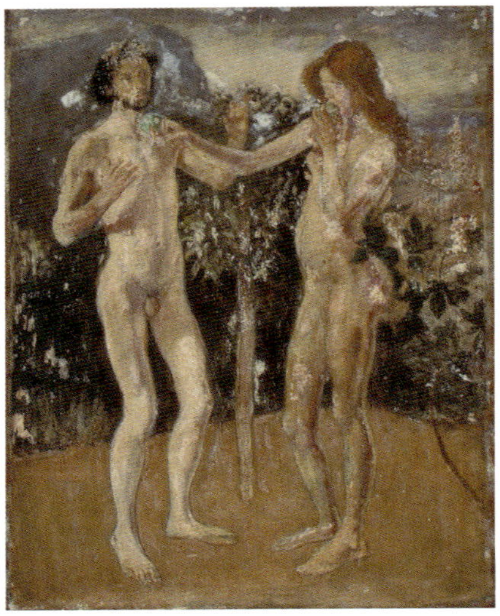

A1129; oil on panel, 45 × 35.4 cm
Presented by Mrs Palmer, 1983; WA1983.54

After Tonks's death, his executor, C.H. Collins Baker, made a bonfire of the contents of his studio. This painting, in very poor condition, was rescued by Mrs Monnington, the donor's sister.

Copy after Tiziano Vecellio, called Titian
(*c.* ?1485/90 – 1576)

The Battle of Cadore

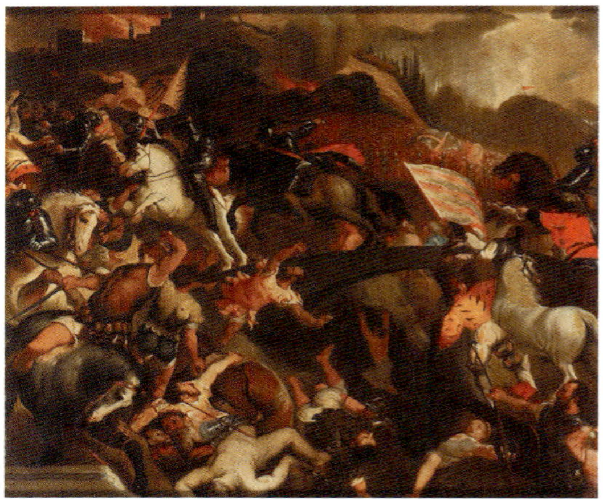

A277; oil on canvas, 81 × 92 cm
Prov.: Josiah Gilbert
Presented by Mrs Josiah Gilbert, 1895; WA1895.10

Titian's painting of *The Battle of Cadore* of 1537–8 in the Sala del Maggior Consiglio in the Palazzo Ducale, Venice, was destroyed by fire in 1577. The composition is known through engravings and through an early painted copy (Uffizi, Florence). According to Ridolfi (1642) there were many painted copies of this famous work. A277 is of good quality and may have been made after the lost painting, rather than after another copy.

Copy after Tiziano Vecellio, called Titian
(*c.* ?1485/90 – 1576)

A Shepherd and a Nymph

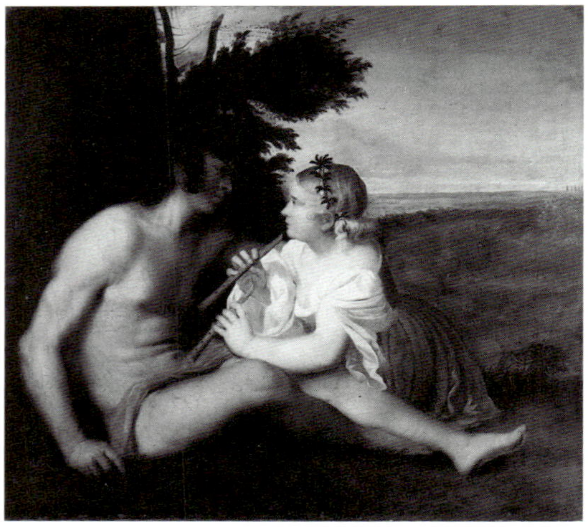

A522; oil on canvas, 81 × 90 cm
Bequeathed by Miss Mabel Price, 1939; WA1939.16

Wethey 1975, under no. 36

A522 is an accurate copy of the group on the left of Titian's painting known as *The Three Ages of Man* in the collection of the Duke of Sutherland which may date from *c.* 1512–13. The original painting left Venice at a relatively early date: in 1568 Vasari described a similar picture owned by a collector in Faenza. A522 could have been made after the original or an early copy, such as that in the Doria collection.

Henry Tonks
(1862 – 1937)

The Birdcage

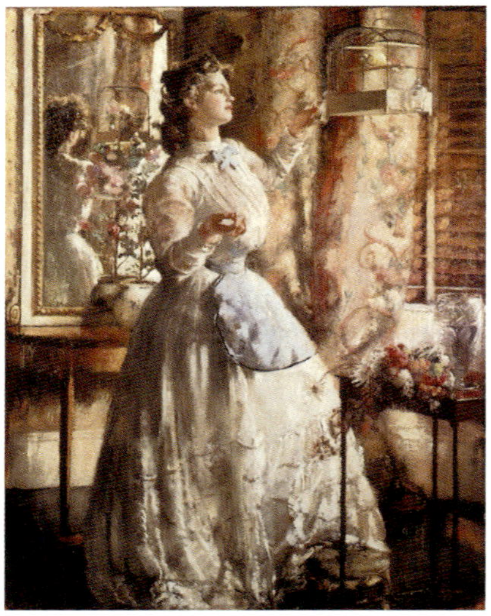

A439; oil on canvas, 140 × 112 cm
Signed and dated: *Henry Tonks 1907*
Prov.: Judge William Evans
Presented by Mrs W.F.R. Weldon, 1935; WA1935.79

Hone 1939, pp. 82–3; Morris 1985, no. 7

Tonks developed a personal kind of Impressionism under the influence of Wilson Steer and it is seen to best advantage in his genre paintings before the First World War. The model in this painting was Ethel N. Burford (1883–1944), who sat to Tonks and many other artists. It was exhibited at the New English Art Club in 1907.

FELICE TORELLI
(1667 – 1748)

The Betrayal of Christ

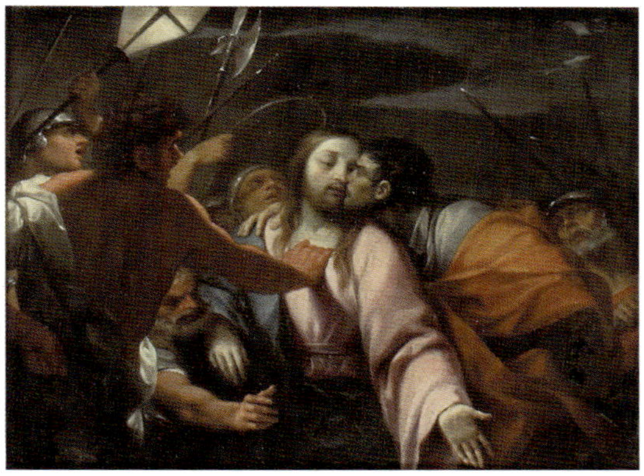

A904; oil on copper, 25 × 33 cm
Prov.: R. Owen Roberts, Lea Manor House, Ilfracombe
Presented anonymously, 1957; WA1957.95

Faietti and Zacchi 1998, under no. 82

Judas betrays Christ to the waiting soldiers by identifying him with a kiss in the darkness of the Mount of Olives. The dramatic nocturnal scene, dating from *c.* 1695–1700, ultimately derives from a painting by Ludovico Carracci of *c.* 1589–90 that made an impact on Bolognese artists, including Guercino. Torelli painted another version of the subject (Pinacoteca Nazionale, Bologna) in a more classicizing mode. A preparatory drawing for A904 is in the Pinacoteca Nazionale.

WILLIAM TOWNSEND
(1909 – 1973)

Bridge over a Stream

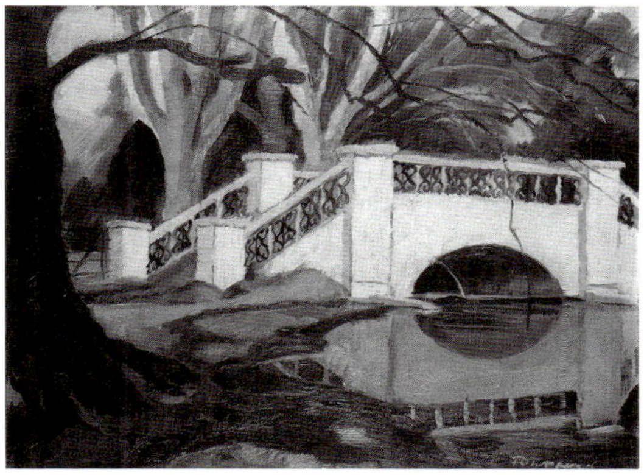

A1143; oil on canvas, 35.5 × 45.5 cm
Signed: *Townsend*
Bequeathed by Dame Helen Gardner, 1986; WA1986.98

Townsend developed a manner of painting naturalistic landscapes, which rely on a careful observation of tone and structure. This is a characteristic landscape of the type, a fluently painted view of a bridge in a quiet park during winter.

JEAN-FRANÇOIS DE TROY
(1679 – 1752)

Portrait of a Woman

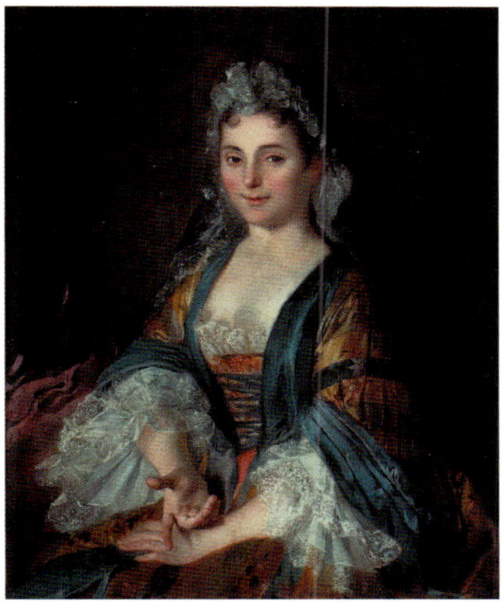

A961; oil on canvas, 91 × 73 cm
Prov.: Dr E. Carter
Madan Bequest, 1962; WA1962.17.3

Leribault 2002, no. P.47

Once thought to be Venetian, A961 was subsequently identified as French, with suggested attributions including that of Jean Raoux. The lady's costume, headdress and lace are datable to *c.* 1710–20. A961 is striking for its directness and informality and a convincing attribution to de Troy around 1710–15 has recently been proposed.

HENRI DE TOULOUSE-LAUTREC
(1864 – 1901)

La toilette (Celle qui se peigne)

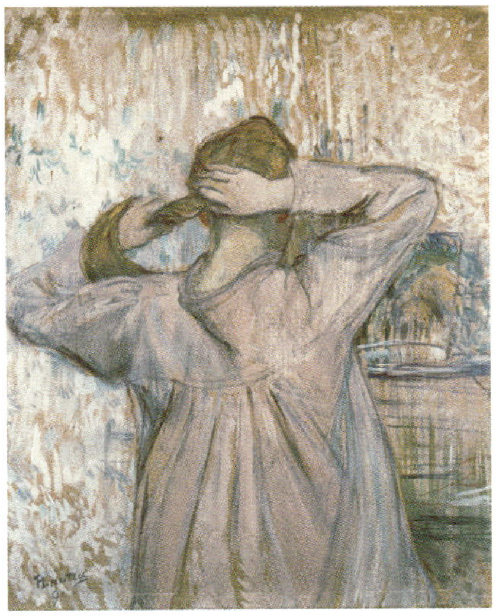

A641; oil on board, 58 × 46 cm
Signed and dated: *T-Lautrec 1891*
Hindley Smith Bequest, 1939; WA1940.1.23

The artist painted several variations of this theme in 1891. The style and subject recall similar works by Degas. Although executed in oil, the absorbent card gives the surface a dry, pastel-like appearance.

Circle of FRANCESCO TREVISANI
(1656 – 1746)

The Baptism of Christ

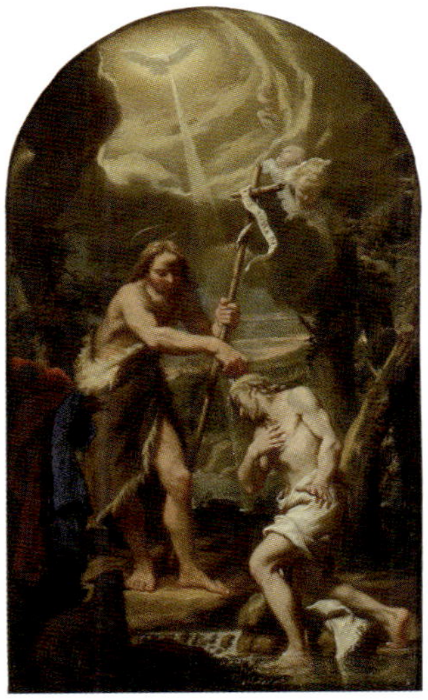

A931; oil on canvas mounted on plywood, 75 × 44 cm
Purchased, 1959; WA1959.60

Christ was baptised by St John in the river Jordan; the Holy Spirit descended in the form of a dove and the voice of God was heard proclaiming his son (Matthew 3: 13–17). Formerly attributed to Francesco Trevisani, A931 is by an artist in his circle in Rome. A plausible attribution has recently been suggested to Girclamo Pesci (1679 – 1759), on the grounds of the strong affinity of A931 with an altar-piece of 1728 in San Pietro, Zagarolo.

GEORGE TUCKWELL
(b. 1919)

Skull

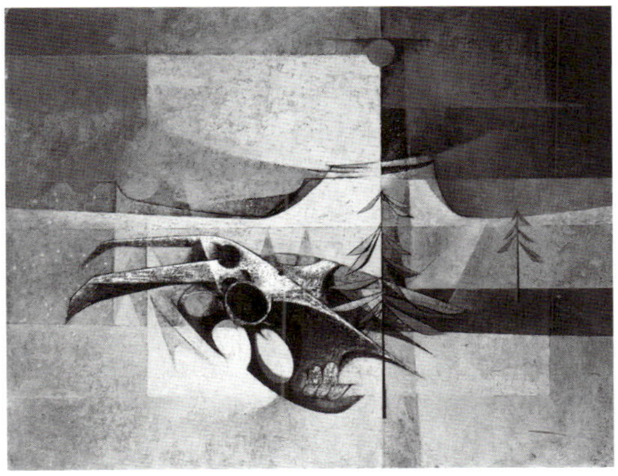

A999; oil on board, 58.2 × 74 cm
Signed in monogram: *GT*
Presented by Miss Elizabeth Watt, 1963; WA1963.31

Tuckwell used surrealistic details in the manner of Graham Sutherland. In this painting a skull is placed in an orange-yellow landscape, indicated through a few horizontal lines, two trees and a sun. The space is built up with stripes of colour forming a geometrical pattern, not related either to the skulls or to the landscape itself.

George Tuckwell
(b. 1919)

Plant Abstract

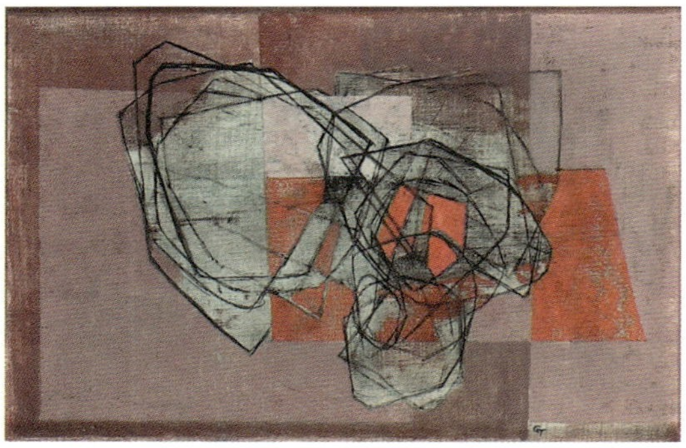

A1241; oil on canvas, 30.5 × 45.5 cm
Signed in monogram: *GT*
Prov.: purchased from the artist by the donor in 1946–7
Presented by Dr and Mrs Peter Barton, 2001; WA2001.72

In this painting Tuckwell explores the effect of building space and form through lines and patterns of colour. Following ideas developed in Germany and France during the 1910s and 1920s, mainly based on Delaunay's colour theory and his awareness of the work of Kandinsky and Klee, Tuckwell tries to find a balance between large patterns of colour and a more dynamic use of line.

William Turner of Oxford
(1789 – 1862)

The Wyndcliffe, Chepstow

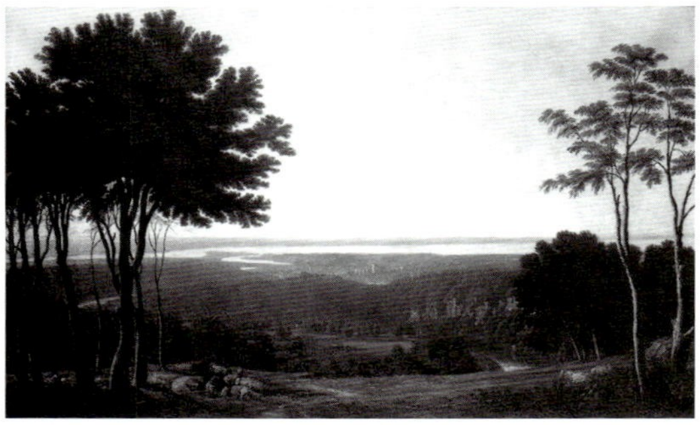

A351; oil on canvas, 95 × 149 cm
Bequeathed by Robert William Raper, 1915; WA1915.62

Wyndcliffe is about two miles from Chepstow, at the mouth of the Wye in Monmouthshire, and a favourite stopping-place for tourists in search of the picturesque in Wales. Turner made his first tour of Wales in 1817 and this oil may have been based on sketches made then.

William Turner of Oxford
(1789 – 1862)

King's Mill on the Cherwell

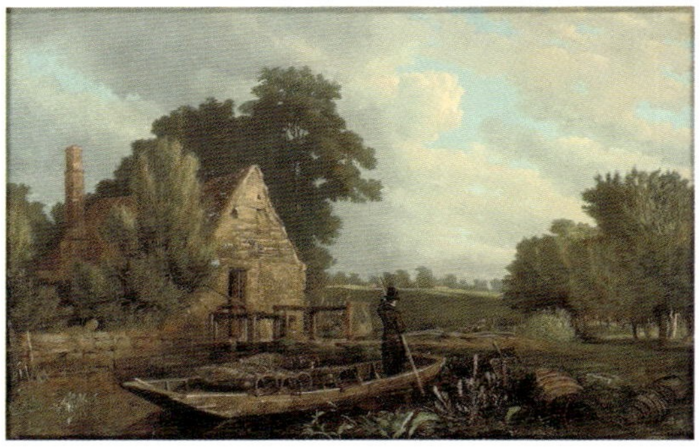

A438; oil on millboard, 51 × 76 cm
Presented by Mrs H.T. Gerrans in memory of her husband, 1934; WA1934.14

The King's Mill, on the River Cherwell in Oxford (now in the University Parks), is recorded in the Doomsday Book and was a working mill until 1825.

William Turner of Oxford
(1789 – 1862)

Woodland Landscape

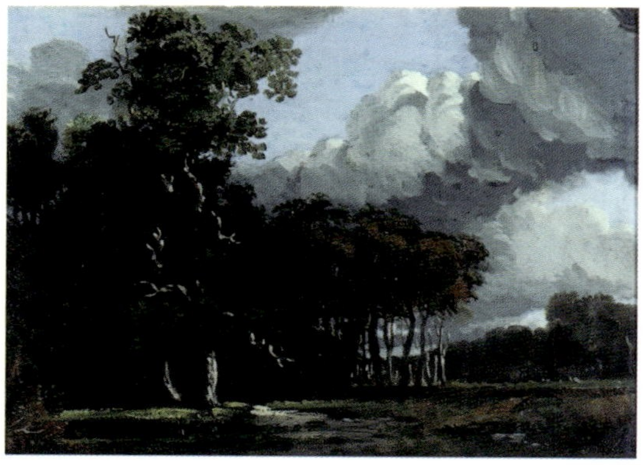

A656; oil on millboard, 22 × 29 cm
Presented by Francis Falconer Madan, 1939; WA1939.53

Titterington and Wilcox 1984–5, no. 30

This freshly painted sketch exploring the effects of strong light on tree trunks against the dark foliage and lowering sky has been dated *c.* 1816–20.

William Turner of Oxford
(1789 – 1862)

Gravel Pit on Shotover Hill, near Oxford

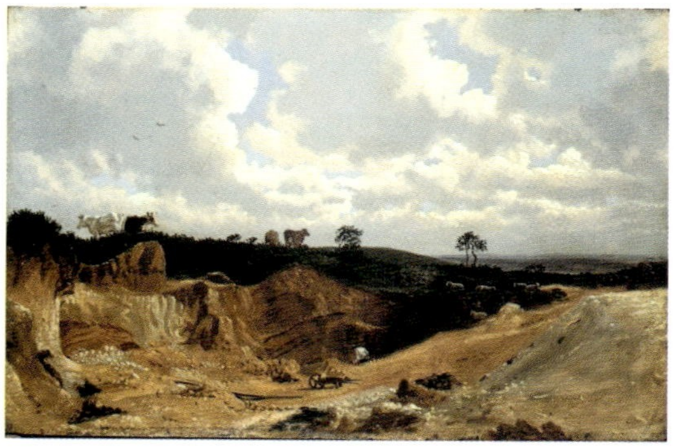

A702; oil on millboard, 27 × 40 cm
Prov.: G.R. Owen
Presented by the Revd Canon the Hon. A.F. Northcote, 1942; WA1942.61

Titterington and Wilcox 1984–5, no. 36

The hills around Oxford had provided building materials from medieval times. Turner's painting inevitably recalls John Linnell's *Kensington Gravel Pits* of 1813 (Tate Britain), and probably dates from *c.* 1818.

William Turner of Oxford
(1789 – 1862)

View of Marston, near Oxford

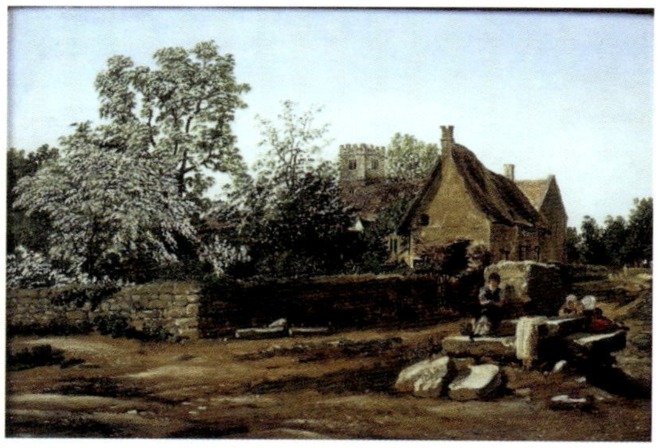

A701; oil on millboard, 27 × 40 cm
Prov.: G.R. Owen
Presented by the Revd Canon the Hon. A.F. Northcote, 1942; WA1942.60

The ancient village of Marston is one of the most picturesque and accessible of those near Oxford.

WILLIAM TURNER OF OXFORD
(1789 – 1862)

View in Bagley Wood, near Oxford

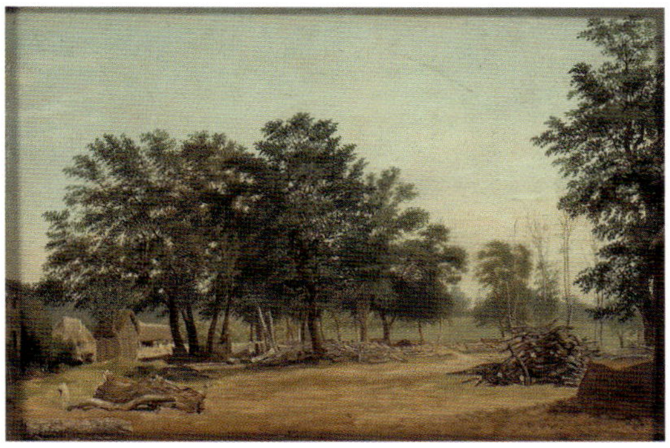

A703; oil on millboard, 27 × 40 cm
Prov.: G.R. Owen
Presented by the Revd Canon the Hon. A.F. Northcote, 1942; WA1942.62

Bagley Wood is about two miles south of Oxford, on the top of Hinksey Hill.

ANONYMOUS TUSCAN ARTIST
(*c.* 1390)

Head of an Angel

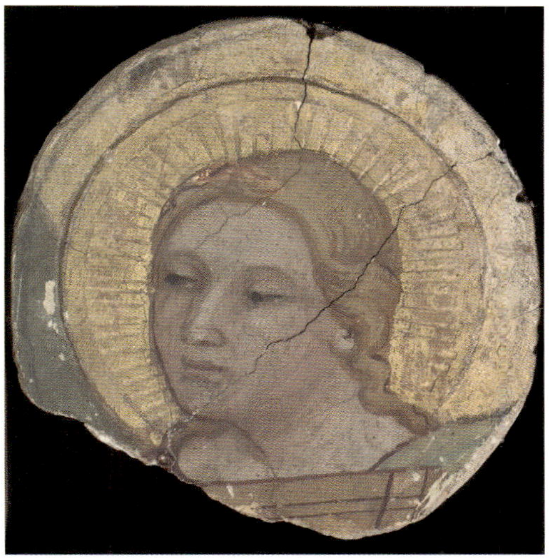

A451C; fresco, 23 cm in diameter
Presented by Mrs Leslie Milne, 1936; WA1936.7

Lloyd 1977, p. 142

A fragment of a fresco, A451C appears to have been retouched in parts. It probably dates from the late 14th century.

ANONYMOUS TUSCAN ARTIST
(*c.* 1480 – 1500?)

Portrait of a Boy

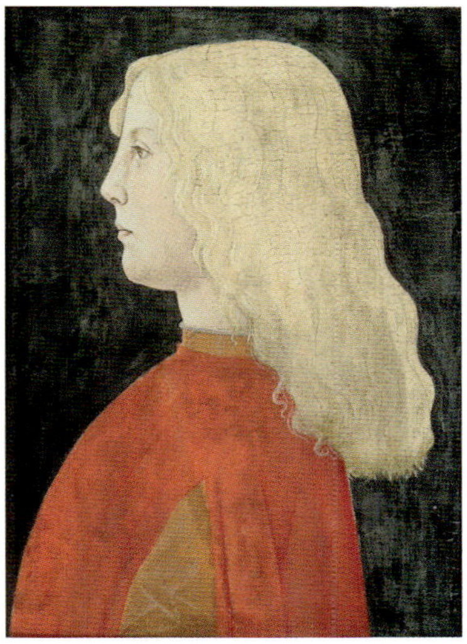

A95; tempera (?) and oil on panel, 36 × 25.8 cm
Fox-Strangways Gift, 1850; WA1850.17

Lloyd 1977, pp. 184–5

See under A94.

WILLIAM TURNER OF OXFORD
(1789 – 1862)

Self-portrait

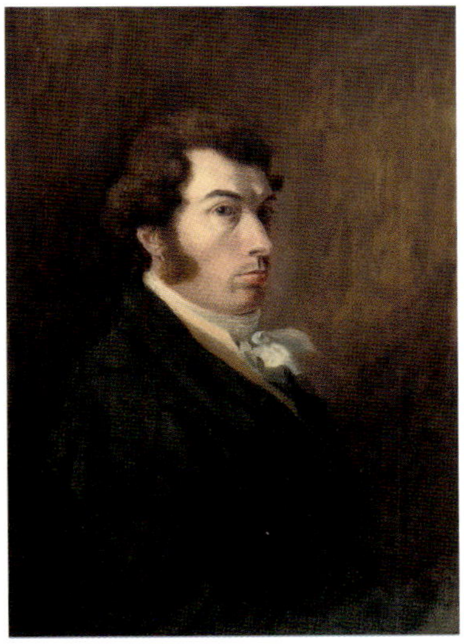

A415; oil on paper on canvas, 55 × 38 cm
Prov.: the Revd T. Archer Turner
Presented by C.E. Turner, 1932; WA1932.78

Titterington and Wilcox 1984–5, no. 43

This is Turner's only portrait in oils and may have been made to commemorate his marriage to Elizabeth Ilott in 1824.

ANONYMOUS TUSCAN ARTIST
(*c.* 1480 – 1500?)

Portrait of a Boy

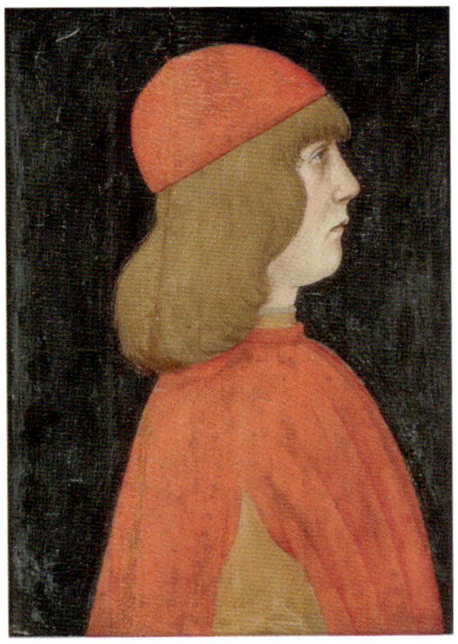

A94; tempera (?) and oil on panel, 36.5 × 25.3 cm
Fox-Strangways Gift, 1850; WA1850.16

Lloyd 1977, pp. 184–5

Traditionally attributed to Gentile Bellini, A94 and A95 were later attributed to an anonymous artist of the school of Verona. Recently the consensus is that these portraits or decorative profile heads are unlikely to be Veronese and instead derive from Tuscan painting of the late 15th century.

Attributed to PAOLO DI DONO, called UCCELLO
(1397 – 1475)

The Annunciation

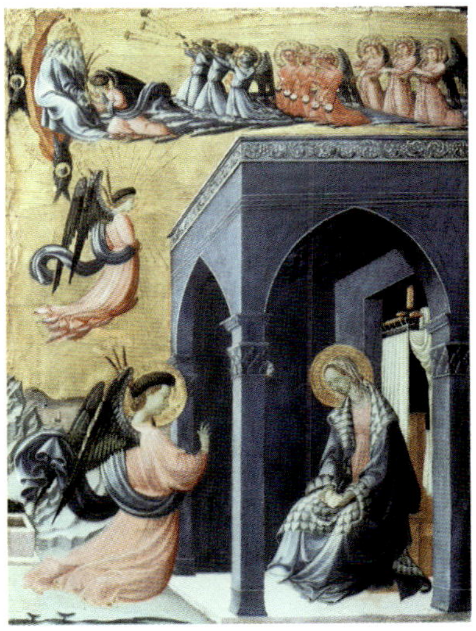

A80; tempera and gilding on panel, 65 × 48 cm
Fox-Strangways Gift, 1850; WA1850.7

Lloyd 1977, pp. 61–2; Borsi 1992, p. 343

The Angel Gabriel is sent by God the Father to announce to the Virgin Mary that she will bear the son of God (Luke 1: 26–8). A80 may have been painted by Uccello in the early 1420s: the figure types, the interest in perspective, the refined, decorative approach and unusual treatment of the subject are all characteristic of his work. Recent examination has revealed a lively underdrawing with *pentimenti*, including a change in the position of the Holy Spirit. With its lavish use of gold and ultramarine, A80 was an expensive image to produce.

Paolo di Dono, called Uccello
(1397 – 1475)

The Hunt in the Forest

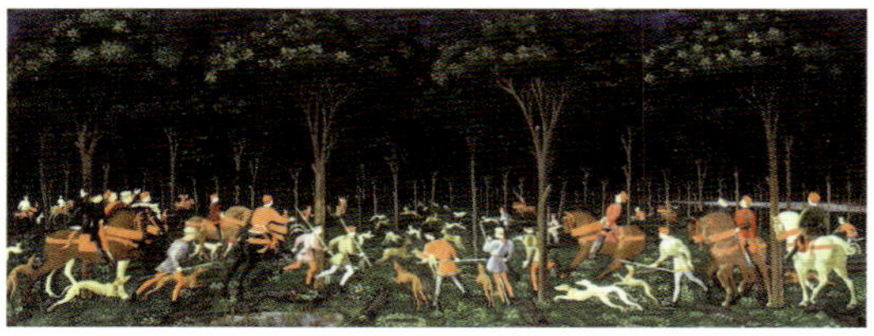

A79; tempera and oil, with traces of gold, on panel, 73.3 × 177 cm
Fox-Strangways Gift, 1850; WA1850.31

Lloyd 1977, pp. 172–5; Kemp and Massing 1991; Whistler 2001

Celebrated in his lifetime as a painter of perspective and of animals and landscape, Uccello was a versatile artist who worked at times on mosaic and stained glass design. A79 is a late work, probably of *c.* 1470. It is a highly original painting, both as a nocturnal landscape and as a brilliantly structured composition. Uccello mapped out a grid on the panel's surface as a guide for his design, fixing a central vanishing point. The devices of the huntsmen's spears, the cut branches and logs and the area of water denote this coherent space, inhabited by the receding forms of men and animals. Uccello's approach is also highly decorative, with bright, clear colours set off against a dark background: the foliage of the trees was once picked out with gold, accentuating the precious, mosaic-like effect. Hunting was an aristocratic pastime with its own rituals (and the crescent moon, symbol of Diana, the chaste goddess of the hunt, appears in the horses' trappings) and the idea here of a hunt by night is playful or symbolic rather than realistic. A79 is a *spalliera* panel painted for a luxurious domestic setting, perhaps in Urbino or in Florence.

Anonymous Umbro-Marchigian Artist
(*c.* 1510)

The Adoration of the Child with St Francis

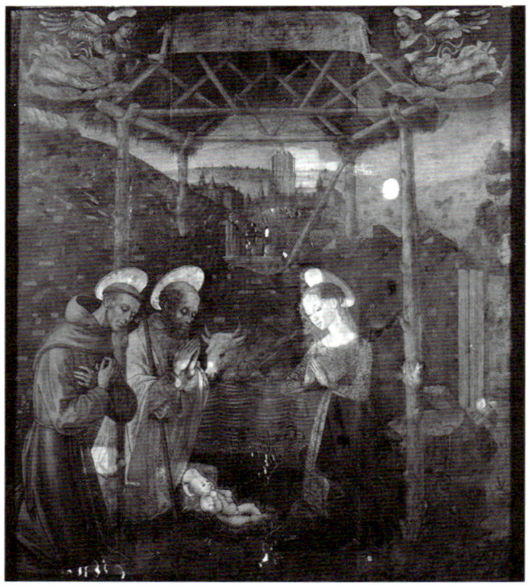

A736; oil and tempera with gilding on panel, 174 × 150.5 cm
Inscribed: *GLORIA IN EXCELSIS DEO E*
Presented by the daughters of James Reddie Anderson, 1947; WA1947.239

Lloyd 1977, p. 200

Although considered in the past to be a fake on the grounds of its composite design and poor condition, this painting may be by a provincial artist working in Umbria and the Marches. It could be by a follower of Ludovido Urbani or Luca di Matelica. The banner held by the angels also has some musical notations.

Charlotte Unger
(first half of 20th century)

St Giles Fair, Oxford

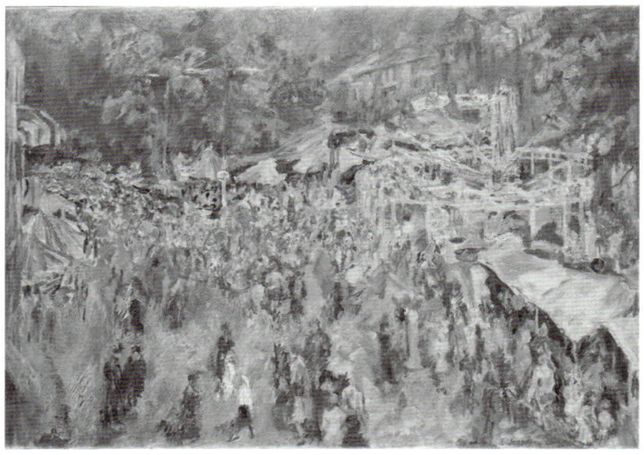

A1128; oil on canvas, 43 × 65 cm
Signed: *Unger*
Presented by the artist, 1983; WA1983.41

A record of the annual city fair which is held in St Giles, Oxford in early September. The view is taken from an upstairs window in the Randolph Hotel, looking north.

Leon Underwood
(1890 – 1975)

Charles Ashdown

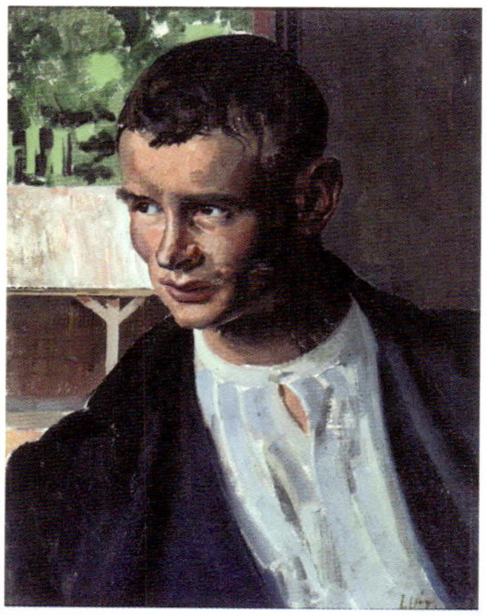

A1201; oil on canvas, 44.5 × 34.2 cm
Signed and dated: *LU'22.*; numbered on the back: *228–63*:
Presented by Garth Underwood, the artist's son, 1996; WA1996.382

Eustace 1999, no.18

In 1921 Underwood, who has little formal training, set up his own art school. He encouraged his pupils to work fast, for the sake of capturing effects of volume and movement. This portrait, made during a summer visit to Ashurst, Kent in 1922, is a typical example of his working methods. With quick and lively brush-strokes it captures a sense of life on the farm in a close-up sensitive study of the young farmer.

Michelangelo Unterperger
(1695 – 1758)

Christ disputing with the Doctors

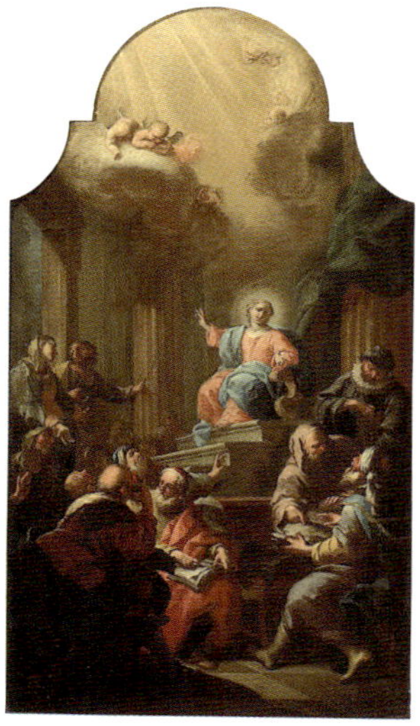

A343; oil on canvas, 90 × 50 cm
Prov.: T.W. Jackson; Joseph Jackson
Purchased, 1915; WA1915.2

Kronbichler and Mich 1995, pp. 85, 88, 89, 211

A343 is related to Unterperger's 1751 altar-piece now in the Augustinian church, Vienna. Three other oil-sketches are known, in the Herzog-Anton-Ulrich-Museum, Braunschweig (probably the *modello*); Castello di Buonconsiglio, Trento (an autograph replica); and Joanneum, Graz (a studio replica). In A343, which displays considerable variations in the design, the artist explored an alternative composition.

Adriaen van Utrecht
(1599 – *c.* 1652)

Still Life of a Lobster, Vegetables, Fruit, and Game

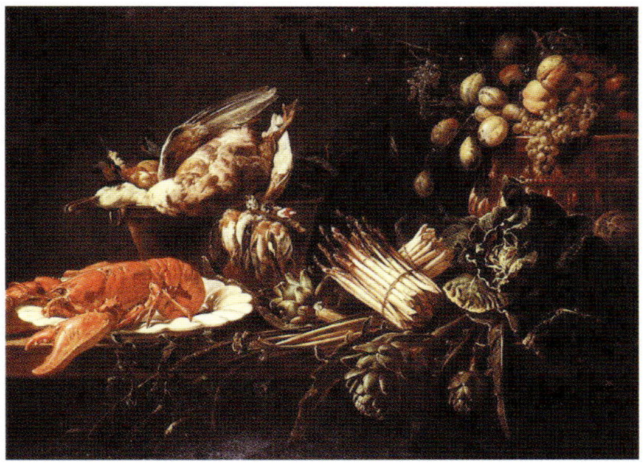

A606; oil on canvas, 88 × 118 cm
Signed: *Adriaen van Vtrecht fecit 1645*
Daisy Linda Ward Bequest, 1939; WA1940.2.82

Meijer 2003, no. 82

Van Utrecht painted live animals as well as still life. This painting includes many of his favourite accessories set in a kitchen interior. It may have been cut down. There is an echo of his interest in the still-life paintings by the followers of Caravaggio which he must have seen in Italy, but it is less noticeable than in other works by him.

Maurice Utrillo
(1883 – 1955)

A Village Street

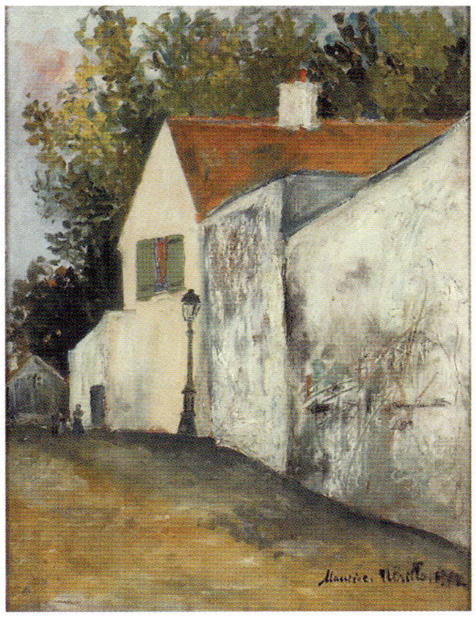

A636; oil on canvas, 45 × 60 cm
Signed and indistinctly dated: *Maurice Utrillo, 19[...]*
Hindley Smith Bequest, 1939; WA1940.1.18

According to an old label this is a view of a street in the Butte de Montmartre, showing the house of the composer Hector Berlioz, at the corner of the rue de l'Abreuvoir and the rue Cortot. The rather muted colours and the characteristic composition show that Utrillo had already freed himself from his earlier Post-Impressionist preoccupations.

Andrea Vanni
(*c.* 1330 – 1413)

The Virgin and Child with the Angel of the Annunciation in the gable

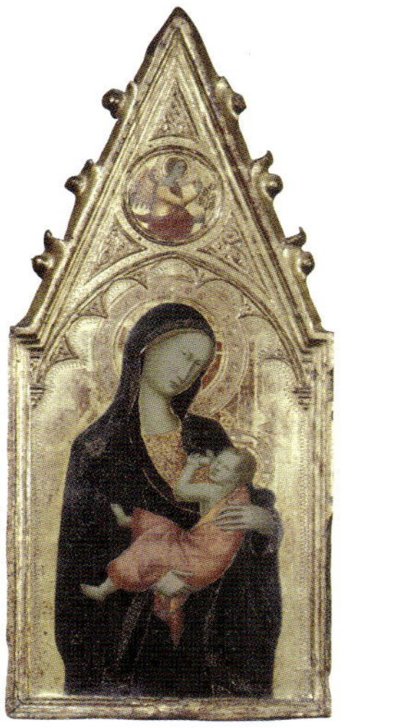

A696; tempera and gilding on panel, integral frame, 58 × 25 cm
Presented by the National Art Collections Fund, 1942; WA1942.48

Lloyd 1977, pp. 178–80; Boskovits and Schleier 1988, p. 9

Hinge-marks on the right side of A696 indicate this is the left wing of a diptych, which could be opened and closed like a book. The right wing, with the *Crucifixion with the Virgin Mary and St John* and *The Virgin of the Annunciation* in a roundel above, is in the Harvard University Art Museum. The Virgin feeds the Child in an image known as the *Madonna del Latte* (of the milk).

Maurice Utrillo
(1883 – 1955)

La Rue des Poissonniers, Montmartre

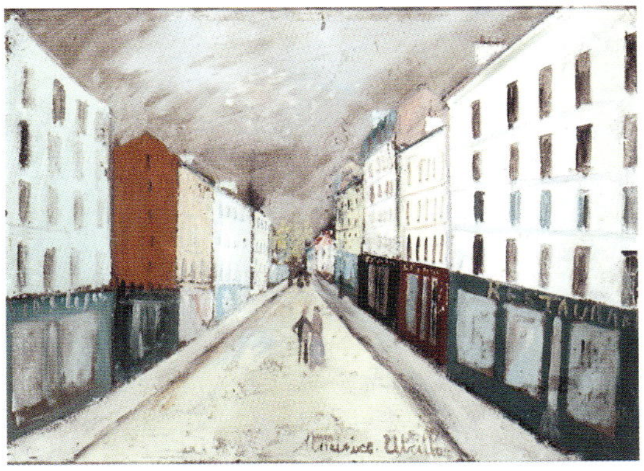

A1195; oil on board, 44.2 × 59.5 cm
Signed: *Maurice Utrillo*
Presented by Colin Cohen in memory of Cdr and Mrs Kenneth Cohen and Carol Liniger, 1996; WA1996.24

Petrides 1964, no. 458

During his so-called white period from 1908 to 1914 Utrillo was able to free himself from the ideas of Sisley and Pissarro and became more self-assured. In this painting he has chosen classically symmetrical perspective, while the buildings at both sides are treated with a new freedom.

Louis Valtat
(1869 – 1952)

Le Quai du Louvre

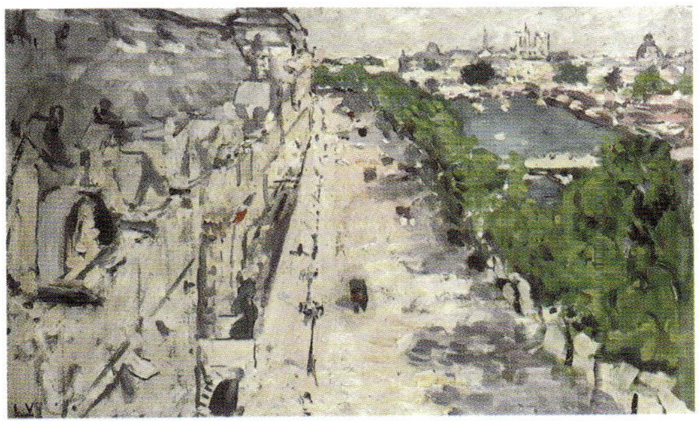

A1069; oil on canvas, 38 × 61 cm
Signed: *LV*
Bequeathed by Lt-Col G.E. Bouskell-Wade, 1972; WA1972.162

According to a label on the stretcher, the painting dates from 1892. The artist took his viewpoint from an upstairs office in the recently completed Pavillon de Flore, looking east along the quayside, with the cathedral of Notre-Dame in the distance.

Giorgio Vasari
(1511 – 1574)

An Allegory of the Immaculate Conception

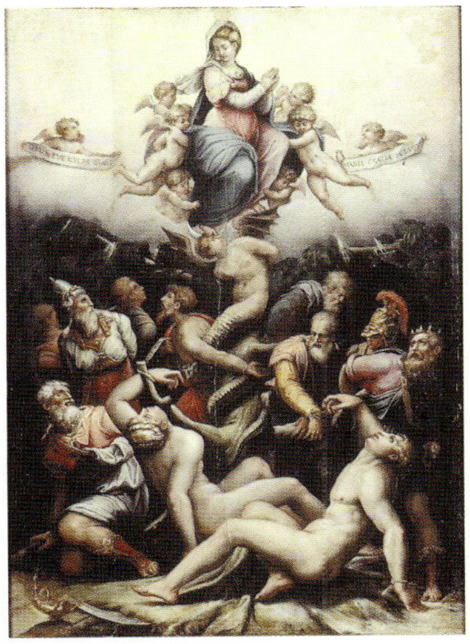

A991; oil on panel, 57 × 41 cm
Inscribed on the scroll carried by angels: *QUOS EVE CULPA DAAVIT / MARIAE GRATIAE SOLVIT*; on that carried by the Baptist: *ECCE AGNIU[S]*; on Abraham's shoulder strap: *UNIUS ONNOSTAAT*
Prov.: Sir Philip Miles, Bt, Leigh Court, Bristol
Purchased, 1962; WA1962.26

Lloyd 1977, pp. 180–2; Corti 1989, under no. 20

Vasari delighted in the complexity of the iconography and design of his celebrated altar-piece of 1540 for the Altoviti chapel in SS Apostoli, Florence. A991 is a small-scale, autograph version. The Virgin Mary is shown as an agent of Salvation, triumphing over Satan and sinfulness represented by Eve, according to the Latin inscriptions carried by angels. Adam and Eve are bound to the Tree of Knowledge, round which the serpent (in female form) is wound; Old Testament prophets and kings are also bound to the Tree, in this gloomy stage of mankind before Salvation, while John the Baptist proclaims the coming of Christ.

Attributed to Antonio Vazquez
(*c.* 1485 – after 1563)

The Crucifixion and the Descent from the Cross

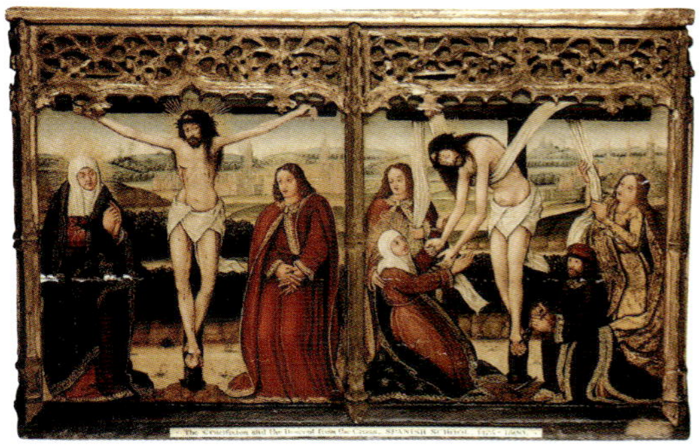

A356–357; tempera and gilding on panel, with an integral frame, 63.5 × 93.3 cm
Presented by Mrs W.F.R. Weldon, 1918; WA1918.2

Gaya Nuño 1958, no. 1689

Formerly attributed to the Master of Mambrillas, this pair of devotional scenes may come from a larger retable. A convincing attribution has recently been suggested to Vazquez, a prolific, conservative artist in Valladolid who worked in a late Gothic tradition. A356–7 share characteristic features of his work such as the continuous Flemish-style landscape, the solidly-modelled, impassive figures, the cool, light tonality and the decorative use of gold in the halos and hair as well as in the costumes.

Adriaen van de Velde
(1636 – 1672)

Italian Landscape with a Girl milking a Cow

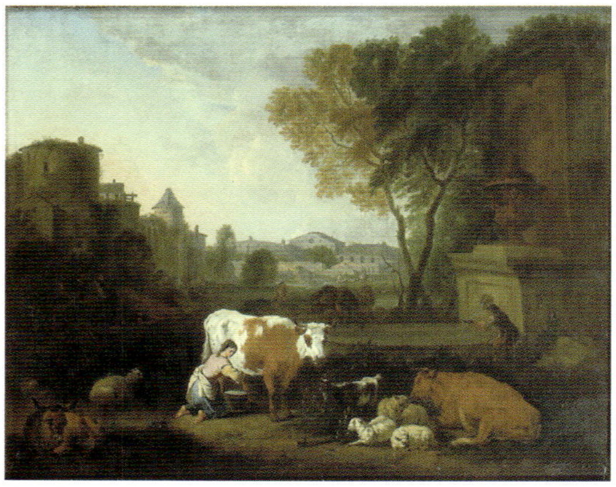

A774; oil on canvas, 32 × 64 cm
Indistinctly signed: *VF*
Bequeathed by the Hon. Miss H.E. Tyrwhitt, 1949; WA1949.185

White 1999, p. 155

One of a group of Italianate subjects which became the artist's predominant theme from the mid-1660s onwards, although he remained based in Amsterdam and does not seem to have visited Italy. It has been dated *c.* 1670 on account of the free brushwork which seems to have been characteristic of his late work.

Jan Jansz. van de Velde III
(*c.* 1620 – 1662 or later)

Still Life with a Clay Pipe

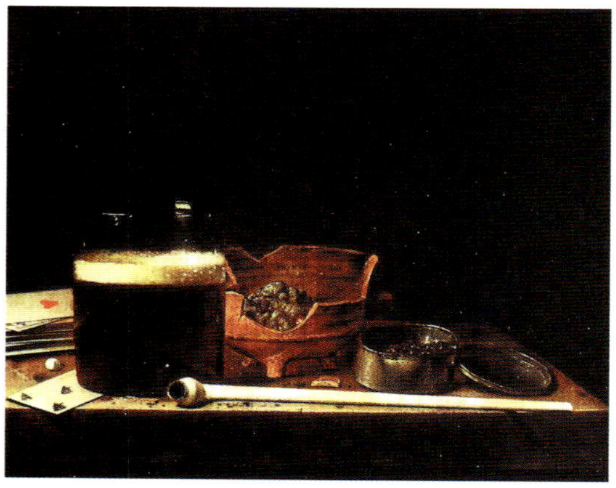

A607; oil on panel, 29.7 × 37.2 cm
Signed and dated: *J. van de Velde Anno 1651*
Daisy Linda Ward Bequest, 1939; WA1940.2.83

Van de Velde was born in Haarlem. The hard, brittle translucency of the drinking glasses which appear in many of van de Velde's still-life compositions is clearly inspired by the Haarlem painter, Willem Claesz. Heda. The accessories in this still life, which include a clay pipe, a glass of beer, a bowl of burning charcoal, playing cards and a piece of chalk, can be found in the work of Jan Jansz. Treck, a painter from Amsterdam whose work would have become familiar to van de Velde after he had settled in Amsterdam.

Jan Jansz. van de Velde III
(*c.* 1620 – 1662 or later)

Still Life with a Pipe-lighter

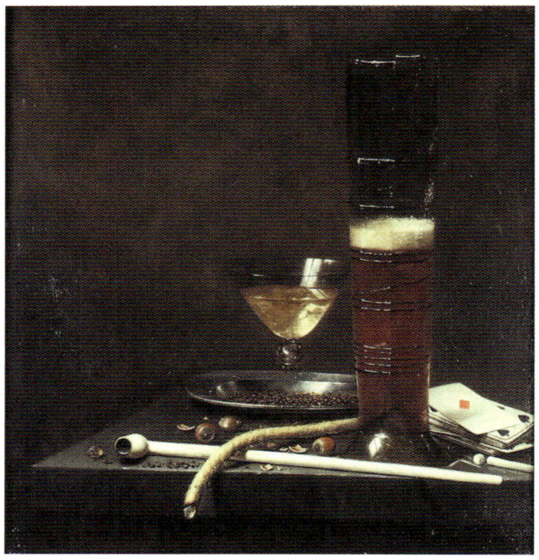

A608; oil on canvas, 43.3 × 40.5 cm
Signed and dated: *J. v. velde Anno 1653*
Daisy Linda Ward Bequest, 1939; WA1940.2.84

Meijer 2003, no. 84

The objects in this painting reappear in many of van de Velde's still-life compositions. The same pewter dish (or one very similar) appears in works extending across the artist's career while the *pasglas* is found in works dating from 1641 onwards. The details refer to the pleasures of the public house: smoking, drinking and playing cards. The chalk would have been used by the card-players to chalk up the score.

Jan Jansz. van de Velde III
(*c.* 1620 – 1662 or later)

Still Life with Strawberries and Cherries

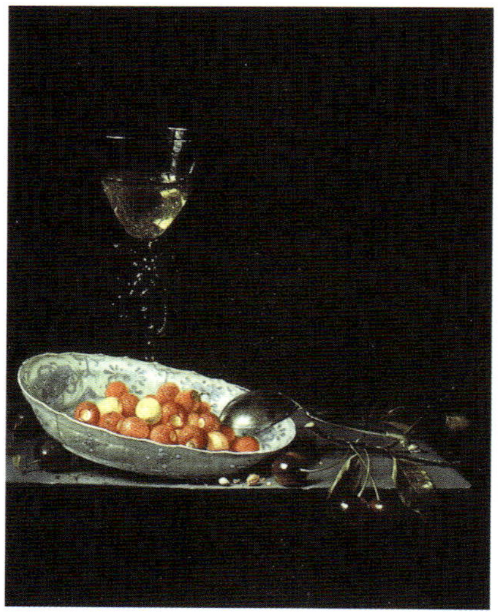

A609; oil on panel, 38 × 30 cm
Signed and dated: *j. vande velde.fecit / Ano.1658*
Daisy Linda Ward Bequest, 1939; WA1940.2.85

Meijer 2003, no. 85

Still-life paintings of fruit are rare in van de Velde's work. This one includes a Wan-li porcelain dish of strawberries, a silver spoon, cherries and a glass fashioned in the Venetian manner. Paintings combining glasses of wine with fruit seem to have been a subject which he took up in the last seven or eight years of his career. These are more colourful than his previous work and were perhaps painted in response to the growing popularity of Jan Davidsz. de Heem's work.

Dionijs Verburgh
(active 1677 – before 1722)

River Landscape

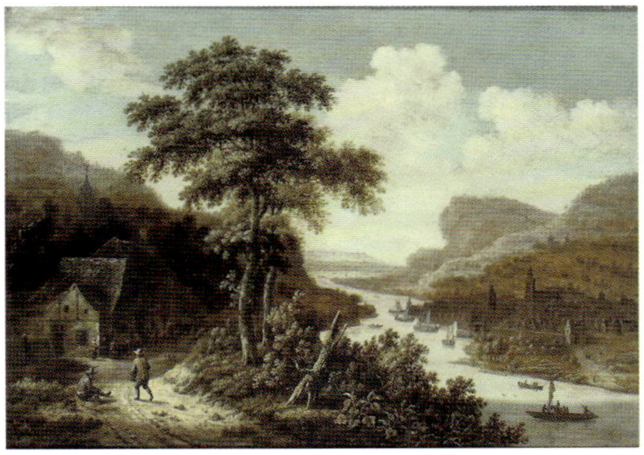

A810; oil on panel, 61 × 84 cm
Signed in monogram: *DVB*
Prov.: Mrs E.C. Burton until 1936
Bequeathed by J. Reginald Jones, 1951; WA1951.51.4

White 1999, p. 156

This is a characteristic painting by Dionijs Verburgh who specialised in river landscapes.

Anonymous Venetian or Veronese Artist
(*c.* 1560 – 1570)

Portrait of a Man and his Secretary

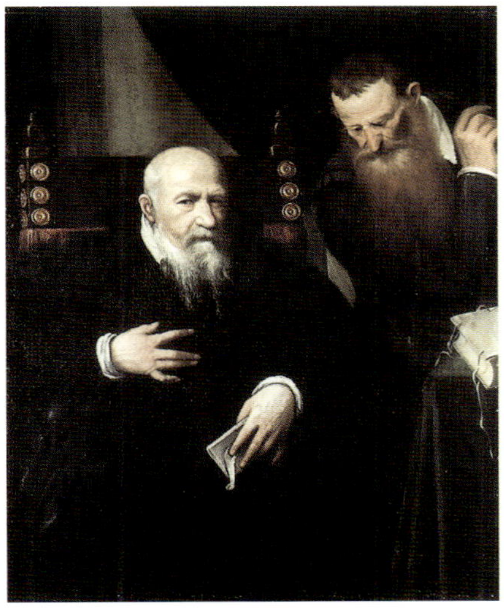

A1080; oil on canvas, 128.5 × 103 cm
Prov.: Sir Frederick Cook, 2nd Bt; by descent to Sir Francis Cook, 4th Bt
Purchased, 1975; WA1975.155

Lloyd 1977, pp. 212–3; Rearick 2001, no. 10

This handsome double portrait has been attributed in the past to various Venetian or Veronese artists. A number of scholars agreed with an attribution to Jacopo Bassano first proposed in 1931, dating A1080 to his maturity. Recently this attribution has been strongly questioned and other candidates suggested, including the Veronese artist Orlando Flacco, datable to *c.* 1560–65.

Anonymous Venetian Artist
(*c.* 1700)

The Adoration of the Magi

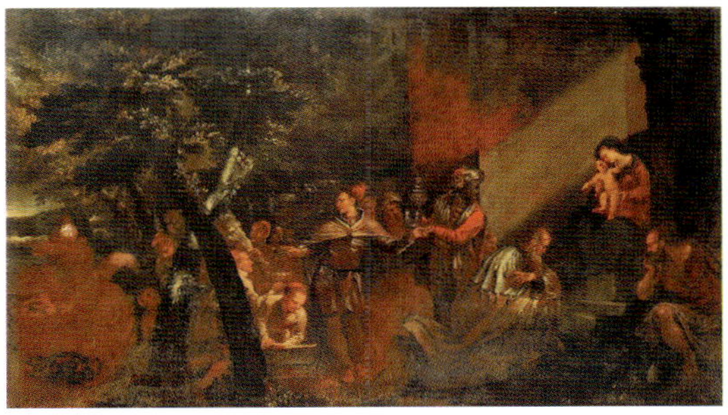

A736e; oil on canvas, 84 × 143 cm
Presented by the daughters of James Reddie Anderson, 1947; WA1947.201.3

The three Magi or wise men with their exotic entourage worship the new-born Christ (Matthew 2: 1–12) in this unfinished and/or damaged painting. The artist was familiar with Venetian art of the 16th and 17th centuries and may have been active in Venice in the late 17th century. Narrative scenes of this shape and subject were placed on the side-walls of chapels: a similar work is that by Francesco Zanella in the Duomo at Padua.

Anonymous Venetian Artist
(*c.* 1510)

Petrarch and Laura de Noves

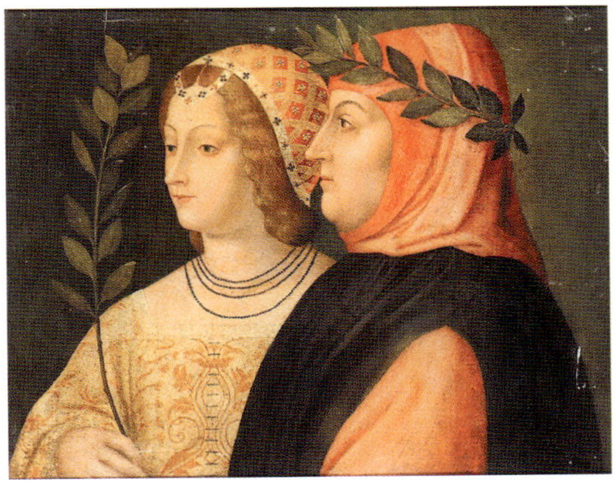

A293; oil on canvas, 56 × 70 cm
Bequeathed by John D. Chambers, 1897; WA1897.22

Lloyd 1977, pp. 183–4

Many portraits are known of the poet Petrarch (1304–1374), from early manuscripts of his work, but none is known of his beloved, Laura (1307/8–1348), here depicted with a laurel branch, an attribute of poetry. The source for the portraits is a 15th-century Tuscan manuscript in which the subjects are depicted separately. The unknown artist, whose style is close to Bartolomeo Veneto, may have known these or copies of them.

Anonymous Venetian Artist
(*c.* 1600)

Hagar and Ishmael

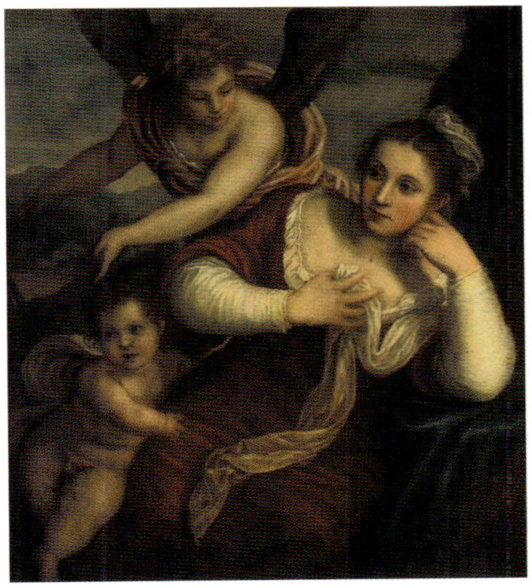

A669; oil on canvas, 113 × 100 cm
Prov.: purchased in Athens before 1901
Bequeathed by Sir Arthur Evans, 1941; WA1941.2

Abraham banished Hagar and her son Ishmael from his house; they were consoled by an angel in the desert who brought them food and water (Genesis 21: 9–19). A669 is probably by an artist close to Domenico Tintoretto who was also familiar with the work of Alessandro Varotari, il Padovanino.

Anonymous Venetian Artist
(*c.* 1850)

The Lagoon and Island of San Giorgio seen from the Molo

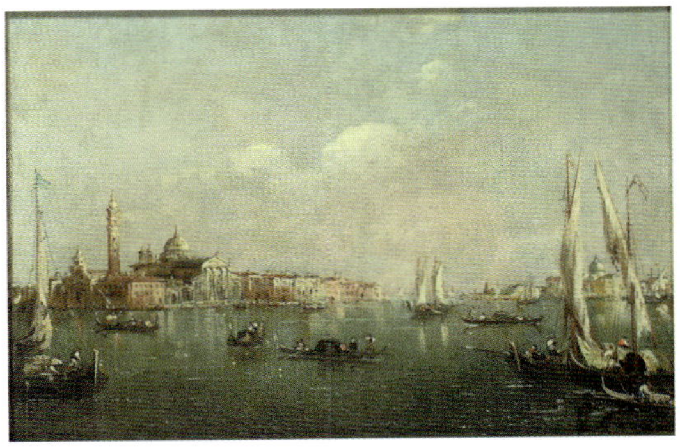

A330; oil on canvas, 38 × 55 cm
Prov.: Catherine Kerr Lawson
Purchased, 1911; WA1911.3

Formerly attributed to Michele Marieschi, this free imitation of Francesco Guardi probably dates from the mid-19th century and was made for the tourist market.

Simon Verelst
(1644 – between 1710 and 1717)

A Vase of Flowers

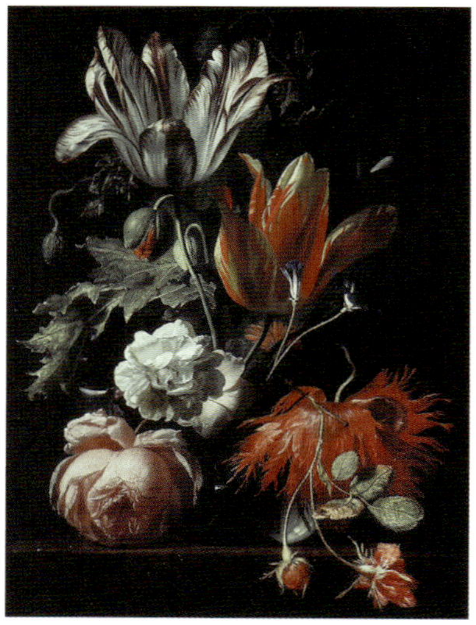

A611; oil on canvas, 44 × 32 cm
Daisy Linda Ward Bequest, 1939; WA1940.2.87

Meijer 2003, no. 86

Born in The Hague, Verelst moved to London in 1669 where his work was admired and where he died at an uncertain date. This painting has been dated to the artist's early years in London. Twisting and complex, the composition is pulled into place by the manipulation of light and colour. Willem van Aelst gave the artist a point of departure but the effect and the composition of this work are particularly inventive.

Simon Verelst
(1644 – between 1710 and 1717)

Still Life of Apple Blossom

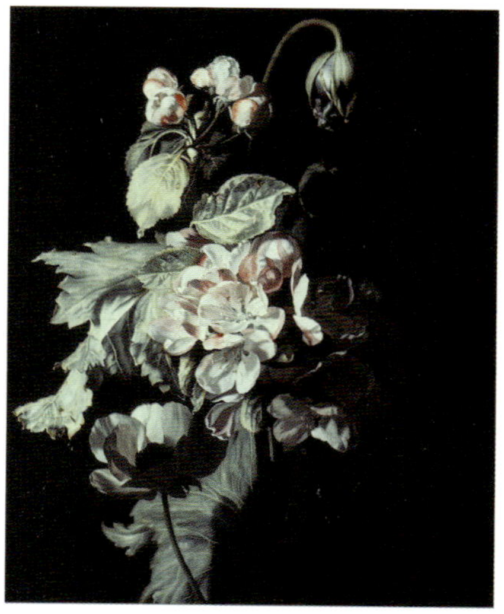

A612; oil on canvas, 35 × 28 cm
Signed: *S Verelst f*
Daisy Linda Ward Bequest, 1939; WA1940.2.88

Meijer 2003, no. 87

This seems to be the only flower painting by Verelst which does not include a vase. The poppy anemone, mixed here with apple blossom, was one of Verelst's favourite flowers. The rarity with which dates appear in his work makes it difficult to follow the development of his style but this still life has been tentatively dated to the 1680s. A similar bouquet mixed with poppies and anemones in the Fitzwilliam Museum in Cambridge may be contemporary with this.

Constantin Verhout
(active 1663 – 1667)

Still Life with a Crab

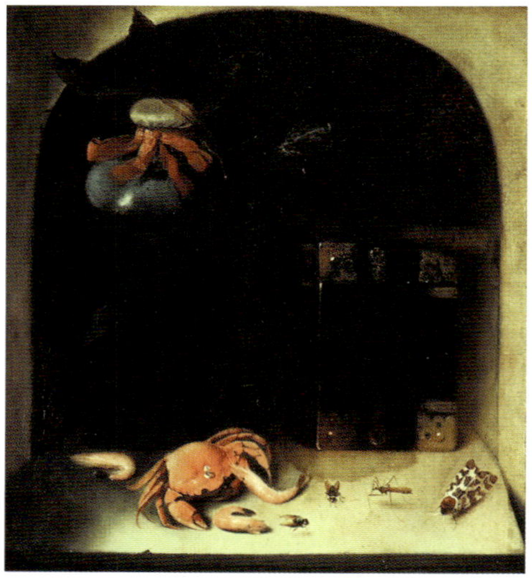

A613; oil on panel, 41 × 33 cm
Prov.: James Simon, Berlin until 1927
Daisy Linda Ward Bequest, 1939; WA1940.2.89

Meijer 2003, no. 88

Almost nothing is known about Verhout. About five paintings, mostly scenes of daily life, have been identified, one of which is dated 1663. The attribution of this still life is based on an inscription on the back of the panel but it is supported by comparison with details of his known work. The combination of the glass, brass-mounted book, recorder, crab, prawns, insects, butterfly, moth and laurel wreath is peculiar and must once have had a particular meaning.

Style of Jan Cornelisz. Vermeyen
(1500 – 1559)

Portrait of a Man holding a Peach

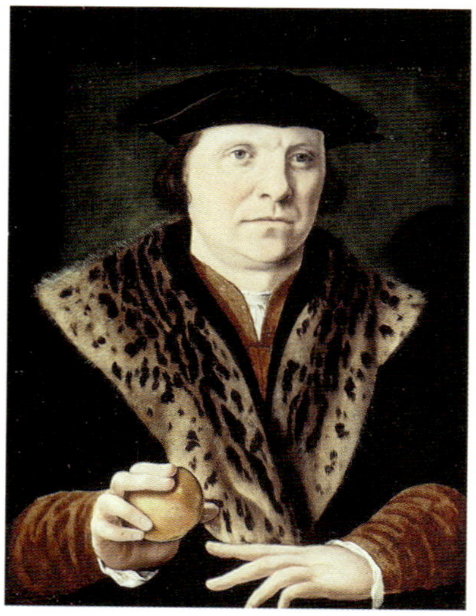

A1047; oil on panel, 33 × 25 cm
Prov.: H.A. Wetzlar
Bequeathed by William W. Spooner, 1968; WA1968.137

White 1999, p. 156

Formerly described as works in the style of Bernaert van Orley, this portrait and the following have more in common with the portraits of Vermeyen who worked for the Regents of the Netherlands and for the Emperor Charles V. They are presumably the work of a follower and probably date from the late 1520s.

Style of Jan Cornelisz. Vermeyen
(1500 – 1559)

Portrait of a Woman

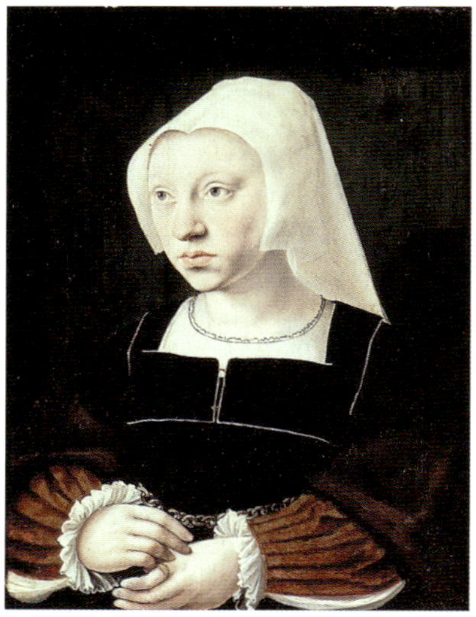

A1048; oil on panel, 33 × 25 cm
Prov.: H.A. Wetzlar
Bequeathed by William W. Spooner, 1968; WA1968.138

White 1999, p. 156

A companion to the previous portrait. The linen headdress, bodice and short, wide sleeves are typical of north European costume of the 1520s.

Claude-Joseph Vernet
(1714 – 1789)

Coastal Scene (La nuit)

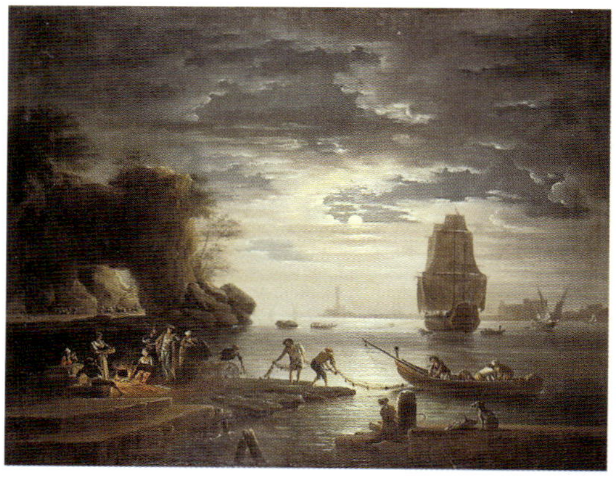

A1036; oil on canvas, 97 × 123 cm
Bequeathed by A.G. Gooch through the National Art Collections Fund, 1967; WA1967.60.1

Ingersoll-Smouse 1926, no. 396

Vernet made his reputation in Rome from 1734–53, attracting an international clientele as a specialist in marine painting. In 1750 he painted a series of four oval *Times of Day* destined for Joseph Leeson, later Lord Milltown. A1036 is a rectangular replica of the fourth scene. Other Grand Tourists in Rome commissioned similar sets from Vernet in the 1750s. A1036 was copied by Charles François Lacroix de Marseille.

Claude-Joseph Vernet
(1714 – 1789)

River Scene with Bathers

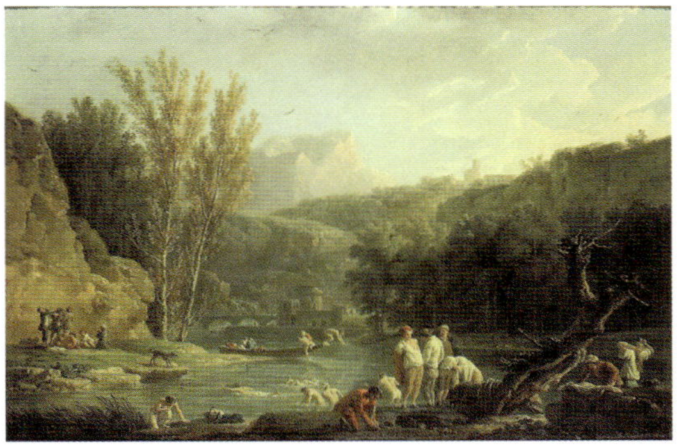

A984; oil on canvas, 67 × 98 cm
Signed and dated: *J. Vernet, F.1770*
Prov.: Probably Jean-Joseph de la Borde; Mrs Scott, Thorpe House, Egham
Madan Bequest, 1962; WA1962.17.26

Ingersoll-Smouse 1926, no. 912; Pichon 1993, pp. 74–5

A984 is probably identifiable with one of a pair of scenes of the same size and subject as commissioned by Jean-Joseph de la Borde in 1768 and paid for in September 1770. These companion pieces showed a morning scene with female bathers and an evening scene with male figures. Exhibited at the Salon of 1771, A984 was described as *Un paysage au soleil couchant*.

Paolo Caliari, called Veronese
(1528 – 1588)

The Holy Family with the young St John the Baptist and St George

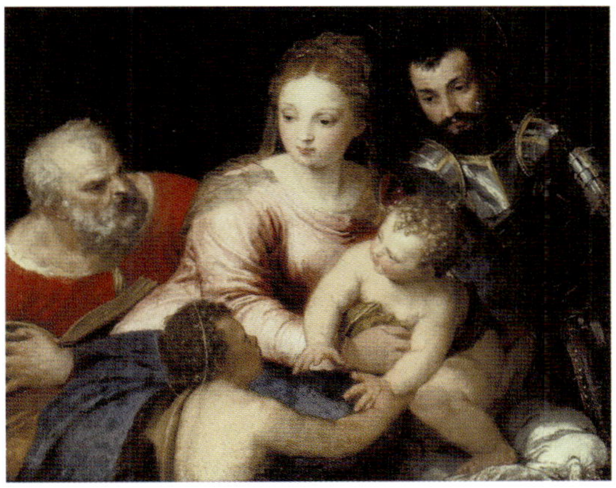

A863; oil on canvas, 41 × 50 cm
Prov.: Sir Richard Green Price, 2nd Bt
Purchased, 1952; WA1952.52

Lloyd 1977, pp. 187–8; Pignatti and Pedrocco 1995, no. 38

The cult of St George, an early Christian soldier and martyr, was popular in Venice, since the state had played a leading role in the Crusades. Veronese's interest in strong, broadly-handled forms and in exploring a range of textures, is characteristic. An early work intended for a private client, A863 probably dates from the early 1550s, soon after the artist moved from Verona to Venice.

Circle of Paolo Caliari, called Veronese
(1528 – 1588)

Judith receiving the Ancients of Bethulia

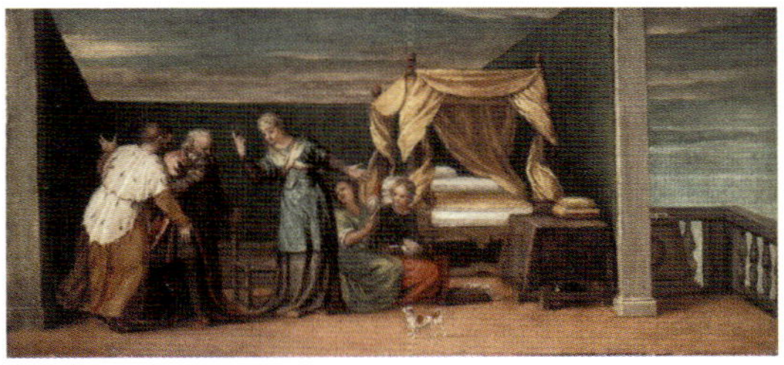

A378; oil on canvas, 27 × 57 cm
Prov.: Sir Paul Methuen; by descent to the 3rd Baron Methuen
Presented by Mrs W.F.R. Weldon, 1926; WA1926.3

Lloyd 1977, pp. 189–90; Pignatti 1976, I, no. A229

Follower of Claude-Joseph Vernet
(1714 – 1789)

Coastal Scene

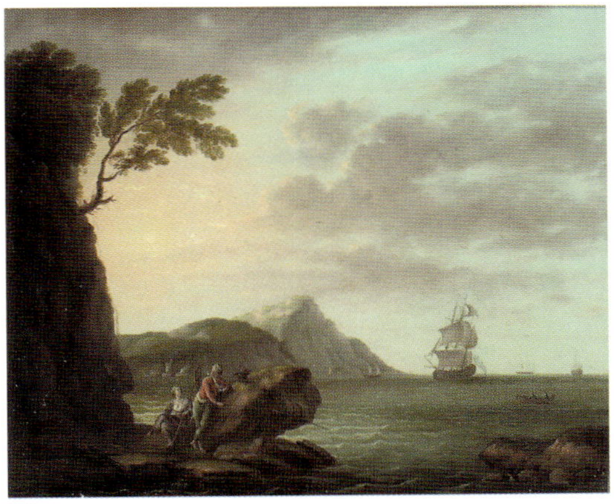

A895; oil on canvas, 76 × 65 cm
Presented by Mr and Mrs H.R. Marshall through the National Art Collections Fund in memory of their son, William Somerville Marshall, 1957; WA1957.43

A picturesque scene of a type popular on the art market in the late 18th century, A895 is by an imitator of Vernet, possibly French or English.

Circle of Paolo Caliari, called Veronese
(1528 – 1588)

The Flight of Achior from the Camp of Holofernes

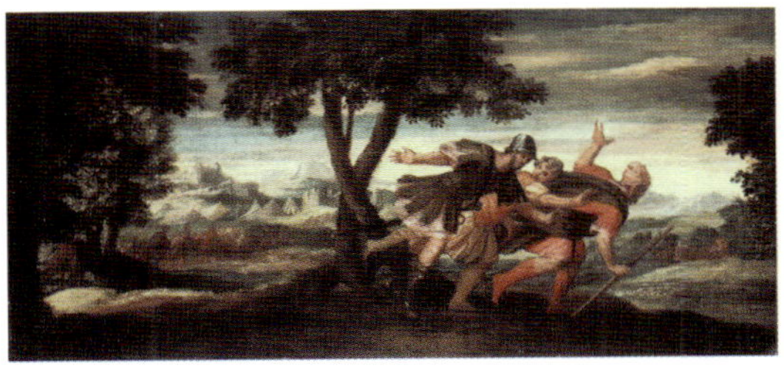

A377; oil on canvas, 27 × 57 cm
Prov.: Sir Paul Methuen; by descent to the 3rd Baron Methuen, Corsham Court, Chippenham, Wiltshire
Presented by Mrs W.F.R. Weldon, 1926; WA1926.2.

Lloyd 1977, pp. 189–90; Pignatti 1976, I, no. A229

Once attributed to Veronese, A377–82 may have been made in his studio. The narrative, from the apocryphal Book of Judith, celebrates the Jewish heroine who saved her people from the tyranny of Holofernes; the subject was especially popular in Venice. Sumptuous narrative panels such as these were often inserted into luxury chests, or formed part of the decoration of a room, perhaps set in a frieze at the level of the cornice.

Circle of Paolo Caliari, called Veronese
(1528 – 1588)

Judith leaving Bethulia

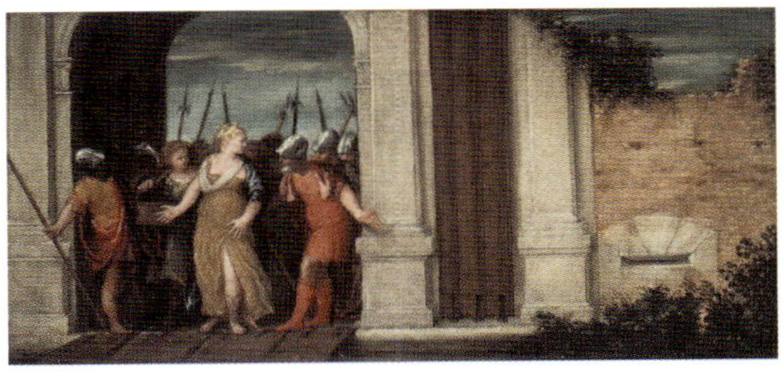

A379; oil on canvas, 27 × 57 cm
Prov.: Sir Paul Methuen; by descent to the 3rd Baron Methuen
Presented by Mrs W.F.R. Weldon, 1926; WA1926.4

Lloyd 1977, pp. 189–90; Pignatti 1976, I, no. A229

Circle of PAOLO CALIARI, called VERONESE
(1528 – 1588)

Judith received by Holofernes

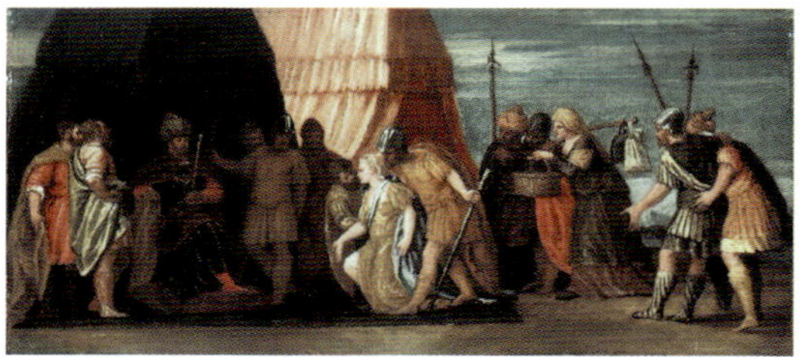

A380; oil on canvas, 27 × 57 cm
Prov.: Sir Paul Methuen; by descent to the 3rd Baron Methuen
Presented by Mrs W.F.R. Weldon, 1926; WA1926.5

Lloyd 1977, pp. 189–90; Pignatti 1976, I, no. A229

Circle of PAOLO CALIARI, called VERONESE
(1528 – 1588)

Judith about to kill Holofernes

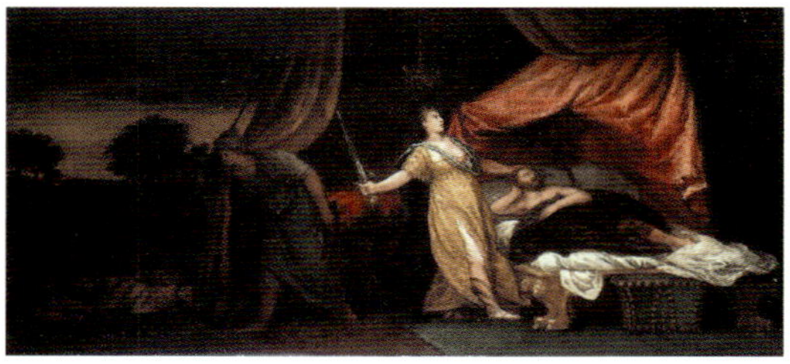

A382; oil on canvas, 27 × 57 cm
Prov.: Sir Paul Methuen; by descent to the 3rd Baron Methuen
Presented by Mrs W.F.R. Weldon, 1926; WA1926.7

Lloyd 1977, pp. 189–90; Pignatti 1976, I, no. A229

JAN VETH
(1864 – 1925)

Girl from Laran with Cornflowers

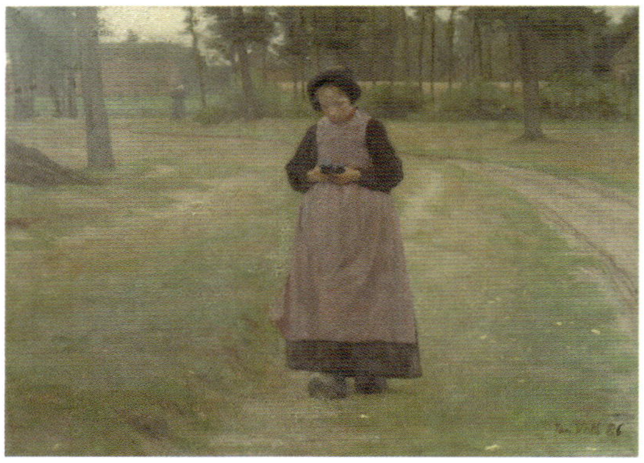

A1187; oil on canvas, 91 × 124 cm
Signed and dated: *Jan Veth 86*
Bequeathed by Professor Edith Bulbring, 1991; WA1993.424

White 1999, p. 157

Veth belonged to a generation of artists in Amsterdam who reacted against the older artists of The Hague School. According to a label on the back, this painting represents a girl from the village of Laran. It has been pointed out that this painting seems to have been influenced by the work of Veth's contemporary, Max Liebermann, who painted similar studies of rustic life in Laran.

Circle of PAOLO CALIARI, called VERONESE
(1528 – 1588)

Judith feasted by Holofernes

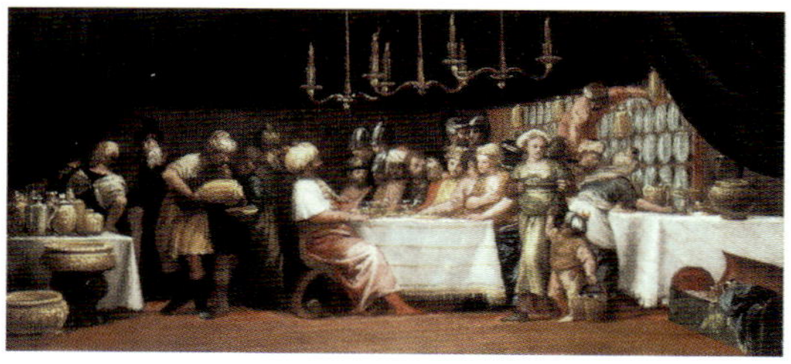

A381; oil on canvas, 27 × 57 cm
Prov.: Sir Paul Methuen; by descent to the 3rd Baron Methuen
Presented by Mrs W.F.R. Weldon, 1926; WA1926.6

Lloyd 1977, pp. 189–90; Pignatti 1976, I, no. A229

Copy after PAOLO CALIARI, called VERONESE
(1528 – 1588)

Moses brought before Pharoah's Daughter

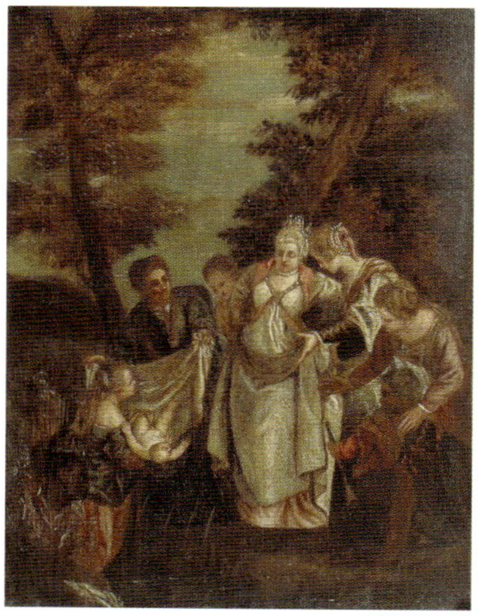

A143; oil on canvas laid on panel, 54.5 × 41.3 cm
Chambers Hall Gift, 1855; WA1855.160

Lloyd 1977, p. 191

Pharoah had ordered all first-born Hebrew sons to be killed; the baby Moses was placed in a rush basket in the Nile, whence he was rescued by Pharoah's daughter (Exodus 2: 3–10). The prototype for A143 is the painting in the National Gallery of Art, Washington (which shows variations in the costume of Pharoah's daughter with respect to the first version of *c.* 1582 in the Prado, Madrid). A143 does not fully replicate the landscape on the left. It may date from the early to mid-18th century.

Attributed to GEORGE VINCENT
(1796 – 1831)

Mousehole Heath, Norfolk

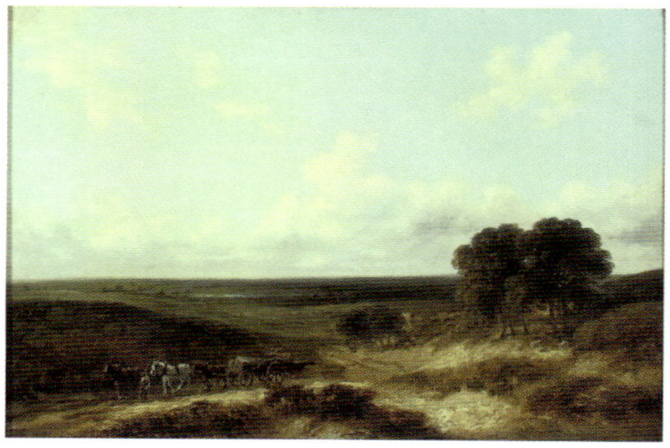

A773; oil on canvas, 43 × 63 cm
Bequeathed by the Hon. Miss H.E. Tyrwhitt, 1949; WA1949.184

Arnout Vinckenborch
(before 1590 – 1620)

The Incredulity of St Thomas

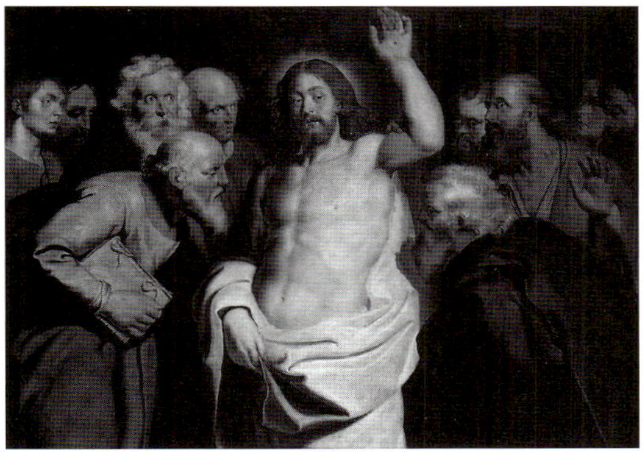

A7; oil on panel, 137 × 190 cm
Bequeathed by the Revd Dr John King, 1737; WA1845.7

White 1999, p. 158

The picture shows the apostle Thomas convinced by the sight of Christ's wounds that Christ has arisen (John 20: 24–9). The painting depends on the example of Rubens. It has been attributed to Vinckenborch by comparison with the paintings supplied by him for St Pauluskerk in Antwerp in *c.* 1617. The back is marked with the brand of the panel-maker, Lambrechts I Steens.

Attributed to Cornelis Visscher
(?1629 – 1658)

St Francis kneeling before the Virgin and Child

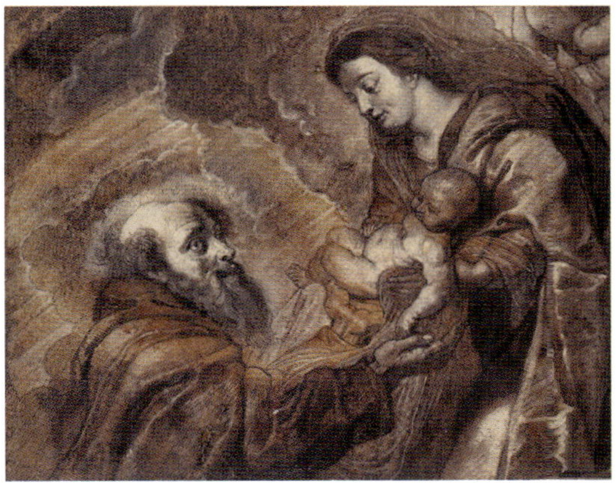

Oil on paper, mounted as a drawing, 20.4 × 25.4 cm
Presented by Sir Thomas Barlow, 1937; WA1937.129

Parker 1938, no. 206

This is a fragment of a design for a print engraved by Cornelis Visscher after a painting in the church of St Antoine in Antwerp supplied by the studio of Rubens. The sketch could have been made after the painting by the engraver but it could also have been supplied by an artist in Rubens's studio.

Attributed to Hendrick Cornelisz. van Vliet
(1611/12 – 1675)

Portrait of a Lady wearing a black Mantilla

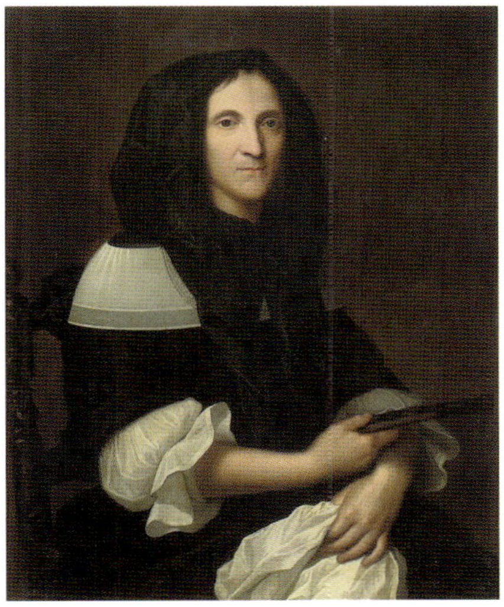

A442; oil on canvas, 81 × 65 cm
Presented by Mr and Mrs Julian G. Lousada through the National Art Collections Fund, 1935; WA1935.6

White 1999, p. 160

Van Vliet was a portrait painter from Delft. The attribution is based on similarities with signed and dated paintings in other collections.

Arnout Vinckenborch
(before 1590 – 1620)

Moses striking the Rock

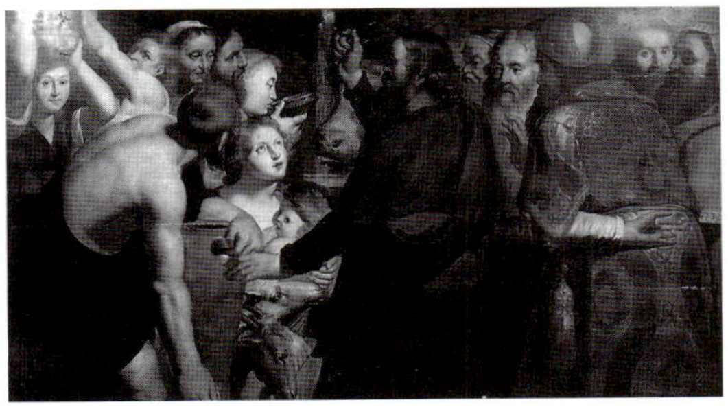

A8; oil on panel, 128 × 227 cm
Bequeathed by the Revd Dr John King, 1737; WA1845.8

White 1999, p. 159

This subject shows Moses causing water to flow from a rock by striking it with his rod (Numbers 20: 7–11). The painting is by the same artist as the previous painting and comes from the same source although it is not the same size and does not form a pair with it. The back is impressed twice with the left hand of Antwerp, the mark of the Antwerp Guild.

Maurice de Vlaminck
(1876 – 1958)

Still Life of Flowers

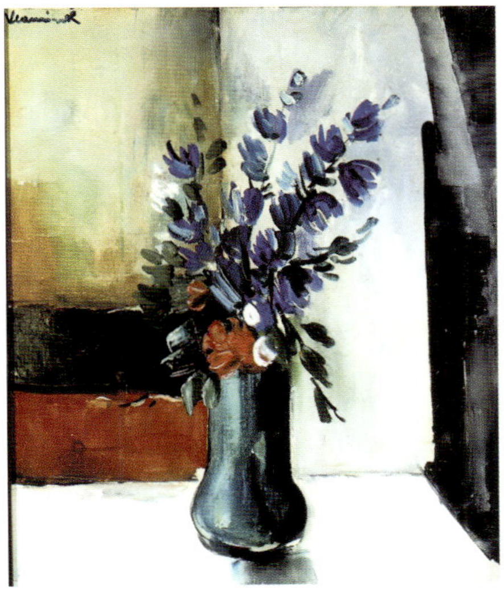

A621; oil on canvas, 55.9 × 47 cm
Signed: *Vlaminck*
Hindley Smith Bequest, 1939; WA1940.1.3

After a short period of Fauvism, when Vlaminck, Derain and Matisse explored the effects of unconventional combinations of colours, Vlaminck returned to a less excited manner, using clearly built structures and more conventional colours. In this instance, he used the corner of a niche to mark the centre of a painting, which is firmly occupied by the vase of flowers.

Antoine Vollon
(1833 – 1900)

Still Life of Herrings suspended on a Wall

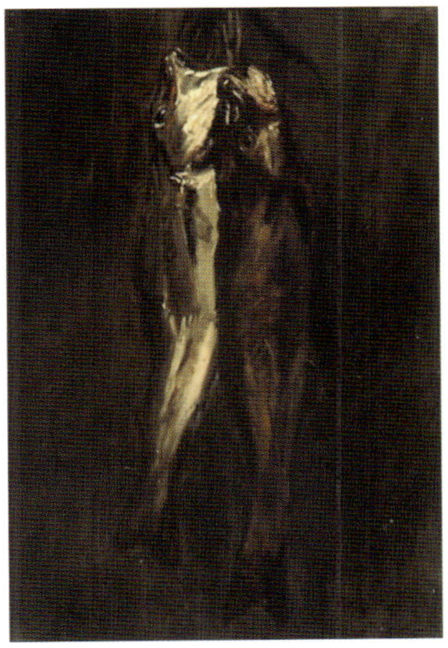

A456; oil on canvas, 47 × 32 cm
Weldon Bequest, 1937; WA1937.36

A characteristic work by an artist who painted many still-life compositions but was also known for his landscapes. The flamboyant technique which is a striking feature of this work and the following was much admired in Vollon's lifetime. These are both probably late works. The striking contrasts of dark paint and highlights with little colour derives from a fashion for 17th-century Spanish art in 19th-century France which was at its height in the 1860s.

Antoine Vollon
(1833 – 1900)

Still Life of white Azaleas

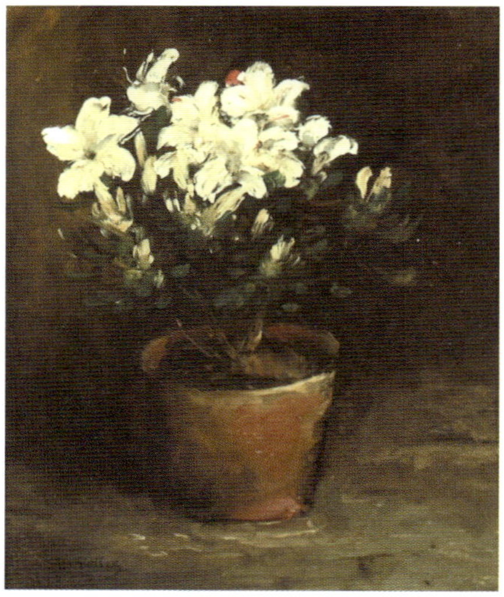

A476; oil on panel, 41 × 33 cm
Weldon Bequest, 1937; WA1937.56

Jan Vonck
(*c.* 1630 – after 1660)

Still Life of Game on a Stone Sill

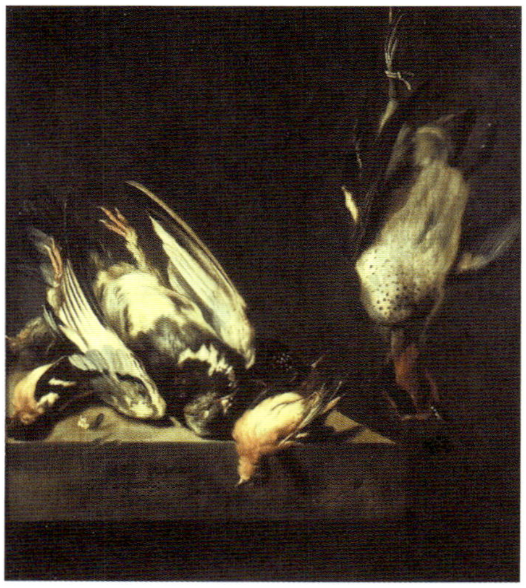

A614; oil on panel, 52 × 45 cm
Signed: *J Vonck fecit / An 16*[*6*.]
Prov.: John Haslam
Daisy Linda Ward Bequest, 1939; WA1940.2.90

Meijer 2003, no. 89

This painting is based on the work of Vonck's father, who was one of the early painters of paintings of dead game in Holland. Unlike his father, who liked to include more exotic birds in his hunting pictures, Jan confined himself to common birds, hares and rabbits. The date is indistinct but the third digit seems to have been a 6, making this a late work in the artist's brief career.

Copy after Cornelis de Vos
(1584/5 – 1651)

Portrait Group of an Unidentified Family

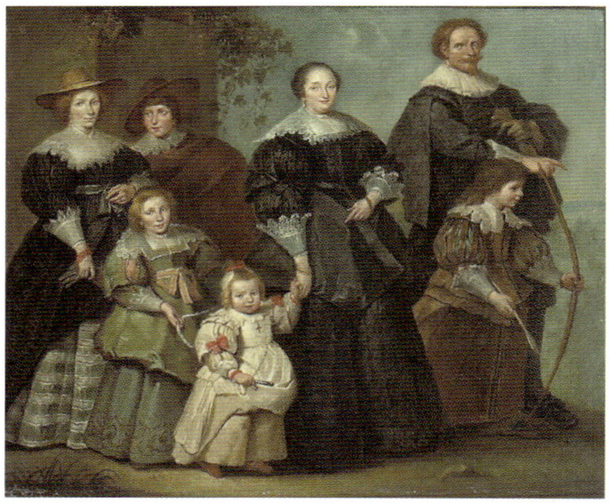

A807; oil on canvas, 53 × 64 cm
Bequeathed by J. Reginald Jones, 1951; WA1951.51.1

White 1999, p. 162

A reduced copy of a painting by de Vos now in the Hermitage State Museum, St Petersburg.

Jan Vonck
(*c.* 1630 – after 1660)

Still Life of Dead Birds

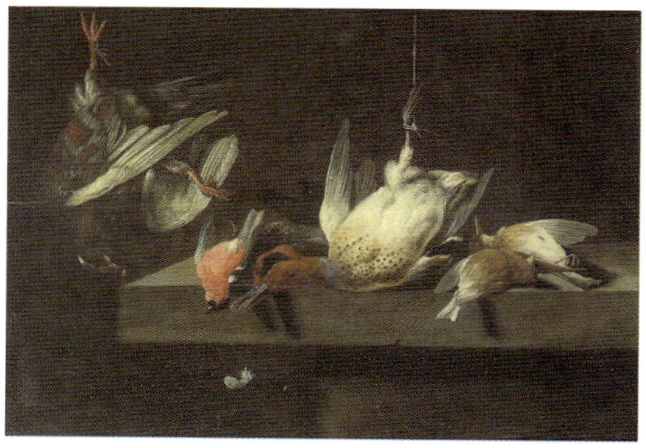

A283; oil on panel, 45 × 63 cm
Signed: *J. Vonck F.*
Presented by Thomas Humphry Ward, 1897; WA1897.6

White 1999, p. 161

Jan Vonck was a still-life painter, based in Amsterdam, who specialised in painting dead birds, game and fish in the manner of his father, Elias Vonck. He also painted a few pictures of live animals, chiefly dogs. This is a characteristic game piece by Vonck.

Cornelis de Vos
(1584–5 – 1651)

Portrait of a Child holding a Rattle

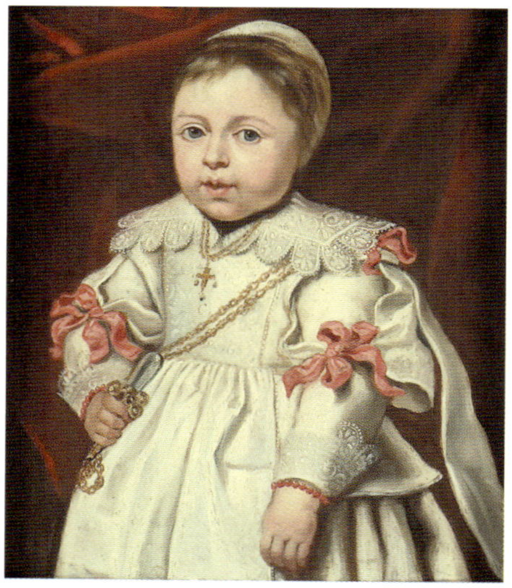

A166; oil on panel, 50 × 39 cm
Chambers Hall Gift, 1855; WA1855.167

White 1999, p. 161

De Vos painted portraits and historical pictures in Antwerp where he was influenced by Rubens and van Dyck. His portraits of children, in particular, are painted with charm and affection. It has been suggested, very tentatively, that this might be a portrait of one of his own children.

Simon Vouet and studio
(1590 – 1649)

The Virgin and Child (of the Column)

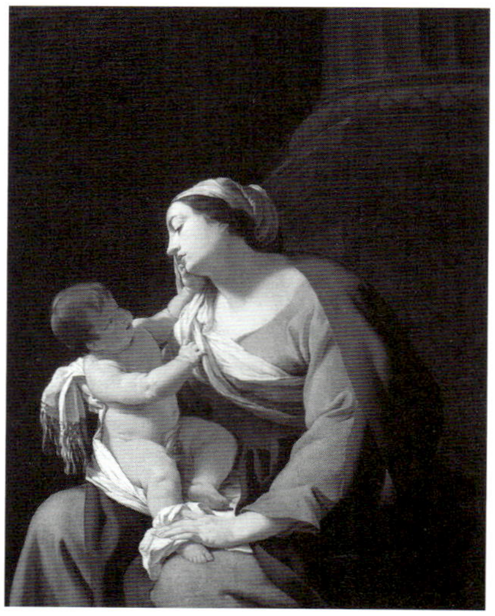

A745; oil on canvas, 135 × 108 cm
Prov.: Thomas Barnard, Bishop of Limerick; his son, Andrew Barnard; Earls of Crawford and Balcarres until 1946
Presented by the National Art Collections Fund, 1948; WA1948.77

Crelly 1962, no. 53; Thuillier *et al.* 1990, under no. 50

A745 is one of a number of versions by Vouet and his studio of a celebrated composition painted *c.* 1639–40. It differs from others in showing more of the fluted column so that the figures are proportionately smaller, and a piece of drapery has been decorously added to cover the Child's nudity. An engraving of 1640 by Pierre

Daret may have been the model for some of the derivations, such as the grisaille by Jan van Kessel the Elder of 1654. A copy of A745 (including the drapery) was on the art market in 1984. The prime version may be the painting, formerly in the Crozat collection, now in the Hermitage State Museum, St Petersburg.

Attributed to Roelof Jansz. van Vries
(*c.* 1631 – after 1681)

A Path leading through a Wood with Figures

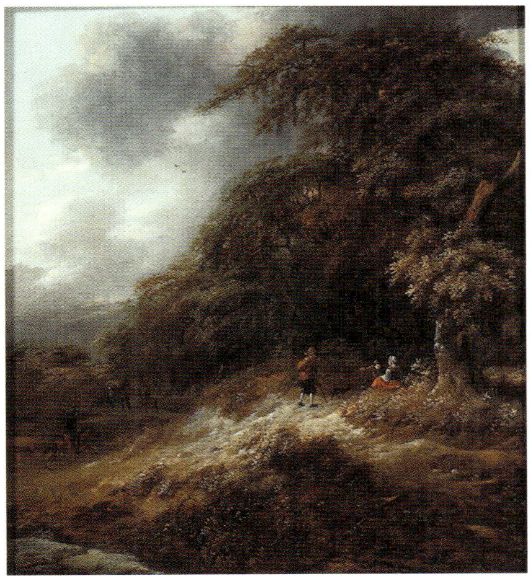

A286; oil on panel, 46 × 41 cm
Presented by Thomas Humphry Ward, 1897; WA1897.9

White 1999, p. 163

Van Vries's master is unknown but his work shows the influence of Jacob van Ruisdael. There are weaknesses in the execution of the figures in this painting but the style is his and the painting may be by him.

Gerrit van Vucht
(active 1658 – 1697)

Breakfast-piece with a Ham

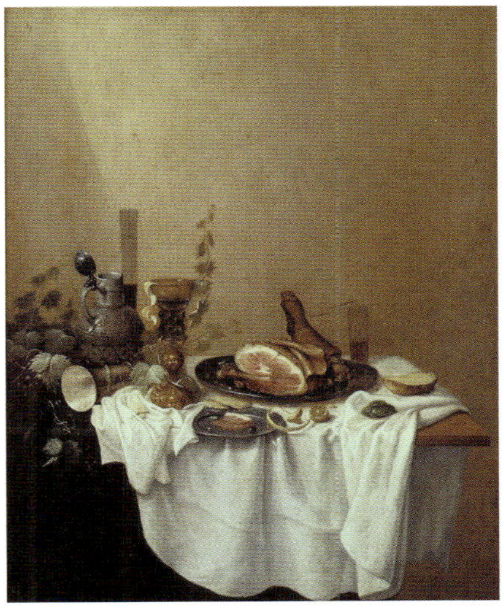

A555; oil on panel, 39 × 32 cm
Daisy Linda Ward Bequest, 1939; WA1940.2.31

Meijer 2003, no. 90

Van Vucht spent his life in the fishing town of Shiedam. His name subsequently fell into obscurity and his work has been attributed to other artists, in particular to Gerrit Willemsz. Heda, son of Willem Claesz. Heda, to whom this painting was formerly attributed. There are affinities with Heda's school which might account for the misattribution. This is one of Vucht's most sumptuous banquet paintings.

Jacobus Vrel
(active 1654 – ?1670)

The Little Nurse

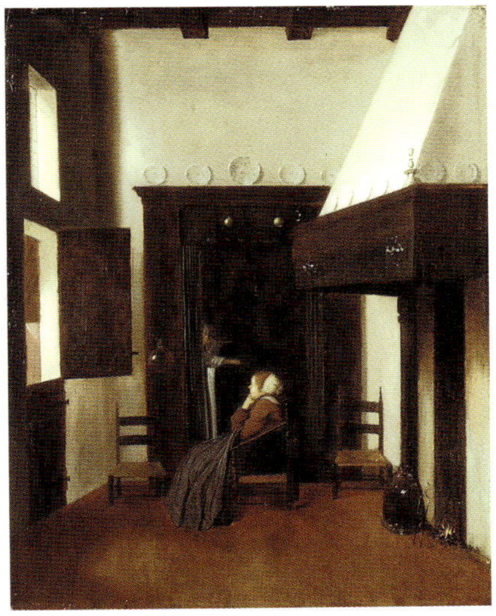

A1070; oil on panel, 54 × 42 cm
Prov.: Frederick Percy; W.C. Alexander and by descent
Presented by the National Art Collections Fund from the Bequest of Miss Jean Alexander, 1972; WA1972.287

White 1999, p. 163

Little is known about Vrel apart from a number of signed works. Three other versions of this painting are known (in the Museum voor Schone Kunsten, Antwerp; the J. Paul Getty Museum, Los Angeles; and the San Diego Museum of Art). His style is spare and simple and seems to owe something to Vermeer.

Style of Hendrick Cornelisz. Vroom
(1566 – 1640)

Three Warships off Flushing

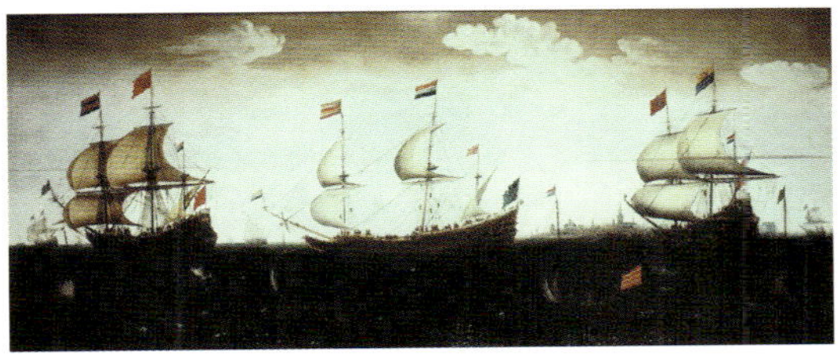

A16; oil on panel, 92.6 × 218.8 cm
Bequeathed by the Revd Dr John King, 1737; WA1845.16

White 1999, p. 165

Vroom was one of the first Dutch painters to specialise in marines. He was much imitated and this painting seems to be the work of a follower, possibly Aert Anthonisz., whose paintings were often confused with those of Vroom. The town of Flushing is located at the mouth of the river Scheldt. The ship on the left appears to fly a flag bearing the arms of the House of Orange. The ship on the right carries the flags of the Province of Zeeland and the city of Flushing.

Gerrit van Vucht
(active 1658 – 1697)

Still Life with a Skull and Books

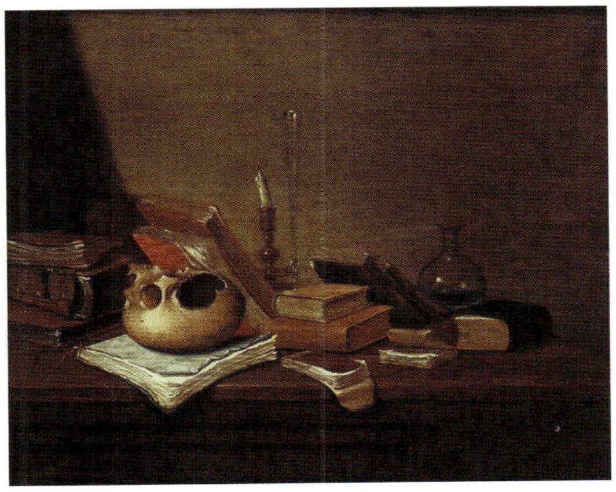

A601; oil on panel, 25 × 31 cm
Daisy Linda Ward Bequest, 1939; WA1940.2.77

Meijer 2003, no. 91

The *vanitas* was one of the artist's favourite subjects. The thick volume with torn leather cover, which appears again in a fully signed *vanitas* in the Muzeum Narodowe, Poznan, was a common symbol of the vanity of human endeavour, along with the skull and the extinguished candle where the symbolism is more obvious. The painting was formerly attributed to Pieter Steenwyck, brother of Herman Steenwyck.

Edouard Vuillard
(1868 – 1940)

Le Déjeuner

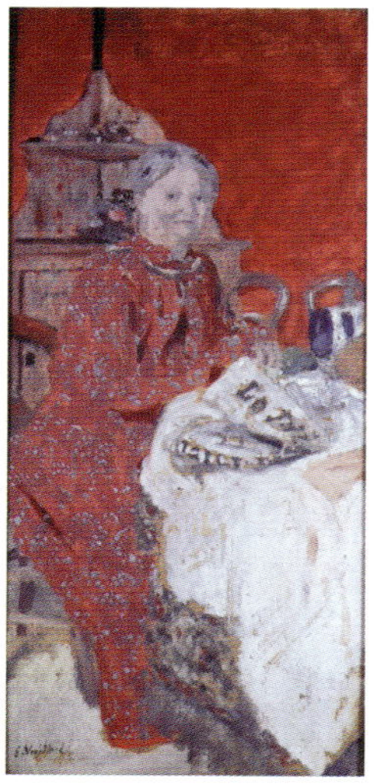

A1190; oil on canvas, 20 × 45 cm
Prov.: Sam Salz; Mrs Hugh Neame
Accepted by H.M. Government in lieu of Inheritance Tax from the estate of Mrs Eve Tooth and allocated to the Ashmolean Museum, 1994; WA1994.3

Vuillard painted many scenes of domestic life which feature his relatives and friends in an intimate setting. This represents his mother, a seamstress, who was a frequent model. The matt colour and flat patterned manner are characteristic of his work in the 1890s.

Kaspar Waldmann
(1657 – 1720)

Gipsy Musicians

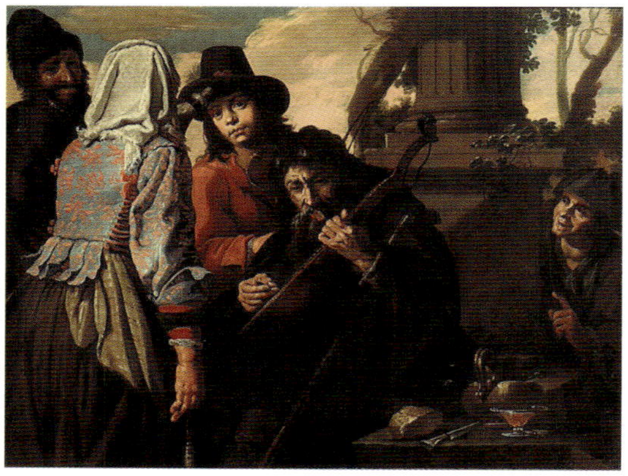

A705; oil on canvas, 85 × 107 cm
Signed: *GASPAR WALDMAN F*
Presented by Percy Moore Turner, 1943; WA1943.2

While Waldmann may have travelled to Italy, much of his career was spent in Innsbruck, where he painted numerous altar-pieces and frescoes. A smaller version of A705, attributed to Ulrich Glantschigg, is in Innsbruck.

Dame Ethel Walker
(1861 – 1951)

Seascape: The coming Storm

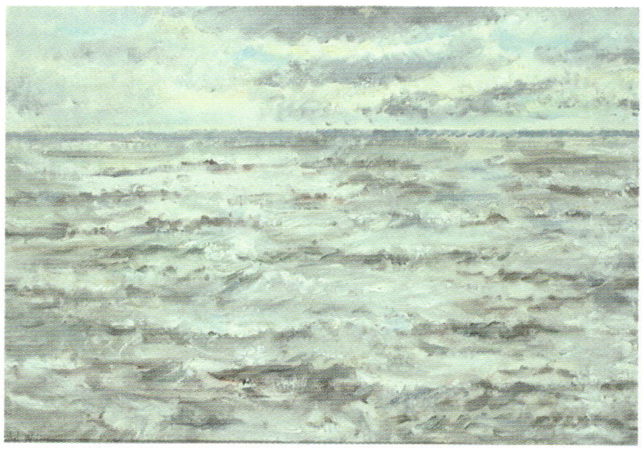

A448; oil on canvas, 63 × 89 cm
Signed: *Ethel Walker*
Presented by Mrs W.F.R. Weldon, 1936; WA1936.49

Probably painted at The White Gate, Robin Hood's Bay, Yorkshire.

Roger Wagner
(b. 1957)

Black Poplar

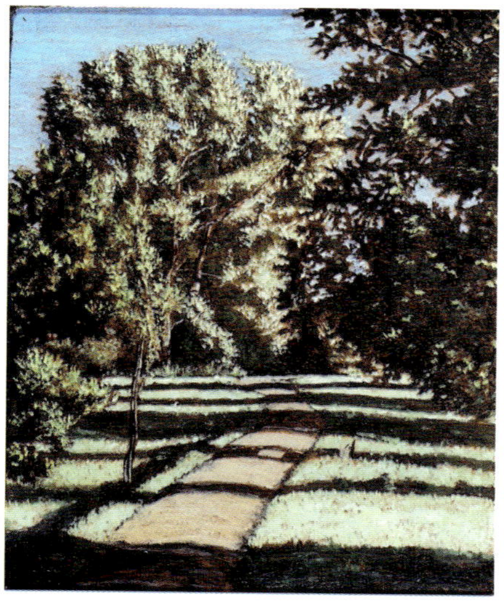

A1193; oil on board, 20.5 × 17 cm
Signed in monogram on the back
Purchased from the artist, 1995; WA1995.68

Oxford 1994, no. 29

While studying at Oxford, Wagner became deeply interested in pastoral landscapes in the tradition of Samuel Palmer. Many of his paintings are charged with a religious meaning although this is sometimes only indirectly indicated. This sunlit path has no obvious religious attributes but may refer to the theme of paradise.

Dame Ethel Walker
(1861 – 1951)

Sun and Wind

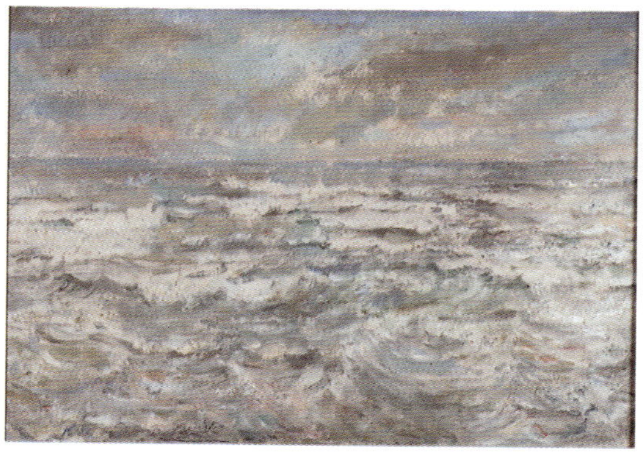

A1026; oil on canvas, 64 × 89 cm
Bequeathed by Mrs W.S.S. Tyrwhitt, 1966; WA1966.42.3

Ethel Walker spent the greater part of her working life between Cheyne Walk, Chelsea and her cottage at Robin Hood's Bay, Yorkshire. Her sea-pieces, painted while on holiday, are studies in light and atmosphere between the sea and the sky, painted in the broad, Impressionist technique she favoured.

Robert Walker
(?1595/1610 – ?1659)

Self-portrait

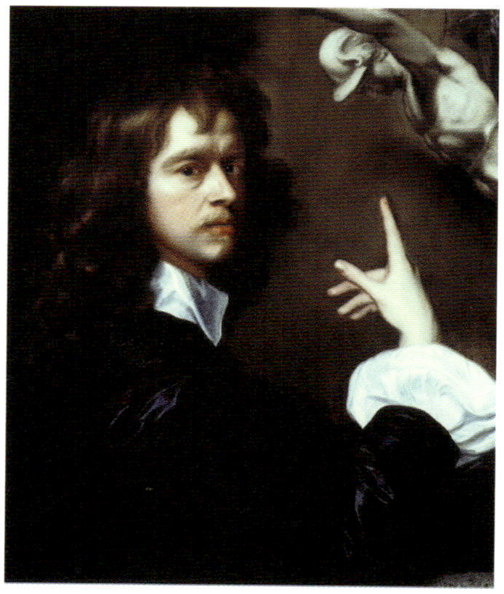

A1; oil on canvas, 75 × 62 cm
Acquired by the Bodleian Library before 1679; WA1845.1

Poole 1912, no. 424

Walker was the leading portrait painter to the parliamentary side during the Civil War. This self-portrait is the most elaborate of several variants (Royal Collection; National Portrait Gallery; Belvoir Castle), which have been dated to the 1640s. It pays ironic homage to van Dyck's *Self-portrait* (Westminster Collection), in which the artist points at a sunflower as a symbol of homage to the King. Here, Walker points to a statue of Mercury as patron of the arts.

Goffredo Wals
(*c.* 1595 – *c.* 1638)

Landscape with pastoral Figures

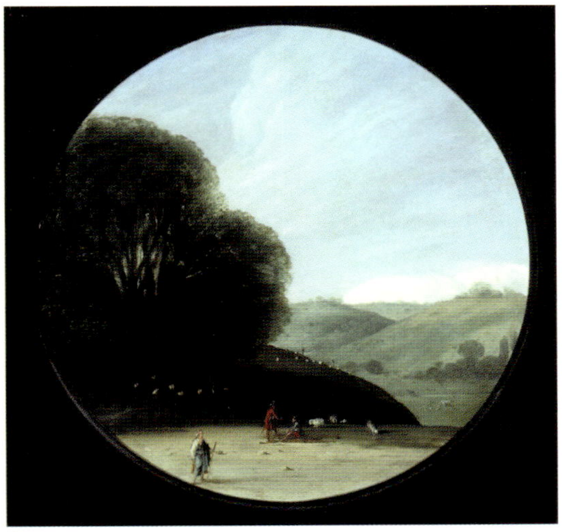

A185; oil on copper, 24 cm in diameter
Chambers Hall Gift, 1855; WA1855.188

White 1999, p. 166

Wals was born in Cologne but studied with Agostino Tassi in Rome and settled in Naples, where he is said to have taught Claude. His work has been reconstructed round a number of small circular landscapes in which the figures are small and the space has been simplified into clearly divided planes.

Henry Walter
(1786 or 1790 – 1849)

A Farm House

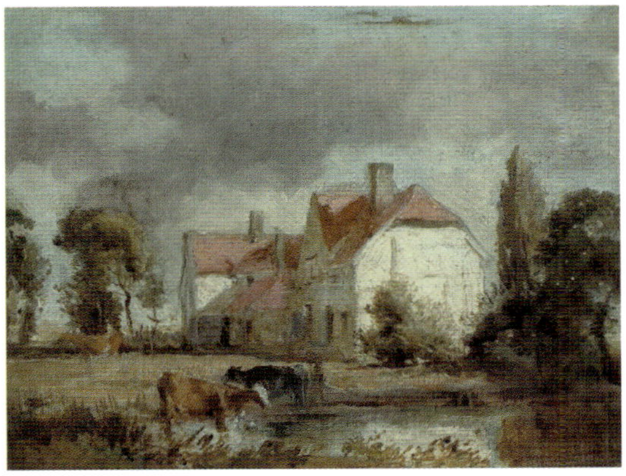

A787; oil on canvas, 20 × 26 cm
Prov.: George Richmond and by descent
Bequeathed by Mrs Hilda Fothergill Medlicott, 1950
WA1950.27

A companion to the preceding.

Daisy Linda Ward (*née* Travers)
(1883 – 1937)

Still Life with a Matchbox

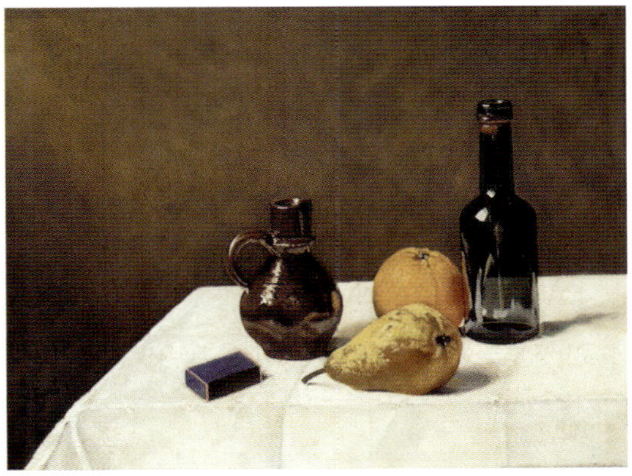

A524; oil on canvas, 36 × 45.5 cm
Signed: *L. Travers*
Daisy Linda Ward Bequest, 1939; WA1940.2.96

Meijer 2003, p. 11

The close angle of vision, the diagonal emphasis and the humble objects placed in isolation on a table which protrudes into the composition all recall Harmen Steenwyck whose work is well represented in the Ward Bequest.

Henry Walter
(1786 or 1790 – 1849)

Cows in a Landscape

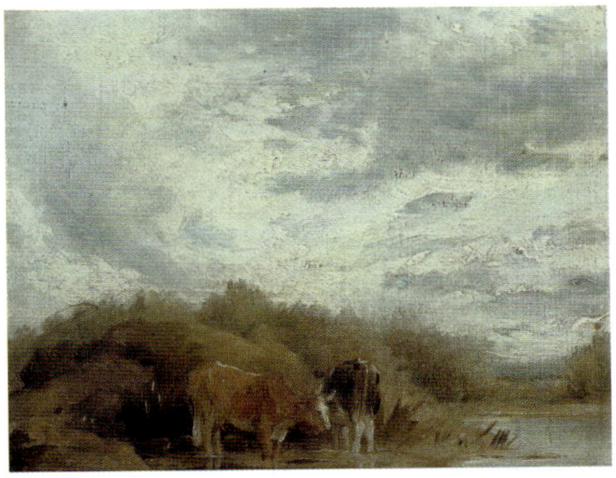

A786; oil on canvas, 20 × 26 cm
Prov.: George Richmond and by descent
Bequeathed by Mrs Hilda Fothergill Medlicott, 1950;
WA1950.26

Walter was one of the 'Ancients', who lived and worked at Shoreham in Kent in the late 1820s. This landscape and its companion were given to his fellow 'Ancient', George Richmond. It depicts the timeless pastoral ideal Walter and his friend, Samuel Palmer, sought at Shoreham.

Daisy Linda Ward (*née* Travers)
(1883 – 1937)

Still Life with Fruit

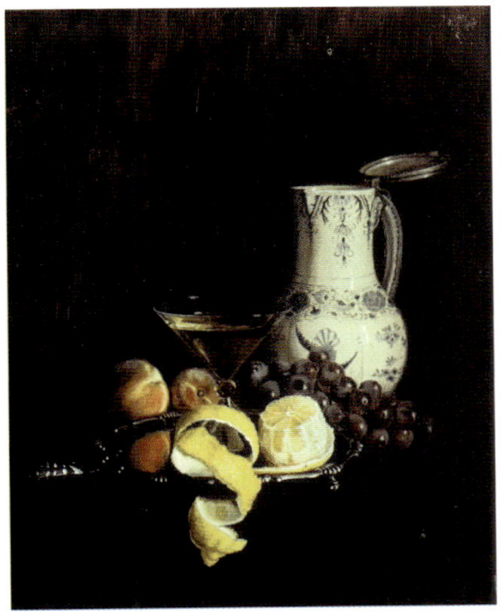

A523; oil on canvas, 34 × 45 cm
Signed: *Linda Travers*
Daisy Linda Ward Bequest, 1939; WA1940.2.95

Meijer 2003, p. 11

The artist appeared at the Royal Academy summer exhibition for the first time in 1925. Her speciality was still life. With her husband, Theodore Ward, she collected the group of Dutch and Flemish still-life paintings which were bequeathed to the Ashmolean in 1939. The effect of reflected light on rich, shining objects set against a dark background, derives from the work of Willem Kalf and his followers.

Attributed to Louis-Etienne Watelet
(1780 – 1866)

A Mill in a mountainous Landscape

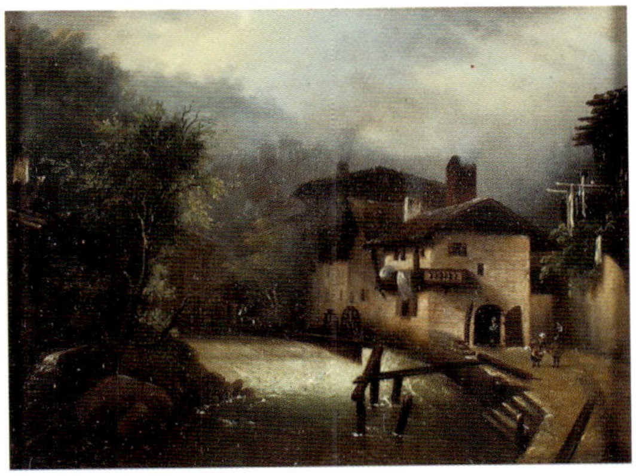

A1194; oil on copper, 7.9 × 10.3 cm
Bequeathed by Cyril Eland, 1996; WA1996.21

The attribution is based on an inscribed label on the back. Watelet began in the tradition of classical landscape painting in early 19th-century France but adopted more rustic subjects in his later work. Mills were a favourite motif.

Jean-Antoine Watteau
(1684 – 1721)

Le Repos Gracieux

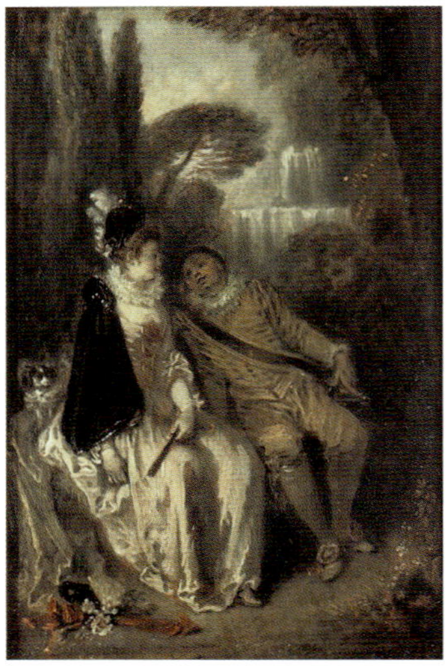

A387; oil on panel, 19.5 × 11.3 cm
Prov.: Thélusson; Solirène; Delaroche; Lord Taunton; E.A.V. Stanley
Presented by Mrs W.F.R. Weldon, 1927; WA1927.2

Grasselli and Rosenberg 1984, no. 27

The figures are dressed as Columbine and Crispin from the Commedia dell'Arte and from French popular drama respectively; they may be actors, off-stage, or lovers in fancy dress. A387 is typical of Watteau's enigmatic paintings, often inspired by theatrical and musical themes; it may date from *c.* 1713. The figures reappear in an engraving by Gabriel Huquier, perhaps based on a lost drawing. An early copy of A387 is at Rennes.

Frederick William Watts
(1800 – 1862)

River Landscape

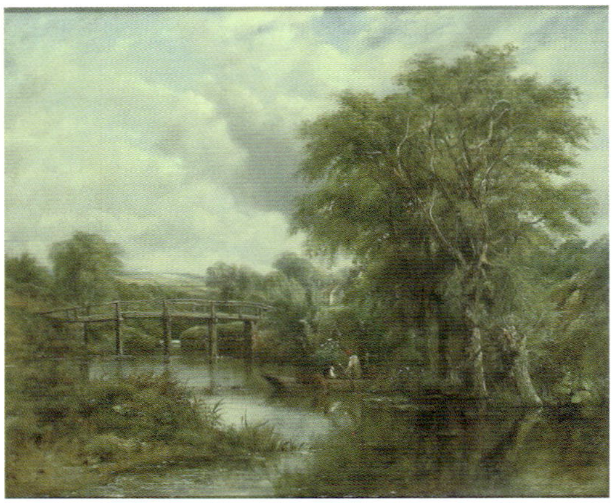

A1012; oil on canvas, 79 × 95 cm
Bequeathed by Major Thomas Bouch, 1963; WA1963.150.9

George Frederic Watts
(1817 – 1904)

Little Red Riding Hood

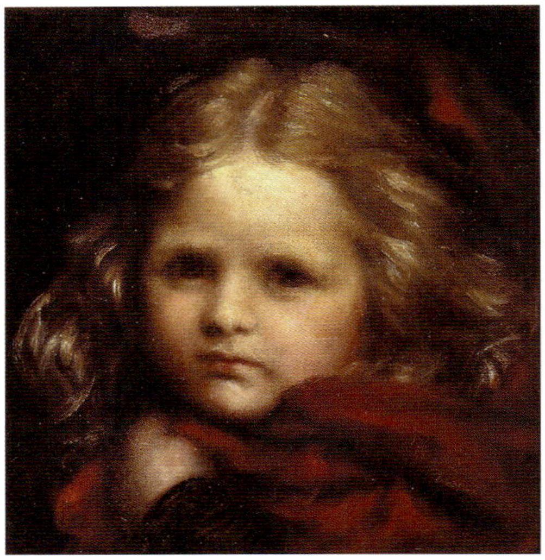

A452; oil on canvas, 26.4 × 25.1 cm
Prov.: Sir William Bowman, Bt
Weldon Bequest, 1937; WA1937.32

This is Watts's first treatment of the theme, an illustration to Perrault's fairy tale. It was painted in 1864 and bought by Sir William Bowman, whose portrait Watts painted in the following year. A full-length version of the subject, painted in 1890, is in Birmingham City Art Gallery.

Frederick William Watts
(1800 – 1862)

Near Epsom

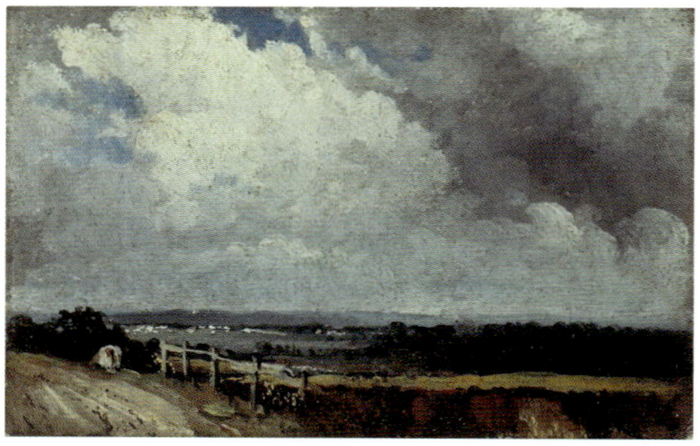

A951; oil on board, mounted as a drawing, 11.3 × 17.3 cm
Bequeathed by J.E. Bullard, 1961; WA1961.31.2

Watts enjoyed a considerable career producing decorative pastiches of Constable, both as oil-sketches, as here, and as full-scale exhibition pieces.

George Frederic Watts
(1817 – 1904)

The Brethren of Saturn delivered

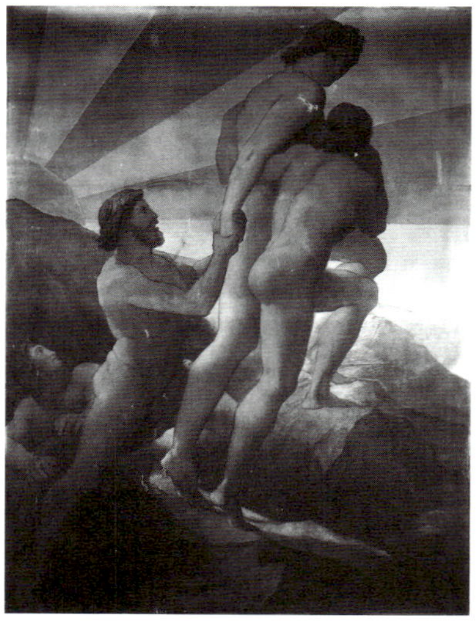

A138; oil on canvas, rolled, 134 × 152 cm
Presented by Dr Henry Wentworth Acland, 1853; WA1853.2

The subject is taken from John Flaxman's plate to Hesiod's *Theogony* and was suggested by the donor for a spandrel for his house in Broad Street, Oxford.

George Frederic Watts
(1817 – 1904)

The Carrara Mountains from Pisa

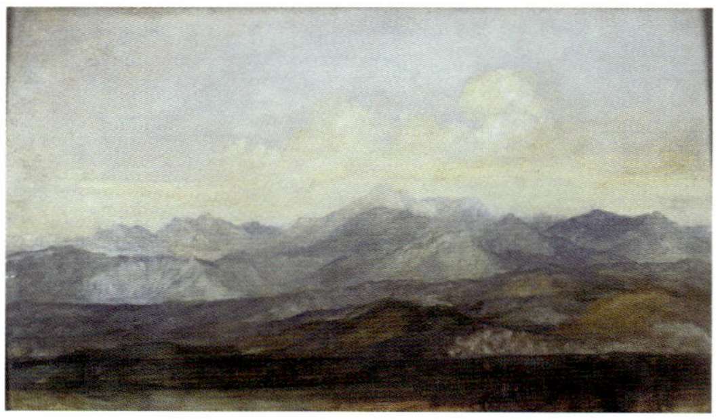

A352; oil on panel, 28 × 45 cm
Signed: *G.F. Watts*
Prov.: Charles Hilditch Rickards
Presented by Mrs W.F.R. Weldon, 1915; WA1915.63

Watts spent the years 1843–7 in Florence. In 1845–6, he made a number of watercolour studies from the top of the leaning tower of Pisa. This small oil-sketch was based on one and served in its turn as the basis for a larger painting exhibited at the Grosvenor Gallery, 1881.

George Frederic Watts
(1817 – 1904)

Edward VII as Prince of Wales

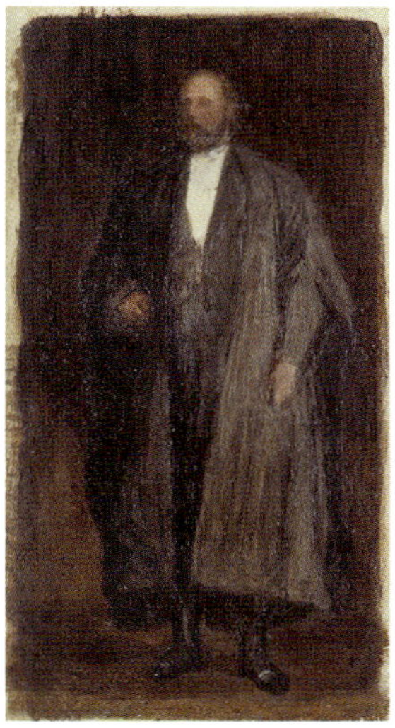

A888a; oil on canvas, mounted as a drawing, 23.5 × 12.4 cm
Prov.: Hon. Clare Stuart-Wortley; Lord Robert Cecil
Purchased, 1956; WA1956.12

Albert Edward (1841–1910), who reigned as King Edward VII (1901–10), was created Prince of Wales soon after his birth. He studied at Christ Church, Oxford, in 1859–60. Watts drew him on several occasions, but found him an unsympathetic sitter. This is a study for the portrait commissioned for the Middle Temple in 1874 (Watts Gallery, Compton). Watts was dissatisfied with the result and reclaimed the painting after it was exhibited at the Grosvenor Gallery in 1882.

George Frederic Watts
(1817 – 1904)

Thomas Carlyle

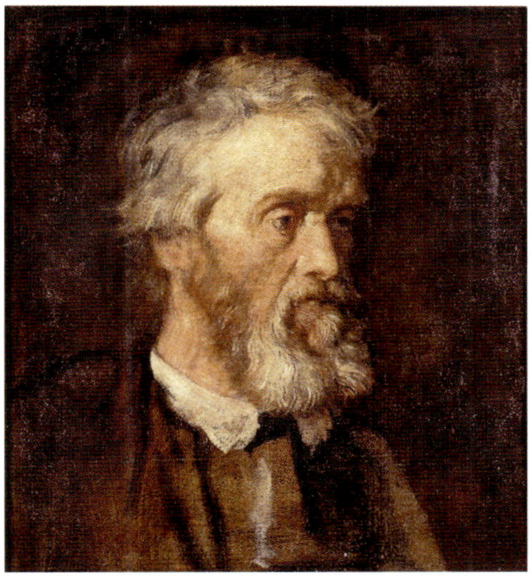

A949; oil on canvas, 48 × 44 cm
Prov.: Mrs Michael Chapman, the artist's adopted daughter
Bequeathed by Miss Katherine Elizabeth Lewis, 1961; WA1961.30

One of three portraits of the Scots historian and essayist, Thomas Carlyle (1795–1881), for which sittings are recorded in 1867–8. Watts found Carlyle a difficult subject because he could not conceal his boredom. For his part, Carlyle complained that Watts had made him look 'like a mad labourer'.

George Frederic Watts
(1817 – 1904)

Miss Eliza Ann Ogilvy

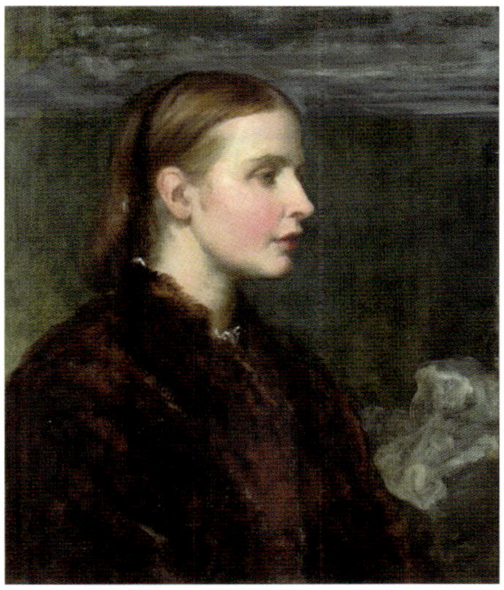

A681; oil on canvas, 61 × 52 cm
Prov.: Louis Huth
Presented by A.B. How, 1941; WA1941.54

Eliza Ann (d. 1872), the daughter of Thomas Ogilvy of Corrimony. This portrait was painted for her sister, Mrs Huth, in 1866, on the eve of her marriage to C.D. van Lennep and departure to Smyrna. Watts was struck by her beauty and sweet nature and touched that the sisters should be separated.

George Frederic Watts
(1817 – 1904)

'All the air a solemn stillness holds'

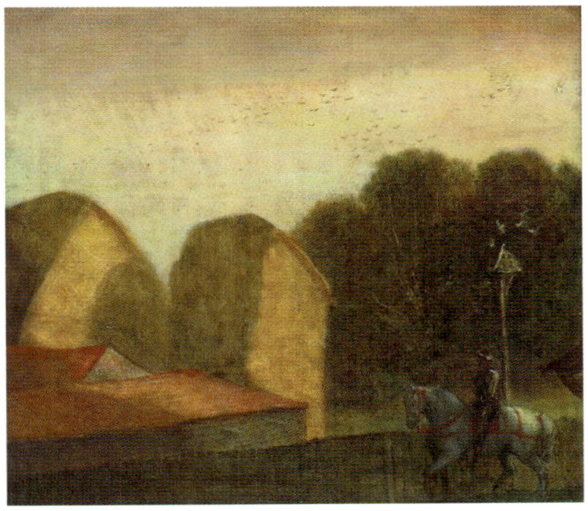

A915; oil on panel, 34 × 38 cm
Prov.: Mrs Michael Chapman, the artist's adopted daughter
Russell Bequest, 1958; WA1958.57.9

This was painted in 1863–4 and depicts part of the grounds of Watts's residence, Little Holland House, in London. The title is taken from Gray's *Elegy in a Country Churchyard*. Watts painted a second version in 1868, replacing the knight with a labourer. The first version was greatly admired by John Ruskin.

George Frederic Watts
(1817 – 1904)

Miss Helen Rose Ogilvy

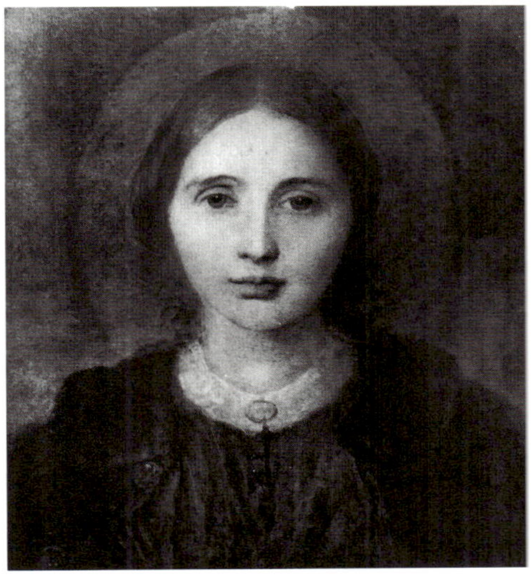

A682; oil on canvas, 61 × 52 cm
Prov.: Louis Huth
Presented by A.B. How, 1941; WA1941.55

Helen Rose Ogilvy (1837–1924) was the daughter of a merchant, Thomas Ogilvy of Corrimony, and sister to Eliza Ann Ogilvy. She married the collector, Louis Huth (1821–1905) and, after his death, A.B. How, Fellow of Exeter College, Oxford. In 1874, Whistler painted her portrait in his *Arrangement in Black No. 2: Portrait of Mrs Louis Huth* (private collection), for which there is a study in the Ashmolean. A682 was recorded missing in 1965.

George Frederic Watts
(1817 – 1904)

Time and Death

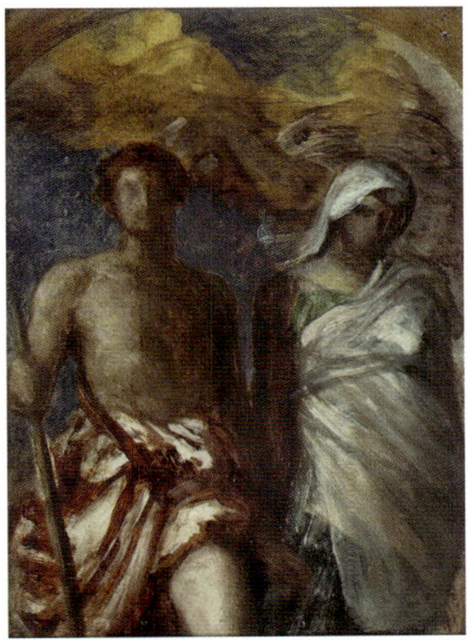

A880; oil on cardboard, 27 × 19 cm
Prov.: Mrs Michael Chapman, the artist's adopted daughter
Presented by A.G.B. Russell, 1955; WA1955.25

The allegorical subject of *Time, Judgement and Death* was one of Watts's chief hopes to be considered a serious intellectual artist. This is an early sketch, painted in *c.* 1868, for the large paintings in the National Gallery of Canada, Ottawa; Tate Britain; and St Paul's Cathedral. Watts also made a mosaic of the subject which he presented to the church of St Jude's, Whitechapel. The figure of Time appears on the left of the sketch, and Death on the right. Judgement has not yet been incorporated.

George Frederic Watts
(1817 – 1904)

The Rider on the Black Horse

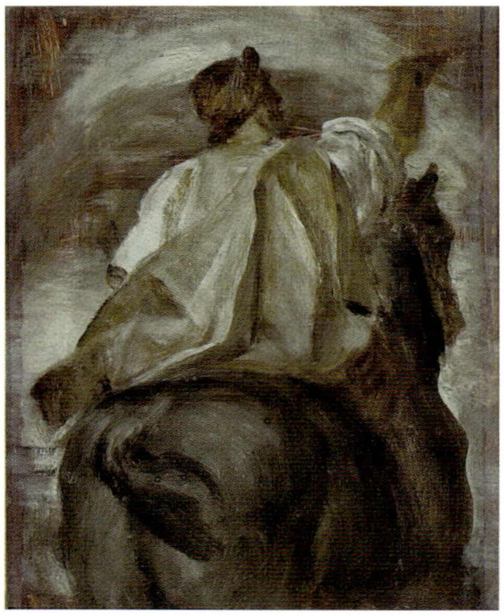

A816; oil on panel, 24 × 19 cm
Prov.: Mrs Michael Chapman, the artist's adopted daughter
Presented by A.G.B. Russell, 1951; WA1951.148

Morris 1996, p. 477

This is a study for *The Rider on the Black Horse*, one of the *Four Horsemen of the Apocalypse* (Walker Art Gallery, Liverpool). The subject was taken from Revelation 6: 1–8. The series was begun around 1868 and exhibited at the Grosvenor Gallery in 1883. Watts probably meant the horses to have allegorical significance: a contemporary suggested that *The Rider on the Black Horse* was the spirit of Commerce.

H. Maria Weerts
(second half of 17th century)

Still Life with Flowers

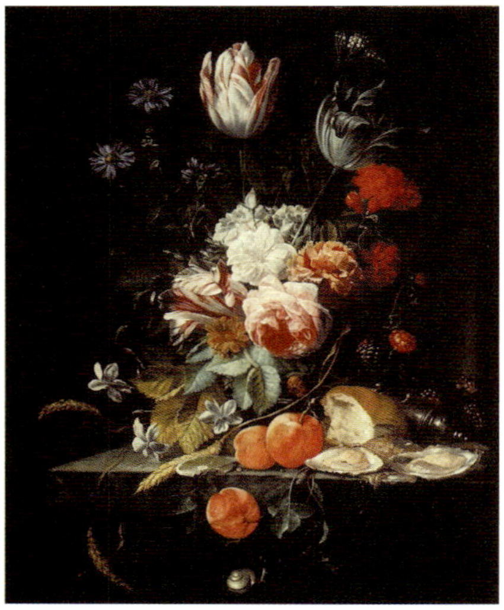

A618; oil on canvas, 53 × 43 cm
Signed: *h weerts f*
Prov.: Rochas
Daisy Linda Ward Bequest, 1939; WA1940.2.94

Meijer 2003, no. 93

The artist is known only known through a handful of signed still-life paintings. A suggestion that the artist might be a certain Henricus van Weert, who seems to have come from Amsterdam, has been doubted. The paintings seem to indicate a link with Antwerp. This painting is an amalgam of motifs taken from Nicolaes van Verendael and the de Heems.

Jan Hendrik Weissenbruch
(1824 – 1903)

Landscape with a Peasant Girl feeding Chicken

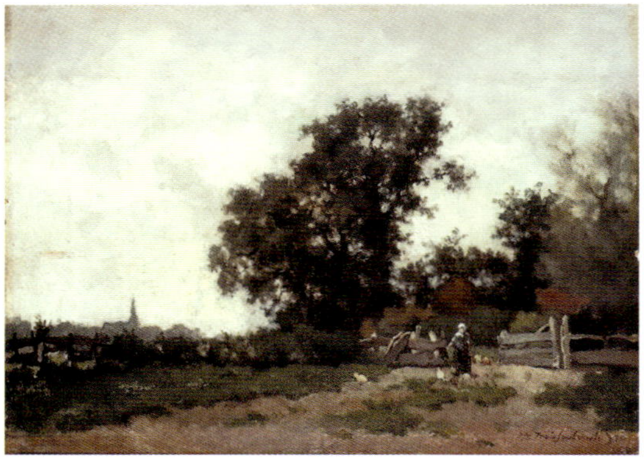

A1147; oil on panel, 29.6 × 39.7 cm
Signed and dated: *J.H.Weissenbruch / 70*
Presented by the children of Mr and Mrs Henry van den Bergh (Mrs Dorrit Talbot, Mrs S. Roskill and Col Donald S. van den Bergh) through the National Art Collections Fund, in memory of Captain Seymour and Major James van den Bergh, 1987; WA1987.41

Weissenbruch's art was, in part, derived from his interest in the art of Ruisdael, Potter and Vermeer. He shared with them a liking for effects of light and weather. The soft, liquid touches in this painting recall the technique of his watercolours.

Jan Weenix
(1642 – 1719)

A Vase of Flowers

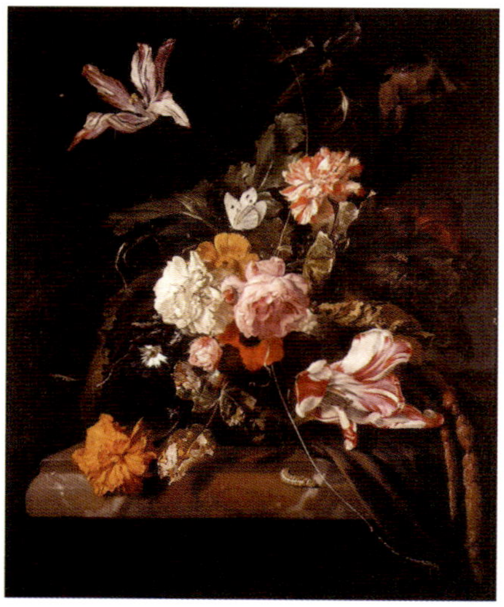

A617; oil on canvas, 62 × 50 cm
Daisy Linda Ward Bequest, 1939; WA1940.2.93

Meijer 2003, no. 92

Weenix lived for most of his career in Amsterdam where he was chiefly known for his hunting pieces. Flowers often appear in his female portraits and in his paintings of game but still-life paintings of flowers by him are rare. The withered leaves do not appear in his work before the 1670s but are common in his later work. A date of about 1680 is suggested by the dark background, the form of the ledge and by the out-of-doors setting in which Weenix placed all his still lifes after *c.* 1680.

Carel Victor Morlais Weight
(1908 – 1997)

Miss Orovida Pissarro

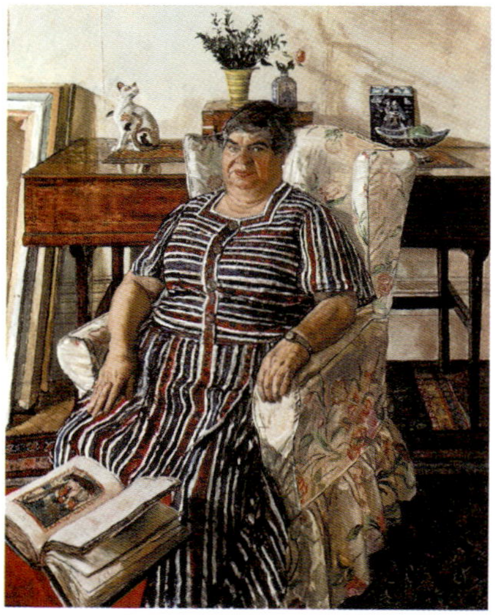

A920; oil on canvas, 91.8 × 71.5 cm
Signed: *Carel Weight*
Presented by Miss Orovida Pissarro, 1958; WA1958.54

Weight 1994, pp. 56–7

Orovida Pissarro (1893–1968) commissioned this portrait from Weight in 1956. Weight painted two different versions: one now in Tate Britain shows the sitter seen from above, while the version in the Ashmolean shows her on the same level. The book open in front of her is her father's *Catalogue de gravures sur bois*, which she bequeathed to the Ashmolean.

Hubert Lindsay Wellington
(1879 – 1967)

Overhanging Tree, Frampton Mansell

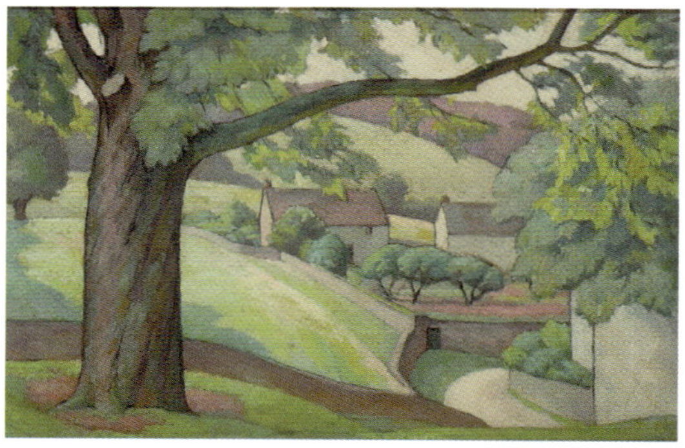

A1013; oil on canvas, 41 × 61 cm
Dated on the back: *1915*
Presented by the artist, 1964; WA1964.35

Gloucester 1968, no. 20

Wellington painted a number of views of the village of Frampton Mansell, near Stroud in Gloucestershire.

Jacob Willemsz. de Wet
(*c.* 1610 – after 1675)

Paul and Barnabas at Lystra

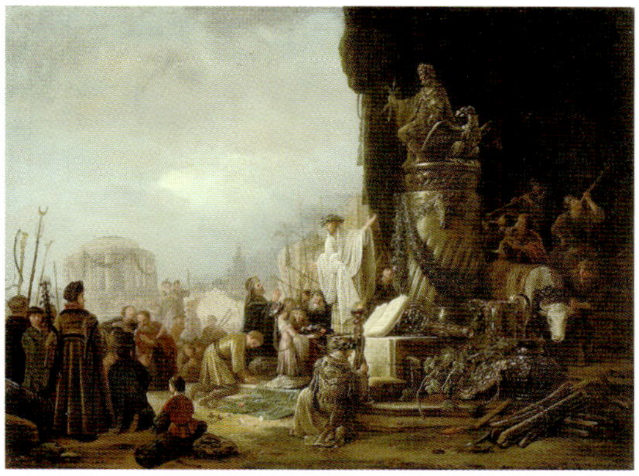

A315; oil on canvas, 67 × 87 cm
Signed: *JdWet*
Presented by Miss Emily Perrin, 1907; WA1907.4

White 1999, p. 168

De Wet worked mostly in Haarlem, painting religious and mythological subjects in a style that suggests contact with Rembrandt in the 1630s. The subject of this painting illustrates the adulation of the people of Lystra who mistook the visitors for gods after Paul had cured a cripple. On the left, Paul and Barnabas tear their clothes in dismay at this misconception (Acts 14: 11–15).

James Abbott McNeill Whistler
(1834 – 1903)

The Shore, Pourville

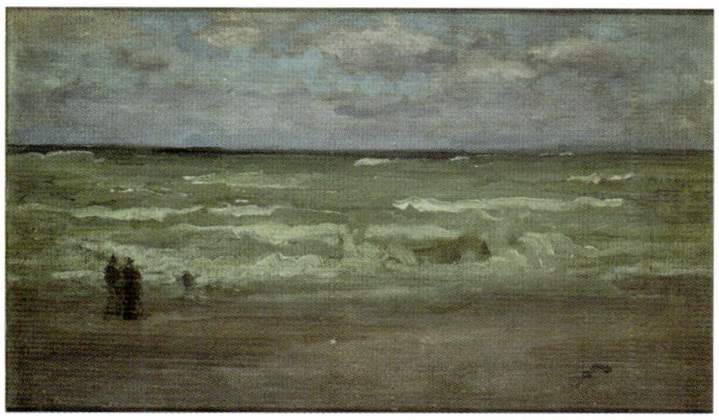

A985; oil on panel, 13.7 × 23.3 cm
Signed with butterfly
Prov.: Miss Rosalind Birnie-Philip
Madan Bequest, 1962; WA1962.17.27

Young, MacDonald, Spencer 1980, no. 521

In the summer of 1899, Whistler stayed with his ward, Rosalind Birnie-Philip, and her mother at the Pavillon Madeleine, Pourville-sur-Mer, near Dieppe, convalescing from a recurrent illness. Apart from brief excursions elsewhere, he remained from the end of July until 26 October. While he was there, he painted a series of nine small seascapes on panel, thinly brushed, and subdued but refined in colour.

Cornelis Claesz. van Wieringhen
(*c.* 1580 – 1635)

Ships in a Squall on the Haarlemmer Meer

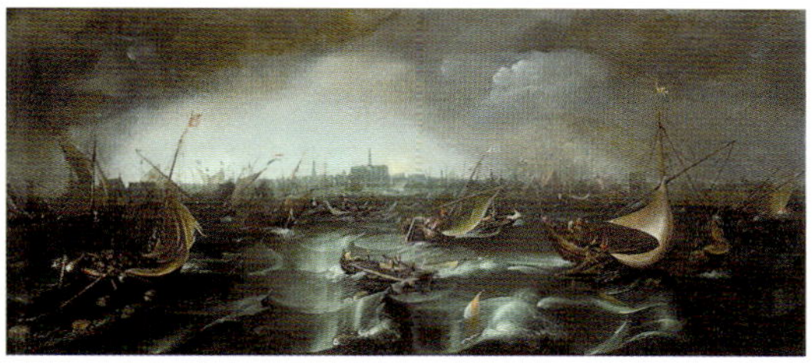

A10; oil on panel, 38.6 × 85.6 cm
Bequeathed by the Revd Dr John King, 1737; WA1845.10

White 1999, p. 169

The city of Haarlem where van Wieringen worked appears in the background of this marine. The Groote Kerk of St Bavo is visible in the centre. Several ships are in difficulty in the heavy sea and some cargo has been lost overboard. This may be a late work influenced by the monochrome style of Jan Porcellis to whom this picture was attributed when acquired by the Bodleian Library.

James Abbott McNeill Whistler
(1834 – 1903)

Portrait of a Man in Evening Dress

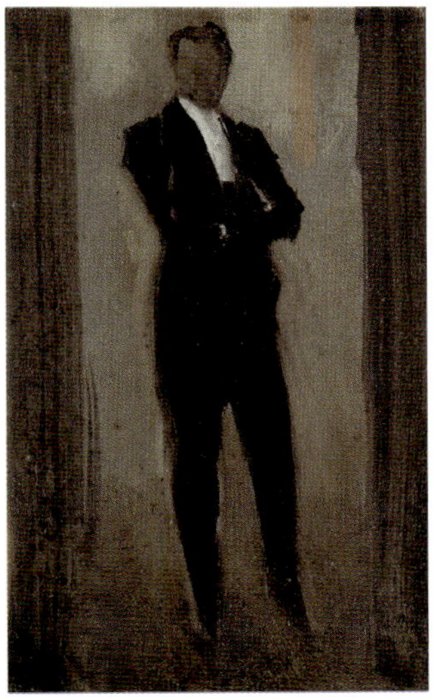

A718b; oil on panel, mounted as a drawing, laid down, 16.1 × 9.2 cm (sight)
Purchased, 1945; WA1945.139

Young, MacDonald, Spencer 1980, no. 316

A date in the mid-1880s has been suggested. The features are not clear, but the actor-manager Herbert Beerbohm Tree (1853–1917) has been proposed as the subject.

Diana White
(1868 – 1950)

Mist in the Valley, Stogumber

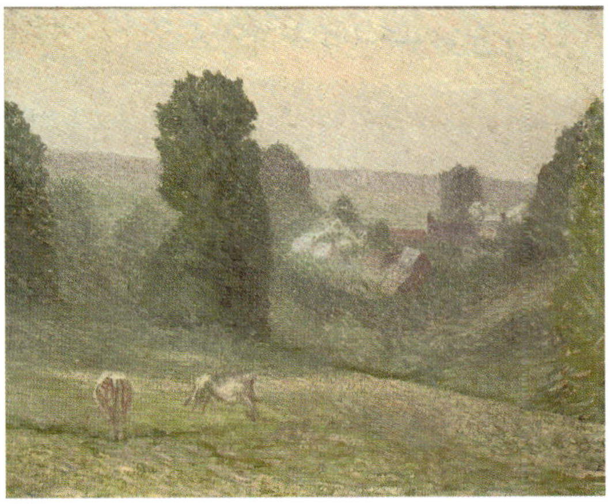

A792; oil on canvas, 46 × 55 cm
Presented by Mrs Lucien Pissarro in memory of the artist, 1950; WA1950.172

A view of the village of Stogumber, in west Somerset, painted in 1911.

Sir David Wilkie
(1785 – 1841)

Blind Man's Buff

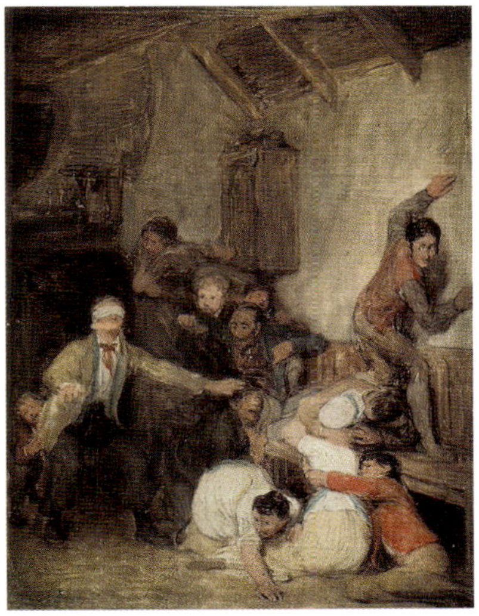

A986; oil on wooden panel, mounted as a drawing, 17 × 13 cm
Prov.: (?)John Wilkie
Madan Bequest, 1962; WA1962.17.28

Brown 1985, no. 2

The original version of *Blind Man's Buff* was commissioned by the Prince Regent and completed in 1812 (Royal Collection). It was based on a sequence of drawings and oil-sketches developed in the previous year. This sketch shows the right half of the composition and corresponds with drawings in Nottingham and Edinburgh. A later oil-sketch of the whole composition, dated 1811, is in Tate Britain.

Sir David Wilkie
(1785 – 1841)

Helen Wilkie, later Mrs William Hunter

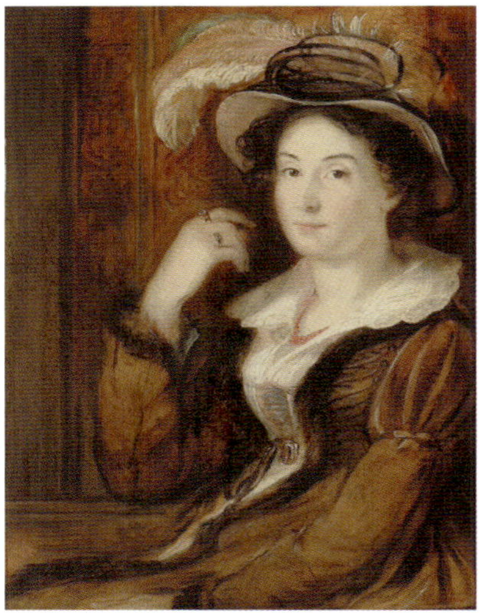

A694; oil on panel, 43 × 32 cm
Presented by Percy Moore Turner, 1942; WA1942.19

Brown 1985, no. 40

Helen Wilkie, the artist's sister, kept house for her brother and frequently served as a model. After his death, she married William Hunter, Surgeon-Major in the Coldstream Guards. This portrait, made around 1830, is one of several of her, including a magnificent large drawing in the Ashmolean.

Sir David Wilkie
(1785 – 1841)

Maria, Lady Callcott

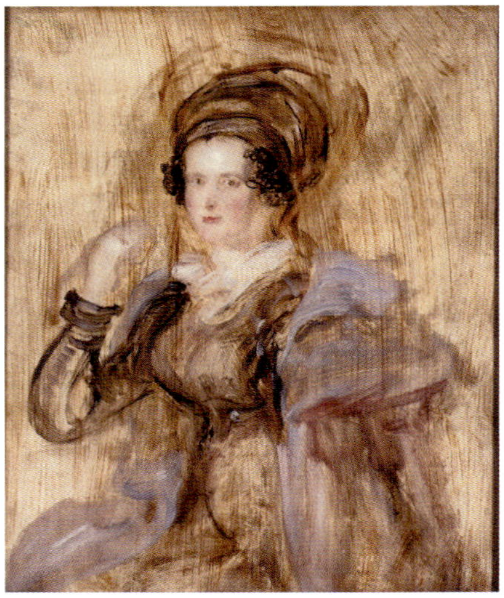

A1119; oil on panel, 38.1 × 31.5 cm
Prov.: Colonel Dundas; James Bridges; John Bryson
Purchased with the assistance of the Museums & Galleries Commission/Victoria & Albert Museum Purchase Grant Fund and the Friends of the Ashmolean, 1981; WA1981.79

Brown 1985, no. 57

Maria Dundas (1785–1842), wife of Capt. Thomas Graham, was an intrepid traveller. After his death, she married the painter, Sir Augustus Wall Callcott (1779–1844) in 1827. This lively sketch was probably made in the late 1830s and shows her wearing the turban-like headdress she affected to conceal a childhood scar.

William Williams
(active 1763 – 1795)

Landscape with a Track and a Man sitting on a Gate

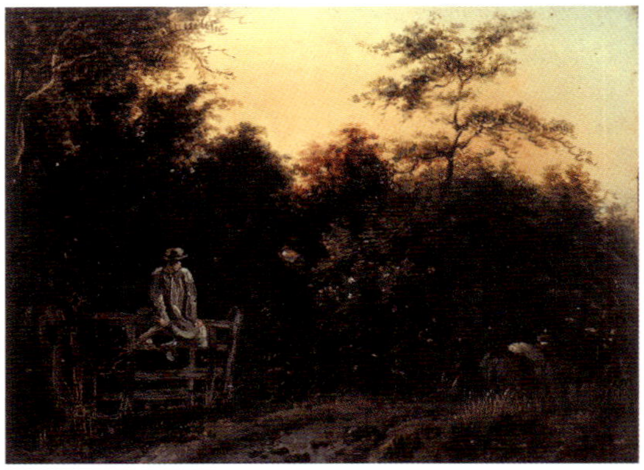

Oil on paper, mounted as a drawing, 24.9 × 32.9 cm
Prov.: Sydney D. Kitson
Presented by the Misses Kitson, 1940; WA1940.8.10

The attribution to this obscure watercolourist is tentative.

Sir David Wilkie
(1785 – 1841)

Nelson writing the Copenhagen Letter

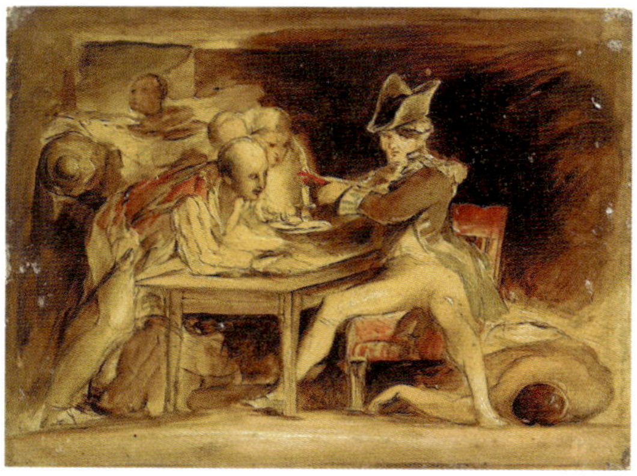

A1059; oil on panel, mounted as a drawing, 17.4 × 22.7 cm
Prov.: (?)Horatio McCulloch
Purchased, 1970; WA1970.115

Brown 1985, no. 42

The Battle of Copenhagen was fought on 1 April 1801 to reduce the Danish fleet. Nelson sent a flag of truce and a letter to the Crown Prince of Denmark which persuaded him to make terms. Wilkie apparently conceived the subject in 1835 as a pendant to *Columbus at the Convent of La Rabida* (North Carolina Museum of Art, Raleigh), but it progressed no further than this dramatically lit oil-sketch and some related drawings.

Adam Willaerts
(1577 – 1664)

Warships off the Coast with a Fishmarket on the Beach

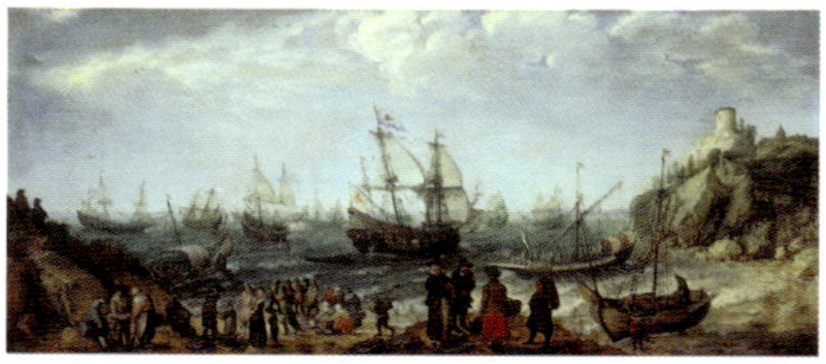

A9; oil on panel, 48 × 106 cm
Signed: *A. WILLARTS*
Bequeathed by the Revd Dr John King, 1737; WA1845.9

White 1999, p. 170

Willaerts was born in Antwerp but settled in Utrecht. Marines were his speciality. The nearest ship fires a salute in honour of a person of distinction, standing on the stern of the galley approaching from the right. The painting has been dated *c.* 1620 by comparison with *Ships off a Rocky Coast*, signed and dated 1621, in the Rijksmuseum, Amsterdam.

Richard Wilson
(1714 – 1782)

A Weir on the River Po near Ferrara

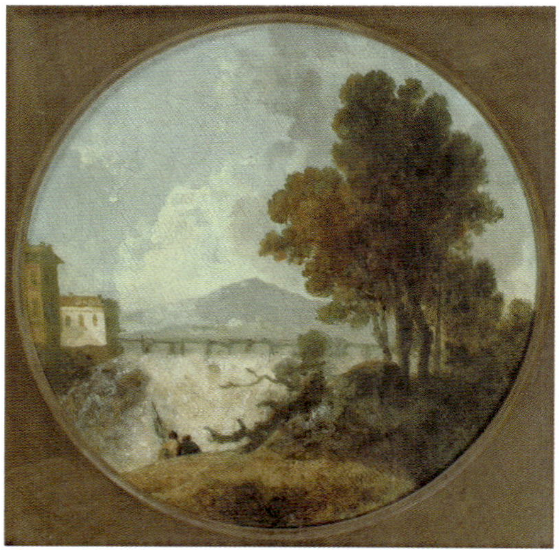

A200; oil on canvas, 23 cm in diameter
Chambers Hall Gift, 1855; WA1855.202

Constable 1953, p. 211; French 1980, no. 73

The title is taken from an old inscription on the back, but the landscape does not resemble the Po Valley near Ferrara. At least six painted versions are known and two drawings. They may be based on the composition of two paintings by Gaspard Dughet.

Richard Wilson
(1714 – 1782)

The Lago di Agnano

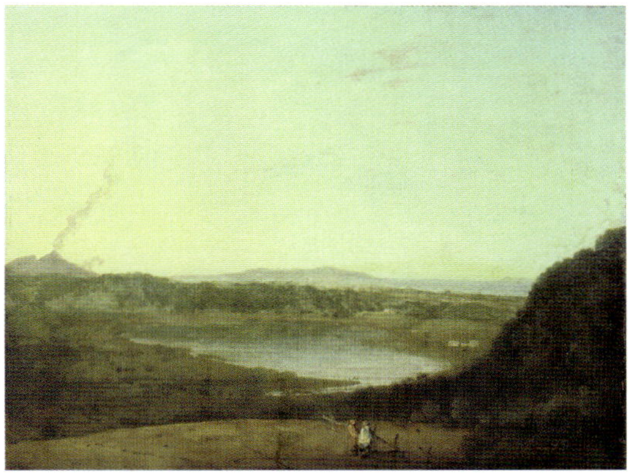

A199; oil on canvas, 43 × 55 cm
Chambers Hall Gift, 1855; WA1855.204

Constable 1953, pp. 190–1

The view is taken looking south towards the Bay of Naples, with Vesuvius on the left. The Lago di Agnano, in a volcanic crater, was drained in 1870. The painting was probably based on a drawing made on a visit in 1752 or perhaps later (Ashmolean; Brown 1982, no. 1892), which also served as the basis for another painting, of which several versions are known, including one in the Yale Center for British Art.

Richard Wilson
(1714 – 1782)

River Scene with Bathers

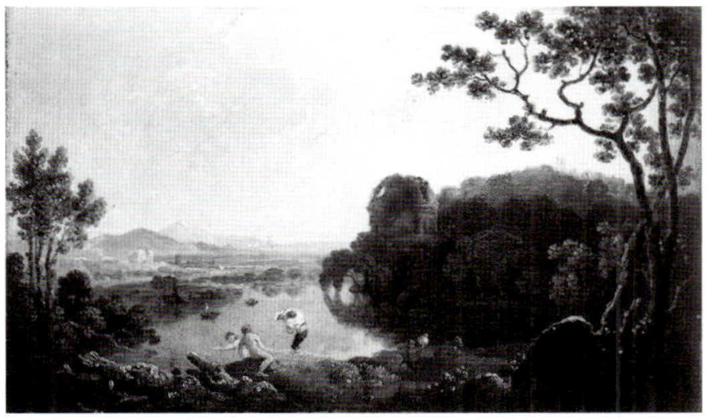

A864; oil on canvas, 80 × 50 cm
Prov.: Sir Charles Biron
Bequeathed by E.H.W. Meyerstein, 1953; WA1953.2

Constable 1953, p. 213

This composition is probably an idealised vision of Italy, painted after Wilson's return to England and incorporating elements found in other works. The temple is based on the temple of Minerva Medica, in Rome. There are numerous versions, of which that in the Huntington Art Gallery is considered the prime and has been dated to the 1760s. This example is more freely painted than some of the others.

Attributed to Richard Wilson
(1714 – 1782)

Aquae Albulae, near Tivoli

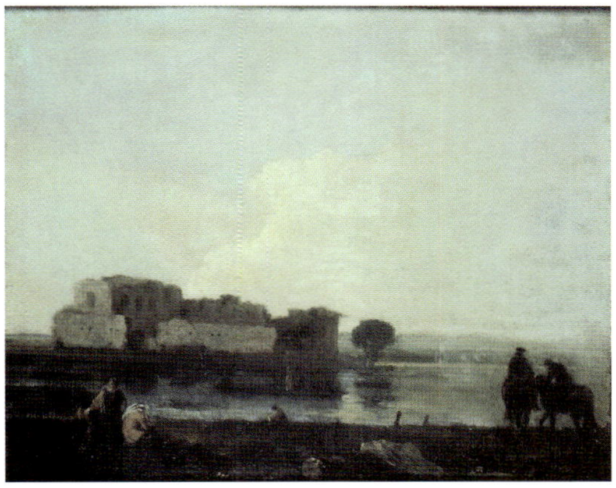

A893; oil on canvas, 33 × 40 cm
Prov.: E.H. Martineau
Bequeathed by Sir Charles Holmes, 1957; WA1957.96

Constable 1953, p. 236

A label identifies the scene as the Aquae Albulae, the small lakes of S. Giovanni and delle Colonalle, near the ruins of the Baths of Agrippa. The attribution of the painting is not certain and John Robert Cozens has been proposed as an alternative.

Richard Wilson
(1714 – 1782)

Pastoral Scene with Musicians by a classical Ruin

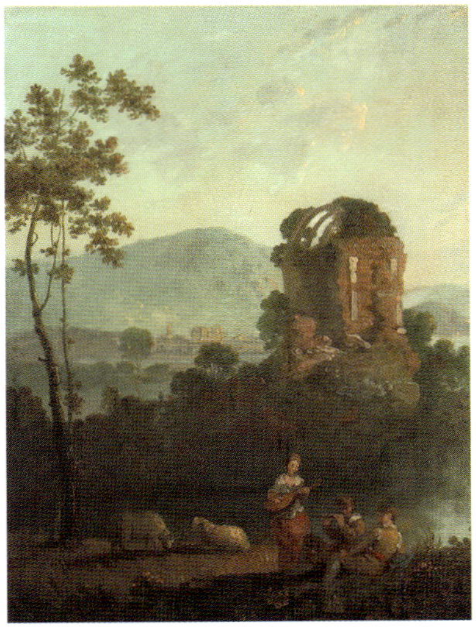

A988; oil on canvas, 69 × 51 cm
Prov.: Samuel Rogers; Baroness Burdett-Coutts; Mrs F.L. Evans
Madan Bequest, 1962; WA1962.17.30

Constable 1953, p. 217; Solkin 1982–3, no. 139

The left half of a composition known in two other versions (Bayerisches Staatsgemäeldesammlungen, Munich; V&A); another version of the right half is also in the V&A. All have been dated to the early 1770s. One was early identified with the ruins near Naples, but the scene is probably a generalised evocation of pastoral contentment rather than topographically accurate.

Richard Wilson
(1714 – 1782)

Rome from the Villa Madama

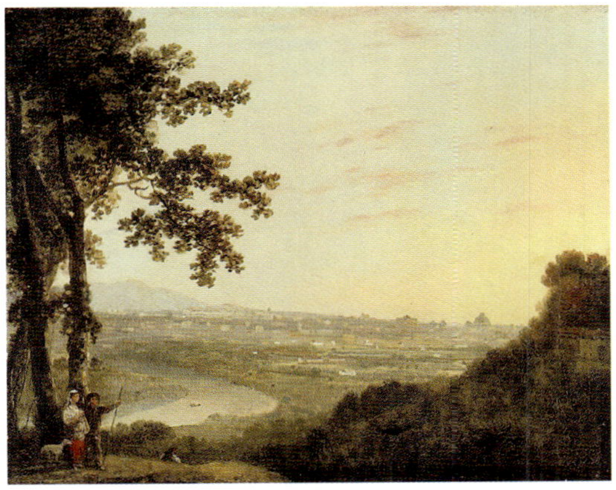

A987; oil on canvas, 44 × 53 cm
Prov.: Col M.H. Grant
Madan Bequest, 1962; WA1962.17.29

Constable 1953, pp. 218–19

From the 17th century, this view was a favourite with artists visiting Rome. It is taken from the gardens of the Villa Madama, on the slopes of Monte Mario, looking towards Rome; the River Tiber meanders through the composition and the dome of St Peter's can be seen on the skyline. This is more freely painted than Wilson's other versions of this composition and includes fewer incidental details.

Attributed to Richard Wilson
(1714 – 1782)

Bridge of Augustus at Rimini

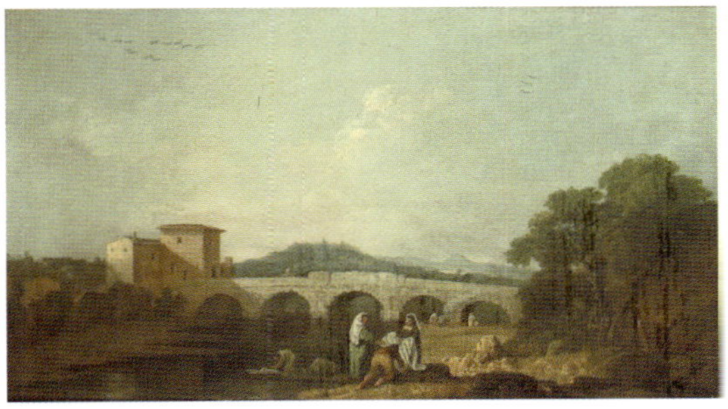

A402; oil on canvas, 40 × 71 cm
Presented by Sir Michael Sadler in memory of Lady Sadler through the National Art Collections Fund, 1931; WA1931.1

Constable 1953, p. 212

Although incidental details are different from those in other versions of this composition, the attribution is doubtful. The Ponte d'Augusto strides the River Marecchia at Rimini in the distance is the hill of the Republic of San Marino. All the numerous versions of this composition are based on drawings made on the spot between 1753 and 1757.

Jacob de Wit
(1695 – 1754)

Triumph of the Three Christian Virtues

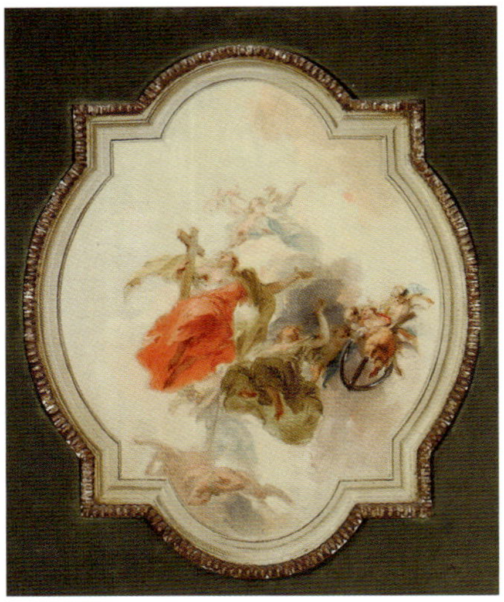

A425; oil on panel, 42 × 35 cm
Presented by the National Art Collections Fund in memory of T.E. Althaus, 1933; WA1933.9

White 1999, p. 171

De Wit worked as a decorative painter in Amsterdam. He was much in demand as a painter of ceilings and as a skillful painter of *trompe l'oeil* reliefs. This must have been made as a model for a ceiling in a church or chapel. Faith, Hope and Charity rise towards God the Father in the clouds while St Michael drives out the rebel angels below.

Thomas Worlidge
(1700 – 1766)

James Smith, Senior

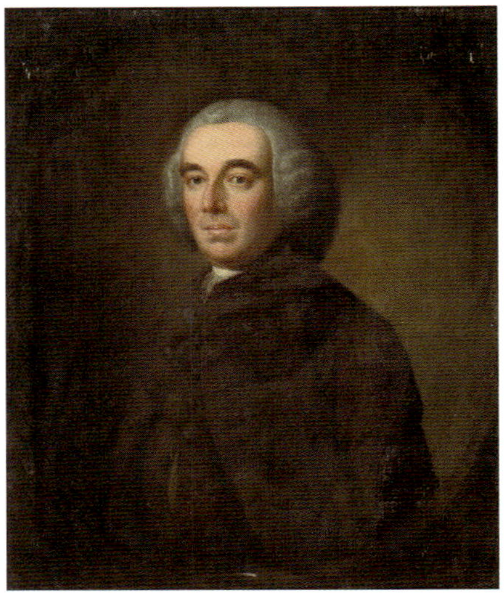

A438b; oil on canvas, 77 × 64 cm
Prov.: by descent from the sitter
Pierrepont Barnard Bequest, 1934; WA1934.419

James Smith, Senior (d. 1795), was a wealthy wool merchant at Norwich. He was a cultivated man, with a good knowledge of French, and a Unitarian. He served as High Sheriff of Norwich in 1745–6, when this portrait may have been made.

Thomas Worlidge
(1700 – 1766)

Frances Kinderley, Wife of James Smith, Junior

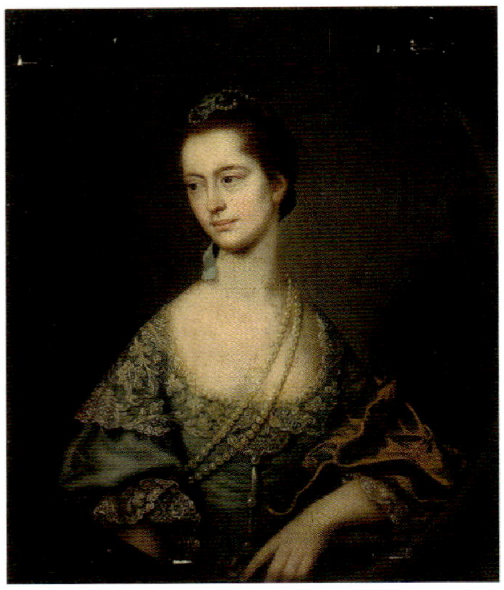

A438d; oil on canvas, 77 × 64 cm
Prov.: by descent from the sitter
Pierrepont Barnard Bequest, 1934; WA1934.421

Frances Kinderley (1731–1820) was the daughter of the Revd John Kinderley (d. 1775), perpetual curate of St Helen's Church, Norwich, and Sarah Raining. One of her sons was Sir James Edward Smith (1759–1828), the botanist and founder of the Linnaean Society.

John Wootton
(*c.* 1681 – 1764)

Young True Blue at Newmarket

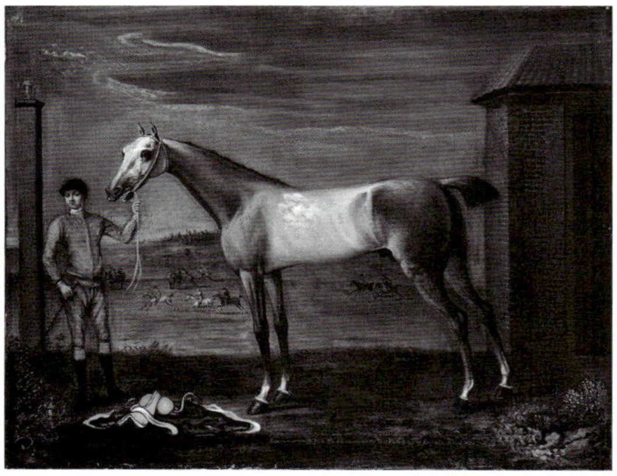

A1110; oil on canvas, 100 × 128 cm
Inscribed and dated: *Young True Blue. 1718 / Mr Honywood's White Arabian was sire of the two True-Blues, our brothers, both grey, who were / both in a very high form. The elder (1710), was the best Plate Horse in England. (N. Pick Vol. 1 page 91)*
Bequeathed by Dr Eric North, 1979; WA1979.71

Young True Blue was a grey colt, foaled in 1718 and sired by Honeywood's Arabian. The view includes the Rubbing-Down House on Newmarket Heath, on which is inscribed the names of the descendants of Honeywood's White Arabian.

Thomas Worlidge
(1700 – 1766)

James Smith, Junior

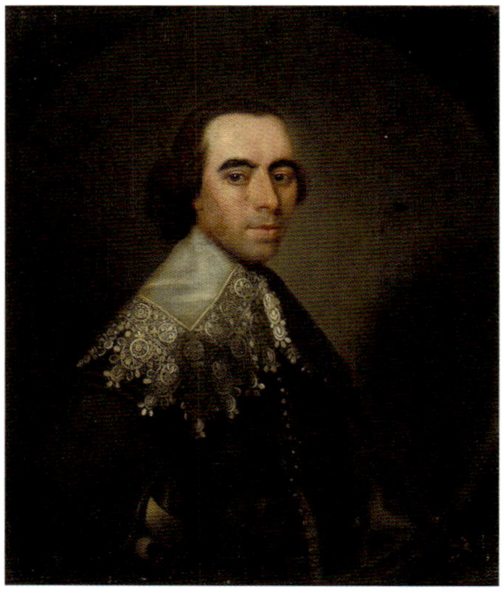

A438c; oil on canvas, 77 × 64 cm
Prov.: by descent from the sitter
Pierrepont Barnard Bequest, 1934; WA1934.420

James Smith, Junior (1727–1795), the son of James Smith, Senior, is portrayed in 17th century costume. This portrait may have been made at the same time as Worlidge's drypoint of his son, J.E. Smith, as a child, i.e. around 1763–4.

Joseph Wright of Derby
(1734 – 1797)

Italianate Lake Scene with Waterfall

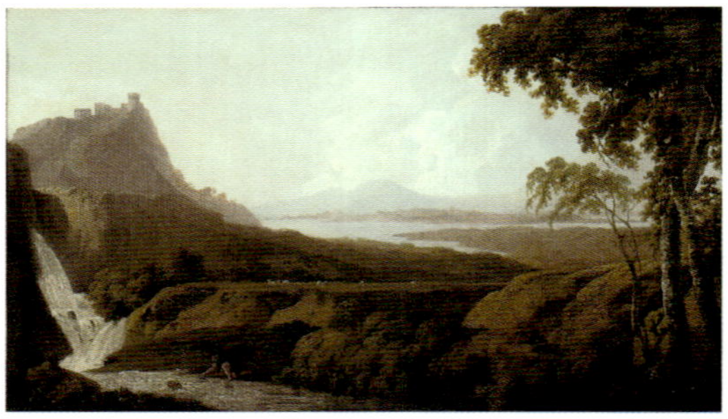

A1109; oil on canvas, 52.5 × 89.5 cm
Prov.: G.W. Bowden; Henry Isherwood Kay
Bequeathed by Mrs Barbara Isherwood Kay, 1979; WA1979.51

Like his elder, Richard Wilson, Wright of Derby was so deeply influenced by the landscape of the Roman campagna that, even after his return from Rome in 1755, he imbued his depictions of English and Welsh landscape with Italianate features. This landscape has not been identified and may be imaginary.

Copy after Joseph Wright of Derby
(1734 – 1797)

Two Boys with a Bladder; Candlelight Effect

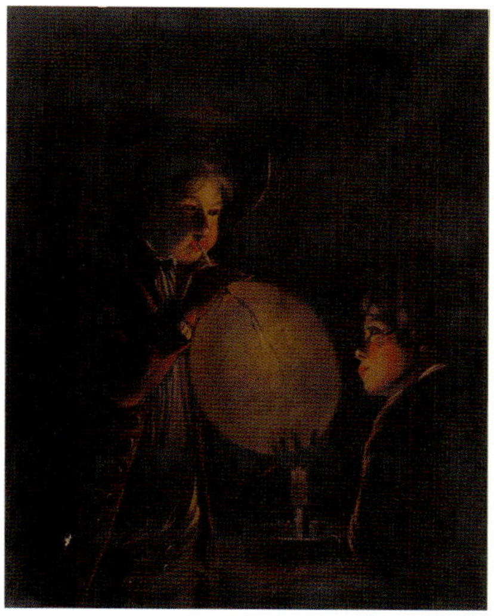

A310; oil on canvas, 91 × 70 cm
Prov.: (?)Charles Fortnum
Fortnum Bequest, 1899; WA1899.CDEF.P14

A mediocre and damaged copy after a lost original of 1769–70, the best version of which is in the Huntington Art Gallery, California (Nicolson 1968, no. 208).

Thomas Wyck
(?1616 – 1677)

Italian Street Scene

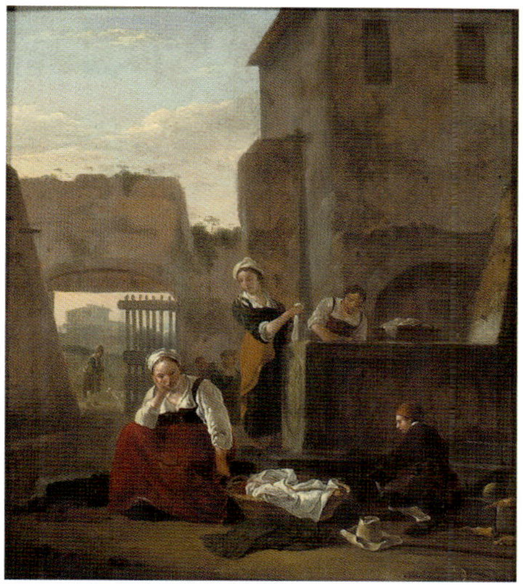

A125; oil on panel, 32 × 26cm
Signed: *T Wÿck*
Bequeathed by the Revd Dr Thomas Penrose, 1851; WA1851.22

White 1999, p. 173

It is not certain whether or not Wyck went to Italy although he used an Italianate background for a number of his pictures, as here, where two women are washing clothes in an antique sarcophagus used as a cistern.

Jack Butler Yeats
(1871 – 1957)

The Open Gate

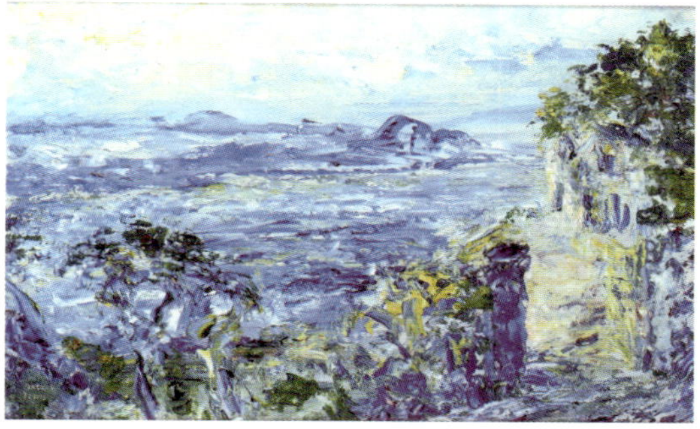

A1225; oil on board, 23.1 × 35.6 cm
Signed: *Jack B Yeats*
Bequeathed by Miss Margaret Miller, 2000; WA2000.75

This rustic scene, painted with much impasto and strong contrasts of light and colour, is typical of Yeats's atmospheric landscapes. The brush-strokes, as often in his later works, are clearly visible and give the painting a structure independent of the subject itself. The unspectacular theme of an open gate may be in Dublin, his preferred setting.

Joachim Antonisz. Wtewael
(1566 – 1638)

The Adoration of the Shepherds

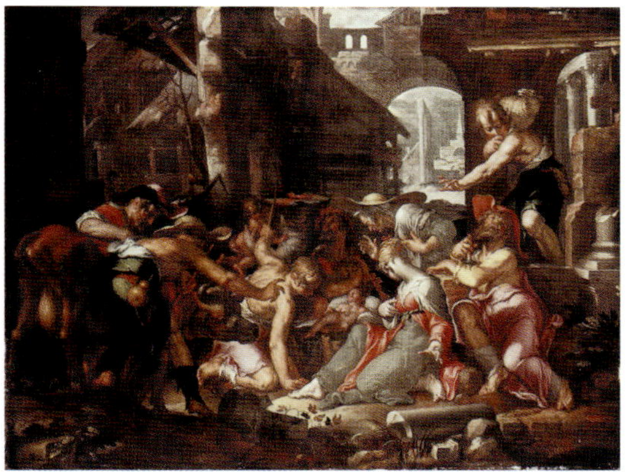

A770; oil on canvas, 75 × 97 cm
Prov.: Lord Kinnaird
Purchased (France Fund), 1948; WA1948.100

White 1999, p. 172

The Adoration of the Shepherds was one of Wtewael's favourite subjects. This version has been dated *c.* 1606 by comparison with a dated *Annunciation to the Shepherds* in the Saul Steinberg Collection, New York.

Jack Butler Yeats
(1871 – 1957)

Dublin Evening

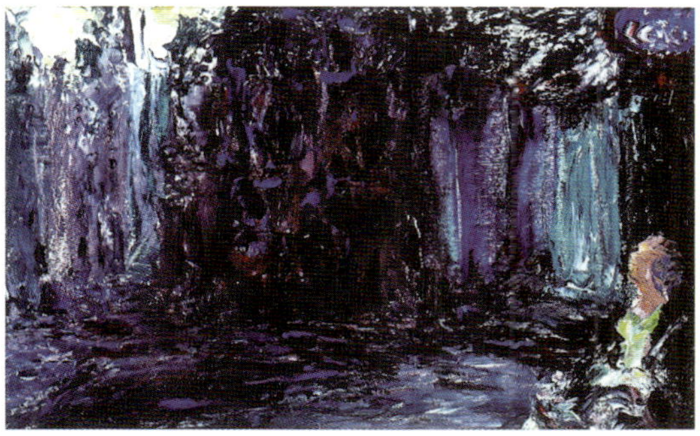

A1224; oil on canvas, 22.8 × 35.8 cm
Signed: *Jack B Yeats*
Bequeathed by Miss Margaret Miller, 2000; WA2000.74

In his early career Yeats mainly worked as an illustrator but shortly after the turn of the century he began to work regularly in oil. The freedom of brushwork which he developed in his oils is exemplified in this small painting. He evokes the atmosphere of Dublin, using expressive impasto and rapidly applied paint to create a romantic, highly personal image which reflects his childhood memories of light and landscape.

Jack Butler Yeats
(1871 – 1957)

Rehearsal

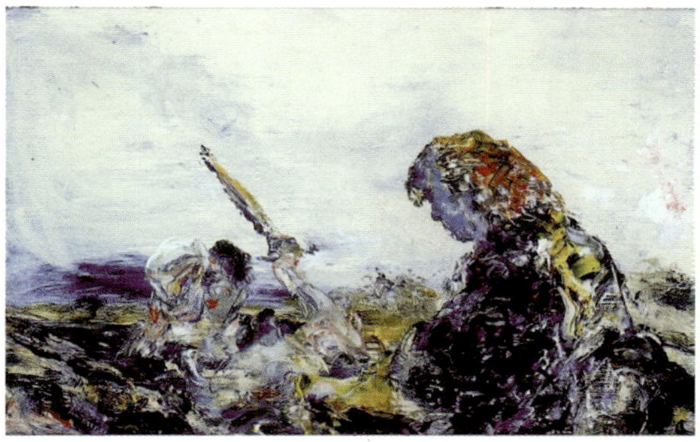

A1226; oil on board, 23.5 × 35.9 cm irregular
Signed: *Jack B Yeats*
Bequeathed by Miss Margaret Miller, 2000; WA2000.76

Many of Yeats's paintings illustrate circus scenes or music-halls. However, rather than being a precise depiction, the subject is instead evoked through brushwork, impasto and vivid colour.

John Butler Yeats
(1839 – 1922)

Miss Margaret Grierson

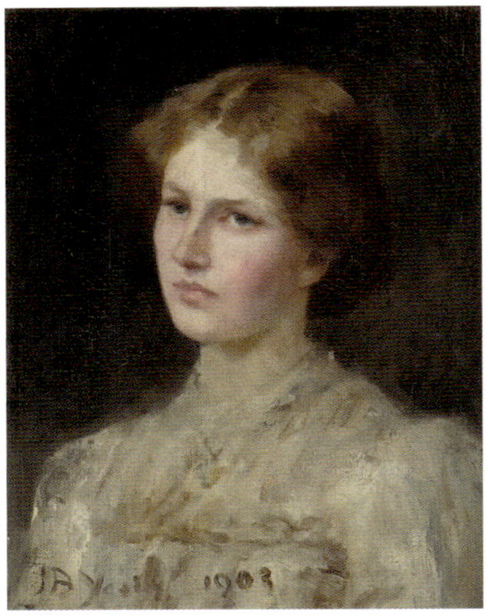

A1018; oil on canvas, mounted on board, 45 × 34 cm
Signed and dated: *JB Yeats 1903*
Presented by Miss Mary Swanzy, 1964; WA1964.71

No details of the sitter's life seem to be recorded.

Frans Ykens
(1601 – 1693)

A Garland of Flowers surrounding a Medallion of the Virgin and Child

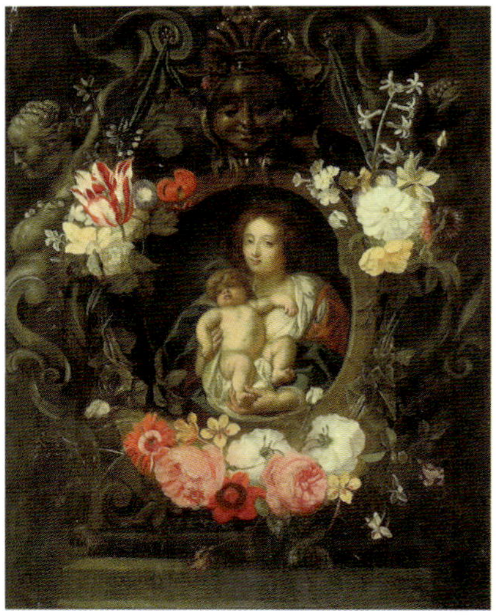

A278; oil on panel, 69 × 54 cm
Presented by Thomas Humphry Ward, 1897; WA1897.1

White 1999, p. 173

Ykens worked mainly in Antwerp and Brussels. He painted a number of religious compositions of this type enclosed within a floral wreath, sometimes in collaboration with other artists. It has been suggested that the figures in this painting might have been painted by Cornelis Schut.

Johan Zoffany
(1733 – 1810)

David Garrick

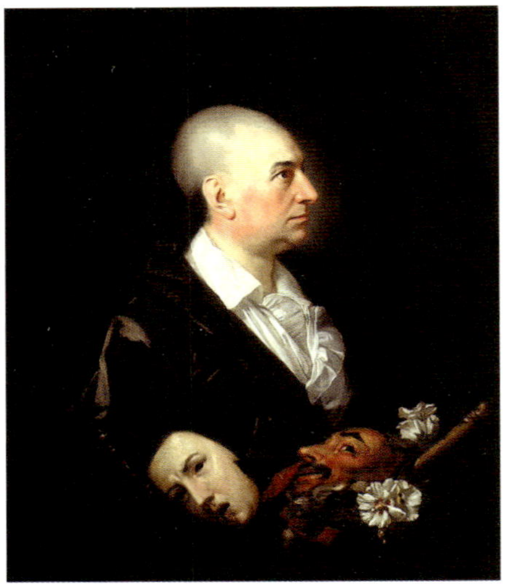

A1219; oil on canvas, 75.2 × 62.7 cm (sight)
Prov.: John Cowper, Carleton Hall, Cumberland; Asher Wertheimer and by descent
Accepted by H.M. Government in lieu of Inheritance Tax from the estate of Mrs Joan Cecily Conway and allocated to the Ashmolean Museum, 1999; WA1999.10

Manners and Williamson 1920, p. 243

The celebrated actor, David Garrick (1717–1779), bought out the young German artist, Zoffany, from his apprenticeship with Benjamin Wilson in 1762, and became one of his most consistent patrons. Most of Zoffany's portraits of Garrick show him either in character on the stage, or in conversation pieces. Here, he is seen in an informal pose without his wig, but with the traditional device of masks of Comedy and Tragedy below. A copy of this portrait in the National Portrait Gallery is dated 1763, making the prototype one of the first of the portraits of Garrick.

Johan Zoffany
(1733 – 1810)

Two Sketches of David Garrick as Abel Drugger in 'The Alchymist'

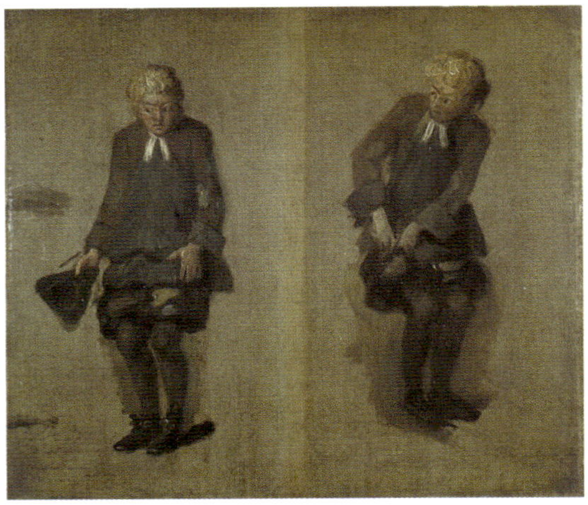

A196–7; oil on canvas, 33 × 38 cm
Prov: (?)William Alexander
Chambers Hall Gift, 1855; WA1855.201

Manners and Williamson 1920, p. 225; Webster 1977, no. 58

Although the attribution has been doubted, these are apparently two sketches taken from life. They show Garrick in one of his most celebrated roles, as Abel Drugger in Ben Jonson's *The Alchymist*. The first sketch was used as a study for *Garrick with Burton and Palmer in 'The Alchymist'*, shown at the Royal Academy in 1770 (formerly at Castle Howard, sold Sotheby's, 29 November 2001, lot 11).

Johan Zoffany
(1733 – 1810)

Mary Thomas, the Artist's second Wife

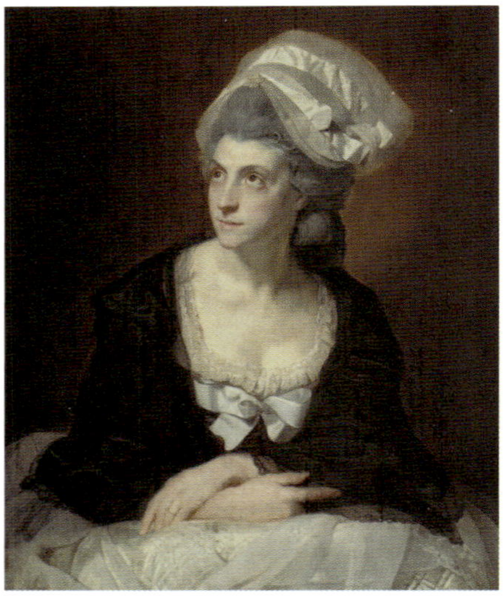

A1111; oil on canvas, 75 × 61.5 cm
Prov.: by descent from the sitter to Miss Claudine Roberts
Purchased with the assistance of the Museums & Galleries Commission/Victoria & Albert Museum Purchase Grant Fund, the National Art Collections Fund and the Friends of the Ashmolean, 1979; WA1979.81

Manners and Williamson 1920, p. 205; Webster 1977, no. 96

Mary Thomas (*c.* 1755–1832) followed Zoffany to Florence in 1772. She bore him a son and the couple were married soon afterwards. In spite of her humble origins, she captivated Anglo-Italian society and became a great favourite with people of all ranks. This portrait was probably painted in England in *c.* 1781–2.

Attributed to Johan Zoffany
(1733 – 1810)

Captain William Hall

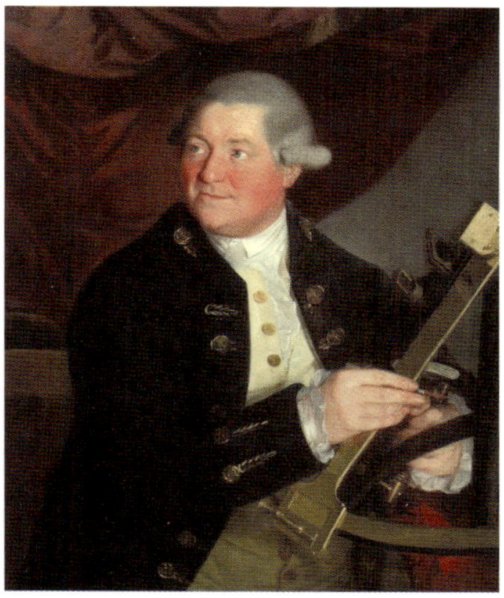

A194; oil on canvas, 82 × 68 cm
Chambers Hall Gift, 1855; WA1855.198

William Hall, the father of Chambers Hall, spent twenty years in the ships of the East India Company, the later years as Captain. He is said to have been instrumental in arranging Zoffany's journey to India in 1783 and this portrait of Hall in the uniform of a Captain in the East India Company probably dates from that period. The attribution is traditional but doubtful.

Marco Zoppo
(1433 – 1478)

St Paul

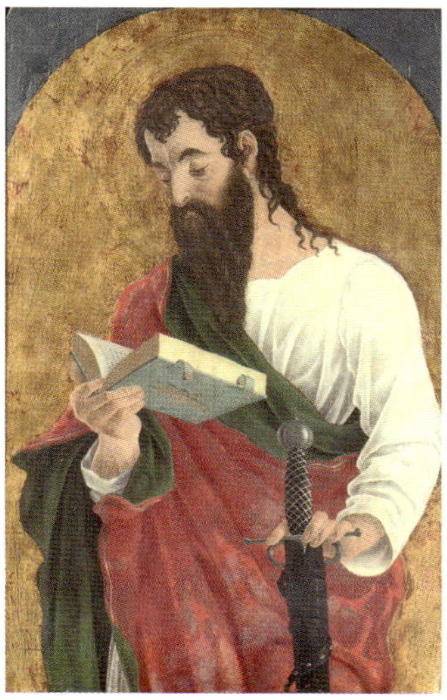

A98; tempera and gilding on panel, 49.5 × 31 cm
Fox-Strangways Gift, 1850; WA1850.34

Lloyd 1977, pp. 191–3; Lucco 1993, pp. 109–14 & p. 173

After his training with Squarcione in Padua from 1453, Marco worked mainly for Venetian and Bolognese patrons. This shaped panel comes from the upper tier of a polyptych, probably that made in 1468 for the church of Santa Giustina, Venice. Three other panels have been identified, *St Augustine*, *St Peter* and *St Jerome*, all from the upper register and all lit from the right. St Paul is shown with a sword, the instrument of his martyrdom, and a book, a reference to his Epistles.

Copy after Francisco de Zurbarán
(1598 – 1664)

The Flight into Egypt

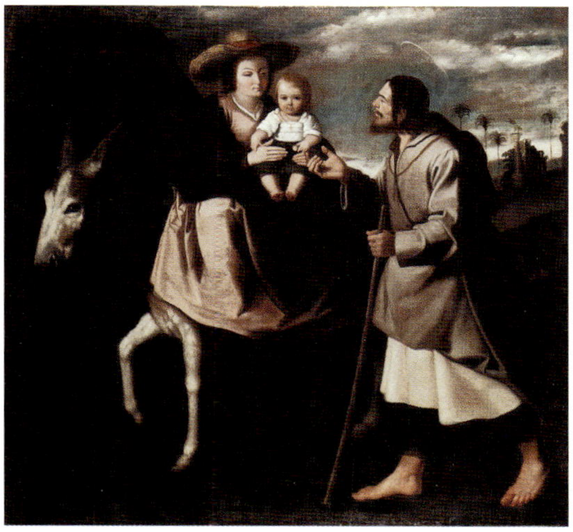

A879; oil on canvas, 155.5 × 162.5 cm
Presented by O.T. Falk, 1955; WA1955.86

Caturla 1994, no. 41

Joseph was warned in a dream by an angel to flee with Mary and the young Child and to remain in Egypt until the death of Herod (Matthew 2: 13–15). A879 is a possibly contemporary version of a composition by Zurbarán sent from Seville to Spanish America *c.* 1650 and formerly in the Franciscan church in Lima, Peru.

Attributed to Johan Zoffany
(1733 – 1810)

Elizabeth Gostling, Mrs William Hall

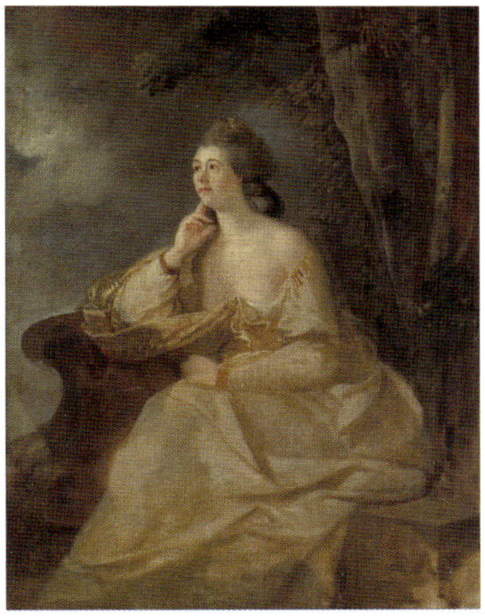

A195; oil on canvas, 66 × 50 cm
Chambers Hall Gift, 1855; WA1855.199

The identifications of both the sitter and the artist were made by the donor, the sitter's son. The portrait is uncharacteristic of the work of Zoffany, even if a sketch, and was clearly not intended as a pendant to the portrait of her husband. No details of Mrs Hall's life are known.

Francesco Zuccarelli
(1702 – 1788)

Landscape with Monks reading

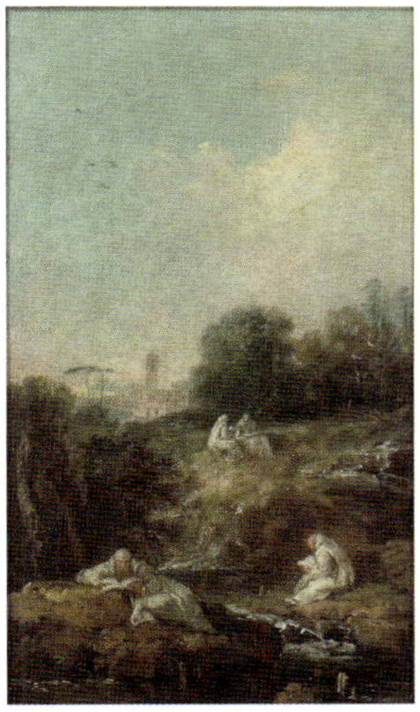

A989; oil on canvas, 36 × 22 cm
Madan Bequest, 1962; WA1962.17.31

Alessandro Magnasco in particular had popularised the subject of hermits or monks in picturesque landscapes and Zuccarelli is known to have painted such scenes on a small scale for collectors.

ICONS

An icon is a venerated image used in churches of the Eastern rites. Many icons were painted on small wooden panels, sometimes embellished with a metal cover cut out to reveal the central part of the picture. As these derive from the Byzantine tradition, the collection of Greek and Russian icons in the Ashmolean is kept in the Department of Antiquities along with other artefacts from the Byzantine world. The first icons to enter the collections of the University are those which were transferred to the Ashmolean from the Bodleian Library at some point before 1908. Others arrived with the bequest of the Revd Greville John Chester in 1892, followed by a group, including several of the most important icons in the collection, bequeathed by Professor Ingram Bywater in 1915. Bywater had been an undergraduate with Walter Pater at Queen's College and spent his life in Oxford as a Fellow of Exeter College, sub-librarian at the Bodleian and Professor of Greek from 1893 until he retired in 1905. His bequest of 4,000 books to the Bodleian Library on the history of classical scholarship included many rarities. His interest in Greece might explain his taste for icons, although the collection seems to have been acquired largely by his wife, Charlotte Bywater, during their travels on the Continent.

Anonymous, Byzantine
(14th/15th century)

The Raising of Lazarus

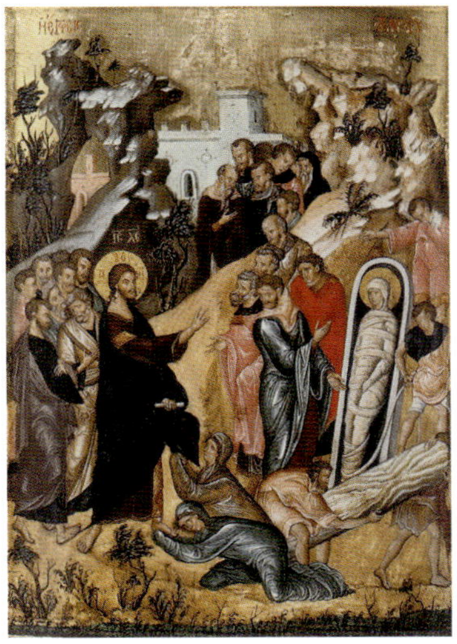

A346; tempera on panel, 45 × 31.6 cm
Prov.: purchased in Venice, 1891
Bywater Bequest 1915; WA1915.13

Mathew 1950, p. 22; Talbot Rice 1958, no. 236; Talbot Rice 1963, no. 264; Talbot Rice 1964, no. 181; Lloyd 1977, pp. 197–8; Gendle 1980, no. 1

The Raising of Lazarus, entitled in Greek at the top, is executed in a Byzantine style, possibly at a date before the fall of Constantinople in 1453. The scene is depicted in the traditional composition of Christ standing opposite the figure of Lazarus revealed in his sarcophagus. Three groups of figures bear witness to the miracle. At Christ's feet are the prostrate figures of Mary and Martha. The setting of rocky landscape, distant architecture and delicate plants, is characteristic of feast scenes such as this from the 13th century on. The painting style may be compared with Palaeologan work such as the icon of the same subject in the Hermitage, St Petersburg where, however, the figures are less elongated and the so-called Cardinal Bessarion's reliquary.

Angelos Akotantos
(active 1436 – 1450)

Embrace of the Apostles Peter and Paul

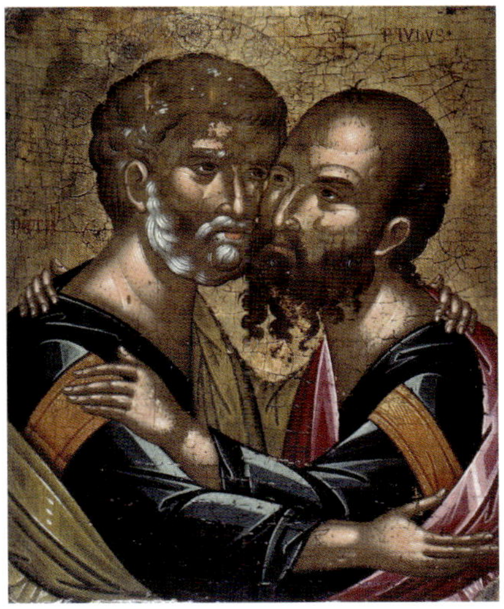

A1125; oil on canvas on wood, 46.4 × 37 cm
Prov.: Humphris sale, Horham Hall, Essex
Bequeathed by James Campbell Thomson, 1982; WA1982.192

Vassilaki 1990, pp. 405–22, fig. 1

The Embrace of the Apostles Peter and Paul, whose names are inscribed in Latin, belongs to a series of nearly identical icons by the Veneto-Cretan painter Angelos Akotantos, two of which are signed. The subject is seen as symbolic of oecumenical peace. More specifically, these icons have been linked to hopes raised at the Council of Ferrara/Florence (1438–9) which unsuccessfully aimed at the union of the eastern and western churches.

Nikolaos Tzafouris
(active 1487 – 1501)

Triptych: Pietà with St Francis and Mary Magdalen

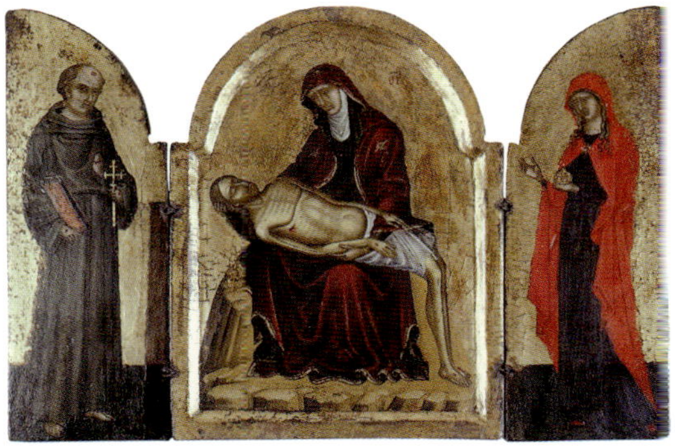

Tempera on wood, 17 × 12 cm
Bywater Bequest 1915; ANT1915.180

Mango 2002, pp. 302–3

The Pietà on the central panel is flanked by St Francis and Mary Magdalen on the wings, all western subjects. The painter Nikolaos Tzafouris is known from Venetian documents to have been active in Crete. Five of his signed icons survive. This icon is executed in the *maniera italiana*, as practised by Cretan painters for western commissions. A larger version of the Pietà panel is in the Benaki Museum, Athens.

Anonymous, Post-Byzantine
(15th/16th century)

St George slaying the Dragon

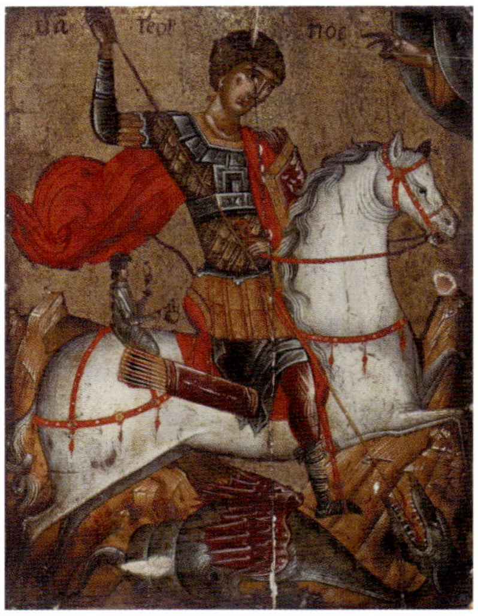

A319; oil on panel, 42 × 31.8 cm
Acquired before 1908; WA1908.204

Talbot Rice 1951, pp. 383–7; Lloyd 1977, p. 195; Gendle 1980, no. 56

St George was revered as a military martyr whose cult was based at Lydda. The legend of his triumph over the dragon probably dates to the 12th century. The small figure behind the saint represents a Christian slave whom the saint rescued. The saint, his armour and horse stylistically resemble comparable features of 15th and 16th-century icons at Mt Sinai and on Cyprus.

Anonymous, Post-Byzantine
(16th century?)

Triptych: St John dictating his Gospel and the Annunciation

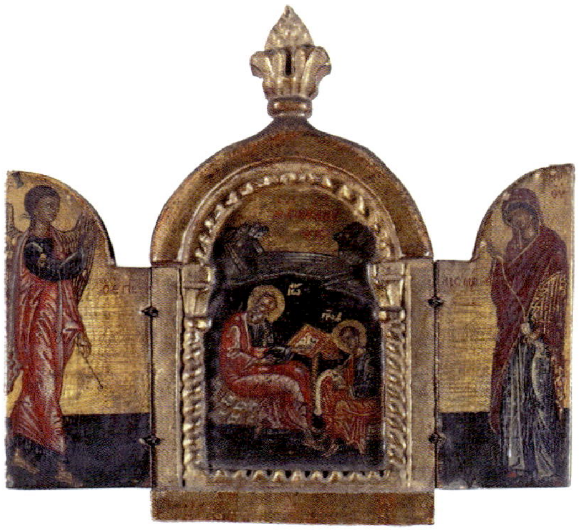

Oil on wood, 19 × 10.2 cm (closed); 21.5 cm (open)
Bywater Bequest, 1915; ANT1915.179

Gendle 1980, no. 61

The triptych has an arched top with finial and its central panel framed by twisted columns. The wings are decorated with an Annunciation and the central panel with St John dictating his Gospel to his disciple Prochoros, before the mouth of a cave on the island of Patmos. Both scenes are identified by Greek inscriptions. A handle projects from the reverse side. A nearly identical icon is in the Walters Art Gallery, Baltimore.

Anonymous, Post-Byzantine
(17th century)

Triptych: The Healing of the Paralytic [wings missing]

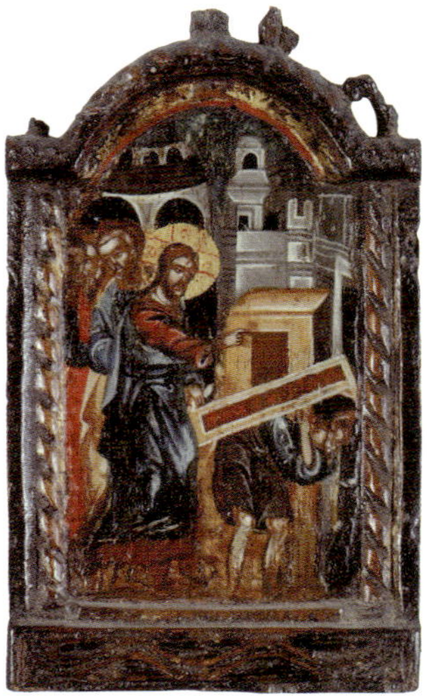

Oil on wood, 14.4 × 8.5 cm
Prov.: purchased in Athens, 1914
Presented by Miss Rosemary Rendel in memory of her parents, Sir George and Lady Rendel, 1988; ANT1988.21

This central panel of a triptych is set within a frame arched at the top, with lateral twisted columns. The Healing of the Paralytic formed part of the Byzantine New Testament miracle cycle sometimes included within the main feasts in monumental art. As portrayed here, Christ and the paralytic, holding his bed (inscribed in Greek 'Take your bed and walk'), fill the main part of the scene with a few observers to the left. The background is filled with a variety of buildings.

Anonymous, Post-Byzantine
(16th century?)

The Virgin and Child

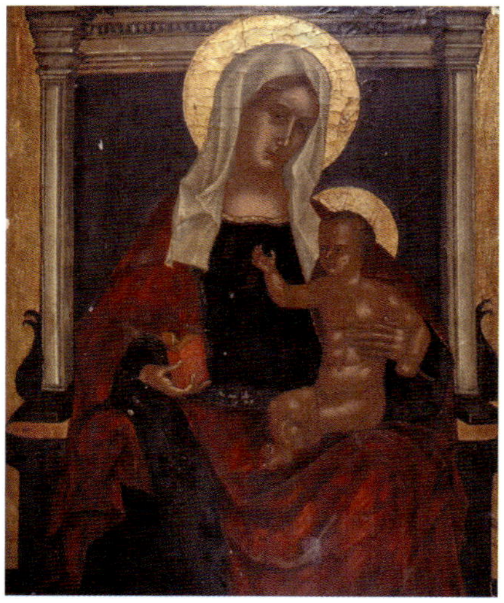

A1061; oil on panel, 49.5 × 39.6 cm
Prov.: purchased in Vienna, *c.* 1935
Presented by Prof C.M. Robertson, 1971; WA1971.47

Lloyd 1977, p. 199

The Virgin and Child are represented here in the Italianate manner of Michael Damaskinos, active in Crete (1574–82). The Virgin, seated in a broad marble throne, holds open a small codex in front of the Christ Child who holds his right hand upwards. His halo is half obscured by the Virgin's shoulder.

Anonymous, Post-Byzantine
(16th/17th century)

The Seven Sleepers of Ephesus

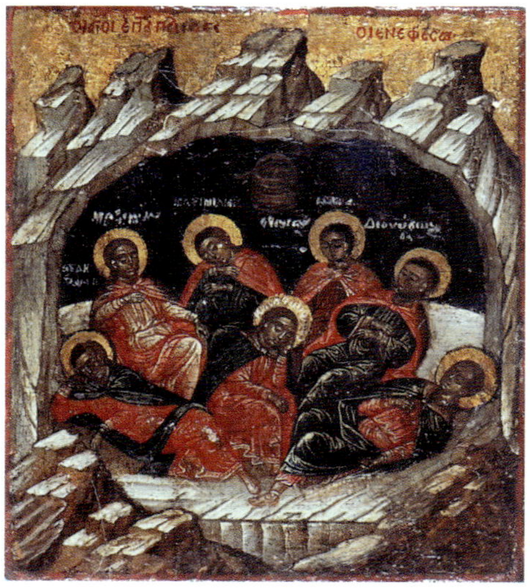

Oil on wood, 15.2 × 13.2 cm
Prov.: purchased in Athens, 1914
Presented by Miss Rosemary Rendel in memory of her parents, Sir George and Lady Rendel, 1988; ANT1988.23

The Seven Sleepers of Ephesus, whose names are given in Greek, are shown reclining inside a cave where a basket of olives hangs from the roof. Jagged mountain peaks rise above the cave. Legend records that the Christian youths seeking refuge in a cave from the persecution of the Emperor Decius in *c.* 200, fell asleep and were miraculously awakened over two hundred years later at the time of the Council of Ephesus (431). This was a popular subject in Cretan icons from the 15th century onwards.

Anonymous, Post-Byzantine
(17th century)

Virgin Blachernitissa

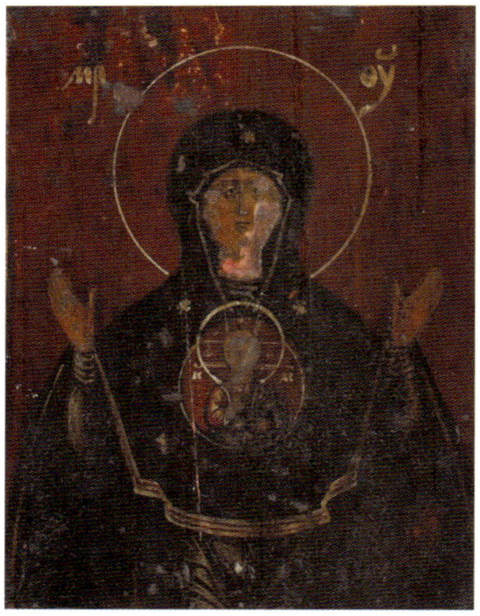

Oil on panel, 16.7 × 13 cm
Prov.: the Revd Greville John Chester
Purchased 1869; ANT1869.14

The Virgin Blachernitissa, sometimes also called Platytera, is so named because the iconographic type originated in the church of the Blachernai at Constantinople. She was portrayed in an orant posture, with a half-figure of the 'pre-eternal' Christ suspended in a medallion in front of her breast. The names of the figures are inscribed in Greek. The red background is characteristic of painting produced in the Near East, where this panel may have originated.

Anonymous, Post-Byzantine
(18th century)

The Annunciation (recto)

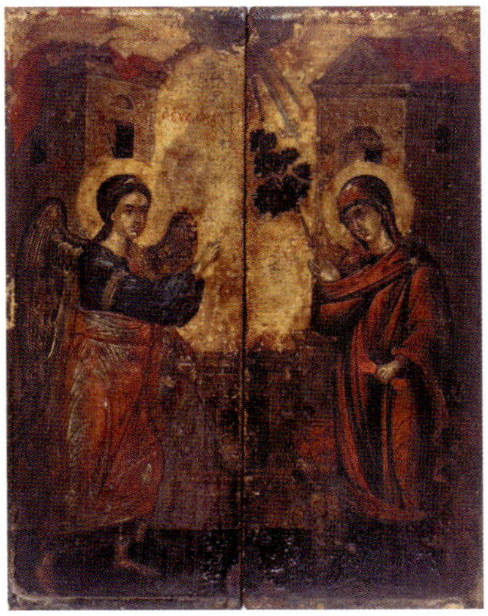

A71; oil on panel painted on both sides, integral frame, 22.8 × 18 cm
Fox-Strangways Gift, 1850; WA1850.23

Lloyd 1977, p. 194; Gendle 1980, no. 58

The panel was cut vertically in two to form the wings of a triptych. With the wings open, the Evangelists (on the left Matthew, Luke; on the right John, Mark) on the reverse would face in towards a central panel, now missing. These figures, shown half length, and The Annunciation on the obverse side of the wings, are inscribed in Greek and are presented in traditional Byzantine iconography combined with a somewhat Italianate style.

Anonymous, Post-Byzantine
(17th century)

The Presentation of the Virgin in the Temple

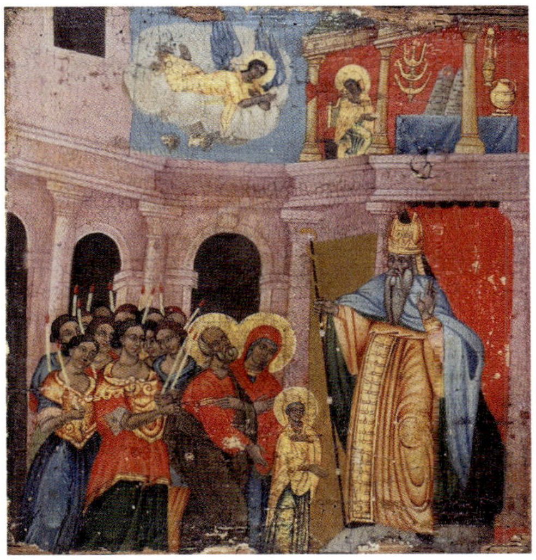

A1045; oil on panel, 31.5 × 29.5 cm
Bequeathed by Thomas Balston through the National Art Collections Fund, 1968; WA1968.28

Lloyd 1977, p. 199

The Presentation of the Virgin in the Temple is rendered in the pastel palette characteristic of the Ionian islands and in a composition based on western spatial concepts. The virgins carrying candles on the left and the priest Zacharias wear western costume. Only the central figures of Joachim, Anna and the Virgin appear in traditional Byzantine form. In Byzantine art, the presentation formed part of the narrative cycle devoted to the Virgin Mary.

'John'
(18th/19th century)

The Annunciation

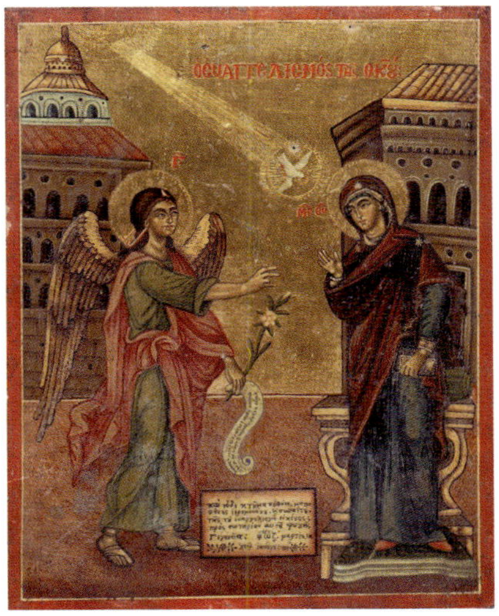

A253; oil on canvas on wood, 30.7 × 23.7 cm
Bequeathed by the Revd Greville John Chester, 1892; WA1892.10

Lloyd 1977, p. 194

The Annunciation, entitled in Greek at the top, is represented in the traditional Byzantine form but set against a background of Italianate architecture. Other western details include the branch and open scroll held by Gabriel and the marble bench behind the Virgin. The framed Greek inscription between the figures records that the icon, painted by John in 1807, was the property of the hieromonk, Metrophanes the Sinaite.

Anonymous, Post-Byzantine
(18th century)

Four Evangelists (verso)

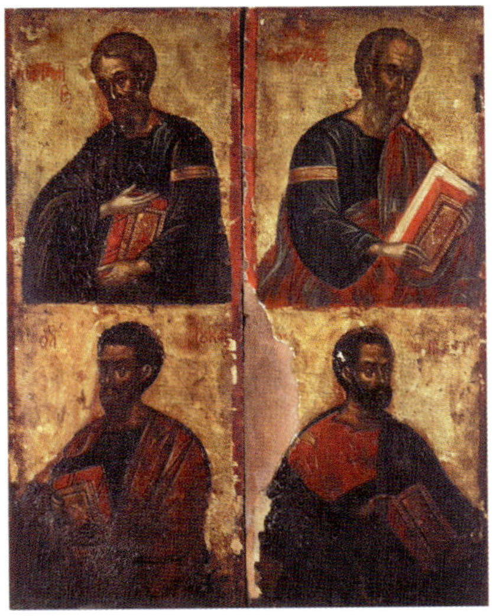

A71; oil on panel painted on both sides, integral frame, 22.8 × 18 cm
Fox-Strangways Gift; WA1850.23

Lloyd 1977, p. 194; Gendle 1980, no. 58

Georgios Chrysolouras
(active 1723 – 1761)

Saints Irene and Lucy

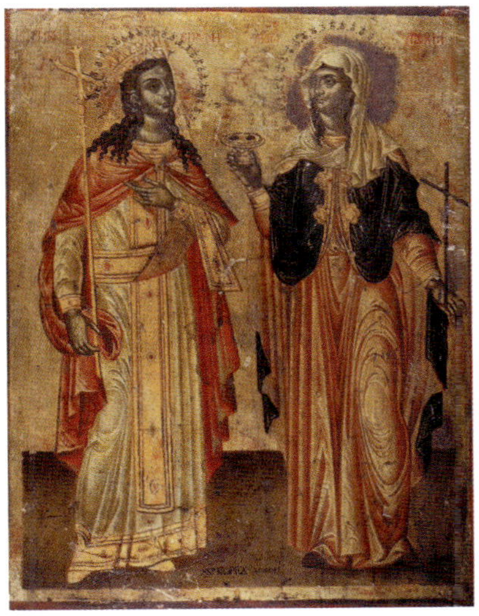

A1095a; oil on board, 46.6 × 36 cm
Prov.: Michel Savier, 1929
Presented by Gerald Reitlinger, 1972; WA1978.37

Piompinos 1984, pp. 410–11

The full length figures of St Irene and St Lucy, identified by Greek inscriptions, hold martyr's crosses. St Irene is dressed in a simplified version of imperial costume. St Lucy, a western saint, raises a dish containing an additional martyrial symbol, her eyes. The painter Chrysolouras was active in Corfu and Venice. Signed icons by him are dated between 1727 and 1755.

Anonymous, Post-Byzantine
(19th century)

St Gerasimos

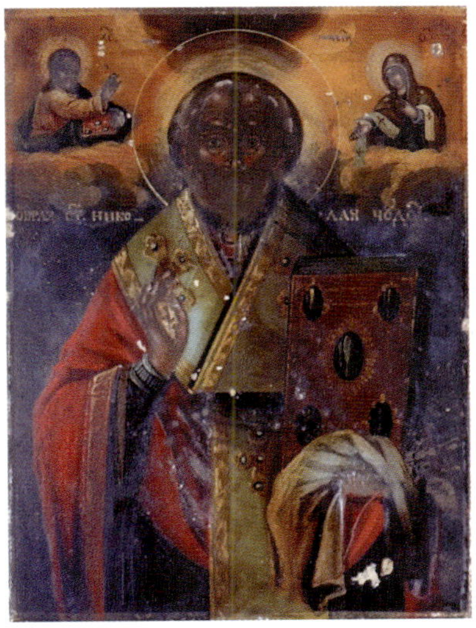

Oil on wood, 11 × 11 cm
Bywater Bequest, 1915; ANT1915.182

The half length figure of St Gerasimos, identified by a Greek inscription, wears monastic dress and holds his left hand upright. The scroll in his right hand bears an edifying Greek text. A silver revetment of this small icon, stamped *delta pi*, is preserved.

Anonymous, Russian
(early 16th century)

The Just entering Paradise

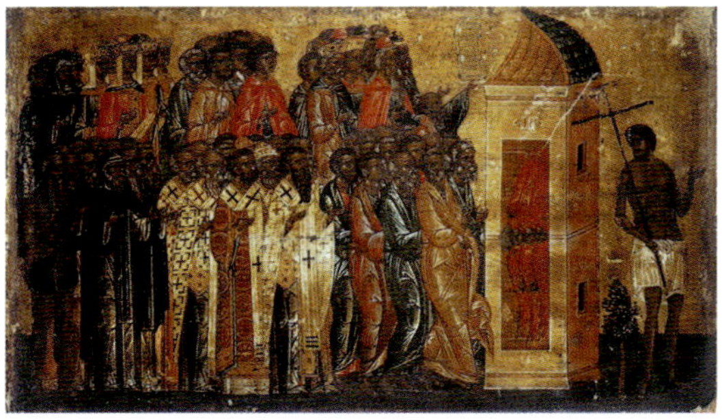

A317; oil on panel, 18.6 × 30.7 cm
Acquired before 1908; WA1908.202

Lloyd 1977, p. 194; Gendle 1980, no. 50

On the left, seven groups of the righteous approach a gate guarded by three cherubim. Beyond the gate stands the Good Thief, the first to enter Paradise. The panel has been cut down. With A318 it formed part of a series showing the Last Judgement, a theme often found on the back wall of medieval churches. Similar figures and the curved roof of the gate are found in the wall paintings of the Ferapontov Monastery near Moscow, executed by and under the direction of the great master Dionysii in 1500–2.

Anonymous, Russian
(15th/16th century)

St Nicholas

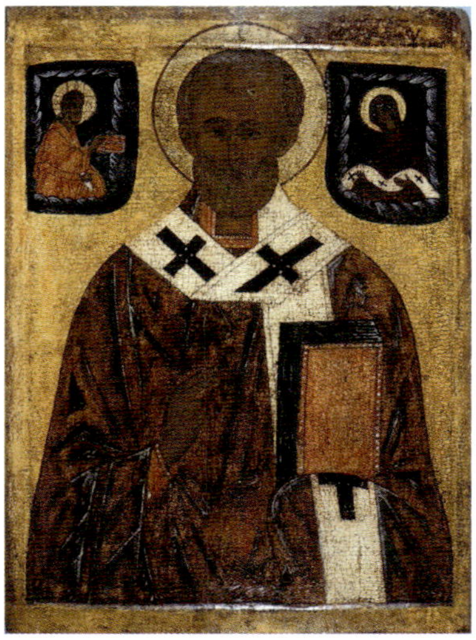

A1126; oil on panel, 63.5 × 45 cm
Bequeathed by James Campbell Thomson, 1982; WA1982.193

St Nicholas, one of the most popular saints of Eastern Orthodoxy, is shown as the Miracle Worker, holding a codex and flanked above by John the Baptist, his name inscribed in Greek on his halo, and by the Virgin. This type of image apparently developed in Novgorod in the 15th century where the thin paint and pale colouring of the background and of St Nicholas's face and robes are typical.

Anonymous, Russian
(16th/17th century)

Pokrov (The Virgin of Refuge) with Saints

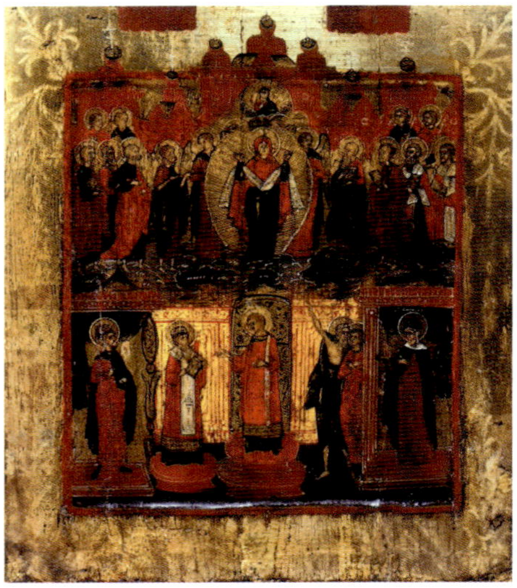

A344; oil on panel, fastened at the back with two horizontal battens, 26.3 × 22.4 cm
Prov.: Herbert Dunlop
Bywater Bequest, 1915; WA1915.14

Lloyd 1977, p. 196

The theme of the refuge offered by the garment of the Virgin Mary originated in Vladimir-Suzdal. It was based on a vision seen in the Blachernai shrine at Constantinople by Andrew 'the Fool for the sake of Christ', who is shown in the lower register with his disciple Epiphanios. Directly below the Virgin is St Romanos the Melode. The small figures are executed in a style associated with Moscow in the 16th-17th centuries.

Anonymous, Russian
(early 16th century)

The Just in Paradise

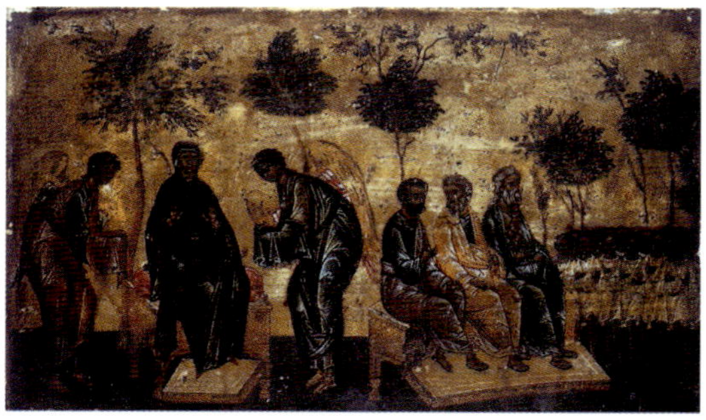

A318; oil on panel, 18.7 × 29.6 cm
Acquired before 1908; WA1908.203

Lloyd 1977, p. 195; Gendle 1980, no. 50

The Just in Paradise includes two scenes: on the left, the Virgin flanked by angels; on the right, Isaac, Jacob and Abraham, the last holding the soul of Lazarus in his bosom, are seated beside the souls of the Just in the guise of boys. Like the preceding icon, this panel preserves two original edges (left and top). Both were apparently cut from two separate panels.

Anonymous, Russian
(15th/16th century)

Elijah fed by a Crow

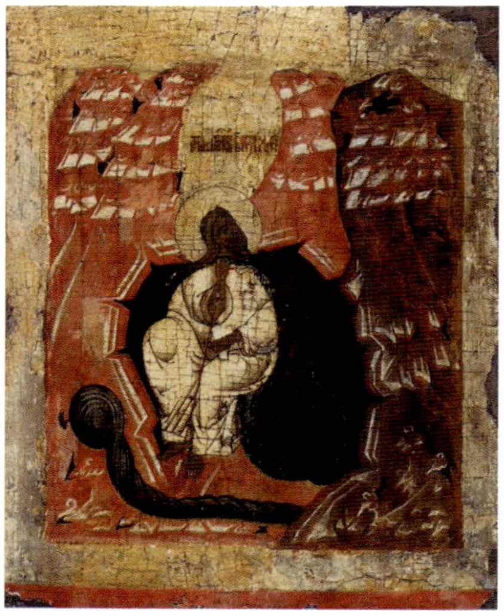

A1127; oil on panel, 25.5 × 21 cm
Bequeathed by James Campbell Thomson, 1982; WA1982.194

The prophet Elijah, identified by a Slavonic inscription, sits in a stark setting of pink and brown rock with a large black cave at the centre. The River Jordan, a dark torrent of water, flows at his feet. He looks up towards the right to the small crow approaching with nourishment. The composition is rendered in bold geometric forms (for example, the fractured rocks) and a muted limited palette characteristic of Novgorod painting. The icon has a later copper revetment *(riza)* decorated with enamel and coloured glass pastes.

Anonymous, Russian
(16th/17th Century)

Triptych: The Twelve Feasts of the Church

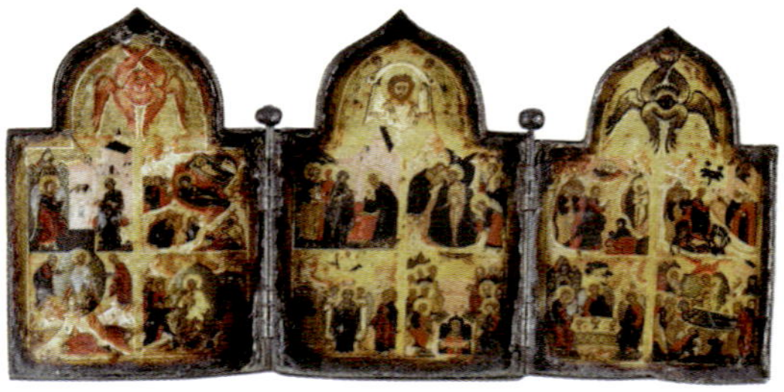

Oil on panel, 13.2 × 27.8 cm (open)
Prov.: purchased in Athens, 1914
Presented by Miss Rosemary Rendel in memory of her parents, Sir George and Lady Rendel, 1988; ANT1988.22

The Dodekaorton 'Twelve Feast Cycle' is portrayed on three panels set within hinged metal frames. At the top is a central Mandylion (the Holy Towel with Christ's face) flanked by seraphs. Above are the Annunciation, Nativity, Presentation in the Temple, Baptism, Raising of Lazarus, Entry into Jerusalem; below, Transfiguration, Anastasis, Ascension, Pentecost, Old Testament Trinity, Dormition. The cycle is executed in fine detail in a figure style reminiscent of the Pokrov icon (A344).

Anonymous, Russian (Strogonov School, Savin family?)
(17th century)

Old Testament Trinity with standing Saints

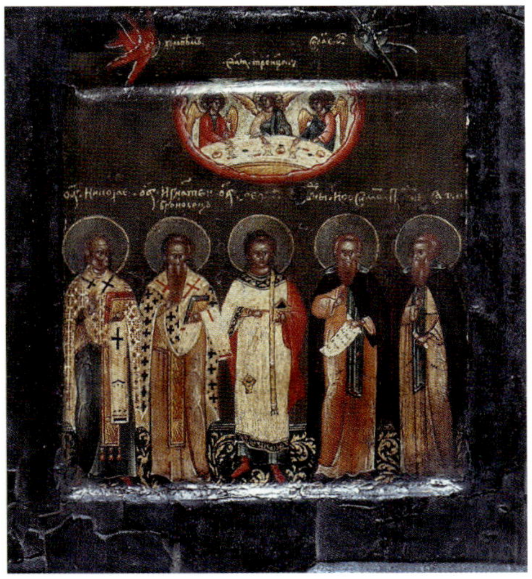

A345; oil on panel, 17 × 15 cm
Bywater Bequest, 1915; WA1915.15

Lloyd 1977, p. 197; Gendle 1980, no. 26

The Old Testament Trinity (also known as the Hospitality of Abraham), which appears in the oval frame, was considered a prefiguration of the Eucharist. The version shown here includes only the three angels who appeared to Abraham and Sarah. Two seraphim appear in the upper border. Below the saints (identified by Slavonic inscriptions, from left Nicholas, Ignatios, Stephen, Symeon, Sabas) stand before a gilded foliate frieze. Talbot Rice attributed the icon to the Savin workshop.

Anonymous, Russian
(18th century)

Virgin Hodegetria surrounded by Saints with Scrolls

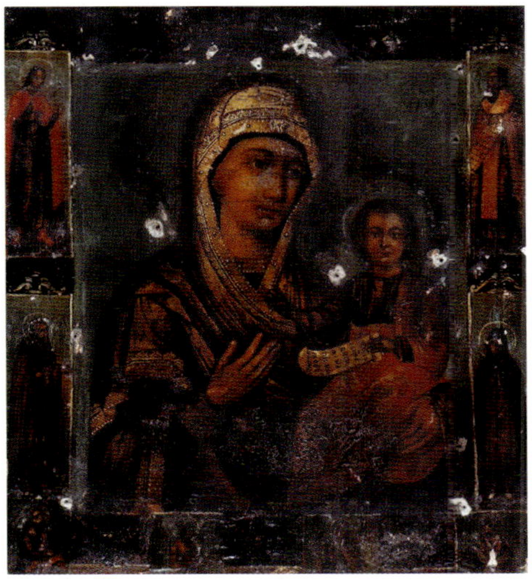

Oil on wood, 27.5 × 24 cm
Bywater Bequest, 1915; ANT1915.186

The Virgin Hodegetria was a popular iconographic type portraying the Virgin who 'shows the way', gesturing to the Child who holds here an open scroll written in Slavonic. These figures are surrounded by small full-length figures of saints (Gabriel, Gerasimos, Blaise, Eudokia, Procopius, Basil, Paraskeve, John) likewise holding open inscribed scrolls. The painting style of the main figures combines traditional and modern treatment of faces and drapery. A silver revetment (*riza*) dated 1778 and a halo dated 1830 are preserved.

Anonymous, Russian
(19th century)

Virgin Hodegetria

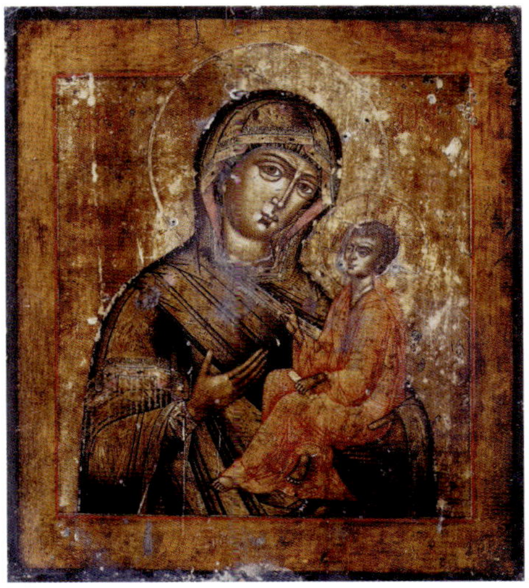

Oil on wood, 32 × 28 cm
Prov.: Bywater Bequest, 1915; ANT1915.190

The Virgin Hodegetria (see ANT1915.186), the figures inscribed in Greek, is represented here in the characteristic pose gesturing towards the Christ Child seated on her left arm. As with the Virgin Eleousa, this Byzantine iconographic type was taken over into Russian art. An unstamped silver revetment *(riza)* added to the icon is preserved.

Anonymous, Russian
(18th century)

Triptych: Extended Deesis with military and other Saints

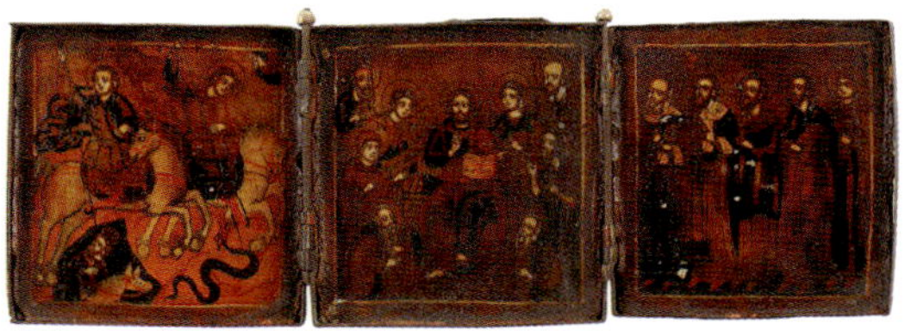

Oil on panel, 7.2 × 21 cm (open)
Bywater Bequest, 1915; ANT1915.187

This small triptych composed of panels set in hinged brass frames combines three types of scene. The central panel contains an extended Deesis (Intercession) with Christ flanked by (in descending order) Saints Peter and Paul, two angels, the Virgin and St John the Baptist and two monks. The left panel depicts two military saints, St Demetrios spearing a Roman emperor (Diocletian or Julian), and St George spearing a serpent. The right panel portrays two bishops, two male and one female saints, all turning towards the Deesis. Figures are inscribed in Slavonic.

Anonymous, Russian
(18th/19th century)

Virgin Eleousa (Vladimir Virgin)

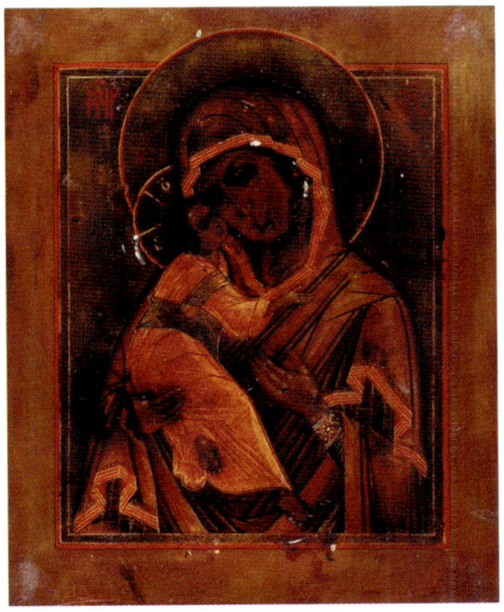

Oil on wood, 26.7 × 21.7 cm
Bywater Bequest, 1915; ANT1915.191

The Virgin Eleousa (of Tenderness) portrays the Mother and her Child with cheeks touching. A Byzantine icon of this type of Virgin, painted in the 11th century, reached Kiev in the 12th and became known as the Vladimir Virgin. The figures in the Ashmolean icon are inscribed in Greek, while a Russian inscription appears on the reverse. A gilt bronze revetment *(riza)* made for the icon is preserved.

Anonymous, Russian
(18th century)

St Nicholas

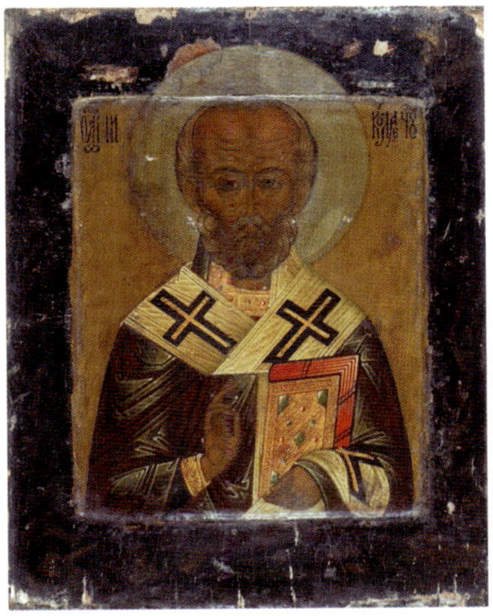

Oil on wood, 31 × 24.8 cm
Bywater Bequest, 1915; ANT1915.188

This icon of St Nicholas is a later iconographic version of the main figure seen in A1126 of the 16th–17th centuries. However, stylistically his facial features, the pronounced highlights of his robes and the gemmed codex cover may originate in a South Russian tradition. The saint's name is written in elaborate Slavonic script.

Anonymous, Russian
(18th/19th century)

St Nicholas

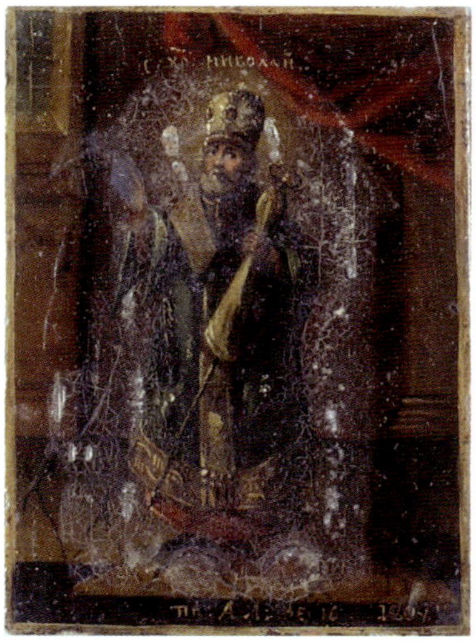

Oil on wood, 8.5 × 6.1 cm
Bywater Bequest, 1915; ANT1915.183

This small icon shows a mitred St Nicholas, his name written in Slavonic, blessing with one hand and holding a staff with the other. He stands in a palatial setting dominated by a red curtain hung against marble walls. At the bottom of the icon a Slavonic inscription gives an illegible painter's name and the date 1808. The painting style is entirely western and modern. A silver revetment *(riza)* datable to 1850 is preserved.

Anonymous, Russian
(19th century)

St Nicholas

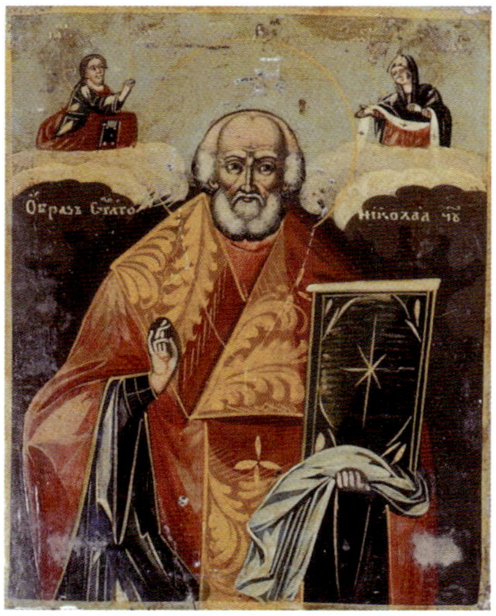

Oil on wood, 17.4 × 13.7 cm
Bywater Bequest, 1915; ANT1915.185

St Nicholas, whose name is inscribed in Slavonic, holds a large codex and is flanked above by cloud-borne figures of Christ and the Virgin, identified in Greek in a pale blue sky. A silver revetment *(riza)* belonging to this icon is preserved.

Anonymous, Russian?
(19th century)

Triptych: God the Father and six Saints

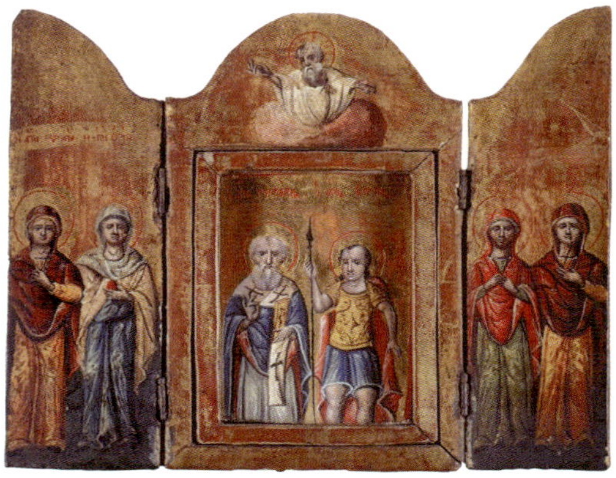

Oil on wood, 18.7 × 22.2 cm (open); 11.5 cm (closed)
Prov.: the Revd Greville John Chester
Purchased, 1868; ANT1872.593

Small gilded wooden triptych with figures inscribed in Greek, has a note on the verso stating 'Greek triptych of Russian make'. The central portion features a western type of God the Father emerging from a cloud above a separate inset panel with the Church Father Gregory of Nazianzus and the military St Sergius. On the wings stand (on the left) St Euphemia and St Irene and (on the right) two other female saints.

Anonymous, Russian
(18th/19th century)

St Nicholas

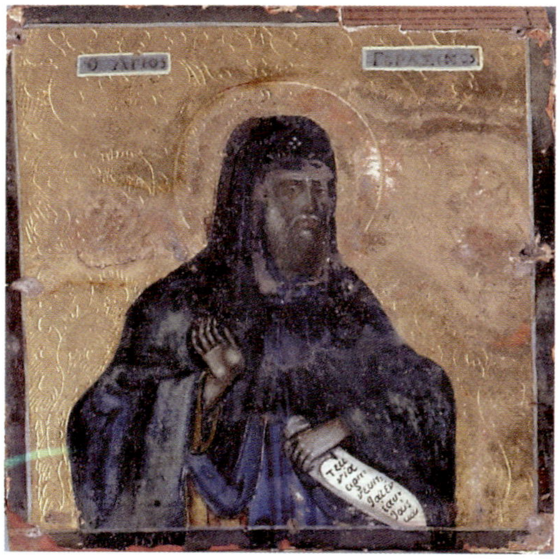

Oil on wood, 16.7 × 12.5 cm
Bywater Bequest, 1915; ANT1915.184

St Nicholas, his name inscribed in Slavonic, holds a large codex with ornamented cover. He is flanked above by clouds from which emerge the figures of Christ and the Virgin, their names given in Greek. A silver revetment *(riza)* belonging to this icon and datable to 1817 is preserved.

Anonymous, Russian
(18th/19th century)

Crowned Virgin and Child 'Joy of those who grieve'

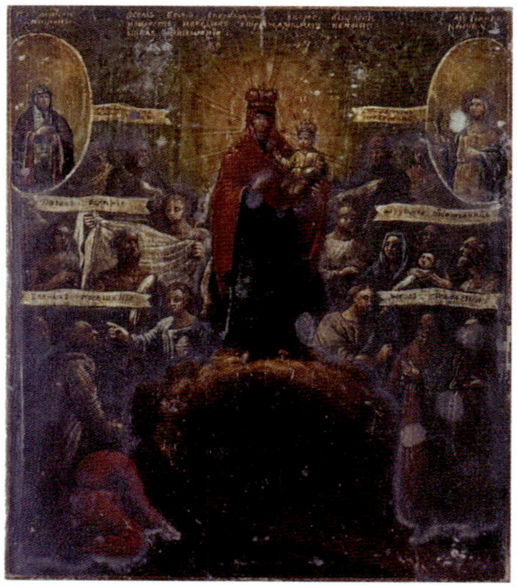

Oil on wood, 18.1 × 15.3 cm
Bywater Bequest; ANT1915.189

The icon portrays in a western, modern style a crowned Virgin and Child standing on a red cloud, the iconographic type entitled in Slavonic 'Joy of those who grieve', introduced in Russia in the 17th century. On either side are groups of figures identified (as the sick, the naked, etc.) by Slavonic inscriptions on horizontal banners. The icon may date to 1815 and a silver revetment *(riza)* dated 1833 is preserved.

Anonymous, Russian
(19th century)

The Virgin and Child

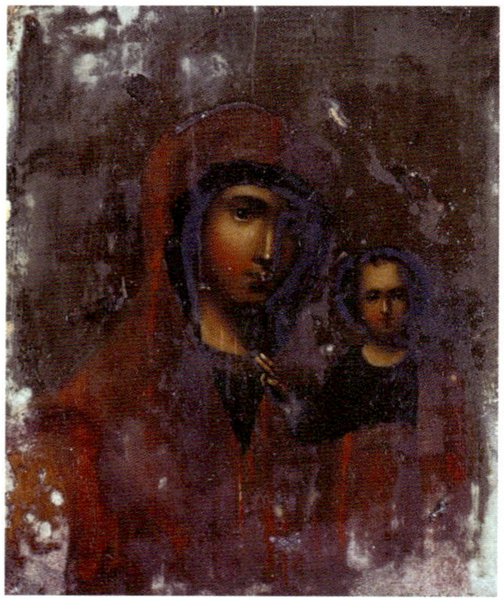

A244; oil on panel, 17 × 14 cm
Presented by the Revd Greville John Chester, 1887; WA1887.1

An icon of which only the faces of the Virgin and Child are fully painted. The rest of the figures, presumably to be covered by a metal revetment *(riza)*, was left in a sketchy condition.

Anonymous, Italian
(16th century?)

Christological Scenes

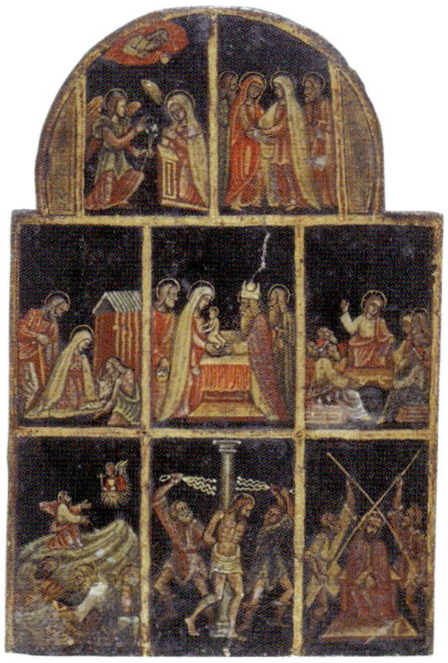

Oil on wood, 16.2 × 10.6 cm and 17.3 × 11.8 cm
Bywater Bequest, 1915; ANT1915.177

This panel and the following are each decorated with eight scenes. Here, the Annunciation, Visitation, Nativity, Presentation, Christ among the Doctors, the Agony in the Garden, Scourging and Mocking of Christ. The scenes in both panels are typically Roman Catholic and follow in the tradition of the works of Giovanni Maria Scupola, active in late 15th to early 16th-century Otranto. A French label on the reverse states they were acquired in Rome in 1858.

Anonymous, Post-Byzantine
(18th century?)

The Virgin and Child

A72; dimensions unknown
Fox-Strangways Gift, 1850; WA1850.24

Recorded missing in 1906.

Anonymous, Italian
(16th century?)

Christological scenes

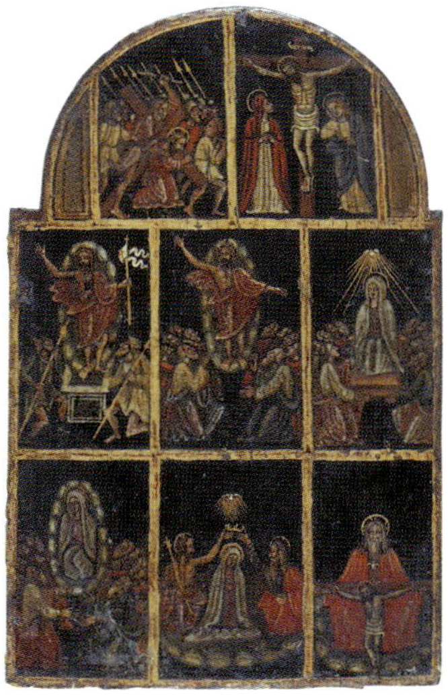

Oil on wood, 16.2 × 10.6 cm and 17.3 × 11.8 cm
Bywater Bequest, 1915; ANT1915.178

A pair to the preceding. The scenes are Carrying of the Cross, Crucifixion, Resurrection, Ascension, Virgin among the Apostles, Assumption, Coronation of the Virgin and the Trinity.

ARTISTS' BIOGRAPHIES

Abbott, John White
(1764 – 1851)
Abbott was an amateur painter. He spent his life in Exeter where he practised as a surgeon. His style of working in watercolour is very close to that of Francis Towne, who was his friend and teacher. He also worked in oil. He exhibited at the Royal Academy from 1793 to 1805 and in 1810 and 1822. In 1825, he inherited the estate of Fordlands near Exeter and was appointed Deputy Lieutenant for Devonshire in 1835.

Aelst, Willem van
(1627 – in or after 1683)
Van Aelst was born in Delft where he became a pupil of his uncle, Evert van Aelst. After travelling in France and Italy, he stopped briefly in Delft in 1656 and settled in Amsterdam in 1657. He became famous for his elaborate still-life compositions of fruit and flowers with silver and glassware. He also specialized in painting game.

Agnolo di Domenico di Donnino
(1466 – *c.* 1513)
According to Vasari, Agnolo was closely associated with Cosimo Rosselli, who strongly influenced his work. He may have trained with Domenico Ghirlandaio. He is best known for his frescoes at the Hospital of S Bonifazio in Florence and in the audience rooms in the Palazzo dell'Opera di S. Jacopo in Pistoia.

Aken, Joseph van
(*c.* 1699 – 1749)
Van Aken is said to have been born in Antwerp. In about 1720 he settled in London. In his early years in England, he painted genre scenes and conversation pieces. From about 1735, he began to specialize in drapery painting. Costumes painted by him appear in many portraits by a number of the leading British painters of the 1730s and 1740s.

Akotantos, Angelos
(active 1436 – 1450)
Greek icon painter from Candia, Crete. His career can be traced through legal documents. His icon of the *Birth of Christ* was singled out for praise by the painter Andreas Pavias. His brother Ioannis (active 1436–1477) converted to Roman Catholicism, but Angelos remained Orthodox.

Alexander, Charles
(exhibited 1893–4)
Little is known about Alexander except that he exhibited in London in the early 1890s when he gave his address as Alderley, Wotton-under-Edge.

Allchin, William T. Howell
(1844 – 1883)
Allchin was organist at St John's College, Oxford from 1876 to 1883. He copied still-life compositions in oil and watercolour and specialized in caricature.

Allori, Alessandro
(1535 – 1607)
Allori was trained in Bronzino's workshop in Florence and became his adopted son. An early visit to Rome confirmed his interest in the muscular figures and energetic poses which appear in the work of Michelangelo and were imitated by Allori. His frescoes include two large histories for the Medici villa at Poggio a Caiano. His last works show a new warmth and softness.

Allori, Cristofano
(1577 – 1621)
The son of Alessandro with whom he studied, Cristofano enjoyed Medici patronage early in his career. He moved to the studio of Gregorio Pagani around 1600, in search of a more naturalistic style; he was deeply influenced by Lodovico Cigoli. Cristofano had a high reputation as a portraitist and his celebrated *Judith with the Head of Holofernes* (several versions), in which the severed head is a self-portrait, inspired numerous copies and derivations.

Alma-Tadema, Sir Lawrence
(1836 – 1912)
Born in Holland, Alma-Tadema settled in London in 1870 and took British nationality in 1873. At first he took his themes from the early history of France and Belgium. A visit to Pompeii in 1863 turned his attention to the Ancient world. Following his move to England, he specialized in scenes from the history and daily life of Ancient Rome. His compositions show a remarkable talent for creating effects of light and for capturing the texture of translucent marble.

Amigoni, Jacopo
(*c.* 1685 – 1752)
Almost certainly born in Venice, Amigoni is mentioned in 1711 as working abroad. He was called to the service of the Elector of Bavaria in 1717, notably painting fresco cycles at Nymphenburg, Schleissheim and the Benedictine abbey of Ottobeuren. In 1728 he travelled to Rome, Naples and Venice, before establishing himself in England from 1729 to 1739 as a portraitist and decorative artist. He worked in Venice from 1739 to 1747, before accepting an invitation to become court painter to Ferdinand VI at Madrid from 1747 until his death in 1752.

André, Albert
(1869 – 1954)
André was born in Lyon and went to Paris as an industrial designer. Contact with Valtat, Ranson and Henry Bataille encouraged him to exhibit at the Salon d'Automne. He became a painter of figures, landscapes, still life and interiors but also illustrated books and designed tapestries for the factory at Beauvais. He worked at first in Paris and in Loudon before settling in Bagnols-sur-Cèze, where he was appointed curator of the local museum.

Andrea di Bartolo Cini
(*c.* 1358–64 – 1428)
Son of the Sienese painter, Bartolo di Fredi, who seems to have influenced his early work. His later work seems to have more in common with Taddeo di Bartolo. There are several signed works but none are dated and the chronology is hypothetical. A large number of panel paintings have been attributed to him, suggesting that he had a large workshop.

Andrea del Brescianino
(*c.* 1487 – after 1525)
Brescianino may have been a pupil of Gerolamo del Pacchia but is first documented working with Battista di Fruosino in Siena. Later, in Florence, he came under the influence of Leonardo and Raphael. After returning to Siena, he continued to respond to the work of Florentine artists, including Andrea del Sarto who became a major influence on his later work.

Andriessen, Henrick
(1607 – 1655)
Probably identical with the artist of this name who became a pupil at the Antwerp Academy in 1637. He specialized in painting still lifes. Most of the few paintings which can be attributed to him are pictures of *vanitas*.

Angel, Philips
(1616 – after 1683)
Philips Angel was born in Middelburg. In 1639, he was registered at the Haarlem guild and was appointed secretary in 1643. By the late 1640s, he was back in Middelburg where he remained for the rest of his life. He specialized in painting still lifes, but also painted barn interiors and live birds.

Angelico, Fra (Guido di Pieri)
(*c.* 1395–1400 – 1455)
Fra Angelico was attached to the Dominican friary at Fiesole, where he became Prior in 1450. Some time after 1436 he began working extensively for the Dominican friary of S. Marco in Florence. He also carried out important commissions for frescoes and altar-pieces in Cortona, Orvieto and Rome where he died. He had many assistants.

Antolinez, José
(1635 – 1675)
A pupil of Francisco Rizi, Antolinez also studied the Venetian and Flemish pictures in the Spanish Royal Collection, particularly the work of Titian and Rubens, and became a brilliant colourist. He painted some portraits and genre scenes and had a reputation as a painter of mythologies (although little has survived) but was famous above all for his religious works and his renditions of the popular theme of the Immaculate Conception.

Apollonio di Giovanni
(*c.* 1416 – 1465)
Apollonio di Giovanni ran a workshop that specialized in *cassone* panels and other domestic paintings in Florence along with Marco del Buono Giamberti. His early work comes out of the tradition of International Gothic but his later work shows the influence of contemporaries like Domenico Veneziano.

Arcangelo di Jacopo del Sellaio
(1478 – 1531)
Son of Jacopo del Sellaio, he inherited his father's workshop in 1493 and was called in to complete an altar-piece in the church of S. Frediano in Florence, left unfinished at the time of his father's death. He seems to have worked in a somewhat old-fashioned style derived through his father from the ambience of Botticelli.

Artz, David Adolphe Constant
(1837 – 1890)
Artz was born in The Hague and became the most gifted pupil of Jozef Israels. In 1865, on leaving the Academy of Amsterdam, he moved to Drenthe and then to Paris in 1866 where he remained until 1874. During this period he also visited England, Scotland, Germany and Italy before returning to The Hague where he spent the rest of his life. Like Israels, he was mainly a painter of beach scenes and subjects from the life of fishing people.

Asse, Geneviève
(b 1923)
Between 1940 and 1942, Asse studied at the Ecole Nationale Supérieure des Arts Décoratifs in Paris. Through the group L'Echelle, she came into contact with Othon Friesz. For a time after the war, she designed fabrics. She also illustrated a number of texts by contemporary authors. Early in her career, she painted still-life compositions of boxes and bottles. In about 1960, she became aware of the work of Morandi and her art became increasingly minimalist.

Ast, Balthasar van der
(1593–4 – *c.* 1657)
Van der Ast was born in Middelburg where he trained in the studio of his brother-in-law, Ambrosius Bosschaert. In 1632, he settled in Delft where he remained for the last twenty-five years of his life. He specialized in painting still-life compositions of fruit and flowers in which the influence of Bosschaert is dominant.

Aubry, Etienne
(1745 – 1781)
Aubry was received into the French Royal Academy in 1775 as a painter of portraits. From the mid-1770s, he began to paint scenes from daily life and illustrations to contemporary literature. Greuze was the main inspiration for his work of this kind.

Austin, Robert
(1895 – 1973)
Austin studied at the Leicester School of Art and the Royal College of Art. From 1927 to 1944 he taught engraving at the Royal College, becoming professor in 1948. He exhibited at the Royal Watercolour Society, of which he became president, and was elected to the Royal Academy in 1949.

Bacchiacca (Francesco Ubertini)
(1494 – 1557)
Bacchiacca was a pupil of Perugino and of Franciabigio and worked frequently for the Medici in Florence. He painted portraits and also religious compositions, derived from Andrea del Sarto, Raphael, Leonardo and Michelangelo. His later work shows some Mannerist tendencies acquired from Pontormo and Rosso.

Backer, Jakob Adriaensz.
(1608 – 1651)
Backer was born in Haarlem. In 1611 he moved to Amsterdam but returned to Friesland in about 1626 and became a pupil of Lambert Jacobsz. at Leeuwarden. By the early 1630s, he was back in Amsterdam where he came under the influence of Rembrandt. He remained in Amsterdam for the rest of his life. His work consists of biblical and mythological subjects and portraits.

Bacon, Sir Nathaniel
(1585 – 1627)
Bacon was an accomplished amateur painter of portraits and dead game. His work suggests that he had studied in the Netherlands, perhaps with Ter Brugghen at Utrecht. His pictures were probably painted only for his own family. He is known also to have painted classical subjects but none of these seems to have survived.

Badalocchio, Sisto
(1585 – after 1619)
A pupil of Agostino Carracci, Badalocchio went to Rome in 1602 where, together with his friend Giovanni Lanfranco, he worked at the Palazzo Farnese as part of Annibale Carracci's workshop, remaining until the master's death in 1609. Badalocchio worked in Rome and in Reggio Emilia in later years, but was mainly based in Parma from 1617. However, few of his paintings are documented, making dating of his work difficult. Annibale Carracci and Lanfranco remain the mainsprings for his style, although there are numerous other influences from Emilia and Ferrara.

Baker, Thomas
(1809 – 1869)
Baker of Leamington, as he was known to distinguish him from other artists of the same name, specialized in painting landscapes with sheep and cattle. He worked mainly in Warwickshire and the Midlands. Work by him appeared at the Royal Academy summer exhibitions in 1831, 1847 and 1858.

Balston, Thomas
(1883 – 1967)
Balston was educated at Eton and Oxford. He studied painting for a brief period in the 1930s with Mark Gertler and exhibited regularly at the Redfern Gallery. He collected the work of his contemporaries and contributed articles to the periodicals *Image* and *Signature*. He also wrote books on various themes, including several on wood-engraving.

Bardwell, Thomas
(1704 – 1767)
Bardwell began his career as a decorative painter in Bungay. In about 1729, be began to paint landscape overmantels and a number of conversation pieces are known from 1736 to 1740. In the 1740s, his portraits increased in size. He travelled in Scotland and Yorkshire and visited London before settling in Norwich in 1759 where he had a successful practice.

Barker of Bath, Thomas
(1769 – 1847)
Barker settled with his family in Bath in about 1782 where his precocious talent was noticed by a wealthy local coach-builder, Charles Spackman. Spackman paid Barker's father a small allowance in exchange for the rights to his son's work. He also paid for a visit to Italy in the early 1790s. Barker's work, in which the influence of Gainsborough is clear, was much admired. His compositions were extensively reproduced in prints. From his earnings, he built Sion Hill in Bath which he decorated with a large mural.

Barna da Siena
(active *c.* 1330 – 1350)
The main work associated with the artist know as Barna da Siena, is the series of frescoes in the Collegiata at S. Gimignano. These show the influence of Simone Martini and Pietro Lorenzetti while his work elsewhere shows his knowledge of Duccio's *Maestà* . Several works in the same Sienese style have been attributed to Barna but the attribution of these has been much disputed. Barna is sometimes identified as Lippo Memmi.

Barocci, Federico
(*c.* 1535 – 1612)
In 1550, Barocci went to Rome where he decorated a ceiling for the Casino of Pius IV in the Vatican Gardens. He then returned to Urbino and painted mainly religious works in which the influence of Raphael and Correggio is combined. His large altar-pieces are marked by a complexity and vitality of composition while his brushwork is soft and his figures are painted with an idealized charm.

Barret, George, the Elder
(*c.* 1728 – 1784)
George Barret was born in Dublin. He was largely self-taught. In 1763, he settled in London where he had some success with his views of North Wales and scenes of country estates. His later work shows the influence of Richard Wilson. His three sons were painters. The younger George Barret (1767–1842) began by painting views of the Thames Valley and the Home Counties, occasionally moving into Wales. He is said to have been exclusively a watercolourist.

Bartolomeo degli Erri
(active *c.* 1430 – 1479)
Bartolomeo and his brother Agnolo (active 1442–1497) worked in partnership with another family of Modenese painters, headed by Antonio and Francesco Azzi. There are a number of paintings which can be assigned to one or other of the Erri brothers on the basis of documents; this makes it possible to distinguish between their styles.

Bartolomeo di Fruosino
(1366 – 1441)
In 1394, Bartolomeo di Fruosino was listed among the pupils of Agnolo Gaddi working in Prato cathedral. In addition to altar-pieces, he also illuminated manuscripts, one of which, a signed and dated Missal of 1421 (Museo di S. Marco, Florence), has formed a basis for attributions.

Bartolomeo, Fra (Baccio di Paolo del Fattorino called Baccio della Porta)
(1472 – 1517)
Fra Bartolomeo was the son of a muleteer. He is recorded as an apprentice to Cosimo Rosselli in 1485 and was particularly influenced by Piero di Cosimo, Rosselli's assistant. After a short spell, he left the workshop to set up a partnership with Mariotto Albertinelli. In 1500 he became a Dominican monk and renounced painting. In about 1504, he returned to painting and became an influential painter of altar-pieces which contributed to the development of the High Renaissance style in Florence.

Basaiti, Marco
(active 1496 – 1530)
Although Basaiti was probably taught by Alvise Vivarini, other Venetian artists such as Giovanni Bellini, Carpaccio and Cima da Conegliano also influenced his style. At a late stage, he began to imitate the manner of Giorgione. There are several signed paintings by him, some of them dated.

Bassano, Jacopo (Jacopo da Ponte)
(*c.* 1510 – 1592)
Jacopo began in his father's workshop but was also a pupil of Bonifazio Veronese. He went to Venice in about 1533 when he entered the circle of Venetian artists round Titian and seems to have been attracted by the Mannerism of Parmigianino and, later, of Tintoretto. Towards 1565, he began to specialize in genre scenes or pastoral interpretations of religious subjects.

Bassano, Leandro (Leandro da Ponte)
(1557 – 1622)
Leandro was the pupil and third surviving son of Jacopo Bassano. He was particularly known as a painter of portraits although he also painted rustic pictures of game and altar-pieces.

Bastien-Lepage, Jules
(1848 – 1884)
After a false start in the postal administration, Bastien-Lepage joined Cabanel's class at the Ecole des Beaux-Arts with a grant from his local council. He exhibited his first peasant subject in 1874 and made his reputation with a painting of haymakers at the Salon of 1877. His rustic pictures and lively brushwork had an immense international influence. He was also a successful painter of portraits.

Batoni, Pompeo
(1708 – 1787)
The son of a goldsmith, with whom he first trained, Batoni left Lucca for Rome aged twenty, in order to study Raphael, Bolognese classicism and the antique. He soon established a high reputation with his history paintings and altar-pieces, which were much in demand. Batoni's major activity, however, was that of portraiture, in which he rivalled his contemporary, Anton Raphael Mengs. He evolved a type of polished, elegant and nonchalant portrait which appealed to Grand Tourists in Rome and became extremely fashionable.

Bayes, Walter John
(1869 – 1956)
Bayes was the son of the artist Alfred Walter Bayes and brother of Gilbert Bayes, the sculptor. He studied in London and Paris and became associated with Walter Sickert and his friends in the Camden Town Group. He also taught at various schools in London before becoming Director of Painting at Lancaster School of Art in 1944. He contributed art criticism to a number of periodicals and wrote several books on art.

Baynes, Keith
(1887 – 1977)
Baynes studied at Cambrdge and then at the Slade School (1912–14). After the war, he entered the circle of Roger Fry and came under the influence of the French Impressionists. He exhibited at the London Artists' Association from 1926 until the Association was disbanded in 1931 and subsequently exhibited with London dealers and overseas.

Beaumont, Sir George Howland
(1753 – 1827)
English collector and amateur painter whose estate at Coleorton in Leicestershire became a centre for writers and artists. He studied art with Alexander Cozens and admired the work of Claude Lorrain. His painting, *Peel Castle in a Storm,* inspired Wordsworth to write a sonnet and Constable was a close friend. Beaumont played an important role in the founding of the National Gallery, to which he presented the best paintings from his collection.

Beert, Osias, the Elder
(*c.* 1580 – 1623)
Beert is known only as a painter of flowers and fruit. As he rarely signed his paintings and never dated them, reconstructing his work is not easy. He was probably born in Antwerp, where he became master of the guild in 1602 and where he died.

Bega, Cornelis
(1631/2 – 1664)
Bega spent his life in Haarlem painting and etching scenes of peasant life. He was a pupil of Adriaen van Ostade. In 1653 he travelled in Germany and Switzerland with the painter Vincent Laurenz. van der Vinne and was accepted into the Haarlem guild the following year.

Bell, Vanessa
(1879 – 1961)
Vanessa Bell was the daughter of the writer, Sir Leslie Stephens and sister of the writer, Virginia Woolf. With her husband, Clive Bell, she was one of the members of the Bloomsbury Group. She studied with Arthur Cope at the Royal Academy Schools and worked with Roger Fry at the Omega Workshops. Apart from her paintings in oil, she designed textiles and ceramics.

Bellini, Giovanni
(*c.* 1431–6 – 1516)
Younger brother of Gentile Bellini and son of Jacopo. The main influence on Giovanni's early style was that of his brother-in-law, Andrea Mantegna. He painted a large number of paintings on the theme of the Madonna and Child which trace the development of his art from the harder work of his early years to the softer late works. In his last years he painted a number of allegorical and mythological works of which the largest and most impressive, *The Feast of the Gods,* was commissioned by Alfonso d'Este. He had many pupils, including Giorgione and Titian.

Bellucci, Antonio
(1654 – 1726)
Bellucci began his career as a soldier, then studied under Antonio Zanchi; his few known early works testify to his interest in Luca Giordano and in Veronese. He worked in Vienna from *c.* 1692 until 1704 for Johann Adam von Lichtenstein; after a brief sojourn in Venice in 1705 he moved to Düsseldorf, working for the Elector Johann Wilhelm on large historical paintings there and at the castle of Bensberg. In 1716 Bellucci went to England, counting James Brydges, first Duke of Chandos, amongst his patrons; he returned to Venice in 1722.

Bendz, Wilhelm
(1804 – 1832)
Bendz studied at the Academy in Copenhagen with Eckersberg. His portraits and interior scenes established him as one of the leading figures of the Danish Golden Age. In 1831, a grant enabled him to travel through Germany to Munich. In 1832, he set out for Rome but died on 14 November in Vicenza.

Benson, Ambrosius
(active 1521 – d. 1550)
Benson was born in Lombardy. He became a master in Bruges in 1519 where he worked under Gerard David. His art combines Flemish motifs, particularly taken from the work of Gerard David, with an Italianate breadth.

Berchem, Nicolaes Pietersz.
(baptized 1620 – 1683)
Berchem was taught by his father, Pieter Claesz., a still-life painter, and by a number of other Dutch artists. He became a member of the Haarlem guild in 1642. He specialized at first in painting and etching Dutch landscapes but later followed fashion by painting more Italianate scenes. He also painted biblical, mythological and allegorical subjects and made designs for maps. It is suggested that he may have visited Italy in the early 1650s. He lived in Haarlem until 1677 when he settled in Amsterdam.

Berrettoni, Niccolò
(1637 – 1682)
Berrettoni apparently began his career as a pupil of Simone Cantarini in Pesaro and *c.* 1670 moved to Rome with the support of a local patron. He was one of the most talented associates of Carlo Maratta and worked principally in Rome but also in his native Pesaro. Berrettoni's frescoes at the Palazzo Altieri, Rome, demonstrate his gifts as a late Baroque painter of secular themes.

Berswordt Master (see Master of the Bielefeld Altar)

Bertin, Jean-Victor
(1767 – 1842)
Bertin was a follower of Valenciennes. He exhibited landscapes at the Salon from 1793 onwards. He seems to have visited Italy between 1806 and 1808 . He became an important teacher of a younger generation of landscape painters, including Corot.

Bevan, Robert Polhill
(1865 – 1925)
Bevan was born in Hove and studied in Paris. Much of his work consists of portraits, animals and landscapes. At the beginning of his career, he specialized in painting horse fairs. Later, he painted Devonshire landscapes. He worked in a faceted style of painting which owes something to Cézanne.

Beyeren, Abraham van
(1620–1 – 1690)
Van Beyeren painted marine subjects at the beginning of his career but is chiefly known as a painter of still life. The first recorded date on one of his still-life compositions is 1653 but a number have been dated earlier on stylistic grounds. He painted sumptuous banquet paintings as well as still-life compositions of sea-fish and a number of flower pieces. He was born at The Hague and worked there for periods of several years at a time, separated by visits to other Dutch towns.

Biagio di Antonio Tucci
(1446 – 1516)
Biagio's art reflected the style of a number of contemporary Tuscan painters. He was trained in Florence and was influenced by Filippo Lippi and by Verrocchio. He worked for many years in Faenza but also travelled. In 1481–2 he collaborated with Cosimo Rosselli in the Sistine Chapel in Rome. His late work shows an interest in the art of Domenico Ghirlandaio. In addition to painting altar-pieces he also produced many *cassone* paintings.

Bibiena, Ferdinando Galli
(1657 – 1743)
The son of the decorative artist Giovanni Maria Bibiena (1625–1665), Ferdinando studied briefly under Cignani and then became a specialist in illusionistic architecture and theatre design. His work was highly influential. Ferdinando, together with his brother Francesco (1659–1739), his three sons and his nephew, formed an extraordinarily talented and consistent team of court architects and designers; singly and in collaboration, they worked for the major courts of Europe, from Vienna to Lisbon.

Bicci di Lorenzo
(active late 1380s – 1452)
Bicci's father, Lorenzo di Bicci and his son, Neri de Bicci, were both painters in Florence. Bicci's early style is marked by the influence of his father but this gave way to the more fashionable style of Lorenzo Monaco and Gentile da Fabriano. He was a prolific painter. It is thought that Masaccio was for a short time apprenticed to him.

Blanche, Jacques-Emile
(1861 – 1942)
Blanche was a pupil of Gervex and an associate of the Impressionists, Manet was a particular influence. He made an early success in the 1890s as a portrait painter at the Salons of the Société Nationale des Beaux-Arts. He painted a wide range of subjects, including many scenes of fashionable life, and wrote several semi-autobiographical novels.

Bloemen, Jan Frans van (Orizzonte)
(1662 – 1749)
Van Bloemen was born in Antwerp where he was a pupil of Antoon Goubau. Around 1648, he went to Italy and settled in Rome. His landscapes, which often feature classical buildings, were much admired and imitated in early 18th-century Rome.

Boel, Pieter
(1622 – 1674)
Boel was born in Antwerp and became a member of the guild in 1650–51. It appears that he had already spent some years in Italy by this date. He was an animal and still-life painter who sometimes collaborated with other artists. His work was influenced by Jan Fijt and Frans Snijders who were probably his teachers. From 1668, he was employed at the Gobelins tapestry works near Paris where he provided designs for animals.

Bollongier, Hans
(*c.* 1600 – 1650)
Bollongier was admitted to the Haarlem guild in 1623. He is recorded at Haarlem in 1636 and again in 1642. He was mainly a painter of flowers. All his known work is painted on panel and dated.

Bolognini, Giacomo
(?1664 – 1734/37)
Bolognini's early career is still obscure. He evolved a lively late Baroque style and contemporary documentary sources praise his talents as a historical and mythological painter. He worked for a range of patrons in Bologna, Piacenza, Imola, Mantua, Verona and Venice, sometimes in fresco and regularly in oil, showing a predilection for secular subjects. His art is characterized by dramatic effects of light and shade and by the distinctive physiognomy of his figures. Bolognini was a founder member of the Accademia Clementina in 1709.

Bomberg, David
(1890 – 1957)
Bomberg was born in Birmingham. His first teacher was Walter Bayes with whom he took lessons at the City and Guilds evening classes. He later studied with W.R. Lethaby at the Central School of Arts and Crafts and with Walter Sickert at the Westminster School of Art. From 1911 to 1913, he studied at the Slade School. Before the war, he worked for Roger Fry's Omega Workshops. His work at this time was influenced by the Vorticists although the influence did not last. In the 1920s and 1930s his extensive travels, notably in Spain and Palestine, inspired a series of expressive landscape paintings.

Bonifazio de' Pitati
(1487 – 1553)
The son of an armourer, Bonifazio possibly trained under Palma Vecchio in Venice. He is first documented in 1528 and from 1529 to 1553 received an important series of commissions for the Palazzo dei Camerlenghi in Venice for biblical narratives and other images. Bonifazio was responsive to central Italian art as well as to the work of Pordenone, Lotto and Titian. His patrons included small confraternities and his busy workshop provided a variety of furniture and other domestic painting. Jacopo Bassano was his most important pupil.

Bonington, Richard Parkes
(1802 – 1828)
Bonington was born near Nottingham. At the age of fifteen, he moved with his family to Calais where the watercolourist, Louis Francia, encouraged him to paint coast scenes. In 1820, he went to Paris where he entered the Ecole des Beaux-Arts and became a friend of Delacroix. At first he worked exclusively in watercolour but extended his range in about 1822 to include marine paintings in oil. In 1825, he visited England with Delacroix and began to paint a series of small historical compositions. He visited Italy in 1826 and found new inspiration among the canals of Venice.

Bonnard, Pierre
(1867 – 1947)
On arrival in Paris in 1888, Bonnard studied at the Académie Julian where he met Sérusier, Maurice Denis and others who formed the Nabis, a group of painters who admired Gauguin. Later, he met Xavier Roussel and Vuillard, whose decorative art struck a sympathetic chord. In 1903, he was one of the founder members of the Salon d'Automne, organized by the Fauves. His work is marked by a strong sense of colour which he combined after 1915 with a clear sense of design.

Boonen, Arnold
(1669 – 1729)
Boonen was born in Dordrecht. He was trained by Arnold Verbuys and Godfried Schalken and specialized in painting portraits. In 1694, he went to Gemany, where he was much sought after as a portrait painter, but returned to Holland in 1696. He died in Amsterdam.

Borès, Francisco
(1898 – 1972)
Born in Madrid, Borès was intended for a career in engineering. In 1925, he transferred to Paris where he became associated with his fellow Spaniards, Miró, Picabia and Juan Gris. His subject matter in this period was taken from the carnival, from dances and from scenes of the crowd which he painted with vigour. In the early 1930s, his brush became more dynamic and his touch became even more improvised but from 1934 onwards, he organized his compositions more carefully and reined in the freedom of his brushwork.

Borman, Johannes
(active 1653 – in or after 1660)
Probably the same Johannes Borman who came from The Hague and became a citizen of Amsterdam in 1659. He is probably also to be identified with the Joannes Borremans who was admitted to the Leiden guild in 1658 and left shortly after. He specialized in painting still life.

Bosboom, Johannes
(1817 – 1891)
Bosboom was born in The Hague into a strict Protestant family and became a student at The Hague Academy at the age of fourteen. Between 1835 and 1839 he travelled in Germany, Belgium and France. He was chiefly famed for painting church interiors, somewhat in the manner of the 17th-century painter Emanuel de Witte.

Bosschaert, Ambrosius
(1573 – 1621)
Bosschaert was born in Antwerp, the son of a painter. In about 1597, his family moved to Middelburg where he remained for most of his career. He married the elder sister of Balthasar van der Ast who became his pupil and adopted son. In the last years of his life, he left Middelburg and worked in Amsterdam, Bergen-op-Zoom, Utrecht, Breda and The Hague, where he died. He was a pioneer in flower painting, often painting on copper. The influence of his work was lasting and extensive.

Both, Jan
(*c.* 1618 – 1652)
Both's teacher was probably Abraham Bloemaert. He spent his life in Utrecht apart from a period in France and Italy. The time he stayed in Rome with his brother Andries from *c.* 1638 until 1641 left a lasting impression on his art. His paintings of travellers and peasants driving cattle along roads lit by a golden light were much admired and imitated by his Dutch contemporaries.

Botticelli, Sandro (Alessandro di Filipepi)
(*c.* 1444–5 – 1510)
Botticelli probably worked under Filippo Lippi, whose style he assimilated in his earliest works. He worked mainly in Florence but painted three frescoes in the Sistine Chapel in Rome (1481–2). Several of his most important works were painted for the Medici family including *The Birth of Venus* and *Primavera*, both executed in a new, mannered and decorative style.

Boudin, Eugène
(1824 – 1898)
Boudin ran a stationery and picture-framing shop in Le Havre where he came into contact with a number of artists visiting the region. He took up painting himself, becoming an advocate of the virtues of painting out of doors. He mainly painted scenes on the beaches, in the ports and sand dunes and among the fishing people along the northern coast of France. His work was included in the first Impressionist exhibition in 1874.

Bowles, Oldfield
(1739 – 1810)
Bowles had an estate at North Aston near Oxford. He was not a professional painter but admired the landscapes of Richard Wilson and took lessons from Wilson's pupil, Thomas Jones. He painted a few portraits but was chiefly a landscapist.

Braque, Georges
(1882 – 1963)
Braque's father was a house painter. In 1900, Braque went to Paris from Le Havre and studied at the Ecole des Beaux-Arts. His links with the Fauves encouraged him to paint with bright colours but the discovery of Cézanne's work at l'Estaque in 1906 led him to develop a more formalist approach to painting. This rapidly developed into Cubism. Until 1914 he worked closely with Picasso. After 1917, he concentrated on still life and later became interested in beach scenes.

Breakspeare, William
(1855 – 1914)
Breakspeare was a founder member of the Birmingham Art Circle. He painted scenes of genre, often set in the 18th century and became a member of the Newlyn School in Cornwall. He had studied in Paris and, as with other artists of the Newlyn group, his work shows a French influence.

Brescianino, Andrea del (see Andrea del Brescianino)

Brett, John
(1831 – 1902)
Ruskin admired Brett's painting, *The Stonebreaker*, at the Royal Academy exhibition in 1858 and prevailed upon the artist to visit Italy. As a result of Ruskin's influence, Brett turned towards subjects of a botanical or geological interest, particularly coastal scenes, which he exhibited at the Royal Academy over a period of forty years.

Bril, Paul
(1554 – 1626)
Paul Bril was born in Antwerp. In 1574, he went to Lyon and later joined his brother, Matthijs, in Rome. He is first recorded there in 1582 when he joined the Accademia di S. Luca. Apart from a visit to Naples in about 1602–3, he spent the remainder of his life in Rome. Paul and Matthijs were mostly painters of landscape. Their art evolved away from the more fantastic conceptions of the 16th century towards a greater naturalism which was taken up by younger painters working in Rome in the early 17th century.

Broeck, Elias van den
(1649/50 – 1708)
Van den Broeck moved with his family from his native Antwerp to Amsterdam at an early age. He was apprenticed to a goldsmith in 1665 and then to the still-life painter Cornelis Kick. In 1669, he became a pupil of Jan Davidsz. de Heem in Utrecht and after a period when he followed de Heem to Antwerp he returned to Amsterdam in 1685. He painted mainly still-life compositions of flowers and fruit in the manner of de Heem.

Bronzino (Agnolo Tori di Cosimo di Moriano)
(1503 – 1572)
Bronzino was Pontormo's adopted son. His paintings are somewhat similar to Pontormo's but are less charged with emotion and are executed with a harder surface. He worked in Florence, mainly for the Medici, particularly after the marriage of Cosimo I and Eleanora of Toledo in 1539. His work covers a wide range of religious and secular subjects. His portraits established a format for court portraits which was taken up at other European courts in the 16th century.

Brook, Peter
(b. 1927)
Peter Brook was born at Holmfirth in Yorkshire. He received tuition at Huddersfied School of Art and Goldsmiths' College School of Art. At first, he painted industrial scenes, then views of the Pennines and, from 1980, Scottish and Lancashire landscapes.

Brooking, Charles
(*c.* 1723 – 1759)
Brooking is said to have been employed at Deptford Dockyard but little detail of his life is known. He may have been self-taught. He painted marine subjects, somewhat in the manner of the van de Veldes whose work he sometimes copied. His work was published in a series of prints by John Boydell in 1753. Shortly after, he painted a large picture of ships for the Foundling Hospital in Greenwich.

Brouwer, Adriaen
(1605/6 – 1638)
Brouwer was probably born in Oudenaarde but is first recorded in Amsterdam in 1626. It is supposed that he was a pupil of Frans Hals in Haarlem in the 1620s. In 1621–2 he moved to Antwerp where he spent the remainder of his life. He is best known for his paintings of drinkers and smokers and scenes of sleeping peasants. He also painted landscapes. His earliest work is more colourful than the later works when he followed the Dutch fashion for monochrome effects.

Brown, Ford Madox
(1821 – 1893)
Brown was born in Calais, son of a half-pay ship's purser. He studied at the art schools of Bruges, Ghent and Antwerp. He spent from 1840 to 1843 in Paris and settled in London in 1844. A visit to Rome in 1845 brought him into contact with the German Nazarenes and he altered his style on returning to England. Through Rossetti, who was briefly his pupil in 1848, he came into contact with the other members of the Pre-Raphaelite Brotherhood. Later he worked as a designer for William Morris.

Brueghel, Jan, the Elder
(1568 – 1625)
Brueghel painted landscapes with mythological, religious and allegorical subjects. He also painted flowers. He often collaborated with other artists, especially with Rubens. He spent from 1590 to 1596 in Italy and then travelled in the Netherlands before he settled in Antwerp where he became court painter to the Archduke Albert and the Archduchess Isabella.

Brueghel, Jan, the Younger
(1601 – 1678)
Jan Brueghel the Younger, son and pupil of Jan Brueghel the Elder, was born in Antwerp. In 1622, he went to Italy, working at first for Cardinal Federico Borromeo in Milan. On the death of his father in 1625, he returned to Antwerp to take over the studio.

Brugghen, Hendrick ter
(1588 – 1629)
Ter Brugghen was taught by Abraham Bloemaert. He spent the years from 1604 to 1614 in Italy where he became familiar with the work of Caravaggio. By 1616 he was back in Utrecht where he joined a group of painters who had acquired a range of subjects and tricks of lighting from Caravaggio's followers in Italy. No certain works have been identified by him before *c.* 1620.

Brundrit, Reginald Grange
(1883 – 1960)
Brundrit was born in Liverpool and studied at the Bradford School of Art and at the Slade School. He also took lessons from the animal painter and sculptor, John M. Swan. He lived at Masham, in Yorkshire. The landscape of Yorkshire was his favourite subject.

Buoneri, Francesco (Cecco del Caravaggio)
(active *c.* 1610 – 1621)
Little documentary evidence exists for this distinctive follower of Caravaggio, who is referred to in 1619 as one of a group of artists decorating the Casino of Cardinal Montalto in 1613–5 and is mentioned *c.* 1617–21 amongst the followers of Caravaggio. Recently Cecco has been convincingly identified as Francesco Buoneri, possibly Lombard in origin, who was said to have been Caravaggio's model for the *Amore Vincitore* of *c.* 1601–2 (Berlin, Gemäldegalerie). Buoneri is documented as having painted an altar-piece for the Guicciardini chapel in Santa Felicità, Florence, which was rejected; this is identifiable with the *Resurrection*, now in Chicago.

Buonsignori, Francesco
(*c.* 1460 – 1519)
Although traditionally said to have trained in Verona, Buonsignori's early works reveal his debt to Venetian art. Around 1490 he was in the service of the Gonzaga court at Mantua; he is later documented there as a court artist in 1506–7. Bonsignori was in Verona in 1514. He was strongly influenced by the art of Andrea Mantegna.

Burne-Jones, Sir Edward Coley
(1833 – 1898)
Burne-Jones came to Oxford in 1854 intending to follow a career in the church. His meeting with William Morris in Oxford and his discovery of the work of the Pre-Raphaelites encouraged him to pursue a career in art. He took lessons with Rossetti and travelled in France and Italy. Until 1859, his work was confined to watercolour and his subjects were chiefly taken from medieval history and literature, but he later extended his range to include subjects from Greek mythology. During this later period, the influence of Italian Renaissance art was marked. As a figure designer he made a substantial contribution to the success of the stained glass, tiles and tapestries produced by the firm of William Morris and Co.

Calderon, Philip Hermogenes
(1833 – 1898)
Calderon was a painter of domestic and historical scenes and leader of the St John's Wood Clique. He was born in Poitiers and educated by his father who was professor of Spanish literature in King's College, London. He studied briefly with Picot in Paris. His earliest work shows a Pre-Raphaelite tendency. After 1870, he turned mainly to painting portraits.

Callcott, Sir Augustus Wall
(1779 – 1844)
Callcott studied at the Royal Academy Schools and took lessons with the portrait painter, John Hoppner. His earliest work was portraiture but he became a specialist in painting somewhat idealized landscapes. He was a prolific painter and held the post of Surveyor of the Queen's pictures for many years.

Calraet, Abraham van
(1642 – 1722)
Calraet spent his life in Dordrecht. He trained as a woodcarver and seems to have taken up painting later. No sculptures by him are known. A group of still-life paintings formerly attributed to Aelbert Cuyp are now recognized as the work of Calraet. Later in his life, he seems to have concentrated on landscape painting.

Calvert, Edward
(1799 – 1883)
Calvert was a friend and follower of William Blake and Samuel Palmer. He was member of the group of artists who gathered round Palmer after he had moved to Shoreham in 1825. During his Shoreham period, Calvert produced a series of woodcuts illustrating Arcadian themes in a highly idealized style. Later, he painted mainly oil pictures of subjects inspired by pagan antiquity.

Cameron, Sir David Young
(1865 – 1945)
Scottish painter and etcher. His early work shows his interest in the work of Velázquez, Whistler and the painters of Barbizon and The Hague School. Later, he took his subjects mainly from the landscape of his native Scotland.

Camuccini, Giovanni Battista
(1819 – 1904)
Camuccini was the son of the history painter Vincenzo Camuccini and probably acquired some knowledge of art from him. In 1839, he began to take lessons with the landscape painter Giambattista Bassi. On the death of his father in 1844, he inherited an extensive art collection. The latest known painting by Camuccini dates from 1852. In 1855, he sold many works to the Duke of Northumberland and married the daughter of the President of the Monte di Pietà Bank. In 1862, he purchased the Cantalupo estate near Rome and acquired the title of Prince.

Canaletto (Giovanni Antonio Canal)
(1697 – 1768)
In 1719–20 Canaletto worked with his father who was a Venetian scene painter. Shortly afterwards he began to paint views of Venice and by the 1730s his work was in demand among the British visitors. He came to England in 1746 and stayed until at least 1755. In 1763, following his return to Venice, he was elected to the Venetian Academy. His last dated work was painted in 1766.

Candlelight Master, The
(active *c.* 1620 – 1640)
A group of Caravaggesque paintings has been associated with this artist whose work often includes an effect of candlelight. For a time, he was identified as Trophime Bigot, an artist from Arles in the south of France who had been to Rome in the 1620s. It is difficult, however, to believe that the signed works by Bigot, several of which remain in Provence, are by the same hand as the author of the candlelit group.

Caporali (Bartolomeo di Segnolo)
(active 1422 – *c.* 1503)
Caporali's art was formed by influences from Benozzo Gozzoli and Fra Angelico and to a lesser degree from Domenico Veneziano He collaborated with Bonfigli on an altar-piece for the church of S. Domenico in Perugia. Works by Caporali are sometimes misattributed to Bonfigli. His art does not seem to have developed much.

Carlevaris, Luca
(1663 – 1730)
Carlevaris was born in Udine and worked mainly in Venice. He specialized in view painting. The strict perspective of his work reflects his training as a mathematician. In 1703, he published a set of one hundred engraved views of Venice which were taken up as a source of ideas by later view painters.

Carline, George
(1855 – 1920)
Carline painted rustic scenes, particularly with a garden setting. He was born at Lincoln and studied in London, Paris and Antwerp. He exhibited at the Royal Academy from 1886 onwards.

Carline, Richard
(1896 – 1980)
Richard Carline was born in Oxford into a family of painters. From 1913–15, he attended Percyval Tudor-Hart's Academy in Paris then studied in London. He served as a pilot with the Royal Flying Corps in the First World War and as a war artist. From 1924 to 1929, he taught at the Ruskin School in Oxford. In 1946–7, he was first art counsellor of Unesco. In his later years, he wrote a number of books on art.

Carline, Sydney William
(1888 – 1929)
Sydney Carline was the son of the painter George Carline and the brother of Richard. He studied at the Slade School. Apart from painting portraits and landscapes, he was an illustrator and a medallic engraver.

Carlone, Carlo Innocenzo
(c.1686 – 1775)
Carlone's father was the sculptor, Giovanni Battista Carlone. He was taught painting by Giulio Quaglio at Como and worked at first in Venice and in Rome before leaving for Austria, where he remained from 1701 to 1725. He then spent from 1727 to 1737 in Germany before he returned to settle in Lombardy. He contributed significantly to the diffusion of the rococo in the German-speaking world as a painter of frescoes.

Carolus-Duran, Charles-Emile-Auguste
(1837 – 1917)
Carolus-Duran trained at first with teachers in his native Lille before moving to Paris in 1853. His work during his first period in Paris between 1853 and 1862 shows a debt to Courbet, Manet and the Realists. He went to Rome with a prize from Lille, returning to Paris in 1866. A visit to Spain between 1866 and 1868 confirmed his interest in Spanish art and he adopted a dark, Spanish manner of painting on his return. He became a successful painter of portraits and an influential teacher. In 1904, he was appointed Director of the French Academy in Rome.

Caroto, Giovanni Francesco
(c. 1480 – c. 1555)
Caroto was a pupil of Liberale da Verona but took his inspiration from Mantegna, Raphael and Giulio Romano. He worked mainly in Verona but also in Casale and Milan.

Casali, Andrea
(1705 – 1784)
A pupil of Francesco Trevisani, Casali began painting Grand Tour portraits in Rome around 1738. Encouraged by Sir Charles Frederick and his friends in Rome, he moved to England in 1741, staying briefly in Paris; he remained in London until 1766. Casali found a ready market for his elegant, suave style, painting portraits and mythological or allegorical decorative works for patrons as diverse as William Beckford, the Howard family and Sir Charles Frederick. He worked in Rome from 1766.

Ceccarelli, Naddo
(documented 1347)
Ceccarelli worked in Siena where he was a pupil of Lippo Memmi. Only one signed and dated work by him is known and few works have been attributed to him.

Cecco del Caravaggio (see Buoneri, Francesco)

Cerquozzi, Michelangelo
(1602 – 1660)
Cerquozzi spent his life in Rome, painting genre scenes, battles, small mythological and religious pictures and still lifes. He joined the Accademia di S. Luca in 1634. He seems to have been particularly close to the Spanish colony in Rome and included a number of Northern artists resident in the city among his friends. His links with Dutch and Flemish artists greatly influenced his own art.

Cerrini, Giovanni Domenico (Il Cavalier Perugino)
(1609 – 1681)
Having had some basic training with Gianantonio Scaramuccia, Cerrini is said to have travelled to Rome to work with Guido Reni. While this is chronologically unlikely, Cerrini certainly studied Reni's art and his early works also reveal his interest in the art of Lanfranco and of Andrea Sacchi. He painted altar-pieces for churches in Rome and in Ascoli Piceno, then moved to Florence c. 1656 to work for the Medici. Cerrini probably spent time in Perugia before returning to Rome in 1661, where he decorated the cupola of S. Maria della Vittoria, working in a manner closer to that of Carlo Maratta.

Cézanne, Paul
(1839 – 1906)
Cézanne's early works, dating from the 1860s, are crude and dark. In the 1870s, his palette lightened as he came under the influence of the Impressionists and landscape became a major interest. He never wholly adhered to the new naturalism of Monet and his friends and from 1883 onwards his work showed an increasing interest in simplified mass and structure. Between 1895 and 1906 he returned to the theme of bathers, painted on a monumental scale. He also continued to paint landscapes, figure subjects and still lifes.

Champaigne, Philippe de
(1602 – 1674)
Born in Brussels, Philippe de Champaigne moved to Paris with his master, Jacques Fouquières, in 1621 and became a French citizen in 1629. His portraits and religious paintings derive from Flemish examples but developed towards a greater simplicity. He became one of the most important painters of portraits working in 17th-century France. He became involved with the Jansenist movement in the 1640s and painted some of his finest works for the Jansenist convent at Port Royal.

Chardin, Jean-Siméon
(1699 – 1779)
Chardin was trained by history painters but specialized in still life and, from the 1730s onwards, in scenes of domestic life. In the 1730s, he received his first commissions for large decorative paintings for the royal residences of Bellevue and Choisy. Many of his still-life compositions are small-scale, relatively modest kitchen, game and fruit pieces. He played an active role in the affairs of the Academy.

Chintreuil, Antoine
(1814 – 1873)
Chintreuil moved from Bresse to Paris in 1838. He entered the studio of Delaroche in 1842. Corot, whom he met in about 1843, encouraged his interest in landscape painting. His first landscapes (c. 1846 to 1850) were mainly painted near Paris. In 1850 he settled at Igny in the valley of the river Bièvre where he painted woodland views and village scenes. He spent his last years in Tournelle-Septeuil in the valley of the Seine.

Chowne, Gerard
(1875 – 1916)
Chowne studied at the Slade School under Fred Brown and became a member of the New English Art Club. He painted landscapes, portraits and flowers. He was killed in the First World War.

Chrysolouras, Georgios
(active 1723 – 1761)
A Greek icon painter from Corfu, born into a family that had its origins in Constantinople. Signed icons by him survive and his principal works can be seen on Corfu and Leukas and in Ioannina.

Churchyard, Thomas
(1798 – 1865)
Churchyard painted the landscape of Suffolk where he lived and practised as a lawyer. He exhibited his work in London from 1830 to 1833. Several of his children were also painters.

Cignani, Carlo
(1628 – 1719)
Cignani was the leading painter in late 17th-century Bologna. He was taught by Albani but his style is closer to that of Guido Reni. In 1711, he became first president of the Accademia Clementina in Bologna.

Cipper, Giacomo Francesco (Il Todeschini)
(1664 – 1736)
The Austrian-born artist was based in Milan from at least 1696. Little is known of his training or patrons, although he began by specializing in still life before turning to genre painting. His favourite subjects were tavern and street scenes, with sturdy, good-humoured inhabitants of poverty-stricken surroundings. Cipper's work has affinities with that of Eberhard Keilhau and with the Bergamesque genre painters Antonio Cifrondi and Giacomo Ceruti.

Claesz., Pieter
(c. 1597 – 1660)
Claesz. was probably born in Flanders. He is first recorded at the baptism of his son, Nicolaes Berchem, in 1620 at Haarlem and remained there for the rest of his life. He is not known to have painted any subjects other than still lifes.

Claeuw, Jacques de
(1623 – after 1694)
Born in Dordrecht, Jacques de Claeuw became a member of the guild in The Hague in 1646. In 1649, he married a daughter of Jan van Goyen. Later, he is recorded as living in Leiden. Apart from a few domestic scenes, he painted still-life compositions of flowers, fruit and game as well as several *vanitas* paintings.

Claude Lorrain (Claude Gellée)
(c. 1604/5 – 1682)
Claude emigrated from his native Chamagne in the Vosges to Rome about 1613. Apart from a year in Nancy in 1625–6 and a period in Naples when he is said to have taken lessons from Goffredo Wals, he remained in Rome for the rest of his life. At first, he worked with Agostino Tassi whose compositions gave him a model for his earliest landscapes. In the late 1630s, he developed a type of ideal landscape in which mythological and historical figures occupy a grandiose countryside based on the scenery of the Tiber valley.

Clausen, Sir George
(1852 – 1944)
Born in London, the son of a Danish sculptor, Clausen studied at the South Kensington Schools. He visited Holland and Belgium in 1876 and exhibited his first work at the Royal Academy in the same year. He worked for a time in Paris and came strongly under the influence of Bastien-Lepage. He worked much out of doors and specialized in scenes of rural life; he also tackled other subjects, including nudes and still life.

Codde, Pieter Jacobsz.
(1599 – 1678)
Codde was born and worked in Amsterdam. He painted small-scale portraits and genre scenes in the manner of Anthonie Palamedes. In 1637, he completed a group portrait left incomplete by Frans Hals. Works with dates are known from 1625 to 1646.

Coghill, Sir Egerton Bushe
(1853 – 1921)
Son of the Irish painter, Sir John Joscelyn Coghill, Egerton studied at Dusseldorf and Paris. He painted figures and landscapes.

Colaert, Johannes
(?c. 1615 – after 1678)
There are two artists of this name. It is assumed that the author of the Ashmolean landscape is to be identified with the Joannes Colaert who worked in Amsterdam. He was a wine-merchant as well as a painter. For two or three years before 1678, he had been confined to the Dolhuis in Amsterdam on account of insanity.

Coldstream, Sir William Menzies
(1908 – 1987)
Coldstream studied at the Slade School of Art (1926–9) and became Slade Professor in 1949. In conjunction with Victor Pasmore and Claude Rogers, he founded the Euston Road School of Drawing and Painting in 1937. He was Official War Artist in the Middle East and Italy in 1943–5.

Collins, Cecil
(1908 – 1989)
Shortly after leaving the Royal College of Art in London where he studied from 1927–1931, Collins married his fellow student Elisabeth Ramsden; she became an important inspiration and his constant model. From 1951, he taught at the Central School of Arts and Crafts. His art has a visionary character and he worked in a number of different media.

Collins, Charles Alston
(1828 – 1873)
Collins came into contact with the Pre-Raphaelites at the Royal Academy Schools and shared their manner of painting in the 1850s. He was particularly close to Millais. Towards the end of the 1850s he gave up painting for writing. His brother was the novelist Wilkie Collins and he married a daughter of Charles Dickens.

Collinson, Robert
(1832 – after 1889)
The details of Collinson's life are obscure. He exhibited genre scenes at the Royal Academy exhibitions from 1858 to 1890.

Conder, Charles
(1868 – 1909)
Conder spent his early years in India and Australia. He went to Paris in 1890 and after 1897 lived mainly in England. He was a founder member of the Society of Twelve. His work includes landscapes and portraits but he is best known for his decorative watercolours on silk.

Connard, Philip
(1875 – 1958)
Connard worked at first as a house painter but took art lessons in the evening and won a scholarship to the Royal College of Art. He was associated with Wilson Steer. From 1916 to 1918, he worked as a war artist to the Royal Navy. He painted portraits and landscapes but also worked as an illustrator and designed textiles.

Constable, John
(1776 – 1837)
The landscape in and around East Bergholt in Suffolk where Constable was born gave him the subjects for many paintings. In 1799, he abandoned work in his father's watermills and entered the Royal Academy Schools. He exhibited at the Royal Academy in 1802 but did not become a full member until 1829. Apart from Suffolk, he worked regularly in Sussex, Hampshire and Salisbury. He came to notice chiefly with a series of large naturalistic river and farm scenes which included the *Haywain* exhibited in London in 1821 and, with greater success, in Paris in 1824.

Constable, Lionel
(1828 – 1887)
Lionel was the seventh and last child of John Constable. His father died when he was nine. In 1847–8, he attended Sass's Academy in Bloomsbury and sent his first landscape to the Royal Academy in 1849. His last painting at the Royal Academy appeared in 1855, after which he appears to have devoted himself to sailing and photography. Many of his paintings have been misattributed to his father.

Cooke, Edward William
(1811 – 1880)
Cooke was the son of the engraver, George Cooke. He was employed by the marine painter Clarkson Stanfield to make studies of rigging and was encouraged by Stanfield to take up painting in oils. He specialized in painting rivers and coastal scenes and travelled extensively.

Cooper, Abraham
(1787 – 1868)
Cooper was largely self taught. His early employment at a circus owned by his uncle gave him the opportunity to study horses and he became well known as a painter of sporting and battle pictures. He painted many historical battles as well as racehorses. John Frederick Herring Senior was one of his pupils.

Coorte, Adriaen
(active 1683 – in or after 1707)
Coorte probably worked in Middelburg. His earliest known works show birds in a landscape in a manner derived from the work of M. d'Hondecoeter, but his chief work consists of still-life paintings of fruit and vegetables, simply posed, sometimes including no more than a single species. He produced few flower paintings and his typical work is small in scale. Dated works range from 1683 to 1707.

Corbet, Edith
(*c.* 1850 – 1920)
Edith Ellenborough married the painter Arthur Murch and lived in Rome where she worked with Giovanni Costa, leader of the Etruscan School. After her second marriage to her fellow Etruscan, the painter Matthew Ridley Corbet, she settled in London. Like her second husband, she painted many views of Italy and scenes of Italian life.

Cornelis Cornelisz. van Haarlem
(1562 – 1638)
Cornelis van Haarlem ranks alongside Goltzius and Karel van Mander as one of the most important representatives of Mannerism in late 16th-century Haarlem. He was taught by Pieter Cornelisz. in Haarlem and by Gillis Coignet in Antwerp. On his return to Haarlem, he received several important commissions from the city and formed the 'Haarlem Academy' with his colleagues.

Corot, Jean-Baptiste-Camille
(1796 – 1875)
Corot's teachers, Achille-Etna Michallon and Jean-Victor Bertin, gave Corot a lasting taste for the Italianate tradition in landscape painting. In 1825 he set out for a first trip to Italy during which he painted numerous studies out of doors. He mainly exhibited larger studio compositions lightly idealized. He also painted a few decorative landscapes for interiors. In the 1850s, his work became more generalized and his colours became more monochromatic. He placed limited value on his small studies but they were taken as a model by many of his younger contemporaries.

Correggio (Antonio Allegri)
(*c.* 1489 – 1534)
Correggio seems to have been influenced by Mantegna in his first works but added to Mantegna's austere art a softness inspired by Leonardo and the rich colour of the Bolognese. In about 1580, he moved to Parma where he was commissioned to paint the ceiling of a room in the Benedictine convent of S. Paolo. In his decorative treatment of illusory space, he showed his recent study of the work of Raphael and Michelangelo in Rome. This was followed by commissions to decorate the dome and apse of S. Giovanni Evangelista (1520–4) and the dome, apse and choir vault of Parma cathedral. The illusionism he employed in these frescoes inspired many later artists.

Cortona, Pietro da (Pietro Berettini)
(1596 – 1669)
Pietro da Cortona trained under Andrea Commodi in Cortona. Following his move to Rome, he received important commissions from the Barberini family, including his most famous work, *The Triumph of the Barberini Family*, painted with extreme illusionism on the ceiling of their Roman palace. He broke off work on the ceiling in 1637 to undertake work in Florence but returned to finish the ceiling in 1639. He returned to Florence in 1641 to finish work which he had begun in the Pitti Palace and undertake a series of new ceilings. From 1647 until his death, he worked again in Rome.

Costa, Giovanni (Nino)
(1826 – 1903)
Costa's early training was at the Collegio Bandinelli in Rome, which he abandoned in 1845 to work in the studios of Coghetti and Podesti. A volunteer under Garibaldi in 1848–9, he continued to be active in the politics of the Risorgimento. As a landscape painter first in the Castelli Romani, then in Tuscany and Umbria, he met numerous foreign artists, developing friendships with George Heming Mason and Frederic Leighton and later exhibiting at the Royal Academy. In 1883–4 a group of Italian and English artists with Costa at their head formed the Etruscan School, favouring a type of landscape imbued with sentiment.

Courbet, Jean-Desiré-Gustave
(1819 – 1877)
Courbet tried a number of subjects before achieving success in 1849 with a rural interior scene inspired by his home in Ornans. He returned to the formula with the *Burial at Ornans* exhibited in 1850. In the mid-1850s he began to paint many landscapes inspired by the countryside of the Franche-Comté. He also painted a number of nudes and seascapes. Following a fine for his involvement in demolishing the Vendôme column in Paris during the Commune, he fled to Switzerland where he painted his last works, sometimes with the help of studio assistants.

Cowden, William
(active 1798 – 1820)
Cowden was an amateur artist. He is said to have been a follower of the genre painter George Morland and exhibited three sea-pieces at the Royal Academy between 1798 and 1820.

Cox, David
(1783 – 1859)
In his youth, Cox worked as a scene painter in Birmingham and London where he received lessons from John Varley. He lived in London from 1829 to 1841 before settling in Harborne, near Birmingham, from where he made annual expeditions into Wales. He is chiefly known as a watercolourist but also worked in oils and wrote a number of treatises on landscape painting in watercolour.

Crespi, Giovanni Battista (Il Cerano)
(*c.* 1575–6 – 1632)
Crespi worked mainly in Milan. From 1586 to 1595 he was in Rome where he became a friend of Cardinal Federico Borromeo, who was his chief patron and with whom he returned to Milan. The Cardinal appointed him head of the painting section of the Accademia Ambrosiana and he played an important role in the artistic regeneration of the city. In 1602 he was commissioned to supply four paintings celebrating the life of Carlo Borromeo for Milan cathedral. In 1610, he added a further six. In addition to painting, he was also a sculptor, engraver, architect and writer.

Crespi, Giuseppe Maria
(1665 – 1747)
Crespi was trained in Bologna. He specialized in genre paintings, lit with striking contrasts of light and shadow, somewhat in the manner of the Carracci. He had a number of distinguished pupils, including Piazzetta and Pietro Longhi.

Crespi, Luigi
(1708 – 1779)
A portraitist, priest, art-dealer and art historian, Luigi was the elder of two sons of Giuseppe Maria Crespi who were assistants in the studio. His early works have been confused with those of his father, whose influence on him was considerable. Luigi developed a more distinctive style as a result of his travels to Venice, Trieste, Vienna and Dresden in 1752–3. Amongst his writings on Bolognese art the *Vite de' Pittori Bolognesi non descritte nella Felsina Pittrice*, Rome 1769, stands out for its polemical tone.

Critz, Emanuel de
(1608 – 1665)
Emanuel de Critz was baptized in London in 1608. He was presumably trained by his father, John de Critz, who was born in Antwerp but settled in London. It is not certain what Emanuel painted apart from a signed and dated portrait of Sir John Maynard of 1657.

Critz, Thomas de
(1607 – 1653)
The younger son of John de Critz, Thomas was baptized in London in 1607 and died there in 1653. He is recorded as undertaking decorative work and restoration for the Crown from 1629 to 1637.

Crivelli, Carlo
(c. 1430–5 – 1494)
The son of a painter, Carlo was already an independent master in Venice by 1457. His art has affinities with the work of Jacopo Bellini and Antonio Vivarini, while he was strongly influenced by Paduan masters, notably Francesco Squarcione. By 1468 Carlo was in Zara and seems to have settled in Ascoli Piceno in the Marches by 1469. He painted some important large polyptychs, now dismembered.

Crivelli, Vittorio
(c. 1444–9 – 1501–2)
Vittorio was probably a younger brother of Carlo Crivelli. His earliest work reveals a debt to Antonio Vivarini but his later work is closer to that of Carlo Crivelli whom he followed to Dalmatia and then to the Marches.

Crome, John
(1768 – 1821)
Crome was born and died in Norwich. He was apprenticed to a coach and sign painter and specialized in painting landscape, influenced by the work of the Dutch painters of the 17th century. He was a founder member of the Norwich Society of Artists in 1803. He was also an etcher and drawing-master.

Dadd, Richard
(1817 – 1886)
Dadd studied at the Royal Academy Schools and became a member of the sketching club, The Clique, with Egg, Phillip, O'Neil and Frith. From 1842–3, he travelled with Sir Thomas Phillips in Italy, Greece, the Middle East and France. On his return to England he began to show symptoms of insanity. In 1843, he murdered his father and spent the rest of his life in confinement. The art from his years of insanity is intense and detailed and deals largely with scenes of fantasy and memories of his travels.

Daintrey, Adrian Maurice
(1902 – 1988)
Painter, illustrator and writer, Daintrey studied at the Slade School in London and then at the Académie de la Grande Chaumière in Paris. He shared his first exhibition with Paul Nash in 1928. He served in the Second World War as a camouflage artist and as art critic for *Punch* magazine.

Daubigny, Charles-François
(1817 – 1878)
Daubigny was given his first lessons in painting by his father, Edmé-François, who, like his son, was a landscape painter. He styled himself a pupil of Corot and was attracted to Corot's atmospheric sketches painted out of doors. In 1857, he launched a floating studio to enable him to paint more directly from nature. He studied effects of light on water chiefly through tone and his palette remained relatively limited.

Daumier, Honoré
(1808 – 1879)
Daumier was a professional and prolific lithographer who seems to have taken up painting for his own pleasure. His caricature, are the work of an accomplished draughtsman with a keen understanding of human physiognomy. He began to contribute political cartoons to the weekly magazine *Caricature* in 1830 and was imprisoned in 1832 for libelling the French king. Most of his paintings probably date from after 1860. Many of these take up the themes of his lithographs.

Decker, Cornelis
(before 1623 – 1678)
Little is known of Decker's life which seems to have been spent in Haarlem. He painted mainly landscapes but also several peasant interiors. There are dated paintings from 1649 onwards. From these, one may surmise that he belonged to a group of painters in Haarlem who followed Jacob van Ruisdael.

Dedreux-Dorcy, Pierre-Joseph
(1789 – 1874)
Dedreux-Dorcy was taught in the studio of Pierre Guérin in Paris where he came into contact with Géricault and the artists of the Romantic generation. He painted portraits, historical scenes and landscapes and worked in pastel as well as in oil.

Delamotte, William Alfred
(1775 – 1863)
Delamotte was born in Weymouth into a family of French refugees. He studied at the Royal Academy Schools and became Drawing Master at Sandhurst Military Academy. He painted views of his travels in Europe in oil and watercolour as well as views in Wales and near Oxford. He also illustrated topographical books.

de l'Ange, Jacques
(documented 1631–2 – 1642)
Jacques de l'Ange was trained by Jan Cossiers. He entered the Antwerp Guild in 1631–2 and is recorded in Antwerp until 1642 with a break in 1639 when he went to Italy. His work was influenced by Cossiers as well as by Jordaens, Matthias Stom and the Utrecht followers of Caravaggio.

Delff, Cornelis Jacobsz.
(1570/1 – 1643)
Cornelis Delff was born in Gouda where he studied with his father, Jacob Willemsz. Delff. He then worked with Cornelis Cornelisz. in Haarlem in about 1595 but was back in Delft by 1610. Delff was one of the earliest painters of still life. In 1637 he painted an overdoor of fruit for Prince Frederik Hendrik's palace in Rijswijk.

Deodato Orlandi
(active 1284 – 1332)
A painter from Lucca, Deodato signed and dated a number of works and died before 1339 when his wife remarried. Nothing is known of his training. His early work, however, displays a close study of Berlinghieri and Cimabue, either through direct knowledge of their paintings or through the work of another artist. His art then reveals some acquaintance with the new naturalism of Giotto. Deodato painted many frescoes, altar-pieces and devotional images, carrying out important work at the Cathedral and Camposanto in Pisa.

Derain, André
(1880 – 1954)
Derain studied engineering in Paris before becoming a painter. He took part in the Fauve Salon of 1905 with Matisse and Vlaminck but his interest in the work of Cézanne and the Old Masters caused him to part company with his colleagues. His work in the 1920s is marked by his return to the classical tradition.

Deverell, Walter Howell
(1828 – 1854)
Deverell was born in Charlottesville in the USA where his father was a schoolmaster. He came to England with his father in 1829 and studied at Henry Sass's drawing school in London where he met Rossetti and also shared a studio with him. He worked in a manner close to the work of the Pre-Raphaelites with whom he was associated. He died young and exhibited only four works at the Royal Academy.

Devis, Arthur B.
(1711 – 1787)
Devis was born in Preston in Lancashire and was taught portrait painting by Peter Tillemans. He specialized in small-scale conversation pieces and modest full-length portraits. In later years, he took up glass painting.

Devis, Arthur William
(1762 – 1822)
Arthur William Devis, the son and pupil of Arthur Devis, was born in London and entered the Royal Academy Schools in 1774. He accompanied an expedition to the East Indies as draughtsman in 1782 and found success as a painter in India. Apart from portraits, he painted a series of works illustrating the arts and manufactures of Bengal. On return to England he painted portraits and a few history pictures.

De Wilde, Samuel
(1748 – 1832)
De Wilde's father was a Dutch joiner who had settled in London by 1748. Samuel was apprenticed to learn joinery with his godfather but left after five years in 1769 to study at the Royal Academy Schools. He exhibited portraits and some paintings of *banditti* at the Society of Artists and at the Royal Academy but became a specialist in painting theatrical portraits. He was introduced to the genre while illustrating John Bell's *British Theatre* in 1790. Subsequently, he exhibited theatrical portraits at almost every exhibition at the Royal Academy from 1792 to 1821.

De Wint, Peter
(1784 – 1849)
After abandoning plans to become a doctor, De Wint was apprenticed to John Raphael Smith. Following his release from his apprenticeship, he took lodgings near John Varley who probably encouraged him to work in watercolour. His early work owes much to Varley and Girtin but he soon developed his own broad, confident sweep and a sense of deep warm colour. He travelled much, especially in Lincolnshire, in the area of the Trent, the Lake District and Wales. He also painted in oils and contributed topographical illustrations to a number of publications. Illness contracted during a sketching expedition in Hampshire in 1843 affected his last years.

Diest, Adriaen van
(1655/6 – 1704)
Van Diest was born in The Hague. He was a landscape and animal painter and etcher. By March 1678, he had moved to England where he became a specialist in painting decorative landscapes.

Disher, Eve
(1894 – 1991)
Eve Disher studied at the Hornsey School of Art. After the First World War she travelled widely. For many years, she shared a studio with Vera Cuningham, whose work influenced her own style. She worked mainly in gouache and specialized in painting portraits, flower compositions and scenes of city life.

Dobson, William
(1611 – 1646)
Dobson was the most distinguished painter of portraits in England in the years immediately after the death of van Dyck, although he also painted subject pictures. About sixty paintings by him are known, mostly dating from 1642 to 1646 when he was painter to the court of Charles I in Oxford. Following the capture of Oxford by the Parliamentarians in 1646, he is believed to have returned to London where he was imprisoned for debt and died.

Dobuzhinsky, Mstislav Valerianovich
(1875 – 1957)
From 1899 to 1901, Dobuzhinsky studied in Munich and completed his training in the Academy of St Petersburg. He became president of the 'World of Art' group, founded by Diaghilev and like several of the artists involved in the group, became a designer for the theatre. In 1920, he left Russia and lived by turn in England, France and the USA, where he continued his career as a designer for the theatre. He also illustrated books.

Dodgson, John
(1890 – 1969)
Dodgson's mother was an amateur painter and his uncle, Campbell Dodgson, was Keeper of the Department of Prints and Drawings in the British Museum. He was a keen Italophile and collector, mainly of contemporary art. From 1946 to 1950, he taught at the Camberwell School of Arts and Crafts and from 1950 to 1958, at Chelsea School of Art. Much of his work was destroyed in a fire in his studio in 1964.

Dolci, Carlo
(1616 – 1686)
Dolci painted many religious subjects as well as portraits. He was based in Florence and rarely left the city. His trip to Innsbruck in 1675 to paint Claudia Felice de' Medici when she married the emperor Leopold was a rare exception. His religious paintings, smoothly painted, have a remarkable intensity and were much admired in his lifetime.

Domenichino (Domenico Zampieri)
(1581 – 1641)
After studying with Denys Calvaert and with Ludovico Carracci in Bologna, Domenichino went to Rome in 1602 and joined the group of artists working with Annibale Carracci at the Palazzo Farnese. He received a number of major decorative commissions in Rome and in the neighbourhood, including work at S. Luigi dei Francesi and S. Andrea della Valle. In 1631, he moved to Naples and worked in the cathedral but was forced to leave in 1634 because of the hostility of local artists.

Dossi, Dosso (Giovanni Luteri)
(1486/7 – 1541/2)
Dossi is first recorded in 1512 at Mantua. By 1514, he was in Ferrara where he spent the rest of his life. He combined the colour and landscape effects of Titian and the Venetians with a personal element of fantasy. In addition to mythological, allegorical and religious compositions, portraits and frescoes, Dossi designed court entertainments, tapestries and other work for the court at Ferrara.

Downman, John
(1750 – 1824)
Downman was a pupil of Benjamin West. His speciality was chalk and watercolour portraits but he also worked in oil. He spent some time in the early 1770s in Italy and in 1777–8 was in Cambridge where he began making small portrait drawings. From 1779 to 1804 he was in London. He moved to Exeter when he married in 1806; he returned to London after his wife's death in 1808 and settled in Chester in 1817.

Downton, John
(1906 – 1991)
Downton studied the history of art at Cambridge before entering the Slade School in London. He travelled widely. The detailed realism of his work and his use of tempera reflected an interest in the art of the Italian Quattrocento.

Drost, Willem
(*c.* 1630 – after 1680)
Drost is said to have been a pupil of Rembrandt. This must have been around 1650. He seems to have been in Italy at some point between 1654 and 1663, staying in Rome and Venice. He is last recorded in 1680 in Rotterdam.

Drummond, Malcolm
(1880 – 1945)
Drummond studied at the Slade School and then at the Westminster School of Art under Sickert. He became a member of the Camden Town Group in 1911. After teaching at the Westminster School, he settled at Moulsford in Berkshire in 1932 and he spent the rest of his life there.

Dubois, Guillam
(*c.* 1610 – 1680)
Dubois is first recorded when entering the Haarlem guild in 1646. In 1652, he travelled with Cornelis Bega, Theodor Helmbrecker and Vincent Laurensz. van de Vinne to Germany and returned to Haarlem in 1653 where he remained for the rest of his life. He belonged to the group of landscape painters who followed Jacob van Ruisdael in Haarlem.

Duck, Jacob
(*c.* 1600 – 1667)
Duck was born in Utrecht where he spent much of his life. He was probably a pupil of Joost Cornelisz. Droochsloot.

Dughet, Gaspard (Gaspard Poussin)
(1615 – 1675)
Dughet was born in Rome. He was the brother-in-law and pupil of Nicolas Poussin and devoted his life to painting somewhat idealized landscapes based on the Roman Campagna. His frescoes illustrating the lives of Elijah and Elisha (1647–51) painted in the church of S. Martino ai Monti in Rome, led to several important commissions for decorative landscapes for the palaces of Rome.

Du Jardin, Karel
(1622 – 1678)
Du Jardin painted portraits, history paintings and landscapes with an Italianate setting of a kind made popular by Berchem. He spent his last years in Italy and had probably been there earlier, to judge by the subjects of his paintings and landscape etchings.

Dupont, Alfred Gainsborough
(1754 – 1797)
In 1772, Dupont was apprenticed to his uncle, Thomas Gainsborough, for seven years. He enrolled at the Royal Academy Schools in 1775. He remained as Gainsborough's assistant until the older artist died in 1788. He inherited his uncle's studio and contents and continued to produce a few portraits. His manner of painting portraits, genre pictures and landscapes is very similar to Gainsborough's.

Dupressoir, François-Joseph
(1800 – 1859)
Dupressoir exhibited at the Paris Salon from 1824 to 1842. His most important work consisted of a series of battle paintings commissioned for the Musée Historique de Versailles. His work otherwise consists of marine subjects, rustic scenes and landscapes painted in the Ile de France and Normandy. He exhibited two views of Edinburgh in 1834.

Dyck, Sir Anthony van
(1599 – 1641)
Born in Antwerp, van Dyck was taught by Hendrik van Balen and worked as an assistant to Rubens. He was in England 1620–1 when he was appointed court painter to James I. In 1621, he left England and went to Italy where he remained until 1627. From 1632 until his death, he was based again in London. He was engaged as court painter to Charles I in this period and was chiefly employed as a painter of portraits.

Eagles, John
(1783 – 1855)
Eagles was a clergyman and amateur painter. He took holy orders at Wadham College, Oxford, and subsequently held a number of livings, mostly at Bristol where he began as curate of St Nicholas and where he died in 1855. He was a member of Danby's Sketching Club and an etcher. He was also an art critic.

Earles, Chester
(1821 – 1905)
Earles exhibited at the Royal Academy from 1842 to 1863. He painted portraits, religious pictures and subjects from Spenser, Shakespeare, Milton, Tennyson and Keats. In 1864, he emigrated to Australia.

Eeckhout, Gerbrand van den
(1621 – 1674)
Eeckhout spent his life in Amsterdam. In the later 1630s, he seems to have been a pupil of Rembrandt, whose influence is evident in his early works. He painted religious subjects as well as genre scenes, portraits and a few landscapes. He also designed and etched pattern books for goldsmiths.

Egg, Augustus Leopold
(1816 – 1863)
Egg was born in London where he attended Henry Sass's drawing school before entering the Royal Academy Schools in 1836. In the late 1830s, he was a founder member of The Clique, a sketching club which included Frith and Dadd. His first subjects were Shakespearean and historical but from 1858, he turned to the type of contemporary themes which also attracted the Pre-Raphaelites in the same decade. In 1863, he travelled to Africa for his health but died in Algiers.

Elford, Sir William
(1747 – 1837)
Elford was born in Devon and exhibited views of Devonshire at the Royal Academy from 1774 to 1837. He became a baronet in 1800 and was an amateur painter in oils and watercolours

Elinga, Pieter Janssens
(1623 – before 1682)
Pieter Janssens was born in Bruges. He went to Amsterdam in 1653 and seems to have settled there. He was a musician (probably a violinist) as well as a painter of still life and of interiors. His banquet pieces were at one time mistaken for those by Willem Kalf.

Elliger, Ottmar
(1633 – 1679)
Elliger was born in Gothenburg. He is said to have been taught painting by Daniel Seghers in Antwerp, although his earliest work shows a debt to Jacob Marrel, who worked in Frankfurt. He probably worked in Copenhagen in the mid-1650s and moved later to Amsterdam. In 1666 he was in Hamburg. He was appointed court painter to the Elector of Brandenburg in 1670. He painted portraits and still-life compositions, mostly of fruit and flowers.

Enslin du Plessis, Hercules
(1894 – 1978)
Enslin du Plessis was born in Standerton in the Transvaal. In the First World War, he was employed as correspondent for the South African press in the Middle East. He took up painting seriously in his thirties and exhibited his work extensively in England from the late 1920s.

Es, Jacob Foppens van
(active *c.* 1616 – 1666)
In 1616 van Es entered the Guild of St Luke in Antwerp where he spent his entire life, although he is said to have been in Rome in 1638. He seems to have worked exclusively as a painter of still life.

Esselens, Jacob
(*c.* 1627 – 1687)
Esselens was born in Amsterdam and was based there all his life. He travelled extensively in England, Scotland, France and Italy. As well as painting, Esselens was also a silk merchant.

Etchells, Frederick
(1886 – 1973)
Etchells studied at the Royal College of Art in London and later in Paris, where he was attracted by the work of the Fauves and Cubists. His work was included in Fry's second Post-Impressionist exhibition. He also participated in the Vorticist movement and contributed drawings to *Blast*. In the 1930s, he abandoned painting for architecture.

Etty, William
(1787 – 1849)
Etty was born in York and entered the Royal Academy Schools in 1807. He continued to work in the life class throughout his career and specialized in subjects of the nude figure. His mature style, which is characterized by rich Venetian colour, was formed during a period in Italy in 1822–3. He retired to York in 1848.

Faed, Thomas
(1826 – 1900)
Born in Kirkudbright in Scotland, Faed taught himself by copying engravings and working out of doors. After his father's death, he entered the Art School of the Board of Manufactures in Edinburgh where his fellow pupils were W. Q. Orchardson and Erskine Nicol. In 1852, he moved to London, where he made his reputation as a painter of Scottish life, specializing in scenes of poverty and misfortune.

Fantin-Latour, Ignace-Henri-Jean-Théodore
(1836 – 1904)
Fantin-Latour was born in Grenoble, the son of a portrait painter. From 1850 to 1856 he studied at the Petite Ecole de Dessin in Paris. He met François Bonvin in 1853 and shared with Bonvin and the artists in his circle an interest in painting scenes from contemporary life without the anecdotal content common in much genre painting at the time. He also painted and exhibited a number of group portraits of contemporary writers and artists. Flower painting was a major preoccupation from the early 1860s onwards. Musical, literary and allegorical themes, treated in a vague, suggestive manner, represent a second strand in his art. This tendency, first seen in his lithographs of the early 1860s, became more common after 1870.

Farthing, Stephen Frederick Godfrey
(b. 1950)
Farthing studied at St Martin's School of Art (1969–73) and at the Royal College of Art (1973–6). His teaching career began as lecturer at the Canterbury College of Art (1977–9). He was Ruskin Master in Oxford from 1990 until 2000, when he left to take up the position of Executive Director of the New York Academy of Art in Manhattan.

Ferrari, Francesco Bianchi
(active 1481 – d. 1510)
Bianchi Ferrari's known paintings are not numerous. His work combines influences from Bologna and Ferrara. He worked in Modena and is said to have been Correggio's first master.

Filippi, Camillo
(*c.* 1500 – 1574)
Camillo Filippi belonged to a family of painters much employed by the Este court in Ferrara. He worked as an assistant to Dosso Dossi and was influenced by Garofalo and Gerolamo da Carpi, with whom he collaborated on occasion.

Fisher, Joseph
1796 – 1890
Joseph Fisher was an etcher and topographical painter. He was apprenticed to the Oxford engraver J. Whessell and worked for a time in London before returning to Oxford in the early 1830s. In 1844 he was appointed the first Keeper of the University Galleries in Oxford and remained in this post until his death.

Fisher, Joseph H. Vignoles
(1864 – 1945)
J.H.Vignoles Fisher's work appeared at the Royal Academy from 1884 until 1939. He exhibited views of the Stour valley, the Mendips and elsewhere in England, interspersed with views of France. After the First World War, he lived in Sussex and regularly exhibited scenes of rural Sussex.

Fisher, William Mark
(1841 – 1923)
Born in Boston, USA, where he painted portraits and figure subjects. In 1861, he went to Paris and took lessons with Charles Gleyre. After a period in Boston, he moved to England in 1872 and showed for the first time at the Royal Academy summer exhibition in 1897. Most of his work consists of animal subjects and landscapes.

Flandrin, Hippolyte-Jean
(1809 – 1864)
Hippolyte and his brother Paul entered the Ecole des Beaux-Arts in Lyon in 1826, and transferred in 1829 to the studio of Ingres in Paris. Following success in the Rome Competition in 1832, Hippolyte spent from 1833 to 1838 in Rome. His work in the chapel of St John in the church of St Séverin in Paris, completed in 1841, resulted in a series of commissions for murals, of which the biblical series in St Germain-des-Prés, begun in 1842, and the procession of saints in St Vincent-de-Paul (1849–53) are the best-known.

Flandrin, Jules
(1871 – 1947)
Jules Flandrin was a pupil of Gustave Moreau from 1895 to 1898 and a close member of the group of artists from Moreau's studio who later formed the Nabis and the Fauves. From 1906, his interest in Fauve colour diminished. Contact with Maurice Denis encouraged him to develop more stylized effects. In the period shortly before the First World War, his work began to show the increased interest in classical order and simplified form which are characteristic of much of his art from 1919 onwards.

Fletcher, William Teulon Blandford
(1858 – 1937)
At the age of sixteen, Fletcher went to study drawing at the South Kensington School of Art, where he stayed for four years. From 1879 to 1883, he studied at the Académie Royale in Antwerp, making regular trips during this period to work in Britanny. Around 1885, on return to England, he was one of the founding members of the group of artists who worked in the Cornish village of Newlyn. He subsequently worked in various rural locations and spent the last years of his life (1915–37) in Abingdon.

Fontebasso, Francesco
(1707 – 1769)
Born in Venice, Fontebasso studied for a time under Sebastiano Ricci. In the early 1760s, he was nominated painter to the court at St Petersburg. He worked mainly in Venice and was appointed president of the Venetian Academy in 1768. He painted religious and mythological subjects and also engraved a set of fantastic images after his own drawings.

Forain, Jean-Louis
(1852 – 1931)
In the early 1870s, through his friendship with Degas, Forain met Manet and the Impressionists who influenced his use of colour and his choice of subject matter. Degas, in particular, introduced him to the themes of the race-course and the ballet. His career as an illustrator began in 1876 and he made his reputation as a social and political cartoonist. About 1900, his colour became subdued and he began to paint biblical and law-court themes. Towards the end of his life he returned to the theme of dance.

Fortescue-Brickdale, Eleanor
(1872 – 1945)
Fortescue-Brickdale studied at the Crystal Palace School of Art and at the Royal Academy Schools. In 1896, she won a £40 prize for designing a lunette for the Royal Academy dining-room. She made her debut at an Academy exhibition the following year. Apart from painting historical and invented subjects, she designed stained glass and illustrated many books. Her work belongs to the last phase of English Pre-Raphaelitism.

Francesco de' Franceschi
(active 1443 – 1468)
Various documents attest to Francesco's activity in Venice, including a painting, now lost, for S. Samuele in 1448. He made his will in 1468 but may still have been alive in 1473. His only secure surviving work is a polyptych of *St Peter and Saints* (Museo Civico, Padua) made in 1447 and other works have been attributed to him on that basis. Francesco was very close in his manner of painting and his figure types to Giambono and to Antonio Vivarini.

Francia, Francesco (Francesco di Marco Raibolini)
(*c.* 1450 – 1517/18)
Francia was born into an ancient Bolognese family which had fallen on hard times. He was apprenticed to a jeweller called Francia whose name he later adopted, and became a successful jeweller and engraver of medals. He was probably taught painting by Lorenzo Costa with whom he collaborated. The earliest dated picture by Francia is from 1494. Subsequently, be became a very prolific and distinctive painter of altar-pieces for the churches of Bologna.

Franciabigio (Francesco di Cristofano)
(1484 – 1525)
Fanciabigio worked in Florence where his style was influenced by Albertinelli, Piero di Cosimo, Fra Bartolomeo and Andrea del Sarto. He collaborated with Andrea del Sarto in the cloisters of SS Annunziata and the Scalzi in Florence.

Frélaut, Jean
(1879 – 1954)
Frélaut was born in Grenoble. At the age of ten, his father retired from the army to the family property near Vannes in Morbihan. In 1897, he entered the Ecole des Beaux-Arts and studied under Fernand Cormon. Frélaut retained strong links with Vannes, where he settled in 1919 and remained until his death. The district round Vannes provided him with many subjects for his paintings, including landscapes, scenes of rural and marine life. As well as painting, he was an etcher and illustrator of books.

Freud, Lucian
(b. 1922)
Born in Berlin, Freud arrived in England at the age of ten and took British citizenship seven years later. He studied at the Central School of Art, the East Anglian School of Art and Goldsmiths' College School of Art and had his first one-man show in 1944. His work, which is characterized by an uncompromising directness, has been exhibited widely. In 1993, he was appointed to the Order of Merit.

Friesz, Emile-Othon
(1879 – 1949)
Friesz was born in Le Havre. In 1905, he associated with Matisse and the Fauves but soon after introduced a more structured order into his paintings under the influence of Cézanne. A visit to Italy in 1909 encouraged him to paint a series of Arcadian themes between 1908 and 1911 which combined modernist tendencies with a sense of the classical past.

FRITH, WILLIAM POWELL
(1819 – 1909)
Frith went to Henry Sass's drawing school before entering the Royal Academy Schools. Most of his early works illustrated literary and historical subjects. He was a founding member of the sketching club, The Clique, with Dadd and Egg. In 1854 he exhibited the first of three panoramic compositions of modern life, illustrating the seaside, the racecourse and the railway station. Both the paintings and the prints after them were extremely popular.

FROST, WILLIAM EDWARD
(1810 – 1887)
Frost went to Henry Sass's drawing school on the advice of Etty. He exhibited at the Royal Academy from 1836 to 1879. He won the gold medal of the Academy in 1839 for a painting of *Prometheus Bound* and another prize in the competition for the Houses of Parliament in 1843. This encouraged him to abandon portraits and become a painter of sylvan and bacchanalian mythology. His choice of subjects and his manner of painting both derive from Etty.

FRY, ROGER
(1866 – 1934)
After graduating from Cambridge, Fry studied painting and art history in Paris and Italy. He became art critic of the *Athenaeum* in 1901 and a founder of *The Burlington Magazine* in 1903. From 1905 to 1910 he was curator of paintings at the Metropolitan Museum in New York. In 1906, his discovery of Cézanne made him a champion of the modern French art which he introduced to London in 1910 and 1912 with his Post-Impressionist exhibitions. His own paintings are tamer than the modern work which he promoted. In 1913, he founded the Omega Workshops, which produced domestic ware and furnishings with the help of members of the Bloomsbury Group.

FULLEYLOVE, JOHN
(1847 – 1908)
Fulleylove was a genre and topographical painter who travelled in Greece, Italy and the Holy Land in search of subjects. He was also a book illustrator.

GAINSBOROUGH, THOMAS
(1727 – 1788)
Born in Sudbury, Suffolk, Gainsborough went to London *c.* 1740 and trained with Gravelot. He subsequently lived and worked, mainly as a portrait and landscape painter, in Suffolk, Bath and London. In 1768 he was a founder member of the Royal Academy. As his rival Sir Joshua Reynolds noted, he was the most versatile and naturally accomplished artist in 18th-century England.

GALLIS, PIETER
(1633 – 1687)
The birthplace of Gallis is unknown. He is reported to have lived in Enkhuizen before moving to Hoorn, where he was the manager of the local pawn-shop and where he died. He had the same occupation at Purmurend from 1679 to 1683. Little else is known of his life; his few dated works are restricted to the period 1667–8 to 1673. Still-life paintings of fruit and flowers were his main subjects.

GANDOLFI, GAETANO
(1734 – 1802)
First listed at the Accademia Clementina, Bologna, in 1751, Gaetano won prizes in the sculpture class. Antonio Buratti, a Venetian merchant, commissioned him to make a series of drawn copies of notable altar-pieces in Bologna and invited him to Venice in 1760, where he spent a year and clearly was impressed by the work of Piazzetta and Tiepolo. He was also open to wider European interests, visiting London in 1787. He became *Direttore di figura* at the Accademia Clementina in 1765.

GANDOLFI, UBALDO
(1728 – 1781)
A prize-winning student, Ubaldo was taught painting at the Accademia Clementina in Bologna by Felice Torelli and subsequently Ercole Graziani the younger (1688–1765), while he studied sculpture and anatomy under Ercole Lelli (1702–1766). His first independent commission dates from 1748 and he provided religious and secular paintings for a discerning local market. From his student days he was a protégé of the Marchese Gregorio Casali. Ubaldo was *Direttore di figura* at the Accademia from 1761 and *Principe* in 1772. He and his brother Gaetano were outstanding draughtsmen.

GARDINER, CLIVE
(1891 – 1960)
Born in Blackburn, Gardiner studied at the Slade School of Fine Art and the Royal Academy Schools and worked as a painter and poster designer. He was head of Goldsmiths' College School of Art from 1929 to 1957.

GARSTIN, NORMAN
(1847 – 1926)
Born in Ireland, Garstin studied in Antwerp and Paris (with Carolus-Duran) and later settled in Cornwall. He was a leading member of the Newlyn School of painters and specialized in scenes from everyday life

GARZI, LUIGI
(1638 – 1721)
Born in Pistoia, Garzi was a pupil of Andrea Sacchi and was trained in the grand classical tradition. He particularly admired the austere late work of Guido Reni. However he was also interested in the more dynamic Baroque style of Lanfranco and was responsive to the colour and brilliance of leading Neapolitan artists such as Giordano and Solimena. Garzi was an important figure in the Roman Academy.

GEROLAMO DA SANTACROCE
(*c.* 1485 – 1556)
Gerolamo was one of a Bergamesque family of artists which may have originated in Istria. He was a pupil of Gentile Bellini in Venice, subsequently working with Giovanni Bellini; his first datable paintings are from 1516. Gerolamo was also interested in the art of Cima da Conegliano and of Palma Vecchio. He painted in a conservative, eclectic manner for a range of patrons in Venice and the Veneto, running a busy workshop with his son Francesco.

GÉRÔME, JEAN-LÉON
(1824 – 1904)
Gérôme studied in Paris with Delaroche and Gleyre and became one of the most successful of Salon painters. His subjects were mainly classical, orientalizing and historical. He was also a sculptor and a teacher at the Ecole des Beaux-Arts.

GERTLER, MARK
(1891 – 1939)
The son of Jewish immigrants, Gertler was brought up in poverty in East London, before going to the Slade School of Fine Art. There he won acclaim as a painter and began a passionate relationship with Dora Carrington. He achieved social success in artistic and literary circles and was a regular visitor to Lady Ottoline Morrell at Garsington, near Oxford. He was elected to the 'London Group', founded by Gilman, of which Bomberg and Wyndham Lewis were prominent members, and developed a forceful and personal style. Depressed by poor health and intermittent success as a painter, he committed suicide in 1939.

GHIRLANDAIO, DAVIDE
(1452 – 1512)
Davide was assistant and then partner to his brother, Domenico, maintaining this important Florentine workshop after his death and training Domenico's son, Ridolfo Ghirlandaio. Davide painted frescoes and panel paintings, but was particularly involved in mosaic designs. His manner of painting owes much to his more celebrated brother.

GHIRLANDAIO, DOMENICO
(1449 – 1494)
Initially trained as a goldsmith, Ghirlandaio was one of the leading artists of late 15th-century Florence, counting the young Michelangelo amongst his pupils. He worked in Rome on frescoes for the Sistine Chapel in 1481 and at S. Gimignano and Pisa. In Florence he enjoyed presigious commissions such as the vivid narrative frescoes of the Tornabuoni chapel at S. Maria Novella. Ghirlandaio could orchestrate large compositions with complex architectural settings in a grand, harmonious manner.

GIAMBONO (MICHELE GIOVANNI BONI)
(*c.* 1400 – 1462)
Giambono was an artist of high repute whose opinion was sought on public works including Donatello's equestrian statue in Padua. He settled in Venice before 1420, working in a late Gothic style in which he was influenced by Jacobello del Fiore and by the art of Gentile da Fabriano and Pisanello, who both visited Venice. Giambono's paintings are characterized by their decorative detail, including rich Venetian textiles and their sinuous, often slightly melancholy figures. He designed some of the mosaics in the Mascoli Chapel, S. Marco, *c.* 1443–50.

GIAQUINTO, CORRADO
(1703 – 1766)
A pupil of Nicola Maria Rossi in Naples, Giaquinto was strongly influenced by Giordano and Solimena. He went to Rome in 1723, where he developed a more classicizing style, with a lighter palette and a decorative approach. He developed a high reputation as a painter of frescoes, altar-pieces and mythological or historical subjects. Giaquinto worked at the court of Turin in the 1730s and was invited to Spain by Fernando VI in 1753, where his frescoes, tapestry designs, paintings and other work proved enormously influential for a generation of Spanish artists including Goya. He returned to Naples to recover his health in 1761.

GILLIG, JACOB
(*c.* 1636 – 1701)
Gillig was born in Utrecht and lived there all his life. He seems to have begun painting in his late twenties. In 1661 he married a daughter of the marine painter Adam Willaerts. He may have been a pupil of the fish-painter Willem Ormea. Reportedly he first worked as a merchant and then became a warden of the prison in Utrecht Town Hall (near the fish market). Although he was quite prolific, he never registered as a master in the Utrecht guild. Apart from occasional portraits, he specialized in still-life paintings with fish. There are dated works from 1663 to 1694.

GILMAN, HAROLD
(1876 – 1919)
Gilman was born in Somerset and studied for a year at Oxford before going to Hastings School of Art and then to the Slade School of Fine Art. In 1907 he met Sickert and became a member of the Fitzroy Street Group; then in 1911 he was a founder-member of the Camden Town Group. He died of influenza.

GINNER, CHARLES ISAAC
(1878 – 1952)
Ginner was born and brought up in France. He settled in London in 1910 and was a founder-member of the Camden Town Group in 1911. He worked as a war artist in both World Wars and painted many pictures of Hampstead scenes.

Giordano, Luca
(1632 – 1706)
A celebrated Baroque artist, Giordano was immensely versatile and prolific. Trained probably with Jusepe de Ribera in Naples, he first went to Rome in 1652 and was inspired by Pietro da Cortona and by the art of Veronese and Rubens. Giordano worked in Florence and Venice as well as Rome and Naples, developing a highly-charged, luminous Baroque style, although he readily produced imitations of the work of other artists. The speed at which he worked earned him the nickname of 'Luca fa presto'. He worked at the court of Charles II in Spain from 1692 to 1702 and had a strong impact on both Neapolitan and Spanish art.

Giorgione (Giorgio da Castelfranco)
(*c.* 1477/78 – 1510)
Although Giorgione was celebrated in his brief lifetime, little of his work is documented. He was a highly original artist who created a new genre of poetic, even mysterious subjects, rich in atmospheric effects and luminosity. He also painted religious works and portraits. Since the mid-16th century he has been viewed as the artist who transformed Venetian painting, developing a sensuous, tactile manner of using oil paint which had an enormous impact on the next generation of artists such as Titian, Paris Bordone and Schiavone.

Giotto di Bondone
(1266/67? – 1337)
A highly original artist and an important teacher, Giotto was praised by Dante, Petrarch and other writers, ensuring his fame beyond his native Tuscany. He was particularly celebrated for his innovative naturalism. Giotto worked at the Arena chapel, Padua, *c.* 1305, and other important frescoes are in the Bardi and Peruzzi chapels in Santa Croce, Florence. He has been traditionally associated with the decoration of the Basilica at Assisi. Giotto also worked in Rome, Naples and Rimini, but much of his output has been lost.

Giovanni Antonio da Pesaro
(documented 1461 – 1511)
Little is known of this artist, who signed his name on two major religious commissions of 1461 and 1463. He seems to have trained in Emilia in a late Gothic manner. He was a conservative artist who studied Venetian paintings by Jacobello del Fiore and other artists of the early 14th century in churches in Pesaro and used them as a source for his figures.

Giovanni di Paolo
(*c.* 1399 – 1482)
A refined, conservative artist, Giovanni worked mainly in Siena and produced important book and manuscript illustrations as well as altar-pieces and small devotional panel paintings. He developed a sophisticated, expressive manner that often deliberately recalls the art of the great Sienese masters of the previous century. He also admired painters such as Gentile da Fabriano and Fra Angelico and sculptors including Jacopo della Quercia and Donatello.

Gogh, Vincent van
(1853 – 1890)
Van Gogh was born in Groot-Zundert, Holland. On leaving school, he was apprenticed to the art dealers Goupil in The Hague and subsequently tried his hand at both teaching and preaching. Around 1880 he decided to become a painter of peasant life. He moved to Paris in 1886 and felt the impact of the work of the Impressionists, such as Seurat, Monet and Pissarro. In 1888 he moved to Arles in the south of France, where he was later joined by Gauguin. At the end of that year he began suffering bouts of mental illness, but continued painting. He shot himself in July 1890 and died two days later. His numerous letters, especially to his brother Theo, provide an extensive commentary on his work.

Gore, Spencer Frederick
(1878 – 1914)
Gore studied at the Slade School of Fine Art and was a founder member both of the Fitzroy Street Group and, in 1911, of the Camden Town Group. He moved to Richmond, Surrey, in 1913 but died of pneumonia in the following year.

Gosse, Sylvia
(1881 – 1965)
Sylvia Gosse, daughter of the critic Sir Edmund Gosse, studied at the Saint John's Wood School of Art and the Royal Academy Schools. She was encouraged as a painter and her style was influenced by Walter Sickert. She was a member of the London Group.

Gotlib, Henryk
(1890 – 1966)
Gotlib was born in Kraków, Poland. He studied painting in Kraków, Vienna and Munich and became a member of the Polish avant-garde 'Formist' movement. After extensive travels, he settled in England in 1939 and joined the London Group.

Gowing, Sir Lawrence Burnett
(1918 – 1994)
Gowing studied painting with William Coldstream at the Euston Road School. He had a many-sided career as painter, teacher, curator, broadcaster and art historian, including periods as Deputy Director of the Tate Gallery and Slade Professor of Fine Art at University College, London.

Goya y Lucientes, Francisco de
(1746 – 1828)
A pupil of Francisco Bayeu in Madrid, Goya travelled to Italy and was interested in Roman and Neapolitan art. By 1776 he was working on tapestry designs for the Spanish court, becoming painter to the king in 1786. A severe illness in 1792 left him permanently deaf. He was active at court and in the Madrid Academy, painting religious works, portraits and scenes of his own invention, especially modern narrative subjects. A superb draughtsman and printmaker, Goya responded with wit and fervour to the radical upheavals in politics and society around the turn of the century. He lived in exile in Bordeaux from 1824.

Goyen, Jan van
(1596 – 1656)
Van Goyen was born in Leiden and trained as a painter there and with Esaias van de Velde in Haarlem. He moved to The Hague in 1632 and lived there for the rest of his life. He travelled extensively in the Netherlands and Germany, producing numerous landscapes of the places he had visited, as well as town views and seascapes. Among his pupils was Jan Steen, who married his daughter.

Graham, Thomas Alexander Ferguson
(1840 – 1906)
Graham trained at the Trustees' Academy in Edinburgh. He was one of the more prominent and successful of Scottish painters of the Victorian period, in some degree influenced by the Pre-Raphaelites. He specialized in scenes of fishing and of country life and also painted portraits.

Granacci, Francesco
(1469/70 – 1543)
Granacci had a close association with Michelangelo, as they were students together in Ghirlandaio's workshop and in the Medici sculpture garden; he later assisted him briefly on the Sistine Chapel ceiling. However, Granacci, who made his career in Florence, was particularly interested in the art of Fra Bartolomeo and Raphael and developed a lively, graceful manner of painting.

Granet, François-Marius
(1775 – 1849)
Granet was the son of a mason in Aix-en-Provence. Having shown precocious talent for drawing, he went to Paris in 1796 and was for a period a pupil of David's. From 1802 until 1824 he lived in Rome, where he painted numerous atmospheric views of ruins and sombre church interiors. In 1826 his friend Auguste de Forbin appointed him a curator in the Louvre. His collection and the contents of his studio are preserved in the Musée Granet in Aix.

Grant, Duncan
(1885 – 1978)
Grant studied art in London, Paris and Italy and from 1910 carried out a number of decorative painting projects, some in collaboration with Vanessa Bell and Roger Fry. In 1911 he exhibited with the Camden Town Group and in 1912 moved to Brunswick Square in Bloomsbury, London, becoming part of the Bloomsbury Group. From 1913 to 1919 he was involved, with Fry and Bell, in the Omega Workshops in Fitzroy Square, producing ceramics, furniture and textiles. In 1919 he became a member of the London Group. During the Second World War he was an Official War Artist and he continued painting into the 1970s.

Greaves, Walter
(1846 – 1930)
The son of a Thames boatman, Greaves and his brother Henry were studio assistants to Whistler from 1863. He developed a style close to Whistler's and made paintings and etchings of scenes on the Thames and in Chelsea. He was given a one-man exhibition at the Goupil Galleries in 1911, but died in poverty as a Poor Brother of the Charterhouse.

Greenham, Peter
(1909 – 1992)
Greenham was born in Streatham, South London and read English at Oxford, before attending the Byam Shaw School of Art from 1936 to 1939. He later became a much-loved teacher at the Royal Academy Schools and, in 1964, Keeper of the Royal Academy.

Grimaldi, Giovanni Francesco
(1606 – 1680)
A pupil of Ludovico Carracci, Grimaldi went to Rome *c.* 1626 and was closely associated with Pietro da Cortona in the 1630s. While he was involved in architectural design, Grimaldi was mainly a landscape painter, working in fresco and oil and producing a variety of landscape drawings and etchings, often based on the work of the Carracci.

Gryeff, Adriaen de
(*c.* 1670 – 1715)
De Gryeff was the son of the Leiden painter Jacques de Claeuw. In 1687 he became a master in Ghent, but he worked mainly in Antwerp and Brussels. In 1690 he lived in Brussels, but after 1694 he lived in Antwerp, where in 1699 he became free master of the Guild of St Luke. He died in Brussels.

Guardi, Francesco
(1712 – 1793)
Francesco was the son of an artist and his brothers Gian Antonio and Niccolò were also painters, although little is known of the latter's work; his sister Cecilia married Giambattista Tiepolo. While Francesco painted some religious subjects, he is best known for his views of Venice, his paintings of festivities and his *capricci* or fantasy landscapes and views. He was praised in his lifetime for his 'magical effects' in paint. Guardi's views of Venice were especially popular with British visitors.

Guercino (Giovanni Francesco Barbieri)
(1591 – 1666)
A long and prolific career gave Guercino lasting international renown. Although he studied with Benedetto Gennari, he was largely self-taught, being greatly impressed by the art of the Carracci (particularly Ludovico), Scarsellino and Guido Reni. His early works are remarkable for their naturalism, boldness of design and handling, and dramatic chiaroscuro. After a sojourn in Rome in 1621–3 he developed a more classicising mode with dignified, monumental figures and a delicate handling of paint. He settled in Cento after the death of Pope Gregory XV, moving to Bologna in 1640. Guercino was an inventive and powerful draughtsman who made many independent drawings as well as preparatory studies and whose drawings were sought after by collectors in his own lifetime.

Guigou, Paul
(1834 – 1871)
Guigou trained as a notary in Apt and Marseilles, but also practised as a painter and exhibited Provençal landscapes in a style influenced by the Barbizon school. In 1862 he gave up notarial work, moved to Paris and became a full-time landscape painter, exhibiting regularly at the Salon.

Guillaumin, Jean-Baptiste-Armand
(1841 – 1927)
Guillaumin grew up in Moulins and made himself a painter despite family opposition. In 1863 he exhibited at the Salon des Refusés and in the 1870s and 1880s at the Impressionist exhibitions. He was mainly a landscape painter, working for periods alongside Pissarro and Cézanne, and remained an influential figure in the development of French painting into the twentieth century.

Gwynne-Jones, Allan
(1872 – 1982)
Gwynne-Jones was born in Richmond, Surrey and trained as a lawyer. From 1913 he exhibited with the New English Art Club. His studies at the Slade School of Fine Art were interrupted by army service in the First World War, but resumed in 1919. From 1923 to 1930 he was Professor of Painting at the Royal College of Art and afterwards taught at the Slade School, including its period of evacuation to Oxford during the Second World War. He painted mainly landscapes, still lifes and portraits and also made some etchings.

Hall, Christopher
(b. 1930)
Hall trained at the Slade School of Fine Art from 1950 to 1954. He is a painter of landscapes and people and especially of buildings and is best known for his scenes of English and Italian towns. He lives in Newbury.

Hals, Dirck
(1591 – 1656)
Born in Haarlem, he was the younger brother of Frans Hals, who may have been his master. Apart from at least two stays in Leiden, in 1641–2 and 1648–9, Dirck Hals was active, mainly as a painter of merry company scenes, in Haarlem, where he died.

Hals, Nicolaes (Claes)
(1628 – 1686)
He was born in Haarlem, a son and perhaps a pupil of Frans Hals. He became a member of the Haarlem guild in 1656. His rare paintings, genre and landscape, show the influence of Jacob van Ruisdael rather than that of his father. He died in Haarlem.

Hambling, Maggi
(b. 1945)
Hambling was born in Suffolk. She trained at Ipswich and Camberwell and from 1967 to 1969 at the Slade School of Fine Art. In 1980–1, she was the first Artist-in-Residence at the National Gallery. She lives and works in London.

Hamilton, Edward
(documented 1805–6)
The only record of Hamilton's work is the landscape given by him to the Bodleian Library in 1805. He was probably an amateur artist.

Hamilton, Gawen
(*c.* 1697 – 1737)
Hamilton was born in Scotland, but from *c.* 1730 made his career in London. He was best known as a painter of 'conversation pieces' and was in his time considered to be one of the main rivals of Hogarth in the genre.

Hanneman, Adriaen
(?1604 – 1671)
Hanneman was born in The Hague and was a pupil of Anthonis van Ravesteyn. In 1626 he went to England, where he worked with Cornelis Janssens van Ceulen and was much influenced by van Dyck. In 1637 he returned to The Hague, where he entered the guild in 1640. He was patronised by the House of Orange, as well as by exiled members of the English court. He died in The Hague.

Hannot, Johannes
(1633 – 1684)
Hannot was born in Leiden, where he became a member of the guild in 1650 and where he was buried in 1684. He was a still-life painter, especially of fruit, inspired by Jan Davidsz. de Heem. His only known dated paintings are of 1654 and 1668. His known *oeuvre* barely exceeeds fifteen paintings. He was also a wine-merchant and most of his still-life paintings include at least one glass of wine.

Harcourt, George Simon, 2nd Earl
(1736 – 1809)
George Harcourt, who succeeded as 2nd Earl Harcourt in 1777, was M.P. for Saint Albans 1749–77 and subsequently Master of the Horse to the Queen, as well as an amateur landscape painter. The family seat was at Nuneham near Oxford.

Harmar, Fairlie (Viscountess Harberton)
(1876 – 1945)
Fairlie Harmar was born in Weymouth and studied at the Slade School of Fine Art, becoming a painter of portraits, figure subjects and landscapes. She married the 7th Viscount Harberton in 1932.

Harpignies, Henri-Joseph
(1819 – 1916)
Harpignies was born to a prosperous background in Valenciennes and showed early talent both in drawing and in music. He spent some years working in the family business before taking up a career as an artist. In 1849 he went to Italy and discovered the landscapes around Rome and Naples. He was a prolific painter of landscape oils in the tradition of Corot and enjoyed success at the Salon and elsewhere. He also made prints and watercolours.

Hassall, Joan
(1906 – 1988)
Joan Hassall was the daughter of the artist John Hassall. While a student at the Royal Academy Schools she discovered wood-engraving, which was to become her main medium, finding its expression in a long series of illustrated books from 1936 onwards. She lived for many years in Malham, North Yorkshire.

Havell, William
(1782 – 1857)
Havell was the son of a drawing master in Reading. He became a landscape painter in oils and watercolours and was a founder member of the Society of Painters in Watercolours. From 1817 to 1825 he lived in India. He was an early experimenter in photography. He died in London.

Haydon, Benjamin Robert
(1786 – 1846)
Haydon was born in Plymouth and went to London in 1804, studying at the Royal Academy Schools. He painted ambitious historical and biblical subjects, as well as more modest genre scenes. He was single-minded and uncompromising as an artist and as a person and an inveterate and vocal opponent of the Royal Academy. He committed suicide after an exhibition he had organized of his own work at the Egyptian Hall, Piccadilly, proved a failure. His diary and autobiography are vivid documents of English Romanticism.

Hayet, Louis
(1864 – 1940)
Hayet was born at Pontoise and self-taught as a painter. After meeting Camille and Lucien Pissarro, he moved to Paris in 1887. From 1889 he was associated with the Neo-Impressionist group. He experimented with wax encaustic painting and was much concerned with theories of colour, but enjoyed little commercial success as a painter. He spent his later years painting stage scenery and writing.

Hayter, Sir George
(1792 – 1871)
Hayter was the son of the miniature-painter Charles Hayter. He studied at the Royal Academy Schools and was successful as a history and portrait painter. In 1815 he was appointed Painter of Miniatures to Princess Charlotte and in 1837 Portrait and History Painter to Queen Victoria, whose State Portrait he painted.

Heda, Willem Claesz.
(1594 – 1682)
Heda was born in Haarlem and in 1631 became a member of the guild there, in which he subsequently held various offices. He was a still life and occasional history painter. Together with Pieter Claesz., he developed the so-called 'monochromatic' style. He died in Haarlem.

Heem, Cornelis de
(1631 – 1695)
Cornelis de Heem, the son and pupil of Jan Davidsz. de Heem, was born in Leiden; in early childhood he moved with his parents to Antwerp, where in 1660–1 he became a member of the Guild of St Luke. In 1667 he stayed briefly at Utrecht, probably moving on to Amsterdam. In 1676 he moved from Ijsselstein to The Hague, where he was a member of the *Confrerie Pictura* until at least 1687. Some time around 1690, he returned to Antwerp. He painted flower pieces, fruit and banquet pieces, often combined. Dated works are known between 1654 and 1690, but dates after 1665 are very rare.

Heem, David Cornelisz. de
(1663 – 1701/14)
David de Heem was born in Antwerp, the son of Cornelis de Heem. He moved with his parents to Holland and was probably trained by his father at The Hague. He married there in 1690. In 1693–4 he entered the Guild of St Luke in Antwerp. Between 1697 and 1701 he is recorded in The Hague and in 1714 his widow claimed she had lived in the same house there for twenty-six years. The date of his death is unknown. The only paintings by him known are still lifes of fruit and flowers; no dated works are known.

Heem, Jan Davidsz. de
(1606 – 1684)
De Heem was born in Utrecht, the son of a musician from Antwerp. In 1625 he moved to Leiden and is recorded there until 1631. His teacher is unknown, but many of his early works show the influence of the Utrecht painter Balthasar van der Ast. By 1635 de Heem had settled in Antwerp, becoming a member of the guild in 1636. In 1665 he was again living in Utrecht; he may have spent time there in the previous years, though he was not a member of the Utrecht guild until 1669. Following the French invasion in 1672, he returned to Antwerp, where he died. He was one of the most successful, original and influential still life and flower painters of the 17th century.

Heemskerk, Egbert van
(1634/5 – 1704)
Van Heemskerk was born in Haarlem and a pupil of Pieter de Grebber and a follower of Adriaen Brouwer. He was active in Holland until 1674, in which year he may have moved to England. He presumably lived for a time in Oxford around 1687, when he painted *The Oxford Election* (Corporation of Oxford). There is some uncertainty about his later biography, since there were apparently two similarly-named artists working in England at the end of the 17th century.

Hennekyn, Paulus
(1611 – 1672)
Hennekyn was born in Antwerp but moved to Amsterdam with his family when he was five months old. He married in Amsterdam in 1636 and remained there until his death. He painted still lifes and portraits influenced by Bartholomeus van der Helst.

Herkomer, Sir Hubert von
(1849 – 1914)
Hubert Herkomer was born in Bavaria, but the family settled in Southampton in 1857. He trained at the South Kensington Schools and achieved success as a painter of social realism, historical subjects, portraits and landscapes. He was Slade Professor of Fine Art at Oxford from 1885 to 1894. He adopted the 'von' in his name after being raised to the German nobility in 1899. He also engraved, wrote music and designed for the stage.

Hervier, Louis-Adolphe
(1818 – 1879)
Hervier was born and died in Paris. He was taught by his father, who was a miniature-painter and had been a pupil of David's. He painted in oils and watercolours and his work was praised by Corot, but he was especially successful as an etcher.

Hill, Derek Arthur
(1916 – 2000)
Hill was born in Hampshire and studied stage design in Munich, Paris and Vienna from 1933 to 1935. He decided to become a painter in 1938. He was primarily a portrait painter, but also worked as a stage-designer, exhibition organizer and writer and was Art Director of the British School at Rome. He lived for many years in Donegal, Ireland.

Hillier, Tristram Paul
(1905 – 1983)
Hillier was born in China and studied art at the Slade School of Fine Art under Tonks and at the Westminster School of Art under Meninsky. He lived for periods in France and Italy and exhibited in Paris as well as in London. He painted landscapes, marine and architectural subjects and still lifes.

Hitchens, Ivon
(1893 – 1979)
Hitchens was born in London and travelled widely before attending St John's Wood School of Art and the Royal Academy Schools. He painted landscapes, still lifes and some abstracts, and was particularly influenced by Cézanne. After his London home was bombed in 1940, he moved to Midhurst, Sussex and took the Downland landscape as his principal subject.

Hoare, William
(*c.* 1707 – 1792)
Hoare was born in Suffolk and studied under Giuseppe Grisoni, who was working in England in the 1720s. Hoare accompanied Grisoni back to Rome in 1728 and continued his studies as a pupil of Imperiali. By 1739, he had settled in Bath where he remained for the rest of his life. He had a successful career as a portrait painter in the city, particularly before Gainsborough's arrival in 1759.

Hodgkin, Eliot
(1905 – 1987)
Hodgkin was born in Purley, Surrey and studied at the Byam Shaw School and the Royal Academy Schools. He subsequently taught at Westminster School of Art and wrote several books. He is best known for his small, meticulous tempera still lifes.

Hoffmann, Carl, the Younger
(1838 – after 1900)
Hoffmann was born in Paris and brought up in Rome. He studied in Düsseldorf from 1863 to 1866. He was back in Rome from 1866 to 1877, then worked in Berlin and Dresden. He was again in Rome in 1891–2. He was still alive in Dresden around 1900.

Hogarth, William
(1697 – 1764)
Hogarth was born in London. He was apprenticed to the silver engraver Ellis Gamble and throughout the 1720s worked as an engraver. In 1729 he married the daughter of Sir James Thornhill. In the 1730s and 1740s he painted several popular series of satirical paintings and made a successful business of publishing engravings after his paintings, as well as practising as a portrait painter. In 1753 he published his theoretical work *The Analysis of Beauty*. In 1757 he was appointed Sergeant-Painter to the King. He died in London and was buried at Chiswick.

Holbein, Hans, the Younger
(*c.* 1497 – 1543)
Hans Holbein the Younger was the son of the painter, Hans Holbein the Elder, who taught both Hans the Younger and his brother Ambrosius in his workshop in Augsburg. The younger Hans arrived in Basle as a journeyman in 1517 and was admitted to the guild in 1519. As Basle became embroiled in the troubles of the Reformation, he went to France in 1524 and then to England in 1526 on the recommendation of Erasmus. He painted a number of portraits in London before returning to Basle in 1528. Again, the religious atmosphere made his life difficult and he returned to England in 1532 where he was employed in particular by the German merchants in London. By 1536, he had entered the service of Henry VIII, for whom he painted mural decorations, miniatures and court portraits and designed jewellery and metalwork.

Holl, Francis Montague
(1845 – 1888)
Holl studied at the Royal Academy Schools and exhibited at the Academy from 1864. In 1870 his *No Tidings from the Sea* was bought by Queen Victoria. From 1877 he enjoyed much success as a portrait painter.

Holland, James
(1799 – 1870)
Holland was born in Burslem, in the Potteries, of a family of china-painters. He went to London in 1819 and changed from painting flowers to landscapes. His early watercolours were much influenced by Bonington. He came to specialize in views of European scenes, especially of Venice.

Holmes, Sir Charles John
(1868 – 1936)
Holmes was born in Preston and educated at Eton and Brasenose College, Oxford. From 1903 until 1909 he was joint-editor of the newly founded *Burlington Magazine*. He was Director of the National Portrait Gallery from 1909 to 1916 and of the National Gallery from 1916 to 1928. He painted landscapes and industrial scenes in an individual style and also wrote several books on art and art history.

Holroyd, Sir Charles
(1861 – 1917)
Holroyd was born in Leeds. He studied and subsequently taught at the Slade School of Fine Art. He exhibited at the Royal Academy from 1885 to 1895 and was also an accomplished etcher. He became the first Keeper of the Tate Gallery and was Director of the National Gallery from 1906 to 1916.

Horton, Percy Frederick
(1897 – 1970)
Horton was born in Brighton. Fom 1916 to 1918 he was imprisoned as a Conscientious Objector. He attended Brighton School of Art before going on to the Central School of Art (1918–20) and the Royal College of Art (1922–5). He taught at Rugby School and the Royal College of Art and from 1949 to 1964 was Master of the Ruskin School of Drawing in Oxford.

Houasse, René-Antoine
(1644/5 – 1710)
A pupil and collaborator of Charles Lebrun, Houasse became a senior figure in the official art world, being prominent in the Paris Academy and becoming Director of the French Academy at Rome in 1699. He enjoyed prestigious commissions for altar-pieces, portraits and decorative schemes at the Tuileries and Versailles.

Houghton, Arthur Boyd
(1836 – 1875)
Houghton studied at Leigh's Art School and became a very successful book illustrator, working for *The Graphic* and making illustrations for books such as Dalziel's *Arabian Nights* (1865). His oil paintings are mainly of contemporary genre scenes.

Houthuesen, Albert
(1903 – 1978)
Houthuesen was born in Amsterdam and moved to London in 1912. In 1923 he won a scholarship to the Royal College of Art. He lived by teaching at the Working Men's College and elsewhere. He painted a wide range of subjects, in oils and later in acrylics.

Howard, George James, 9th Earl of Carlisle
(1843 – 1911)
George Howard, who succeeded as 9th Earl of Carlisle in 1889, was an amateur topographical painter in oils and especially in watercolours, having been taught by Legros and by Giovanni Costa. He had a wide circle of literary and artistic friends including Tennyson, Leighton, Morris and Burne-Jones. He was a long-serving and influential Trustee of the National Gallery.

Hughes, Arthur
(1832 – 1915)
Hughes was born in London and in 1847 went to the Royal Academy Schools. In 1850 he became an associate of the Pre-Raphaelites, although he did not become a member of the Brotherhood. In 1857 he took part in the project to decorate the Oxford Union. Apart from his work as a painter, he was a prolific book illustrator.

Hughes, Malcolm
(1920 – 1997)
Malcolm Hughes was born and studied art in Manchester, then attended the Royal College of Art from 1946 to 1950. He taught art at Bath Academy, at Chelsea College of Art and at the Slade School of Fine Art. His abstract paintings and constructions were exhibited at the Institute of Contemporary Arts, the Victoria & Albert Museum, the Tate Gallery and elsewhere.

Hughes, William
(1842 – 1901)
William Hughes was a pupil of George Lance and William Henry Hunt. He was a still-life painter and lived in London and Brighton. He exhibited at the Royal Academy between 1866 and 1901. His major work was a set of five large bird pictures in Lord Calthorpe's house in Grosvenor Square.

Hulst, Frans de
(*c.* 1610 – 1661)
Hulst was born in Haarlem. He was a landscape painter in the style of Jan van Goyen and Salomon van Ruysdael.

Hulton, William Stokes
(1851 – 1921)
Hulton exhibited at the Royal Academy betwen 1882 and 1889, including scenes in France and in Venice. He died in Venice.

Hunt, Alfred William
(1830 – 1896)
Hunt was the son of the painter Andrew Hunt and brought up in Liverpool. He went to Corpus Christi College, Oxford, where he was a fellow from 1853 to 1861. He exhibited at the Royal Academy from 1854, where his landscapes in the Pre-Raphaelite manner were championed by Ruskin. He married in 1861 and moved to London in 1862. He painted landscapes in oils and was a prolific watercolourist.

Hunt, William Holman
(1827 – 1910)
Holman Hunt was born in London and entered the Royal Academy Schools in 1844. There he became a close friend of Millais and then Rossetti; in 1848 these three artists formed the Pre-Raphaelite Brotherhood. In 1853 he painted *The Light of the World*, which was purchased by Thomas Combe and later presented to Keble College, Oxford. After the dissolution of the Brotherhood, Hunt continued to paint in accordance with its principles. In 1905 he published *Pre-Raphaelitism and the Pre-Raphaelite Brotherhood.*

Inchbold, John William
(1830 – 1888)
Inchbold was born in Leeds. He went to London in his teens and worked for the lithographers Day and Haghe. He entered the Royal Academy Schools in 1847. About 1852 he began painting landscapes in the Pre-Raphaelite style, which were admired by Ruskin. He spent much of his later life abroad. He wrote poetry and was a friend of poets such as Swinburne.

Ingalton, William
(1794 – 1866)
Ingalton was the son of a Surrey shoemaker. He lived for a long time at Eton, where he painted domestic and rural scenes and made lithographs of Eton. He exhibited at the Royal Academy between 1816 and 1826. About 1826 he ceased to practise as an artist and became an architect and builder. He spent the last years of his life in the Isle of Wight.

Isabey, Louis-Eugène-Gabriel
(1803 – 1886)
He was the son of the painter Jean-Baptiste Isabey and brought up at the heart of the Paris art world. He began as a painter of landscapes, but later painted genre scenes, marine subjects and large history paintings, becoming one of Louis-Philippe's principal court painters. He also made topographical watercolours and lithographs.

Isenbrandt, Adriaen
(active 1510 – d. 1551)
Isenbrandt may have been born in Antwerp and was a master in Bruges in 1510. He is said to have been trained by Gerard David. Contemporary documents indicate he became prosperous and successful, but none of the pictures attributed to him are signed or documented.

Israels, Isaac
(1865 – 1934)
Isaac was the only son of Jozef Israels. He studied at The Hague Academy alongside George Breitner, who influenced his style. After 1886, when he moved to Amsterdam, he painted almost exclusively modern subjects. He died in The Hague.

Israels, Jozef
(1824 – 1911)
Israels was born into a traditional Jewish family in Groningen. In 1845 he moved to Amsterdam, studying at the Royal Academy and then under J.W. Pieneman. Between 1845 and 1847 he was in Paris, where he learnt to paint chiefly historical scenes and portraits. From 1855 he turned to painting the scenes of village scenes and family life for which he is best known. In 1871 he settled in The Hague and was considered the leading member of The Hague School.

Ivanov, Alexander Andreyevich
(1806 – 1858)
Ivanov was born in St Petersburg and trained at the Academy of Arts in the city. From 1830 to 1857 he lived mainly in Rome, where there were several other Russian artists active and where he was a friend of Nikolay Gogol. He was a man of intense religious fervour and the foremost religious painter in 19th-century Russia. His principal work, *Christ Appearing to the People* (Tretyakov Gallery, Moscow), took him twenty years to paint and was finally exhibited in 1857. He died in St Petersburg.

Jackson, Francis Ernest
(1872 – 1945)
Jackson was born in Huddersfield in Yorkshire. He was apprenticed to a firm of printers as a lithographer. In 1895, he went to Paris with help from his employer to study at the Académie Julian and at the Ecole des Beaux-Arts. In 1900, he settled in London where he promoted interest in lithography as an art form. He taught lithography at Croydon, Camberwell, Chelsea and especially at the Central School of Arts and Crafts, where he also gave lessons in life drawing. Between 1926 and 1940, he was principal of the Byam Shaw School. In addition to his work as a lithographer, he painted in oil and tempera and designed posters.

Jackson, John
(1778 – 1831)
Jackson was born in Lastingham in the North Riding of Yorkshire. At the age of nineteen, he turned to miniature painting and was taken up by the Earl of Carlisle and by Sir George Beaumont who employed him as a copyist. He was elected to the Royal Academy in 1817. In 1819, he went to Rome with Sir Francis Chantrey. Following his return to England he became an established painter of portraits.

Jacomb-Hood, George Percy
(1857 – 1929)
Jacomb-Hood studied at the Slade School before going to Paris. He exhibited the first of many genre paintings at the Royal Academy in 1879. He was also a prolific portrait painter and contributed illustrations to *The Graphic* and *The Illustrated London News.* His work for *The Graphic* took him to India for the Durbar in 1902 and he returned again in 1905 and 1911.

Jacque, Charles-Emile
(1813 – 1894)
In the 1830s and 1840s Jacque worked as an illustrator in Paris and London. Following a visit to Burgundy in 1838, he discovered a love of the countryside and rustic themes became the subject of his etchings and his first paintings. He made contact with Jean-François Millet in the 1840s and went with him to the village of Barbizon in 1849 during an outbreak of cholera in Paris. In the following years, Jacque divided his time between Paris and his two studios at Barbizon and Montrouge, painting barnyard scenes, sheep and cattle. He also became involved in a succession of speculative but unprofitable commercial ventures.

Jamieson, Alexander
(1873 – 1939)
Born in Glasgow, Jamieson studied art in Glasgow at the Haldane Academy where he won a scholarship to Paris. He visited Spain in 1911 and served in France during the First World War. He painted landscapes, town scenes and portraits. His early work has affinities with the work of the Glasgow colourists.

Jeaurat, Etienne
(1699 – 1789)
A pupil of Nicolas Vleughels, with whom he went to Rome in 1724, Jeaurat was received into the Paris Academy in 1731. He had a successful career at the Academy and was a noted history painter, while also painting portraits and still lifes. Jeaurat is best known for his genre scenes of Parisian street life (which have affinities with Hogarth's prints) and domestic interiors, many of which were reproduced in engravings.

John, Augustus Edwin
(1878 – 1961)
John trained at the Slade School in London from 1894 to 1898 where he acquired a fluency in drawing and a taste for French art; Puvis de Chavannes was an early influence on his work. He found the subject matter of his first paintings among the Romany gypsies for whom he felt a close affinity. After the First World War, he became a prolific and successful painter of portraits.

Jones, Ernest Yarrow
(1870 – 1951)
Jones was born in Liverpool and studied at the Westminster School of Art and at South Kensington. He also went to the Académie Julian and the Atelier Colarossi in Paris. He was a sculptor and painter who divided his time between Hythe in Kent and Paris.

Jones, George
(1786 – 1869)
Jones went to the Royal Academy Schools in 1801 but his studies were interrupted by service in the army, chiefly in the Peninsular War and later with the army of occupation in Paris. When he returned to painting, he took his subjects mainly from military themes and in particular from the campaigns in which he had served. He was Librarian of the Royal Academy from 1834 to 1840 and Keeper from 1840 to 1850.

Jones, Thomas
(1742 – 1803)
Jones studied under Richard Wilson from 1763 to 1765 and became a landscapist in Wilson's manner. He exhibited Welsh and Italian views in London, based upon his travels. From 1776 to 1783 he was in Italy, visiting Rome and Naples which he recorded in a series of oil-sketches. These sketches were painted in the open air with a directness, simplicity and luminosity which are not found in his larger studio compositions.

Jongkind, Jean-Berthold
(1819 – 1891)
Jongkind studied in The Hague under Andreas Schelfhout. In 1846, he moved to Paris where he became associated with the painters of the Barbizon School. His bright, atmospheric marines and river scenes were admired by Boudin and Monet but, unlike them, he habitually painted in the studio, using watercolour studies as his models. His later career was disrupted by alcoholism and increasing mental instability, ending in madness.

Jonson, Cornelius
(1593 – 1661)
Cornelius Jonson (Cornelis Janssens van Ceulen) was born in London of Flemish parents. He may have been trained in portrait painting in the Netherlands but the earliest of his many identified works are of English sitters. His first portraits are simple head and shoulders but he later painted three-quarter and full-length figures. In 1643, he left England for the Netherlands where he continued his career painting portraits in Amsterdam, Middelburg, Utrecht and elsewhere.

Jordaens, Jacob
(1593 – 1678)
Jordaens was taught in Antwerp by Adam van Noort, Rubens's master. He was admitted to the guild in 1615 as a tempera painter which allowed him to paint cartoons for tapestries. His early work is indebted to van Dyck and Rubens although he added his own sense of the burlesque and the commonplace. He was mainly a painter of myths and religious themes. Following the death of Rubens in 1640, he became the chief painter of Antwerp, completing a number of commissions left unfinished by Rubens and undertaking similar large-scale paintings in The Hague, Amsterdam and elsewhere. At the end of his life, he became a Protestant but continued to accept commissions from Catholic churches.

Kalf, Willem
(1619 – 1693)
Kalf was born in Rotterdam, the son of a prosperous textile merchant. By 1641, he was living in Paris but was back in Rotterdam by 1646. By 1653, he had moved to Amsterdam, where he died. After painting a number of barn interiors in the early 1640s, he devoted himself to painting luxury still-life compositions. His earliest dated work is from 1642 and the latest from 1679–80. He seems to have given up painting in his last years to concentrate on art dealing.

Kandinsky, Wassily
(1866 – 1944)
Kandinsky was born in Moscow. In 1893, he was appointed to a post at the Faculty of Law. The impact made upon him by an exhibition of French Impressionists in 1895, however, encouraged him to leave Russia to study painting in Munich. He took part in several avant-garde movements in the city and was the central figure in the summer colony of artists which met in Murnau outside Munich. These artists formed the nucleus of the Blaue Reiter group, formed in 1911. After the outbreak of war, he returned to Russia and became involved in administrative matters. In 1921, he left to take up a teaching post at the Bauhaus where he remained until it was closed in 1933. His early decorative and strongly coloured works developed between 1910 and 1913 into the first purely abstract works.

Karlowska, Stanislawa de
(1876 – 1952)
Karlowska was born in Poland and studied in Warsaw and Kraków. In 1896 she went to the Académie Julian in Paris where she met her future husband, Robert Bevan. In 1898, she settled in England and became a member of the Camden Town Group, adopting the Camden Town manner of painting. Her interiors and landscapes are strongly constructed and painted with a light, colourful touch.

Keilhau, Eberhard (Bernard Keil called Monsù Bernardo)
(1624 – 1687)
The son of a German artist at the court of Denmark, Keilhau was apprenticed to Maarten von Steenwinckel there. He subsequently lived in Amsterdam, studying with Rembrandt in 1640–2. By 1651 Keilhau was in Italy, working first in Venice and then settling in Rome from 1656. He painted religious subjects and portraits, working with a broad, sketchy technique. He developed a type of genre scene in Rome for which he became famous, where groups of children and adults are depicted engaged in an activity such as sewing or lace-making.

Kessel, Jan van, I
(1626 – 1679)
Kessel was born in Antwerp. He was a pupil of his father, Hieronymous II van Kessel and probably of his uncle, Jan Brueghel II. He became a member of the Antwerp guild in 1645 and died there in relative poverty. He painted floral bouquets, fruit pieces and animal paintings. He also made cartoons for the floral borders of tapestries but is now best known for his little paintings on copper of insects, flowers and shells.

Kettle, Tilly
(1735 – 1786)
After studying at Shipley's and the St Martin's Lane Academy in London, Kettle worked in Oxford and the Midlands as a painter of portraits. His portrait types are somewhat similar to those of Reynolds. From 1768 to 1776, he worked in India, where he was in demand among the native nobility as well as among the administrators of the East India Company. He had less success on his return to England and set out again for India but died on the voyage.

Key, Willem
(*c.* 1515 – 1568)
Key was taught by Peter Coecke van Aelst and Lambert Lombard and entered the Antwerp guild in 1542. He was chiefly a portrait painter but also painted altar-pieces, mostly destroyed. It is said that he died of chagrin caused by the execution of counts Egmont and Horn.

Keyser, Thomas de
(1596 – 1667)
After training with his father, the architect and sculptor, Hendrick de Keyser, Thomas worked as municipal architect to the city of Amsterdam from 1662 until his death. He was also a prolific painter of portraits, including small-scale, full-length figures set in an interior and group portraits. During the 1640s, he traded in marble and his output declined somewhat but he continued to carry out important commissions late in his career.

Kick, Cornelis
(1631/4 – 1681)
Cornelis Kick was a pupil of his father Simon Kick and is said to have started his career as a portrait painter. According to his biographer, Houbraken, the success of Jan Davidsz. de Heem inspired Kick to turn to painting flowers and fruit. Elias van den Broeck served as Kick's apprentice for four years from 1665.

Kick, Simon
(1603 – 1652)
Little is known of Kick's life. He was born in Delft and by 1624 had moved to Amsterdam where he worked with Pieter Codde, Jacob Duck, Willem Duyster and others. He painted genre scenes, military subjects, banqueting scenes and merry companies.

Kinley, Peter
(1926 – 1988)
Kinley was born in Vienna and arrived in England in the late 1930s. After some years in the army, he studied at the Düsseldorf Academy in 1948–9 and at St Martin's School of Art in London from 1949 to 1953. The exhibition in London of the work of the French painter Nicolas de Staël had a lasting effect on his work.

Kirkby, Thomas
(active 1796 – 1847)
Little is known about Kirkby apart from the forty-three works which he exhibited at the Royal Academy between 1796 and 1846. Most of his later works were portraits. He also exhibited landscapes and figure compositions. He is recorded at addresses in London and in Litchfield.

Knijff, Wouter
(*c.* 1607 – after 1693)
Born in Wesel, Knijff lived in Haarlem from 1639 until at least 1675. He became a member of the Guild of St Luke in 1640. He was a landscape painter who worked in the style of the Haarlem painters, Jan van Goyen and Salomon van Ruysdael.

Koenig, Johann
(1586 – 1642)
Koenig was born in Nuremberg, the son of a goldsmith, Arnold Koenig. He studied in Augsburg and moved to Rome in 1610, where he became a member of the circle of Adam Elsheimer. He chiefly painted small-scale genre scenes and historical compositions on copper in the manner of Elsheimer. In 1616, he returned to Augsburg but moved to Nuremberg in about 1629 where he remained until his death.

Koninck, Philips
(1619 – 1688)
Koninck was born in Amsterdam. He trained with his brother, Jacob, in Rotterdam but by 1653 was back in Amsterdam. He is said to have been a pupil of Rembrandt, whose work certainly influenced his own style of painting. He produced portraits and genre pictures but is chiefly known for his landscapes, which usually show vast panoramas of the flat Dutch countryside beneath an expanse of lively clouds.

Korovin, Konstantin Alekseevich
(1861 – 1939)
Korovin graduated from the Moscow School of Painting, Sculpture and Architecture where he studied landscape under Savrasov and Polenov. He joined the 'World of Art' group and worked mostly as a landscape painter in an Impressionist style. From 1885 to 1891, he worked for Savva Mamontov's opera as a designer and later for the Imperial Opera in Moscow and St Petersburg. From 1923 he lived in Paris.

Lance, George
(1802 – 1864)
Lance studied under Benjamin Robert Haydon. He specialized in still life and exhibited extensively at several London venues, including the Royal Academy and the British Institution. His work appeared regularly at the Liverpool Academy, of which he was an honorary member. He also painted occasional works of historical genre.

Lande, Willem van de
(*c.* 1610 – active 1650)
Van de Lande is recorded in Delft in 1635 but was in Amsterdam by about 1650. Very little is known about his life or his work. He was a genre painter and etcher. Only one signed painting, a merry company in the open air, has been recorded.

Landseer, Sir Edwin Henry
(1802 – 1873)
Landseer was taught by the academic painter Benjamin Robert Haydon. He specialized in subjects which gave a prominent place to animals. Following a visit to the Highlands of Scotland in 1824, he began to paint scenes of deer and deer hunting and returned there every autumn to hunt and sketch. He became a favourite painter of the royal family. In 1840, he suffered a nervous collapse and the rest of his life was blighted by alchoholism and mental illness. The design of the four bronze lions round Nelson's column in Trafalgar Square in London, commissioned in 1857 and unveiled in 1867, was the chief work of his last years.

Lanfranco, Giovanni
(1582 – 1647)
Lanfranco, a pupil of Agostino Carracci, worked with Annibale Carracci from 1602 at the Palazzo Farnese in Rome and made contact with important Roman patrons. He moved to Parma in late 1610, where the work of Correggio was a major influence. Lanfranco then established his career in Rome in 1612, in competition with Domenichino and Reni, painting numerous altar-pieces and frescoes. He developed a strongly Baroque style in the 1620s. He worked for the Jesuits in Naples in 1634 and remained there for twelve years, returning to Rome in 1646.

Lanyon, Peter
(1918 – 1964)
Lanyon was born in St Ives in Cornwall and remained closely linked with the town. In 1936–7, he attended the Penzance School of Art and had lessons in 1938 at the Euston Road School. From 1940 to 1945, he served in the Royal Air Force and after the war made an international reputation with his near-abstract landscapes. He took up gliding in 1959 to give him a better understanding of the Cornish landscape and died as the result of a gliding accident.

László, Philip Alexius de
(1869 – 1937)
De László was born in Budapest and was at first apprenticed to a scene painter but left after a few months to study at the Budapest Academy and in Paris. He established a successful portrait practice in Austria-Hungary. In 1900, he married a member of the Guinness family and subsequently worked in England and Ireland. He filled the place left vacant by Sargent's death as a fashionable portrait painter and became a British citizen in 1914.

Laurence, Samuel
(1812 – 1884)
Laurence based in London, and specialized in portrait drawings in chalk. He exhibited at the Royal Academy from 1836 to 1882.

Laurencin, Marie
(1883 – 1956)
Laurencin was born in Paris and was largely self-taught. She came into contact with Picasso and the Cubists through the poet Apollinaire and exhibited with them in 1907 and 1909–13. Her work has little in common with Cubism and is characterized by her use of pastel colours and a preference for subjects of dancers and actresses painted in a self-consciously feminine style.

Laurens, Jean-Paul
(1838 – 1921)
Laurens was born in the Haute-Garonne in France where he received his first lessons from a visiting painter from Piedmont. He then went to the art school at Toulouse where he won a scholarship in 1858 which enabled him to complete his studies in Paris. He came to notice in 1872 with the first of a long series of history paintings which often deal with somewhat sinister subjects from the Dark Ages. From 1877 to 1880 he painted a series of works on the life of St Geneviève for the Pantheon in Paris, the first of numerous public commissions. He also illustrated books. He was appointed to a Professorship at the Ecole des Beaux Arts in 1886 and was elected to the Académie des Beaux-Arts in 1891.

Lawson, Cecil Gordon
(1851 – 1882)
Born in Wellington in Shropshire, Lawson moved to London with his family in 1861. He was taught by his father, William Lawson, a portrait painter. In 1869, his family moved to Cheyne Walk where he painted a series of pictures of the River Thames. He achieved success in 1878 with *The Minister's Garden*, inspired by Goldsmith's *The Deserted Village*, which was exhibited at the Grosvenor Gallery. He continued to exhibit at the Grosvenor Gallery until his death.

Lear, Edward
(1812 – 1888)
At the age of sixteen, Lear began work as an illustrator of birds and animals. In 1837, he set out for Rome, where he earned his living giving lessons and selling drawings. In 1841, he published his first book of Roman views. His *Book of Nonsense* appeared in 1846. In 1850, he entered the Royal Academy Schools and in 1852 met Holman Hunt, who gave him some instruction in oil painting. Over the next years he travelled extensively in the Near East, recording the sites in many drawings and watercolours. These gave him materials for his travel books and many landscapes.

Lee, William
(1809 – 1865)
Lee specialized in painting rural and coastal scenes, mainly in watercolour. He exhibited at the Royal Academy from 1844 to 1854. He was a member and secretary of the Langham Sketching Club.

Lees, Derwent
(1885 – 1931)
Lees was born in Melbourne and was educated there and in Paris. In 1905, he went to London and studied under Brown and Tonks at the Slade School. In 1908, he joined the staff of the Slade as drawing master. He travelled widely, painting landscapes in France, Germany, Spain, Belgium, Italy and Russia, but fell ill in about 1918 and spent the last thirteen years of his life in a mental hospital.

Legros, Alphonse
(1837 – 1911)
Legros may have attended classes at the art school in his native Dijon before going to Paris in 1851. He took lessons with Lecoq de Boisbaudron at the Petite Ecole and later at the Ecole des Beaux-Arts. The first of his many hundreds of etchings dates from 1855. With Whistler and Fantin-Latour he founded the Société des Trois and became a prominent member of a tendency in the 1860s to paint darkly coloured scenes of popular life. In 1863, he visited London and became a naturalized British citizen in 1880. In 1876, he succeeded Poynter as Professor of Fine Art at the Slade School and from this position extensively influenced a generation of British artists who.

Leighton, Frederic, Lord
(1830 – 1896)
Leighton was born in England but educated in Germany and Rome. His debut at the Royal Academy exhibition in 1855 with *Cimabue's Madonna carried in Procession* made him famous. From the 1860s, he specialized in painting scenes from antique history and literature based on his mastery of academic figure drawing. He became President of the Royal Academy in 1878 and was made a peer the day before his death.

Lely, Sir Peter
(1618 – 1680)
Lely was born in Westphalia and trained under Pieter de Grebber in Haarlem. He came to London in about 1643 and painted a number of historical and mythological themes before turning to portraiture. Lely became the dominant portrait painter in England, filling the gap left by van Dyck's death. His position was confirmed after the Restoration of the monarchy in 1660, when he became Court Painter to Charles II.

Lemon, Arthur
(1850 – 1912)
Born on the Isle of Man, Lemon spent his youth in Rome. For ten years, he worked as a cowboy in California, where he made studies of Indians. He then studied under Carolus-Duran in Paris and later lived in England and Italy. He was mainly a painter of genre and specialized in Italian pastoral views.

Leonardo da Vinci
(1452 – 1519)
A painter, sculptor, architect, scientist and engineer, Leonardo was one of the most influential figures in European art from his lifetime onwards. Having studied under Andrea Verrocchio in Florence, he worked there and in Milan and Rome, moving to the court of France in 1517. Relatively few of his paintings survive, in some cases because of his experimental technique and much of his output of sculpture has been lost. However, his ideas and inventions are known through his drawings and through copies and adaptations by students and followers. In his writings on art he developed ideas about naturalism and expressiveness that became the basis of teaching in academies of art. Similarly his profound interest in anatomy and in the workings of the human body had an inspirational effect.

Lépine, Stanislas-Victor-Edouard
(1835 – 1892)
Lépine was initially self-taught. He later took advice from Corot and Jongkind and the influence of both can be seen in his port scenes and many tranquil river landscapes. He also painted views of Paris often under a silvery overcast sky. He exhibited at the first Impressionist exhibition in 1874 and shared a number of concerns and motifs with the Impressionists, but was not obviously influenced by them.

Le Sidaner, Henri-Eugène-Augustin
(1862 – 1939)
Le Sidaner was born Port-Louis in Mauritius and went to Paris in 1880. He enrolled at the Ecole des Beaux-Arts in 1884. In 1898 and 1899 he visited Brussels and stayed in Bruges. He found many of his subjects on the canals of Bruges and Venice, painting effects of evening light in particular. In 1930, he was elected to the Institute.

Levitan, Isaak Il'ich
(1860 – 1900)
Levitan was born in the village of Kibarti near Verzhbolovo. From 1873, he studied at the Moscow School of Painting, Sculpture and Architecture and taught there from 1898. He specialized in landscape painting in a somewhat Impressionist style and exhibited both with the Wanderers and with the artists of the 'World of Art' movement.

Licinio, Bernardino
(*c.* 1490 – after 1549)
A member of a family of artists from Bergamo, Licinio is first documented in 1511. He was impressed by contemporary Venetian art, particularly that of Giorgione and Titian, while the art of Lorenzo Lotto was also important for his later career. Licinio is best known as a portraitist, particularly for his half-length portrait groups which are characterized by a sober naturalism. However, he also painted religious works and some large altar-pieces.

Linnell, John
(1792 – 1882)
Linnell went to the Royal Academy Schools in 1805. His early work consisted of portraits and watercolours . Later, he specialized in painting landscape in oils. In 1852, he moved from London to Redhill in Surrey, where he remained for the rest of his life. He was a friend and patron of William Blake and father-in-law of Samuel Palmer. Many of his landscapes are based on the Surrey countryside.

Lippi, Fra Filippo
(*c.* 1406 – 1469)
Lippi took his vows as a Carmelite in 1421 and is first mentioned as a painter in 1431. He was employed by the Medici and worked in Padua, Prato and Spoleto, as well as in Florence where both Botticelli and his son Filippino Lippi were his pupils. Filippo was strongly impressed by the art of Masaccio and developed an early interest in Flemish art. While much of his output was of religious subjects, he was also an important portrait painter.

Lippi, Lorenzo
(1606 – 1665)
Lippi was a pupil of Matteo Rosselli in Florence and a great admirer of the austere Santi di Tito, whose work he copied well into his career. Baldinucci, the principal source for his life and reputation, praised Lippi's truth to nature and gracefulness, although his increasingly simplified style was not always admired. A friend of Salvator Rosa, with whom he collaborated, Lippi wrote poetry, including a mild parody of Tasso's epic *Gerusalemme Liberata*.

Locatelli, Andrea
(1695 – 1741)
Andrea studied with the marine painter known as Monsù Alto and subsequently under Bernardo Fergioni. Giovanni Ghisolfi and Salvator Rosa were major influences. Locatelli's reputation was established in Rome by 1723, although he was to some extent overshadowed by van Bloemen and Panini. As a specialist in landscape and genre, Locatelli occasionally collaborated with history painters. His admirers included Cardinal Ottoboni and Filippo Juvarra, who commissioned pictures from him for the courts of Turin and Spain.

Loiseau, Gustave
(1865 – 1935)
Loiseau was born in Paris and trained at the Ecole des Arts Décoratifs. He was drawn towards the Impressionists and from 1890, worked at Pont-Aven and at Pouldu. He met Gauguin through his friendship with Maufra but was not attracted by the more doctrinaire aspects of the Pont-Aven school. His work was chiefly influenced by Monet. In 1895, he settled at Moret-sur-Loing but travelled in Nomandy, Brittany, the Dordogne, and especially along the river banks of the Ile de France. He often returned to Pont-Aven, painting in an Impressionist style which changed little.

Long, Edwin Longsden
(1829 – 1891)
Long's first pictures were Spanish subjects of the kind painted by his teacher John Phillip. He later turned to subjects from the Bible and ancient history, specializing in Egyptian themes, which he painted in a manner that owed much to Alma-Tadema. His work was popular and sought after: his huge *Babylonian Market*, exhibited at the Royal Academy in 1878, sold for 7,000 guineas.

Longhi, Pietro
(1702 – 1785)
Longhi was the son of a Venetian silversmith. He probably studied painting with G.M. Crespi in Bologna. From about 1732 onwards, he lived in Venice where he carried out a few fresco commissions but was chiefly known for his small pictures of contemporary life. He was a friend of the playwright, Carlo Goldoni. His own scenes of fashionable life have a theatrical, sometimes mildly satirical character.

Lorenzo di Credi
(*c.* 1457 – 1536)
The son of a goldsmith, Lorenzo trained in the studio of Andrea Verrocchio in Florence and was a fellow pupil of Leonardo, by whose work he was to some extent influenced. Lorenzo took over the workshop after Verrocchio left for Venice. Like others of his generation, he was extremely interested in Flemish art, of which many examples could be seen in Florence. While he is best known for his altar-pieces and devotional works, he also painted portraits and was a versatile draughtsman.

Loutherbourg, Philip James de (Philippe Jacques)
(1740 – 1812)
Loutherbourg was educated in Strasbourg and was an established artist in Paris by the time he came to London in 1771. He designed for the theatre and made his reputation in England with sublime and picturesque landscapes and compositions of dramatic action. He developed a type of peep-show, incorporating landscapes with lighting effects, called the Eidophusikon, which he exhibited with success in London in 1782.

Lowinsky, Thomas Esmond
(1892 – 1947)
Lowinsky was born in India and educated at Eton and Oxford before studying art at the Slade School from 1912 to 1914. In addition to painting scenes of fantasy, Lowinsky painted portraits in a style which reveals a debt to the art of the Renaissance.

Luny, Thomas
(1759 – 1837)
Luny was apparently a pupil of Francis Holman in London. He specialized in painting naval actions, coast scenes and naval dockyards. He was a prolific artist. Following his retirement to Teignmouth around 1810, he continued to paint despite being crippled in both his hands and legs.

Lupton, Nevil Oliver
(1828 – after 1877)
Lupton was the son of Thomas Lupton, an engraver and painter of miniatures. He exhibited pictures of landscapes and rural genre from 1851 until his death.

Lust, Abraham de
(active *c.* 1650 – after 1659)
The painter Abraham de Lust who was living in Leeuwarden in 1659 and seems to have then left to work in Germany, is probably the author of a group of still-life paintings signed: *a.d.lust*. In 1656, a painter named Lust is recorded in Lyon. There is some evidence that he was later active in Amsterdam.

Luttichuys, Simon
(1610 – 1661)
Luttichuys was born in London to Dutch parents who returned to the Netherlands when Simon was young. He was in Amsterdam by 1649 and remained there for the rest of his life. There are dated pictures from 1644 to 1657, mostly banquet pieces and *vanitas* pictures.

MacColl, Dugald Sutherland
(1859 – 1948)
Born in Glasgow, MacColl was educated at London and Oxford. He attended art classes at Westminster School of Art and studied at the Slade School under Legros from 1884 to 1892. He was a member of the New English Art Club. Through his work as an art critic on *The Spectator* and *The Saturday Review*, he encouraged interest in the work of the Impressionists. He was Keeper of the Tate Gallery from 1906 to 1911 and of the Wallace Collection from 1911 to 1924.

Maes, Nicolaes
(1634 – 1693)
Maes was born in Dordrecht where he received his first lessons. In about 1650, he became a pupil of Rembrandt. In 1653, he returned to Dordrecht, where he remained until 1673. He then returned to Amsterdam. He is said to have visited Antwerp in the late 1660s for the purpose of studying the work of Rubens and his followers. His early work includes biblical scenes, but he later painted genre subjects and finally specialized in portraits.

Maffei, Francesco
(*c.* 1605 – 1660)
Trained in the studio of the Maganza family in Vicenza, Maffei also absorbed the lessons of 16th-century art, particularly that of Jacopo Bassano, Tintoretto and Veronese. He visited Venice *c.* 1638–40 and was stimulated by the work of Strozzi, Johann Liss and Domenico Fetti, the three foreigners there who were transforming the Venetian baroque. He was a successful and highly original artist.

Magnasco, Alessandro
(1667 – 1749)
Magnasco studied under Filippo Abbiati in Milan in around 1681–2 and became a specialist in figure painting, often collaborating with specialists in landscape or perspective designs. He explored unusual kinds of genre subjects from 1695, painting Quaker meetings and scenes with beggars and gypsies or Capuchin friars, with a muted palette and fragmentary brush-strokes. Magnasco worked at the Medici court in Florence from *c.* 1703–9 and in Genoa in 1735, but otherwise made his career primarily in Milan. He was a prolific draughtsman.

Mahoney, Charles Cyril
(1903 – 1968)
After studying at the Royal College of Art (1922–6), Mahoney took up teaching posts at the Royal College (1928–53), the Byam Shaw School (1954–63) and the Royal Academy Schools (1961–8). His murals at Morley College (1928–30) led to further mural commissions at Brockley School in Kent and at Campion Hall in Oxford. He took inspiration for his flower paintings from his own garden.

Maillol, Aristide-Joseph-Bonaventure
(1861 – 1944)
Maillol was born at Banyuls in the Pyrénées Orientales and studied in Paris as a painter. In 1883, he became a friend of the sculptor Bourdelle and met Gauguin. In 1886, he began a small tapestry workshop in Banyuls. In 1893, he came into contact with the Nabis and exhibited with them. After the turn of the century he took up sculpture and devoted his life to sculptures of the female nude.

Maino, Juan Bantista
(1581 – 1641)
Maino visited Italy in the early 1600s, where he studied the work of Annibale Carracci, Caravaggio and Guido Reni. His earliest known work is an altar-piece of 1608 in Pastrana. By 1611 he was in Toledo, where he enjoyed the patronage of the Dominican friars of St Peter Martyr (he joined the Dominican order). Having been drawing master to the future Philip IV, Maino became an influential court artist: his major work is the *Recapture of Bahia* (Prado) of 1634–5.

Mair von Landshut
(active 1485 – d. 1510)
Mair's name appears on twenty-one engravings and a woodcut. His Christian names are unknown and the suffix, Landshut, was added on account of the coat of arms of the town of Landshut which appears in one of his prints. He seems to have assisted Jan Polack in painting an altar-piece in the church of St Peter in Munich in *c.* 1490. He also painted a lunette with scenes from the life of Christ for the sacristy of Freising Cathedral.

Maistre, Roy de
(1894 – 1968)
Born at Bowral in New South Wales, de Maistre studied music and painting in Sydney from 1913. He went to Paris in the 1920s with a scholarship and exhibited at the Salon of 1924. He had his first one-man show in London in 1929 in the studio of Francis Bacon. He painted figure compositions and still life subjects with a controlled sense of colour and a debt to Cubist forms.

Maitland, Paul Fordyce
(1863 – 1909)
Maitland studied at the Royal College of Art under Theodore Roussel who was friendly with Whistler. Maitland's paintings of landscapes, parks and town views, painted with a reticent touch and a delicate harmony of tones, show Whistler's influence. He was Art Examiner to the Board of Education, 1893–1908, but suffered from ill-health and died at a fairly early age in London.

Manet, Edouard
(1832 – 1883)
After giving up a career in law, Manet set out on a voyage to Rio de Janeiro. On returning to Paris in 1850, he entered the studio of Thomas Couture. His early work shows a strong debt to Spanish art. His modern life *Lunch on the Grass*, based on a composition designed by Raphael, was refused admission at the Salon of 1863 and appeared at an exhibition of rejected works. His *Olympia*, exhibited in 1865, developed this synthesis of the old with the new. In the 1870s, contact with the Impressionists led to a lightening of his palette and a more direct treatment of contemporary themes.

Manson, James Bolivar
(1879 – 1945)
Manson was born in London and studied at Heatherley's, Lambeth School of Art and the Académie Julian in Paris. He was much influenced by the Impressionists. He became a member and secretary of the Camden Town Group in 1911 and exhibited with the New English Art Club from 1915. In 1920, he founded the Monarro Group with his close friend Lucien Pissarro with the aim of promoting Impressionist ideas. He was Director of the Tate Gallery, 1930–8, and wrote several books on art.

Mansueti, Giovanni
(active 1484 – d. 1526–7)
First documented as a pupil of Giovanni Bellini in Venice, Mansueti remained in the Bellini workshop in the 1480s. He painted numerous small devotional works and some large scenes including two for the confraternity or Scuola di S. Giovanni Evangelista of the mid-1490s and three for the Scuola di S. Marco of *c.* 1518–26, which reveal his talents in orchestrating narrative scenes in complex architectural settings.

Maratta, Carlo
(1625 – 1713)
A pupil of Andrea Sacchi in Rome from 1637, Maratta remained close to his master until Sacchi's death in 1661. He evolved a powerful yet graceful decorative style, which remained strongly classical. He enjoyed prestigious papal and imperial commissions and worked for an international clientele; he was also a distinguished portraitist. By the 1680s Maratta was the most important artist in Rome and an influential teacher.

Marchand, Jean Hippolyte
(1882 – 1941)
Marchand studied at the Ecole des Beaux-Arts from 1902 to 1906 and at the Académie Vitti under Henri Martin in 1909. He experimented with Cubism but his interest in Cézanne encouraged him to adopt a more naturalistic and traditional approach to painting. He lived for two years in Syria and the Middle East in the late 1920s and executed two decorative murals for the Palais de la Résidence in Beirut and for the Syrian pavilion at the Colonial Exhibition in Vincennes during this period. He was also a book illustrator.

Marco del Buono Giamberti
(?1403 – after 1480)
Marco del Buono Giamberti worked in Florence. He joined the Guild of S. Luca in 1424 and formed a partnership with Apollonio di Giovanni to produce cassone panels. The survival of a fragmentary workshop book has enabled many paintings to be attributed to Apollonio di Giovanni but none has yet been securely attributed to Marco del Buono himself.

Maris, Jacob
(1837 – 1899)
Maris was a prominent member of The Hague School. He attended classes in the Hague Academy from 1850 until 1854 when he went to Antwerp. His brother, Mattijs, joined him in the city, where they shared a house with Alma-Tadema. In about 1865, Jacob visited Barbizon in France and absorbed much of the French manner of painting. After returning to The Hague in 1871, he rarely painted figures but specialized in landscape views and townscapes painted with an increasingly vigorous touch.

Maris, Willem
(1844 – 1910)
Apart from some instruction from his brothers, Jacob and Mattijs, and some evening classes at The Hague Academy, Willem Maris was self-taught. In 1862, on a visit to Oosterbeek, he met Anton Mauve with whom he established a long friendship. Scenes with cows and ducks became his constant theme. Despite the occasional excursion to Germany, Paris and Norway, his career was largely centred on The Hague.

Marmion, Simon
(*c.* 1425 – 1489)
Marmion trained in Amiens, assisting his father Jean and worked as an illuminator and panel painter. His patrons included Philip the Good, Duke of Burgundy. Although no signed or documented works by Marmion survive, a group of paintings have been attributed to him which share a vivid sense of colour, a distinctive approach to landscape and somewhat stiff figures with thin limbs.

Marq, Charles
(b. 1923)
Marq was trained as a philosopher. In 1949, he married the painter Brigitte Simon and set up a workshop with her for making stained glass windows. His paintings tend to be simple, abstract and monochromatic.

Marrel, Jacob
(1614 – 1681)
Marrel was born in Frankfurt where he took lessons with Georg Flegel. By December 1632, he had settled in Utrecht but was back in Frankfurt in 1637. In 1641, he married in Utrecht but later settled in Frankfurt where he died. Marrel was a painter of flowers and still-life compositions. He produced tulip books in watercolour and did a few etchings. There are dated works by him from 1643 to 1681.

Martin, John
(1789 – 1854)
Martin was born in Northumberland. He made his reputation with *Joshua commanding the Sun to stand still*, exhibited in 1816, the first in a series of large paintings with cosmic and apocalyptic themes. He also did illustrations to the Bible in a similar vein. His work was widely popularized through prints and he exercized a particular fascination for French writers.

Martin, William
(active 1765 – 1831)
Born in Norwich, Martin entered the Royal Academy Schools in 1772. He was pupil and assistant to Cipriani until at least 1784. He occasionally painted portraits but his work was mainly devoted to historical subjects in the tradition of Angelika Kauffmann. In 1810, he was given the title of History Painter to King George III.

Martineau, Robert Braithwaite
(1826 – 1869)
Martineau gave up his studies in law to take lessons at the Royal Academy Schools. Here he became friendly with Holman Hunt, with whom he shared a studio around 1851–2. He began to exhibit at the Royal Academy in 1852, specializing in genre and literary scenes. He continued to share a studio with Hunt until his marriage in 1865. At his early death in 1869, he was working on a large composition of *Christians and Christians*.

Martino da Verona
(documented 1396 – 1410)
Martino based his style on that of his celebrated master Altichiero, repeating compositional schemes and individual motifs. He worked mainly in fresco, although some panel paintings are known and he also painted miniatures in manuscripts. He is documented in Verona, but, like Altichiero, probably also worked for Paduan patrons.

Maso da San Friano (Manzuoli, Tomasso d'Antonio)
(1531 – 1571)
Probably a pupil of Pier Francesco Foschi in Florence, Maso enjoyed a high reputation by 1560. His engagement with the art of Andrea del Sarto and Pontormo was fundamental to his style, which alternates between a classical restraint and a more convoluted Mannerism. Maso worked for a variety of Florentine patrons including the Medici and was a founder member of the Accademia del Disegno in Florence

Master of the Ashmolean Predella
(active mid to late 14th century)
This anonymous master worked with both Andrea di Cione (Orcagna) and his younger brother Jacopo, in Florence. He collaborated with Jacopo on the *Crucifixion* altar-piece in the National Gallery, London. Sometimes he has been identified with other anonymous masters, such as the Master of the Golden Gate.

Master of Baldraccani
(active *c.* 1480 – 1510)
The artist's name derives from an altar-piece formerly in the Muti-Bussi collection, Rome, which carries the arms of the Baldraccani family from Forlì. While his style has close affinities with that of Giovanni Santi, he may have travelled to Florence and Rome, since his art displays some knowledge of the work of Antoniazzo Romano and of Domenico Ghirlandaio.

Master of the Bielefeld Altar
(active *c.* 1400 – *c.* 1435)
An anonymous artist, named after an altar-piece in the Neustädter Marienkirche in Bielefeld, now partly dismembered. The frame is said to have been dated 1400. The same artist has been linked with a *Crucifixion* of 1431 in the Marienkirche in Dortmund which bears the arms of the Berswordt family. Hence he is sometimes identified as the Berswordt Master. All paintings which have been grouped round these works are derived from the work of other masters, notably Master Bertram and Conrad von Soest.

Master of Charles III of Durazzo
(active *c.* 1390)
A Florentine artist whose patrons included Neapolitans (or Florentines living in Naples), this anonymous artist has been given various names by art historians. He was active towards the end of the 14th and beginning of the 15th century, working in the figurative style of Orcagna and his followers. His known work is mainly *cassone* panels and birth salvers; his name derives from a *cassone* panel now in the Metropolitan Museum of Art, New York depicting the conquest of Naples by Charles III of Durazzo in 1381. Recently a possible identification with Francesco di Michele, documented between 1385 and 1395, has been proposed.

Master of Dominican Effigies
(active 1336 – 1345)
This anonymous artist painted an unusual subject, *Christ and the Virgin attended by seventeen Dominican Blessed and Friars* c. 1336 in the sacristy of S. Maria Novella, Florence. On the basis of this picture, various works have been attributed to him. The artist is notable for his vivacious small-scale narrative paintings and was a successful painter of miniatures in manuscripts.

Master of Marradi
(active *c.* 1500)
This unidentified, conservative artist was close to Domenico Ghirlandaio and painted a variety of religious works.

Master of San Martino alla Palma
(active *c.* 1310 – *c.* 1335)
The output of this master has been reconstructed on the basis of an altar-piece of *The Madonna and Child with Angels* from the church of S. Martino alla Palma, Scandicci, which largely derives from the Maestà by Giotto (Uffizi, Florence). His style is close to that of Bernardo Daddi.

Matisse, Henri
(1869 – 1954)
Matisse was born in Picardy. In 1892, he abandoned his studies in law to study art in Paris. He worked in the Académie Julian and also with Gustave Moreau at the Ecole des Beaux-Arts where he met Georges Rouault and others who were later associated with him in the Fauve movement. His early work was mostly landscapes and still lifes, painted in a low key. In 1899, he adopted Neo-Impressionist colour and techniques. His art was never abstract but the simplification of his forms and his improvised use of colour often gives an impression of abstraction. After 1918, his art became more naturalistic but in his last works he returned to a larger, more simplified manner, culminating in a series of paper cut-outs in the early 1950s.

Matteis, Paolo de
(1662 – 1728)
A talented pupil of Luca Giordano in Naples, de Matteis also studied in Rome from 1680 to 1682 with Gianmaria Morandi. He was strongly influenced by the art of Carlo Maratta and his followers. He returned to Naples in late 1682 after his most important patron in Rome, the Marchese del Carpio, became Viceroy there. With a growing international reputation, he was invited to Paris in 1702–5 and again to Rome 1723–6. In Naples, Paolo worked for a wide range of patrons including members of the Arcadian circle of intellectuals who appreciated his graceful classicism. While not as famous or influential as Solimena, Paolo provided an elegant alternative to his more robust style.

Matteo di Giovanni
(active 1452 – d. 1495)
Probably born in Sansepolcro, Matteo worked in Siena from 1452, remaining active there and in Sansepolcro. He may have trained with Domenico di Bartolo. While retaining a traditional Sienese emphasis on line and pattern in his painting, Matteo was also stimulated by the art of Piero della Francesca and by new developments in Florentine art.

Mauve, Anton
(1838 – 1888)
Mauve was first taught by the animal painter Pieter Frederik van Os and he remained chiefly a painter of animals in his later career. In 1858, he met Willem Maris, who became an influential friend. From 1871, he was based in The Hague until he moved to Laran in 1885. In 1881–2, van Gogh, who was a cousin of his wife, worked in his studio. In his last years at Laran, he painted more peasant subjects than before, partly influenced by his admiration for the work of Jean-François Millet.

McFadyen, Jock
(b. 1950)
Born in Paisley, Scotland, McFadyen studied at the Chelsea School of Art 1973–7 and became a part-time teacher at the Slade School. In 1981, he was Artist-in-Residence at the National Gallery in London. His art, usually based on themes of modern urban life, is painted with raw paint and a strong sense of colour.

Medley, Robert
(1905 – 1994)
Medley studied at the Byam Shaw School, the Royal Academy Schools and the Slade School from 1923–6 and spent the years 1926–8 in Paris. On his return to London, he worked with Duncan Grant and Vanessa Bell. He also worked as a designer in the theatre. He taught at Chelsea School of Art and at the Slade School and was Head of the Fine Art department at Camberwell School of Arts and Crafts, 1958–65. From 1967 to 1977 he was Chairman of the Faculty of Painting at the British School at Rome.

Meegeren, Han van
(1889 – 1947)
Van Meegeren studied art at The Hague Academy, graduating in 1914. As early as 1923, he seems to have produced his first forgeries of 17th-century paintings. In 1932, he retired to the south of France where he produced a long series of fakes, most notably eleven compositions purporting to be early works by Vermeer. He confessed to forgery after the Second World War when accused of selling a painting by Vermeer to Hermann Goering.

Meissonier, Ernest
(1815 – 1891)
Meissonier was born in Lyon but moved with his family to Paris in 1818. He took lessons with A.-J. Potier, and, briefly, with Léon Cogniet but was largely self-taught. He developed his talent for small-scale, detailed compositions by working as an illustrator. His earliest known painting dates from 1834, the first in a series of works based upon the fine manner of the 17th-century Dutch and Flemish genre painters. In 1859, he attended the Battle of Solferino and afterwards became increasingly interested in Napoleonic subjects. He occupied many important positions in the art world and was the first artist to receive the Grand Croix of the Legion of Honour.

Melone, Altobello
(*c.* 1490 – d. before May 1543)
Altobello combined an interest in both German and Venetian art and was influenced by northern European prints. He emulated the painterly qualities of Giorgione and Titian and the strong expressive forms of Gerolamo Romanino, with whom he was closely associated from *c.* 1508. He worked on a major cycle of frescoes at Cremona Cathedral from late 1516.

Mengs, Anton Raphael
(1728 – 1779)
Mengs studied in Rome from 1740–4 and 1746–9, copying antiquities and the work of Raphael in particular and studying Venetian and Bolognese art. He worked at the Dresden court as a portraitist and painter of altar-pieces, eventually making his career in Rome from 1751 with Grand Tourist portraits and religious and historical paintings. He was invited to Madrid in 1761 where he became First Painter to Charles III. A close friend of Winckelmann, Mengs was a highly influential artist and writer on art whose views were promoted by academies of art throughout Europe.

Meninsky, Bernard
(1891 – 1950)
Shortly after his birth in the Ukraine, Meninsky came to England. He studied at the School of Art in Liverpool and at the Slade School. In 1913, he worked for Gordon Craig's theatre school in Florence and then at the Central School of Arts and Crafts. In 1920, he took up a teaching post at Westminster School of Art. He taught at the Oxford City School of Art from 1940 and at the Central School of Art in London from 1945. He was a skilled figure draughtsman.

Meulen, Adam Frans van der
(1632 – 1690)
Van der Meulen was trained by Pieter Snayers in Brussels. He moved to Paris *c.* 1665 where he worked chiefly as a designer of tapestries for the Gobelins Factory. He accompanied Louis XIV on his campaigns and the sketches he made on the spot were later used by him for the compositions which were woven at the works. He was also a painter of genre and landscapes sometimes incorporating hunting parties and scenes of rustic feasting.

Michel, Georges
(1763 – 1843)
Michel was poor and unsuccessful in his own career, but his art was greatly appreciated by French realist landscape painters of the mid-19th century. Until *c.* 1789 he made a living as a drawing master; he exhibited at the Salons from 1791 to 1814 and worked as a restorer of the Dutch and Flemish paintings at the Louvre. His subject was the countryside around Paris an early biographer named him 'The Ruisdael of Montmartre'.

Michelangelo Buonarroti
(1475 – 1564)
Sculptor, draughtsman, architect, painter and poet, Michelangelo was one of the most influential European artists of all time. He trained briefly under Ghirlandaio in Florence and studied sculpture in the Medici garden. His early masterpieces include the Vatican *Pietà* (1498–1500) and the *David* (1501–4) (Accademia, Florence). He worked mainly in Florence and Rome, where he was called in 1505 by Julius II. Amongst his major achievements are the Sistine Chapel ceiling decoration (1508–12) and the *Last Judgement* there (1536–41), together with the Medici Chapel (1519–33) and Library (begun *c.* 1524) in Florence and his designs for St Peter's, Rome, from 1546. Though many commissions remained unfinished in the course of his long career – including the ambitious sculptural project of the tomb of Julius II – Michelangelo's ideas can be traced in the large corpus of drawings which has survived.

Mignon, Abraham
(1640 – 1679)
Mignon was born in Frankfurt-am-Main where he took lessons with Jacob Marrel. Probably in 1650, Marrel took Mignon with him on one of his visits to Utrecht. In the early 1660s, he moved permanently to Utrecht, where he was strongly influenced by Jan Davidsz. de Heem, with whom he worked and whose studio he took over. Mignon chiefly painted still life compositions of fruit and flowers and dead birds.

Millais, Sir John Everett, Bt
(1829 – 1896)
Millais entered the Royal Academy Schools at the age of eleven. There he came into contact with Holman Hunt and Rossetti, and with them and a few colleagues, founded the Pre-Raphaelite Brotherhood in 1848. His work in the early 1850s shows a mastery of the highly detailed naturalism which the Brotherhood based in part on the writings of John Ruskin. Following his marriage in 1854 to Ruskin's former wife, he began to paint in a freer manner and parted company with the Pre-Raphaelites. In 1896, he became President of the Royal Academy.

Millet, Jean-François (Francisque)
(1642 – 1679)
Relatively little is known of Millet's development and career. Born in Antwerp of a French father, he trained with Laureys Franck, then moved to Paris in 1659 and was a member of the Academy in 1673. He travelled to England and Holland. Millet studied and copied the work of the Carracci, Titian and others, notably Poussin, and made his reputation with austere classical landscapes in the manner of that master. Some of these were engraved at an early date, providing virtually the only documentation for his work.

Millet, Jean-François
(1814 – 1875)
Millet was born into a family of farmers in Normandy. He studied with Delaroche in Paris and painted a range of small pastoral pictures in the 1840s before discovering his subject matter among the peasants who lived in and around the forest of Fontainebleau. He acquired a studio in the village of Barbizon in 1849 and became one of the chief artists of the so-called Barbizon School.

Milne, Hilda Lucy
(*c.* 1870 – 1960)
Milne's father was an amateur artist and Chairman of the Manchester City Art Gallery Sub-Committee from 1900 to 1910. Her brother was the painter, Malcolm Milne. Her own career in art does not appear to have been documented.

Milne, Malcolm Midwood
(1887 – 1954)
Trained as an architect, Milne abandoned his chosen career through ill-health and turned to art. He studied from 1908 to 1911 at the Slade School and then at the Westminster School with Sickert. After war service, he joined the New English Art Club and exhibited there regularly. He travelled extensively, working often in pen and watercolour. He was converted to Roman Catholicism in 1943. In 1949 he was commissioned to paint a series of Stations of the Cross for the church of St Catherine Labouré in Glasgow; these were still unfinished when he died in Oxford in 1954.

Minderhout, Hendrick Van
(1632 – 1696)
Minderhout was mainly active in the Southern Netherlands. He was based in Bruges from 1652 but moved to Antwerp in 1672. He painted mostly sea-pieces in the tradition of Jan Baptist Weenix amd Johannes Lingelbach. His subjects included imaginary sea-ports as well as views of Antwerp.

Moeyaert, Claes Cornelisz.
(*c.* 1590 – 1655)
In 1605, Moeyaert moved to Amsterdam with his family and worked there as an etcher before becoming known as a painter. His work is largely devoted to biblical and historical themes. His earliest work was influenced by Pieter Lastman and Jan and Jacob Pynas. From the mid-1630s, he began to respond to the work of Rembrandt and his touch became correspondingly more lively.

Mola, Pier Francesco
(baptized 1612 – 1666)
The son of Giovanni Francesco Mola, an architect, stuccoist and writer, Mola travelled and worked in the north of Italy, studying the art of the Bassano, Titian, Guercino and Albani (in whose studio he worked, probably *c.* 1634–5). He established himself in Rome in 1647, painting small cabinet paintings with attractive landscape settings. Mola studied the work of Poussin, whom he knew and whose landscapes he particularly admired. He received some important public commissions, with his later style becoming more powerful and dramatic. Mola was also a talented and lively draughtsman.

Molenaer, Jan Miense
(c. 1610 – 1668)
Nothing is known of Molenaer's training but he worked in Haarlem and was heavily influenced by Frans Hals. He painted genre, portraits and allegories. In 1626, he married Judith Leyster. They moved to Amsterdam when his property was confiscated to pay debts. From the 1640s, he specialized in low-life scenes of the kind associated with Adriaen van Ostade.

Momper, Joos de
(1564 – 1635)
Momper entered the Antwerp guild in 1581 and probably went to Italy in the same year. He was back in Antwerp in 1590. His earliest landscapes are panoramic views relating to works by Pieter Brueghel I. He collaborated with several figure Flemish painters. His approach to landscape bridged the transition from the more imaginary landscapes of the 16th century to the naturalism of the early 17th century.

Monet, Claude
(1840 – 1926)
Monet was encouraged to paint out of doors by Boudin, whom he met in Le Havre in 1856–7. After military service, he entered the studio of Charles Gleyre in 1861 where he met Renoir, Sisley and Bazille. In 1869, while working with Renoir on the Seine at La Grenouillière, he began to paint with the freedom and colour which became characteristic of Impressionism in the 1870s. In 1885, he moved to Giverny, where he constructed a garden and used it as the model for an extensive series of paintings of water-lilies. In the 1890s, he painted a number of motifs in series, including poplars, grain-stacks and Rouen Cathedral.

Montagna, Bartolomeo
(c. 1450 – 1523)
Documented in Venice in 1469, Montagna may have worked in Bellini's studio; he was also influenced by the art of Andrea Mantegna, Antonello da Messina and Alvise Vivarini, which he could have studied in Venice. By 1474 he was established in Vicenza, where he became the leading artist, working also in Padua. Montagna's paintings are characterized by their imposing, expressive figures and strong feeling for landscape.

Moor, Carel de, the Younger
(1655 – 1738)
Born in Leyden, Carel de Moor was taught by Gerrit Dou, Frans van Mieris, Godfried Schalken and Adriaen van den Tempel. He was a successful painter of portraits. His portraits of Prince Eugene and the Duke of Marlborough, commissioned for the Imperial ambassadors, earned him enoblement. He also painted historical scenes and was an engraver of portraits.

Moore, Henry
(1831 – 1896)
Elder brother of the painter, Albert Joseph Moore, Henry Moore was taught by his father, William Moore, and later at the York School of Design and the Royal Academy Schools. His early landscapes are painted with a certain Pre-Raphaelite detail, but in about 1857, he turned to marine painting, which became a speciality.

Morales, Luis de
(c. 1520 – after 1585)
Morales spent his career in Badajoz, working on commissions for churches in the area, especially along the border of Extremadura and Portugal. The majority of his pictures are small devotional works of an intensely pious spirit, for which he became famous (and was known as 'El Divino'). Some of his paintings reveal contacts with contemporary writings on mysticism. Little is known of his training, but he certainly knew the work of Italianate Flemish artists such as Quentin Massys.

Morelli, Domenico
(1826 – 1901)
A pupil of Costanzo Angelini and Camillo Guerra in Naples, Morelli was active in politics, taking part in the Insurrection of 1848. He also studied in Rome and Florence. He painted literary or historical subjects often with Christian or patriotic allusions: in this he was influenced by Francesco Hayez and, after visiting Paris in 1855, by contemporary French painting. In his later career he was inspired by his study of the Bible, the Koran and mystical literature.

Moretto da Brescia (Alessandro Bonvicino)
(c. 1498 – 1554)
Influenced by Lombard and Venetian art, Moretto combined strong realism with a soft, painterly handling. He came from a family of artists and probably travelled to Venice early in his career; otherwise he worked for clients in Brescia, Bergamo and Milan. Moretto's religious works are solemn and imposing, while his portraits are often innovative in design. He was a highly influential artist.

Morland, George
(1763 – 1804)
Morland learned his art while serving a seven-year apprenticeship to his father, Henry Robert Morland, during which he was made to copy and forge Dutch landscapes. Morland specialized in small, sentimental scenes of children up to about 1788, then turned to rustic scenes and pictures of smugglers and wreckers. His work was much popularized through prints.

Moroni, Giovanni Battista
(c. 1520 – 1578)
A pupil of Moretto, Moroni worked mainly in Bergamo, except for an important sojourn in Trent in the late 1540s and early 1550s at a time of religious debates about the reform of the Catholic church. His religious art reveals a striking naturalism and simplicity of approach which seems in accord with this new religious climate. His portraits, striking for their cool tonality, often have a direct, intimate air.

Morsberger, Philip
(b. 1933)
Morsberger studied at Maryland Institute College of Art, the Carnegie Institute of Technology and the Ruskin School of Drawing in Oxford, where he graduated in 1958. On return to the USA, he took a post at Miami University in Ohio. In 1968, he became Artist-in-Residence at the Rochester Institute of Technology, New York. In 1971, he returned to the Ruskin School as Ruskin Master. After leaving Oxford in 1984, he held posts at Dartmouth, Berkeley, the San Francisco Art Institute and the California College of Arts and Crafts before moving to Augusta State University in 1996 as the William S. Morris Eminent Scholar in Art.

Mortel, Jan
(c. 1650 – 1719)
Mortel was born in Leyden. He was registered as a member of the Guild of St Luke from 1675 to 1713. In 1690, he was appointed Official Draughtsman in the University Garden, and Painter in the Garden in 1711. He painted some portraits early in his career but specialized in fruit and flower still lifes influenced by Jan Davidsz. de Heem and Abraham Mignon.

Moynihan, Rodrigo
(1910 – 1990)
Moynihan was born in Santa Cruz in the Canary Islands and divided his early days between England, America and Italy. He attended classes at the Accademia Rosso in Rome and at the Slade School (1928–31). From 1933 to 1936, he was a leading member of the Objective Abstractions Group and later worked with the Euston Road School. His style and subjects varied from abstraction to works of detailed realism. He painted numerous portraits.

Muirhead, David
(1867 – 1930)
After abandoning a career in architecture in Edinburgh, Muirhead studied at the Royal Scottish Academy Schools in Edinburgh and later at the Westminster School under Fred Brown. He settled in London in 1894 and exhibited at the Royal Academy. He was chiefly a painter of landscapes, figures and buildings in both oil and watercolour.

Müller, William James
(1812 – 1845)
Müller was born in Bristol. His father was a refugee from Prussia. He was briefly apprenticed to J.B. Pyne and painted views in and around Bristol. He also travelled extensively in Wales (1833) and in Germany, Swtzerland and Italy (1834–5). In 1838–9, he visited Greece, Egypt, Malta and Naples. On return, he settled in London and became a member of the Clipstone Street Society. In 1840, he visited France and in 1843–4, he went to Turkey. He died prematurely in 1845.

Mullins, George
(active 1763 – 1775)
Mullins was a pupil of James Mannin in Dublin. He painted landscapes which he exhibited in Dublin from 1765 to 1769. He went to London in 1770 and painted decorative ceilings for Chirck Castle in 1773. He probably died in London two years later.

Munnings, Sir Alfred James
(1878 – 1959)
Munnings was born in Suffolk. His work is chiefly inspired by the Suffolk countryside. He was employed as a lithographer for a few years in Norwich while studing at the Norwich School of Art. In 1903–4, he studied at the Académie Julian in Paris. He became President of the Royal Academy in 1944. He specialized in painting landscapes with horses.

Mura, Francesco de
(1696 – 1782)
A pupil of Domenico Viola in Naples, de Mura's formative years were spent from 1708 in Solimena's studio where he closely imitated the master's style. By the 1730s he had developed a lighter palette and a more delicate touch. De Mura was a leading artist in Naples, with major patrons including the Benedictines at Montecassino and the new Bourbon king; he also worked at the Turin court, 1741–3. His later style is more classicizing, with radiant colours and elegant, solid forms.

Murry, Richard Arthur Crosthwaite
(1902 – 1984)
Following a period at the Central School of Arts and Crafts, where he studied book production, Murry attended the Slade School. He was for many years secretary of the Art Workers' Guild and librarian at the Central School. Apart from painting, Murry was also an etcher, illustrator and teacher.

Naish, Richard Ellis
(1912 – 1988)
Naish went to the Royal College of Art in 1932 and the Ruskin School of Drawing in Oxford in 1934. After the Second World War, he moved to Oxfordshire. Many of his paintings, which he usually executed in the open air, were based on the landscape of Oxfordshire. He was Ruskin Master at Oxford from 1964 to 1971.

Naldini, Giovanni Battista
(1537 – 1591)
A pupil of Pontormo in Florence, Naldini also admired the art of Andrea del Sarto and of Bronzino. He worked with Vasari as one of a team of artists on commissions for the Medici, including the *studiolo* at the Palazzo Vecchio, but had many patrons in Florence and Tuscany. Naldini went to Rome in the late 1570s and was responsive to the demands of the Counter-Reformation for a more direct kind of religious art, while remaining an idiosyncratic Mannerist artist.

Nash, John Northcote
(1893 – 1977)
John Nash took up painting with encouragement from his brother, Paul. He was largely self-taught. In 1918 he was made an Official War Artist. He also served as War Artist to the Admiralty in the Second World War. He taught at the Ruskin School in Oxford from 1922 to 1927 and for periods before and after the Second World War at the Royal College of Art. From 1944, he lived near Colchester and found a source of subjects in the East Anglian countryside. He was mainly a landscape painter but also illustrated books.

Nash, Thomas Saunders
(1891 – 1968)
Nash studied at the Slade School from 1909 to 1912 where he came into contact with Wadsworth, Nevinson and Stanley Spencer. From 1920, he shared a house with Gilbert Spencer. His work deals mainly with rural and biblical themes.

Nasmyth, Patrick
(1787 – 1831)
Patrick Nasmyth was the eldest son of the Scottish landscape painter, Alexander Nasmyth. He exhibited in Edinburgh from 1808 to 1814, although he had moved to London in 1808 and began to exhibit at the Royal Academy in 1811. He was known as 'the English Hobbema' on account of the Dutch manner in which he worked.

Nason, Pieter
(1612 – 1688–90)
Nason was born in The Hague and studied under Jan van Ravesteyn. He painted portraits and miniatures as well as still life. In 1666 he was working at the court in Berlin. He died in The Hague.

Nazari, Bartolomeo
(1693 – 1758)
Nazari's early training is unknown, but in 1717 he was in the studio of Angelo Trevisani in Venice. He studied in Rome from 1717 to 1723 with Benedetto Luti and Francesco Trevisani. Nazari then worked in Venice mainly as a portraitist from 1724 to 1736, counting Grand Tourists amongst his clients. He returned to his native Bergamo, but re-established himself in Venice by 1745, becoming effectively the official State portraitist. He was admired for his realism and his ability to characterize his sitters.

Neefs, Pieter, the Elder
(1578 – 1656/61)
Neefs was born in Antwerp and remained there for the rest of his life. He was probably a pupil of Henrik van Steenwyck the Elder. He entered the Guild of St Luke in 1609 and specialized in painting church interiors in which the figures were often added by other artists. He employed his sons, Lodewijk and Pieter the Younger, to assist in his compositions, and their works are not easily distinguished.

Neer, Aert van der
(1603–4(?) – 1677)
Aert took up painting in Amsterdam in the 1630s. In 1639, he set up as an innkeeper but was declared bankrupt in 1662 and thereafter presumably depended upon painting for a living. His early work is close to the work of the Camphuysen brothers. His later paintings are characterized by subtle effects of light and atmosphere. He specialized in winter and moonlight scenes and also painted sunsets.

Neri di Bicci
(1419 – 1492)
The son of Bicci di Lorenzo and grandson of Lorenzo di Bicci, Neri was the last artist member of the Florentine family. A painter of modest talent, he nevertheless had a wide range of patrons and taught talented artists such as Cosimo Rosselli. Neri kept a workshop diary from 1453 to 1475, the *Ricordanze*, which provides an unrivalled source of information on the business of producing painted images, secular and devotional, at this time in Italy.

Neve, Cornelis de
(?1594 – after 1664)
Cornelis de Neve's name is included with his father's in a list of aliens living in London in 1594. Judging by his style, he may have trained under Mierevelt in the Netherlands. He is known only as a portrait painter and is last documented when painting a portrait of Elias Ashmole in 1664.

Nevinson, Christopher Richard Wynne
(1889 – 1946)
Nevinson was born in London and studied at St John's Wood School of Art and at the Slade School (1908–12). He then went to Paris to study at the Académie Julian and became a member of Matisse's Cercle Russe. He also studied lithography under Ernest Jackson. He became involved with the Italian Futurists and exhibited with the Vorticists. His work as a War Artist was marked by both movements. After the Second World War, he found a new source of modern urban inspiration in New York.

Nicholson, Ben
(1894 – 1982)
Son of Sir William Nicholson, Ben Nicholson was married first to the painter, Winifred Nicholson and then to the sculptor, Barbara Hepworth. He studied at the Slade School from 1910 to 1911 then travelled extensively. In 1928, he made his first visit to Cornwall, where he discovered the work of the naïve painter, Alfred Wallis, who decisively influenced his own work. Meetings with Brancusi, Picasso, Mirò and Mondrian in the early 1930s encouraged him to work in a simplified and carefully constructed manner. His paintings and reliefs, which often seem purely abstract, are based on still life and landscape motifs.

Nicholson, Sir William
(1872 – 1949)
While studying at Herkomer's school in Bushey in 1888–9, Nicholson met the painter James Pryde, with whom he collaborated in the 1890s in designing posters. He spent 1899 at the Académie Julian in Paris where he admired the work of Manet and Velázquez. On return to England, Nicholson married Pryde's sister, Mabel, who was also a painter. In the 1890s his wood-engravings appeared in a number of publications. In the early 1900s, he designed sets for the theatre. Afterwards, he turned to painting still lifes, landscapes and portraits.

Nicola di Maestro Antonio d'Ancona
(active 1472 – 1510)
The artist's name is known from a signed and dated altar-piece of 1472 (Carnegie Institute, Pittsburgh) which provides the basis for attributing other paintings. His style displays affinities with the art of Carlo Crivelli, who worked extensively in the Marches, and of artists such as Cosmè Tura and Marco Zoppo.

Nollekens, Joseph Francis
(1702 – 1748)
Nollekens was born in Antwerp and worked for several years in London. He is said to have arrived England in 1733 and worked with Peter Tillemans. He painted pastoral and genre scenes somewhat in the manner of Watteau. Joseph Nollekens, the sculptor, was his son.

Nomé, François de
(*c.* 1593 – after 1644)
For a long time de Nomé's art was confused with that of Didier Barra in art-historical literature, because the work of both had been described in 1742 under the single name of Monsù Desiderio. De Nomé travelled from his native Metz to Rome around 1602 and worked with a Maestro Baldassare, possibly the Flemish artist Balthasar Lauwers; he moved to Naples in 1610 and enjoyed considerable success there. He specialized in architectural fantasies, cataclysms and ruins, and his images have affinities with northern European prints.

Opie, John
(1761 – 1807)
Opie was discovered by the writer, John Walcot, in Cornwall and taken by him to London in 1781. Opie's work was much admired. His direct manner of painting, touched with considerable charm, made him a popular painter of genre scenes and portraits. He also undertook a few history paintings, including several commissioned by John Boydell.

Orcagna, Andrea di Cione
(*c.* 1315/20 – 1368)
Trained as a painter, Andrea also worked as a sculptor and architect in Florence. Some of his important frescoes have not survived, such as those at the Capella Maggiore of S. Maria Novella of 1348–52. By then he was a prominent artist in Florence, working with his brothers Nardo and Jacopo. In 1352 he took on a commission for Orsanmichele of a monumental architectural tabernacle, to house a miracle-working image. This iconographically complex and sculpturally rich tabernacle was a collaborative work with other sculptors and artisans. Andrea was also closely involved with the design of Florence Cathedral.

Orioli, Pietro di Francesco degli
(1458 – 1496)
Orioli was probably a pupil of Matteo di Giovanni in Siena and was an independent artist from the 1480s. Renowned for his religious devotion as well as his artistic skill, he painted almost exclusively sacred subjects. His paintings were previously attributed to Giacomo Pacchiarotto.

Orpen, Sir William
(1878 – 1931)
Orpen studied at the Dublin School of Art before attending classes at the Slade School from 1878 to 1879 where he was the contemporary of Augustus John. His early figure paintings and portraits combined intense preparatory drawing with brilliant technique. He served as an Official War Artist during the First World War. After the war, he became a highly successful painter of portraits.

Orsi, Lelio
(1508/11 – 1587)
The son of a painter, Bernardino Orsi, Lelio was familiar with the art of Giulio Romano at Mantua and with that of Correggio; he also travelled to Rome. He painted many frescoes in Reggio Emilia and his native Novellara, both illusionistic façade paintings and interior decoration, but relatively little has survived. Orsi developed a distinctive idiosyncratic style, with a visionary approach to religious subjects, reminiscent of Michelangelo.

Os, Jan van
(1744 – 1808)
Van Os was born in Middelharnis and studied under Aert Schouman before moving to The Hague. He painted a few early sea-pieces but later specialized in richly detailed still-life paintings of flowers and fruit with dead birds and insects which are clearly indebted to the example of Jan van Huysum.

Osona, Rodrigo de
(active 1463 – 1513)
One of the leading artists in Valencia, Rodrigo was familiar with both Flemish and early Renaissance Italian art, perhaps as a result of travelling to Italy or viewing pictures in private collections. He received numerous important religious commissions in Valencia. His son Francisco (*c.* 1465–*c.* 1514) was an artist of lesser talent who worked in his studio; their paintings have often been confused.

Ostade, Adriaen van
(b. 1610 – 1684)
According to his first biographer, van Ostade was taught in Haarlem by Frans Hals. Adriaen Brouwer, who is also said to have been in Hals's studio at this time, was a more obvious influence on his art. Van Ostade spent his life in Haarlem, entering the guild by 1654 and becoming its Dean in 1662. His early genre scenes feature carousing or quarrelling peasants in barns and taverns while his later work is more colourful and less boisterous. He made many watercolour drawings and over fifty etchings.

Ostade, Isack van
(1621 – 1649)
Isack van Ostade was taught by his brother, Adriaen, in Haarlem. He may also have studied landscape painting with Salomon van Ruysdael, who sued him in 1640 for board and tuition fees. His early work follows the example of his brother but from 1643, the year he entered the Haarlem guild, he absorbed elements of the Italianate manner brought back to Holland by Pieter van Laer and his colleagues. Interior scenes became less common in his work in this period.

Pacchia, Gerolamo del
(1477 – after 1533)
After working in Florence and Siena, Gerolamo moved to Rome in about 1500. In 1508, he was back in Siena where he collaborated in particular with Pacchiarotto. The two artists subsequently went to France and executed paintings in the Château de Gaillon.

Palma Vecchio (Jacopo Negretti)
(*c.* 1480 – 1528)
Palma settled in Venice by 1510, where he was probably apprenticed to Andrea Previtali, who was also from Bergamo. He became celebrated for his devotional images with groups of half-length saints gathered around the Virgin and Child and for his idealized portraits of beautiful women, which relate to themes in contemporary poetry. Palma was interested in both central Italian art and Venetian art, responding in particular to the innovations of Giorgione and Titian. He was an important teacher in Venice.

Palmer, Samuel
(1805 – 1881)
Through John Linnell, Palmer met William Blake about 1824 and adopted several features of Blake's art. The simplified images of rustic life which he drew and painted during the period he spent in Shoreham in Kent (1826–35) are works of a visionary imagination, illustrating themes from the Bible, Milton, Shakespeare and Virgil. Following his marriage to Linnell's daughter, his work became more conventional. On return from a protracted honeymoon in Italy (1837–9) he earned his living as a teacher. He took up etching in mid-career and his etchings and a number of strongly coloured late watercolours recapture something of the dream-like quality of his early work.

Pan (Jacqueline Regina Ward)
(b. 1923)
Jacqueline Regina Monziols was born in Nice. She married Theodore A.J. Ward in 1955. Work by her has appeared in exhibitions in several countries.

Panini, Giovanni Paolo
(1691 – 1765)
Panini studied perspective in Piacenza probably with Ferdinando Bibiena, Giuseppe Natali and Giovanni Battista Galluzzi; he went to Rome in 1711 and studied under Benedetto Luti. He entered the Accademia di S. Luca in 1719 and taught perspective; meanwhile his circle of patrons grew to include Roman cardinals and noble families, while he had extensive contacts with French artists and visitors to Rome. He specialized in view paintings, scenes of official festivities and *capricci* or fantasy views.

Paolini, Pietro
(1603 – 1681)
Paolini studied from 1619 under Angelo Caroselli in Rome and was greatly impressed by the northern European followers of Caravaggio active in Rome in the 1620s. He settled in his native Lucca in 1631, specializing in allegorical and musical subjects and exploring the new subject of still-life painting. Paolini opened a private academy around 1650.

Parsons, Alfred William
(1847 – 1920)
While studying at the South Kensington Art School, Parsons worked as a post office clerk. He exhibited extensively at various venues, incluing the Royal Academy, where he made his debut in 1871. In addition to his fresh landscapes, he painted plants and gardens. He was also a watercolourist and illustrator.

Pasmore, Victor
(1908 – 1998)
Pasmore was a part-time amateur until he was persuaded by Kenneth Clark to take up painting as a career. In 1938, he founded the Euston Road School with William Coldstream and Claude Rogers. He taught at the Camberwell School of Art, 1943–9. In the late 1940s, he abandoned his Impressionistic manner for abstraction and began to work in relief. From 1954 to 1961 he was Director of Painting at the Department of Fine Art at Newcastle University.

Patel, Pierre, the Elder
(*c.* 1605 – 1676)
Patel was established in Paris by 1635, where he gained a high reputation as a landscapist. He also worked on decorative schemes for aristocratic patrons. Between 1668 and 1670 he painted a series of topographical views of royal palaces. Although he apparently never travelled to Italy, his speciality was an Italianate type of classical landscape, based on pictures arriving from Rome that he could study in Parisian collections. He was called 'The Claude Lorrain of France' in the mid-18th century.

Patenir, Joachim
(active 1515 – d. before 1524)
Patenir was admitted to the Antwerp guild in 1515 and may have previously taken lessons from Gerard David. He specialized in painting landscapes. His compositions are either panoramic views seen from a high viewpoint or vertical images with tall, fantastic rock formations. Both types of landscape were invariably used as the settings for figures which were sometimes inserted into his paintings by other artists. He was one of the first European artists to specialize in painting landscapes and his work had a lasting influence on his successors.

Pater, Jean-Baptiste
(1695 – 1736)
A pupil and close imitator of Watteau, whom he may have met in Valenciennes in 1709–10, Pater was the son of a sculptor and art dealer. He was placed with a local artist, J.B. Guidé, before following Watteau to Paris, probably *c.* 1710–11. Like his master, Pater worked mainly for amateurs rather than seeking official commissions. He was received into the Academy in 1725 as a painter of *fêtes galantes*; these were his principal subjects, together with scenes of military campaigns and genre scenes deriving from Flemish art.

Patrick, J.
(first half of 19th century)
Almost nothing is known about this artist except that he exhibited an unidentified portrait in the Royal Academy in 1808 and two portraits in 1813, each described as 'portrait of a lady'.

Peeters, Clara
(active 1607 – after 1621)
For an artist of distinction, the life of Clara Peeters is surprisingly ill-documented. From the character of her work, it is supposed she was born in or near Antwerp. Her dated works range from 1607 to 1621 but she may have continued working into the 1620s.

Pellegrini, Giovanni Antonio
(1675 – 1741)
The son of a Paduan glovemaker, Pellegrini trained with Paolo Pagani, whom he accompanied to Moravia and Vienna, returning to Venice in 1696. A sojourn in Rome in 1699–1701 allowed him to study the high Baroque art of Pietro da Cortona and Giovanni Battista Gaulli. He worked in England, 1708–13, where his light palette, sketchy handling and elegant manner found favour with patrons. Pellegrini then led a peripatetic career as a painter of imaginative and colourful decorative schemes, altar-pieces and easel paintings, in Düsseldorf, Paris, Antwerp, England, Würzburg, Dresden, Vienna and Mannheim, punctuated by periods in Venice.

Penny, Edward
(1714 – 1791)
After training with Thomas Hudson in London, Penny left for Rome in the early 1740s, where he took lessons with Marco Benefial. In 1745, he returned to England and became a successful painter of portraits. He also painted a number of moral scenes from ancient and recent history as well as moralizing genre pictures. He was one of the founder members of the Royal Academy in 1768.

Perugino, Pietro (Pietro di Cristoforo Vannucci)
(documented 1469 – 1523)
Perugino apparently trained in the studio of Verrocchio, and, according to Vasari, with Piero della Francesca. He developed a harmonious classical style and was in particular demand as a painter of altar-pieces. An important commission was that of group of frescoes in the Sistine Chapel, Rome, *c.* 1479–82. He was based mainly in Florence in the 1490s, when his reputation was at its peak, running a busy workshop, while from *c.* 1495 he moved to Perugia. Perugino's art was viewed as old-fashioned later in his career.

Peruzzini, Antonio Francesco
(*c.* 1668 – 1724)
A landscape specialist from Ancona, Peruzzini was strongly influenced by the art of Salvator Rosa and painted wild, atmospheric landscapes and stormy marine pictures; he also knew the art of Pietro Mulier, il Tempesta. He often collaborated with figure painters, notably Alessandro Magnasco and Sebastiano Ricci. Little is known of Peruzzini's early career, but he was active in Bologna by the mid-1680s, collaborating with Ricci there in 1687–8. He worked mainly in Milan, with an important sojourn at the court of Florence in the early 1700s.

Pettie, John
(1839 – 1893)
At the age of sixteen, Pettie entered the Trustees' Academy in Edinburgh, where he became a member of a group of colourists, including William MacTaggart, Tom Graham and W.Q. Orchardson, with whom he shared a studio in London. He painted many episodes from British history. He also worked as an illustrator for *Good Words*. In his later years, he turned more to portraiture.

Phillips, Thomas
(1770 – 1845)
Phillips was trained as a glass painter. On arrival in London in 1790, he worked on the windows of St George's Chapel in Windsor. He entered the Royal Academy Schools in 1791 and painted a few history pictures but went on to become a highly successful painter of portraits.

Phillips, Tom
(b. 1937)
Phillips studied Anglo-Saxon literature at Oxford (1957–60) before moving to Camberwell School of Arts and Crafts. He taught at Bath Academy, 1966–7, and showed at the Venice Biennale in 1971. His activities cover many fields, including music, graphics, sculpture, writing and designing books.

Philpot, Glyn Warren
(1884 – 1937)
Born in London, Philpot attended Lambeth Art School and then went to the Académie Julian in Paris in 1905, where he came under the influence of Charles Ricketts and was converted to Roman Catholicism. He became a successful portrait painter. In the 1930s, he changed his style in response to contemporary trends in France.

Picasso, Pablo
(1881 – 1974)
Born in Malaga, Picasso studied with his father and at the art schools at Corunna and Barcelona. From 1900 to 1904, he moved between Spain and Paris, painting images of mothers, circus people and paupers in a predominantly blue range of colour. In 1904, he moved to Paris and added pink to his palette. Following his meeting with the Fauves and his discovery of African sculpture, his art became more distorted and fragmented. In 1907, this developed into Cubism. After 1920, he reverted to more classical forms, combined in the 1930s with a darker, more expressive element. After the Second World War, he moved to the south of France and produced an abundance of work in different media, including prints, painted ceramics and sculpture. His last paintings were brash and colourful.

Piero di Cosimo
(1461 – 1522)
The son of a goldsmith, Piero took the name of his master, Cosimo Rosselli, with whom he went to Rome in 1481–2. While he worked in fresco at the Sistine Chapel, Piero specialized in panel paintings on his return to his native Florence, painting altar-pieces, devotional images, portraits and historical or mythological scenes. He was particularly admired for his inventive fantasy, and his *spalliera* panels for private patrons are often of unusual subjects; Piero was also in demand as a designer of pageants. An original and innovative artist, he was familiar with the art of Leonardo and Michelangelo and played an important role in the formation of artists such as Andrea del Sarto, Fra Bartolomeo and Pontormo.

Pietro degli Ingannati
(active 1529 – 1547)
A follower of Giovanni Bellini in Venice, Pietro specialized in half-length groups of saints with the Virgin and Child (a subject known as a *sacra conversazione*), which he made for private patrons. He may have been trained with Alvise Vivarini; however, he looked to Bellini for his compositions and figure types and probably spent time in the workshop of the elderly artist. Pietro remained true to this heritage, still producing *sacra conversazione* paintings in a conservative style as late as 1548.

Pintoricchio, Bernardino (Bernardino di Betto)
(*c.* 1452 – 1513)
Born in Perugia, Pintoricchio collaborated with Perugino at the Sistine Chapel in 1481–2. He developed a distinctive style characterized by a richness of decorative detail and a delicacy of touch that has affinities with late Gothic art. However, he was also interested in antique decoration and in Flemish art. Pinturicchio's major fresco commissions include the decoration of the Borgia apartments at the Vatican, 1492–94, and the Piccolomini Library in Siena Cathedral, 1507–8. He also painted numerous religious works and was an important miniaturist.

Piper, John
(1903 – 1992)
From 1921 to 1926, Piper studied law before attending art classes at the Kingston School of Art and at the Royal College. After visiting Paris in the mid-1930s he took up abstract painting but later returned to representational work. He wrote extensively for periodicals, published his own quarterly review, *Axis*, produced travel guides and designed for the theatre. Much of his work is based upon architecture. He also designed windows, notably for Coventry Cathedral.

Pissarro, Camille
(1830 – 1903)
Pissarro was born at St Thomas in the Danish West Indies. He went to Paris in 1855, where he admired Corot's work. From about 1859, he attended the Atelier Suisse, where he met Monet. He began to produce his first Impressionist landscapes after he moved to Louveciennes in 1869 and continued when he moved to London in 1870 and to Pontoise in 1871. In the early 1880s, figures became more important in his work. In 1884, he settled at the village of Eragny in Normandy. After meeting Seurat in 1885 he experimented with the pointillist manner of the Neo-Impressionists but returned to a more improvised technique in the 1890s. In the last decade of his life he worked mainly in the countryside around Eragny but also in Rouen, Le Havre, Dieppe and Paris. Several of his Paris views were painted in series.

Pissarro, Félix
(1874 – 1897)
The third son of Camille Pissarro, Félix worked first as a carpenter and then took up painting with some tuition and encouragement from his father. To avoid military service he joined his brothers Georges and Lucien in England where they worked together. In 1894, Georges and Félix went to Belgium but they returned to England in 1896 where Félix painted many landscapes on the south coast. He was always in financial difficulties and died of tuberculosis at his studio in Kew the following year.

Pissarro, Lucien
(1863 – 1944)
Lucien Pissarro's art was strongly marked by the work of his father Camille Pissarro. Several of his early paintings use a Neo-Impressionist technique. In 1890, he moved permanently to London. From 1894 until 1914, he devoted much time to designing and printing books for his Eragny Press, which he set up with help from Ricketts and Shannon. After the press closed, he devoted his time to painting. He participated in the New English Art Club, the Fitzroy Street Group and the Camden Town Group.

Pissarro, Ludovic-Rodolphe
(1878 – 1952)
Ludovic-Rodolphe was Camille Pissarro's fourth son. In 1894, he published his first wood-engravings. His early work was influenced by the contemporary decorative tendencies in Belgian art and had some affinities with the Fauves, with whom he exhibited. He painted urban views, especially in London, where he spent much time. With Lucien, he founded the Monarro Group to promote the work of the Impressionists in England. His art was much influenced by his father and he spent over twenty years writing a catalogue of his work.

Pissarro, Orovida
(1893 – 1968)
Orovida was Lucien's only child. She was born in Epping in England and worked briefly with Sickert. At an early stage she turned away from her father's Impressionism and adopted a decorative style combining, at times, gold-leaf and tempera and taking her subjects from exotic sources. Wild animals are a constant theme in her paintings and in her etchings. By the mid-1930s, she turned to subjects of contemporary life. Her later works are marked by a return to naturalism and by the use of oil paint, which she took up during the Second World War, apparently because eggs for tempera were in short supply.

Pittar, Barry
(1880 – 1948)
Pittar was born in Kent and became chief architectural artist to the Royal Doulton Potteries at Lambeth. He also supplied illustrations to *The Graphic* and *The Illustrated London News*. He was chiefly a painter and etcher of architectural subjects but also painted landscapes.

Pittoni, Giambattista
(1687 – 1767)
Pittoni learned the basics of his profession in Venice under his uncle, Francesco Pittoni, but his real mentors were Antonio Balestra, Giambattista Piazzetta and Sebastiano Ricci. Unlike Amigoni or Tiepolo, Pittoni did not travel abroad, except possibly a trip to Paris in 1720. His style was closer to contemporary French art than that of his Venetian contemporaries. He enjoyed an international market for his pictures, whether cabinet paintings or altar-pieces, particularly with Austrian, German and to some extent English clients. He was President of the Academy in Venice in 1758.

Pittuck, Douglas Frederick
(1911 – 1993)
Pittuck studied at the Ruskin School of Drawing in Oxford part-time from 1931 to 1939 and again as a full-time student after the Second World War. He lived at Barnard Castle in County Durham where he painted a mural for the Glaxo laboratories.

Poole, Vera Ellen
(1890 – 1965)
Vera Poole (*née* Dendy) was born in Melbourne, Australia. In 1905, she moved to Weybridge in England. She studied at the Lambeth School of Art in 1909 and took lessons with Sickert in 1910. She spent 1912 to 1914 in Paris. In 1917, she settled in Oxford where she took up a teaching post at the Oxford School of Drawing. From 1916 to 1922 she exhibited landscapes at the New English Art Club. After 1931, she painted little.

Porcellis, Jan
(*c.* 1584 – 1632)
Porcellis was born in Ghent but moved to Holland where he worked in many Dutch cities. He specialized in painting marine subjects. He introduced a new interest in atmospheric effects into Netherlandish pictures of ships at sea. Many of his sea-pieces represent storms and ship-wrecks.

Pordenone (Giovanni Antonio de Sacchis)
(1483 – 1539)
The son of a master mason, Pordenone, named after his native town, was an innovative and influential artist, becoming a rival to Titian in the 1530s. He painted numerous illusionistic frescoes on palace façades, most of which are lost, together with important frescoes in Cremona cathedral from 1520; he also painted some notable altar-pieces. Pordenone was familiar with central Italian art as well as with German painting and northern European prints. He was an important draughtsman.

Porter, Frederick James
(1883 – 1944)
Porter was born at Auckland, New Zealand, where he studied art before moving to Melbourne and Paris. He studied at the Académie Julian in Paris before settling in England. From 1924 to 1944, he taught at the Central School of Arts and Crafts and was closely associated with the Bloomsbury Group.

Poussin, Gaspard (see Dughet, Gaspard)

Poussin, Nicolas
(1594 – 1665)
Having trained under Quentin Varin, Poussin spent his formative years in Paris from 1612 to 1623, where he became friends with the poet Giovanni Battista Marino. He settled in Rome in 1624, returning to France to work for Louis XIII in 1640–42. Part of the erudite circle of Cassiano dal Pozzo in Rome, Poussin studied the antique and the art of Raphael and Titian. A deeply learned artist, he could visualize the mysteries and passions of the antique world, producing paintings of classical and Christian subjects of extraordinary emotional intensity and rational control. His work was enormously influential.

Predis, Giovanni Ambrogio de'
(*c.* 1455 – after 1508)
The half-brother of Cristoforo, a well-known illuminator, Giovanni Ambrogio first worked as a miniaturist *c.* 1474. He is then documented in 1482 in the employment of the Duke of Milan: he produced a variety of portraits for the Sforza and Este courts and also worked for the Milanese mint. De Predis was able to study the art of Leonardo in Milan and collaborated in the execution of the London *Virgin of the Rocks*. He was in the service of the Emperor Maximilian I in Innsbruck in 1493–4.

Preti, Matia
(1613 – 1699)
Born in Calabria, Preti had some training in Rome under his brother, Gregorio (*c.* 1603–72), but the influence of Caravaggio was fundamental to his artistic formation. He was also interested in Guercino, Lanfranco and Venetian art: he travelled to Florence, Emilia and the Veneto in the late 1630s. He became a knight of the Order of Malta and enjoyed numerous important religious commissions in Rome. Preti worked in Naples from *c.* 1653, settling in Malta in 1661, where his great achievement was the fresco decoration of the Cathedral of S. Giovanni in Valletta.

Prinsep, Valentine Cameron
(1836 – 1904)
Born in India, Prinsep was destined to become a civil servant like his father but was encouraged by G.F.Watts to take up painting. He studied under Watts and turned towards the Pre-Raphaelites following a meeting with Rossetti. He participated in the decoration of the walls of the Oxford Union in 1857 and later studied under Gleyre in Paris, where Whistler, Poynter and Du Maurier were fellow students. He was the model for Taffy in Du Maurier's *Trilby*. He later travelled in Italy with Burne-Jones and in India where he found subjects for a number of his later pictures.

Prout, Margaret Millicent Fisher
(1875 – 1963)
Margaret Prout was taught by her father, Mark Fisher, and studied at the Slade School. She exhibited landscapes, animal paintings and figure compositions at the New English Art Club and many other venues.

Pryde, James Ferrier
(1866 – 1941)
Pryde was born in Edinburgh and studied at the Royal Academy Schools and in Paris. In 1893, he collaborated with his brother-in-law William Nicholson in designing posters under the pseudonym of The Beggarstaff Brothers. After working as an actor, Pryde returned to painting in 1905. His characteristic work, featuring dark interiors or architectural inventions, has a theatrical quality. He abandoned painting about 1929.

Pulzone, Scipione
(1544 – 1598)
Born in Gaeta, Pulzone was mainly active in Rome, where he was possibly a pupil of Jacopino del Ponte; he worked also in Naples and Florence. He admired the portraits of Raphael and of Flemish artists, becoming a notable portraitist whose work was characterized by its naturalism. In his religious art Pulzone also strove for a direct, naturalistic approach, a type of art encouraged by the Council of Trent.

Pury, Edmond Jean, Baron de
(1845 – 1911)
De Pury was a born at Neuchâtel and studied under his fellow countryman, Charles Gleyre, in Paris. He found many of his subjects among the picturesque peasants of Rome, Capri and Venice. He was also a prolific etcher.

Raeburn, Sir Henry
(1756 – 1823)
Raeburn seems to have been self-taught. He received his first commission for a portrait in 1776. Following his marriage in 1778, he went to Italy, meeting Reynolds in London en route. On returning to Scotland, he settled in Edinburgh and dominated the production of portraits in the capital for the next forty years. He painted directly onto the canvas, using square brushes which have left a visible and characteristic mark in many of his portraits. He was knighted by George IV in 1822.

Ramsay, Allan
(1713 – 1784)
Ramsay was born in Edinburgh. His father was the poet, Allan Ramsay. He studied in London under the Swedish portrait painter Hans Hysing and completed his studies in Italy in1736–7, studying with Imperiali in Rome and with Solimena in Naples. He returned to a successful practice in London and found sitters chiefly among the Scottish aristocracy. He was in Rome, 1754–7, where he studied the art and the antiquities of the city. On his return to London, his success continued and he took up writing. In 1760, he was appointed painter to George III. In 1775 he abandoned painting and returned to Rome to pursue his antiquarian interests.

Raphael (Raffaello Santi)
(1483 – 1520)
The son of an artist at the Urbino court, Giovanni Santi, Raphael was traditionally said to have studied with Perugino, with whom he had a close association in his early career. He worked for patrons in Città di Castello and Perugia; in Florence in 1504–8 he studied the art of Leonardo and Michelangelo while painting portraits and devotional works for Tuscan and Umbrian patrons. In Rome from 1508 he worked on fresco decoration in the Vatican Stanze for Popes Julius II and Leo X, as well as altar-pieces, portraits and other paintings for a range of patrons. Raphael ran a major workshop, designing tapestries and buildings as well as paintings, and was a superb draughtsman, with many of his drawings reproduced as prints in his own lifetime. His art became a touchstone of high quality for artists and collectors down to modern times.

Read, David Charles
(1790 – 1851)
Read exhibited rustic subjects and landscapes in London. He was also a lively watercolourist and etcher. He lived in Salisbury, where his patron Chambers Hall also lived. Many of his works were given to the University Galleries in Oxford by Chambers Hall in 1855.

Reader, William
(active 1672 – 80)
Reader was born in Maidstone in Kent. He was a pupil of Gerard Soest and is known to have lived for some time in the house of a nobleman. His earliest known portrait is dated 1672. It is said that he ended his days in poverty.

Rembrandt Harmensz. van Rijn
(1606 – 1669)
Rembrandt was born in Leiden and educated at the Latin School and briefly at the University. He learned painting with the history painters, Jacob van Swanenburgh and Pieter Lastman in Amsterdam. Following his return to Leiden, he painted his first small biblical and historical works. He had already begun the long series of self-portraits which he painted regularly throughout his career, and made his first etchings. In 1631–2, he moved to Amsterdam. By 1639, he had many pupils and bought a large house where he kept his art collection. He was much in demand as a painter of portraits for most of his time in Amsterdam. In the 1640s, partly in response to the work of Titian, his subjects became less theatrical, his canvases became larger and his manner of painting became increasingly bold. In 1656, probably as a result of financial mismanagement, he had to sell his house and contents and he died insolvent.

Reni, Guido
(1575 – 1642)
Reni trained in Bologna under Denys Calvaert along with Domenichino and Albano and, like them, transferred to the more fashionable studio of the Carracci in 1594–5. By 1601, he had moved to Rome where he was employed by the Borghese family. He was influenced briefly by the work of Caravaggio but the influence of Raphael became more important to him. In 1614, he returned to Bologna where he painted a series of major religious compositions. In his later works, his touch became thinner and more sketch-like and his colour became much lighter. According to his contemporary biographer, Malvasia, he had a neurotic and quarrelsome character.

Renoir, Pierre-Auguste
(1841 – 1919)
Renoir worked as a porcelain painter before entering the studio of Charles Gleyre in 1861, he studio he met Sisley, Bazillle and Monet, who formed the nucleus of the Impressionist movement. In the 1870s, he painted sunlit landscapes, gardens, portraits and scenes of modern urban life. In 1881, he went to Italy, and adopted a less improvised manner of working on his return. In 1905, he settled at Cagnes on the south coast of France and his art became more expansive and more warmly coloured. Paintings of nudes and bathing women became a major theme after 1880.

Reynolds, Sir Joshua
(1723 – 1792)
Reynolds was born in Plympton in Devon and trained under Thomas Hudson in London. He earned his living painting portraits before going to Italy in 1751 to study the art and antiquities of Rome. On his return to London he became the foremost English painter of portraits and first President of the Royal Academy, on its foundation in 1768.

Reynolds, Samuel William, the Younger
(1794 – 1872)
Reynolds was chiefly a painter of portraits although he also exhibited a few genre pictures at the British Institution. He was the son of the painter and engraver Samual William Reynolds and father of the portrait painter Frank Reynolds. Like his father, he worked in mezzotint.

Rhoades, Geoffrey Hamilton
(1898 – 1980)
Rhoades studies at Clapham Art School, 1915–17 and, after the First World War, at the Slade School under Henry Tonks. In the 1920s, he undertook a series of works at Stoke Rochford House in Lincolnshire. From 1953 to 1972, he taught at the Ruskin School of Drawing in Oxford. His favourite subjects are drawn from the natural world, including figures, landscapes and flowers.

Ribot, Augustin-Théodule
(1823 – 1891)
Ribot came to Paris in 1845 where he worked as a gilder for a frame-maker and took lessons with Auguste-Barthélémy Glaize. He supported himself with many different jobs through the 1850s. In 1861, he exhibited the first of a number of paintings of cooks and went on to paint religious subjects, genre scenes, portraits and still life in a manner marked by his taste for Rembrandt and the painters of 17th-century Spain. He fell ill in the late 1870s and gave up painting.

Ricard, Louis-Gustave
(1823 – 1873)
Ricard studied at the art school in Marseille before transferring to the studio of Léon Cogniet in Paris. He was in Paris by 1843 but he had already embarked on his long artistic engagement with the Old Masters. He spent from 1844 to 1848 travelling in Italy, Belgium, Holland and England, studying and copying the work of the Venetians, Rubens, Rembrandt, Reynolds and others. His portraits, exhibited from 1850 to 1859 and again in 1872, are marked by the influence of these artists to which he added an air of mystery and introspection.

Ricci, Marco
(1676 – 1730)
Trained with his uncle Sebastiano, Marco fled Venice after a brawl, working in Split (Dalmatia) with a landscape artist. This became his speciality, together with scene-painting for the Venetian theatre. In Florence from 1705 to 1707, he collaborated with Magnasco. Together with Giovanni Antonio Pellegrini he went to England in 1708 to work on scenery at the new opera house in Covent Garden and there painted landscapes and genre scenes. Marco returned to Venice in 1715. He is best known for his small, freshly-painted pastoral or rugged landscapes in tempera on kid-skin.

Ricci, Sebastiano
(1659 – 1734)
Ricci trained under Federico Cervelli in Venice, before travelling widely (often as the result of amatory escapades) in northern Italy, where he studied Emilian art in particular. In Rome, financed by the Duke of Parma, he was profoundly influenced by the art of Annibale Carracci and Pietro da Cortona. He worked at the Medici court in Florence from 1706 to 1707. In Venice he led a Veronese revival, marked by his altar-piece for S. Giorgio Maggiore of 1708. Sebastiano joined his nephew Marco in England 1712–15, where the young Earl of Burlington was a major patron. Ricci enjoyed a high international reputation.

Richmond, George
(1809 – 1896)
Richmond met Samuel Palmer while studying at the Royal Academy Schools. Together with Edward Calvert, he joined the group of Blake's followers, the 'Ancients', who gathered round Palmer at Shoreham in Kent in the mid-1820s. Blake influenced his early work but there is little trace of this in his later work when he became a successful portrait painter. Paintings by him appeared at the Royal Academy exhibitions from 1825 to 1884.

Richmond, Sir William Blake
(1842 – 1921)
William Blake Richmond was George Richmond's son. He had some tuition from Ruskin before he went to the Royal Academy Schools in 1857. He exhibited at the Academy summer exhibitions for the first time in 1861 and had a long career as a successful painter of portraits. Following the death of his first wife in 1864, he went to Italy where he met Leighton and Costa, both of whom had a decisive influence on his art.

Ricketts, Charles de Sousy
(1866 – 1931)
Ricketts was born in Geneva and lived for most of his life in London. He was closely associated with Charles Shannon, whom he met at Lambeth School of Art in 1882 and with whom he worked until his death in 1931. The Vale Press which they managed produced a series of books illustrated, designed and printed by themselves. Ricketts was a prolific wood-engraver, illustrator and theatrical designer as well as a painter.

Rielly, James
(b. 1956)
Rielly was born in Wales and studied at the Gloucestershire College of Art and Design, 1975–8, and at Belfast College of Art, 1980–1. He held a succession of fellowships in the 1980s and 1990s, including the Momart Fellowship at the Tate Gallery, Liverpool in 1995. His work has appeared in many group shows as well as in numerous solo exhibitions in Britain and elsewhere.

Rigaud, John Francis
(1742 – 1810)
Rigaud was born in Turin of a French father. He was trained in Turin, Florence and Bologna. During two years spent in Rome he met James Barry and returned to England with him in 1771. He was much sought-after in England for decorative schemes, portraits and historical compositions. Most of his decorative work has been destroyed. He contributed to Boydell's *Shakespeare Gallery* and to Macklin's *Poets' Gallery* and painted many small-scale pictures of history somewhat in the style of Hamilton and Cipriani.

Riley, John
(1646 – 1691)
Riley was taught by Isaac Fuller and Gerard Soest. In 1682, he entered the Painter-Stainers' Company and had a successful career as a portrait painter in the following decade. After the Revolution of 1688, he was appointed chief painter to the king along with Kneller. He had an arrangement to collaborate on portraits with John Closterman which seems to have foundered on the unequal division of the earnings.

Rivière, Briton
(1840 – 1920)
Rivière was taught by his father, William and then by John Pettie and W.Q. Orchardson. Animals were his chief theme. He acquired his skill in painting animals by studying at London Zoo. He painted many genre and historical scenes in which animals, usually dogs, were prominent.

Rivière, William
(1806 – 1876)
William Rivière exhibited genre pictures and portraits at the Royal Academy from 1826 to 1869. He held the post of Drawing Master at Cheltenham College before moving to a studio in Park Town in Oxford. He was father of the animal painter, Briton Rivière.

Roberts, Clare
(second half of 20th century)
The artist was a student at the Ruskin School of Drawing in the mid-1970s, when in 1975 she won the Coghill landscape prize. She later studied at the Royal College of Art, graduating in illustration.

Roberts, William
(1895 – 1980)
Roberts was born in London and studied at St Martin's School of Art and at the Slade School, 1910–13. He travelled in France and Italy and was influenced by Picasso. In 1914, he became a member of the Vorticist Group. In 1917–18, he worked as a war artist. He published a number of polemical pamphlets and, apart from his many portraits, painted scenes of contemporary social life in a tightly drawn, highly formalized manner. He taught at the Central School of Arts and Crafts from 1925 to 1960 with a break during the Second World War when he taught at the Oxford Technical School.

Rogers, Claude Maurice
(1907 – 1979)
Rogers spent his early years in London and in Buenos Aires. He studied at the Slade School from 1925 to 1928 where he was a contemporary of William Coldstream, Roderigo Moynihan and Geoffrey Tibble, with whom he was associated in founding the Euston Road School in the late 1930s. His style remained true to the principles of the School. He was visiting lecturer at the Slade from 1948–63, and Professor of Fine Art at the University of Reading, 1968–72.

Romanelli, Giovanni Francesco
(*c.* 1610 – 1662)
A pupil of Domenichino in Rome, Romanelli then moved to the studio of Pietro da Cortona, with whom he became closely associated. Like Cortona he enjoyed Barberini patronage, painting frescoes and making tapestry designs at the Vatican. At the death of Urban VIII (Barberini) he left for Paris to work for Cardinal Jules Mazarin 1646–8; he later returned to Paris in 1655–8. Romanelli's style is graceful and assured, characterized by rich colouring and his work had some impact on public art in late 17th-century France.

Romney, George
(1734 – 1802)
After beginning his career as a painter of portraits in Kendal and Lancaster, Romney moved to London in 1762. He visited Paris in 1764 and spent 1773–5 in Italy. He had ambitions to be a painter of historical compositions but made his reputation as a painter of portraits. He returned to Kendal in 1796 and remained there for the rest of his life.

Rooke, Thomas Matthews
(1842 – 1942)
At the age of twenty-nine, Rooke was employed as a designer by William Morris's firm and became assistant to Burne-Jones. He was also employed by Ruskin who sent him to the Continent each year to make drawings of ancient buildings. In the earlier part of his career, he painted a number of biblical subjects, portraits and landscapes in the Pre-Raphaelite manner.

Roos, Johann Melchior (Rosa da Tivoli)
(1659 – 1731)
One of a numerous family of painters who worked mostly in Italy, Roos was born in Frankfurt and later settled in Nuremberg. He painted landscapes and portraits and, later in life, specialized in animal scenes and landscapes.

Rosa, Salvator
(1615 – 1673)
Trained by Francesco Francanzano, Rosa probably completed his studies with Aniello Falcone, although the art of Ribera was of great importance in his formation. He mainly worked in Rome, with a sojourn in Florence, 1640–9, where he worked for Giovan Carlo de' Medici. Rosa was a poet, actor, printmaker and satirist, as well as becoming famous for his wild landscapes and often macabre learned subjects. He also painted religious works and portraits. An ambitious artist, he resented the popularity of his landscapes.

Rothenstein, Sir William
(1872 – 1945)
Rothenstein was born in Bradford. He studied at the Slade School in 1888 and at the Académie Julian, in Paris, from 1889–93. In 1893, he visited Spain and Morocco and settled in London in 1895. In 1912, he moved to Stroud in Gloucestershire. He was an official war artist with the British army in 1917–18 and with the Canadian army in 1919. He was principal of the Royal College of Art from 1920 to 1935 and was knighted in 1931.

Royen, Willem Frederiksz. van
(*c.* 1645 – probably 1723)
Van Royen is said to have been born in Haarlem but is first recorded in The Hague in 1661 as a pupil of Arnoldus van Ravesteyn. In 1669, he was summoned to the court of Friedrich Wilhelm, Elector of Brandenburg, in Berlin. He was one of the founders of the Berlin Academy in 1696 and became Rector in 1698. He painted still lifes of fruit and flowers as well as hunting pieces.

Rubens, Sir Peter Paul
(1577 – 1640)
Born at Siegen in Westphalia in1577, Rubens trained in Antwerp, chiefly with Otho van Veen. He was in Italy from 1600 to 1608 and then mostly in Antwerp where he set up his studio. In 1609 he was appointed painter to the Archduke Albert of Austria and his wife Isabella, governors of the Southern Netherlands. Between 1609 and 1621, he undertook a series of major commissions in Antwerp, including altar-pieces for the cathedral, tapestry designs and altar-pieces and ceiling panels for the new Jesuit Church. In 1622–5, he completed a cycle of paintings celebrating the life of Marie de Médicis, for the Luxembourg Palace in Paris. After 1626, he was increasingly involved in diplomatic work which brought him further commissions from Philip IV of Spain and Charles I of England. He spent the last four years of his life in his country manor, Het Steen.

Ruisdael, Jacob van
(1628/9 – *c.* 1682)
Ruisdael was born in Haarlem, where he was probably trained by his father Isaac Jacobsz. van Ruisdael and his uncle, Salomon van Ruysdael. In 1650, he visited Bentheim in Germany with Nicolaes Berchem. He was a landscape painter whose favourite themes were rushing streams, empty expanses of fields and forests. His work was a source of inspiration to many other artists, including Hobbema, who was his pupil.

Ruoppolo, Giovanni Battista
(1629 – 1693)
Ruoppolo's father was a painter of maiolica in Naples, while his brother Carlo painted maiolica and pictures. Giovanni Battista specializing in still-life paintings, working for a market of wealthy Neapolitans and Flemish merchants and bankers. A pupil of Giacomo Recco, a Caravaggesque flower painter, Ruoppolo first painted in a strongly naturalist style. His mature works are more Baroque, with an emphasis on elaborate compositions and lavish decorative effects.

Ruysch, Rachel
(1664 – 1750)
Ruysch was born in The Hague. Her father was a botanist who had settled with his family in Amsterdam by 1667. She seems to have been taught still-life painting by Willem van Aelst. From 1708 to 1716, she was court painter to the Elector Palatine Johann Wilhelm in Düsseldorf but remained in Amsterdam. Dated works by her are known between 1681 and 1747.

Ruysdael, Salomon van
(1600/3? – 1670)
Ruysdael is recorded as a member of the Haarlem guild in 1623. He remained in Haarlem for the rest of his life. His early landscapes are somewhat monochromatic but his later work is broader and more colourful. His work has affinities with the work of his contemporary, Jan van Goyen.

Sajó, Gyula
(1918 – 1989)
Born in Hungary, Sajó studied art and architecure at the Academy of Applied Art in Budapest, 1933–41. In 1956, he came to England. From 1959, he lived at Worthing in Sussex where he founded the Atelier Art Group. His work is characterized by a strong sense of colour.

Sandby, Paul
(1731 – 1809)
Sandby worked mainly in watercolour and gouache. He went from Nottingham to London with his brother, the architect Thomas Sandby, in 1747. From 1747 to 1752, he worked with the Survey of Scotland and learned etching in Edinburgh. He was one of the first artists to use the aquatint process in England. He was an influential teacher in watercolour. His oils tend to date from his last years.

Sands, Ethel
(1873 – 1962)
Born at Newport, Rhode Island, Sands came to London in 1879 with her parents. With her friend Nan Hudson she went to Paris and studied under Eugène Carrière from 1896 to 190. She lived in Garsington in England from 1900 until 1920, when she moved to London. She became associated with Sickert and exhibited with the Fitzroy Street Group and had her first London exhibition with Nan Hudson in 1912.

Sandys, Frederick
(1829 – 1904)
Sandys's father was a painter from Norwich. He studied under George Richmond and Samuel Laurence at the Royal Academy Schools and acquired from them his talent for drawing in chalks. He made his debut at the Royal Academy summer exhibition in 1851 and became friendly with Rossetti and Swinburne, through whom he became an associate of the Pre-Raphaelites. His paintings of idealized women are derived from Rossetti. After about 1880, he concentrated mostly on portraits in chalk. He was also a prolific illustrator in woodcut.

Sano di Pietro (Ansano di Pietro di Mencio)
(1405–6 – 1481)
A prolific painter and illuminator from Siena, Sano di Pietro was probably trained by Sassetta. He left many dated works, displaying an awareness in his early maturity of the art of Paolo Uccello and of Fra Angelico. After the 1450s, when he was much in demand, his works tend to be more repetitive and conservative, satisfying the demands of his clients. He had numerous assistants. Sano's illuminations for manuscripts are of consistently high quality.

Sargent, John Singer
(1856 – 1925)
Sargent was born in Florence where his father had retired from a medical practice in Philadelphia. He travelled extensively in Europe and studied with Carolus-Duran in Paris. In 1886, he settled in London and achieved great success as a portrait painter. From 1890, he carried out a series of murals for the Boston Public Library. He also painted many landscapes and topographical views on his travels, at first in oil, latterly largely in watercolour.

Sarto, Andrea del
(1486 – 1530)
One of the most important Florentine painters of the early 16th century, Andrea taught a generation of artists including Pontormo, Rosso, Salviati and, briefly, Vasari, while his work was widely copied by mid- and late-16th-century painters. The son of a tailor, he trained with Piero di Cosimo and studied the work of Leonardo, Michelangelo, Fra Bartolomeo and Raphael. He probably visited Rome *c.* 1511 and he was invited to the court of Francis I, working in Paris in 1518–19. Sarto's paintings share a sense of grandeur, an emotional intensity and brilliant colouring and soft handling. He was a sensitive portraitist and an influential draughtsman.

Sassoferrato (Giovanni Battista Salvi)
(1609 – 1685)
After some training in the Marches with his father, Tarquinio, Sassoferrato made his career mainly in Rome where he settled in 1641. Although he painted some distinguished altar-pieces and portraits, he is best known for his expressive devotional images of the Virgin and Child, often on a relatively small-scale and exquisitely painted. Many variations were produced by his studio, and Sassoferrato's work was also widely copied.

Savery, Roelandt
(1576 – 1639)
Born in the Southern Netherlands, Savery migrated with his family to the North where he practised as a painter of landscapes and flowers. In 1603, he went to Prague, probably to work for the Emperor Rudolf II. Most of his surviving work dates from the time he spent in central Europe. The Emperor's menagerie gave him models for the many animals that populate his work. In 1613, he returned to the Netherlands and settled in Utrecht.

Scarsellino, Lo (Ippolito Scarsella)
(*c.* 1550 – 1620)
The son of a painter, Scarsella made study visits to Bologna and Venice, where he is said to have spent four years in the studio of Veronese. His intense colouring and his approach to landscape reflect his interest in Titian, Tintoretto and Veronese. The art of Parma and of his native Ferrara also provided points of reference for his style, Parmigianino and Dosso Dossi being the most important. Scarsellino's career is sparsely documented, making chronology difficult. In the early 1590s he worked closely with the Carracci, including decorative painting at the Palazzo dei Diamanti at Ferrara, and he remained strongly impressed by Ludovico Carracci.

Schalcken, Godfried
(1643 – 1706)
In 1654, Schalken's family moved to Dordrecht where he became a pupil of Samuel van Hoogstraten and, after 1662, of Gerard Dou. He worked at Dordrecht from 1675 to 1691 and then at The Hague, where he died in 1706. He painted portraits and domestic genre scenes, often featuring a candle.

Schedoni, Bartolomeo
(1578 – 1615)
The son of a mask-maker employed at the Este and Farnese courts, Schedoni was taken up by Duke Ranuccio Farnese who sent him to Rome at the age of seventeen to train under Federico Zuccaro; illness forced his early return to Parma in 1595. The major influence on Schedoni's style was Correggio, while he was also aware of the naturalism of the Carracci and probably of the dramatic range of Caravaggio. Schedoni's brawls and court cases are well documented and he may have committed suicide. He painted altar-pieces and frescoes (mainly lost) but is best known for his small, delicate devotional works.

Scheggia, Giovanni di Ser Giovanni called Lo
(1407 – 1486)
Scheggia trained with Bicci di Lorenzo in Florence from late 1420, while he was closely associated with his brother, Masaccio. His only signed work is a fresco of 1457. Many of the paintings that can be attributed to him are small-scale devotional works, or domestic pictures including *cassone* panels and birth salvers. His best known work is the highly elaborate salver of *The Triumph of Fame* commisioned to celebrate the birth of Lorenzo de' Medici in 1449 (Metropolitan Museum of Art, New York). Scheggia also made designs for intarsia work.

Schiavo, Paolo (Paolo di Stefano Badaloni)
(1397 – 1478)
Schiavo's signed and dated frescoes of 1436 and other signed paintings reveal him to have been very close to his master Masolino in style. He was active in Florence and Pisa, concentrating on small-scale devotional works in his early career, while also working on miniatures in manuscripts and on embroidery designs.

Schut, Cornelis
(1597 – 1655)
Trained probably by Wenceslas Coeberger, Schut became a pupil of Rubens and after Rubens's death was one of the leading artists in Antwerp. He painted religious compositions but was also an engraver.

Scott, Samuel
(*c.* 1702 – 1772)
Scott was born in London. He began his painting career imitating the work of the marine painter, Willem van de Velde the Younger. He also became a specialist in painting views of the London river-front which were in demand as overdoors. His health declined after 1765 and he painted little afterwards.

Scott, William Bell
(1811 – 1890)
Scott studied under his father, an Edinburgh engraver, and at the Trustees' Academy. He moved to London in 1837 and entered the competition for the Westminster Hall murals. In 1843, he was appointed Master of the Government School of Design in Newcastle. Through Rossetti, whom he met in 1847, he became an associate of the Pre-Raphaelites and painted somewhat in their manner. He returned to London in 1858.

Secante, Sebastiano
(active 1518 – 1576)
Sebastiano was related to Pomponio Amalteo, a pupil and collaborator of Pordenone and probably trained with him. He was one of a family of artists active in Friuli down to the mid-17th century. However documentary information on this artist has to be treated with caution as there may have been more than one Sebastiano working as a painter. An important signed and dated work by this artist is an altar-piece of the *Virgin and Child with Saints* of 1558 at Gemona and various works can be attributed to the same hand.

Seddon, Thomas
(1821 – 1856)
Son of a cabinet-maker, Seddon entered the Pre-Rapahelite circle through his friendship with Holman Hunt, whom he accompanied to the Holy Land in 1853–4. In 1856 he returned to Cairo, where he died. His work is highly detailed in the Pre-Raphaelite manner. Because of his early death, his output was small.

Segonzac, André Dunoyer de
(1884 – 1974)
Dunoyer de Segonzac studied under Luc-Olivier Merson. In 1908, he discovered St Tropez, which he painted frequently and where he settled in his last years. His work was marked by his interest in Cézanne and by the return to naturalism characteristic of a number of French artists in the 1920s. In 1919, he took up etching and then turned to watercolour in 1920. Etching and watercolour became his preferred media and he painted only the occasional oil after about 1925. He also designed for the theatre and illustrated many books.

Sellaio, Arcangelo di Jacopo del (see Arcangelo di Jacopo del Sellaio)

Sequeira, Domingos António de
(1768 – 1837)
Trained in Lisbon under Francisco da Rocha, Sequeira travelled to Italy in 1788 and was elected to the Accademia di S. Luca in Rome in 1793. On his return to Lisbon, he attempted unsuccessfully to set up a similar academy. He was a court painter in Lisbon from 1802, painting portraits and allegories, and during the Peninsular Wars was briefly imprisoned. He designed a magnificent silver service as a royal gift for the Duke of Wellington, 1812–16 (Apsley House). Of liberal views, Sequeira chose exile in Paris in 1823; from 1826 onwards he lived in Rome.

Serangeli, Gioacchino Giuseppe
(1768 – 1852)
A pupil of David, Serangeli and his fellow students demanded the master's release from prison in 1794. He painted grand Napoleonic subjects, history paintings and numerous portraits and exhibited at the Salon from 1796 to 1817. Serangeli worked in Milan from 1812 to 1824; called to Turin in 1824, he remained there as a successful and prolific court painter until his death.

Severn, Joseph
(1793 – 1879)
From 1813 to 1819, Severn studied at the Royal Academy Schools, winning the Gold Medal for historical painting in his final year. He went with Keats to Rome in 1820 and became a successful portrait painter of Roman society. He returned to London in 1841 but was sent back to Rome as British Consul in 1860 and remained there for the rest of his life.

Shannon, Charles Haslewood
(1863 – 1937)
Shannon studied wood-engraving at the Lambeth School of Art; there he met Charles Ricketts with whom he set up a life-long partnership. They collaborated in book illustration and in the Vale Press, which produced a series of finely printed and illustrated books. In the later 1890s, he turned to painting in a late Romantic style with echoes of the French artists whom he admired. He also produced lithographs. He was incapacitated in his last years as the result of a fall from a ladder in 1929.

Shaw, Joshua, of Bath
(1776 – 1861)
Shaw exhibited landscapes at the British Institution from 1810 to 1841. He lived in Bath, Somerset, from 1802 to 1817. At some point, he emigrated to North America and he died in New Jersey.

Shirley Smith, Richard
(b. 1935)
A meeting with David Jones at Harrow School had a lasting influence on Shirley Smith's work as an engraver and painter. He studied for four years at the Slade School under Anthony Gross from 1956 to 1960 and then spent two years in Rome. He has worked extensively as a book illustrator and as a muralist in Kensington Palace, the Guardian Royal Exchange and elsewhere. His work is akin to Rex Whistler's, incorporating visual puns and a touch of Surrealism.

Siberechts, Jan
(1627 – 1703)
Siberechts was born and worked in Antwerp. His earliest landscapes are influenced by the work of his Italianate contemporaries but his manner changed in the 1660s, his figures and animals became larger, the setting became less idealized and he developed a new interest in the effects of daylight. He was brought to England by the 2nd Duke of Buckingham in about 1672 and travelled extensively, painting panoramic views of country estates and river valleys. The latest dates found on his work are from the late 1690s. He died in England.

Sickert, Walter Richard
(1860 – 1942)
Sickert's father was a Danish painter and illustrator. He was born in Munich and came to England with his parents in 1868. He first studied acting but moved to the Slade School in 1881 and became a pupil of Whistler. From 1887 to about 1899, he painted a series of music-hall subjects. He lived in Dieppe from 1899 to 1905. Following his return to England he became leader of the Camden Town Group and painted a number of subjects taken from the more humble and lurid areas of urban life. Much of his later work, illustrating contemporary themes, was based upon press photographs.

Simon, Brigitte
(b. 1926)
Simon was taught by her father, a glass painter, and divided her life between painting glass and painting landscapes. From 1945 to 1949, she worked for Le Corbusier. In 1949, she married the painter, Charles Marq, and through him came into contact with the artists in his circle, Roger de Bissière, Serge Poliakoff, Raoul Ubac and others. She also illustrated books. The rocky landscape of the Ardèche became a favourite theme in her painting from 1959 onwards, treated in a monochrome, near abstract style.

Simone dei Crocifissi (Simone di Filippo Benvenuti da Bologna)
(active 1355 – 1399)
A pupil of Jacopo di Dalmasio, Simone was a master painter in Bologna by 1355. He worked side by side with Vitale da Bologna in 1359 at S. Maria dei Servi, while he was also acquainted with Venetian painting, particularly the work of Paolo Veneziano. His nickname derives from the four great painted crosses made from *c.* 1360 to 1380. Simone was the dominant artist of his day in Bologna and his studio produced numerous devotional images.

Sinnott, Kevin
(b. 1947)
Sinnott was born in Wales and studied at Cardiff College of Art, 1967–8; Goucester College of Art, 1968–71 and the Royal College of Art from 1971 to 1974. He later taught at the Ruskin School of Drawing in Oxford and at St Martin's School of Art.

Sisley, Alfred
(1839 – 1899)
After a false start in commerce in London, Sisley's father allowed him to enter the Paris studio of Charles Gleyre. Renoir, Monet and Bazille were among his fellow students. He painted landscapes at St Cloud, Chailly, Marlotte, Honfleur and elsewhere in the 1860s. Following the death of his father in 1870, Sisley had to rely on painting for an income. He contributed work to four Impressionist exhibitions between 1874 and 1886. Unlike his fellow Impressionists, who painted figure subjects as well as landscape, Sisley confined himself to painting landscapes, including many river views, in which effects of light and weather constitute the chief interest.

Skippe, John
(1742 – 1811)
Skippe was born into a landed family from Herefordshire and went to Oxford University in 1760. On leaving University, he travelled in Italy, making many drawings after the work of the Old Masters. He is chiefly known for the series of wood-engravings in chiaroscuro done in imitation of the work of early Italian artists. Some bistre drawings by Skippe of other subjects are known.

Slechtenhorst, J. van
(active before 1662 – after 1669)
Several paintings, signed SL Horst, have recently been identified as the work of the painter, J. van Slechtenhorst, whose full signature is recorded on a few landscapes and one still life. The latest known work is the still life in the Ashmolean dated 1670; the earliest, dated 1662, was once in a collection in Düsseldorf. Apart from these few works, his life is undocumented.

Smetham, James
(1821 – 1889)
Smethan began painting portraits in Shropshire before moving to London and entering the Royal Academy Schools. Ruskin and Rossetti supported him but he had little success and fell prey to insanity in the last twelve years of his life. He was devoutly religious and painted biblical subjects as well as imaginary landscapes and literary themes. He was also a critic and writer on art and one of the first to recognize the importance of the work of William Blake.

Smith, Colvin
(1795 – 1875)
Colvin Smith was born in Scotland and studied at the Royal Academy Schools. After visiting Italy, he set up as a portrait painter in Raeburn's former studio in Edinburgh and enjoyed some success.

Smith, Sir Matthew Arnold Bracy
(1879 – 1959)
Matthew Smith studied at the Slade School and then for a short period in Paris where he came into contact with Matisse and the Fauves. He painted nudes, still lifes and landscapes in a manner which derived from the work of the Fauves and developed into a distinctively rich, free and colourful style. He spent much of his life up to 1940 in Paris.

Smith, William
(active 1815 – 1859)
William Smith's life is not well documented. He lived in London and at Newport in Shropshire. Between 1813 and 1859, he exhibited portraits, pictures of animals and landscapes.

Smits, Theodoor
(active before 1657 – after 1658)
Smits entered the Antwerp guild in 1658–9. His life is not well documented. Dated works are known from the late 1650s. He painted simple still-life compositions, often including crabs.

Snijers, Pieter
(1681 – 1752)
Snijers was born in Antwerp where he became a pupil of Alexander van Bredael in 1694. He registered at the Brussels guild in 1705 and at the Antwerp guild in 1707. It is said that he was in England some time between 1720 and 1726 where he painted many portraits. He returned to Antwerp to settled for the remainder of his life. His work includes genre subjects, landscapes, still life and portraits. He was also a printmaker.

Solario, Andrea
(*c.* 1465 – before 1524)
One of a family of architects and sculptors from near Lugano, Andrea shared a workshop with his brothers. He visited Venice early in his career and was influenced particularly by the work of Antonello da Messina and Andrea Mantegna. In Milan, he was associated with Leonardo da Vinci and adopted his language of gesture and expression. Solario was also interested in northern European painting and prints. Having worked for Cardinal d'Amboise in Normandy from 1507 until 1509 or later, Solario was afterwards based mainly in Milan.

Solimena, Francesco
(1657 – 1747)
Trained first by his father Angelo, Solimena studied the art of Luca Giordano and Mattia Preti in Naples, where he was based from 1674. He became the dominant figure in Neapolitan 18th-century art, running a major studio and working for international clients, since his paintings were in demand from different European courts. He also produced altar-pieces and fresco decoration for Neapolitan churches. Solimena developed a style based on dramatic chiaroscuro and rich, fluent handling of paint, becoming more moderate and classical after a trip to Rome in 1701.

Somov, Konstantin Andreevich
(1869 – 1939)
Son of the Keeper of the Department of Paintings at the Hermitage Museum in St Petersburg, Somov was brought up in an artistic environment. He studied under Repin at the Academy of Fine Arts and became a member of the 'World of Art' group. He painted portraits and genre scenes, often set in the 18th century, and was a prolific illustrator. In 1924 he emigrated to America and then settled in Paris.

Soreau, Isaak
(1604 – d. after 1645)
Soreau was born in Hanau, near Frankfurt. Like his twin brother, Peter Soreau, he specialized in still life. They were probably taught by their father Daniel Soreau and also by Sebastian Stosskopf, Daniel's pupil. He is last recorded in Hanau in 1626 and subsequently is only known from dated paintings of 1638 and 1645. His work shows a relationship with the work of the Antwerp painter Jacob van Hulsdonck and he may have spent time in Antwerp in his later years.

Spencer, Gilbert
(1892 – 1979)
Brother of the painter, Stanley Spencer, Gilbert Spencer is chiefly known as a painter of landscapes. He studied at the Camberwell School of Arts and Crafts and at the Slade School from 1913 to 1920 with a period of war service. From 1940 to 1943, he was an Official War Artist. From 1934 to 1936, he executed a series of murals in Holywell Manor, Oxford. He taught at the Royal College, at the Glasgow School of Art and at Camberwell and turned to writing in his later years.

Spencer, Sir Stanley
(1891 – 1959)
Spencer was born and lived in the village of Cookham in Berkshire. After studying at the Slade School from 1908 to 1912 he returned to Cookham and began work on the series of biblical pictures set in contemporary surroundings which occupied him throughout his life. He also painted landscapes and portraits. He worked at first in a clear detailed manner but, in the 1930s, he combined this with an increasingly distorted sense of space and figure drawing. In 1940, he was sent as War Artist to the Glasgow shipyards. He spent his last years in Cookham working on religious compositions.

Spitzweg, Karl
(1808 – 1885)
After an early career as a pharmacist, Spitzweg took up painting relatively late. Visits to France and England introduced him to the work of English and French humourists as well as to the work of the French Romantics, Baron, Diaz and Lami. He specialized in small-scale genre subjects touched with wry humour.

Spruyt, Johannes
(*c.* 1627 – 1671)
Spruyt is first mentioned as a painter on the occasion of his marriage in 1659. He appears to have been based in Amsterdam. He was mainly a painter of live birds but also painted still-life compositions of dead birds and a few portraits. A few history paintings are mentioned in documents but now are not known.

Stanfield, William Clarkson
(1793 – 1867)
Stanfield entered the Merchant Navy in 1808. He was subsequently pressed into the Royal Navy from which he was discharged in 1818. He worked at first as a scene painter in London and also in Edinburgh, where he met David Roberts, a fellow scene painter who became his close friend. In 1834, he gave up scene painting and became a specialist in views of shipping.

Stark, James
(1794 – 1859)
Stark was born in Norwich and studied under John Crome. Like Crome, he painted mainly English landscapes with animals and rustic figures. He entered the Royal Academy Schools in 1817 and exhibited at the Royal Academy from 1831 to 1859. He also exhibited extensively at the British Institution. On account of ill health, he returned to Norwich; he remained there for twelve years but finally settled in London in 1830.

Steenwyck, Harmen van
(1612 – after 1656)
Like his elder brother, Pieter Steenwyck, Harmen specialized in painting still life. He was born in Delft but studied under his uncle, David Bailly, in Leyden. He joined the Delft guild in 1636. In 1654–5 he sailed with the Dutch merchant fleet to the East Indies. He is last recorded in Delft in 1656. All his known works, including a number of barn interiors and market scenes, include some element of still life.

Steer, Philip Wilson
(1860 – 1942)
Steer studied at the Gloucestershire School of Art and then at the Académie Julian in Paris in 1882. His early work consists of scenes on the coast, painted mainly at Walberwick and in France. In 1886, he joined the New English Art Club where he exhibited for many years. After 1900, he painted landscapes in a style which combines Impressionist brushwork with a debt to Constable. He made annual sketching tours, often in Yorkshire. For forty years he taught painting at the Slade School.

Stoffe, Jan Jacobsz. van der
(*c.* 1611 – 1682)
Stoffe is recorded at Leiden from 1644 until his death in 1682. His work has been confused with that of Esaias van de Velde, in whose style he worked. He was a painter of hunting scenes and cavalry engagements.

Strang, William
(1859 – 1921)
Strang was a Scottish painter and etcher of portraits and figure subjects. In 1875, he went to London and studied under Legros at the Slade School. He concentrated at first on etching but also worked in lithography, line engraving, mezzotint, aquatint and woodcutting. In the 1890s, he began to work more in oils and watercolour and won a first class medal for painting at the Dublin International Exhibition in 1897. He lived for most of his life in London and died in Bournemouth.

Streek, Juriaen van
(1632 – 1687)
Van Streek is first recorded in Amsterdam in 1653. He appears to have spent his life in Amsterdam, painting mainly still life subjects. A few genre pictures are known. He is said to have given up painting in about 1680 and became an inn-keeper. None of his surviving works are dated.

Striep, Christian Jansz.
(1634 – 1673)
Striep was born in s'-Hertogenbosch, married in Amsterdam in 1655 and took Amsterdam citizenship in 1656. Most of his work consists of still-life paintings in the style of Willem Kalf. A few woodland still-life compositions are known.

Stroiffi, Ermanno
(1616 – 1693)
Having received some training in Padua under his father, an artist of Flemish origin, Stroiffi became a pupil of Bernardo Strozzi in Venice. He also travelled to Rome via Bologna and Florence, and Guercino became an important source for his art. Stroiffi took holy orders in 1647, becoming a member of the order of the Filippini in 1653 and of the Congregazione dell' Oratorio in Venice in 1661. His limited output consists mainly of religious works and portraits of members of his rder, in a style closely based on that of Strozzi.

Strong, Charles Edward
(exhibited 1851 – 1856)
Little is known about this artist. He painted marines and shipping pictures and exhibited four works at the Royal Academy and a further four at the British Institution. He lived in Gravesend, Kent.

Strozzi, Bernardo (Il Prete Genovese)
(1581/2 – 1644)
Strozzi's style was formed in Genoa not so much by his early teacher Pietro Sorri, but by the influx of major artists or their works to the city, so that the art of Rubens, Federico Barocci, Giulio Cesare Procaccini and later Orazio Gentileschi and van Dyck all made an impact. Strozzi became a Capuchin friar *c.* 1597, but obtained permission *c.* 1609–10 to leave his convent and pursue his profession as an artist. After a serious rift with his order he took refuge in Venice in 1633, where he worked successfully for the remainder of his career and had many followers. Strozzi produced still lifes and genre painting as well as magnificent portraits and important religious and historical works.

Strij, Jacob van
(1756 – 1815)
Jacob van Stry was brother of the painter Abraham van Stry. He was taught by André Lens in Antwerp. He was chiefly a landscape painter. His style was much affected by his taste for the work of Paul Potter and Hobbema and especially Cuyp.

Sully, Thomas
(1783 – 1872)
Born at Horncastle in England, Sully followed his parents, who were actors, to the United States in 1789. He studied painting at Charleston and set up a practice in Richmond as a painter of portraits. Subsequently, he studied with West and Lawrence in London. In 1838, he settled in Philadelphia. He painted historical compositions, genre subjects and landscapes, but was primarily a painter of portraits.

Sumner, Maud
(1902 – 1985)
Sumner was born in Johannesburg of English parents. She went to Oxford in 1922 to read English but subsequently turned to art. In 1925, she went to the Westminster School of Art where she was taught by Frank Dobson and Bernard Meninsky. Her life was divided between London, Paris and South Africa. Her first work is influenced by French Post-Impressionism. Later, she painted religious subjects. Much of her work is inspired by the landscape and skies of Africa.

Susenier, Abraham
(*c.* 1620 – between 1666 and 1672)
Susenier was born in Leiden. He is recorded in The Hague in 1640; he became a member of the Dordrecht guild in 1646 and probably settled there. He was mainly a painter of still life, including *vanitas* and compositions of fish. No dated work after 1666 is known.

Sustris, Lambert
(*c.* 1510–15 – after 1560)
Sustris travelled to Italy as a young man, visiting Rome before settling in Venice *c.* 1535, where he was associated with Titian. He painted frescoes near Padua in 1542–3 and went to Augsburg with Titian where he made various portraits of German sitters in 1548 and 1552. Little is known of his career in Venice after 1553, but the art of Schiavone, Tintoretto and Veronese were all important influences.

Suttermans, Justus (Sustermans)
(1597 – 1681)
Sustermans was a pupil of Willem de Vos and of Frans Pourbus II. He became court painter to Cosimo II in Florence in 1620. In 1624, he was sent to Vienna where he was ennobled. Most of his work consists of portraits although he also painted religious compositions.

Sweerts, Michiel
(1618 – 1664)
Sweerts was born in Brussels and worked from 1643 to 1656 in Rome, where he came into contact with the Bamboccianti, the circle of genre painters round Pieter van Laer. His paintings have a subdued character. In 1656, he returned to Brussels and went shortly afterwards to Amsterdam. In 1661, he joined a missionary group which set out for the East but was dismissed at Tabriz by the bishop in charge. It is said that he died in Goa.

Swynnerton, Anna Louisa
(1844 – 1933)
Anna Robinson was born near Manchester and studied at the Manchester School of Art and then in Paris and Rome. She lived in Rome until the death of her husband, the sculptor, Joseph Swynnerton, in 1910. She painted allegorical and symbolical paintings, influenced by Watts but also by the colour of contemporary French art. She became an Associate of the Royal Academy in 1922.

Teniers, David, the Younger
(1610 – 1690)
Teniers's early paintings show some influence from his father-in-law, Jan Brueghel, and from Frans Francken II. His peasant subjects are derived from Brouwer's. In 1645, he became a member of the Antwerp guild and shortly afterwards was appointed court painter to Archduke Leopold Wilhelm of Austria in Brussels. He was also made curator of the Archduke's art collection. In this capacity he painted views of the galleries and small copies of a number of the pictures. He was a prolific artist and worked in a number of genres, but is best known for his scenes of rustic life.

Terbrugghen, Hendrick (see Brugghen, Hendrick ter)

Testa, Pietro
(1611 – 1650)
Born in Lucca, Testa studied in Rome from *c.* 1630 with Domenichino and Pietro da Cortona and was greatly influenced by Poussin. He made copies of ancient sculpture for Cassiano dal Pozzo. A prolific draughtsman and printmaker, Testa produced relatively few paintings. His intellectual interests are apparent in his unusual treatment of familiar subjects and in his highly inventive approach to new ones. He was not a great success as a history painter and apparently committed suicide by drowning in the Tiber.

Thielen, Jan Philip van
(1618 – 1667)
Born in Malines, van Thielen was taught in Antwerp by his brother-in-law Theodor Rombous and then by Daniel Seghers. In 1641–2 he became a member of the Guild of St Luke. In 1660 he returned to Malines where he was admitted to the guild and where he died in 1667. He was a flower painter who collaborated with other painters, often adding floral garlands to figure subjects.

Thomas, Johannes
(1617 – 1678)
Thomas was born at Ypres. He may have been taught by Rubens. He accompanied Abraham van Diepenbeeck to Italy and entered the Antwerp guild in 1648. In 1654, he left Antwerp to be court painter to the bishop of Mainz. In 1656, he is recorded in Vienna and in 1658, was court painter at Frankfurt. In 1663, he returned to Vienna where he died.

Thornhill, Sir James
(1676 – 1734)
Born in Dorset, Thornhill studied under Thomas Highmore but learned his art chiefly from studying and probably assisting Verrio and Laguerre. He began painting scenery in 1705. From 1708 to 1727, he was occupied in decorating the Painted Hall in Greenwich Hospital. He also painted decorative works at Hanbury Hall, Blenheim Palace, Charborough Park, St Paul's Cathedral and elsewhere. In 1711 he became a director of Kneller's Academy. In 1720, he succeeded Highmore as Serjeant Painter and was knighted. He became Member of Parliament for Weymouth in 1722 and ran an academy in his house.

Tiepolo, Giovanni Battista
(1696 – 1770)
Trained by Gregorio Lazzarini in Venice, Tiepolo was also impressed by the innovations of Sebastiano Ricci and Giambattista Piazzetta; like them, he looked back to the achievements of 16th-century Venetian artists: the influence of first Tintoretto and then Veronese can be seen in his work. Tiepolo worked mainly in Venice and the north of Italy, gaining a European reputation as an expressive religious artist and an innovative painter of allegorical and mythological fresco decoration. He travelled to the courts of W_rzburg (1750–53) and Madrid (1762–70) to paint frescoes and altar-pieces together with his two artist sons, Domenico and Lorenzo.

Tindle, David
(b. 1932)
Tindle was born in Huddersfield, Yorkshire and studied at the Coventry School of Art from 1945 to 1946. He taught at Hornsey College of Art, 1959–74, and at the Royal College of Art, 1972–83, and was subsequently appointed Master of the Ruskin School of Drawing in Oxford. Much of his work is executed in egg tempera, which suits his carefully controlled sense of detail and delicate colour.

Tintoretto, Domenico (Robusti)
(1560 – 1635)
Trained in the family workshop in Venice, together with his sister Marietta and brother Marco, Domenico assisted his father Jacopo particularly on commissions for the Palazzo Ducale, Venice. Apart from trips to the courts of Ferrara (1592) and Mantua (1595) to paint portraits, he worked in Venice, with religious commissions dominating later in his career. His portraits are frank and direct in approach, while he was interested in the landscapes of artists like Paolo Fiammingo, who collaborated with his father.

Tintoretto, Jacopo (Robusti)
(1518 – 1594)
The son of a cloth-dyer (*tentor*), Tintoretto was a prolific and influential artist. He worked for a wide range of patrons in Venice, becoming virtually the official state painter and making only one trip away for a Gonzaga commission at Mantua. His best known works are in the Palazzo Ducale and the Scuola di S. Rocco, Venice. Tintoretto was deeply interested in the expressive figures of Michelangelo and the art of Schiavone and Titian, although his own dynamic compositions with elongated figures and rhythmic patterns denote a different trajectory. His lack of finish was sometimes controversial. Tintoretto ran a large studio, including northern European artists, and was an active draughtsman.

Titian (Tiziano Vecellio)
(*c.* ?1485–90 – 1576)
The greatest of Venetian painters, Titian was pre-eminent in portraiture as in religious art and history painting, while he made independent landscape drawings which were often engraved. Little is known of his early career, but he was in the orbit of Giovanni Bellini and Giorgione; the great *Assumption* altar-piece at the Frari, Venice (1519) established his reputation as a highly innovative and powerful artist. His patrons included the emperor Charles V, Pope Paul III and the courts of northern Italy, while late in life he worked almost exclusively for Philip II of Spain. Artists such as Rubens, van Dyck and Velázquez were deeply impressed by his free, sensuous painting technique, his naturalism and his psychological sensitivity.

Tonks, Henry
(1862 – 1937)
Born at Solihull, Warwickshire, Tonks first studied medicine and became a Fellow of the Royal College of Surgeons in 1888. While practising as a surgeon, he went to the Westminster School of Art, where he worked under Fred Brown. He took up art full-time in 1893, becoming Brown's assistant at the Slade School, and succeeded him as Slade Professor in 1918. He was an influential teacher. His work covers a wide range of figure work and landscapes and is characterized by a style of blurred Impressionism.

Torelli, Felice
(1667 – 1748)
A pupil of Santo Prunati in Verona, Torelli moved to Bologna to study under Gian Gioseffo dal Sole, whose art made a strong impact on his style. He also studied the work of the Carracci. Torelli painted a few remarkable portraits and many large-scale works in a dark, powerful manner. He was a co-founder of the Accademia Clementina in 1709. Although he hardly left Bologna, his reputation quickly spread and he supplied altar-pieces and history paintings to clients in central and northern Italy.

Toulouse-Lautrec, Henri de
(1864 – 1901)
Toulouse-Lautrec was left deformed by accidents in his youth. He was encouraged by his uncle to take up painting and studied under Léon Bonnat and Fernand Cormon in Paris. In 1885, he set up studio in Montmartre and began to supply magazines with illustrations. At first he painted mostly sporting subjects but from about 1888 he took his subjects from the theatres, music-halls and café life of Paris. In 1890, he went to the Moulin Rouge for the first time and began to design posters and paintings of the performers. In 1888, he met Gauguin and acquired an interest in Japanese colour prints. The influence of these is particularly evident in his lithographs.

Townsend, William
(1909 – 1973)
Townsend studied at the Slade School, 1926–30, before travelling extensively in Europe and the Near East. He followed his colleagues from the Slade to the Euston Road School in the late 1930s. After the Second World War, he taught at Camberwell School of Art and the Slade School. In 1951, he went to the Banff School of Fine Arts in Canada to teach the summer session and later became visiting professor at the University of Alberta. He also wrote books on a number of favourite themes, including *Canterbury* and *Canadian Art Today*.

Travers, Daisy Linda (see Ward, Daisy Linda)

Trevisani, Francesco
(1656 – 1746)
Trained in Venice under Antonio Zanchi, Trevisani moved to Rome *c.* 1678. He became part of the circle of Carlo Maratta, studying Emilian and Roman classicism. However, he was also impressed by the dynamic art of Solimena. Trevisani was a distinguished portraitist and painted a variety of altar-pieces, historical and allegorical subjects. He counted Grand Tourists among his clients in Rome.

Troy, Jean-François de
(1679 – 1752)
Trained by his father in Paris, de Troy studied in Rome from 1699 to 1706, making lengthy sojourns in Florence and Pisa. He was received into the Paris Academy in 1708 as a history painter and in 1738 was Director of the French Academy in Rome. In addition to history paintings, de Troy painted portraits, designed tapestries for the Gobelins factory and produced genre scenes on contemporary fashions and manners that were extremely popular.

Tuckwell, George
(b. 1919)
Born at Burwell in Cambridgeshire, Tuckwell studied art at the Sir John Cass College and Goldsmiths' School of Art. From 1940 to 1946, he served in the Royal Air Force. After the War, he became an art teacher for the London County Council.

Turner, William
(1789 – 1862)
Turner of Oxford, as he was known to distinguish him from his better-known namesake J.M.W. Turner, was brought up by an uncle at the Manor House in Shipton-on-Cherwell and studied watercolour under John Varley. Until 1815, he worked in the southern counties, often painting near Bristol, and then went on excursions to the Lakes, North Wales, Derbyshire, Devon and the New Forest. From 1838, he visited the west coast of Scotland. His later views are characterized by a neat, colourful naturalism. In about 1833, he settled in Oxford where he was an influential teacher. He also worked in oil.

Tzafouris, Nikolaos
(active 1487 – 1501)
A Greek icon painter working in Venetian Crete. He introduced western themes and motifs such as the Man of Sorrows, the Pietà and the Kneeling Virgin into the religious iconography of the Orthodox east.

Uccello, (Paolo di Dono)
(1397 – 1475)
First documented as a painter in Florence in 1414. Uccello trained with Lorenzo Ghiberti at a time when his workshop was producing the first set of bronze doors for the Florence Baptistery. Uccello was a versatile artist, designing mosaics in Venice in 1425–7 and, later in Florence, stained glass. Although much of his work is lost or damaged, his interest in both the new science of perspective and in the decorative values of late Gothic art is evident. Uccello worked for a range of religious and secular patrons in Florence, Padua and Urbino and had a high reputation. Soon after his death, he was described as a great master of animal and landscape painting who understood perspective well.

Underwood, Leon
(1890 – 1975)
Underwood studied at the Regent Street Polytechnic and the Royal College of Art. After the First World War, he completed a series of paintings for the Imperial War Museum. He returned for a year to the Slade in 1919–20, chiefly studying life drawing. In 1921 he opened the Brook Green School and concentrated on printmaking. During the 1920s, he travelled extensively and illustrated several books. In the 1930s, he took up sculpture. In the 1950s, following a break during the Second World War and a visit to West Africa, he returned to sculpture.

Unger, Charlotte
(first half of 20th century)
Charlotte Unger is said to have come to England in the late 1930s as a refugee. Her career in art does not appear to have been documented.

Unterperger, Michelangelo
(1695 – 1758)
Trained by Giuseppe Alberti, Unterperger possibly travelled to Venice. He was established in upper Austria by 1730 and settled in Vienna in 1737. He painted altar-pieces and history paintings for a range of patrons, enjoying important Jesuit commissions. His art has some affinities with that of Venetians such as Amigoni and Pittoni, while his colouring is rich and warm. Unterperger's appointment as Rector of the Vienna Academy in 1751 indicates his high standing.

Utrecht, Adriaen van
(1599 – *c.* 1652)
Adriaen van Utrecht was born in Utrecht. In 1614 entered the studio of Herman de Rijt. He travelled in France, Italy and Germany and was back in Antwerp by 1625 when he entered the guild. He was a painter of live animals and still life subjects, including fruit, vegetables, flowers, fish and game, somewhat influenced by Frans Snijders.

Utrillo, Maurice
(1883 – 1955)
Utrillo was the son of the painter Suzanne Valadon. He took up painting at the age of nineteen as a therapy for alcoholism. His first subjects were found in the village of Montmagny, north of Paris, where he painted many landscapes in 1903–4. These are sombre in colour and heavily impasted. From 1909 until *c.* 1914, he mixed his paint with glue, plaster or cement which gave his works a chalky whiteness. As his health deteriorated, he withdrew into nursing homes, where he worked from post cards of his favourite views in Montmartre.

Valtat, Louis
(1869 – 1952)
Valtat belonged to the group of painters from the studio of Gustave Moreau who later formed the nucleus of the Fauves. In the mid-1890s, he absorbed ideas from Impressionism, van Gogh and the Pointillists and collaborated with Toulouse-Lautrec in designing for the stage. From 1899 to 1914, he divided his time between Paris and Anthéor, near Le Lavandou, where he built a house; he also travelled in North Africa, Italy, Spain and the French provinces. After 1914, he moved between Paris, Versailles and Rouen, painting scenes of contemporary life, flowers, seascapes and landscapes in a strongly patterned and colourful style. He also made prints, notably wood-engravings.

Vanni, Andrea
(*c.* 1330 – 1413)
Vanni was prominent in public life in Siena from 1368 to 1385, travelling to Avignon and Naples on behalf of the Sienese Commune. He painted many frescoes and altar-pieces for the Cathedral and churches of Siena. Essentially he continued to work in the manner of Simone Martini, producing paintings rich in narrative detail, with attention to textural effects. He also worked as an illuminator.

Vasari, Giorgio
(1511 – 1574)
Trained in Arezzo by Guillaume de Marcillat, Vasari moved to Florence to the workshops of Andrea del Sarto and Baccio Bandinelli. He was in Rome in 1532 in the service of Cardinal Ippolito de' Medici and Medici patronage was to mark his entire career. A versatile artist, Vasari worked as a painter, draughtsman and architect, mainly in Florence but with important sojourns in Venice, Bologna and Naples. By his own account he began work on his series of biographies of artists in the mid-1540s, publishing his *Vite* in 1550 and a revised edition in 1568: these volumes set the tone for art-historical writings in Italy for several generations. Vasari was also innovative in assembling an extraordinarily rich collection of drawings.

Vázquez, Antonio
(*c.* 1485 – after 1563)
One of the most important painters in 16th-century Valladolid, Antonio was a prolific, conservative artist. His style owes much to that of Pedro Berruguete and Juan de Borgogna.

Velde, Adriaen van de
(1636 – 1672)
Adriaen van de Velde is said to have been first taught by his father Willem van de Velde I and then by Jan Wijnants in Haarlem. By 1657, he is recorded in Amsterdam, where he remained for the rest of his life. He chiefly painted meadow scenes and Italianate landscapes but also coastal scenes, forests, winter scenes, portraits in a landscape setting and a few biblical and allegorical compositions. His earliest known works are six etchings of 1653. He was an accomplished painter of figures and animals and was often asked to add these to the work of other artists.

Velde III, Jan Jansz. van de
(*c.* 1620 – 1662 or later)
Jan Jansz. van de Velde was born in Haarlem, the son of the engraver and landscape painter of the same name. He was probably taught by his father but is not known to have painted any subjects other than still life. His earliest paintings, dated 1639 and 1640, show the influence of contemporary Haarlem painters, Pieter Claesz. and Roelof Koets.

Verburgh, Dionijs
(active 1677 – before 1722)
Verburgh was a painter of river landscapes who was active in Rotterdam in the mid 17th century. He travelled in Surinam between 1703 and 1710.

Verelst, Simon
(1644 – between 1710 and 1717)
Verelst was born in The Hague where he was taught by his father. In 1663 he became a member of the society of painters, the *Confrerie Pictura*, in The Hague and moved soon after to Voorburg along with his brother, Herman, who also painted flower pieces. In 1669, he moved to London. He is said to have been in Paris in 1680 but is recorded in London between 1685 and 1710. His paintings of flowers were greatly admired in England. He also painted some still-life compositions of fruit and game and portraits of the nobility. He appears to have suffered from manic depression and, despite his success, is said to have died in poverty.

Verhout, Constantin
(active 1663 – 1667)
Little is known about Verhout. According to Houbraken, he painted 'modern histories' at Gouda. Only about five paintings can now be attributed to him, mostly simple genre scenes, one of which is dated 1663.

Vermeyen, Jan Cornelisz.
(1500 – 1559)
Vermeyen was principally a painter of portraits although he painted several religious and historical compositions. He was born in Beverwijk, near Haarlem and trained in the workshop of Bernaert van Orley in Brussels. He was chiefly employed by the Habsburg court, working for Margaret of Austria, Mary of Hungary and Charles V, whom he accompanied to Tunis on his campaign of 1535. The drawings which he made on this occasion were used later as the basis for tapestries commemorating the campaign.

Vernet, Claude-Joseph
(1714 – 1789)
Trained initially in Avignon and with Jacques Viali in Aix, Vernet made his reputation in Rome from 1734 to 1753, attracting the attention of French and British patrons as a specialist in marine painting. His scenes were generally imaginary, composed from his observations of places including the gardens of Rome, Tivoli, the Campagna and the picturesque coastline between Rome and Naples. His landscapes met with acclaim at the Paris Salon, where he exhibited from 1746; from 1753 to 1762 he travelled in France with a royal commission to paint views of its ports. He settled in Paris and continued to work for an international clientele until his death.

Veronese (Paolo Caliari)
(1528 – 1588)
The son of a stonecutter, Veronese trained in Venice with Antonio Badile IV and Giovanni Caroto, rapidly making his reputation with patrons in Verona, Mantua and Venice. He settled in Venice from 1553, where his best-known works are ceiling paintings in the Palazzo Ducale, cycles of paintings for S. Sebastiano and a series of grand-scale biblical feasts for convent refectories. He was also prominent in villa decoration, notably that of the Palladian Villa Barbaro at Maser. As well as being a supreme colourist, Veronese was an important portraitist and draughtsman. His family workshop with his brother Benedetto and sons Gabriele and Carletto continued painting in his manner after his death.

Veth, Jan
(1864 – 1925)
Veth was trained by August Allebé at the Academy in Amsterdam. Among his fellow pupils were George Brietner, Willem Witsen and Jacobus van Looy, with whom he formed the so-called 'Amsterdam School'. In about 1886, he studied landscape painting under Anton Mauve and was briefly attracted to peasant subjects. In 1888, he settled in Baarn and devoted himself to painting portraits. His art now became more linear. The same style appears in the many lithographic portraits which he made in the 1890s for various periodicals. Veth was also known as a poet and art critic.

Vincent, George
(1796 – 1831)
Vincent's father was a weaver and shawl manufacturer from Norwich. At an early age, Vincent was drawn into the lively art world of early 19th-century Norwich, exhibiting his first paintings with the local Society of Artists in 1811. He received tuition from John Crome and made his debut at the Royal Academy exhibition in 1814. In 1816, he went to Paris with Crome's son and settled in London on return. His landscapes were admired but he fell into financial difficulties in the 1820s and spent from 1824 to 1827 in prison for his debts.

Vinckenborch, Arnout
(before 1590 – 1620)
Vinckenborch was born in Alkmaar but by 1615 was living in Antwerp, where he remained. Between 1616 and 1620 he was closely associated with Rubens's studio.

Visscher, Cornelis
(?1629 – 1658)
Visscher was probably taught by Pieter Soutmans in Haarlem. In 1649–50, he made many portrait engravings for print series published by Soutmans. In 1653, he was admitted to the Haarlem guild but moved to Amsterdam shortly afterwards. Between 1651 and 1658, he produced numerous engravings of biblical and historical subjects, landscapes and genre scenes, both after other artists and of his own invention. His work as a portrait engraver and draughtsman constitutes the most important part of his work.

Vlaminck, Maurice de
(1876 – 1958)
Vlaminck's parents were musicians who lived near Paris. He also studied music and later played the double-bass. From 1892, he turned to painting while working as a mechanic and racing cyclist. After his marriage, he took up music again, giving violin lessons and playing the violin in popular orchestras. Vlaminck was self-taught as a painter but was inspired by van Gogh's work, which he saw in 1901, and became drawn into the Fauve movement. From 1907 to about 1910, his art became more structured in response to his interest in Cézanne. He had no sympathy for Cubism and from 1917, when he settled at Valmondois, he developed a distinctive form of naturalism in which country roads are seen in a dramatic, stormy light. He was also a book illustrator and prolific writer of novels, poems and reminiscences.

Vliet, Hendrick Cornelisz.van
(1611/12 – 1675)
Van Vliet is said to have been taught in Delft by his uncle Willem van Vliet and Michiel van Mierevelt. Like his masters, he worked at first as a painter of portraits. In about 1651, he began to paint church interiors in the manner of Emanuel de Witte. Many of his interior views of the 1650s and early 1660s include a framing archway or *trompe-l'oeil* curtain to enhance the illusion. His later works are numerous but tend to be stiffer and more careless than the earlier paintings.

Vollon, Antoine
(1833 – 1900)
Vollon worked for a maker of enamelled metalwork and engraver in Lyon before attending classes at the city art school. In 1859, he moved to Paris, where he met François Bonvin and Théodule Ribot, who encouraged him to paint genre scenes and still lifes. In 1864, a kitchen scene exhibited at the Salon was purchased by the state. He was best known as a painter of still life, vigorously painted and strongly coloured.

Vonck, Jan
(*c*. 1630 – after 1660)
Vonck was born in Poland, son of the Amsterdam still-life painter, Elias Vonck. By 1639, the family was back in Amsterdam, where Jan married in 1653. He worked in the manner of his father, painting still-life compositions of birds and fish and a few live animals, mainly dogs. His dated paintings extend from 1653 to 1663. As his widow remarried in 1665, he must have died about 1664.

Vos, Cornelis de
(1584–5 – 1651)
Born in Hulst, de Vos moved with his family to Antwerp in 1596 and became a pupil of David Remeeus. In 1608, he was admitted to the Antwerp guild. In 1616, when he became a citizen of Antwerp, he was described as a dealer. In the early 1620s, be came to attention as a painter of portraits, several of which feature carefully detailed background interiors. From about 1626, he began to paint large-scale family groups as well as several important biblical and historical compositions. He assisted Rubens in the decoration of one of the triumphal arches erected in 1635 to mark the entrance of the Cardinal-Infante Ferdinand into Antwerp and assisted him again from 1636 to 1638 in painting compositions to decorate the hunting lodge of Philip IV of Spain.

Vouet, Simon
(1590 – 1649)
The son of a painter, Vouet went to England in his youth then to Constantinople (1611–12), Venice (1612–13) and Rome (1614–27), with brief trips elsewhere in Italy. In Rome he worked on prestigious commissions for frescoes, altar-pieces and smaller paintings and was president of the Accademia di S. Luca in 1624. Caravaggio, the Carracci and contemporary Bolognese painting were all important influences on his style. His elegant yet vigorous manner was successful in his native Paris, where he worked from 1627, running a large workshop and training a generation of artists, including Le Sueur and Le Brun.

Vrel, Jacobus
(active 1654 – ?1670)
Apart from a group of some thirty-eight paintings of interiors and street scenes, several of which are signed, nothing is known about Jacobus Vrel. On account of a certain kinship with the work of Vermeer, to whom Vrel's work was at one time attributed, it has been suggested that Vrel, like Vermeer, worked in Delft. His work is remarkable for the quiet simplicity of his subjects and for the air of emptiness and anonymity which pervades his art. One of his street scenes has a near-illegible date which may be read as 1670.

Vries, Roelof Jansz. van
(*c*. 1631 – after 1681)
Van Vries was born in Haarlem. His master is not known but his art suggests a debt to Jacob van Ruisdael. He was admitted into the Leiden guild in 1653. In 1657, he was back in Haarlem and by 1659 he was in Amsterdam, where he appears to have settled. He is last mentioned there in 1681. In 1688, his wife was described as a widow.

Vroom, Hendrick Cornelisz.
(1566 – 1640)
Vroom was born in Haarlem but, trained in Delft. He travelled extensively in Europe as a painter of faience before settling in Haarlem in 1592. In the same year, he designed a set of tapestries commemorating the defeat of the Spanish Armada for Lord Howard of Effingham. Subsequently, he specialized in paintings of naval events, setting the pattern for the development of marine painting in Holland.

Vucht, Gerrit van
(active 1658 – 1697)
Vucht is first recorded in Schiedam, near Rotterdam, in 1658. He appears to have remained there for the rest of his life. He was a painter of still-life compositions of kitchen utensils, breakfast, *vanitas* and fruit.

Vuillard, Edouard
(1868 – 1940)
Vuillard was brought up in Paris, where his mother and elder sister worked as dress-makers. At school, he met Maurice Denis and Xavier Roussel, who persuaded Vuillard to follow him into the studio of Diogène Maillart. In 1886, he went to the Académie Julian where he became associated with the Nabis. In the 1890s Vuillard executed a series of small works in a flat decorative style based on his domestic surroundings and influenced by Japanese woodcuts. His art lent itself to theatre decoration and this brought him important commissions for large-scale work from private patrons in the 1890s. After 1900, he became a successful portrait painter and continued his work in supplying decorative panels, of which the largest was a monumental mural commissioned for the League of Nations building in Geneva.

Wagner, Roger
(b. 1957)
After reading English at Lincoln College, Oxford from 1975 to 1978, Wagner studied under Peter Greenham at the Royal Academy Schools from 1978 to 1981. Much of his art is biblical or has a religious character. His work is small-scale and carefully detailed in oil or acrylic. His treatment of sacred subjects, based on familiar landscapes, is in the tradition of Samuel Palmer and Stanley Spencer.

Waldmann, Kaspar
(1657 – 1720)
Born in Innsbruck, Waldmann was trained by his father, Michael Waldmann I (*c.* 1605–1658) and then learned fresco painting with Egid and Johann Paul Schor. He may have travelled to Italy. He is recorded in 1684 as a citizen of Innsbruck and in 1692 was a member of the city council. He painted numerous altar-pieces and ceiling frescoes in and around Innsbruck.

Walker, Dame Ethel
(1861 – 1951)
Ethel Walker decided to study art after seeing an exhibition of oriental art in Edinburgh. She went to the Putney School of Art, then to the Westminster School of Art and to the Slade School from 1892 to 1894. On a visit to Spain in 1884, she admired Velázquez's art and in Paris was impressed by the work of Manet and the Impressionists. In 1898, she acquired a studio in Cheyne Walk in London and remained there for the rest of her life. Apart from flower paintings, she executed a number of large decorative compositions in which she expressed spiritual ideas through classical themes.

Walker, Robert
(?1595/1610 – ?1659)
Although Walker based several of his portraits on the work of van Dyck there is no evidence that he was van Dyck's pupil. He borrowed ideas also from Italian sources and was known as a successful copyist. He was much employed during the Commonwealth, particularly for his portraits of Oliver Cromwell, which were widely copied and reproduced in prints.

Wals, Goffredo
(*c.* 1595 – *c.* 1638)
Wals was born in Cologne. It is said that when he was very young he went to Naples and then worked in Rome with Agostino Tassi around 1616–18. He spent the following years in Naples, Genoa and Savona before returning to Naples. He died in an earthquake in Calabria. The works by which he is now known are mostly small, circular landscapes with simple motifs and delicate effects of light.

Walter, Henry
(1786 or 1790 – 1849)
Walter was a painter of landscapes and rural genres. He exhibited six works at the Royal Academy, including two studies from nature and one of a beech tree painted on the spot. He died in Torquay.

Ward, Daisy Linda
(1883 – 1937)
Daisy Linda Travers was possibly born in New Jersey but little is known about her early life. She moved with her parents to Newcastle upon Tyne and married Theodore Ward there in 1908. She was trained as a painter at the Slade School and, like her sister, had a career in music. She sang at Covent Garden in 1919–20 and exhibited still-life paintings at the Royal Academy from 1925 onwards. The collection of still-life paintings which she formed with her husband was given to the Ashmolean Museum in her memory by Theodore Ward in 1939.

Watelet, Louis-Etienne
(1780 – 1866)
Although self-taught, Watelet is said to have gone to the studio of Valenciennes and he worked at first in this tradition. He made his début at the Salon in 1800 with a picturesque sunset. He last exhibited in 1857. He travelled much, exhibiting views of Normandy, Picardy, Belgium, the Tyrol, Italy, Savoy and the Dauphiné. He had many pupils and published a series of lithographs after his own studies in 1829.

Watteau, Jean-Antoine
(1684 – 1721)
Born in Valenciennes Watteau was apprenticed either to Jacques-Albert Gérin or to the sculptor Antoine-Joseph Pater, before settling in Paris, where he worked *c.* 1702 for a dealer. By *c.* 1705 he was painting theatrical subjects with Claude Gillot and then fashionable interior decoration with Claude Audran III. On a sojourn in Valenciennes in 1709–10 he painted military genre scenes. He developed the *fête galante*, a subject involving elegant gatherings in a parkland setting with music and fancy-dress, to which he brought a new psychological sensitivity and refinement of touch. He was received into the Paris Academy in 1717 in a category of *fêtes galantes*, invented to accommodate him. A skilled and prolific draughtsman, his work was widely collected.

Watts, Frederick William
(1800 – 1862)
Constable, who lived in Hampstead at the same time as Frederick Watts, had a major influence on Watts's work. Unlike Constable, however, Watts was an assiduous traveller particularly in the south and west of England. In the 1820s, he worked much in Wales and the west country. In the 1840s, he painted many river scenes, particularly along the Thames.

Watts, George Frederic
(1817 – 1904)
Watts studied under the sculptor William Behnes before entering the Royal Academy Schools in 1837. A prize won in the Westminster Hall Competition in 1843 enabled him to visit Florence, where he remained until 1847. On his return to England, his many portraits ensured him a livelihood while he undertook a series of universal allegories inspired by his ambition to revive heroic painting. In the late 1860s, he turned to sculpture. An equestrian statue commissioned by the Marquess of Westminster in 1870 gave him the starting point for a monumental allegory of Physical Energy on which he worked until the end of his life.

Weenix, Jan
(1642 – 1719)
Weenix was born in Amsterdam, son of Jan Baptist Weenix, with whom he studied in Utrecht. He was cousin of the animal and still-life painter, Melchior d'Hondecoeter, who was also trained by Jan Baptist. He entered the Utrecht guild in 1664. Some time after 1668, he moved to Amsterdam. From about 1702 to 1714, he was court painter to the Elector Palatine, Johann Wilhelm, in Düsseldorf, for whom he painted a series of game pieces as decorations for the prince's hunting lodge. He died in Amsterdam. His work consists of landscapes, portraits, figures, flower pieces, still lifes and especially hunting pieces.

Weerts, H. Maria
(second half of 17th century)
The painter is known only from a handful of signed still-life paintings, mainly of flowers. It has been suggested that the artist is to be identified wth a Henricis van Weert who was empowered by the art dealer Uylenburgh to collect certain dues at Genoa in 1667.

Weight, Carel Victor Morlais
(1908 – 1997)
Weight was born in London and studied at the Hammersmith School of Art, 1928–30, and at Goldsmiths' College School of Art, 1930–33. He served in the Second World War and was appointed a War Artist in 1945. He painted murals for the Festival of Britain's Country Pavilion in 1951 and another for Manchester Cathedral in 1963. In 1947 he was appointed to a teaching post at the Royal College of Art, becoming Professor of Painting ten years later. He retired from the Professorship in 1973.

Weissenbruch, Jan Hendrik
(1824 – 1903)
Weissenbruch's early paintings show a debt to the landscape painters, Bartholomeus J. van Hove, who was his master and Andreas Shelfout. Weissenbruch also looked back to the work of Ruisdael, Potter and Vermeer whose work he copied and whose light effects he imitated. From 1875, he made regular visits to the villages of Noorden and Nieuwkoop in south Holland where he painted waterside views. His work shows a predominant interest in light and sky. He was less concerned with the human figure than his Hague School contemporaries. Apart from his landscapes, he also painted a number of street scenes in The Hague which were carefully adjusted for the sake of harmonizing the composition.

Wellington, Hubert Lindsay
(1879 – 1967)
Wellington was born in Gloucester and studied at the Gloucester School of Art, 1895–8, the Birmingham School of Art, 1898–99, and at the Slade School of Art, 1899–1900. Through Spencer Gore, who was also at the Slade, he became involved with the Camden Town Group. After the First World War, he was appointed a lecturer at the National Gallery, where he remained until 1922. He taught at the Royal College of Art for ten years and was principal of the Edinburgh College of Art from 1932 to 1942. In 1942, he retired to Oxfordshire but was invited to return to the Slade School as lecturer in the late 1940s. Wellington contributed to several periodicals and wrote a number of books. He was chiefly a landscape painter.

Wet, Jacob Willemsz. de
(*c.* 1610 – after 1675)
De Wet painted mostly biblical and mythological subjects. His early work shows a debt to Jan Pynas and Pieter Lastman but in the early 1630s the influence of Rembrandt is more evident, indicating that he might have been a pupil of Rembrandt. In his later work, landscape plays a more notable role and the figures become smaller.

Whistler, James Abbott McNeill
(1834 – 1903)
In 1855, after learning etching as a US navy cartographer, Whistler went to Paris to study painting with Charles Gleyre. He acquired a taste for Velázquez and oriental art and met Courbet, who influenced his early paintings. After settling in London in 1859, he met Rossetti and Swinburne and his art was affected by Rossetti's aestheticism. His links with the Pre-Raphaelites also inspired his Peacock Room (1876–7, now Freer Gallery of Art, Washington, DC) commissioned by F.R. Leyland, which bridged the gap between William Morris and Art Nouveau. A libel action brought by him against Ruskin contributed to bankrupting him in 1879. In 1880, he left for a year in Venice, working on a series of etchings for the Fine Art Society. He continued to paint portraits in his later years and spent more time making lithographs, watercolours and etchings, as well writing combative pamphlets and letters to the press.

White, Diana
(1868 – 1950)
Diana White was associated with Lucien Pissarro at the Eragny Press from 1903 onwards and painted in a manner similar to his. She was also a writer.

Wieringhen, Cornelis Claesz. van
(*c.* 1580 – 1635)
Van Wieringhen's shipping pictures derive closely from the work of Hendrick Vroom, who may have been his master. He was based in Haarlem and took an active part in the affairs of the Guild of St Luke in the city. He received commissions from the city of Haarlem, the Admiralty in Amsterdam and others. Apart from these politically-inspired compositions, van Wieringhen painted a number of smaller panel pictures of ships at sea.

Wilkie, Sir David
(1785 – 1841)
Wilkie was born at Cults in Fifeshire and entered the Trustees' Academy in Edinburgh. He supported himself painting portraits and painted his first genre painting, a view of Pitlessie Fair, in 1804–5. In 1805, he moved to London and exhibited a series of scenes of rustic life, partly based on 17th-century Dutch examples, but with an added freshness and whimsicality and an understanding of the varieties of physiogonomy which ensured their success. In 1824, he set out on a European tour to recover from a nervous breakdown. After three years, he returned to England and introduced a new breadth into his technique and a new amibition into his subjects. In 1840, he set out on a tour of the Holy Land but died on the return jouney.

Willaerts, Adam
(1577 – 1664)
Willaerts was born in Antwerp but, like many other Protestants in this period, he emigrated to the northern Netherlands, where he settled in Utrecht. His earliest known painting, dated 1608, derives from the example of Hendrick Vroom. Many of his works also show familiarity with the work of Jan Brueghel I. Most of his marine paintings are coastal scenes with foreground figures, sometimes with a biblical theme and flanking rocks, trees and other motifs. Animals appear in the 1620s; after 1650, when he began to collaborate with Willem Ormea the still-life painter, a catch of fish, painted by Ormea, sometimes appears on the beach. Several of his works celebrate contemporary events.

Williams, William
(active 1763 – 1795)
A little-known painter of landscapes and portraits who lived in Birmingham. Williams exhibited at the Royal Academy and at the British Institution.

Wilson, Richard
(1714 – 1782)
From 1729 to 1735, Wilson studied under the portrait painter Thomas Wright in London. He was supported after the death of his father, a Welsh clergyman, by Sir George Wynn, who was related to his mother. In 1737, he began to paint landscapes and donated two landscapes to the Foundling Hospital collection in 1746. In 1750, he set out for Italy, apparently with the intention of improving himself as a painter of portraits. He worked at first in Venice and was in Rome by about 1752. He stayed in Rome for about five years, studying landscape. His Roman landscapes were influenced by Dughet and Rosa and in particular by Claude. On return to England he specialized in landscape painting, repeating Roman views and composing views of English and Welsh scenery in the Claudian manner. He also painted several ambitious historical landscape compositions. After 1770, his circumstances declined and he retired to Wales in 1781.

Wilde, Samuel de (see De Wilde, Samuel)

Wint, Peter de (see De Wint, Peter)

Wit, Jacob de
(1695 – 1754)
At the age of nine, de Wit was apprenticed to Albert van Spiers, a ceiling painter who had worked with Gérard de Lairesse. In 1711–12, he made copies after Rubens's ceiling paintings in the Jesuit church in Antwerp, which provided valuable evidence after the originals were destroyed by fire in 1718. In 1713, he entered the Guild of St Luke and then moved to Amsterdam. As he was a Roman Catholic he was given commissions by the Catholic authorities in Amsterdam but also worked for the Reformed Church and the Baptists. His decorative work was initially influenced by Rubens but he adopted a lighter style in his later work. Apart from his ceilings, he was famed for painting *trompe-l'oeil* grisailles, usually featuring putti.

Wootton, John
(*c.* 1681 – 1764)
Wootton may have received some training from Jan Wyck in the 1680s but his origins are not clear. By 1710, he was well established as the leading English horse painter. He painted horse portraits, scenes of racing at Newmarket and hunting pictures. For much of his earlier work, he took his models from Dutch and Flemish predecessors but later introduced borrowings from Claude and Dughet into the background. He also painted a few battle pictures. He gave up painting in about 1760 and sold his extensive art collection in 1761.

Worlidge, Thomas
(1700 – 1766)
Worlidge was born at Peterborough in Cambridgeshire. He took drawing lessons from the Genoese painter Alessandro Grimaldi and went with Grimaldi's son Alexander to Birmingham in about 1736. He worked there as a glass painter. In the mid-1730s, he moved to London and lived in Covent Garden, where he drew and painted a number of theatrical portraits. In the 1750s and 1760s he worked in the area of Bath making portraits in pencil, crayon and oil. As an etcher he copied and imitated Rembrandt above all.

Wright of Derby, Joseph
(1734 – 1797)
Wright was born in Derby and trained in London as a portrait painter with Thomas Hudson. He earned his living at first by painting portraits in his native Derby and elsewhere in the Midlands. In the 1760s, he began to paint subject pictures, lit by candles and lamps. The largest of these illustrate contemporary scientific themes. In 1773, he set out for Italy and spent two years in Rome studying the Sistine Chapel and classical antiquities. He also painted landscapes in the Campagna and views of Vesuvius erupting and continued to paint these following his return to England. After two years in Bath he settled permanently in Derby. A number of literary subjects date from his later years.

Wtewael, Joachim Antonisz.
(1566 – 1638)
Wtewael is said to have been trained in his father's glassworks in Utrecht. He spent from about 1588 to 1592 in Italy and France where he seems to have absorbed some ideas from the art of Parmigianino and the School of Fontainebleau. On return to Utrecht he came under the influence of the local Mannerists, Hendrick Goltzius, Cornelis van Haarlem and Karel van Mander, acquiring their taste for turbulent compositions of muscular figures in exaggerated and contrasted poses. He was mainly a painter of biblical and mythological subjects. Several portraits by him are known. He was also a flax merchant and politician and served several times on the Utrecht town council; he was a founder of the St Luke's Guild of painters in Utrecht in 1611.

Wyck, Thomas
(?1616 – 1677)
Wyck visited Italy before he appears as a painter in Haarlem in 1642. From about 1660 to 1668 he was in England, where he painted port scenes, marines and scenes set in laboratories as well as views of London, including some of the Fire of London in 1666. His best-known work consists of scenes of Roman life, probably of the early 1640s.

Yeats, Jack Butler
(1871 – 1957)
The son of the painter John Butler Yeats and brother of the writer W.B. Yeats, Jack Butler Yeats was inspired by the light and landscape of County Sligo to become a painter. He worked initially as a black and white illustrator. He also wrote a series of plays on Irish themes. His first paintings were in watercolour and he did not work regularly in oils until he was over thirty. In the mid-1920s, his style became freer and his colours more luminous. He was a prolific painter taking his subjects mainly from the Irish countryside and life in Dublin.

Yeats, John Butler
(1839 – 1922)
In 1867, after studying law in Dublin, Yeats moved to London where he enrolled at Heatherley's Art School. For the first twenty years of his career, he painted genre pictures, landscapes and illustrations. In the 1880s, he began to specialize in portraits, particularly in pencil.

Ykens, Frans
(1601 – 1693)
Ykens was apprenticed to his uncle, the still-life painter Osias Beert and entered the Antwerp guild in 1631. He travelled in Provence after his apprenticeship, probably in about 1629. He is known only for his still-life paintings. There are dated works from 1635 to 1663. These include flowers, fruit, game and fish with accessories, painted in various styles. Under the influence of Daniel Seghers, he painted many garlands of flowers around votive images painted by other artists.

Zoffany, Johan
(1733 – 1810)
Zoffany was born in Frankfurt. He studied painting at Regensburg and then in Rome where he was taught by Agostino Masucci. He had arrived in London by 1760, where he was encouraged by David Garrick to illustrate theatrical scenes. By 1764, he had received commissions for portraits from the royal family and for two elaborate group portraits, one showing the members of the Royal Academy gathered in the life-class and the other showing the scholars and tourists of Florence grouped in the Tribuna. He subsequently spent six years in India.

Zoppo, Marco (Marco di Antonio di Ruggero)
(1433 – 1478)
An assistant from 1453 to Francesco Squarcione, the most prominent painter in Padua, Marco moved to Venice in 1455. He was to work for patrons in Bologna and Venice and enjoyed a high reputation. His sinuous figures, delineated with incisive contours, have a strong sculptural presence. He was also an important and expressive draughtsman.

Zuccarelli, Francesco
(1702 – 1788)
Having studied the frescoes of Andrea del Sarto in Florence, Zuccarelli trained in Rome under Paolo Anesi and Giovanni Maria Morandi. After settling in Venice *c.* 1730, he became a landscape painter, specializing in decorative, arcadian scenes and experimenting occasionally with Dutch-style landscapes. His pictures were engraved by Francesco Bartolozzi. Encouraged by his patron Joseph Smith, he worked in England from 1752 to 1773, where his landscapes were popular; he became a founder member of the Royal Academy.

Zurbarán, Francisco de
(1598 – 1664)
The son of a trader, Zurbarán trained in Seville with Pedro Díaz de Villanueva and studied polychrome sculpture. Little survives of his early work, but by the late 1620s he was working for the Dominican and the Mercedarian orders in Seville, painting forceful, realistic figures bathed in strong light. He made numerous religious works which were often copied, and produced remarkable still-life paintings. In Madrid in 1634, Zurbarán collaborated on the decoration of the Buen Retiro palace. Major patrons from the late 1630s include the Carthusians at Jerez de la Frontera and the Hieronymites of Guadalupe. In the late 1640s he sought a new market in Spanish America; he returned to Madrid in 1658.

APPENDIX OF ORIGINAL FRAMES IN THE ASHMOLEAN MUSEUM

Timothy Newbery

The original or first frame a painting receives to embellish it, is the basis of all further understanding of how frames relate to paintings, their styles, dates, hanging locations of framings and significance. These frames are not always contemporary with their paintings, because pictures are sometimes either framed with existing earlier frames or not framed until some years after their date, for a variety of reasons. The identification of original frames depends on a complex network of comparative material.

Original gilt composition frame, made in England, *c.* 1895
Charles Alexander, *L'amateur chez lui*
A299a

Original gilt composition and veneer frame, made in England, 1878
Sir Lawrence Alma-Tadema, *A Hearty Welcome*
A881

Original carved and gilt triptych, made in Rome, *c.* 1430
Studio of Fra Angelico, *Virgin and Child with Angels and a Dominican Saint*
A77

Possibly original plaster Carlo Maratta style frame, made in England, *c.* 1959
Thomas Balston, *Interior with an Arum Lily*, 1939
A928

Original engaged frame, made in Siena, *c.* 1350–75
'Barna da Siena', *The Crucifixion and Lamentation*
A73
Newbery 2002, no. 2

Possibly original Alma-Tadema frame, made in England, *c.* 1879
Jules Bastien-Lepage, *Laura, Lady Alma-Tadema*, 1879
A1020

Original carved and gilt frame, made in England, *c.* 1764
Pompeo Batoni, *David Garrick*, 1764
A61
Newbery 2002, no. 19

Original gilt composition ornament Carlo Maratta frame, made in England, *c.* 1815
Sir George Howland Beaumont, *Woodland Scene with Gipsies*
A42

Original silver and gilt moulding, made in Denmark, 1832
Wilhelm Bendz, *The Church of Ramsau, Austria*, 1832
A1244

Possibly original bronzed and painted moulding, made in England, *c.* 1921
Robert Polhill Bevan, *Showing at Tattersalls*, *c* 1919
A898

Original three-ply board, oak, varnish frame, made in England, *c.* 1912–14
David Bomberg, *Procession*, *c.* 1912–14
A1120
Newbery 2002, no. 31

Original gilt composition frame, made in France, *c.* 1862
Eugène Boudin, *The Jetty at Trouville: Sunset*, 1862
A475

Original plaster and gesso, water-gilt frame, made in France, *c.* 1880
Eugène Boudin, *The Estuary*
A633
Newbery 2002, no. 27

Original gilt composition frame, made in France, *c.* 1860–70
Eugène Boudin, *A Beach Scene at Trouville*, *c.* 1860s
A963

Original black and gold cassetta frame, made in England, 1587–8
Anonymous, British Artist, *Portrait of a Man, called Sir Francis Drake*, 1587
A21a

Original black and gold 'Tradescant' frame, made in England, *c.* 1640
Anonymous British Artist, *John Lowin*, 1640
F741

Original provincial 'Lawrence' frame, made in England, *c.* 1845
Anonymous, British Artist, *Landscape with two Figures walking along a Track*
A419b

Original lime(?) water-gilt frame, made in England, *c.* 1840
Ford Maddox Brown, *Mrs James Maddox*, 1840
A936a
Newbery 2002, no. 22

Original carved and gilt frame, made in England, *c.* 1853
Ford Maddox Brown, *The Seeds and Fruits of English Poetry*, 1845–53
A360
Newbery 2002, no. 23

Original gilt oak frame, made in England, *c.* 1880–90
Ford Maddox Brown, *Lady Rivers and her Children*, 1887–9
A1087

Original gilt composition tabernacle frame, made in England, *c.* 1870–80
Philip Hermogenes Calderon, *Broken Vows*, 1857
A967

Probably original carved and gilt Louis XV-style frame, made in Glasgow(?), late 19th century
Sir David Young Cameron, *The Hills of Provence*, 1922–4
A478

Possibly original gold and silver moulding, made in England, *c.* 1919
Sydney William Carline, *Over the Hills of Kurdistan: Flying above Kirkuk*, 1919
A398

Original gilt plaster frame, made in France, *c.* 1870
Charles-Emile-Auguste Carolus-Duran, *M. Berthon*, 1870
A764

Original engaged frame, made in Siena, *c.* 1340–50
Attributed to Naddo Ceccarelli, *The Virgin and Child*
A1062

Original reverse black and gold octagonal cassetta, made in Rome, *c.* 1640
Michelangelo Cerquozzi, *Spring (Flora)*, *c.* 1630s?
WA.L.99.8

Original reverse black and gold octagonal cassetta, made in Rome, *c.* 1640
Michelangelo Cerquozzi, *Summer (Ceres)*, *c.* 1630s?
WA.L.99.11

Original gilt composition frame, made in England, *c.* 1910
Gerard Chowne, *Still-life: A Bowl of mixed Flowers*, 1907
A473

Original water-gilt composition frame, made in England, 1851
Charles Alston Collins, *Convent Thoughts*, 1851
A273
Newbery 2002, no. 24

Possibly original palisander veneer frame, made in Holland, *c.* 1690
Adriaen Coorte, *Still Life with Hazel-nuts*, 1696
A545

Original gilt frame, made in England, *c.* 1870
Giovanni Costa, called Nino, *View of Monte Amiata, Tuscany*, *c.* 1880?
A410

Original silvered frame, made in England, *c.* 1960
Adrian Maurice Daintrey, *Beach Scene, Totland Bay*
A1097

Set of 7 original dark brown polished frames, made in Holland, *c.* 1640s
Attributed to Jacques de l'Ange, *The Seven Deadly Sins*, *c.* 1640s
A22-8

Probably original gilt composition frame, made in England, *c.* 1925–30
John Downton, *Susan Saneon*, *c.* 1948
A1214

Original black and gold 'Tradescant' frame, made in England, *c.* 1640
Copy after Sir Anthony van Dyck, *Thomas Howard, later Fifth Duke of Norfolk, when a Boy*
F669

Possibly original carved and gilt Louis XV-derived frame, made in England, *c.* 1835
William Etty, *The penitent Magdalen*, 1835
A422

Original brown polished moulding, made in England, 1987
Steven Frederick Godfrey Farthing, *The Last Day in the Old House*, 1987
A1227

Possibly original gilt composition moulding, made in England, *c.* 1890–1900
Joseph H. Vignoles Fisher, *Summer Evening*
A737

Original black and gold cassetta frame, made in France, *c.* 1525–30
Anonymous Flemish (?) Artist, *The Battle of Pavia*, *c.* 1525–30
F664

Original blue, gilt and carved frame, made in England, *c.* 1920
Eleanor Fortescue-Brickdale, *Time the Physician*
A1159

Original Roman 17th-century style gilt cassetta frame, made in England, *c.* 1933
Roger Fry, *La Salle des Caryatides in the Louvre*
A424

Original silver-gilt plaster frame, made in England, *c.* 1925
Mark Gertler, *Young Girlhood, No.2*, 1925
A925

Probably original gilt plaster Louis XIV provincial frame, made in England, *c.* 1930
Mark Gertler, *Thomas Balston*, 1921
A1038

Original Watts-derived frame, made in England, *c.* 1921
Mark Gertler, *Staffordshire Group*, 1921
A1039

Original gilt moulding, made in England, *c.* 1925
Mark Gertler, *Apples in a Bag*, 1925
A1040

Original gilt inner frame, made in Florence *c.* 1477–8. Gilt and cartapesta outer frame, made in the Veneto, *c.* 1550
Domenico Ghirlandaio, *Portrait of a young Man*, *c.* 1477–78
A83

Original engaged gilt frame, made in Siena, early 14th century
Studio of Giotto di Bondone, *The Virgin and Child*, *c.* 1310
A332
Newbery 2002, no. 1

Original sculpted plaster frame, made in England, *c.* 1920s
Charles Isaac Ginner, *Hampstead Heath – Spring*, 1932
A1042

Probably original southern Italian silver-gilt style frame, late 18th century
Sylvia Gosse, *Versailles*
A1028

Original grey-painted 'Whistler' frame, made in England, *c.* 1890
Sir Lawrence Burnett Gowing, *Lady with Book*, *c.* 1942
A718a

Possibly original grey Louis XIV-style frame, made *c.* 1929
Duncan Grant, *Interior*, 1929
A649

Original oil-gilt reeded frame, made in England, *c.* 1890
Attributed to Walter Greaves, *Symphony in Silver and Grey*
A916

Original plaster Louis XV-derived frame, made in England, *c.* 1970–75
Peter Greenham, *Mrs Lia Ralli*
A1200

Original polished walnut frame, made in England, *c.* 1985
Maggi Hambling, *Francis Bacon*, 1985
A1248

Original 'Barbizon' frame, made in France, *c.* 1860
Louis-Adolphe Hervier, *The Outskirts of a Village*, 1852
A651

Original engaged black and gold tondo, made in eastern Spain, *c.* 1550
Anonymous Hispano-Flemish Artist, *The Virgin and Child*
A336

Original white paint pine frame, made in England, *c.* 1925–30
Ivon Hitchens, *A Border Day (Morning, Bankshead)*, 1925
A1146
Newbery 2002, no. 33

Original gilt and off-white frame, made in England, *c.* 1975
Eliot Hodgkin, *Study of Asparagus*, 1975
WA1976.23

Original gilt oak frame, made in England, *c.* 1911
Sir Charles John Holmes, *Coniston Old Man from Levens Water*, 1911
A328

Original gilt oak frame, made in England, *c.* 1911
Sir Charles John Holmes, *Saddleback from the South-west*, 1911
A775

Original gilt composition frame, made in England, *c.* 1880
Arthur Hughes, *The Eve of St Agnes*, 1855–6
A708

Original gilt composition Régence-style frame, made in England, *c.* 1850
William Holman Hunt, *A converted British Family sheltering a Christian Missionary from the Persecution of the Druids*, 1850
A265

Original gilt composition frame, made in England, *c.* 1859
William Holman Hunt, *The School-Girl's Hymn*, 1859
A266

Original gilt composition frame, made in England, 1861
William Holman Hunt, *The Afterglow in Egypt*, 1861
A267

Original gilt carved composition tabernacle-style frame, made in England, 1863
William Holman Hunt, *London Bridge on the Night of the Marriage of the Prince and Princess of Wales*, 1863–6
A268

Original carved and gilt frame, made in England, *c.* 1866
William Holman Hunt, *The Festival of St Swithin (The Dovecot)*, 1866–75
A269

Original water-gilt composition frame, made in England, *c.* 1877
William Holman Hunt, *Plain of Esdraelon from the Heights above Nazareth*, 1875–7
A270
Newbery 2002, no. 25

Possibly original 16th century North European-style cassetta frame, made in England, *c.* 1856
John William Inchbold, *Cuillin Ridge, Skye, from Sligachan*, 1855
A326

Probably original gilt plaster frame, made in N. Germany, *c.* 1888
Jozef Israels, *Girl on a Dune*, early 1890s
A1182

Original oak and gilt frame, made in N. Germany, *c.* 1905
Jozef Israels, *A Fishergirl on a Dune, knitting*
A1183

Original carved and gilt rococo-style frame, made in England, *c.* 1930
Francis Ernest Jackson, *Lindsay M. Gladstone*, *c.* 1940
A1198

Original carved and gilt Venetian *c.* 1720-style frame, made by Chapman Bros in London, *c.* 1930
George Percy Jacomb-Hood, *A Summer's Day*
A401a

Original polished oak frame, made in England, *c.* 1929
Augustus Edwin John, *T.E. Lawrence*, 1929
A726

Original Louis XIV-style gilt composition frame, made by Foord & Dickinson in London, *c.* 1850
George Jones, *An Archway at Bologna, with the Piazza Maggiore beyond*, between 1820–1830s
A237

Original gilt frame, made in England, 1851–2
George Jones, *Turner's Burial in the Crypt of St Paul's*, *c.* 1851–2
A243

Original Louis XIV-style gilt composition frame, probably made by Foord & Dickinson in London, *c.* 1854
George Jones, *The Battle of the Alma*
A236

Original gilt plaster 'Barbizon' frame, made in France, *c.* 1864
Jean-Berthold Jongkind, *View of Notre-Dame, Paris*, 1864
A489

Possibly original carved and gilt Carlo Maratta frame, made in England, *c.* 1778
Tilly Kettle, *Mrs Drewry Ottley*, 1768
A308

Original gilt neo-classical frame, made in England, 1872
Edward Lear, *Thermopylae*, 1872
A1205

Original gilt composition frame, made by Foord & Dickinson in London, 1880
Edward Lear, *The Plains of Lombardy from Monte Generoso*, 1880
A353

Original carved gilt and composition frame, made in England, *c.* 1870
Frederic Lord Leighton, *Acme and Septimius*, 1867–8
A1089
Newbery 2002, no. 26

Possibly original carved and gilt frame, made in England, *c.* 1937
Thomas Esmond Lowinsky, *Miss Avril Turner*, 1937
A766

Original gilt composition ornament frame, made in England, *c.* 1870
Nevil Oliver Lupton, *The Harvest Field*, 1857–8
A706

Original grey-painted frame, made by Alfred Stiles & Sons in London, *c.* 1960
Charles Cyril Mahoney, *Yellow Ox-eye Daisies*
A1082

Original silver frame, made in England, *c.* 1980
Charles Marq, *Antichambre*, 1977
A1153

Original gilt composition neo-renaissance-style frame, made in England, *c.* 1855
Robert Braithwaite Martineau, *Katherine and Petruchio*, 1855
A798

Original gilt composition cassetta frame, made in England, 1864
Robert Braithwaite Martineau, *The Knight's Guerdon*, 1864
A799

Original gilt composition frame, made in England, *c.* 1868
Robert Braithwaite Martineau, *Girl with a Hoop*, 1868
A801

Original engaged carved and gilt inner frame, made in Lombardy, *c.* 1490. Carved and gilt outer frame, made in Bologna, *c.* 1640
Attributed to the Master of Baldraccani, *Portrait of an unknown Lady*
A711

Original gilt plaster frame, made in France, *c.* 1880
Style of Anton Mauve, *Shepherd and Sheep, Evening*
A1186

Original mahogany polished softwood frame, made in England, 1990
Jock McFadyen, *Limehouse Basin*, 1990
A1249

Original pine frame, made in England, *c.* 1988
Robert Medley, *Maggi Hambling*, 1988
A1250

Original gilt composition bunched-leaf-style frame, made in England, 1851
Sir John Everett Millais Bt, *The Return of the Dove to the Ark*, 1851
A271

Original gilt frame, made in England, *c.* 1912
Christopher Richard Wynne Nevinson, *The Towpath*, 1912
A499

Original black and white frame, made in England, *c.* 1945
Ben Nicholson, *Still Life with Flag*, 1945
A1202

Original gilt plaster ripple frame, made in England, *c.* 1917
Sir William Nicholson, *The Rose-Crested Cockatoo*, 1917
A728

Probably original Salvator Rosa-derived gilt frame, made in England, *c.* 1930
Sir William Orpen, *The Chess Players*
A465

Original grey painted moulding, painted by the artist and integral, made in England, *c.* 1980
Tom Phillips, *The Artist's Mother at 18 and 88*
A1222

Original grey and white frame, made in England, *c.* 1934
Glyn Warren Philpot, *Man with a Gun*, 1922
A1140

Original plaster, white paint and gilt pine frame made in England, *c.* 1928
Glyn Warren Philpot, *Gabrielle and Rosemary*, 1928
A1023a
Newbery 2002, no. 32

Possibly original grey painted moulding, made in England, *c.* 1890
Félix Pissarro, *The Rat*
A829

Original grey painted frame, made in England, *c.* 1923
Lucien Pissarro, *Mme Camille Pissarro*, 1923
A796

Original silver moulding, made in England, *c.* 1931
Orovida Pissarro, *The Archer's Return*, 1931
A1050a

Original gilt composition Louis XIV-style frame, made in France, *c.* 1925–35
James Ferrier Pryde, *The Slum*, 1916
A943

Original gilt 'Richmond' frame, made in England, *c.* 1840
George Richmond after Raphael, *The Archimedes Group from 'The School of Athens'*, 1839
A680

Original gilt cassetta frame, made in England, *c.* 1910–20
Charles Ricketts, *Jephthah's Daughter*, *c.* 1905–7
A729

Possibly original gilt moulding, made in England, *c.* 1920–30
Charles Ricketts, *Tobias being comforted by the Angel*
A913

Original polished walnut and white frame, made in England, *c.* 1997
James Rielly, *Trainerspotting*, 1997
A1251

Original carved and gilt limewood frame, made in England by Grinling Gibbons, *c.* 1681–2
John Riley, *Elias Ashmole*, *c.* 1681–2
F730
Newbery 2002, no. 13

Original gilt and limewood frame, made in England in the studio of Grinling Gibbons, *c.* 1682
John Riley, *King Charles II*
F731

Original gilt and limewood frame, made in England in the studio of Grinling Gibbons, *c.* 1682
John Riley, *James, Duke of York, later King James II*
F732

Original gilt composition and oil-gilt 'Watts' frame, made in England, *c.* 1889
Briton Rivière, *Prometheus*
A363 1889

Original carved and gilt frame, made in England, *c.* 1815
William Rivière, *William Young Ottley*
A507

Original gilt plaster frame, made in England, *c.* 1925
William Roberts, *T.E. Lawrence as Aircraftman Shaw*, 1923
A727

Unfinished original carved frame, made in England, 1785–90
George Romney, *Mrs Siddons*, *c.* 1784
A391

Original engaged gilt and punched moulding, made in Siena, *c.* 1470–80
Sano di Pietro, *The Virgin and Child with St Jerome, St Catherine of Alexandria and two Angels*, *c.* 1470
A76

Probably original gilt oak frame, made in England, *c.* 1875
William Bell Scott, *Keats's Grave*, 1873
A263

Probably original gilt oak frame, made in England, *c.* 1875
William Bell Scott, *Shelley's Grave*, 1873
A264

Original gilt composition frame, made in England, *c.* 1855
Thomas Seddon, *View on the Nile*, 1855
A708a

Original gilt oak frame, made in England, *c.* 1910
Charles Haslewood Shannon, *The Apple Gatherers*
A683

Original white gold and painted cassetta frame, made in England, 1996
Richard Shirley Smith, *Still-life with Marble Foot*, 1996
A1203

Probably original gilt oak frame, made in England, *c.* 1890
Walter Richard Sickert, *The Bridge of Sighs, Venice*, *c.* 1901
A1234

Original plaster water-gilt Italian 17th century style frame, made in England, 1907
Walter Richard Sickert, *Gaieté Montparnasse, dernière galerie de gauche*, *c.* 1906
A1230
Newbery 2002, no. 30

Original silver moulding, made in England, *c.* 1950
Brigitte Simon, *Au Delà*, 1977
A1155

Original silver moulding, made in England, *c.* 1980
Brigitte Simon, *Tryptique: Tombeau de Charchoune*
A1156

Original frame, made in England, *c.* 1959
Kevin Sinnott, *Wrestlers II*, 1959
A1252

Possibly original Louis XIV provincial plaster frame, made in England, *c.* 1930
Sir Matthew Smith, *Still-life of Flowers*, mid 1920s
A626

Original gilt composition frame, made in England, *c.* 1837
William Smith, *Philip Eury Duncan*, 1837
A518

Original red and gold double-sided engaged frame, made in S. Germany, late 15th century
Anonymous, South German Artist, *St Sebastian*
A426

Original octagonal ebony and brass cassetta frame, made in Augsburg, *c.* 1590–1600
Anonymous Spanish Artist (?), *St Teresa of Avila in Ecstasy*
A908a

Original off-white and stippled paint frame, made in England, *c.* 1920
Gilbert Spencer, *Pegwell Bay, Kent,* 1921
A441

Probably original gilt composition frame, made in England, *c.* 1835
James Stark, *The Willow Stream,* between 1819–1840
A762

Possibly original brown polished pearwood veneer cassetta frame, made in Holland, 1635
Harmen van Steenwyck, *Still Life of Fruit on a Ledge,* mid 1640s
A598

Probably original Carlo Marratta-derived gilt composition frame, made in England, *c.* 1902
Philip Wilson Steer, *Stroud: View over the Plain,* 1902
A935

Original gilt frame, made in England, *c.* 1915
William Strang, *The Fisherman's Home,* 1905
A684

Original gilt composition frame, made in England, *c.* 1835
Thomas Sully, *The Love Letter,* 1834
A313

Original gilt plaster frame, made by Chapman Bros in London, *c.* 1903
Anna Louisa Swynnerton (née Robinson), *Head of a Bacchante,* 1903
A511a

Original buff painted English *c.* 1690-style moulding, made in England, *c.* 1975
David Tindle, *Portrait,* 1975
A1189

Original gilt composition frame, made in England, *c.* 1805
William Turner of Oxford, *Woodland Landscape, c.* 1816–20
A656

Original carved and gilt frame, made in Siena, late 14th century
Andrea Vanni, *The Virgin and Child with the Angel of the Annunciation in the gable*
A696
Newbery 2002, no. 3

Possibly original gilt composition Louis XIV-style frame, made in France, *c.* 1840
Antoine Vollon, *Still Life of white Azaleas*
A476

Original 'Watts' frame, made in England, *c.* 1860
George Frederic Watts, *Time and Death, c.* 1868
A880

Original 'Watts' frame, made in England, *c.* 1865
George Frederic Watts, *The Rider on the Black Horse*
A816

Original gilt composition oak 'Watts' frame, made in England, *c.* 1870–75
George Frederic Watts, *The Carrara Mountains from Pisa*
A352

Possibly original gilt composition frame, made in Holland, *c.* 1880–90
Jan Hendrik Weissenbruch, *Landscape with a Peasant Girl feeding Chicken,* 1870
A1147

Original inner engaged modello frame, made in Holland, *c.* 1730. Carved and gilt neoclassical outer frame, made in England, *c.* 1790
Jacob de Wit, *Triumph of the three Christian Virtues*
A425

Original gilt oak frame, made by Combridge & Co., Dublin, *c.* 1903
John Butler Yeats, *Miss Margaret Grierson,* 1903
A1018

Original carved and gilt neo-classical frame, made in England, *c.* 1790
John Zoffany, *Captain William Hall, c.* 1780s
A194

BIBLIOGRAPHY

Ainsworth 1992
Maryan Ainsworth, 'New observations on the working technique in Simon Marmion's panel paintings', in T. Kren, ed., *Margaret of York, Simon Marmion and The Visions of Tondal* (Los Angeles, 1992)

Aldeburgh and Bristol 1966
Charles Brooking 1723–1759: Paintings, Drawings and Engravings (exh. cat., Aldeburgh Festival and Bristol City Art Gallery, 1966)

Allderidge 1974
Patricia Allderidge, *The Late Richard Dadd* (exh. cat., Tate Gallery, London, 1974)

Anderson 1997
Jaynie Anderson, *Giorgione. The Painter of 'Poetic Brevity'* (New York, 1997)

Angulo Iñiguez 1957
Diego Angulo Iñiguez, *José Antolinez* (Madrid, 1957)

Angulo Iñiguez and Pérez Sánchez 1969
Diego Angulo Iñiguez and Alfonso E. Pérez Sánchez, *Historia de la pintura española. Escuela Madrileña del primer tercio del Siglo XVII* (Madrid, 1969)

Arisi 1986
Ferdinando Arisi, *Gian Paolo Panini e i fasti della Roma del '700* (Rome, 1986)

Armstrong 1901
Walter Armstrong, *Sir Henry Raeburn* (London 1901)

Arnáiz 1981
José M. Arnáiz, *Eugenio Lucas, su vida y su obra* (Madrid, 1981)

Athill and Goodchild 1980–81
Philip Athill and Anne Goodchild, *William Strang R.A. 1859–1921, Painter-Etcher* (exh. cat., Graves Art Gallery, Sheffield, Glasgow Museums, National Portrait Gallery, London, 1980–81)

Aubrun 1985
Marie-Madeleine Aubrun, *Jules Bastien-Lepage, 1848–1884: Catalogue raisonné de l'oeuvre* (Paris, 1985)

Bailey 1987
Colin J. Bailey, *Ashmolean Museum, Oxford. Catalogue of the Collection of Drawings, V, German Nineteenth Century Drawings* (Oxford, 1987)

Baker 1998
Christopher Baker, 'Paintings', *Effigies and Ecstasies: Roman Baroque Sculpture and Design in the Age of Bernini* (exh. cat., ed. Aidan Weston-Lewis, National Gallery of Scotland, Edinburgh, 1998, pp. 80–84)

Balboni Brizza 1995
Maria Teresa Balboni Brizza, *Stipi e cassoni. Museo Poldi Pezzoli di Milano* (Milan, 1995)

Ballarin 1994
Alessandro Ballarin, *Dosso e Battista Dossi: la pittura a Ferrara negli anni del ducato di Alfonso I*, 2 vols (Venice, 1994)

Ballarin 1995
Alessandro Ballarin, *Jacopo Bassano Scritti 1964–1995*, ed. Vittoria Romani, parts I and II (Padua, 1995–6)

Baron 1973
Wendy Baron, *Sickert* (London, 1973)

Baron 1979
Wendy Baron, *The Camden Town Group* (London, 1979)

Bartoli 1999
Roberta Bartoli, *Biagio d'Antonio* (Milan, 1999)

Baticle and Marinas 1981
Jeanine Baticle and Cristina Marinas, *La Galerie espagnole de Louis-Philippe au Louvre, 1838–1848* (Paris, 1981)

Beckett 1949
R.B. Beckett, *Hogarth* (London, 1949)

Beckett 1951
R.B. Beckett, *Lely* (London, 1951)

Begni Redona 1988
Pier Virgilio Begni Redona, *Alessandro Bonvicino, il Moretto da Brescia* (Brescia, 1988)

Bellosi and Haines 1999
Luciano Bellosi and Margaret Haines, *Lo Scheggia* (Florence, 1999)

Benati 1988
Daniele Benati, *La Bottega degli Erri e la pittura del Rinascimento a Modena* (Modena, 1988)

Benati 1990
Daniele Benati, *Francesco Bianchi Ferrari e la pittura a Modena fra' 4 e '500* (Modena, 1990)

Berardi 1988
Paride Berardi, *Giovanni Antonio Bellinzoni da Pesaro* (Fano, 1988)

Bevan 1965
Robert Bevan, *Robert Bevan: A Memoir by his Son* (London, 1965)

Biagi Maino 1995
Donatella Biagi Maino, *Gaetano Gandolfi* (Turin, 1995)

Biagi Maino 1996
Donatella Biagi Maino, *Idea Prima: Disegni e modelli preparatori, pittura di tocco dal '500 al '700* (Bologna, 1996)

Biard 2003
Bernard Biard, *Francisque Millet. La peinture de paysage en France de 1650 à 1700* (Dijon, 2003)

Bills 1998
Mark Bills, *Edwin Longsden Long, R.A.* (London, Madison and Teaneck, 1998)

Binyon 1925
Laurence Binyon, *The Followers of William Blake* (London, 1925)

Blunt 1966
Anthony Blunt, *The Paintings of Nicolas Poussin. A Critical Catalogue* (London, 1966)

Boisclair 1986
Marie Nicole Boisclair, *Gaspard Dughet: Sa vie et son oeuvre* (Paris, 1986)

Bologna 1958
Francesco Bologna, *Francesco Solimena* (Naples, 1958)

Bonnici 1989
Claude-Jeanne Bonnici, *Paul Guigou 1834–1871* (Aix-en-Provence, 1989)

Bonsanti 1998
Giorgio Bonsanti, *Beato Angelico: Catalogo completo* (Florence, 1998)

Borsi 1992
Franco and Stefano Borsi, *Paolo Uccello* (Paris, 1992)

Boskovits and Schleier 1988
Miklós Boskovits and Erich Schleier, *Gemäldegalerie Berlin. Katalog der Gemälde. Frühe Italienische Malerei* (Berlin, 1988)

Bowness 1973
Alan Bowness, *Ivon Hitchens* (London, 1973)

Brettell & Lloyd 1980
Richard Brettell and Christopher Lloyd, *A Catalogue of Drawings by Camille Pissarro in the Ashmolean Museum, Oxford* (Oxford, 1980)

Brown 1975
David Brown, 'Turner, Callcott and Thomas Lister Parker: New Light on Turner's *Junction of the Thames and Medway* in Washington', *The Burlington Magazine*, CXVII (1975), pp. 721–2

Brown 1981
David Blayney Brown, *Augustus Wall Callcott* (exh. cat., Tate Gallery, London, 1981)

Brown 1982
David Blayney Brown, *Ashmolean Museum, Oxford, Catalogue of the Collection of Drawings, IV, The Earlier British Drawings: British Artists and Foreigners working in Britain born before c. 1775* (Oxford, 1982)

Brown 1985
David Blayney Brown, *Sir David Wilkie: Drawings and Sketches in the Ashmolean Museum* (exh. cat., Ashmolean Museum; Morton Morris & Co., London, 1985)

Brown 1987
David Blayney Brown, *The Pre-Raphaelites in Oxford* (exh. cat., Tokyo, 1987)

Brown 1987
David Alan Brown, *Andrea Solario* (Milan, 1987)

Browse 1956
Lillian Browse, *Sickert* (London, 1956)

Browse 1960
Lillian Browse, *William Nicholson* (London, 1960)

Buckman 1973
David Buckman, *James Bolivar Manson: An English Impressionist, 1879–1945* (London, 1973)

Bull 1999
Malcolm Bull, 'Notes on Poussin's Egypt', *The Burlington Magazine*, CXLI (1999), pp. 537–41

Busiri Vici 1976
Andrea Busiri Vici, *Andrea Locatelli e il paesaggio romano del Settecento* (Rome, 1976)

Butlin and Joll 1984
Martin Butlin and Evelyn Joll, *The Paintings of J.M.W. Turner*, revised edn, 2 vols (New Haven and London, 1984)

Cadogan 2000
Jean Cadogan, *Domenico Ghirlandaio Artist and Artisan* (New Haven and London, 2000)

Carvalho 1996
José Alberto Seabra Carvalho in *Sequeira 1768–1837. Um português na mudança dos tempo* (exh. cat., Lisbon, 1996)

Casteras 1995
Susan P. Casteras, *James Smetham: Artist, Author, Pre-Raphaelite Associate* (Aldershot, 1995)

Caturla 1994
María Luisa Caturla, *Francisco de Zurbarán*, translated and edited by Odile Delenda (Paris, 1994)

Chappell 1984
Miles Chappell, *Cristofano Allori* (exh. cat., Florence, 1984)

Christian 1989
John Christian, *The Last Romantics: The Romantic Tradition in British Art: Burne-Jones to Stanley Spencer* (exh. cat., Barbican Art Gallery, London, 1989)

Christiansen *et al.* 1988
Keith Christiansen, Laurence Kanter and Carl Brandon Strehlke, *Painting in Renaissance Siena* (exh. cat., The Metropolitan Museum of Art, New York, 1988)

Clark and Bowron 1985
Anthony M. Clark, *Pompeo Batoni. A Complete Catalogue of his Works*, ed. E. Peters Bowron (Oxford, 1985)

Clover 1999
Catherine Clover, 'Documentation on Naldini's Ascension for S. Maria del Carmine in Florence, *The Burlington Magazine* CXLI (1999), pp. 615–617

Cocke 1972
Richard Cocke, *Pier Francesco Mola* (Oxford, 1972)

Cohen 1996
Charles E. Cohen, *The Art of Giovanni Antonio da Pordenone*, 2 vols (Cambridge, 1996)

Cohen 2001
David Cohen, *Jock McFadyen – a book about a painter* (London, 2001)

Colantuono 1996
Anthony Colantuono, 'Interp_eter Poussin. Métaphore, similarité et 'maniera magnifica'', *Nicolas Poussin (1594–1665). Actes du colloque organisé au musée du Louvre* [1994], Paris 1996, pp. 649–65

Company i Climent and Berg Sobre 1995
Ximy Company i Climent, Judith Berg Sobre *et al.*, *El Mundo de los Osuna ca 1460–ca 1540* (exh. cat., Valencia, 1995)

Confalone 2002
Maria Confalone in *Natura morta italiana tra Cinquecento e Seicento* (exh. cat., ed. Mina Gregori and Johann Georg Prinz von Hohenzollern, Munich, 2002)

Constable 1953
W.G. Constable, *Richard Wilson* (London, 1953)

Constable and Links 1989
W.G. Constable and J.G. Links, *Canaletto*, 2nd edn (Oxford, 1989)

Corti 1989
Laura Corti, *Giorgio Vasari: catalogo completo* (Florence, 1989)

Coural 2001
Natalie Coural, *Les Patel. Pierre Patel (1605–76) et ses fils. Le*
paysage de ruines à Paris aux XVIIe siecle (Paris, 2001)

Crelly 1962
William R. Crelly *The Paintings of Simon Vouet* (New Haven and London, 1962)

Crookshank and Glin 2002
Anne Crookshank and the Knight of Glin, *Ireland's Painters 1600–1940* (New Haven and London, 2002)

Cropper 1984
Elizabeth E. Cropper, *The Ideal of Painting: Pietro Testa's Düsseldorf Notebook* (Princeton, 1984)

Cummings and Staley 1968
Frederick Cummings and Allen Staley, *Romantic Art in Britain: Paintings and Drawings, 1760–1840* (exh. cat., Detroit Institute of Arts; Philadelphia Museum of Art, 1968)

Cust 1917
Lionel Cust, 'A 17th Century Portrait by an Unknown Painter', *The Burlington Magazine*, XXX (1917), p. 167

Dalli Regoli *et al.* 2001
Gigetta Dalli Regoli, Romani Nanni and Antonio Natali, *Leonardo e il mito di Leda* (exh. cat., Palazzina Uziella del Museo Leonardiano, Vinci, 2001)

Darracott 1980
Joseph Darracott, *The World of Charles Ricketts* (London, 1980)

Dauberville 1965–74
Jean and Henry Dauberville, *Bonnard: Catalogue raisonné de l'oeuvre peint*, 4 vols (Paris, 1965–74)

Dearden 1999
James Dearden, *John Ruskin: A Life in Pictures* (Sheffield, 1999)

De Benedictis 1979
Cristina de Benedictis, *La pittura senese 1330–1370* (Florence, 1979)

De Grazia 1996
Diane de Grazia, 'Tiepolo e l"arte" del ritratto', in *Giambattista Tiepolo 1696–1996* (exh. cat., ed. Keith Christiansen, Ca' Rezzonico, Venice, 1996), pp. 254–73

De Grazia and Garberson 1996
Diane de Grazia and Eric Garberson, *Italian Paintings of the Seventeenth and Eighteenth Centuries. The Collections of the National Gallery of Art. Systematic Catalogue* (New York and Oxford, 1996)

Delaney 1990
J.G.P. Delaney, *Charles Ricketts: A Biography* (Oxford, 1990)

Della Chiesa and Baccheschi 1976
Bruno della Chiesa and Edi. Baccheschi, 'I pittori da Santacroce', in *I pittori bergameschi dal XIII al XIX secolo. Il Cinquecento*, II (Bergamo, 1976), pp. 1–83

Di Provvido 1997
Sandra di Provvido, in *Vittorio Crivelli e la pittura del suo tempo nel Fermano*, ed. Stefano Papetti (Milan, 1997)

Dublin 1978
William Orpen 1878–1931: A Centenary Exhibition (exh. cat., National Gallery of Ireland, Dublin, 1978)

Earland 1911
Ada Earland, *John Opie and his Circle* (London, 1911)

Easton and John 1975
Malcolm Easton and R. John, *Augustus John* (exh. cat., National Portrait Gallery, London, 1975)

Edinburgh 1992
James Pryde (exh. cat., Scottish National Gallery of Modern Art, Edinburgh, 1992)

Elzea 2001
Betty Elzea, *Frederick Sandys 1829–1904: A Catalogue raisonné* (Woodbridge, 2001)

Erbentraut 1999
Regina Erbentraut, in *Von Venedig bis Neapel. Renaissance und Barock in Italien. Sammlungen Malerei, Zeichnung, Plastik, Majolika, Staaliches Museum Schwerin* (exh. cat., Schwerin, 1999), pp. 69–70

Erickson 1992
Kristen L. Erickson, 'Orovida Pissarro: Painter and Print-maker with a catalogue raisonné of Paintings' (unpublished dissertation, University of Oxford, 1992)

Eustace 1999
Katherine Eustace, *Twentieth century paintings in the Ashmolean Museum* (Oxford, 1999)

Fahy 1993
Everett Fahy, 'Late Fifteenth-Century Florentine Painting in Florence', *The Burlington Magazine*, CXXXV (1993), pp. 170

Fahy 1994
Everett Fahy, 'Florence and Naples: A cassone panel in the Metropolitan Museum of Art', in *Hommage à Michel Laclotte: Études sur la peinture du Moyen Age et de la Renaissance* (Milan and Paris, 1994), pp. 231–43

Faietti and Zacchi 1998
Marzia Faietti and Alessandro Zacchi, eds, *Figure: Disegni dal Cinquecento all'Ottocento nella Pinacoteca Nazionale di Bologna* (Milan, 1998)

Fantin-Latour 1911
Mme Fantin-Latour, *Catalogue de l'oeuvre complet (1849–1904) de Fantin-Latour* (Paris, 1911)

Farr 1958
Dennis Farr, *William Etty* (London, 1958)

Ferrari 1990
Oreste Ferrari, *Bozzetti italiani dal Mannierismo al Barocco* (Naples, 1990)

Ferrari and Scavizzi 1992
Oreste Ferrari and Giuseppe Scavizzi, *Luca Giordano: L'Opera completa*, 2nd edn (Naples, 1992)

Filippini 1992
Cecilia Filippini, 'Tematiche e soggetti rappresentati su forzieri, spalliere e deschi da parto', in *Maestri e Botteghe: Pittura a Firenze* (exh. cat., Palazzo Strozzi, Florence, 1992–3), pp. 232–37

Finaldi and Kitson 1997
Gabriele Finaldi and Michael Kitson, *Discovering the Italian Baroque: The Denis Mahon Collection* (London, 1997)

Flores d'Arcais 1995
Francesca Flores d'Arcais, *Giotto* (Milan, 1995)

Franco 1998
Tiziana Franco, *Michele Giambono e il monumento a Cortesia da Serego* (Venice, 1998)

Franklin 2001
David Franklin, *Painting in Renaissance Florence 1500–1550* (New Haven and London, 2001)

French 1980
Anne French, *Gaspar Dughet called Gaspar Poussin (1615–175)* (exh. cat., Kenwood, London, 1980)

Funnell and Warner 1999
Peter Funnell and Malcolm Warner, *Millais Portraits* (exh. cat., National Portrait Gallery, London, 1999)

Gaskell 1984
Ivan Gaskell, 'Vermeer, Judgement and Truth', *The Burlington Magazine*, CXXVI (1984), pp. 557–61

Gaya Nuño 1958
José Antonio Gaya Nuño *La Pintura Espanola fuera de España* (Madrid, 1958)

Gemin and Pedrocco 1993
Massimo Gemin and Filippo Pedrocco, *Giambattista Tiepolo: Opera completa* (Venice, 1993)

Gendle 1980
Nicholas Gendle, *Icons in Oxford: Byzantine, Greek and Russian Icons* (exh. cat., Christ Church, Oxford, 1980)

Genty 1979
Jean Genty, *Pier Francesco Mola pittore* (Lugano, 1979)

Gere 1953
J.A. Gere, 'William Young Ottley as a Collector of Drawings', *British Museum Quarterly*, XVIII (1953), pp. 44–53

Gibson 1914
Frank Gibson, *Charles Conder: His Life and Work* (London, 1914)

Gibson 1984–5
Robin Gibson, *Glyn Philpot 1884–1937: Edwardian Aesthete to Thirties Modernist* (exh. cat., N.P.G., London, 1984–5)

Girtin and Loshak 1954
Thomas Girtin and David Loshak, *The Art of Thomas Girtin* (London, 1954)

Gloucester 1968
Hubert Wellington Memorial Exhibition (exh. cat., Gloucester City Museum, 1968)

Goldberg 1978
Norman L. Goldberg, *John Crome the Elder*, 2 vols (Oxford, 1978)

Gowing 1971–2
Lawrence Gowing, *Hogarth* (exh. cat., Tate Gallery, London, 1971–2)

Gowing 1982
Sir Lawrence Gowing, *Lucian Freud* (London and New York, 1982)

Gowing and Sylverster 1990
Lawrence Gowing and David Sylvester, *William Coldstream 1908–1987* (exh. cat., Tate Gallery, London, 1990)

Grasselli and Rosenberg 1984
Margaret Morgan Grasselli and Pierre Rosenberg, *Watteau 1684–1721* (exh. cat., National Gallery of Art, Washington; Grand Palais, Paris; Charlottenburg, Berlin, 1984)

Gregori 1979
Mina Gregori, 'Giovanni Battista Moroni', in *I pittori Bergameschi. Il Cinquecento*, III (Bergamo, 1979), pp. 95–377

Greig 1911
James Greig, *Sir Henry Raeburn, R.A.: His Life and Works* (London, 1911)

Grundy 1933–8
C. Reginald Grundy, *A Catalogue of the Pictures and Drawings in the Collection of Frederick John Nettlefold*, 4 vols (n. pl. 1933–8)

Hardie 1908
Martin Hardie, *John Pettie, R.A., H.R.S.A.* (London, 1908)

Hayes 1981
John Hayes, *Thomas Gainsborough* (exh. cat., Tate Gallery, London, 1980–1)

Hayes 1982
John Hayes, *The Landscape Paintings of Thomas Gainsborough*, 2 vols (London, 1982)

Hedberg 1975
Gregory Hedberg, 'In favor of Nicola di Maestro Antonio', *The Minneapolis Museum of Art Bulletin*, I (1975), pp. 84–99

Heimbürger 1988
Minna Heimbürger, *Bernardo Keilhau detto Monsù Bernardo* (Rome, 1988)

Held 1980
Julius Held, *The Oil Sketches of Peter Paul Rubens: A Critical Catalogue* (Princeton, 1980)

Hellebranth 1976
Robert Hellebranth, *Charles-François Daubigny 1817–1878* (Morgues, 1976)

Hewison 1996
Robert Hewison, *Ruskin and Oxford: The Art of Education* (exh. cat., Ashmolean Museum, Oxford; City Museum and Mappin Art Gallery, Sheffield, 1996)

Hogarth 1975
Paul Hogarth, *Arthur Boyd Houghton* (exh. cat., Victoria and Albert Museum, London, 1975)

Hogarth 1981
Paul Hogarth, *Arthur Boyd Houghton* (London, 1981)

Hone 1939
Joseph Hone, *The Life of Henry Tonks* (London, 1939)

Hoozee 1979
Robert Hoozee, *L'Opera completa di Constable* (Milan, 1979)

Hudson 1949
Derek Hudson, *James Pryde 1866–1941* (London, 1949)

Humfrey 1983
Peter Humfrey, *Cima da Conegliano* (Cambridge, 1983)

Ingersoll-Smouse 1926
Florence Ingersoll-Smouse *Joseph Vernet, peintre de marine 1714–89* (Paris, 1926)

Ingersoll-Smouse 1928
Florence Ingersoll-Smouse, *Jean-Baptise Pater* (Paris, 1928)

Jaffé 2003
David Jaffé, ed., *Titian* (exh. cat., National Gallery, London, 2003)

Kanter 1994
Laurence Kanter, *Italian Paintings in the Museum of Fine Arts, Boston*, I (Boston, 1994)

Kemp and Massing 1991
Martin Kemp and Ann Massing, 'Paolo Uccello's "Hunt in the Forest"', *The Burlington Magazine*, CXXXIII (1991), pp. 164–78

Kidson 1999
Alex Kidson, *Earlier British Paintings in the Lady Lever Art Gallery* (Liverpool, 1999)

Kidson 2002
Alex Kidson, *George Romney 1734–1802* (exh. cat., Walker Art Gallery, Liverpool; National Portrait Gallery, London; Henry E. Huntington Library and Art Gallery, 2002)

Knox 1995
George Knox, *Antonio Pellegrini 1675–1741* (Oxford, 1995)

Kronbichler and Mich 1995
Johann Kronbichler and Elvio Mich, *Michelangelo Unterperger* (Trento, 1995)

Krückmann 1990
Peter O. Krückmann, *Carlo Carlone 1686–1775: Der Ansbacher Auftrag* (exh. cat., Ansbach, 1990)

Land 1999
Norman E. Land, ed., *The Samuel H. Kress Study Collection at the University of Missouri* (Columbia and London, 1999)

Langedijk 1981
Karla Langedijk, *The Portraits of the Medici*, revised edn, 5 vols (Florence, 1981)

Laughton 1971
Bruce Laughton, *Philip Wilson Steer 1860–1942* (Oxford, 1971)

Lecchini Giovannoni 1991
Simona Lecchini Giovannoni, *Alessandro Allori* (Turin, 1991)

Leribault 2002
Christophe Leribault, *Jean-François de Troy* (Paris, 2002)

Lightbown 1978
Ronald W. Lightbown, *Botticelli, Life and Work*, 2 vols (London, 1978)

Lines 1966
Vincent Lines, *Mark Fisher and Margaret Fisher Prout, Father and Daughter: A Record of a Hundred Years of Painting* (London, 1966)

Lipke 1967
William Lipke, *David Bomberg: A Critical Study of his Life and Work* (London, 1967)

Lister 1981
Raymond Lister, *George Richmond: A Critical Biography* (London, 1981)

Lister 1988
Raymond Lister, *Catalogue raisonné of the Works of Samuel Palmer* (Cambridge, 1988)

Lloyd 1977
Christopher Lloyd, *A Catalogue of the Earlier Italian Paintings in the Ashmolean Museum* (Oxford, 1977)

Lloyd 1993
Christopher Lloyd, *Italian Paintings before 1600 in the Art Institute of Chicago* (Chicago and Princeton, 1993)

Loire 1996
Stéphane Loire, *Musée du Louvre, Département des Peintures. École Italienne, XVIIè siècle, I, Bologne* (Paris, 1996)

London 1958
Sir James Thornhill (exh. cat., Guildhall A.G., London, 1958)

London 1961
Paintings and Drawings by Sir Edwin Landseer, R.A., 1802–1873 (exh. cat., Royal Academy of Arts, 1961)

London 1973
A Loan Exhibition of Drawings, Watercolours, and Paintings by John Linnell and his Circle (exh. cat., P.&D. Colnaghi, London, 1973)

London 1988
The Painters of Camden Town 1905–1920 (exh. cat., Christie's, London, 1988)

London 1989
Retrospective Exhibition of Paintings and Graphic Works by Gyula Sajó, 1918–1989 (exh. cat., Institute of Education, University of London, 1989)

London 1992
Mark Gertler: Paintings & Drawings (exh. cat., Camden Arts Centre, London; Castle Museum, Nottingham; Leeds City Art Gallery, Leeds, 1992)

London 1996
Frederic Leighton 1830–1896 (exh. cat., Royal Academy, 1996)

London, Paris, Boston 1980–81
Pissarro (exh. cat., Hayward Gallery, London; Grand Palais, Paris; Museum of Fine Arts, Boston, 1980–81)

Lorquin 2001
Olivier Lorquin *et al.*, *Maillol peintre* (exh. cat., Fondation Dina Vierney-Musée Maillol, Paris, 2001)

Lowe 1966
Ian Lowe, *Retrospective Exhibition of Paintings and Drawings by Malcolm Milne (1887–1954)* (exh. cat., Ashmolean Museum, Oxford, 1966)

Lucco 1993
Mauro Lucco, 'Marco Zoppo nella pittura veneziana', in Berenice Giovannucci Vigi, ed., *Marco Zoppo e il suo tempo* (Cento, 1993), pp. 107–20

Lucie-Smith 1977
Edward Lucie-Smith, *Fantin-Latour* (Oxford, 1977)

Lutyens 1984
Mary Lutyens, 'Walter Howell Deverell (1827–1854)', in *Pre-Raphaelite Papers*, ed. Leslie Parris (London, 1984), pp. 76–96

Lyles 1999
Anne Lyles, review of Graham Reynolds, 'The Early Paintings and Drawings of John Constable', *The Burlington Magazine*, CLXI (1999), pp. 181–3

Macandrew 1967
Hugh Macandrew, 'Vouet's Portrait of Giulio Strozzi and its Pendant by Tinelli of Nicolo Crasso', *The Burlington Magazine*, CIX (1976), pp. 266–71

Macandrew 1980
Hugh Macandrew, *Catalogue of the Collection of Drawings, III, Italian Schools: Supplement* (Oxford, 1980)

Magani 1995
Fabrizio Magani, *Antonio Bellucci: Catalogo Ragionato* (Rimini, 1995)

MacGregor 1983
Tradescant's Rarities: Essays on the Foundation of the Ashmolean Museum 1683, with a Catalogue of the surviving early Collections, ed. Arthur MacGregor (Oxford, 1983)

Mango 2002
Oxford History of Byzantium, ed. Cyril Mango (Oxford, 2002)

Manners and Williamson 1920
Lady Victoria Manners and G.C. Williamson, *John Zoffany R.A.: His Life and Works, 1735–1810* (London and New York, 1920)

Mannings 2000
David Mannings, *Sir Joshua Reynolds: A Complete Catalogue of his Paintings*, 2 vols (New Haven and London, 2000)

Marani 1989
Pietro C. Marani, *Leonardo: Catalogo completo* (Florence, 1989)

Marshall 1997
David R. Marshall, 'Early Panini Reconsidered: The Estergom *Preaching of an Apostle* and the Relationship between Panini and Ghisolfi', *Artibus et Historiae*, 36, XVIII (1997), pp. 137–99

Martineau 1924
Helen Martineau, 'A Pre-Raphaelite Painter', *The Studio*, LXXXVII (1924), pp. 206–8

Martineau 1947
Helen Martineau. 'Echo of a Pre-Raphaelite Painter', *The Studio*, CXXXIV (1947), pp. 78–9

Martineau 1981
Jane Martineau, ed., *Splendours of the Gonzaga* (exh. cat., Victoria and Albert Museum, London, 1981)

Mayes 1971
I. Mayes, *The De Wildes* (exh. cat., Northampton Central Art Gallery, 1971)

McConkey 1980
Kenneth McConkey, *Sir George Clausen, R.A., 1852–1944* (exh. cat., Cartwright Hall, Bradford; Bristol City Art Gallery; Laing Art Gallery, Newcastle, 1980)

McConkey 1995
Kenneth McConkey, *Impressionism in Britain* (exh. cat., Barbican Art Gallery, London, 1995)

McCorquodale 1981
Charles McCorquodale, *Painting in Florence 1600–1700* (London, 1981)

McKerrow 1982
Mary McKerrow, *The Faeds: A Biography* (Edinburgh, 1982)

McNairn 1997
Alan McNairn, *Behold the Hero: General Wolfe and the Arts in the Eighteenth Century* (Montreal etc., 1997)

MacDougall 2002
Sarah MacDougall, *Mark Gertler* (London, 2002)

Mathew 1950
Gervase Mathew, *Byzantine Painting* (London, 1950)

Mazzoni 2001
Giuseppe Mazzoni, *Quadri antichi del Novecento* (Vicenza, 2001)

Meijer 2003
Fred G. Meijer, *The Ashmolean Museum, Oxford. Catalogue of the Collection of Paintings. The Collection of Dutch and Flemish Still-Life Paintings bequeathed by Daisy Linda Ward* (Zwolle, 2003)

Mérot 1990
Alain Mérot, *Nicolas Poussin* (London, 1990)

Miles 1982
Frank Miles, 'Refusal to flatter: Samuel Laurence (1812–184)', *Country Life* (27 May 1982), pp. 1604–5

Millar 1992
Oliver Millar, *The Victorian Pictures in the Collection of Her Majesty the Queen*, 2 vols (Cambridge, 1992)

Milner 1926–7
J.D. Milner, 'Tilly Kettle, 1735–1786', *Walpole Society*, XV (1926–7), pp. 47–104

Mitchell 1944
Charles Mitchell, 'Benjamin West's *Death of Wolfe* and the Popular History Piece', *Journal of the Warburg and Courtauld Institutes*, VII (1944), pp. 20

Mitchell 1999
James Mitchell, *Julius Caesar Ibbetson (1759–1817): 'The Berchem of England'* (London, 1999)

Miziolek 1996
Jerzy Miziolek, ' "Florentina libertas". La "Storia di Lucrezia romana e la cacciata del tiranno" sui cassoni del primo Rinascimento', *Prospettiva*, 83–4, (1996), pp. 159–76

Moatti 2000
Emmanuel Moatti, *Giovanni Battista Camuccini 1819–1904. Oil Sketches of the Roman Countryside* (New York, 2000)

Morassi 1973
Antonio Morassi, *Guardi*, 2 vols (Venice, 1973)

Moreau-Nélaton 1921
Étienne Moreau-Nélaton, *Millet raconté par lui-même* (Paris, 1921)

Moro 1997
Franco Moro, 'Due fratelli, due differenti percorsi: Martino e Alberto Piazza', *Studi di Storia dell'Arte*, 8 (1997), pp. 69–184

Morris 1996
Edward Morris, *Victorian and Edwardian Paintings in the Walker Art Gallery and at Sudley House: British Atists born after 1810 but before 1861* (London, 1996)

Morris 1985
Lynda Morris, *Henry Tonks and the 'Art of Pure Drawing'* (exh. cat., Norwich School of Art Gallery, 1985)

Mortari 1995
Luisa Mortari, *Bernardo Strozzi* (Rome, 1995)

Muraro 1992
Michelangelo Muraro, *Il libro secondo di Francesco e Jacopo Bassano* (Bassano, 1992)

Muti and De Sarno Prignano 1994
Laura Muti and Daniele de Sarno Prignano, *Alessandro Magnasco* (Faenza, 1994)

Nappi 1991
Maria Rosaria Nappi, *François de Nomé e Didier Barra: l'enigma Monsù Desiderio* (Milan, 1991)

Negro and Pirondini 1995
Emilio Negro and Massimo Pirondini, ed., *La Scuola dei Carracci: I seguaci di Annibale e Agostino* (Modena, 1995)

Negro and Roio 1998
Emilio Negro and Nicosetta Roio, *Francesco Francia e la sua scuola* (Modena, 1998)

Negro and Roio 2000
Emilio Negro and Nicosetta Roio, *Bartolomeo Schedoni 1578–1615* (Modena, 2000)

Neilson 1979
Nancy Ward Neilson, *Camillo Procaccini Paintings and Drawings* (New York and London, 1979)

Newall 1989
Christopher Newall, *The Etruscans* (exh. cat., Stoke-on-Trent, 1989)

Newall 1993
Christopher Newall, *John William Inchbold: Pre-Raphaelite Landscape Artist* (exh. cat., Leeds City Art Galleries, 1993)

Newall 1995
Christopher Newall, *The Grosvenor Gallery Exhibitions: Change and Continuity in the Victorian Art World* (Cambridge, 1995)

Newbery 2003
Timothy Newbery, *Frames and Framings in the Ashmolean Museum*, Ashmolean hanbook (Oxford, 2003)

Newcome 1993
Mary Newcome, 'Oil Sketches and Drawings by Bernardo Strozzi', *Antichità Viva*, XXXII (1993), 6, pp. 14–24

Newman and Watkinson 1991
Teresa Newman and Raymond Watkinson, *Ford Madox Brown and the Pre-Raphaelite Circle* (London, 1991)

Nicolson 1968
Benedict Nicolson, *Joseph Wright of Derby*, 2 vols (New York and London, 1968)

Nicolson and Vertova 1990
Benedict Nicolson, *Caravaggism in Europe*, 2nd edn, revised and enlarged by Luisa Vertova (Turin, 1990)

Noakes 1985
Vivien Noakes, *Edward Lear 1812–1888* (exh. cat., Royal Academy of Arts, London, 1985)

Noon 1991
Patrick Noon, *Richard Parkes Bonington: 'On the Pleasure of Painting'* (exh. cat., New Haven and London, 1991)

Noris 1982
Fernando Noris, 'Bartolomeo Nazari' in *I pittori bergameschi dal XIII as XIX secolo. Il Settecento*, I (Bergamo, 1982), pp. 199–267

O'Connell 1988
Sheila O'Connell 'Lord Shaftesbury in Naples' *The Walpole Society*, LIV (1988), pp. 149–214

Offner 1981
Richard Offner, *A Critical and Historical Corpus of Florentine Painting. A Legacy of Attributions*, ed. Hayden B.J. Maginnis (New York, 1981)

Olson 2000
Roberta Olson, *The Florentine Tondo* (Oxford, 2000)

O'Neill 1981
M. O'Neill, *Les peintures de l'école française des XVIIe et XVIIIe siècles. Musée des Beaux Arts d'Orléans* (Nantes, 1981)

Ormond 1975
Leonée and Richard Ormond, *Lord Leighton* (London, 1975)

Owen and Brown 1987
Felicity Owen and David Blayney Brown, *A Collector of Genius: Sir George Beaumont* (New Haven and London, 1987)

Owen and Stanford 1981–2
Felicity Owen and Eric Stanford, *William Havell 1782–1857* (exh. cat., Spink & Son, London; Reading Museum and Art Gallery; Abbot Hall Art Gallery, Kendal, 1981–2)

Oxford 1964a
An Exhibition of the Works of Egerton Bushe Coghill, 1853–1921: An Irish Impressionist (exh. cat., Ashmolean Museum, Oxford, 1964)

Oxford 1964b
Catalogue of Paintings and Drawings by Percy Horton (exh. cat., Ashmolean Museum, Oxford, 1964)

Oxford 1971
Mark Gertler, 1891–1939 (exh. cat., The Minories, Colchester, and other venues, 1971)

Oxford 1987
The Christopher Hewett Collection (exh. cat., Ashmolean Museum, Oxford, 1987)

Oxford 1994
Roger Wagner, Paintings – 1982–1994 (exh. cat., Ashmolean Museum, Oxford, 1994)

Pantin 1937
W.A. Pantin, 'The recently demolished houses in Broad Street, Oxford', *Oxoniensia* II (1937)

Pagnotta 1988
Laura Pagnotta, in *La Pittura in Italia: Il Cinquecento*, ed. Giuliano Briganti, 2 vols (Milan, 1988)

Palluchini and Rossi 1982
Rodolfo Palluchini and Paola Rossi, *Tintoretto, le opere sacre e profane*, 2 vols (Venice, 1982)

Papi 2001
Gianni Papi, *Cecco del Caravaggio* (Soncino, 2001)

Paris 1999–2000
Chardin (exh. cat., Grand Palais, Paris, and other venues, 1999–2000)

Parker 1938
K. T. Parker, *Catalogue of the collection of drawings in the Ashmolean Museum, I, Netherlandish, German, French and Spanish Schools* (Oxford, 1938)

Parker 1956
Karl Parker, *Catalogue of the Collection of Drawings in the Ashmolean Museum, II, Italian Schools* (Oxford, 1956)

Parris 1984
Leslie Parris, *The Pre-Raphaelites* (exh. cat., Tate Gallery, London, 1984)

Parris and Fleming-Williams 1982
Leslie Parris and Ian Fleming-Williams, *Lionel Constable* (exh. cat., Tate Gallery, London, 1982)

Paulson 1989
Ronald Paulson, *Hogarth's Graphic Works*, third edn (London, 1989)

Pavière 1950
Sydney H. Paviere, *The Devis Family of Painters* (Leigh-on-Sea, 1950)

Payne 1993
Christiana Payne, *Toil and Plenty: Images of the Agricultural Landscape in England, 1780–1890* (exh. cat., Nottingham University Art Gallery; Yale Center for British Art, New Haven, 1993–4)

Pedrocco 2001
Filippo Pedrocco, *Titian. The Complete Paintings* (London, 2001)

Pepper 1984
D. Stephen Pepper, *Guido Reni: A Complete Catalogue of his Works with an Introductory text* (Oxford, 1984)

Pestelli 1990
Pestelli, Lord Shaftesbury e Paolo de Matteis: *Ercole al bivio* tra teoria e pratica, *Storia dell'arte*, 68 (1990), pp. 95–121

Petrides 1964
Paul Petrides, *L'oeuvre complet de Maurice Utrillo* (Paris, 1964)

Phillips 2000
Tom Philips, 'A portrait of my mother' *The Ashmolean*, no. 38 (Spring, 2000), pp. 2[illegible]–2

Pichon 1993
Yann le Pichon, *Le Musée retrouvé de Denis Diderot* (Paris, 1993)

Pietrangeli 1961
Carlo Pietrangeli, *Villa Paolina*, Quaderni di Storia dell'Arte, *XI* (Rome, 1961)

Pignatti 1974
Terisio Pignatti, *L'Opera completa di Pietro Longhi* (Milan, 1974)

Pignatti 1976
Terisio Pignatti, *Veronese*, 2 vols (Venice, 1976)

Pignatti and Pedrocco 1995
Terisio Pignatti and Filippo Pedrocco, *Veronese* (Milan, 1995)

Pignatti and Pedrocco 1999
Terisio Pignatti and Filippo Pedrocco, *Giorgione* (NewYork, 1999)

Piompinos 1984
Piompinos, *Hellenes hagiographoi mexri to 1821* (Athens, 1984)

Pissarro and Venturi 1939
Ludovic-Rodo Pissarro and Lionello Venturi, *Camille Pissarro: Son art et son oeuvre*, 2 vols (Paris, 1939)

Poole 1912
Mrs Reginald Lane Poole, *Catalogue of Portraits in the Possession of the University, Colleges, City, and County of Oxford, I* (Oxford, 1912)

Postle 1995
Martin Postle, *Sir Joshua Reynolds: The Subject Pictures* (Cambridge, 1995)

Pressly 1984
'Facts and Recollections of the XVIIIth Century in a Memoir of John Francis Rigaud Esq., R.A. by Stephen Francis Dutilh Rigaud', ed. William L. Pressly, *The Walpole Society*, L (1984), pp. 1–164

Reale and Succi 1994
Isabella Reale and Dario Succi, eds, *Luca Carlevarijs e la veduta veneziana del Settecento* (exh. cat., Padua, 1994)

Rearick 2001
W. Roger Rearick, 'The Portraits of Orlando Flacco', *Venezia Cinquecento*, XI, (2001), pp. 137–54

Reggio Emilia 1987
Lelio Orsi 1511–1587, dipinti e disegni (exh. cat., Reggio Emilia, 1987)

Rewald 1996
John Rewald, *The Paintings of Paul Cézanne, A Catalogue Raisonné*, 2 vols (New York, 1996)

Reynolds 1984
Graham Reynolds, *The Later Paintings and Drawings of John Constable*, 2 vols (New Haven and London, 1984)

Reynolds 1996
Graham Reynolds, *The Early Paintings and Drawings of John Constable*, 2 vols (New Haven and London, 1996)

Reynolds 1995
Simon Reynolds, *William Blake Richmond: An Artist's Life 1842–1921* (London, 1995)

Richmond 1996
Spencer Gore in Richmond (exh. cat., Museum of Richmond, 1996–7)

Robaut 1905
Alfred Robaut, *L'oeuvre de Corot: Catalogue raisonné et illustré* (Paris, 1905)

Roberts and Wildman 1997
Leonard Roberts and Stephen Wildman, *Arthur Hughes: His Life and Works* (Woodbridge, 1997)

Robertson 2003
Bruce Robertson ed., *Sargent and Italy* (Princeton, 2003)

Roethel-Benjamin 1982
Hans K. Roethel and Jean K. Benjamin, *Kandinsky: Catalogue raisonné of the Oil Paintings*, 2 vols (London, 1982)

Roethlisberger 1961
Marcel Roethlisberger, *Claude Lorrain: The Paintings*, 2 vols (New Haven and London, 1961)

Roethlisberger 1968
Marcel Roethlisberger, *Claude Lorrain: The Drawings*, 2 vols (Berkeley, 1968)

Roettgen 1999
Steffi Roettgen, *Anton Raphael Mengs 1728–1779* (Munich, 1999)

Rogers 1878
J.J. Rogers, *Opie and his Works* (London, 1878)

Roli 1977
Renato Roli, *Pittura Bolognese 1650–1800. Dal Cignani ai Gandolfi* (Bologna, 1977)

Roland Michel 1984
Marianne Roland Michel, *Lajoue et l'art rocaille* (Neuilly-sur-Seine, 1984)

Romani 1984
Vittoria Romani, *Lelio Orsi* (Modena, 1984)

Rosci 2000
Marco Rosci, *Il Cerano* (Milan, 2000)

Rosenberg 1979
Pierre Rosenberg, *Chardin 1699–1779* (exh. cat., Grand Palais, Paris; Cleveland Museum of Art; Museum of Fine Arts, Boston, 1979)

Rossi 1991
Paola Rossi, *Francesco Maffei* (Milan, 1991)

Rothenstein 1938
William Rothenstein, *Life and Death of Conder* (London, 1938)

Rouart and Wildenstein 1975
Denis Rouart and Daniel Wildenstein, *Édouard Manet. Catalogue raisonné*, 2 vols (Lausanne, 1975)

Royal Academy 1974–5
Turner, 1775–1851 (exh. cat., Royal Academy, London, 1974–5)

Ruda 1999
Jeffrey Ruda, *Fra Filippo Lippi, Life and Work* (London, 1999)

Russell 1987
Francis Russell, *Portraits of Sir Walter Scott: A Study of Romantic Portraiture* (London, 1987)

Rylands 1988
Philip Rylands, *Palma Vecchio* (Cambridge, 1988)

Schleier 2001
Erich Schleier, *Giovanni Lanfranco. Un pittore barocco tra Parma, Roma e Napoli* (exh. cat., Milan, 2001)

Salmina-Haskell 1989
Larissa Salmina-Haskell, *Russian Paintings in the Ashmolean Museum* (Oxford, 1989)

Sandby 1892
William Sandby, *Thomas and Paul Sandby, Royal Academicians* (London, 1892)

Sendai/Tateshima/Utsunomia 2003
Marie Laurencin: A Retrospective (exh. cat., Mediatheque Art Gallery, Sendai; Musée Marie Laurencin; Utsunomiya Museum of Art, Utsunomiya; Tokyo Metropolitan and Teien Art Museum, Tokyo, 2003)

Sestieri 1994
Giancarlo Sestieri, *Repertorio della pittura romana della fine del Seicento e del Settecento* (Turin, 1994)

Sewter 1951
A.C. Sewter, *Glyn Philpot 1884–1937* (London, 1951)

Schmit 1973
Robert Schmit, *Eugène Boudin, 1824–1893*, 3 vols (Paris, 1973)

Schmit 1993
Robert and Manuel Schmit, *Stanislas Lépine 1835–1892: Catalogue raisonné de l'oeuvre peint* (Paris, 1993)

Sharp 1892
W. Sharp, *The Life and Letters of Joseph Severn* (London, 1892)

Sheffield and elsewhere 1996–7
John Downton 1906–1991: Temperas and Drawings (exh.cat., Sheffield and elsewhere, 1996–7)

Simonetti 1986
Simonetta Simonetti, 'Profilo di Bonifacio de'Pitati', *Saggi e Memorie di Storia dell'Arte*, XV (1986), pp. 83–134

Simpson 2001
Juliet Simpson, *Jules Flandrin (1871–1947): The other fin de siècle* (exh. cat., Ashmolean Museum, Oxford, 2001)

Smart 1999
Alastair Smart, *Allan Ramsay: A Complete Catalogue of his Paintings*, ed. John Ingamells (New Haven and London, 1999)

Smith 1992
Bill Smith, *D.Y. Cameron: The Vision of the Hills* (Edinburgh, 1992)

Smith 1982
Hammond Smith, *Peter De Wint 1784–1849* (London, 1982)

Solís Rodríguez 1999
Carmelo Solís Rodríguez, *Luis de Morales* (Badajoz, 1999)

Solkin 1982–3
David Solkin, *Richard Wilson: The Landscape of Reaction* (exh. cat., Tate Gallery, London, 1982–3)

Solkin 1986
David H. Solkin, 'Portraiture in Motion: Edward Penny's *Marquis of Granby* and the Creation of a Public for English Art', *Huntington Library Quarterly*, XLIX (1986), pp. 1–23

Spalletti 1979
Ettore Spalletti, *Gli Uffizi: Catalogo Generale* (Florence, 1979)

Spear 1982
Richard Spear, *Domenichino* (New Haven and London, 1982)

Spike 1999
John Spike, *Mattia Preti: Catalogue raisonné of the Paintings* (Florence, 1999)

Spinosa 1986
Nicola Spinosa, *Pittura napoletana del Settecento dal Barocco al Rococò* (Naples, 1986)

St Ives 1978
Norman and Alethea Garstin: Two Impressionists, Father and Daughter (exh. cat., Penwith Gallery, St Ives; Bristol City Art Gallery; National Gallery of Ireland, Dublin; Fine Art Society, London, 1978)

Staley 2001
Allen Staley, *The Pre-Raphaelite Landscape* (New Haven and London, 2001)

Stein *et al.* 2003
Adolphe Stein, Janine Sinizergues, François Lorenceau, Sylvie Brame, *Jongkind 1819–1891: Catalogue critique de l'oeuvre* I, *Peintures* (Paris, 2003)

Stirling 1965
Sir D.Y. Cameron Centenary Exhibition (exh. cat., Stirling, 1965)

Strachey 1907
The Letters of Edward Lear, ed. Lady Strachey (London, 1907)

Swanson 1990
Vern G. Swanson, *The Biography and Catalogue raisonné of the Paintings of Sir Lawrence Alma-Tadema* (London, 1990)

Sudbury 1995
John Dodgson: Paintings and Drawings (exh. cat., Fine Art Society; Gainsborough House, Sudbury, 1995)

Sumner and Smith 2003
Thomas Jones (1742–1803): An Artist rediscovered, ed. Ann Sumner and Greg Smith (exh. cat., Cardiff, Manchester, London, 2003–4)

Talbot Rice 1951
David Talbot Rice, 'The Accompanied S. George', *Actes du VI congrès international d'études byzantines*, II (Paris, 1951)

Talbot Rice 1958
David Talbot Rice, *Byzantine Art* (Edinburgh, 1958)

Talbot Rice 1963
David Talbot Rice, *Art of the Byzantine Era* (London, 1963)

Talbot Rice 1964
David Talbot Rice, *Byzantine Art and European Art* (Athens, 1964)

Talley 1976–8
M.K. Talley, 'Thomas Bardwell of Bungay, Artist and Author, 1704–1767', *Walpole Society*, XLIV (1976–8), pp. 91–163

Tartuferi 1998
Angelo Tartuferi, 'Trecento lucchese. La pittura a Lucca prima di Spinello Aretino' in *Sumptuosa tabula picta. Pittori a Lucca tra gotico e rinascimento*, ed. Maria Teresa Filieri (exh. cat., Museo Nazionale di Villa Guinigi, Lucca, 1998)

Tempestini 1992
Achille Tempestini, *Giovanni Bellini* (Florence, 1992)

Ter Kuile 1976
O. ter Kuile, *Adriaen Hanneman 1604–1671: Een Haags Portretschilder* (Alphen aan den Rijn, 1976)

Thomas 1995
Annabel Thomas, *The Painter's Practice in Renaissance Tuscany* (Cambridge, 1995)

Thorold 1983
Anne Thorold, *A Catalogue of the Oil Paintings of Lucien Pissarro* (London, 1983)

Thorold and Erickson 1993
Anne Thorold and Kristen Erickson, *Camille Pissarro and his Family: The Pissarro Collection in the Ashmolean Museum*, Ashmolean handbook (Oxford, 1993)

Thuillier *et al.* 1990
Jacques Thuillier, Barbara Brejon de Lavergné, Denis Lavalle, *Vouet* (exh. cat., Grand Palais, Paris, 1990)

Tinterow *et al.* 1996
Gary Tinterow, Michael Pantazzi, Vincent Pomarède, *Camille Corot* (exh. cat., Grand Palais, Paris; National Gallery of Canada, Ottawa; Metropolitan Museum, New York, 1996–7)

Titterington and Wilcox 1984–5
Christopher Titterington and Timothy Wilcox, *William Turner of Oxford (1789–1862)* (exh. cat., Oxfordshire County Museum, Woodstock; Bankside Gallery, London; Museum and Art Gallery, Bolton, 1984–5)

Todini 1989
Filippo Todini, *La Pittura umbra dal Duecento al primo Cinquecento*, 2 vols (Milan, 1989)

Turner 2000
Nicholas Turner, *Federico Barocci* (Paris, 2000)

Vassilaki 1990
Maria Vassilaki, 'A Cretan Icon in the Ashmolean: The Embrace of Peter and Paul', *Jahrbuch der Österreichischen Byzantinistik*, 40

Volpe 2002
Alessandro Volpe, *Giotto e i Riminesi: Il gotico e l'antico nella pittura di primo Trecento* (Milan, 2002)

Walker 1985
Richard Walker, *National Portrait Gallery: Regency Portraits*, 2 vols (London, 1985)

Waterhouse 1946
Ellis K. Waterhouse, 'Gainsborough's Fancy Pictures', *The Burlington Magazine*, LXXXVIII (1946), pp. 134–40

Waterhouse 1958
Ellis K. Waterhouse, *Gainsborough* (London, 1958)

Webster 1977
Mary Webster, *Johan Zoffany 1733–1810* (exh. cat., National Portrait Gallery, London, 1977)

Weight 1994
Carel Weight: A War Retrospective (exh. cat., Imperial War Museum, London, 1995)

Wethey 1971
Harold E. Wethey, *The Paintings of Titian, II, The Portraits* (London, 1971)

Wethey 1975
Harold E. Wethey, *The Paintings of Titian, III, The Mythological and Historical Paintings* (London, 1975)

Whistler 1997
Catherine Whistler, 'An exchange of gifts between David Garrick and Richard Kaye', *The Burlington Magazine* (1997), pp. 329–330

Whistler 2001
Catherine Whistler, *The Hunt in the Forest by Paolo Uccello* (Oxford, 2001)

Whistler 2002
Catherine Whistler, in *Gaetano e Ubaldo Gandolfi, opere scelte*, ed. Donatella Biagi Maino (exh. cat., Turin, 2002)

Whistler 2003
Catherine Whistler, 'Las series al óleo basadas en los Toros de Burdeos. Dos escenas de tauromaquia en Oxford' in *Goya y lo goyesco la Fundación lázaro Galdino*, ed. Mercedes Agueda Vilar (exh. cat., Segovia, 2003), pp. 1–16

Whistler and Bomford 1999
Catherine Whistler and David Bomford, *The Forest Fire by Piero di Cosimo* (Oxford, 1999)

White 1999
Christopher White, *Ashmolean Museum Oxford, Catalogue of the Collection of Paintings: Dutch, Flemish, and German Paintings before 1900 (excluding the Daisy Linda Ward Collection)* (Oxford, 1999)

Whiteley 1991
Jon Whiteley, '"Faces in the Fire" by Frank Holl' *The Ashmolean*, 21 (1991), p. 15

Whiteley 2000
Jon Whitely, *Ashmolean Museum, Catalogue of the Collection of Drawings, VII, French School*, 2 vols (Oxford, 2000)

Wildenstein 1974
Daniel Wildenstein, *Claude Monet, biographie et catalogue raisonné*, 4 vols (Lausanne and Paris, 1974–85)

Wildman 1983
Stephen Wildman, *David Cox 1783–1859* (exh. cat., Birmingham City Art Gallery, 1983)

Wilson 1996
Carolyn C. Wilson, *Italian Paintings 14th to 16th Centuries in the Museum of Fine Arts, Houston* (Houston and London, 1996)

Wilson 1988–9
Jeremy Wilson, *T.E. Lawrence* (exh. cat., National Portrait Gallery, London, 1988–9)

Wilson 2003
Timothy Wilson, ed., *The Battle of Pavia* (Oxford, 2003)

Wine 1994
Humphrey Wine, *Claude: The Poetic Landscape* (exh. cat., National Gallery, London, 1994)

Woodward 1998
Christopher Woodward, 'Hogarth's Marriage Contract', *Apollo* (1998), pp. 13–14

Wright 1985–86
Christopher Wright, *Masterpieces of Reality: French seventeenth- century Painting* (exh. cat., Leicestershire Museums and Art Gallery, 1985–86)

Young, MacDonald, Spencer 1980
Andrew McLaren Young, Margaret MacDonald, Robin Spencer, *The Paintings of James McNeill Whistler* (New Haven and London, 1980)

Zampetti 1986
Pietro Zampetti, *Carlo Crivelli* (Florence, 1986)

Zava Bocazzi 1979
Franca Zava Bocazzi, *Pittoni* (Venice, 1979)

Zeri 1986
Federico Zeri, 'Schede romagnole 1. Il Maestro dei Baldraccani', *Paragone*, 441 (1986), pp. 22–6

CHANGES IN ATTRIBUTION SINCE 1980

2004	1980
A152 Anonymous British Artist (*c.* 1830)	Anonymous, Anglo-Flemish School (*c.* 1540–49)
A429 Anonymous British Artist (*c.* 1555)	Anonymous, (?)Anglo-Flemish School (*c.* 1560)
A860 Anonymous British Artist (*c.* 1650)	Anonymous, Anglo-Flemish School (*c.* 1650)
F680 Anonymous British Artist (*c.* 1500)	Anonymous, British School, 16th century
F672 Anonymous British Artist (*c.* 1575–1600)	Anonymous, British School (1574–1597)
F743 Cornelis de Neve	Anonymous, British School (*c.* 1670)
F656 Anonymous British Artist (*c.* 1620?)	Anonymous, British School, 17th century
?F691 Anonymous British Artist (*c.* 1580?)	Anonymous, British School, 17th century
A201 Anonymous British(?) Artist (*c.* 1720)	Anonymous, British School, later 18th century
A6 Pieter Nason	Anonymous, Dutch School (*c.* 1675)
A7 & A8 Arnout Vinckenborch	Anonymous, Flemish (Antwerp) School (*c.* 1615–30)
A961 Jean-François de Troy	Anonymous, French School (*c.* 1720)
A673 Attributed to Pietro Paolini	Anonymous, Italian School, early 17th century
A29 Follower of Carlo Maratta	Anonymous, Italian School, 17th–18th century
A396 Circle of Luigi Garzi	Anonymous, Italian School, 17th–18th century
A107 Copy after Carlo Dolci	Anonymous, Italian School, 17th or 18th century
A91 Attributed to Giovanni di Ser Giovanni, called Lo Scheggia	Anonymous, Italian (Florentine) School (*c.* 1420–30)
A80 Attributed to Paolo di Dono, called Uccello	Anonymous, Italian (Florentine) School (*c.* 1420–30)
A366 Studio of Andrea Orcagna	Anonymous, Italian (Florentine) School (*c.* 1380–90)
A334 Attributed to Paolo Schiavo	Anonymous, Italian (Florentine) School (*c.* 1430–50)
A338 Attributed to Francesco Granacci	Anonymous, Italian (Florentine) School, late 15th century
A231 Master of Charles III of Durazzo	Anonymous, Italian (Neapolitan) School (*c.* 1400–20)
A336 Anonymous Hispano-Flemish Artist	Anonymous, Spanish School, 16th century (?)
A879 Copy after Francisco de Zurbarán	Anonymous, Spanish School, 17th century (?)
A525 Style of Willem van Aelst	Willem van Aelst
A527 Copy of Willem van Aelst	Willem van Aelst
A944 Anonymous Roman Artist	Follower of Francesco Albani
A732 Attributed to Martino da Verona	Follower of Altichiero
A90 Apollonio di Giovanni and Marco del Buono Giamberti	Studio of Apollonio di Giovanni
A92 Apollonio di Giovanni and Marco del Buono Giamberti	Studio of Apollonio di Giovanni
A93 Bartolomeo and Agnolo degli Erri	Bartolomeo degli Erri
A1080 Anonymous Venetian or Veronese Artist	Jacopo da Ponte, called Bassano
A531 Style of Osias Beert the Elder	Osias Beert the Elder
A302 Circle of Giovanni Bellini	Attributed to Giovanni Bellini
A289 Copy after Nicolaes Pietersz. Berchem	Nicolaes Pietersz. Berchem
A781 Anonymous French Artist	Giovanni Lorenzo Bernini
A693 The Candlelight Master	Trophine Bigot
A670 Style of Jan Frans van Bloemen, called Orizzonte	Jan Frans van Bloemen, called Orizzonte
A736 Anonymous Umbro-Marchigian Artist	Formerly attributed to Benedetto Bonfigli
A451a Studio of Bonifazio de' Pitati	Bonifazio de' Pitati
A730 Studio of Bonifazio de' Pitati	Bonifazio de' Pitati
A914 Studio of Bonifazio de' Pitati	Bonifazio de' Pitati
A276 Copy after Richard Parkes Bonington	Formerly attributed to Richard Parkes Bonington
A459 Style of Richard Parkes Bonington	Formerly attributed to Richard Parkes Bonington
A480 Style of Richard Parkes Bonington	Formerly attributed to Richard Parkes Bonington
A85 Attributed to Arcangelo di Jacopo del Sellaio	Follower of Francesco Botticini
A488 Anonymous British Artist	Attributed to Henry Bright
A541 Attributed to Jan Brueghel the Younger	Jan Brueghel the Elder
A812 Style of Jan Brueghel the Elder	Jan Brueghel the Elder
A147 Giovanni Antonio da Canal, called Canaletto	Style of Giovanni Antonio da Canal, called Canaletto
A296 Studio of Giovanni Antonio da Canal, called Canaletto	Style of Giovanni Antonio da Canal, called Canaletto
A451b Francesco Buoneri, called Cecco del Caravaggio	Attributed to Francesco Buoneri, called Cecco del Caravaggio
A347 Attributed to Francesco Buonsignori	Attributed to Giovanni Francesco Caroto
A867 Ippolito Scarsella, called Lo Scarsellino	Annibale Carracci
A711 Attributed to the Master of Baldraccani	Attributed to Baldassare Carrari
A937 Pier Francesco Mola	Follower of Giovanni Benedetto Castiglione
A675 Anonymous Florentine Artist	Sebastiano Conca
A405 Lionel Constable	John Constable
A493 Attributed to John Constable	John Constable
A968 Style of John Constable	John Constable
A469 Style of John Constable	Formerly attributed to John Constable
A646 Anonymous British Artist	Formerly attributed to John Constable
A765 Forgery of John Constable	Formerly attributed to John Constable
A393 Anonymous French Artist	Jean-Baptiste-Camille Corot
A110 Copy after Antonio Allegri, called Correggio	Antonio Allegri, called Correggio
A389 Attributed to Luigi Crespi	Attributed to Giuseppe Maria Crespi
F667 Attributed to Thomas de Critz	Attributed to Emmanuel de Critz
F684 Attributed to Thomas de Critz	Attributed to Emmanuel de Critz
F707 Attributed to Thomas de Critz	Attributed to Emmanuel de Critz
A760 Attributed to John Crome, after Gainsborough	Formerly attributed to John Crome, after Gainsborough
A892 Copy after John Crome	Formerly attributed to John Crome
A942 Style of John Crome	Formerly attributed to John Crome
A547 Attributed to Abraham van Calraet	Aelbert Cuyp
A17 Anonymous British Artist	Attributed to Bartholomew Dandridge
A1092 Anonymous Dutch Artist	Attributed to Jan de Bray
A647 Anonymous Bolognese Artist	Domenichino (Domenico Zampieri)
A970 Attributed to Giovanni Francesco Grimaldi	Attributed to Domenichino (Domenico Zampieri)
A974 Style of Karel Du Jardin	Attributed to Karel Du Jardin
A172 Copy after Sir Anthony van Dyck	Sir Anthony van Dyck

2004	1980
A173 Style of Sir Anthony van Dyck	Sir Anthony van Dyck
A174 Copy after Sir Anthony van Dyck	Sir Anthony van Dyck
A177 Copy after Sir Anthony van Dyck	Sir Anthony van Dyck
A179 Copy after Sir Anthony van Dyck	Circle of Sir Anthony van Dyck
F739 or 670 Copy after Sir Peter Lely	Copy after Sir Anthony van Dyck
A181 Copy(?) after Sir Peter Paul Rubens	Attributed to Justus van Egmont
A616 Cornelis Kick	Ottmar Elliger
A917 William Etty	Attributed to William Etty
A419a Studio of Francesco Francia	Francesco Francia
A180 & A551 Pieter Boel	Jan Fyt
A88 Attributed to Gerolamo del Pacchia	Gerolamo del Pacchia
A2 Anonymous British Artist	Attributed to Marcus Gheeraerts the Younger
A934 Follower of Corrado Giaquinto	Corrado Giaquinto
A777 Circle of Giorgione	Attributed to Giorgione
A868 Anonymous Flemish Artist	Jan Gossaert
A433 & A434 Follower of Francisco de Goya y Lucientes	Francisco de Goya y Lucientes
A520f Attributed to Thomas Alexander Ferguson Graham	Thomas Alexander Ferguson Graham
A148 Follower of Francesco Guardi	Manner of Francesco Guardi
A150 Follower of Francesco Guardi	Manner of Francesco Guardi
A386 Francesco Guardi	Manner of Francesco Guardi
A330 Anonymous Venetian Artist	Imitator of Francesco Guardi
A936 Anonymous British Artist	Attributed to Hugh Douglas Hamilton
A1050e Studio of Adriaen Hanneman	Copy after Adriaen Hanneman
A994 Style of Willem Claesz. Heda	Willem Claesz. Heda
A11 Style of Pieter Claesz.	Attributed to Willem Claesz. Heda
A560 Copy after Jan Davidsz. de Heem	Jan Davidsz. de Heem
A776 Copy after Egbert van Heemskerk	Egbert van Heemskerk
A186 Attributed to William Hogarth	Manner of William Hogarth
A561 J. van Slechtenhorst	Attributed to S. Horst
A877 Arnold Boonen	Jan van Huysum
A411 Anonymous British Artist	Julias Caesar Ibbetson
A1030 Style of Charles-Émile Jacque	Formerly attributed to Charles-Émile Jacque
A229 & A230 Style of Samuel Scott	William James
A233 & A234 Style of Samuel Scott	Attributed to William James
A66 Anonymous Flemish Artist	Formerly attributed to Cornelius Johnson
A183 Anonymous Anglo-Flemish Artist	School of Cornelius Johnson
A976 Studio of Jacob Jordaens	Jacob Jordaens
A569–72 Jan van Kessel I	Attributed to Pieter Van Kessel
A305 Style of Thomas de Keyser	Attributed to Thomas de Keyser
A418 Anonymous Bohemian Artist (?)	Johann Kupezky
A428 Anonymous German Artist	Attributed to Jacques de Lajoue
A118 Follower of Philippe de Champaigne	Attributed to Claude Lefebvre
A790 & A503 Studio of Leonardo da Vinci	Following of Leonardo da Vinci
A574–5 Abraham de Lust	Antoni de Lust
A359 Alessandro Magnasco and Antonio Francesco Peruzzini	Alessandro Magnasco
A1046 Attributed to Mair von Landshut	Mair von Landshut
A356–7 Attributed to Antonio Vazquez	Attributed to the Mambrillas Master
A84 Davide Ghirlandaio	The Master of the St Louis Altarpiece
A99 Agnolo di Domenico di Donnino	The Master of Santo Spirito
A873 Style of Matteo di Giovanni	Formerly attributed to Matteo di Giovanni
A579 Anonymous Dutch Artist	Attributed to Gabriel Metsu
A431 Attributed to Georges Michel	Georges Michel
A505 Copy after Raphael	Studio of Michele di Ridolfo
A582 Copy after Abraham Mignon	Abraham Mignon
A500 Attributed to Sir John Everett Millais, Bt	Sir John Everett Millais, Bt
A782 Attributed to Claes Cornelisz. Moeyaert	Claes Cornelisz. Moeyaert
A306 Style of Jan Miense Molenaer	Attributed to Jan Miense, Molenaer
A311 Anonymous British Artist	Formerly attributed to George Morland
A484 Copy after John Constable	William James Müller
A371 Copy(?) after Pieter Neefs the Elder	Pieter Neefs the Elder
A74 Master of the Ashmolean Predella	Studio of Andrea di Cione Orcagna
A1047 & A1048 Style of Jan Cornelisz. Vermeyen	Manner of Bernaert van Orley
A938 Attributed to Lelio Orsi	Lelio Orsi
A759 Style of Jan van Os	Formerly attributed to Jan van Os
A930 Pietro Orioli	Jacopo Pacchiarotti
A451 Copy(?) after Joachim Patenir	Attributed to Joachim Patenir
A437 Style of Sir Joshua Reynolds	Formerly attributed to Revd Matthew William Peters
A63a Attributed to Thomas Phillips	Thomas Phillips
A348 Attributed to Neri di Bicci	Formerly attributed to Fiorentino Pier Francesco
A992 Attributed to Jacob Duck	Hendrick Gerritsz. Pot
A1073 Style of Willem Key	Frans Pourbus the Elder
A18 Anonymous Flemish Artist	Manner of Frans Pourbus the Younger
F703 & A704 Anonymous British Artist	Attributed to Johan Priwitzer
A887 Attributed to Giovanni Battista Crespi, Il Cerano	Camillo Procaccini
A511 Anonymous French or Italian Artist	Pierre-Paul Prud'hon
A804 Style of Rembrandt Harmensz. van Rijn	Attributed to Rembrandt Harmensz. van Rijn
A383 Copy after Giovanni Domenico Cerrini, called il Cavalier Perugino	Formerly attributed to Guido Reni
A806 Anonymous, British Artist	Augustin-Théodule Ribot
A717a Attributed to Antonio Francesco Peruzzini	Attributed to Marco Ricci
A111 Style of Johann Melchior Roos (Rosa da Tivoli)	Attributed to Johann Melchior Roos (Rosa da Tivoli)

2004	1980
A261 Anonymous Italian artist	Formerly attributed to Johann Melchior Roos
A998 Follower of Salvator Rosa	Formerly attributed to Salvator Rosa
A154 Style of Sir Peter Paul Rubens	Sir Peter Paul Rubens
A160 Copy after Sir Peter Paul Rubens	Sir Peter Paul Rubens
A805 Copy after Sir Peter Paul Rubens	Studio of Sir Peter Paul Rubens
A587 Elias van den Broeck	Rachel Ruysch
A589 Copy after Rachel Ruysch	Rachel Ruysch
A294 Studio of Giovanni Battista Salvi, called Sassoferrato	Giovanni Battista Salvi, called Sassoferrato
A591 Theodoor Smits	Attributed to Dirck Sauts
A408 Style of Roelandt Savery	Roelandt Savery
A939 Attributed to Sebastiano Secante	Sebastiano Secante
A983 Style of Jan Siberechts	Jan Siberechts
A298 Anonymous British Artist	Formerly attributed to Paul van Somer
A594 Isaak Soreau	Jan Soreau
A601 Gerrit van Vucht	Attributed to Pieter van Steenwyck
A3 Anonymous British Artist	"Summers" (?William Sonmans)
A859 Style of Michiel Sweerts	Michiel Sweerts
A121 & A122 David Teniers the Younger	Eighteenth century imitations of David Teniers the Younger
A235 Anonymous Dutch Artist	Charles Theunissen
A605 Style of Jan Philip van Thielen	Jan Philip van Thielen
A169 Copy after Sir Peter Paul Rubens	Attributed to Sir James Thornhill
A653 Anonymous Northern European Artist	Attributed to Nicholas Tournier
A931 Circle of Francesco Trevisani	Francesco Trevisani
A82 Biagio di Antonio Tucci	Attributed to Biagio di Antoinio da Frienze Utili
A770 Joachim Antonisz. Wtewael	Joachim Antonisz. Uytewael
A69 Studio of Giovanni Paolo Panini	Vanvitelli (van Wittel)
A610 Elias van den Broeck	Simon Pietersz. Verelst
A377–A382 Circle of Paolo Caliari, called Veronese	Paolo Caliari, called Veronese
A669 Anonymous Venetian Artist	Formerly attributed to Paolo Caliari, called Veronese
A142 Attributed to Francesco Fontebasso, after Veronese	Copy after Paolo Caliari, called Veronese
A615 Philips Angel	Jan Vonck
A807 Copy after Cornelis de Vos	Attributed to Cornelis de Vos
A618 H. Maria Weerts	Henricus van Weerts
A198 Anonymous British Artist	Formerly attributed to Richard Wilson

Changes in Location

A325 Edward Francis Burney *Dr Charles Burney, (after Reynolds)* transferred to the Music Schools
A932a William Carter *Portrait of Howard Carter* transferred to the Griffith Institute
A520a Kenneth Green *Portrait of Francis Llewellyn Griffith* transferred to the Griffith Institute

INDEX OF SELECTED SUBJECTS

Old Testament, Apocrypha and related subjects

New Testament and related subjects

Mythology

LITERARY SOURCES

ALLEGORY

GENRE

Topography

INDEX OF PREVIOUS OWNERS

INVENTORY NUMBERS

Painting Number	Museum Accession Number	Artist Name
1	WA1845.1	Robert Walker
2	WA1845.2	Anonymous British Artist (*c.* 1620)
3	WA1845.3	Anonymous British Artist (*c.* 1700)
4	WA1845.4	Anonymous British Artist (1562)
5	WA1845.5	Anonymous British Artist (late 17th century)
6	WA1845.6	Pieter Nason
7	WA1845.7	Arnout Vinckenborch
8	WA1845.8	Arnout Vinckenborch
9	WA1845.9	Adam Willaerts
10	WA1845.10	Cornelis Claesz. van Wieringhen
11	WA1845.11	Style of Pieter Claesz.
12	WA1845.12	Anonymous British(?) Artist (*c.* 1700)
13	WA1845.13	Anonymous British Artist (*c.* 1680?)
14	WA1845.14	Anonymous British Artist (*c.* 1680?)
15	WA1845.15	Anonymous British Artist (17th century)
16	WA1845.16	Style of Hendrick Cornelisz. Vroom
17	WA1845.17	Anonymous British Artist (1711)
18	WA1845.18	Anonymous Flemish Artist (early 17th century)
19	WA1845.19	Hendrick van Minderhout
20	WA1845.20	Anonymous Florentine Artist (*c.* 1550–1570)
21	WA1845.21	Pieter Jacobsz. Codde.
21a	WA1845.68	Anonymous British Artist (1587)
22	WA1845.22	Attributed to Jacques de l'Ange
23	WA1845.23	Attributed to Jacques de l'Ange
24	WA1845.24	Attributed to Jacques de l'Ange
25	WA1845.25	Attributed to Jacques de l'Ange
26	WA1845.26	Attributed to Jacques de l'Ange
27	WA1845.27	Attributed to Jacques de l'Ange
28	WA1845.28	Attributed to Jacques de l'Ange
29	WA1845.29	Follower of Carlo Maratta
30	WA1845.30	Thomas Bardwell
31	WA1845.31	Anonymous Franco-Flemish Artist (late 17th century)
32	WA1845.32	Anonymous Franco-Flemish Artist (late 17th century)
33	WA1845.33	Anonymous Franco-Flemish Artist (late 17th century)
34	WA1845.34	Anonymous Franco-Flemish Artist (late 17th century)
35	WA1845.35	Anonymous Franco-Flemish Artist (late 17th century)
36	WA1845.36	Anonymous Franco-Flemish Artist (late 17th century)
37	WA1845.37	Edward Penny, after Van Dyck
38	WA1845.38	Edward Penny, after Van Dyck
39	WA1845.39	Edward Penny, after Van Dyck
40	WA1845.40	William Martin
41	WA1845.41	George Simon, Second Earl Harcourt
42	WA1845.42	Sir George Howland Beaumont, Bt
43	WA1845.43	John Skippe
44	WA1845.44	John Skippe
45	WA1845.45	Copy after Raphael
46	WA1845.46	Sir Joshua Reynolds
47	WA1845.47	Imitator of Claude Gellée (Le Lorrain)
48	WA1845.48	Sir William Elford, Bt
49	WA1845.49	Edward Hamilton
50	WA1845.50	William Cowden
51	WA1845.51	Oldfield Bowles
52	WA1845.52	Copy after Raphael
53	WA1845.53	Copy after Raphael
54	WA1845.54	Copy after Raphael
55	WA1845.55	Copy after Raphael
56	WA1845.56	Copy after Raphael
57	WA1845.57	Copy after Raphael
58	WA1845.58	Copy after Raphael
59	WA1845.59	Copy after Raphael
60	WA1845.60	Copy after Rembrandt Harmensz. van Rijn
61	WA1845.61	Pompeo Batoni
62	WA1845.62	Samuel William Reynolds the Younger
63	WA1845.63	After René-Antoine Houasse
63a	WA1845.69	Attributed to Thomas Phillips
64	WA1845.64	Sir Joshua Reynolds
65	WA1845.65	Anonymous British Artist (*c.* 1760)
66	WA1846.310	Anonymous Flemish Artist (*c.* 1630)
66a	WA1845.66	Thomas Kirkby
66b	WA1845.67	William Smith
66c	WA1846.309	Attributed to Michelangelo Buonarroti
67	WA1846.11	Attributed to Francesco Ubertini, called Bacchiacca
68	WA1847.2	Anonymous British Artist (1794)
69	WA1847.1	Studio of Giovanni Paolo Panini
70	WA1849.2	Anonymous Florentine Artist (*c.* 1580s–1590)
71	WA1850.23	Anonymous Post-Byzantine (18th century)
72	WA1850.24	Anonymous Post-Byzantine (18th century?)
73	WA1850.9	'Barna da Siena'
74	WA1850.6	Master of the Ashmolean Predella
75	WA1850.19	Andrea di Bartolo Cini

Painting Number	Museum Accession Number	Artist Name
76	WA1850.22	Sano di Pietro
77	WA1850.5	Studio of Fra Angelico
78	WA1850.25	Follower of Fra Angelico
79	WA1850.31	Paolo di Dono, called Uccello
80	WA1850.7	Attributed to Paolo di Dono, called Uccello
81	WA1850.8	Fra Filippo Lippi
82	WA1850.28	Biagio di Antonio Tucci
83	WA1850.15	Domenico Ghirlandaio
84	WA1850.12	Davide Ghirlandaio
85	WA1850.1	Attributed to Arcangelo di Jacopo del Sellaio
86	WA1850.11	Francesco de'Franceschi
87	WA1850.10	Francesco de'Franceschi
88	WA1850.2	Attributed to Gerolamo del Pacchia
89	WA1850.26	Bicci di Lorenzo
90	WA1850.27	Apollonio di Giovanni and Marco del Buono Giamberti
91	WA1850.29	Attributed to Giovanni di Ser Giovanni, called Lo Scheggia
92	WA1850.30	Apollonio di Giovanni and Marco del Buono Giamberti
93	WA1850.18	Bartolomeo and Agnolo degli Erri
94	WA1850.16	Anonymous Tuscan Artist (*c.* 1480–1500?)
95	WA1850.17	Anonymous Tuscan Artist (*c.* 1480–1500?)
96	WA1850.20	Nicola di Maestro Antonio d'Ancona
97	WA1850.21	Nicola di Maestro Antonio d'Ancona
98	WA1850.34	Marco Zoppo
99	WA1850.14	Agnolo di Domenico di Donnino
100	WA1850.13	Francesco Granacci
101	WA1850.13.1	Francesco Granacci
102	WA1850.33	Copy after Andrea del Sarto
103	WA1850.4	Lorenzo di Credi
104	WA1850.3	Copy after Fra Bartolomeo
105	WA1850.32	Agnolo Bronzino
106	WA1850.35	Anonymous Italian Artist (17th century)
107	WA1850.36	Copy after Carlo Dolci
108	WA1850.37	Copy after Pietro Perugino
109	WA1850.38	Anonymous North Italian Artist (*c.* 1600)
110	WA1850.39	Copy after Antonio Allegri, called Correggio
111	WA1850.40	Style of Johann Melchior Roos (Rosa da Tivoli)
112	WA1850.41	Charles Edward Strong
113	WA1851.12	Anonymous North Italian Artist (*c.* 1650)
114	WA1851.10	Giovanni Paolo Panini
115	WA1851.11	Giovanni Paolo Panini
116	WA1851.13	Andrea Locatelli
117	WA1851.14	Andrea Locatelli
118	WA1851.9	Follower of Philippe de Champaigne
119	WA1851.15	David Teniers the Younger
120	WA1851.16	David Teniers the Younger
121	WA1851.17	David Teniers the Younger
122	WA1851.18	David Teniers the Younger
123	WA1851.24	Adriaen van Ostade
124	WA1851.21	Attributed to Simon Kick
125	WA1851.22	Thomas Wyck
126	WA1851.23	Jacob van Strij
127	WA1851.25	Attributed to William Hogarth
128	WA1851.7	Sir Joshua Reynolds
129	WA1851.8	Sir Joshua Reynolds
130	WA1851.3	Style of Thomas Gainsborough
131	WA1851.2	Anonymous British Artist (*c.* 1775)
132	WA1851.5	Sir Augustus Wall Callcott, after Joseph Mallord William Turner
133	WA1851.1	John Opie
134	WA1851.6	George Morland
135	WA1851.4	Sir Augustus Wall Callcott
136	WA1851.19	Philip James de Loutherbourg
137	WA1851.20	Pierre-Joseph Dedreux-Dorcy
138	WA1853.2	George Frederic Watts
139	WA1854.1	Colvin Smith
140	WA1854.2	Antonio Bellucci
141	WA1855.582	Anonymous Lombard Artist (*c.* 1520–30)
142	WA1855.159	Attributed to Francesco Fontebasso, after Veronese
143	WA1855.160	Copy after Paolo Caliari, called Veronese
144	WA1855.219	Copy after Giovanni Antonio de Sacchis, called Pordenone
145	WA1855.208	Anonymous Bolognese Artist (*c.* 1730–40)
146	WA1855.187	Giovanni Antonio da Canal, called Canaletto
147	WA1855.186	Giovanni Antonio da Canal, called Canaletto
148	WA1855.182	Follower of Francesco Guardi
149	WA1855.183	Francesco Guardi
150	WA1855.184	Follower of Francesco Guardi
151	WA1855.185	Francesco Guardi
152	WA1855.197	Anonymous British Artist (*c.* 1830)
153	WA1855.170	Sir Peter Paul Rubens
154	WA1855.177	Style of Sir Peter Paul Rubens
155	WA1855.161	Sir Peter Paul Rubens
156	WA1855.179	Sir Peter Paul Rubens
157	WA1855.176	Sir Peter Paul Rubens
158	WA1855.178	Sir Peter Paul Rubens
159	WA1855.222	Sir Peter Paul Rubens
160	WA1855.166	Copy after Sir Peter Paul Rubens
161	WA1855.163	Attributed to Sir Peter Paul Rubens
162	WA1855.175	Copy after Sir Peter Paul Rubens
163	WA1855.189	Style of Sir Peter Paul Rubens
164	WA1855.164	Style of Sir Peter Paul Rubens
165	WA1855.168	Style of Sir Peter Paul Rubens
166	WA1855.167	Cornelis de Vos
167	WA1855.162	Attributed to Sir Peter Paul Rubens
168	WA1855.165	Anonymous Dutch Artist (17th century)
169	WA1855.169	Copy after Sir Peter Paul Rubens
170	WA1855.573	Style of Sir Peter Paul Rubens
171	WA1855.171	Sir Peter Paul Rubens
172	WA1855.228	Copy after Sir Anthony van Dyck
173	WA1855.225	Style of Sir Anthony van Dyck
174	WA1855.180	Copy after Sir Anthony van Dyck
175	WA1855.172	Sir Anthony van Dyck
176	WA1855.173	Sir Anthony van Dyck
177	WA1855.190	Copy after Sir Anthony van Dyck
178	WA1855.570	Cornelis Schut
179	WA1855.571	Copy after Sir Anthony van Dyck
180	WA1855.181	Pieter Boel
181	WA1855.221	Copy(?) after Sir Peter Paul Rubens
182	WA1855.174	Anonymous Flemish Artist (17th century)
183	WA1855.196	Anonymous Anglo-Flemish Artist (*c.* 1630)
184	WA1855.212	David Teniers the Younger
185	WA1855.188	Goffredo Wals
186	WA1855.192	Attributed to William Hogarth
187	WA1855.195	William Hogarth
188	WA1855.194	Attributed to Gawen Hamilton
189	WA1855.193	William Hogarth
190	WA1855.583	William Hogarth
191	WA1855.158	Sir Joshua Reynolds
192	WA1855.157	Sir Joshua Reynolds
193	WA1855.191	Sir Joshua Reynolds.
194	WA1855.198	Attributed to Johan Zoffany
195	WA1855.199	Attributed to Johan Zoffany
196-7	WA1855.201	Johan Zoffany
198	WA1855.203	Anonymous British Artist (*c.* 1780)
199	WA1855.204	Richard Wilson
200	WA1855.202	Richard Wilson
201	WA1855.584	Anonymous British Artist (*c.* 1720)
202	WA1855.585	John Constable
203	WA1855.205	John Linnell
204	WA1855.223	John Linnell
205	WA1855.206	David Charles Read
206	WA1855.207	David Charles Read
207	WA1855.213	David Charles Read
208	WA1855.214	David Charles Read
209	WA1855.215	David Charles Read
210	WA1855.216	David Charles Read
211	WA1855.217	David Charles Read
212	WA1855.218	David Charles Read
213	WA1855.220	David Charles Read
214	WA1855.224	David Charles Read
215	WA1855.226	David Charles Read
216	WA1855.227	David Charles Read
217	WA1855.574	David Charles Read
218	WA1855.575	David Charles Read
219	WA1855.576	David Charles Read
220	WA1855.577	David Charles Read
221	WA1855.578	David Charles Read
222	WA1855.579	David Charles Read
223	WA1855.580	David Charles Read
224	WA1855.581	David Charles Read
225	WA1857.5	John Eagles
226	WA.OA903	Copy after Tiziano Vecellio, called Titian
227	WA.OA904	Copy after Guido Reni
228	WA1859.1	Copy after Raphael
229	WA1861.2	Style of Samuel Scott
230	WA1861.1	Style of Samuel Scott
231	WA1864.1	Master of Charles III of Durazzo
232	WA1869.1	Sir Anthony van Dyck
233	WA1870.2	Style of Samuel Scott

Painting Number	Museum Accession Number	Artist Name
234	WA1870.3	Style of Samuel Scott
235	WA1870.1	Anonymous Dutch Artist (19th century)
236	WA1873.17	George Jones
237	WA1873.19	George Jones
238	WA1873.18	George Jones
239	WA1873.20	George Jones
240	WA1881.347	George Jones
241	WA1881.348	George Jones
242	WA1881.349	George Jones
243	WA1881.350	George Jones
244	WA1887.1	Anonymous Russian (19th century)
245	WA1887.3	Paul Sandby
245a	WA1908.202	Anonymous British Artist (19th century)
246	WA1889.1	John Francis Rigaud
247	WA1879.1	George Barret the Elder
248	WA1891.2	Sir Hubert von Herkomer
249	WA1891.3	Sir Hubert von Herkomer
250	WA1891.4	Sir Hubert von Herkomer
251	WA1891.5	Sir Hubert von Herkomer
252	WA1891.6	Sir Hubert von Herkomer
253	WA1892.10	'John'
254	WA1892.9	Anonymous Italian Artist (*c.* 1800–1820)
255	WA1892.8	Simone dei Crocifissi
256	WA1892.2	Copy after Scipione Pulzone
257	WA1892.1	Follower of Carlo Cignani
258	WA1892.3	Anonymous Bolognese Artist (*c.* 1750)
259	WA1892.4	Anonymous Central Italian Artist (*c.* 1570–1590)
260	WA1892.5	Anonymous Spanish Artist (17th century)
261	WA1892.6	Anonymous Italian artist (early 18th century)
262	WA1892.7	Carl Hoffmann the Younger
263	WA1893.3	William Bell Scott
264	WA1893.2	William Bell Scott
265	WA1894.1	William Holman Hunt
266	WA1894.2	William Holman Hunt
267	WA1894.3	William Holman Hunt
268	WA1894.4	William Holman Hunt
269	WA1894.5	William Holman Hunt
270	WA1894.6	William Holman Hunt
271	WA1894.8	Sir John Everett Millais, Bt
272	WA1894.9	Sir John Everett Millais, Bt
273	WA1894.10	Charles Alston Collins
274	WA1894.11	Charles Alston Collins
275	WA1894.12.1	James Holland
276	WA1894.12.2	Copy after Richard Parkes Bonington
277	WA1895.10	Copy after Tiziano Vecellio, called Titian
278	WA1897.1	Frans Ykens
279	WA1897.2	Jacob Esselens
280	WA1897.3	Guillam Dubois
281	WA1897.4	Johannes Colaert
282	WA1897.5	Jan Jacobsz. van der Stoffe
283	WA1897.6	Jan Vonck
284	WA1897.7	Cornelis Gerritsz. Decker
285	WA1897.8	Attributed to Willem Van de Lande
286	WA1897.9	Attributed to Roelof Jansz. van Vries
287	WA1897.10	Wouter Knijff
288	WA1897.11	Cornelis Bega
289	WA1897.12	Copy after Nicolaes Pietersz. Berchem
290	WA1897.14	Altobello Melone
291	WA1897.14.1	Altobello Melone
292	WA1897.21	Gerolamo da Santacroce
293	WA1897.22	Anonymous Venetian Artist (*c.* 1510)
294	WA1897.20	Studio of Giovanni Battista Salvi, called Sassoferrato
295	WA1897.15	Gaspard Dughet
296	WA1897.16	Studio of Giovanni Antonio da Canal, called Canaletto
297	WA1897.19	Follower of Simon Marmion
298	WA1897.17	Anonymous British Artist (17th century)
299	WA1897.18	Attributed to Étienne Jeaurat
299a	WA1899.3	Charles Alexander
299b	WA1899.4	Charles Alexander
300	WA1899.CDEF.P3	Master of San Martino alla Palma
300a	WA1899.5	Studio of Andrea Orcagna
300b	WA1899.6	Studio of Andrea Orcagna
301	WA1899.CDEF.P27	Vittore Crivelli
302	WA1899.CDEF.P1	Circle of Giovanni Bellini
303	WA1899.CDEF.P10	Bernardino Pintoricchio
304	WA1899.CDEF.P2	Anonymous Central Italian Artist (late 18th century or early 19th century)
305	WA1899.CDEF.P4	Style of Thomas de Keyser
306	WA1899.CDEF.P24	Style of Jan Miense Molenaer
307	WA1899.CDEF.P7	Anonymous British Artist (*c.* 1660)
308	WA1899.CDEF.P26	Tilly Kettle
309	WA1899.CDEF.P9	John Opie
310	WA1899.CDEF.P14	Copy after Joseph Wright of Derby
311	WA1899.CDEF.P8	Anonymous British Artist (*c.* 1790)
312	WA1899.CDEF.P6	William Ingalton
313	WA1902.3	Thomas Sully
314	WA1903.1	Carlo Crivelli
315	WA1907.4	Jacob Willemsz. de Wet
316	WA1907.3	Arthur Hughes
316a	WA1907.2	Sir William Blake Richmond
316b	WA1907.1	John Riley
317	WA1908.202	Anonymous Russian (early 16th century)
318	WA1908.203	Anonymous Russian (early 16th century)
319	WA1908.204	Anonymous Post-Byzantine (15th/16th century)
320	WA.OA906	Anonymous British Artist (19th Century)
321	WA.OA907	Copy after Carlo Dolci
322	WA.OA909	Copy after Sir Peter Paul Rubens
323	WA.OA910	Joseph Fisher
324	WA.OA911	Joseph Fisher
324a	WA.OA282	Copy after Sir Joshua Reynolds
326	WA1909.1	John William Inchbold
327	WA1909.2	Ford Madox Brown
328	WA1911.1	Sir Charles John Holmes
329	WA1911.2	Follower of Pietro Longhi
330	WA1911.3	Anonymous Venetian Artist (*c.* 1850)
331	WA1912.1	Sir Hubert von Herkomer
332	WA1913.1	Studio of Giotto di Bondone
333	WA1913.2	Giovanni di Paolo
334	WA1913.3	Attributed to Paolo Schiavo
335	WA1913.4	Anonymous Ferrarese Artist (*c.* 1510–30)
336	WA1913.5	Anonymous Hispano-Flemish Artist (*c.* 1500)
337	WA1913.6	Master of the Bielefeld Altar
338	WA1913.7	Attributed to Francesco Granacci
339	WA1914.1	George Mullins
340	WA1914.2	Alfred William Hunt
341	WA1914.3	Charles de Sousy Ricketts
342	WA1915.1	Franciabigio
343	WA1915.2	Michelangelo Unterperger
344	WA1915.14	Anonymous Russian (16th/17th century)
345	WA1915.15	Anonymous Russian (Strogonov School, Savin family?) (17th century)
346	WA1915.13	Anonymous Byzantine (14th/15th century)
347	WA1915.11	Attributed to Francesco Buonsignori
348	WA1915.12	Attributed to Neri di Bicci
350	WA1915.61	Attributed to Frans de Hulst
351	WA1915.62	William Turner of Oxford
352	WA1915.63	George Frederic Watts
353	WA1916.39	Edward Lear
353a	ANT1916.23	Thomas Luny
353b	ANT1916.24	Thomas Luny
354	WA1917.2	Jan Porcellis
355	WA1917.1	Nicolaes Maes
356-7	WA1918.2	Attributed to Antonio Vazquez
358	WA1919.2	Alfred William Hunt
359	WA1919.30	Alessandro Magnasco and Antonio Francesco Peruzzini
360	WA1920.3	Ford Madox Brown
361	WA1920.4	Paulus Hennekyn
362	WA1920.1	Copy after Giovanni Battista Tiepolo
363	WA1920.5	Briton Rivière
364	WA1921.1	Nicolaes (Claes) Hals
365	WA1921.2	Follower of Deodato Orlandi
366	WA1921.3	Studio of Andrea Orcagna
367	WA1921.4	Formerley attributed to Salvator Rosa
368	WA1921.5	Formerley attributed to Salvator Rosa
369	WA1921.6	Joseph Severn
370	WA1921.7	Attributed to Andrea del Brescianino
371	WA1923.1	Copy(?) after Pieter Neefs the Elder
372	WA1923.2	Frederick Sandys
373	WA1923.3	Henry Moore
374	WA1924.1	Samuel de Wilde
374a	WA1924.11	Anonymous British Artist (*c.* 1630)
374b	WA1924.12	Anonymous British Artist (*c.* 1630?)
375	WA1925.1	John Constable
376	WA1926.1	Claude Gellée (Le Lorrain)
377	WA1926.2	Circle of Paolo Caliari, called Veronese
378	WA1926.3	Circle of Paolo Caliari, called Veronese
379	WA1926.4	Circle of Paolo Caliari, called Veronese
380	WA1926.5	Circle of Paolo Caliari, called Veronese
381	WA1926.6	Circle of Paolo Caliari, called Veronese

Painting Number	Museum Accession Number	Artist Name
382	WA1926.7	Circle of Paolo Caliari, called Veronese
383	WA1926.9	Copy after Giovanni Domenico Cerrini, called il Cavalier Perugino
384	WA1926.10	Adriaen de Gryeff
385	WA1926.11	Adriaen van Diest
386	WA1927.1	Francesco Guardi
387	WA1927.2	Jean-Antoine Watteau
388	WA1927.3	Jean-Siméon Chardin
389	WA1927.4	Attributed to Luigi Crespi
390	WA1929.1	Willem Drost
391	WA1929.2	George Romney
392	WA1929.3	Alfred Gainsborough Dupont
393	WA1929.4	Anonymous French Artist (early 19th century)
394	WA1929.5	Sir David Young Cameron
395	WA1929.7	John Singer Sargent
396	WA1929.8	Circle of Luigi Garzi
397	WA1929.9	Copy after Jacopo Tintoretto
398	WA1929.30	Sydney William Carline
399	WA1929.32	John Constable
400	WA1929.33	George Richmond
400a	WA.OA281	Attributed to Pietro degli Ingannati
401	WA1929.34	John Linnell
401a	WA1930.9	George Percy Jacomb-Hood
402	WA1931.1	Attributed to Richard Wilson
403	WA1931.2	Jean-Baptiste-Camille Corot
405	WA1931.3	Lionel Constable
406	WA1931.4	Philip Wilson Steer
407	WA1931.16	Joos de Momper
408	WA1931.17	Style of Roelandt Savery
409	WA1931.18	Bartolomeo Nazari
410	WA1931.57	Giovanni Costa, called Nino
411	WA1931.58	Anonymous British Artist (*c.* 1780)
412	WA1931.62	David Cox
413	WA1932.1	Studio of Sandro Botticelli
414	WA1932.2	Samuel Palmer
415	WA1932.78	William Turner of Oxford
416	WA1932.195	Jean-Francois (called Francisque) Millet
417	WA1932.196	Edward Calvert
418	WA1932.199	Anonymous Bohemian Artist (?) (*c.* 1720)
419	WA1932.200	John Jackson
419a	WA1932.215	Studio of Francesco Francia
419b	WA1932.216	Anonymous British Artist (*c.* 1830)
420	WA1933.2	Piero di Cosimo
421	WA1933.3	Richard Parkes Bonington
422	WA1933.4	William Etty
423	WA1933.7	John Constable
424	WA1933.8	Roger Fry
425	WA1933.9	Jacob de Wit
426	WA1933.22	Anonymous South German Artist (15th century)
427	WA1933.23	Anonymous Flemish Artist (*c.* 1500)
428	WA1933.24	Anonymous German Artist (*c.* 1770–1780)
429	WA1933.25	Anonymous British Artist (*c.* 1555)
430	WA1934.5	Ignace-Henri-Jean-Théodore Fantin-Latour
431	WA1934.6	Attributed to Georges Michel
432	WA1934.8	Giovanni Battista Ruoppolo
433	WA1934.9	Follower of Francisco de Goya y Lucientes
434	WA1934.10	Follower of Francisco de Goya y Lucientes
435	WA1934.11	Willem van Aelst
436	WA1934.12	Pietro Testa
437	WA1934.13	Style of Sir Joshua Reynolds
438	WA1934.14	William Turner of Oxford
438a	WA1934.418	John Opie
438b	WA1934.419	Thomas Worlidge
438c	WA1934.420	Thomas Worlidge
438d	WA1934.421	Thomas Worlidge
438e	WA1934.422	John Opie
438f	WA1934.423	John Opie
438g	WA1934.65.249	Anonymous British Artist (*c.* 1765)
438k	WA1934.414	Attributed to Valentine Cameron Prinsep
438L	WA1960.76	Allan Ramsay
439	WA1935.79	Henry Tonks
440	WA1935.60	Adriaen Isenbrandt
441	WA1935.76	Gilbert Spencer
442	WA1935.6	Attributed to Hendrick Cornelisz. van Vliet
443	WA1935.65	Sir Edwin Henry Landseer
444	WA1935.40	Joseph Francis Nollekens
445	WA1935.97	Leandro Bassano
446	WA1935.160	Giovanni Battista Moroni
447	WA1936.48	Jean-Desire-Gustave Courbet
448	WA1936.49	Dame Ethel Walker
448a	WA1936.31	Benjamin Robert Haydon
448b	WA1936.229	John Martin
449	WA1936.30	Augustus Edwin John
450	WA1936.39	Anonymous North Italian Artist (*c.* 1600)
451	WA1936.36	Copy(?) after Joachim Patenir
451a	WA1936.170	Studio of Bonifazio de' Pitati
451b	WA1936.222	Francesco Buoneri, called Cecco del Caravaggio
451c	WA1936.7	Anonymous Tuscan Artist (*c.* 1390)
451d	WA1936.6	William Hughes
452	WA1937.32	George Frederic Watts
453	WA1937.33	Richard Arthur Crosthwaite Murry
454	WA1937.34	Albert André
455	WA1937.35	Barry Pittar
456	WA1937.36	Antoine Vollon
457	WA1937.37	Gilbert Spencer
458	WA1937.38	William Etty
459	WA1937.39	Style of Richard Parkes Bonington
460	WA1937.40	Henri-Joseph Harpignies
461	WA1937.41	Ignace-Henri-Jean-Théodore Fantin-Latour
462	WA1937.57	Charles-François Daubigny
463	WA1937.42	Ignace-Henri-Jean-Théodore Fantin-Latour
464	WA1937.43	Augustin-Théodule Ribot
465	WA1937.45	Sir William Orpen
466	WA1937.46	Georges Michel
467	WA1937.47	Philip Wilson Steer
468	WA1937.48	Philip Wilson Steer
469	WA1937.49	Style of John Constable
470	WA1937.50	Jean-Desire-Gustave Courbet
471	WA1937.51	Henri-Eugène-Augustin Le Sidaner
472	WA1937.52	David Muirhead
473	WA1937.53	Gerard Chowne
474	WA1937.54	Ignace-Henri-Jean-Théodore Fantin-Latour
475	WA1937.55	Eugène Boudin
476	WA1937.56	Antoine Vollon
477	WA1937.58	Augustin-Théodule Ribot
478	WA1937.59	Sir David Young Cameron
479	WA1937.60	Alfred Sisley
480	WA1937.61	Style of Richard Parkes Bonington
481	WA1937.62	Louis-Eugène-Gabriel Isabey
482	WA1937.63	Thomas Gainsborough, after Van Dyck
483	WA1937.64	Sir William Rothenstein
484	WA1937.65	Copy after John Constable
485	WA1937.66	Ignace-Henri-Jean-Théodore Fantin-Latour
486	WA1937.67	Ignace-Henri-Jean-Théodore Fantin-Latour
487	WA1937.68	Lionel Constable
488	WA1937.69	Anonymous British Artist (*c.* 1830)
489	WA1937.70	Jean-Berthold Jongkind
490	WA1937.71	Edward Calvert
491	WA1937.72	Lucien Pissarro
492	WA1937.73	Camille Pissarro
493	WA1937.74	Attributed to John Constable
494	WA1937.75	Thomas Churchyard
495	WA1937.76	Philip Connard
496	WA1937.77	Stanislas-Victor-Édouard Lépine
497	WA1937.78	William Etty
498	WA1937.79	Jean-Louis Forain
499	WA1937.499	Christopher Richard Wynne Nevinson
500	WA1937.81	Attributed to Sir John Everett Millais, Bt
501	WA1937.82.1	Richard Arthur Crosthwaite Murry
502	WA1937.82.3	Arthur B. Devis
502a	WA1937.82.2	William Etty
503	WA1937.102	Studio of Leonardo da Vinci
504	WA1937.103	Jacopo Negretti (Palma Vecchio)
505	WA1937.299	Copy after Raphael
506	WA1937.105	Ignace-Henri-Jean-Théodore Fantin-Latour
507	WA1937.106	William Rivière
508	WA1937.107	William Powell Frith
509	WA1937.108	Philip Alexius de László
510	WA1937.110	Sir James Thornhill
511	WA1937.113	Anonymous French or Italian Artist (early 19th century)
511a	WA1937.118	Anna Louisa Swynnerton
511b	WA1937.119	Alexander Jamieson
512	WA1937.122	Anonymous Italo-Flemish Artist (*c.* 1560–1570)
513	WA1937.123	Anonymous Flemish Artist (16th century)
514	WA1937.124	Francesco Solimena
515	WA1938.1	Gianantonio Pellegrini
516	WA1938.2	Attributed to Sebastiano or Marco Ricci and a collaborator
517	WA1938.3	Thomas Faed

Painting Number	Museum Accession Number	Artist Name
518	WA1938.4	William Smith
519	WA1938.6	Anonymous Flemish Artist (*c.* 1500)
520	WA1938.5	Anonymous Flemish Artist (*c.* 1500)
520a	WA1938.64	Thomas Churchyard
520b	WA1938.84	Thomas Churchyard
520c	WA1938.125	Copy after Agnolo Bronzino
520d	WA1938.126	Master of Marradi
520f	WA1938.85	Attributed to Thomas Alexander Ferguson Graham
521	WA1939.1	Gilbert Spencer
522	WA1939.16	Copy after Tiziano Vecellio, called Titian
522a	WA1939.18.1	John White Abbott
523	WA1940.2.95	Daisy Linda Ward (née Travers)
524	WA1940.2.96	Daisy Linda Ward (née Travers)
525	WA1940.2.1	Style of Willem van Aelst
526	WA1940.2.2	Willem van Aelst
527	WA1940.2.3	Copy of Willem van Aelst
528	WA1940.2.4	Willem van Aelst
529	WA1940.2.5	Henrick Andriessen
530	WA1940.2.6	Balthasar van der Ast
531	WA1940.2.7	Style of Osias Beert the Elder
532	WA1940.2.8	Abraham van Beyeren
533	WA1940.2.9	Abraham van Beyeren
534	WA1940.2.10	Abraham van Beyeren
535	WA1940.2.11	Abraham van Beyeren
536	WA1940.2.12	Abraham van Beyeren
537	WA1940.2.13	Hans Bollongier
538	WA1940.2.14	Johannes Borman
539	WA1940.2.15	Ambrosius Bosschaert
540	WA1940.2.16	Elias van den Broeck
541	WA1940.2.17	Attributed to Jan Brueghel the Younger
542	WA1940.2.18	Pieter Claesz.
543	WA1940.40.19	Pieter Claesz.
544	WA1940.2.20	Jacques de Claeuw
545	WA1940.2.21	Adriaen Coorte
546	WA1940.2.22	Adriaen Coorte
547	WA1940.2.23	Attributed to Abraham van Calraet
548	WA1940.2.24	Cornelis Jacobsz. Delff
549	WA1940.2.25	Ottmar Elliger
550	WA1940.2.26	Jacob Foppens van Es
551	WA1940.2.27	Pieter Boel
552	WA1940.2.28	Pieter Gallis
553	WA1940.2.29	Jacob Gillig
554	WA1940.2.30	Johannes Hannot
555	WA1940.2.31	Gerrit van Vucht
556	WA1940.2.32	Cornelis de Heem
557	WA1940.2.33	David Cornelisz. de Heem
558	WA1940.2.34	Jan Davidsz. de Heem
559	WA1940.2.35	Jan Davidsz. de Heem
560	WA1940.2.36	Copy after Jan Davidsz. de Heem
561	WA1940.2.37	J. van Slechtenhorst
562	WA1940.2.38	Pieter Janssens Elinga
563	WA1940.2.39	Willem Kalf
564	WA1940.2.40	Jan van Kessel I
565	WA1940.2.41	Jan van Kessel I
566	WA1940.2.42	Jan van Kessel I
567	WA1940.2.43	Jan van Kessel I
568	WA1940.2.44	Jan van Kessel I
569	WA1940.2.45	Jan van Kessel I
570	WA1940.2.46	Jan van Kessel I
571	WA1940.2.47	Jan van Kessel I
572	WA1940.2.48	Jan van Kessel I
573	WA1940.2.49	Cornelis Kick
574	WA1940.2.50	Abraham de Lust
575	WA1940.2.51	Abraham de Lust
576	WA1940.2.52	Simon Luttichuys
577	WA1940.2.53	Nicolaes Maes
578	WA1940.2.54	Jacob Marrel
579	WA1940.2.55	Anonymous Dutch Artist (third quarter of 17th century)
580	WA1940.2.56	Abraham Mignon
581	WA1940.2.57	Abraham Mignon
582	WA1940.2.58	Copy after Abraham Mignon
583	WA1940.2.59	Abraham Mignon
584	WA1940.2.60	Jan Mortel
585	WA1940.2.61	Clara Peeters
586	WA1940.2.62	Willem Frederiksz. van Royen
587	WA1940.2.63	Elias van den Broeck
588	WA1940.2.64	Rachel Ruysch
589	WA1940.2.65	Copy after Rachel Ruysch
590	WA1940.2.66	Rachel Ruysch
591	WA1940.2.67	Theodoor Smits
592	WA1940.2.68	Godfried Schalcken
593	WA1940.2.69	Pieter Snijers
594	WA1940.2.70	Isaak Soreau
595	WA1940.2.71	Johannes Spruyt
596	WA1940.2.72	Harmen van Steenwyck
597	WA1940.2.73	Harmen van Steenwyck
598	WA1940.2.74	Harmen van Steenwyck
599	WA1940.2.75	Harmen van Steenwyck
600	WA1940.2.76	Harmen van Steenwyck
601	WA1940.2.77	Gerrit van Vucht
602	WA1940.2.78	Juriaen van Streek
603	WA1940.2.79	Christian Jansz. Striep
604	WA1940.2.80	Abraham Susenier
605	WA1940.2.81	Style of Jan Philip van Thielen
606	WA1940.2.82	Adriaen van Utrecht
607	WA1940.2.83	Jan Jansz. van de Velde III
608	WA1940.2.84	Jan Jansz. van de Velde III
609	WA1940.2.85	Jan Jansz. van de Velde III
610	WA1940.2.86	Elias van den Broeck
611	WA1940.2.87	Simon Verelst
612	WA1940.2.88	Simon Verelst
613	WA1940.2.89	Constantin Verhout
614	WA1940.2.90	Jan Vonck
615	WA1940.2.91	Philips Angel
616	WA1940.2.92	Cornelis Kick
617	WA1940.2.93	Jan Weenix
618	WA1940.2.94	H. Maria Weerts
618a	WA1940.1.92	Walter Richard Sickert
619	WA1940.1.1	Philip Wilson Steer
620	WA1940.1.2	Frederick James Porter
621	WA1940.1.3	Maurice de Vlaminck
622	WA1940.1.4	Pierre-Auguste Renoir
623	WA1940.1.5	Duncan Grant
624	WA1940.1.6	Édouard Manet
625	WA1940.1.7	Emile-Othon Friesz
626	WA1940.1.8	Sir Matthew Smith
627	WA1940.1.9	Pierre Bonnard
628	WA1940.1.10	Pierre Bonnard
629	WA1940.1.11	Henri Matisse
630	WA1940.1.12	Camille Pissarro
631	WA1940.1.13	Jean-Baptiste-Camille Corot
632	WA1940.1.14	Jean-Baptiste-Camille Corot
633	WA1940.1.15	Eugène Boudin
634	WA1940.1.16	Pablo Picasso
635	WA1940.1.17	Walter Richard Sickert
636	WA1940.1.18	Maurice Utrillo
637	WA1940.1.19	André Dunoyer de Segonzac
638	WA1940.1.20	André Derain
639	WA1940.1.21	Georges Braque
640	WA1940.1.22	Louis-Gustave Ricard
641	WA1940.1.23	Henri de Toulouse-Lautrec
642	WA1940.1.24	Jean-Baptiste-Camille Corot
643	WA1940.1.25	Pierre-Auguste Renoir
644	WA1940.1.26	Vanessa Bell
645	WA1940.1.27	Antoine Chintreuil
646	WA1940.1.28	Anonymous British Artist (*c.* 1830)
647	WA1940.1.29	Anonymous Bolognese Artist (*c.* 1610)
648	WA1940.1.30	Jean Frelaut
649	WA1940.1.31	Duncan Grant
650	WA1940.1.32	Duncan Grant
651	WA1940.1.33	Louis-Adolphe Hervier
652	WA1940.1.34	Jean Hippolyte Marchand
652a	WA1940.1.35	Copy after Guido Reni
653	WA1939.50	Anonymous Northern European Artist (*c.* 1620–1630)
654	WA1939.51	Copy after Giovanni Francesco Barbieri, called Guercino
655	WA1939.52	Charles-François Daubigny
656	WA1939.53	William Turner of Oxford
657	WA1939.54	Richard Dadd
658	WA1940.3	Charles Conder
659	WA1940.4.1	Camille Pissarro
660	WA1940.4.2	Walter Richard Sickert
661	WA1940.5.1	Alphonse Legros
662	WA1940.5.2	Alphonse Legros
663	WA1940.8.1	William Havell
664	WA1940.8.2	William Havell
664a	WA1940.8.2.2	Peter de Wint
665	WA1940.20	Karel Du Jardin
666	WA1940.21	Samuel Palmer
667	WA1940.22	Lorenzo Lippi

Painting Number	Museum Accession Number	Artist Name
668	WA1941.1	Jakob Adriaensz. Backer
669	WA1941.2	Anonymous Venetian Artist (*c.* 1600)
670	WA1941.3	Style of Jan Frans van Bloemen, called Orizzonte
671	WA1941.4	Attributed to Giacomo Francesco Cipper, Il Todeschini
672	WA1941.5	Copy after Agnolo Bronzino
673	WA1941.6	Attributed to Pietro Paolini
674	WA1941.7	Anonymous Dutch Artist (mid-17th century?)
675	WA1941.8	Anonymous Florentine Artist (*c.* 1675–1695)
676	WA1941.14	Master of the Dominican Effigies
677	WA1941.14	Master of the Dominican Effigies
678	WA1941.15	Camillo Filippi
678a	WA1941.18	Jacopo Robusti, called Tintoretto
679	WA1941.28	Arthur Hughes
680	WA1941.29	George Richmond after Raphael
680a	WA1941.21.1	George James Howard, 9th Earl of Carlisle
681	WA1941.54	George Frederic Watts
682	WA1941.55	George Frederic Watts
683	WA1941.57	Charles Haslewood Shannon
684	WA1941.58	William Strang
684a	WA1941.58.1	Glyn Warren Philpot
684b	WA1941.58.2	John Pettie
685	WA1941.61	Robert Braithwaite Martineau
686	WA1941.65	Thomas Matthews Rooke
687	WA1941.89	William Edward Frost
687a	WA1941.120	Walter Howell Deverell
688	WA1941.157	George Morland
689	WA1941.158	Augustus Leopold Egg
690	WA1941.159	José Antolinez
690a	WA1941.162	Sir George Hayter
692	WA1942.16	William Etty
693	WA1942.18	The Candlelight Master
694	WA1942.19	Sir David Wilkie
695	WA1942.20	Anonymous Italian Artist (*c.* 1600)
696	WA1942.48	Andrea Vanni
697	WA1942.56	Augustus Leopold Egg
698	WA1942.57	George Lance
701	WA1942.60	William Turner of Oxford
702	WA1942.61	William Turner of Oxford
703	WA1942.62	William Turner of Oxford
704	WA1943.1	Jan Both
705	WA1943.2	Kaspar Waldmann
705a	WA1943.117	Anonymous Flemish Artist (17th century)
706	WA1943.3	Nevil Oliver Lupton
707	WA1944.11	Patrick Nasmyth
708	WA1944.13	Arthur Hughes
708a	WA1944.31	Thomas Seddon
709	WA1944.100	Federico Barocci
710	WA1944.101	Hendrick ter Brugghen
711	WA1945.61	Attributed to the Master of Baldraccani
712	WA1945.62	Ambrosius Benson
713	WA1945.63	Copy after Giovanni Ambrogio de' Predis
714	WA1945.73	Gerbrand van den Eeckhout
715	WA1945.74	Authur Boyd Houghton
716	WA1945.75	Sir William Rothenstein
717	WA1945.98	Attributed to Lambert Sustris
717a	WA1945.99	Attributed to Antonio Francesco Peruzzini
718	WA1945.100	Johann Koenig
718a	WA1945.101	Sir Lawrence Burnett Gowing
718b	WA1945.139	James Abbott McNeill Whistler
719	WA1946.197	Philips Koninck
720	WA1946.198	Jacopo Robusti, called Tintoretto
721	WA1946.199	Bernardino Licinio
722	WA1946.200	Bartolomeo Montagna
723	WA1946.201	Bartolomeo Montagna
724	WA1946.202	Bartolomeo Montagna
725	WA1946.265	Giovanni Paolo Panini
726	WA1946.266	Augustus Edwin John
727	WA1946.267	William Roberts
728	WA1946.268	Sir William Nicholson
729	WA1946.269	Charles de Sousy Ricketts
730	WA1946.270	Studio of Bonifazio de' Pitati
730a	WA1946.376	Frederick Etchells
731	WA1946.271	Domenico Robutsti, called Tintoretto
732	WA1947.246	Attributed to Martino da Verona
733	WA1947.243	Francesco Bianchi Ferrari
734	WA1947.203	Anonymous Florentine Artist (*c.* 1470–1490)
735	WA1947.202	Attributed to Marco Basaiti
736	WA1947.239	Anonymous Umbro-Marchigian Artist (*c.* 1510)
736a	WA1947.244	Anonymous Italian Artist (perhaps 16th century)
736b	WA1947.201	Attributed to Giovanni Mansueti
736c	WA1947.202.1	Attributed to Bartolomeo di Fruosino
736d	WA1947.201.2	Attributed to Bartolomeo di Fruosino
736e	WA1947.201.3	Anonymous Venetian Artist (*c.* 1700)
736f	WA1947.201.4	Anonymous British Artist (*c.* 1830)
737	WA1947.267	Joseph H. Vignoles Fisher
738a	WA1947.314	James Smetham
738b	WA1947.315	James Smetham
739	WA1947.233	Jacques-Émile Blanche
740	WA1947.318	James Smetham
741	WA1947.270	Domingos António de Sequeira
742	WA1947.161	Sisto Badalocchio
743	WA1947.168	Samuel Palmer
744	WA1948.155	Jean-Baptiste Pater
745	WA1948.77	Simon Vouet and studio
750	WA1948.72	Keith Baynes
751	WA1948.67	Sir William Menzies Coldstream
752	WA1948.73	Hercules Enslin du Plessis
753	WA1948.70	Rodrigo Moynihan
754	WA1948.68	Victor Pasmore
755	WA1948.69	Victor Pasmore
756	WA1948.71	Claude Maurice Rogers
757	WA1948.32	Sir Edward Coley Burne-Jones, Bt
758	WA1948.33	Jan Van Os
759	WA1948.34	Style of Jan Van Os
760	WA1948.35	Attributed to John Crome, after Gainsborough
761	WA1948.37	Patrick Nasmyth
762	WA1948.36	James Stark
763	WA1948.101	François-Joseph Dupressoir
764	WA1948.102	Charles-Émile-Auguste Carolus-Duran
765	WA1948.178	Forgery of John Constable
766	WA1948.80	Thomas Esmond Lowinsky
767	WA1948.81	Ethel Sands
768	WA1948.116	Adam Frans van der Meulen
769	WA1948.76	Giambattista Pittoni
770	WA1948.100	Joachim Antonisz. Wtewael
771	WA1949.5	Jacopo da Ponte, called Bassano
772	WA1949.6	Luca Carlevaris
773	WA1949.184	Attributed to George Vincent
774	WA1949.185	Adriaen van de Velde
775	WA1949.186	Sir Charles John Holmes
776	WA1949.202	Copy after Egbert van Heemskerk
777	WA1949.222	Circle of Giorgione
779	WA1949.313	Isaak Il'ich Levitan
780	WA1950.6	Bernardo Strozzi
781	WA1950.10	Anonymous French Artist (*c.* 1620–1630)
782	WA1950.20	Attributed to Claes Cornelisz. Moeyaert
783	WA1950.21	Giovanni Francesco Caroto
784	WA1950.22	Gaetano Gandolfi
785	WA1950.23	Gaetano Gandolfi
785a	WA.OA881	John Opie
786	WA1950.26	Henry Walter
787	WA1950.27	Henry Walter
788	WA1950.47	Sir William Blake Richmond
789	WA1950.74	Bartolomeo Schedoni
790	WA1950.166	Studio of Leonardo da Vinci
791	WA1950.169	Nicolas Poussin
792	WA1950.172	Diana White
793	WA1950.179	Tommaso d'Antonio Manzuoli, called Maso da San Friano
794	WA1950.184	Camille Pissarro
795	WA1950.186	Camille Pissarro
796	WA1950.188	Lucien Pissarro
797	WA1950.189	Lucien Pissarro
797a	WA1951.226	Anonymous British Artist (*c.* 1815)
797b	WA1951.50	Cristofano Allori
798	WA1951.197	Robert Braithwaite Martineau
799	WA1951.198	Robert Braithwaite Martineau
800	WA1951.199	Robert Braithwaite Martineau
801	WA1951.200	Robert Braithwaite Martineau
802	WA1951.161	Juan Bautista Maino
803	WA1951.7	Attributed to Bartolomeo Caporali
804	WA1951.8	Style of Rembrandt Harmensz. van Rijn
805	WA1951.9	Copy after Sir Peter Paul Rubens
806	WA1951.48	Anonymous British Artist (late 19th century)
807	WA1951.51.1	Copy after Cornelis de Vos
808	WA1951.51.2	Nicolaes Pietersz. Berchem
809	WA1951.51.3	Charles-Émile Jacque
810	WA1951.51.4	Dionijs Verburgh
811	WA1951.51.5	Jan van Goyen
812	WA1951.51.6	Style of Jan Brueghel the Elder

Painting Number	Museum Accession Number	Artist Name
813	WA1951.51.7	Adriaen Coorte
814	WA1951.51.8	Ambrosius Benson
815	WA1951.51.9	Dirck Hals
816	WA1951.148	George Frederic Watts
817	WA1951.49	Andrea Solario
819	WA1952.6.1	Camille Pissarro
820	WA1951.225.1	Camille Pissarro
821	WA1952.6.2	Camille Pissarro
822	WA1951.225.2	Camille Pissarro
823	WA1951.225.3	Camille Pissarro
824	WA1952.6.3	Camille Pissarro
825	WA1951.225.4	Camille Pissarro
826	WA1951.225.5	Camille Pissarro
827	WA1952.6.4	Camille Pissarro
828	WA1951.225.6	Félix Pissarro
829	WA1951.225.7	Félix Pissarro
830	WA1951.225.8	Félix Pissarro
831	WA1951.225.9	Félix Pissarro
832	WA1951.225.10	Félix Pissarro
833	WA1951.225.11	Félix Pissarro
834	WA1952.6.5	Félix Pissarro
835	WA1952.6.6	Lucien Pissarro
836	WA1952.6.7	Lucien Pissarro
837	WA1952.6.8	Lucien Pissarro
838	WA1952.6.9	Lucien Pissarro
839	WA1951.225.12	Lucien Pissarro
840	WA1951.225.13	Lucien Pissarro
841	WA1952.6.10	Lucien Pissarro
842	WA1952.6.11	Lucien Pissarro
843	WA1951.225.14	Lucien Pissarro
844	WA1951.225.15	Lucien Pissarro
845	WA1951.225.16	Lucien Pissarro
846	WA1951.225.17	Lucien Pissarro
847	WA1951.225.18	Lucien Pissarro
848	WA1952.6.12	Lucien Pissarro
849	WA1952.6.13	Lucien Pissarro
850	WA1951.225.19	Lucien Pissarro
851	WA1952.6.14	Lucien Pissarro
852	WA1952.6.15	Lucien Pissarro
853	WA1951.225.20	Lucien Pissarro
854	WA1952.6.16	Ludovic-Rodolphe Pissarro
855	WA1952.6.17	Orovida Pissarro
856	WA1952.6.18	Orovida Pissarro
856a	WA1952.6.9	Orovida Pissarro
857	WA1951.225.21	Orovida Pissarro
858	WA1952.63	William Hogarth
859	WA1952.64	Style of Michiel Sweerts
860	WA1952.66	Anonymous British Artist (*c.* 1650)
861	WA1952.116	George Jones
862	WA1952.117	George Jones
863	WA1952.52	Paolo Caliari, called Veronese
863a	WA1952.123	Anonymous Cremonese Artist (*c.* 1570–90)
864	WA1953.2	Richard Wilson
865	WA1953.67	Alphonse Legros
866	WA1953.84	Louis Hayet
867	WA1953.77	Ippolito Scarsella, called Lo Scarsellino
868	WA1953.23	Anonymous Flemish Artist (early 16th century)
869	WA1953.148	Anonymous Roman Artist (*c.* 1690–1740)
870	WA1954.85	Walter Richard Sickert
871	WA1954.52	Luis de Morales
872	WA1954.84	Pier Francesco Mola
872a	WA1954.70.164	Karl Spitzweg
872b	WA1954.81	Thomas Jones
873	WA1955.93	Style of Matteo di Giovanni
874	WA1955.3	Bartolomeo Montagna
875	WA1955.66	Jacob van Ruisdael
876	WA1955.67	Giovanni Battista Tiepolo
877	WA1955.63	Arnold Boonen
878	WA1955.62	Thomas Gainsborough
879	WA1955.86	Copy after Francisco de Zurbarán
880	WA1955.25	George Frederic Watts
881	WA1955.60	Sir Lawrence Alma-Tadema
882	WA1955.78	Giovanni Antonio da Pesaro
883	WA1955.28	Cornelis Cornelisz. van Haarlem
884	WA1955.68	William Lee
885	WA1956.18	Sir George Clausen
886	WA1956.15	Attributed to Dosso Dossi
887	WA1956.13	Attributed to Giovanni Battista Crespi, Il Cerano
888	WA1956.44	Jean-François Millet
888a	WA1956.12	George Frederic Watts
889	WA1957.59.1	Sir Peter Paul Rubens
890	WA1957.59.2	Anonymous Genoese Artist (?) (*c.* 1650–1680)
891	WA1957.59.3	Anonymous Dutch Artist (mid-17th century)
892	WA1957.59	Copy after John Crome
893	WA1957.96	Attributed to Richard Wilson
894	WA1957.42	Anonymous Flemish Artist (17th century)
895	WA1957.43	Follower of Claude-Joseph Vernet
896	WA1957.14.1	Robert Polhill Bevan
897	WA1957.14.2	Robert Polhill Bevan
898	WA1957.14.3	Robert Polhill Bevan
899	WA1957.15	Malcolm Drummond
900	WA1957.16	Harold Gilman
901	WA1957.17	Charles Isaac Ginner
902	WA1957.18.1	Spencer Frederick Gore
903	WA1957.18.2	Spencer Frederick Gore
903a	WA1957.105	James Bolivar Manson
904	WA1957.95	Felice Torelli
905	WA1957.89	Copy after Jacopo Bassano
906	WA1957.84	Percy Frederick Horton
907	WA1957.47	Copy after Jean-Siméon Chardin
908	WA1957.44	Anonymous German Artist (*c.* 1500–1525)
908a	WA1957.80.18	Anonymous Spanish Artist (?) (*c.* 1620)
909	WA1957.85.1	Percy Frederick Horton
910	WA1958.57.4	Robert Collinson
911	WA1958.57.5	Charles Conder
912	WA1958.57.7	Thomas Phillips
913	WA1958.57.8	Charles de Sousy Ricketts
914	WA1958.57.1	Studio of Bonifazio de' Pitati
915	WA1958.57.9	George Frederic Watts
916	WA1958.57.10	Attributed to Walter Greaves
917	WA1958.57.6	William Etty
918	WA1958.57.3	Copy after Sir Joshua Reynolds
919	WA1958.57.2	Attributed to Niccol Berrettoni
920	WA1958.54	Carel Victor Morlais Weight
921	WA1958.10	Attributed to Rodrigo de Osona
922	WA1958.22	Francesco Maffei
923	WA1959.4.1	Alexander Jamieson
924	WA1959.4.2	Alexander Jamieson
924a	WA1959.43.2	Clive Gardiner
924b	WA1959.43.1	Thomas Balston
925	WA1959.54.2	Mark Gertler
926	WA1959.54.1	Derwent Lees
927	WA1959.54.3	Thomas Saunders Nash
928	WA1959.54.4	Thomas Balston
929	WA1959.3	Richard Arthur Crosthwaite Murry
930	WA1959.6	Pietro Orioli
931	WA1959.60	Circle of Francesco Trevisani
932	WA1959.20.1	Samuel Laurence
933	WA1960.6	Chester Earles
934	WA1960.32	Follower of Corrado Giaquinto
935	WA1960.37	Philip Wilson Steer
936	WA1960.52	Anonymous British Artist (*c.* 1790)
936a	WA1960.53	Ford Madox Brown
937	WA1960.73	Pier Francesco Mola
938	WA1960.70	Attributed to Lelio Orsi
939	WA1960.56	Attributed to Sebastiano Secante
940	WA1961.1.1	Attributed to Philip James de Loutherbourg
941	WA1961.1.2	Attributed to Philip James de Loutherbourg
942	WA1961.1.3	Style of John Crome
943	WA1961.2	James Ferrier Pryde
944	WA1961.8	Anonymous Roman Artist (*c.* 1700–1720)
945	WA1961.15	Robert Polhill Bevan
946	WA1961.20	Sir Henry Raeburn
947	WA1961.23	William Holman Hunt
948	WA1961.28.1	Walter Richard Sickert
949	WA1961.30	George Frederic Watts
950	WA1961.31.1	Mark Fisher
951	WA1961.31.2	Frederic William Watts
952	WA1961.31	Paul Fordyce Maitland
953	WA1961.36	William Alfred Delamotte
954	WA1961.46	Harold Gilman
955	WA1961.47	Thomas Barker of Bath
956	WA1962.4.1	Ernest Meissonier
957	WA1962.4.2	John William Inchbold
958	WA1962.15	Sir Egerton Bushe Coghill, Bt
959	WA1962.17.1	Anonymous Flemish Artist (16th century)
960	WA1962.17.2	Anonymous Flemish Artist (17th century)
961	WA1962.17.3	Jean-François de Troy
962	WA1962.17.4	Joseph van Aken
963	WA1962.17.5	Eugène Boudin

Painting Number	Museum Accession Number	Artist Name
964	WA1962.17.6	Copy after Paul Bril
965	WA1962.17.7	Charles Brooking
966	WA1962.17.8	Adriaen Brouwer
967	WA1962.17.9	Philip Hermogenes Calderon
968	WA1962.17.10	Style of John Constable
969	WA1962.17.11	Claude Gellée (Le Lorrain)
970	WA1962.17.12	Attributed to Giovanni Francesco Grimaldi
971	WA1962.17.13	William Etty
972	WA1962.17.14	Giovanni di Paolo
973	WA1962.17.15	Jan van Goyen
974	WA1962.17.16	Style of Karel Du Jardin
975	WA1962.17.17	Cornelius Jonson (Cornelis Janssens van Ceulen)
976	WA1962.17.18	Studio of Jacob Jordaens
977	WA1962.17.19	Paul Fordyce Maitland
978	WA1962.17.20	Paul Fordyce Maitland
979	WA1962.17.21	Attributed to Carel de Moor the Younger
980	WA1962.17.22	Alessandro Bonvicino, called Moretto da Brescia
981	WA1962.17.23	François de Nomé
982	WA1962.17.24	Jacob van Ruisdael
983	WA1962.17.25	Style of Jan Siberechts
984	WA1962.17.26	Claude-Joseph Vernet
985	WA1962.17.27	James Abbott McNeill Whistler
986	WA1962.17.28	Sir David Wilkie
987	WA1962.17.29	Richard Wilson
988	WA1962.17.30	Richard Wilson
989	WA1962.17.31	Francesco Zuccarelli
990	WA1962.18.1	Sir George Hayter
991	WA1962.26	Giorgio Vasari
992	WA1962.35.1	Attributed to Jacob Duck
993	WA1962.35.2	John Downman
994	WA1962.35	Style of Willem Claesz. Heda
995	WA1962.58.1	Arthur Hughes
996	WA1962.78	Francisco Borès
997	WA1963.1	Attributed to Sir William Orpen
998	WA1963.27	Follower of Salvator Rosa
999	WA1963.31	George Tuckwell
1000	WA1963.44	James Bolivar Manson
1001	WA1963.56	Stanislawa de Karlowska
1002	WA1963.63	Ermanno Stroiffi
1002a	WA1963.89.48	Sir Edwin Henry Landseer
1003	WA1963.122	John Linnell
1004	WA1963.150.1	Charles-François Daubigny
1005	WA1963.150.2	Jean-Baptiste-Armand Guillaumin
1006	WA1963.150.3	Gustave Loiseau
1007	WA1963.150.4	Thomas Baker
1008	WA1963.150.5	William Havell
1009	WA1963.150.6	Cecil Gordon Lawson
1010	WA1963.150.7	Sir Alfred James Munnings
1011	WA1963.150.8	Sir Alfred James Munnings
1012	WA1963.150.9	Frederic William Watts
1013	WA1964.35	Hubert Lindsay Wellington
1014	WA1964.41.1	Giovanni Battista Naldini
1015	WA1964.46	Ivon Hitchens
1015a	WA1964.48	Jacopo Amigoni
1016	WA1964.59	James Bolivar Manson
1017	WA1964.60	Copy after William Dobson
1018	WA1964.71	John Butler Yeats
1019	WA1965.22.1	Orovida Pissarro
1020	WA1965.15.2	Jules Bastien-Lepage
1021	WA1965.49.1	Reginald Grange Brundrit
1022	WA1965.62	Ferdinando Galli Bibiena
1022a	WA1966.13.1	Sir Lawrence Alma-Tadema
1022b	WA1966.132	Abraham Cooper
1022c	WA1966.24	William Breakspeare
1023a	WA1966.28	Glyn Warren Philpot
1023b	WA1966.37	John Pettie
1024	WA1966.42.1	Fairle Harmar, Viscountess Harberton
1025	WA1966.42.2	Margaret Millicent Fisher Prout
1026	WA1966.42.3	Dame Ethel Walker
1027	WA1966.43	Antonio Bellucci
1027a	WA1966.51	Edwin Longsden Long
1028	WA1966.60	Sylvia Gosse
1029	WA1966.65	Bernhard Keilhau, known as Monsù Bernardo
1029a	WA1966.87.1	John Downman
1029b	WA1966.87.2	John Downman
1030	WA1966.96	Style of Charles-Émile Jacque
1031	WA1967.24	Copy after Bernardo Strozzi
1032	WA1967.34.1	Walter John Bayes
1032a	WA1967.34.2	Walter John Bayes
1033	WA1967.52.1	Circle of Francesco Guardi
1034	WA1967.52.2	Circle of Francesco Guardi
1035	WA1967.52.3	Follower of Francesco Guardi
1035a	WA1967.52.40	David Teniers the Younger
1035b	WA1967.52.41	David Teniers the Younger
1036	WA1967.60.1	Claude-Joseph Vernet
1036a	WA1967.60.2	Tristram Paul Hillier
1036b	WA1967.60.3	Tristram Paul Hillier
1037	WA1968.20	Harold Gilman
1038	WA1968.21	Mark Gertler
1039	WA1968.22	Mark Gertler
1040	WA1968.23	Mark Gertler
1041	WA1968.24	Mark Gertler
1042	WA1968.25	Charles Isaac Ginner
1043	WA1968.26	Gilbert Spencer
1044	WA1968.27	Stanley Spencer
1045	WA1968.28	Anonymous Post-Byzantine (17th century)
1046	WA1968.136	Attributed to Mair von Landshut
1047	WA1968.137	Style of Jan Cornelisz. Vermeyen
1048	WA1968.138	Style of Jan Cornelisz. Vermeyen
1049	WA1968.139	Stanislawa de Karlowska
1050	WA1968.457	Dugald Sutherland MacColl
1050a	WA1968.471	Orovida Pissarro
1050b	WA1968.472	Orovida Pissarro
1050c	WA1968.474.1	Copy after Sir Peter Lely
1050d	WA1968.474.2	Anonymous British Artist (*c.* 1670–80)
1050e	WA1968.474.3	Studio of Adriaen Hanneman
1051	WA1969.7	Malcolm Midwood Milne
1052	WA1969.8	William James Müller
1053	WA1969.19	Arthur Lemon
1054	WA1969.20	Edith Corbet
1055	WA1969.21	Edmond Jean de Pury
1056	WA1969.138	John Piper
1057	WA1969.139	Bernardo Strozzi
1058	WA1970.78	Luca Giordano
1059	WA1970.115	Sir David Wilkie
1059a	WA1970.128	William Stokes Hulton
1060	WA1971.46	Philip Wilson Steer
1061	WA1971.47	Anonymous Post-Byzantine (16th century?)
1061a	WA1971.107	Hilda Lucy Milne
1062	WA1971.258	Attributed to Naddo Ceccarelli
1062a	WA1971.267	William Teulon Blandford Fletcher
1063	WA1971.387	Gioacchino Serangeli
1064	WA1972.7	Isack van Ostade
1065	WA1972.8	Salomon van Ruysdael
1066	WA1972.18	Vincent van Gogh
1067	WA1972.160	Jean-Louis Forain
1068	WA1972.161	Aristide-Joseph-Bonaventure Maillol
1069	WA1972.162	Louis Valtat
1070	WA1972.287	Jacobus Vrel
1071	WA1973.4	William Stokes Hulton
1072	WA1973.5	Domenico Morelli
1073	WA1973.104	Style of Willem Key
1074	WA1974.3	Justus Suttermans (Sustermans)
1075	WA1975.69	Charles Brooking
1076	WA1975.72	Thomas Gainsborough
1077	WA1975.73	Pan (Jacqueline Regina Ward)
1078	WA1975.108	Maud Sumner
1079	WA1975.125	Mstislav Valerianovich Dobuzhinsky
1080	WA1975.155	Anonymous Venetian or Veronese Artist (*c.* 1560–1570)
1081	WA1976.6	Peter Brook
1082	WA1976.63	Charles Cyril Mahoney
1083	WA1976.70	Sir Edwin Henry Landseer
1084	WA1976.260	Konstantin Andreevich Somov
1085	WA1976.261	Konstantin Andreevich Somov
1086	WA1977.21	Ford Madox Brown
1087	WA1977.22	Ford Madox Brown
1088	WA1977.23	Arthur Hughes
1089	WA1978.7	Frederic Lord Leighton
1090	WA1978.25	Attributed to Francesco de Mura
1091	WA1978.32	Anonymous British Artist (*c.* 1800)
1092	WA1978.33	Anonymous Dutch Artist (17th century)
1093	WA1978.34	Edward Calvert
1094	WA1978.35	William Etty
1095	WA1978.36	Joshua Shaw of Bath
1095a	WA1978.37	Georgios Chrysolouras
1096	WA1978.38	Attributed to Spencer Frederick Gore
1097	WA1978.39	Adrian Maurice Daintrey
1098	WA1978.64	Marie Laurencin
1099	WA1978.67	John Northcote Nash
1100	WA1978.75	Anton Raffael Mengs

Painting Number	Museum Accession Number	Artist Name
1101	WA1978.76	George Carline
1102	WA1978.106	Giacomo Bolognini
1103	WA1958.119	Thomas Barker of Bath
1104	WA1978.122	Albert Houthuesen
1105	WA1978.123	Mattia Preti
1106	WA1979.3.1	Clare Roberts
1107	WA1979.8	Anonymous North Italian Artist (*c.* 1530)
1108	WA1979.49	Thomas Gainsborough
1109	WA1979.51	Joseph Wright of Derby
1110	WA1979.71	John Wootton
1111	WA1979.81	Johan Zoffany
1112	WA1980.2	Geoffrey Hamilton Rhoades
1113	WA1980.79	Paul Cézanne
1114	WA1980.80	Édouard Manet
1115	WA1980.81	Claude Monet
1116	WA1980.92	Paolo de'Matteis
1117	WA1980.93	Allan Gwynne-Jones
1118	WA1980.136	Andrea Casali
1118a	WA1981.11.1	Édouard Manet
1119	WA1981.79	Sir David Wilkie
1120	WA1981.604	David Bomberg
1121	WA1982.35	Peter Kinley
1122	WA1982.36	Ubaldo Gandolfi
1123	WA1982.38	Alessandro Allori
1124	WA1982.40	Maud Sumner
1124a	WA1981.623	Bernard Meninsky
1125	WA1982.192	Akotantos Angelos
1126	WA1982.193	Anonymous Russian (15th/16th century)
1127	WA1982.194	Anonymous Russian (15th/16th century)
1128	WA1983.41	Charlotte Unger
1129	WA1983.54	Henry Tonks
1130	WA1983.168	Ernest Yarrow Jones
1131	WA1984.61.1	Roy de Maistre
1132	WA1984.148	Philip Morsberger
1133	WA1984.149	Michele Giovanni Boni, called Giambono
1134	WA1985.29	Giovanni Lanfranco
1135	WA1985.174	Robert Austin
1136	WA1985.192	Vera Ellen Poole
1137	WA1985.198	Adrian Maurice Daintrey
1138	WA1986.73	John Linnell
1139	WA1986.76	Etienne Aubry
1140	WA1986.80	Glyn Warren Philpot
1141	WA1986.96	Peter Greenham
1142	WA1986.97	Peter Greenham
1143	WA1986.98	William Townsend
1143a	WA1987.3	Christopher Hall
1144	WA1987.17	Jean-Louis Forain
1145	WA1987.26	Giovanni Bellini
1146	WA1987.37	Ivon Hitchens
1147	WA1987.41	Jan Hendik Weissenbruch
1148	WA1987.44	Charles-François Daubigny
1149	WA1987.67	Hippolyte-Jean Flandrin
1150	WA1987.68	Samuel Palmer
1151	WA1987.87	Geneviève Asse
1152	WA1987.88	Geneviève Asse
1153	WA1987.138	Charles Marq
1154	WA1987.139	Charles Marq
1155	WA1987.182	Brigitte Simon
1156	WA1987.183	Brigitte Simon
1157	WA1988.229	Lucian Freud
1158	WA1988.230	Richard Carline
1159	WA1988.231	Eleanor Fortescue-Brickdale
1160	WA1988.288	Pierre-Auguste Renoir
1161	WA1988.289	Pierre-Auguste Renoir
1162	WA1988.290	Pierre-Auguste Renoir
1163	WA1988.291	Eugène Boudin
1164	WA1988.292	Salomon van Ruysdael
1165	WA1988.293	Jean-Baptiste-Camille Corot
1166	WA1988.294	Francesco Guardi
1167	WA1988.295	Honoré Daumier
1168	WA1988.361	Augustus Leopold Egg
1169	WA1989.74	Sir Peter Paul Rubens
1170	WA1990.123	Anonymous French Artist (*c.* 1800)
1171	WA1991.12	Alexander Andreyevich Ivanov
1172	WA1991.27	Orovida Pissarro
1173	WA1991.184	Francis Montague Holl
1174	WA1991.345	Peter Greenham
1175	WA1991.433	Charles de Sousy Ricketts
1176	WA1991.437	Henryk Gotlib
1177	WA1993.333	Gyula Sajó
1178	WA1993.328	Jean-Victor Bertin
1179	WA1993.416	David Adolphe Constant Artz
1180	WA1993.417	Johannes Bosboom
1181	WA1993.418	Isaac Israels
1182	WA1993.419	Jozef Israels
1183	WA1993.420	Jozef Israels
1184	WA1993.422	Jacob Maris
1185	WA1993.423	Willem Maris
1186	WA1993.424	Style of Anton Mauve
1187	WA1993.424	Jan Veth
1188	WA1993.541	David Tindle
1189	WA1993.542	David Tindle
1190	WA1994.3	Edouard Vuillard
1191	WA1994.43	Anonymous Spanish Artist (?) (?19th century)
1192	WA1994.141	Augustus Edwin John
1193	WA1995.68	Roger Wagner
1194	WA1996.21	Attributed to Louis-Etienne Watelet
1195	WA1996.24	Maurice Utrillo
1196	WA1996.385	John Dodgson
1197	WA1996.34	Francis Ernest Jackson
1198	WA1996.35	Francis Ernest Jackson
1199	WA1996.36	Peter Greenham
1200	WA1996.37	Peter Greenham
1201	WA1996.382	Leon Underwood
1202	WA1996.459	Ben Nicholson
1203	WA1996.482	Richard Shirley Smith
1204	WA1997.3	Han van Meegeren
1205	WA1997.14	Edward Lear
1206	WA1997.26	François-Marius Granet
1207	WA1997.33	Wassily Kandinsky
1208	WA1997.38	J. Patrick after François-Marius Granet
1209	WA1998.10	Arthur Derek Hill
1210	WA1998.52	Aert van der Neer
1211	WA1998.54	John Martin
1212	WA1998.55	Sir William Menzies Coldstream
1213	WA1998.83	John Downton
1214	WA1998.84	John Downton
1215	WA1998.178	Anonymous Danish (?) Artist (19th century)
1216	WA1998.185	Anonymous North Italian Artist (?) (*c.* 1750)
1217	WA1998.217	John Brett
1218	WA1999.9	David Teniers the Younger
1219	WA1999.10	Johan Zoffany
1220	WA1999.21	Roger Fry
1221	WA1999.54	William Clarkson Stanfield
1222	WA2000.19	Tom Phillips
1223	WA2000.20	Joan Hassall
1224	WA2000.74	Jack Butler Yeats
1225	WA2000.75	Jack Butler Yeats
1226	WA2000.76	Jack Butler Yeats
1227	WA2000.77	Stephen Frederick Godfrey Farthing
1228	WA2000.85	Tiziano Vecellio, called Titian
1229	WA2001.19	Giovanni Battista Camuccini
1230	WA2001.28	Walter Richard Sickert
1231	WA2001.29	Walter Richard Sickert
1232	WA2001.30	Walter Richard Sickert
1233	WA2001.31	Walter Richard Sickert
1234	WA2001.32	Walter Richard Sickert
1235	WA2001.33	Walter Richard Sickert
1236	WA2001.34	Walter Richard Sickert
1237	WA2001.35	Walter Richard Sickert
1238	WA2001.45	Jean-Léon Gérôme
1239	WA2001.53	Jules Flandrin
1240	WA2001.54	Cecil Collins
1241	WA2001.72	George Tuckwell
1242	WA2001.151	Paul Guigou
1243	WA2002.43	Sir Peter Paul Rubens
1244	WA2002.44	Wilhelm Bendz
1245	WA2001.176	Peter Lanyon
1246	WA2001.183	Copy after Giovanni Antonio da Canal, called Canaletto
1247	WA2002.55	Sir Anthony van Dyck
1248	WA2002.65	Maggi Hambling
1249	WA2002.66	Jock McFadyen
1250	WA2002.67	Robert Medley
1251	WA2002.68	James Rielly
1252	WA2002.69	Kevin Sinnott
1253	WA2002.288	John Northcote Nash
1254	WA2003.94	Percy Frederick Horton
1255	WA2003.96	Lucien Pissarro
1256	WA2003.139	Giovanni Costa, called Nino

Painting Number	Museum Accession Number	Artist Name
F476	WA1898.31	William Reader
F634	WA1898.7	Attributed to Emanuel de Critz
F635	WA1908.224	Sir Nathaniel Bacon
F637	WA1898.4	Copy after Hans Holbein the Younger
F643b	WA1908.225	Anonymous Dutch Artist (*c.* 1690)
F655 or 745	WA1898.28	Studio of Sir Peter Lely
F656	WA1898.35	Anonymous British Artist (*c.* 1620?)
F657	WA1898.24	Cornelis de Neve
F658	WA1898.23	Attributed to Emanuel de Critz
F659	WA1898.8	Attributed to Emanuel de Critz
F661	WA1898.2	Anonymous Flemish Artist (early 17th century)
F662	WA1898.15	Anonymous British Artist (*c.* 1645)
F663	WA1898.12	Attributed to Emanuel de Critz
F664	WA1908.226	Anonymous Flemish (?) Artist (*c.* 1525–1530)
F665	WA1898.30	Anonymous British Artist (*c.* 1670–79)
F667	WA1898.11	Attributed to Thomas de Critz
F668	WA1898.32	Copy after Sir Anthony van Dyck
F669	WA1898.33	Copy after Sir Anthony van Dyck
F670	WA1898.38	Copy after Sir Anthony van Dyck
F671	WA1898.13	Anonymous British Artist (*c.* 1644)
F672	WA1898.6	Anonymous British Artist (*c.* 1575-1600)
F676	WA1898.27	Anonymous British Artist (*c.* 1625–1640)
F677	WA1898.34	Anonymous British Artist (*c.* 1640)
F680	WA1898.1	Anonymous British Artist (*c.* 1500)
F684	WA1898.10	Attributed to Thomas de Critz
F685	WA1898.26	Anonymous British Artist (*c.* 1635)
?F691	WA1898.3	Anonymous British Artist (*c.* 1580?)
F692	WA1898.9	Anonymous British Artist (1638)
F703	WA1898.16	Anonymous British Artist (*c.* 1638)
F704	WA1898.17	Anonymous British Artist (*c.* 1638)
F706	WA1898.14	Copy after Cornelius Jonson (Cornelis Janssens van Ceulen)
F707	WA1898.14	Attributed to Thomas de Critz
F730	WA1898.36	John Riley
F731	WA1898.39	John Riley
F732	WA1898.40	John Riley
F737	WA1898.42	Copy after Hans Holbein the Younger
F739 or 670	WA1898.37	Copy after Sir Peter Lely
F740	WA1898.21	Cornelis de Neve
F741	WA1898.22	Anonymous British Artist (1640)
F743	WA1898.25	Cornelis de Neve
F746	WA1898.18	Anonymous British Artist (*c.* 1594)
F747	WA1898.19	Anonymous British Artist (*c.* 1630)
F748	WA1898.20	Anonymous British Artist (1646)
	WA1863.262	Anonymous Dutch Artist (early 17th century)
	WA1863.287	Jan Thomas
	WA1918.7.1	Alfred William Hunt
	WA1932.197	Edward Calvert
	WA1932.198	Edward Calvert
	WA1937.13	Edward Calvert, after Titian
	WA1937.44	Edward Calvert
	WA1937.128	Francesco Solimena
	WA1937.129	Attributed to Cornelis Visscher
	WA1939.56	Carlo Innocenzo Carlone
	WA1940.8.10	William Williams
	WA1940.109	Carlo Maratta
	WA1946.338	Bernardo Strozzi
	WA1949.164	Alfred William Parsons
	WA1950.178.442	Frederic Lord Leighton
	WA1951.40	Anonymous French or Italian Artist (17th century)
	WA1954.80.8	Sir Charles Holroyd
	WA1955.31	Anonymous Bolognese Artist (*c.* 1600)
	WA1959.48	Edward Calvert
	WA1960.36.3	Konstantin Alekseevich Korovin
	WA1960.36.4	Konstantin Alekseevich Korovin
	WA1960.36.5	Konstantin Alekseevich Korovin
	WA1960.36.6	Konstantin Alekseevich Korovin
	WA1960.36.7	Konstantin Alekseevich Korovin
	WA1960.36.8	Konstantin Alekseevich Korovin
	WA1960.36.9	Konstantin Alekseevich Korovin
	WA1960.36.10	Konstantin Alekseevich Korovin
	WA1960.36.11	Konstantin Alekseevich Korovin
	WA1963.54	John Linnell
	WA1965.30.1	Jean-Paul Laurens
	WA1965.31	Richard Ellis Naish
	WA1965.44.9	John Fulleylove
	WA1966.20.2	William T. Howell Allchin

Painting Number	Museum Accession Number	Artist Name
	WA1966.22	John Brett
	WA1967.39.1	John Pettie
	WA1967.52.5	Edward William Cooke
	WA1968.37	Thomas Saunders Nash
	WA1971.384	Copy after Sir Henry Raeburn
	WA1976.23	Eliot Hodgkin
	WA1976.148	Edward Calvert
	WA1978.33.1	Eve Disher
	WA1978.107	William Hoare
	WA1979.86	Malcolm Hughes
	WA1980.120	Norman Garstin
	WA1980.121	Norman Garstin
	WA1980.122	Norman Garstin
	WA1981.562	Douglas Frederick Pittuck
	WA1981.605	David Bomberg
	WA.C.I.44	Cornelisz Schut
	WA.OA411	Anonymous Italian Artist(?) (19th century)
	WA.OA412	Anonymous Italian Artist(?) (19th century)
	WA.OA413	Anonymous Italian Artist(?) (19th century)
	WA.L.99.6	Paul Bril
	WA.L.99.7	Pietro da Cortona
	WA.L.99.8	Michelangelo Cerquozzi
	WA.L.99.10	Guiseppe Maria Crespi
	WA.L.99.11	Michelangelo Cerquozzi
	WA.L.99.12	Domenico Zampieri, called Domenichino
	WA.L.99.13	Gaspard Dughet
	WA.L.99.14	Giovanni Francesco Barbieri, called Guercino
	WA.L.99.15	Pierre Patel the Elder
	WA.L.99.16	Giovanni Francesco Romanelli
	WA.L.99.17	Ippolito Scarsella, called Lo Scarsellino
	WA.L.99.18	Bernardo Strozzi
	ANT1869.14	Anonymous Post-Byzantine (17th century)
	ANT1872.593	Anonymous Russian? (19th century)
	ANT1915.177 & 178	Anonymous Italian (16th century?)
	ANT1915.179	Anonymous Post-Byzantine (16th century?)
	ANT1915.180	Nikolaos Tzafouris
	ANT1915.182	Anonymous Post-Byzantine (19th century)
	ANT1915.183	Anonymous Russian (18th/19th century)
	ANT1915.184	Anonymous Russian (18th/19th century)
	ANT1915.185	Anonymous Russian (19th century)
	ANT1915.186	Anonymous Russian (18th century)
	ANT1915.187	Anonymous Russian (18th century)
	ANT1915.188	Anonymous Russian (18th century)
	ANT1915.189	Anonymous Russian (18th/19th century)
	ANT1915.190	Anonymous Russian (19th century)
	ANT1915.191	Anonymous Russian (18th/19th century)
	ANT1988.21	Anonymous Post-Byzantine (17th century)
	ANT1988.22	Anonymous Russian (16th/17th century)
	ANT1988.23	Anonymous Post-Byzantine (16th/17th century)
	ANT1990.101	Anonymous British Artist (18th century)
	HCR1980.6.13	Arthur William Devis
	HCR1980.9.1	Arthur William Devis

PHOTOGRAPHIC ACKNOWLEDGEMENTS

Every effort has been made to trace all copyright owners and seek their permission for the inclusion of their works. If any copyright owner has been overlooked, they should notify the Museum, any errors or omissions can then be corrected in future editions. The Ashmolean Museum wishes to thank all those who have given permission for works to be reproduced, acknowledging specifically the following:

p. 3, André: © ADAGP, Paris and DACS, London 2003; p. 6, Asse: © ADAGP, Paris and DACS, London 2003; p. 6, Austin: © Rachel Austin; p. 11, Baynes: © Sir John Baynes nephew of the artist, and his sons; p. 11, Bell: © 1961 Estate of Vanessa Bell, courtesy Henrietta Garnett; p. 16, Blanche: © ADAGP, Paris and DACS, London 2003; p. 18, Bomberg: © The artist's family; p. 20, Bonnard: © ADAGP, Paris and DACS, London 2003; p. 20, Borès: © ADAGP, Paris and DACS, London 2003; p. 22, Braque: © ADAGP, Paris and DACS, London 2003; p. 33, Brook: © Oxford University Press; p. 38, Cameron: © For information about the copyright position enquiries should be addressed to Professor D. Cameron Watt or to his estate; p. 40, Carline: Nancy Carline; p. 46, Coldstream: © The Bridgeman Art Library, London; p. 59, Derain: © ADAGP, Paris and DACS, London 2003; p. 63, Drummond: © Estate of the artist; p. 70, Etchells: © Estate of the artist; p. 73, Farthing: © Stephen Farthing; p. 74, Flandrin: © ADAGP, Paris and DACS, London 2003, p. 80, Frelaut: © ADAGP, Paris and DACS, London 2003; p. 81, Freud: © The artist; p. 81, Friesz: © ADAGP, Paris and DACS, London 2003; p. 82, Fry: © The artist's estate; p. 86, Gertler: © Luke Gertler; p. 90, Gosse: © The Bridgeman Art Library, London; p. 90, Gowing: © The estate of Sir Lawrence Gowing; p. 92, Grant: © 1978 Estate of Duncan Grant, courtesy Henrietta Garnett; p. 93, Greenham: © The Bridgeman Art Library; p. 96, Gwynne-Jones: © The Bridgeman Art Library; p. 96, Hall: © Oxford University Press; p. 97, Hambling: © The artist, courtesy Marlborough Fine Art; p. 98, Hassall: © Brian North Lee; p. 99, Hayet: © ADAGP, Paris and DACS, London 2003; p. 102, Hill: © The executors of the estate of Derek Hill; p. 102, Hillier: © Mrs L.M. Hillier; p. 103, Hitchens: © Jonathan Clark Fine Art; p. 103, Hodgkin: © Mrs Mimi M. Hodgkin; p. 106, Horton: © The Trustees of Percy Horton; p. 107, Houthuesen: © The Trustees of the Albert Houthuesen Trust; p. 115, Jackson: © John Standen; p. 117, John: © The Bridgeman Art Library, London; p. 120, Kandinsky: © ADAGP, Paris and DACS, London 2003; p. 120, Karlowska: © Mrs R.A.P. Bevan; p. 123, Kinley: © Estate of the artist; p. 126, Lanyon: © Sheila Lanyon; p. 127, László: © The Bridgeman Art Library, London; p. 127, Laurencin: © ADAGP, Paris and DACS, London 2003; p. 130, Le Sidaner: © ADAGP, Paris and DACS, London 2003; p. 132, Loiseau: © ADAGP, Paris and DACS, London 2003; p. 135, MacColl: © Estate of the artist; p. 136, Mahoney: © Elizabeth Bulkeley, the artist's daughter; p 136, Maillol: © ADAGP, Paris and DACS, London 2003; p. 136, Maistre: © Estate of Roy de Maistre; p. 143, Matisse: © Succession H. Matisse/DACS 2003; p. 144, McFadyen: © Jock McFadyen; p. 144, Medley: © The estate of Robert Medley; p. 145, Meninsky: © Nora West, cousin of the late Nora Meninsky; p. 151, Morsberger: © Philip Morsberger; p. 152, Munnings: © The Sir Alfred Munnings Art Museum, Dedham, Essex, England; p. 153, Nash: © Artistic Trustee of the John Nash Estate; p. 156, Nevinson: © The Bridgeman Art Library; p. 156, Nicholson, B.: © Angela Verren-Taunt 2003. All rights reserved, DACS; p. 156, Nicholson, W.: © Elizabeth Banks; p. 162, Pan: © Mrs J.R. Ward; p. 163, Pasmore: © Victor Pasmore Estate, courtesy Marlborough Fine Art; p. 166, Phillips: © Tom Phillips 2003. All rights reserved, DACS; pp. 166–7, Philpot: © Rosemary Newgas (niece of the artist); p. 167, Picasso: © Succession Picasso/DACS 2003; p. 168, Piper: © The Piper estate; p. 177, Pittuck: © John Pittuck, elder son of the artist; p. 177, Poole: © Catherine Dupré; p. 191, Rielly: © courtesy Spencer Brownstone Gallery: p. 192, Roberts, C.: © Oxford University Press; p. 193, Roberts, W.: © courtesy William Roberts Society; p. 193, Rogers: © Crispin J. Rogers; pp. 194–5, Rothenstein: © The Bridgeman Art Library; p. 200, Sajó: © Mrs E.B. Sajó; p. 201, Sands: © The Christopher Sands Trust; p. 205, Segonzac: © ADAGP, Paris and DACS, London 2003; p. 205, Shannon: © Mrs Quintin Bridge; p. 206, Shirley Smith: © Richard Shirley Smith; pp. 206–8, Sickert: © Estate of Walter R. Sickert 2003. All rights reserved, DACS; p. 208, Simon: © DACS 2003; p. 209, Sinnott: © Kevin Sinnott; p. 213, Spencer, G.: © The Bridgeman Art Library; p. 213, Spencer, S.: © Estate of Stanley Spencer 2003. All rights reserved, DACS; pp. 215–6, Steer: © Tate; p. 224, Tonks: © Family of the Artist; p 229, Utrillo: © Association Maurice Utrillo, ADAGP, Paris and DACS, London 2003; p. 229, Valtat: © ADAGP, Paris and DACS, London 2003; p. 235, Vlaminck: © ADAGP, Paris and DACS, London 2003; p. 238, Vuillard: © ADAGP, Paris and DACS, London 2003; p. 238, Wagner: © Roger Wagner; p. 238, Walker: © The Bridgeman Art Library; p. 239, Ward: © Mrs J.R. Ward; p. 242, Weight: © Estate of the artist.